The Macintosh Bible

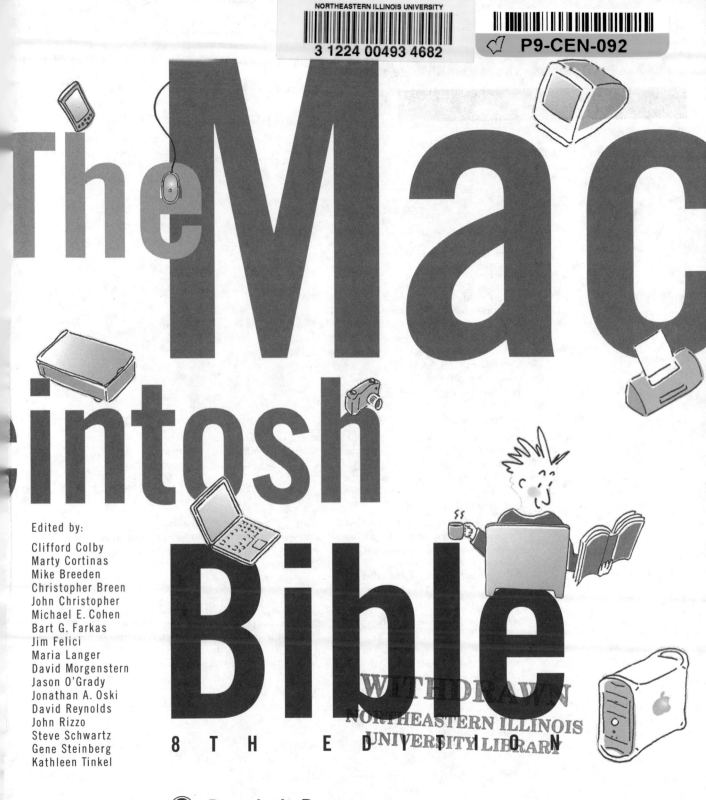

Edited by:

Clifford Colby
Marty Cortinas
Mike Breeden
Christopher Breen
John Christopher
Michael E. Cohen
Bart G. Farkas
Jim Felici
Maria Langer
David Morgenstern
Jason O'Grady
Jonathan A. Oski
David Reynolds
John Rizzo
Steve Schwartz
Gene Steinberg
Kathleen Tinkel

8TH EDITION

Peachpit Press

The Macintosh Bible, 8th Edition

Edited by Clifford Colby and Marty Cortinas

Peachpit Press

1249 Eighth Street
Berkeley, CA 94710
(510) 524-2178
(800) 283-9444
(510) 524-2221 (fax)

Find us on the World Wide Web at: www.peachpit.com

To report errors, please send a note to errata@peachpit.com

Peachpit Press is a division of Pearson Education

Editors: Clifford Colby and Marty Cortinas
Production coordinator: Connie Jeung-Mills
Copy editors: Gail Nelson (chief), Elissa Rabellino, and Kathy Simpson (proofreader)
Compositor: Owen Wolfson
Cover illustration and margin icons: John Grimes
Cover design: Gee + Chung Design
Indexer: Rebecca Plunkett
Tech readers: Jeffy Milstead, Kevin O'Connor

Notice of Rights

Notice of Liability

4-10-02

Trademarks

ISBN 0-201-70899-X

9 8 7 6 5 4 3 2 1

Printed and bound in the United States of America

If there were no Macintosh, it would be necessary to invent one.

—*Michael E. Cohen*

Contents at a Glance

Table of Contents

1978	**1979**		**1981**	**1982**
Apple begins game-machine project, code-named Annie.	Apple Chairman Mike Markkula asks Jef Raskin to take over Annie project. Raskin, instead, proposes creating an easy-to-use personal computer. Raskin becomes manager of the	renamed Macintosh project. The machine will ship in September 1981 and sell for $500. Steve Jobs and other Apple employees visit Xerox PARC.	Steve Jobs takes charge of Macintosh project.	Apple finishes Macintosh enclosure design; the company inscribes signatures of Macintosh team members inside the case.

1984		**1985**		
Apple introduced the Macintosh with the "1984" commercial.	The Macintosh 128K sells for $2,495 and includes MacWrite and MacDraw.	Apple airs the "Lemmings" commercial.	Microsoft releases Word for the Mac.	Nashoba Systems ships its FileMaker database.

Steve Wozniak leaves Apple.	Apple rolls out the first LaserWriter printer.	Aldus unveils PageMaker.	Steve Jobs leaves Apple to start NeXT.	Microsoft ships Excel; it's available only for the Mac.

1986			**1987**	
Apple releases the Mac Plus, the first Mac with SCSI.	Adobe releases its first fonts for the Mac.	Steve Jobs purchases Pixar from Lucasfilm.	Adobe Illustrator ships.	QuarkXPress ships.

Chapter 3: System Software 137

				1988
Apple introduces the Mac II, its first expandable Mac.	ACI releases 4th Dimension database in the U.S.	Microsoft releases first version of Windows.	Apple announces HyperCard.	Aldus rolls out FreeHand.

1988			**1989**	
NeXT unveils its first computer.	WordPerfect for the Mac ships.	Claris ships its first version of FileMaker after acquiring the database from Nashoba.	Adobe licenses from John and Thomas Knoll the software that will become Adobe Photoshop.	Apple rolls out the Macintosh Portable. At 15.8 pounds, it weighs more than the stationary workhorse Mac IIci (13.6 pounds), which also debuts in 1989.

		1990	1991	
NeXT releases NeXTstep OS (12 years later, Apple uses the NeXT OS as the foundation of its own Mac OS X).	Microsoft ships Office 1.0 for the Mac.	Adobe Photoshop 1.0 ships.	System 7 ships.	Apple unveils the PowerBook 100. Weighing 5.1 pounds, it is Apple's first real portable.

1991	*1992*			
System 7.1 ships.	Apple releases QuickTime.	Windows 3.1 ships.	BBEdit first ships.	Apple unveils Newton PDA project.

1993			**1994**	
Apple releases AppleScript.	Apple board makes Michael Spindler CEO, replacing John Scully, who leaves Apple in October.	Apple rolls out first Netwon MessagePad.	Apple announces Copland, the code-name for its star-crossed attempt to rewrite its operating system. The modern OS will ship mid-1995, Apple says.	Apple introduces the first PowerPC systems, the Power Macs. The Power Mac 6100, 7100, and 8100 use PowerPC 601 chips running at 60 to 80 MHz.

1994				
System 7.5 ships.	Netscape releases first public beta of its "network navigator."	First 100-MHz PowerPC machine, the Power Mac 8100/100.	Apple announces plans to license the Mac OS to third-party hardware vendors.	Netscape releases Navigator 1.0.

1995				
Mac OS-licensee Power Computing ships first Mac OS-compatible clone.	Apple demonstrates Copland and says the modern OS will be available in the middle of 1996.	Apple rolls out first PCI-based Power Mac, the Power Mac 9500, with System 7.5.2.	Apple announced ill-fated PowerBook 5300.	Apple reports a "safety problem" with Power-Book 5300 and halts production. Within a month, Apple resumes shipping PowerBook 5300 and cuts its price.

Part 2: Getting Productive

1995		1996		
Apple shows off Newton 2.0 operating system.	Apple releases OpenDoc 1.0, the company's dazzling but little-used scheme for building applications from software components.	Microsoft releases first public beta of Internet Explorer for the Mac.	Apple board makes Dr. Gilbert F. Amelio chairman and chief executive officer of Apple, replacing Michael Spindler.	Apple releases System 7.5 Update 2.0.

Apple loses $740 million in its second quarter. The figure marks the low point in a bruising string of bad fiscal quarters.	Apple pushed back release of Copland to mid-1997.	Microsoft ships first version of Internet Explorer for Macintosh.	Cyberdog 1.0 released, Apple's Internet toolkit based on OpenDoc.	Apple releases System 7.5.3 Revision 2.

Chapter 12: Personal and Business Management **453**

1996				
Apple releases System 7.5 Version 7.5.3.	Ellen Hancock becomes chief technology officer of Apple. She had previously worked for 28 years at IBM.	Apple cancels first developer release of Copland and decides instead to release its MIA operating system piecemeal in upcoming releases of the Mac OS.	Apple releases first 200-MHz system, the Power Macintosh 9500/200.	Apple releases System 7.5.5 Update.

1997

Apple says it will buy NeXT Software for $400 million. Apple gets NeXT's operating system and Steve Jobs, NeXT's chairman and CEO.	At a grinding three-hour keynote address at the January Macworld Expo in San Francisco, Apple CEO Gil Amelio unveils Rhapsody, the code-name for Apple's	upcoming operating system based on NeXT and Apple technologies. Apple says Rhapsody will be released to customers within 12 months.	Apple ships Mac OS 7.6 and Mac OS Runtime for Java 1.0.	Macromedia acquires FutureWave Software, maker of FutureSplash. Macromedia rechristens the software Flash.

Part 3: Getting Creative

1997				
Apple rolls out PowerBook 3400.	Apple lays off 2,700 employees and pulls the plug on several of its technologies, including OpenDoc.	Apple ships first 300-MHz system, the Power Mac 6500.	Mac OS 7.6.1 released.	Apple releases Cyberdog 2.0, an update to its suite of Internet tools.

Apple unveils new OS roadmap to its developers. At the end of the road is Rhapsody, which Apple says customers will get in 1998.	Twentieth Anniversary Macintosh ready to ship.	Dr. Gilbert F. Amelio, Apple's chairman of the board and chief executive officer, and Ellen Hancock, Apple's executive vice president of technology, resign.	Apple releases Mac OS 8. Users outraged because the new OS uses Charcoal as the default system font.	At Macworld Expo in Boston, Bill Gates pledges Microsoft's support of Apple and shows it by investing $150 million in Apple.

1997

Apple remakes board of directors: Mike Markkula and Gilbert Amelio leave; Larry Ellison joins board.	Apple buys assets of clone-vendor Power Computing, effectively putting an end to Apple's short-lived Mac OS licensing plan.	Steve Jobs become interim Apple CEO, or iCEO.	Apple debuts its "Think Different" commercial during the TV premiere of *Toy Story*.	Apple releases Rhapsody to software developers and reiterates that new OS will ship to customers in 1998.

Apple launches Newton MessagePad 2100.	Apple unveils first PowerPC G3 Power Macs.	Apple opens Apple Store, its online e-commerce site.	Apple says it has added the Mac OS compatibility environment (called the Blue Box) to Rhapsody.	Macromedia releases Dreamweaver.

1998				
Claris becomes FileMaker Inc. New company keeps FileMaker Pro database and hands off ClarisWorks to Apple, which renames software suite AppleWorks.	Apple pulls plug on Newton handheld devices.	Mac OS 8.1 available.	iMac and the redesigned, stylish PowerBook G3 announced.	Apple rejiggers its OS strategy and abandons its Rhapsody plans. Instead, Apple announces Mac OS X, which will ship to customers in Fall 1999, Apple says.

Part 4: Extending Your Reach

			1999		
iMac ships with 56K modem.	AppleWorks 5 ships.	Mac OS 8.5 ships. Apple engineering T-shirt declares the OS "sucks less" than Mac OS 8.	Adobe releases InDesign.		Blue-and-White Power Mac G3s and five colors of iMacs debut.

1999

| Apple ships first 400-MHz system, with the new Power Macs. | Final Cut Pro released. | Apple says Mac OS X will ship early in 2000. | Mac OS 8.6 ships. | Sears says it will sell iMacs. |

iBook announced with AirPort wireless networking.	iMovie and Mac OS 9 ship.	Apple releases the first PowerPC G4-equipped systems, the Power Mac G4.	**2000** Jobs shows off Mac OS X at Macworld Expo in San Francisco. Tells conventioneers Mac OS X will be available as shrink-wrapped software product in the summer.	Jobs becomes Apple CEO.

2000				**2001**
Apple announces the first 500 MHz system, with the latest round of Power Macs.	Apple tells developers Mac OS X will be available January 2001.	Power Mac G4 Cube announced.	Apple releases Mac OS X public beta. Apple says Mac OS X will be released in early 2001.	Apple releases iTunes and iDVD and says Mac OS X will ship March 24.

Apple announces first 600-MHz and 700-MHz system with new versions of the Power Mac G4.	Apple ships Mac OS X.	Mac OS X Server 2.0 released.	The QuickSilver Power Mac G4s ship: first 800-MHz systems.	Mac OS X 10.1 released.

Introduction

By Clifford Colby and Marty Cortinas

Welcome to *The Macintosh Bible.*

If you are new to the *Bible,* the 22 chapters, appendix, and glossary of this book are chock-full of timely and useful information compiled by the smartest Mac people we know.

And if you've used previous editions of the *Bible,* this one will seem very familiar. The eighth edition is brimming with advice, insights, and opinions from nearly 30 of the most knowledgeable and trusted authorities in the Mac community (including many folks who contributed over the past 15 years to earlier versions of the *Bible*).

In This Book,
You'll Find out About...

Mac OS X 10.1 and Mac OS 9.2.1, including directions for using Apple's newest operating systems.

Apple's desktop and portable machines, and guidance on which system to buy.

Software for the home and office, plus helpful advice for using design and productivity software.

Troubleshooting tips on everything from when you have trouble starting up your Mac to sharing files with a Windows machine.

And much more that you need to know to use Macintosh applications and hardware effectively.

We started work on this version of *The Macintosh Bible* not too long after the last edition shipped to bookstores in 1998—right after Apple released the first iMac and announced Mac OS X.

We knew this *Bible* had to include information on Mac OS X, so we planned to release the book early in 2000, when Apple initially said it would ship the new operating system. But Apple for a year and a half inched back the release of Mac OS X, and we inched back with it.

Life went on. From the time we started work on the *Bible* until we finished, entire families started up and reproduced: Three *Bible* folks got married (Kristina DeNike, Gail Nelson, and David Reynolds); four had babies join their families (Christopher Breen, John Christopher, Bart Farkas, and David Reynolds); one (perhaps less adventurously) bought a helicopter (Maria Langer).

Through it all, it's been a labor of love and—most of the time—fun. Which is the first commandment of *The Macintosh Bible:* "This is the Mac. It's supposed to be fun."

What to Look for

A glance through *The Macintosh Bible* 8th edition will show some major differences from—and similarities to—earlier editions.

Who wrote what. With this edition of the *Bible,* we've returned to having a group of contributors create the book. Each chapter lists who was its editor and writers. You'll see the initials of the people who wrote each entry in the entry headline or subheadline. (Skip ahead a few pages to see the bios of the sharp folks who helped write and edit this edition.)

Icons to help you find specific kinds of information. As in earlier editions of the *Bible*, you can use the icons in the margins to direct you to hot tips, good features, Mac OS X advice, and other kinds of information. (Turn the page to see a guide to the icons.)

Editors' polls. This edition of the *Bible* is divided into four sections, and each section starts off with an editors' poll that is tied to the section. For example, to kick off the section on creative software, we asked the editors to weigh in on whether the Web has changed how designers approach their work.

About each chapter. Each editor had a free hand in determining how to approach the topics he or she was responsible for. We just asked everybody to use the pages they were allotted to say the most important things about that topic they could think of. Generally though, each chapter includes a basic introduction to the topic, pointers to products you should know about in the category, and tips and advice to make your life easier. The chapter introductions and tables of contents will give you an overview of what each editor decided to highlight.

We've included an index and glossary in the back of the book. We try to explain Macintosh terms the first time they come up in a chapter, but come on: Who knows what order you're going to read the chapters in, and we can't define each term each time. So, if you come across a term you're not familiar with, head to the glossary and index.

Finally, when we discuss a product, we include its price and company's Web address. However, Web addresses, prices, and version numbers are like San Francisco bus schedules: They change all the time. We checked everything right before we sent the book to the printer, but with all the products we talk about in this book, we are pretty sure *something* will have changed by the time you read this.

Companion Web site. As with previous editions of the *Bible,* we'll provide periodic news, updates, and tips to keep this edition up to date. We used to send out these quarterly updates in the mail; now we do it on the Web. Check out www.macbible.com for *Macintosh Bible* updates.

Guide to the Icons

The icons you see in the margins of this book serve as signposts on your trip through the chapters. Use them as beacons to direct you to information you are interested in.

 Hot Tip. When you see this icon, you'll find next to it a piece of advice, a bit of insight, or some sort of information that will make your computing life a little easier.

 Good Feature. This points you to a well-thought-out part of an application or piece of hardware.

 Bad Feature. On the other side of the coin, the passage next to this icon alerts you to a problem with a piece of software or hardware—or something especially dumb a product does. We like how this icon looks.

 Mac OS X. This guides you to a passage on Apple's new operating system. Throughout the *Bible* we discuss the similarities and differences between Mac OS X and Mac OS 9 and cover how to perform tasks on both operating systems.

 Portable. This label appears next to information about Apple's PowerBooks and iBooks.

 Warning. You won't have your Mac taken away from you if you ignore the information next to this icon, but you will be a lot happier if you pay attention when you see this sign.

The Macintosh Bible Editors and Contributors

Timothy Aston (TA) is the technical services manager for the Hartford Courant Company (a Tribune Publishing Company). He is responsible for desktop and server deployment as well as network infrastructure support.

Ruffin Bailey (RB) is a hard-core Microsoft SQL 7.0 sellout when contracting for the National Oceanic and Atmospheric Administration, but in his spare time he's a Mac games aficionado. He's worked for www.xlr8yourmac.com and Inside Mac Games, covering game news over the last two-plus years, and has owned a Mac for more than a decade.

Mike Breeden (MB) is the Webmaster of AccelerateYourMac! (www. xlr8yourmac.com), a popular Web site with reviews, tips, guides, and news on getting the most out of your Mac. The site also includes searchable databases of Mac owner reports on CPU upgrades and drives of all types as well as a topic-based FAQ.

Christopher Breen (CB) is a contributing editor for *Macworld* magazine and has been writing about the Mac since the Reagan administration. He pens *Macworld*'s Mac 911 column.

John Christopher (JC) is a data-recovery engineer at DriveSavers in Novato, California, where he retrieves data from drives and other storage devices that have crashed and burned (sometimes literally). In the past seven years, John has recovered data for Apple alumni Steve Wozniak and Guy Kawasaki. (He is still waiting for Steve Jobs's drive to crash.) His other celebrated recoveries include writers and producers for *The Simpsons* and HBO's *Sex and the City* and band members from the group Nine Inch Nails. Over the years, John has also managed to find time to write for various Macintosh publications, including *Macworld*, *MacUser*, Tidbits, and *MacHome Journal* and was a contributing editor for the sixth edition of *The Macintosh Bible*. Send e-mail to him at johnchristopher@mac.com.

Michael E. Cohen (MEC) has produced and programmed multimedia titles for the Voyager Company and Calliope Media. Currently the Webmaster and interactive media specialist for UCLA's Center for Digital Humanities, he still owns the memory board from his Apple Lisa and remembers reading *Inside Macintosh* when it was in loose-leaf notebooks.

Clifford Colby is a senior editor at Peachpit Press and has worked at a handful of now-dead computer magazines, including *eMediaweekly*, *MacWEEK*, *MacUser*, and *Corporate Computing*. For several years, he worked at the White House.

Marty Cortinas (MC) is a San Francisco-based freelance editor and writer. He is the author of several columns about Apple computers published in TechWeb and Byte.com. He is the editor of several Peachpit Press books, including *Sad Macs, Bombs, and Other Disasters.* Marty became a Mac pro in 1993, when he joined the staff of *MacWEEK* as a copy editor. Marty worked there until its closure in 1999, by which time he had become managing editor. Before he joined the technology industry, Marty was an editor at several newspapers, including *The Oakland Tribune,* The Alameda Newspaper Group, *The Modesto Bee,* and the *Mesa Tribune.* From April to October, he can be found in Section 105, Row 23, Seat 2, in Pacific Bell Park.

Kristina DeNike (KD) has been working in the Macintosh market for ten years. Although she has covered a wide variety of hardware and software, her true passion is storage. She has tested, evaluated, and written about everything from floppies to Fibre Channel RAID arrays. She is currently the director of product evaluation for *Macworld.* Previously she was test manager at *MacUser* and *MacWEEK* labs, where she helped develop and beta test multiple versions of MacBench. She is a frequent guest on TechTV's *Call for Help* and *Screen Savers.* Miraculously, she has never owned a computer.

Andrea Dudrow (AD) is a writer based in New York. Her work has appeared in *Macworld, MacWEEK, Publish, Print,* and *Red Herring* magazines as well as in the *San Francisco Chronicle.*

Michael M. Eilers (ME) is a freelance writer and video editor whose love of computers (and computer games) began when software came on a cassette tape. He is the senior news editor for Inside Mac Games and a regular contributor to *MacHome Journal.*

Bart G. Farkas (BF) lives in the icy climes of the great white north in Calgary, Alberta, Canada, and is kept warm by his wife, Cori, two kids (Adam and Derek), and a pair of fuzzy felines. A die-hard Macintosh enthusiast, Bart coauthored the once-definitive work for Mac gaming: *The Macintosh Bible Guide to Games* (Peachpit Press). Bart was also editor in chief of *Inside Mac Games* magazine for a few years in the late 1990s. Currently, Bart works as a full-time strategy guide author for games of all races, colors, and creeds.

Jim Felici (JF) was on the startup team at *Macworld* and *Publish* magazines and served for years as *Computer Currents'* Mac adviser. He's the author of *The Desktop Style Guide* (ITC/Bantam), and he's worked in publishing since before you were born.

Erfert Fenton (EF) is a technical writer and horse wrangler who lives in the fabled Silicon Valley. An early employee of *Macworld* magazine, she became smitten with Macintosh fonts when she saw the first LaserWriter printer. Erfert is the author of *The Macintosh Font Book* (Peachpit Press), which has been in print for more than a decade.

Phil Gaskill (PG) has been in the publishing/typesetting business since 1971, on both the editorial and production sides. He actually didn't start using Macs until late 1987; since then, however, he has been an unabashed "Mac person." In 1988, he was hired as a support technician at Aldus Corp. in Seattle, doing telephone support for PageMaker 3.01 and, shortly thereafter, the late, lamented Aldus Persuasion 1.0 (he was one of the original team of five Persuasion support technicians). He later became the technical writer for the PageMaker engineering department. Then he moved to New York (where he still lives) in 1992, working at first for Hearst Magazines, then for a couple of book packagers, then for a now-defunct design firm/Web-site developer, doing both desktop publishing and HTML work. He has written on type and typesetting/desktop publishing for *Aldus* and *Adobe* magazines, *MacUser, Publish, MacAddict,* and probably several other magazines and has edited, technical-edited, authored, or coauthored numerous books on QuarkXPress and PageMaker, the best-known probably being *QuarkXPress Tips and Tricks* (Peachpit Press) with David Blatner.

Greg Kramer (GK) is a former senior editor of Inside Mac Games and has contributed his Mac gaming expertise to the magazines *MCV USA, MacAddict,* and *MacHome Journal.* He is also the author of more than 20 Prima Games strategy guides, most recently *American McGee's Alice and Oni.*

Maria Langer (ML) is the author of more than 40 computer books, including best-selling books on the Mac OS, Microsoft Word, and Microsoft Excel. She is a columnist for *Mac Today* and *FileMaker Pro Advisor* and writes for *MacAddict.* She recently became a commercial helicopter pilot and offers tours and aerial photography services in Wickenburg, AZ.

Tara Marchand (TM) manages the Web design team at the University of California, Berkeley, Extension Online. In a past life, she worked in the trenches as a Mac tech-support provider.

David Morgenstern (DM) is a freelance writer, editor, and branding consultant based in San Francisco. With long experience on the Mac platform, Morgenstern was editor of *MacWEEK* and *eMediaweekly*; his recent writing can be found at *Macworld*, MacInTouch, and Creativepro.com. He has also held positions at startups in the color calibration, display, and Internet video fields. He can be reached at www.davidmorgenstern.com.

Jason D. O'Grady (JOG) is editor in chief of O'Grady's PowerPage (www.ogrady.com) and a mobile-technology consultant based in Philadelphia. Jason is also a contributing editor for ZDNet, CNet's News.com, and *MacPower* magazine in Japan, and is a member of the Macworld Expo Conference faculty.

Jonathan A. Oski (JO) is manager, Professional Services, for Callisma, a network consulting firm based in Palo Alto, California. He's proudly used Macs since 1984 and been a contributing editor for MacInTouch and *MacWEEK* as well as a contributor to prior editions of *The Macintosh Bible.*

Karen Reichstein (KR) is an associate editor at Peachpit Press. Over the years, she's worked as a waitress, alternative-culture writer, BBS intern, technical-book buyer, produce-company office assistant, computer book rep, and retail marketing manager. Her first computer was a Macintosh Color Classic, which she bitterly regrets selling. She can often be found rummaging for old planters and abandoned compact Macs in various Northern California East Bay flea markets.

David Reynolds (DR) was editor in chief and one of the founding editors of *MacAddict* magazine. He lives in San Francisco with his wife, Susan, and son, Jacob, as well as a dog and three cats. His first Mac was a Mac Plus that he bought in 1987.

John Rizzo (JR) is publisher of the MacWindows.com, a columnist for CNet, and author of *How the Mac Works*. He was an editor for seven years at the wonderful *MacUser* magazine.

Steve Schwartz (SS) is a veteran computer-industry writer, dating back to the days of the Apple II. He has been a regular contributor to *Macworld* since its inception as well as to more than a dozen other computer magazines. He is the author of more than 40 books on computer and game topics, including the *FileMaker Pro 5 Bible* (Hungry Minds), *Macworld AppleWorks Bible* (Hungry Minds), *Running Office 2001: Mac* (the official guide) (Microsoft Press), and Visual QuickStart Guides from Peachpit Press on Internet Explorer and Entourage. You can visit Steve's official Web site (www.siliconwasteland.com) to learn more about his Mac books.

Gene Steinberg (GS) first used a Mac in 1984. He is a fact and science-fiction writer and a computer software and systems consultant. His more than two dozen computer-related books include *Upgrading and Troubleshooting Your Mac: Mac OS X Edition* (Osborne/McGraw-Hill 2001) and *The Mac OS X Little Black Book* (The Coriolis Group 2001). He is also a contributing editor for CNet, and a contributing writer for *MacHome Journal,* and his online column, "Mac Reality Check," appears in the Arizona Republic (www.azcentral.com/steinberg/computing). His Mac support Web site, The Mac Night Owl (www.macnightowl.com), receives thousands of visits from Mac users each day. In his spare time, Gene and his son, Grayson, are developing a new science-fiction adventure series, Attack of the Rockoids (www.rockoids.com).

Phil Strack (PS) is the manager of Network and Desktop Support Services for Time Warner Trade Publishing, the book-publishing division of AOL Time Warner. He has had several years' experience implementing and managing a wide variety of electronic mail and messaging systems and has been using and supporting the Macintosh platform since 1986.

Kathleen Tinkel (KT) bought a 128K Macintosh in April 1984 and never looked back. Within three years, her Tinkel Design studio, based in Westport, Connecticut, was doing all its in-house production on the Mac. She started writing about design and typography for the lamented *Personal Publishing*; became a founding contributing editor for *Step-by-Step Electronic Design* newsletter in 1989; coedited the weekly fax newsletter *MacPrePress*; wrote regularly for *Aldus* and *Adobe* magazines and irregularly for *MacUser, Macworld, Publish,* and several graphic arts publications; and had a column called "Print Clearly" in the last year of *MacWEEK.* She has also been a manager of CompuServe forums dedicated to graphic design, typography, and desktop publishing since 1990 and can still be found daily at http://go.compuserve.com/pubproduction?loc= us&access=public (now free to all).

Daniel Drew Turner (DT) swore off computers after getting a humanities degree at M.I.T. and an M.F.A. in creative writing. Of course, this led to a job at *MacAddict* magazine; from there he worked at *eMediaweekly, MacWEEK,* ZDNet and other computer-related publications. In addition, he has written (sometimes even about nondigital topics) for Salon, Feed, Nerve, I.D. and other well-known media outlets. He's all too well aware of the old saying "To a hammer, everything looks like a nail."

Bob Weibel (BW) is a former technical editor for *Publish* magazine and a past contributor to *The Macintosh Bible.* For a day job he's the publishing manager of Musician's Friend, the world's largest catalog and Web direct-mail retailer of musical gear.

PART 1

Looking at the Mac

Editors' Poll: What Makes a Mac a Mac?

CB: The Great Cloning Experiment of the late 1990s demonstrated that a Mac is more than a hunk of plastic, wires, and circuits stamped with an Apple logo. What made these beige boxes Macs was the Mac OS. Although the clones are gone and Apple has gussied up its designs, what continues to make a Mac a Mac is an operating system that makes sense from the tips of its toes to the top of its pointy little head. The Mac OS has a consistency of design and ease of use that allows people to concentrate on the work they're doing with the computer rather than on the computer itself.

DM: Two qualities mark the Mac platform: its deep integration of hardware and operating system and its tradition of user-centric values. First, Macs just work, and that's not just an accident; rather, it's the result of hardware and software engineering working together from the beginning of the design process. That's impossible on the Wintel side. From the beginning, the Mac was intended to be easy to set up, use, and manage—and for the most part Apple has delivered on that goal (forgetting the horror of the round iMac mouse). Hey, I almost wept when I first opened the side panel of the current Power Mac enclosure. Everything is open and accessible. That's the Mac way.

MC: That furshlugginer one-button mouse. Now you might consider that a flip, smart-aleck response—and it was—but after some thought, I stick by it. On the one hand, you've got simplicity, the Mac's hallmark. You can't press the wrong mouse button if there's only one. Beautiful. On the other hand, you've got Apple's stubbornness. Clearly, there are uses for a second button on a mouse. But does Apple make one or even offer one with its computers? No, of course not. So the one-button mouse, to me, is the perfect symbol for the Macintosh.

BF: After all these years, for me it's still the interface and ease of use. When I got my first iMac, I was absolutely stunned at how easy it was to set up, and that ease of use transfers through to all aspects of the Macintosh experience.

DR: It's kind of a Zen answer, but the whole of the Mac really is more than the sum of its parts. Ease of use, great integration, a sense of style, powerful software and hardware—a Mac has to have all of these things to be what it is.

MEC: The friendly smile it gives you every time you turn it on (although you see it much less often with Mac OS X, because you have to reboot so rarely!).

SS: Even with the introduction of Mac OS X, the Mac remains a Mac because of the intuitive way we can perform common (and not-so-common) tasks and because of consistency. Whether we're working on the Desktop or within almost any major program, we're seldom forced to guess how things work or to learn a whole new paradigm.

JO: It sounds corny, but to me the entire user experience is what makes a Mac. Having used PCs for as long as I've used a Mac, I really appreciate the consistency I get (most of the time) with a Mac that I can't count on when using a PC. Like many users, I like to start using an application or game before cracking open the manual. The consistency of the Macintosh user experience makes this possible nine times out of ten. Another great aspect of the Macintosh is the community. Some call us crazy zealots, but our passion for the computer is part of what makes the community so supportive of one another.

JF: As opposed to a Wintel PC? Well, it's sort of like what makes a Yankee a Yankee instead of a Met, or a White Sock instead of a Cub. As PCs have become easier to use and Macs more difficult (I use both), the main difference I see these days is the attitude of the person at the keyboard. Sometimes I think that the only thing that gives the Mac its Macness is the fanatical devotion of its users. Without that, there would be no Macs at all.

1

Working with Your Mac

David Reynolds (DR) is the chapter editor and author.
Karen Reichstein (KR) contributed to the chapter.

Back in 1984, when the Macintosh first hit the scene, there was nothing else like it. Its easy-to-understand system of folders, files, and menus meant you didn't have to be a rocket scientist to accomplish amazing things with a Mac. But that was nearly two decades ago, and the Macintosh interface has caught on with nearly every computer and operating-system maker out there. Now almost every computer sold—whether it's running Windows, Unix, or the now departed BeOS—has its own graphical user interface with files, folders, and menus. When you can't beat 'em, join 'em.

Still, the Macintosh is, in our humble opinion, the best combination of hardware (the physical Macintosh) and software (the Macintosh operating system) on the market. Compared with PCs running Windows (or Unix, for that matter), the Macintosh is far more elegant, easy to use, and creatively powerful.

That doesn't mean Apple hasn't made any changes over the years. The latest version of the Mac OS, Mac OS X, is quite a bit different from any of its predecessors—both on the surface and under the hood.

 By the way, the *X* in Mac OS X is a roman numeral, not a letter—hence it's pronounced "ten."

Apple released Mac OS X in the spring of 2001 (after many, many years of development), and it now comes preinstalled on all new Macintoshes. If you own a Macintosh with a G3 or G4 processor and you don't have Mac OS X, you can buy a copy. Although Mac OS X has a lot of similarities to earlier versions of the Mac OS (namely, Mac OS 9 and earlier), they are most definitely not the same.

We cover the differences here and in other chapters, and we let you know what features are specific to Mac OS 9 and earlier or to Mac OS X when we talk about them. For now, though, let's take a look at the basics—what makes a Mac a Mac.

In This Chapter

The Macintosh Desktop (DR)

Whether you're running a brand-new Mac with the latest version of Mac OS X installed or you're using an older Mac with Mac OS 8.0, you see the same basic thing when you start up your Mac—the famed Macintosh Desktop. Macs use the desktop metaphor to provide a familiar setting—a desk, essentially—for Mac users to command their machines. At its heart, the Macintosh Desktop works a lot like a desk in the real world. It has a space in which you open folders and work with documents and storage areas where you can organize your documents in folders. You can also use those storage areas to hold other devices that help you do your work, such as a calculator, a spreadsheet, or even a CD player.

On the Macintosh, a specialized program called the *Finder* creates the Desktop. The Finder is so named because it helps you find and work with your files—but that's not all it does. Besides maintaining a place for you to do your work, the Finder opens folders (showing you what's inside), launches the right program when you open a file, and lets you organize your workspace by moving things around. The Finder also manages windows and can even send a few commands to the system software—for example, telling it to shut down.

Below are two versions of the Macintosh Desktop—the one you'll find in Mac OS 9 and earlier (**Figure 1.1**), and the one you'll find in Mac OS X (**Figure 1.2**). Odds are, if you've used your Mac for any length of time, your Desktop won't look like the ones we picture. You may have moved your icons around, or perhaps you're not using the Launcher. Still, you should be able to follow along pretty easily.

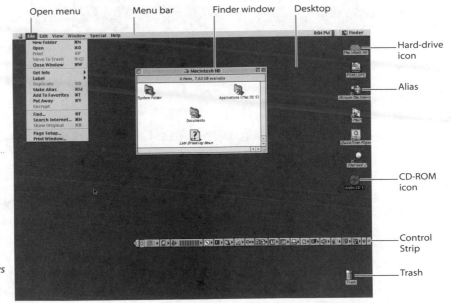

Figure 1.1

The Mac OS 9.2.1 Finder presents the interface you'll use to boss your Mac around. It holds sway over the Desktop as well as the various icons, menus, and windows you'll encounter on your Mac.

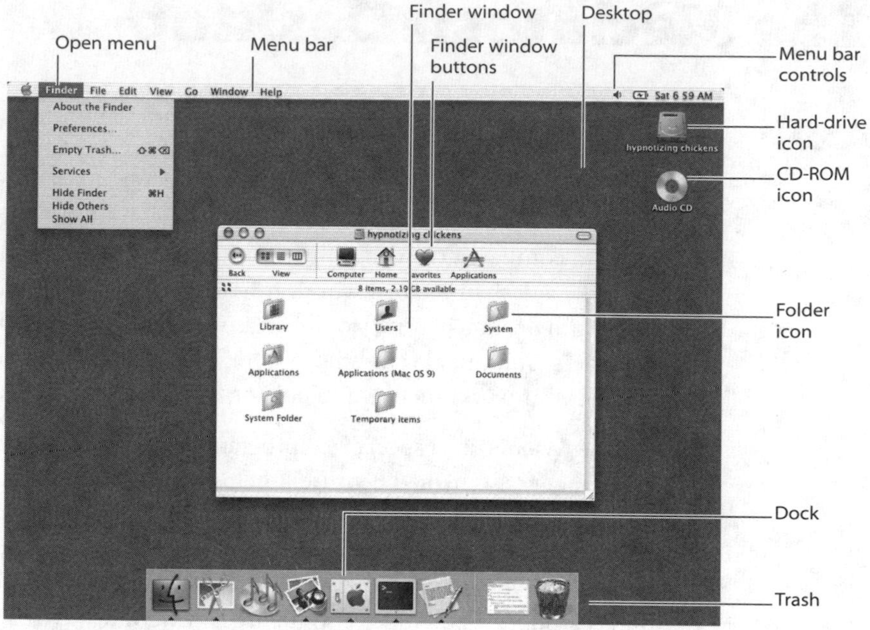

Open menu   Menu bar   Finder window

Finder window buttons   Desktop

Menu bar controls

Hard-drive icon

CD-ROM icon

Folder icon

Dock

Trash

Figure 1.2

The Mac OS X Desktop looks like a rounded, blue, three-dimensional version of its predecessors. All of the familiar elements are there—such as menus, icons, and windows—but it has a couple of new elements, too: a toolbar in each Finder window and the Dock at the bottom of the screen.

There's an easy way to find out whether you're using Mac OS 8, Mac OS 9, or Mac OS X—take a look at the top-right corner when you first turn on your Mac (**Figure 1.3**). If you use Mac OS 8 or 9, you'll see a little icon to the right of the clock—Mac OS X has no such icon. This icon represents the Application menu, used to switch between running programs (more on that later).

Figure 1.3

By looking at the menu bar in the top-right corner of the screen, you can tell at a glance which operating system you're using. In Mac OS 8 or 9, you'll see an icon and sometimes a program name to the right of the clock; in Mac OS X, the clock appears all the way to the right.

The Desktop in Mac OS 9 and Earlier

Over the years, Apple tweaked and refined the Desktop you see in Mac OS 9.2.1, but it's still the same basic environment introduced with the original Macintosh in 1984. In it, you'll find the menu bar and the basic Finder menus (used to work with files, folders, and the system itself) as well as a couple of icons (small pictures): a hard-drive icon (one for each hard drive you have), the Trash icon, and a CD icon (if you have a CD in your CD drive). You'll also see the pointer, which most often looks like an arrow pointing up and to the left, although it can change in appearance. The pointer is your link to the mouse. Move the mouse, and the pointer moves along with it.

The Desktop in Mac OS X

Although Mac OS X looks and acts a lot like Mac OS 9 and earlier, it's a brand-new user interface for a brand-new operating system, and there are some differences—this applies to the Desktop, too. The Mac OS X Desktop has many of the same elements as the one in Mac OS 9 and earlier, such as hard-drive icons, a Trash icon, a menu bar with a clock, menus, and a pointer, but it also has a feature with no real equivalent in previous Mac OSs—the Dock. In Mac OS X, the multitalented Dock hangs out at the bottom or on one side of the screen and keeps track of what programs are running. It also serves as a handy place to put shortcuts to programs, folders, and documents. You can also change some system settings here, and it even serves as a resting place for minimized windows. We'll be covering the Dock in more detail in the "Mac OS Desktop Elements" section below.

In Mac OS X, the Finder and the Desktop are not parts of the same thing, as in Mac OS 9 and earlier, where the Finder maintains the Desktop. Instead, the Finder is the part of Mac OS X that works with windows and files, while the Desktop is, well, the part of Mac OS X responsible for maintaining the Desktop, meaning that although they work very closely, they are independent parts of the operating system. This distinction isn't that important right now, but it may matter a lot in the future. Apple has hinted that the Finder might become an optional part of the Macintosh experience. After all, if you only use your Mac to check e-mail, why do you need the Finder at all? You don't, and it may one day be possible to set up your Mac so that when you start up, all you see is your e-mail program and not your Desktop.

The Varied and Wonderful Pointer

The mouse pointer—usually in the shape of a small black arrow—is the little graphical doodad onscreen that connects the mouse to your Macintosh's software. When you move the mouse, the pointer moves along with it. With this powerful tool, you can move files or folders around, select menu items and commands, rearrange and resize windows, and push buttons—pretty much anything you *wouldn't* type on a keyboard. It's known as a pointer mostly because you point at things with it. Of course, you can do a lot more than just point, but you get the idea.

Types of Pointers

Most of the time, the pointer appears either as an arrow or as an I-beam. You use the arrow to move items around, and the I-beam lets you select and manipulate text.

Depending on the habitat in which the pointer finds itself, it can change its shape to suit its surroundings and tell you what you can do with it at any given moment. The pointer can take *lots* of different shapes. Besides the arrow and the I-beam, it can appear as a wristwatch, a spinning beach ball, or a swirling rainbow circle. Here's a look at the most common pointers you might encounter—they appear in Mac OS 9 and in Mac OS X unless otherwise indicated (**Figure 1.4**).

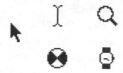

Figure 1.4

Five of the pointers you'll see as you use your Mac (clockwise, starting with the arrow): the pointer, I-beam, magnifying glass, wristwatch, and beach ball.

Arrow. This is the basic pointer in the shape of a black arrow. You use it mostly for manipulating objects, such as files, folders, menus and menu items, and buttons.

I-beam. Use the I-beam to select text and to place the insertion point—the flashing pointer that marks where text appears when you start typing.

Wristwatch. When you see the watch pointer, that means your Mac is thinking really hard and you'll have to wait until it's done.

Beach ball. OK, so it doesn't resemble an actual beach ball anymore than 'N Sync resembles entertainment. Still, it does evoke that vinyl toy used to whack concertgoers everywhere. In the Mac OS, it works a lot like a wristwatch pointer—it means a program is busy thinking and you'll have to wait a minute until it's done. (Although Mac OS X is fully multitasking, it does sometimes get stuck for a second, and you may still see the wristwatch—especially if you're using an older Mac program in Mac OS X.)

Rainbow circle. This is the Mac OS X version of the wristwatch. It means that Mac OS X is busy and you can't work in whatever program puts it up. Because Mac OS X has preemptive multitasking (which means it's generally more responsive to your clicks, not locking you out of using your Mac while it's thinking), you can usually move into a different program and continue working while Mac OS X works things out.

Magnifying glass. You'll see this pointer when you've done the click-and-a-half mouse move, which we'll cover in a minute. It's a way of drilling down through folders to see what's inside them, closing up folders behind you. This one you'll only find in Mac OS 9 and earlier, though.

Although that covers most of the pointers you'll encounter, it doesn't show them all. Programs can have their own custom pointers, and technically minded users of Mac OS 9 and earlier can modify them to suit their whims with a special program called ResEdit.

Hot Spots

Each pointer has a special region called a hot spot. This is the teeny, tiny part of the pointer where the action takes place when you click the mouse button. For example, the hot spot for the arrow is right at the tip, not at the base—just as you'd expect. For the I-beam, the hot spot is located just below where the top arms meet the middle vertical bar, and it determines exactly where text is selected when you click and drag—especially noticeable when the I-beam spans two lines of text and you're trying to select text on just one. Some pointers—such as the wristwatch, rainbow circle, and beach ball—don't have a hot spot. That's because they're there to indicate that your Mac is busy, so clicking with them doesn't do anything.

Mouse Moves

Now that you know everything you'd ever care to about pointers, it's time to dig in and start actually using the mouse. Aside from rolling the pointer around the screen and pointing at things, you can perform one of six basic mouse moves:

Point. As you might think, pointing refers to moving the pointer to a specific item or place using the mouse.

Press. Pressing refers to clicking and holding down the mouse button while pointing to an item onscreen. For example, you press a menu to reveal its commands or you click and hold a Control Strip item to show what commands it contains.

Click. Clicking refers to pressing and releasing the mouse button in fairly quick succession, usually when you're pointing to something.
To select an icon, for example, you click it.

Double-click. This one's easy. Double-clicking is clicking twice in fairly rapid succession. You double-click to perform an action, such as launching a program, selecting a word in some text, or opening a document. You can't move the mouse while double-clicking or leave too much time between clicks, or your Mac might interpret them as two single clicks.

Click-and-a-half. A click-and-a-half means you start to double-click, but instead of releasing the mouse button at the end of your second click, you keep pressing it to drill down through folders. The pointer then turns into a magnifying glass, and when you hold it over a hard drive, CD, or folder, that item will open after a short pause. You can continue by moving the pointer over a folder inside the open item—that folder will open after a pause. If you move the magnifying glass outside the currently open window, the window just opened while hovering will close. When you release the mouse button, the last window you opened using the magnifying glass will stay open, but the others will close—assuming that you kept the magnifying glass over the last window when releasing the button.

Drag. You drag by pressing and holding the mouse button while moving the mouse. You can drag icons to move them, drag the I-beam pointer across text to select it, or drag the arrow across a series of icons to select them.

Mac OS Desktop Elements

Besides the pointers, you're going to encounter several other items in your cruise around the Desktop. Most of these are icons—graphical representations of files, hard drives, programs, and the like. These icons let you see at a glance what you're working with. (Older operating systems used text alone to represent these items.) Unless you've been moving things about on your Mac, you'll encounter just a few icons on your Desktop. You can put more there or remove the existing ones if you like.

Files

Files are a lot like their paper counterparts in the real world. Their main job in life is to hold information. Typical files are such things as digital photos or letters you've written. Each file has a parent program that launches when you double-click the file; you can tell what that program is by looking at the file's icon (**Figure 1.5**).

Figure 1.5

The icons on these documents show what kind of documents are in them (such as text or a picture) as well as what program can open them.

Report   Screen shot   Read Me

Clippings

Clippings are a special kind of file created when you drag some text or a picture from a document to a Finder window or the Desktop (**Figure 1.6**). While you

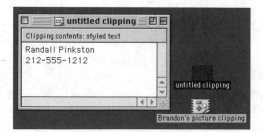

Figure 1.6

Clippings are a great way to store snippets of text and pictures quickly and easily.

must open most files using a program, you can view and open clippings without *any* specialized program—the Finder handles them, showing you the text or image inside the clipping. Clipping icons show what kind of information is inside (such as text or picture clippings), and text clippings take their file name from the first few words in the selection, tacking the word *clipping* onto the end. A clipping looks like a ragged-edge representation of what the file is—whether that's lines of text or a teeny graphic. Mac OS X doesn't have Clippings, but when you drag a bit of text or an image to the Desktop, Mac OS X will create a file that contains that text or image. In Mac OS X, though, you'll need a program to open that file.

Folders

Folder icons look like what they're supposed to represent—the traditional file folder (only they're not manila—on the Mac, they're blue) (**Figure 1.7**).

Figure 1.7

Folders serve as the primary way to organize your hard drive. You can put almost anything you like inside a folder, even another folder.

A Folder

A Folder

Folders hold files, programs, and even other folders and provide a way to organize the items on your hard drive. To create a new folder, from the File menu, choose New Folder (⌘N in Mac OS 9 and earlier, ⌘Shift N in Mac OS X). The new folder will appear with the imaginative name "Untitled Folder," but you can change that to almost any name you want (see "Working With Icons," later in this chapter).

Programs

Program icons come in all shapes and colors, and they're carefully crafted to let you know at a glance what program (also known as applications) they represent—witness Adobe Photoshop's eye or Microsoft Word's *W*. These icons represent a bunch of programming code that, when run on your Macintosh, let you actually *work* with all of those files you have on your disk. Don't worry—you don't have to know the specifics of what a program icon represents to use it (**Figure 1.8**).

Figure 1.8

Program icons tell you at a glance what program you're dealing with, and if you're lucky they might give you a hint as to what that program does.

QuickTime Player

Adobe Photoshop

QuickTime Player

Microsoft Word

Internet Explorer

Sherlock

URLs

URL (Uniform Resource Locator) files store Internet addresses—such as a Web page's address or an FTP site's location (**Figure 1.9**).

Figure 1.9

When you drag text in the form of a URL—such as an e-mail address or a Web page—to another folder (or to the Desktop), it turns into a URL file. Double-click this, and your Mac will either take you to the Web site or create a new preaddressed e-mail message.

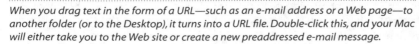
www.apple.com

Volumes

Volume icons represent a place to store files, folders, and programs. They appear on the Desktop in a column on the right side of the screen (although in Mac OS X they don't have to—you have the option of not having your hard-drive icons show up on your desktop). Here's a list of typical volume icons (**Figure 1.10**):

Figure 1.10

Here are four common kinds of volumes you might encounter (from left): CD-ROMs, network volumes, hard drives, and DVDs.

 Audio CD File server Macintosh HD MYSTMEN

Hard drives. Hard drives (or hard disks) are the volume icons you'll most commonly encounter. Although most Macs have only one hard drive, they *can* have several, producing several volume icons—one for each hard drive. You can also divide a hard drive into several volumes (or partitions), which gives that hard drive several volume icons, each representing a single storage area. This is only useful in a few specific situations. Most of the time, a hard drive has a single volume associated with it.

CDs. CD icons come in several flavors, including CD-ROMs and audio CDs. They appear as disc-shaped icons on the right side of the screen. Sometimes CD-ROMs have their own custom icons, which can appear as almost anything. A CD-ROM can contain files, folders, and programs, just like hard drives; audio CDs contain only audio files.

Zip disks and other removable volumes. Disks you can remove from your Macintosh—such as Zip disks, Jaz disks, Compact Flash cards, and SmartMedia cards—appear in the right column on the Desktop, just like hard drives and CDs. The one difference here is that you can remove these disks from your Mac. Removable volumes typically have custom icons that look like the physical disks.

iDisks and other servers. Just about every Mac ever made can connect to other Macs (and even to Windows and Unix machines) over a network. Apple's iDisks (part of Apple's iTools package at http://itools.mac.com/itoolsmain.html) are a prime example of volumes that show up over a network. Network volumes are displayed along the right side of the screen, just as hard drives are. Typically, server volume icons appear with a little wire connected to them, emphasizing their network abilities. (They can, however, have any custom icon.)

DVDs. Like CDs, DVDs show up on the right side of the screen, and they even share the same disclike generic icon. The difference with DVDs is that you most likely can't open them yourself unless you have the special software for playing back DVDs.

Aliases

Aliases are icons that point to items on your hard drive. When you click an alias, the original file actually opens. Aliases are ideal when you want to get to a much-used file, folder, or program quickly but don't want to move that item. It's like having the same file in two places at once. To find the original item to which an alias points, select the alias and choose Show Original under the File menu (⌘R). The window containing the original item will open before your eyes.

Read Me

Read Me alias

Alias icons look exactly like their originating file, folder, program, or disk except for two defining features: First, the file-name appears in italics; second, a little right-curving arrow at the bottom of the icon identifies an alias so you can tell the difference between it and the real deal (**Figure 1.11**). On a fresh installation of Mac OS 9 and earlier, you'll find a few aliases already on your Desktop:

Browse the Internet. Opens your Web browser.

Mail. Opens your e-mail program.

QuickTime Player. Plays music and movies.

Sherlock 2. Helps you find files and Web pages.

On a fresh Mac OS X installation, you won't find any aliases. Instead, you'll find several items in your Dock, which serves the same purpose in this case—offering quick access to a few often-used items. The items in your Dock *are* aliases, but because they're in the Dock, they take on a different appearance. Here's what you'll find:

Finder. The program that helps you work with files. It's always running, so it's always in the Dock.

Mail. Opens Mail, an e-mail program.

Internet Explorer. A Web browser for using the Internet.

iTunes. Apple's own music player that plays CDs and MP3 files.

Sherlock. Helps you find files and Web pages.

System Preferences. Lets you change your Mac's settings.

QuickTime Player. Plays video and music.

Mac OS X URL. Takes you to Apple's Mac OS X Web page.

Trash. Holds files you may be throwing away.

Desktop Printers

Figure 1.12

In Mac OS 9 and earlier, printers show up on the Desktop, just like hard-drive icons.

In Mac OS 9 and earlier, printers you've selected in the Chooser appear on the Desktop, and they're called Desktop Printers, logically enough. Desktop Printers take care of printing, letting you see what files you've sent to the printer and how those print jobs are going (**Figure 1.12**). If you don't see a Desktop Printer on *your* Desktop, don't worry; either Desktop Printing has been turned off on your Mac or you don't have a printer selected in the Chooser.

The Trash

Figure 1.13

The Trash is where you put files when you no longer want them on your hard drive. Mac OS X has updated the Trash's look and put it in the Dock.

The Trash in the lower-right corner of the screen is where you send files, folders, and programs when you want to erase them. You can do this by dragging the item to the Trash icon or pressing ⌘Delete (**Figure 1.13**). The Trash in Mac OS 9 and earlier doesn't always work so intuitively, though. When you want to eject a removable disk, you drag it to the Trash. Don't worry—this doesn't erase the disk. Instead, your Mac will eject the disk and remove it from the Desktop. Yeah, we didn't think that was too intuitive, either. (To eject a disk in Mac OS X, simply select the disk and then choose Eject from the File menu or press ⌘E. You can also drag it to the Trash to eject it.)

The Control Strip

Users of Mac OS 9 and earlier will probably also encounter one item that's not an icon—the Control Strip (**Figure 1.14**). Originally part of the system software created specifically for PowerBooks, the Control Strip is a little six-sided item at the bottom of your screen that floats over the Desktop as well as over any windows that happen to be near it. The Control Strip lets you change all kinds of system settings through various Control Strip modules—adjusting your Mac's audio volume and the monitor's color depth and resolution, turning file sharing off or on. Many third-party developers have created their own Control Strip modules, so don't be surprised to find some non-Apple controls lurking in there. In Mac OS X, there is no Control Strip; the Dock and menu bar items take over many of its duties.

Figure 1.14

Originally meant for PowerBooks, the Control Strip has become a useful widget for all Macs running Mac OS 9 and earlier.

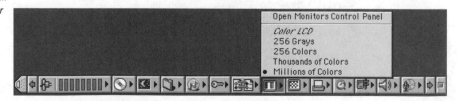

New Menu Bar Items

In Mac OS X 10.1, Apple added a handful of little widgets that show the status of your Mac and let you make minor system adjustments. These controls—reminiscent of Control Strip modules—control AirPort connections, handle speaker volume, show battery life on portables, display a clock, and control AppleScript. Clicking one of these widgets will reveal a menu full of actions that you can perform using it.

How Hard Drives Are Organized

The first time you start up a Mac with Mac OS 9 or later installed (but not Mac OS X), you'll find that the hard drive already contains some items. When you first open the hard-drive icon, you'll see three folders:

- The System Folder contains the system software that makes your Mac run.
- The Applications (Mac OS 9) folder (in Mac OS 9 only) holds programs.
- The Documents folder holds the documents you'll create—plus it has a few already in it.

You'll also see a fourth item called Late Breaking News, which contains information about Mac OS 9.1 or 9.2.1, or whichever version you have.

 Mac OS X also has some organizing folders preinstalled, and the structure of these is even more important to understand. It has five folders:

- The Applications folder holds your Mac OS X programs.
- The Library folder holds files your Mac needs to run properly, such as fonts, preferences, and even Web pages your Mac can serve up.
- The System folder holds your Mac's system software.
- The Users folder holds home folders for users of your Mac, including one with your name on it as well as one titled Shared, which users can share over a network. Folders in the Users folder allow individual users to have a secure place for files, fonts, and preferences. Other users who log in to the same Mac OS X computer can't get at the items in those folders. Inside each user's folder are several other folders that hold documents, movies, pictures, and music. Each folder also contains a Library folder, which contains fonts, sounds, screensavers, and other system-related items specific to that user.

    If you've installed Mac OS 9.2.1 with Mac OS X, you will also see several of its folders, including the System Folder and Applications (Mac OS 9) folder.

The Mac OS X Dock

The Dock in Mac OS X is a catch-all feature that has a bazillion functions. It serves:

- As a place to put aliases.
- As a status bar that shows all running programs and minimized windows.
- As a Control Strip replacement where you can quickly change your Mac's settings.
- As an area where you can add your own files and folders for quick and easy access.

The Dock looks like a series of icons in a translucent rectangle along the bottom or a side edge of your screen. The Dock is very customizable, too—you can change its size and hide it when it's not in use, and it can even magnify its icons for easier viewing when you pass the pointer over them.

When you add icons to the Dock, it grows horizontally to include the new items. If it grows large enough to reach the edges of the screen, it shrinks the size of the icons so that it fits onscreen. When you move the mouse over a Dock item, the item's name pops up above or beside it. We'll tell you more about the Dock later in this chapter in "Using The Dock."

Working with Icons

Now that you know what the various icons on your Desktop look like, it's time to find out what you can actually *do* with them. After all, these icons—combined with your mouse pointer—are the gateway to opening documents, arranging files, and the like.

Selecting Icons

Before you can do anything with an icon, you first have to select it. Once an icon is selected, you can apply a menu command to it, move it, or open it using the mouse. To select a single icon, you just click it—the icon will turn black to show it's selected. You have two other, often more useful, ways to select icons, especially when you want to select more than one.

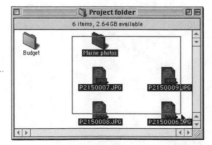

Figure 1.15

By dragging the pointer across several icons, you can select them all at once.

Drag-select. You can drag the mouse over an area to select several icons. To do this, click in an area of the window or Desktop where there are no icons and then drag the mouse over the icons you want to select. The pointer will draw a rectangle (a dark gray outline in Mac OS 9 and earlier (**Figure 1.15**), a translucent gray box in Mac OS X), with one corner where you first pressed the mouse button and the diagonal corner connected to the mouse pointer. This selects all of the icons within or touching the rectangle, whether that means one icon or several hundred. If the window is too small to show all of a folder's contents, you can drag the pointer to the window's edge, scrolling the window to reveal more of its contents.

Shift-select. To select a group of icons you can't easily surround with a rectangle, in Mac OS 9 and earlier you can hold down [Shift] and then click the individual icons to select them. With [Shift] held down, every icon you click stays selected.

In Mac OS X this works a little differently. You can still use [Shift] in the manner described, but if you're viewing a window in list or browser view, this method selects every icon between the first two icons you click while holding down [Shift]. To cherry-pick only the icons you want to select in Mac OS X, you must hold down [⌘] while clicking.

Type a name. You can also select an icon by typing the first few letters of the icon's name—provided that the window containing the icon is in front. Once you have an icon selected in this manner, you can select the nearest icon in any of four directions—up, down, right, or left—by pressing the appropriate arrow key on your keyboard.

Moving Icons

Moving an icon (or a whole mess of icons once they're selected) is easy—just click the icon you want to move and then drag the pointer. The selected icon will follow the pointer as you move it. A translucent gray version of the selected icon will follow your pointer around, and when you release the mouse button, the icon will move to whatever location the pointer hovers over—whether that's another window or the Desktop. If you move an icon onto a folder, that icon goes inside that folder. If you drag an icon onto a different hard drive (or another volume), your Macintosh copies the file, folder, program, or even the entire volume onto that hard drive.

Opening Icons

Other than moving icons around onscreen (which, let's face it, gets boring after a while), most often what you'll do with icons is open them. To open an icon, you can click it, then select Open from the File menu ([⌘O]). More commonly, though, you'll open an icon by double-clicking it. Opening an icon means different things depending on what *kind* of icon you have selected.

Volumes and folders. If you open a folder or volume icon, your Mac will present you with a window that shows all of the files and folders *inside* the icon you just opened. (The same is true of the Trash, incidentally.)

Program icons. If on the other hand, you open a program icon, your Mac will start running that program. There will be a pause of a few seconds—sometimes longer—as the program goes through the process of setting things up. In Mac OS 9 and earlier, you can't do much during that pause; in Mac OS X, though, you can go on working in other programs while one is launching. We'll cover this in depth in "Launching and Quitting Applications."

File icons. Opening a file icon releases a one-two punch that no other operating system can match in terms of accuracy. When you open a file (or document) icon, your Mac first launches the program that created the file. Next, the program reads the file you opened, making it ready for you to work on. There are some differences between how this works in Mac OS 9 and in Mac OS X, which we'll discuss in "Launching and Quitting Applications."

Aliases. Opening an alias is the same as opening the original file from which you created the alias.

Desktop printers. Opening a Desktop Printer in Mac OS 9 and earlier brings up a specialized window that shows all of the items currently printing and gives you the opportunity to pause or cancel the print job—handy when you've sent that 65-page manifesto to your printer by mistake.

Renaming Icons

Unlike your parents, your Mac doesn't stick you with a set of names you have to live with. Instead, you can change the moniker attached to almost any icon to pretty much any name you like. The only limitations you face are the colon and the slash—in Mac OS 9, you can't use the colon; in Mac OS X, you should stay away from the colon and the slash in filenames. That's because they're reserved by Mac OS to denote path names—that is, the path from a hard drive's name through folders to a given file or folder.

Figure 1.16

When you're renaming an icon, your pointer will change to show you the name is editable. You can use the pointer to select portions of the name to change.

To change an icon's name, click the icon to select it and then press [Return] or [Enter]. The icon's name changes from white text in a black box to black text in a colored box, usually blue. (We can't be too specific here because you can change the color of selected text—it's blue by default.) At that point, the icon's name is editable, and you can change it to whatever you like. You can also click the icon's name—after a short pause, it becomes editable. How can you tell? Again, instead of white text on a black rectangle, you see black text on a colored rectangle. (The color of this rectangle may vary if you've done some customization.) The pointer changes from the arrow-shaped pointer into the I-beam. This lets you know that you can select and edit the text underneath the pointer (**Figure 1.16**).

This colored text is selected, which means you can change it by typing or by using menu commands. When you start typing, the selected text will disappear, and whatever you type will replace it. If you only want to change part of an icon's name, you need to select that portion of the name using the I-beam pointer. With the icon's text selected and editable, drag the pointer over the portion of text you want to change—whether it's a single letter or every bit except for a letter at one end or the other. Now when you type, you'll replace only the selected portion of the text.

A few mouse moves can help out with shortcuts for text selection:

Click. A single click in editable text places a vertical black line (the insertion point) in the text where you click. This insertion point is where new letters will appear when you type them. If you put the insertion point to the left of any text, you'll push that text further to the right as you type. You can also use the arrow keys on your keyboard to move the insertion point up or down one line (by pressing ⬆ or ⬇, respectively), or left or right one character (by pressing ⬅ or ➡, respectively).

Double-click. A double-click when you're using the I-beam pointer selects the whole word underneath the pointer. In most programs (including the Finder), this only selects the word—it doesn't select any spaces before or after the word.

Drag. As we mentioned before, dragging involves holding down the mouse button while moving the pointer. With text, you'll start selecting where you first click the mouse button, and you'll end the selection when you release the button. You can select up, down, left, or right from your starting point.

 A triple-click when you're using the I-beam pointer selects an entire line or even an entire paragraph of text, depending on the program you're using. In the Finder, however, it acts like a double-click, selecting only a single word.

 If you've totally messed up an icon's name while editing it and you want to return it to its previous name, select *all* of the name's text, press Delete, and then press Return. Since you can't have an unnamed file, the Finder changes the icon's name back to the previous one.

 Macintosh filenames are case insensitive—that is, your Mac sees the names "My great American novel" and "mY GREat amerIcaN NOVEl" as the same. It doesn't distinguish between uppercase and lowercase letters.

Of course, there are some differences between naming files in Mac OS 9 and earlier and in Mac OS X. Here are the basics:

Mac OS 9 and earlier. Icon names in Mac OS 9 and earlier are limited to 31 characters, so although you can be somewhat descriptive, you can't write a novel underneath a folder's icon. Also, file extensions don't mean much to this OS, so you can give an icon any file extension you want—for example, you could give a word-processing document a .jpg extension—without risk of confusing your Mac—unless you take the file to a computer running Mac OS X or Windows. (A file extension is a three- or four-letter chunk of text that stands for what kind of file it is—for example, .jpg after a file's name indicates that it's a JPEG image file.)

Mac OS X. Icon names in Mac OS X can be very, very long. In fact, they can be much longer than you'd probably ever want, so you don't have to worry about running out of space. What you *do* have to worry about, at least a bit, is file extensions. The reason for worry is that Mac OS X uses these to under-stand what kind of item (a folder, file, program, and so forth) a given icon is. File extensions, which consist of a period followed by three or four characters tacked on the end of the filename, help Mac OS X launch the correct program to handle a given file when you open it.

This means if you create a new folder and give it the name My Poetry.jpg, Mac OS X will tell you that adding the .jpg extension to the name means the system may interpret the item as an image file—not a folder. And you may not get a warning, either. So be careful when you add file extensions or you may get unexpected results, such as Preview launching when you double-click your word-processing document. Here is a brief list of file extensions you might come across:

File Extensions

.app	Tells Mac OS X the item is actually an application or program. Mac OS X won't let you give an item the .app file extension on a whim, so you can't easily turn a folder into a program—and that's a good thing. (You won't often see this extension.)
.rtf	Indicates a Rich Text Format file, used by word-processing pro-grams to store text and information on how to format that text.
.pdf	Indicates a Portable Document Format file, a document that looks the same no matter what computer you view it on—Mac OS, Windows, or Unix.
.jpg or **.jpeg**	Indicates a JPEG image, commonly found in digital photos and on Web pages.
.gif	Indicates a GIF image, also popular on Web pages.
.tif or **.tiff**	Indicates a TIFF image, used mostly in print graphics.

Beware of using the forward slash (/) character when creating file or folder names in Mac OS X. Mac OS X's Unix underpinnings use this character to define file paths, basically lists of nested folders that show in which folders a file is located, such as Macintosh HD/Users/bill/myfile.doc. Although using a slash in Mac OS X icon names won't crash your computer, it *may* cause some

weirdness—for example, you may create new folders without meaning to—so you should avoid it. In Mac OS 9 and earlier, a similar problem arises when you use a colon (:) in a filename, because the colon does the same thing in the older OS that a slash does in Mac OS X. In Mac OS 9 and earlier, though, the Finder changes any colons you try to use into hyphens to avoid the problem altogether.

Using the Trash

The Mac OS Trash is where you put files and folders you want to remove from your hard drive. In Mac OS 9 and earlier, the Trash looks like a svelte little receptacle with its lid neatly on top—that is, when it's empty. Drop an item *in* the Trash (either by dragging it onto the Trash icon or selecting it and pressing ⌘Delete), and the can's lid appears by its side, while the can itself appears to be overflowing with garbage. That indicates you've got something in the Trash waiting for erasure from your hard drive (**Figure 1.17**).

Figure 1.17

Whether you're in Mac OS 9 or Mac OS X, the Trash's appearance changes to let you know when there's something inside it, waiting for deletion.

Just putting an item in the Trash doesn't delete it. You have to tell your Mac specifically that you want to erase the item by emptying the Trash. To do so, choose the Special menu in Mac OS 9 and earlier and the Finder menu in Mac OS X, then Empty Trash, and your Mac will ask if you're really sure you want to delete permanently the items in the Trash. If you really want to go through with it, click OK, and your Mac removes the offending items from your hard drive forever. If you've changed your mind, click Cancel, and the files remain in the Trash.

 If you're using Mac OS 9.1 or later (including Mac OS X) and you want to empty the Trash with a keyboard command, press ⌘Shift Delete.

If you've decided you just can't live without an item you've thrown in the Trash, you can still retrieve it—that is, if you haven't yet emptied the Trash as described above. To go Dumpster diving and retrieve the item, open the Trash icon by either double-clicking it or selecting it and choosing Open from the File menu. The Trash pops open like any other window, and you can drag the contents wherever you like.

 Your Mac can put files back where they belong with one simple command: in Mac OS 9 it's Put Away, which you will find in the Special menu; in Mac OS X it's Undo Move or Redo Move, found in the Edit menu. In Mac OS 9 and earlier, to put an item or items currently in the Trash back where they came from, select them and choose Put Away from the Special menu.

The Mac OS X Trash is very similar to the one in Mac OS 9 and earlier, except that it always appears in the Dock. Otherwise it behaves the same way, showing wrinkled papers inside the icon when it holds items waiting for deletion, and you can open it to drag items out. Because it's in the Dock, though, you can open it with a single click. To empty the Trash in Mac OS X, from the Finder menu select Trash (or press ⌘ Shift Delete).

Once you empty the Trash, its contents are gone forever. There's no Undo command, and there's no easy way to get those files back. A few utility programs, such as Symantec's Norton Utilities for Macintosh (www.symantec.com), *can do* the job with some degree of success, but even that method isn't guaranteed to work.

Ejecting Disks

Desktop Macs—from the earliest models to the latest G4—have some sort of removable media, which simply refers to a disk or volume you can unmount and remove from your computer. (Unmounting simply means taking a volume's icon off the Desktop.) For older Macs, it's the floppy disk; for newer ones, it's the CDs and DVDs. In either case, the method for removing a disk from your Mac is simple, if unintuitive, in Mac OS 9 and earlier—drag it to the Trash can. Don't worry—this won't erase the disk. Instead, it will unmount the volume and eject the disk from your computer. You can also eject a selected removable disk by choosing Eject Disk from the Special menu or by pressing ⌘ E.

Ejecting a disk in Mac OS X is the same as in Mac OS 9 and earlier. You either drag the disk icon to the Trash or select the disk's icon and then choose Eject from the File menu. The Trash icon in Mac OS X will change to an eject-button icon when you're dragging something that can be ejected. This helps eliminate confusion.

Working with Windows

The Mac OS uses *windows* to let you look at an item's contents, whether that item is a folder, a volume, or even a file. Windows frame the contents of a folder or file, and controls nestled in that frame let you manipulate a window by changing its size, closing it, or moving its contents around to view whatever you like.

Anatomy of a Window in Mac OS 9 and Earlier

Although the Mac OS 9 window has been around in various forms for a long time, it hasn't changed a lot over the years. You'll find certain elements in every Finder window you open (**Figure 1.18**):

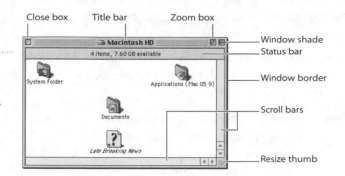

Figure 1.18

Mac OS 9 Finder windows offer a view on what's inside hard drives, folders, and files. Each window has several controls.

Close box. This small box in the top-left corner closes the window when clicked.

Title bar. This broad horizontal border along the top provides a solid handle with which you can drag the window around. The text in the title bar reflects the name of the folder or volume you're looking at. A small icon to the left of the text shows whether the window represents a volume, a folder, the Trash, or a Desktop Printer. The small icon acts as a proxy icon—that is, if you drag the little icon in the title bar to a new place, you'll also move the item connected to that window.

Zoom box. This icon on the right side of the title bar, which looks like a box within a box, lets you quickly resize a window. Click it once, and the window resizes so it's big enough to show all of its contents, if possible. Click it again, and the window resumes its previous size. This behavior can be a bit confusing at first. If the window is too small to show everything, it will grow larger when you click the zoom box; if the window is larger than it needs to be to show everything, it will shrink when you click the zoom box.

Window shade. The rightmost box—the one with the horizontal bar through it—is the window-shade control, and clicking it will roll up the window so only the title bar is visible (known as *minimizing* a window). Click it again, and the window unrolls to its original size.

Status bar. This line of text below the title bar tells you at a glance how many items are in a given folder or volume and how much space is left on the hard drive that contains the window.

Scroll bars. Every window has two of these—one horizontal scroll bar and one vertical. You can use these to move the contents of a window around if it's not big enough to show all of the contents at once. (If all of a window's contents are visible, the corresponding scroll bar will be gray and inactive.) Each scroll bar has four elements: two Scroll arrows, the scroll-bar thumb, and the gray bar in which the scroll-bar thumb sits.

Resize thumb. This square with three diagonal lines in the lower-right corner resizes the window when dragged.

Window border. You can also use the thin gray border around the left, right, and bottom of a window to drag a window to a new location—just as you would do with the title bar.

Because programs have their own window resources, a given program's windows might be missing some—or all—of these features. In a few extreme cases (in most MP3 player programs, for instance), windows may not look like windows at all. They can look like sculptures, rocks—almost anything.

Pop-up Windows

You can view Mac OS 8 and 9 windows in two ways—as the standard windows we all know and love and as pop-up windows, which show up as tabs along the bottom of the screen. Pop-up windows aren't really all that different from regular windows, except that they're attached to the bottom of the screen. When you drag a window's title bar to the bottom of the Desktop, its outline will change shape—instead of a square window hanging off the bottom of the screen, it converts to a pop-up window, which has a tab at the top instead of a menu bar.

When you release the mouse button after this transformation, the window's title bar snaps to the lower edge of the screen, showing nothing but the window's title and icon on a tab at the bottom of the desktop. Click the tab (or drag an item onto the tab), and the window pops up into view, showing its contents (**Figure 1.19**). Click the tab again (or move something *out* of the window), and the window snaps shut, showing just its tab once more. If you'd rather have your old standard window back, drag the window's tab up and away from the bottom of the screen.

Figure 1.19

Pop-up windows attach themselves to the bottom of the screen, and instead of title bars, they have tabs. Clicking a pop-up window's tab makes it jump up, revealing its contents.

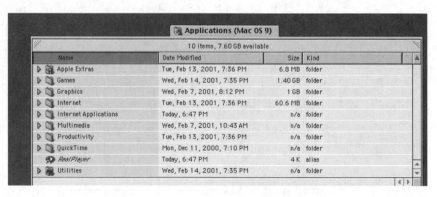

You can make just about any Finder window (including a Desktop Printer window) into a pop-up window by dragging it to the proper location. You can also use the View menu to change a regular window into a pop-up window and vice versa: In the View menu, select As Window or As Pop-up Window.

Anatomy of a Window in Mac OS X

The user interface for Mac OS X—called Aqua—does introduce some new features to the Macintosh window (or at least they *look* new). Instead of the tried-and-true square boxes that Mac OS 9 and earlier provides to handle basic window operations, Mac OS X windows have candylike round widgets (**Figure 1.20**). Here's a look:

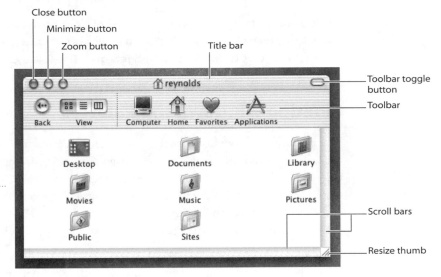

Figure 1.20

Mac OS X's sleek, rounded windows contain even more controls than their Mac OS 9 counter-parts.

Close button. The red button in the upper-left corner is the close box. Click it to close the window.

Minimize button. The yellow button shrinks the window and moves it to the Dock at the lower edge of the screen, using an impressive effect that looks like a genie coming out of (or going into) a bottle. This is called the Genie Effect, as you might have guessed.

Zoom button. The green Mac OS X zoom button works like the Mac OS 9 and earlier zoom box. It's a quick way to resize a window to the smallest possible size at which you can still see all of its contents. Click the zoom button a second time, and the window returns to its original size.

Title bar. The Mac OS X title bar shows the name of the currently open item. You can move the window by dragging its title bar—in Mac OS X, you can't drag a window by grabbing the side or bottom borders.

Toolbar. The toolbar is full of buttons that give you quick access to various folders and commands. It is customizable—you can change what buttons appear there. See the "Mac OS X Window Toolbar" sidebar below for more information.

Toolbar toggle button. This button toggles the window's toolbar on and off.

Scroll bars. Mac OS X scroll bars work just like their counterparts in Mac OS 9 and earlier except they're now three-dimensional and colorful. These scroll bars can move a window's contents if it's not big enough to show everything. Each scroll bar has four elements: two scroll arrows, the scroll-bar thumb, and the gray bar in which the scroll-bar thumb sits.

Resize thumb. Mac OS X windows also have a resize thumb in the lower-right corner that you can use to change the size of a window.

 Don't count on Mac OS X window button colors to be the same on every Mac—learn their positions as well. Apple has also introduced a Graphite color scheme that turns all of the widgets gray. They always appear in the same places, though.

Floating Windows and Palettes

Not all Macintosh windows look and act like standard windows. There is a class of Mac window called a *floating window* (sometimes referred to as a palette). Floating windows often resemble regular windows (with a menu bar, close box, zoom box, and window-shade controls for Mac OS 9 and earlier, and close, minimize, and maximize buttons in Mac OS X), except that all of their elements are smaller (**Figure 1.21**).

Floating windows float above all other windows (hence the name). That means you can't cover up floating windows with other windows from the same application—floating windows always end up on top. Floating windows are typically filled with buttons, text boxes, pop-up menus, and other controls—they constitute a tool palette (hence the *other* name). (Not all floating windows are control palettes; some display chat text or a string of news headlines.) These windows float above other windows so the controls they contain are always accessible.

Figure 1.21

Whether they allow quick access to formatting controls (left) or display a list of all the programs you can quit (right), floating windows maintain a position above all others because of their importance.

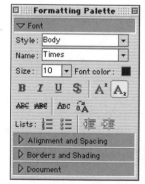

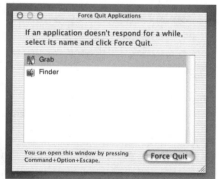

Opening and Closing Windows

Opening a window is a piece of cake—just double-click any icon other than a document or application icon, and a window will open, showing you what's inside the item. Closing a window is just as easy—click the window's close button (or press ⌘W), and the window will close.

 If you hold down the Option key while closing a window, *all* the open windows close. This little tidbit works in both Mac OS 9 and earlier and Mac OS X.

Moving and Resizing Windows

To move a window, drag it by its title bar to its new location and then release the mouse button. In Mac OS 9 and earlier, a rectangular outline will represent the window as you drag it. This is a holdover from many years ago when the Mac just didn't have the processing horsepower to draw the window as it moved (and redraw all the areas behind the window erased by its passing). Dragging an outline saves graphics power. In Mac OS X (and with very fast modern computers), there's no need to conserve power like that. The window moves along with the mouse pointer when dragged—no outline necessary.

 Windows can be layered on top of each other so that one window partly or totally covers another window. If you want to move a window that's behind another window without disturbing this stacking order, hold down ⌘ and drag the window. It will stay in its place in the stack while you drag it. This trick works in both Mac OS 9 and earlier and Mac OS X.

To resize a window, drag the resize thumb in the bottom-right corner of the window. In Mac OS 9, a dotted outline will form, showing the size of the window as it will be when you release the mouse button; in Mac OS X, the window itself resizes as you drag the thumb. The reasons for this are the same as the reasons for the old outline mode of dragging a window—faster computers and modern operating systems have made it possible to do *live resizing*.

Minimizing Windows in Mac OS 9 and Earlier

In Mac OS 9 you can minimize windows (or make them take up less screen real estate) by clicking the window-shade control in the upper-right corner. Clicking this item causes the window to roll up so that only its title bar is visible. This trick is incredibly useful if you need to move a window out of the way but don't want to close it or move it offscreen entirely. To unroll a minimized window, click the window-shade widget again, and the window will return to normal.

 The Appearance control panel in Mac OS 9 has an option that allows double-clicking a window's title bar to trigger the window-shade effect.

Minimizing Windows in Mac OS X

In Mac OS X you can also move windows quickly out of the way, but you do so differently than in Mac OS 9 and earlier. In Mac OS X, clicking the minimize button (the yellow button on the left side of the title bar) makes the window shrink down to squeeze itself in the Dock. Once the window has assumed its place in the documents and folders area of the Dock, it stays there until you click it again, at which time it resumes its former position. The plus side to this new minimization method is that it clears up a cluttered screen quickly. The minus side is that you can't manipulate the windows when they're minimized.

Apple has put a lot of effort into minimizing windows, and it works so well with high-powered machines that QuickTime movies will continue to play even while you're squeezing them down into a Dock-size square.

If you want to see the Genie Effect in slow motion, hold down ⎇Shift⎇ **when you click the Minimize button. Great fun at parties!**

Zooming Windows

The zoom box lets you quickly resize a window so you can see all of its contents without having to scroll. A second click returns the window to its original size and shape. This can get a bit confusing. Most of the time, clicking a zoom box in a window that's too small will make it get bigger so you can see what's inside. However, if you click a zoom box in a window that's already larger than is necessary to display all of its contents, it will actually shrink to the minimum size required. So clicking a zoom box can make a window grow or shrink, depending on its state when you click it.

If you want to enlarge a window so that it takes up almost the entire screen, hold down ⎇Option⎇ **while clicking the zoom box.**

Scrolling Windows

Unless a window has relatively few items in it, you'll probably have to scroll it to see all of its items. Scrolling moves the window's contents up, down, left, or right, depending on which scroll controls you click. Each window has two scroll bars, a vertical one and a horizontal one. The vertical scroll bar scrolls the contents up and down, and the horizontal one scrolls the window right and left. A window's contents have to be too large for viewing in a given direction (horizontally or vertically) to make that scroll bar active.

You have three ways to scroll a window's contents (**Figure 1.22**). Clicking a scroll-bar arrow scrolls the window in that direction just a little bit, and pressing a scroll arrow makes the window's contents scroll by at a moderate clip until you release the mouse button. Clicking the gray bar between the scroll arrow and the scroll-bar thumb makes the window's contents move faster than clicking, and pressing that area (clicking and holding) makes the window's contents fly by at breakneck speed. Dragging the scroll-bar thumb along the scroll bar makes the contents scroll by as fast or as slowly as you drag the thumb; this is called *live scrolling*.

Mac OS X uses a proportional scroll-bar thumb to indicate how much of a window's contents you're viewing. The larger the scroll-bar thumb, the more of the window's contents you can see. Mac OS 9 and earlier *can* use proportional scroll-bar thumbs, but you have to set that option in the Appearance control panel.

Figure 1.22

Scroll bars are made up of three parts: the scroll arrows, the scroll bar thumb, and the space between the arrows and the thumb. Clicking in any of these areas will result in scrolling.

 You can also "grab" a window's contents in Mac OS 9 and earlier by holding down ⌘ and dragging any part of a window's contents—as long as you don't click an icon. When dragging the mouse in this state, you'll drag the window's contents around.

Window Views

Windows let you look at things in several ways. By default, you see a window's contents as a series of icons you can place just about anywhere. But that's not the only way you can look at a window's contents—it's like a Zen painting that way. You can view a window in icon, small icon, list, or button mode, and Mac OS X also has its own special browser view mode. Each mode has its advantages in particular situations, but you can use any mode you like at any time.

Icon view. This is the default view that made the Macintosh famous—a series of squarish pictures that represent actual files, programs, and folders. In Mac OS 9 and earlier, these icons are 32 by 32 pixels; in Mac OS X, they're much larger, a maximum of 128 by 128 pixels (**Figure 1.23**).

Figure 1.23

Icon view is best used when a folder only contains a few items—otherwise you might get confused or lose files in a sea of icons.

List view. List view puts a window's contents into a vertical list using small icons (**Figure 1.24**). This view shows lots of information, such as the sizes and the last modification dates of items, in columns, and you can sort the lists by clicking a column. You can also resize columns in a list view by dragging the edge of each column. Folders appear in the list view with a small triangle (called a *disclosure triangle*) next to them. If you click a folder's triangle, it reveals that folder's contents in the same list without opening a new window. In Mac OS 9 and earlier, a window in list view has a button in the upper-right corner resembling a small pyramid of horizontal lines. When clicked, this button reverses the window's sort order so that, for example, a list sorted by filename will read from *Z* to *A*. Clicking it again sets things right. You can achieve the same effect by clicking the column name in Mac OS X. This flips the window's sort order and also flips a little triangle in the column name to let you know that the sort order has changed.

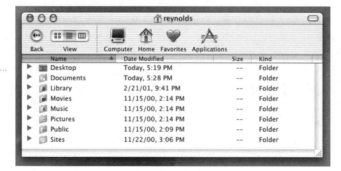

Figure 1.24

If you have more than a few items in a folder, consider using the list view, which provides built-in organizational tools.

Button view (in Mac OS 9 and earlier only). The button view looks a lot like the icon view, except that the icons sit on a slightly larger gray square (**Figure 1.25**). Buttons take just a single click to open, so if you want to select a button, you'll have to draw a box around it with the pointer.

Browser view (in Mac OS X only). Mac OS X introduces the browser view, which actually has its roots in another operating system, NextStep. In the browser view, the window is divided into a series of columns that show the file path (the series of nested folders) leading to the selected item (**Figure 1.26**). The column series starts with the hard drive on the left and works its way through the folders you click, expanding toward the right to show you the selected item's contents. One really cool thing about the browser view is that you're never more than a couple of clicks away from any folder on your hard drive, and you don't have to keep more than one window open at a time. A second, even cooler thing is that you get a preview of selected files (such as text documents, pictures, or even movies) right in the browser view.

Figure 1.25

For times when you want to access items with a single click, the button view (unique to Mac OS 8 and Mac OS 9) is the way to go.

Figure 1.26

The browser view is unique to Mac OS X. It lets you view your entire hard drive's folder structure in a single window. When you select a file, it gives you a preview of that file. It will even play back QuickTime movies.

You can change the size of icons in the icon view in both Mac OS 9 and earlier and in Mac OS X. In Mac OS 9 and earlier, choose View Options from the View menu. This brings up a window where you can select small or large icons. (It also lets you customize many other aspects of the window display.) In Mac OS X, choose Show View Options from the View menu. This also brings up a view-customization window in which you can change the size of a window's icons using a slider control.

To change views in Mac OS 9 and earlier, just choose the kind of view you want to use from the View menu; to change Mac OS X views, you can either click the icons in the window's toolbar or select the type of view you want from the View menu.

The Mac OS X Window Toolbar

Every window in Mac OS X has a set of buttons held in a *toolbar* along the top of the window. By default, the toolbar contains a couple of controls (a back button and three buttons that switch between icon, list, and browser views) and four buttons that "jump" a window to a new location—the Computer folder, the Home folder, the Favorites folder, or the Application folder. Clicking one of the jump buttons instantly moves the window to the new location, just as if you'd opened a window in that location.

The buttons along the top of the window don't have to be visible. If you want to get rid of them, click the oblong toggle button on the right side of the window's title bar.

If you don't like the arrangement of buttons in your windows, you can change which buttons appear there by choosing Customize Toolbar from the View menu. This makes the window larger and temporarily changes its contents to show all of the possible buttons you can drag on and off the toolbar. You can choose from 20 possible buttons and also select whether just buttons, just their names, or both buttons and names appear in the toolbar by selecting one of these options from a pop-up menu (**Figure 1.27**).

Once you've made all the changes you like to the toolbar, click the Done button at the bottom to return the window to the working state (so you can't accidentally change the buttons)—along with its shiny new toolbar. If you don't like the toolbar changes you've made, you can use the default button set at the bottom of the customization window to return things to their original state.

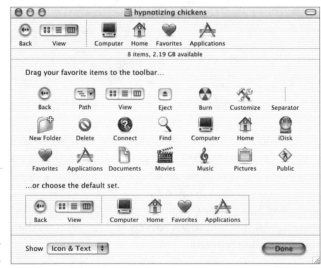

Figure 1.27

By dragging buttons from the special customization area into a Finder window, you can create a button bar to meet your needs.

Menus and Dialog Boxes

Menus and dialog boxes are the way you and your Mac talk to each other. You use menu commands (the individual items in a menu) to tell your Macintosh what you want it to do; your Mac uses dialog boxes to tell you what it's doing and ask for guidance now and then. You'll be using menus and dialog boxes for a fair bit of work on your Mac, so you need to become adept at using them. It's easy.

All About Menus

The menu bar across the top of the screen is home to all of your Mac's menus; each word in the menu bar is a menu. When you click a menu, it opens downward, revealing all of its individual menu commands or items. The Finder has its own menu bar, as does almost every program you launch. These menus contain commands appropriate for the program that's running—after all, it wouldn't make much sense to have the Finder's menus (which deal mostly with folders and files and systemwide services) when you're using a word processor to write a letter. When you switch to a different program, the menus in the menu bar change to reflect the new environment.

Figure 1.28

The Mac OS X File menu has a mix of enabled and disabled menu commands, and groups its commands into logical sections.

Menus organize menu commands into related groups, and typically a menu's title describes the relationship of the commands listed underneath it. For example, the File menu (which almost every Mac program, including the Finder, has) lists a series of commands for dealing with files—creating a new file, opening an existing file, or printing a file (**Figure 1.28**). In Mac OS 9 and earlier, programs also put the Quit command in the File menu, which doesn't make as much sense. In Mac OS X, the Quit command is in the Application menu. This organizational scheme also breaks down when a program uses a menu with a generic name, such as Tools, which serves as a catch-all for any menu command one might consider a tool, from spelling checks to e-mail account management. Still, Mac menus are remarkably consistent across the board, and if you're looking for a particular command, the menu's name will usually lead you to it.

In a general sense, there are two kinds of menu commands: those that require you to first select an item and those that don't care whether you have anything selected. Menu commands that require a selection—whether it's an icon, some text, or part of an image—act on whatever you have selected (for example, the Finder's Make Alias command makes an alias of whatever icons you have selected). Menu commands that don't require a selection, known as *global* commands, act on the currently running program or—in the case of the Finder—on the Mac itself (for example, the Shut Down command from the Mac OS 9 Special menu, which tells your Mac to turn itself off).

When you pull down a menu (by clicking it in the menu bar), it opens to reveal all of its commands. Aside from the short command phrases, you'll often see thin gray horizontal lines between groups of commands. These dividers organize a menu's commands into even smaller logical groups. For example, the third set of commands in the Mac OS 9.2.1 Finder's File menu—Find, Search Internet, and Show Original—are all about looking for an item, whether it's a file or folder on your hard drive, a specific Web page, or the original item to which an alias points.

 Some items in the menu bar aren't actually menus, such as the clock in the upper-right corner or the battery icon for PowerBook users. Although these items won't produce a list of menu commands when clicked, they might change functions. Click the clock in the Mac OS 9 menu bar, for example, and it shows the date briefly.

The Finder Menus

Over the years, Apple has added to and changed several items in the menu bar. With Mac OS 9.1, Apple settled on six menu items for the Finder: File, Edit, View, Window, Special, and Help (**Figure 1.29**). (The Window menu is new to Mac OS 9.1.) We'll be covering the Apple menu later, because of its unique status as a systemwide menu—it appears in all applications with menus, not just the Finder. Here's something about each of the others:

Figure 1.29

Mac OS 9.1's Finder menu bar boasts six menus—plus the ubiquitous Apple menu on the left. Earlier versions of the Mac OS are missing the Window menu.

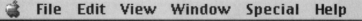

File. The Finder's File menu is chock-full of menu commands for working with files and folders. These commands let you create new folders, open and print documents, and find files and Web pages. The File menu also includes a cluster of commands for working with specific icons (to get more information about an item, give it a label, make a copy or alias of it, and other options).

Edit. The Edit menu is a short list of editing commands, such as cut, copy, paste, and clear. This menu is mostly for working with text and graphics in the Finder, which is limited primarily to icons and icon names. One curious thing: the Preferences command, nestled at the bottom of the menu, opens the Finder's Preferences window, in which you can change how the Finder behaves, otherwise known as editing the Finder's preferences.

View. Remember when we talked about the various views you can use in your Finder windows? This menu lets you select a view for a given window and contains some tools for cleaning up and arranging window contents in an orderly fashion. The View Options command at the bottom of this menu opens a window in which you can tweak and twiddle the look of a particular window.

Window. New to Mac OS 9.1, the Window menu displays a list of all open windows (including pop-up windows), putting a check next to the active window.

Special. The Special menu is a catch-all menu for commands that don't quite fit in with any of the other menus. Besides one file-related menu item—Empty Trash—most of its commands are actually System commands, affecting your entire Macintosh, not just files and folders. The Special menu commands let you eject and erase disks, shut down or restart your Mac, or even log out of your Mac (if you have it set up to handle multiple users).

Help. Short and sweet (at least when the Finder is the active program), the Help menu is your gateway to getting assistance with your Mac. From the Help menu, you can launch your Mac's Help Center (which contains all kinds of helpful information about the Mac OS and some of the programs installed on your Mac), plus you can zip directly to Macintosh tutorials or help files. This menu also lets you access balloon help, useful for finding out what a specific widget or menu does.

In Mac OS X, the Finder has seven menus: Finder, File, Edit, View, Go, Window, and Help (**Figure 1.30**). Here's an overview:

Figure 1.30

Mac OS X's Finder menu bar is home to seven menus as well. The system puts the Apple menu up on the left, and the Finder doesn't hold any sway over it.

Finder. The Finder menu is only visible when the Finder is the active program. That's because it's linked to the Application menu, a revamped menu in Mac OS X showing commands that work on the active program as a whole. The Finder menu lets you get some information about the Finder, set how the Finder behaves by changing its preferences, and hide and show the Finder (as well as other programs).

File. The old standby from Mac OS 9 and earlier, the File menu holds commands for dealing with files and folders in Mac OS X.

Edit. The Edit command is largely unchanged from Mac OS 9 and earlier. It holds commands (such as cut, copy, and paste) used when editing text, pictures, video, and audio. In Mac OS X, the Edit menu no longer includes the Finder's preferences as it did in Mac OS 9. It has a systemwide Undo command now too.

View. The Mac OS X View menu lists all of the possible view modes for a given window and contains options to clean up and organize windows as well as hide or show their toolbars. The Show View Options command at the bottom of the menu opens a window where you can tweak how views look.

Go. The Go menu connects your Mac to several locations, including the Home, Favorites, iDisk, Applications, Documents, and Users folders; plus it keeps track of any folders you've recently opened. Finally, the Go menu has a command called Connect to Server that opens a connection to a file server.

Window. The Window menu in Mac OS X is a little more evolved than the one introduced in Mac OS 9.1—besides listing the currently open windows, it also contains a command to minimize a window and a command to bring all the Finder's windows to the front.

Help. This menu gives you quick access to your Macintosh help.

Special Menus

As we mentioned earlier, Mac OS 9 and earlier and Mac OS X both have two menus that are worth a closer look—the Apple menu and the Application menu. These menus are present no matter what program is active. Although these menus go by the same name in both operating systems, they have different functions in each.

The Apple menu. In Mac OS 9 and earlier, the Apple menu is home to a potpourri of items, including small utility programs (such as the Calculator, AirPort utility software, and the Chooser) and special folders (which hold control panels, favorites, or recently opened programs). Accessing any one of these programs or folders (which act like submenus) is easy—just select it from the Apple menu, always visible in the upper-left corner of the menu bar. The Apple menu in Mac OS 9 and earlier is completely customizable—you can remove items and add new ones (Chapter 3 covers the specifics).

 In Mac OS X, the Apple menu is in the same place, but instead of the old six-color version popular in the 1980s and 1990s, the Mac OS X version is glossy blue. Instead of a mélange of gadgets and widgets, you'll find system-wide commands under the Mac OS X version of the Apple menu—such as setting your Mac's system preferences, controlling how the Dock behaves, and shutting down your Mac. Many of the commands here are taken from the Special menu in Mac OS 9.

The Application menu. In Mac OS 9 and earlier, the Application menu sits on the far right side of the menu bar, and its job is to list all running programs. You can switch between programs by selecting the one you want from the menu—the currently active one has a checkmark next to it. This menu also has three commands you can use to make running programs visible or to hide them, windows and all. These commands hide the currently open program, hide all other running programs, or show all hidden programs.

 You can tear off the Application menu in Mac OS 9 and earlier to form a floating window (or palette) by clicking the Application menu and dragging the pointer off the bottom of it while the menu is still pulled down, tearing off the menu. This palette, which floats above all other windows, has buttons that allow you to select each of the currently running programs.

 In Mac OS X, the Application menu is on the left side of the menu bar, and instead of showing a list of running programs (as it does in Mac OS 9 and earlier), it contains a list of commands that apply to the currently active program. In the Finder's case, these commands can open the Finder's preferences and hide or show the Finder and other running programs (**Figure 1.31**).

Figure 1.31

Although they share the same name, the Application menus in Mac OS 9 and in Mac OS X are two very different animals. They contain different commands and serve different purposes.

 So how *do* you see which programs are currently running in Mac OS X? For that you'll have to refer to the Dock. Running programs have a small upward-pointing black triangle at the bottom of their icons in the Dock.

Selecting a Menu Item

Selecting a menu item is a simple affair. Click the menu that contains the item you want to select (such as the Edit menu), and then move the pointer over the desired menu item. Moving the pointer over items in a menu highlights them one at a time. When the menu item you want is highlighted, click the mouse button a second time to execute the menu command.

 In older versions of the Mac OS (before Mac OS 8), menus weren't sticky— that is, they didn't stay down when clicked. To select a menu item, users had to click a menu and then keep holding down the mouse button while moving the pointer to the desired menu item, releasing the button only when the pointer was over the command. Otherwise, the menu would disappear.

The Common Menus

In Mac OS 9 and earlier, you'll see five menus almost all the time: the Apple menu, File, Edit, Help, and the Application menu. (There are exceptions to this, mostly games, but it's true in most cases.) The system software actually provides the Apple, Help, and Application menus, so they are almost always the same no matter what program is active. The Apple menu has a list of miscellaneous gadgets and folders available no matter what program is running. Help provides quick access to whatever help you need, such as balloon help or the Mac OS Help Center. (The Help menu changes its contents somewhat to provide help options specific to the active program, but some of its commands stay the same.)

Finally, the Application menu in the far-right corner of the menu bar can have one of two looks: either a small icon showing the currently active application or an expanded version (to get this, drag the vertical bar with four tiny dots in it to the left). The Application menu shows a list of currently running programs. Plus it has three commands at the top that let you hide the current program, hide all programs *except* the current program, or show all programs.

The File and Edit menus, also present in almost every program, work a little differently. The system software doesn't supply these menus—instead, each program provides its own File and Edit menus, so although they may *look* the same, they're customized to meet the needs of the active program.

Mac OS X has its own set of consistent menus that show up everywhere, and the list contains a few familiar entries: the Apple menu, Application, File, Edit, Window, and Help. The last four menus are similar to their counterparts in Mac OS 9.1 and 9.2.1 in that they show up in just about every program with a similar set of menu commands. However, the Apple and Application menus have changed. The Apple menu takes on the task that used to belong to the Special menu in Mac OS 9 and earlier—it handles system commands, such as starting up and shutting down your Mac. The Application menu no longer lists what applications are running. Instead, it takes on the name of the currently running program (such as the Finder) and provides commands appropriate to the program as a whole (such as changing its preferences, hiding or showing it, or quitting the program).

These changes to Mac OS X's menus make the menu commands a little more logical for new users. Old Mac hands may struggle with the new arrangement a bit before it becomes second nature.

Different Kinds of Menu Items

Although every line of text in a menu is a menu item, you'll find lots of variations. These include whether a menu item is selectable (that is, executable), as well as special characters that indicate how menu items work (**Figure 1.32**).

Enabled. Enabled menu items are menu commands you can execute at that moment. Sometimes you can't select a menu item because it's not appropriate for the situation—for example, a Save menu item isn't enabled unless you have a file open and therefore have something to save. Enabled menu items appear in solid black text.

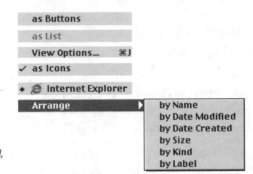

Figure 1.32

Menus are home to several kinds of menu items, and each item can have several characteristics. Some of these, from top to bottom, are: enabled, dimmed, ellipsis, checkmark, diamond, and submenu.

Dimmed. The flip side of the enabled menu item, a dimmed menu item (or disabled menu item) can't be selected, and thus turns gray. (That's where the term *dimmed* comes from.) Programs sometimes disable menu items or even whole menus when you can't use them in the situation at hand—for example, you can't use the Cut command from the Edit menu when you don't have anything selected, so Cut appears in a dimmed form.

Ellipsis. An ellipsis (…) at the end of a menu item means selecting that particular menu item brings up a dialog box, in which you can change some settings or tweak some controls. Usually that dialog box also contains a button to cancel any changes, so in effect you get a chance to change your mind before executing the command. Menu commands *without* ellipses take place immediately, with no intermediate dialog box.

Checkmarks. Some menu items are called *toggle items,* because selecting them toggles an option (such as guides in a page-layout program) on or off. These menu items use a checkmark to indicate whether the option is on or off. If a checkmark appears next to the item, the option it represents is turned on, and selecting the item turns the option off and makes the checkmark disappear. If there's no checkmark, selecting the menu item turns the option on and puts a checkmark next to that item.

Diamonds. Diamonds occasionally appear next to menu items that need your attention. This happens most often in the Application menu in Mac OS 9 and earlier, when a program requests that you switch to it (perhaps a dialog box has popped up while you were working in another program.) When this happens, a diamond appears to the left of the program's name.

Submenus. Sometimes a menu item encompasses too many options to fit neatly in a dialog box, or too *few* to justify a dialog box's existence. That's when you encounter a submenu. Submenus are indicated by right-facing triangles to the right of menu items; when you point to a such a menu item, another menu appears to its right. Submenus can have submenus of their own, although stacking too many menus in this fashion is considered bad form. To select an item in a submenu, click the menu that contains it, and then move the pointer over the submenu item until the second menu pops up to the right. Slide the pointer horizontally until you're in the submenu, and then move it over the desired menu item. Click the mouse button a second time over that item, and you're on your way.

If your Mac runs out of space along the right to display submenus, they'll appear on the *left* side of the menu, on top of whatever menu previously occupied that space.

Scrolling menus. When there are too many items to fit in the vertical space your Mac's monitor allows (sounds crazy, but it happens, particularly with the Fonts menu), menus take on the ability to scroll so you can see all of the available selections. A scrolling menu has a black triangle at the top or bottom (or both), showing which direction has more content (**Figure 1.33**). Holding the pointer over a triangle makes the menu scroll in that direction—slowly, if the pointer is near the center of the menu, vertically, or quickly, if the pointer is at the menu's upper or lower edge. To select an item in a scrolling menu, click the menu, scroll through the list by holding the pointer over the appropriate triangle until you reach the desired menu item, and then click that item.

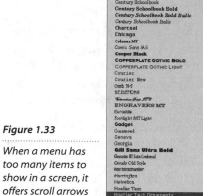

Figure 1.33

When a menu has too many items to show in a screen, it offers scroll arrows so you can scroll through its contents.

Keyboard Equivalents

You may have noticed something else in your menus that we haven't covered yet—letters and strange-looking characters to the right of some menu commands. These are called *keyboard equivalents,* and they let you issue menu commands directly from your keyboard. Each keyboard command has a letter preceded by one, two, or three of four basic symbols that stand for the keys you need to hold down while pressing a particular character on the keyboard. These four keys— ⌘, Option, Shift, and Control—are known as *modifier* keys. The most commonly used modifier for ⌘-key equivalents is the ⌘ key itself.

Most of the time, keyboard equivalents appear in menus with the ⌘ symbol and then a letter, which often stands for the command given (for example, ⌘S for Save). Sometimes, though, you'll see two or three of these symbols in a row before the letter. In this case, you have to press all

Key Command Symbols

⌘	Command
Control	Control
Shift	Shift
Option	Option

those keys simultaneously before you press the letter key. For best results when using keyboard equivalents, first press and hold the modifier key or keys. With those keys held down, press the appropriate letter. Your Mac executes the command as if you had selected the menu item itself.

Common Menu Commands

Thanks to nearly two decades of attention to human interface design, the Mac has an incredibly consistent set of controls across all of its programs, and this consistency goes down to the menu command level. Almost all programs—in Mac OS 9 and earlier and Mac OS X alike—share consistent menu items and keyboard equivalents. Here are several of the most common ones:

Common Menu Commands

Command	Keyboard Equivalent	What It Does
File, New	⌘N	Creates a new document. In the Finder, it creates a new folder.
File, Open	⌘O	Opens a document or an item.
File, Close	⌘W	Closes a document or window.
File, Save	⌘S	Saves a document. (The Finder doesn't have this command.)
File, Print	⌘P	Prints the active document or Finder window.
File, Quit	⌘Q	Quits the active program. (In the Finder, it logs out the current user.)
Edit, Undo	⌘Z	Undoes the last thing you did. This command is a lifesaver!
Edit, Cut	⌘X	Cuts the currently selected item and puts it on the Clipboard, removing the original item.
Edit, Copy	⌘C	Copies the currently selected item onto the Clipboard, leaving the original untouched.
Edit, Paste	⌘V	Pastes whatever is on the Clipboard into the currently active document.
Edit, Select All	⌘A	Selects everything in the currently active window.

Contextual Menus

Although we'd like to think the Macintosh side of personal computing had all of the good ideas, it's just not true. Occasionally Apple engineers borrowed a couple of user interface ideas from Windows, such as *contextual menus,* borrowed from the Windows right-click technique (in both Mac OS 9 and X).

A contextual menu is a menu full of options that apply to a specific item or location. These menus make selecting menu commands easier—you don't have to dig through various menus for them (**Figure 1.34**). To invoke a contextual menu, hold down [Control] (which adds a little rectangular object resembling a menu to the pointer's lower-right corner) and then click the object to see a

Figure 1.34

This contextual menu shows all of the menu commands you can apply to the [Control]-clicked folder.

list of commands you can apply to it. For example, in Mac OS 9, if you [Control]-click the Trash, a short menu of possible commands pops up right over it—commands such as Help (for help on using the Trash), Empty Trash (to erase its contents), and Add To Favorites (which puts the Trash in your Favorites submenu), among other commands. All of these commands work with the Trash, and you would have to go to three different menus to find them it weren't for contextual menus.

The Finder has built-in contextual menus, but not all Macintosh programs offer them, so you'll have to experiment by [Control]-clicking in your favorite programs. Don't worry if the pointer doesn't take on its familiar contextual-menu look when you press the [Control] key—some programs don't make this visual change even though they're capable of using contextual menus.

All About Dialog Boxes

Now that you've learned how to tell your Mac what to do with menu commands and double-clicks, it's time to learn how to listen to some feedback from your Mac. The primary way this happens is through dialog boxes, which serve a couple of purposes: to tell you about some event you may not know about (such as a program crashing in the background), and to solicit more information so your Mac can complete a task (such as printing a word-processing file).

Dialog boxes come in two major flavors: *modal* and *nonmodal*. Modal dialog boxes put your Mac in a specific mode, and they don't go away until you deal with them—by either dismissing them or providing the information they ask for. You can't get away from a modal dialog box until you fulfill its needs. A nonmodal dialog box is a friendlier dialog box (some might call it a pushover) that won't stop you from working on other things—it waits patiently in the background for you to get around to it, if you ever do. Most dialog boxes—especially in Mac OS X—are of the nonmodal variety. That's because modern operating systems strive not to come to a total halt for a single event, such as your Mac asking you how many copies of your party invitation it should print.

Outside these two groups, dialog boxes are difficult to categorize. They come in all shapes and sizes, from a screen-filling, show-stopping print dialog box, to a polite little floating window telling you your AppleTalk network has gone down, to a little speech bubble coming from Microsoft Office's animated Assistant.

Dialog Boxes Explained

Dialog boxes range from the dead simple to the hideously complicated, depending on what they're designed to do. A dialog box can contain anything from a few words of text (such as "Your AppleTalk network is now available") to an array of controls (such as pop-up menus, text boxes, buttons, check boxes, and so on), arranged to help you finish a complicated task such as printing a document (**Figure 1.35**). Here's a look at some of the items you might encounter inside a dialog box:

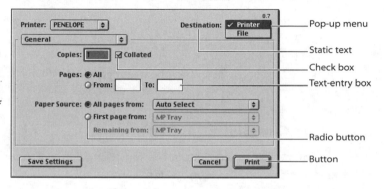

Figure 1.35

The Print dialog box contains a variety of controls you should become familiar with, because you'll see them in lots of other places.

Static text. This is plain-vanilla text that sits inside a dialog box. It's there to pass along a message from your Macintosh to you—such as the text "Your AppleTalk network is now available."

Text-entry box. If your Macintosh needs some information from you (such as the name or size of a font), you'll often respond in a text-entry field, typically a rectangle in which you type the information your Mac is looking for.

List box. A list box provides a place to show a list of items you can select, such as filenames in an Open dialog box. Typically, what you choose in a list box affects what happens when you dismiss the dialog box. List boxes resemble a Finder window in list view mode.

Buttons. These items look and work like their real-world counterparts on machines. Press a button to make something happen. Usually labels on the button itself (say, Print or Cancel) indicate what will happen.

Radio buttons. Radio buttons let you select a single item from a list of choices by clicking the button next to the choice you want. Clicking another button in the list deselects the first one and selects the one you click. Radio buttons take their name from the mechanical buttons on car radios. When you punched one to tune in a favorite radio station, the previously pushed button would come out because you can only tune in one radio station at a time.

Check box. A check box lets you choose one or more items from a list of choices by clicking the check boxes next to the ones you want. When you do so, a checkmark will appear in the box. You can choose as many check boxes in a group as you like.

Pop-up menus. Pop-up menus, like radio buttons, let you choose a single option from a list. You'll see pop-up menus instead of radio buttons in cases where the list of options is very long (more than three or four options). That's because pop-up menus take up a lot less space than a list of radio buttons—only one menu choice at a time has to be visible with a pop-up menu.

Tabs. These hang out at the tops of some dialog boxes, providing access to more than one set of controls. They work like the physical tabs found in reference books (dictionaries, for example), which let you quickly locate a new section in the book. In a dialog box, tabs group closely related controls in the same view, and they often appear in dialog boxes where you set preferences.

Save Clarus! (KR)

Longtime Mac users might notice something different in the Mac OS X page setup dialog box. The dogcow is missing.

This strange-looking half-dog, half-cow icon is familiar to Macintosh users worldwide as Clarus (all cows, by nature, are female). Some say Clarus first came to life in the late 1980s as a character in Apple's Cairo font. Others insist she didn't truly emerge as a dogcow until a few years later, when she started appearing in various page setup dialog boxes. Nevertheless, for the past fifteen years the humble dogcow has inspired underground mouse pads, t-shirts, wristwatches, fan Web sites, and a few irreverent Apple developer tech notes.

We hope Apple's Mac OS X team will reconsider Clarus's place in history and put her back in the Mac. Moof!

Dismissing Dialog Boxes

Dialog boxes pop up when you select a menu item with an ellipsis after it. This ellipsis indicates that the menu command will bring up a dialog box, because the menu command is too complex or has too many options for a simple menu command to suffice. Selecting such a menu item brings up a dialog box full of controls, which you tweak to customize the menu command you just issued. After you've finished fiddling with the controls in a dialog box, you have two ways to make it go away: by clicking either the OK button or the Cancel button along the bottom of the box. Clicking the OK button accepts all of the settings in the dialog box and then executes the menu command that brought it up in the first place, using your settings. Clicking the Cancel button cancels the menu command altogether—none of the settings you've changed take effect.

Dialog boxes have a default button, selected when you press (Return) on your keyboard. In Mac OS 9 and earlier, the default button is the one with the thick border around it; in Mac OS X, the default button is even harder to miss—it pulses blue (or gray, if you've changed your Mac OS X color scheme). The default button can be the OK button, Cancel button, or another button altogether, depending on what button would be picked most of the time.

Alerts

Alerts are specialized dialog boxes in which your Mac provides some vital bit of information, such as telling you a program has crashed or a network has become available. These dialog boxes don't pop up in response to a menu command you've selected; rather, they reflect your Mac's internal state of affairs. You might see a few types of alerts:

Alert. Before Mac OS 9 came on the scene, alerts occurred in three flavors: Stop, Caution, and Note. A Stop alert, which shows a red stop sign next to some text, comes up to alert you of a problem so big that your Mac can't complete an action. You dismiss Stop alerts by clicking the OK button at the bottom. A Caution alert, which shows a yellow caution triangle, pops up to tell you that something undesirable might happen if you continue, and gives you the option of continuing or canceling the action. A Note alert, with a Note icon (usually a face with some bubble text), comes up to tell you about a minor error or other bit of information that won't wreak havoc if left as is. Most Note alerts have a single OK button at the bottom that dismisses them, although a few have two or more buttons offering you a choice of actions to take.

Notification. A Notification alert—a small floating window with a gray border, a yellow background, and black text—pops up in the upper-right corner of the screen. This modeless Notification alert was introduced with Mac OS 9.0 and is produced by the notification manager. Notifications are reserved for times when your Mac (or some other program running in the background) has something to tell you—just like an old-style alert. (You can still encounter both kinds in Mac OS 9.) For example, when a previously unavailable AppleTalk network comes back online, it may send you a notification; a shareware program may use one to remind you to pay up. Notifications can also tell you that another program needs your attention—for example, when the Finder has noticed a program crash or when your e-mail program has received new messages. (When a background program asks for attention like this, a diamond will appear next to that program in the Application menu.) To dismiss an alert in a floating window, simply click its close box.

Mac OS X alerts. Alerts in Mac OS X are similar to Mac OS 9 alerts in that they give you information, tell you about minor problems, and alert you to major errors. Instead of popping up as windows as they do in Mac OS 9, Mac OS X alerts often slide out as sheets, a new kind of Mac OS X dialog box. At heart, though, they're still the same—a message from your Mac, an icon to tell you how serious the problem is, and a button (or two) with choices on how to deal with the alert.

Mac OS X Sheets

Mac OS X uses a slick new way of handling dialog boxes (such as Force Quit alerts or Save dialog boxes in which you save a file on your hard drive), called *sheets*. Sheets slide out from under a window's title bar, revealing the dialog box's controls. A sheet is always tied to the window where the action that brought it up took place. For example, when you save a document, a sheet slides out under the title bar of the window, showing the document you're saving (**Figure 1.36**).

Sheets are cleverly designed. If the window is too small to contain a sheet, the sheet enlarges as it comes out from under the title window until it reaches its full size. If the window is too close to the edge to allow display of the whole sheet, the window and the sheet slide to the right or left to make room for the whole thing.

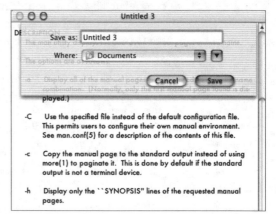

Figure 1.36

Instead of the old-fashioned Save dialog box in Mac OS 9, Mac OS X employs sheets to serve the same purpose. These sheets slide out from under the title bar, and you can expand them by clicking the downward-pointing arrow to reveal a file browser.

Beyond the Desktop

If the Macintosh consisted of just the Finder and the Desktop, it would amount to a very expensive and moderately amusing toy that would wear thin quickly. Fortunately, the Desktop and the Finder are just the start of things when it comes to using your Mac. They let you run programs, which is how you make *real* use of your Mac by sending e-mail, editing video, browsing the World Wide Web, writing short stories or papers, manipulating photos, and so on. The list of possibilities is nearly endless.

Commercial Software, Shareware, and Freeware—Paying for Software

There are lots of ways to differentiate the thousands of programs available for the Mac. One very useful way for those of us on a budget is according to how those programs are sold—whether they are commercial products, they are shareware programs, or they come free of charge.

Commercial programs are typically sold in computer stores or via mail-order catalogs, and they're almost always the most powerful programs in their categories. You pay for all that power, though—commercial programs are typically the most *expensive* in their categories as well. Commercial software is most often created by software companies (such as Adobe, Microsoft, and Macromedia) that employ lots of programmers to do the job—hence the high cost.

Shareware programs are usually smaller in scale and ambition than their commercial counterparts, mainly because they're most often the creations of individuals or very small groups who know how to write Macintosh programs. You can usually download shareware from the Internet or copy it from a CD-ROM and use it before you have to pay any money at all. Then, if you like the software (or find it useful), you register your shareware by paying for it.

It typically costs much less to register shareware than to purchase commercial software, but you face a couple of trade-offs. First of all, shareware is almost never as powerful as a commercial program in the same category. Second, shareware typically focuses on a specific task, not a general mode of working. For example, a shareware program might be great for creating text-only documents, but a commercial program might do that *and* let you lay out a newsletter, complete with multiple fonts and pictures. You often get what you pay for, but if you need a program for a specific task, shareware is a great way to go. (If you use shareware, don't be a chiseler: Pay the shareware fee.)

Freeware programs are generally programs that an individual (or a small group) writes and then gives away free of charge. Sometimes people release freeware as an act of kindness, as when a programmer recognizes the need for some bit of software, writes it, and gives it away. Other times, freeware forms part of a company's larger strategy, as in the case of Netscape Communicator and Microsoft Internet Explorer, both of which are Web browsers given away to gain some control over the Internet. Some freeware programs released by software companies fall in the category of player programs, used to play movies, music, and live Internet broadcasts.

Applications and Documents

Other than volumes (such as hard drives and CDs) and folders, you'll encounter two common kinds of items while using your Macintosh: applications and documents. Applications (also known as programs) are the active force behind all those wonderful things your Mac is capable of—they make things happen on your Mac.

Your Mac comes with several programs already installed on its hard drive that let you view Web pages, write text documents, watch movie clips, listen to

MP3-based music, and check your e-mail. These programs are just the tip of the iceberg—thousands more applications cover just about everything you can imagine when it comes to using your Mac. Companies and individuals other than Apple create most of these programs and sell them in software packages you can buy at your local Mac-friendly computer store.

Documents are the passive counterpart to applications—that's where you store information created using an application. You use applications on your Mac to create and change documents. Also commonly known as files, documents are where your Mac stores data of a specific kind, such as a digital photograph of your dog, that term paper you wrote last fall, or a QuickTime movie trailer of an upcoming blockbuster.

Not all programs create and edit documents. In games, you fire up a program just to play around, whether that means a rousing round of solitaire or a death match in Unreal Tournament. Most of the time, though, programs have the ability to open and save documents of some sort. This even applies to Web browsers. At first glance, you might think they don't do anything but browse the Web. However, what a Web browser actually *does* when it shows a Web page is open a special file (called an HTML file) that's sitting on another computer somewhere else on the globe. A browser operates via your modem and telephone line—or if you're one of the lucky folks with high-speed Internet access, your cable modem or DSL connection.

Classic, Carbon, and Cocoa

The two Macintosh operating systems in widespread use—Mac OS 9 and earlier and Mac OS X—have given rise to three flavors of applications that run on one or both operating systems. These application types are called Classic, Carbon, and Cocoa, and you should know a few things about each kind of program.

Classic. A Classic application is a program written to run in Mac OS 9 and earlier only—although almost all Classic programs will run in Mac OS X. When running in Mac OS 9 and earlier, Classic applications run normally; when running in Mac OS X, Classic applications have to run in a special *Classic environment*. Classic programs running in Mac OS X don't have Mac OS X's new features, such as its rounded buttons and stylish windows, or the crash protection and responsiveness that other application types—such as Carbon and Cocoa—have.

Carbon. A Carbon application is a Classic application that has been modified to run in Mac OS X and take advantage of its new user interface, crash protection, and responsiveness. The beauty of Carbon applications (also called Carbonized applications) is that they run in Mac OS 9 just fine. Carbon applications offer the best of both worlds.

Cocoa. A Cocoa application (yes, the name is a bit goofy) is an application written specifically for Mac OS X. While it benefits from Mac OS X's new user interface, crash protection, and improved responsiveness, a Cocoa application can't run at all in Mac OS 9 and earlier. Few programs are Cocoa applications, and many of those ship with Mac OS X.

We'll be talking more about Classic, Carbon, and Cocoa programs, as well as the Classic environment, in Chapter 3. We'll also show you how to tell the difference between Classic applications and newer Carbon and Cocoa applications.

Launching and Quitting Applications

To use a program, you'll first need to launch—or open—it. There are a couple of ways to do this:

- Double-click the application icon.
- Select the application icon, and choose Open from the File menu or press ⌘O.

Either approach works whether you're using Mac OS 9 and earlier or Mac OS X, and they result in the same basic event—your Mac will start running the selected program.

In Mac OS 9 and earlier, when a program launches, the first thing you'll see is a rectangle that zooms out in all directions from the application's icon, and then the name of the program you just launched will appear in the menu bar. During this time, the freshly launched program initializes—that is, it creates its menus, sets up special structures in your Mac's memory, and generally gets things ready. Once that's done, the program's name shows up in the Application menu, its menus appear in the menu bar, and any windows the program uses—including palettes or blank document windows—pop up. While a program is busy launching, you can't do anything else with your Mac—you have to wait for initialization to complete.

You launch an application in Mac OS X the same way as in Mac OS 9 and earlier. Select the program you want to launch, and select Open from the File menu (or press ⌘O). You can also double-click the program's icon. Once this happens, the application initializes (by building menus and creating structures in memory) and then puts its menu bar across the top. While a program is launching in Mac OS X, its icon appears in the Dock, bouncing up and down like a rubber ball on concrete. Once a program has finished launching, a small black triangle appears under or next to the icon in the Dock to indicate that the app is active.

Program icons may appear in the Dock even if those programs aren't running. That's because the Dock serves as a placeholder for icons of all types—programs, documents, and folders. If you've already put a program's icon in the Dock for easy access, it will start jumping up and down immediately when clicked (or when you otherwise launch the program).

There's one other way to launch a program, and that's by opening a document. When you open a document (by double-clicking it, by selecting it and choosing Open from the File menu, or by pressing ⌘O), this signals your Mac to open the program that created the document (or at any rate, one that *can* open the document). Once that program is running, it opens the document in a new window so that you can view it, print it, or work on it.

Finally, you can open a document by dragging it onto the icon of a program that can open it (for example, dragging an image document onto PictureViewer, a program for viewing pictures.) This method, called *drag and drop,* launches the program, which in turn opens the document. This way you can choose which program opens a given document.

Once you've launched a program and are done working with it, you should probably *quit* it. Quitting programs frees up memory and processor power and guards against crashes (at least when working in Mac OS 9 and earlier; Mac OS X manages its resources differently so quitting isn't quite so important but still recommended). To quit a program you're no longer using, select Quit under the File menu in Mac OS 9 and the Application menu in Mac OS X or press ⌘Q, which sends a quit command to the currently active program (the one whose menus appear in the menu bar). The program will stop running, freeing up any memory or other resources on your Mac that it may be using. If you have any unsaved documents open (or you've made changes to those documents since you last saved), the program will ask if you want to save before quitting.

Using the Launcher

Mac OS 9 and earlier has a simple way to help you open programs, files, and even folders—the Launcher, a small program that keeps a single window open. This window, which looks like a standard Finder window, holds a series of buttons with icons taken from documents, folders, and applications on your hard drive. Click a button in a Launcher window, and the program, document, or folder represented by that icon opens. It only takes a single click to launch a program from the Launcher, as opposed to the double-click required to open a standard application icon. That's because the items in a Launcher window are actually buttons, not icons (**Figure 1.37**).

Figure 1.37

With the click of a button in the Launcher, you can open any program or document that has an icon in its window.

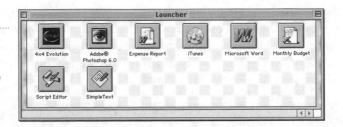

You can add your own buttons to the Launcher so it offers access to the applications, folders, and documents you use most. To add a button to the Launcher, drag an item to the open Launcher window. A button with the item's name and icon appears in the window—the original item stays put, so you won't actually be moving it with this little drag operation. The Launcher window arranges items in alphabetical order.

To remove a button from the Launcher, drag it *by its name* to the Trash. The button will disappear from the window. If you try to drag the item out of the window by grabbing the button itself, you'll be disappointed—the button won't drag. If you drag the button elsewhere (that is, not to the Trash), an alias to the original item will appear where you release the mouse button, but the Launcher button will disappear from the Launcher window.

The Launcher doesn't appear by default on your Mac—you have to turn it on. To do so, open the General Controls control panel by choosing the Apple Menu, then Control Panel, then General Controls, and check the box next to the "Show Launcher at system startup" item. The next time you start your Mac, the Launcher window will appear.

Using the Dock

Besides handling a host of other features, the Dock in Mac OS X serves as a quick-access placeholder for icons of all kinds—folders, applications, and documents alike. You can open items in the Dock with a single click rather than a conventional double-click.

When you start up your Mac the very first time, icons for various programs and documents already on your hard drive fill the Dock. You can add your own by dragging items to the Dock—programs go on the left side of the thin white vertical line; documents and folders go on the right. If you try to drag an item to the wrong side of the Dock, the icons won't move aside and the Dock won't accept the item. When you drag an item to the Dock, the icons already there slide aside to make room for the new item. The icon is actually an *alias* to the original item, which stays put. Once an item has an icon in the Dock, you can drag it to a new position there.

When a program is launching, its icon appears in the Dock (if it's not already there), and it bounces up and down until the program has finished launching (**Figure 1.38**). All running programs have an icon in the Dock (whether you put them there or not), as well as a small black upward-pointing triangle at the bottom of the icon.

Figure 1.38

When you launch an application, its icon bounces in the Dock. And when you look in the Dock, you can tell a program is running because it will have a small black upward-pointing triangle beneath its icon.

Removing an item from the Dock is simplicity itself. Just drag the icon up and away from the Dock, and release the mouse button. The icon disappears in a puff of smoke, and the other icons around it close the gap.

Besides being a handy program manager, the Dock serves several other purposes, including the following (**Figure 1.39**):

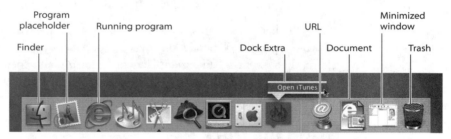

Figure 1.39

Mac OS X's Dock is a tremendously powerful user interface feature that shows you what programs are running and holds icons of documents and programs so they're just a click away. The Dock also serves as a place to change your Mac's settings and to store minimized windows. The Trash and Finder icons always appear on either side of the Dock for quick access.

Control Strip. Like the Control Strip in Mac OS 9 and earlier, the Dock can hold various Mac OS X settings panels (called Dock Extras), which let you change settings by clicking the Dock Extra and choosing a setting from the menu that pops up.

Window holder. When you minimize a window in Mac OS X by clicking the yellow minimize button (or pressing ⌘M), the window shrinks to fit into the Dock. Besides providing a simple place for minimized windows to land, these windows are live—that is, any changes that happen while a window is minimized show up in its Dock icon. The beauty of this is that you can minimize a clock window, a battery gauge, or any other indicator showing the status of some item on your Mac and keep an eye on it without sacrificing all that screen space.

Moving Between Applications

Since the early 1990s, Macs have had the ability to run more than one program at one time. Usually programs are thought of as running in layers—that is, the program you're actively using is the one *in front,* and all other programs run *behind* that program (or *in the background*). When you have more than one program running at once (and the Finder does count as a program), you need a way to switch between running programs. Fortunately, your Mac provides several:

The Application menu. In Mac OS 9 and earlier, all running programs are listed in the Application menu in the upper-right corner of the menu bar. The currently active application (the one that's in front) has a checkmark to the left of its name when you pull down the menu. To switch to a different program, select its name from the Application menu.

 The Dock. In Mac OS X, all running programs have an icon in the Dock (complete with a small black triangle at the bottom), and you can switch between running programs by clicking the appropriate application's icon in the Dock, which brings it to the front. Note that if you click the icon of a program that is *not* running, you'll launch that program.

Pressing ⌘Tab. Both Mac OS 9 and earlier and Mac OS X have the ability to cycle through open programs using a key combination—⌘Tab. This brings the next program to the front, moving the currently active one to the background. Mac OS 9 and earlier determines the next program alphabetically; Mac OS X selects the next program depending on its placement in the Dock, going from left to right. ⌘Shift Tab moves you backward through your open programs.

Double-clicking the open program's icon. When you double-click a program's icon, your Mac opens that program. If the program is already open, it becomes the active program. Choosing Open from the File menu or pressing ⌘O with the program's icon selected does the same thing.

How to Tell Which Application Is in Front

It's easy to tell which program is up front in Mac OS 9 and earlier—besides seeing that program's name and icon in the Application menu and its menus in the menu bar, you'll see all of the currently active application's windows on top of everything else.

 Things are a bit different in Mac OS X. Bringing a program to the front in Mac OS X doesn't bring all of that program's windows up front, but the program's name still shows up in the Application menu and its menus will appear in the menu bar.

Clicking a program's window. If you click a window in the background, the program that opened that window will come to the foreground, and the window will become active.

In any case, a program you've concealed using the Hide command in the Application menu becomes visible again when you make it active.

The Order of Windows

Window order—the layering of open windows on the screen—differs between Mac OS 9 and earlier and Mac OS X, and that's going to cause some confusion, especially for those who are used to how Mac OS 9 handles things. Mac OS 9 groups together all of a program's open document windows (and any other windows that belong to that program). That is, when you bring a given program to the front, *all* of its windows (documents and palettes alike) come into the foreground, jumping in front of all other programs, including the Finder.

 This isn't the case in Mac OS X, which can interleave a program's windows with those belonging to other programs. Bringing a given program to the front does *not* make all of its windows move to the front. They remain layered with other windows—similar to the way the four suits in a deck of cards stay shuffled when you put a heart on top of the deck. If you want to bring all of a program's windows to the front, choose Bring All to Front from the Window menu.

 Some specialized utility programs—called *background applications*—always run in the background; you can't ever bring them to the front. A couple of examples are Login (a small program in Mac OS 9 that keeps track of who is currently logged in to your Mac) and Application Switcher (another tiny program that handles switching between programs).

The Open/Save Dialog Box

One basic dialog box is important in dealing with files, whether you're opening a file or saving one. It's called the Open/Save dialog box, and it has two variations: one for opening a file and one for saving a file. The reason they're so similar is that they're flip sides of the same function—navigating through your hard drive's folders when you want to open or save a file. These are two different dialog boxes, but they're so similar in form and function, we grouped them together. First, let's tackle the Open dialog box. There are several variations on the basic Open dialog box, but they all share a few characteristics—even the Mac OS 9 and the Mac OS X versions (**Figure 1.40**).

Open and Cancel buttons. These are the two basic Open dialog box controls. The Open button opens the file selected in the list field (or if you've selected a folder in the list field, it opens that folder, showing you what's inside). The Cancel button closes the Open dialog box *without* opening a file.

The Open button is the default, which means that pressing Return or Enter is the same as clicking the Open button. In Mac OS X, the Open button only opens a file, since the list field uses a browser view. This browser view lets you scoot through your hard drive's folders without having to open them one at a time. The older list view only shows the contents of a single folder, so you're stuck opening folders to get to where you want to go.

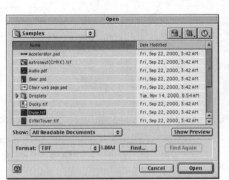
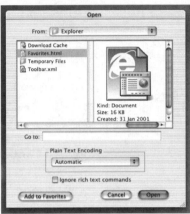

Figure 1.40

The Mac OS 9 (left) and Mac OS X Open dialog boxes let you navigate your hard drive in search of files to open.

List field. This is the largest part of an Open dialog box. In it, you'll see a list of everything in the current folder. When opening a file, you'll see two kinds of items in this list field—black (or active) folders and files and disabled files and applications (which are grayed-out in the list). The reason? You can open folders here, as well as files the program is capable of reading. However, you can't open the wrong kinds of files—for example, graphic files in a word-processing program—or other applications. In Mac OS X, the list field is actually a browser field, which shows your current location in a series of columns, going all the way back to your hard drive.

Folder menu. This pop-up menu shows you which folder the Save dialog box is currently looking into. When you press the Folder pop-up menu, one of two things will happen, depending on whether you're using Mac OS 9 and earlier or Mac OS X. If you're using Mac OS 9 and earlier, pressing the Folder menu shows a list of all the folders enclosing the current folder, all the way to the Desktop. If you want to move up one or more levels in the folder list, just select the target folder, and the Save dialog box looks inside *that* folder. In Mac OS X, pressing the From pop-up menu shows the current folder, a list of Favorite Places (also folders), and a list of Recent Places (recently visited folders), along with other items.

Other controls. Depending on the program you're using, your Open dialog box may offer other controls, including the ability to see a preview version of files you select and a pop-up menu that can filter out certain files (for example, in a graphics program you might want to see only JPEG-format graphics).

The Save version of this dialog box also has common characteristics in all of
its versions (**Figure 1.41**):

Figure 1.41

*The Mac OS 9 (left)
and earlier Mac OS
X Save dialog boxes
let you navigate
your hard drive to
find a place for your
new document.*

Save and Cancel buttons. These are the two basic controls in any Save
dialog box. The Save button saves your file, and the Cancel button closes the
Save window *without* saving the file. When you save a file, it goes in the folder
you're currently viewing in the list field, using the name you've typed in the
filename field. The Save button is the default button, which means that pressing Return or Enter has the same effect as clicking the Save button.

List field. This is the largest single feature of a Save dialog box. In it, you'll
see a list of everything in the current folder that the Save dialog box is pointing
to—usually this is one of a few default locations: the folder where the program
lives, your Documents folder, the Desktop folder, or the last folder in which
you saved or opened a file. Some programs let you customize this default location. When saving a file, you'll see two kinds of files in this list field—black
(active) folders and grayed-out (disabled) file and application icons. The reason
for this is simple—you can open folders in the Save dialog box, but you can't
open applications or files here. When you select a folder in the list field, the Save
button changes to read Open. Clicking this button now (or double-clicking a
folder) will open the selected folder, revealing all of *its* contents in the list field.
In Mac OS X, this list field is actually a browser field, which shows your current
location in a series of columns, going all the way back to your hard drive, but
it works in the same manner.

Filename field. To give a file a name, type it in this field. When you first open
a Save dialog box, you'll probably find some text already in this field (something imaginative, such as "Untitled document"). You can (and probably should)
replace it with a name of your own (that is, unless you *meant* to title your great
American novel "Untitled"). By default, the name in this field is selected when
the dialog box first appears, so you can just start typing your new filename without having to select the text first.

Folder pop-up menu. This pop-up menu is almost identical to the one in the Open dialog box. In Mac OS 9 and earlier, it shows a list of the nested folders containing the current folder, going all the way to the Desktop.

New Folder button. Click the New Folder button, and your Mac creates a new folder in the current location shown in the Save dialog box. After you click the button, a small dialog box pops up, asking you to give the new folder a name. Do so and click the Create button. Your Mac creates a new folder in that location, and then the Save dialog box puts your file there. This little button saves a lot of time by not forcing you to exit the program just to create a new folder.

Besides Open and Save flavors, the Open/Save dialog box comes in three basic variations, depending on the age of the program in question as well as the operating system you're using.

Old-style dialog boxes. Open/Save dialog boxes found in older Mac applications are simple affairs, with just basic controls for finding the locations and files you need. They're found only in programs written for Mac OS 9 and earlier—you won't find an old-style dialog box in a program written with Mac OS X in mind.

Navigation Services Open/Save dialog box. Newer Mac applications use Navigation Services dialog boxes. These newfangled dialog boxes are much more powerful than their predecessors. Besides containing the basic controls for getting around your hard drive, these Open/Save dialog boxes have a title bar, can be moved around like other Mac windows, and have a resize thumb at the bottom. Their list fields show both filenames and the last modification dates for those files, and you can sort the window by name *or* date by clicking the appropriate column. If you click the Sort icon (it looks like four horizontal lines forming a pyramid), that reverses the current sort order. Three buttons appear at the top of each Open/Save dialog box: Shortcuts, which lets you select a volume from the list; Favorites, which shows you items in your Favorites folder (Chapter 3 covers this); and the Recent Items pop-up menu, which shows you a list of items you've opened recently. Finally, each Navigation Services–based Open/Save dialog box has a Help button (a circle with a question mark in it) that lets you get help with one click.

 Mac OS X sheets. Mac OS X emphasizes the difference between Open and Save dialog boxes a little more than Mac OS 9 and earlier, but the two are still closely related. In its simplest form, a Save sheet in Mac OS X asks for two bits of information—a filename and a location chosen from a pop-up menu of several predetermined folders. These folders—your Favorites (or Favorite Places)—are simply folders you frequent. This simple Save sheet also has Cancel and Save buttons so you can cancel the Save command or save the file, respectively. If you need more flexibility than this (say you want to navigate to a folder that doesn't appear in the pop-up menu or create a new folder), you can do so by clicking the button with the downward-pointing triangle. This expands the sheet to show a small browser view, in which you can navigate to any location on your hard drive. This expanded window also features two new buttons—New Folder and Add to Favorites—that let you create a new folder or add the current location to your Favorite Places list, respectively. A Mac OS X Open dialog box contains the same elements but doesn't share the Save sheet's compressed form.

Creating Documents

If you want to create an entirely *new* document, first you have to launch the program in question. Once it's open, select New from the File menu (⌘N in most programs). This tells the program to create a new blank document. Some programs open a dialog box when you create a new document, asking for a few specifics. For example, a graphics program might ask for the dimensions of your new document, while a video-editing program might ask what kind of video camera you'll be using.

Opening Documents

Opening programs is a fine pastime for a Sunday afternoon when there's nothing but golf on, but sooner or later you'll want to do more than that. You'll probably want to start working with documents so you can write reports, balance budgets, play with digital photos, and edit movies. Just about everything else on your Mac—the operating system, the programs, and the folders—exists so you can create, view, and change documents of all kinds.

Before you can work with a document, you must first open a program that can read it—whether or not that program created the document in question. Once the program is running, you can open the document. Fortunately, your Mac takes care of much of this for you, so you don't have to first open a program and then journey all the way back to the Finder to open the document (although you can go about it that way if you want). Here's a look at the myriad ways to open documents using the Mac:

Double-clicking. The most basic—and efficient—way to open a document is to double-click it. This first opens the program that created the file, and then opens the document itself. Selecting the icon and choosing Open from the File menu (or pressing ⌘O) does the same thing.

Drag and drop. You can also open a document by dragging it on top of a program's icon (the program has to be able to open a file of that type). If the program can handle the file, its icon turns black. When you release the mouse button, the program launches and then opens the document you dropped on it.

Opening files from inside the program. You can also open a document from within a program by first launching the program and then selecting Open from the File menu (or pressing ⌘O). The Open command, along with its keyboard equivalent, appears in the File menu of just about every Mac program ever written. When you give the Open command from within a program, an Open dialog box pops up. You can use the controls in this dialog box to navigate through the folders on your hard drive and find the document.

What to Do When Double-Clicking a Document Doesn't Open an Application—or Opens the Wrong One

Double-clicking a document to open it is all well and good when you have the program that created it on your Mac, but it's a whole different game when you don't. Perhaps someone sent you a file he or she made using a program you don't own, or maybe you took it off your hard drive. Whatever the reason, your Mac is well equipped to deal with such an emergency.

In Mac OS 9 and earlier, documents have two characteristics that help them work properly with applications: a type and a creator. A document's *type* indicates the general kind of document it is—whether it's a picture in JPEG format or a text file. A document's *creator,* on the other hand, indicates what program created it. Many documents can be opened by more than one program, which is a real benefit. If you don't have exactly the right program, your Mac relies on the document's type to match it to a program that *can* handle it.

With Mac OS 9 and earlier, your Mac relies on the File Exchange control panel, which offers a choice of programs that might be able to read the document (**Figure 1.42**). When you see the list of programs that File Exchange provides, all you have to do is choose the one you want and then click the OK button.

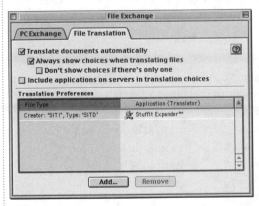

Figure 1.42

Using the File Exchange control panel—part of Mac OS 9 and earlier—you can link files of a certain type to the program of your choice.

Mac OS X tells you it doesn't have a program to open the document in question and then asks if you'd like to choose one. If you decide to, it presents a browser in which you can choose a program. Alternatively, you can select the document and then choose Show Info from the File menu. In the window that pops up, choose Application from the Show menu and then click the Change Application button. This presents you with the same browser.

Some documents, such as graphics and text files, are generic and standard enough so that any of several programs can open them. Other documents use *proprietary* file formats—that is, the documents have a secret structure that prevents other programs from easily opening them.

Saving Documents

When you have a changed document (either a brand-new document or an existing one you've altered), you can save the changes you've made onto your hard drive. If the document is new (that is, you've never saved it onto your hard drive), select Save from the File menu (or press ⌘S). This brings up the Save dialog box, which you'll probably notice bears a strong resemblance to the Open dialog box. That's because they share a very similar function. Save dialog boxes look into a particular folder on your hard drive and allow you to save a document there.

If you're working with a document that already exists on your hard drive, saving changes is easy. All you have to do is select Save from the File menu (or press ⌘S), and your Mac will save the file without showing the Save dialog box at all.

Sometimes, though, you'll *want* to see that Save dialog box again—particularly when you want to save a copy of the file with a new name. That's when it's time to take advantage of the Save As command. Located in the File menu and often given the ⌘ Shift S keyboard equivalent, the Save As command opens a Save dialog box as if you'd never saved the file before. In it, you can give the file a new name or save it in a different location. Afterward you'll be working with the new copy—the Save As command closes the original without saving any changes you made to it since the last save.

Closing Documents

Most of the time, closing a document is a lot like closing a Finder window. You can go about it in three ways: Click the close box in the upper-right corner, select Close from the File menu, or press ⌘W, which is the same as selecting the Close command.

One of two things will happen when you close a document. If you haven't made any changes to it since you opened it, the document's window just closes—no muss, no fuss. If you've made *any* changes to the file, the program asks if you want to save them and most likely gives you three choices in the form of buttons: Don't Save, Save, or Cancel (**Figure 1.43**).

Figure 1.43

If you try to close a document you haven't saved, your Mac warns you before you throw away the contents of your document.

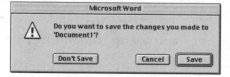

If you choose Don't Save, the document closes and any changes you've made evaporate into nothing. If you choose Save, that saves the changes on your hard drive—and if this is a new document, your Mac presents you with the Save dialog box so you can enter a name. If you choose Cancel, the dialog box disappears and you end up back in your document. (By the way, the same sequence of events happens when you *quit* a program—

before it quits, all of its open windows close, and if a document has unsaved changes, the program asks if you want to save them.)

There's one important concept you should know—closing all of a program's windows does *not* quit the program, which can pose a bit of a problem. When you switch from one program without any open windows to another program, it's easy to forget the first program is running—and even without any windows open, it's still taking up system resources unnecessarily. This is more of a problem in Mac OS 9 and earlier than in Mac OS X (because Mac OS X is much better at managing system resources), but it's still a good idea to quit any programs you're not using. In Mac OS 9 you can see a list of running programs by clicking the Application menu in the upper-right corner; in Mac OS X you can identify currently running programs by the upward-pointing triangles that appear below their icons in the Dock.

Moving Information Between Documents

Open documents are not worlds unto themselves. In fact, you can move data from document to document even if they weren't created in the same program. For example, you can create a graphic in a drawing program and move it to a word-processing document, even though the two documents serve different purposes and are created by different applications. Your Mac gives you two main ways to go about this—cut, copy, and paste; and drag and drop. (You can also use these commands to move stuff around in the same document.)

Selecting Information in a Document

Before you start moving things around inside and between documents, you have to tell your Mac exactly what it is you want to select. You make a selection with the pointer. In practice, this is just like selecting icons or text in the Finder, and you can use the same techniques—usually dragging the pointer over the area you want—to select a region of text or a specific area in a painting document. Often your Mac takes care of changing the pointer so you can select whatever's underneath, but sometimes (especially when you're using a graphics program) you have to select the right pointer from a tool palette to make a selection. Here's a glimpse of a few different selections you can make:

Text selection. When you're working with text, you're working with the I-beam pointer, which lets you select text by dragging over the letters, words, or lines you want. You can also double-click a word to select it (this doesn't select spaces to either side, though this varies from program to program), and in some programs you can triple-click to select an entire line or paragraph.

Image selection. When you're working with an image using QuickTime or SimpleText, you can select a portion of the image by dragging the pointer over the area you want. This draws a selection rectangle starting where you first click the mouse button and ending where you release it. If you're using an image-editing program (such as Adobe Photoshop or GraphicConverter) to open the image, you'll probably have your choice of selection pointers (also known as tools) for selecting circles, rounded rectangles, polygons, or even freeform shapes.

Sound or movie selection. When you're working with real-time media (mostly video or sound files) in QuickTime, you can select a portion of the file by holding down ⓢⓗⓘⓕⓣ and dragging in the timeline above the play controls. If you're using a video- or audio-editing program, you'll probably need to use a special tool to select a section of the file.

Cut, Copy, and Paste

These three basic commands have been around since the Mac first came on the scene, and they appear in the Edit menu of almost every Mac program ever written. With them, you can cut or copy something you've selected in one document, then paste that selection in another. The Mac OS has a feature called the Clipboard that holds your selection while it's in transition. You can think of the Clipboard as a temporary holding place for whatever you cut or copy—some text, a picture, a movie clip, or a snippet of music. Putting something new on the Clipboard erases what was previously there, and when you shut down your Mac, the contents of the Clipboard go away. You use cut and copy to put something *on* the Clipboard; you use paste to move the contents of the Clipboard into the active document.

Cut. Use the cut command (Cut from the Edit menu, or ⌘X in almost every program) when you want to move a selected item from one place to another. The cut command cuts whatever you have selected (whether that's a paragraph of text or part of a digital photograph) out of the document and puts that data on the Clipboard. It's a lot like cutting an item out of a newspaper or magazine and putting it on a clipboard so you can carry it somewhere else for another use.

Copy. The copy command (Copy from the Edit menu, or ⌘C in almost every program) is best used when you want to put a copy of a selected item in another place. The copy command places a copy of whatever you have selected (text, graphics, video, audio—you name it) on the Clipboard, leaving the original selection intact.

Paste. The paste command is the flip side of cut and copy. It pastes the contents of the Clipboard into the currently active document. If the document has an insertion point (such as the little vertical line in a word processing document where characters appear when you type), the item you're pasting in appears to the left of the insertion point, and everything to the right of the insertion point gets pushed to the right. If you're working with an image and you have an area selected, the item you're pasting should appear in that area. If you don't have anything selected, the application chooses where the selection appears, but you can move it where you like.

You can use the paste command as many times in a row as you like without erasing the contents of the Clipboard. This makes short work of writing "I will not talk in class" 500 times! Just copy the phrase, put the pointer where you want it, paste the selection 500 times, and you're done. (Or if you really want to speed it up, paste 10 copies, select those 10, copy them to the Clipboard, and then paste those 10 copies 49 times—and you're all done.)

Sometimes you'll find the paste command grayed out, even though you know you copied *something* to the Clipboard. This often means the program into which you're trying to paste doesn't know how to handle the kind of data you've got on the Clipboard. This can happen if you try to paste text into an open image document. Sometimes you can get around this limitation if the program has an appropriate tool for the data. For example, if your graphics program has a text tool and you use that to create a text box on top of the image, you should then be able to paste text into that box.

 Several shareware utilities can give your Mac more than one Clipboard so you can copy multiple items without erasing the Clipboard's contents. You can find Lazy Mountain Software's ClipDoubler at www.lazymountainsoftware.com/ products.html, and Script Software's CopyPaste at www.scriptsoftware.com.

Drag and Drop

Mac programs offer another way of moving information around in the same document (or between documents). It's called *drag and drop,* and it works just as the name implies. With drag and drop, you simply drag a selection to a new location (whether that's inside the same document or in a different document) and drop it there. Your Mac makes a copy of the selection in the receiving document—another document created by the same program or even one created by a different program. All that's required is two open windows and some item you've selected to drag between them. (Of course, you can drag things around in the same window, too.)

Not all programs support drag and drop, but most that have been updated in the last few years do. To test whether a specific program supports it, select some text or part of an image, then click and hold in the middle of the selection. Drag the pointer over to the Desktop and release the mouse button. If a new clipping file appears on the Desktop where you released the mouse button, your program supports drag and drop. If you want to move data between documents with this method, *both* programs have to support drag and drop, and the receiving document has to be able to understand the kind of data you're dragging onto it. Otherwise, your drag bounces back and nothing happens.

Undo Is Your Friend

One of the first things every Mac user should learn is that the undo command is your friend. Undo (accessible in most Mac programs via Undo from the Edit menu or by pressing ⌘Z) does what its name implies—it undoes your last action. This can be especially useful if you've accidentally erased everything in a 50,000-word document. A simple ⌘Z will undo the deletion, restoring things to the way they were. Some programs only undo the very last thing you did, so if you accidentally erase everything in a document and then type *Oops,* you can only undo your typing of the word. The lesson: Don't do *anything* after you've made a horrendous mistake. Select Undo from the Edit menu right away to see if that fixes things.

Some programs have a multiple undo feature, which lets you step backward in time by selecting Undo over and over again. With each undo command you issue, your program undoes one more action; in some cases you can go back hundreds of steps.

A few programs (including SimpleText and the Finder in Mac OS 9 and earlier) have a disabled Undo command in the Edit menu. That's because these programs haven't implemented undo, even though it shows up in the menu, and pressing ⌘Z won't do any good. You've been warned. Mac OS X, however, *does* have a version of undo that applies mostly to moving and renaming items. You can undo those commands with a quick trip to Undo from Edit.

Other Features of Applications

These days, many programs have tools you won't find in the Finder: *tool palettes, control palettes,* and *button bars.* (Button bars have made it into Mac OS X Finder windows, but that's a pretty recent thing.)

Tool palettes are floating windows containing several different tools—essentially different pointers—that you can use on an open document. (For example, a graphics program might have a tool palette with an airbrush, a paint bucket, a pen, a pencil, and an eraser.) To use a tool, click it in the palette, and either click inside an open document with it or drag the tool around in an open document—the technique varies depending on the tool you're using. For example, you might click with a text cursor tool to place a text cursor, but you might drag with a paintbrush tool to paint inside a document.

Like tool palettes, control palettes are small floating windows, but instead of different pointer tools, they contain a selection of settings for controlling what happens in a document. For example, a control palette for a word-processing program might have controls that let you select a font, a font size, text alignment (such as left-aligned or centered text), and text styles (such as bold or italic).

Finally, button bars hang out above or to the left of a program's main windows, and they're typically attached to the edges of the screen—although you can move some around wherever you like. Button bars typically provide one-click access to menu commands. For example, many button bars have cut, copy, and paste buttons with the same functions as menu commands that have the same names. Some people find pressing buttons easier than selecting menu commands.

Finder Tips

 As you start working your way around the Finder, you'll learn various short-cuts and tips for how to do things more easily and more quickly. To accelerate that process and make you a superuser right away, we've compiled some of the best Mac OS Finder tips for your perusal.

Common Finder Commands

You should get familiar with a few Finder commands if you want to convince others of your Macintosh guru status—or if you just want to work more efficiently.

Power key. Pressing the power key on your Mac's keyboard (if your keyboard doesn't have one, press the power key on the Mac itself) brings up a dialog box with four choices: Restart, Sleep, Cancel, and Shut Down. Shut Down is the default choice, so if you press Return or Enter, your Mac shuts down—it's the same thing as choosing Shut Down from the Special menu, and it only takes two quick presses on your keyboard.

Select All. To select every item in the currently active Finder window, choose Select All from the Edit menu (or press ⌘A). This trick is especially handy when you have a couple hundred files you'd like to move from one place to another and you don't relish the thought of dragging your mouse that far.

New Folder. Odds are you'll outgrow the basic folder structure on your hard drive pretty quickly, and you'll want to create new folders. To do so, open the window where you want the new folder to appear and select New Folder from the File menu (⌘N in Mac OS 9 and earlier, ⌘Shift N in Mac OS X). When you issue this command, a freshly minted folder appears with its name selected and ready to edit. Just type the name you want to give the folder, followed by Return to make it stick.

Move to the Trash. To move something to the Trash without dragging it there, select the item in question and select Move To Trash from the File menu (or press ⌘Delete).

Make Alias. When you select an item or items in the Finder and select Make Alias from the File menu (⌘M in Mac OS 9 and earlier; ⌘L in Mac OS X), your Mac makes an alias of the selected icon in the same window and tacks the word *alias* onto the end. The icon's name is also in italic text.

Reveal Original. This command is only available when you've selected an alias in the Finder. Select Reveal Original from the File menu (or press ⌘R), and your Mac opens the folder that contains the original item and selects that item so there's no mistaking the alias's origin.

Cancel. Pressing ⌘. will cancel most actions already in progress.

Put Away. When you've just moved an item to a new folder, you can send it back to its original location by choosing Put Away from the File menu (or pressing ⌘Y). This makes the Finder move the item back to the folder where it came from, and that includes moving items out of the Trash. The Put Away command only shows up in Mac OS 9 and earlier. Mac OS X does, however, have an equivalent in its Undo command, which can undo moving an item to a different location.

Get Help. In Mac OS 9 and earlier, you can call up Macintosh Help while you're in the Finder by pressing ⌘?, which is the same as ⌘Shift/, because the forward slash (/) and the question mark (?) are located on the same key. ⌘/ will also invoke help, thanks to some quick thinking on the part of Apple's interface designers. That way, if you forget the Shift key, you'll still get help.

Force quit. At times in every Mac user's life, programs may crash or freeze, and it may happen more often than you like. Sometimes a program just stops responding, even though you can still move the mouse, and sometimes *everything* (pointer included) freezes. If this happens, you can try *force-quitting* the program by pressing ⌘Option Esc. This brings up the Force Quit dialog box. In Mac OS 9 and earlier, this dialog box offers two choices: Cancel and Force Quit. Clicking Cancel returns your Mac to its previous state (great if you pressed this key combination by accident), and clicking Force Quit forces the troublesome program to go away. When you force-quit a program in Mac OS 9 and earlier, you should restart your Mac as soon as possible because it may now be unstable. In Mac OS X, the Force Quit dialog box shows *all* running programs on your Mac, including a few background programs you might not even know about, and it has one button at the bottom labeled Force Quit (unless you select the Finder; you then see a Relaunch button). Select the troublesome program and click this button. Your Mac will give you a chance to back out, noting that you might lose any unsaved changes in the program you're force-quitting. Click Force Quit again and the rebel program will go down (or Cancel if you want to back out). In Mac OS X, though, there's no need to restart your Mac, thanks to its advanced crash protection. We'll cover crashes and troubleshooting techniques in much more detail in Chapter 8.

Soft restart. Then there are the times when your Mac crashes so hard that you can't do anything. It's time for a soft restart. To execute this, press ⌘Ctrl-Power. Your Mac *immediately* restarts, and anything you may have been working on is gone.

Do not use this command unless you have no other choice. You won't get a chance to change your mind, and your Mac will take much longer to restart, because it has to check its disk structure for any errors that might have occurred because of the quick restart. Again, there'll be more on dealing with crashes in Chapter 8.

Modified Drags

Figure 1.44

Your pointer can assume four forms, depending on what keys you hold down. Clockwise from upper left: copy, make alias, contextual menu, and grab.

When you're using the Finder, you may notice that the pointer sometimes takes on a little extra icon, depending on what keys you're holding down while you click or drag. These modified pointers tell you that instead of a plain-vanilla click or drag, you're actually going to issue one of four commands—copy an item, make an alias, open a contextual menu, or grab the contents of an open window to move them (this last one's a bit tricky.) These are modified drags, and they serve as shortcuts for Finder menu commands. Here's a bit about each (**Figure 1.44**):

Copy. If you hold down Option while dragging a file, the pointer arrow acquires a little plus sign (+) in the lower-right corner. When you release the mouse button, the Finder will make a copy of the dragged item in the location where you release the mouse button.

Make an alias. Hold down ⌘Option while dragging an item, and a small, right-curving arrow appears in the pointer's lower-right corner. When you release the mouse button, the Finder creates an alias—or pointer—to the original file in the location where you let go.

Open a contextual menu. Hold down Control (without clicking anywhere), and a small rectangle appears in the pointer's lower-right corner. This means if you click an item (or even the Desktop itself), you'll invoke a contextual menu with choices specific to that item. We'll cover contextual menus later in this chapter.

Grab a window's contents. This fourth modified click creates an all-new kind of pointer—the gloved hand, reminiscent of a certain famous animated mouse's hand. By dragging in a window while holding down ⌘ in Mac OS 9 and ⌘Option in Mac OS X you can drag the window's contents around, saving you a trip to the scroll bar. At least one of the window's scroll bars has to be active for this to work. It's like scrolling without using the scroll bars.

Navigating by Keyboard

Believe it or not, you can navigate through your Mac, opening folders and launching programs, without ever leaving the comfort of your keyboard. Here are a couple of tricks you'll need:

Typing names. If you start typing an item's name, the Finder will do its best to match an icon in the currently active window (or on the Desktop) to the name you're typing. The Finder makes a selection after you enter the first few characters, picking the first item in alphabetical order that matches the characters you've typed. Once an item is selected, you can use other Finder commands on it (such as Open or Move To Trash).

Arrow keys. These let you select an icon to the left, right, above, or below the currently selected icon, depending on which arrow key you press.

Modified arrow keys. If you hold down ⌘ and press ⬇, the Finder opens the selected item, whether it's a folder, file, or icon. It's the equivalent of selecting Open from the File menu or pressing ⌘O. Hold down ⌘ and press ⬆, and the Finder will open the folder that holds the folder you're viewing the contents of. (Unfortunately, the latter trick doesn't work in Mac OS X.) Finally, holding down Option while using these shortcuts closes the window that contained the item you're moving from. For example, when you open the hard drive and then hold down Option while opening the Documents folder, the hard-drive window will close and the Documents folder will open.

Get Info

The Get Info command in Mac OS 9 and earlier is your key to understanding an item on your hard drive. It tells you how big an item is, where it's located, and when it was modified, among other things. The Get Info window (**Figure 1.45**) changes depending on whether you've selected a file, a folder, an application, or a volume. To find out more about an item on your Mac, select it and press ⌘I (under the File menu, select Get Info and then General Information) to bring up the Get Info window. (In Mac OS 9 and earlier, each item on your Mac can have its own Get Info window.) Here's what you can expect to see in a Get Info window for each basic item type:

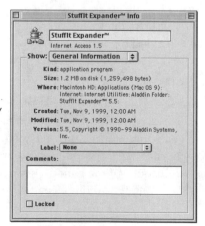

Figure 1.45

The Get Info window serves up lots of tasty information about the item to which it refers. It has a pop-up menu that lets you switch between different functions.

Documents. The document's name, which application created it, how big it is, where it's located, when it was created, and when it was last modified.

Folders. The folder's name, its size (and how many items are inside it), where the folder is located, when it was created, and when it was last modified.

Applications. The application's name, its size, where it's located, when it was created and last modified, and its version. This last piece of information can be useful if you don't know exactly which version of a program you have on your hard drive.

Volumes. The volume's format, how much information it's capable of holding, how much space is available, how much is already in use, the number of items on the volume, the volume's location (including some details about its physical interface to your Mac), when the volume was created, and when it was last modified.

Most Get Info windows have a couple of common elements, including a pop-up menu that lets you select a label for the item, a field for comments (if you want to jot down a few notes about what's in an item), and a Show pop-up menu. This last feature lets you set who can see the item over a network via file sharing, as well as the amount of memory a program gets when you launch it. We'll cover these details in future chapters.

Mac OS X has a similar Info window that does the same basic thing (**Figure 1.46**). You call up the Info window by selecting Show Info from the File menu (or pressing ⌘I). You can only have one Info window open at a time in Mac OS X, and it changes its contents to reflect what you have selected in the Finder.

It also has the pop-up menu at the top that lets you change how items are shared over a network—this menu has different items in it depending on the kind of icon selected. For example, if you select a document, you can choose a program to open it; if you select an application, you can turn on different languages the program is capable of using.

Figure 1.46

Mac OS X has updated the venerable Get Info feature, changing it to Show Info and giving it new abilities. The pop-up menu in the Info window lets you switch between various modes. Only one Info window can be visible at a time.

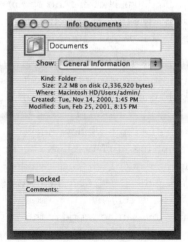

Tips for Working with Files

 When you spend some time working with the files on your hard drive, you'll develop your own techniques for doing things quickly. Here are a few tools to help you on your way:

Locking and unlocking files. If you want to protect an important file or program from changes, you can lock that document so no one can rename or change it when it's open and it's harder to delete from your hard drive. To lock a file or application, select it, and then from the File menu select Get Info, General Information (in Mac OS 9 and earlier); select File, Show Info (in Mac OS X); or press ⌘I. In the window that pops up, check the Locked check box at the bottom and close the window. The item's icon will now sport a little lock in the lower-left corner, and users won't be able to change the item's name or alter the item (although they can still open it), nor can they delete the file without first unlocking it. The aim of this is to keep you from accidentally deleting an important document, not to provide solid security. That's because it's easy to unlock an item. To do so, open its Get Info or Show Info window, and uncheck the Locked check box in the lower-left corner.

Trashing locked icons. Occasionally you'll throw away a locked item you really *do* want to get rid of, or worse yet, you'll throw away a passel of locked files, and when you try to empty the Trash, your Mac will tell you it can't delete the locked files. (Mac OS X will not let you put locked items in the Trash at all, so you can only try this trick with Mac OS 9 and earlier.) To get around this, hold down Option and select Empty Trash from the Special menu. Your Mac will obediently erase everything in the Trash without asking any questions. Be careful, though, because with Option held down, choosing this option empties the Trash. Your Mac won't ask if you're really sure you want to throw everything away, and that's true of both Mac OS 9 and earlier and Mac OS X.

Turning off the Trash warning. In Mac OS 9 and earlier, if you don't want your Mac to ask if you're sure you want to delete items in the Trash when you choose Empty Trash, you can turn off this warning by selecting the Trash icon and, from the File menu, choosing General Information, Get Info (or pressing ⌘I). In the Trash's Get Info window, uncheck the check box next to the words "Warn before emptying." In Mac OS X choose Preferences from the Finder menu to bring up the Finder Preferences window. Uncheck the box "Show warning before emptying the Trash" near the bottom of the window. Now, when you empty the Trash, its contents just go away. This also means you don't get a warning, so be sure you want to get rid of the Trash's contents before you select the Empty Trash command. You can't undo it.

Encrypting an item. In Mac OS 9, if you want to protect an item from prying eyes, you can do so by selecting the item (this doesn't encrypt a folder full of items, by the way) and then choosing Encrypt from the File menu. Your Mac asks for a password and encrypts the item. If you want to open an encrypted item, you'll first have to type in the password. It's important not to forget your password—if you do, there's no way to unencrypt your file. Encrypting an item also makes it smaller, so if you're dying for a little hard-drive space, you can encrypt a few items you don't use on a regular basis. Mac OS X doesn't have this kind of built-in encryption.

Creating stationery. The Mac provides special documents called stationery, which act conceptually like pads of paper with preprinted designs, and when you open stationery, it's like ripping the top sheet off. You still have the pad for later use, but you can work with the sheet you just ripped off, and you don't have to go through the trouble of adding items that are used every time, such as a logo or address. Opening a stationery document opens a copy of the document, complete with all of that document's contents—text, pictures, and the like. For example, stationery is useful for items such as letterhead, which has your name, address, and company logo on it but is otherwise blank. Opening your letterhead stationery opens a copy of the letterhead document, leaving the original untouched, ready for the next time you need to write a letter. You can make stationery out of any document by selecting its icon and, from the File menu, selecting Get Info and then General Information (in Mac OS 9 and earlier); selecting File, Show Info (in Mac OS X); or pressing ⌘I. Check the Stationery Pad check box and close the window. The document's icon should now look like a pad of paper instead of a single sheet. When you open that document, you'll get an untitled document with the same content as the stationery document. To turn stationery into a regular document, open its Get Info or Inspector window and uncheck the Stationery Pad check box.

Tips for Working with Windows

We've shown you the basics of working with your Mac's windows, but now it's time to pick up a few advanced techniques.

Cleaning up a window's contents. After a short time, you might find that a window in icon or button view might start looking a little, well, disheveled. After all, it's hard for humans to move items around with machinelike accuracy. You can fix your messy windows with a quick menu command: Clean Up from the View menu. This makes your Mac square up all the icons in the currently active window according to a grid, making order out of chaos. The problem with this command is that it sometimes doesn't arrange icons sensibly. To make up for that, use View's Arrange submenu in Mac OS 9 and earlier, which offers you the choice of arranging by name, date, label, size, or kind. In Mac OS X, go to View; Show View Options to pick how to arrange the icons.

Customizing window views. If you want to *really* keep your windows looking their best, open the View Options window, which lets you set how the window looks—the size of icons, how they're arranged (and whether they snap to an invisible grid), and what columns appear in a list view. To open the

View Options window, choose View Options from the View menu (in Mac OS 9 and earlier) or Show View Options from the View menu (in Mac OS X). The keyboard equivalent in either case is ⌘J. This pops open a window with controls that let you change how the contents of the currently active window behave.

Finding the path to a window. In Mac OS 9 and earlier and Mac OS X, you can take a look at the folder path (the list of folders in which the currently open window is nested) by ⌘-clicking the window's title bar. This creates a pop-up menu showing each folder that lies between the current window and the Desktop, and you can open any of these intermediate folders by selecting it from the menu. Some programs, such as Microsoft Word and Internet Explorer, also support this trick.

Closing a window when you open something in it. If you hold down Option while double-clicking an item, that window closes when the item opens. It's a handy way to keep your Desktop tidy when drilling down through a series of folders.

Hiding an application. If you want to hide the currently active application without going to the Application menu, you can do so by holding down Option and clicking another program's windows (or clicking the Desktop). The currently active application disappears, and the program for the item you clicked becomes active.

Dragging an inactive window. To drag a window that's behind another window without bringing it to the front, hold down ⌘ and drag the window by its title bar. When you release the mouse button, the window stays behind the other windows.

Using characters to sort files in list view. Although your Mac does a fair job at sorting items alphabetically in list view, sometimes you want just one file or folder to show up in a different place—say, at the top or bottom of the list. You can achieve this by adding a character to the beginning of a file's name. To get a file to bubble up to the top of an alphabetically sorted list, put a space at the beginning of its name. While the name *looks* almost the same, a file named this way pops to the top of an alphabetically sorted list. To keep a file at the bottom of a list, put a bullet in front of its name (press Option 8 to get a bullet). A file named this way sinks to the bottom of an alphabetical list. You can also use numbers in front of filenames to arrange files in the desired order (**Figure 1.47**).

Figure 1.47

Putting a space in front of the Raw Files folder's name places the folder at the top of an alphabetically sorted list. It would otherwise appear second to last. The bullet in front of the Done folder's name pushes that folder to the bottom of the list.

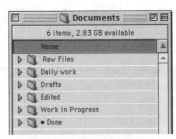

2

The Macintosh Family

Clifford Colby is the chapter editor.

Mike Breeden (MB), Christopher Breen (CB), David Morgenstern (DM), Jason O'Grady (JOG), and Daniel Drew Turner (DT) are the chapter coauthors.

Sharon Zardetto Aker (SA) was the editor of the seventh edition of **The Macintosh Bible,** *from which portions of this chapter are taken.*

At first, picking which Mac to buy was a snap: In 1984 you paid $2,495 for the original Macintosh, and Apple threw MacWrite and MacPaint in with the deal. Your big choice: Did you want an Apple carrying case for $99?

Ten years later, your choices were more varied—and bewildering. For example, just in the Performa line, at one time or another you could pick from (or wade through) the Performa 520, the Performa 5320CD, the Performa 630CD DOS Compatible, the Performa 6218CD, the Performa 6360, and 50-something other Performa models.

To make sense of any of it, you had to know processor speeds, if you wanted PCI or NuBus slots, how fast the CD-ROM drive read data, how big the hard drive was, and a dozen other speeds and sizes. In the past three years, Apple has whittled down its products to four trim lines—one portable model for consumers and another for professionals; one desktop model for consumers and another for professionals. As a Mac shopper, however, you still have to pick from removable storage options, networking transfer rates, battery lives, and of course, processor speeds. This chapter will get you going on what all that hardware inside your Mac does and help you sort through the machines that make up Apple's four hardware categories. (Other chapters—including Chapter 4, "Memory;" Chapter 5, "Storage;" Chapter 7, "Peripherals;" and Chapter 20, "Networking"—go much further. And for more guidance on what is the right Mac for you, check out Appendix A, "Buying Macs.")

In This Chapter

Mac Innards (DM)

Before launching into an examination of the various species of Macintosh, we would do well to briefly describe its genus: the personal computer. In other words: What are the common elements found in any computer, whether it's housed in a desktop, notebook, or even personal digital assistant?

All computers require a central processing unit, or CPU, that runs the machine's instructions and data; an amount of random-access memory (RAM) to hold the data during manipulation; a startup program to start up the device; a means of displaying the data to the user; one or more storage devices; and perhaps one or more input-output, or I/O, interfaces that can send and receive instructions. (Of course, we can't forget software: the operating system and applications that transform the hardware from an expensive doorstop to a productivity tool. We cover the essential system software component in the first and third chapters of *The Macintosh Bible*.)

Understanding the CPU (DM/SA)

The central processing unit is a type of integrated circuit (IC), or chip, a little silicon wafer with microscopic circuits etched into it. Blocks of wafers are sometimes sold at mineralogical fairs or flea markets. In a computer, you don't see or touch the actual chips, since they're encased in plastic or ceramic blocks with metal connectors protruding from them.

A computer uses many kinds of chips for specialized tasks such as RAM, graphics, and I/O. So-called embedded processors also add computer processing functions to all digital devices and even cars.

The CPU, also referred to as a microprocessor, or just a processor, processes instructions. The processor handles and routes millions of instructions every second—of course, it's all submicroscopic so we never directly witness this miracle of computing. The performance of this component is so vital that some people say "CPU" when they mean a whole computer. Apple focuses much of its branding on the CPU by naming its Power Macintosh line after the generation of PowerPC chip used in the box—that's the G in G4.

A Metaphor a Day (DM)

To help us non-electrical-engineering types understand how computers work, well-meaning writers have compared computers to a wide range of things, using metaphors from the common brain and body to the Los Angeles freeway system. My current, best comparison is an oven, perhaps influenced by my addiction to the *Iron Chef* television show. The computer user combines ingredients (raw data) and a recipe (software and OS) with an oven (memory) and heat (processor) to create food (data files, images, the result), which is then consumed. What is the fridge? A Zip cartridge? So maybe the cooking resemblance only goes so far.

Information marches through a processor chip—as well as all the other components on a computer logic board—to the beat of a different drum: an oscillator, usually a quartz crystal, that vibrates in response to an electric current. The pulses are so rapid that they're measured in megahertz, or millions of cycles per second. This *clock* determines the speed of your processor: a 500 MHz clock beats 500 million times a second.

Common sense suggests that to compare computers, all one has to do is check the processor clock rates. Most computer users believe this to be true. Unfortunately, and despite its common use in almost all marketing materials, clock speed is no measure of the actual performance of a particular computer or even between competing computers using the same processor.

Too many other variables can affect real world performance: how well a processor can crunch different types of data such as streaming media or large sets of records, and the relative speeds and architectures (or lack of same) of the other components housed on and off the logic board. As Intel keeps boosting megahertz of the Pentium 4 (with a technology demo heading past 3 GHz), Apple and even manufacturers of Intel-compatible CPUs such as Advance Micro Devices refer to this long-held folk wisdom among users as the "Megahertz Myth." (See www.apple.com/g4/myth/ for Apple's take on this.)

Memory and RAM Caches (DM)

RAM provides working space for applications and instructions. RAM is used in several important places. The first is in a series of caches for frequent use; the other is the primary system RAM, placed in upgradable slots on the logic board.

A memory cache is an area of memory set aside for data that the processor will need imminently and frequently. Cache memory is closely connected to the processor and uses a faster route than the system RAM. Computers can have more than one memory cache—in fact most have a couple. The caches on a given Mac are determined by the processor and model; years ago, some Mac models were differentiated by their cache architecture.

The three levels of cache memory are:

Level 1 (also called L1 or data), a small piece of memory in the processor that holds the latest information.

Level 2 (L2), a larger cache that may or may not be incorporated in the chip itself.

Level 3 (L3), which is always physically separate from the processor chip and usually runs at a slower speed.

After checking the L1 cache for needed information, the processor will next look at the L2 cache and subsequently the L3 cache—anything to avoid having to request data from the main system memory, which offers the slowest memory access—except for recalling something that's been *paged* to the hard drive with virtual memory. But that's a different story (see Chapter 4, "Memory"). In some older Macs, the L2 cache was separate, like today's L3 cache, and occasionally upgradable.

For example, the current PowerPC G4 processor (which Motorola calls the MPC7450) integrates a small 32 Kbyte Level 1 cache and a 256 Kbyte Level 2 cache into the processor chip itself, working at full speed, meaning it transfers data back and forth with the processor at the clock rate that the processor runs at. This is called *on-chip* cache. Motorola states that the chip also can handle either a 1 MB or 2 MB Level 3 cache, dubbed *backside cache.* On some Power Mac G4 (QuickSilver) models, Apple offers a 2 MB backside cache, which runs at a quarter of the processor speed, in the 200 MHz range.

The Mac's primary system memory is located on the logic board using one or more industry-standard, dual in-line memory module (DIMM) expansion slots. Each module is a small circuit board that holds an array of memory chips. Although complying with a standard specification, the modules are not necessary interchangeable between Mac models, and some cost more than others. Thus, the modules for a PowerBook are smaller and more expensive than those used in a desktop machine. Some older Macs used SIMMs, or single in-line memory modules.

But even similar Mac models can have problems with exchanging RAM. One example, the Power Mac G4 (QuickSilver), has three slots for 168-pin synchronous dynamic RAM (SDRAM) DIMMs; as of this writing it can support as much as 1.5 GB of RAM, or three 512 MB modules. The *synchronous* part means that the memory will automatically match its clock speed to that of the processor when data is moved around—a very good thing, since mistiming requires the CPU to wait. As with traffic on the freeway (the darned metaphors again), a slight delay can cause a longer backup. However, Apple says the parts must be PC133-compliant, pointing to the JEDEC Solid State Technology Association, an industry standards body formerly known as the Joint Electron Device Engineering Council. So RAM from earlier models— PC100-compliant modules—won't work. (To learn much more about RAM, see Chapter 4.)

 For more technical details on memory, including what kind of RAM your Mac needs, you can refer to the "Memory Questions" section of Accelerate Your Macintosh's FAQs (www.xlr8yourmac.com), check on MacFixIt (www.macfixit.com), or look up your model at the Chip Merchant (www.thechipmerchant.com). (DT)

Starting Up Your Mac (DM)

After you press the power button, a computer runs a set of instructions. It's usually stored in a *ROM,* or read-only memory. This type of small, memory-based instruction package is called *firmware.* The small program checks the hardware, runs diagnostic routines on memory and other hardware elements, and sets values that will be needed by programs, the operating system, and hardware. It also loads drivers, special small low-level programs for hardware devices connected to the machine. In the Windows/Intel world this startup ROM is known as the *BIOS,* or Basic Input and Output System. The Mac ROM uses Open Firmware, the IEEE 1275-1994 standard to regulate the startup procedure.

In the past, the Mac ROM held the code necessary to start up the computer, as well as the Mac ToolBox, a collection of small software pieces that were available for Mac programs to use. Following the introduction of the iMac, the ROM has conformed to Apple's NewWorld Architecture. [*For those who can't get enough of this stuff, Apple outlines the NewWorld Architecture in Technical Note 1167, which you can find at http://developer.apple.com/technotes/tn/tn1167.html.—Ed.*] This scheme focused the ROM on the low-level startup process—under this plan, the new name for the Mac ROM is the Boot ROM.

The higher-level ToolBox items were moved to a file located on the primary hard drive called the ToolBox ROM Image. When a Mac OS 9 and earlier application wants a ToolBox item, it's loaded into the main system RAM and works just like the old versions stored in the ROM. Apple also calls this mechanism the ROM-in-RAM architecture.

A variety of other user-related system settings required by your Mac are stored in the parameter RAM, or PRAM, a small memory chip located on the logic board. There's also an Extended PRAM, but it's really all the same thing.

You can reset the PRAM at startup time by holding down ⌘ Option P R; this action is called "zapping the PRAM." PRAM runs off a battery, and some problems can arise when the battery runs out of power, which happens eventually, after a few years.

Why the Mac ToolBox? (DM)

Back in 1983, when the Mac was invented, RAM was terribly expensive. Placing a set of shared high-level routines on a relatively less expensive ROM was more efficient for Mac programs and the Mac OS and saved everyone money. That's hard to imagine nowadays, when a 512 MB module costs less than $100. However, in 1986, a 512 KB (yes, kilobyte) memory upgrade was $1,000. Ouch, indeed.

A Bus Runs Through It: Graphics/Video and I/O (DM/DT)

Although the processor is critical to the performance, there's much more to a logic board than the CPU. A data bus connects the processor to other subsystems that provide display and graphics; I/O (input/output) connectors for storage and networking; and other ways to expand the capabilities of the computer. There's no way that the main processor could control all the functions of the computer; instead, each subsystem has its own set of integrated circuits.

When bits and bytes flow through the various components of your Mac, they do so through a data bus. Just as a wider pipe allows a greater flow of water, a wider bus makes for faster data transmission. Current Power Mac G4s have a 128-bit bus for connecting the processor and RAM; earlier Macs have used 16-, 32-, and 64-bit buses. However, the bus also branches out to connect with the different subsystems at different speeds and widths.

Speaking of Bits (DM)

Confusion can often arise between binary and decimal measurements of computer technologies. The bit is the smallest binary unit, representing a zero or 1; and 8 bits equal a byte. The common decimal reading of a kilobyte is 1,000 bytes; however, some smarty-pants said that a kilobyte should be counted as 1,024 bytes, or 2 to the 10th power. Fortunately, several years ago industry standards groups agreed to use the decimal definition, so a kilo is a kilo. You can find more discussion on the subject at www.seagate.com/support/kb/disc/bytes.html.

Here are the common subsystems and I/O ports found on today's Macs:

Video. To handle the image on the screen, all computers employ a graphics subsystem, usually with its own memory and ICs. The video circuitry can be found on a removable card in a dedicated slot or simply integrated on the logic board and often accelerates display performance by independently processing 2D and 3D graphics routines. In bygone Macs, the video circuitry was sometimes on the logic board and sometimes with a slot used to add special video RAM modules.

Depending on its capabilities, the video subsystem can also support more than one display. Today's desktop Macs offer two types of external ports for video: the familiar DB-15 VGA and a recent proprietary connector, called the Apple Display Connector.

Expansion slots. Most computers offer one or more ways to expand their hardware capabilities, usually through some industry-standard card interface. Mac and Windows desktop machines have several PCI (Peripheral Component Interconnect) slots, and portables often provide a PC Card interface.

The current Power Mac PCI slots can handle 6.88-inch and 12.283-inch PCI cards running at 33 MHz with a power requirement of 3.3 volts (V) or 5V. Apple's PCI slots support the PCI Local Bus Specification, Revision 2.1.

PCI-SIG has more information than you ever wanted to know about PCI technology: www.pcisig.com/home.

Storage I/O. Most computers use a separate subsystem to handle I/O devices inside and outside the case, such as hard drives and optical mechanisms. The latest Mac I/O controller, called KeyLargo, supports a wide range of storage standards, including the Ultra DMA/66 (AT Attachment-5) interface for hard drives and ATAPI-4 (AT Attachment Packet Interface) for optical formats such as CD-Rewritable, DVD, or DVD-Recordable.

USB. Intel spearheaded the development of Universal Serial Bus (USB) to encompass separate interfaces needed for the keyboard and mouse as well as for serial and parallel devices. Now it's used for a wide variety of external devices such as digital cameras, printers, scanners, and MP3 players. Apple's USB ports handle data throughput of 12 Mbps.

FireWire. Apple invented FireWire in the early 1990s; its standard name is IEEE 1394a, a slight revision to the first 1394 specification, which was 1394-1995. Sony and its partners call it i.Link, but it's still the same thing. The goal for FireWire was to succeed flavors of the venerable SCSI interface for digital video cameras and players, scanners, and storage devices. It provides speeds as fast as 50 MBps, can connect as many as 62 devices, lets devices receive power through the cable, and allows users to plug and unplug devices without shutting down (USB also has this hot-swapping capability).

The 1394 Trade Association is the place for more about FireWire: www.1394ta.com.

Networking. Many computers support networks with an add-on card or integrated interface. Most Macs come standard with an Ethernet port; the latest models offer a single interface supporting the Gigabit Ethernet standard, or IEEE 802.3. In addition, all current Macs provide a slot for wireless networking using the 802.11b standard, branded by Apple as AirPort.

Name That Connector (MB)

Over the past few years, Apple has offered several ways to connect peripherals to your Mac.

FireWire

FireWire is a high-speed (400 Mbps or 50 MBps) serial interface with *potential* transfer rates higher than those of Ultra SCSI (40 MBps). In reality, as with any interface, the physical device is usually the limiting factor. One huge advantage FireWire has over SCSI is that with FireWire, you don't have to deal with any device IDs or termination settings. Like USB, FireWire allows you to connect and disconnect devices with the power on and without requiring a restart. (For drives, however, make sure you drag them to the Trash or use the Put Away command before disconnecting them.) FireWire is also an ideal way to import movies, since many digital camcorders now include a FireWire port. (Note that some camera vendors may refer to FireWire as IEEE 1394 or i.Link.) FireWire is also a popular interface for CD recorders.

FireWire can daisy-chain 60-some devices using cable lengths as long as 14 feet. Powered FireWire hubs and repeaters can provide even more connections and an extended range. Mac FireWire ports are the larger six-pin (U-shaped) connector type. Check your equipment type to see if you need a 6-pin-to-6-pin cable (common for hard drives and CD-ROM recorders) or a 6-pin-to-4-pin cable (for devices such as DV camcorders that don't use FireWire bus power).

For more information on FireWire, see www.apple.com/FireWire/.

USB

USB, or Universal Serial Bus, has a maximum interface rate of 12 Mbps, so it is best used for devices that don't require a high-speed connection. (Common USB devices include keyboards, mice, graphics tablets, game controllers, and lower-speed CD-ROM recorders.)

USB is also a popular interface for transferring data to your Mac from PDAs (personal digital assistants), digital cameras, and portable MP3 audio players that include a USB port.

Theoretically, you can connect as many as 127 devices at once, but in reality that's not practical. You can buy a hub to provide more ports if you use a lot of USB devices and don't like switching cable connections.

You can get a USB-to-ADB adapter from a third-party source such as Griffin Technology (www.griffintechnology.com) if you need to connect ADB devices to USB Macs. For more information on USB, see www.apple.com/usb/.

SCSI

SCSI (Small Computer Systems Interface) was the standard storage interface included on the logic boards of Macs through the first Power Mac G3 series.

The SCSI interfaces of Mac logic boards prior to the Beige Power Mac G3 series included an external 25-pin connector with a 5 MBps maximum rate (SCSI-1) and an internal 50-pin interface with a maximum speed of 10 MBps (SCSI-2, or Fast SCSI). Both ports could handle a maximum of seven devices each (using SCSI IDs 0 to 6; ID 7 is the SCSI controller.) The onboard SCSI was 8 bits wide (called Narrow SCSI). Faster PCI cards feature 16-bit interfaces (Wide SCSI) at much higher clock rates.

continues on next page

Name That Connector continued

The Beige G3's onboard SCSI interface was not only the last seen on new Macs but also one of the slowest. The 5 MBps onboard SCSI had a single channel for both internal and external connections. Therefore, you had to ensure that your external devices did not have the same SCSI ID as that used for an internal device. (This was not a problem with previous models, which had separate inter-faces for external and internal SCSI connections.) Some Beige G3s shipped with an optional PCI SCSI card and Wide SCSI drives for higher performance.

For more information on the various types of SCSI, see the reference articles and white papers at SCSI manufacturers' Web sites, such as those of Adaptec (www.adaptec.com), Quantum (www.quantum.com), and Granite Digital (www.scsipro.com).

I/O in the Looking Glass (DM)

In late 2001, various industry groups started promoting technologies that could become the next generation of PCI and AGP (Accelerated Graphics Port). The list included Arapahoe—also called 3GIO (for third-generation IO, see developer.intel.com/technology/3gio/), HyperTransport (www.hypertransport.org), and RapidIO (www.rapioio.org). Each has its proponents. All aim to avoid performance bottlenecks within future high-speed computers, servers, and network switches. Some are being designed to reach speeds upwards of 10 Gbps.

Arapahoe is supported by a consortium including Dell and Intel. It looks to be a shoo-in for the PCI replacement and was placed before the PCI SIG in late summer 2001. According to reports, 3GIO is about two years away from arrival in products. HyperTransport is supported by Advanced Micro Devices, Apple, Cisco Systems, Sun Microsystems, and nVidia, among others. According to analysts, HyperTransport is currently incorporated in graphic card vendor nVidia's latest chip set. RapidIO is boosted by a consortium including Alcatel, Cisco, EMC, IBM, Lucent, and Motorola, but analysts said its most logical application is in embedded applications.

The Ages of the Desktop Macintosh (DM)

The easiest way to assess Macintosh design is by processor. However, it's also the most likely to lead you astray, because much of the time, differences in machine performance are a result of cache architecture, expansion ports, and graphics capabilities. Nevertheless, here, going from newest to oldest, are the three major processor ages of desktop Macintosh:

Modern Macs. The CPUs compatible with Mac OS X, spanning the Power Mac G3 (Blue and White) and Power Mac G4 series (as well as a couple of strays).

RISC Pioneers. Macs that used the first generations of the PowerPC processor.

The Golden Age. Machines that ran a Motorola 680X0 processor (starting with the original Mac).

Aside from the colorful industrial design that we now appreciate, modern Mac desktops are very different on the inside from their forebears. Today's Macs use more industry-standard parts and connectors instead of the home-grown technologies Apple used to favor. For example, the familiar USB and PCI replaced proprietary and pricey Apple buses. This approach has reduced the expense of development and manufacturing as well as provided a larger market for upgrades and peripherals, because PC vendors can now offer their devices on the Mac side often by just writing a Mac driver.

In addition, Apple has reduced the number of logic boards used in its machines. Following Steve Jobs' now-classic grid of professional and home markets, Apple uses one logic-board design for professional desktop models and the other for iMacs. In the past, each machine had its own design team, making things difficult (and expensive) on the compatibility front for Apple's own system-software team and third-party developers.

Why a Desktop? (DM)

This question has no relationship to the Marx Brothers koan: Why a duck? Instead, it points to the increasing perception among computer buyers—fostered by marketing—that desktop and portable computers now are somewhat equivalent in features and capabilities. Or enough alike that it really doesn't matter. If only it were true.

Notebook computers are designed first to be portable and then powerful. They trade performance for size and heat. Comparable desktop machines are designed for performance; can run faster processors; hold more, and less expensive, RAM; generate better graphics; and provide slots for expansion and storage. Still, you can't carry a desktop easily into the neighborhood coffee shop.

The Thoroughly Modern Mac: The Power Mac G4 Series (DM)

The Power Mac G4 series brought several important technologies to the platform: the PowerPC G4 processor; the revival of multiprocessing; and the Accelerated Graphics Port (AGP), an industry-standard connector for improving graphics.

The PowerPC G4, or the PowerPC 74xx series, incorporates what Apple calls Velocity Engine and Motorola calls AltiVec. Whatever the moniker, it's a special vector execution unit that lets the processor subdivide a task and work on each part simultaneously. Applications such as 3D graphics, image and video processing, and audio encoding use vector data and can benefit from this parallel engine and some of its multimedia-specific routines.

Nothing ever comes free, however, and applications must be tuned to take advantage of the Velocity Engine. And many common functions of a computer can't be accelerated with the scheme. Still some tasks can run as much as 10 times faster on a PowerPC G4 than a PowerPC G3 at the same speed.

The first models of the Power Mac G4 came with the PPC7400 processor. Later models graduated to the 7410 and then in 2001 to the 7450, a version with higher speeds, longer pipelines, and a 256 Kbyte on-chip cache. [*Pipelines allow a processor to execute several instructions, or different parts of an instruction, at the same time. Among its advantages, a longer pipeline helps a processor run at a higher frequency.—Ed.*]

In addition, the PowerPC G4 can handle symmetric multiprocessing, or the use of two processors instead of just one. (Several 1990s Macs came equipped with dual processors, but that capability was set aside with the arrival of the PowerPC G3 processor, which Apple used in the first of the modern Macs.) Just as some applications can be accelerated with AltiVec, others can be tuned to take advantage of two CPUs.

The Power Mac G4 series also switched video connections from PCI to the Accelerated Graphics Port (AGP). AGP improves the Mac's performance for 3D graphics capabilities, such as textures, alpha buffers, and z-buffers.

Here's the Power Mac G4 series, in reverse order of introduction:

Power Mac G4 (QuickSilver). QuickSilver refers to the slight changes in the enclosure's front bezel.

Power Mac G4 (Digital Audio). Introduced a digital audio port.

Power Mac G4 (Gigabit Ethernet). Introduced 10/100/1000 Ethernet port.

Power Mac G4—AGP Graphics. Introduced the AGP card slot.

Power Mac G4—PCI Graphics. Lower-end models.

Several versions were also sold as servers, one with Mac OS X Server software.

Interestingly, the first lower-end models, with 350- and 400-MHz processors, used a logic board code-named Yikes! It provided a PCI slot for graphics, rather than the AGP logic board, which was code-named Sawtooth. Apple gave users an "easy" way to distinguish the models: On Yikes! machines the microphone and sound-output ports on the rear panel are placed sideways.

Meanwhile, Apple's series-branding scheme, fully developed with the Power Mac G4, continues to cause confusion for users, developers, and especially technical writers and editors. The company designates a series of machines with a name; so a G4 model is a G4 model, and don't sweat the small stuff such as changes in the enclosure, version of the processor, logic-board architecture, and support for peripherals. For example, the Power Mac G4 (Digital Audio) January 2001 documentation warns users to check a green light on the logic board when installing PCI cards. The Power Mac G4 (QuickSilver), released six months later in July, tells of a red light.

You can get some answers by checking the readout in the Apple System Profiler application. In addition, the dated Apple Spec documentation at www.info.apple.com often provides answers; however, its documentation can suffer from amnesia about the exact version of the PowerPC processor used in a model (it will just list a 350 MHz G4 processor instead of a 350 MHz PowerPC 7400). The excellent EveryMac site offers this information at www.everymac.com/systems/apple/.

G4 Cubed (DM)

One of the most controversial models in many years, the Power Mac G4 Cube debuted in July 2000. The system featured a PowerPC G4 processor and AGP graphics in a striking 8-inch enclosure, about a quarter of the size of most PCs. It was marketed with Apple's equally high-style flat-panel displays. Some pundits complained about PCI expansion slots stripped from the Cube's logic board, others barked about its lack of support for removable media and its cost. Although more than 100,000 Cubes were sold, Apple had expected much more. Steve Jobs told financial analysts in early 2001 that the Cube had been accepted by the market. "The disappointment to us was the market wasn't as big as we thought," he said.

The Arrival of the PowerPC G3 (DM)

The landing of the PowerPC G3 processor on the Mac platform was vitally important to the company and to the Mac user community. Naturally, it provided a big step forward in performance from the first generations of PowerPC machines; the G3 was more than 30 percent faster than the speediest chip of the preceding generation.

One-Time Wonder (DM)

In the spring of 1997, before the introduction of the Power Mac G3 models, Apple released a special-edition Mac to commemorate the company's founding 20 years earlier. The Twentieth Anniversary Macintosh was a bold design, incorporating a 12.1-inch flat-panel screen, television tuner, stereo speakers, and a CD-ROM drive. Its power supply was separate and contained the subwoofer. Its custom components were expensive, but potential purchasers considered it underpowered, given its $7,500 price tag.

In addition, the Power Mac G3 models heralded the introduction of the important FireWire interface to the desktop; and along with the earlier iMac, they showed Apple's willingness to rile important market segments by abandoning ADB, SCSI, and serial interfaces.

The PowerPC G3 (or PowerPC 750), so named for the third generation of the line, offered high performance with low power; it was much smaller than the top-of-the-line PowerPC 604e processor that preceded it. Code-named Arthur, the CPU used a built-in Level 2 cache controller with a separate bus for a backside cache, allowing it to handle instructions, talk with the cache, and send data over the system bus simultaneously.

The first three models—desktop, minitower, and a large, tooth-shaped all-in-one version—were similar in design to previous machines. Today they are known as the Beige G3 models.

PowerPC G3 and G4 Macs

Model	Processor	Chip Speed (MHz)	PCI Slots	AGP	ADB	FireWire	USB	Ethernet	Intro.
Power Mac G4 (QuickSilver)	G4	733/ 800 dual/ 867	4	1	-	2	2	10/100/1000	7/01
Power Mac G4 (Digital Audio)	G4	466/ 533 dual/ 667/733	4	1	-	2	2	10/100/1000	1/01
Power Mac G4 Cube	G4	450/500	-	1	-	2	2	10/100	7/00
Power Mac G4 (Gigabit Ethernet)	G4	400/ 450 dual/ 500 dual	3	1	-	2	2	10/100/1000	7/00
Power Mac G4 (AGP Graphics)	G4	350/400/ 450/500	3	1	-	3	2	10/100	9/99
Power Mac G4 (PCI Graphics)	G4	350/400	4	-	-	3	2	10/100	9/99
Power Mac G3 (Blue and White)	G3	350/400/ 450	4	-	1	2	2	10/100	1/99
Power Mac G3 All-In-One	G3	233/266	3	-	1	-	-	10	4/98
Power Mac G3 Desktop	G3	266/300	3	-	1	-	-	10	11/97
Power Mac G3 Mini Tower	G3	266/300	3	-	1	-	-	10	11/97

With the 1999 introduction of the Power Macintosh G3 (Blue and White), the shape of modern Macs became evident. The enclosure was colorful and provided easy access to the interior. But the most important changes were on the inside with its Yosemite logic-board design. Primarily, the new model offered a much different set of interfaces than high-end Mac users were used to.

First, Apple offered FireWire as a replacement for SCSI, a connector that had been standard on the platform since 1986. Today it's easy to see the advantages of FireWire for video and even storage, and a whole market has grown up around it. But at that time, few FireWire peripherals were available. This move away from SCSI alarmed professional users with a heavy investment in SCSI technology.

In addition, Apple replaced serial, printer, and Apple Desktop Bus (ADB) interfaces with USB. Of course, many users had serial modems and printers and even older LocalTalk networking. And although ADB was primarily used for a keyboard and mouse, it was commonly brought into play with software copy protection dongles outside the U.S.

The Golden Age and Pioneer Power Macs (DM/SA)

For those Mac users who missed the original Macintosh in action, it's difficult to understand the impact it had on the public following its 1984 release. "Electrifying" comes close to the mark. The lightweight, all-in-one box had a tiny black-and-white screen, but it showed fonts and pictures. Instead of entering commands, users could physically interact with its interface via a mouse. It was simply amazing.

For the first decade of its life, the Macintosh platform was based on the Motorola 68000 family of processors. The chip was so named because it had 68,000 transistors etched on it. The PowerBook 190 was the last model to be manufactured with a Motorola 68000-series processor. Here's a list of the CPUs:

- The 68000 was used for the first Macs. The PowerBook 100 used a special low-power version, the 68HC000.

- The 68020 handled 32-bit chunks internally and had a 256-byte instruction cache.

- The 68030 added a 256-byte data cache, and its two 32-bit data paths could handle twice the information traffic. It also featured a paged memory management unit (PMMU) needed for virtual memory.

- The 68040 had larger instruction and data caches as well as a built-in math coprocessor. The 68LC040 was a low-cost version without the math functions.

The earliest Macs were all based on a closed, semiportable design with an integrated handle and were passively cooled.

The original Mac—later dubbed the 128K—was launched with the famous "1984" Super Bowl ad. The Mac 128K aimed to be the first computing appliance, a relatively low-cost and accessible computer. The $2,495 Mac was a wild success. Although its 128 Kbytes of memory was generous at the time, it still wasn't enough to meet the demands of a graphical interface. Even a simple file copy would require users to spend many minutes swapping 400 Kbyte floppy disks in and out of the drive. Later that year, Apple released the Mac 512K, also called the Fat Mac.

In 1986, Apple offered the Mac Plus, the first real update to the platform. It addressed the primary shortcomings: slots for RAM upgrades and a SCSI port, the first use of the interface on any desktop computer.

One stroke of genius on the early Macs was AppleTalk, the networking protocol built in to every Mac. When combined with the PostScript-capable LaserWriter, the small Mac Plus suddenly became a digital publishing workstation out of the box.

A year later Apple offered the Macintosh SE (code-named Aladdin), the first Mac to feature an internal hard drive and a cooling fan as well as an Apple Desktop Bus connector. Unlike the simple dedicated cables used on earlier Macs and PCs, ADB was a standard bus that could be used by a variety of devices, much as USB is today. The SE also featured the Mac's first upgrade slot, called the Processor Direct Slot.

Apple in 1989 also updated its all-in-one line with the faster 68030 processor. Its small monochrome screen required scant overhead, when compared with the Mac II series and its larger displays. The result was a screaming little box that became a favorite among AppleTalk network managers.

Days of Rectangular Pixels (DM)

The Mac didn't spring full-blown from the brain of Steve Jobs and his band of programming pirates on the Apple campus. Some of the groundwork was laid with Apple's Lisa, a high-performance business workstation with a graphical user interface and mouse. The machine used the 68000 processor but featured a larger screen, as much as 512K of RAM, and a built-in hard drive. It would be years before the Mac came up to the Lisa's capabilities. In 1985, the Lisa models were renamed the Macintosh XL and came with a 10 MB hard drive. And yes, its pixels weren't exactly square.

Opening the Closed Box (DM/DT)

Yet, the Mac was still a closed box, a situation Apple addressed in 1987 with the Mac II. Running a 68020 processor, the desktop model offered color graphics, an internal hard drive, and a set of six expansion slots using NuBus, an advanced connector technology. Like today's PCI, Apple's NuBus was self-arbitrating, meaning it registered the cards automatically with the Mac at startup time. The upgrade slots on DOS machines required users to adjust tiny DIP switches and jumpers when adding an expansion card. The connector was also sturdy and secure, something PCI could still learn.

A series of Mac II models followed:

IIx. The IIx introduced the 68030 chip and included a floating point unit; it also was the first to use 1.4 MB floppy drives.

IIcx. The smaller IIcx (1989) was a slightly faster version of the IIx but with only three NuBus slots.

IIci. The IIci (1989) ran at 25 MHz instead of its predecessors' 16 MHz. This model was well built and a favorite of Mac fanatics, with its built-in video circuitry and a slot to expand the cache memory. It was a workhorse known for its longevity.

IIsi. The IIsi (1990) offered affordable performance with a single NuBus slot and a low-profile "pizza box" case. It featured a sound-input port and came with a microphone.

IIvx. The IIvx (1992) came with an internal CD-ROM drive.

A Macintosh by Any Other Name (DM)

In 1990 and 1991, Apple decided to rebrand its desktop lines, based on market segment, processor, and channel. Apple aimed certain lines at certain markets— such as education, SOHO (small office/home office), and enterprise—and then confined the distribution of each brand to its own channel. The result was a complicated sales picture.

GeoPort: Now You See It … (DM)

Some of the machines of this time offered the GeoPort, Apple's proprietary serial-port technology, designed to replace modems. The connector sported an extra pin hole supplying power, and in conjunction with a special adapter and telecommunications software, it could replace most modem functions. However, the cost of standalone modems fell and their performance outstripped the GeoPort scheme. The Power Mac 5200 and the Performa 5200 and 6200 have an extra pin on their modem ports, yet are not GeoPorts. Go figure.

The Macintosh Quadra series was based on the 68040 chip (quad equals 4, get it?); the Macintosh Centris was a line of middle-of-the-road systems; and Macintosh LCs were low cost, aimed primarily at the education market. The company also revived the all-in-one form factor with several Macintosh Classic models and even a Color Classic.

In 1992, Apple expanded this structure with the Macintosh Performa, a new brand aimed at consumers, and sold at mass-market retailers such as Sears. The models came bundled with a variety of software, similar to today's iMac. The hardware, however, was identical to the members in other brands, albeit with some slight variations in memory, hard-disk size, or cache. The Performa naming scheme, which tried to inform customers of processor, speed, and extras, grew complicated for retailers and users alike.

Name Game: Differentiating the Performa Siblings

Performa	Alternate
200	Classic
250	Color Classic
275	Color Classic II
400	LC II
405/410/430	LC II (with modem and larger hard drive)
450	LC III
460/466/467	LC III+
475/476	LC 475/Quadra 605
520	LC 520
550/560	LC 550
575/577/578	LC 575
580CD/588CD	LC 580
600/600CD	IIvx (but with no cache card and FPU)
630	LC 630

Dorm Entertainment (DM)

In 1993, Apple offered the Macintosh TV, a machine aimed at college students. Using the Mac LC 530 case and integrating a TV tuner, the model's case was black instead of the usual white/platinum.

PowerPC Macs   Includes models sold only in the United States.

Performa	Processor	Chip Speed (MHz)	L2 Cache	PCI Slots	NuBus	Introduced
6400	603e	180/200	Opt/256 KB	2	-	8/96
6360	603e	160	Opt	1	-	10/96
6320CD	603e	120	256 KB	-	-	4/96
6300CD	603e	100	256 KB	-	-	10/95
6290CD	603e	100	256 KB	-	-	1/96
6230CD	603	75	256 KB	-	-	7/95
6220CD	603	75	256 KB	-	-	7/95
6218CD	603	75	256 KB	-	-	7/95
6216CD	603	75	256 KB	-	-	7/95
6214CD	603	75	256 KB	-	-	8/95
6210CD	603	75	256 KB	-	-	10/95
6205CD	603	75	256 KB	-	-	8/95
6200CD	603	75	256 KB	-	-	7/95
6118CD	601	60	Opt	-	1	11/94
6117CD	601	60	Opt	-	1	11/94
6116CD	601	60	Opt	-	1	7/95
6115CD	601	60	Opt	-	1	11/94
6112CD	601	60	Opt	-	1	11/94
6110CD	601	60	Opt	-	1	11/94
5400CD	603e	120	Opt	1	-	4/96
5300CD	603e	100	256 KB	-	-	10/95
5260	603e	120	Opt	-	-	10/96
5260CD	603e	100	Opt	-	-	4/96
5215CD	603	75	256 KB	-	-	7/95
5200CD	603	75	256 KB	-	-	7/95

Apple phased out these brands over time, especially as the company shifted its machines to the PowerPC processor and away from the 68040. The Performa had the most staying power, but Apple finally retired the Performa brand in 1997. It used the Power Mac name for all desktop machines until it introduced the iMac in 1998.

680X0 Macs   Includes models sold only in the United States.

Quadra/Centris	Processor	Chip Speed (MHz)	Slots	Introduced
Quadra 950	68040	33	5	5/92
Quadra 900	68040	25	5	10/91
Quadra 840AV	68040	40	3	7/93
Quadra 800	68040	33	3	2/93
Quadra 700	68040	25	2	10/91
Quadra 660AV	68040	25	1	10/93
Centris 660AV	68040	25	1	7/93
Quadra 650	68040	33	3	10/93
Centris 650	68040	25	3	2/93
Quadra 630	68040	33	-	7/94
Quadra 610 DOS Compatible	68040	25	-	2/94
Quadra 610	68040/68LC040	25	1	10/93
Centris 610	68LC040	20	1	2/93
Quadra 605	68LC040	25	-	10/93

Performa	Processor	Chip Speed (MHz)	Slots	Introduced
640CD DOS Compatible	68LC040	66	-	5/95
638CD	68LC040	66	-	7/94
637CD	68LC040	66	-	7/94
636/636CD	68LC040	66	-	7/94
635CD	68LC040	66	-	7/94
631CD	68LC040	66	-	7/95
630/630CD	68LC040	66	-	7/94
600/600CD	68030	32	3	9/92
580CD	68LC040	66	-	5/95
578	68LC040	66	-	2/94
577	68LC040	66	-	2/94
575	68LC040	66	-	2/94
560	68030	33	-	1/94
550	68030	33	-	10/93
476	68LC040	50	-	10/93
475	68LC040	50	-	10/93
467	68030	33	-	10/93
466	68030	33	-	10/93
460	68030	33	-	10/93
450	68030	25	-	4/93

Performa	Processor	Chip Speed (MHz)	Slots	Introduced
430	68030	16	-	4/93
410	68030	16	-	10/93
405	68030	16	-	4/93
400	68030	16	-	9/92
250	68030	16	-	2/93
200	68030	16	-	9/92
LC	**Processor**	**Chip Speed (MHz)**	**Slots**	**Introduced**
LC 630 DOS Compatible	68LC040	66	-	4/95
LC 630	68LC040	66	-	7/94
LC 580	68LC040	66	-	4/95
LC 575	68LC040	66	-	2/94
LC 550	68030	33	-	2/94
LC 520	68030	25	-	6/93
LC 475	68LC040	50	-	10/93
LC III+	68030	33	-	10/93
LC III	68030	25	-	2/93
LC II	68030	16	-	3/92
LC	68020	16	-	10/90
Macintosh TV	68030	32	-	10/93
II	**Processor**	**Chip Speed (MHz)**	**Slots**	**Introduced**
IIvx	68030	32	3	10/92
IIsi	68030	20	1	10/90
IIfx	68030	40	6	3/90
IIci	68030	25	3	9/89
IIcx	68030	16	3	3/89
IIx	68030	16	6	9/88
II	68020	16	6	3/87
All-in-One	**Processor**	**Chip Speed (MHz)**	**Slots**	**Introduced**
Color Classic	68030	16	-	2/93
Classic II	68030	16	-	10/91
Classic	68000	8	-	10/90
SE/30	68030	16	-	1/89
SE	68000	8	-	3/87
Plus	68000	8	-	1/86
512Ke	68000	8	-	4/86
512K	68000	8	-	9/84
128K	68000	8	-	1/84

Today, Apple uses four brands for its computers—Power Macintosh, iMac, PowerBook, and iBook—and each corresponds to a market segment. The big difference is that Apple manufactures usually four (sometimes five) logic boards for its models, rather than the dozen or so that it tried to mix and match between brands.

PowerPC Pioneers (DM)

For the first decade of its existence, the Mac platform ran processors using CISC (complex instruction set computing, technology still used today for most processors in the world). In 1994, Apple changed tack and based its computers on the PowerPC chip, which instead uses a RISC (reduced instruction set computing) architecture. According to theory, RISC is inherently more efficient than CISC, because each additional instruction set makes the chip bigger, more complicated, and hence, slower. Apple, IBM, and Motorola formed an alliance, called AIM, to engineer and manufacture the chip.

In addition to pure speed, the PowerPC offered other technologies that could benefit the Mac platform. First, some versions could handle multiprocessing, a performance-boosting technology that appeals to Mac users in the scientific and video fields. Second, the alliance produced flavors of the processor for mobile computing, letting Mac notebooks perform faster than comparable-speed Intel versions. And Apple would benefit from economies in production, since the alliance believed that the PowerPC would be used widely in computers and servers running the Windows and Unix operating systems, as well as Mac clones.

Did a Meteor Kill the Mac Clones? (DM)

Long after the sinking of Atlantis and before the rise of Amazon.com was the Golden Age of Macintosh. In common reckoning: around 1990. Readers may argue the assertion—after all, isn't the Mac *everywhere?* However, the historical record shows that through much of the 1990s, Apple took a series of strategic missteps that moved the company from a position of industry leadership to the brink of destruction.

In bygone days, the Mac was the sole desktop computer with an easy-to-use graphical user interface. No other platform offered such an elegant integration of machine and software; indeed, the same circumstance still exists to this day. The Mac was also used widely in big business—some sites had more than 30,000 Macs.

Apple then was a vastly larger company than it is today. The development efforts of Apple, modeled on its competitor IBM, encompassed a wide range of technologies. In addition to Macs, Apple worked on peripherals, including digital cameras and printers; consumer and business programs; and interfaces such as FireWire. And like Big Blue, Apple maintained a division for basic R&D, dubbed the Advanced Technology Group, which explored arcana from agent technology to basic human interface design.

As 1990 came around, Apple's strategy came into focus: The company envisaged its long-term success not in hardware sales but from software products and licensing. The quick adoption of Microsoft's Windows 3.0 following its early 1990 release convinced Apple management of the correctness of its new path. Still, almost all of Apple's business was hardware of some kind.

A year and a half later, Apple and IBM shocked the high-tech industry by forming a collection of jointly funded companies and technologies: The PowerPC Initiative would manufacture a next-generation processor based on the reduced instruction set computing (RISC) design; Kaleida would create a new multimedia software architecture; and Taligent would develop a next-generation, high-performance operating system with a Mac look and feel. Taligent aimed to finish an Apple project code-named Pink. Motorola joined up to design and manufacture the chips.

According to IBM, the traditional, complex (CISC) processor design—the architecture used by Intel for its processors—would soon become obsolete and the PowerPC's novel scheme would provide more than twice the performance, with less heat and at a much lower price. Although Apple would be a solid customer, IBM expected that the price/performance benefit of the PowerPC chip would immediately attract manufacturers of Intel desktop systems and servers; these buyers would make up more than 75 percent of the total market.

(In hindsight, the assumptions for RISC never panned out. Intel's Pentium engineering has more than matched the PowerPC megahertz for megahertz; only recently has any vendor strayed from the Intel standard. The PowerPC's Velocity Engine and IBM's ground-breaking microprocessor manufacturing methods should keep Macs steady with the rest of the industry. But the Mac's continued success has been more due to its great software engineering, integrated hardware, and spiff industrial design rather than Apple's choice of processor.)

Of course, making an announcement is easy. Building new companies and shipping products out the door takes years. Apple discovered roadblocks to its software-centric goal as an engineering brain-drain took a toll on continuity within the company. Talented Mac programmers were shifted to the joint ventures just as Apple increased its project list with new versions of the Mac OS, dubbed Copland; QuickTime; and OpenDoc, a novel cross-platform "compound-document" architecture that would let a user cobble together an application feature-by-feature by adding small modules. (Kaleida and Taligent eventually proved fruitless—the only survivors from this time are QuickTime and some of Copland's interface elements.)

On the market front, Apple saw the widespread defection of large enterprise sites to Windows. In the fall of 1994 (when Apple had a record $2.94 billion quarter), bad-news stories in the PC trade press predicted the quick demise of the Mac and quoted industry bigwigs saying Apple was a takeover target. More important to Apple was the way the Mac platform was shedding third-party developers. As markets for the Mac contracted, developers saw expanding opportunities for Windows programs and programmers. Mac developers demanded that Apple find new customers for their products.

continues on next page

Did a Meteor Kill the Mac Clones? continued

Tears of a Clone

At this moment, Apple responded: Send in the clones! Apple said licensing the Mac OS would grow the Mac's market share from 10 percent to 18 percent by 1998. After a trial period using Apple-derived motherboard designs, the licensees would gain freedom with the use of the Common Hardware Reference Platform that could run the Mac OS, IBM's OS/2, Apple's flavor of Unix, Windows NT, Novell's NetWare, and Sun's Solaris. Analysts predicted that corporate America would go gaga over this flexible box and the Apple/IBM/cloner crowd would quickly rise to a 30 percent market share.

As the Mac industry waited for a big name to join the Mac OS licensee ranks, the field was taken up with small newbies. The cloners were able to win the backing of Mac users through excellent compatibility, good prices, and even better performance. The smaller companies wooed performance aficionados by beating Apple to market with the highest-speed processors, albeit in very, very small batches.

The clone makers also brought excitement back to the Mac market. Mike Rosenfelt, Power Computing's brash marketing maven, unveiled a string of brilliant marketing efforts that reassured the Mac community. And software developers hailed the cloners for providing them with opportunities to bundle and comarket products. This type of arrangement was virtually impossible with Apple; it was busy hawking bundles of its own consumer wares.

Meanwhile, Apple's plan was unraveling. As cloners gained increasing market and mind share, Apple's huge software projects proved unworkable. Finally, in late 1996, Apple pulled the plug on Copland, a project that had employed a 500-man team for years. With quarterly losses hitting $700 million, the company brought back Steve Jobs and his OpenStep OS to save the day.

Jobs had learned much while in exile at Next—a lot more money was to be made from selling both software and hardware. And he knew that most Mac owners would want the performance boost promised by the forthcoming PowerPC G3 processor. This upgrade market was too ripe a fruit to share with the cloners. In the summer of 1997, even as Apple negotiators inked tentative agreements with cloners for final-stage licensing, Jobs himself pulled the plug on all deals and later bought out some for pennies on the dollar. He told the faithful at the Macworld Expo in Boston that summer: "Trust me for a few months."

And it was all over. These days, the only traces of the Mac clones can be found in flea markets.

Pippin (DM)

In 1994, Apple hoisted its flag in the game market with a PowerPC-based design called Pippin. As the market changed, so did the product's positioning: Sometimes it was an Internet appliance and thin-client computer and other times it was a game console. Licensed to the Japanese company Bandai (www.bandai.com), the devices were offered for $599. Unfortunately, the company ran into production delays, and manufacturing costs ran over budget. Apple shelved plans for a second version during a bruising 1997 restructuring.

Here's a list of the first PowerPC generations:

601. The first-generation processor used in Apple transition models.

603/603e. Designed to be inexpensive and energy efficient, the 603 was used in PowerBooks and low-end desktop Macs. This and the 604 are the G2 processors.

604/604e. Bigger and faster than the 603s, the 604 sported larger caches and multiprocessor capabilities.

Early PowerPC Macs also brought the PCI bus to the Mac platform, and Apple incorporated faster flavors of SCSI. The combination of performance, expandability, and options for integrated A/V technology helped maintain the Mac platform in the important markets for multimedia and print-content creation and in scientific data analysis. Some popular A/V configurations were offered with S-video and RCA video input/output connectors.

Here's a rundown of the first generation of the PowerPC models:

4400. Based on the Tanzania logic-board design originated for AIM licensing, the model used a desktop case and many industry-standard parts to lower production costs.

5200/5260. A 603-based CPU with an elegant all-in-one enclosure. The similar 5300 used a 603e processor.

5400/5500. Also an all-in-one box, the 5400 changed to the Alchemy logic board; the 5500 used the Gazelle board.

6100/6200/6300. It used a low-profile desktop enclosure similar to the Centris 610. Also known as the Performa 6xxx series and Work Group Server 6xxx.

6400. It used a minitower enclosure and an SRS 3D surround-sound system with integrated subwoofer.

6500. Based on the Gazelle board, the line used a tower case with an integrated Zip drive.

7100/7200/7220/7300. With a high-profile desktop case, the 7100 was based on the BHA logic board; the 7200 used the Catalyst board; and the 7220 used the Tanzania design. The 7300 graduated to the TNT architecture used on the 7500.

7500/7600. With a similar case to the other 7xxx models, these models used the high-performance TNT board design. The 7500 came with a 601 CPU.

8100/8115/8200/8500/8515/8600. Encased in a tower enclosure, the 8100/80 was based on the Cold Fusion logic board design. The 8200 used the Catalyst architecture, and the 8500 and 8600 stepped up to a board code-named Nitro.

9500/9600. The 9500 offered six PCI slots in a tall tower case. The later 9600 and 8600 used a larger tower chassis, called K2 (for the Chogori mountain peak), that provided a hinged side-panel door holding the fan and easy access to the board and seven storage bays.

PowerPC Macs   Includes models sold only in the United States.

Power Mac	Processor Chip	Speed (MHz)	L2 Cache	PCI Slots	NuBus	Introduced
9600	604e	200/200 Dual/ 233/300/350	512 KB/l MB	6	-	2/97
9500	604e	200/180 Dual/	512 KB	6	-	8/96
9500	604	120/132/150	512 KB	6	-	5/95
8600	604e	200/250/300	256 KB/l MB	3	-	2/97
8500	604	120/132/150/180	256 KB	-	3	8/95
8100	601	80/100/110	256 KB	-	3	3/94
7600	604	120/132	256 KB	3	-	4/96
7500	601	100	Opt	3	-	8/95
7300	604e	180/200	256 KB	3	-	2/97
7200	601	75/90/120	Opt	3	-	3/96
7100	601	66/80	Opt/256 KB	-	3	3/94
6500	603e	225/250/275/300	256 KB/512 KB	2	-	2/97
6400	603e	200	256 KB	2	-	10/96
6100	601	60/66	Opt/256 KB	-	1	3/94
5500	603e	225/250	256 KB	1	-	2/97
5400	603e	120/180/200	Opt/256 KB	1	-	4/95
5300	603e	100	256 KB	-	-	8/95
5260	603e	100/120	Opt/256 KB	-	-	8/96
5200	603	75	256 KB	-	-	8/95
4400	603e	200	256 KB	2	-	2/97
4400	603e	160	Opt	3	-	11/96
Twentieth Anniversary Mac	603e	250	256 KB	1	-	6/97

Who's Calling Whom a Butt Head? (DM)

Apple engineers gave the Power Mac 7100's logic board the code name Sagan. Following a *MacWEEK* report of the honor, Carl Sagan decided to sue the company. So the code name was changed to BHA, which some wags claimed was an acronym for Butt Head Astronomer. Try to prove that!

The iMac: Back in Fashion (CB)

The iMac—the cute-as-a-bug Macintosh phenom—is credited with single-handedly saving Apple's bacon in 1998. And little wonder. Apple iCEO Steve Jobs had recently returned to an Apple that more closely resembled its cookie-cutter-PC competitors than the innovative dynamo of the mid-1980s. At that time of the Second Coming of Steve, Apple's products were more expensive and less powerful than Mac-compatible models manufactured by the likes of Power Computing, Umax, and Motorola. Apple was dabbling in everything from handheld computers to TV-console systems to online services, and its market share—thanks to a Microsoft operating system that "borrowed" substantially from the Mac's—was eroding at an alarming rate. In short, Apple was in deep distress.

When Jobs pulled the cover off the iMac in May 1998, it marked more than the unveiling of a new, inexpensive computer. It signaled the return of innovation at Apple and the beginning of a new design philosophy that valued form as much as function.

Despite the concerns of many industry pundits that the iMac's nonexpandable, all-in-one design was a step backward, the iMac sold in record numbers—not only ensuring that Apple would live to fight another day but also demonstrating that Steve Jobs still had the Midas touch.

Look and Feel

At first blush, the obvious difference between the iMac and its predecessors is the playful design. No previous computer—Mac or PC—was so approachable, so much fun to use. The iMac's friendly appearance paid off in significant sales to new computer users—seniors and students in particular. Apple also benefited from more than a little free advertising when iMacs popped up in countless TV programs, were featured in national newsmagazines, and adorned the showrooms of trendy furniture outlets.

Thanks to the iMac, for the first time in a long time, it was cool to own a Mac.

But the iMac was far more than an indication that Apple was interested in making unique-looking computers. It was also a pronouncement that Apple intended to break from the past and spearhead (or at least embrace) the latest technical innovations.

There's No Future in the Past

Once people got over the initial shock of seeing such an unusual computer, the first question that came to mind was, "Where's the floppy drive?" Yes, unlike every other Mac since the beginning of time, the iMac lacked a slot for floppy disks. Horror of horrors!

Apple's response: "Get over it. The floppy's dead."

Our reply: "But we've got a bunch of important Microsoft Word documents on floppies, and we'd really love to use them on our spiffy new iMacs!"

Apple's rejoinder: "Oh, very well. If you need to use floppy disks, you can add an external floppy drive via the iMac's built-in USB port."

Our riposte: "Oh, OK, we'll just add a floppy drive to the … WHAT?! What the heck is a USB port?"

And then we opened the little side door on the iMac, looked at the ports in residence, turned the iMac around and around to be sure we weren't missing something, and returned to the side door with a look of dumb dismay.

Floppy drive—gone. Modem (GeoPort) port—gone. Printer port—gone. ADB port—gone.

In their place we found two USB, or Universal Serial Bus, ports, an Ethernet connector, a sound-input port, a sound-output port, a modem connector, a couple of tiny holes for accessing the reset and interrupt buttons, and something called the mezzanine port; on the front of the iMac—two headphone jacks, a CD-ROM drive, and an IrDA (infrared) port (**Figure 2.1**).

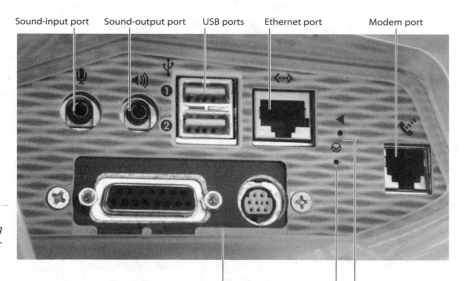

Sound-input port　Sound-output port　USB ports　Ethernet port　Modem port

Figure 2.1

The ports of the first iMac, including the enigmatic mezzanine port.

Mezzanine port (with Griffin Technology's iPort adapter)　Interrupt button　Reset button

Making Connections

As supportive of Apple's latest forays into the wonderful world of industrial design as we'd all like to be, it's a bit irksome to awaken one day to discover that thousands of dollars' worth of peripherals are no longer supported on current Mac models. What are you supposed to do with all your old serial, SCSI, and ADB devices now that Apple has omitted these ports from the iMac?

Either buy adapters or move on, that's what. Take a look:

ADB. I'll stop using my ADB Apple Extended Keyboard II when Apple pries it out of my cold, dead hands. The keyboard bundled with the first iMacs is execrable, and I don't like the current Apple Pro Keyboard much better. Thankfully, I can use the Extended Keyboard II with any USB Mac, thanks to Griffin Technology's iMate USB-to-ADB adapter (www.griffintechnology.com). This $39 doodad allows you to continue using your favorite mouse, trackball, trackpad, tablet, or ADB dongle.

Serial. Because the iMac includes a modem, you don't need to make your old modem work with your new Mac, but printers are another story. I've found Farallon's iPrint Ethernet-to-serial adapters to be useful. The $102 EtherMac Adapter iPrint LT supports LocalTalk printers, and the $83 EtherMac iPrint Adapter SL works with Apple's StyleWriter printers. Check Farallon's Web site (www.proxim.com) for a list of supported printers.

MIDI interfaces. Items with a MIDI interface that depend on serial ports may need to be replaced with USB or FireWire models. Regrettably, USB-to-serial adapters for the iMac don't support the kind of timing data necessary for MIDI to work.

SCSI. SCSI is a tougher nut to crack. Some SCSI-to-USB adapters are available, but they tend to work only with things such as external SCSI drives. Throw a SCSI scanner into the equation and you'll quickly learn the meaning of "SCSI hell." When it comes to SCSI devices, I believe you're better off replacing what you've got. IDE and FireWire drives are not terribly expensive, and USB scanners are downright cheap.

The Puck

There is no clearer example of Apple's newfound desire to create great-looking computers—and willingness to sacrifice functionality to achieve that desire—than the Puck, Apple's now-retired round USB mouse. Although the Puck was a beautiful-looking mouse, it takes no more than a few minutes of pushing the thing around your mouse pad to realize what a totally hopeless input device it is. To begin with, because it was round, you couldn't tell by touch which end was up. Invariably you grabbed the thing, moved it to the right, and found the pointer drifting off to the southeast because you were holding the Puck at an angle. (Apple later addressed this problem by placing a small indentation in the mouse button on subsequent models of the Puck.)

Also, the Puck was an open invitation for the carpal-tunnel fairy to come a-callin'. The Puck was too short to offer any support for an adult-size hand. Therefore, you had to crab up your hand to operate the mouse, causing more stress to the wrist and arm.

continues on next page

The Puck continued

Despite the screams of protest about this wretched device, Apple continued to include it with all desktop models for a full two years. Why is this? Did Apple truly believe that the Puck was a superior input device that the Great Unwashed simply had to get used to? Not a chance. From all appearances it was stubbornness, pure and simple.

How else can you explain the fact that during one Macworld Expo keynote speech, Steve Jobs himself used a Puck with an attached extension that returned his input device to the oblong shape to which we've all grown accustomed?

Finally, in the summer of 2000 (and two years after the first iMac shipped), Apple replaced the Puck with the oblong Pro Mouse.

Looking Forward

Apple was prepared for users' concerns about legacy peripheral devices and their skepticism about this new USB port. During the iMac's unveiling, Jobs announced that a handful of USB devices—floppy drives, input devices, and adapters that would allow you to use many of your old peripherals—would be available when the iMac was released. And many were. Imation's SuperDisk (www.imation.com) allowed you to read 1.44 MB floppy disks as well as higher-density 120 MB disks; several alternative mice and keyboards arrived on the scene; and a host of adapters—USB to serial, USB to ADB, even USB to SCSI—appeared in short order. In addition, USB-native devices such as printers and scanners began to pop up—some in eye-catching colors that matched the iMac. And although Apple's pronouncement of the floppy's demise inconvenienced some software publishers, major developers had been distributing software on CDs for quite some time.

Suddenly the loss of the floppy drive didn't seem so bad.

She Comes in Colors

January 5, 1999, saw the release of a new line of iMacs in five new colors—Strawberry (pink), Blueberry (blue), Grape (purple), Lime (green), and Tangerine (orange). Due to this fruity naming scheme, the world never saw a yellow iMac—I mean, honestly, would Apple dare call one of its iMacs a Lemon?

These first colorful models were slightly faster than the Bondi Blue models—offering a PowerPC G3 processor that, at 266 MHz, was 33 MHz faster than its predecessor—and had a hard drive with 2 GB of additional space and a slightly spiffier ATI graphics card. Mostly, however, the five new flavors of iMacs were noteworthy because of what they lacked rather than what they included. With this generation of iMacs, the mezzanine and IrDA ports were now *portis non gratis* (**Figure 2.2**).

Neither port was particularly missed. Most vendors took heed of Apple's warning not to develop for the mezzanine port, so except for employees of Griffin Technology and Micro Conversions (see the sidebar "The Mezzanine Port"), few folks mourned its departure. More might have missed the iMac's IrDA port if it hadn't been an inappropriate port to include in the first place. After all, how many iMac owners had also dropped several thousand dollars on an IrDA-bearing PowerBook? And why would Palm owners bother hot-syncing their PDAs via IrDA when using a USB cradle was so much easier and faster?

Sound-input port   FireWire ports   Modem port   USB ports   Ethernet port

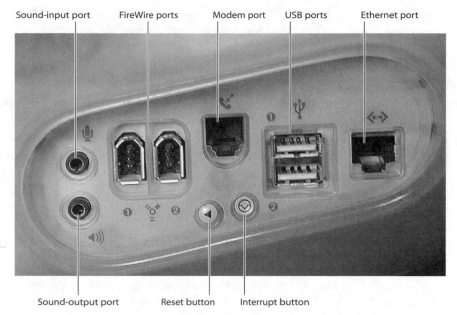

Figure 2.2

Port side with the slot-loading iMacs.

Sound-output port   Reset button   Interrupt button

The Mezzanine Port

The first Bondi Blue iMacs (Revs. A and B) included the mysterious "mezzanine" port—a rectangular port that was visible (if you removed the blue metal plate) on the right side of the iMac. Typically tight-lipped, Apple never bothered to explain the purpose of this port; all it would say was that the port was "for internal purposes only." Developers were warned in no uncertain terms that this was an unsupported port—if any of them developed a product for it, they were on their own.

A couple of intrepid developers forged ahead anyway. Griffin Technology produced something called the iPort that fit in the mezzanine slot. This capable card provided a serial port as well as a 15-pin video-output port that allowed you to run a second monitor at resolutions greater than the three available on the iMac.

continues on next page

The Mezzanine Port *continued*

Micro Conversions also produced a card for the mezzanine port—the Game Wizard, a video gaming card that carried a then-state-of-the-art 3dfx Voodoo2 processor. Considering the lackluster gaming performance of the ATI graphics chip included with the iMac, the Game Wizard was a godsend for gamers.

The mezzanine port met its maker with the release of the five fruit-colored iMacs in early 1999. While Griffin had a broad enough product base to bear the loss, Micro Conversions regrettably did not—the company disappeared a few months later. Griffin continues to offer the iPort for $79. The Game Wizard, like its maker, has gone the way of the dodo.

Jumping Ahead

Since the colored iMacs were released, the iMac has gone through several more iterations. Some of these models have introduced different color schemes and, like the first fruit-colored iMacs, faster processors and higher-capacity hard drives. Others have proved more useful. FireWire was at last included with the iMac DV, in the fall of 1999. This iMac also included AirPort capabilities, a VGA output port, a DVD–ROM drive, and a more capable graphics card—the ATI Rage 128. These were also the first iMacs to include Apple's revolutionary entry-level video-editing application, iMovie. The Special Edition iMacs of this and other DV models were largely notable for their unique color schemes—Graphite and—shudder—Snow.

The next really worthwhile iMacs were released in the winter of 2001. The two most expensive iMacs of this series carried CD-RW (Compact Disc–Rewritable) drives—devices that allow you to record your own CDs. These same two iMacs were also conspicuous for their unique color schemes—Flower Power and Blue Dalmatian. Some people loved these new patterned iMacs. Of course, some people also enjoy pickled pig's feet and consider "Who's the Boss?" to be a complete hoot.

With the July 2001 Macworld Expo came expectations that Apple would scrap the original iMac. The form factor was now three years old, and sales of the diminutive desktop computer were flagging. Regrettably, those hoping to see Steve Jobs pull the cover off a new iMac on the morning of July 18 were disappointed. Rather than a completely new iMac, Jobs announced new iMac models that were little more than minor upgrades. These machines offered more-expansive hard drives, more RAM, faster processors, and a CD-RW drive on all models. To the relief of some, they also lacked the Flower Power and Blue Dalmatian color schemes. Instead, Apple brought back the Snow and Graphite cases for the midpriced and most expensive models and retained Indigo for the entry-level iMac.

iMac

Model	Release Date	Processor/ Speed (in MHz)	Ports	Colors
Mac Rev. A (Bondi Blue)	8/98	PowerPC G3/233	USB (2), 10/100Base-T, modem, sound input, sound output, headphones (2), IrDA (infrared), mezzanine	Bondi Blue
iMac Rev. B (Bondi Blue)	11/98	PowerPC G3/233	USB (2), 10/100Base-T, modem, sound input, sound output, headphones (2), IrDA, mezzanine	Bondi Blue
iMac Rev. C (five flavors)	1/99	PowerPC G3/266	USB (2), 10/100Base-T, modem, sound input, sound output, headphones (2)	Strawberry, Lime, Grape, Blueberry, Tangerine
iMac Rev. D (five flavors)	4/99	PowerPC G3/333	USB (2), 10/100Base-T, modem, sound input, sound output, headphones (2)	Strawberry, Lime, Grape, Blueberry, Tangerine
iMac (slot loading)	10/99	PowerPC G3/350	USB (2), 10/100Base-T, modem, sound input, sound output, headphones (2)	Blueberry
iMac DV (slot loading)	10/99	PowerPC G3/400	USB (2), 10/100Base-T, modem, sound input, sound output, headphones (2), FireWire (2), AirPort, VGA output (mirroring)	Strawberry, Lime, Grape, Blueberry, Tangerine
iMac DV Special Edition (slot loading)	10/99	PowerPC G3/400	USB (2), 10/100Base-T, modem, sound input, sound output, headphones (2), FireWire (2), AirPort, VGA output (mirroring)	Graphite
iMac (summer 2000)	7/00	PowerPC G3/350	USB (2), 10/100Base-T, modem, sound input, sound output, headphones (2)	Indigo
iMac DV (summer 2000)	7/00	PowerPC G3/400	USB (2), 10/100Base-T, modem, sound input, sound output, headphones (2), FireWire (2), AirPort, VGA output (mirroring)	Ruby, Indigo
iMac DV+ (summer 2000)	7/00	PowerPC G3/450	USB (2), 10/100Base-T, modem, sound input, sound output, headphones (2), FireWire (2), AirPort, VGA output (mirroring)	Ruby, Sage, Indigo
iMac DV Special Edition (summer 2000)	7/00	PowerPC G3/500	USB (2), Ethernet 10/100Base-T, modem, sound input, sound output, headphones (2), FireWire (2), AirPort, VGA output (mirroring)	Graphite, Snow
iMac (early 2001)	2/01	PowerPC G3/400	USB (2), 10/100Base-T, modem, sound input, sound output, headphones (2), FireWire (2), AirPort, VGA output (mirroring))	Indigo

continues on next page

iMac   *continued*

Model	Release Date	Processor/ Speed (in MHz)	Ports	Colors
iMac (early 2001)	2/01	PowerPC G3/500	USB (2), 10/100Base-T, modem, sound input, sound output, headphones (2), FireWire (2), AirPort, VGA output (mirroring)	Indigo, Flower Power, Blue Dalmatian
iMac Special Edition (early 2001)	2/01	PowerPC G3/600	USB (2), 10/100Base-T, modem, sound input, sound output, headphones (2), FireWire (2), AirPort, VGA output (mirroring)	Graphite, Flower Power, Blue Dalmatian
iMac (Summer 2001)	7/01	PowerPC G3/500	USB (2), 10/100Base-T, modem, sound input, sound output, headphones (2), FireWire (2), AirPort, VGA output (mirroring)	Indigo, Snow
iMac (summer 2001)	7/01	PowerPC G3/600	USB (2), 10/100Base-T, modem, sound input, sound output, headphones (2), FireWire (2), AirPort, VGA output (mirroring)	Graphite, Snow
iMac Special Edition (summer 2001)	7/01	PowerPC G3/700	USB (2), 10/100Base-T, modem, sound input, sound output, headphones (2), FireWire (2), AirPort, VGA output (mirroring)	Graphite, Snow

PowerBooks: Macintosh to Go (JOG)

Perhaps the most versatile Macintosh in the Apple lineup, the PowerBook has become a tool coveted by everyone from writers to creative types to CEOs. Who wouldn't want a portable Macintosh? The only problem with the original PowerBooks was that they were expensive, underpowered afterthoughts compared with their more powerful desktop cousins.

When the Macintosh first came out, computer users adopted it with open arms. The easy-to-use interface and applications made the Mac a hit with novices and professionals alike. The Mac hardware differed from most other computers in its innovative all-in-one industrial design.

Combining the CPU and monitor in one box was a piece of engineering genius. Andy Hertzfeld, an original member of the Mac design team, said fellow Mac designer Jef Raskin came up with the all-in-one Macintosh design, which lent itself naturally to portable versions.

Students liked this design because they could quickly pick up the machine and move it around. Study session at the room down the hall? No problem! Group project in another dorm? Just grab your Mac by its convenient handle and go.

Although the original Mac was fairly portable, it wasn't really what we think of as a portable computer. It was heavy, and its lack of a battery limited its use to locations near an electrical outlet. (This didn't stop people from toting their Macs into local eating establishments and coffee shops, though.) And while in theory you could have used the original Mac in a car, a train, or (heaven forbid) an airplane, it didn't exactly suit such purposes.

After five years on the market, when consumer demand had grown to sufficient levels, Apple started to consider a truly portable Mac. IBM and other PC manufacturers were creating portable computers, and Mac users demanded an equivalent on their own beloved platform. Apple rushed out its first portable system: the Mac Portable. (For more info on the Macintosh Portable—or Mac Luggable, as people affectionately, or not so affectionately, called it—see the "Early PowerBook Models" section later in this chapter.)

Honey, I Shrunk the Mac!

A PowerBook is just a smaller Macintosh, with basically the same components: a CPU, monitor, keyboard, and memory. The major difference between a desktop Mac and a PowerBook is that the latter miniaturizes everything to fit it inside a smaller enclosure—and this adds a premium to the price.

Previously, this price gap was as much as 300 percent—I paid almost $6,000 for my PowerBook 5300ce/117 in 1996—but Apple has since realized that prices had to be more in line with those of PC notebooks to remain competitive. Today, the price of a PowerBook G4 Titanium is about the same as the equivalent Sony Vaio notebook—unthinkable just a year ago.

Displays

The most expensive part of a PowerBook is the display. Today's Thin Film Transistor (TFT) color active-matrix displays can cost as much as the rest of the machine put together. The original Mac Portable shipped with a simple 1-bit (nonbacklit) black-and-white display. A backlit model, which you could use in the dark, soon followed.

Apple introduced the first color PowerBook, the 165c, in 1993. Unfortunately, it came with a passive-matrix screen. If you haven't had the displeasure of working with such a display, imagine a screen on which variation and dimming of color near the edges makes images practically unviewable unless you look at them straight on. In addition, the pointer would often disappear while you were moving the mouse because the screen could not redraw fast enough (critics dubbed this flaw *submarining*). For early adopters and Mac diehards, though, the 165c was the only color option available, and it was arguably better than the black-and-white alternative.

A scant four months later Apple released the first PowerBook with an active-matrix display, the 180c. Although it represented an evolutionary upgrade for the product line, users hailed its bright, crisp display as revolutionary. Active-matrix and TFT displays are much brighter and sharper than their passive cousins, with better color depth and wider viewing angles. Today, all PowerBooks and most PC notebooks ship with active-matrix displays.

 If you are buying a used PowerBook (or any notebook, for that matter), avoid models with passive-matrix displays. Passive displays, also called "dual-scan" or "DSTN" (Double-layer SuperTwist Nematic), are much cheaper than active-matrix models, but if you spend the extra money, you'll thank yourself later for making a worthwhile investment.

Apple broke new ground with the display in the Titanium PowerBook G4. The machine's 15.2-inch active-matrix display is the best ever in a PowerBook, and its massive 1152-by-768-pixel resolution is 128 pixels wider than the PowerBook G3s. The wider display is perfect for editing an HTML document and previewing it in an adjacent browser window, crunching numbers in a large spreadsheet, or even keeping two word-processing documents open side by side. Those who spend a lot of time in palette-happy graphics applications such as Adobe Photoshop will love this display, as the palettes tend to take over valuable screen space.

Input Devices

Another defining attribute of a PowerBook is its input device, which is smaller than a desktop system's. Keeping a PowerBook as small and light as possible requires tradeoffs. Sure, it would be nice to have access to an Apple extended keyboard with a full numeric keypad, but it just isn't practical in coach. People try, though. (Don't laugh: A friend brought a full-size keyboard with his PowerBook on a flight to a Macworld Expo because his notebook's keyboard wasn't working.)

PowerBook keyboards will seem flimsy to experienced touch typists because they don't have much key travel (up and down movement of keys) or feedback (the audible click a key makes when depressed) compared with a desktop keyboard. You have to remember that PowerBooks were designed for productivity in the cramped quarters of the coach seat on a commercial airliner. If you are using a PowerBook as your main computer, you will probably want to purchase an external ADB or USB keyboard (depending on your notebook model) for use at the office or at home.

PowerBook G3 and G4 keyboards leave faint marks on the display from everyday use, but don't panic! The marks are only visible with the backlighting turned off, and Apple claims that the marks are "not permanent and can be removed by gently wiping off the display with a clean cloth." Apple goes on to say that "periodically wiping off the keyboard and display will reduce the visibility of any marks on the display." You can easily remove the marks with special LCD screen wipes (about $5 for a pack of six) from Fellowes (www.fellowes.com) and other companies. ID East End in Japan (www.id-ee.co.jp/) sells a cool slice of silicone that prevents the marks—the BookMark 4—but a simple piece of white paper or silk handkerchief does the job as well: Simply lay it over the keyboard before closing the lid.

Batteries

The other defining attribute of a portable computer is that it has its own power supply and, unlike a desktop system, doesn't require access to electrical outlets. The venerable rechargeable battery is an indispensable commodity for mobile technology. Although it's improving technologically, the battery remains the weakest link in the mobile computer system. Running out of power reduces your computer to an expensive paperweight.

Battery technology has made great strides in the past several years. The new lithium-ion (LiIon) batteries in the PowerBook G4 Titanium are specified to last as long as 5 hours, though 3 to 4 is more realistic in everyday use. Within the next few years, expect battery run time to increase to as much as 8 to 12 hours with the advent of new technology such as lithium-polymer batteries and more-efficient processors and memory.

Battery life is so crucial for some users, especially those who often travel by airplane, that it may be the single most important reason to upgrade to the newest PowerBook model. By the same token, take care when considering the purchase of a used PowerBook. Older models often suffer from weak battery life (5 to 30 minutes), so you could end up with a PowerBook that requires a constant AC connection.

Battery types. The original PowerBook 100 used lead-acid batteries, like the ones in cars, but these were not efficient for their weight. Apple switched to nickel-cadmium (NiCd) batteries starting with the PowerBook 140, and stayed with this technology for the rest of the 100 series because it yielded a run time almost double that of lead-acid batteries at the same weight.

Both lead-acid and NiCd batteries suffer from the memory effect, a condition that occurs when you partly charge a battery to the same level several times consecutively. The battery develops a chemical memory of the level and will not allow charging past that point, resulting in run times of less than 20 minutes.

If this occurs, allow the battery to discharge completely and then charge it until the Control Strip module indicates a full charge. Repeat this process three times and see if the battery functions normally. If it does not, replace the battery.

 The nickel—metal hydride (NiMH) cell includes a small microchip with an energy monitoring module circuit that detects the battery's capacity and tells the computer when it requires charging. As NiMH battery technology improved over the years, Apple released updated cells: Type I is the original, and Types II and III are its successors.

The PowerBook Duo 210, the PowerBook 500, the PowerBook 190 and 5300 models, and the PowerBook 1400 use NiMH batteries. Some third-party vendors sell NiMH cells for the PowerBook 3400, but the superior LiIon cells provide more-reliable power via intelligent charging circuitry inside the battery itself. The PowerBook 500 was the first to ship with a smart battery.

(The PowerBook table in this section includes basic specifications for every PowerBook model, and Apple's TIL article 16168—www.info.apple.com/kbnum/n16168—identifies the AC adapters and battery and gives recharger information for all PowerBooks and iBooks.)

 EMMpathy 2.0 from VST Technology (www.vsttech.com), is a small, free application that tests and repairs memory-related errors in smart batteries. If your PowerBook 500-series smart batteries are giving you trouble—that is, they won't charge, they get hot when they do charge, they don't show up in the Control Strip—EMMpathy can probably fix them. VST last updated EMMpathy to version 2.1 in 1996 and no longer supports it. A little digging in a search engine such as Google should help you find it.

Current G3 and G4 PowerBooks ship with the latest LiIon batteries—these are among the most efficient batteries on the market today, with an excellent power-weight ratio. LiIon batteries typically last 2 to 4 hours and can recharge in about half their run time (1 to 2 hours). They're also lighter than their predecessors, and—like NiMH—they allow recharging at any point during their life cycle.

The Future of Batteries

Batteries form the weakest link in mobile technologies because of their run time and weight. Several companies are leading the charge to create a battery for portable electronic devices that will run for a full day (8 to 12 hours) without requiring a recharge.

Even more exciting are the advances in lithium-polymer batteries from companies such as Moltech (www.moltech.com), Valence (www.valence-tech.com), and Lithium Tech (www.lithiumtech.com). Lithium-polymer technology has three major advantages:

First, the batteries are light—they essentially consist of putty packed in either a flat foil or plastic bag.

Second, they can assume a variety of shapes. Theoretically, this offers a great advantage for a notebook battery, as it allows development of a polymer pack with a single cell, reducing manufacturing costs.

Third, lithium-polymer batteries are safer than current LiIon ones—they are less likely to ignite or explode.

Power Management

No discussion of batteries would be complete without looking at how to squeeze every last precious minute out of them—especially if you want to use your notebook on commercial flights. (As I write this section, I am sitting on a Northwest Airlines 747 en route to Japan to cover Macworld Expo Tokyo 2001.)

Preparing for a flight with your PowerBook is quite easy, actually—it just requires some simple calculations. First determine the length of your typical flights to approximate your battery needs. Most domestic flights in the lower 48 states are 1 to 5 hours (not counting connections and layovers). This means you should carry one or two LiIon batteries if you want to stay productive during a coast-to-coast flight from, say, Philadelphia to San Jose, California.

Although a direct flight may take 5 or more hours, a third of that time might be spent boarding, taxiing, taking off, and landing. Add to that a meal service and possibly a nap, and you may only net 2 to 3 hours of actual PowerBook use.

Make sure all of your batteries are fully charged before you depart, and remember that batteries charge fastest when your PowerBook is shut down, second fastest when it is asleep, and slowest when it is in use.

 To maximize your battery's run time, dim the backlighting on your PowerBook's LCD—set it just one notch above completely off. This will increase your run time by about 10 to 15 percent and is a perfectly comfortable level for use, especially on a dark plane.

The Energy Saver Control Panel and Pane

You can dramatically improve your battery's run time by using the Energy Saver control panel in Mac OS 9 and earlier, and the Energy Saver pane in System Preferences in Mac OS X (**Figure 2.3**).

The first tab—Sleep Setup in Mac OS 9 and Sleep in Mac OS X—allows you to set when your PowerBook will go to sleep, dim the display, and spin down the hard drive. You can also adjust these settings based on whether you are connected to AC power or running off the battery. When using the battery, I usually set my PowerBook to general sleep in 5 minutes, display sleep in 2 minutes, and hard-drive sleep in 2 minutes. When it's connected to AC power, I set all three options to Never.

The other important tab in the Mac OS 9 Energy Saver control panel is Advanced Settings. Most times when traveling, I use my PowerBook for word processing and e-mail—not exactly reaching the limits but productive nonetheless. If you don't need to push pixels in Photoshop or edit that film you shot over the weekend, you can extend the run time by dropping the speed of your processor.

Figure 2.3

Mac OS 9's handy Energy Saver control panel (left) and Mac OS X's Energy Saver System Preferences pane (right).

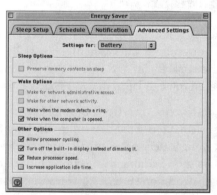
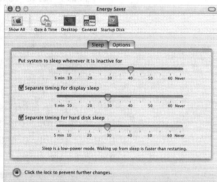

To squeeze the most life out of your battery, check all four options under the Other Options heading : "Allow processor cycling," "Turn off the built-in display instead of dimming it," "Reduce processor speed" and "Increase application idle time." Some of these options are PowerBook specific and will not appear in the Energy Saver control panel on a desktop Mac. (Mac OS X, as of Version 10.1, does not offer these settings.)

File Synchronization

You have two ways to store files offline: *archiving,* which means you move the files to the destination disk and then *delete* them from your hard drive; and *backing up,* which means you move the files to the destination disk and then *keep* the files on your hard drive. You'll use the first if you create a lot of data, don't need constant access to it, and do need to conserve hard-drive space; the second is a precautionary measure to minimize your downtime in the event of data loss.

This is probably the most important tip in *The Macintosh Bible:* If you have not done so already, purchase an external hard drive, CD-RW drive, or digital linear tape (DLT) device and make regular backups of your main documents or data folder. You can also back up to another Mac, if you have more than one, but a dedicated storage device is better because you don't use it for other purposes, which makes it less likely to crash or become corrupted. Unfortunately, most Mac users don't back up their data regularly or at all. Usually it takes a major data loss (as in a hard-drive crash) to convince users to schedule regular backups. Don't be a victim—make a backup of your data today. [*See Chapter 5, "Storage," and Chapter 8, "Prevention and Troubleshooting," for more on backing up and what to do if—heaven help you—you do lose data—Ed.*]

The simplest way to back up your data is to drag and drop it to another hard drive mounted on the Desktop. The only problem is that in subsequent back-ups, you have to replace all of the files on the destination disk, even if you only created one new file.

Apple has addressed this problem in Mac OS 9 and earlier with the File Synchronization control panel (**Figure 2.4**). File Synchronization lets you specify pairs of documents, folders, or disks and synchronize them, saving the most recently modified versions of your files in both places (newer versions write over older ones). File Synchronization replaces the PowerBook's File Assistant application.

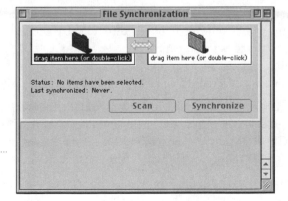

Figure 2.4

The File Synchronization control panel.

Although it's better than backing up manually, File Synchronization can only handle small to medium backups (fewer than 500 files). If you routinely back up more than 500 files, you should investigate third-party software.

If you prefer to drag and drop your backups—after all, that's the easiest way— Connectix's CopyAgent ($39; www.connectix.com/products/cca.html) is an excellent method. CopyAgent is a suite of tools designed to copy, back up, and synchronize your data automatically. The package also includes Connectix's Network Copy, which can boost network-copy speeds by as much as two times according to the company.

CopyAgent's most useful feature is something the Mac OS lacks: an intelligent file-replacement utility called SmartReplace. Rather than replacing every file on the destination disk, SmartReplace asks if you would prefer to replace only those files that have changed since your last backup. It automatically copies any new files. CopyAgent does its magic by comparing the modified dates of both files and only copying a file if it has a newer modified date than the file on the destination disk. It can also copy files in both directions—this is called synchronizing—as you would do with a PDA and your Mac.

Expansion Bays

Expansion bays are convenient slots in PowerBooks that allow you to extend the feature set of your machine easily by swapping out media devices, such as floppy drives, SuperDrives, magneto-optical drives, CD and DVD drives, and batteries. Expansion bays add a new level of hardware customization not available in early PowerBooks.

Expansion bays debuted with the dual-battery bays in the PowerBook 500 series, released in May 1994. The revolutionary dual-bay design meant you could use your PowerBook for an extended run time and even change a battery without putting the machine to sleep. By far the most popular expansion-bay device for the PowerBook 500 was the card cage, a small battery-shaped enclosure that contains two PC Card slots.

The 5300 and 190 series PowerBooks also featured an expansion bay, filled with a floppy drive from Apple, but its different size and shape made previous expansion-bay devices incompatible. The PowerBook 1400 featured expansion bays as well but placed them on the front of the machine—again frustrating consumers with a different form factor that didn't accept earlier devices.

The PowerBook 3400, and subsequently the original PowerBook G3, shipped with an expansion bay, but it rarely held anything other than a factory-installed floppy or CD-ROM drive. The 3400 had the same expansion bay as the PowerBook 5300/190 series, allowing them to share devices.

The trend continued with the PowerBook G3 series—but this time Apple heeded customer complaints about compatibility, or at least attempted to listen.

The PowerBook G3 series released in 1998 (also called Wall Street because that was its code name while it was in development) and its successor (Wall Street II or PDQ) had the same expansion-bay dimensions and thus could share devices. When Apple revised the PowerBook G3s, it made the form factor significantly thinner, necessitating another change to expansion-bay architecture.

You can easily identify the newer, thinner PowerBook G3s released in 1999 (code-named Lombard) and 2000 (code-named Pismo) by their bronze-colored keyboards. These models can share expansion-bay devices with each other but not with earlier PowerBook G3s that have black keyboards. Still confused? The Apple Tech Info Library article "PowerBook: Proper Method for Exchanging Expansion Bay Modules," should shed additional light (http://docs.info.apple.com/article.html?artnum=45055).

PowerBook Upgrades

If you are like me, you will eventually own several PowerBooks and will have a small entourage of family and friends carrying around your old models. The best way to upgrade is to buy a new model and sell the old one to a friend. That way you have a new machine with a new warranty—the problem is, this is also the most expensive option.

With most PowerBooks, as with most computers, RAM and hard drives are the most commonly purchased upgrades because they pack the most bang for the buck. My rule of thumb is to figure out the maximum amount of RAM I think I'll ever need—then *double* the number. And I opt for the largest hard drive I can afford. Memory and storage prices have never been lower, and you won't regret an investment in RAM. Of course, the amount of hard-drive space you need is relative to the amount of data that you need immediately available to you. You'll appreciate having a little extra room so you can create an extra partition for Mac OS X.

The other way to upgrade a PowerBook is to switch out the processor for a faster one. You can only accomplish this on PowerBooks that have the processor on a daughtercard (this means the CPU is on a separate card that you can remove from the main motherboard). CPU-upgradable PowerBook models include the PowerBook 500, 1400, 2400, and G3 series.

PowerBook 500. Because the PowerBook 500 ships with a 68040 processor, you're probably best off selling it and getting a new PowerBook. If you cannot afford a new one, Newer Technology's 167 MHz PowerPC upgrade is worth a look. Unfortunately, not many accessories are made for the wonderful PowerBook 500 anymore, so you will have to go through used-equipment channels, such as auction Web sites or the PowerPage message boards (www.ogrady.com).

PowerBook 1400. Although this model is much newer than the PowerBook 500, the same rule applies. Consider carefully before spending any money on this machine. It lacks USB and FireWire connections and will not run Mac OS X—you're probably better off selling it and buying a used PowerBook G3. If that doesn't discourage you, check out the Sonnet Crescendo G3/PB upgrade card, which replaces the original 117, 133, or 166 MHz PowerPC 603e processor with a PowerPC G3 processor running at 333 or 400 MHz with 512 Kbytes or 1 MB of backside cache, respectively.

The upside is that the low-power copper IBM PowerPC G3 processor in the Crescendo can extend the PowerBook 1400's battery life by 30 percent. These upgrades sell for $300 to $400 on the auction sites.

PowerBook 2400. The 2400 is a PowerBook with cult status in Japan. Originally developed under the code name Comet, the 2400 was the closest thing to an Apple subnotebook since the PowerBook 100. The 2400 originally shipped with a 180 MHz PowerPC 603e processor; a subsequent model shipped with a 240 MHz CPU, but only in Japan. Newer Technology manufactured a 240 MHz G3 upgrade card for the 2400, but the company ceased operations in December 2000. Interware (also known as Vimage), a Japanese firm, manu-factured the Booster 400 MHz G3 upgrade for the PowerBook 2400—this upgrade shipped with 1 MB of backside cache for around $1,400. Again, the best place to find such cards is on the used market.

PowerBook G3. You can upgrade the processors on all PowerBook G3s, with the exception of the original model, (which carried the Kanga code name and has a 250 MHz G3 in the PowerBook 3400 enclosure). Logic dictates that you won't want to upgrade the latest PowerBook G3s (Lombard and Pismo) because they already have the faster processors in them, but you may want to look into your options if you own a 233, 250, 266, 292, or even 300 MHz PowerBook G3 (denoted by Family Number M4753, which you can find by flipping your PowerBook over and looking at the bottom label). The PowerLogix Blue Chip G3, a processor upgrade for the above models, comes in 466 or 500 MHz clock speeds. Both cards come with 1 MB of backside cache and sell for around $600.

Travel Survival Tips

If you own a PowerBook, you probably like to travel (or at least roam around your home or apartment). PowerBook ownership implies that you're indepen-dent, mobile, and always on the move. That may not *always* be the case—but let's face it, you are much more likely to take a PowerBook on a trip to Big Sur than to lug along a Blue and White Power Mac G3.

That said, follow a few rules of the road when you're preparing for a trip—they'll save you a lot of hassle while you're traveling. First, do not overpack.

Some people have the tendency to bring the kitchen sink on a weekender to the Delaware shore, then don't end up so much as breaking the safety seal on the PowerBook bag throughout the whole trip. Be realistic and know your limitations. Are you really going to work on that book and balance your accounts on the flight? Or is *Meet the Parents* on DVD more in line?

The Old Soft Shoe

OK, it's not really a PowerBook tip, but here's another oft-overlooked travel suggestion—bring a comfortable pair of shoes, especially if you are sightseeing or going to a trade show. Whether you are schlepping around Chappaqua, New York, to visit friends or flying to Whistler, British Columbia, for a week of snowboarding, you will be carrying a lot of gear, especially if you take your PowerBook. The more weight you carry, the more you will fatigue your feet and back. A comfortable pair of walking shoes will pay huge dividends over the course of your trip.

What to Bring

The well-stocked PowerBook bag should contain these items:

A bootable system CD. Make sure that it is current and that it starts up your specific PowerBook (not all will), and keep it in a safe place.

Two RJ-11 cables and an RJ-11 coupler. Why two? Although 6 feet is good for most locations, you will probably need a 12- to 25-foot cable in most hotel rooms. You don't want to be chained to the desk when you really want to surf and watch *The Sopranos* from bed. The coupler is useful for times when you need both cables or when the phone line is hardwired to the wall.

Ethernet and crossover cables. If your model supports Ethernet, this is a great way to share files with someone else quickly. Bring both cables if you have a G3 or earlier PowerBook; G4 and iBook Dual USB users need only a regular (or "straight") Ethernet cable because those machines will auto-sense whether they are connected to another machine or to a hub.

A mouse. A mouse will increase your efficiency if you plan to work for an extended period of time. Most optical mice will work on any available surface— even your pants leg!

Tools. Pack a miniature Torx 8 and Torx 10, a Phillips-head screwdriver, and a small pocketknife in your checked luggage. You can often mitigate PowerBook accidents that happen while you're traveling—for example, spilling a soda on your keyboard—by taking the keyboard and battery out, washing them off, and letting the machine dry open and upside-down overnight.

Earphones or headphones. Nothing is worse than having to listen to every ping and boing someone's computer makes on a cramped plane or train—not to mention your blaring Godsmack MP3s. Do everyone a favor and bring a pair of earphones. If you are traveling with a loved one, bring a second pair of earphones and a ⅛-inch headphone splitter so you can both watch *The Big Lebowski* on DVD (or listen to your Godsmack MP3s together).

Power Management and Other Issues

The most important aspect of traveling with a PowerBook is proper power management. Bring enough batteries to last the duration of your flight, and about 50 percent extra for unexpected delays and cancellations. (For more battery tips, see "Batteries," earlier in this section.) Also bring a reliable, working power supply and even an airline EmPower adapter (EmPower is a new form of electrical outlet found in business-class seats on some flights) or a cigarette-lighter adapter.

If you expect to need all of your electronic devices, having the right batteries, cables, and AC adapters is paramount—forget one and you may be out of luck. If you are flying, pack as much of the electronics as possible in your checked luggage—you don't need your hot-sync cradle and power adapter in your carry-on bag.

 Back up all of your data before you go. In fact, it is a great idea to drop a copy of your important presentation (or report or résumé for that matter) on an FTP server or an Apple iDisk before you depart—that way, you should be able to make your presentation even after the worst possible scenario. Traveling is risky, and anything can and will happen—your PowerBook can get lost, stolen, or damaged easily while you are on the road. Replacing your PowerBook is simple, but replacing your data is not. You have been warned.

 Even if you don't travel often, you may want to consider insurance for your PowerBook. AppleCare (www.apple.com/applecare) insurance is economical (about $300 for three years) when you compare it with the cost of any PowerBook repair, but it does not cover theft or accidental damage that occurs when you drop your computer. Some homeowner's policies will cover computers outside the home, but always check with your insurance agent before taking a chance. SafeWare (www.safeware.com) sells insurance policies especially designed for computers and even has policies that cover theft and accidental damage.

Early PowerBook Models

The PowerBook began life as an entirely different machine—the Mac Portable—a large, clunky, and somewhat non-Macintosh machine that couldn't be further from a modern-era PowerBook. But Apple's first portable is an important part of Apple history—it allowed the company to get a product out to market and helped Apple learn from its mistakes. Amazingly, Apple's next portable, the first real PowerBook (the PowerBook 100), was a complete departure from the Mac Luggable. It was light, had a small footprint, and is still considered by some to be the best PowerBook of all time.

The Mac Portable

Apple released the Mac Portable, the first portable Macintosh and the grandparent of them all, on September 20, 1989, at $6,500 (or around $7,300 with a hard drive). At 15.8 pounds, the original Mac Portable wasn't much smaller or lighter than a desktop Mac—but it did run on a battery. Some unique features of the Mac Portable included support for dual floppy drives or one floppy and one 3.5-inch hard drive, a lead-acid battery with a life of 5 to 10 hours, and a cool keyboard with a swappable trackball and numeric keypad. Today Mac Portables are collector's items.

The PowerBook 100, 140, 170

Realizing the errors of its ways, Apple went back to the drawing board to create a truly portable Mac. This time the company came back with a really cool model—the PowerBook. Apple launched the 100, 140, and 170 models with much fanfare in October 1991. The PowerBook 100—the first genuinely portable Mac—was also the first Apple hardware to bear the PowerBook moniker. Lexicon Branding in Sausalito, California, came up with the term "PowerBook" for Apple; Sony manufactured the first model, the 100.

The PowerBook 100 had the same relatively slow processor (16 MHz Motorola 68000 processor) as the Mac Portable but was the first (and as of this writing the only) PowerBook to feature an instant-on feature that allowed you to open the machine and begin using it almost immediately. PowerBooks running Mac OS 9 and earlier have to wake from sleep—a process that can take anywhere from 30 seconds to a couple of minutes, depending on your model and configuration. This is less than beneficial when inspiration strikes. The good news is that PowerBooks wake from sleep in less than 1 second in Mac OS X.

Following the PowerBook 100 (16 MHz 68HC000) were the PowerBook 140 (16 MHz 68030) and the PowerBook 170 (25 MHz 68030). The 100 and 140 had 1-bit passive-matrix screens, and the 170 had a 1-bit active-matrix screen.

In the years to come, Apple continued to enhance the line and release other 68030-based PowerBooks: the 145, 145b, 150, 160, 165, 165c, 180, and 180c. True to Apple style, prices remained about the same (with the exception of color models, which cost more) with each new model but Apple added features with each revision.

The PowerBook Duo

The PowerBook Duo was one of Apple's most innovative ideas in mobile computing. It stripped the PowerBook down to the bare essentials: keyboard, monitor, trackball, and only the basic ports (power, ADB, and modem). The idea was to strip away any excess weight not absolutely required for productivity and deliver a machine thinner and lighter than any of the PowerBooks before it.

Sure, video out and networking are nice, but at the time Apple didn't consider them essential requirements—and besides, you could add the missing pieces by strapping on a dock that met your needs. The market agreed, and the PowerBook Duo was a success. The Duo series ranged in weight from 4.2 pounds for the minimalist black-and-white Duo 210, 230, 250, and 280 to 4.8 pounds for the color 270c and 280c, released in 1993 and 1994, respectively.

The PowerBook 500

In 1994, Apple released the first 68040-based PowerBooks, the PowerBook 520, 520c, 540, and 540c, all of which used Motorola's 68LC040 processor. The 500 series had a radically different case design and introduced an input device still used in modern laptops (yes, even some Intel-based notebooks)— the *trackpad*. This device allowed the pointer to follow the movement of your finger on a special pad.

The PowerBook 5300

In September 1995 Apple started a new chapter in PowerBook history: It announced the PowerBook 5300, the first PowerBook based on Motorola's PowerPC processor. However, quality problems plagued the 5300 (and the 190 series)—motherboard issues, breaking plastics around the lower LCD bezel, and defective AC connectors. The model faced a handicap even before it was shipping in quantity, following reports that a prototype's LiIon battery caught fire in Apple's labs.

Motherboard problems with the 5300 and the 190 series prompted Apple to institute a repair-extension program that extended the warranty period for these machines. You can find out more about this on Apple's Web site (http://product.info.apple.com/pr/product.updates/1996/q3/960606.pr.up.repair.html).

The PowerBook 1400

The PowerBook 1400 was an evolutionary step for Apple, building on the 5300's strengths and repairing its weaknesses. The 1400 holds the distinction of being the first notebook computer to ship with a built-in CD-ROM. The 1400 also shipped with a unique changeable "book cover" that allowed users to switch the standard black cover for a clear cover and insert colored panels underneath it for a new personality. You even got several colorful sample inserts and a template for creating your own designs on any printer.

From a PowerBook Kludge to a Powerful Web Site

The PowerBook 5300's many problems also inspired my Web site, Go2Mac (www.go2mac.com), originally called O'Grady's PowerPage. I started it because I am a PowerBook fanatic and I couldn't get my Global Village PC Card modem to work with my new PowerBook 5300.

After buying a 5300ce/117 for about $6,000 with accessories, I was extremely annoyed to find that I could not send e-mail in Eudora using my trusty Global Village combo Ethernet-and-modem PC Card. After calling Global Village and getting bounced from one technician to another for about an hour, I finally reached someone who recognized the problem.

"So you have a 5300?"

"Yes."

"Well, you have to go to this FTP site and download the PowerBook 5300 kludge."

After navigating to the FTP location (which was about 100 characters long), I downloaded and installed "kludge for broken 5300 Ethernet card" (the real filename!). Then—and only then—I could send mail in Eudora 2.1.4b10. Imagine that.

I knew I couldn't possibly be the only person having this problem. So I got to thinking—I had a Power Mac 8100 and a practically empty T1 line in my office for the Web shop I was starting, Odyssey Systems. A little Photoshop and BBEdit later, O'Grady's 5300 PowerPage was born. The rest, as they say, is history.

The PowerBook 2400

Codesigned with IBM Japan, the PowerBook 2400 was Apple's first small PowerBook since the Duo series. At 4.4 pounds, the 2400 fell just outside the technical specifications for a subnotebook (it must weigh less than 4 pounds), but many still consider it one. Designed only for the U.S. and Japanese markets, the 2400 is not covered by warranty in other countries.

The 2400 shipped with a reduced-size keyboard, which featured the first inverted-T cursor-key configuration, now standard on all PowerBooks. The 2400 lacked a built-in floppy or CD-ROM drive, but customers didn't seem to mind, especially in Japan, where it became highly popular.

The PowerBook 3400

Code-named Hooper, the 3400c was a full-size PowerBook that featured a PowerPC 603ev processor running at 180, 200, or 240 MHz, making it the fastest portable in the world. Apple based the 3400 on a new PCI motherboard and used its industrial design as the form factor for the original PowerBook G3.

The 3400 was unique because it featured a domed lid that housed two additional speakers for a total of four. The 3400 also accepted expansion-bay devices from the older 5300/190 PowerBooks and was the first PowerBook to take advantage of the faster 1 MB IrDA infrared standard.

Mac Portables Prior to the G3 Series Includes models sold only in the United States.

PowerPC Models	Processor Chip	Speed (MHz)	Display Type	Colors	Weight (lbs.)	Introduced
5300ce/117	603e	117	active	color	6.2	8/95
5300cs/100	603e	100	passive	color	6.2	8/95
5300c/100	603e	100	active	color	6.2	8/95
5300/100	603e	100	passive	grays	5.9	8/95
3400c	603e	180/200/240	active	color	7.2	2/97
2400c	603e	180/240	active	color	4.4	5/97
1400cs	603e	117/133/166	passive	color	6.7	10/96
1400c	603e	117/133/166	active	color	6.6	10/96

680XO Models	Processor Chip	Speed (MHz)	Display Type	Colors	Weight (lbs.)	Introduced
540c	68LC040	66	active	color	7.3	5/94
540	68LC040	66	active	grays	7.1	**5/94**
520c	68LC040	50	passive	color	6.4	5/94
520	68LC040	50	passive	grays	6.3	5/94
190cs	68LC040	66	passive	color	6.3	8/95
190	68LC040	66	passive	grays	6	8/95
180c	68030	33	active	color	7.1	6/93
180	68030	33	active	grays	6.8	10/92
170	68030	25	active	B&W	6.8	10/91
165c	68030	33	passive	color	7	2/93
165	68030	33	passive	grays	6.8	8/93
160	68030	25	passive	grays	6.8	10/92
150	68030	33	passive	grays	5.8	7/94
145B	68030	25	passive	B&W	6.8	6/93
145	68030	25	passive	B&W	6.8	8/92
140	68030	16	passive	B&W	6.8	10/91
100	68000	16	passive	B&W	5.1	**10/91**
Portable	68000	16	active	B&W	15.8	9/89

Duo Models	Processor Chip	Speed (MHz)	Display Type	Colors	Weight (lbs.)	Introduced
Duo 2300c	603e	100	active	color	4.8	8/95
Duo 280c	68LC040	66	active	color	4.8	5/94
Duo 280	68LC040	66	active	grays	4.2	5/94
Duo 270c	68030	33	active	color	4.8	10/93
Duo 250	68030	33	active	grays	4.2	10/93
Duo 230	68030	33	passive	grays	4.2	10/92
Duo 210	68030	25	passive	grays	4.2	10/92

The PowerBook G3

The release of the original PowerBook G3 in 1997 changed everything and opened a new chapter in mobile computing for Apple. Building on the successes of previous "world's fastest" notebooks, the first PowerBook G3 introduced a new level of price and performance in a portable that even the most vehement PowerBook detractors could not ignore. Finally, true desktop power had migrated to the laptop.

PowerBooks were long the mainstay of senior creatives and executives immune from corporate budget limitations. In addition to offering greater speeds, this generation of PowerBooks—the G3s—cost significantly less than its predecessors. At last, Apple's coveted portables were within reach of consumer-level buyers.

PowerBook G3 Scorecard

Model	Speed (MHz)	Code Name	Introduced	Family	Feature
PowerBook G3	250	Kanga	10/97	M3553	G3 processor
PowerBook G3 Series	233, 250, 292	Wall Street	5/98	M4753	Thin form factor
PowerBook G3 Series	233, 266, 300	PDQ	9/98	M4753	Speed bump
PowerBook G3 Series	300, 400	101, Lombard, Bronze	5/99	M5343	USB only
PowerBook G3	400, 500	102, Pismo	2/00	M7572	FireWire, USB

The PowerBook G3 (Kanga)

Apple introduced the PowerBook G3 in October 1997 as a logical extension of its wildly popular line of desktop Power Mac G3s. Packed in the same enclosure as the PowerBook 3400, the PowerBook G3 marked the first time Apple had squeezed so much horsepower into such a small package. At this machine's heart was the zippy 250 MHz PowerPC 750 (or G3) processor with a fast 512 Kbyte backside cache running at 100 MHz.

The PowerBook G3 signified a revolution for Apple—for the first time, the PowerBook line was on par with its desktop counterparts. No longer a slower cousin, it instead had evolved into the desktop's speedy little sibling in the top bunk.

The PowerBook G3 Series 1998
(Main Street, Wall Street, PDQ)

Apple announced the PowerBook G3 Series in May 1998 (at the same time as the iMac debut), calling it—you guessed it—the PowerBook G3 Series (see the sidebar "A PowerBook by Any Other Name? A Good Idea!" for more on Apple's disastrous PowerBook G3 naming conventions).

The PowerBook G3 Series I models, aka Main Street (233 MHz) and Wall Street (250 and 292 MHz), featured a new style of enclosure and were the first PowerBooks that offered numerous built-to-order options. You could pick from a 233, 250, or 292 MHz PowerPC G3 CPU and a 12.1-inch passive-matrix, 13.3-inch TFT, or 14.1-inch TFT display at a price range of $2,500 to $6,000.

In summer 1999 Apple revved the PowerBook G3 series to 233, 266, and 300 MHz under the code name PDQ, which stands for Pretty Damned Quick. Now *that's* what I call a name!

The PowerBook G3 Series 1999
(101, Lombard, Bronze)

In May 1999 Apple released yet another PowerBook G3 series, running at 333 and 400 MHz and code-named 101, or Bronze after its beautiful translucent mocha-colored keyboard. The new PowerBook G3 Series looked similar to the model it replaced, but closer inspection revealed that it was 20 percent thinner and almost 2 pounds lighter. In addition, Lombard featured a pair of stacked USB ports—a PowerBook first, essentially killing ADB ports in the line.

A PowerBook by Any Other Name? A Good Idea!

Although most commercial products have unique names—mostly to differentiate the newest model from the one it replaced—PowerBooks work a little differently. Since 1997, Apple has more or less called them all PowerBook G3s, leaving consumers and tech-support reps alike confused.

In the early and middle 1990s, Apple incremented product names by a few digits to differentiate models—a widely criticized move (it's hard to tell what a Performa 5430 is, for example), but it usually allowed you to tell which model was newer. When Steve Jobs returned to Apple in 1997, he streamlined the number of product offerings, which was a good thing. He may have taken the process too far with the PowerBook line, however. The issue got so confusing that Apple had to issue a Tech Info Library article (http://docs.info.apple.com/article.html?artnum=24604) to help people identify which model they had.

The original PowerBook G3 had one of the best code names around—Kanga. Apple called the PowerBook G3 Series Wall Street and PDQ (for Pretty Damned Quick) in the labs; it called the next model 101 or Lombard, for the names of the overall project and the logic board, respectively. Wall Street and Lombard are much friendlier names than PowerBook G3 Series/300, and I wish Apple had considered a similar naming convention for its PowerBooks.

The PowerBook 2000 (102, Pismo, FireWire)

Apple announced the last professional PowerBook G3 in February 2000 at Macworld Expo Tokyo. The new model shipped with the same form factor as the previous PowerBook G3, but it ran at either 400 or 500 MHz, and Apple replaced the long-in-the-tooth HDI-30 SCSI port with dual 400 Mbps FireWire ports. Additionally, the system featured a new Unified Motherboard Architecture (UMA) that ran at a sizzling 100 MHz (up from 66 MHz).

The new motherboard also included an AirPort wireless networking slot under the keyboard, an AGP-based ATI Rage 128 graphics chip set, and a 6X DVD-ROM drive. The PowerBook G3 with FireWire came in two configurations: the 400 MHz G3 processor, 64 MB RAM, 6 GB hard-drive model for $2,499; and the 500 MHz, 128 MB, 12 GB model for $3,499.

The PowerBook G4

The PowerBook G4 2001 (code-named Mercury) set the entire computing world on its ear in January 2001 when Apple announced it at Macworld Expo San Francisco. The newest PowerBook was a speed demon because of its 400 or 500 MHz PowerPC 7410 (or G4) processor, and it was also a total design departure for Apple, ushering in a new generation of portable Macs.

Previous PowerBooks were solid, curvy, and functional, but they always contained compromises. Whether it was size, weight, performance, or battery life, users always found something to complain about in their PowerBooks. The PowerBook G4 threw all those complaints out the window.

The PowerBook G4 came wrapped in a spectacular enclosure that was an incredibly slim 1 inch thick and weighed a paltry 5.3 pounds. The new machine was thinner than even the smallest Sony portable, giving Apple major bragging rights in the marketplace. Another outstanding feature was the PowerBook G4's beautiful 15.3-inch (1152-by-768-pixel) wide-screen display. On top of all this, it came in a beautiful enclosure crafted of titanium, which—as Steve Jobs pointed out—is stronger than steel and lighter than aluminum.

PowerBook G4

Model	Speed (MHz)	Code Name	Introduced
PowerBook G4	400, 500, 550, 667	Mercury	1/01

The iBook

The iBook, announced in July 1999 at Macworld Expo New York, was Apple's first real foray into the consumer portable market. It may have been the most anticipated Apple portable in history, with the PowerBook G4 Titanium coming in a close second.

The iBook filled the empty consumer-portable quadrant in Steve Jobs' two-by-two product matrix. The iBook sat directly under the wildly successful iMac in the matrix—the Apple doesn't fall far from the tree.

A completely new class of PowerBook, at only $1,299 the iBook brought the power of the G3 processor to the masses in an attractive, portable package.

Borrowing design cues from the iMac, the iBook attempted to appeal to everyone from students of all ages to computer novices to early adopters (or die-hard users) who had to have every new Apple model. Its Blueberry and Tangerine color schemes took a page from the iMac book.

The iBook offered several innovations—AGP graphics, UMA, AirPort wireless networking, a 6-hour LiIon battery, and a handle. (For more on AirPort networking technology, check out Chapter 20, "Networking.")

To achieve the desired price point, however, Apple had to make some compromises: The iBook lacked a PC Card slot, IrDA, video out, audio in, and high-speed connectivity (either through SCSI or FireWire).

Apple priced early iBooks at a premium that was out of the reach of many customers. The company switched gears and brought prices down to $2,500 for the entry-level model—a major step in the right direction. But $2,500 (and even the $1,800 price that model eventually reached) was too much for the average student. Enter the iBook at $1,599 ($900 less than the least expensive PowerBook)—who *wouldn't* want one?

However, even the first-generation iBook had its detractors. Some early critics found it too big and heavy for students or small children and considered the screen too small at 12.1 inches and 800 by 600—all valid points, as the iBook was larger than the professional PowerBook G3. Adding fuel to the fire, some PC-oriented journalists characterized it as girlish, saying it looked like a purse or makeup compact.

With the iBook Special Edition, announced in February 2000, Apple bumped the base RAM from 32 to 64 MB and increased the hard drive's size from 3.2 to 6 GB.

The second-generation iBook arrived in September 2000 and came in two flavors—regular and extra crispy…that is, Special Edition. The new iBook added a new, faster 366 MHz PowerPC 750CX (aka the G3e) processor that featured an on-chip Level 2 cache running at the same speed as the processor. It also shipped with a FireWire port and a video output and came in two new colors: Indigo and Key Lime. The SE version included a DVD-ROM drive and a 466 MHz processor and came in Graphite and Key Lime.

Apple changed everything again in May 2001 with the announcement of the iBook Dual USB. The new iBook amazed customers and silenced the critics with a totally redesigned enclosure—a chip off the block of the amazing PowerBook G4. Significantly smaller and lighter (4.9 versus 6.6 pounds), it looked nothing like the previous iBook. The new iBook is square and compact, as opposed to the round and curvy original design.

What's Your iBook?

Model	Introduced	Speed (MHz)	RAM	HD	Code Name	Price	New
iBook	7/99	300	32 MB	3.2 GB	P1	$1,599	Everything!
iBook SE	2/00	300	64 MB	6 GB	Rev. b	$1,799	64 MB RAM, 6 GB hard drive
iBook 2nd Edition	9/00	366	64 MB	10 GB	Rev. c	$1,499	PowerPC 750 CX, FireWire, video out, Indigo and Key Lime colors
iBook SE 2nd Edition	9/00	466	64 MB	10 GB	Rev. c	$1,799	DVD, Graphite and Key Lime colors
iBook Dual USB	5/01	500, 600	128 MB	10 GB	Marble	$1,299–$1,699	Smaller design, optional DVD/CD-RW

Personal Digital Assistants

Although Apple canceled its handheld line early in 1998, Mac users haven't stopped using the handy devices. A personal digital assistant, or PDA, provides an easy way to link your Macintosh with a sleek handheld computer that you can carry along daily. The advantages include access to all your phone numbers, contacts, calendars, and to-dos at all times. In addition, you can synchronize any data you've added or changed on either machine by performing the convenient synchronize—or as Palm calls it, HotSync—function. PowerBook users can even synchronize via infrared.

The evolution of these devices over the past few years has been toward more choices for consumers, including audio, video, expansion options, and color. Palm led the way with its series of

PDAs, creating a strong user base and embracing many third-party accessories and software, although others have followed with their own handheld devices. Handspring and Sony, for example, have licensed the Palm operating system and incorporated its speed and simplicity into their products.

One of the great features of having an organizer is the ability to easily add, delete, and share information with other PDA folks. Using the infrared port on the handheld, you can simply beam a recipient your electronic business card or your favorite game. More important (at least for *Macintosh Bible* purposes), the Palm also synchronizes with your Macintosh, providing the convenience and security of storing your important data in two places at once. To sync data, simply place your handheld in the included cradle and press the HotSync button on the cradle. You'll need to purchase a USB or serial connection kit to adapt the cradle's parallel port for the Macintosh. The infrared port can also share data with your PowerBook while you're on the road, though this requires a little planning.

You might find it easiest to enter your address book using your Mac's keyboard, but Graffiti, the handwriting-recognition application for Palm OS, provides an alternative to scraps of paper covered with indecipherable notes. Using simple strokes that form the basis for capital letters, you can enter memos, to-dos, and contacts while you're away from your desktop.

Are you reluctant to change from your current calendar program? The Palm desktop application, though it's appealing, does not necessarily have to replace your program of choice. Palm's import feature works well, but Palm OS can also function in the background, transferring data from Power On Software's Now Up-To-Date and Microsoft's Entourage calendars to your handheld device without even requiring that you launch these applications. Actually, you can use any commercial software application that has a Palm conduit (a small translator program) in conjunction with your handheld; if you are unsure, ask the software developer.

Expansion

Expansion is a great way to add all kinds of capabilities to your handheld. Use a wireless or wired modem and leave your laptop at home while you are on the road.

Cameras, memory, MP3 players, business card scanners, and expandable keyboards are just a few of the many expansion opportunities available. One disadvantage to expansion with Palm-powered devices is that they all use different types of media. Palm uses Secure Digital (SD), Handspring uses the Springboard module, Sony uses its Memory Stick technology.

With one of the new generation of pocket-sized Palm keyboards you can easily take notes at your next meeting or write reports on an airplane.

The Palm Portable Keyboard, $99 from the Palm store (https://store.palm.com/), weighs in at less than eight ounces. This full-size keyboard folds into a small package just slightly bigger than a Palm organizer itself, making it a practical enhancement if you need speedy data entry that only a keyboard can provide. Simply install the Palm Portable Keyboard software, set your Palm organizer in the custom docking cradle, and start typing.

Upgrades (MB)

Upgrades are a great way to extend the useful life of your Mac. Although we can't cover all of the many upgrade possibilities, we can list the most popular ones. For more information, we point you to Web sites to help you wade through the many choices.

RAM

RAM (or main memory) is the first upgrade you should make to your Mac unless it came with a large amount. RAM is a primary factor in overall system performance and stability. Without enough RAM, a fast CPU, a new graphics card, and other upgrades can't perform at their best. Think of RAM as your computer's oxygen supply. A fast CPU with too little RAM is like a sprinter running with a plastic bag over his head or a Ferrari with a one-pint gas tank.

(For more information on memory, RAM types, and system compatibility, see Chapter 4, "Memory.")

If you own a Power Mac G3 series or later Mac that uses SDRAM, keep in mind that prices for this type of memory are lower than ever. At the time we wrote this, 128 MB SDRAM DIMMs were selling for less than $50.

For More Information

To find out what type of RAM your Mac uses, start with the Apple Memory Guide; go to http://kbase.info.apple.com and search for *Apple Memory Guide*. The memory guide stops at November 2000, so Apple suggests you search its Knowledge Base, using the product name and memory as your search criteria, for newer models.

Storage

The variety of storage-related upgrades available for the Mac is bewildering. Hard drives (both SCSI and ATA/IDE) have continued to get larger, faster, and more affordable. Dozens of vendors also offer FireWire and USB hard drives (both AC powered and portable), CD recorders, and removable-media drives. If your Mac didn't ship with USB or FireWire and you have an available PCI slot, you can buy a card to add these interfaces. The same holds true for IDE and SCSI—upgrade cards can add faster IDE or SCSI capability to almost any PCI-slot Mac.

If you're replacing an ATA/IDE hard drive in your Mac or PowerBook, FireWire case kits are a great way to reuse the original drive. For illustrated guides on FireWire case kits, see www.xlr8yourmac.com/firewire.html.

For More Information

For a drive-compatibility database that's searchable by Mac model, drive type (hard drive, CD-RW, DVD-ROM, DVD-RAM, removable, tape drive, and so forth), interface type, and drive brand, see http://forums.xlr8yourmac.com/drivedb/ search.drivedb.lasso. The entries in this database usually include comments on compatibility and performance.

You'll find installation guides for hard drives and CD-ROMs for Power Macs (as well as PowerBooks) at the ATA/IDE, FireWire, and SCSI articles pages at www.xlr8yourmac.com. Apple also has some installation guides for later Mac models at www.info.apple.com/support/cip/.

CPU Upgrades

The CPU is the engine, or data pump, for your Mac and plays a primary role in how fast programs run. Although the system memory speed and the graphics card's capabilities are also factors in some cases, a CPU upgrade can dramatically boost your Mac's performance.

You can't upgrade or replace the CPU on all Macs. Many older Macs had the CPU chip soldered on the logic board, although in some cases specialized CPU upgrades such as PCI cards or Level 2 (L2) cache slots can work around this limitation.

Also be aware that for applications and 3D games that move a lot of data over the system bus, no CPU or graphics-card upgrade can match the performance of the latest Mac models, which have faster memory, system-bus speeds, and graphics-card interfaces. If you're considering upgrades to the CPU, graphics card, and hard drive, often it makes more sense to sell your older Mac and spend the funds on a faster and more capable later model.

CPU upgrades are readily available for Power Mac G3 and G4 models. (PowerPC 604 upgrades have not been manufactured since about 1998.) Some upgrades can adjust for bus speed and CPU speed; others cannot. Typically, upgrades from Sonnet Technology (www.sonnettech.com) are plug and play (non-adjustable), whereas those from XLR8 (www.xlr8.com) and PowerLogix (www.powerlogix.com) have switch settings that allow you to change card speeds. The adjustable cards usually ship with a default setting that should work fine but let you change settings if you want to experiment with higher speeds. Not all settings are reliable, and *overclocking* (running the CPU at higher-than-rated speeds) may lead to data corruption or premature failure.

The design of the Catalyst motherboard used in some Mac OS clones renders G4 CPU upgrades incompatible with these systems. Verify that the CPU upgrade you are considering is compatible with your Mac model. The dealer's or manufacturer's product pages should list compatible Macs for each of its CPU upgrades. The documentation includes important hardware and software installation notes you should read. Most current CPU upgrades ship with software to address potential issues.

If you're upgrading the CPU of a pre-G3 Power Mac with a PowerPC G3 or G4 card, it's usually best to remove the L2 cache DIMM on the logic board (also called the motherboard). Oftentimes the faster bus speeds or the different timing of the upgrade card can cause problems with the original system's L2 cache DIMM. Some Power Macs, such as the 9500 and 9600 series (except the 9600/300 and 9600/350), and some Mac OS clones, such as the Umax S900, have soldered-in L2 cache, which you cannot remove. However, this is not a problem for most CPU upgrades.

Types of CPU Upgrades

What type of CPU card upgrades a Macintosh will accept depends on the slots available—this varies from one model to another.

PDS models. NuBus and older Macs often have a PDS (Processor Direct Slot), which vendors have used to upgrade the CPU. Many vendors of these upgrade cards are no longer in business, but Sonnet Technology has the widest selection.

PCI models. In late 2000, Sonnet Technology released the first CPU upgrade for the Power Mac 7200 and 8200 series, which have no CPU card slot. Total Impact (www.totalimpact.com) offers expensive and specialized multiple-processor PCI CPU upgrade cards that are out of the price range of most users.

CPU card models. Many older PCI Macs have the original CPU on a removable card.

ZIF (Zero Insertion Force) socket models. The Power Mac G3 (also known as the Beige Power Mac G3), G3 All-in-One, G3 (Blue and White), and G4 PCI models have the CPU on a small circuit board called a ZIF module. The logic board has a ZIF socket, which allows you to upgrade easily to a faster CPU by replacing the existing processor. There are many brands of ZIF CPU upgrades, including PowerPC G3 and G4 types.

Some ZIF upgrades are OEM (original equipment manufacturer), with no speed adjustments on the module. (The same is true of the ZIF CPU modules that shipped in G3 Macs.) These modules rely on the logic board's jumper settings to determine their operating speeds. If you're buying a ZIF CPU module that

doesn't have a name brand such as Formac, Newer Tech, Metabox, PowerLogix, XLR8, or Sonnet, chances are it is an OEM model that will require changes to the logic board's jumper settings.

For More Information

For reviews of a large variety of CPU upgrades (from PowerPC 604 to G3 and G4 models), see www.xlr8yourmac.com/cpucards.html. A searchable database (by Mac model and upgrade brand) of more than 5,000 owner reports on CPU upgrades is available at http://forums.xlr8yourmac.com/cpureview.lasso.

For a review of the ZIF module, with links to installation guides and jumper settings, see www.xlr8yourmac.com/G3CARDS/OWCmercury/.

Some Beige Power Mac G3s shipped with a VRM (voltage regulator module) that Newer Technology claims can damage a G4 ZIF upgrade if used in those Macs. For a guide to determine what model VRM you have installed in your Beige G3, see www.kiechle.com/vrm/index.htm.

Blue and White Power Mac G3s with certain firmware versions cannot run a G4 CPU upgrade without a patch to the firmware. Most G4 ZIF upgrades ship with a patch and instructions on how to install it. An example and guide is available at www.xlr8yourmac.com/G4CARDS/XLR8_G4_400Z/.

PCI Cards

PCI is the standard for the add-in cards Apple has used in Macs since the company moved away from the slower (10 MHz) NuBus slots found in the Mac II through the Power Mac 6100, 7100, and 8100 series. Standard PCI slots run at 33MHz with an interface that's 32 bits wide, allowing 132 MBps rates (actual rates vary depending on the logic board controller and other factors). With the Power Mac G3 (Blue and White) in 1999, Apple began to include PCI slots compatible with higher-performance 64-bit cards. The Power Mac G3 (Blue and White) and Power Mac G4 PCI models also included one 32-bit, 66 MHz PCI slot, used for the graphics card. Later Power Mac G4 desktop systems replaced the 66 MHz PCI slot with an AGP slot for the graphics card.

Although we can't cover in this space the many types of PCI upgrades, here are some examples:

Graphics cards. Faster and more capable cards (with three-dimensional acceleration, video input, video capture, and so on) are available from many manufacturers. Modern graphics cards from ATI (www.ati.com), Formac (www.formac.com), and others offer 3D hardware acceleration, higher resolutions, and other features such as DVI (Digital Video Interface) for connecting to digital flat-panel LCD displays. Within the limits of your CPU and system, these cards offer faster drawing of screen contents along with improved 3D and game performance. PCI graphics cards such as the ATI Radeon, ATI Orion, ATI Nexus128, and Formac Proformance III are compatible with both 33 MHz and 66 MHz PCI slots. Although the 66 MHz PCI slot has twice the clock speed of a standard 33 MHz PCI slot, you'll typically see only about 10 percent faster performance due to other limiting factors.

Video-capture cards. PCI video-capture cards are available in several price ranges, with capabilities that may include importing (capturing) analog video from devices such as video tape decks and camcorders. The best-known manufacturers are Media100 (www.media100.com), Aurora Video Systems (www.auroravideosys.com), and Pinnacle Systems (www.miro.com).

SCSI controllers. Many high-performance SCSI controllers are available, with much faster transfer rates than those of the onboard 8-bit SCSI interface. These cards offer much higher clock rates and 16-bit data paths to the hard drive. Adaptec (www.adaptec.com), Atto (www.attotech.com), and Initio (www.initio.com) are the best-known manufacturers of high-performance PCI SCSI controllers for the Macintosh. Ultra SCSI (40 MBps), Ultra2 SCSI (80 MBps), and Ultra 160 (160 MBps) models are available. Keep in mind that the actual drives you're using with these cards are the limiting factor, as no single drive currently available can sustain the transfer rates of the fastest SCSI controllers. Connecting a fast PCI SCSI card to the drive that shipped in an older Mac won't get you anywhere, since those drives had lower performance than the original onboard SCSI interface's limits.

For More Information

For reviews of many of the most popular past and present PCI graphics cards for PCI Macs, see www.xlr8yourmac.com/video.html.

For reviews and related articles on PCI SCSI controllers for the Mac, see www.xlr8yourmac.com/scsi.html.

ATA/IDE controllers. Most pre-G3 series Macs don't have an onboard ATA/IDE controller (there are exceptions, such as some Performa models and some clones). Acard (www.acard.com), Sonnet, and VST (www.vsttech.com) offer Mac-compatible PCI IDE controllers with dual ATA/66 (66.6 MBps maximum) ports that allow you to connect as many as four IDE drives (if there's enough space inside your Mac). Both Acard and Sonnet also offer an IDE RAID card that makes multiple ATA/IDE drives appear as a single drive without requiring RAID software. (Note that PCI ATA/IDE controllers and attached drives appear as SCSI to the Mac OS due to the card's firmware.) One problem you'll often encounter when you install PCI ATA/IDE controllers in pre-G3 Macs is stuttering audio during playback from the IDE drive.

FireWire and USB controllers. You can add FireWire and USB capability to your PCI-based Mac with PCI cards available from sources such as OrangeMicro (www.orangemicro.com), FireWireDirect (www.firewiredirect.com), and FireWireDepot (www.fwdepot.com). Some models also include USB or even SCSI on the same card.

 Many PCI FireWire cards sold for PCs also work in Macs. If the box notes that the card is OHCI compliant, it should work in Macs using Apple's FireWire drivers, available at www.apple.com/firewire/. (Mac OS 8.6 or later is required for FireWire support.)

For More Information

For more on IDE-related reviews and articles, see www.xlr8yourmac.com/IDE.html.

For reviews of FireWire controllers and comments from owners of FireWire-USB combo cards, see www.xlr8yourmac.com/firewire.html.

For more information on PCI Cards for Macintosh, see http://msproul.rutgers.edu/macintosh/PCIcards.html and Apple's PCI Expansion Bus Architecture Description (http://karchive.info.apple.com/article.html?orig=til&artnum=17732).

For a guide to buying a Mac audio card, see www.xlr8yourmac.com/audio/issue47.html. There are more than 60 articles on Mac audio hardware and software at www.xlr8yourmac.com/audio/.

Audio/Midi Interfaces. Since the onboard audio capability of Macs is limited, several manufacturers offer add-in PCI cards for professional audio use.

From the perspective of a general or home user, a sought-after audio card is the Mac Sound Blaster Live from Creative Labs ($100). See www.soundblaster.com/products/macintosh/ for details.

Networking. Macs prior to the Blue and White series of G3s have at best a 10Base-T (10 Mbps) Ethernet interface. If you need 100Base-T (100 Mbps) or wireless (AirPort-compatible) networking capability for PCI Macs, see sources such as Proxim (www. proxim.com) and Asanté (www.asante.com).

AGP Cards

Intel originally developed AGP (Accelerated Graphics Port) as a dedicated expansion slot to replace PCI for use with high-performance graphics cards. Unlike PCI, AGP is a dedicated interface that does not share bandwidth with other cards or slots. AGP has a direct path to main system memory and is a higher-performance interface that has become the standard for onboard graphics in new PowerBooks, iBooks, and iMacs as well as upgrade cards.

The Macs with AGP graphics released in 1999 and 2000 use a 2x AGP inter-face (this has a 66 MHz clock speed but triggers on both the rising and the falling edge of the clock pulse for an effective 133 MHz rate). The 2001s Power Mac G4 models are the first Macs with an even faster 4x AGP slot. If you have a 1999 Power Mac G4 system and wonder whether it's a PCI or an AGP model, look at the graphics card's connector on the logic board. PCI connectors are white; AGP connectors are brown. (A PCI card cannot fit into an AGP slot and vice versa, as the connectors are different.)

For More Information

Apple has a guide to determining your Power Mac G4 model at http://docs.info.apple.com/article.html?artnum=58418.

Since only the 1999 Power Mac G4 AGP and later G4 models have an AGP slot, the current installed base is small, which is one reason why few retail AGP graphics cards are available for the Mac. For a review of Mac AGP graphics cards, including the ATI Radeon and ProMax DH-Max, see www.xlr8yourmac.com/video.html.

For more information on AGP definitions and standards, see Intel's AGP Technology page at http://developer.intel.com/technology/agp/info.htm. (This page refers mainly to the company's own processors and chipsets but has links to basic information on AGP.)

3

System Software

David Reynolds is the chapter editor and author.

Although your Mac's hardware is well designed and put together, it's the system software running your Mac that makes it distinct. After all, if Microsoft wanted to put the effort into it, the Redmond company *could* write a version of Windows that would run just fine on your Mac. (Of course, it would *still* be Windows, despite the great hardware it was running on.)

As we discussed in Chapter 1, Apple offers two versions of Macintosh system software: Mac OS 9 and Mac OS X. Mac OS 9.2.1 is the latest incarnation of the original Macintosh system software, which has a lineage going all the way back to 1984, making it exceptionally mature—and exceptionally vulnerable to certain kinds of crashes. Mac OS X, on the other hand, is a brand-new operating system that has its roots in Unix, not in the original Mac OS. Using the Classic compatibility environment, Mac OS X can run Mac OS 9.2.1 almost as if it were another program; this enables older programs written for Mac OS 9 and earlier to run in Mac OS X, but they run inside the copy of Mac OS 9 that's hosted in Mac OS X. Yes, it's conceptually a little complicated, but fortunately, it all works almost transparently. (For those who are technically minded, in Classic, Mac OS 9 runs in a virtual machine inside of Mac OS X.)

Here are a few tasks your system software does:

*   It starts up your Mac.
*   It lets your Mac's hardware components (its memory, hard drive, processor, and so on) talk to each other.
*   It draws windows, menus, and other widgets on the screen.
*   It handles requests you make using the keyboard or mouse (such as clicking an icon or opening a window).
*   It handles requests from running programs (for memory or processor time).
*   It does pretty much everything else that makes your Mac run.

In This Chapter

The Operating System

Every personal computer ever made has an operating system at its heart. An operating system (often abbreviated as OS) is a highly specialized program that tells the computer's hardware components how to behave and talk to each other. It also takes care of the user interface—the part of the software that handles interaction with a computer's users. This latter part of the system software gets all of the attention, mostly because it's the most visible part of the operating system. Operating systems go much deeper than their user interfaces, though.

Under your Mac's serene surface area of windows and icons is a labyrinth of programming code that's busily moving data between the hard drive, the memory, and the monitor, all the while keeping track of what programs are running, which windows are open, and what network connections it needs to maintain. Add to *that* keeping track of every key press and mouse click, and you start to understand why operating systems get so big and complex. And that's just the start of things. Fortunately, you don't have to become too intimately acquainted with the inner workings of your Mac's operating system, but it's a good idea to understand the basics of how it all works. That way, when you run into a problem or need to do some tweaking beyond moving a few folders around, you're more likely to have the knowledge required to take care of things yourself.

System Software

The Macintosh OS, often referred to as the Mac's system software, is what really makes a Macintosh a Macintosh. In fact, you can run other operating systems (such as Linux) on your Macintosh and never install the Mac OS at all. In Mac OS 9 and earlier, the system software consists of the System file (the core of the Mac OS), the Finder (which provides the interface between you and your Mac), and lots of add-ons such as fonts and extensions that enhance what your Mac can do. In Mac OS X, the system software is less easy to categorize, in part because it's both more complex and more modular. At its heart, Mac OS X has a core system (called Mach) that handles memory, hard-drive connections, and other really low-level stuff. On top of that is a flavor of Unix, and on top of *that* is the user interface.

Version Numbers

The Mac OS has been around for nearly 20 years now, and it's grown and changed a lot since its inception. Software—system software included—uses *version numbers* to keep track of what came first. It's like naming your children after yourself—you have Charles, Charles the second, Charles the third, and so on. If Charles were software, the naming would go like this: Charles (or Charles 1.0), Charles 2.0, Charles 3.0, and so on. The Mac OS is now at version 10—and that's a *long* time by system-software standards.

The first number (the one before the decimal) is the main version number—changes to that number indicate huge changes to the software, major new features, and so on (**Figure 3.1**). A change to the first number after the decimal (say, from 5.0 to 5.1) usually indicates a few new features and some bug fixes—you'll likely find the software a little more useful and stable, but it doesn't boast a slew of new abilities. Finally, a change to a second number after a decimal (say, from 9.0.3 to 9.0.4) indicates some bug fixes but no new features. Of course, these rules aren't hard and fast, and some companies ignore them entirely, such as when Windows 3.1 went to Windows 95, to represent a year, not a version number. And not all programs have a second decimal place—they just use a first-decimal place replacement.

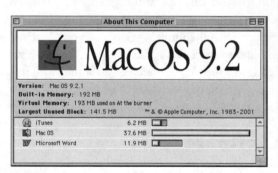

Figure 3.1

In Mac OS 9.2.1 and earlier, you can call up the About This Computer window by choosing About This Computer from the Apple menu with the Finder active. This window (left) tells you what version of the Mac OS you're running, and it also tells you how much memory each program is using. The process is similar in Mac OS X. Choose About This Mac from the Apple menu to bring up the About This Mac window (right), which shows you what version of Mac OS X you're running and the total amount of real memory you have installed.

The Mac OS falls into six major groups according to its version-number scheme:

System 1 to 6.0.8 (1984–91). This is the first set of releases, back when it was simply known as the System, followed by a number. The original series of Mac operating systems lasted from 1984 to 1991 and demanded little from the hardware that ran it. The entire operating system could fit comfortably on a floppy disk and required less than 1 MB of RAM to run.

System 7 to 7.5 (1991–97). Released in 1991, System 7 brought multitasking (the ability to run more than one program at a time) to the Macintosh. With System 7's new abilities came a new need for power: System 7 required 4 MB of RAM to work well, four times what its predecessor used. Apple made some tweaks to System 7 over the years, but no major changes hit the operating system through version 7.5.3, released in 1996. That's because Apple engineers were concentrating on the next Mac operating system, code-named Copland, which was never released. After years of development that drained resources from System 7, it was clear that Copland was in trouble. In late 1996, Apple announced that it had purchased Next, a computer company founded by Steve Jobs (who also cofounded Apple in 1976), and that OpenStep (formerly named Nextstep) would become the basis for the next OS.

Mac OS 7.6 (1997). In 1997, Apple released Mac OS 7.6 as part of its plan to clean up the operating-system mess. Mac OS 7.6 represented a name change— from System to Mac OS—as well as the start of regular system-software updates. With version 7.6, the Mac OS has had grown considerably since its ancestor first made the scene in 1984—it could no longer operate from a floppy disk, and it needed 16 MB of RAM to operate well. By this time, Apple had also announced the impending release of its next-generation operating system, based on recently acquired technology from Next, with the code name Rhapsody. Apple promised more updates to the now-venerable Mac OS before Rhapsody's release.

Mac OS 8 to 8.6 (1997–99). With the release of Mac OS 8 in 1998, parts of the ill-fated Copland project saw the light of day in release form as Apple engineers salvaged parts of Copland by grafting them onto the original Mac OS. These parts included the ability to make multiple file copies simultaneously and a simplified installer. Mac OS 8 was the biggest thing to happen to the Macintosh system software since the introduction of System 7 in 1991. Mac OS 8 was also the first operating system that required a PowerPC chip— stranding all Macs built before 1994 (and a few built after that) at Mac OS 7.6. Mac OS 8.6 shipped in 1999 (with Mac OS 8.1, 8.5, and 8.5.1 in between), and while this series of releases added modern niceties such as indexed file searches, much of those improvements centered on under-the-hood tweaks for speed and stability. In the meantime, the Rhapsody project, renamed Mac OS X, promised to cure the ills of the now-aging Mac OS while still letting users run their old programs on their Macs—some ten years old or older.

Mac OS 9 to 9.1 (1999–2001). By the time Mac OS 9 hit the scene in late 1999, the original Mac OS had seemingly undergone as much refinement as possible. Remarkably stable and capable, Mac OS 9 still relies on the tech-nology of the original 1984 release. Mac OS 9 set the stage for its successor, Mac OS X, by including such features as multiple user support (a way of letting several people use the same Mac at different times without messing up each others' workspaces).

Mac OS X (2001–present). Mac OS X is the first totally new Macintosh operating system since the original in 1984. Although it took nearly ten years (Apple started the Copland project in the early 1990s), Apple engineers man-aged to marry the brute strength of Unix (on which Nextstep was also based) with the best parts of the traditional Mac OS to produce Mac OS X. This power-house of an operating system can act as a Web and file server while it helps you send e-mail and listen to MP3-based music. Over the years, the system require-ments have grown from a measly 400 Kbyte floppy disk and 128 Kbytes of RAM to 1 GB of hard-drive space and 128 MB of RAM—that's more than 2,000 times the hard-drive space and 1,000 times the memory needed for the first Mac OS.

Mac OS X Server

Throughout the 1990s, Apple engineers worked feverishly on a brand-new version of the Macintosh operating system. Code-named Copland, it was supposed to be thoroughly modern —more stable, more responsive, with a whole new look and feel.

Unfortunately, it proved to be *too* modern for most Mac software, causing many programs to stop working altogether. So after spending tons of money and years of effort on Copland, Apple shifted gears by purchasing the Next computer company, with plans to use its OpenStep oper-ating system as the basis of Mac OS X. Code-named Rhapsody, this new attempt to rewrite the Mac operating system for more stability and responsiveness offered one compelling advantage over Copland: Existing Macintosh programs could run on Rhapsody in a carefully controlled, boxed-off portion of the operating system. To take advantage of Rhapsody's crash protection and responsiveness, though, developers would have to rewrite their programs from the ground up.

Since most developers were unwilling to do this, Apple changed plans and came up with Mac OS X. Developers could take advantage of Mac OS X's new benefits by *tweaking* instead of com-pletely rewriting their software. Thus Rhapsody became Mac OS X. Mac OS X also provides a way to run older, unmodified programs, called the Classic environment.

Along the way, Apple released an operating system called Mac OS X Server. Released on March 16, 1999, Mac OS X Server was a halfway step between Mac OS X and the original versions of Mac OS and OpenStep. Built on Unix, it was primarily meant as a server for Web pages and QuickTime movies. Mac OS X Server didn't have Mac OS X's Classic compatibility layer, which lets unmodified Mac OS 9 and earlier programs run side by side with Mac OS X programs. Instead, any programs written for the original Mac OS ran in the Blue Box, a version of Mac OS 8 that ran *inside* Mac OS X Server. To use those programs, you had to switch to a new screen—Mac OS 8 and Mac OS X Server programs could never appear onscreen at the same time. Mac OS X Server also couldn't run Carbon applications, specially tweaked to run in Mac OS 9 *and* Mac OS X.

In May 2001, Apple released a revamped Mac OS X Server, version 2.0, that looked and behaved like the client edition of Mac OS X but came with industrial-grade server parts—three discs' full, actually.

How Mac OS X Differs from Mac OS 9 and Earlier

Although Mac OS 9 and Mac OS X can run a lot of the same software and look similar on the surface, the two are actually entirely different operating systems that share very little in the lower levels. However, Mac OS X does have the capability to *host* Mac OS 9, letting you run programs for both Mac OS X *and* Mac OS 9 without restarting your Macintosh. This capability is known as the Classic environment, and we'll be covering that in detail later in the section "The Classic Layer." Here are some of the differences you should be aware of between Mac OS 9 and Mac OS X.

Underpinnings. Mac OS 9 (and the versions of the Mac OS leading up to it) is largely a *monolithic* operating system, which means it's difficult to separate into parts or layers. With programming code and concepts that date back to 1984 and even earlier, Mac OS 9 is its own animal and has little in common with other operating systems at its most basic level. This structure (or architecture) is one of the reasons Mac OS 9 seems so long in the tooth from a technical standpoint. Programs can access your Mac's hardware directly (generally a bad thing), and the system doesn't have many built-in mechanisms to keep one program from corrupting another's memory—both of these faults lead to crashes. To add new capabilities to Mac OS 9 (such as OpenGL and QuickTime), engineers mostly have to use extensions and shared libraries, which bring their own set of problems.

Mac OS X, on the other hand, has fairly well-defined parts that give it some serious power. At its heart, Mac OS X is built on the Mach kernel, an itty-bitty operating system in its own right. The Mach kernel is the only part of the operating system that works directly with hardware, managing the operation of hard drives, memory, video cards, and the like. It's this separation that makes Mac OS X so stable—Mach knows how to handle all the hardware, and all other programs have to ask Mach to do things with that hardware. This way, programs aren't sneaking around behind Mach's back, making hardware demands Mach doesn't know about—a situation that can result in a crash, as often happens in Mac OS 9 and earlier.

On top of the Mach kernel sits a version of Berkeley Standard Distribution (BSD) Unix, a Unix flavor that's popular in education and as a server operating system—it runs a *lot* of Web servers. Several new technologies (graphics and networking, mostly) are built into Mac OS X at a fairly low level, giving your Mac amazing power without adding a single crash-inducing, memory-swilling extension to the mix. Finally, on top of all of this is the brand-new Aqua interface, with its rounded buttons, translucent menus, and gorgeous drop shadows.

Graphics. Mac OS has always been known for its graphics capabilities. After all, the desktop-publishing revolution of 1985 catapulted the Mac to the top design-tool position, where it remains very strong today. Over the years Apple added new graphics capabilities to the Mac (such as QuickTime, OpenGL, and ColorSync), largely via extensions. At its core, Mac OS 9 still uses QuickDraw to handle graphics, and QuickDraw came on the scene in 1984 with the original Mac.

Mac OS X has all-new graphics capabilities, using Adobe's Portable Document Format (PDF) as the basis for two-dimensional graphics and OpenGL for three-dimensional graphics. Along with that sits the latest version of QuickTime, the über-media format that can play back almost any audio or video file, including MP3 audio, MPEG video, and even interactive Flash files. All of this means Mac OS X can do amazing graphics tricks, and graphics designers, gamers, and video producers alike will find this system very powerful. To tie all of its graphics panache together, Apple engineers created Quartz, which lets all of these graphics capabilities work seamlessly—allowing you to, for example, drag a translucent, miniaturized QuickTime movie over an active OpenGL animation while the movie plays, showing you the composited pixels (with the animation showing through the transparent movie, still playing) without missing a beat. Now *that's* power. Add to this the ability to save files as PDF documents, and you have an unmatched graphics powerhouse.

Memory use. Of all the ways in which Mac OS 9 and Mac OS X differ, memory use is at the top of the list. When a program launches in Mac OS 9, it gets a fixed slice of the available memory; the user is responsible for setting how much memory each program receives. Programs have a default amount assigned by the programmer, but this amount is just a best guess—it's often not enough, especially when you're working with graphics, sound, or video programs. When a program doesn't get enough memory, it may crash more often. Mac OS 9 and earlier has a version of virtual memory (hard-drive space that acts like RAM), but again the user has to set how much hard-drive space to use as virtual memory in the Memory control panel. You can turn off virtual memory in Mac OS 9, but then your programs generally take up more RAM.

In Mac OS X, on the other hand, the operating system handles all memory needs for programs, using virtual memory (which is always on and grows and shrinks to meet memory needs) to keep things running smoothly. Mac OS X users never have to adjust the memory use of any Carbon or Cocoa program, and if one application needs more memory, Mac OS X is smart enough to take it from programs that aren't using their share. (Because programs in the Classic environment are still running under a version of Mac OS 9, which runs inside Mac OS X, *those* programs may require the user to adjust their memory use—even though the memory ultimately comes from Mac OS X anyway.)

Responsiveness. Both Mac OS X and Mac OS 9 and earlier can perform more than one task at a time—for example, running a word processor, a photo editor, and an e-mail program, all while downloading files from the Internet. They go about this in different ways, though. Mac OS 9 uses *cooperative multi- tasking,* in which the active application gets to say how much of your computer's resources it wants to use, while all of the other running programs must make do with what's left over. This means a single program can hog your Mac, preventing you from doing the simplest things (such as pulling down menus) while it's working—bad news if that program takes a few minutes or hours to complete a task.

Mac OS X approaches the problem of sharing a single Mac among several programs with *preemptive multitasking.* Instead of relying on the programs to divvy up available time on your Mac's CPU, the system software schedules each task, leaving some room for basic jobs such as switching between pro- grams, moving the pointer, and using menus. The net result is that Mac OS X feels more responsive than Mac OS 9 when several programs are vying for your Mac's attention, and you'll never have to deal with a rogue program taking over your entire system again.

Crash protection. Because the Macintosh operating system was originally designed to run just one program at a time, it didn't have any built-in mecha- nisms to keep a bug in one program from running roughshod over the memory another program was using. This wasn't a problem until the early 1990s, when System 7 gave every Mac the ability to run more than one program at a time. Despite ten years of work on the problem, Mac OS 9.2.1 still can't pre- vent one running program from corrupting another's memory space, and that includes the system software. This weakness can—and does—lead to some spectacular crashes.

Mac OS X *can* prevent one program from taking down another program—or the entire system. Through a feature called *protected memory,* Mac OS X sepa- rates the memory used by the operating system and by each running program. If a program tries to write over another program's memory, Mac OS X shuts the first program down, leaving the rest of the system untouched. You don't even have to restart your Mac!

Installation

Installing a new operating system may be the Mac equivalent of a personality transplant, but the prospect isn't nearly as daunting as it sounds. After all, Apple *intended* your Mac to undergo an occasional personality overhaul in the form of an operating-system upgrade, and its engineers have made installation pretty easy. Also, if your current installation has gone bad and you just *can't* set it right using any other troubleshooting method, reinstalling your Mac's operating system may be your last hope.

Installing Mac OS 9 and Earlier

Despite the fact that you're replacing the software that makes your Mac an active, happy member of computing society, installing Mac OS 9 is pretty easy, thanks to the amazing engineering work of Apple folks. Just ask anyone who's ever had to install Linux or an older version of Windows, and you'll realize just how good you have it.

Getting ready. The first part of installing your Mac's operating system is to use the CD with the system-software installer on it as the startup volume. That's because the software on the CD hasn't been subjected to the wear and tear of everyday Mac use and doesn't have any third-party extensions that might cause problems during installation.

To start your Mac using this CD, first put the disc in your CD drive and then hold down ⓒ while restarting. Your Mac should start from the CD rather than from your hard drive. This may not work on older Macs; in that case try holding down ⌘ Control Option Delete just after you press the power button.

You can also start up using your regular hard drive and then open the Startup Disk control panel, where you can select the system-software CD as your startup volume (**Figure 3.2**). Close the window and restart your Mac. It should now start up from the CD.

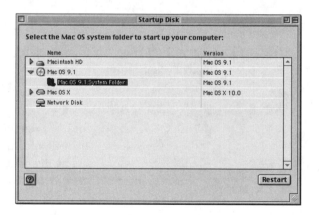

Figure 3.2

The Startup Disk control panel in Mac OS 9 lets you choose a System Folder from which to start up your Mac. By choosing the system-software installer CD, you ensure that your Mac will start up from that CD, which makes for an easy installation. In earlier versions of the Mac OS, this control panel lets you choose a startup volume but not an individual System Folder.

Finally, if you have a Mac that's only a few years old, hold down Option when starting up. Your Mac will show you pictures of all of the disks from which it can start up, and you can select the disk to use as your startup volume. Once you've started up your Mac from the CD, double-click the Mac OS Install icon to get the ball rolling.

 Almost every installer screen has a Go Back button in the lower-right corner that lets you step back a screen to change some settings if you're having second thoughts.

The four-step installation. The first window you see when installing (aside from the splash screen that briefly pops up) is a welcome window that gives you an overview of the installation process. All you have to do is select where you're going to install the Mac OS, read a document that tells you things you really *should* know about installing, agree to Apple's license agreement, and *then* actually install the software. When you click Continue, the installer starts its work. Here's how it goes from there:

Destination disk. The next screen contains a pop-up menu with a list of hard drives on which you can install your copy of the Mac OS (**Figure 3.3**). It also shows how much space an installation will take and whether you have enough room for it. If you click Options at the bottom of the window, you can perform a clean install (see the section "Clean Install" below). Clicking Select takes you to the next screen, which is chock-full of nutritious information.

Figure 3.3

The first thing you'll do when installing is choose a destination for the system software.

Read the "Before You Install" message. Although it may seem as tedious as Ben Stein reading the Unabomber's manifesto, take the time to read the information in this screen (**Figure 3.4**). It may contain a tidbit that will save your Mac's life—and save *you* from pulling out your hair when things go wrong. You can save or print this document for later perusal.

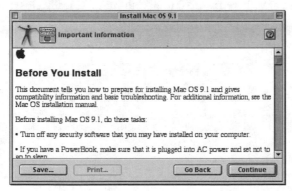

Figure 3.4

When installing, you really should read the information presented after you choose a destination disk. It can save you a lot of heartache.

License agreement. Before you go installing Apple's software on your hard drive, you should at least glance at the Mac OS license agreement, a scintillating bit of legalese likely to put you to sleep and containing words such as *subsidiary* and *nuclear facilities* (**Figure 3.5**). You can save or print this document. Click Continue and you'll see a no-nonsense dialog box: Agree or Disagree. Click Agree to continue to the actual installation screen; click Disagree to drop the whole matter and cancel installation.

Figure 3.5

More reading—wuff! This bit of text isn't nearly so gripping as the last, but it may be worth perusing if you want to find out what you're legally agreeing to when installing your system software.

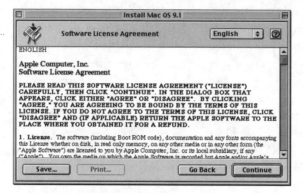

Installation time. Finally! You're now presented with the Install Software screen—it has four buttons along the bottom, one of which is labeled Start (**Figure 3.6**). If you click that button, the installer will begin an Easy Install (one that includes all the default components). Click the Customize button, and the installer window changes to the Custom Installation and Removal screen, in which you can select just the components you want to install onto your hard drive. (You can also remove components here.) Finally, if you click Options, you can tell the installer whether it should update the hard-disk drivers (you'll almost always want to do this), and whether you want the installer to create a text file that logs installation progress.

Once you've clicked Start and the actual installation process has begun, your Mac takes anywhere from 10 to 30 minutes (typically closer to 10) to install the Mac OS on your hard drive. After the installation is done, you can restart the Mac using your new system software.

Figure 3.6

OK—it's time! Click Start to begin installing your system software.

Make sure you've selected the disk with the newly installed system software in the Startup Disk control panel. This ensures that your Mac uses the correct disk when it starts up.

Easy versus custom installation. Mac OS installs come in two flavors: easy and custom. An easy installation is a sort of hands-off install, where the installer takes care of everything, including what software packages are chosen (**Figure 3.7**). A custom installation puts those choices in your hands, letting you choose which software packages to install as well as what *portions* to include. This allows some truly magnificent customization, but it also means you'll have to wade through a slew of check boxes and pop-up menus, plus you'll have to know enough about the Mac OS to select all of the items you need.

Figure 3.7

An easy installation (left) is just that—one click and you're off. A custom installation (right) is full of pop-up menus and check boxes, so be ready to spend some time fiddling before you install. In the end, though, you'll get exactly the operating system you want.

If you're feeling brave enough to attempt a custom installation, click Customize in the Install Software screen, which presents you with a list of software packages. Each item in the list (which covers the base system software, Internet access software, Java, text-to-speech software, and so on) has a check box to its left and a pop-up menu to its right. Selecting the check box tells the installer to include that software package. The pop-up menu on the right lets you either choose the recommended installation of a given package or select what parts to install. (You can also use this pop-up menu to remove components.) Finally, click the information icon at the far right (a small *i* in a button) to find out more about what a given software package does. You can use this window to trim your installation to the minimum amount of software you need or to add a component that didn't get installed previously.

Update install. Unless you've recently installed a brand-new hard drive (or erased your existing hard drive), you probably already have an operating system installed. So instead of doing a regular installation, you'll need to do an *update install,* in which the installer software updates all of the system-software components to newer versions. The process is almost the same as in a regular install: You start up from a system-software CD, run the installer program, and go through the same series of screens in which you choose the drive on which to update the system software. Then you read important information, agree to the license agreement, and finally install the darned software. Once you're done, just restart your Mac using the appropriate disk. When you update your system software, your Mac keeps most of its previous settings, such as TCP/IP and your file-sharing user name and password.

Update with caution. When you're considering an update to your operating system, think long and hard. The downside to system-software updates is that they can cause some of your favorite programs or extensions to stop working, especially if they haven't been updated for a few years. (Sometimes developers will release a newer version that *will* work.) That's because programs rely on parts of the Mac OS to behave in a certain way, and if the operating system changes enough, those programs may stop working.

The best thing to do is to wait a short while after the release of a new Mac OS version to see what others report as broken and find out about any potential disasters that may result from rearrangement of system features. If none of your essential software or hardware gets hit, go ahead and upgrade. You can follow what people are saying about a new version of the Mac OS by visiting the excellent MacFixIt and MacInTouch troubleshooting sites at www.macfixit.com and www.macintouch.com.

Before we start sounding like Eeyore without his Prozac, we should add that there *is* an upside to updating your system software—quite a few, actually. First, system-software updates typically contain lots of bug fixes, which should make your Mac less crash prone. Second, updates often contain lots of goodies—added features that let your Mac do new and interesting things.

Clean install. Occasionally things will go horribly wrong with your system software, and the only cure is a *clean install*. Unlike a regular install or an update install (both of which work with an existing System Folder to add and update components), a clean install starts from scratch, creating a brand-new System Folder with all-new components. It gives the existing System Folder the name Previous System Folder so you don't lose everything you had in that folder. The tricky part about clean installs is that you have to merge the folders, moving items such as preferences, browser bookmarks, and fonts from your old System Folder to the new one. Because of this daunting task of sifting through hundreds of files, clean installs are typically a last resort.

Note that it's possible to install Mac OS 9 and earlier without starting up from a system-software CD-ROM, but you should take a few precautions first. Start your Mac with only the standard Mac OS extensions enabled, and if you're installing on a PowerBook, make sure that it's plugged into AC power and that you've changed the settings in the Energy Saver control panel so it won't go to sleep. Also turn off file sharing and any virus protection you may have installed. If you're upgrading from Mac OS 8.1 or earlier to Mac OS 9.1 or later, you should start up using Mac OS 8.5 or later, according to Apple (although you *may* be able to upgrade without doing so).

Setup Assistant. Once you've finished installing the Mac OS and restart your Mac, Setup Assistant will greet you after you see the Desktop. This helpful utility holds a kind of interview—it asks some questions about how you'll use your Mac and changes settings based on your answers (**Figure 3.8**). Setup Assistant presents 11 screens of questions, asking which regional settings you prefer (for example, if you want to use a Brazilian keyboard layout); your name and organization; the current date and time, including your time zone; and a few questions about the network to which your Mac is connected, if any. Once you've answered all of the questions, Setup Assistant changes settings in several control panels to reflect your answers.

Figure 3.8

Mac OS Setup Assistant interviews you and changes your Mac's settings based on the answers you give. It's a real time-saver.

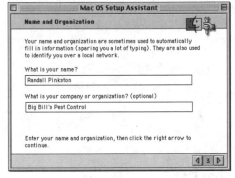

The last screen of the Setup Assistant asks if you want to configure your Internet settings using Internet Setup Assistant. This second assistant asks all kinds of questions about your Internet settings, including your e-mail address, account password, and other settings your ISP should provide (**Figure 3.9**). If you don't *have* an ISP, the Internet Setup Assistant can find one for you by connecting to a database at Apple and letting you choose one.

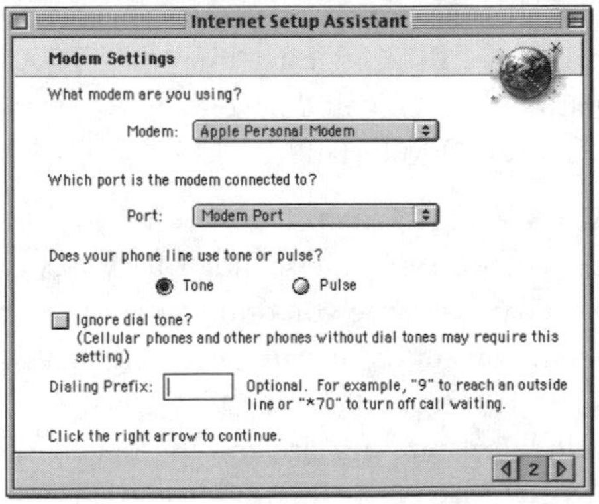

Figure 3.9

After you've completed the standard Setup Assistant, you'll have an option to complete the Internet Setup Assistant, which changes your Internet settings based on your answers to its questions.

Installing Mac OS X

After years of all-nighters and gallons of Mountain Dew, Apple's engineers have come up with an easy-to-use, easy-to-install version of Unix—an accomplishment for which we should laud them. Installing Mac OS X is surprisingly easy given its size and scope.

Getting ready. To get started installing Mac OS X, insert the system-software CD. When it mounts, it should pop open a window that says "Welcome to Mac OS X." Inside that window a couple of documents talk about Mac OS X, and several folders contain the same documents in several other languages. One of these folders has some utilities that can erase your hard drive and set the startup disk, if you like.

Finally, at the top of the window is an Install Mac OS X icon. Double-click this icon to start the installation process. When you do, the installer puts up a window with some text and a single button labeled Restart (**Figure 3.10**). Clicking this button restarts your Mac from the Mac OS X CD and begins the installation process.

Figure 3.10

When you launch the Mac OS X installer from inside Mac OS 9, you'll see an impressive-looking screen with one button—Restart. Click it, and your Mac starts up from the Mac OS X installation CD. Then the real fun begins.

You can also start up from the Mac OS X CD by putting it in your CD drive and starting up with Ⓒ held down. This method is great if you want to install Mac OS X on a second hard drive. Because the Mac OS X installer won't run in the Classic compatibility layer, you'll have to either start up in Mac OS 9 or start from the Mac OS X CD to install Mac OS X a second time.

The actual Mac OS X installation. Despite that you're working with a far more high-powered operating system, installing Mac OS X is actually easier than installing Mac OS 9. That's because you don't have to worry about what parts of the operating system you should install—you only have a couple of choices. Once your Mac has restarted from the Mac OS X CD-ROM, you'll see a happy Mac and a small multicolor spinning circle in the upper-left corner. This is your indication that your Mac is starting up into Mac OS X for the first time.

This initial startup from the CD may take a while, so you might want to have a snack or take a little walk. Don't worry—nothing much will happen without you.

Once your Mac finishes getting its act together, it will start up into the Mac OS X installer. The first window you face is the Installer window, in which you'll work through your installation.

 If you change your mind and want to go back a step, you can always click the Go Back button in the installer.

Select a language. In the first installer window, you have your choice of several languages to use as Mac OS X's main language. Choose one and click Continue.

Welcome. Now you're in the installer proper. The first screen is simply a welcome screen, in which Apple sends its warmest wishes. Click Continue.

Read-me file. That's right—this installer also has an important information section, and although it looks a little boring, you really should take the time to read through this document. It might save your bacon during installation. Once you've read it, click Continue.

License agreement. What installation experience would be complete without a long legal document to read through and agree to? Apple has thought of this and included the software license agreement, in which you agree to any number of legally binding items. Once you've thoroughly gone through this, click Continue. Just to make *sure* you know you're agreeing to the license agreement, the installer puts up another window asking you to agree or disagree. If you click Disagree, you're done—the installer exits. If you click Agree, the installation continues.

Choose a location. The installer looks for any available hard drives on which to install Mac OS X and lists them in this window. Click the desired hard drive to select it. Although you don't have to, you can erase the disk where you're installing Mac OS X. If you want to do so, select the "Erase destination and format as" check box at the bottom of the screen. This item also has a pop-up menu in which you can select a volume format for your newly formatted disk: Mac OS Extended or Unix File System. Unless you *know* you want Unix File System, select Mac OS Extended. Click Continue.

Choose your installation. By default, the installer does an easy installation, which installs everything Apple thinks Mac OS X needs to run properly. Most folks should go with the easy installation. If you want to customize your Mac OS X installation, click Customize at the bottom. This presents you with the Custom Install screen, in which you can check or uncheck the parts of the operating system. Actually, you'll only have the opportunity to uncheck a few items: BSD Subsystem, which contains certain optional parts of Mac OS X's Unix underpinnings, and additional printer drivers. If you plan to install the developer package, you should check the BSD box. (An easy install includes BSD Subsystem by default.) This window tells you how much disk space you'll need to complete the installation—if you don't have enough, Mac OS X won't install. Click Install to continue.

Install. The installer will go to work, copying software from the CD and moving things around on the hard drive. This process can take anywhere from a few minutes to half an hour, depending on your CD-drive speed and Mac processor. The installer will keep you apprised of how long the process will take, but don't take the installer at its word until the final stages—this number can vary wildly. This is another good time for a snack or a trip to the rest room.

Wrap up. Once the installer has completed its job, it tells you it's done. Your Mac automatically restarts after a set amount of time; you can click Restart if you're feeling impatient. That's it! You've installed Mac OS X.

Setting up your installation. You're not done yet, though. The next step is filling in a set of forms Mac OS X will use to create a user account, set up Internet access, and make other basic tweaks to your Mac's settings. During this process, you'll also be asked to register Mac OS X with Apple. This registration information gets sent to Apple the next time you connect to the Internet. Here's a quick look at the process:

Welcome. In a beautiful blue movie reminiscent of the video United Airlines plays just before takeoff, Apple welcomes you to Mac OS X and asks what country you live in. Select your country and click Continue.

Keyboard selection. The next step in your setup is to choose a keyboard layout. These layouts are listed by country, and there are a lot of them. Once you've selected your keyboard, click Continue. If you don't see the keyboard you want to use, check the Show All check box at the bottom.

Product registration. Setup Assistant now asks for your name, address, phone number, e-mail address, and company or school. Most of this information is *not* optional, and you can't proceed without entering it. If you try, the Assistant marks the mandatory fields with a red icon indicating items you missed. After you fill in this information, click Continue.

More registration. The next screen asks how you plan to use your Mac and what your occupation is. You have to answer these two questions from pop-up menus or you can't proceed with your setup. The screen also asks permission for Apple and other companies to contact you with news and information about related products—this is optional. Once you've entered your answers, click Continue. The final registration screen tells you that your registration information will be sent to Apple the next time you connect to the Internet. Click Continue.

Account setup. Again, the Assistant asks you to enter your name, as well as a short name, or Unix-style nickname, that you can use when entering a user name and password, but the installer will fill in these two bits of information based on the information you entered previously. You'll also need to enter a password and a hint, used to create a Mac OS X account for you—every installation has at least one account. Click Continue.

Internet selection. In this screen, you can tell Mac OS X whether you would like to use your existing ISP or would rather not set up your Internet settings at the moment. Click the radio button next to your choice, and then click Continue.

Connection method. Next, Mac OS X asks how you connect to the Internet—via modem, LAN, cable, DSL, or AirPort. (You'll only see this section if you elect to use your existing ISP.) Depending on which of these you select, the next couple of screens will walk you through the specific settings for your ISP—you'll need to get that information from your service provider. Click Continue in each screen to move on to the next setting.

Set up iTools. Apple gives you the opportunity to sign up for an iTools account, which gives you a free e-mail account and 20 MB of server space on one of Apple's servers. You can also find out more about iTools in this screen. Click Continue.

Send in your registration. Now that you've completed your Internet setup, Mac OS X connects to Apple's servers and sends in your registration information. If you cancel this process before it finishes, Mac OS X won't send your information, but you can continue to set up your Mac.

Set up e-mail. In the final round of questions, Mac OS X asks whether you'd like to use a mac.com e-mail address or set up another address. If you choose to set up another account, the setup assistant asks for your e-mail address, your incoming mail server, account ID, e-mail password, and outgoing mail server.

Select a time zone. The next question's an easy one—this screen asks you to select a time zone on a nifty map.

Set the date and time. Getting down to the minutiae, this screen asks you to set the current date and time for your Mac.

Congratulations! When you move on from setting the date and time, the next thing you'll see is your Mac OS X desktop.

Installing Mac OS 9 along with Mac OS X. Most people will probably want to run their Mac OS 9 and earlier programs on Mac OS X. To do so, you'll need to install a copy of Mac OS 9.1 on your Mac—fortunately, the boxed copy of Mac OS X includes a Mac OS 9.1 CD. To install both operating systems, simply start up from the Mac OS 9.1 CD and install it as described earlier. You can install Mac OS 9.1 and Mac OS X on the same hard-drive partition if you like, or you can separate them on two or more partitions. After installing, you can then update to Mac OS 9.2.1 (the updater comes with the Mac OS X 10.1 package).

 If you're installing Mac OS 9 and Mac OS X on the same partition, install Mac OS 9 first—you may run into trouble if you try to install it later. If your installer says you can't install Mac OS 9 without starting up from the system-software CD, but you've already done so, try a clean install.

Installing developer tools. If you plan to take advantage of all the Unix software available for downloading, install the Mac OS X developer tools. This software package lets you compile source code into working Unix applications. (These tools also let you create your own programs using Apple's programming tools.) The developer tools come on a second CD that ships with Mac OS X. To install them, start up from Mac OS X, put the developer CD in the drive, and double-click the Developer.pkg icon to launch the installer. Follow the onscreen instructions to install the tools.

Updating Hard-Disk Drivers

An important but often-overlooked component of installing a new version of the Mac OS is updating your hard disk's driver. Every hard drive has a little section devoted to driver software, which is how it and your Mac communicate at a basic level. You can't see hard-disk drivers as files in the Finder—they make their home on a special part of the hard drive that's not normally visible.

Any installation of the Mac OS updates your hard-disk drivers with new information, which usually includes some bug fixes and maybe even some performance enhancements at a very basic level. Updating hard-disk drivers is almost always a good idea, so if you're asked, go ahead and do it. One note— if you have a non-Apple hard drive (that is, one that didn't come with your Mac), you can't update its drivers via the installer. You'll have to use the utility software you used to format it in the first place.

Adding and Removing Components

You can use the Mac OS installer to add components to your current Mac OS installation (giving your Mac more abilities) or remove previously installed components (to free up valuable hard-drive space and memory). You can also remove system components in Mac OS 9 and earlier by putting the appropriate extensions, control panels, and preferences in the Trash, but it's hard to make sure you've thrown away all of the files necessary to remove the component completely from your system. You're better off letting the Mac OS installer handle the job.

To add or remove operating-system components in Mac OS 9 and earlier, you start up from your installer CD and launch the installer. You'll see the same welcome screen that appears when you're installing a new version of the operating system, but after you select the hard drive with the System Folder you want to update and click Select, the installer will notice that the selected hard drive already has that system software installed. At this point, it asks if you want to reinstall your system software or add and remove components from your current installation (**Figure 3.11**). Click Add/Remove. This brings up the Custom Installation and Removal window, in which you select the individual packages to add or remove and choose what actions to perform when you click Start: Recommended Installation, Customized Installation, or Customized Removal.

Figure 3.11

When you select a disk that already has the version of the Mac OS you want to install, you'll be asked whether you want to reinstall that version or add or remove components.

Recommended Installation. This mode installs the set of extensions, control panels, and so on that give you most of what you need to make the selected component work well, with the bonus of not having to know what the individual items do.

Customized Installation. If you really know what you're doing and want to install just the software you need and no more, choose this option, which lets you pick exactly what bits of software to install. For example, if you're installing Mac OS 9.2.1's video software components and you *know* you're not going to need the 7200 graphics acceleration extension, you can make sure it's not selected in the list presented during a customized installation of Mac OS 9.2.1.

Customized Removal. If you just don't need some parts of your system software, you can select Customized Removal from this pop-up menu, which lets you choose already installed operating-system components to leave facedown in the proverbial ditch.

Unlike Mac OS 9, Mac OS X doesn't allow you to remove part or all of the operating system. To uninstall Mac OS X, you'll simply have to start up in Mac OS 9 and delete the Mac OS X System folder and all other folders Mac OS X puts on your hard drive. This can be a problem, because Mac OS X creates many invisible folders—you'll either have to make these visible using a tool such as ResEdit and then deleting them or back up that hard drive and format it to get rid of everything and then restore your files from the backup. Although it takes a good deal of work, the latter option will ensure that you get rid of every vestige of Mac OS X.

Updating Your OS

With the advent of Mac OS 9, Apple introduced a way to update your system software automatically, called Software Update. This imaginatively titled program connects to the Internet (either at your command or on a schedule you set) and then looks to see if Apple has released any operating-system updates. If it finds any, it downloads them to your hard drive and installs them—no muss, no fuss.

To use Software Update, under the Apple menu choose Control Panels and then Software Update, which brings up the Software Update control panel. This simple control panel features a large Update Now button in the center—when clicked, it starts your Mac on a software-seeking journey (**Figure 3.12**). The bottom portion of this control panel contains a check box that lets you set a schedule for software updates so you can tell your Mac to, say, look for new software every Thursday morning at 3:47 a.m.

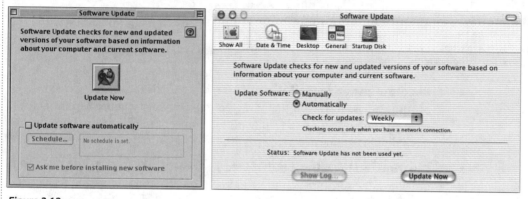

Figure 3.12

The primary feature of the Software Update control panel (left) is a fat Update Now button—when you click it, your Mac contacts Apple's servers to see if any new system software is available. Mac OS X's Update Now button is more subtle (right).

Be aware that earlier versions of Software Update were a bit flaky—they tended to either crash or fail to download and install updates completely. The latest versions are much more reliable and usually do the job.

Mac OS X also has a Software Update program that checks for updates every week. You can change Software Update's settings in Mac OS X by opening System Preferences, clicking the Show All icon (if you don't see everything), and then clicking the Software Update icon. Instead of checking every week, you can check daily or monthly, or you can set Software Update to do the work manually (when you click the Update Now button). You can also check Software Update's log to see what it's been up to.

What Disk Format to Use (HFS, HFS+, UFS)

When you're preparing a hard drive for use (in other words, formatting it with Drive Setup), you'll need to choose a *volume format,* a fancy term for the framework in which you save files.

You have three choices: HFS (Hierarchical File System), HFS+, or UFS (Unix File System). HFS—also known as Mac OS Standard Format—was first introduced well over a decade ago. This file system lets you nest one folder inside another—hence the name. HFS was cutting-edge in its day, but several limitations keep it from being the best choice now. That's why Apple introduced HFS+—also known as Mac OS Extended Format—in Mac OS 8.1. HFS+ has a couple of big advantages—it uses disk space more efficiently, and it lets your Mac understand filenames longer than 31 characters. Given this choice, go with HFS+.

The third option, UFS, only works with Mac OS X (or its cousin, Mac OS X Server). Use UFS for your volume format only if you plan to use Mac OS X as a Unix installation, without Mac OS 9.2.1 installed at all. Mac OS 9.2.1 and earlier can't use UFS disks, and you can't run programs in Mac OS X's Classic compatibility layer if those programs are on a UFS disk.

Bottom line—go with HFS+ and you can't go wrong. For those of you who use Mac OS X in a Unix environment and who don't need Mac OS 9 and earlier programs at all—you know who you are—consider UFS instead.

The System Folder in Mac OS 9 and Earlier

Most every Mac has a special folder with a blue Mac OS face on its front, located on one of the hard drives. This folder, called the System Folder, contains all of the system software's files and programs. Inside the System Folder you'll find the actual system software, the Finder, all of your fonts, your desktop pattern—everything that makes your Mac run. Get a grip on how the System Folder works and what's inside it, and you're well on your way to becoming a Mac expert.

The System and Finder Files

There are two very special files inside your Mac named System and Finder. The System file is fairly meaty (in Mac OS 9.2.1, it weighs in at 16.1 MB), and it contains most of the information your Mac needs to start up and run properly. The System file handles your memory, your hard drive, and your graphics chip—in short, it makes sure all the hardware is working together in harmony, and it gives the Finder access to that hardware.

The Finder is your interface with your Mac. It's responsible for drawing your Desktop, creating your icons, and moving files around on the hard drive when you drag them to different places. It also launches programs when you double-click them and links double-clicked documents to the appropriate programs. The Finder is the public face of your Mac's system software.

Figure 3.13

These two files—the System file (left) and the Finder file (right)—make up the core of the Mac OS 9 system software.

System

Finder

Together, the System and the Finder run your Mac, and their presence in a folder makes it special—*blessed,* in Apple jargon (**Figure 3.13**). The Finder finds out what you want and passes that on to the System, which then enacts your command on the hardware level—whether that means writing a file on the hard drive or shutting down the Mac.

The System file. Despite its placid appearance, the System file contains hundreds of resources your Mac needs to run properly—everything from icons, to text strings you might see in an error message, to the Application menu. The System is a *suitcase* file—that is, you can open it and put stuff inside it, just as if it were a real suitcase. In the old days (say, in System 7.0), if you wanted to add a sound or a font to your Mac, you opened the System file and dropped it in. Fonts have moved out into their own room—a Fonts folder inside the System Folder—but the System file still houses your system sounds and keyboard layouts. (System sounds are the beeps your Mac makes to alert you that it needs your attention; keyboard layouts let you change your Mac keyboard layout from the standard QWERTY to DVORAK or any number of other layouts for other languages such as German, Italian, or Japanese.)

Figure 3.14

The Mac OS 9 System suitcase contains system sounds and keyboard layouts; you can add and remove these files to create a custom System.

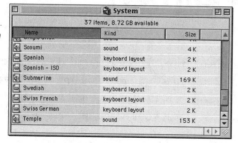

To see what's inside the System suitcase, open the System Folder and double-click the System file. This opens a window showing all of the keyboard layouts and system sounds installed in your Mac (**Figure 3.14**). You can remove any sounds or keyboard layouts by dragging them from the window to the Trash. You can *add* sounds and keyboard layouts by dragging them to this window (or dragging them to the System suitcase).

The Finder file. The other special denizen of the System Folder is the Finder. Unlike the System suitcase, the Finder can't be opened or modified, except by technically minded folks using special software. As we've said before, the Finder is responsible for your Mac's user interface. It draws windows, moves files, shows icons, launches applications—it handles the basics.

Special files. Besides the System and the Finder, the System Folder contains a handful of special files that provide services or otherwise make your Mac experience a great one. Here are a few you might encounter:

Clipboard. The Clipboard file is where your Mac stores data you cut or copy using Cut or Copy from the Edit menu. If you want to know what the Clipboard currently holds, double-click the Clipboard file and a window will open, showing you its contents.

Login. The Login file, with its Finder-like icon, lets your Mac provide a multiple-user environment, where each person who uses the Mac has to sign in. Besides providing more security, Login keeps each user's workspace separate—including documents, desktop patterns, and even Web browser bookmarks. You can't open the Login file by double-clicking it.

Mac OS ROM file. Older Macs had a special set of chips called the Mac OS ROM containing basic instructions on how a Mac should start up and run. Newer Mac models (starting with the iMac) keep most of this set of instructions in the Mac OS ROM file in your System Folder.

MacTCP DNR. This odd file appears in the System Folder because some older Internet programs that rely on its resources need to have it in that location or they won't work. You can't open the MacTCP DNR file yourself.

Panels. The Panels file provides an alternative to the Finder. That's right—your Mac doesn't absolutely *have* to have the Finder to function correctly. The Panels interface is a simple Finder, with program and file buttons arranged in neat panels. You can't open Panels—it's strictly for the System's use.

Scrapbook. The Scrapbook is a holding place for snippets of text, movie clips, sound files, or pictures you've come across and would like to keep for a while. To put something in the Scrapbook, select the item and copy it to the Clipboard (choose Cut or Copy from the Edit menu). Then choose Scrapbook from the Apple menu to open the Scrapbook window. Paste the item you put on the Clipboard by choosing Paste from the Edit menu. You can use your Scrapbook items by scrolling to the one you want, copying it to the Clipboard, and then pasting it where you want.

System Resources. After years of development, the System file was packed so full of resources that Apple reached the limit for resources in a single file. So engineers created the System Resources file to hold some of those additional resources. You can't open System Resources—only the System uses it.

Suitcases

Suitcases are special files that hold other files. In practice, they're a lot like folders except that you can put only certain kinds of items in a suitcase. Although Mac OS used to have several kinds of suitcases, now it commonly uses only two—the System suitcase and font suitcases, which hold fonts.

Font suitcases are a way of organizing related fonts into one easy-to-manipulate file. When you open a Font suitcase, a window opens, listing any fonts in that suitcase. Many font suitcases contain only one font, but some hold several variations on a font (such as bold and italic versions) (**Figure 3.15**), and others may hold all the fonts a particular program uses.

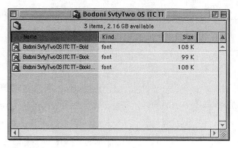

Figure 3.15

In Mac OS 9 and earlier, font suitcases can contain several variations on the same font.

Special Folders

The System Folder is also home to several special folders that hold files your Mac needs to go about its business. These folders hold hundreds of files—fonts, desktop patterns, and items that launch when your Mac starts up.

Appearance. The Appearance folder is where your Mac stores all the files it needs to present a pretty face. Specifically, this folder stores your desktop pictures as well as theme files and sound sets. *Themes* are files that govern the color and shape of windows, buttons, and controls. Apple Platinum is the only appearance theme that comes with a Macintosh, but you *can* download other themes out there if you want to customize your Mac. Sound sets provide a soundtrack for your Mac by assigning sounds to button presses, menu choices, opening and closing windows, and so on.

 If you want to save a little space, you can throw away pictures you've got in the Desktop Pictures folder that you never plan to use as desktop images.

Apple Menu Items. Any items you place in the Apple Menu Items folder show up in the actual Apple menu—this is an incredibly powerful and customizable feature. You can put programs, files, folders, and even aliases to other items in here. If you put a folder in the Apple Menu Items folder, it appears as a hierarchical menu in the Apple menu, showing off its contents for all the world to see.

Application Support. When you install programs, they sometimes put items they need in this folder. It's just a convenient storage place that programs use—you probably won't need to open this folder at all.

ColorSync Profiles. The Mac's color-management software, ColorSync, makes sure graphics professionals get the colors they expect in every aspect of their work—on the monitor and from the printer. ColorSync saves profiles that show how an individual piece of hardware handles color.

Contextual Menu Items. This folder contains files that add items to your Mac's contextual menus. You can add a ton of additional contextual-menu commands to your Mac by putting them here.

Control Panels. The Control Panels folder contains a special set of files called *control panels,* which can change settings on your Macintosh (for the nitty-gritty of what this means, see "Control Panels" later in this chapter). You can tweak a *lot* of settings here; a standard Mac OS 9.2.1 installation includes more than 30 control panels, which let you set up your AppleTalk network, change your Desktop picture, control how quickly your mouse moves the pointer, and even share a USB printer over a network.

Control Strip Modules. This folder holds items that show up in your Mac's Control Strip. These modules offer an easy way to change your Mac's settings; they contain a subset of the controls you'll find in certain control panels. Although they contain fewer settings than the corresponding control panels, they're easier to access. A standard Mac OS 9.2.1 installation has tons of Control Strip modules, which let you turn AppleTalk on or off, choose a different printer, control audio CD playback, change monitor resolution, and so on.

Extensions. The Extensions folder holds all of your Mac's extensions—you'll become intimate with these as you get used to your Mac. Extensions are special files that add new abilities to your Mac, and they must be in this folder to load properly.

Favorites. This underused folder contains a quick way to get at folders, files, URLs, and applications. Items put in the Favorites folder (whether they're the real thing or just aliases) appear in the Favorites submenu under the Apple menu, as well as next to the Favorites button in the Open or Save dialog box, if the program in question can use them. For example, the Favorites button in Microsoft Word's Open dialog box shows you those documents Word can open as well as any folders its Open dialog box can point to. To open an item in your Favorites folder, choose Favorites from the Apple menu and select an item.

Fonts. The Fonts folder holds all of the fonts available to your Mac. To add a font in Mac OS 9 and earlier, drop it on the closed System Folder and your Mac puts the font in the Fonts folder; or you can drop new fonts directly on this folder. To remove a font, simply drag it out of this folder to a new location. Any program running at the time you add those fonts can't use them until you quit and relaunch it. To remove fonts, you'll have to quit all of the programs so the only thing running is the Finder, and then move the fonts you no longer want out of the Fonts folder. Each font installed takes up a little bit of your Mac's memory.

Help. This folder holds your Mac's help files. When you go to the Help menu and choose a topic, these files provide information about your Mac and the software installed on it. Mac help files are mostly plain HTML files that you can read with a Web browser, if you're so inclined, but there's no need to do so, as the built-in Help Viewer program pops up automatically when you open a topic from the Help menu.

Internet Plug-Ins. The Internet Plug-Ins folder holds plug-ins for Internet programs that give your Web browser new abilities. Each browser also maintains its own plug-ins folder, so it's unlikely you'll find anything other than the QuickTime plug-in here.

Internet Search Sites. This folder contains Sherlock plug-ins, which enable your Mac's built-in search program to scour the Internet for whatever you request. You can add new Sherlock plug-ins by putting them in this folder (see the "Sherlock" section, later in this chapter).

Language & Region Support. The items in this folder let your Mac work well with multiple languages, such as Chinese, Finnish, Japanese, and even Swedish.

Launcher Items. Items you put in the Launcher Items folder (including aliases to other items) show up in the Launcher window.

Preferences. The Preferences folder is where programs store specialized *preference* files, which contain settings for a given program. It's not uncommon for the Preferences folder on a Mac you've been using for a while to have hundreds of items in it.

PrintMonitor Documents. When you print a document, your Mac creates a file that represents this print job and puts it in the PrintMonitor Documents folder. The program that handles background printing is called PrintMonitor, and it looks to this folder for any waiting print jobs. You probably won't ever need to open this folder, unless you're having some difficulty with a print job.

Scripting Additions. This folder holds scripting additions files, which give AppleScript more power. Mac OS 9 has several scripting additions by default, and you can add more of your own by putting them in this folder.

Scripts. The Scripts folder is a convenient place to store AppleScripts, and if you drop an AppleScript on the System Folder, it'll go here. By default, this folder contains Folder Action Scripts, which holds a group of AppleScripts you can attach to a folder. These scripts run when the folder to which they're attached changes. We'll tell you more about AppleScript, including Folder Action Scripts (see the "AppleScript" section, later in this chapter).

Servers. This folder holds aliases to servers that open whenever your Mac starts up. You can remove these autoconnecting servers by removing their aliases from this folder—you can delete them if you're sure you no longer need them, or you can move the aliases to another location, where you can double-click them to open the servers they represent.

Shutdown Items. Any items in this folder (including aliases) open when your Mac shuts down. A good example is an AppleScript that backs up your Documents folder whenever you switch off your Mac.

Startup Items. Any items in this folder (including aliases) open when your Mac starts up. For example, if you *always* launch a particular program when you start up your Mac, put its alias in here and your Mac will launch it for you.

Text Encodings. This folder contains items that help your Mac convert one type of text (say, English) into another (say, Hebrew).

Your Mac's System Folder is a smart folder. If you drop an item on it that belongs in one of its special folders (such as a font, a control panel, or an extension), your Mac asks if you want to put that item in the appropriate folder inside the System Folder. You almost always do.

Extensions

Extensions are special files that extend your Mac's abilities—hence the name. A typical extension might let your Mac talk to a new hardware peripheral, add the ability to listen to a new music file format, or even change the way your Mac's menus look. Thousands of extensions are available, ranging from the subtle to the sublime. At startup, your Mac loads those it finds in the Extensions folder (**Figure 3.16**).

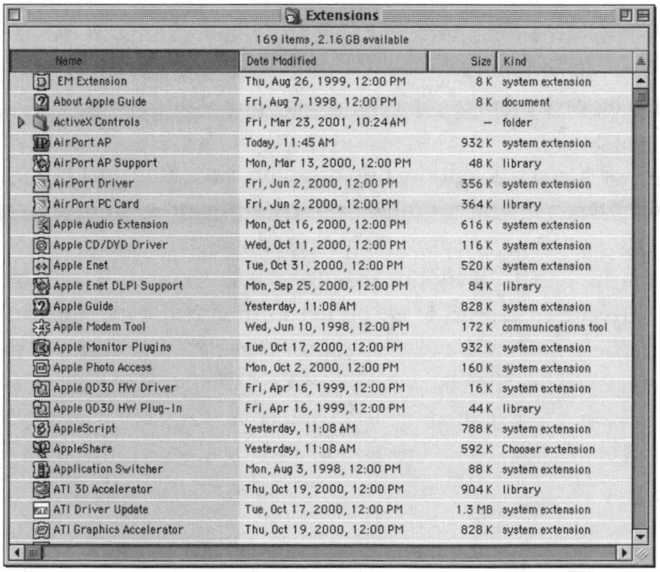

Figure 3.16

The number of extensions installed on your Mac is most likely long and varied—most are part of the standard Mac OS installation.

Extensions are different from applications in that they're *global,* whereas applications generally aren't. That means extensions change your whole Macintosh experience, no matter what program you're using, and applications have an impact only when they're active. And although extensions resemble control panels (they both load bits of code into the Mac OS at startup), control panels let you easily change their settings, and extensions might rely on a sibling in the control panel to do that work for them. Many extensions don't allow you to change their settings at all.

 You can generally tell which files are extensions because of their icons, which look like interlocking puzzle pieces.

Types of extensions. You'll find a couple of types of items in your Extensions folder: extensions and libraries. Extensions are active bits of code that load when your Mac starts up, and libraries are passive bits of code that other programs go to when they need to do certain things. For example, the QuickTime extension modifies your Mac so it can play music and videos with ease, and the DrawSprocketLib provides a way for other programs to draw onscreen. Libraries just need to be present in the background—they don't have to load during startup.

Extension memory use. When they load while your Mac is starting up, extensions take up some of your Mac's memory. Although a single extension may take less than a few hundred kilobytes, by the time you've loaded 30 or so extensions, you've added several megabytes to the amount of memory your Mac needs for system software—sometimes as much as 15 or 20 MB. If your Mac doesn't have a lot of memory, you might experiment with disabling some extensions to free some up.

Problems extensions can cause. Extensions are powerful things—they essentially replace little bits of the operating system with their own programming code. For example, an extension might replace the part of the Mac OS responsible for drawing windows with its own code, drawing windows with a pink stripe through the title bar. This isn't such a bad thing in itself, but it can cause some serious problems. First, if the programmer hasn't done the job just right, the extension might not do what it's supposed to, resulting in a crash. Second, if another extension tries to modify the same bit of the system software or expects to encounter unmodified code, this will probably also cause a crash. Known as an *extension conflict,* this is one of the leading causes of Mac crashes. (By the way, Mac OS X doesn't use extensions, which is one reason it's so darned stable.) We'll cover how to take care of extension conflicts in Chapter 8, "Prevention and Troubleshooting."

How extensions load. When your Mac starts up, it first goes through a series of tests and then finds a hard drive with system software on it, from which it starts loading the system software. This is what's happening when you see the splash screen in Mac OS 9 and earlier. Next, your Mac looks inside the Extensions folder and starts loading the extensions it finds there. It loads these items alphabetically, which means you can change when extensions load by altering their names. Put a space in front of an extension's name and it will load early; put a *z* (or a bullet) in front of an extension's name and it will load near the end. The reason you might want to change an extension's load order is that certain extensions crash unless they load first—or last.

A few items load before items in the Extensions folder (such as MacsBug or enabler software for processor upgrade cards). These early startup items also load alphabetically, but they do so before regular extensions. So if you find an extension that loads before any of the others even though its name comes up later alphabetically, this is probably why.

Selected extensions and what they do. Your Mac's Extensions folder is chockablock with files—a clean install of Mac OS 9.2.1 will put nearly 150 items in this folder. Although this folder may intimidate would-be spelunkers, it's worth getting to know some of the items in your Extensions folder—just in case you need to move them around. Here's a sampling of what you might find in a Mac OS 9 and earlier System Folder, and what each item does:

EM. This part of the Extension Manager software lets you control which extensions load. This extension has a space at the beginning of its name to ensure that it loads early on, and that's the reason we listed it here—it's the first extension you'll see when you open your Extensions folder.

AirPort extensions. This set of extensions lets your Mac work with the AirPort wireless networking card.

Apple Audio. This file updates audio capabilities for PCI-based Macs.

Apple CD/DVD Driver. This enables your Mac to use a CD or DVD drive.

Apple Enet. This tells your Mac how to communicate across an Ethernet network.

Apple Photo Access. This enables your Mac to read Photo CD–format CD-ROMs.

AppleScript. This extension lets you write text scripts that tell your Mac what to do, such as copy the contents of your Documents folder to another hard drive when you shut down the Mac.

AppleShare. This Chooser extension lets your Mac connect to AppleShare servers on a network.

Application Switcher. This extension tells your Mac to switch to another program when you press ⌘Tab.

Audio CD Access. This enables you to play audio CDs in your Mac's CD-ROM drive.

Authoring Support. This enables Macs equipped with a CD-R or DVD-R drive to write CDs or DVDs.

CarbonLib. This extension provides all of the necessary code to let certain programs written for Mac OS 9 and earlier run on Mac OS X.

Color Picker. This lets you use one of several methods of choosing a highlight color.

ColorSync. This extension makes your Mac superaccurate about how colors look when displayed on a monitor and when printed. This ensures that artistic folks get the colors they're expecting when they print.

Contextual Menu. This gives your Mac the ability to show and use a contextual menu when you Control-click an item.

Control Strip. This is part of the software that puts the Control Strip onscreen.

Desktop Printer Spooler. Part of the Desktop Printer software, this item lets your Mac *spool* documents to the PrintMonitor queue, where a specialized program handles them.

Desktop PrintMonitor. The other side of the Desktop Printer software, this program prints a document in the background when you use a Desktop Printer.

DVD extensions. This set of extensions lets your Mac play DVD video disks, if it has the proper hardware.

FBC Indexing Scheduler. This extension schedules when Sherlock indexes your hard drive. Indexing a hard drive speeds up searching for specific text in a variety of documents.

File Sharing. This lets your Mac share files and folders over a network.

File Sharing Library. This extension provides a library of code to help your Mac share files and folders over a network.

Find By Content. This extension lets your Mac go through all of the text-based documents on its hard drive, creating an index of significant words for quick searching.

FireWire extensions. These let a Mac with built-in FireWire ports communicate with DV cameras, hard drives, and other FireWire-based devices.

Folder Actions. These let you attach AppleScripts to folders on your Mac's hard drive. These Folder Actions are AppleScripts that launch when you change the folder (by moving the folder or putting something inside it).

FontSync. This extension makes sure that fonts with the same name really *are* the same fonts.

Foreign File Access. This lets your Mac read CD-ROMs that don't use standard Macintosh file systems.

High Sierra File Access. This lets your Mac use CD-ROMs that use the High Sierra file system.

ISO 9660 File Access. This extension lets your Mac read CD-ROMs that use the ISO 9660 file system.

LaserWriter 8. This Chooser extension connects your Mac to most laser printers.

Location Manager. Part of the Location Manager software, this extension lets you quickly change certain settings on your Mac (for the network, modem, and so on) that often depend on your location.

MacinTalk extensions. These let your Mac speak to you with a variety of computer-generated voices.

Macintosh Guide. This was the old way of providing help with certain tasks on your Mac. Most new programs don't use Macintosh Guide files to provide help. (The Mac OS now uses HTML-based files.)

Multi-User Startup. This extension provides some security and privacy (when enabled) by making users log in and keeping their workspaces separate.

Open Transport extensions. These provide a way for your Mac to communicate over a network. Open Transport is important when it comes to using the Internet.

OpenGL extensions. These let your Mac use OpenGL-based 3D graphics programs, which are mostly games.

PrintingLib. This extension provides a library of prefabricated code for programs that need to print.

PrintMonitor. If you're *not* using Desktop Printing for your printing needs, PrintMonitor handles background printing tasks for you.

QuickDraw 3D extensions. These let your Mac work with QuickDraw 3D objects and games. They now mostly go unused in favor of OpenGL.

QuickTime extensions. This fat set of extensions and libraries enables your Mac to play and edit all kinds of multimedia files, including video, audio, and even MIDI files.

Security extensions. This collection of extensions and libraries lets you store your passwords in a keychain file.

Software Update Engine. The driving force behind the automatic updating of your Mac's system software, Software Update Engine searches special Apple servers over the Internet for the latest operating-system components.

Software Update Scheduler. This extension lets you schedule when your Mac connects to the Internet to look for new system software.

SOMobjects for Mac OS. This extension provides a library of tools for certain programs. Few applications rely on this library any longer.

Sound Manager. This extension updates your system software to get the best sound capabilities out of your Mac.

Speakable Items. This extension enables your Mac to do simple tasks based on voice commands.

Speech Manager. Lets your Mac speak selected text.

Speech Recognition. This enables your Mac to recognize your voice.

Text Encoding Converter. This helps your Mac use text that's been formatted in a format not native to the Mac—such as text found on the Internet.

Time Synchronizer. This extension provides a way for your Mac to set its internal clock by checking with a time server over the Internet.

Type 1 Scaler. This enables Type 1 PostScript fonts to work properly with certain applications.

UDF Volume Access. This extension enables your Mac to read and write volumes that use the Universal Disk Format (UDF) file system.

USB Device. Helps your Mac make use of USB devices that you plug into it.

USB Printer Sharing. This lets your Mac share a USB-based printer with other Macs on the same network.

USB Software Locator. This extension helps your Mac track down USB driver software by contacting an Apple server and comparing the hardware with a list of drivers on that server.

Trashing extensions. You can't just throw extensions away as you can most files on your Mac's hard drive. That's because when your Mac loads an extension at startup, it marks the file as *in use*. Your Mac can't discard these files because it believes it's using them for something important. The same thing happens if you have a file open in, say, a word processor, and you try to throw it away. Try to empty the Trash when it contains in-use files and you'll get a dialog box that says essentially, "Put that extension down—I'm using it. You can't throw it away!" (**Figure 3.17**).

Figure 3.17

If you try to throw away an extension that Mac OS 9 is using, the OS will tell you in fairly polite terms that you can't. To do the trick, you'll have to restart while that extension is in the Trash and then empty it.

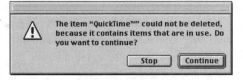

If you're sure you want to throw an extension away, you can, but you'll have to restart your Mac. Move the extension into the Trash, and then choose Restart from the Special menu. When your Mac starts up again, the extension in the Trash won't load, so it won't be marked as in use, and you can finally throw it away.

Holding down Option and emptying the Trash won't get rid of an in-use extension.

Control Panels

Control panels are bits of software that let you change settings on your Mac. Whether that means adjusting your speaker volume or changing your TCP/IP network settings, the Control Panels folder has a slew of software bits to do the job. Control panels come in a couple of flavors—some act like small applications, and some act like extensions. The ones that act like applications appear in the Control Panels folder more as a matter of convenience than out of necessity. They can replace parts of the operating system and load at startup, just like extensions.

In practice, there's little difference between the two, because both let you tweak your Mac's settings. When you launch a control panel by choosing it from the Control Panels submenu (or double-clicking it in the Control Panels window), that panel will put up a small window full of controls. You can change these, and when you close the window, those settings are saved and the control panel quits.

Some control panels and what they do. You can install hundreds of control panels on your Mac, and like extensions they give your Mac amazing new abilities. Unlike extensions, control panels also let you exercise some measure of control over how they act. Here's a selection of Mac OS 9 control panels you might run across and a brief bit about what each one does (see Chapter 2 for control panels specific to PowerBooks and iBooks):

Appearance. This lets you alter how your Mac looks and sounds by changing your Mac's scroll arrows, the fonts it uses for menus and filenames, your desktop pattern, and even the sounds your Mac makes when you open a menu or close a window.

Apple Menu Options. This control panel lets you turn on submenus in your Apple menu and choose whether to track recently opened applications, documents, and servers.

AppleTalk. This contains a few networking options you can tweak, such as how your Mac connects to an AppleTalk network (Ethernet, remote access, and so on) and your default AppleTalk zone.

ColorSync. This is the front-end control software for Apple's color-management software. It makes sure that the color you see onscreen is what comes out of a printer.

Control Strip. This lets you hide or reveal the Control Strip, as well as set the font for Control Strip modules.

Date & Time. You can use this control panel to set your Mac's clock and tell it what time zone you're in. There's also an option to let your Mac set its own clock by getting the time from an Internet time server.

DialAssist. This control panel's main job in life is to make using your modem easier. It remembers your area code, any prefixes you might have to dial for an outside line, and any suffixes (such as a calling-card number) you might want to use.

Energy Saver. This conserves energy by reducing the amount of electricity your Mac needs. This control panel can also make your Mac start up and shut off on a schedule.

Extensions Manager. This control panel enables and disables extensions, control panels, and startup items. We'll go into more depth regarding this control panel (see the "Extensions Manager" section, below).

File Exchange. This lets you control what types of documents are linked to what programs. For example, you can set the File Exchange control panel to open all MPEG movie files with QuickTime Player.

File Sharing. This controls what services your Mac offers over a network. You can use this control panel to share files and programs over a network; you can also assign user names and passwords to yourself and selected guests so that not just anyone can connect to your Mac.

File Synchronization. This control panel provides an easy way to make sure that two folders contain the same files—great for backing up important documents.

General Controls. The catch-all of control panels, General Controls governs whether the desktop is visible in the background, how many times a menu item blinks when you select a menu command, how fast the insertion point blinks, where the Open or Save dialog box opens by default, and whether the Mac checks and fixes the disk when you shut down your machine incorrectly.

Internet. This lets you set some common Internet preferences, such as your e-mail address, your default Web page, and your news server's particulars.

Keyboard. This control panel alters your Mac's keyboard layout to match different languages—plus you can set function keys to launch specified programs and documents.

Keychain Access. This sets the passwords stored in your keychain. Once you unlock the keychain, programs can retrieve any passwords stored there without your having to type them.

Launcher. This control panel doesn't actually control anything. Instead, it opens the Launcher, a window full of buttons you can customize to launch programs and documents quickly.

Location Manager. Useful for PowerBooks and iBooks, the Location Manager control panel lets you change your Mac's settings (mostly network and modem ones) to match your location.

Memory. This lets you tweak how your Mac uses its memory by setting the size of your disk cache, how much virtual memory your Mac uses, and whether your Mac uses some portion of memory as a RAM disk.

Modem. This control panel lets you set which modem your Mac uses, how it dials in, and whether its speaker is on or off.

Monitors. This controls your screen's resolution and color depth. If you have more than one monitor hooked up, you can arrange which parts of your Desktop they show here.

Mouse. You set the speed of pointer movement and double-clicks with this control panel. You can also set your pointer to leave temporary tracks so it's easier to see.

Multiple Users. Use this control panel to set up user accounts for people. These accounts keep each person's documents and preferences separate.

Numbers. This lets you set a format for numbers based on a region (such as the United Kingdom, Italy, or the United States). You can also create custom number formats in this control panel.

QuickTime Settings. This controls how QuickTime acts, including the speed of your Internet connection, whether QuickTime starts playing CDs when you insert them, and whether it checks for software updates.

Remote Access. Use this control panel to connect to the Internet (or AppleTalk remote access server) via your modem.

Software Update. This checks for new versions of your system software, plus it lets you set a schedule for checking and downloading those updates.

Sound. Here you set alert sounds as well as audio-input sources and speaker volume.

Speech. This controls how your Mac talks and listens. Here you can set your Mac's speaking voice, whether it reads your alerts aloud, and whether it's listening for your voice commands.

Startup Disk. This sets which System Folder your Mac should use when it starts up.

TCP/IP This control panel contains all of your Mac's TCP/IP network settings, mainly used to connect your Mac to the Internet.

Text. Here you select a script style (such as Roman) and a regional behavior (such as English or Brazilian) for your text. This controls how text is sorted and converted.

Web Sharing. This control panel turns your Mac into a basic Web server so others can look at Web pages on your hard drive via an Internet connection. You can use this control panel to tell your Mac where the Web pages are located on your hard drive and how much memory the Web server gets.

Extensions Manager

Since extensions can cause so many troubles—with crashes, memory use, and so on—Apple saw fit to provide an easy way to control which extensions load when your Mac starts up. Extensions Manager, which is itself a combination extension and control panel, lets you choose which extensions and control panels to load. (It also works on startup and shutdown items as well as on items that are loose in your System Folder—that is, items that aren't in any of the specialized folders.) The way it works is pretty basic—Extensions Manager moves the items you don't want to load out of the Extensions and Control Panels folders—but the slick interface makes it easy to weed out problem extensions.

Using Extensions Manager. To use Extensions Manager, from the Apple menu choose Control Panels and then Extensions Manager. This brings up the Extensions Manager window, which lists all of your Mac's control panels, extensions, shutdown items, startup items, and any other items in the System Folder. It does this in a list view, dividing the list into five columns—On/Off, Name, Size, Version, and Package. You can sort the list by clicking any of the column headings (by default, it's sorted by Name.) Here's some information about each column (**Figure 3.18**):

On/Off. This column of check boxes lets you set whether an extension is on or off—that is, whether it loads at startup. If you're viewing a line for a folder (such as the Control Panels folder), this check box probably has a minus sign in the box, which indicates that *some* of the items inside are enabled.

Name. This column shows you every item's name and lets you sort the list accordingly. These names are the same ones you'll see in the Finder.

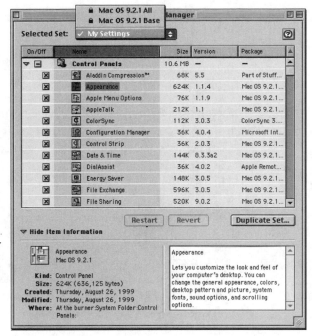

Figure 3.18

Extensions Manager lets you enable or disable extensions, create extension sets, and get information on a given extension.

Size. If you're curious about how much space an item or folder occupies on your hard drive, take a look here. You can also sort this list by size if you want to cleanse your hard drive of the biggest items.

Version. This shows the version number of every item—if it has one. This is tremendously useful for finding out whether you have the latest version of a given item.

Package. This shows the larger group to which an item belongs. For example, each of the AirPort extensions in Mac OS 9.2.1 shows up as part of the AirPort Install package. You can sort your list of items by package—just click the Package column head.

 If you select an item, a short description of it shows up in the Item Information box.

The Extensions Manager window lists five folders—Control Panels, Extensions, Shutdown Items, Startup Items, and the System Folder—that mark the five kinds of things you can enable or disable.

Control Panels. This entry lists all of the items in the Control Panels folder.

Extensions. This lists all of the items in the Extensions folder.

Shutdown Items. This lists all of the items in the Shutdown Items folder. These items open when you shut down your Mac.

Startup Items. This lists all of the items in the Startup Items folder; these items open when you start up your Mac.

System Folder. This folder shows active items that are loose in your System Folder—for example, a startup screen that sits in your System Folder but not inside any of the special folders.

Extension Sets. So you don't have to run through a list of hundreds of control panels and extensions each time you need to change your set, Extensions Manager uses *extension sets*—sets of enabled extensions that have a unique name and that you can choose as a group in the Selected Set pop-up menu. The Mac OS 9 Extensions Manager comes with three prebuilt extension sets: Mac OS 9 Base (the basic set for Mac OS 9), Mac OS 9 All (all of the Mac OS 9 extensions, but no more), and My Settings (a set you can tweak to your heart's content).

To change an extension set, choose it from the Selected Set pop-up menu and close Extensions Manager. When you restart your Mac, the selected set of extensions will load. To create a *new* extensions set, first select the set on which you want to base the new one and then click Duplicate Set in the lower-right corner. This creates a new set and asks you for a name. Your new set becomes part of the Selected Set pop-up menu, and you can make changes to that set without affecting any other sets. There'll be more on using Extensions Manager in Chapter 8.

Apple Menu Items

One other especially interesting feature of the System Folder is the contents of the Apple Menu Items folder. Items in this folder show up in the Apple menu, which you can access from almost any program. Although the contents of this folder are a hodgepodge, they're powerful and useful. Here's a quick look at what you'll find:

Apple System Profiler. This powerful utility program tells you *everything* there is to know about your Mac, such as what processor you have, how much memory you have, what USB devices are connected, and even specifics about the system software you're running.

Calculator. Not much of a tool by today's standards, Calculator has remained pretty untouched for more than 15 years. It adds, subtracts, multiplies, and divides—and that's about it.

Chooser. Chooser lets you choose a printer or an AppleTalk network connection. Network Browser has largely replaced the AppleTalk portion of Chooser.

Favorites. This folder stores favorite files, folders, and URLs; you can open them by choosing them from the Apple menu.

Key Caps. This small utility shows you all of the characters in a given font on a virtual keyboard. When you press a modifier key (such as Option or Shift), all of the characters change to show you what you'll get when you combine that key with another one—an invaluable tool for figuring out the key combination for a special character such as a bullet (•) or an accented *e* (é).

Network Browser. This utility lets you browse through your network, looking for servers to which you can connect your Mac. Network Browser shows both AppleTalk and some TCP/IP-based servers.

Recent Applications. By default, this tracks the last ten applications you've launched. You can adjust how many applications, documents, and servers it tracks (or whether it tracks them at all) in the Apple Menu Options control panel.

Recent Documents. This tracks the last ten documents you've opened.

Recent Servers. This tracks the last ten file servers to which you've connected.

Scrapbook. Scrapbook works like its real-world namesake by providing a place to keep bits and pieces you might want to use in other places. You can use Scrapbook to hold almost anything you can put on the Clipboard—sound clips, text, pictures, and even 3D objects.

Sherlock 2. You can use Mac OS 9's powerful Sherlock search utility to search your hard drive or the Internet.

Stickies. This electronic notepad provides small windows in which you can write chunks of text—memos, reminders, lists, and so on. The windows look remarkably like Post-it notes, as you may have guessed. [*Stickies and the 68K emulator are two of Apple's finest software accomplishments. —Ed.*]

Mac OS X System Folder

The Mac OS X system software is fundamentally different from earlier versions of the Mac OS, and that difference goes from its plumbing to its user interface. That's because it's actually a melding of three operating systems: OpenStep (a product of Steve Jobs's previous company, Next), BSD Unix (a powerful flavor of Unix), and Mac OS. This hybrid makes Mac OS X a powerful beast, but it also introduces a few quirks and some evil magic necessary to make the whole mélange work together properly.

Unlike Mac OS 9, Mac OS X doesn't put all the system components in a single blue folder. Instead, it has many invisible files and folders in various places on your hard drive—you'll probably never need to see or do anything with these—along with a few folders you can see and manipulate. Read on for a look at Mac OS X's files and folders.

Special System Folders

Like Mac OS 9, Mac OS X has its own set of special folders that contain items the operating system needs to work properly. In this case, though, you probably won't need to add items to or delete items from these folders—in fact, Mac OS X makes it exceedingly difficult to do so. One special folder is the Library folder, which lives in the System folder. It contains shared resources that your Mac can use. Although 40-some folders nest in the Library folder, you only need to know about a few of them:

CoreServices. This folder holds many of the widgets you use all the time in Mac OS X, including BootX (which lets you select whether to start up in Mac OS 9 or Mac OS X), the Dock program, the Mac OS X System and Finder files, Help Viewer, and the Software Update engine.

Fonts. This folder holds system fonts—not those you use in your regular documents.

PreferencePanes. This folder contains System Preferences files, such as Dock, Mouse, and QuickTime preferences.

Screen Savers. Modules for the Mac OS X screensaver live in this folder.

Sounds. System beeps reside in this folder—they're simple AIFF files.

Other Special Folders

Besides the special folders in the System folder, Mac OS X has a few *other* special folders you'll find at the top level of the hard drive as well as in each person's home folder. Here are the folders you'll see at the top level of your hard drive:

Applications. This folder holds your Mac OS X applications. You don't *have* to put them here; it's just a convenient holding place.

Applications (Mac OS 9). This folder holds your Mac OS 9 programs. Again, they don't have to be here; it's just a prefab place for them. This only applies if you're using the Classic environment (see the section "The Classic Layer," later in this chapter).

Documents. This folder is a holdover from Mac OS 9 and earlier. In Mac OS X, it's easier and more secure to use the Documents folder you'll find inside your home folder.

Library. This folder contains lots of folders that hold your Mac's fonts, browser plug-ins, desktop pictures, and receipts for items you've installed.

System. This contains the inner workings of the Mac OS X system. (This is not a file as in Mac OS 9.)

System Folder. The good old Mac OS 9 System Folder; it won't be present unless you install Mac OS 9.1 or 9.2.1 on your hard drive as well. This System Folder is used to provide Mac OS X with its Classic compatibility layer.

Users. This folder contains a special folder for each user account you've set up in Mac OS X. Each user's folder is protected so other users can't access it (**Figure 3.19**). These folders are known as *home folders*.

Figure 3.19

When you install Mac OS X, the installer creates some folders to store various programs and files, plus it sets up a special Users folder that holds each user's documents and preferences. These are also known as home folders.

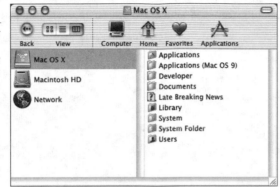

The home folder is a special folder created inside the Users folder, and it's given the short name (the Unix nickname that you entered when installing Mac OS X). This folder is also created when you create a user account. Each user's home folder contains a special set of folders (**Figure 3.20**). There are eight of these:

Desktop. Through the strange magic of Mac OS X, the Desktop folder contains the items that appear on a user's Desktop. If you add an item to the Desktop folder, it appears on your Desktop, and vice versa. Remove an item from your Desktop folder, and it disappears from your Desktop.

Documents. This is a handy folder for all of your documents.

Library. This folder contains your personal fonts, sounds, screensaver modules, mailboxes, browser plug-ins, preferences, and other such items.

Movies. Got a movie? Drop it in here.

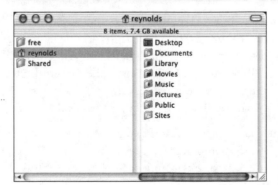

Figure 3.20

Each user's home directory contains a set of folders for organizing and storing that individual's files.

Music. This is the perfect folder for your MP3s.

Pictures. Still images go here. When you plug in a digital camera, it automatically downloads the images to this folder.

Public. Any user on your Mac can open the Public folder, unlike the other folders in your user folder (**Figure 3.21**).

Sites. If you turn on Mac OS X's built-in Web server, it can serve up the Web sites located in this folder, if someone connects to your Mac using a Web browser.

Figure 3.21

If you try to get into another user's home folder, you'll see a series of folders with red "do not enter" signs. You can't open those folders, but you can open the Public and Sites folders. That's how you can trade files with other users—put the files you want to exchange in the Public folder.

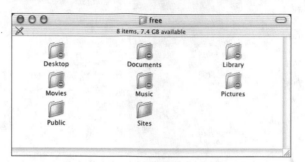

Invisible Folders

Mac OS X is rife with invisible folders that let the Unix part of the operating system work properly. You'll almost never encounter these, but they may occasionally come into play. For example, invisible folders titled etc, tmp, and var are familiar to Unix users.

System Preferences

Mac OS X doesn't have extensions and control panels in the same sense as Mac OS 9 does, which makes it much more stable. Mac OS X *does* have something similar to control panels called *system settings.* The System Preferences window lets you change how your Mac behaves. This window has three main parts— the Show All button, the shelf, and a content area that shows the controls in a specific group.

When clicked, the Show All button in the upper-left corner shows 23 icons in the content area (**Figure 3.22**). These icons are the various groups of controls, and they often correspond to control panels in Mac OS 9 and earlier, such as Energy Saver, Keyboard, and QuickTime. The System Preferences window is divided into four groups: Personal, Hardware, Internet & Network, and System. Here's what each of the preference panes does:

Classic. The Classic pane features two tabbed areas that let you choose which Mac OS 9 System Folder to use with Classic. You can also start, restart, or shut down the Classic environment here (more on this in the "Classic Layer" section).

ColorSync. This pane lets you set how ColorSync color management works—great for publishing pros.

Date & Time. In this pane you set the current date, time, and time zone, plus you can control whether your Mac sets its own clock using a network time server and how the clock in the menu bar behaves.

Desktop. This pane lets you set your Desktop pattern using the images that come with the system or those you have in another folder.

Displays. Choose your monitor's resolution, geometry, and color depth. If you have more than one monitor, you can arrange them all here.

Dock. Set the Dock's size, magnification, and position as well as whether the Dock automatically hides.

Energy Saver. This pane controls when your Mac components (the system, monitor, and hard drive) go to sleep.

General. Here you can set whether to use Blue or Graphite as the color for windows and widgets as well as the highlight color. You can also choose whether clicking in the scroll bar makes the window scroll or jump to the clicked location.

International. This pane lets you set your preferred languages and how Roman and Japanese script behave. You can also set your date, time, and currency formats as well as what keyboard layouts appear in the Keyboard menu.

Internet. This contains settings for your iTools account, e-mail account, Web-browser preferences, and news preferences.

Figure 3.22

To change your Mac OS X system settings, click one of the icons in the System Preferences window. This brings up the settings for that particular area of the system.

Keyboard. This pane lets you set how long it takes a key to repeat when you hold one down as well as at what rate a repeating key puts characters on the screen.

Login. Here you choose what items launch when you log in—the equivalent of Startup Items in Mac OS 9 and earlier—as well as whether you get logged in automatically when you start up. You can also tweak some of the login panel's preferences here.

Mouse. Set mouse and trackpad speed and double-clicking characteristics. You can also set whether your trackpad allows you to click and drag without pressing the trackpad button.

Network. This big panel has four sections where you set your TCP/IP settings as well as PPP, proxy, and modem settings. You can also create multiple locations and configurations for Ethernet, modem, and AirPort connections. You can even create several configurations to use on a single port.

QuickTime. Home to five settings, including your connection speed, QuickTime browser plug-in settings, whether QuickTime updates automatically via the Internet, which music synthesizer to use, and any media keys you may have. (Media keys are keys that let you use restricted media, such as watching a pay-per-view video.)

Screen Saver. Simple at heart, the built-in screensaver exposes its controls here, including which modules it's using and how long it takes to pop up.

Sharing. This pane lets you turn on file sharing and Mac OS X's built-in Web server as well as remote access and FTP services.

Software Update. This contains a schedule of when Software Update checks with Apple's server for updates. You can also peek at Software Update's log to see what it's been up to.

Sound. This pane contains a nice set of volume controls that let you set system volume and balance as well as alert volume. You can also choose your system beep here.

Speech. This controls your Mac's speech-recognition capabilities and the voice your Mac uses when it talks to you.

Startup Disk. This lets you choose which system software on which disk to use when you start up your Mac.

Universal Access. This pane lets you tune how you use the keyboard and mouse if you have difficulty using the standard mouse and keyboard settings.

Users. In this pane, you create new user accounts and set options for each account (for example, the user name and password).

The Classic Layer

Apple realized that most people would want to run their old (Mac OS 9 and earlier) software—especially early on in Mac OS X's life—because not too many companies had written or rewritten their programs to run specifically on the new operating system. The company's solution: the Classic compatibility layer. This clever engineering feat lets you run your older programs unmodified in Mac OS X—as long as those programs don't use hardware directly (as hard-drive utilities and certain games do). The reason for this restriction is that giving programs access to hardware without going through Mac OS X would make the operating system prone to crashes.

Despite this restriction, Classic works surprisingly well, running almost every program written in the last ten years—and in some cases even older programs.

How Classic works. The way Apple implements this amazing compatibility is by running Mac OS 9 in a *virtual machine.* This means Mac OS X creates a kind of software Macintosh inside its own memory and then runs Mac OS 9 on that virtual machine. The result—when you launch a program written for Mac OS 9 or earlier and not rewritten for Mac OS X, Mac OS X actually starts up a copy of Mac OS 9 and then runs that program inside the virtual operating system. Mac OS 9 and earlier program icons show up in the Dock alongside those for Mac OS X programs. Classic application windows appear right next to Mac OS X windows, and you can switch between Classic and Mac OS X programs just by clicking their windows or their icons in the Dock.

When a Classic application first launches, a window pops up with a progress bar that represents Mac OS 9 starting up inside Mac OS X (**Figure 3.23**). Click the little disclosure triangle in this window to see the Mac OS 9 startup screen and extensions as they load. This process takes about as long as starting up Mac OS 9 on a real-world Mac—anywhere from 30 seconds to a few minutes. Once this process is done, the Classic program launches as it would in Mac OS 9 (**Figure 3.24**). The Classic environment only needs to start up once—when it's open, all Classic programs run in this virtual environment, and they launch in about the same amount of time they would take in a real-world Mac OS 9 environment (Classic programs also *run* almost as fast in Mac OS X as they do in Mac OS 9, by the way).

Figure 3.23

The first time you run Classic in Mac OS X, it will ask if you want to add certain resources to your Mac OS 9 System Folder. Go ahead and do so—Classic won't run properly without them.

Some Classic-specific resources need to be added to or updated in your System Folder on Macintosh HD. These changes should not affect your ability to use your System Folder with native Mac OS 9.

Do you want to add to or update them?

Quit   OK

Figure 3.24

Look familiar? It's
the Classic version
of Mac OS 9 starting
up in a window. You
can follow along as
your Mac-within-a-
Mac starts up.

Although Classic programs can run in Mac OS X, they don't benefit from any of Mac OS X's nifty advantages, such as the Aqua user interface or crash protection. Instead, Classic programs use the old set of windows and scroll bars as well as the old-style menu bar with the Application menu and clock. One misbehaving Classic program can take down every single running Classic program. Fortunately, this is limited to the Classic layer—at worst, you'll have to use the Classic pane in the System Preferences application to restart your Classic environment. (No more trips to the coffee shop while you're starting up a crashed Mac!)

Classic applications also have the old-style Apple menu, complete with its set of control panels and the like (**Figure 3.25**). You can use these control panels to tweak some of what happens in Classic programs, but don't count on them to change everything. For example, the Appearance control panel can change how scroll bars appear in Classic programs, but it won't let you change your Desktop picture.

It's pretty easy to tell whether you're working with a Classic program or a Mac OS X–native program. If you see Mac OS 9–style windows, menus, and scroll bars, the program is a Classic application. If you're looking at candylike Aqua buttons and widgets, you're using a Mac OS X–native program.

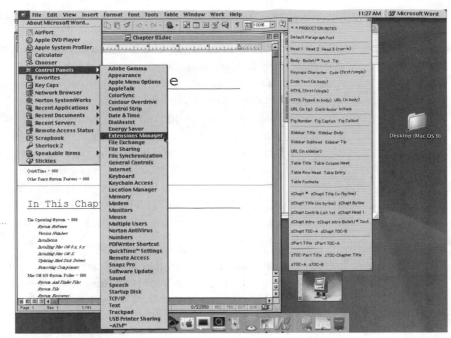

Figure 3.25

When running a program in Classic, you can see and use the other bits of Mac OS 9 that aren't part of that application, such as the Apple menu.

Configuring Classic. Mac OS X contains a few tools for working with Classic in the Classic pane of the System Preferences program. To configure Classic, launch System Preferences and click the Classic pane. This presents two tabs—Start/Stop and Advanced (**Figure 3.26**).

Figure 3.26

The Classic System Preference pane lets you choose a System Folder for Classic, as well as stop and start the Classic environment (left). It also lets you troubleshoot and tweak how Classic starts up (right).

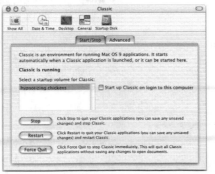 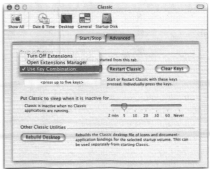

Start/Stop contains some simple controls that let you choose which Mac OS 9 System Folder runs Classic applications—this System Folder doesn't have to live on the same disk as your Mac OS X system software. This tab also contains a check box that lets you set whether the Classic environment launches when you start up your Mac. The bottom of this window contains three buttons that let you start and stop Classic, restart Classic (which quits all Classic programs and relaunches the Classic environment), or force-quit your Classic environment—something you may have to do if it locks up.

The Advanced pane holds a few tools that let you troubleshoot Classic and control how it works with the operating system. At the top of the pane is a menu that lets you restart Classic with extensions off, with the Extensions Manager open during startup (if you're having trouble with an extension), or with a certain key combination held down (such as a key that disables a specific extension). In the center of the pane is a slider that can put Classic to sleep if it's inactive for a specified period of time. This improves performance in Mac OS X programs, but it can take some time for Classic programs to wake up if the Classic environment goes to sleep. If you plan on using a lot of older programs that can't run natively in Mac OS X, move this slider all the way over to Never. Finally, at the bottom of the panel is a Rebuild Desktop button that rebuilds the Classic Desktop to correct the wrong icons being displayed or problems with the wrong program launching when you double-click a document. You can rebuild the Desktop without starting the Classic environment.

A word about Carbon. In its thoughtfulness, Apple provided a way for developers to get their programs ready to run natively on Mac OS X without rewriting them from the ground up. This technology is *Carbon,* and a Mac OS 9 and earlier program tweaked to run natively in Mac OS X is *Carbonized.* The beauty of Carbonized programs is that they can also run unmodified in Mac OS 9 or later using the Carbon Library (or CarbonLib). For example, AppleWorks 6 is one of the first Carbonized programs, and it can run unmodified in both Mac OS 9 and Mac OS X.

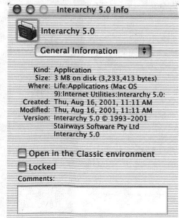

Figure 3.27

By selecting a check box in the Show Info window, you can tell a program to launch in the Classic layer instead of as a Mac OS X–native program. Do this when you're having trouble running the program natively.

Launching a program in Classic or in Carbon. Carbonized programs can run natively in Mac OS X, or they can launch in the Classic compatibility layer—which you might prefer if the program doesn't work quite right in Mac OS X (**Figue 3.27**). To change this option, with the Finder active select the program's icon and choose Show Info from the File menu (⌘ I). In the window that pops up, you can select whether the program launches in the Classic environment or whether it launches as a native Mac OS X program.

Switching Between Mac OS 9 and Mac OS X

If you've installed Mac OS X, odds are you'll also be installing Mac OS 9— if you haven't already done so. After all, the Mac OS X box contains a Mac OS 9 CD for just this purpose. If so, you can start up your Mac using *either* Mac OS 9 or Mac OS X. So why would you want to use Mac OS 9 if you're already using Mac OS X? Compatibility, mainly. Although Apple engineers have done a phenomenal job making most Mac OS 9 programs work well with Mac OS X, a few just won't function. In this case you can restart, using Mac OS 9 to run the finicky program, and then going back into Mac OS X when you're done. As developers update their programs to work natively in Mac OS X, this problem will gradually go away. You have a few ways to go about switching back and forth.

Starting up into Mac OS 9 from Mac OS X. Open the System Preferences program and click the Startup Disk icon in the top row. (If it's not there, click the Show All icon and then click the Startup Disk icon.) The System Preferences window will show all of the volumes currently mounted on your Mac, as well as the valid System folders on each of those volumes—both Mac OS 9 and Mac OS X flavors (**Figure 3.28**). Select the Mac OS 9 System Folder you want— there can be both a Mac OS 9 and a Mac OS X System folder on a single volume—and restart your Mac. You'll start up in Mac OS 9.

Figure 3.28

The Mac OS X version of the Startup Disk control panel looks a lot like the Mac OS 9 version. In it, you can choose the system software you want to use when starting up your Mac.

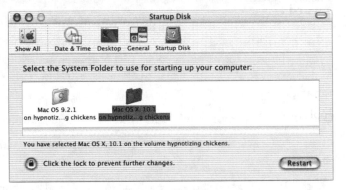

Starting up into Mac OS X from Mac OS 9. If you're running Mac OS 9 and you want to restart in Mac OS X, you can do this via the Startup Disk control panel. Open it by going to the Apple menu and choosing Control Panels and then Startup Disk; when the Startup Disk window opens, select your Mac OS X System folder. Close the Startup Disk window (which writes your selection into a special part of the Mac's memory), and restart your Mac. It'll now start up using Mac OS X.

Yes, we know folders aren't disks, but the reason this control panel is named Startup Disk is that until recently you could only have one System Folder per volume. Now, though, you can have a Mac OS 9 System Folder *and* a Mac OS X System folder on the same disk, so you can choose either one to start up your Mac.

You should always select a startup disk in the Startup Disk control panel or System Preferences panel. This will speed the startup process. If you *don't* have a startup volume selected, your Mac will spend some time looking for one— even if there's only one to begin with.

Using Option. Newer Macintoshes let you select a startup volume before you've started up your Mac by pressing the power button and then holding down Option. Your Mac will scan the available hard drives for valid system software and then present you with a series of icons representing the startup volumes. You will also see two arrows onscreen—a circular arrow that scans for valid startup drives and a right-pointing arrow that tells your Mac to continue starting up. Click the volume icon you want to use, and then click the right-facing arrow. Your Mac will now start up using the volume you selected.

Included Mac OS X Applications

Mac OS X ships with a handful of small and tremendously useful programs that you can use to send and receive e-mail, open pictures, connect to the Internet, browse the Web, maintain a list of addresses—all kinds of things. These programs live in your Applications folder. Here's a look at some of the more common ones:

Address Book. This program stores names, addresses, phone numbers, and e-mail addresses for various people. It coordinates with your e-mail program so that when you're writing an e-mail message, Address Book entries appear automatically.

Calculator. This simple utility lets you add, subtract, multiply, and divide.

Chess. Your Mac can play chess with you using this program, and it's a pretty good opponent!

Clock. This program shows a small analog or digital clock in the Dock. It can also display a clock in a window, if you like.

Image Capture. This utility downloads pictures from a digital camera to your hard drive.

iMovie. Your favorite home-movie-maker.

Internet Connect. This lets you set how your modem or AirPort card connects, including a phone number, user name, and password.

Internet Explorer. Microsoft's popular Web browser is included in a Mac OS X–native version.

iTunes. Apple's music player runs on Mac OS X.

Mail. Apple's nifty and flexible e-mail client lets you send and receive e-mail from several accounts.

Preview. This opens and displays still images, such as JPEG, TIFF, and PDF files.

QuickTime Player. This program plays QuickTime-supported video and sound files—which includes most of them.

Sherlock. The Mac OS X–native version of the powerful search utility helps you find files and information on the World Wide Web as well as on your Mac's hard drive.

Stickies. Digital sticky notes make your computing experience complete.

System Preferences. This lets you set how Mac OS X behaves.

TextEdit. A basic text editor, TextEdit lets you write documents using all of your system's fonts. It also includes basic formatting controls (such as bold and centered text), and you can even check your spelling.

Utilities

Mac OS X ships with a folder full of utilities that let you manage and configure your Mac OS X installation. Here's a quick look at some of them:

Apple System Profiler. When launched, it tells you tons about your Mac, including what processor is inside and how much memory is installed.

Applet Launcher. This item launches and runs Java applets.

CPU Monitor. This utility shows you how much of a load your Mac's CPU is carrying and what programs are taking up most of your processor cycles. It's pretty to watch, too!

Disk Copy. This utility lets you create and open disk images.

Disk Utility. Combining Drive Setup and Disk First Aid, Disk Utility lets you verify and repair disks as well as format them.

Grab. This utility can take screen shots in Mac OS X. You can still use the good old ⌘ Shift 3 key combination too.

Installer. This installs Mac OS X application packages.

Key Caps. Similar to the Key Caps program in Mac OS 9, this utility shows you all of the characters in a given font as well as which keys you press to produce them.

Keychain Access. Use this utility to edit keychains, specialized files that store passwords.

Print Center. This connects your Mac to a printer.

ProcessViewer. This utility lists in a window all running programs. Mac OS X relies on a lot of background programs to do its work, so you may be surprised at how many programs appear when you launch this.

StuffIt Expander. This is a Mac OS X–native version of the popular file-decompression utility by Aladdin Systems Inc.

Terminal. This application opens up a Unix command-line terminal, which lets you use Unix commands directly in Mac OS X.

AppleScript

First released in 1993, AppleScript is a quirky but powerful automation utility that lets you give your Mac a list of tasks to do. AppleScript is powerful enough to be considered a programming language, but it's simple enough so that mere mortals who don't relish the thought of learning to program can still use it. AppleScript is a standard part of every recent Mac OS version in the last five years.

Besides providing a list of tasks for the Finder to do, AppleScript can tell many other applications what to do, and it can even make two programs that understand AppleScript work together. That's powerful stuff! Of course, there's one caveat—to use programs with AppleScript, they must understand it. Otherwise you can't use AppleScript at all. There are three levels of AppleScript comprehension when it comes to applications: scriptable, recordable, and attachable.

Scriptable applications. This is the most basic level of AppleScript compatibility. A scriptable application might only understand the most basic of commands (such as open and close); on the other hand, it might comprehend hundreds of commands, covering every single one of its features. The only way to tell for sure is to take a look at its AppleScript dictionary (see the "Using a Dictionary" section, below). The majority of programs that work with AppleScript are scriptable.

Recordable applications. In the case of recordable applications, you can record a series of actions into an AppleScript just by using a recordable application, taking an I'll-show-you-what-to-do approach. Because it's harder to make a program recordable than it is to make it scriptable, there are fewer of these types of applications. By default, a recordable application is also scriptable.

Attachable applications. This is the rarest category of AppleScript-capable programs. Attachable applications are those that let you add AppleScripts to their menus, making the scripts part of the program. Very few programs are attachable; Microsoft Outlook is one.

 Mac OS X 10.1 and its edition of AppleScript (version 1.7) supports XML-RPC and SOAP protocols, which allows you to script applications across the Web.

Figure 3.29

The small Script Runner application (top) lets you run scripts by choosing them from its menu; through Script Menu (bottom), you can get to scripts from the menu bar.

AppleScript in Mac OS 9 and Mac OS X. AppleScript works about the same way in Mac OS 9 as it does in Mac OS X. Each has a set of AppleScript commands that it understands, and each creates scripts in a program called Script Editor. Mac OS X 10.1 contains two additional items that make your scripting life easier—Script Runner and Script Menu. The small Script Runner program provides a floating window that lets you launch AppleScripts by clicking the window and then selecting a script from the list that pops up. Script Menu gives you access to AppleScripts (as well as Perl and Shell scripts) from the menu bar (**Figure 3.29**). (To use Script Menu, go the www.apple.com/applescript/macosx/script_menu/ and download Script Menu. Drag the Scriptmenu.menu file up to the right side of your menu bar.)

Creating an AppleScript

You have two ways to go about creating an AppleScript—writing it or recording it. Both of these methods involve using Script Editor (which you'll find in the Apple Extras folder in Mac OS 9 and earlier, and in the Applications folder in Mac OS X). To create an AppleScript, start by launching Script Editor. Script Editor is a simple affair, with only a few controls: a place to describe the script, four control buttons (Record, Stop, Run, and Check Syntax), and a text area in which you can write AppleScripts (**Figure 3.30**).

Figure 3.30

Those with a flair for programming can make their Macs jump through hoops with a few lines of code. Those without such aptitude can still do the trick by recording their Mac's actions.

Writing an AppleScript. Most of the time, you'll create an AppleScript by writing it in the Script Editor window. A simple AppleScript might look like this:

```
tell application "Finder"
    activate
    select folder "Applications (Mac OS 9)" of startup disk
    open selection
end tell
```

This script tells the Finder to select and open the folder titled Applications (Mac OS 9) on whatever disk starts up the Mac that the script is running on.

As you write your script, you can click Check Syntax to ensure that what you're writing makes sense as an AppleScript. You can also test out the script by clicking Run or stop a running script by clicking Stop.

Besides giving applications a laundry list of instructions to carry out, scripts can also put up dialog boxes that gather information from you, making AppleScript a useful way to write small programs called *applets*.

 You can find all kinds of AppleScript information, including beginner's tutorials, at www.apple.com/applescript/.

Recording an AppleScript. The second—and easier—way to create an AppleScript is to record it rather than write it. Of course, this requires that you use a recordable application, so don't hold your breath—there aren't many of these. One great exception to this is the Finder in Mac OS 9.2.1, which *is* recordable—and since this is the most-used program on the Mac, that's a great benefit. (In Mac OS X 10.1 it's not scriptable.)

To record a script, click Record in the open Script Editor window and then run through the actions you want to record. As you do this, a list of AppleScript commands appears in the Script Editor window. When you're done recording, click Stop in the Script Editor window. You've just created an AppleScript without writing a line of scripting code.

 Recording an AppleScript and looking it over is a great way to learn how one works.

Saving an AppleScript

Once you have a script recorded, you'll probably want to save it, which brings you face to face with a few choices. You can save an AppleScript in one of three formats: text, compiled script, or application, and these scripts can work across Mac OS X and Classic. You can also save scripts as stationery or as regular documents (**Figure 3.31**).

Text. Saving an AppleScript as text simply saves the text in the Script Editor's window. You won't be able to run the script without first opening it in the Script Editor.

Figure 3.31

You can save three flavors of AppleScripts —text only, compiled scripts, and applications.

Compiled script. You still have to run a compiled script using the Script Editor, but the Script Editor has already checked it out to make sure that everything works and that its instructions have been converted into a form your Mac can understand.

Application. When you save a script as an application, it will run in Mac OS 9 and Mac OS X.

You can also save an AppleScript as a run-only script so others can't open your script to make changes to it. To do this, choose Save As Run Only from the File menu. This brings up a Save dialog box (you won't be able to save the script as text or as stationery) (**Figure 3.32**).

Figure 3.32

When you save an AppleScript, you can choose what flavor you want to use from the Format pop-up menu in the Save window.

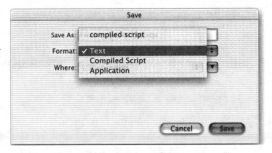

Running an AppleScript

As with creating an AppleScript, you have two ways to run a script. Which method you choose depends on how you've saved the script. If it's text or a compiled script (or if you've never saved it at all), you'll have to run it by opening it in the Script Editor and clicking Run (or choose the Control menu and then Run, which is the same as ⌘ℝ). If you've saved the script as an applet (either Classic or Mac OS X), just double-click it to run it.

Using a Dictionary

Although engineers have tried to make AppleScript easy to use, you'll probably need to look at a program's AppleScript dictionary to find out what commands it can understand. You have a couple of ways to do so. You can drop the program's icon on the Script Editor icon, which opens the command dictionary. Alternatively, you can open the Script Editor and choose Open Dictionary from the File menu. In the resulting Open dialog box, navigate to the application in question. When you open the application, it will present its AppleScript dictionary to you (**Figure 3.33**).

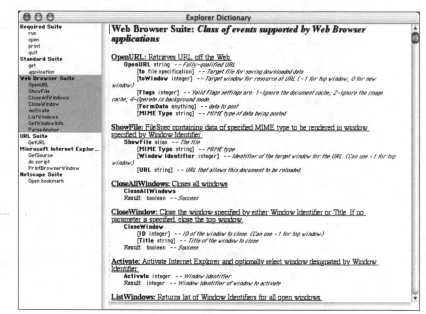

Figure 3.33

To see what commands a program understands, open its dictionary and click one of the terms in the left column.

Sherlock

With the introduction of Sherlock in Mac OS 8.5, Apple applied its engineering abilities to make it easy to find items using your Mac—whether that meant searching for a specific file, a word or phrase *inside* a file, or even information on the Internet. Sherlock is the answer to all of that—you can use it to look for just about anything.

Opening Sherlock

To launch Sherlock, with the Finder active choose Find from the File menu (⌘F). (In Mac OS 9 and earlier, you can also choose Sherlock 2 from the

Apple menu; in Mac OS X, click the Sherlock icon in the Dock.) The Sherlock window is divided into four major parts: Channels, search controls, a volume or plug-in list, and a summary information area (**Figure 3.34**).

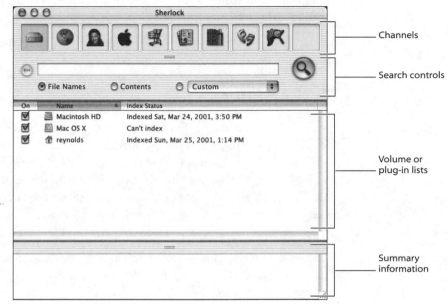

Figure 3.34

Sherlock is a killer utility for finding files on your hard drive and information on the Internet. It's divided into several areas.

Channels. Sherlock has nine channel icons across the top—Files, Internet, People, Apple, Shopping, News, Reference, Entertainment, and My Channel. These channels let you search for items in the areas they cover, and you can customize My Channel by enabling only the plug-ins you want to use (such as to create a Mac-only channel). The first channel is a file search; the next eight search the Internet for information. Clicking a channel makes Sherlock's interface change to fit the kind of search you're doing.

Search controls. The area directly below the list of channels contains Sherlock's search controls. You can enter search terms here, plus you can set whether searches look *for* files or *inside* them. Finally, you can create a custom file search for all kinds of file-related parameters, such as modification dates and visibility.

List. The list area shows one of two things. If you're using the Files channel, it shows all of the available volumes to search for a given file, and you can check or uncheck volumes to speed up and narrow your search. This list view gives you a little information about each volume, showing whether Sherlock has indexed the volumes. If you're using any of the other Sherlock Internet channels (such as Internet, People, Shopping, News, Apple, Reference, or Entertainment), the list area shows a list of Sherlock plug-ins you can enable or disable. Each plug-in represents an Internet-based search engine that can look for information of the desired type. The list area also changes to contain the items Sherlock finds.

Summary. The bottom part of the Sherlock window also shows one of two things, depending on the type of search you're doing. If you're looking for a file, this area shows you where it is located. If you're looking for an item on the Internet, this pane shows a summary of the items Sherlock finds.

When you're doing an Internet search, a fifth space at the bottom holds a banner ad. The only thing you'll get when you click this is a quick trip to the advertiser's Web site.

Finding Files

One of the most common things you'll be doing with Sherlock is looking for files. Given the size of hard drives today, it's easy for a file to hide deep inside your hard drive in places you'd never think to look. To search for a file, open Sherlock and click the Files channel—it's the one on the far left with the hard-disk icon. You can do three types of searches for files: a filename search, a content search, or a custom search. Each search type has a radio button next to it; click the button next to the type you want to perform. Here's a bit about each type:

Filename search. This type of search looks through your hard drive for a file with a given name. Type part of the file's name into the text box at the top and click the Search button, and Sherlock looks through your hard drive, gathering a list of any files that match what you've typed. This search is case insensitive, so searching for My Manifesto and my mANIFeSTo will produce the same results.

Content search. Sherlock can also search through all of the text-based files (such as text files and HTML files) on your hard drive for a specific word or phrase contained in the file. Before doing a content search, you'll have to index all of the files on your hard drive so Sherlock knows what's inside them (see the "Indexing Your Hard Drive" section, below). To perform a content search, type the word or phrase you're looking for, click the Contents radio button, and then click the Search button. Sherlock will look through all of the files it has indexed, returning a list of those that contain the word or phrase. It will even rank your search, depending on how many occurrences of the word or phrase it finds in each file.

Custom search. Finally, if you want to do a more advanced search, click the Custom radio button. This triggers a custom search, where you can choose one of four prefabricated types of custom searches in the pop-up menu next to the radio button: applications (this limits your search to applications with a given name), items larger than 1 MB, items modified today, or items modified yesterday. You can also remove a custom search from this list, if there's an option you never use.

Finally, if you know a *lot* about the kind of file you'd like to find, you can do a totally customized search by clicking Edit (or choosing Edit from the pop-up menu in Mac OS X). Choosing Find and then More Options, or typing ⌘M, will do the same thing in both Mac OS 9 and Mac OS X. This opens up a window with a plethora of search criteria you can use when looking for a file—a file's size, kind, version number, whether it has a custom icon, or even whether it is visible (**Figure 3.35**). Once you're done setting search criteria, click OK and then click the Search button. These search criteria are arranged a bit differently in Mac OS 9 and earlier and in Mac OS X.

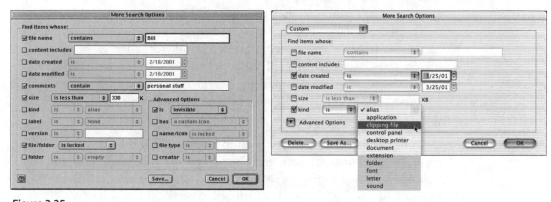

Figure 3.35

Sherlock in both Mac OS 9 (left) and Mac OS X (right) lets you customize your file searches using a variety of controls.

 If you perform a particular custom search on a regular basis, you can click Save in the advanced search screen to save your search to the Custom pop-up menu.

When a file search is finished, Sherlock presents a list of results, showing file-names, dates modified, and sizes, among other bits of information. This list works a lot like a Finder window in list view. You can open files from this window by double-clicking their icons; you can move them by simply dragging them to a new location.

 You can save a search by choosing Save Search Criteria from the File menu. To do the same search later, just open the saved search.

Indexing Your Hard Drive

Before you can search the contents of the items on your hard drive, you first have to index the files on it, which can take a very long time, depending on the drive's size. In the indexing process, the Mac OS looks inside every text-based document and builds an index of the words it finds. Later, when you search by contents, your Mac refers to that index, which is *much* faster than searching through the files one at a time.

To index your hard drive, open Sherlock and choose Index Volumes from the Find menu (⌘L) in Mac OS 9, Index Now from the File menu in Mac OS X. This starts the indexing process right away. In Mac OS 9, the Index Volumes window pops up. Select the volume you want to index and then click the Create Index button, and Sherlock goes to work. Remember—this process can take many hours for large hard drives, and it'll slow your Mac to a crawl, so do this when you don't need your Mac.

You can set an indexing schedule for Sherlock (**Figure 3.36**). With the Index Volumes window open in Mac OS 9, check the Use Schedule check box next to the volume's name and then click Schedule at the bottom. In the window that pops up, you can set a time and day or days for Sherlock to index the hard drive. In Mac OS X, you can't set a schedule for indexing, but there's usually no need—when you tell Sherlock to index a hard drive by choosing Index Now in Sherlock's Find menu, Sherlock goes to work, but it doesn't take over your whole Mac—it does its work very nicely in the background.

In Mac OS 9.2.1 and earlier, you can index a portion of your hard drive by selecting the files or folders you want to index and control-clicking those items. In the contextual menu that appears, choose Index Selection, and your Mac will go to work creating an index of the selected items. In Mac OS X, Sherlock indexes each user's home directory on the fly.

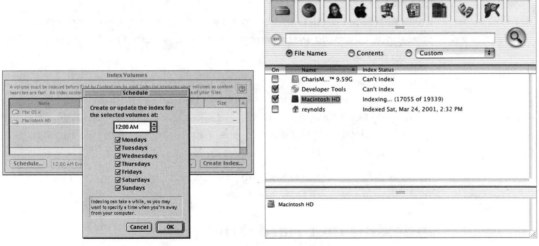

Figure 3.36

In Mac OS 9, you can tell Sherlock when to index your hard drive—this comes in handy because your Mac is almost unusable while it's indexing (left). In Mac OS X (right), there's no need for an indexing schedule, because Sherlock indexes in the background, letting you do other things.

Searching the Internet

Sherlock shines when it comes to searching the Internet for all kinds of information depending on the channels you have selected. Sherlock has eight Internet-related search channels (these are the same as the ones we mentioned earlier; **Figure 3.37**):

Figure 3.37

When you perform an Internet search using Sherlock, some of the search sites will return relevance information—indicating how relevant the results are to your search—when giving you the results.

Internet. Use this channel when you're searching the Internet for general information, such as why the sky is blue or where swallows go in the winter. This channel utilizes several popular Internet search engines at once.

People. If you're looking for someone's e-mail address or phone number, use this channel. It's a great way to find long-lost friends.

Shopping. When you're in a buying mood, use the Shopping channel to search for the best prices and availability on various e-commerce Web sites, such as Amazon.com and Barnes & Noble.com (www.bn.com).

News. If you're looking for that story about emus you just *know* you read last week, try a search in the News channel. It searches sites such as CNET.com, E! Online (www.eonline.com), and CNN.com.

Apple. The Apple channel searches four sections of Apple's Web site for all kinds of good Macintosh information.

Reference. Looking for quick answers to factual questions? The Reference channel can probably deliver via Britannica.com, Roget's Thesaurus (www.thesaurus.com), or the Internet Movie Database (www.imdb.com).

My Channel. Blank by default, My Channel lets you create your own collection of Sherlock plug-ins. Add the plug-ins you want by putting them in the My Channel folder. In Mac OS 9, this folder lives in the Internet Search Sites folder of the System Folder; in Mac OS X, look in the Users menu under your user name, then Library, then Internet Search Sites.

Entertainment. The Entertainment channel lets you search for entertainment-related information on the Internet through sites such as E! Online and RollingStone.com. You'll have to add your own entertainment-related items to the Entertainment folder, which lives in the System Folder under Internet Search Sites.

These channels use Sherlock plug-ins (see the "Finding and Installing Sherlock Plug-Ins" section, below). To search a channel's subject area, click the channel icon, revealing a series of plug-ins (you can select just the plug-ins you want to use here). Then type the search term, and click the Search button. After connecting to the Internet, Sherlock returns a list of items you may want to look at, whether it's a series of Web pages or a list of CDs at Amazon.com. Select an item in the list, and you'll see a summary in the summary information view at the bottom of the window.

Finding and Installing Sherlock Plug-Ins

Sherlock searches the Internet by virtue of its plug-ins—little bits of software that tell Sherlock how to use an Internet search site. Apple maintains a list of Sherlock plug-ins at www.apple.com/Sherlock/plugins. To add a plug-in to Sherlock, download the desired plug-in and then drag and drop it on the list area of Sherlock's main window. You can also drag and drop it on the appropriate channel.

Sherlock can also automatically add plug-ins, if you have an Internet connection.

QuickTime

QuickTime is one of the biggest Apple success stories. Since its introduction in the early 1990s as a way to watch video on your Macintosh, QuickTime has grown to encompass just about every kind of media available—whether that means audio, video, or still images. QuickTime is unsurpassed in the number of file formats it can handle, and it makes those capabilities available to all kinds of programs, which rely on QuickTime for the heavy lifting. QuickTime is available for both Macintoshes and Windows-based PCs, and it can play streaming video and audio as well as files on your hard drive.

 For all things QuickTime-related, visit Apple's QuickTime Web site at www.apple.com/quicktime/.

QuickTime Software

Mac OS 9 and earlier enables QuickTime through a group of extensions. The standard installation of QuickTime 5.0.2 (the current version as we wrote this chapter) installs more than 20 extensions and one control panel that help your Mac understand just about any media format available, plus the extensions let QuickTime work with FireWire-based digital video and even Java. As we explained earlier (in the section "Control Panels"), the QuickTime control panel sets how all of these extensions work together. QuickTime also installs two multipurpose programs for working with both dynamic media and still images: QuickTime Player and PictureViewer.

QuickTime Player. The QuickTime Player program handles all *dynamic media*—files that change over time, such as sound files, movies, and Flash animations. It consists of a window with a content area for viewing the file; a timeline showing where you are in the currently playing file; a volume slider; five playback controls (start of file, rewind, play and pause, fast forward, and end of file); and a TV button that shows a series of channels to which you can connect via the Internet, including Disney, NPR, MTV, HBO, and TechTV (**Figure 3.38**). These channels are *streaming media*—and with the arrival of cable modems and DSL, you can finally look forward to listening to and viewing streaming-media channels, such as Internet radio or a movie trailer, on your home computer.

Figure 3.38

QuickTime Player lets you play movies and sound in just about any format out there. Player can also tune in to streaming broadcasts.

You can also add your favorite QuickTime items (either Internet sites or files on your hard drive) in the Player window. By the way, if you launch the latest version of QuickTime Player by double-clicking the icon, it attempts to connect to the Internet and load the Hot Picks movie, which gives you a preview of all kinds of QuickTime content.

For more on what you can do with QuickTime, see Chapter 16, "Multimedia.'

 If you want to create your own custom interface for the QuickTime Player (what Apple calls a Media Skin), visit www.apple.com/quicktime/products/ tutorials/mediaskins/.

Figure 3.39

QuickTime's PictureViewer lets you open and view image files of almost any format.

PictureViewer. PictureViewer is QuickTime Player's less accomplished sibling (**Figure 3.39**). Its sole purpose in life is to display still images, and it can handle just about any image file format out there: JPEG, TIFF, GIF, BMP, PICT, and on and on. Besides helping you view image files, PictureViewer lets you rotate the image and zoom in and out.

Standard Versus Pro Versions

QuickTime comes in two versions—standard and pro. The standard version lets you play back QuickTime-based content, and you can download it for free from Apple's Web site. The pro version, on the other hand, lets you unlock QuickTime's editing capabilities. With it, you can save, edit, and translate movie and sound files, even adding special effects. That power costs something, however—the professional version goes for $29.95. To upgrade, visit www.apple.com/quicktime/. In Mac OS 9, open the QuickTime Settings control panel, and choose Registration from the pop-up menu at the top. In Mac OS X, open the QuickTime System Preferences pane and click the Registration button, which unrolls a sheet. With either one, click the Register On-line button. This opens your Web browser and points it to Apple's QuickTime purchase page. The upgrade price is worth it.

Installing QuickTime

Mac OS 9 and earlier and Mac OS X come with QuickTime preinstalled. If for some reason you need to reinstall it, go to www.apple.com/quicktime/ and download the installer. Unlike most other software installers, it's a network installer—that is, it connects to the Internet, downloads the files it needs, and installs those, ensuring that you get the latest version. During this process, you can choose whether to install the minimum installation for playing back some media files; the standard installation, which covers most bases; or the Custom installation, which lets you install every single QuickTime file. Remember—the more you install, the longer the files take to download.

Updating QuickTime

Besides QuickTime Player and PictureViewer and a few other files, QuickTime ships with one other program: QuickTime Updater. This program connects via the Internet to an Apple server and looks for updates to QuickTime. If it finds any, it downloads them to your hard drive and installs them. You can also set QuickTime to download *codecs* (bits of software used to encode and decode audio and video) on the fly. If you try to play a movie QuickTime doesn't understand, it'll connect to Apple's servers and look for an update that lets you play back the movie.

QuickTime Settings

The QuickTime Settings control panel in Mac OS 9 contains a ton of settings that control how QuickTime acts. You can change QuickTime's settings in any of 11 areas by choosing an area from the pop-up menu in the Control Panel window:

AutoPlay. This setting lets QuickTime automatically play back audio CDs and some specific CD-ROMs when you insert them. When turned on, these options leave your Mac vulnerable to an AutoStart worm, a type of virus. Because of that, we never turn these features on by checking their boxes.

Browser Plug-in. This controls how the QuickTime Web browser plug-in works—for instance, determining whether movies embedded in Web pages play back automatically and get saved in the browser cache.

Connection Speed. This option tells QuickTime what your connection speed is so that it can choose the best version of an Internet-based file to play back.

Language. Here you can set your preferred language for Internet-based QuickTime files, if a choice is available.

Media Keys. If you have access to private media files, your keys to those files are stored here.

Music. This option lets you select a music synthesizer from a list, if you have more than one installed on your hard drive.

QuickTime Exchange. Here you can choose whether to enable QuickTime Exchange, which lets you open movies created on systems other than Macs.

Registration. Register QuickTime to unlock the pro version.

Streaming Proxy. If you use a proxy server to connect to the Internet, you can enter the particulars here.

Streaming Transport. This option allows you to choose what protocol and port QuickTime uses to connect to a QuickTime stream. Use this only if you're having trouble connecting to a QuickTime stream.

Update Check. Use this screen to set the manner in which QuickTime checks for updates to its software via the Internet.

 In Mac OS X, you find similar settings in the QuickTime System Preferences pane. Mac OS X organizes the settings into five tabs: Plug-In, Connection (includes transport settings), Music, Media Keys, and Update. It lacks AutoPlay settings because iTunes now handles audio CD playback for the system.

4

Memory

. . . .

Mike Breeden is the chapter editor and author.

This chapter covers the types of memory in your Macintosh. The primary focus is on practical, useful information rather than technical details. I examine each of the memory types: DRAM (Dynamic Random Access Memory), cache, virtual memory, and special cases such as NVRAM (Non-Volatile RAM) and ROM (read-only memory). I also include links to memory-related guides and other resources on the Web. The goal is to give you the information you need to get the most out of the memory you have and to be able to add more RAM to your Mac. When I refer to *main memory,* I'm talking about DRAM (the RAM memory modules installed in your Mac).

RAM is one of the primary factors affecting system performance, and it's usually the first thing you upgrade unless your Mac shipped with a large amount of it. Regardless of your CPU (central processing unit) speed, too little RAM suffocates your machine's performance. Adding RAM is probably the most universally beneficial upgrade for your Mac, as it is a core component used by every application. If you run more than one program simultaneously, adequate RAM also reduces crashes and lockups.

If you own a PowerPC G3 or G4 Mac, there's never been a better time to buy memory. I recently bought a 256 MB DIMM (memory module) for less than I paid for a 16 MB module for my Power Mac 8500 three years ago.

In This Chapter

The Types of Memory

Memory comes in all sorts of configurations and packages, and you want to make sure you are referring to and using the appropriate kind of memory to ensure everything works right. Here's a listing of the types of memory in your Macintosh, with basic descriptions of their function and purpose.

In Mac OS 9 and earlier, you have quite a bit of control over how your system and applications use memory. Mac OS X handles memory quite differently and gives you much less control over what to do with it. So just about all the information I cover in this chapter about memory settings and allocations pertain to Mac OS 9 and earlier. If a bit of information applies to Mac OS X too, I say so.

About Mac OS X and Memory

Here's a brief overview of how Mac OS X's memory handling differs from that of previous Mac OS versions.

Protected Memory

Unlike previous Mac OS versions, Mac OS X has protected memory, which means that a misbehaving program cannot write to other memory areas—an action that could crash the system or other applications. Although a program can still crash, it should not affect other running programs or the OS. With Mac OS X you can force-quit a frozen or crashed program and not have to restart the entire system.

Automatic Allocation of Virtual Memory

Mac OS X (like Unix and Windows) automatically and dynamically handles virtual-memory allocation to programs. This means the user doesn't have to adjust RAM allocations for native Mac OS X programs, as is the case with previous Mac OSs. It's one less thing for the user to mess with (possibly causing problems such as allocating too little or too much RAM to a program).

If you're not upgrading to Mac OS X yet, never fear. Current versions of the Mac OS will be supported and useful for many years to come, because software developers know it's the OS used by the vast majority of Mac owners (their customers). In my opinion, Mac OS X will take years to approach the installed base of users running earlier versions. And as with any new OS release (especially one as radically different as Mac OS X), it will be some time before Mac OS X has all the functionality you enjoy with Mac OS 9 and earlier software.

DRAM (Dynamic Random Access Memory)

Most references to memory pertain to the main system RAM that your programs and system software use. (When you see the term *RAM* used here, I'm referring to DRAM—the memory modules that you can install in your Mac.) It's called *Random Access* because individual pieces (locations) of RAM can be read or changed. It is *volatile,* which means it retains its contents only while power is on (or while the system is in sleep mode). The contents of RAM are maintained by refreshing (powering) the memory in repeating cycles. If you forget to save your work before shutting down the computer or if a power outage occurs, the contents in RAM (the main system memory where programs and the OS are loaded) are gone. (Operating system and applications code can be reloaded from disk, but any changes to data files you were working on that were not saved to disk will be lost.)

 With the current cost of a UPS (uninterruptible power supply) relatively low, I recommend that you buy one for protection from power outages, line surges, and lightning strikes.

Many users overlook the importance of adequate RAM; instead, installing CPU or other upgrades but forgetting the primary role that memory plays in performance and stability. In one lab I know, a low-cost RAM upgrade for a slew of 32 MB iMacs resulted in a dramatic reduction in system lockups and support costs, with better performance and user productivity. In the not-so-distant past, 128 MB was a lot of RAM, but current Mac OS versions and popular applications use a lot more memory, and many users run several programs simultaneously. With memory prices at an all-time low, if you own a modern Mac with less than 64 MB of RAM, this should be your first upgrade, unless you use only one program at a time. And if you are using Mac OS X, 128 MB of RAM should be your minimum installation.

DRAM is normally added via small circuit boards called DIMMs (Dual Inline Memory Modules, used in Power Macs and slot CD drive iMacs), SIMMs (Single Inline Memory Modules, used in older Macs), or SODIMMs (Small Outline DIMMs, used in modern PowerBooks, iBooks, and early iMacs). I cover the types and sizes in more detail later in this chapter. (Most older PowerBooks use nonstandard memory modules, which are too varied to cover here.)

How do I find out which type of RAM my Mac uses? The type and size of compatible memory vary by Mac model. I provide details later in this chapter.

How do I determine how much RAM I have? To see how much memory you have installed in your system, switch to the Finder, and from the Apple menu select About This Computer in Mac OS 9 and earlier and About This Mac in Mac OS X. The amount of physical RAM installed is listed as Built-in Memory in Mac OS 9 and earlier (**Figure 4.1**) and as Memory in Mac OS X.

In Mac OS 9, the Virtual Memory size (if enabled) is listed underneath. As the name implies, virtual memory is not really physical RAM (I cover it later in this chapter).

How do I make the most of the RAM I have? In Mac OS 9 and earlier, the first step is to minimize the amount of RAM your system is using. (Because of the way Mac OS X handles memory for each application, you have much less control over how to make the best use of RAM.) Enabled control panels and extensions consume memory, so first use the Extensions Manager control panel to create a backup set (I call it Trimmed) just in case you want to revert back to your original set. Then disable any extensions you don't need or use in the Trimmed extensions set. Later OS versions install a lot of extensions I don't need (in Mac OS 9, for instance, I always disable the Multiple Users extension and control panel, Web Sharing, and so on, because I never use them). Trimming extensions can reduce RAM use by the system as well as save CPU cycles, and that improves performance. Some applications install extensions you may not need (Toast 4.x, for instance, installs USB and FireWire extensions, which you don't need if your CD-Rewritable drive is not USB or FireWire). I also get rid of the myriad of printer drivers installed that I don't need. I avoid running screen savers or appearance add-ons—these consume RAM and CPU resources. (Modern monitors don't need screen savers to prevent burn-in. For LCD, or flat-panel, displays, use the Energy Saver control panel to turn off the display instead because that extends the life of the display backlight.) Decreasing the disk cache can also save RAM, but very low settings will degrade disk performance to such an extent that it is noticeable even in the Finder.

If you're confused about what all those extensions in your System Folder are for, or you need a little help managing them, you might want to give Extension Overload a try ($25, single user; www.extensionoverload.com). This shareware includes descriptions of more than 4,000 extensions, control panels, and Control Strip modules from System 7 to Mac OS 9.2.1.

When you're trying to manage memory, don't arbitrarily increase memory allocation to applications that don't need it. Consider which applications you use most heavily before making any changes. For instance, I typically have many windows open in my Web browsers, so I increase their RAM allocation a bit for improved stability. Don't go overboard, however. If you allocate more RAM to a program than it needs, that's memory you won't have available for other uses. If the program you're using doesn't allow you to open another document, freezes often, or displays a low-memory warning, you need to increase its allocation. I'll go over how to check and change a program's memory use in more detail later in this chapter.

If you own a very old Mac that already has the maximum RAM installed, or memory upgrades are no longer available (or horribly expensive), consider using a RAM compression utility such as Connectix's RAM Doubler ($29; www.connectix.com). With older Macs, you should carefully evaluate your OS upgrades—they usually require more RAM and may not add any functionality you need. OS upgrades can also introduce conflicts with older software, third-party drivers, and utilities. If your Mac doesn't have enough RAM for a high-end program, consider alternatives that may require much less memory. Instead of an expensive commercial program, you may find a shareware or alternative one that uses less RAM, runs better on older machines, and still does the tasks you need. VersionTracker.com (www.versiontracker.com) is a great source for shareware programs or demo versions you can try before you buy.

How do I change the memory allocated to applications? Make sure you've quit the program, because you can't change the memory allocation while the program is active. From the Finder, select the program's icon (not an alias of it) and then press ⌘⃣Ⅰ⃣ or choose Get Info in the Finder's File menu. In the Get Info dialog box, select Memory from the Show pop-up menu (**Figure 4.2**). You'll see three fields with memory amounts listed: Suggested Size, Minimum Size, and Preferred Size. The Suggested Size is the software author's recommendation of how much RAM to allocate to the application for general use; the Minimum Size is the smallest recommended setting. The Preferred Size usually defaults to the Suggested Size and is the field you should use to allocate more memory to the program. Using the Preferred field rather than the Minimum field lets the program use more if it's available but still retain the ability to run in less memory (the Minimum Size). You can reduce the Minimum Size, but you may experience problems if you do.

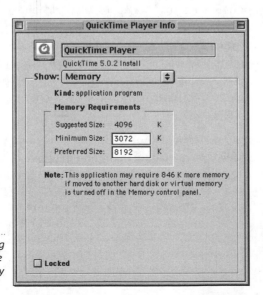

Figure 4.2

In the Get Info dialog box you can change a program's memory allocation.

How much RAM should I allocate to applications? First, you never want to allocate more than your installed physical RAM to any single application, even with virtual memory enabled. In many cases, increasing the default allocations can help stability and performance with programs using large files or many open windows. Don't go overboard and waste precious RAM, however. If you allocate more memory than the program needs, the excess won't be available for other programs or system use. One way I check this is, while running the program with my typical work files loaded, I switch back to the Finder and select the About item in the Apple menu (**Figure 4.3**). This shows each running application, the size of its allocation (in megabytes), and how much of the allocated memory is actually being used. If you see that the program is not using most of its allocation (its bar is only partially filled in), you can reduce the program's Preferred Size setting. (You must quit the program to change its memory settings.) Use caution in reducing the Minimum Size setting, however, because that is more likely to cause problems. As I discuss in more detail later in this chapter, enabling virtual memory will also reduce program (and system) memory requirements.

In Mac OS X, you can watch the percent of memory applications and processes are using in the ProcessViewer application. It's located in the Utilities folder inside the Applications folder. It doesn't clearly label all applications. TextEdit is listed as TextEdit, for example, but iTunes is shown as LaunchCFMApp. And you can't change memory allocations; instead, you can watch the system do it for you.

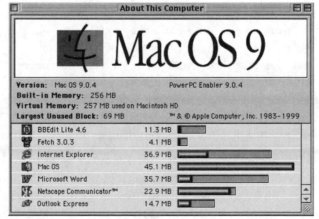

Figure 4.3

About This Computer shows how memory is put to use—the bars show how much of its allocation each running application is using.

The memory information shown in Figure 4.3 indicates that most applications are using only a fraction of their partition size. (I intentionally overallocated memory for some applications for illustrative purposes.) Notice that Netscape Communicator is using almost all of its allocation, however, so I would consider increasing its amount. BBEdit Lite and Fetch don't normally deal with large data files, so their allocations are wasting a lot of RAM and should be reduced to about a quarter of the current amount, based on the information shown. Remember, though, that memory use will vary depending on such factors as the number of open windows in the application and the size of data files loaded. Check usage during worst-case conditions after extended use and with your largest work files loaded before making final determinations on what changes, if any, are needed. If you are having problems opening large files or additional windows, or you are experiencing freezes, these are sure signs that you need to increase the memory allocated to that program.

My Microsoft Word, Outlook Express, and Internet Explorer memory allocations are larger than usual because I often use these programs with many windows open and with several large files. I've found that these programs are more reliable with extra memory allocated for my particular work pattern and needs. With 256 MB of RAM installed in my computer, the benefits of stability are worth the extra memory use.

For best results with Adobe Photoshop, an old rule of thumb is to allocate memory to the program up to five times the size of the image you will be working on (assuming you have more than that in physical RAM in your Mac). This helps avoid Photoshop's using its own virtual memory (called a *swap file*). Once Photoshop hits the swap file, performance takes a nosedive. The performance benefit from Photoshop's running at 100 percent efficiency can be as great as adding a faster hard drive or CPU in some cases, depending on the image size and system.

For 3D games, avoid a common cause of problems: Don't allocate most of your installed RAM to the game, especially with virtual memory off. Remember that the game, operating system, and OpenGL all consume memory. I'd suggest your Mac have a minimum of 256 MB of RAM installed if you want to run OpenGL games such as Quake III or Unreal Tournament. Mac OS 9 can use 40 MB to 70 MB of RAM on a 256 MB system, depending on whether virtual memory is enabled and how many applications are running. The more applications you run simultaneously, the more RAM the OS will consume. Enabling virtual memory helps, but that has other tradeoffs.

What is memory fragmentation? How can I avoid it? Memory fragmentation occurs when you run several programs and then quit one or more. Let's say you have 128 MB of RAM free (after the Mac OS's usage) and launch programs A, B, and C. Program A uses 32 MB, Program B uses 28 MB, and Program C uses 40 MB (total usage is 100 MB, with 28 MB available). Let's say you then quit program B, which leaves a hole in memory that is now free but may not be enough to run another program, depending on its requirements. Even though you now have 56 MB of RAM (total) available, the largest contiguous block of available RAM is only 28 MB; if a program's minimum requirements are more than 28 MB, you won't be able to launch it. The solution is to exit program C. (You could exit and restart program C to eliminate the hole in memory left by exiting program B, making all free memory contiguous.)

To minimize fragmentation, I launch the largest programs (and those I use for the longest duration) first. That way I'm less likely to exit those programs, and I have the maximum possible contiguous memory available.

How much RAM do I need? That depends on the types and number of applications you want to run simultaneously. As I noted earlier, serious Photoshop users should consider adding as much RAM as possible, but even today's 3D games require large amounts of RAM (often 100 MB or more for the game alone). If you're a casual user on Mac OS 9 and earlier just running applications such as AppleWorks and a Web browser, 64 MB is the absolute minimum I would suggest—preferably 128 MB. If you are running Mac OS X, 128 MB is the minimum. If your Mac is a G3 or later model (that uses SDRAM memory modules), this is affordable now. For 3D applications or Photoshop (even for nonprofessional use) on a Mac OS 9 system, I like to have at least 256 MB of RAM installed. In my Power Mac G4, on which I run LightWave 3D and other professional applications, I have the luxury of 1 GB of RAM. As of mid-2001, the two 512 MB DIMMs cost less than $100 each. Unfortunately, Fast-Page Mode RAM (which I detail later in this chapter) for older Macs is much more expensive (typically more than $100 for a 64 MB module).

Cache Memory

Since the advent of personal computers, CPUs have outpaced memory technology in operating speeds. High-speed memory, called *cache,* is used between the CPU and main system memory to minimize the time the CPU waits when reading or writing data. Cache memory allows the CPU to run faster and more efficiently without being a slave to the speed of main memory. The CPU's caches store data and instructions that the CPU is working on at the time or is predicted to need (a technique called *branch prediction,* in which the CPU prefetches data or code into the cache based on educated guesses of what will be needed next). Having code or data in the cache allows the programs to execute in many fewer CPU clock cycles than if it had to be fetched from main memory. Cache is also used to store data written from the CPU to avoid waiting on much slower main memory. In general, the larger the cache the better, since it can hold more program code and data for high-speed access by the CPU. If the CPU can't find the data it needs in the cache, it has to wait for it to be fetched from main memory (called *wait states*). The more often the CPU finds the data it needs in the cache, the faster the program will execute.

Cache memory is referred to by *levels,* generally denoting how close the cache memory is to the CPU. For instance, Level 1 cache (often called L1 cache) is normally a part of the CPU chip itself and is very high speed. Level 2 (L2) cache most often resides external to the CPU, although the latest Mac models use new PowerPC designs such as the PowerPC 750CX (G3) and PowerPC 7450 (G4), which have on-chip 256 Kbyte L2 caches running at the full processor speed. The higher-end 2001 Power Mac G4 models with PowerPC 7450 (G4) CPUs also have a Level 3 (or L3) cache external to the processor. External L2 cache is located on the CPU module or main logic board (for models that do not have the CPU on a separate module/daughtercard).

L1 cache runs at the full CPU clock speed. L2 cache (except for the PowerPC 750CX and 7450 chips) normally runs at a ratio or divisor of the CPU speed (such as 1:2 or 1:4) for G3 and G4 Macs or at the system bus speed in pre-G3 models. The Level 3 cache in the 2001 G4 Macs with PowerPC 7450 CPUs runs at one-fourth the processor clock speed. [*Whew. —Ed.*]

The L3 cache chips in the PowerPC 7450-equipped Macs are double-data-rate (DDR), which means the effective rate is twice the actual clock speed.

The so-called Mach 5 or Kansas Power Mac 8600/250, 8600/300, 9600/300, and 9600/350 systems use a 604ev processor with an inline L2 cache on the CPU card running at 100 MHz, twice their main system bus speed of 50 MHz. These Mach 5 CPU cards are not usable in any other Mac model.

If you're upgrading the CPU of a pre-G3 (PowerPC 604/603/601 CPU) series Power Mac with a PowerPC G3 or G4 CPU upgrade card, it's usually best to remove the L2 cache DIMM on the logic board (motherboard), if present. Often the faster bus speeds or different timing of the CPU upgrade card can cause problems with the original system's L2 cache DIMM. Some Power Macs, such as the 9500 and 9600 (except the Mach 5 models just noted), and Mac OS clones, such as the Umax S900, have soldered-in L2 cache that you cannot remove. However, the soldered-in cache is usually not a problem for most CPU upgrades. For a guide to getting at the cache DIMM on the 8500, the most difficult-to-access Mac model, see www.xlr8yourmac.com/8500cache.html.

Related Links

For tests of L2 cache–size effects on performance, see:

G4/350 CPU upgrade—1 MB versus 2 MB L2 tests at www.xlr8yourmac.com/G4CARDS/G4_1MBvs2MB.html.

G3 CPU upgrade—512 Kbyte versus 1 MB L2 cache Photoshop tests at www.xlr8yourmac.com/G3CARDS/g3cachetest.html.

Power Macintosh—L1 and L2 cache explained (does not cover 2001 systems as of this writing) at http://til.info.apple.com/techinfo.nsf/artnum/n14750.

The disk cache. The other type of cache your Mac uses is the system disk cache. The system disk cache is allocated from main memory (RAM) to increase performance of disk operations by storing portions of the hard drive's contents in RAM for faster access. When you first access the drive to load a file or program, the contents are held in memory for quick retrieval should they be needed again. RAM has access times much faster than mechanical devices such as hard drives. (RAM access time is measured in nanoseconds; disk-drive access times are in milliseconds.) In Mac OS 9 and earlier, you adjust the system disk-cache size in the Memory control panel (**Figure 4.4**). In later Mac OS versions, the disk-cache size defaults to a percentage of the installed RAM (up to a maximum of about 8 MB). You can override this setting and designate your own preferred size by selecting the "Custom setting" option; however, I've seen no real benefit to doing so except for video-capture applications with pre-G3 series Macs. (A tip for better video-capture performance with older Macs is to run the smallest possible disk cache size.)

Figure 4.4

The Memory control panel lets you manipulate disk-cache settings.

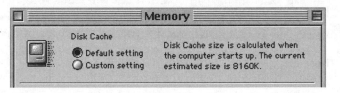

In general use for Mac OS 9 and earlier, the larger the disk-cache setting, the better for performance, with diminishing returns once sizes exceed about 4 MB. Simple disk caches can't help for random data access patterns (for example, searching a huge database or searching for files across an entire disk) since the cache can't hold the entire contents of the disk. If you use video-capture programs with older (pre-G3) Mac models, set the disk cache to the smallest size possible for higher capture rates. (Older Macs' RAM write speeds seem to be a bottleneck and writing the captured data directly to the hard drive usually results in higher capture rates. Some capture-card owners note that this is unnecessary for the latest Mac models.) Using a 1998 G3 series PowerBook I got approximately three times the EditDV capture rate with the disk cache set to the minimum size versus the default setting, so you may want to experiment with different cache sizes. Small disk-cache settings have also been useful for Photoshop, but I don't see any need to lower the disk-cache settings if you have allocated enough RAM to Photoshop that it doesn't use its swap file.

More on Disk Cache

For an article evaluating performance with various disk-cache sizes in an older Mac, see www.xlr8yourmac.com/tips/cachestudy.html.

Virtual Memory

Virtual memory, as the name implies, is not actually RAM at all. It's the term for assigning part of the hard drive's disk space for use as if it were physical RAM. Power Macs (those with PowerPC CPUs) have better virtual-memory capabilities and performance than the early 680X0-based Macs. PowerPC Macs use a virtual-memory feature called *file mapping* that reduces the amount of physical RAM required to run an application.

In Mac OS 9 and earlier, the Get Info dialog box for an application usually shows the reduction of RAM requirements from enabling virtual memory.

Without virtual memory enabled, the program's temporary data storage (called the stack), dynamically allocated storage (called the heap), and all executable code must load into the application's partition (set in the memory section of the Get Info dialog box). With virtual memory enabled, only the program's stack and heap load into the partition, and this will reduce program load times as well as memory requirements. Sometimes the savings can be substantial—for instance, Adobe GoLive 5.0 uses 4.7 MB less RAM with virtual memory enabled.

There are negatives to using virtual memory, however; the most universal is its effect on audio. Several parts of Mac OS 9's sound software are hindered by enabling virtual memory, causing delays in sound effects, for instance. Virtual memory can also affect overall performance, most noticeably in older Macs with slower hard drives or in cases where there is little physical memory installed.

I don't recommend using virtual memory for pro audio applications or for video capture. I've also seen negative effects even in modern Macs with plenty of RAM while importing digital video into iMovie. With virtual memory enabled on a PowerBook G3/500 FireWire model, the movie's audio was distorted and useless. Disabling virtual memory and reimporting the video solved the problem. (Restarting is required for any changes in virtual memory to take effect.)

Virtual Memory Pros and Cons

Pros	Cons
Reduces application RAM requirements	Has negative effects on audio and video capture
Program load times are decreased	Consumes disk space
Mac OS RAM use is reduced (especially when running multiple programs simultaneously)	No substitute for physical memory for applications that require a large amount of RAM
	Performance is reduced
	May cause delayed sound effects in games

In Mac OS 9 and earlier, turn on and adjust virtual memory in the Memory control panel (**Figure 4.5**). If you have one drive that is much faster than another, you can select that drive to hold the virtual-memory swap file using the Select Hard Disk pop-up menu. Any changes take effect only after restarting. Best overall performance is usually obtained by setting virtual memory to 1 MB more than the installed RAM size (which is the default setting).

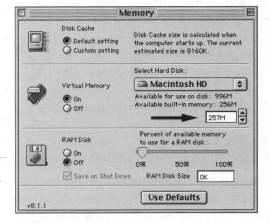

Figure 4.5

Set your virtual-memory configuration in the Memory control panel.

Connectix's RAM Doubler is an alternative to Apple's virtual memory. With more than 1 million copies sold over the years, it's clearly been popular. However, if you own a G3 series or later Power Mac, I'd recommend getting more RAM instead. (As of this writing, 128 MB of SDRAM sells for under $30.) For older Macs with more expensive RAM, RAM Doubler may be worth a look. RAM Doubler uses a compression scheme and other tricks to increase the amount of apparent RAM in your system by up to a factor of three. Since the CPU has to handle the compression, performance is affected to some extent. Performance degrades further if you allocate more RAM to an application than you have physically installed in your Mac. RAM Doubler doesn't have to use the hard drive, and this can increase battery life for portables, compared with conventional virtual memory. For more information on RAM Doubler, including important compatibility information, see www.connectix.com/products/rd9.html.

Related Links

For a technical discussion of how virtual memory differs in Power Macs versus older 680X0 CPU-based models, see http://til.info.apple.com/techinfo.nsf/artnum/n15854.

Video RAM

Often called VRAM for short, video RAM is memory dedicated for use by the graphics card or onboard graphics chip. (If your Mac doesn't have a graphics card installed, it has a graphics chip on the logic board—called *onboard video*.) The graphics chip uses VRAM to store the display's frame buffer, which holds the contents of the monitor's screen images. The amount of memory required primarily depends on the display mode and color depth set in the Monitors control panel. The more VRAM the better, in general, as higher resolutions and color depths increase the amount of VRAM required. Each pixel of the display mode uses varying amounts of VRAM, depending on the color depth. In 256-color mode, each pixel uses 1 byte of memory; thousands-of-colors mode uses 2 bytes per pixel; and millions-of-colors uses 4 bytes. Three-dimensional software and games also use additional amounts for buffering, texture storage, and display-page flipping (holding a second screen already calculated in VRAM to allow rapid changing of the display for animation, for instance).

You cannot increase the amount of VRAM on graphics cards, in all but rare cases. Modern graphics cards for the Mac include anywhere from 8 MB to 64 MB of VRAM. Many onboard-video Macs, such as the Power Mac 7300/7500/7600/8500/8600 series, have VRAM slots on the logic board. For those models you can add VRAM up to a maximum of 4 MB via special SIMMs available from Apple dealers or through mail order. Check prices, however—you may be able to add more performance and functionality by adding a graphics card rather than upgrading the onboard VRAM. Adding VRAM won't add 3D graphics acceleration to the onboard-video chip or make it faster; it will only allow your computer to run higher resolutions and color depths. If you have a second monitor handy, connecting it to the graphics card will allow you to run dual displays (using the onboard video for one monitor and the graphics card for the other). The Mac OS will treat both monitors as one wide desktop area.

Related Links

For reviews and performance tests of Macintosh graphics cards, and related articles, see www.xlr8yourmac.com/video.html. If you have a PCI or AGP (Accelerated Graphics Port) slot model, you can see how your Mac may perform with a new graphics card by searching the systems/video-card performance database at http://forums.xlr8yourmac.com/fpsdb/.

PRAM

Your Mac stores settings for such system elements as the startup disk, AppleTalk, and the Chooser in a special type of memory called NVRAM (Non-Volatile RAM). NVRAM chips are used to store settings in the PRAM (Parameter RAM) on the Mac. (Don't confuse PRAM, the name for the area where your system settings are stored, with NVRAM, which is a chip type used.) This small amount of memory has its contents preserved, even when the computer power is off, by means of the logic-board battery. The battery is typically a nicad or lithium-ion type good for five years or more. If you ever notice that your Mac doesn't retain settings such as the date when powered off, it's time to replace the battery. Apple dealers and electronics stores such as Radio Shack usually carry replacements.

The PRAM (Parameter RAM) contents include the status of AppleTalk, date, serial-port configuration and port definition, alarm-clock setting, application font, serial-printer location, keyboard repeat rate and delay, speaker volume, alert sound, double-click rate, cursor-blink time (insertion-point rate), mouse scaling (mouse speed), startup disk, menu-blink count, monitor depth, 32-bit addressing (only on older 680X0 CPU Macs), virtual-memory settings, RAM-disk settings, and disk-cache settings.

Clearing, or zapping, the PRAM. Sometimes you may want to reset the PRAM contents when you're troubleshooting a problem to make sure no corrupted settings are stored there. (This technique can also help if you have problems after replacing a graphics card, for instance.) The common term for this is *zapping the PRAM.* To do this, press the system power button and then quickly hold down the ⌘ Option P R key combination. You must press this key combination before the gray screen appears. For best results, hold down the keys until you hear the Mac's startup bong repeat three times. This will clear the startup-disk selection, so you may see a flashing question mark, but after some delay the system disk will be found and the Mac will start up. Remember to reset your control panels, such as Startup Disk, Date, and AppleTalk, to their preferred settings.

Another way to clear the PRAM settings is to use the logic-board reset button (called the CUDA on pre-G3 Macs). This is also recommended when upgrading older Macs with a different type of CPU card, such as a PowerPC G3 or G4 upgrade, or in extreme troubleshooting cases in which zapping the PRAM does not fully clear contents. (The instruction manual for the CPU upgrade usually shows the location of the reset button, often near the CPU card slot.) In some severe cases, removing the logic-board battery overnight is another way to clear the NVRAM/PRAM contents.

ROM

When a computer is powered on, the main memory of the system contains no data or code. To allow the system to start up (or boot), access the hard drive for loading the operating system, and perform other low-level system functions, instructions are permanently stored in memory called *ROM,* or *firmware.* (On PCs this is often called the BIOS—basic input/output system.) It's called read-only memory because it cannot be written to or modified, since erasing or changing this basic low-level code and instructions could render the system inoperable. The Blue and White Power Mac G3 and later Macs can have the ROM updated with special Apple system software (and button-press sequences) to allow firmware updates that address bugs and increase performance or to provide for things such as future OS support. The system's boot ROM is not to be confused with the Mac OS ROM file that is in later versions of the System Folder. Without the boot ROM, the computer would not be able to access the higher-level Mac OS ROM file stored on the hard drive. (On modern Macs, Apple System Profiler—found in the Apple Menu in Mac OS 9 and earlier and in the Utilities folder inside the Applications folder in Mac OS X—will list your firmware version, Mac OS ROM file version, and boot ROM version if available.)

The RAM Disk

Another feature of the Memory control panel allows you to use a portion of main memory to create a RAM disk that is treated just like a hard drive (although it's much faster). Unless you have huge amounts of RAM installed, it can't substitute for a real hard drive; however, it can be useful in some situations, such as holding a Web browser's cache, which speeds up Web surfing. RAM disks on later Mac OS versions with modern Macs can retain their contents even when the computer is powered off. (The contents are written to the hard drive before shutting down and copied back when you start back up.) Remember that a RAM disk is not the safest place to put important files and documents—it's best used as fast temporary storage. Should your system freeze, the data in the RAM disk is more likely to be lost or corrupted than if it were stored on the hard drive. (A shareware utility called ramBunctious offers security options such as write-through to the hard drive that are not found in Apple's RAM disk. For more on ramBunctious, see below.)

To create a RAM disk, open the Memory control panel, and in the Ram Disk panel select the On radio button. Then adjust the slider or enter the size of the disk you'd like to create (**Figure 4.6**). If your Mac OS has the option, select the Save on Shut Down check box to preserve the RAM disk's contents even when the computer is powered down.

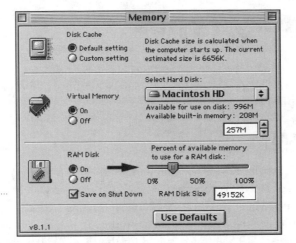

Figure 4.6

Open the Memory control panel to create a RAM disk.

When you move the slider (or type a number) to increase the RAM-disk size, the "Available built-in memory" number in the Virtual Memory panel and the Disk Cache figure are reduced. These reflect that the RAM disk is using memory that was available for the system. (In Mac OS 8.5 and later, the disk cache-size defaults to a percentage of available RAM.) Also note that the size of the RAM disk is reflected in the amount of memory the Mac OS is using when you select the About option in the Finder.

After you've selected the desired size and options, restart the Mac and you'll see the RAM-disk icon on the desktop. You use the RAM disk just as you would a normal drive except that it's noticeably faster. Dragging the RAM disk to the Trash has no effect; it can only be turned off from the Memory control panel. If the RAM disk contains any files, the options in the Memory control panel are grayed out and can't be changed. You must empty the contents or use the Finder's Erase Disk command before you can turn off the RAM disk.

The shareware RAM-disk utility ramBunctious ($25; www.clarkwoodsoftware.com/ rambunctious/) has customizable options for speed, security, safety, and versatility. For instance, you can set it to write through to a file on a real disk for safety in the event of a crash. It also allows the simultaneous use of multiple RAM disks. Most notably, ramBunctious uses the same memory that applications use, so the memory is instantly available for other applications when the RAM disk is put away.

RAM Memory Types

Macs through the years have used various types and sizes of RAM. Here's a technical rundown of the types of memory modules used in Macs, through the mid-2001 models.

SDRAM

SDRAM (Synchronous Dynamic Random Access Memory) is the most common type of RAM manufactured as well as the most widely used and lowest in cost (due to high production volumes). Starting with the first Power Mac G3 (often called the Beige G3 or Platinum G3), Apple began using SDRAM in all models. SDRAM was required for the faster main system-bus speeds, which contributed to better overall performance. All Mac-compatible SDRAM modules must be 3.3-volt, unbuffered, 8-byte, nonparity, non-ECC types. (These are actually the most common.) Parity DIMMs use an extra bit as an error check and are not compatible, nor are ECC (Error Correcting Code) DIMMs. (ECC RAM is often used in non-Mac servers or workstations.)

In addition to the memory chips, SDRAM modules contain a small chip that is basically a ROM with the module's characteristics and timing. The system reads this information to identify the module type. This chip is called the SPD (Serial Presence Detect). Information contained in the SPD includes the speed rating (PC133, PC100) and the memory timing parameters, such as CAS (Column Address Strobe) timing and latency. Most common or lower-cost PC133 and PC100 DIMMs have CAS timings of 3-2-2, although the lower-latency 2-2-2 DIMMs are available often for the same price (at least in the PC100 variety) if you shop around. The slowest SDRAM timing made currently is 3-3-3.

CAS timing is often referred to as a "CL" rating. For instance, you may see 2-2-2 SDRAM referred to as CL2 and 3-3-3 referred to as CL3. The Apple System Profiler on 2001 PowerPC systems, for instance, will report CL2 or CL3 instead of the 222 or 333 ratings it shows on earlier models.

SDRAM is made up of four banks; each has its own internal clock synchronized with the system-memory bus. When one bank is active and switches to the adjacent bank for input/output, there is a switching delay before continuing I/O operations. For the slowest speed code (3-3-3) SDRAM, this means that when switching from one bank to another, the CPU has to wait three clock cycles. With the fastest speed code (2-2-2) SDRAM, the CPU only has to wait for two clock cycles.

Although 2-2-2 is the lowest-latency (or the shorter-delay) SDRAM, the difference in real-world performance between 2-2-2 and 3-2-2 SDRAM that I have seen in testing is small—about 2 percent in Photoshop tests on a PC100-based system with a 10 MB image file. The difference between 2-2-2 and 3-3-3 would be greater, however, and those insisting on maximum efficiency will want to buy only 2-2-2 SDRAM. The good news is, if you shop around, it doesn't always cost more than the more common 3-2-2 types.

By the way, the memory controller in the Beige and Blue and White Power Mac G3s runs all DIMMs at the CAS timing of the slowest installed module. I have not seen test results on the later models to determine if the controller in the later Core99 or Uni-N chipset operates the same way.

For owners of the iMac 350 MHz and up; iBook; PowerBooks with FireWire; PowerBook G4; and Power Mac G4s with AGP, Apple's System Profiler will report your memory's CAS timing. **Figure 4.7** shows a clipping from the Apple System Profiler (under the Apple menu), taken from a PowerBook FireWire model. To the right of the "Built-in memory" size is "PC100-222S," which denotes that PC100 modules with 2-2-2 timing (fastest) are installed.

Figure 4.7

For Macs made since 1999, Apple System Profiler will show your memory's rating.

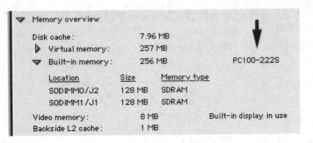

Apple System Profiler shows CAS timing on 2001 Power Mac G4 models as a single CL2 or CL3 rating rather than the full 222, 322, or 333 ratings shown with the Power Mac G4 Cube, pre-2001 Power Mac G4s, PowerBook G3 (FireWire), and slot-loading iMacs. Only 1999 and later model Macs will show memory timing in Apple System Profiler.

SDRAM is available in two physical sizes: 168-pin DIMMs for desktops; and the smaller, 144-pin SODIMMs (Small Outline DIMMs) for the PowerBook G3 series, early iMacs (233 MHz through 333 MHz), iBooks, and the 2001 PowerBook G4.

There are several grades of SDRAM named by their bus-speed rating (see the "Mac Models and Compatible SDRAM Types" section):

PC133. As the name implies, these modules are designed for computers with a 133 MHz system bus. They are 168-pin DIMMs commonly available in 64 MB, 128 MB, 256 MB, and 512 MB sizes. The 2001 Power Mac G4s are the first Macs to use PC133 RAM. Apple refers to the early 2001 Power Mac G4s as Power Mac G4 (Digital Audio) to differentiate them from previous Power Mac G4 models of 1999 and 2000, which used PC100 memory and 100 MHz bus speeds. The Power Mac G4 (QuickSilver) models introduced in the summer of 2001 also use PC133 RAM.

PC100. Rated for 100 MHz system buses. They are available in 168-pin DIMMs for desktops and 144-pin SODIMMs for notebooks (and early iMacs). In systems that use PC100 RAM, faster types such as PC133 can be used, with the exceptions I note in the listing of systems that follow. Installing PC133 RAM in a PC100-based system won't make the RAM run faster, however, since memory bus speeds are controlled by the Mac's logic board. An analogy would be putting 133 mph–rated tires on a car has a maximum speed of 100 mph. The higher-rated tires can't make the car go faster. One benefit of buying PC133 is that it's usable in the 2001 Power Mac G4s, should you buy a new system later.

PC66. Rated for 66 MHz system buses. Available in 168-pin DIMM and 144-pin SODIMM modules. PC66 memory is rarely made now, as systems moved to faster bus speeds years ago. (See below for compatibility notes on using PC100 or PC133 RAM in Macs originally designed for PC66 memory.)

Mac Models and Compatible SDRAM Types

Power Mac G4 (QuickSilver). Introduced in July 2001, the QuickSilver version of the Power Mac G4 use the same PC133 RAM Apple first used in the Power Mac G4 (Digital Audio) models. These machines have three DIMM slots and can accept DIMM sizes of 128 MB, 256 MB, and 512 MB, for a maximum of 1.5 GB of RAM.

Power Mac G4 (Digital Audio). In January 2001, Apple announced a new line of Power Mac G4 systems using a 133 MHz system bus and requiring PC133 RAM. The Digital Audio G4s have three DIMM slots, as opposed to four in the previous G4 towers. Compatible DIMM sizes are 32 MB, 64 MB, 128 MB, 256 MB, and 512 MB. The system has a maximum of 1.5 GB of RAM. For more information on the 2001 Power Mac G4 RAM specifications, see http://til.info.apple.com/techinfo.nsf/artnum/n58763.

Power Mac G4 AGP Graphics. In fall 1999, Apple released its first systems with an AGP graphics-card slot. In summer 2000 it made Gigabit Ethernet standard, replacing the 10/100-Mbps Ethernet of the original models. You can tell if your Power Mac G4 is a Gigabit model by the small silver heat sink on the networking chip on the logic board. These systems have four DIMM slots for PC100 RAM. Compatible DIMM sizes are 32 MB, 64 MB, 128 MB, 256 MB, and 512 MB. The maximum addressable RAM (in Mac OS 9) is 1.5 GB.

Power Mac G4 Cube. The G4 Cube uses a 100 MHz system bus and PC100 (or faster) SDRAM DIMMs. Compatible sizes are 32 MB, 64 MB, 128 MB, 256 MB, and 512 MB. The G4 Cube has three DIMM slots for a maximum of 1.5 GB of RAM.

Power Mac G4 PCI Graphics. This system, introduced in September 1999, is based on the same logic board (or motherboard) as the Blue and White Power Mac G3 and uses PC100 SDRAM. PC133 SDRAM should also work if the DIMM is composed of memory chips that are 128 Mb or less density. Compatible sizes are 32 MB, 64 MB, 128 MB, and 256 MB. (Note: 256 MB DIMMs will only be fully recognized if they are constructed of 128 Mb chips. If a 256 MB DIMM has only 8 chips, it's using 256 Mb memory chips and would not be compatible.) No 512 MB DIMMs are compatible, as they are composed of 256 Mb chips.

The Power Mac G4 PCI Graphics systems had a short production life and were discontinued after three months with the release of the first Power Mac G4 AGP Graphics systems. If you're unsure if your Power Mac G4 is the PCI or AGP model, look at the graphics-card slot (the slot closest to the middle of the logic board). If the connector on the logic board for the graphics card is white, the computer is a PCI Graphics box. If it's brown, it's an AGP Graphics model.

Power Mac G3 (Blue and White). The Blue and White Power Mac G3 was the first Mac to use a 100 MHz system bus, three 64-bit PCI slots, and one 66 MHz 32-bit PCI slot. It uses PC100 SDRAM DIMMs, although PC133 SDRAM should also work if the DIMM is composed of memory chips with 128 Mb or less density. Compatible sizes are 32 MB, 64 MB, 128 MB, and 256 MB, with the same chip-density restrictions noted for the Power Mac G4 PCI Graphics model. The motherboard has four DIMM slots, for a maximum RAM capacity of 1 GB using compatible 256 MB DIMMs. The 512 MB DIMMs are not compatible, as they are composed of 256 Mb chips.

Power Mac G3 Desktop, Mini Tower, and All-In-One (commonly called the Beige Power Mac G3s). These were the first SDRAM-based Macs and have a 66 MHz system bus. PC66 RAM is hard to find now, and most owners buy PC100 DIMMs. The PowerMac G3 uses the same memory controller as the Blue and White Power Mac G3 and Power Mac G4 PCI Graphics models and cannot fully address memory chips denser than 128 Mb. Compatible sizes are 32 MB, 64 MB, 128 MB, and 256 MB. (Some 256 MB DIMMs may use eight 256 Mb chips instead of sixteen 128 Mb chips. Only the latter is compatible.) No 512 MB DIMMs are compatible with these models. The motherboard has three DIMM slots, for a maximum RAM capacity of 768 MB using compatible 256 MB DIMMs.

Installing RAM in G3s

The maximum DIMM height for Power Mac G3 Desktop models is 1.15 inches. For a guide to installing RAM (or VRAM) in a Beige G3, see www.xlr8yourmac.com/G3-ZONE/G3_RAM.html.

PowerBook G4. The low-end PowerBook G4 uses the same PC100 SODIMMs as the FireWire model but has a 1.5-inch maximum module height. The higher-end models have 133 MHz system buses and use PC133 SODIMMs. Compatible sizes are 32 MB, 64 MB, 128 MB, 256 MB, and 512 MB. Make sure that the modules you're buying are 1.5 inches or less in height (this is especially important to verify when you are looking at 256 MB or 512 MB modules). The PowerBook G4 has two memory slots under its keyboard for a maximum of 1 GB or RAM.

PowerBook G3 (FireWire). The FireWire model PowerBook, rolled out in February 2000, was the first Mac portable to use PC100 SODIMMs and a 100 MHz system bus. Compatible sizes are 32 MB, 64 MB, 128 MB, 256 MB, and 512 MB. It has two available slots (one under and one on top of the CPU module). Maximum RAM is 1 GB.

PowerBook G3 series (1998–1999). These models used PC66 SODIMMs, with the exception of the PowerBook G3/250 MHz and G3/292 MHz (1998), which used an 83 MHz bus speed and needed faster RAM. Code names for these models were Wall Street (1998 G3/233 to G3/300) and Lombard (1999 G3/333 and G3/400 with the Bronze keyboard). Since PC100 SODIMMS are the most common (and lowest in cost), it's best to buy those types. Available sizes are 32 MB, 64 MB, 128 MB, and 256 MB. Because of the memory controller used in these models (the same as the Power Mac G3 noted earlier), 512 MB modules cannot be used. The low-profile 256 MB modules I've owned use a trick of stacking 128 Mb chips to allow them to fit on the smaller SODIMM. There are two expansion slots (one under and one on top of the CPU module). Compatible sizes are 32 MB, 64 MB, 128 MB, and 256 MB (specials). Maximum RAM is 512 MB using two compatible 256 MB SODIMMs.

The bottom slot supports low-profile 1.25-inch memory modules only; the top slot supports up to 2-inch memory modules. 256 MB low-profile modules available at sources such as TransIntl.com (www.transintl.com).

PowerBook G3 first model (aka 3500/Kanga). Unlike the later PowerBook G3s, this model uses a nonstandard memory-module design. The logic board has 32 MB of RAM soldered in and one RAM expansion slot. The maximum RAM is 160 MB (32 MB onboard plus a 128 MB module).

iBooks. As of Fall 2001, the low-end iBook has a 66 MHz bus speed and requires PC66 (or faster) SDRAM SODIMMs. The higher-end iBooks have 100 MHz system buses and use PC100 SODIMMs. The iBooks have either 32 MB or 64 MB of RAM soldered on the logic board with one expansion slot. Commonly available sizes are 32 MB, 64 MB, 128 MB, and 256 MB. Although scarce at the time this was written, there are sources of 512 MB iBook compatible SODIMMs from vendors such as TransIntl.com (www.transintl.com). This high-density module is listed there as compatible with every iBook model made and allows them to exceed Apple's original maximum memory limits. (Apple's info was written before the high-density modules were available.) Since there's only one expansion slot, the maximum RAM depends on the iBook model's base RAM on the logic board. (You can add a SODIMM to complement the onboard soldered-in RAM).

iMacs—350 MHz and faster. The iMac G3/350 and faster models use standard PC100 SDRAM DIMMs. They have two RAM slots, which are easily accessible without disassembly (unlike earlier iMac models). Compatible sizes are 32 MB, 64 MB, 128 MB, 256 MB, and 512 MB, for a maximum of 1 GB of installed RAM. (These iMacs use the same chipset as the Power Mac G4 AGP Graphics systems and can therefore use 256 Mb chip–based modules.)

iMacs—233 MHz to 333 MHz. The original iMac series uses the same SDRAM SODIMM modules as the PowerBook G3 series and actually has a similar CPU module design. (The RAM slots are on the CPU module as in the PowerBook G3 series.) These iMacs have a 66 MHz bus and use PC66 or faster SODIMM modules. As with the PowerBook G3 series, the bottom slot supports low-profile 1.25-inch memory modules only, and the top slot supports up to 2-inch memory modules. There are 256 MB 1.25-inch modules available at sources such as TransIntl.com. Otherwise, the maximum SODIMM size is 128 MB.

FPM and EDO RAM

The memory configurations of the pre-Power Mac G3 series Mac models are too numerous and varied to cover individually here. Apple frequently updates its Memory Guide, which lists Mac models and RAM compatibility. You can download the guide as an Adobe Acrobat PDF file at http://asu.info.apple.com/ swupdates.nsf/artnum/n10084. You may notice that in some cases, such as the PowerBook G3 FireWire, I've put maximum RAM sizes higher than Apple's guide lists. This is because the guide does not reflect the use of higher-capacity modules. Another great RAM-compatibility guide is Newer Technology's GURU application. Although the company is no longer in business, GURU is still available at http://eshop.macsales.com/Tech/index.cfm?load=newertech.html.

GURU does not include information on the latest high-density memory modules, so the maximum RAM size listed may not be accurate for SDRAM-based Mac models. (The same is true of Apple's current Memory Guide also.) Its primary benefit in my opinion is for researching older Mac models.

A utility more up to date than GURU is available. Called MacTracker, it lists RAM information for all Mac models and information on Apple's displays and printers. There's even a Mac OS X version with an Aqua interface. Find MacTracker at http://plaza.powersurfr.com/mactracker/.

The Apple Memory Guide includes an index of Apple Mac models, notes on memory types and sizes, and even logic-board diagrams showing where the RAM slots are for each model. Refer to this guide before purchasing or adding RAM to your Mac.

If in doubt, consult the Apple guide—or for clones, check sites such as www.everymac.com—and a reputable dealer of Macintosh memory.

Pre-PowerPC G3 Mac Memory Tips

Here are a few performance and upgrading tips for pre-G3 series Mac owners.

Memory Interleaving

Many Power Macs (7300 to 9600) and Mac OS clones (Power Computing PowerTower Pro and PowerWave, Umax SuperMac S900 and J700) can use interleaved RAM. Even though the system data bus is 64 bits wide in these models, the memory controller can handle 128-bit data read/write operations by interleaving data between corresponding DIMMS. Interleaving memory provides higher effective transfer rates (called *bandwidth*) between the CPU and main memory. The benefits vary by application, and the highest gains are seen with programs or games that move a lot of data over the bus. For a performance comparison of interleaved RAM, see www.xlr8yourmac.com/RAM/. Power Mac G3 series and later Macs use SDRAM and don't support memory interleaving by DIMM pairs. (SDRAM interleaves RAM on each DIMM and has much higher bandwidth due to higher clock speeds.)

For Macs that can use it, you interleave RAM by installing identical (size and type) DIMMs in matching A/B slots (for example, A1/B1, A2/B2, and so on). So, if you install a 32 MB DIMM in slot A1 and a matching 32 MB DIMM in slot B1, the Mac will interleave access to those DIMMs.

RAM Tips for CPU Upgrades

If you're considering a CPU upgrade, be aware that some upgrade cards may not be stable with interleaved RAM. I've not had this problem when using matched DIMMs (same manufacturer, 60-nanosecond speed rating) with **any** CPU upgrade I've tested personally. However, some visitors to my Web site have had this problem, due to the almost infinite variety of older RAM types and speeds found in many Macs. The design of the CPU-upgrade card can also affect stability. For thousands of owner reports on CPU upgrades in older Macs, search the database at http://forums.xlr8yourmac.com/cpureview.lasso.

Owners of Macs with six PCI slots considering a Newer Technology CPU upgrade should note that Umax was the first to report an issue with certain types of buffered RAM. Full details on the issue and how to check the memory you have were originally in the Umax knowledge base but have been removed. See the CPU Upgrades or Memory Questions section of the AccelerateYourMac FAQ (http://forums.xlr8yourmac.com/faq.lasso) for details.

2K Refresh and 4K Refresh Memory

Main memory has to be refreshed to maintain the memory contents. You'll often hear *2K refresh* or *4K refresh* in discussions about older Mac RAM. This refers to the number of refresh cycles required for all sections of the memory array. It is determined by the number of row addresses on the module. For example, a 4-Mb by 4-bit wide memory chip can be configured as either 2K or 4K refresh. Memory with 4K refresh has 12 row addresses and 10 column addresses, and 2K refresh has 11 row addresses and 11 column addresses. For more information on refresh rates, see the Power Macintosh: Memory FAQ at http://til.info.apple.com/techinfo.nsf/artnum/n20575.

Apple's RAM Installation Guides

If you own an iMac, iBook, PowerBook G3 series or later (including the PowerBook G4), or Power Mac G4, Apple provides online guides to RAM installation at www.info.apple.com/support/cip/.

 The 1999 and early 2000 Power Mac G4 AGP Graphics models have a motherboard similar to that of the Power Mac G4 Gigabit Ethernet model introduced in summer 2000, so memory installation is identical.

Memory-Buying Tips

Here are a few things to keep in mind before you buy memory for your Mac. Most of the memory sold by reputable Mac dealers is generally of good quality and with proper handling should last as long as your Mac will.

Compatibility. Always verify that the memory you are buying will work with your specific Mac model. Many times the lowest prices on the Web will be from generic memory dealers. Most of the time the memory will be fine, but as I noted earlier, in several cases certain types or sizes of RAM are not compatible with some Mac models. A dealer that sells memory listed for use with Macs should be able to verify that what you're buying is correct for your model.

Pricing. Always compare the total *delivered* cost. Many times the lowest price comes with a large shipping and handling fee. Consider the dealer's reputation also—RAM is not the place to cut corners on quality as it is critical to your system's stability and reliability. The difference in price can seem trivial if the RAM is not reliable and causes crashing, return shipping costs, and phone calls. You can save a bundle over catalog and retail-store prices on the Web and still get quality RAM, but beware of deals that seem too good to be true.

Warranty. Many dealers back their memory with a lifetime warranty. I personally would never buy memory with a shorter warranty. Dealers offering less make me wonder if that's because they have a higher return rate (failure rate) or have little confidence in the memory they're selling.

Name-brand versus generic RAM. Most of the memory I've bought over the years has been generic—meaning it was not sold with the brand-name label of a major manufacturer such as Kingston or Crucial. I'd guess that 90 percent of the RAM sold in the world is generic, and this is not necessarily a sign of lesser quality. The components used in generic memory modules are usually from major manufacturers using proven circuit boards. Although there's always a chance of problems with any memory, if you buy from a reputable Mac dealer that's been around for years, you should be fine.

Precautions for Handling Memory

Memory modules are sensitive to static electricity. Never touch the metal contacts on the module or the pins on the memory chips. Leave the memory in the antistatic bag it ships in until you're ready to insert it into the Mac. Static electricity is easily generated in the typical home environment and is the No. 1 cause of component failure. Levels that may not destroy the part can still shorten its life. For maximum protection, wear an antistatic wrist strap available from computer and electronics-supply stores, and always discharge yourself by touching a metal part of the Mac's chassis before touching, inserting, or removing any parts inside the computer.

See your owner's manual or the Apple guides referred to in this chapter for other precautions. If you're not comfortable with installing RAM, a local dealer can do this for a nominal fee.

5

Storage

John Christopher (JC) is the chapter editor and coauthor.

Kristina DeNike (KD) and David Morgenstern (DM) are the chapter coauthors.

Sharon Zardetto Aker (SA) and Henry Norr (HN) edited earlier editions of
The Macintosh Bible, *from which portions of this chapter are taken.*

If you're like most computer users, you aren't much more interested in computer storage than in bookcases. After all, hard disks, floppies, CD-ROM drives, and tape backup units don't actually *do* much—they just provide a place to store the files you've created and collected.

In reality, nothing is more critical to the performance and reliability of your computer system than your storage devices. If your drive is slow, you'll be staring at the wristwatch pointer and twiddling your thumbs when you should be working or having fun. If your hard disk crashes, you could lose hours or years of your work, and if you haven't taken the necessary precautions, you may never get those files back. Problems like those can make you rue the day you ever heard of the computer's great benefits and timesaving abilities.

No one can guarantee you'll never have such hassles—but in this chapter we aim to improve your odds by providing background information and tips to help you understand how storage devices work; teaching you what to look for when purchasing a new drive; and showing you how to manage your devices effectively to avoid the worst.

In This Chapter

Hard Disks (JC)

Hard disks are truly precision instruments that rely on principles of aerodynamics, electricity, and magnetism to operate. What follows are the gruesome anatomical details of hard-disk innards. While the following descriptions may seem somewhat technical, they will help you understand exactly what is happening as you use your Mac and prepare you for our "Hard-Disk Buyers' Guide," later in this chapter.

Hard-Disk Anatomy

The numerous moving parts inside a hard disk work together for the sole purpose of reading and writing data. The main components—the platters, spindle, and actuator assembly—are contained inside a sealed housing to protect them from dust and other airborne contaminants (**Figure 5.1**).

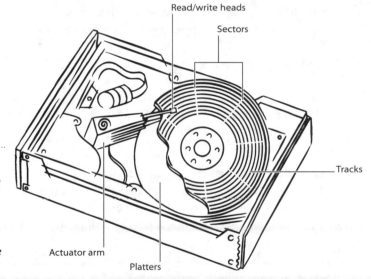

Read/write heads

Sectors

Tracks

Actuator arm

Platters

Figure 5.1

Inside a hard disk mechanism. The platters are stacked on a spindle that spins rapidly as the read/write heads, attached to the actuator arm, move back and forth.

Platters. The word *platter* might conjure up thoughts of serving a Thanksgiving feast. When it comes to your hard disk, the platter serves up your data. Platters are flat and circular, manufactured from a durable material. The term *hard disk* was coined because of the rigid material used in the platter itself. Every hard disk contains at least one platter; modern high-capacity drives usually have more than one. A magnetic material coats both sides of a platter, allowing it to function as a receptacle for your data.

Spindle. At the heart of the hard-disk assembly is a spindle where the platters are stacked like old-fashioned phonograph records. A built-in high-speed motor rotates the platters at a constant rate—typically 7,200 revolutions per minute (rpm). Many new hard disks spin even faster—some disks spin as fast as 15,000 rpm.

Actuator. The actuator includes a flexible arm that extends the diameter of the platter and moves rapidly across it at a speed greater than 60 miles per hour. A set of read-write heads are mounted at the end of the arm, one head for each side of the platter. These miniature heads read and write your data.

This is how it all works together: When you switch on your Mac, electrical current spins up the spindle motor. When the motor reaches the correct speed, the actuator arm unlocks and air pressure pushes the heads up above the platters, allowing them to ride on a cushion of air. The heads' flying height is less than the width of a human hair.

The read-write heads store your data by giving bits of the magnetic coating a positive or negative magnetic charge, corresponding to the 1s and 0s of digital data; they read the data by checking to see what the charges are.

 Is it a hard disk or a hard drive? Does your Macintosh have a hard drive or a hard disk? You may wonder what the difference is. In fact, they mean the same thing—you can use these terms interchangeably.

Logically Speaking

Beyond the physical characteristics of hard disks are their logical attributes— the features that make a hard disk usable with a Macintosh computer. Next we'll describe some technical details on the creation of a Mac hard disk and how it affects your data.

Formatting and initializing disks. Every type of storage media used with a Mac must be formatted to set up the file system and keep track of stored data; this process is sometimes called *initialization*. A special disk utility known as a *hard-disk formatter* carries out these tasks. The fundamental process of preparing your hard drive breaks down into two steps: the creation of a new directory— your disk's table of contents—and the installation of a disk driver to enable the Mac to communicate with the disk.

The formatting process may also include some other options—setting up multiple partitions, zeroing out all sectors (erasing the entire disk), or perform-ing a low-level format, a task exclusive to SCSI drives.

Tracks and sectors (SA). A disk's surface is divided into concentric rings called *tracks;* the tracks are subdivided into areas called *sectors.* These divisions aren't initially present on a disk but actually get written to the surface. When you first format a disk, the hard-disk formatter creates the dividers—little mag-netic fences—so your Mac can use the disk.

Disk drivers. The disk driver is an invisible program that gets written to a hard disk during initialization—it manages all communication between your hard disk and your Mac. Whenever you start up your Mac, it reads the disk driver from your hard disk and loads that into memory. The hard disk's icon appears on the Desktop courtesy of the driver. Anytime you open or save a file, the disk driver moves the data between the Mac's memory and the hard disk—it's a kind of conveyor belt for information.

To upgrade disk drivers, you use a hard-disk formatter such as Apple's Drive Setup (**Figure 5.2**). In most cases you can simply select the formatter's Update or Install command to replace the current disk driver with a different version.

Upgrading disk drivers is important when you're moving up to a new version of the operating system or adding new storage devices. Apple's Installer program automatically updates the driver whenever you install a new operating system. However, if you haven't formatted your hard disk with Apple's Drive Setup, you may receive a message stating that the program couldn't update the driver. In that case you should purchase a third-party formatter that's compatible with the new OS.

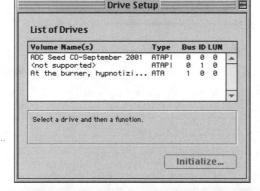

Figure 5.2

Apple's Drive Setup waiting for you to pick a drive.

File systems. To store data efficiently, your Mac must rely on a filing system. Just as you would organize folders in a real-world file cabinet, your Mac has its own method called HFS (Hierarchical File System). HFS uses a treelike hierarchy to keep track of stored files.

HFS (Mac OS Standard Format). In the early days of the Mac, HFS was an efficient method for file management. As hard disks grew in capacity and the number of files expanded, HFS eventually needed an overhaul. Its main problem lay in the *allocation blocks*. HFS required that all data stored on a hard disk be spread out over a set number of blocks—65,536, to be exact. This method was fine for 10 or 20 MB drives, but as drives increased in capacity, the structure of HFS created a real problem because it forced small files to use large blocks of space.

HFS+ (Mac OS Extended Format) (SA). Apple introduced HFS+ in Mac OS 8.1. The new file structure allowed many more allocation blocks per disk. It had a limit of 4.2 billion blocks, resulting in smaller allocation-block sizes: 4 Kbytes regardless of the drive's size. HFS+ makes much better use of the space on your hard disk, especially if the disk is larger than 1 GB. This is now the default format for hard disks in new Macs (**Figure 5.3**).

You can't use disks formatted for HFS+ with system versions prior to Mac OS 8.1. Hook up an HFS+ disk to an earlier system, and you won't be able to access its contents. All you'll see is a single file named Where Have All My Files Gone. This SimpleText document explains to the uninitiated (that's not you anymore) that only Mac OS 8.1 and later can read the disk.

Figure 5.3

When you format a disk with the Finder's Erase command in Mac OS 9 and earlier, you can choose between Mac OS Standard and Mac OS Extended format.

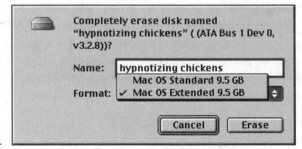

Before switching to HFS+ format, consider the following:

•   The disk must be at least 1 GB in size to achieve any real benefit.

•   If you're partitioning a newly formatted drive with Drive Setup, you can format some partitions as HFS and others as HFS+.

•   The majority of your files should be on the small side. If your work consists mostly of word processing, spreadsheets, programming, and Web pages, your disk is a good candidate for HFS+. If you do high-end graphics, sound, or video, your large files aren't wasting that much space to begin with, so there's not much point in changing formats.

•   For externals and removables, use the HFS format if there's even the *slightest* chance you'll be using the disk on a machine that's not running Mac OS 8.1 or later.

Allocation blocks (SA). As you already know, a disk is divided into tracks and sectors. But there's another division, too—the aforementioned allocation block. It's not a physical area of the disk but rather a logical division, providing a way for the Mac to treat a group of sectors as a single unit.

The allocation block is the smallest unit the Mac uses in storing a file. A block can't store two different files; if a file (or part of a file that has spilled over from other storage blocks) doesn't completely fill it, the remaining space stays empty. Putting a very small file into a very large block wastes a lot of space. The larger the disk, the more room a file takes. The actual size of an allocation block depends on the size of the disk; larger disks have larger blocks, because an HFS disk allows only 65,536 blocks at most. Disks under 60 MB use 1 Kbyte for each allocation block; for every 32 MB of disk capacity, the size of an allocation block grows by .5 Kbyte.

UFS. Beginning with Mac OS X, Apple added UFS (Unix File System) for the Mac. The original Unix, developed in 1969 by AT&T, was created to support multiple users in a multitasking environment. Many Web servers on the Internet currently run under the Unix operating system. Apple built Mac OS X on a Unix foundation. When you install Mac OS X, you can choose to erase your hard disk and create either UFS or HFS+ volumes.

Realistically, you probably want to avoid formatting your hard disk as UFS unless you intend to use your Mac as a server on a network that will support many users or connect to other Unix computers.

Hard-disk formatters. You're not likely to use a hard-disk formatter every day, but it is vital to your hard disk's functionality. It not only formats and initialize the drive but becomes an absolute necessity when your Mac's hard drive crashes.

Apple includes its hard-disk formatter, Drive Setup, on its system-installer CD. Mac OS X users have a radically different version of the program incorporated into the Disk Utility application (**Figure 5.4**). You'll find both Drive Setup and Disk Utility included on your hard disk as part of the usual operating-system installation as well as located in the Utilities folder.

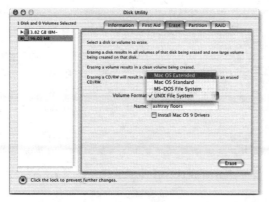

Figure 5.4

Disk Utility can initialize and format nearly every modern hard disk, except of course your startup disk.

Several companies publish universal hard-disk formatters that work with just about every kind of drive and most removable media. The best of the crop are FWB Software's Hard Disk ToolKit, LaCie's Silverlining, and CharisMac's Anubis Utility. These programs offer features that let you control every aspect of hard-disk performance and security. You'll also benefit from their ability to use a single disk driver to communicate with all your storage devices.

Partitioning—the logical divide. Partitioning means dividing a single physical disk into two or more logical volumes—individual sections that the Mac regards as completely separate hard disks. Partitioning allows you to minimize the amount of space a file uses on a drive and configure options for controlling access to specific data.

It used to be that if you wanted to squeeze every iota of performance you could possibly get from your hard disk, you could reduce its access time by creating partitions. When hard-disk capacity usage rarely exceeded a single gigabyte, partitioning was an absolute necessity to obtain high-speed performance and use space efficiently by reducing the size of allocation blocks. The real benefits to partitioning drives these days come in the form of convenience and flexibility. Here are a few ideas to help you decide if partitioning is for you.

If you use Adobe Photoshop, you may be aware of the *scratch-disk setting*. The program allocates logical space on your hard disk to store data temporarily. If you create a separate partition dedicated to Adobe Photoshop, some scratch-disk operations might speed up because your temporary data will not become fragmented. Photoshop 4.0 and later supports as much as 2 GB of scratch-disk space on a total of two volumes; Photoshop 5 and later supports 200 GB of scratch-disk space on a total of four volumes.

Having a separate partition can come in really handy when you need to perform maintenance or recovery following a crash. Just create a 200 MB "system-rescue" partition and copy the disk utilities and System Folder into that area. That way you can start up your Mac from that partition and run your software. Although this method is easier than running utilities from a bootable CD or DVD, it won't help if your drive suffers mechanical failure.

Finally, you might consider using a separate partition to control access to sensitive data on your Macintosh. After you've created an independent partition, you can set options to lock it for read-only access, password-protect it to keep unauthorized parties out, and manually mount it on the Desktop only when you desire.

At the burner

Here are a few things to consider before partitioning your hard disk:

hypnotizing chickens

You'll have to reformat to increase the size of partitions. Some hard-disk formatters allow you to increase the size of a lone partition as long as you have free space on your drive. However, in most cases you will likely have to reformat the entire hard disk to adjust sizes. Don't forget to back up first!

ashtray floors

Figure 5.5

Partitions look and act like independent hard disks, but they're not. Don't use them to back up.

Don't use partitions for backing up! As we mentioned at the beginning of this chapter, hard disks are mechanical devices that can fail without warning (**Figure 5.5**). Do not use a partition to back up your critical files. Invest in a backup device (see "Back Up, Back Up, Back Up!" later in this chapter).

Hard-Disk Buyers' Guide (JC)

Let's face it—your hard disk is full. How do we know? Well, if you're like us, you've probably built up a massive collection of MP3s and digitally edited a cinematic masterpiece of your vacation in Hawaii, and now you don't have enough space to install the latest version of Quicken. Even if you don't fall into that category, in general you need more disk space to do more things. But should you buy an internal hard disk to replace the shrinking one you currently own, or simply add another hard disk and use them both? Perhaps you want to connect your new drive externally to one of your Mac's peripheral ports. Buying a new hard disk is a hard choice, but sit tight as we help you make an informed decision.

What's Inside?

If you don't already know what kind of hard drive you have installed inside your Mac, your first mission is to find out. Knowing this will aid in choosing the proper interface and help you decide whether you need an internal or external drive.

The manual that shipped with your Mac is a good place to start, as Apple frequently provides details on storage-expansion capabilities. If your manual is missing in action, you can get a copy from Apple Support at www.info.apple.com/manuals/manuals.taf. (You'll need Adobe Acrobat Reader to open the file—download the software free from www.adobe.com/products/acrobat/readermain.html.) Find more details at Apple's Tech Info Library (http://til.info.apple.com).

Another useful tool to assist in your quest is the Apple System Profiler, installed as part of your system software. It provides detailed information about your Mac, its components, and your installed software. Find it in the Apple menu in Mac OS 9 and earlier and in the Utilities folder in Mac OS X.

To get technical information about your hard disk, launch the Apple System Profiler and select the Devices And Volumes tab. Click the triangle next the hard drive to reveal details like capacity and interface. Note that your Mac's internal hard drive is either an ATA or a SCSI device.

 Many Macs have a bar-code label affixed on the back that details what's installed inside, such as memory configuration, processor speed, and cache size, hard-drive capacity.

Besides your internal hard disk, your Mac has other ways of addressing storage devices. These technologies may include SCSI, USB, or FireWire. Again, the Apple System Profiler is likely the best way to find out what kind of connections your Mac supports. Beyond that, you can also inspect your Mac visually and check out its expansion ports.

The Eternal Question: Internal vs External

One burning question that frequently crosses the minds of storage-seeking Mac users is what kind of hard drive to buy, internal or external.

Internal drives are installed inside your Mac. Sometimes known as hard-disk mechanisms, they are self-contained units—that is to say, they come equipped with everything they need to function. As you've probably discovered, your internal hard disk uses only one of two types of interface for communication—ATA or SCSI.

It may surprise you to know that Apple doesn't actually manufacture your hard disk. As is the case with many other components, Apple buys drives from all the major vendors—Western Digital, Seagate, Quantum, IBM, and others—and brands them with an Apple label before installing them inside your Mac. So if you decide to replace your internal hard drive tomorrow, rest assured that whatever brand of drive mechanism you choose, it will likely be fully Mac compatible.

Sometimes choosing an internal drive means you must simultaneously replace your current hard disk and move your data to a new drive (for more on this subject, see "Backup Devices and Removable Storage," later in this chapter). This is true if you own an iMac, an iBook, or a PowerBook because these models don't offer any internal space for an additional hard drive.

No matter which Mac you own, you have options for connecting external drives. An external drive houses the hard-disk mechanism in a box known as an *enclosure*. A drive with this extra feature typically costs $70 to $100 more than an internal, uncased hard-disk mechanism. The enclosure has a fan, a power supply, and sometimes additional electronic circuitry to run the drive. Because you can attach external drives to your Mac via the USB, SCSI, or FireWire port, you have your pick of a wide variety of devices.

Although they cost slightly more, external drives offer some real advantages over internal models. Specifically, you can transport the drive easily if you need to move large amounts of data between Macs. Adding an external drive is also easier than installing an internal one, and when you graduate to a new Mac, you won't have to remove the drive—just unplug it and go.

What's an Interface?

The *interface* refers to the method by which peripherals connect to your Macintosh. In this case we're talking exclusively about storage devices. USB, SCSI, ATA, and FireWire devices use different kinds of interfaces to communicate with your Mac.

Each of these technologies is unique and has its own set of benefits and limitations. The following section offers an overview of the various storage interfaces. The sidebars expand on useful technical tidbits.

ATA and IDE. If you've bought a Macintosh in the last eight years, it probably has a built-in IDE hard disk connected to the ATA bus. Sometimes known as ATA or EIDE (Enhanced Integrated Drive Electronics, the second generation of IDE) drives, these devices are the least expensive type (current prices hover around $200 for 20 GB and up), offering high capacity at a low cost. An excellent value, they provide moderate to very good performance.

SCSI. Die-hard Mac fanatics are already familiar with the many faces of SCSI (pronounced *scuzzy,* even though it isn't). The most significant advantage SCSI drives have over ATA drives is performance, but you may not notice if you use your Mac for commonplace tasks like Web browsing or word processing. The key to SCSI's performance is throughput (something we cover in more depth below).

Realistically, you should invest in a SCSI drive if you crave maximum performance. These drives are almost a necessity for digital-audio and video editing, 3D rendering, and other disk-intensive applications. Performance comes at a price, as always, so expect these drives to cost roughly $200 more than more-economical IDE drives with identical capacities. You might also have to add a PCI SCSI card, which ups the price a bit more.

ATA and IDE: Simple but Limited (KD)

Apple introduced its first ATA drive on a Mac in 1994. ATA (AT Attachment; the "AT" is a vestige from the early PC days) and IDE (Integrated Drive Electronics) are interchangeable terms. The first ATA drives, though plentiful and inexpensive, were slower than the SCSI drives Apple had been using. However, newer generations of ATA are substantially faster.

ATA is cheaper because it integrates the controller onto the disk drive itself. PC (meaning non-Mac) manufacturers adopted this cost-efficient technology early on in the development of the personal computer. Since parts always cost less when a vendor can make many simultaneously, ATA drive prices kept falling as the technology became more popular. You can now buy an ATA drive for $100 less than a SCSI drive with the same rotation speed and capacity.

ATA comes in different types. The first version of ATA supported one or two hard drives on a 16-bit interface. ATA-2, also known as Fast ATA or Enhanced IDE (EIDE), is faster and supports ATAPI, a protocol for attaching CD-ROM, Zip, tape, and other non-hard drives. Ultra-ATA, also called Ultra-DMA, ATA/33, or DMA-33, supports multiword DMA and can transfer data at as fast as 33 MBps. (A "word" is 2 bytes, so a single-word DMA moves data a word at a time. Multiword DMA moves data in bursts.) ATA/66 doubles ATA's throughput to 66 MBps. Apple currently includes ATA/66 in its latest systems. Although the specifications for a 100 MBps version of ATA are not final, ATA/100 drives and chips are on the market, and it is only a matter of time before Apple incorporates them into new Macs.

continues on next page

ATA and IDE: Simple but Limited *continued*

Although originally designed as a simple way to install a single hard drive in a computer, ATA currently supports as many as four devices—a master and a slave on each of two ATA channels. The master drive doesn't actually dominate the slave drive; these are simply distinguishing names. The first Mac to allow slave drives was the beige Power Macintosh G3 with the second motherboard revision. The simplest way to find out if you can add a slave drive to your beige G3 is to run the Apple System Profiler. If the ATI graphics chip on your motherboard is an ATI Rage Pro chip, not a plain ATI Rage, you can add a slave drive.

Adding a second internal ATA drive is a fabulous way to increase your storage for a reasonable price. A Power Macintosh typically comes with the hard drive on the first channel and the CD-ROM drive on the second. You can use the Apple System Profiler to check how many ATA or ATAPI devices you already have. You should add the second drive to the same channel as the first drive. Set your startup drive as the master and the second drive as the slave by changing their jumper connections. Often the drive has a small diagram showing you the proper jumper settings. If not, consult the drive manufacturer's Web site. Once you've set the jumpers properly, you can connect them in any order.

When it comes to ATA drives, Mac users needn't feel PC envy—practically every current ATA hard drive is Macintosh compatible. You can purchase a drive at outlets ranging from Costco to an online retailer such as Outpost.com (www.outpost.com). Like SCSI, ATA is backward and forward compatible, meaning you can put an ATA/33 or ATA/100 drive on your ATA/66 bus. Once you've added a new drive, use Apple's Drive Setup in the Utilities folder to format it. For more tips on installing an ATA drive, check the Macworld Web site (www. macworld.com) or Accelerate Your Mac (www.xlr8yourmac.com).

Unless you decide to add an internal hard drive or replace your CD-ROM drive, you may never have to worry about your ATA bus at all. All of the drive utilities (with the exception of RAID software) work the same way with ATA and SCSI drives. ATA is a convenient, straightforward technology for use inside your computer, but for external connectivity, FireWire, USB, or even SCSI is a better choice.

SCSI: Gone but Not Forgotten (KD)

In 1986, when Apple built SCSI into the Mac Plus, it was a revelation in connectivity. SCSI was the first easy way to connect multiple devices such as hard drives, scanners, or printers to a computer. However, as peripherals became faster and more plentiful, SCSI aged less than gracefully. Since 1999 Apple has been abandoning the familiar SCSI DB-25 connector. In its place are USB and FireWire connectors for external devices and ATA for internal drives.

Although Apple had good reasons to forgo SCSI, reasons remain for considering it. Anyone with an older computer can continue to use this handy connection option. Those who have recently purchased a newer system may want to preserve their investment in SCSI devices. Last, the latest versions of SCSI, though expensive, are blindingly fast.

continues on next page

SCSI: Gone but Not Forgotten *continued*

People often refer to configuring SCSI as black art or voodoo. Don't let them scare you; the basic rules are simple. However, the more devices you add to your SCSI chain, the more likely you are to encounter troubles with termination and cable length.

Each SCSI device must have a unique SCSI ID between 0 and 6. Most external devices provide a simple dial or wheel to set the ID. On an internal drive, you use jumpers the size of a grain of rice. On older systems—made before Apple switched to ATA for internal devices—both internal and external SCSI devices use the same SCSI bus, with the internal hard disk set to ID 0 and the internal CD-ROM to ID 3.

Rules of SCSI Termination

You must terminate the first and last devices on a SCSI bus. Termination stops the electrical data signal when it gets to the end of the SCSI chain, thus preventing it from reflecting back across the bus and causing data errors.

If the first device on the Macintosh is an internal hard disk, you must terminate that device. Apple installs internal drives with termination.

SCSI also has restrictive cable rules. The faster the type of SCSI, the shorter the allowed cable lengths. SCSI I, the type of SCSI on the back of the Macintosh, transfers data at a maximum 5 MBps and allows as much as 18 feet of cable. However, the more modern Ultra SCSI—which supports 20 MBps—allows a total cable length of just 3 feet.

SCSI comes in two major types, Narrow and Wide, which describe both the bus and the type of device. Wide is double the speed of standard SCSI and uses denser cables and connectors. Wide also allows as many as 15 devices. The fastest flavor of SCSI is Wide Low Voltage Differential Ultra 3, which can move data at a blazing 160 MBps. That translates into 1,280 Mbps, making FireWire's 400 Mbps look pokey. Before you get dizzy at the thought of all that speed, remember that you can only use it if you have peripherals that also go 160 MBps.

As SCSI has gone through many generations, it has managed to remain backward and forward compatible. You can put an old, slow device on the newest SCSI card. Likewise, you can connect a new device to your old Mac. Although you won't get optimum speed if you mix generations, this compatibility does preserve your investment in peripherals. One exception—don't hook up a Wide device to a Narrow card.

If you have an older computer with built-in SCSI, you may not want to invest in new SCSI devices. The SCSI on the back of your Mac transfers data at 5 MBps, much slower than FireWire or current SCSI. Also, when you do buy a newer system, you will have difficulty moving over your SCSI devices. A better idea is to buy a PCI FireWire card for less than $100 and then get the latest FireWire devices.

continues on next page

SCSI: Gone but Not Forgotten *continued*

SCSI Cards

If you own a desktop Mac such as a Power Mac G3 or G4, you've got lots of room for PCI-card expansion, including a high-speed SCSI card (sometimes known as a SCSI adapter). SCSI cards fill the void Apple left when it abandoned SCSI as its standard drive interface in favor of low-cost IDE drives.

In the last few years, Apple has made SCSI cards an option on many of its G3 and G4 models. But if you weren't lucky enough to get one when you bought your Mac, you can easily add it later. Adaptec (www.adaptec.com), ATTO Technology (www.attotech.com), and other third-party manufacturers offer SCSI cards with transfer rates as fast as 160 MBps.

FireWire. Also known as IEEE 1394, FireWire is capable of moving data at 400 Mbps, but realistically most of today's drives can't deliver this kind of performance. FireWire drives plug into the external FireWire port (although some Power Mac G4 models offer an internal port as well). High-capacity drives start around 20 GB and increase from there.

You can hot-swap FireWire drives—that is, unplug or plug them in while the Mac is running—and they don't involve the hassles of ID, termination, and limited cable lengths. FireWire drives offer decent performance, are supereasy to hook up and use, and are available at modest prices.

USB. This is currently the slowest method of moving your data, but it may be your only option if you own an early iBook or iMac with a USB port. Most USB hard drives can move data at a top speed of just 1.5 MBps, which is very slow when you compare it with any of the other technologies we've described. But USB drives offer some real benefits. For one thing, they tend to cost less than any other type of external drive, and like FireWire they are extremely easy to hook up and use. A new USB specification (USB 2.0 or Hi-Speed USB) promises to push performance up to 480 Mbps (60 MBps).

Capacity. After figuring out how your new hard disk will connect to your Mac, you should next think about *capacity*—the amount of storage space you need for current data and free space you require for future expansion. First and foremost, purchase the largest-capacity drive you can afford, especially if you work with graphics, databases, and video or sound files. Buying a hard disk with more space than you currently need is a good idea, since your requirements will keep expanding.

When looking at the capacity of a new hard disk, keep in mind that some areas of the disk contain directories and other data, so you never get to use the drive's entire capacity. It's not uncommon to lose about 5 percent of the total capacity on an initialized (formatted) drive.

FireWire: Setting the Macintosh Ablaze (KD)

Apple has pushed SCSI out of the nest in favor of FireWire. This standard has a lot going for it, including speed and ease of use. Many computer companies agree with Apple—it has become very common on the PC side as well.

Although this Apple-developed technology was adopted as a standard in 1995, Apple didn't include FireWire on a Macintosh until January 1999. The first Macintosh with FireWire was the Blue-and-White Power Macintosh G3. Apple has included FireWire on subsequent Power Macintoshes, as well as the iMac DV, iBook (FireWire), and the second-generation PowerBook G3. You can add FireWire to older Macs by installing a PCI card or PC Card.

FireWire cabling is simple and hot swappable. The cables are thin and come in more-generous lengths than SCSI ones. FireWire also frees you from termination and setting IDs. FireWire is much faster than USB, which operates at only 12 Mbps—FireWire operates at 400 Mbps. If that isn't fast enough for you, 800 and 1,600 Mbps versions of FireWire are on the drawing board.

The maximum cable length between devices is 4.5 meters; from the computer to the last device the limit is a whopping 72 meters. Although FireWire supports 63 devices, it will only connect 16 devices or hubs in a row. You can reach 63 devices by adding hubs. For example, after connecting 14 devices in a row, you could add a 5-port hub, putting all devices connected to that hub just 16 hops from the computer. FireWire also provides limited power—as much as 60 watts—over the cable. Low-power devices, such as small hard drives, don't need an external power source.

FireWire particularly suits consumer-oriented digital products, including digital camcorders, because it provides both high-bandwidth and isochronous transfers. When you copy a file to a hard drive, you probably won't notice if the transfer pauses for half a second. However, if your favorite song stops for this long, it's infuriating. Isochronous transfers guarantee that a stream of data will get a certain amount of bandwidth, so that the stream won't get interrupted.

Today you can buy FireWire hard drives, scanners, printers, camcorders, and CD-R drives. However, many of these devices contain a bridge chip that translates from the device's native interface—for instance, IDE—to the FireWire interface. This extra bit of electronics means that you pay a modest premium for FireWire devices and that they may not deliver their maximum performance.

The FireWire specifications include peer-to-peer connections, which offer the potential for a slew of convenient and powerful features. Someday soon, you may be able to connect a FireWire camcorder to a FireWire hard drive and start a download—without a CPU. You can use FireWire in place of Ethernet to connect computers to each other or to a shared peripheral. Indeed, FireWire may be the home-electronics connection of the future, connecting your stereo, TV, DVD player, and game console.

So What's ATAPI?

Earlier we mentioned the Apple System Profiler as an important tool, useful for identifying the type of hard drive you have installed. If you had an opportunity to look at the information provided, you may have noticed that it lists your CD-ROM, DVD-RAM, and even DVD-ROM drives as ATAPI (AT Attachment Packet Interface) devices.

ATAPI is a low-cost interface that relies on an ATA connection and almost exclusively serves removable-media drives. The basic facts are as follows: You can have just one ATAPI device in your Mac, and in most cases it is a CD-ROM, DVD-RAM, DVD-ROM, or Zip drive. Drives that use ATAPI are typically inexpensive and require internal installation.

Sizes and shapes (HN, JC). Two physical dimensions commonly categorize drives: the diameter of the platters inside and the height of the whole sealed mechanism. Known as the *form factor,* these dimensions constitute the standard sizes that make units from different manufacturers interchangeable.

There are five form factors: full height, 5.25-inch diameter; half height, 5.25-inch diameter; half height, 3.5-inch diameter; low profile, 3.5-inch diameter; and low profile, 2.5-inch diameter.

Most modern hard disks are 3.5-inch low-profile models only 1 inch high; you'll find these inside almost every desktop Mac from the SE/30 to the Cube and beyond. The 2.5-inch drives are installed inside PowerBooks and iBooks. Removable drives such as CD-ROM and DVD-ROM are half-height 5.25-inch devices.

Drive performance (HN). There's no single index for measuring hard-disk performance. If you care about maximum speed, pay attention to several variables and weigh them differently depending on your Mac and what you plan to do with it.

The simplest variables are the *average seek time* and the *average access time,* both measured in milliseconds (ms). The average seek time is how long it takes the heads to move to the desired track; nowadays, it can be anywhere between 3 and 12 ms, depending on the type of drive interface (SCSI or ATA). The average access time is the sum of that figure plus an additional, smaller amount (normally about 2 to 3 ms) for *latency,* the average wait for the desired sector to come around under the heads once they get to the right track. Unfortunately, many vendors use these terms inconsistently; some will even tell you they mean the same thing. If milliseconds matter to you, make sure you're using the same standard when comparing products. A drive with an average *access* time of 15 ms is actually faster than one with an average *seek* time of 12 ms.

Throughput or transfer rate. *Data transfer rate* is a measure of how fast a drive can deliver data to the Mac once it gets to the sectors it's looking for. The transfer rate is counted in megabytes per second (or sometimes, just to confuse things, megabits per second). Today's drives have transfer rates from 5 all the way up to 320 MBps. This figure depends on the interface—ATA or SCSI, for example.

If you deal mostly with small files like word-processing documents, transfer rate is less important than seek or access time, because your drive will spend more time getting to the data you need than transferring it to the Mac. When you open a letter created in Word, your Mac doesn't have to read large amounts of data, so even large differences in the transfer rate have negligible consequences. But if you work with large scanned images in Adobe Photoshop or with big QuarkXPress layouts or giant QuickTime files, transfers actually take whole seconds, so differences in the transfer rate matter—in terms of seek or access time, you won't encounter differences of more than a few thousandths of a second.

There's also a difference between *burst transfer rates* and *sustained transfer rates*. The former measures how fast a drive can pump out a small amount of data loaded into memory buffers on the drive controller; the latter is how fast it can deliver larger amounts even after the buffers are empty. Burst rates are much higher, so some vendors focus on those, but for most purposes the sustained rate is more important because it is a better indicator of real-world performance.

Spindle speed. The standard spindle speed—the rate at which a hard disk's platters rotate—used to be 5,400 rpm. In the last few years drive manufacturers have been delivering drives that spin at 7,200, 10,000, even 15,000 rpm. The extra speed reduces latency, but its main benefit is to boost sustained transfer rates: The faster the disks are spinning, the faster the drive should read in all the data it's after. You'll notice the difference mainly with big files.

Reliability. Drive manufacturers measure the durability of their drives in terms of *mean time between failures* (MTBF)—the number of average power-on hours a drive will last before some component gives out. For most new drives the figure runs from about 500,000 hours to 1.2 million hours.

However, 500,000 hours works out to 57 years and 1.2 million hours adds up to 137 years, so these claims are not based on actual field experience—lab testers derive them by running a bunch of drives simultaneously and extrapolating from the rate of breakdown during the test period.

Still, MTBF probably means something, at least as an indicator of relative reliability, so it's worth considering when you are choosing a product. But try to supplement this rating with reviews in Mac publications and first-hand reports from users.

Warranty. The length of time a drive remains under warranty is an extremely important consideration. Expect a warranty period of at least one year for most drives and as long as five years for some.

Should the drive mechanism or any components inside an external case fail (the power supply, fan, and so forth), the vendor will typically replace the drive at no charge. It will not, however, cover the cost to recover or re-create any data lost as a result of a drive failure, so back up your hard drive *religiously.*

Disk Images: So Real, You Just Click (SA)

Disk images often serve as the medium of transfer for software downloads from Web sites: You obtain the disk image, put it on a floppy or mount it as a virtual floppy, and access the information.

The Disk Copy utility that comes with your system software creates and later interprets all disk images. The file Disk Copy makes and interprets is called a *disk image file.* Its icon looks like a document (it has a turned-down corner) with an image of a floppy icon on it. Disk Copy can also make disk images of floppy disks and CD-ROMs.

Backup Devices and Removable Storage

We hadn't even invented computers when Murphy's Law (anything that can go wrong, will go wrong) became a popular adage. Nevertheless, it rings doubly true in the case of computer technology. Always be prepared for the worst to happen, and *protect your data.*

To avoid running smack into disaster, follow this simple rule of thumb: Whenever you use your Macintosh, back up your critical data. This is especially urgent if you rely on your computer for business purposes. The time involved in backing up seems minuscule when you consider the hours of frustration and effort that reinputting or re-creating the data would involve.

Back Up, Back Up, Back Up!

Hard disks are mechanical devices that can only operate for a certain amount of time before they break down. There is no early-warning system when a hard disk fails, so to protect yourself from losing everything you've ever created on your computer, you've got to back up.

What to back up. Backing up creates a copy of your critical files on a completely separate storage device or media. That means your data resides somewhere else in addition to your hard disk.

Once you commit to performing backups, you need to decide what you will back up. Your ultimate goal is to be able to restore your data effortlessly in the event of a hard-drive crash so you can get on with your work. You can focus selectively on your most important files, or you can pick the safest route, which is to back up the entire drive—applications, System Folder, and all.

Tailor backups to your needs. Your basic backup can be as simple as copying a handful of critical files to a floppy disk or other storage device. But that won't take care of the rest of your data and other information, such as preferences and settings, e-mail, and Internet Bookmarks or Favorites. You can always reinstall applications from their CDs, but you could miss an awful lot if you simply grab a few essential files. To be brutally honest, you should invest in a backup device and software if you can afford them—that will make your backup tasks easier and more efficient.

Use multiple media. Another adage—"Don't put all your eggs into one basket"—holds a lot of truth when it comes to backing up. Don't put your data on just one cartridge, floppy disk, CD-RW, or whatever. After all, what if your backup disk gets mangled, stolen, or destroyed? When you buy your backup device, make sure you have plenty of disks, tapes, and so forth, because you'll want multiple copies of your important data, and it may consume several disks or tapes.

Configure and schedule. The first time you connect your backup device, you'll need to take it out for a spin. Hook it up, peruse the manual, and get acquainted with it. Run some test backups to ensure that things are working properly.

The same goes for your backup software. Learn how to schedule backups so they won't interrupt your work flow. A good time is right after you stop work. Do you leave your office at 5 p.m. every day? Set up your backup to run automatically at 5:15 p.m. All you have to do is configure the program and make sure media is available.

If your backup software has a verification option, make sure it is turned on. That way the software will check every file it has backed up against the original to make sure the copy is accurate. This can double the time required to complete a backup, but it's worth it.

Rotate your media. Earlier we mentioned that you should have your data on multiple pieces of media. Now we'll explain why. You're going to create *incremental* backups. Some backups will encompass only the files you've created or modified since the last full (and time-consuming) backup. For this purpose (among others), a good backup utility makes life much simpler.

Basically, you should change your backup media every day so you're never more than one day from your last backup. If your hard disk crashed right now, you could restore from the backup you did yesterday, the day before, or even the day before that, if need be. However diligently you make your incremental backups, it's still a good idea to do a full backup from time to time.

Store your backups offsite. OK, so you've been good about backing up, but there is one thing you may not have thought of—the destruction or theft of your computer and all the data it holds. For this reason, *always* keep a backup someplace outside your office. When you leave at day's end, take a backup with you. If you work at home, store a backup offsite and replace it frequently. Of course, you should always leave media in your device so it can complete that night's backup.

Check your backups. Your backups need occasional checkups. Don't back up religiously for months, only to discover that the backup device never transferred a single file to your media. Restore a few critical files and make sure they work. You should check your backups every month or so.

Archive old data and applications (SA). You make backups of active files so you can get right back to work if something happens to the originals. But you may want to keep another kind of backup, too: an *archival* backup of inactive files you want to keep it around—just not on your hard drive, where they take up too much room. Archival backups can also offer the advantage of longevity, depending on what media you use—CD-ROMs, for instance, stay viable longer than magnetic-based media such as floppy disks.

When you archive your old data and applications, make multiple copies. Keep a copy in your office for convenience, another at home, and perhaps one more in a safe-deposit box at a bank or elsewhere.

Keep in mind that newer versions of applications and newer hardware may not be able to read or open older files. Most applications can open documents only one or two versions back. When you upgrade to newer versions of the parent application, resave old documents in an updated format and then rearchive them as necessary.

Backup software. The backup process doesn't have to be a tedious, time-consuming thing. A few companies publish software that simplifies the entire backup process by automating when, what, and where you back up. There are several software solutions:

- Dantz Development (www.dantz.com) specializes in backup software—that's all the company does, and it does the job well. For years many tape drives have bundled its **Retrospect Desktop Backup** ($174.95). But Retrospect isn't just for tape—it supports all kinds of devices, including Zip, Jaz, and DVD-R. If you don't want to use a tape drive for backup, Dantz Development's **Retrospect Express Backup** ($49.95) is capable of handling all types of drives and media except tape, so you can save yourself a few dollars. For multiple users on a network, you'll need **Retrospect Workgroup Backup** ($339.95) which supports as many as 20 users.

- Charismac Engineering's Backup Mastery (www.charismac.com) supports practically all SCSI tape drives as well as floppy, optical, Zip, Jaz, and SyQuest media or any mounted volume.

- Intego's **Personal Backup** ($39.95; www.intego.com) and Connectix Corporation's **Copy Agent** ($39; www.connectix.com) are file-syncing programs that offer scheduled copy operations and work with removable media and hard disks. Although these products are handy and easy to use, they don't offer incremental backups.

Choosing Backup Storage

Once a quiet corner of the computer industry, the removable-storage market now changes at a breakneck pace. Over the past several years, some brands familiar to the Mac market departed the scene or were supplanted by new technologies. Instead of facing a desktop littered with floppies, Iomega Zip disks, and removable SCSI-based hard disks, today's Mac user can choose from a growing stack of external storage technologies, including writable and rewritable CD and DVD discs, a new class of portable hard drives, disks, tape drives, and PC Card disks.

There's no easy decision as to which secondary or removable-storage technology to buy. Each format offers a different price, performance, and usability configuration. Compounding the choice are the many popular new applications that can do double duty as backup software—for example, iTunes can store digital audio on writable and rewritable optical discs; iMovie, Final Cut Pro, and iDVD can put digital video on DVD-Recordable and FireWire hard drives; and digital photography and cameras can store images using a variety of media formats.

Each drive offers a varying mix of features—no one removable-storage technology will meet all your storage needs for backup and application support. Another headache for prospective buyers are the weekly announcements of new models and technologies, each claiming to outdo the competition.

Device price tag vs media cost. Before purchasing any removable device, look at the cost of the drive as well as that of its media (calculated in cost per capacity—for example, the price per megabyte or gigabyte). Drives can cost from about $200 to $5,000, with media costs of less than $0.10 per megabyte to $1 per gigabyte. Reconditioned or used products can cost much less.

The relationship of a drive and its removable media resembles that of razors and blades. To gain market share in the storage industry, sometimes manufacturers lower the price (and thereby the profit) for a drive—the razor—knowing that owners will more than make up the difference as they buy the media—the blades—over the drive's lifetime. In addition, vendors who maintain backward compatibility for their products will ensure repeat business at upgrade time.

Media cost becomes critical when you create more than one set of backup media, perhaps daily, weekly, or semimonthly. Keeping data integrity in mind, the safest course of action is to back up daily, with each day receiving its own set of media. How you choose to handle your own backups depends on the volume of data you need to copy and the cost of the media required.

Reliability. Data reliability also factors into a removable drive's overall performance, especially for long-term archival storage of files. For example, on CD-R and CD-RW discs, minute scratches can build up on the thin protective layer that covers their writable dye. Although almost invisible, these tiny cuts can degrade reading accuracy. To avoid this problem, some formats house platters in hard plastic shells, as in superfloppies and the cartridges for removable hard disks.

Media longevity. Industry figures regarding media longevity are based on certain abstract criteria, which may change under real-life conditions—for example, in some situations multiple users or frequent transportation might shorten media life. Magneto-optical and tape media are considered to have a longer shelf life than floppy-based media. The jury appears to be out on the longevity of writable optical media such as CD-R, CD-RW, and DVD formats; certainly some manufacturers' claims of decades and even a century remain unconfirmed.

 Almost all removable media are susceptible to heat damage, especially writable CD and DVD media, whether they're sitting in the car or placed on top of a monitor. You're better off storing archive discs and backup sets in a safe designed specifically for data; safes designed for paper records or money won't do the job—the flash point for paper is 451 degrees Fahrenheit (remember reading *Fahrenheit 451* in English class?), and most media can lose data at temperatures below 150 degrees. Sentry Group (www.sentrysafe.com) offers several models of media vaults and claims its boxes will keep removable media cool in a fire, withstanding temperatures of 1,700 degrees for half an hour. That's about the temperature of my car's interior after a day in a Silicon Valley parking lot.

Convenience. The two keys to removable-media convenience are the availability and capacity of media. Some media, such as CD-R discs, are widely available in consumer stores; most computer stores have Iomega-compatible cartridges. However, other formats such as tape are difficult to come by; you must order them by mail or over the Internet. In either case, make sure you have enough free capacity on hand before beginning a backup operation.

Removable-Storage Technologies

You have a lot of choices when it comes to removable media. Here are the finer points of each type.

CD, CD-R, and CD-RW. Designed more than 20 years ago as a consumer-targeted audio format, the shiny 120 mm, 650 MB CD is now the dominant digital-media format, with a reach even greater than the Internet's. All computers ship with some form of CD-compatible drive, and most desktops—and increasingly often, laptops—come with a writable CD mechanism.

CD technology uses one or more infrared laser beams to read a disc instead of the magnetic heads that read a hard-disk platter. A single spiral track runs from the CD's inner diameter to its outer edge. High and low spots on the reflective layer produce differences in reflectivity that the drive's optical assembly can read. The commercial audio and data media is a mass-produced, stamped sandwich of plastic, with a reflective material and protective coatings.

A single CD can hold roughly 650 MB of data or 74 minutes (up to 80 minutes on some media) of digitized audio. CD drives come in four flavors: CD-ROM (Compact Disc–Read-Only Memory); CD-R (Compact Disc–Recordable); CD-DA (Compact Disc–Digital Audio); and CD-RW (Compact Disc–Rewritable).

In the early 1990s, vendors offered the first recordable CD-ROM drives. With the write-once CD-R discs, a high-intensity laser beam burns tiny pits in a photoreactive dye that emulates the high and low areas of the stamped discs. The initial models were expensive ($4,000 to $5,000) and slow, but the technology quickly moved into the consumer arena. CD-R drives today range from $200 to $400.

More common now are CD-RW drives, which can use special rewritable media as well as burn CD-R discs. The reusable media is more expensive, perhaps $3 each, versus less than $1 for a CD-R disc. Instead of a dye, the rewritable media uses a *phase-change* layer whose crystalline structure is altered when heated by the laser. Reheating returns the material to its original state—but for a limited number of times, perhaps a thousand cycles. Since the phase-change material is less reflective than CD-R media's, only compatible drives can read CD-RW media, so some older drives may have problems reading the discs.

Figuring out the performance factor of CD-RW drives can be confusing. Usually, vendors cryptically express the speed in a set of three numbers separated by an *X,* as in 16X10X40X. The numbers correspond to recording, rewriting, and reading speeds, respectively. The meaning of the *X* comes from prehistory; it's based on the first CD-ROM players, which had a data-transfer rate of 150 KBps. So a 4X drive is supposedly four times faster than that prototypical player. These ratings don't guarantee a certain level of performance, since other factors, such as the software, data bus, and hard drive, influence the total recording time. Of course, faster drives cost more.

CD-RW drives now come in a wide variety of sizes, colors, and interfaces, including FireWire, USB, or both. In 2001 several vendors released new low-power models that draw their power from the FireWire bus.

The benefits of CD-R and CD-RW are evident: You can use these inexpensive, ubiquitous drives and media for backup and iTune audio compilations. CD-R discs are readily available in most consumer-targeted music shops, a real boon when you need a blank disc late at night or on a weekend.

What's not to like? CD-R and CD-RW face some capacity constraints compared with today's enormous hard drives, and this makes backing up a 60 GB drive a time-consuming process. Although users assume almost flawless compatibility with all devices when it comes to manufactured CD audio and data discs, it's a different story for home-brewed discs and drives. And as mentioned above, the discs are susceptible to damage.

 Time for spring cleaning: When a CD-R or CD-RW disc suddenly becomes unreadable, the culprit may not be the media. Dust sometimes builds up on the drive's lens; you can easily remove it with a CD-cleaning kit.

Toasting Your Own CDs

When you invest in a CD-R or CD-RW drive, you get some CD-creation software along with it. Roxio's **Toast** software (www.roxio.com) comes bundled with many drives. You can also upgrade to the **Toast Titanium** version ($89.95), which includes some nice extras that let you turn digital photos into video slide shows, burn iMovies onto Video CDs playable on most DVD players, and print custom labels and cases for your new CDs.

Charismac Engineering's **Discribe** ($74.96; www.charismac.com) allows you to write CDs in a couple of clicks. The company offers a free demo of the program on its Web site, and if you own a competing product you can upgrade for as little as $40.

In conjunction with Apple's iTunes, the **Disc Burner** program is a no-frills utility that works with built-in CD-RW drives as well as some third-party ones. If you're running Mac OS 9.1 and later, take a peek inside your Utilities folder and see if it's installed. If not, you can download it free from Apple's site (http://asu.info.apple.com).

Mac OS X has a Burn Disc command on its Edit menu, and you can add a Burn icon to the toolbar.

DVD drives. Life in the optical-storage business is seldom easy, and that's the case when it comes to DVD technologies. A trio of consortiums is facing off with competing formats for recordable DVD: DVD-R (Digital Versatile Disc–Recordable), DVD-RAM (Digital Versatile Disc–Random-Access Memory), and DVD-RW (Digital Versatile Disc–Rewritable). In the past, each format offered different capacity points on the familiar 120 mm disc, but now all have settled on 4.7 GB per side (DVDs come in single- and double-sided flavors). They are mostly incompatible with each other.

Exciting news for DVD-R occurred in early 2001 when Apple added a SuperDrive to the high-end Power Mac G4. Manufactured by Pioneer (the mechanism is called the DVR-A03 DVD/CD), the technology is based on a cyanine dye similar to the one used in CD-R and writes DVD-Video and DVD-ROM formats as well as CD-RW discs. Several vendors announced summer releases for FireWire versions sporting a price tag of about $1,000. A pack of five discs costs $50.

A consortium including Hitachi and Matsushita/Panasonic supports the DVD-RAM standard, which uses a rewritable phase-change technology. Earlier versions of the drive only supported capacities of 2.6 GB, but it joined the 4.7 GB camp in its second-generation model. DVD-RAM drives can't write DVD-R discs yet—the manufacturer announced a future mechanism that also supports DVD-R—and most DVD drives can't read DVD-RAM discs. DVD-RAM does offer a data-integrity bonus, however, by letting users choose between bare discs and media housed in cartridges. Offered by a growing number of vendors in the Mac market, the drives cost less than $500 and are available in both SCSI and FireWire models; the single- and dual-sided discs cost about $30 and $55, respectively.

For more than three years, a consortium including Hewlett-Packard, Philips, and Sony have talked up a DVD+RW rewritable format (an older DVD standard got there first with the DVD-RW name, hence the plus sign). The group said it expects to ship a drive this year, but it has told a similar story in previous years. In addition to handling the rewritable DVD+RW discs, the drives will be able to write DVD-R and CD-RW media. Current DVD-ROM drives, as well as the competing DVD-R and DVD-RAM drives, won't read DVD+RW discs.

Do You DVD?

Apple's high-end Power Mac G4s come with a drive capable of recording DVD video. The built-in SuperDrive, in conjunction with Apple's included iDVD software, allows you to create DVDs that most consumer DVD players will accept. Just edit your masterpiece, burn the DVD, and share it with friends and family. As an added bonus, you can also burn CD-RW discs.

Super-Duper SuperDrive

Everything in storage is super, if you believe the vendors. Apple used its SuperDrive branding once before for an early floppy drive that appeared in the Mac Plus.

Imation owns the SuperDisk (that's a sexier name for its defunct LS-120 drive). And don't forget that Apple introduced the Mac at the Super Bowl!

Writable and rewritable DVD drives show plenty of promise, with high capacity and performance. Owners can easily transfer the experience they've gained with these drives' CD cousins, and DVD-RAM discs mount on the desktop just like hard drives. The discs offer high capacity and let users author their own DVD-Video titles.

The price tag of the stand-alone drives may put off all but the early adopter, however, and other customers may be concerned with the format questions hanging over the technology. In addition, at this time you can't use DVD-R discs as the source for DVD-Video or DVD-ROM production. But there's little doubt that the SuperDrive and DVD-RAM drives have pretty, er, *super* possibilities.

Removable cartridge drives. Removable cartridge drives have been a longtime favorite of Mac users, since the days of the Mac Plus. First popularized by the SyQuest 44 MB drive, the technology delivers speedy, high-capacity storage along with robust removable media.

Currently Iomega (www.iomega.com) is trying to reinvigorate this category, which has suffered from the wave of portable FireWire drives. In the summer of 2001 Iomega shipped the **Peerless,** a FireWire removable-storage system with high-capacity hard-drive media in 10 GB and 20 GB capacities.

Peerless cartridges come sealed, holding both the platters and the read-write heads. A base station contains the electronics and a FireWire port powers the unit. The drives provide sustained data-transfer rates of up to 12 MBps. Previous hard-disk cartridges were open because the drive contained the head assemblies—only the platters were portable. Of course, in a portable hard drive, everything goes along for the ride.

The shipping contenders in the category are Castlewood Systems' 2.2 GB **Orb** ($149.95–$199.95; www.castlewood.com) and Iomega's 2 GB **Jaz** drive (external, $349.95; internal, $274.95). Both drives use 3.5-inch cartridges. According to the specifications, the Orb edges out the Jaz in performance, with sustained data-transfer rates of 12 and 8.7 GBps, respectively.

Several third-party vendors now offer FireWire versions of the Orb. Iomega uses a proprietary connector on its drive, letting users choose between FireWire, USB, and SCSI adapters.

The specs for Iomega's Peerless sound great, but it's an untested technology. It remains to be seen whether the cartridges will prove more robust than a comparable portable FireWire hard drive. As for the others, while removable hard-disk cartridges are faster and offer higher capacities than CD-R and CD-RW, FireWire drives now dominate the market in terms of high-speed portable storage and top capacity. And 2 GB is less than half what a DVD-RAM disc holds.

The Dead SyQuest Scrolls

Not very long ago, SyQuest Technology was a leading manufacturer of removable storage devices. But hard times rolled around and the company was forced to declare bankruptcy. In an effort to pay off creditors, it sold its assets to its biggest competitor—Iomega Corporation. SyQuest no longer owns its trademark name and no longer manufactures drives.

Iomega has stated that it has no intention of manufacturing SyQuest drives or cartridges but will offer support for existing customers through the SyQuest Web site at www.syquest.com. You can still purchase cartridges and replace your drive when it goes belly up. In addition, you can get your drive repaired via www.syquestrepair.com, and you'll find help in resolving problems through a public message board at www.syquestsupport.com.

Zip drives and superfloppies. High-capacity floppy technologies incorporate hard-disk read-write heads with floppy-based media. Although this is not a new technology, the drives were popular for years in the Mac market. With a large installed base of drives still connected to machines, the formats are still useful for sneakernet and casual backup.

The most familiar name in the category is Iomega's **Zip,** now offered in two versions: the original 100 MB classic cartridge ($69.95–$149.95) and an updated 250 MB format ($149.95–$199.95). While the 250 delivers backward compatibility by reading 100 MB cartridges, don't look for it to win any speed contests. Both models come with USB interfaces; the higher-speed drive is also available in SCSI.

Zip drives are probably the most popular removable drives on the planet. You can walk into almost any print or copy shop and find a Zip drive at every station.

You may see advertisements and editorial for Imation's **SuperDisk** (www.imation.com), also called the LS-120. This drive can read and write PC and Mac 1.4 MB floppy disks as well as a special 120 MB floppy. However, with the cutbacks in the technical sector, Imation discontinued the product. No buyer for the technology had come forward as of this writing.

Zip-to-Go

In the past Iomega's Zip drives came with hefty power cubes you plugged into a wall outlet. But with their 250 USB-powered **Zip** drive ($179.95) you get an ultra-slim design that lends itself to portability. Since it's USB-powered, it needs no external power and no power cube. Its increased capacity of 250 MB and backward compatibility with 100 MB disk make it an excellent choice for Zip drive fans.

Tape drives. When backing up files, Mac owners have traditionally eschewed tape for spinning storage, such as removable hard drives and writable CD formats. In spite of this history—and in the face of a quickly growing amount of data requiring backup and archiving—users are taking a closer look at the venerable tape-drive technology.

Tape drives involve a lot of confusing terminology—everything has an acronym and nobody seems to remember what the letters stand for. And the (albeit helpful) practice of offering support for older formats means that many acronyms include a Roman numeral or a plus sign (+).

The primary tape technologies now offered in the Mac market are AIT+ and AIT II (Advanced Intelligent Tape), an 8 mm format; DAT (Digital Audio Tape) drives, which use 4 mm DDS-3 and DDS-4 (Digital Data Storage) formats; DLT (Digital Linear Tape), a pricey high-capacity format from Quantum (www.quantum.com); DPF (Discreet Packet Format), a new technology from Ecrix (www.ecrix.com); and the Travan linear tape format. Each format is incompatible with the others.

Tape drives are designed for backup and require an intermediary program such as Retrospect, which often comes bundled with them. Capacities also vary—most tape drives offer firmware compression, which doubles the native capacity of each tape. Speeds can also vary depending on the type of data and the number of files you're recording.

AIT+ drives offer a native capacity of 35 GB and a backup data-transfer rate of 4 MBps with compression. The costlier AIT II drive supports a 50 to 100 GB capacity per cartridge. AIT cartridges have a small chip that keeps track of the index for faster file access.

DAT drives offer a native capacity of 12 GB per DDS-3 cartridge, with a backup speed of about 2 GBps. The newer $1,200 DDS-4 models with an LVD SVSI interface have a 20 GB native capacity.

The expensive DLT usually gets sold to the server market; however, this format is currently required for transporting DVD images to production houses. The latest DLT 8000 mechanism, also called Super DLT, features tapes that sport a native 40 GB capacity, providing a 6 MBps backup rate.

Ecrix's DPF is more commonly known by its drive name, the VXA-1. The cartridges, dubbed VXAtape, have a 33 GB native capacity, and the drive provides a backup rate of 3 MBps.

The new Travan format offers a 20 GB native capacity with a speed of 1 MBps.

You may see articles and marketing for OnStream's Echo 30 drive. At this writing the company is bankrupt, so you should look elsewhere for your storage needs.

If your data collection is growing, consider a tape drive, especially for digital-video projects. You can use tape only for backup, however, and its media isn't readily available.

Floppy disks. Floppy disks (also called *disks* or *floppies*) are one of the oldest storage media for personal computers; today's generation of Macs has made them an anachronism. When USB arrived on the Mac in 1998, it relegated the built-in floppy drive to the realm of external peripherals. Floppies have a hard plastic exterior, but the encased media is made of a soft, flexible coated plastic.

To answer the demand for third-party floppy drives, many storage venders are offering USB floppy drives for just under $100. VST's version (www. vsttech.com), which comes in all the iMac colors, includes five snap-on panels so you can make it match whatever Mac you own. Teac (www.teac.com) has also joined the fray with its USB drive, available in Graphite and Blueberry. Imation's USB floppy drive comes in Ice-and-Blue and gets power from the USB port. Most of the drives derive their power from USB, so you won't need a power adapter.

Early Macs could use 400 Kbyte and 800 Kbyte disks; in 1988 Apple introduced the SuperDrive (not to be confused with the Apple DVD-R drive), which added a 1.4 MB Mac format as well as support for 720 Kbyte or 1.4 MB disks formatted for PCs. Mac OS 8.1 orphaned the 400 Kbyte format, and the only Mac formats current USB drives can read and write are 1.4 MB disks.

Although short on capacity, floppies are still the easiest method of moving a few small files between Macs or even PCs—most of which still *do* have a floppy drive. To make a floppy PC compatible, use the Erase Disk command to format the disk in the DOS 1.4 MB format.

 There's some debate over Mac OS 9 and higher support for 800 Kbyte floppies, since no USB drive currently supports the format. The 800 Kbyte capability required a multispeed mechanism that's no longer produced. Owners with data on floppy disks should find an older Mac with a built-in floppy drive and migrate the data to a more modern format.

Digital film. Odds are pretty good that if you own a digital camera, you may already have either a CompactFlash or a SmartMedia card. These tiny solid-state storage cards can store your camera's images.

Although you may initially consider only memory-card formats for these applications, vendors have also developed rotating memory—little hard drives and superfloppies. Some have capacities and price points appropriate for casual backup. Most of this type of storage requires a reader or dock to connect with your computer.

IBM (www.storage.ibm.com) offers the **MicroDrive** in 340 MB, 512 MB, and 1 GB capacities ($199–$379). The disks fit into a PC Card holder.

DataPlay is a forthcoming format from Imation with a 500 MB disk that is just a smidgen larger than a quarter. Due to ship in late 2001, the drive will cost about $300 with adapters for CompactFlash and SmartMedia interfaces.

Iomega rebranded Clik. Now dubbed **PocketZip,** the small cartridge holds 40 MB ($49.95).

The Q Factor

Storage devices continue to evolve in remarkable ways. One area that is getting more attention is solid-state technology. Agaté Technologies (www.agatetech.com) has introduced a device it calls the Q USB hard drive. But unlike a hard drive it contains no moving parts. It plugs directly into your Mac's USB port, mounts its icon on your desktop, and acts like any other storage device.

What makes this device so appealing is its size. It fits on your keychain! Currently available in 16, 32, 64, and 128 MB capacities, the Q is the ultimate backup device for PowerBook and iBook owners when they're on the road.

Magneto-optical (HN, DM) Also known as MO, these drives read and write data to 3.5-inch or 5.25-inch removable discs enclosed in a hard plastic case. The media inside consists of a rigid plastic or glass substrate coated by several kinds of metallic alloy in layers. One of the characteristics of the coating is that its polarity can change only at very high temperatures. When you write data to a magneto-optical disc, a laser heats a tiny spot on the media to about 300 degrees Fahrenheit, at which point an electromagnet located underneath that spot can change its polarity. Areas of the surface with different polarities reflect light differently, and that's how the laser reads the information.

Once touted as the most durable method of storage, magneto-optical drives have struggled to survive in a market dominated by cheaper technology. Still, manufacturers of these devices keep on keepin' on, introducing larger-capacity media every few months and slowly lowering prices to keep up with other types of devices in the removable-storage market.

Fujitsu Computer Products of America (www.fcpa.com) offers its **DynaMO** family of drives in USB, FireWire, and SCSI with capacities of 640 MB and 1.3 GB ($299–$399). The company claims its cartridges are impervious to dust, magnets, moisture, and shock.

With as much as 9.1 GB on a single cartridge, Sony's magneto-optical drives (www.storagebysony.com) lead in capacity.

USB Plus FireWire Equals Flexibility

If all this dialogue about USB and FireWire has your head spinning and you're not sure what kind of drive you should buy, consider a hybrid drive that combines USB and FireWire. These days you can purchase a single external hard drive that features a USB port and a FireWire port. This is the ultimate in convenience if you have multiple Macs and move your data around a lot.

LaCie (www.lacie.com) offers its sleek, compact **PocketDrive** in a 10 to 48 GB capacities ($249–$279), likely to be even higher by the time you read this. The device's small size means you can take it on the road with your PowerBook as well as keep it at home with your Power Mac. Either way, you won't need to mess with an external power adapter when using it with FireWire—this baby gets what it needs right off the bus.

Combining high capacity and portability, VST Technologies sizes things up with its stylish SmartDisk VST USB/FireWire Thin Drive hybrid drive, currently available in sizes ranging from 3 GB to 30 GB ($199.95–$549.95). You can expect to see even greater capacities as the market grows.

6

Printing

Jim Felici (JF) is the chapter editor and coauthor.

Bob Weibel (BW) and Gene Steinberg (GS) are the chapter coauthors.

Sooner or later someone says, "Can you print that out for me?" This means getting what's on your screen out of your Mac and into a printing device of some sort.

The printer slaps some black or colored stuff onto paper or plastic, and there you are.

Whether your "hard copy" looks better or worse than what appears on your Mac screen depends on whether you've chosen the right printer for the job, plugged it in correctly, and set it up with the right software on your Mac.

As you'll see, a printer that does a snazzy job with black-and-white text, for example, may make smudge work out of scanned photos that look just great onscreen. And type that looks lumpy onscreen usually looks better when printed out, even on today's cheap printers.

It's all part of the art and science of WYSIWYG (what you see is what you get), the concept that Macintosh rode in on a decade and a half ago.

In This Chapter

QuickDraw: Type and Graphics Unite! (BW)

Macintosh was the first computer to make it easy and affordable to mix type and graphics onscreen. It did this through system software known as QuickDraw. QuickDraw is actually a computer language that "draws" to the Mac screen, although as you'll see a little later, it can also draw to a printer. In addition to plain ol' QuickDraw, you may hear about QuickDraw 3D, designed to quickly draw three-dimensional scenes onscreen, and QuickTime VR (Virtual Reality), designed to draw interactive panoramic pictures onscreen. In this chapter we'll stick to plain ol' QuickDraw.

The important thing about QuickDraw is that it works as a standard way to get things onscreen. The Mac OS and your applications—word processing, database, graphics, whatever—all use QuickDraw to write to the screen. Things were different in the IBM PC world at the time the Mac made its debut. Most applications—especially graphics—wrote to the screen in their own proprietary manner. And fonts were written to the screen one way and graphics another, so it was tough to get both united on a page. WYSIWYG wasn't even dreamed of on the typical PC desktop. QuickDraw made WYSIWYG a reality.

Digital Printing: By the Dots

QuickDraw and most other computer display and printing systems don't really draw, at least not the way people do, using pencils and pens. Computers draw by laying down rows of tiny dots that end up looking like type, illustrations, and pictures. Your Mac screen, for example, lays down about 72 to 100 rows of dots per inch (dpi). Early Mac printers such as the ImageWriter printed relatively big dots—typically 72 dpi—and you could usually see the individual dots that made up the printed text or graphics. These were called *dot-matrix* printers because they created type characters out of, well, a matrix of dots, instead of working like electric typewriters and daisy-wheel printers. Later, dot-matrix models went to 128 dpi, and the printed image looked smoother but still "computery," because the average human eye can still pick out the separate dots at this resolution. Printouts from such printers weren't considered professional, and businesses specified "no dot-matrix computer printouts, please" when soliciting résumés, reports, or other documents.

The first laser printers—such as Apple's LaserWriter—could create images at 300 dots per inch, fine enough to print fairly good-looking type and graphics from the Mac (**Figure 6.1**). If you looked closely, you'd still see some jagginess in small text and delicate graphics. But 300 dpi was deemed professional, and you could pay professional prices of $2,000 to $5,000 for the privilege of owning a laser printer.

Almost all computer printers these days still use this same dot-matrix concept, from the El Cheapo inkjet printer to the expensive color laser printer. The only difference between them and the old ImageWriters is that the dots these days are so small and close together that you barely notice them.

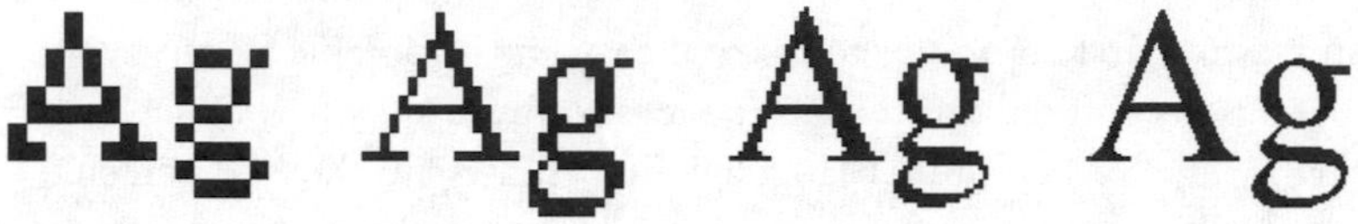

Ag Ag Ag Ag

Figure 6.1

All printer output is made up of dots, and the smaller the dots, the smoother the image. The letters at the left show 12-point type imaged at 75 dpi, as on an ImageWriter. The samples to the right are the same text at 150 dpi, 300 dpi, and 600 dpi.

What Happens When You Hit Print (BW)

Hitting the Print button starts a long chain of events that should (in principle, at least) get your document data out of your Mac and down to a printer. The printer will then pound, blast, bake, or spray the correct dots onto the page, and it'll look great.

But first your application has to gather together the data you've selected to print and then send it to the Mac operating system, which acts as a sort of printing service for all the applications you use.

Let 'Er RIP

But first, back to dots. Somewhere along the line in the printing process, the computer data describing the text and graphics you want to print has to get converted into dots, since most of what you print doesn't start out that way. For example, as you'll read in Chapter 18, "Fonts," TrueType and PostScript printer fonts are composed of mathematical "outline" descriptions of typeface characters. Ditto for graphics from Adobe Illustrator and other draw-type programs (see Chapter 14, "Graphics"): They're mathematical shape data, not dot data.

Something has to convert those curves and outlines—and the "fill" inside the outline—into printer dots. That something is called a *raster image processor* (RIP). *Raster* is simply a technical term for images composed of dots, just like those produced by the dot-matrix printers described above. A TV and Mac display screen, laser printer, and inkjet printer all make images out of dots, so they're all known as raster devices, technically speaking.

A printer RIP may be a separate box connected to a printer, an array of computer chips built inside a printer, or even software running on your computer. But whether the RIP runs as software on a computer or *firmware* inside a printer, it does the same thing: It converts computer data into the raster data—dots—needed to print on a particular printer, from desktop inkjet printer to high-resolution laser imagesetter.

You've already seen that the Mac OS uses QuickDraw to build the images you see onscreen. And you've seen that computer screens build images out of dots, just like printers and TVs. So if you're thinking that QuickDraw must also be a raster image processor, you're right. It can work that way, mainly for inexpensive printers that don't have their own RIPs. Your Mac, using QuickDraw and software called a *driver* from the printer vendor, builds the dot-pattern data that the printer needs to print a page.

PostScript Printing

QuickDraw works as a sort of universal language for writing to the Mac screen, and it helps printers that don't have their own RIPs. But the demands of professional graphics and page design call for a more accurate and versatile universal printing language than QuickDraw. *PostScript* is that language. Developed and licensed by Adobe Systems, PostScript made its first commercial appearance in the Apple LaserWriter back in the mid-1980s.

PostScript is called a *page description language* (PDL), because it can describe everything you'd want on a page, including fancy type and photographic-quality pictures. Any program you use on the Mac can use PostScript to describe the appearance of the pages it creates. PostScript is complex, but fortunately it usually works quietly in the background making high-quality text, line art, and scanned pictures mix together on a page. The original Apple LaserWriter and the PostScript printers that have come on the market since then can read PostScript language data, interpret it, and convert it into the necessary printer dots.

Beyond all the fancy type and graphics, though, the real magic of PostScript is that without any special effort in preparing your pages, you can print them on any PostScript printer—whether color, black and white, laser, inkjet, or imagesetter—and everything on that page will print correctly. The output quality will vary depending on the capabilities of the printer, of course, but everything you put on the page will appear where and as it should. The type will be the same size, so the line endings will be the same, not wrapped differently. Pictures will all appear scaled and rotated the way you intended them.

PostScript's ability to print the same page on a wide variety of printers is called *device independence*. The term means that the data describing the text and graphics has nothing to do with any particular type of printing machine. Instead, the PostScript data stands ready to run on any machine, regardless of make, model, or manufacturer, provided the machine has a PostScript RIP to do the image processing for it.

Device independence is the foundation of what started as desktop publishing but has now, in fact, become publishing, period. Through this innovation, you can create fancy documents on a lowly personal computer screen with PostScript fonts and graphics, and then proof them—with the same fonts and graphics—on a desktop PostScript laser or inkjet printer. You can then also have them printed on high-resolution laser imagesetters—same fonts, same graphics—for magazine or book-quality production. I've had the experience of starting pages on a Mac in QuarkXPress, printing rough drafts on a $900 PostScript laser printer, then printing color proofs on a $40,000 Xerox color copier with PostScript RIP, and finally sending the files to a commercial printer's PostScript printing-plate maker. It's a mighty experience to stand beneath a $10 million, two-story offset web press and realize that PostScript drove the process all the way. That's device independence.

Printing with Adobe Type Manager

A key part of PostScript is its Type 1 font technology, which lets you scale the type from a single font to any size you need, whether it's to display onscreen or to print on a page. Before the TrueType font format was introduced, in fact, Type 1 was the principal scalable font technology on the Mac. (For more about font technologies and font formats, see Chapter 18.) When PostScript first arrived, only PostScript printers could scale PostScript fonts. Scaled fonts could not be used on the Mac screen until Adobe released Adobe Type Manager (ATM). ATM is basically a PostScript font RIP that only renders PostScript Type 1 fonts and not all the other graphics and images of a full-blown PostScript RIP.

But ATM will also work with non-PostScript-printer drivers to scale fonts for non-PostScript printers. That means if you've got PostScript Type 1 fonts installed on your Mac, you can use them to print on inexpensive printers that lack PostScript RIPs.

Adobe Type Manager and Mac OS X (GS)

You can almost forget everything you know about the need for ATM when it comes to Mac OS X. That's because Apple's new operating system includes built-in support for Type 1 fonts. So you can happily view and print documents with PostScript fonts from any Mac OS X application, regardless of whether it's a PostScript or a QuickDraw-type printer, and everything will look fine.

When I say "almost," I mean Classic applications. For those, you still need ATM. Never expect things to come so easy in Mac OS X, especially when it comes to juggling the needs of two operating systems.

In the Mac OS 9 Classic environment of Mac OS X, ATM Deluxe can manage your font library. But it will not work with the font libraries you use for your native Mac OS X applications. Why? In Mac OS X, Apple decided to include much of the work ATM performs. (The Quartz 2D imaging model in Mac OS X is based on PostScript and provides many of the same capabilities.) Because of Mac OS X's PostScript-like features, Adobe is not rewriting ATM Deluxe for Apple's new OS.

Adobe PostScript vs PostScript Clones

When Adobe first licensed PostScript RIP designs to printer manufacturers, it charged a bundle for the privilege. Within a year, folks in labs and garages across the land were hard at work trying to reverse-engineer PostScript so that they could offer "PostScript-clone" printers that worked just like Adobe PostScript printers but cost less.

But cost wasn't the only driving factor. Some printer vendors were interested in creating high-resolution laser printers capable of printing 1,000 dpi or more, and Adobe seemed reluctant, at first, to offer the necessary technology. So these firms also went about creating PostScript clones.

A true PostScript clone would have to be an identical copy of an Adobe PostScript RIP—something you can't do legally without permission from Adobe. So clone makers had to re-create PostScript RIP designs from scratch, making systems that interpreted and *ripped* PostScript code just as an Adobe-licensed printer would.

After a rocky start, things eventually settled down—PostScript clones became very reliable and worth a little risk if (a) you could get one really cheap, or (b) the clone offered features (such as superhigh resolution) that Adobe-licensed printers didn't. Adobe kept clone makers hopping by introducing new versions of PostScript. Level 1 gave way to major performance and feature advancements in Level 2. Just about the time when healthy Level 2 clones emerged, Adobe released its current PostScript 3 with additional prepress features and the ability to directly render Acrobat PDF files, not just straight PostScript code (more on that later). PostScript 3—don't call it Level 3—has proved hard to clone. I've yet to encounter a PostScript 3 clone in any equipment I've used, though PostScript 2 clones are still common.

PostScript Printers' Built-in Fonts

The original Apple LaserWriter shipped with 13 PostScript outline fonts stored in ROM (Read-Only Memory) chips inside the printer. The idea was to create a core set of fonts that every PostScript printer would have, assuring at least some degree of font compatibility across all PostScript printers. When you printed a page that used any of these fonts, the LaserWriter copied them from the ROM chip into its processor memory and munched away, rasterizing the outline font into the necessary printer dots.

These core fonts consisted of four styles (roman, bold, italic, and bold italic) of Times, Helvetica, and Courier, plus Symbol. The LaserWriter Plus expanded that selection to 35, adding (again in four styles each) ITC Avant Garde Gothic, ITC Bookman, ITC New Century Schoolbook, and Palatino, plus ITC Zapf Chancery Medium Italic and ITC Zapf Dingbats. (ITC stands for International Typeface Corp., from which these typeface designs were licensed.)

Many PostScript printers on the market now come with more than 50 fonts, some stored on internal hard drives instead of ROM chips.

Getting Your Printer Wired (BW)

Like all new hardware, your printer first needs a physical connection to your Mac. That connection relies on a hardware interface (that is, a plug socket in your Mac) and some cabling that works with that interface. In the Mac world you'll find five basic types of interfaces: *serial, LocalTalk* (a special kind of serial), *EtherTalk, SCSI* (Small Computer System Interface), and *USB* (Universal Serial Bus, found on iMacs, the Blue and White Power Mac G3s, and Power Mac G4s). Here's a brief profile of each.

Serial. Before the iMac, all Macs had two serial interface connectors—the modem and printer plugs on the rear panel, marked with obvious icons. Technically, both of these will work with a serial printer, but the printer connector doubles as a LocalTalk network connector. If you're not connected to a LocalTalk-interface printer or a LocalTalk network, you can modify the Printer connection to function as a "normal" serial connection, as described below.

LocalTalk. This is a low-speed network connection described in detail in Chapter 20, "Networking." The printer connection on pre-iMac Macintoshes runs AppleTalk network protocols over LocalTalk cabling. A printer with a LocalTalk connection can be daisy-chained to a LocalTalk network connecting a number of Macs, all of which can share the printer.

Serial and LocalTalk printers aren't supported under Mac OS X. Fortunately, you have several options. Replacements for your old serial printer are usually inexpensive, with some models going for less than fifty dollars (except for the possible need to get a USB card), and you can find LocalTalk to Ethernet adapters (from such companies as Asanté and Farallon) that will allow your old printer to work on a modern computer network.

EtherTalk. Many PostScript printers either come equipped with EtherTalk interface connections or offer them as options. These printers can be plugged right into an Ethernet-based network running AppleTalk, TCP/IP, or other network protocols. It's a much higher-speed connection than LocalTalk or serial.

SCSI. Some non-PostScript color printers sport SCSI connectors, since they need the high speed this standard affords to transfer lots of prerasterized page and picture image data from the Mac to the printer hardware. SCSI is related to the *parallel* interface used on many PCs.

USB. The newest Macs, by order of Chairman Steve, have moved away from low-speed serial connections to USB, which boasts a higher speed but still lets you daisy-chain multiple printers and other devices, just as you would on a LocalTalk network.

The Ins and Outs of the Chooser (BW)

The first step on the long journey to printing a page successfully is telling your Mac which printer to use for a particular job. In Mac OS 9 and earlier, the place to do this is in the Chooser.

Chooser Basics

The Mac Chooser desk accessory, tucked away under the Apple menu, works as a sort of switching center for choosing and setting up the printer you want to use for a particular job. It's especially handy if you have more than one printer, which is often the case in workgroup settings. The Chooser also lets you make connections to network file servers and other computer devices connected to the Mac via serial ports and USB ports.

Open the Chooser, and you'll see that its window has two parts (**Figure 6.2**). The left pane displays a set of printer icons (plus an AppleShare icon, if you're on a network) and possibly icons for other devices or services you can use. These icons represent pieces of software, often called *drivers*. These drivers are Chooser software extensions that tell the Mac operating system how to use a particular piece of hardware, such as a printer. Look at it this way: The printer cable is the hardware link between your Mac hardware and your printer; the driver is the software link between your Mac OS software and your printer.

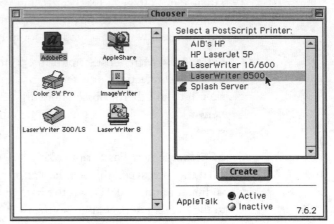

Figure 6.2

The Chooser is divided into two zones. On the left are icons of drivers, pieces of software that allow your Mac to communicate with certain types of devices or services. On the right is a list of specific devices that will work with the driver you've selected. In this case, the PostScript driver is selected, so all available PostScript printers are listed on the right.

The right-hand pane of the Chooser is called the Connect To window. It shows a list of devices currently connected to your Mac—machines that can actually do a job, whether they're printers, network file servers, or something else. These devices will only appear in the pane if they're connected to the Mac, powered on, and ready to roll.

If the name of your printer shows up in the Connect To window of the Chooser when you click the correct driver icon in the left-hand pane, hurray! That means you've installed the right printer software, correctly hooked up the printer cables, and turned on the printer. You can't get just part of this right— you've got to get it all. If you've connected your printer correctly but you haven't installed the printer's software driver, then you won't see any trace of your printer in either Chooser pane. If you *have* installed the correct driver but you've forgotten to turn on your printer, you'll see the correct icon in the left-hand window, but the printer's name won't be listed in the right. If you've got the correct driver selected, and the printer is turned on but it's still not listed in the right-hand pane, then there's a problem with your wiring— probably a loose connection.

The Chooser and Mac OS X (GS)

Although Mac OS X users will have to get accustomed to a new way of selecting and configuring a printer (see the section "Print Center Basics"), Mac OS X's Classic environment, because it's just Mac OS 9, still uses the Chooser. You still need it (and the appropriate printer drivers) to select a printer to handle any document that you print from the Classic environment.

Print Center Basics (GS)

In Mac OS X, Apple replaced portions of the Chooser with Print Center (**Figure 6.3**). Print Center acts somewhat like the Chooser: It lists all printers available to your Mac and lets you define which printer is your default (the first one listed in the Print dialog box). Unlike the Chooser, however, it can't connect your Mac via a network with another computer (you do that through Mac OS X's Go menu and its Connect to Server command).

In addition, Print Center takes over some (but not all) of the desktop printer-functions found in Mac OS 9: You can view the print jobs sent to a printer, check their status, and manage them (more or less).

Figure 6.3

The Chooser is dead in Mac OS X, and Print Center is its (and PrintMonitor's) replacement.

The printers you select and configure under Print Center are only available with Mac OS X applications. You must select printers used for Classic applications the old-fashioned way, via the Chooser.

Beginning with Mac OS X 10.1, Apple made it easier for you to configure a USB printer. As long as the correct drivers are installed, and the printer is connected to your Mac and running, it'll show up in the Print dialog box. No need to make a setting in Print Center, except to change the default printer. If you only have one available printer, that one is always the default.

Print Center handles three types of printer hookups. The first is the one Mac users are most familiar with, AppleTalk. Your standard networked laser printer, attached to your Mac's Ethernet port, will appear in that category. The second, LPR Printers using IP, allows you to select a printer via its IP number (but you have to know the number before you can configure the printer). The third option is the simplest—USB—because these printers should automatically appear in that list.

Here's how to add and configure a printer using Print Center:

1. Locate the Print Center application (it's in the Utilities folder), and launch it.

2. If you haven't configured any printers, you'll see a dialog box reminding you that no printers are available. If that happens, just click Add to proceed. If at least one printer is available, you'll see the Printer List instead, in which case click Add Printer.

Another way to add a printer is via the Print dialog box. Just choose Edit Printer List from the Printer pop-up menu, and Print Center will launch before your very eyes.

3. In the next sheet that pops down, choose the type of printer connection you want from the pop-up menu (AppleTalk, LPR Printers using IP, or USB).

 If you choose AppleTalk and AppleTalk hasn't been activated, you'll see a dialog box offering to take you right to the AppleTalk tab in the Network panel of System Preferences. Since AppleTalk isn't turned on by default under Mac OS X, don't be surprised when this dialog box appears. In addition, Print Center also has a Printer Model pop-up menu at the bottom of the AppleTalk dialog box where you can specify the proper PPD file for your printer (Auto, the default setting, will usually work if the right PPD file has been installed).

4. To make a printer a default—the one that appears first on the list in the Print dialog box—select its name and choose Make Default from the Printers menu. As you'll see when we explore the Mac OS X dialog box, you can easily switch between all available printers directly from the Print dialog box without revisiting Print Center after everything has been configured.

5. If you want to configure a printer to connect via TCP/IP, choose LPR Printers using IP from the Printer List pop-up menu. Here the setup gets a little more complicated.

6. With the LPR option displayed (**Figure 6.4**), enter the IP number of your printer in the LPR Printer's Address field.

Figure 6.4

Configure an LPR printer here, by entering its IP number and selecting the proper PPD file.

LPR Printers using IP

LPR Printer's Address:
Internet address or DNS name

☑ Use Default Queue on Server

Queue Name:

Printer Model: HP LaserJet 8000 Series

Cancel   Add

 How do you find the number? Check your printer's startup or configuration page. If you have a print utility application to configure your printer, see if it has an option to display the IP number. Not all network printers can be set up this way, so you may need to check the manual or contact the manufacturer if you can't find an IP number to use.

7. If you want your printer identified by name rather than number, unselect the Use Default Queue on Server check box and give your printer a Queue Name.

8. Under the Printer Model pop-up menu, choose a PPD file for your printer from the ones listed. If the right PPD isn't listed, stick with Generic for now. (See the section in this chapter on adding PPDs under Mac OS X for information on how to locate and add the one that fits your printer.)

9. All done? Quit Print Center. From here on, unless you want to change a default printer, you'll only need to use Print Center to manage your print queue.

Using Print Center to Track Your Job (GS)

The first time you print a document with a Mac OS X application, you may find something lacking. There's no PrintMonitor window and no desktop-printer icon around. So how do you track the job?

Did you notice the appearance of a familiar icon in the Dock within a few seconds after you issued the Print command? That's Print Center, which (like PrintMonitor) automatically launches to process your document.

Beginning with Mac OS X 10.1, Print Center's Dock icon has changed. As the document is processed by Print Center, you'll see a numeric display in the Dock indicating how many pages remain to be processed. You will also see a warning or exclamation point displayed if there's a problem with one of your print jobs.

When you click the Print Center icon, you'll see a list of the jobs being processed (**Figure 6.5**). To change the print order of a job not being processed, select the job by its name and click Priority. This will move it up or down through the queue.

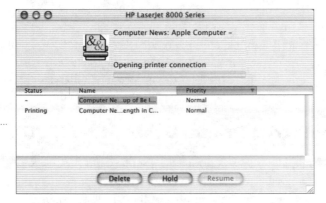

Figure 6.5

Print Center puts up a PrintMonitor-like face when you use it to track your print jobs.

The three buttons at the bottom of the Print Center queue window perform the advertised functions: Delete, Hold, or Resume. The Queue menu offers the same commands, plus a Stop Queue option that halts the process entirely (after which it toggles to Start Queue).

If there's a problem with a job, you'll see a status message above the job's progress bar. Unfortunately, the messages are apt to be no more illuminating than the ones you'd see in PrintMonitor or the desktop-printing window in Mac OS 9 and earlier.

PostScript Printer Drivers (BW)

PostScript printers are a special breed. From a Chooser and printer-selection standpoint, PostScript printers have some particular issues that we'll look at before we get into more advanced topics related to the Mac Chooser.

The first thing to know is that because most PostScript printers connect to Macs via a LocalTalk or EtherTalk network, you can easily have several PostScript printers available to you at the same time. If you have access to six brands and models of PostScript printer over a local area network (LAN), and each brand of PostScript printer requires its own printer driver, you could end up with six drivers to juggle in the Chooser.

This potential problem leads to the second main point about PostScript printers: Fortunately, with some exceptions noted below, you usually don't need a separate printer driver for each model of PostScript printer. Instead, a single PostScript driver, like the one that ships with your Mac operating system, will generally work with all the PostScript printers to which you're connected. If Apple's LaserWriter 8 PostScript driver, for example, is installed on your system, you should see the LaserWriter icon in the left-hand pane of the Chooser. When you click this icon, the pane on the right will list all the PostScript printers currently connected to your Mac—at least all the ones that are turned on and ready to print.

Some specialized PostScript printers come with custom PostScript drivers that look and act like the standard issue but that also activate some special features in the printer (access to a second paper tray, for example). If you don't need those special features, then the regular PostScript drivers will work perfectly well. Conversely, you can often use a printer's custom PostScript driver with your other less specialized PostScript printers. Chances are it will support their features as well, as described in the next section.

PostScript Printer Description (PPD) Files (BW)

Although all PostScript printers can understand the PostScript page-description language, they're not all created equal. PostScript printers differ from each other in tons of ways: in their number of built-in fonts, their PostScript version and revision, their print resolution and printable page areas, their configuration of input and output paper trays, their internal memory and hard-disk space (if any), and much more.

When it comes time to print, and you've got a PostScript printer hooked to your Mac, you'd ideally like to be able to select any of the printing options that your particular model may offer. You'd also like the application from which you're printing to know something about the limitations of the printer, so that its Print dialog box only offers print options that the currently selected printer really has. If your printer can print on 11-by-17-inch paper, for example, you'd like to have that choice in the Print dialog box. On the other hand, if the largest paper size on which it can print is 8.5 by 11 inches, you don't want to be offered the choice of 11 by 17 inches.

So how is one PostScript printer driver supposed to know all this stuff about every PostScript printer you use? How can it help you handle all the options? The answer is that the PostScript driver gets some help from little things called *PostScript printer description* (PPD) files. PPDs act like specialty sidekicks for the main PostScript driver. They are, in fact, little PostScript programs that provide a PostScript driver the information it needs to address a particular feature of a PostScript printer.

It sounds complicated, but it actually makes life simple: Instead of having to get a separate PostScript driver for every PostScript printer, you generally need only a single driver. PPD files will take care of handling the variations in features among PostScript printers. The Apple LaserWriter and the AdobePS PostScript drivers, though fairly generic, are designed to work with PPD files to provide functions specific to a particular printer. The bottom line is that PPDs let you get away with less choosing in the Chooser.

Installing PPDs (BW)

If you want to take full advantage of your PostScript printers' features, you'll need a PPD file for each model you use. You'll usually find these on the installation floppy disks or CD-ROM that came with your printer and on the company's Web site. Normally, the installation software that came with your printer automatically installs the PPD file for you.

If for some reason a PPD file doesn't install properly, you can easily install it yourself. You drag the PPD file into the Printer Description folder, which you'll find inside the Extension folder, which is inside the System Folder in Mac OS 9.

Once a PPD file is safely inside the Printer Description folder, any Mac software that needs it will find it there. If it's not there, it may be somewhere else on your hard drive, so use Sherlock (or the Find command under the Apple menu in Mac OS 8 and earlier) to locate it. If you don't find the PPD on your hard drive, check the printer installation discs, or download it from the printer vendor's Web site. Note that Adobe's Web site (www.adobe.com/support/downloads/pdrvmac.htm) offers a slew of PPDs, organized by vendor, that you can download for free.

 Another great source of PPD files is Macromedia FreeHand, a favorite illustration application for many Mac users. In version 10, which runs on Mac OS 9 and earlier and on Mac OS X, we counted 111 PPDs, including many for high-end output devices used in the printing industry.

PPDs and Mac OS X (GS)

Under Mac OS X, PPD files are still a necessity. In fact, you can use the same ones that you installed in your copy of Mac OS 9 or earlier.

(And no, sorry, Mac OS X's Print Center doesn't see the PPD files stored in your Classic Mac OS System Folder.)

Fortunately, Mac OS X 10.1 comes with a decent supply of PPD files; it's not just limited to Apple's long-departed printer line anymore. Mac OS X includes PPD files for popular printer models from HP, Lexmark, Tektronix (the files all bear a TKP at the beginning of the file name), and Xerox (with an EF3 or XRN in the name).

If you want to add a PPD file under Mac OS X, you can hope the manufacturer will just produce an installer. If not, you place it in the en.lproj folder. (The what? Mac OS X with its multilanguage capabilities has a separate folder for each language it can handle.) So where's that folder? Just use the following path: Library/Printers/PPDs/Contents/Resources.

Can't copy a file to that folder? Make sure you have administrator access to your Mac.

Choosing Direct-Connect vs Networked Printers (BW)

The Chooser works a bit differently in selecting printers depending on whether you're choosing a printer that's directly connected to your Mac via serial or USB port or you're choosing one connected via a LAN.

To select a directly connected printer in the Chooser, first check that the printer is turned on.

1. In the left-hand pane of the Chooser, click the icon of the printer you want to use.

2. In the right-hand pane, click the icon of the serial port (printer port or modem port) to which you've connected the printer (**Figure 6.6**). The little icons embossed in the plastic housing above the ports on the back of your Mac match the ones in the Chooser window.

3. Click the printer you want in the Connect To pane.

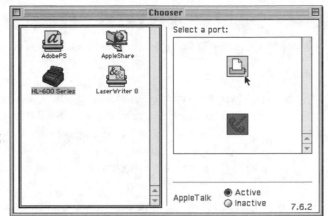

Figure 6.6

When you select the driver for a serial printer in the left-hand window of the Chooser, you then have to specify in the right-hand window which port the printer is connected to: the Printer port or the Modem port.

Most networked printers in the Mac world are PostScript printers, although some inexpensive QuickDraw printers also sport AppleTalk network connectors. As you'll discover in Chapter 20, LANs are shared data connections between computers, printers, file servers, modems, and other devices. Over this shared highway, folks on different computers can share the same printer or several printers.

Selecting a network printer from the Chooser is a little different from selecting a directly connected printer:

1. The printer has to be turned on and fully initialized (PostScript printers take a minute or two to initialize before the system actually "sees" them on the network).

2. Click the printer icon of your choice in the left-hand pane. For a PostScript printer, that would be the LaserWriter driver or the AdobePS driver (if it came with your printer or with some Adobe software you've bought or if you downloaded that driver from Adobe's Web site).

3. If the LAN is divided into AppleTalk zones, the Connect To window will have a list of network-zone names at the bottom. If the printer you want to select doesn't appear in the upper portion of the Connect To window, then click another zone name to see if the printer resides there. Think of AppleTalk zones as different hallways off a main corridor. Clicking a zone name in the Chooser lets you see down that other hall.

4. Click the printer name in the Connect To window.

Desktop Printing in Mac OS 8 and Mac OS 9 (BW)

In System versions before Mac OS 8, you selected a printer pretty much as described above. Every time you needed to print to a different printer, you took a trip to the Chooser. Things changed with Mac OS 8, though, and now you don't always have to go through this step. To save this time, though, you have to spend a little more time up front in setting up your printer so that you can bypass the Chooser.

Starting with Mac OS 8, the Chooser can set up what's called a *desktop printer* for every printer you select in the Chooser's Connect To window. That means that the first time you select a printer from the Chooser in one of these System versions, the Chooser will probably start prompting you with options concerning desktop printers. A lot of folks get baffled at this point, because they aren't expecting this "help." They installed their printer driver, plugged in their printer, and thought they were ready to print. Well, almost.

So what is a desktop printer, anyway? Apple introduced the concept back in System 7.5, when desktop printers were part of an optional operating-system extension called QuickDraw GX. The QuickDraw GX addition didn't catch on in a big way (or even a small way, for that matter), so it was dropped in Mac OS 9, but desktop printers are here to stay. With Mac OS 8.0, Apple made them an integral part of the operating system.

Think of desktop printers as virtual printers. They exist only as software, visible exclusively on your Mac desktop as special printer icons (**Figure 6.7**). Put another way, desktop printers don't fit on the desk or table, next to your Mac—they live on your computer screen and function as stand-ins for the real printers you select in the Chooser.

Figure 6.7

When you create a desktop printer, an icon like this one appears on the right side of your desktop. In this example, the little page symbol in front of the printer image indicates that printing is in progress.

Once you've set them up, desktop printers give you the opportunity to choose between different printers that use the same driver—usually PostScript printers—*without* going through the Chooser. It's faster, easier, better. You can even print by simply dragging a document file icon onto a desktop-printer icon. Mac desktop printers also make it quick and easy to monitor print jobs in progress, as we'll see below.

Creating a Desktop Printer

Creating a desktop printer is easy to do, as long as you're familiar with using the Chooser and the concept of PPD files (see above). In many cases, the process can occur almost automatically when you select a printer in the Connect To window of the Chooser. So don't get nervous. The setup differs a bit depending on whether you're setting up a directly connected printer from the Chooser or setting up a networked PostScript printer:

1. Select the Chooser from the Apple menu.

2. In the left-hand pane of the Chooser, click the printer-driver icon of the printer you want to select.

   If the printer is properly connected to your Mac and turned on, its name should appear listed in the right-hand pane of the Chooser. Assuming that you've never created a desktop printer for this physical printer, you'll only see the printer name listed, without an accompanying icon. If you do see an icon, someone's already created a desktop printer for it.

3. Click the printer name in the right-hand Chooser pane. The button just below the pane will change to Create. Click the Create button. (If someone's already created a desktop printer for you, you'll see a Setup button instead of a Create button.)

   For PostScript printers, clicking the Create button in the Chooser opens a "Setting up" dialog box, which begins to perform an electronic check to identify the printer. The setup routine will usually automatically select the right PPD file for that printer. I say *usually*, but this isn't always the case. Sometimes the setup routine can't figure out which PPD to use, and the barber-pole "wait" indicator in the "Setting up" dialog box will spin indefinitely (**Figure 6.8**). If this happens, go on to the next step.

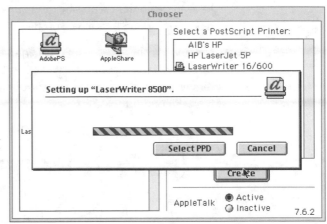

Figure 6.8

It's normal to see the barber-pole progress bar while a PPD file is being installed, but when it stays onscreen for a long time, you have a problem, probably a missing or defective PPD file. In this case, click the Cancel button and make sure the PPD file is in its appointed place.

4. If for a PostScript printer you need to manually select the PPD file or change a selection, click the Select PPD button under the barber pole. The Select a PostScript Printer Description File dialog box appears, showing you all the PPDs stored in the Printer Descriptions folder

(**Figure 6.9**). Scroll down until you find the right PPD file for your model printer. If you don't find it, you should quit the Chooser, locate the PPD file on your printer-installation disk (or download it, if necessary, as described earlier), and then copy the PPD file into the Printer Descriptions folder.

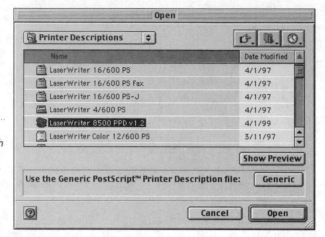

Figure 6.9

When one printer driver can work with several printers, the Chooser offers a list of PPD files for specific printers from which you can choose.

What About Desktop Printing in Mac OS X? (GS)

It's not there. In the initial releases of Mac OS X through 10.1 (the version shipping when this book went to press), the system didn't provide support for desktop printing. What about the Classic environment of Mac OS X? Not there either. When you print from a Classic application, it brings up the print-queue application, PrintMonitor.

So basically, when you run the Classic environment under Mac OS X, you have to be content with selecting and configuring printers separately. But desktop printing isn't a part of the picture.

Fortunately, the version of Print Center that shipped with Mac OS X 10.1 puts up a Dock icon showing print status messages (such as how many pages remain to be processed in the current job), which will help you keep tabs on how the print process is going.

Setting Up Your Pages (BW)

With your printer properly set up, it's time to print. Well, almost time.

You don't necessarily print the same kinds of documents the same way every time you print. For example, you might want to print on large paper one time, letter-size paper the next time. You may want to print a color page as black and white or print a scaled-down version of a large page. In short, once your printer is set up and you're ready to print, it's time to set up the *page* so that it prints the way you want. To set up a page for printing, you'll use the Mac's Page Setup and Print dialog boxes.

Frankly, I find it confusing that the Mac divides your printing options between two dialog boxes—Page Setup and Print—because I think they overlap. The Page Setup dialog box mainly deals with your options for paper size, scaling, orientation (wide or tall—that is, *portrait* or *landscape*), and other things that affect how your page will fit on paper. You can set Page Setup options long before you ever print. The Print dialog box covers more immediate issues: your choice of paper tray, the number of copies and the range of pages you want to print, and print-quality options. You do all this just before you print.

But you'll also find some Page Setup options that affect the quality of your printout. So, basically, you need to go into both dialog boxes to set up a print job properly. Let's look at them one at a time.

Page Setup Dialog Box in Mac OS 9

Whether you're printing from the Finder or from an application, you'll almost always find a Page Setup command under the File menu. But that's about as standard as it gets, since the Page Setup dialog box may look and work differently depending on the printer you've chosen and the application you're printing from. Still, you'll find some basic things in most variants of the Page Setup dialog box. And you'll notice two basic kinds of Page Setup options: those for QuickDraw printers and those for PostScript printers.

QuickDraw Printer Page Setup. The Page Setup dialog box for QuickDraw printers, such as the Apple StyleWriter, is pretty simple. You'll see the following main options, though they vary a lot from vendor to vendor.

Page Size. Read this as "paper size," the size of the sheet of paper you intend to print on. Click this pop-up menu, and you'll see an assortment from 8.5-by-11-inch letter size to 8.5-by-14-inch legal size, up to 11-by-17-inch tabloid or larger, plus a load of smaller pages, envelopes, and whatever else the printer you've selected can handle.

Layout. This indicates how many separate pages (say, from your word processor) you want to print on one piece of paper (the size of which you selected under Page Size). You'll see options such as 1 Up and 2 Up, which refer to how many page images will appear on a sheet. For example, 2 Up means that two pages will print in reduced size on each sheet of paper (**Figure 6.10**).

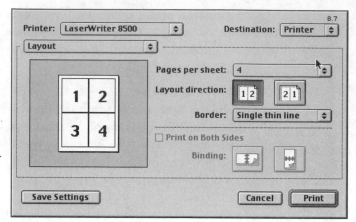

Figure 6.10

Use the Layout options of the PostScript printer driver to print several document pages on a single sheet. This saves paper if you are printing postcards or other small documents, or if you simply need smaller, thumbnail views of a publication's layout pages.

Border. The Border option appears when you select Layout in the pop-up menu above. From the pop-up menu, you can select a border that will print around the 1-up, 2-up, whatever-up pages you print using the Layout options.

Orientation. You can select either the portrait icon on the left (with the little person standing tall) or the landscape icon (with the little person rotated at 90 degrees). If you want to print horizontally along the width of the paper, click the landscape icon.

Scaling. Most printers can print your pages larger or smaller than normal. "Normal" is 100 percent, 50 percent is half-size, and 200 percent is twice as big. If, for example, you have a small picture in your graphics program and want it to fill the printed page more completely, you can do that by increasing the Scaling percentage above 100 percent. Likewise, if you want to print a tabloid page on letter-size paper, you can scale it down.

If you scale something larger than the printer can print on the selected paper size, only part of the page will appear on the paper; the excess will be clipped off. Some applications offer additional options for automatically scaling a print job to fit on the sheet of paper you've selected. Scaling will slow down printing.

PostScript Printer Page Setup. PostScript printer drivers offer quite a few more setup options than QuickDraw printers. To keep these from overwhelming you, the Page Setup dialog box for the Apple LaserWriter and AdobePS printer drivers divide your options into two categories: Page Attributes and PostScript Options. A pop-up menu lets you select which category to view.

Page Attributes

Page Attributes shows you the same options described above, but the AdobePS driver offers this one addition:

Format for. This pop-up menu relates to the rather techie subject of PostScript encoding. You'll generally see a selection for your PostScript printer plus a selection for an alternative type of PostScript coding suitable for use when capturing a PostScript print job as a file rather than letting it go to the printer. This option is covered later in the chapter.

PostScript Options

Select PostScript Options from the pop-up menu. You'll find a set of option boxes that you can click on or off. They're divided into two sections: Visual Effects and Image & Text. You'll also see an icon of a printed page displaying a funny creature known in Mac legend as a *dogcow*. The dogcow page icon shows how the Visual Effects options affect the way your page will print (**Figure 6.11**).

Figure 6.11

With the Flip Vertical and Invert Image options selected in the Page Setup dialog box, the dogcow preview shows how these choices will affect the printed page.

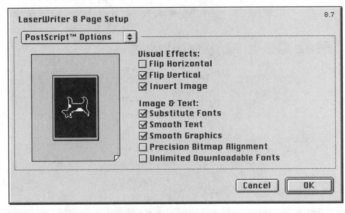

Here are options you'll find.

Flip Horizontal. This prints a mirror image of your page.

Flip Vertical. This prints your page upside down.

Invert Image. This prints a negative image of your page: White turns black and black turns white.

Substitute Fonts. This automatically switches non-PostScript Mac fonts (namely New York, Geneva, and Monaco) to similar-looking PostScript fonts: Times, Helvetica, and Courier, respectively.

Smooth Text. This tries to make text based on non-PostScript bitmapped fonts print without jagged edges, making them look smoother. (See Chapter 18 for more about bitmapped fonts.) It may be smoother, but it still looks crummy.

Smooth Graphics. This reduces jaggies in printed graphics, making them look smoother.

Don't use this option with high-resolution printers or imagesetters, as it causes printing to slow down drastically.

Precision Bitmap Alignment. Tries to make bitmapped images (see Chapter 14) line up dot for dot with the printer dots of the printer. This can prevent annoying crosshatch patterns that result when dots stored in a bitmapped image don't align evenly with the dot pattern of a printer.

Unlimited Downloadable Fonts. Removes any limits on the number of automatically downloaded fonts permitted for a document (see the "Managing Printer Fonts" section below). This may or may not be a good idea, depending on the memory capacity of your printer to store fonts for a page and the time it may take to continually download fonts during the page-printing process. Your alternative is to determine how many fonts the page needs, and manually download them to the printer before printing your pages.

As you make your selections, check the appearance of the dogcow to see if you've selected the right options for your job, and then click OK.

Mac OS X Page Setups (GS)

A look at the Mac OS X Page Setup box (**Figure 6.12**) shows that all those familiar Mac OS 9 printer-effects options are no longer available (which doesn't, of course, mean they won't return in a future version of Mac OS X).

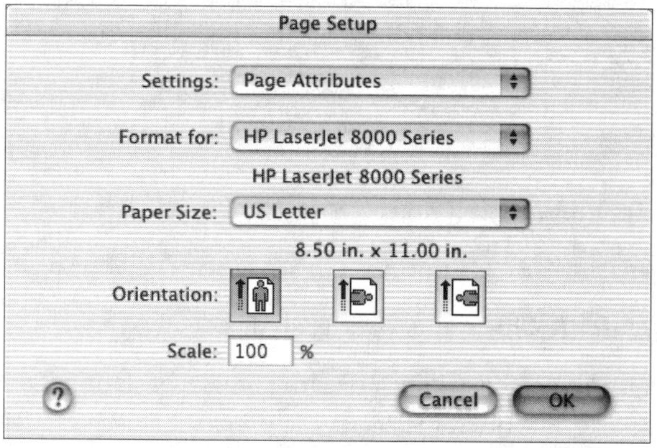

Figure 6.12

Mac OS X's Page Setup box is missing all those printer-effects choices that are part of Mac OS 9 and earlier.

Let's take a quick tour.

Settings. Choose Page Attributes or Summary (which simply lists the options you've selected).

Format for. Choose the name of the printer from this pop-up menu if you want to use a custom paper size or setup. That way your printer's custom options will be available.

Paper Size. Pick the paper size from the pop-up menu.

 If a paper size supported by your printer isn't listed, make sure the right model is selected in the Format for pop-up menu. If it's a PostScript printer, make sure the proper PPD file was installed.

Orientation. Portrait or two forms of landscape (pointing east or west).

Scale. Specify the number, just as you did in Mac OS 9.

Application Page Setup Options (BW)

For Mac OS 9 and X, in addition to the general Page Attributes and PostScript Options Page Setup choices covered above, you'll generally find options in these dialog boxes provided by the application from which you're printing. If, for example, you select Page Setup from the File menu in Microsoft Word, the pop-up list in the Page Setup dialog box will also offer a Microsoft Word selection. Ditto for the Finder, Microsoft Excel, AppleWorks, and most other applications. Check your manuals for these application-specific details.

Background Printing (BW)

 If you're printing long documents, or even short documents on a slow printer, you don't want to be stuck looking at the Print dialog box waiting for the printer to finish its work. Fortunately, you don't have to, if you turn on the Background Printing option for your printer. This quickly captures your print job after you've hit the Print button and stores it on your hard drive. Your application thinks it's finished printing, closes the Print dialog box, and lets you get back to work. Meanwhile, your Mac feeds the print job to your printer, sort of secretly, in the background. Generally, it works without your even knowing it, although you may notice that your Mac slows down a little during printing.

In Mac OS 9, there are a couple of ways to turn on Background Printing, depending on whether you're using a QuickDraw or a PostScript printer. For a QuickDraw printer, do the following:

1. Open the Chooser under the Apple menu.
2. Next to the Setup button under the Chooser's Connect To window, select On under Background Printing.

From that point on, all print jobs sent to that printer will get stored on your hard drive, and then be fed to the printer as a background task.

For PostScript printers, the Print dialog box lets you turn Background Printing on or off for each print job (**Figure 6.13**). No visit to the Chooser is needed, plus you have more options for controlling jobs printing in the background.

 In Mac OS X, background printing is always on.

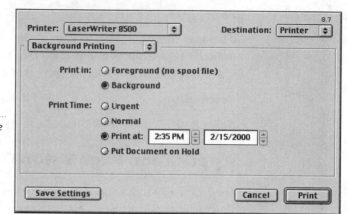

Figure 6.13

Background printing controls let you move your "Urgent" job to the head of the queue of documents waiting to be printed. If you have a job that you know will take a long time to print and monopolize the printer, you can have it print in the dead of night or during your lunch hour.

Hitting the Print Button (Finally!) (BW)

All applications that print have a Print command under their File menu, but you'll also find a Print button in the Page Setup dialog box of many printer drivers. The actual contents of Print dialog boxes can differ. That's because most printers—PostScript printers excluded—use different drivers; and the look, feel, and function of a Print dialog box depend on what the printer vendor wrote into the printer-driver software. That said, you'll find the following general features in most QuickDraw and PostScript Print dialog boxes:

QuickDraw Print Dialog Boxes

Here are the principal options you see in the Print dialog box when you're *not* using a PostScript printer (they'll vary from printer to printer).

Page Range and Number of Copies. Self-explanatory, yes?

Quality. Inkjet printers have a variety of printing methods that affect quality. Higher-quality settings generally print more slowly and use more ink.

Paper/Media Type. Selecting among bond, coated, glossy, transparency, or other media sets the printer driver to adjust its printing method for optimal results on that type of surface.

Print Grayscale/Color. Color printers often let you force color documents to print in black and white (or gray).

Print Back to Front. Prints the last page of the document first so that if pages emerge from the printer face up, the first page ends up on top. In effect, this is an auto-collating feature.

Notification. Sounds an alert to let you know the document has finished printing.

PostScript Print Dialog Box

The Apple LaserWriter 8 and AdobePS 8.6 PostScript drivers offer very similar Print dialog boxes (**Figure 6.14**). Both sport a Printer pop-up menu that lets you select among any of the PostScript printers for which you've created a desktop printer (as described earlier). The other Print dialog box option settings are divided into several main categories, which you select from a pop-up menu directly under the Printer menu at the top of the Print dialog box. The ones you'll use most often are listed here:

General. You can enter the number of copies and the page range you want to print.

Paper Source. Lets you choose which paper trays to use. You can specify a separate tray for a first-page letterhead paper, for example.

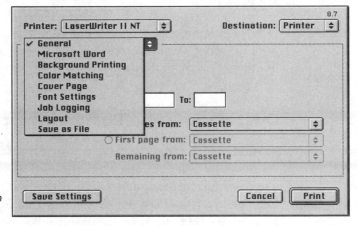

Figure 6.14

The Print dialog box for Apple's generic PostScript driver, simply named LaserWriter, is actually nine dialog boxes in one, and you access each portion through a pop-up menu.

Background Printing

Print In. Specifies whether to print the document first to a spool file on the Mac hard drive (that is, to print it in the background), or to pipe the job straight to the printer. If you're printing to a print server or a printer with a large memory buffer for holding incoming jobs, then you might not need background printing.

Print Time. The Urgent button puts the current job ahead of others waiting in the background printing queue. The Hold option puts the job in the queue but doesn't let it print.

Color Matching

Print Color. This lets you choose whether to print a job as color or grayscale. It also lets you choose between color-correction methods: correction based on ColorSync color-management profiles or correction based on PostScript Level 2 or PostScript 3 color-lookup tables.

Printer Profile. Selecting the ColorSync option above activates this pop-up menu so that you can choose the ColorSync profile of your printer.

Cover Page

Print Cover Page. This gives you the choice of slipping (or not slipping) a cover page in before or after the job prints. A cover page helps separate jobs in the printer's output tray, which is handy in workgroups using shared printers.

Cover Page Paper Source. This option lets you choose from which paper tray to draw the cover page sheet (you don't want to waste good bond paper for a mere cover sheet, do you?).

Layout

Here you can elect to print multiple document pages on a single sheet of paper. You can specify how many pages per sheet, with some control over how you'd like them ordered on the page. You can also specify a border to print around each page.

Destination: File/PostScript Options

Format. This lets you choose among several PostScript file formats. Choose PostScript Job when creating a "print-to-disk" PostScript file to submit to a service bureau (a process described in detail later in this chapter). Select the EPS option for creating a graphic image of your page that you can place inside another page (EPS stands for Encapsulated PostScript). The PDF option creates an Adobe Acrobat PDF file, which is described in the Printing to Disk section below.

PostScript Level. Select Level 1 Compatible if you have a PostScript printer with a Level 1 PostScript RIP (or intend to send your file to someone who has one). Otherwise, select the Level 2 and 3 option.

Data Format. Most PostScript code is written in ASCII (text-only) format, but this isn't an efficient way to describe photographic images. If your files contain photographs or images from paint programs, choose the Binary option.

Font Inclusion. If you're sending your PostScript file to a service bureau, you should probably select All, which will include all of the document's fonts in the PostScript file. That way, the service bureau won't have to bother downloading them (or worry about not having any of them). The option called All But Standard 13 excludes the 13 fonts mentioned in the "PostScript Printers' Built-in Fonts" section earlier (virtually all PostScript printers contain these fonts, so this is usually a safe choice). The final choice is All But Fonts in PPD Files, which includes all fonts except those specified as built-in or otherwise permanently resident, according to the printer's PPD file. (If you're sure which printer you'll be sending your file to and you know which fonts it contains, this is the logical choice.)

Monitoring Background Printing

With Mac OS 8 and Mac OS 9, you can use the desktop printers described earlier to check on the progress of jobs printing in the background. When a print job is in progress, a desktop-printer icon displays a document sticking out the top of it. Double-click the desktop printer icon, and you'll open a tidy little print monitor that lists the job currently printing as well as the jobs waiting in line. You can select a job and specify via the red (stop) or the green (go) icons that it be held or released (**Figure 6.15**). You can also set a specific time to start printing a job. The Special menu on the Desktop menu bar lets you start and stop the entire queue. If another PostScript printer is idle, you can select one or more jobs and drag them from the busy printer into the idle printer's queue. It's handy.

Figure 6.15

Double-clicking a desktop-printer icon opens a print monitor window, where you can delete jobs from the queue; hold them until a specified time; or as shown here, put the entire queue on hold.

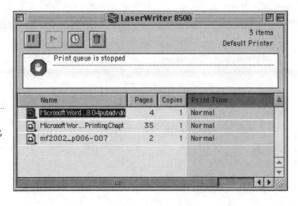

Mac OS X's Print Dialog Box (GS)

If you can use Mac OS 9 and earlier's Print dialog box, you should be able to print a job with a Mac OS X application without missing a beat. The Print dialog box (**Figure 6.16**) has the Mac OS X look, but the choices are not that different.

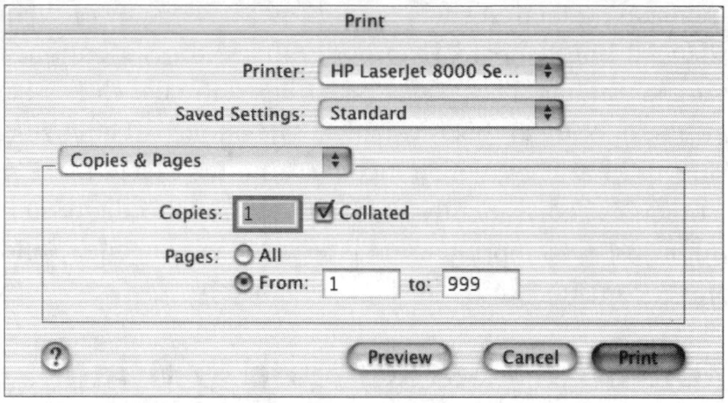

Figure 6.16

The familiar Print dialog box has an Aqua interface and familiar options.

Here's a brief summary:

Printer. Choose a printer from the pop-up list. The model automatically displayed at the top of the list is the one you selected as your default printer in Print Center. The final entry in the pop-up menu, Edit Printer List, opens Print Center so you can configure more printers.

Saved Settings. If you've created a custom setup for outputting a job, you can retrieve it here.

After you have configured the Print dialog box the way you want, choose Save Custom Setting from the pop-up menu described next.

Copies & Pages. Click this pop-up menu to see a list of Print dialog box options (**Figure 6.17**). Depending on the application and printer you're using, the options will differ. Figure 6.17 shows those for a PostScript printer and a PostScript illustration program (in this case, Macromedia FreeHand 10).

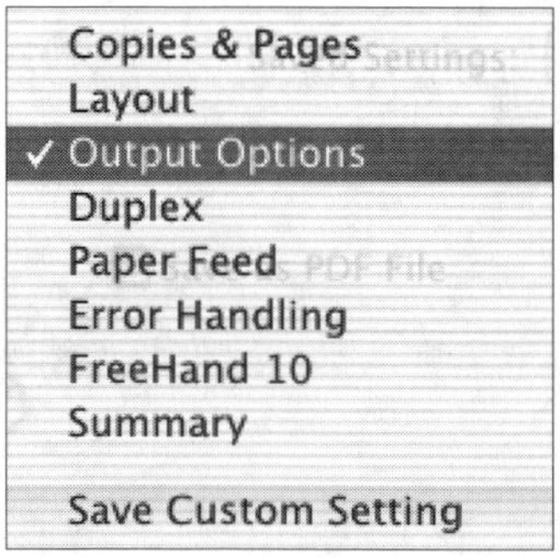

Figure 6.17

Choose your document options from the pop-up menu.

If you want to make a PDF copy of your document, choose Output Options and select Save as PDF File. You'll see one of Mac OS X's Save As dialogs, where you can name the PDF file and select where it's stored. Another way to make a PDF file is to click the Preview button in a Print dialog. The document will open in Mac OS X's Preview application, where you can see how it'll look when converted to PDF. If it looks all right, use the Save As PDF command in Preview's File menu to finish the job.

Copies and Pages. As with the Mac OS 9 Print dialog box, you can choose the number of copies and which pages to print.

Printing to Disk (BW)

It may surprise you to know that a print job doesn't necessarily have to go to a printer after you click the Print button. It can also get routed to your hard drive, to be stored as a file. This is often called *printing to disk*. People mainly do this to send PostScript files to a service bureau using expensive PostScript imagesetters, color printers, printing presses, or other equipment that we common folk can't afford to own. Often the most reliable way to get your PostScript job to such a bureau is to set up your print options so that you can capture on disk the PostScript code that would normally go to your printer. You can then send the PostScript file to the service bureau, which doesn't need the application that created the file (QuarkXPress, Word, whatever) in order to print it. (More on service bureaus later.)

Call your service bureau and ask for any special Page Setup and Print dialog box settings it requires for your PostScript job. Also make sure it sends you any special PostScript drivers and PPDs for the equipment it will use to print your job. Remember: In creating your disk file, you're printing your pages as though you were printing on the service bureau's equipment. The only difference is that you're interrupting the process to grab the PostScript and ship it over to the bureau before the printing continues. So you need to install the same drivers that the bureau uses and set up your print options like it does.

1. When your document is in its final form and ready to print, select the correct PostScript driver from the Chooser.
2. Select Page Setup under the File menu, and check that you've made all the necessary option settings the service bureau requires.
3. Select Print under the File menu to open the PostScript Print dialog box.
4. From the Destination pop-up menu, select File (the default is Printer).
5. Select PostScript Job from the Format pop-up menu (**Figure 6.18**).

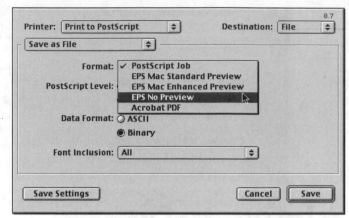

Figure 6.18

With your Destination in the Print dialog box set to File, you're ready to print a PostScript job to disk, which saves your print job as a file. After choosing Save as File in the pop-up menu, you can select just which kind of PostScript file you want to create.

6. Set the PostScript Level, Data Format, and Font Inclusion options to match the service bureau's requirements. Typically it will recommend PostScript Level 2 and 3, Binary, and All, respectively.

7. Select Background Printing from the pop-up options menu. Set the Print In option to Foreground (no spool file).

8. You should notice that the Print button at the lower right of the Print dialog box has changed to a Save button. Click it. A fairly standard Save File dialog box should then open. Rename the file if necessary, and navigate to the folder in which you want to save the file.

To print to disk in Mac OS X, choose Print from the File menu. In the Print dialog, be sure you've selected a printer, and from the pop-up menu that shows Copies & Pages, choose Output Options. Turn on the Save as File check box and choose a format—PDF or PostScript—from the Format pop-up menu. When you click the Save button, you get a Save dialog box.

Printing to Disk Using the Apple Desktop Print Utility

You can create a print-to-disk shortcut in Mac OS 9's Print dialog box by setting up a special print-to-disk desktop printer using the Apple Desktop Printer utility, which ships along with Apple's LaserWriter software. You can also download it from Apple's Web site: http://asu.info.apple.com/swupdates.nsf/artnum/n10466.

Here's how to use it for printing PostScript to disk:

1. Launch the Apple Desktop Printer Utility, and select New under the File menu.

2. The With pop-up menu lets you select a PostScript driver, typically either the Apple LaserWriter or AdobePS driver.

3. Select Translator (PostScript) from the Create Desktop menu, and click OK.

4. The PostScript Printer Description (PPD) File section at the top of the next dialog box lets you select a PPD file. Scroll down the list, highlight the PPD file your service bureau recommended, and then click the Select button.

5. Click the Change button in the Default Destination Folder section of the main utility dialog box. In the Choose a Folder dialog box that appears, select the disk volume and folder into which you want the PostScript file to end up, and click the Choose button.

6. When you're satisfied with your PPD and default destination selections, click the Create button at the bottom of the Printer Utility's dialog box. A standard Save File dialog box appears. Give the specialized desktop printer you just created a name, such as Print to PostScript, and save it to a useful location on your hard drive (which is usually the Desktop).

You can now select this Print to PostScript printer from the Printer pop-up menu of any Print dialog box when you've selected its PostScript driver in the Chooser. With this desktop printer selected, the File option becomes the default setting. In most applications, you still have to click the Save button in the Print dialog box, despite the default destination setting in the desktop printer.

Yeah, yeah, it *is* a lot of work, but you only have to do it once. Once you've got it set up, printing to disk is as easy as drag-and-drop.

PDF Print Jobs

Once you've gotten your PostScript file on disk, you might think about going a step further and converting it to an Adobe Acrobat PDF (Portable Document Format) file. There are several ways to create an Acrobat PDF file from your document pages but you end up with a more compact and manageable form of your PostScript-based document. Acrobat PDF is gaining popularity as a vehicle for getting PostScript jobs to service bureaus because it has the following advantages over PostScript print-to-disk files:

- Compared with raw PostScript code, PDF is more standardized and compact, and it processes more reliably on high-resolution imagesetters and platesetter RIPs.

- PDF files can be edited at the last minute at a service bureau, using one of several PDF utilities. You usually can't do this with PostScript files.

- PDF files can employ various types of image and graphic compression, so you can sharply reduce the size of files you submit to service bureaus; this is also great for online transfers.

 Mac OS X lets you save your print jobs as PDF files. Although you don't get the extensive range of options provided with Adobe Acrobat, such as advanced color settings, the Mac OS X PDF settings should be sufficient for most documents printed on home and office printers.

Managing Printer Fonts (BW)

QuickDraw printers generally get all their font processing done right on your Mac. The QuickDraw printer-driver software uses the TrueType or—with the help of Adobe Type Manager (ATM) in Mac OS 9 and earlier—PostScript Type 1 scalable outline fonts stored on your hard drive, and it generates the right pattern of dots for a particular typeface at the size you want. In other words, when using a QuickDraw printer, you don't have to worry about printer font management.

Things are generally different with PostScript printers. The font processing usually happens down at the printer, not in your Mac. Unless the font you need is built into a ROM (Read-Only Memory) chip, the actual outline font file has to get from your Mac's hard drive down into the printer's memory.

Moving font files from a computer to a printer is called *font downloading*. There are three basic strategies for downloading fonts.

Automatic Downloading

Most applications use automatic downloading: When a document needs to print with a certain font, your Mac automatically downloads the font to the printer. This is great if you're not using too many fonts and if you've got a fast connection to your printer. But over a LocalTalk or serial connection, this constant font downloading eats up time. With automatic downloading, fonts are only temporarily downloaded and get erased from the printer's memory each time the printer starts a new print job. On the other hand, since this downloading happens automatically, you don't spend any time fiddling with fonts, which is not a bad thing.

Hard Drive and FlashROM Font Storage

Many PostScript printers come with a built-in hard drive or SCSI port for attaching a hard drive. This hard drive stores fonts that the printer can quickly load into its own memory when needed. The fonts don't have to download over the relatively slower printer cable or network. Some printers have special programmable ROM chips called FlashROM. You can store fonts in these chips and later on erase them and load in different ones, basically creating your own sets of "built-in" fonts. Printers with these facilities come with simple downloading programs for copying your Mac-based fonts into your printer's particular storage device.

Manual Downloading

If you're printing with the same set of fonts for most of the day, you can download the fonts so that they stay in memory until you turn off the printer.

In font-management terms, this is called *permanent downloading,* even though the fonts aren't installed permanently. You do this type of manual download in Mac OS 9 with the Adobe Downloader utility, in version 5.05 at press time (**Figure 6.19**). In Mac OS 9, here's how to use it:

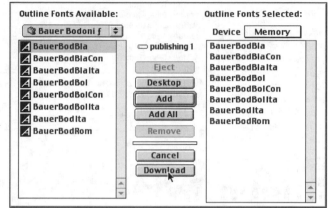

Figure 6.19

To copy fonts into your printer memory, hard drive, or FlashROM using Adobe's Downloader, you simply browse your hard drive to find the printer fonts you want (shown on the left), copy them into the download list (on the right), and click Download.

1. Go to the Chooser and select the printer to which you want to download the fonts.

2. Launch Adobe Downloader. No windows will open; you'll just see the menu bar change.

3. Select Download Fonts under the File menu.

4. Use the Outline Fonts Available list on the left of the dialog box to locate the folder containing the font files you want to download.

5. Select a font you want to download, and click the Add button. The font name will then also appear in the Outline Fonts Selected list at the right. Unfortunately, the only way to select multiple fonts in the Outline Fonts Available list is to click the Add All button. [Shift]-click or [⌘]-click operations don't work for selecting multiple fonts.

6. Once you've added to the list all the fonts you want to download, click the Download button.

If you're wondering which fonts have already been downloaded to memory, which are built into the printer's ROM chips, or which are stored on the printer's hard drive (if it has one), here's what to do.

1. Select Printer Font Directory under the Special menu.

2. You have a choice of printing a font list to your Mac's screen or to the printer. If you choose Printer, your printer cranks out a list of fonts currently residing in memory.

3. If you choose Screen, you'll get a Font Directory dialog box with a font list at the top and a Device pop-up menu at the lower right (**Figure 6.20**). The Device menu lets you choose to display fonts stored in Memory, ROM, Disk, or even FlashROM. But it won't list them all at once.

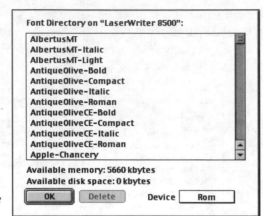

Font Directory on "LaserWriter 8500":

AlbertusMT
AlbertusMT-Italic
AlbertusMT-Light
AntiqueOlive-Bold
AntiqueOlive-Compact
AntiqueOlive-Italic
AntiqueOlive-Roman
AntiqueOliveCE-Bold
AntiqueOliveCE-Compact
AntiqueOliveCE-Italic
AntiqueOliveCE-Roman
Apple-Chancery

Available memory: 5660 kbytes
Available disk space: 0 kbytes

OK   Delete   Device   Rom

Figure 6.20

Adobe Downloader lets you look into your PostScript printer to see which fonts are there, in ROM, in memory, in FlashROM, or on the printer's hard drive.

Printer Talk (BW)

Understanding a printer is easier than understanding a computer—there just aren't as many variables, features, and jargon terms involved. And a printer only has to do one thing well, which you can judge with your own eyes.

But it goes without saying that when it comes to computer equipment, nothing goes without saying. So here's a primer on the basic printer technologies, along with an explanation of the language used to describe printers and how they work.

Resolution

Virtually all desktop printers create images out of dots, and the resolution of a printer is measured in *dots per inch* (dpi). In theory, the higher the resolution of a printer, the smoother its type and graphics will look. In fact, though, the quality of your printed pages also depends on the marking technology used to print them. For example, a laser-printed 600-dpi page will look better than an inkjet-printed 600-dpi page. And a 1200-dpi page from an imagesetter will look better than one from a 1200-dpi laser printer (more on that in a minute). But the general rule of resolution is "The more dots, the better."

Most printers you'll see advertised have the same resolution in both vertical and horizontal directions, but sometimes you'll see machines that tout, say, 600-by-1200-dpi resolution. These are generally 600-dpi printers that have been altered to put twice as many dots horizontally as they do vertically. Usually they do this by doubling the rate at which dots are imaged as the marking device travels along the width of the page. In the case of our example, the dots would be the same size as those on a 600-dpi printer (they have to be, to maintain the 600-dpi vertical resolution); they're just allowed to overlap. This makes the edges of the dots less visible, reducing the dreaded "jaggies." This is an economical way to increase resolution without using a more expensive imaging mechanism, because the finer the jet of ink or the laser beam used to image a page, the more expensive the printer.

But as with monitors, the proof of a printer's quality is in the viewing, and the best test of a printer's resolution is to see how well it represents the kinds of pages you produce.

 Before buying a printer, test it with some of your own pages. This is doubly important if you're buying a printer for images captured with your snappy new digital camera.

Printing Speed

Printers are rated in terms of how many pages they can print per minute (often abbreviated as ppm). This is usually very different from how many pages they actually do print per minute, especially in the case of PostScript printers.

The page-per-minute speed of a printer refers to the speed at which its gears and rollers can push paper, and it doesn't take into account what has to be printed on that paper. (Blank pages will typically print at blinding speed.) Often, the most time-consuming part of printing a page is the processing needed to create the bitmapped image of it (see "Let 'Er RIP," earlier in this chapter).

In the case of QuickDraw printers, this imaging is done by your Mac. With PostScript printers, it's done by a special PostScript interpreter, a computer inside the printer. Because your Mac has a much more powerful microprocessor than most PostScript printers, and because QuickDraw is a simpler imaging technology than PostScript, QuickDraw printers will typically print at closer to their rated speeds than will PostScript printers. But in either case, pages with a lot of graphics, a lot of typeface changes, and a lot of ink to be laid down will take more time to print than simple business letters.

Rated printing speeds, then, are not to be taken literally. Consider them more as relative guides to the potential speed of a particular machine—a frame of reference by which to compare one printer with another.

Memory

The amount of memory in a printer means different things depending on whether the machine in question is a PostScript printer or a QuickDraw printer. Because QuickDraw printers rely on your Mac to process images for them, they don't need much memory. But if they have enough, they can absorb one part of a page image from your Mac while they print the previous one. If there's enough memory, the printer can print at very close to its rated speed because it can always be taking its printing instructions from memory instead of waiting for them to come down the wire from your Mac. Two megabytes is generally enough.

PostScript printers are another story entirely, and how much memory one should have varies according to its rated speed, the size of the pages it can create, and its resolution.

The faster a PostScript printer can push pages, the faster it has to create the dots that make up the page images. The bigger the pages and the higher the resolution, the more dots it has to create. It takes a megabyte to store a letter-size bitmap at 300 dpi—four times that for a 600-dpi page—16 times that for a 1200-dpi page. Get the idea? And ideally, a printer should be working on processing one page while it prints another. On top of that, there has to be room to store downloaded fonts (see "Managing Printer Fonts," earlier in this chapter).

The last point is important, because the memory available for font storage is separate from that used to image the page. In other words, you don't have the option to say, "Hey, use some extra memory for font storage; I don't mind if you print a little slower." So when you're looking at PostScript printers, it's important to ask how much memory is available for fonts.

How much do you need? Figure 50 to 60 Kbytes per font, and you'll see that half a megabyte doesn't get you very far—eight typefaces on a page, and you're just about maxed out. A megabyte is better.

So let's talk minimums: What's a practical minimum amount of memory for a PostScript laser printer, assuming a normal, letter-size page? Figure 2 MB for 300 dpi, 8 MB for 600 dpi, and 16 MB for 1200 dpi at a reasonable (say, eight pages per minute) print speed.

Image-Enhancement Technologies

Printing technologies such as Apple's PhotoGrade (for photographic images) and FinePrint (for type) can vary the size of a dot created by a laser printer. They don't change the printer's resolution; they just shorten the amount of time the laser is turned on for particular dots. This creates a less intense laser flash and results in a smaller dot. Very clever. The smaller dot, when placed along the edge of a printed character, makes the edge seem smoother, as if it were imaged at a higher resolution. **Figure 6.21** shows schematically how this works.

Likewise, for photographic images, the smaller dots create the same effect as using a finer halftone screen. This in turn creates a wider range of grays, smoother color blends, and overall clearer images.

These are great technologies, and they're not available just from Apple. You can also get them in printers from Hewlett-Packard (REt) and GCC Technologies (AccuGray). You want one.

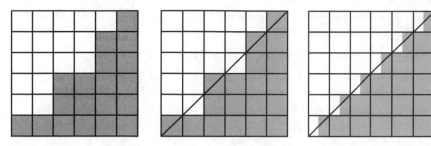

Figure 6.21

The grid on the left represents an array of pixels as they might appear along the edge of a bitmapped character. The edge is quite jagged. The center grid shows the same pixels with the ideal contour of the letter that the bitmap is trying to represent. The grid on the right shows FinePrint at work, using half-pixels to smooth the edge and reduce the jaggies.

Hard-Drive Storage

If you or the colleagues in your workgroup use a lot of fonts, having a hard drive in (or attached to) your PostScript printer can be a boon. This is because PostScript printers need font information, and it's much more efficient when they have the fonts right there inside them. Memory can hold only a handful of fonts. A hard drive can hold thousands.

A printer's hard drive doesn't have to be terribly big, and it's likely that the capacity of the smallest one you can buy these days will be measured in gigabytes. A 1 GB drive will hold maybe 20,000 fonts. This should suffice.

Any printer that comes with a hard drive will ship with a utility program for downloading fonts onto that drive. If you add a hard drive later, though, you can use Adobe's Font Downloader to do the job. Old versions of Apple's LaserWriter Font Utility (discontinued in Mac OS 9) will also work.

Printer Types (BW)

Apple has divided "the rest of us" into two classes: those who can afford the newest, slickest hardware it ships, and the rest of us, who have to make do with last year's—or last decade's—equipment. If you're in the latter group, fear not—this section will talk about all Mac printers, past and present.

ImageWriters

The ImageWriter was the first Mac printer, and while it didn't break any new ground technologically speaking, it seemed revolutionary at the time because it was so adept at printing graphics. All it was really doing, though, was reproducing dot-for-dot what you saw on the Mac screen. Whatever the Mac could image onscreen, the ImageWriter could print.

You can buy a used ImageWriter for next to nothing, because these *dot-matrix* printers are essentially obsolete. ImageWriters use inked ribbons like a typewriter and a print head consisting of a bundle of pins that look like tiny cigarettes in a pack. These pins are thrust forward in various patterns against the ribbon to make a typewriter-like impression on the paper. Each pin corresponds to 1 pixel onscreen.

The original ImageWriters had a resolution of 72 dpi. The ImageWriter II upped that to 144 dpi by overlapping the dots without decreasing their size. This was referred to as *near-letter quality*. The type is perfectly legible, it's just not very pretty—a triumph of function over form. You can still buy ribbons for these old dears, so if you see one at a garage sale, it might just be worth grabbing for a few bucks. If you see one offered on eBay as an antique, don't bite.

It's unlikely that you'll come across an ImageWriter LQ (which stands for—er, stood for—*letter quality*). These higher-resolution versions of the older machines were discontinued because of technical problems and competition from Apple's new baby: the LaserWriter.

ImageWriters are essentially serial printers, but you can also use them over an AppleTalk network with the AppleTalk ImageWriter driver. Since Apple stopped supporting them years back, the ImageWriter-compatible market has dried up and blown away.

LaserWriters and Other PostScript Laser Printers

The LaserWriter was the first desktop PostScript printer, and it almost single-handedly created the desktop-publishing revolution. The product line is now in mothballs, the model 8500 being the last and greatest.

LaserWriters were never cheap, not just because they were from Apple but also because they had an onboard computer to turn the PostScript code they received into printable images. In fact, when the LaserWriter first came out, it contained the most powerful computer Apple had made to date.

Laser printers work like photocopying machines. First a rotating drum receives an electrostatic charge from a heated wire called a *corona wire* (see the "Troubleshooting" section below for instructions on how to clean this). A fine laser beam scans back and forth along the length of this drum as it turns, with the laser blinking on and off as it goes. The width of the laser beam defines the resolution of the printer—the beam of a 300-dpi printer is roughly $\frac{1}{300}$ inch wide. Each blink creates one printed dot.

The laser beam changes the electrical charge on the drum where it hits it. Essentially, the beam is drawing an image of the page using electrical charges instead of ink. The charged drum then passes over a trough containing very fine grains of pigment called *toner powder*. The toner is attracted by the electrical charge on the drum, and this pattern of toner creates the image of the page. The toner is then offset onto the paper, which is sandwiched between the toner drum and a heated roller that melts the toner particles onto the paper. Amazing.

This process explains a lot about the results you get when you use one of these printers. If the density control is set too high, for example, you'll get too much toner attracted to the drum and too much "ink" on the paper. Likewise, if the setting is too light, or the toner reservoir is running low, the printed image will appear faint. It also explains why you should never, ever print on anything that isn't approved for use in a laser printer. Self-adhesive labels and plastic sheets, for example, could easily melt in there. As could your fingers.

Color laser printers are still somewhat of a rara avis, mainly because they're so expensive. They work in essentially the same way as black-and-white models, but their toner cartridges contain toners of the same four colors as commercial offset printing presses.

The principal charm of laser printers is their durability. Many original LaserWriters and LaserWriter IIs are still in service, 10 or 15 years after they were first sold. Their initial purchase costs are high, but eventually their low per-page cost pays off, making them an economical choice.

Most laser printers use replaceable toner cartridges that contain not only additional toner but also a new toner drum, as the surface of the drum wears out after all that scorching and abuse by corona and laser beam. They are expensive to replace, and you're lucky to find a new one for much less than $100. (Cartridges for the 8500 go for more than $200.) For this reason, an industry has popped up that refills once-used cartridges and resells them. This doesn't sound as dicey as it may seem, because it turns out that most cartridges go empty before the toner drum is worn out. Most can have a second full life cycle by being cleaned and refilled. Recycled toner cartridges sell for about half the price of new ones. But before you buy one, make sure that your printer's warranty allows it. Some vendors insist that to keep the warranty in effect, only new cartridges can be used.

Laser printers have been a standard Mac appendage for so long that just about any kind will work with a Macintosh as long as it has the appropriate interface— either a network or a Universal Serial Bus (USB).

StyleWriters and Other Inkjet Printers

If laser printers appeal on the basis of durability, inkjet printers seduce with their price. You can get a 600-dpi inkjet printer for less than a quarter of the price of a 600-dpi laser printer. The difference is even more dramatic when you talk about color, where the price ratio of laser to inkjet is about 10 to 1.

But there are hidden prices to pay for using inkjet printers. First, they're slow: One page per minute is not uncommon. Second, the *replenishables*—that is to say the ink refills—cost about $25 a pop, and these machines burn through ink. Third, they're mechanically not very robust—I would say that they're tinny, but there's hardly any metal to be found in one of these things. When they need repair, it's often cheaper to throw them away than to have them fixed.

This makes them better suited as personal printers or occasional printers than workgroup printers. They're indispensable, though, for use with digital cameras (if you like to see prints of your photos, that is). The higher-priced ones (especially those from Epson) are increasingly favored by graphics arts professionals as color-proofing tools and are used to anticipate how a professionally printed color document will look.

Two similar technologies are lumped together under the inkjet name: *inkjets* and *bubble-jets.* Both use a nozzle to spray ink onto the page through an array of tiny holes (analogous to that of a dot-matrix printer). Inkjets send a squirt onto the page for each printed dot, but bubble jets blow a tint bubble at the end of each nozzle aperture, and the bubble pops onto the page. It sounds bizarre, but the bubble-jet technique can actually create a finer and more controlled dot than a regular inkjet. Because inkjets have a tendency to splatter and splutter instead of squirting neat drops, some more expensive models use a continuous stream of ink that's permitted to hit the page only at certain times. This *continuous flow* technology keeps the nozzle from clogging (as all nozzles are wont to do), and the overflow ink is recycled for later use.

Inkjets use ink cartridges that clip onto the back of the printhead, and this mechanism slides back and forth across your page spraying ink onto it. Inkjet printers can use a one-color cartridge, a three-color cartridge (cyan/blue, magenta/red, yellow), or a four-color cartridge (the other three plus black). The four-color cartridges create the richest color images, as they imitate the ink system used by commercial offset-printing equipment.

In choosing an inkjet printer, you should opt for one that gives you the option of using a one-, three, or four-color ink cartridge. You want to avoid printing text using a multicolor head, because if it's a three-color head, you have to use all three colors to create black. Very inefficient. If you use a four-color printhead, you'll deplete the black reservoir of the cartridge prematurely. Needless to say, if you're going to be doing all this cartridge swapping, you want the process to be as easy as possible, and this isn't always the case unless you have the hands of a surgeon (or of a small child).

Another important factor in choosing an inkjet printer is the kind of paper it uses. Toner used by laser printers stays exactly where it's put, but ink sprayed onto a page has a tendency to spread, especially on absorbent paper that acts like a blotter. Make sure the print samples you're shown are on a kind of paper you can afford to use on a daily basis.

The Exotics: Thermal Transfer and Dye Sublimation

These kinds of color printers are expensive and headed for likely extinction. Color inkjet printing has made such quality strides in the last few years that these technologies are being shunted aside in all markets but high-end professional color proofing. And even there they're not safe.

Thermal transfer printing uses special sheets coated with a waxy pigmented material that's offset onto your pages by means of a heated printhead. It's sort of like a very refined iron-on T-shirt transfer. Only one color can be printed at a time, so a four-color page (cyan/magenta/yellow/black, or *CMYK* for short) has to be printed four times before the final page emerges from the printer. The colors are gorgeous, but the costs of the machine, the transfer sheets, and the special paper required have put this technology on the endangered-species list.

Dye-sublimation printers still have a place in the market because they can create continuous-tone images. That is, when they print a photographic image, it's not composed of an array of tiny colored dots; they actually blend continuous areas and shades of color one into the next. Mechanically speaking, the process works with transfer sheets similar to those used in wax-transfer printers, but the dyes are essentially airbrushed onto the page, as the pigment is gasified before being applied to the paper. It's slow and expensive, but it provides the best-quality proofs of any color printer.

The only problem is that the color from dye-sub printers is so smooth, it looks better than what comes from an offset press. Many professional proofing systems use special software to force these printers to create halftone dots that match those you'll get from your final offset-printed page.

Imagesetters

Unless you have $30,000 or $40,000 burning a hole in your pocket, you're not likely to jump for one of these, but if you aspire to having any of your pages professionally printed, you have to know about them.

Imagesetters are a special breed of laser printer that create their images on photographic surfaces rather than plain paper. Their laser beams aim directly at photographic paper (which creates a positive print), photographic film (for a film negative), or even an offset printing plate (which also uses a photographic emulsion as a printing medium). Virtually all of them use PostScript to image their pages.

Because the photosensitive surfaces of these media are so fine, the image created by the laser is extremely crisp. Resolutions of these machines usually start at

1270 dpi (which is a nice, round 500 dots per centimeter, if you're wondering why it's such a weird number).

Imagesetters don't know anything about color, so to create color pages on such a machine, those files have to be *color separated.* Commercial printing presses typically use only four ink colors (our friends cyan, magenta, yellow, and black) to create the entire rainbow of printed colors, so color images have to be *screened* (broken down into an array of dots) and then separated into four images, one for each color. When these four images are printed one on top of the other, all the superimposed dots blend into the proper range of colors. For every color page you send to the imagesetter, four come out.

Your usual experience of an imagesetter is when you bring your Mac files to a service bureau or print shop to have them prepared for commercial printing. Unless you're a publishing pro, you'll probably hand over a disk and stand back until the final printed pages, books, brochures, or whatevers are ready for you.

But what's on that disk is critical, because running an imagesetter is expensive, and you want everything to go right the first time. Otherwise the bills can be shocking. Here are some tips to follow to make your imagesetting experiences uneventful:

- Even before you start preparing your files, talk to your service bureau or printer and explain the nature of your job. They may well hand you a checklist of things to do to prepare your file. If you don't do what these pros recommend, it will cost you.

- Make sure you have all the components of your file together. When you import a graphic into many applications, for example, the program doesn't actually build it into your file. Instead, it merely creates a link to it so it can find it later, to display it onscreen or to print a page containing it. If you give one of those files to a service bureau without all the linked files that go with it, you're going to end up with holes in your page or a file that won't print.

- The safest way to deliver files for imagesetting is as Portable Document Format (PDF) files. PDF is a special, compact form of PostScript that eliminates a lot of potential printing problems. If your service bureau prefers, you can alternatively send the bureau a PostScript disk file. (How to make one is covered in "Printing to Disk" earlier in this chapter.) Unless your service bureau specifically says it has all the fonts you used in your document, you should embed those fonts in the PostScript or PDF file.

- If you deliver an application file to the service bureau (a file from QuarkXPress, say, or Adobe PageMaker), make sure the bureau has the same version of the program that you used. And once again, make sure you give them all the graphics files and fonts they might need.

- Leave enough time for problems. Just because your pages printed perfectly on your desktop PostScript printer doesn't mean they'll do so on an imagesetter. Graphics that print fine at 300 or 600 dpi, for example, may prove so complicated to process at 3000 dpi that the imagesetter's RIP can't handle it.

Troubleshooting: When Bad Things Happen to Good Pages (JF)

You labored and toiled to get your document to look right onscreen. Just one final tap of the finger—Print!—and your job should be done. But it doesn't print, or it prints wrong, or your Mac starts barking at you as if you've done something wrong. This was supposed to be the easy part!

Printing is fraught with potential problems because it involves not only software conflicts that can arise inside your Mac but also hardware problems outside your Mac: cables, inks, toners, paper, and that most primitive of nemeses: moving parts.

There are a million things that can stand between you and a perfect printout, but they're all variations of a limited number of basic problems, and it's these we'll be taking a look at.

Nothing Happens

There are different kinds of nothing, but all these nonevents have this feature in common: No paper comes out of your printer. Almost all printing error messages are generated by your Mac's operating system, and different versions of the Mac OS use slightly different language to describe these problems. But the language used below is generic, so you'll easily be able to relate your own disaster to the message you get from your Mac (if you're lucky enough to get one, that is).

Missing printer. You may get a message that your printer is missing or unavailable. This points to one of four problems:

- The printer is not turned on or hasn't warmed up long enough to initialize (that is, it's awake but still groggy).

- There's a break in the cabling somewhere between your computer and printer. LocalTalk cabling plugs are notorious for coming loose at the slightest provocation. The solution is to wiggle the wires to make sure they're connected securely. If you're in a workgroup, check with others in the group to see if they're having a problem, too. If some are and some aren't, you'll find the break in the cabling where the have group meets the have-nots. If no one can get at the printer, the problem is at the printer, or maybe even *in* the printer.

- There's a mismatch in the Chooser between the driver you've chosen and the specific printer you want to use (a single PostScript driver can be used with many printer models). You may think you're printing to one machine but you're actually connected to another.

- The printer could be hung up. PostScript printers from time to time choke on a job and become immobilized. This generally happens if a printer is fed a job that overtaxes its memory supply. When this happens, the printer can become comatose and unresponsive. The solution is to *recycle* it—a fancy way of saying turn it off and then back on again. After it reinitializes itself, it will come back online.

"This document cannot be printed." An error message to this effect could mean that the printer has choked on your job, a problem that most commonly occurs with PostScript printers. If you get an error message that says there was an "offending PostScript command," it could mean two things. The first is that you're trying to print using a version of PostScript that your printer doesn't support. There are three versions of PostScript (Levels 1 and 2 and PostScript 3), and a Level 1–compatible machine may not be able to process a job that contains code from a later version of PostScript. In this case, the offending command may actually give a clue as to why the printer balked (maybe not to you or me, but to a trained tech-support person). If PostScript-version incompatibility is a problem, save your file in PDF and specify Level 1 compatibility in the Create PDF dialog box (see "Printing to Disk," earlier in this chapter). This will create a printable file, although you'll need Adobe Acrobat software to print it.

But more commonly you'll get this message if the printer has run out of memory. The "offending command" is simply the code the printer was processing when it hit the memory wall. The two most common causes of this are (a) too many fonts used in the document, or (b) graphics that take so much memory to process that the printer runs out of RAM. If the problem is too many fonts, you can select Unlimited Downloadable Fonts under PostScript Options in the Page Setup dialog box. This will allow only one font to download into the printer's memory at a time. This will slow down printing, but the job will print. If the problem lies with the graphic, you'll have to simplify it somehow. Your graphics program's manual will explain this.

The printer's light blinks but nothing happens. This indicates one of two things: (a) You're being impatient, or (b) the printer is caught in an endless looping calculation and can't free itself. Sometimes in the latter case you'll get an error message, or the printer may "time out," which means that even it realizes the job is taking too long, and it abandons that job. If you've chosen Unlimited Downloadable Fonts as mentioned above, a job can indeed take a very long time to print, as the printer could be spending 10 seconds every time it has to download a font. For a document with more than 100 font changes (not uncommon!), we're talking about 20 minutes to print it.

It's also possible that your Mac is trying to tell you there's a problem you haven't noticed. In Mac OS 9's Print Monitor's Preferences dialog box (which you get to from its Edit menu; **Figure 6.22**), you can set your Mac to give you the subtlest of all warning signs: a gentle blinking in the Applications menu. If you want a more forceful warning, you can opt for the in-your-face warning that will interrupt whatever work you're doing to alert you to a printing problem.

Figure 6.22

In the Print Monitor's Preferences dialog box, you can select the kind of warning you receive if there's a printing problem, ranging from a subtle dot appearing next to the PrintMonitor name in the Applications menu to a warning box that pops up in front of your current work.

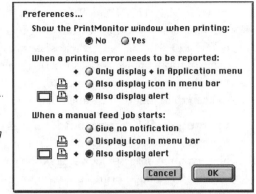

"File is O.K., but it can't be printed." Small consolation. This error is often generated by a corrupted printer driver. Like any System file that gets used and read often (fonts are another good example), drivers risk becoming damaged or corrupted. If you get these messages, try removing your printer's driver and installing a fresh version from the disk that came with your printer.

Unexpected Things Happen

The problems in this category arise when you have indeed printed a page, but what's on it isn't what you expected.

Wrong typefaces. Lots of possibilities here. If you get Courier instead of the typeface you wanted, it's because the printer font for the face you wanted wasn't available. Make sure it's in the Fonts folder, or if you're using a font-management program, check that it's properly loaded into the font set you're using, and that the necessary font set has been activated.

If the type looks sort of right but it's lumpy, bumpy, or otherwise misshapen, the problem is probably that your printer is imaging the page using a screen font instead of a printer font. The printer tries to make these pretty at its higher resolution, but it's a lost cause. Again, the solution is to make sure the printer fonts are where they should be.

If most of the type is right, but the italics, bolds, or bold italics (or all three) are missing, it means your printer only has access to the *regular* or *roman* version of the font family. Onscreen, your Mac can use the screen fonts for the regular member of a typeface family to fake italics, bolds, and bold italics, tricking you into thinking that all the fonts are actually on hand. At print time, though, when these turn up missing, your printer will use what it has available: the regular font.

If you get an incorrect typeface on your printed page but it's rendered clearly and properly, you have had the luck to be smitten by a rare problem: a font ID conflict. Fonts have names, but they also have hidden ID numbers, and there is a possibility that you'll wind up with two fonts with the same ID number on your Mac. That's rare. What makes this problem rarer is that most Mac software is savvy to the possibility of this problem and renumbers fonts temporarily to avoid it. Nevertheless, you may be the lucky one who gets nicked. The solutions are to use a font-management program that adjusts conflicting font ID numbers (see Chapter 18, "Fonts"), or to isolate the conflicting fonts to keep them out of the same document.

Crummy-looking graphics. The most common reason for this is over-optimism. Most desktop printers simply cannot make graphics—especially photographic images—look as good on paper as they do onscreen. Printers can do only two things: print a dot or not print a dot. Some can vary their dot size slightly, but none can print grays or midtones. Color blends or gradations of gray that look great onscreen, then, tend to look coarse and banded on a printed page unless the printer has very high resolution (such as 1000-plus dpi).

Another common cause of bad-looking graphics is trying to print EPS graphics on a non-PostScript printer. A lot of clip art, for example, comes in EPS format. EPS files contain a preview image (usually in PICT or TIFF format) that can be viewed onscreen. When you print an EPS image to a PostScript printer, the image data in the file is used to generate the print image. But on a non-PostScript printer, the screen-preview image will be print instead. It won't be pretty.

My Work Looks Good, but ...

This is where you get to put your hands on your hips and blame sinister outside forces for ruining the looks of your printed page. Right—these problems are not your fault. Not directly, at least.

Faint or fading images. These are generally caused by an inkjet cartridge or a laser printer's toner cartridge running low. Also, inkjet-cartridge nozzles (the jets, in effect) can become clogged with guck (technical term, sorry), in which case they have to be cleared. Inkjet printer drivers usually offer a head-cleaning option that essentially turns up the pressure during printing and blows the guck free of the printhead and onto the page. Printer manufacturers often recommend that you do this de-gucking at regular intervals, but the paranoid among us suspect this is just a way to make the inkjet cartridges empty faster (the cleaning process uses way more ink than normal printing). These suspicious types say that you only need to de-guck when guck becomes a problem.

Just because a laser printer's toner cartridge is getting low (the little warning light on your printer may even go on), that's no reason to replace it yet. Instead, turn the printer off, take the cartridge out of the printer, and rock the cartridge gently to and fro and from side to side. This redistributes the toner powder inside the cartridge, where it may have been sticking to various surfaces. Doing this can greatly extend the life span of your cartridges.

Streaking. In inkjet printers, this can also be caused by guck buildup, as mentioned above. But in laser printers it generally means that the corona wire is dirty. The corona wire creates an electrical charge on the toner drum, onto which toner is attracted and later used to image your pages. Laser printers come with a little brush for cleaning the corona wire, but if you don't have one, you can use a cotton swab. Be careful! Make sure the printer has been turned off for a while before you stick your hands inside it. Some pieces in there get hot as hell, and the corona wire is one of them. It's also very fragile, being tightly strung like a very thin guitar string. Dust off the wire with only the slightest pressure. Better yet, buy one of those little cans of compressed air that photographers use to clean their lenses, and give the wire a good blast.

Weird distortions on laser printer output. If you start to see fun-house mirror effects on your laser-printed pages, look out. Swirly patches, fish-eye effects, and disjointed patches of page images point to a problem with the printer's fusing roller. This roller gets very hot and actually melts the toner particles onto your page. The surface of this roller gets fatigued after a while and can start to bubble and pull away from the roller. These bubbles cause the image distortions. There's nothing you can do about this but take the machine in for repair.

Bad colors. Bad colors on inkjet printers usually arise from a weakness in one of the component inks. The printhead could be clogged with guck (see "Streaking," above), or one of the color wells could be running dry, causing a weakness in that hue and shifting all composite colors in the opposite direction.

More likely, the printer driver isn't doing a great job of matching the colors you see onscreen to those on the printed page. This is a job for color management. In Mac OS 9, if your printer driver permits it, switch to the System's Color Matching pane in your Print dialog box and choose ColorSync Matching to specify an ICC profile for your specific printer (**Figure 6.23**). These profiles allow an application (in this case, the System) to understand the printing capabilities of a printer so it can make adjustments to the color intensities used to image the page. This allows the page to better match what's on the screen. Most color printers come with ICC profiles, and they should be installed in the ColorSync Profiles folder in the System Folder (tons of them come with Mac OS 9, so take a look before you assume you don't have the one you need).

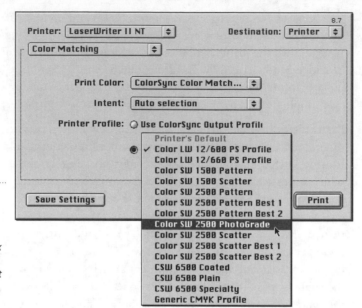

Figure 6.23

You can get more faithful printed colors by selecting Color Matching in the Print dialog box and then choosing a ColorSync Output Profile for your printer.

 In Mac OS X, you can also set profiles with the ColorSync Utility.

Miscellaneous Headaches

These are problems that fall into the category None of the Above.

Slow printing. It is a scientific fact that when you are in a hurry, printers run more slowly. This derives from the same natural principle that explains why a watched pot never boils. But there may be other reasons for slow printing.

First, not all printers print at the same speed, and older ones, like older Macs, just run slower. Two otherwise identical printers may run at different speeds if one has more built-in memory. In the case of QuickDraw printers, for which your Mac does the page processing, if you're asking your Mac to do some heavy-duty work in the foreground (image processing, say, or database thrashing), the work it's doing in the background (that is, printing) is going to slow down, too. Likewise, a lot of traffic on your workgroup's LAN will slow down the communication between your Mac and your printer.

More often, though, the cause of slowness is your own file. If you're printing photographic images, make sure they don't contain more data than your printer can use. Sending a 300-dpi, 8-bit scan to a desktop printer is throwing far more data at it than it can print. It's going to spend a lot of time throwing away data it can't use to *downsample* your image to something it can handle. Consult your image-editing program's manual for more information on how to slim down your images for your printer's resolution.

Rotated photographic images also take a long time to process, because the image-processing software has to remap all the pixels off their original 90-degree grid and onto one that's cocked at an angle. This is complicated stuff and takes a lot of computing energy (and time).

Images with *clipping paths* and layers also print slowly. A clipping path is a shape that works like a stencil to allow part of a background image to show through into the foreground. Calculating this kind of image is complicated, and your image file contains all of the data for the part of the image that's masked out, not just the part you see. Ditto for layered images. You may only see a single flat image, but the file itself may contain gobs of data for parts of images that don't print but still have to be dealt with, even if they're hidden behind another layer.

Using lots of fonts in a document will also slow down printing. When you're using a PostScript printer, unless those fonts are stored in the printer, they'll have to be downloaded to it, and this takes time. If the printer doesn't have enough memory to hold them all, you'll have to select Unlimited Downloadable Fonts under PostScript Options in the Print dialog box. This slows things down to a crawl, as it will force a font download for every typeface change in the document.

Wrinkled envelopes. Most printers aren't built to handle envelopes. The most common problem with such printers is that they wrinkle the envelopes as they print them. You can reduce this effect if you use a brayer to flatten the edges of the envelopes before printing. A teaspoon also works well, or a fingernail, if you have any left. If you can alter the paper path of your printer to straighten it (some printers have a *back door*), that will help a lot, too. Printers that cause media to take a path that doubles back on itself do the worst damage to envelopes.

Lost Chooser selections. You may notice sometimes that in Mac OS 9 and earlier, the Chooser seems to have contracted amnesia and doesn't remember the settings you gave it the day before. There are two related possibilities here. Your Chooser settings are held in a special part of your Mac's memory called *Parameter RAM* (PRAM). These memories, along with others for such things as your mouse and clock settings, are kept alive by a battery that supports the PRAM. If this battery runs down (as it eventually will), your Mac will start to forget things. The clock will go wrong and your Mac will forget what year it is. Your mouse may slow down. And your Chooser will have to be continually reminded of what it's supposed to be doing. Apple does not recommend that you try to replace this battery by yourself. You have to bring your Mac into an authorized dealer.

If your clock and mouse seem to be in good working order, it is also possible that the PRAM itself has been corrupted, in which case you have to reset it. You can do this by holding down four keys at once while you restart your

Mac: ⌘Option PR. You'll hear the little Mac start-up chime sound a second time to signal that the deed has been done. After you've done this, you'll have to use your control panels to reset your Mouse and General settings.

Care and Feeding of Your Printer (JF)

A little bit of TLC will help your printer last a long time. The No. 1 rule of printer maintenance is to carefully read your printer's manual. Stop whining! If you fail to follow the operating and maintenance procedures outlined in the manual, any guarantee, warranty, or service agreement you may have with the printer's manufacturer is null and void, blotto, gone, history. You have to care about this.

Most manufacturers go so far as to specify that you have to use supplies bought from them and no one else. You really can't blame them, as you can't expect them to guarantee their printers against problems caused by some cheapo ink cartridges, refurbished laser-toner cartridges, or whatever. You're free, of course, to suspect that their real motives are to keep you hooked on buying their expensive supplies.

The smart money says to play by the rules and not take any risks as long as your warranty is active.

Keep It Clean

The best thing you can do to extend the life of your printer is to keep it clean. Use a dust cover whenever the machine is turned off. Those little cans of compressed air from photo-supply shops are great for giving the guts of your printer a quick and occasional blow-out. Paper dust, airborne dust, and ink and toner dust all accumulate inside a printer, and none of them does the printer any good in there.

If you have a laser printer, find some way of recycling your printed pages other than sending them through the printer a second time to be printed on the back. Duplex printers—those capable of printing on both sides of a sheet—have mechanisms for cleaning both sets of rollers inside the printer. But one-sided laser printers usually only clean the rollers that face the printing side. When you send recycled sheets through with the printed side down, you run the risk of having old toner particles build up on those other rollers, and this can eventually gum up the works. Unless your printer specifically says two-sided printing is OK, assume that it isn't.

And if you're a smoker, put your ashtray as far away from your printer as your reach will allow. The smoke is bad enough, but the ashes are a real killer.

The Substrate Question

Substrate is the $2 replacement for the 50-cent word *medium*. Most printers are quite accommodating when it comes to what substrates you can print on.

For laser printers, most restrictions are based on the heat used inside these machines to bond—literally to melt—the toner particles to the substrate. This means any nonpaper substrate you use in your laser printer has to be specifically approved for use with either a laser printer or a photocopier (which uses the same basic technology). Acetate sheets and self-adhesive labels that you can use on an inkjet printer may melt inside a laser printer, with fatal results for the printer.

Thick papers also don't work particularly well in laser printers because the heat applied by the fusing roller to melt the toner onto the paper is diffused by the thicker paper. The result is that the toner doesn't adhere as well and has a tendency to chip off. Anything thicker than fine bond paper is likely to suffer this chipping. If you want to use thicker paper, such as card stock for business cards or invitations, you may find it necessary to spray the pages with acrylic fixative (available in art-supply stores), which actually remelts the toner chemically and bonds it firmly to the surface.

Inkjet printers are more forgiving about what they'll print on, but again, make sure any plastic or self-adhesive materials you use with them are specifically approved for that use. For color-proofing purposes, use a coated paper or one that's supercalendered (that is, pressed *really* hard) to give it a very hard, almost polished surface. This will keep the ink from spreading out, blotterlike, from where it was originally applied. This creates a much crisper image and prevents unwanted color blending.

7

Peripherals

John Christopher is the chapter editor and author.

Sharon Zardetto Aker (SA), Brad Bunnin (BB), Andreu Cabré (AC),
Caleb Clark (CC), John Kadyk (JK), Joe Matazzoni (JM), Susan McCallister (SM),
and Arthur Naiman (AN) contributed to earlier editions of **The Macintosh Bible**,
from which portions of this chapter are taken.

Your Mac relies on peripheral devices to carry out your commands. Your mouse, keyboard, and monitor are peripherals—take them away, and all you have is a nice-looking box.

Although you may be perfectly happy with those basic peripherals, odds are pretty good you'll want to add some new ones in the future. Maybe you'd like a scanner to restore those photos of distant relatives—or to remove certain people completely from your photos. Perhaps you are considering a digital still camera or even a camcorder for sharing the big events in your life with family and friends.

If you're not so happy with your current peripherals, you can get better ones. Don't like your mouse? Consider a trackball. Want a big-screen monitor but don't have room for a standard CRT model? Get an LCD display. Is your keyboard too noisy or too quiet, or do you want one that suits you better ergonomically? Replace it.

Welcome to the world of peripherals. You've got lots of choices, and this chapter talks about them all.

In This Chapter

Peripheral Connections: Getting on the Right Bus

For some reason, every time I hear the acronym USB, I start playing Scrabble in my head. Besides making entertaining anagrams, USB stands for Universal Serial Bus. Developed by Microsoft, IBM, and other companies, USB is a multiplatform standard that lets peripheral devices communicate at high speed with any personal computer. Apple rolled out the first Macs with USB when it introduced the iMac. Since then, every new Mac has incorporated at least one USB port and sometimes two.

Parlez-Vous USB?

The USB specification is impressive. First off, it is a true plug-and-play interface. You simply plug in your peripheral (a printer, scanner, or hard drive, for example), turn it on, and away you go—no terminators or ID switches to set. However, initially you will likely have to install some type of software driver so your Mac can communicate with your peripheral device. Thanks to some extra magic in Mac OS 9 and later, whenever you plug in a new USB device, if you don't have the necessary software installed, a dialog box will appear, guiding you to the Internet, where you can download the driver.

Amazingly, USB is capable of connecting as many as 127 devices with the aid of special hubs (see "Adapter, Adapter" later in this chapter for more about hubs). Most can operate without an AC adapter—the bus carries all the power required.

Performance-wise, USB pushes the envelope, with speeds nearly 50 times faster than those of serial connections. Realistically, though, the current crop of low-speed USB devices can only send 1.5 Mbps through the port. A new version of the USB specification is under development. USB 2.0 will offer a maximum transfer rate of 480 Mbps (60 megabytes per second).

The ever-expanding USB universe of peripherals includes digital cameras, mice, keyboards, speakers, microphones, printers, scanners, gamepads, joysticks, and storage devices. The sheer number of peripherals grows every month, because USB devices can run on any type of computer system, not just on Macs. One great place to explore USB peripherals for the Mac is http://guide.apple.com/uscategories/usb.html.

Finally, USB devices are hot-pluggable, or hot-swappable, which means you can disconnect and reconnect a USB peripheral without shutting down your Macintosh and starting it back up again.

The ABCs of ADB

Just a few years ago, every Macintosh produced (except for the Macintosh Plus) featured ADB—Apple Desktop Bus, the forerunner to USB. ADB ports connected the keyboard, mouse, and other devices to the Macintosh.

The last series of Macs that incorporated ADB exclusively were the beige Power Mac G3s in both the minitower and desktop models. The first generation of Blue-and-White Power Mac G3s provided the best of both worlds, integrating ADB and USB ports. This allowed owners of ADB peripherals to hang on to them just a little longer.

ADB allows you to connect roughly 16 devices in a chain to the Macintosh, with a total length not to exceed 16 feet. Realistically, you probably won't want to use more than 3 devices, because the longer the chain, the more the signal will degrade.

Unlike USB, ADB does not allow you to hot-swap devices while the Mac is running. Although it may be possible to plug or unplug an ADB device with the Macintosh on, the device's performance will likely slow down enough to require restarting. In addition, Apple does not recommend hot-swapping ADB devices, as it may damage the ADB controller chip on the logic board.

ADB devices have grown somewhat scarce as USB has gained popularity, but a variety are still available (see "ADB Keyboards" and "Mice and Other Pointing Devices" later in this chapter).

Aye, Aye, iMate

So you forked over the cash and bought yourself a brand-spanking-new Macintosh. Everything was totally cool until you discovered that your USB-equipped Mac was about to force your collection of ADB peripherals into early retirement.

Enter the **iMate** from Griffin Technology ($39; www.griffintechnology.com). This little device preserves your investment by letting ADB keyboards, mice, trackballs, cameras, bar-code readers, special hardware dongles, or what have you speak USB. The product is even compatible with AppleVision monitors, which rely on ADB for ColorSync and onscreen geometry settings.

The Good Old Serial Bus

If you have an older Mac—say older than a Blue-and-White Power Mac G3— it likely has a serial port. For years Macs used serial ports to connect printers, modems, and other devices. Like Apple's ADB port, serial ports and serial devices have disappeared in favor of speedier USB peripherals. Rated at a top speed of 230 Kbps, most serial devices could only move data at 115 Kbps.

Although serial devices are harder to come by new, you can purchase PCI cards to add serial ports to the newest desktop Power Macs or USB adapters so you can use the newest peripherals with older Macs.

Of Keyboards, Mice, and More

Whether you're thinking of replacing your current keyboard, mouse, or other navigational device or you never had one to begin with, this section discusses the major considerations in looking for new equipment.

Evaluating Keyboards (JC, JK)

Picking a keyboard that's right for you can be a daunting task. The information here will help you do a worthwhile comparison and decide what features are most important to you. Then you can find a keyboard in a store or catalog or through an online retailer that meets your needs. If possible, try it out or get one that offers a money-back guarantee. You can't really judge a device's performance until you've used it with your own Mac for awhile.

Two of the most important considerations when choosing a keyboard are:

Key feel. Each keyboard has a slightly different feel. Do you prefer a hard, solid keystroke or a softer, mushier one? You'll need to do some hands-on testing to decide.

Ergonomics. The correct and comfortable positioning of hands, fingers, and wrists is critical when using a keyboard. The combination of improper positioning and uninterrupted typing sessions puts you at risk for various injuries, some of which can become permanent disabilities. If you're a marathon typist, you should seriously consider purchasing a specially built ergonomic keyboard designed to avoid injuries.

The options you can find in keyboards vary greatly; here are some you'll need to consider:

The numeric keypad. Practically all new keyboards come with a numeric keypad or at least let you easily add one. The keypad saves a huge amount of time for people who enter lots of numbers and who can touch-type the ten-key layout.

Built-in trackballs. Some keyboards offer a built-in trackball, which saves you the expense of buying one separately. But don't assume a keyboard trackball will work the same way as one you might purchase to replace your mouse. Built-in trackballs tend to be smaller and harder to control. Whenever possible, try before you buy.

Built-in trackpads. A few keyboards on the market provide built-in track-pads so you can work as you would on a PowerBook keyboard. The trackpad lets you use your index finger to control mouse movement. Using a keyboard with a built-in trackpad can save space on your desk as well as frequent moves back to the mouse.

Key arrangement. The basic alphanumeric keys on a keyboard are always the same, but the placement of the power, ⌘, Control, and Option keys tends to vary. Some keyboards have unique layouts you may find convenient or annoying. You might, for instance, prefer a larger Delete or Return key. Again, it's ideal to try before you buy—or at least get a money-back guarantee.

USB Keyboards

USB keyboards are standard issue on all modern Macs. Apple's own first-generation USB keyboard was compact and stylish and didn't claim much real estate on your desk. Those used to spreading out on an extended keyboard, though, may have found it too small.

The good news is that you don't have to stay married to any particular keyboard. Since USB is a cross-platform standard, multitudes of manufacturers make fully Mac-compatible USB keyboards.

Adesso (www.adessoinc.com) manufactures a large variety of USB keyboards. Its **MCK-560 USB Basic Mac** ($59.95), a full-size keyboard in the Graphite color, includes two bus-powered USB ports and comes with removable wrist support as well as a three-year warranty.

Another full-size keyboard worth considering is MacAlly Peripherals' translucent **iKey** ($49; www.macally.com), designed to match newer Macs in two-tone Ice-and–Bondi Blue or Ice-and-Graphite color combinations. MacAlly includes a 5-foot USB cable and comes with a lifetime warranty.

Going Pro with the Apple Pro Keyboard

If you're looking for a keyboard that's as solid as it is stylish, the **Apple Pro Keyboard** ($59; www.apple.com) may be the one for you. Its Graphite housing matches the Power Mac G4, and the black keys have a nice cushiony feel with a subdued sound (for those of us who don't like to hear a resounding click). It's compatible with any Macintosh that offers a USB port and is running Mac OS 9 and later.

It has 15 Function keys and a height-adjustment bar but lacks a power button, so for startup you'll have to rely on the button on your Mac's front. But where it has removed keys, Apple has also added some new ones: volume up, volume down, mute, and media eject.

Other minor quirks include a shorter-than-normal USB cable (somewhat inconvenient if you keep your Mac on the floor) and no Caps Lock indicator light.

ADB Keyboards

Though these days USB peripherals can be had by the boatload, at the time this was written some manufacturers were still making ADB keyboards, and they were readily available. One of our favorites, **Kensington's Keyboard-in-a-Box** ($49.99; www.kensington.com), comes highly recommended. Kensington even offers a 90-day, no-risk trial. Like all of the company's products, the keyboard comes with a lifetime replacement warranty.

Adesso's **AEK-405 EasyTouch for Mac** ($59) has 105 keys and two extra ADB ports. Its design is not unlike that of Apple's own AppleDesign keyboard, which makes it an ideal low-cost replacement for the keyboards on pre-iMac or platinum-colored Macs. This model has been around for some time, and Adesso claims it will maintain production as long as there is a demand for it.

Ergonomic Keyboards

An ergonomic keyboard is friendly to your wrists and fingers, letting them stay in a more natural position while you type. If you spend long hours at your keyboard, you need one of these. Ergonomic keyboards are designed differently from your typical Mac keyboard. Generally, the alphanumeric keys are split down the middle so your hands can stay farther apart; the two key sections are at a slight angle to each other, and the keyboard is bowed in the middle, with a built-in wrist rest—although some don't include the bow or wrist rest. Altogether, these details add up to a less painful typing experience.

 Because of their unusual shape and size, ergonomic keyboards take up more space in your work area. Take this into consideration when choosing one, especially if you use a keyboard drawer.

Most keyboards on the market have some form of ergonomic support built in, such as height adjustment or softer keys. All of the keyboards mentioned in this section, however, have additional features that qualify them for the ergonomic category.

Adesso leads the keyboard market when it comes to ergonomic models. Its **EKB-2100 Tru-Form** USB ($79.99) is contoured for comfort and breaks the keyboard layout and keypad into three main pieces. The neutral Ice color coordinates with any Mac. But if you want to go Graphite, you should consider the **EKB-888 Nu-Form Basic USB** ($69.95).

Kinesis's contoured keyboard ($225; www.kinesis-ergo.com) is designed to correct the awkward postures that can lead to repetitive stress injuries. According to independent studies cited by Kinesis, as well as reports from users, it really works.

This keyboard's left- and right-hand keys are set in two concave bowls, separated by several inches of empty surface. The keys are arranged so your thumbs are higher than the rest of your hand and your palms turn slightly toward each other. This keeps your hands and arms in a natural position, and very little finger movement is necessary to push down each key. If you want to see some unique keyboards, check out Kinesis's **Maxim** and **Evolution** designs.

One-handed typing (CC). Infogrip's **BAT Personal Keyboard** ($199; www.infogrip.com) is a seven-button keyboard that lets you type one-handed: it has one key for each of your four fingers and three for your thumb. You press combinations, or *chords,* of the seven keys to produce various keyboard characters. For example, for the letter *g* you press the thumb and the middle and ring-finger keys simultaneously.

Standard keyboards are faster than the BAT for straight typing, but this device is convenient for layout and text editing because you can keep one hand on the keyboard and one on the mouse without looking away from the screen. The BAT has a palm rest and ergonomically designed keys, and it doesn't take long to get used to.

The Keyboard Control Panel

Your Mac's Keyboard control panel (Mac OS 9.1 and later) is keeping something from you— an important feature that lets you customize the way you use your keyboard (**Figure 7.1**).

Want to launch an application with the touch of a single button? Just assign a Function key to the task.

Open your Keyboard control panel and click the Function Keys button. A customization panel will appear. Now simply click the Function key you want to use, locate the application, and you're done. Mac OS X 10.1 gives you a limited version of this in its Keyboard System Preferences pane.

Figure 7.1

Press one of the Function keys on your keyboard, and you'll get this prompt.

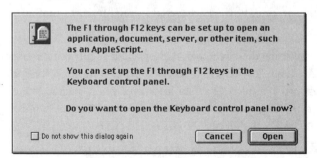

The F1 through F12 keys can be set up to open an application, document, server, or other item, such as an AppleScript.

You can set up the F1 through F12 keys in the Keyboard control panel.

Do you want to open the Keyboard control panel now?

☐ Do not show this dialog again   [Cancel] [Open]

Mice and Other Pointing Devices

Mice are one of the Mac's great innovations. They give you more-direct control over what's onscreen than any keyboard can. The mouse controls the pointer, which gives you the ability to select objects on the screen and control cursors in word processors, paintbrushes in art programs, and paddles in shuffleboard games.

Most of the rules for purchasing a keyboard apply to buying a mouse. You'll spend a great deal of time moving around your Mac's screen and clicking, so the most important criterion is comfort. Whenever possible, take a potential new mouse for a spin.

Apple's **Pro Mouse** ($59) lets you say adios to your mouse pad. It has no rollers or tracking mechanism to clog and no mouse ball to clean. Instead, its optical sensor provides precision tracking. Once you get your hand on one, you'll notice that something's missing—the mouse button. Instead, the entire body pivots up and down to activate the click mechanism.

Kensington's **Mouse-in-a-Box USB/ADB** ($39.99) is great for both old and new Macs. You can connect it to either a USB or an ADB port. It comes with a five-year warranty and an amazing 90-day no-risk trial. If you have an older mouse or need ergonomic support, this is a good choice.

The Kensington folks also make the **Mouse-in-a-Box Optical Pro** ($39.95), the only mouse we know of that comes with a taillight! It works using optical technology, which means you get improved tracking on any surface—and there's no mouse ball to clean. It plugs into your USB port and has four programmable buttons and a handy scroll wheel.

Logitech (www.logitech.com) has been manufacturing mice and other peripheral hardware since 1981. In early 2001 it introduced the **Cordless MouseMan Optical** ($69.95), which combines optical technology with a wireless design. You no longer need to be tethered to your Mac with this ingenious mouse—you can work anywhere within 6 feet of the receiver. It offers a convenient built-in thumb button and a scroll wheel for speedy scrolling.

Trackballs

Trackballs are a bit like upside-down mice. You roll a ball that sits inside a stationary holder, so they require less desk space than mice. Trackballs control the pointer more precisely than mice do (particularly important for graphics). They all have at least two buttons: one that's like a normal mouse button, and one that can lock in the down position so you can drag objects or menus without holding it.

It is practically impossible to say the word *trackball* without uttering the name *Kensington* before it. This company has been manufacturing some of the best-designed trackballs for almost as many years as there's been *The Macintosh Bible.* Some of its recent contributions include the new dynamically designed **Orbit USB/ADB** ($49.99), which features a shape so appealing that it fits in your hand like melted butter. Seriously, though, the Orbit is both functional and—like many other Kensington products—totally cool.

Another of our favorites is the **Kensington Expert Mouse Pro** ($99.99). This top-of-the-line trackball has four programmable mouse buttons and six special direct-launch buttons that provide instant access to Web sites and applications. As if that weren't enough control, a built-in scroll wheel lets you move rapidly through documents and Web pages. With its numerous features, the Expert Mouse Pro is truly the Swiss Army knife of trackballs.

Logitech specializes in uniquely designed, exceptionally functional trackballs. Its **Cordless TrackMan FX** ($79.95) offers superior control of your Mac. It employs digital radio technology with a 6-foot range and even has an adjustable wrist pad for comfort. Its particular shape enhances productivity—the big red ball is easy to manipulate and maneuver with your fingertips. If you want freedom and ergonomic comfort, this device is worth a look.

Adapter, Adapter

Before Macs (or any computers for that matter) became popular, your intrepid editor used to make frequent visits to my neighborhood Radio Shack. Besides the free batteries the store gave away, I always seemed to need a particular adapter for my stereo, reel-to-reel deck, or what have you. I'm still searching for adapters of some kind, but now typically they're for my Mac. You'll find the items mentioned in this section useful for adapting older hardware to your current Mac as well as for expanding what you may add in the future. (By the way, you won't find this stuff at Radio Shack.)

USB hubs. Because USB devices live in such excellent harmony with your Macintosh, you may eventually want to add to your collection. But with only two ports (or sometimes even just one), things get slightly complicated. That's when you need to purchase a USB hub to expand the number of available ports.

Think of a USB hub as Grand Central Station for your peripherals. You simply connect the hub to one of the USB ports on your Macintosh and then connect all your USB peripherals to the hub. Because USB offers only two types of cables and connectors, hooking things up isn't confusing. If you start running out of ports again, you can simply add another hub. In fact, you can daisy-chain USB hubs to accommodate as many as 127 USB devices. We can't recommend one hub over another, but if you're contemplating a purchase, consider those made by **Belkin** ($69.95; www.belkin.com), **Keyspan**

($39; www.keyspan.com), and **MacAlly** ($39; www.macally.com). These prices are for their four-port hubs.

Serial-to-USB adapters. As we mentioned earlier, USB devices provide higher rates of data transfer than serial ones, and current Macs only offer USB for peripheral connections. Your options are somewhat limited if you want to use serial devices such as printers and modems in a USB world.

Keyspan makes a dual-port serial-to-USB adapter, the **USB Twin Serial Adapter** ($79). This one is extremely useful if you own an iMac, PowerBook, or iBook and want to continue using legacy serial devices. For PDAs such as the Palm Organizer, the company's **USB PDA Adapter** ($39) can save the day.

USB-to-SCSI adapters. You really do have every reason to stay in love with your SCSI devices. After all, if you're a longtime Mac user, you grew up with SCSI. If you own a SCSI device such as a scanner or external hard drive and you have a USB-only Mac, you can breathe life into those SCSI devices.

Belkin and Microtech International (www.microtechint.com) both manufacture USB-to-SCSI adapters. Belkin's **USB SCSI Adapter** ($59.95) features a hublike design with five shells in different colors, which you can snap on to make the device match your Mac. The **USB XpressSCSI** ($59) from Microtech International connects SCSI devices via a standard 25-pin connector (a 50-pin high-density model is also available for $59). All of these devices deliver a maximum data-throughput rate of 1.2 MBps.

The iDock II

The **iDock** II from CompuCable ($259.99; www.compucable.com) is an ingenious peripheral device. It includes a floppy drive as well as serial, USB, and ADB ports for your iMac. The unit sits underneath your Mac on a small base so you can turn and twist it at different angles.

Serial bus expansion. Serial devices live on. Modems, printers, and PDAs such as the Palm Pilot are examples of a few popular ones. Once you step up to a new Mac that offers USB ports, you can forget about using your serial devices, unless you purchase an adapter or an expansion card.

Keyspan's **SX Pro Serial Card** ($179), outfitted with four serial ports, installs inside any Mac that has an available PCI slot and is running Mac OS 8 and later. The SX Pro worked seamlessly in our tests and enabled us to use an external modem and an ancient CoStar Labelwriter without a hitch. The company's compatibility list is large and confirms support for numerous printers, graphics tablets, digital cameras, PDAs, and much more. It's a good idea to review the list on Keyspan's Web site to ensure that your serial device is fully supported. If your new Macintosh suffers from serial-port separation anxiety, make it happy again with the SX Pro.

Also worth mentioning is Griffin Technology's Port group of products: the **gPort** ($49), **g4Port** ($49), and **CubePort** ($49). Using the modem slot on the Power Mac G3 and G4 (or the Power Mac G4 Cube, if you bought one before Apple shelved the line), they provide compatibility for printers, MIDI devices, and other serial devices as well as offering LocalTalk file sharing and printing. If you own a single serial device, you can economize with one of these outstanding cards.

Monitors and LCD Displays

Buying a display. Not all monitors are made alike. In this section, we'll describe what to look for in a monitor and an LCD display. You'll find out which ones will work with your Mac and run through some of the many choices on the market.

These days you have a couple of choices when it comes to the type of display you can use on your Mac. The most common and least expensive displays use a cathode ray tube (CRT). Users have relied on this type of display since the computer's inception; it works on the same principle as a television.

The second type is the liquid crystal display (LCD). This technology employs liquid crystals sandwiched between sheets of polarized material. Light from behind the sheets passes through the crystals. LCDs are rapidly becoming standard issue in the computer world.

Size matters (BB, JK). Before rushing out to purchase a new display, you should first think about how much physical space you have on your desk to park it. If you're working in close quarters, you might want to consider investing in a flat-panel LCD screen.

Most monitors fall into one of three size categories, based on their shape and diagonal screen measurement. Don't attach too much importance to a screen's physical size, as it rarely matches the viewable image area—the actual area you see onscreen. The viewable image area is always listed in the manufacturers specifications and frequently posted on their Web sites.

Small (15-inch) monitors are fine for typical home uses: writing letters, surfing the Web, using personal-accounting software, playing games, and so on.

Midsize (17- and 19-inch) monitors allow you to display quite a bit more. They're tall enough to show the full length of a letter-size page with margins or wide enough to show two adjacent pages.

Large (21-inch to 24-inch) monitors display two full letter-size pages side by side, so they're great for desktop publishers. They're also useful for graphic artists and people who create large spreadsheets or keep a lot of documents open.

Pixel particulars (JC, JK). The image you see on a Mac's screen is made up of thousands of tiny dots called *pixels,* a term formed from the words *picture elements.* One or more dots make up a single pixel. The amount of information that fits onscreen is directly related to the number of pixels that screen can display. This is known as *screen resolution.*

The standard resolution for your monitor will vary based on its size. For example, the default resolution for the 15-inch monitor built in to an iMac is 800 by 600 pixels. But you can change the resolution to meet your needs and personal preferences. When you set your iMac monitor to a resolution of 832 by 624, you're putting a lot more pixels in the same area, so the monitor uses smaller pixels. As a result, icons, folders, and all other elements appear smaller. Moving the resolution in the opposite direction to, say, 640 by 480 increases the size of images onscreen.

Change Resolution on the Fly

Mac OS 9's Control Strip offers two ways to change monitor settings. The Monitor Bit Depth and Monitor Resolution Control Strip modules let you change these settings instantly as well as quickly launch the Monitors control panel (**Figure 7.2**). The Monitor control in Mac OS X's menu bar gives you similar access.

This is particularly handy if you are playing a game that requires setting the number of colors to 256. Or you could change the resolution to see an entire Web page or document on a small monitor.

Figure 7.2

Change colors on the fly in Mac OS 9 using the Monitor Bit Depth and Monitor Resolution Control Strip modules (left). In Mac OS X, you can use the Display control in the menu bar (right).

72 dots (SA). No matter how many pixels your monitor packs into an inch, the basic Mac measurement is still 72 dots per inch (dpi). Every 72 dots onscreen equal an inch in a printout. If you're using a program with a ruler in it, the ruler's inch marks will occur at every 72 dots, no matter what the true onscreen measurement is.

As odd as it might sound, this quirky rule of measurement ensures that as you move from one Mac to another or change monitors on your own system, the intended design in your document stays the same. It also means that the higher your monitor's resolution, the smaller the 72-dpi measurement. On an 86-dpi screen, for instance, a ruler inch actually measures about .84 inches; on a 65-dpi screen, a ruler inch's actual measurement is about 1.11 inches.

Color and bit depth (JK, AN). On color monitors, each pixel can be black, white, or any of more than 16.7 million colors, including grays—creating an image of almost photographic quality. You select which level of color you want in the Monitors control panel (in Mac OS 9 and earlier) or in the Displays pane (in Mac OS X).

The richness of the color palette available with a given Mac and monitor setup is called its *bit depth* and refers to the number of bits the Mac's memory assigns each pixel. A 1-bit color setting gives you just black and white, 8-bit gives you 256 colors or shades of gray, 16-bit gives you more than 32,000 colors or shades of gray, and 24-bit gives you 16.7 million. The bigger the monitor, the more pixels it has, and the more memory is required for a given bit depth.

Refresh rate (BB, JK, AN). A monitor's refresh rate—how often it redraws the image onscreen—helps determine how steady and solid the image looks. (Don't confuse the refresh rate with the screen's ability to keep up with the mouse when you move a graphic around onscreen; the latter depends on the speed of the Mac and its graphics acceleration, if it has any.)

The refresh rate is measured in hertz (one million times per second)—abbreviated Hz. If a screen refreshes too slowly, you get *flicker* (also called *strobe*). The larger the screen, the more likely the flicker will bother you, so larger monitors usually have higher refresh rates. The refresh rate is also linked to the monitor's resolution, so a given monitor can have different refresh rates depending on which resolution you're using.

VGA monitors and SVGA monitors can run as low as 60 Hz or even 56 Hz, although some Macs let you increase the refresh rate of SVGA monitors to 70 Hz or 72 Hz in the Monitors control panel by clicking the Options button or in the Mac OS X Display pane.

 Peripheral vision is particularly sensitive to flicker, so if you're in doubt about a screen, turn away from it and see how it looks out of the corner of your eye.

Dot pitch—the smaller the better. Several other factors contribute to image quality. *Dot pitch,* the distance between individual dots of phosphor on the screen, affects the overall clarity of the image. Generally, anything below .30 mm is acceptable, and most monitors fall below that.

With color monitors, *sharpness* depends partly on the ability of the display tube to focus the three-color beams so they hit the right spots onscreen (this is called *convergence,* and a few monitors let you adjust for it—a very good feature). *Distortion* refers to a screen's tendency to misrepresent shapes—to display straight lines as bowed, for example. It's often most noticeable at the edges and corners of the screen, and it's more common on large monitors.

Monitor Terminology

Here are a few terms used in relation to monitors:

RGB. The three primary colors on a monitor are red, green, and blue—abbreviated together as RGB.

Interlacing. Mac monitors draw their images one line at a time, from top to bottom; this is a *noninterlaced* setup. Television screens and some monitors for other computer systems draw lines onscreen in alternating patterns: the odd-numbered lines on one pass, the even-numbered lines on the next. This is called *interlacing,* and it reduces flicker on monitors that aren't as fast as the Mac's.

Degaussing. Does your monitor have automatic or manual degaussing, and what the heck is it? If you move your display and put it down a little roughly or just bump into it, you may find that the colors change because the jarring shifts the magnetic field. Degaussing corrects the colors by resetting the field.

Convergence. This is a way to focus the three-color beams so they work together. A monitor that lets you adjust convergence without opening up the case is a very good thing.

ELF, VLF. Your monitor produces *extremely low frequency* (ELF) and *very low frequency* (VLF) electromagnetic emissions. Although some health concerns regarding this radiation have emerged in recent years, no conclusive evidence has ever definitively linked it to cancer or other problems.

Energy Star. Under this voluntary program set up by the U.S. Environmental Protection Agency in 1992, computer equipment that meets EPA energy-conservation requirements can receive the Energy Star stamp of approval. Although the program started with computers and monitors, the EPA has extended the project to other electricity users, including clothes washers, TVs and VCRs, heating and cooling equipment, and buildings.

The Right Monitor for the Job

In this section we describe some of the current monitor types and models available. You don't want to pay for a bigger monitor than you need to get the job done, so consider how you'll be using your monitor—and how much space you have for it on your desktop.

What's my size? Monitor sizes are measured on the diagonal, from the top-left corner to the bottom-right corner, for example. A monitor's viewable area, however, is usually smaller and is the area of the screen actually lit up and displaying something.

Small color monitors. Most people opt for 15-inch color monitors—they're reasonably priced, they don't take up too much space on the desk, and they meet the typical user's needs. At the time of this writing, you could get a decent 15-inch model for around $180.

The Trinitron picture tube from Sony is almost legendary for its quality and sharpness. With Sony's 15-inch color **Multiscan Computer Display CPD-E100**

($199; www.ita.sel.sony.com/products/displays) you get high quality at a decent price. The screen is visually flat, which makes it perfect for graphics—and everything else.

Another value-oriented 15-inch monitor is the **NEC-Mitsubishi AccuSync 50M** multimedia monitor ($189; www.nectech.com/monitors/index.htm). It provides a slightly smaller viewable image (13.8 inches) and front-panel controls. NEC has an outstanding three-year warranty period that covers parts, labor, and—most important—the picture tube itself.

Medium color monitors (BB, JC). Not only do 17- and 19-inch color monitors boast a bigger screen size but they also have a bigger footprint (the space they take up on the desktop), weight, and bulk than the 15-inchers, and they cost more. Visually speaking, though, they do give you more space onscreen.

Leading the pack in 17-inch models is the **Sony Multiscan G220S** ($399.99). Once again, Sony's Trinitron tube provides superior color and sharpness. You also get 16 inches of viewable screen area. You probably won't want to move it after setting it up, as it weighs 41 pounds.

Also worth a look is the **NEC-Mitsubishi Diamond Plus 73** ($250) with 16 inches of usable screen space. It utilizes an onscreen help manager and is covered by NEC's three-year warranty. You can even get an advance replacement if it happens to go belly up.

In the 19-inch category, you can trust Sony, NEC-Mitsubishi, and ViewSonic to deliver high-quality products. Sony pitches its **Sony CPD-G400** ($499.99) to corporate users, but graphic artists and home users will be just as satisfied with its 18 inches of superclear viewing.

Another fine pair of monitors worth considering are the **NEC MultiSync FP955** ($510) and the **ViewSonic GS790** ($340; www.viewsonic.com). Both provide 18 inches of viewable screen space. The FP955 has a flat screen surface that helps eliminate glare. The GS790 manages to provide a larger screen with a footprint closer to that of a 15-inch monitor, and ViewSonic's three-year limited warranty also gives you peace of mind.

Large color monitors. You can now buy 20-, 21-, 22-, and even 24-inch color monitors. Take note—you may need to install extra video RAM (VRAM) or a third-party display card to use one of these giants. Sony and NEC dominate once again in this area, but don't overlook ViewSonic and Samsung.

 Only buy a large monitor if you genuinely need the large screen and have a place to put it; you'll find its presence overwhelming unless you can sit well back from it.

The **NEC MultiSync FP1375X** ($1,050) is loaded with features such as NEC's Opticlear coating, a multilingual onscreen help program, and a large 20-inch viewable screen, and it's covered by a three-year warranty.

In the expensive-but-worth-it category is the **Sony GDM-FW900** ($1999.99). This monster offers 22.5 inches of viewable screen area in a 24-inch model. Designed for engineers, animators, and other high-end professional users, it has a .23 mm dot pitch that provides extraordinarily accurate colors and crystal-clear images.

Flat-panel displays. In the past, when you wanted a big-screen monitor, you had to sacrifice a good portion of your desk to accommodate the behemoth. These days Apple and a few other display manufacturers are letting you reclaim your workspace and have your monster monitor, too.

Flat-panel LCDs have taken root on the desks of Mac owners, and it looks as if they're here to stay. Flat panels offer all the features of standard CRT displays without the investment in real estate. They're also exceptionally sharp and use considerably less energy than equivalent-size CRTs.

Apple's LCDs are superstylish and—dare we say it—affordable. Its 15-inch ($599, www.apple.com/displays) and 17-inch ($999) **Studio Displays** are reasonably priced and work well for home users and demanding professionals alike. Of course we can't forget the granddaddy of them all—the 22-inch Apple **Cinema Display** ($2,499). If you've ever seen these displays up close, you can appreciate their sharpness and color saturation, all viewable from almost any angle. If you own a Power Mac G4 that includes an Apple Display Connector, take a closer look at these.

Keep It Tidy

Apple's flat-panel monitors use the Apple Display Connector (ADC), which combines the video, USB, and power signals in one cable. The cable certainly keeps things neat behind your Mac, but you can't use the cable to hook the Apple monitors to non-Mac computers and older Mac models. (The **Dr. Bott DVIator**—$149 on the Apple Store Web site—lets you hook up ADC-connector displays to the previous generation of Power Mac G4 that used a DVI connection.) New Macs do include a VGA connector, so you can still use monitors from companies other than Apple.

The Not-So-Friendly Ghost and Your LCD

Even though you left your old CRT monitor behind for a flashy new LCD display, you still need to think about screen burn-in. Images left on the screen for prolonged periods of time—24 hours or so—can leave a ghost image, depending on how bright the image is.

Eventually the LCD will recover and the ghostly image will fade away. It can take twice as long for the ghost image to disappear as it took for it to appear. To avoid this situation, Apple recommends putting your Mac to sleep or shutting it down when you're not using it. Screensavers may help, but they drain the battery on a PowerBook or iBook.

Monitor Controls (SA)

The Monitors control panel in Mac OS 9 and earlier and the Display pane in Mac OS X let you set the number of colors you want displayed onscreen and choose a resolution if your monitor provides more than one (**Figure 7.3**).

The number of grays or colors available in the Color Depth section depends on three factors: the monitor, its support (internal or add-on card), and the amount of VRAM available. The color bars beneath the list of choices change to show what you'll get at different color depths. To select a new resolution, just choose from the list. The options vary depending on the Mac and the monitor.

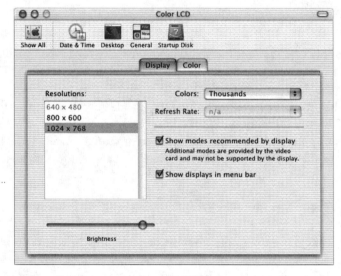

Figure 7.3

Mac OS X's Display pane allows you to set the number of colors and the resolution for your monitor.

Caring for a Monitor (SA)

You may have noticed that a quick swipe with a tissue doesn't help much with your dusty screen—in fact, sometimes it makes things worse because the ensuing static buildup attracts more dust.

A screen needs a damp wiping for it to do any good—damp, not wet. You should use a special monitor-cleaning solution, because any abrasive cleaner can damage the glare-reduction coating on most screens. If you're using a spray, don't spray it on the screen, where it might drip down into the casing; spray the cloth. As for the cloth, the finer the better; cloths made for monitors or for eyeglasses are best. You can find premoistened wipes at almost any computer or office-supply store.

Calibration

Beyond the external controls on your monitor or display, you can make precise adjustments by clicking the Calibrate button in the Monitors control panel (in Mac OS 9 and earlier) or in the Display pane (in Mac OS X).

Calibration settings allow you to control brightness, contrast, white point, gamma, and other settings, depending on your particular model (**Figure 7.4**). Calibration sets up the display for your personal preferences, and it ties in nicely with Apple's ColorSync.

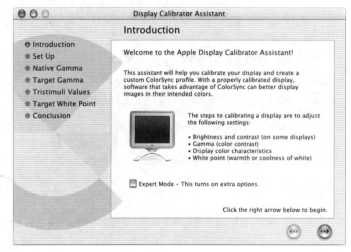

Figure 7.4

The calibration wizard simplifies the process, taking you through each setting step by step.

Scanners and Tablets

Scanners are devices that convert images—typically photographs or other artwork—into digital form so they can be stored and manipulated by computers. When used in conjunction with OCR (optical character recognition) software, they can also convert a page of text into an editable document on your computer.

Mac-compatible scanners range in price from less than a hundred dollars to thousands of dollars. The ones less than $1,000 are great for jobs that don't require precise detail or color reproduction, but they can't compete with high-end equipment when it comes to demanding jobs such as color photographs in slick publications.

You'll find numerous scanners on the market today. The models change frequently and can vary from one individual unit to another, even within the same line—so in addition to the reviews of particular models in the next section, we explain in general terms what to look for when evaluating scanners.

How Scanners Work (JC, JM)

A scanner reflects light from or passes it through the artwork and focuses it onto CCDs (charge-coupled devices—basically, light sensors) that convert the light energy to electricity. Color scanners use colored filters (or sometimes a prism) to read red, green, and blue values separately and then combine the three single-color scans to yield a full-color image. Though the principle is the same for all scanners, units differ in how many readings per inch they take (resolution); how much color information they capture at each reading (bit depth); whether they take separate passes of the light source to read the red, green, and blue values (these are three-pass scanners) or take all the readings in a single pass, minimizing the chance for misregistration and speeding up the scanning process; and the quality of the scanning software they bundle.

Bit depth. Most people use 24-bit color scanners (256 shades each of red, green, and blue for a total of more than 16 million colors).

Some scanners read 36 or 48 bits of information at each sample point, even though their final product is a 24-bit file. This reduces the amount of noise (inaccurate data) that CCDs inherently produce. (The less noise there is in relation to the total data collected, the more usable information the scanner can deliver.)

This extra information doesn't go to waste. Information loss is a common problem when you alter scans—if you brighten colors, for example, you might lose image detail. But when you scan 48 bits, you can tell the scanner to digitally convert, say, only the brightest 16 million colors, so that the final 24-bit image contains the best information.

Resolution. A scanner's resolution refers to the number of sample points per inch it can capture (often expressed as dpi, although spi is actually more accurate). Some scanners are also rated in terms of total resolution, the maximum number of points they can sample. To compare these two figures, divide the total resolution by each dimension of your intended output and then average the two figures. For example, a scanner whose total resolution is 2000 by 3000 dots can output a 5-by-7-inch image at a resolution of about 415 dpi (2000 divided by 5 equals 400; 3000 divided by 7 equals 428.6; the sum of 400 and 428.6 divided by 2 equals 414.3).

Types of Scanners

The two most common types of scanners are flatbed and transparency scanners. Flatbed scanners operate like photocopiers; you place the artwork on a glass surface, and a scanning head and light source move across it under the glass. Flatbeds can scan almost anything that has at least one flat side, even a slab of marble. Most can't scan transparencies or slides, but a growing number of manufacturers offer attachments for that purpose. All flatbeds will scan up to at least 8.5 by 11 inches, and some go up to 11 by 17 inches.

As their name suggests, transparency scanners scan transparent materials such as 35 mm slides, negatives, and larger photographic transparencies (4 by 5 inches or 8 by 10 inches).

Evaluating Scan Quality

Evaluating scanners is easy if you will only be displaying your scanned images onscreen; just run some test scans and compare the results on a monitor like the one you'll be using. The best images for testing contain fine detail and a mixture of bright and muted colors; a human face is ideal, since small tonal shifts can make it look totally wrong.

If you'll be printing scanned images, don't try to evaluate them onscreen. Scans that look dull onscreen may actually contain better data for printing than those that look bright and colorful. It usually isn't possible to make a scan and then print it on the output device you're planning to use, but you can at least avoid some of the most obvious and common problems by running a few test scans.

In the end, the quality of your scans will depend as much on your skill in processing them as on how good a scanner you used. Just about every scan needs brightening and sharpening in software, and no scanner program can take the place of a good image-editing program such as Adobe Photoshop. Also remember that differences in quality generally don't matter as much as differences in convenience. Small color imbalances probably won't bother you if you're producing newsletters, but a slow scanner will annoy you every time you use it.

The scanner should provide a Photoshop plug-in or some other software that enables you to scan directly into your image-editing package. Because all scans need correction, most people find this the most convenient way to work.

Which Scanner to Choose

Perhaps because so many scanners are on the market, models come and go quickly. Epson, Microtek, and Umax are dependable, reputable manufacturers whose scanners have consistently received good reviews. Check Mac publications for information and reviews of current products.

Despite the nearly infinite number of choices, we managed to whittle our picks for flatbed scanners to the following, based on reviews in Mac publications and word of mouth.

The **Epson Perfection 640U** ($149; www.epson.com) has an optical resolution of 600 by 1200 dpi and a maximum bit depth of 36. It uses the USB interface on your Mac and comes bundled with a decent variety of software. This is a good scanner for a small or home office.

In the midrange for price, the **Microtek ScanMaker X12USL** ($299.99; www.microtek.com) can scan legal-size documents and connects to either a USB or a SCSI interface. It's capable of 42-bit color and 1200 by 2400 dpi scans and comes with Adobe Photoshop LE.

Rounding out our top picks is the **Umax PowerLook III** design scanner ($549; www.umax.com). This high-resolution scanner targets professionals in electronic publishing and graphic arts. It can scan slides, transparencies, negatives, and reflective originals. It comes with a SCSI card and includes a full version of Adobe Photoshop.

Graphics Tablets (SA, AC, JC)

Sometimes a mouse just doesn't cut it—especially when you want to *really* draw, using a pencil or pen. The solution is a pressure-sensitive tablet that lets you use a special pen to draw on its surface, with the motions translated into mouse moves. Other than a driver for the tablet, you don't need any special software—once it's up and running, you can use it in any graphics (or other) program you want.

The pens that accompany tablets have gone from wired, to wireless and battery powered, to wireless and battery free. Wired or not, the artistic freedom a tablet provides is invaluable if you constantly do battle with the mouse when you're trying to work in a graphics program.

The Wacom way. Wacom (www.wacom.com)—the industry leader in graphics tablets for some time—has a full line of **Intuos** tablets (ranging from 4 by 5 to 12 by 18 inches, at $179 to $859). The Intuos can interpret as many as 1024 pressure levels; its featherweight stylus, the **Intuos Pen**, has a programmable switch for assigning different functions. The best thing about the Intuos tablets is that you can completely customize stylus and tablet performance, saving different sets of preferences for every program so you don't have to waste time switching options back and forth. The Custom Pressure Curve adjustment lets you control the tablet's response to different pressure levels, so you can, for example, obtain a softer and more sensitive virtual brush.

Audio-Visual Peripherals

It seems that over the years the gap between audio-visual products and computers has closed. If you produce video, still images, or what have you, your Mac can be the medium. Check out the corral of AV gear we've gathered for you here.

Speakers

It seems that no matter what Mac you own, it can always have better-sounding speakers. Except for maybe the Twentieth Anniversary Macs, high-quality audio on the Mac has never really been a reality. Sure, Apple's gotten better at pumping out sound through speakers designed for tiny transistor radios, but what if you want high-fidelity audio? Thankfully for audiophiles, manufacturers such as Harmon Kardon have developed speakers exclusively for the Mac.

For those of us who can never have enough bass, there is the Harmon Kardon **iSub** ($59; http://store.apple.com/). This 20-watt powered subwoofer operates using the USB port on slot-loading iMacs with CD-ROM, DVD-ROM, and CD-RW drives running Mac OS 9 and later. It's also compatible with the Power Mac G4 models when used with the Apple Pro Speakers.

Are you ready for Harman Kardon's **SoundSticks** ($199)? This clear-plastic three-piece speaker system is designed for USB-equipped Macs. Set up the two freestanding speakers on either side of your monitor; plug in the iSub and let 'em rip. They're even Mac OS X ready.

Finally we have evidence that our world is getting flatter. TVs, LCD displays, PowerBooks, and now even speakers are flat (or very close to it). Take, for example, the **iM-700 Flat Panel Audio System** from Monsoon ($169). The compact 4-by-8-inch satellite speakers are incredibly flat, yet they project sound better than just about any commercially available computer speakers. The 5.25-inch powered subwoofer is a force to reckon with—now you can blast your office mates right out of their cubicles.

Microphones

There may come a time when you want to talk to your Mac. (No, we don't mean subjecting it to an angry tirade when your Web browser crashes.) You can control what your Mac does by using the built-in Speakable Items (part of the Speech control panel in OS 9 and earlier and Speech System Preferences in Mac OS X), or even dictate an entire chapter for the next edition of *The Macintosh Bible*.

Many Macs ship with Apple's less-than-exciting but functional unidirectional **PlainTalk** microphone ($15 if yours is missing in action). This external mic sits on top of your monitor and does a decent job for most applications. However, for dictation you'll want a headset-style microphone such as the **Andrea NC-71** ($39.95; www.andreaelectronics.com; it frequently comes bundled with dictation software). It's lightweight and has a flexible metal boom to adjust the microphone to the perfect distance from your mouth.

If you already own a high-quality microphone you want to use, or don't have a sound input port on your new Mac, we suggest Griffin Technology's **iMic** ($35). This little doohickey lets you connect almost any microphone or sound-input device to your Mac's USB port. Why would you want to do that? High-frequency noise from many sources can degrade a computer's audio input and output quality. USB audio improves the sound in and out of the computer. The iMic will give you exceptional sound as well as adapt whatever input source you care to connect to it.

Digital Still Cameras

Digital cameras have revolutionized the world of photography. By substituting memory chips for film, you can capture pictures and save them on your Mac. From there you can manipulate your images, selectively print and e-mail them, and much more. If you're thinking of jumping into the digital-photography pool, there's a lot to consider before you make a purchase.

Your first consideration should be what you plan to do with your images. This is significant because the result will define the type of camera you require as well as how much you'll need to spend. And although the initial investment in the camera itself seems small when you consider you'll never need to buy film, remember that you *will* need to purchase a color printer and plenty of inkjet photo-quality paper to print your images.

Features. Most digital cameras share the characteristics of typical point-and-shoot film cameras, such as automatic exposure, focus, and flash. However, high-end professional models are capable of overriding all the automatic operations in favor of manual tinkering. Beyond these fundamentals, digital cameras have some unique features as well.

The most striking difference is what makes digital cameras—well, *digital.* They store images on reusable flash-memory cards instead of on consumable film. The resolution and quality of the images taken affects the number of images you can store on the card. Cards come in varying capacities, from 2 MB up to 64 MB. You can also get a high-capacity IBM Microdrive in sizes starting at 1 GB.

Many digital cameras incorporate a small color LCD viewfinder to preview your subject before you shoot; this doubles for reviewing pictures you've taken and stored on the camera's flash-memory card. The LCD also allows precise framing of the subject, which is important because the optical viewfinder (the one you look through) is incapable of "seeing" exactly what the lens does.

Unfortunately, the LCD viewfinder can rapidly drain your camera batteries, so you should use it sparingly or keep an ample supply of (preferably rechargeable) batteries on hand.

Another handy feature is an optical-zoom lens that lets you zoom in on your subject for close-ups. Many cameras now include a digital zoom that boosts the zoom power by two or even three times the optical lens's range. The expanded range comes at a price—it degrades picture quality, as software built into the camera simply magnifies the center of the zoomed image.

Macintosh compatibility. Without a doubt the most important feature in any digital camera is the ability to function with a Macintosh. Most manufacturers currently offer fast USB connections compatible with any USB-equipped Mac. If your Mac doesn't include a USB port, some thoughtful camera makers also include a serial cable that attaches to the modem or printer port. FireWire is catching on as another method of transferring pictures from the camera to the Mac, so look for models that feature the IEEE 1394 interface as an option. Most important, look for the phrase "Macintosh compatible" on the box or in promotional materials for the camera that interests you.

Megapixel equals mega quality. The first time you hear the word "megapixel," it will likely impress you—naturally, as it represents a million pixels. This represents the number captured by the CCD, the chip that grabs the images. The more pixels captured, the higher the resolution and the better the image quality. Current models of digital cameras are available in 1 million, 2 million, and 3 million megapixel configurations—4 million megapixels and higher are just around the corner, so stay tuned.

Resolution. Another significant feature is the camera's resolution. This is completely different from the number of megapixels. In this case resolution has to do with the final output of your images. Check out the specifications and find the description for resolution, typically listed as something like 640 by 480. Remember that the higher the resolution, the larger the images will appear on your monitor and in print. A resolution of 640 by 480 will yield fairly small images on paper, so look for higher numbers. An image with a resolution of 1152 by 832 will provide a printed image of 8 by 10 inches.

Which model's right for you? The lowest-priced digital cameras are the 1-megapixel models, frequently offered for as little as $150 to $250. These are good starter cameras, best suited for viewing images on your monitor, adding them to a Web site, or e-mailing them to friends. Pictures taken with these cameras look fine displayed on your monitor, but quality may become an issue if you print them. The greatest benefit of 1-megapixel models is their low cost, but you may sacrifice features—such as a zoom lens—and print quality.

The next step up are the 2-megapixel cameras, priced around $300. They typically offer more features and improved image quality. Priced accordingly, these models are a good choice if you desire more than just basic features. If you want to print photos larger than 8 by 10, don't consider anything less than one of these models.

If you're accustomed to professional photographic gear and have an eye for superior images, you should spend the big bucks for a 3-megapixel or higher model. Although you'll certainly pay a premium for one of these cameras, they do offer high-quality photo reproduction.

Digital-Video Camcorders

As a child I spent countless hours in my darkened bedroom reeling 8 mm film onto tiny spools and painstakingly sticking the pieces together with toxic glue. So when the home-video era began, I was overjoyed at the prospect of shooting hours of tape and watching it all on my television.

Apple stepped up to the plate and gave us two products that improved the entire home-video industry. The first was FireWire (also known as IEEE 1394), which allowed easy transfer of digitized video to the Mac. The second was the iMovie program, which simplified the entire editing process.

With a small investment in software and a digital camcorder, you can now produce professional-looking videos from your not-so-darkened bedroom.

Digital-video formats. Consumer-level digital video is driven by two tape formats: Digital 8 and MiniDV. Both are capable of capturing 60 minutes of digitized video.

Digital 8 camcorders use standard 8 mm videotapes (Hi8 is recommended). They bridge the gap as you move from analog to digital, allowing you to play your previously recorded 8 mm tapes. A 120-minute Hi8 videotape yields a 60-minute video when used with a Digital 8 camcorder.

MiniDV tapes are slightly more expensive than Hi8 tapes. For a while, MiniDV cameras led the way in picture quality with up to 500 lines of horizontal resolution. But Sony has updated its Digital 8 technology and leveled the playing field, providing identical specifications.

Digital 8 vs. MiniDV. Sony is currently the only manufacturer of Digital 8 cameras, generally priced around $100 less than MiniDV models. But MiniDV camcorders have an advantage over the Digital 8 models—their compact size. You can practically put one in your pocket.

Digital-video camcorders. Digital-video camcorders work exactly the same way as any home-video camera. The big difference is that they digitize and compress the information before committing it to tape. The key advantage is that the copy doesn't experience any loss of signal or quality degradation compared to the original. All digital camcorders rely on FireWire to move video and audio to and from your Mac.

Features. You have a lot to consider when choosing a digital camcorder. The most common feature set includes fold-out LCD screens (measuring anywhere from 2 to 4 inches); image stabilization (this helps you overcome the shakes); digital zoom (this extends the range of the camera's optical zoom); a color or black-and-white viewfinder; and one or more CCDs, which digitize whatever you photograph.

In addition, you can choose cameras that offer extra features, such as the ability to capture still images on a separate flash-memory card; and night vision, which bounces infrared beams off your subject so you can record images in total darkness.

CCDs and resolution. As with a digital still camera, in a digital-video camera the quality of video images recorded relates directly to the number of CCDs a camera has and the number of pixels it can capture. Most consumer-level camcorders have just one CCD. In theory, the higher the resolution, the better the picture quality—the majority have resolutions between 200,000 and 500,000 pixels.

Camcorder brands and pricing. Sony and Canon offer some of the most popular camcorders on the market. That doesn't necessarily make these companies the best out there, but they do offer some great options and high-quality products.

Those looking to go digital who already own an analog 8 mm camcorder can easily pick the Digital 8 route and ensure compatibility without converting older tapes. Current Sony pricing for its Digital 8 family runs from $540 to $1,170.

It shouldn't cost you a bundle to buy into the MiniDV revolution, but if you want lots of features, they'll add up quickly. Currently you can buy MiniDV camcorders for as little as $500, and they go all the way up to $2,000. Watch for prices to fall as manufacturers develop new models. [*For more on the software end of digital filmmaking, including iMovie, see Chapter 16, "Multimedia." —Ed.*]

Web Cameras

A few years ago before the Internet really became popular, I wrote a sidebar on the only Web camera made at the time (the Connectix QuickCam). It was the coolest thing ever, even if it only produced gray-scale images.

The current batch of Web cameras offer full color, and many can record sound through built-in microphones. You can use one of these cameras to make a video phone call and capture still images or entire clips.

Kensington's **VideoCam VGA** ($69.99) plugs into your USB Mac and provides images as large as 640 by 480 pixels. It has a swivel base for easy positioning and includes CU-SeeMe software so you can connect with other Web-camera users anywhere in the world.

The iRez **KritterUSB** with Claw ($60.95) is an egg-shaped Web camera that looks like an iMac's offspring. Available in Blueberry, Tangerine, Ice, and Black, it features clawlike legs that allow it to grip anything you attach it to. It delivers 320-by-240 pixel images, but does not include a microphone. A new FireWire version of the Kritter should be shipping by the time this book gets into your hands.

8

Prevention and Troubleshooting

John Christopher (JC) is the chapter editor and author.

*Ted Landau (TL) edited earlier editions of **The Macintosh Bible**, from which portions of this chapter are taken.*

Computers are not to be trusted. They *can* be your best amigo, helping you work productively and accomplish amazing feats in practically no time. But they can also cause incredible grief and agonizing frustration when they go amiss. Although Macs are the friendliest of all computers, they can still ruin your day—especially when they greet you with a flashing question mark in the middle of the screen or when your happy Mac just isn't happy.

But let's start on an optimistic note. Keep in mind that you can avoid most of the terrible things that might happen to you and your Mac if you follow the advice we divulge in our first section, "Prevention: Keeping Your Mac Happy."

There's no troubleshooting like "Effective Troubleshooting." This is the section where we show you the ropes and clue you in on investigating the usual suspects.

When you *really* need our help, the "Common Problems and Solutions" section virtually holds your hand until you and your Mac are in harmony.

As a parting gift, we give you some useful resources for more assistance in "Ask the Experts"—how to get help, a list of Mac-savvy Internet links, and where to go when you've lost everything.

So don't wait for your Mac to crash before you visit this gratifying chapter. Buckle up your data safety belt and proceed to "Prevention." Trust us, it'll keep your best friend smiling.

In This Chapter

Prevention: Keeping Your Mac Happy

There are plenty of things you can do to prevent your Mac from crashing—or to lessen the damage of a crash after it happens.

Back It Up—Right Now!

You may view backing up your data as one of those responsibilities that rates somewhere between flossing your teeth and checking the air in your tires—necessary but tiresome. If you haven't backed up your data recently, stop reading this colossal book and do it now! If you've never backed up your data or are unfamiliar with the term *backup,* proceed immediately to Chapter 5, "Storage," for the intricate details on what, when, and how to do it.

If rule No. 1 is back up your data, rule No. 2 is check your backups. Backing up won't do you much good if you later discover that your critical data is damaged or that the backup program or device failed. To avoid the future shock of a failed backup, restore a few critical files from your backup and then open and view them to make sure they remained intact. However, do be careful if you are restoring from a backup to the hard disk where the data resides. You could potentially overwrite more recent versions of your files with older data you have backed up.

Fight Corruption with Disk Utilities

Just as the table of contents in a book references pages and chapters, the Mac's directory structure maintains the location of files and programs stored on your hard disk. It can be damaged if you shut down your Macintosh improperly or even during a simple freeze while you're using your favorite application. There's almost no way to prevent directory corruption, so use a disk utility regularly to keep your Mac purring like a cheetah. All disk utility programs are capable of repairing minor directory damage, and some even have built-in features to prevent it from ever occurring. You'll find a lengthy discussion of disk utilities and how to use them in the "Troubleshooters' Toolbox" section down the road in this chapter.

Defragment Your Hard Disk

During the typical day-to-day operation of your Macintosh, you create, save, and delete files. As your hard disk fills up, files become fragmented—broken up into pieces, which your Mac writes to different locations. This is known as *disk fragmentation*. When your files get too fragmented, activities such as opening or saving may slow down, as the hard disk must locate every piece of the file you are working on.

Defragmenting reassembles the file fragments on the disk, locating the pieces of a file in contiguous disk segments so your Mac can locate them faster. Speed Disk in Norton Utilities, Alsoft's DiskExpress Pro, and Micromat's TechTool Pro can all defragment your data and improve performance.

As part of Symantec's Norton Utilities for Macintosh, **Speed Disk** works in two ways. It can defragment files individually or optimize the hard disk by organizing system files, applications, and data files into specific areas to increase performance (**Figure 8.1**).

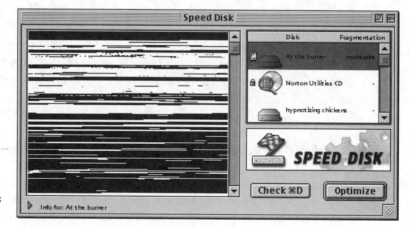

Figure 8.1

Norton Utilities Speed Disk can defragment your hard disk as well as individual files.

DiskExpress Pro ($90; www.alsoft.com) provides intelligent optimization routines as it monitors the way you work. Instead of requiring that you regularly defragment your hard disk, the program operates in the background. It automatically places frequently used files in specific areas to improve performance and increase speed. The product has received numerous accolades from various Mac publications and enjoys continued popularity.

Invest in an Antivirus Package

It seems like every few months or so we hear about a new kind of computer virus that spreads via the Internet—wreaking havoc on computers, rendering them helpless, and destroying the files they store. In most cases, the owners of PCs running Windows seem to suffer the most. But the reality is it's just plain luck that a seriously evil virus hasn't plagued the Macintosh platform.

Safety counts—so you should invest in and install an antivirus software package, and above all download monthly antivirus updates to shield your machine against new virus strains. We describe the functions of Norton AntiVirus in the "Troubleshooters' Toolbox" section later in this chapter.

A Bug Is a Bug, and a Virus Is a Virus

So that you're crystal clear, here's the difference between a virus and a bug: A bug occurs when a programmer makes a mistake while creating the software product. This in turn may cause the program to crash when used.

A virus is a malicious program typically created for the purpose of destroying data, frustrating users, and providing its creator with some twisted sense of gratification.

Keep Your Software Up to Date

Keeping the software on your hard disk up to date with the latest downloads and patches is more important than you might think. Control panels and system extensions (part of Mac OS 9 and earlier) often change to accommodate new versions of the operating system as well as resolve problems and add features.

In the past, the only way to learn about software updates was to wait for notification by snail mail, read your favorite Mac publication, or simply hear about them by word of mouth. The Internet has greatly improved the delivery of updates by allowing you to visit the Web sites of software makers for just about every program you have installed on your hard disk.

Some ingenious companies have designed convenient methods for keeping you and your software current. VersionTracker (www.versiontracker.com) takes full advantage of the Internet's power, featuring links to companies' sites as well as the ability to download files directly from its Web site. In addition, you can install its **TechTracker Pro** software, which scans your hard disk automatically and alerts you of updates and downloads (**Figure 8.2**). You can also subscribe to the company's notification list and receive e-mail whenever an update is available for a product you own.

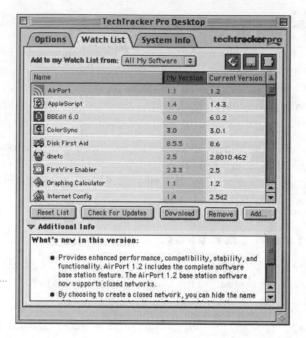

Figure 8.2

TechTracker Pro alerts you of recent software updates.

Symmetry Software Corp. provides its free **Version Master** program, which works in conjunction with the companion Web site (www.versionmaster.com). Once you've installed Version Master on your hard disk, it builds a list of your installed software. When you connect to the company's online database, it retrieves information on current versions and compares them to your own. The service is free, but for $19.95 you get an annual subscription, which gives the program the ability to display direct links to Web and FTP sites.

Third-party companies are not the only ones offering update solutions. Apple has become increasingly aware of customers' need to have easy access to system-software fixes and changes. The Software Update control panel built in to Mac OS 9 and included in System Preferences for Mac OS X connects you to Apple's Internet site and displays recent additions (**Figure 8.3**).

Figure 8.3

Mac OS 9's Software Update control panel (left) or Mac OS X Sofware Update pane (right) keeps you current. It can automatically retrieve the latest Apple software for your Mac.

You may selectively choose which updates you desire or pick them all, and the scheduling feature can connect and install updates automatically. Keep in mind that some updates may not always be available using Software Update, so occasional visits to Apple's Software Download area (http://asu.info.apple.com) can fill in any gaps.

Do You Need an Update or an Upgrade?

The similar-sounding terms *upgrade* and *update* have created a lot of confusion over the years. A software update differs significantly from an upgrade. An update patches or fixes programming problems—commonly known as bugs. In many cases updates are available at no charge and may be downloaded directly from the software company's Web site. Updates are especially desirable if you have experienced bug-related freezes or crashes.

An upgrade incorporates new features and often involves the rewriting of a program from the ground up. Upgrades are almost never free and frequently cost as much as one-third to one-half of the off-the-shelf product price. Buy an upgrade when you feel confident that you will benefit from the additional features or for compatibility with a new operating system.

Desktop Rebuilding—No Hammer Required

If you've owned a Mac for a while—or even if you just got one—you're about to learn the benefits of rebuilding the Desktop. Every Macintosh hard disk running under Mac OS 9 and earlier contains invisible files that support various functions of the operating system. Among them are the Desktop DB and Desktop DF files. These two database files are responsible for maintaining information about all the applications and files stored on your hard disk. Specifically, they ensure that icons appear for each program; that files remain associated with their creator applications; and that aliases can find the path to a file, folder, application, or what have you.

Mac OS X does not require any Desktop rebuilding because the invisible DB and DF files are not part of this operating system. However, the files may still exist on your hard disk because Mac OS 9 is also installed to run Classic Mac applications (those not rewritten to work with Mac OS X).

If you have Mac OS X installed and you discover that icons from Mac OS 9 and earlier are missing or corrupt, you can rebuild the Classic environment's Desktop: Just choose System Preferences from the Apple Menu, select the Classic pane, and click the Advanced tab. You'll see the Rebuild Desktop button near the bottom portion of the pane (Figure 8.4).

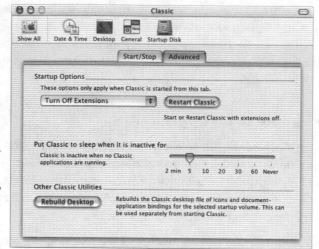

Figure 8.4

Mac OS X's Rebuild Desktop button rebuilds the Desktop icons and alias paths for programs that are running in the Classic environment.

Because files and applications can change frequently, you should rebuild the Desktop once a month. Most of the time, simply holding down ⌘ Option during startup and acknowledging the dialog box works just fine. However, the Apple-approved method requires an added step or two: Before rebuilding the Desktop, you must first use Extensions Manager to turn off all the system extensions and control panels running on your Mac. Follow these steps to accomplish the task:

1. Use Extensions Manager to save the current set of running extensions. From the Apple menu, choose Control Panels and then open the Extensions Manager control panel. Click the Sets pop-up menu and choose New Set. When the Save Set dialog box opens, type a name for your currently selected extensions, such as Current Set. The name of your set will appear in the pop-up menu.

2. Now you must disable all the extensions by clicking the Sets pop-up menu and choosing All Off.

3. Before proceeding, you must turn on one specific control panel using Extensions Manager: Place a checkmark next to the File Exchange control panel.

4. Restart your computer while holding down ⌘ Option.

5. A dialog box should appear with the message "Are you sure you want to rebuild the desktop file on the disk 'Macintosh HD'?" (or whatever you've named your hard disk). Release the keys and click the OK button (**Figure 8.5**).

Figure 8.5

Ready to rebuild? Click OK to confirm the rebuilding of your Mac's Desktop.

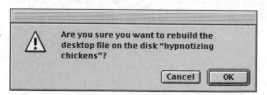

6. When the progress bar shows that the Desktop rebuild has finished, go back to the Apple menu and choose Control Panels and then open the Extensions Manager control panel.

7. Reactivate your extensions and control panels by selecting your previously saved set—Current Set (or whatever you named it) in the Sets pop-up menu.

8. Restart your Mac to activate the extensions and control panels in the current set.

If these steps prove too tedious, plenty of software programs do an exceptional job of rebuilding the Desktop. Among them is **TechTool** from Micromat. This free utility is the smaller sibling of the full-blown TechTool Pro, which offers much more (see the "Troubleshooters' Toolbox" section later in this chapter).

Plug and Play—with Caution

The term *plug and play* means a lot when you own a Mac, but you should rarely *unplug* because *play* could become *pay*. USB devices, for example, allow hot-plugging, which means you may remove their cables from your Mac with the devices turned on without encountering any problems.

This makes perfect sense for USB keyboards and mice but not for storage devices that rely on constant communication with your Mac.

If you need to disconnect a USB or FireWire drive, select its icon on the Desktop and drag it to the Trash. In Mac OS 9 and earlier, a dialog appears, asking you to confirm that you want to dismount the volume. Click OK. Once the icon disappears from the Desktop, turn off the drive and disconnect it. Wait a few moments before picking up an external hard disk. Moving it while it is running or spinning down could cause damage.

Keep in mind that other devices attached to your Macintosh do not allow hot-plugging at all. You never, ever want to plug (or unplug) an ADB or SCSI cable into the back of your Mac while the machine is on. This could cause your Mac to freeze, and you could even damage its electronic circuitry.

Keyboard Protection

If you work in a dusty, damp, or dirty environment—an auto shop, wood shop, or ceramic studio, for example—you may want to protect your keyboard by purchasing a molded plastic skin. **ComputerSkins** (www.computerskins.com) manufactures covers and seals that create a barrier to prevent dust, dirt, and even liquid from finding its way into your Mac keyboard. Its keyboard covers, which you can leave on while you're typing, cost about $15.

Mouse Maintenance

It is a proven fact that Macintosh mice can be furry on the *inside*. We're talking about the dust and fuzz that build up inside your mouse and cause skips, jumps, and other erratic behavior. The tiny ball inside must roll smoothly for the mouse to work properly. Your best bet for keeping the ball free of dirt is to clean it every so often and use a mouse pad. Of course, if you own Apple's Pro Mouse, you can pretty much ignore this tip, because it uses optical tracking and doesn't have a mouse ball to collect gunk. (For details on the Pro Mouse, see Chapter 7, "Peripherals.")

Follow these steps to clean your roller-ball mouse:

1. Unplug your mouse and turn it upside down. Rotate the plastic retaining ring on the bottom counterclockwise to release it. Note that Apple's USB mouse (a round mouse resembling a hockey puck) has the ability to lock the plastic retaining ring in place. If the ring will not budge when you apply finger pressure, you may need to unlock it by inserting a straightened paper clip into the small hole in the retaining ring.

2. Turn the mouse over, and remove the ball and retaining ring.

3. Locate the three small rollers inside the mouse and clean them with a cotton swab moistened with water. If material has built up on the rollers, use your fingernail to remove it gently.

4. Give your mouse ball a bubble bath. Wash the ball in warm water with mild soap such as a dishwashing liquid. Rinse and dry the ball thoroughly.

5. Blow into the mouse housing to remove any free-floating dust particles.

6. Reassemble the mouse by replacing the ball in the case and then reattaching the plastic retaining ring.

Working Under the Hood

When you're upgrading hardware or just looking around your Mac's interior out of curiosity, always protect yourself and your Mac from static electricity. Whether you're installing additional memory or a new hard disk, you need to behave cautiously around the sensitive electronic components. Static electricity can permanently damage the chips and circuits.

You can neutralize the static electricity we all carry in our bodies by touching a metal part inside your Mac. Unplug the computer before you open its case, and then touch the largest metallic piece you see inside—usually the power supply. (Don't worry, you won't get electrocuted.) This will temporarily neutralize static so you won't put your Mac at risk while touching any of its inner workings.

Be extra cautious inside PowerBooks, as they have few metal parts to prevent static discharge. When you're exploring the insides of PowerBook G3 models, Apple recommends touching the metal bar that runs across the top of the hard-disk cage to neutralize yourself. Check the documentation that came with your PowerBook for details.

Many hardware vendors, particularly of memory sticks or hard disks, supply disposable wrist straps with their products. Just wrap the band around your wrist, clip it to a metal area inside the Mac, and you're good to go.

The shocking truth about electricity and your Mac. If you've been acquainted with computers for a while, you may have read about the benefits of using a surge suppressor to protect your Mac from a power surge. You may not think you need one because you live in an area that rarely has thunderstorms or blackouts—but think differently. Speaking from personal experience, we have found that a power event can knock your Mac off its feet and derail your productivity. It could also end up costing you a pretty sum in repairs, as you may have to replace damaged components such as the power supply, motherboard, and memory chips.

To protect your Mac from surges, spikes, brownouts, and other power events, use a surge suppressor. If you run a small business and require your Macintosh to function 24 hours a day, seven days a week, you should invest in an uninterruptible power supply (UPS). A UPS has a built-in battery capable of powering your Mac for several minutes if your area experiences a complete power loss. If the blackout occurs while you are in front of your Mac, you can gracefully shut it down instead of suffering a violent power cut. **American Power Conversion** offers some of the most robust UPSs we've seen, and its Web site (www.apcc.com) offers further insight into power problems and how to handle them.

Is it hot in here—or is it just my Mac? Comfort is always a requirement when you're using your Macintosh. However, you may not have considered the comfort of your Mac in excessively hot or cold environments.

When it comes to heat, you can work safely on most Macs all the way up to a balmy 104 degrees Fahrenheit—usually too uncomfortable for most people to tolerate. The real concern is when the temperature swings in the opposite direction—a Mac may be called on in winter to function in a chilly environment, possibly less than 50 degrees.

Generally speaking, you should review your Mac's documentation, which describes proper operating temperatures. Pay careful attention when transporting an iBook or PowerBook in cold temperatures. You should give them a chance to warm up to room temperature before starting them up.

Protect Your Programs and Your Data

You've been a diligent Macintosh user and probably have all your important data files backed up. So now we're going to talk about a different kind of backup that protects your investment in software. Today you could spend

$420 on the latest version of Microsoft Office, $600 for Adobe Photoshop, and $700 on Quark's QuarkXPress. If you use your Macintosh as a business tool, you might have several thousand dollars' worth of software sitting right on the shelf in your office. In fact, the replacement value of the software may even exceed the cost of your Macintosh!

You need to protect your software just as you would any other piece of valuable property. Store the original CDs and disks at an alternate location—safe deposit boxes at banks and other institutions are an excellent choice for just such a task. You'll have a real sense of security if you protect your software from theft, loss, and damage by keeping it safely offsite. Obviously, it may not seem convenient when you need to reinstall software, but you also have some options when that need arises.

 Whenever you install new software, you are provided with a license agreement that entitles you to use the program. It typically includes a statement granting you permission to make one backup copy of the software. Apple's **Disk Copy** is a free utility that creates disk-image files from all kinds of storage media, including CD-ROM discs, the current standard for installing commercial software. You simply launch Disk Copy, drag and drop the CD icon onto the window, and presto—you have an exact image that you can store as a file on your hard disk or anywhere else. You can use your disk-image to reinstall your software if need be. Before you download Disk Copy from Apple's Web site, check the Utilities folder on your hard disk—you might have a copy already.

If you own a drive that can write to CD-Recordable or CD-Rewritable discs, you can make a complete duplicate of your software using the **Roxio Toast** program that comes bundled with most new drives. We offer some buying advice on CD-R and CD-RW devices in Chapter 5, "Storage," along with information on creating your own CDs and further details on Apple's Disk Copy utility.

Troubleshooting

Just as with any task in life, you need the right tools for the job. The following items represent everything you should have on hand for a Mac emergency. If you own the system-installer CD that shipped with your Mac, you already have three out of the four tools you'll need to resolve problems.

Troubleshooters' Toolbox

Fill your toolbox with the following:

- You'll need a CD containing the system software for starting up your Mac in case the hard disk fails. Most Apple computers ship with a wallet that contains CDs of all the programs installed on your Mac before it ships. Specifically, you'll use two CDs for troubleshooting—software restore and system install. You can start up your Mac from either of these CDs. For most situations mentioned here, you will use the system-installer CD. Every Mac with a CD or DVD drive originally came with a system-installer CD. If you do not have the original CD, you must purchase a system CD from your Mac dealer.

- Apple's Disk First Aid (known simply as First Aid in Mac OS X's Disk Utility program) is an excellent utility designed to check your hard disk and resolve minor problems and directory corruption. If Disk First Aid cannot fix a problem, graduate to a commercial utility such as Symantec's Norton Utilities (see the "Disk Utilities" section later in this chapter to decide which program will work best for you).

- Keep a copy of the hard-disk formatter originally used to set up the hard disk. In most cases, Apple's Drive Setup formats and initializes your Mac's hard disk. If you're unsure which hard disk formatter was used, see our discussion of hard-disk formatters in Chapter 5, "Storage."

- A paper clip—yes, you really should have one handy at all times. You'll find the paper clip an invaluable tool, great for restarting first-generation iMacs and early PowerBooks as well as removing CDs, removable cartridges, or floppy disks that get stuck in their drives.

Other Useful Utilities

The following items are not critical to the troubleshooting process, but they certainly make it a lot easier. For resolving startup problems—such as freezes—you'll need Apple's **Extensions Manager** or Casady & Greene's superb **Conflict Catcher** ($79.95; www.casadyg.com). Either one will help you resolve extension conflicts in Mac OS 9 and earlier. Conflict Catcher has some powerful features that make it one of the best troubleshooting tools you can buy.

Tucked away in the Apple menu of nearly every Macintosh is Apple's **System Profiler**. (Mac OS X users will find the program in the Utilities folder.) This unique little utility provides information on almost every critical component of your Macintosh. Best of all, you can print out the details of your configuration for safekeeping and review it if needed when trouble develops. Make sure you have version 2.1 or later of the Profiler installed on your Mac, as earlier renditions lack some advanced features.

Disk Utilities

A plethora of disk utilities exists to battle directory damage and prevent other problems from delivering a knockout punch to your Mac.

Disk First Aid and Disk Utility. To fix minor directory corruption, Apple includes a program called **Disk First Aid** with the system-installer CD that ships with your Mac. In some versions of the operating system, the program appears in the Utilities folder on your hard disk. In Mac OS X, Apple rolled Disk First Aid's capabilities into a program known as **Disk Utility** (**Figure 8.6**). The First Aid component in Disk Utility works exactly like Disk First Aid.

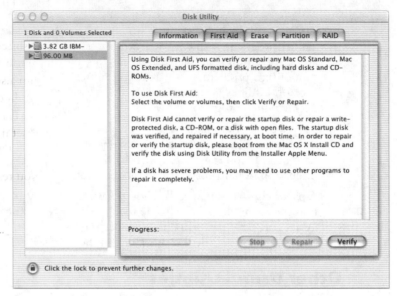

Figure 8.6

First Aid is your first line of defense for disk maintenance and repair.

These low-power, no-frills disk utilities are your first line of defense when it comes to repairing directory damage. You should always elect to use them first before turning to any third-party utility. Other utility software may fix problems that Disk First Aid or First Aid cannot, but Apple's programs offer the safest method by far.

Disk First Aid to the Rescue

If you're running Mac OS 9 and earlier, you may have noticed that following a crash, this message appears during startup: "Your computer did not shut down properly. Disk First Aid is checking your hard disk and will repair any problems" (**Figure 8.7**).

Figure 8.7

Disk First Aid automatically checks for any directory corruption that may occur when your Mac crashes or shuts down improperly. Although we don't recommend doing so, you can turn off this feature: In the General Controls control panel, uncheck the box next to "Warn me if computer was shut down improperly" in the Shut Down Warning pane.

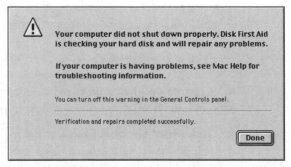

Norton Utilities. The granddaddy of all disk utilities, Symantec's **Norton Utilities** ($95; www.symantec.com) is a collection of programs designed to help your Mac out of a jam as well as improve its performance. Owners of the product are likely to be familiar with the all-powerful Disk Doctor, and some may ignore the other eight—mostly useful—components: UnErase, Volume Recover, Speed Disk, System Info, FileSaver, Fast Find, Wipe Info, and Live Update.

Still, it's easy to see why Disk Doctor gets all the attention, since the functionality of the entire package weighs heavily on its ability to repair directory corruption (**Figure 8.8**). Besides running fix-it routines, the program also scans your disk looking for bad sectors, fixes incorrect creation and modification dates, and identifies damaged files, which could contribute to future crashes. Version 6 of the program is capable of mending Mac OS X volumes set up in the HFS+ (Mac OS Extended) format but not those in UFS—the Unix File System format.

For serious crash recovery, the UnErase function helps you rescue data instead of fixing the damaged directory. You should always try to recover data from a crashed hard disk rather than attempt to fix existing corruption.

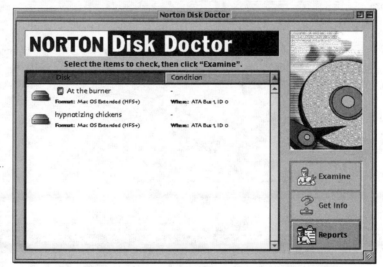

Figure 8.8

Disk Doctor is in. For years Mac users have relied on Norton Disk Doctor to aid with disk maintenance and emergencies.

Norton SystemWorks Gets It Together

Symantec was thinking ahead when it released its **Norton SystemWorks** software ($129.95). The all-inclusive package contains a suite of utilities designed as a complete set of disk-maintenance tools. The CD includes Norton Utilities and Norton AntiVirus for virus protection as well as Dantz Development's Retrospect Express for backup and Aladdin's Spring Cleaning to spruce up your hard disk.

TechTool Pro. Without a doubt, **TechTool Pro** ($90, www.micromat.com) from Micromat contains more bells and whistles than any other piece of Macintosh utility software (**Figure 8.9**). Although the program certainly qualifies as a disk utility, its feature set extends far beyond that of similar programs. Mending damaged directories is just a subset of TechTool Pro's capabilities. It also offers protection against viruses and can optimize disks, but testing the intricate hardware components inside your Mac is what the program is really about. Whether you're dealing with a suspect modem or a malfunctioning keyboard, TechTool Pro can test almost every hardware component inside your Mac.

Two specialized versions of TechTool Pro also exist—the freeware TechTool and TechTool Deluxe, a light version of the program (Apple includes the latter as part of its AppleCare Protection Plan). The freeware version tests the Mac's PRAM, efficiently rebuilds Desktop files, and more. The Deluxe version falls somewhere in the middle, adding some of the fix-it routines that the full-blown Pro product offers. You can download the freeware version from Micromat's Web site (www.micromat.com).

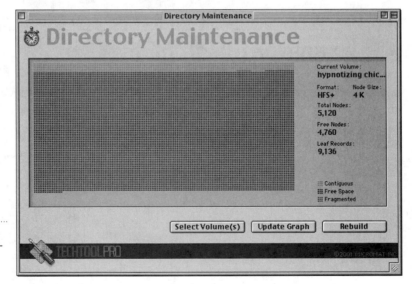

Figure 8.9

Many users like TechTool Pro's complete set of integrated disk tools.

Drive 10 Debuts

As we were going to press, Micromat had just released Drive 10, the first disk utility that fully supports Mac OS X. According to the promotional materials, Drive 10 offers automatic backups and can scan and repair damage on hard disks set up in HFS+ format.

Drive 10 is good news for fans of the company's TechTool Pro software. At first glance, the new program appears to perform many of the same tests.

DiskWarrior. On nearly the exact opposite end of the bells-and-whistles scale lies Alsoft's **DiskWarrior** ($69.95; www.alsoft.com). Designed for ease of use, DiskWarrior focuses its efforts on just three things: recovering your data when you experience disk corruption, optimizing disk directories to improve speed, and preventing directory damage before it gets written to the hard disk (**Figure 8.10**).

One of DiskWarrior's best features is its Preview button, which lets you see exactly what changes and fixes the program has made to your hard disk before permanently committing to them. If you want a simple, powerful product that comes highly recommended, go for DiskWarrior.

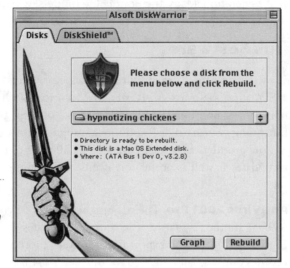

Figure 8.10

Alsoft's DiskWarrior may be the easiest-to-use disk utility on the planet. It offers both power and simplicity.

Rewind. The concept behind Power On Software's **Rewind** ($89.95; www.poweronsw.com) is simple: When your Mac suffers a severe crash—you get a flashing question mark at startup, for example—you can simply "rewind" back to a time or day when everything was copacetic. The same idea applies to files or anything you may have inadvertently deleted. Rewind is easy to use and offers about the only way we know of to travel back in time and recover your data. The geniuses at Power On even let you download the program and throw in a 30-day money-back guarantee.

The Mac's Most Versatile Utility?

Once upon a time, some engineers devised the world's most brilliant troubleshooting tool. It was so ingenious that they believed nearly every Macintosh user would want to have one constantly at their disposal. Behold the venerable paper clip! From the 128K Macintosh to the iMac and beyond, this minuscule piece of twisted wire has proved itself to be your very best friend whenever your Mac freezes up or simply won't spit out a CD-ROM.

Unfortunately, the cost of producing high-quality paper clips has soared, so Apple has never included them with its Macs. We're kidding, of course, but seriously—never leave home without a paper clip, especially if you own an iBook or PowerBook. Desktop-bound Macs can benefit as well, since you can't effectively restart first-generation iMacs (the Bondi Blue models) without a paper clip.

Antivirus Software

At the time of this writing, three antivirus software products were available to Mac users: Symantec's Norton AntiVirus for Macintosh, Network Associates' Dr. Solomon's Virex, and Intego's VirusBarrier. All of these programs are capable of scanning your hard disk and inoculating it against new viruses. Featurewise, the products are pretty equal—they all offer one-click downloads of antivirus updates as well as protection against infected files delivered via the Internet.

Norton AntiVirus 2001 Pro. The major advantages of Symantec's antivirus package ($59.95) are the regularity of its antivirus updates and its excellent support (**Figure 8.11**). You can expect updates every month, sooner if a major new virus comes out. Updates are free for one year; a small annual fee of $3.95 applies thereafter. Besides technical support, Symantec's Web site includes its AntiVirus Research Center, which describes what specific viruses do and alerts you to newly discovered ones.

Figure 8.11

Norton AntiVirus offers automatic, frequently updated virus protection.

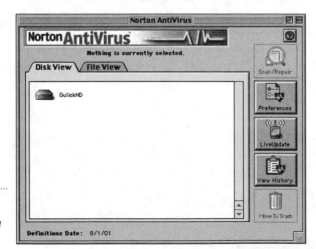

Dr. Solomon's Virex. One of our old favorites is this speedy program offered by PC software giant Network Associates ($49; www.mcafee-at-home.com). Virex is just as powerful as Norton AntiVirus and excels when it comes to scanning your hard disk rapidly for viruses and preventing suspect programs from running. It is available through various Mac mail-order companies and may be downloaded from Dr. Solomon's Web site.

VirusBarrier. This one ($49.95; www.intego.com) is the new kid on the block, but just because it's green doesn't mean you should ignore it. The program effectively protects your Mac the same way AntiVirus and Virex do, and it's the least expensive of the three. We found Intego's virus updates timely and its support exceptional. Download a ten-day trial version of the program from the Intego Web site.

The Worm, the Virus, the Trojan Horse, and Your Mac

The world of computers has a dark side. No, we're not taking cheap shots at Windows users. This little tidbit is about computer viruses. To begin with, your Mac won't get a virus if you happen to sneeze on it. It could pick one up, though, if you download files off the Internet, move documents across a network, or even install a commercial software package. By definition a virus is a piece of software that can self-replicate—that is, it reproduces until it makes a nuisance of itself.

The term *virus* generically describes any type of computer virus. In reality, various forms of viruses can infect your Mac: A *Trojan horse* masquerades as a useful program and infects a file or system when launched. A *worm* can automatically spreading without any user interaction.

A virus can affect your Mac in different ways. You may not be able to open certain files, or the flashing question mark may appear onscreen as you attempt to start up your machine. If you suspect you have a virus, do not share any files until you've eradicated it using antivirus software.

Effective Troubleshooting

Troubleshooting your Macintosh is easier than you might think. You can solve the most common problems on your own without any prior experience or computer knowledge. You only need a little time, some patience, this chapter at your side, and maybe a paper clip.

Troubleshooting Procedures

Fundamentally speaking, you can't get past square one without knowing the fundamentals for effective troubleshooting. If you've been using a Mac for a long time and are already familiar with these tasks, feel free to skip to the section "Common Problems and Solutions," later in this chapter.

What went wrong? Whenever something appears to have gone wrong while working on your Mac, stop and review the following steps to resolve whatever ails your Mac:

- Take notes! Refamiliarize yourself with pen and pad.
- Don't get in too deep! Take a break after 20 minutes.
- Think about what you were doing just before and while the Mac crashed.
- What has changed since the last time you used the system?
- What software or hardware did you recently install?
- How would you describe the problem?

Question the usual suspects. Before you do any troubleshooting, always start here. Although these suggestions may seem obvious, you'd be surprised how often they solve the problem. When you can answer "yes" to each of these questions—and only then—proceed to the next section.

- Is everything plugged in? Believe it or not, this is the most common reason that a component doesn't work. Do yourself a favor and make sure all your cables are securely attached and snug in their sockets. Go ahead and check them out—we'll wait here for your return.
- Are the keyboard and mouse plugged in? (OK, who unplugged the mouse? Oh, that's right—it was me, doing some late-night spring cleaning.)
- Are the monitor, external drive, scanner, and all other external devices plugged in and switched on? Do you see any dark indicator lights? If you have external peripherals, you need to do double duty to ensure that your devices are properly attached and are getting power.

If you are using any external SCSI devices, ask yourself these questions too:

- Are the SCSI devices properly terminated? (We describe the rules of termination in Chapter 5, "Storage.")
- Does each SCSI device have its own separate address? If you're not sure what this means, you really need to visit Chapter 5 now.

How to force-quit an application. If your Mac experiences a crash and the cursor is not frozen, you can try using the force-quit command to close the application.

 This is the preferred method if you are running Mac OS X: Press and hold ⌘Option and then, holding them down, press Esc.

If you are running Mac OS 9 and earlier, the message in the dialog box will read: "Are you sure you want to Force Quit?" Click OK. Once the offending program has quit, you should restart your Mac to guard against further crashes. Be aware that you will lose any unsaved changes or additions made to a document you had open during the crash.

Mac OS X users have a real advantage here. Specifically, Mac OS X features protected memory, which means you can quit a frozen application and continue working as though nothing happened. Use the same key combinations listed above to force-quit an unruly application, or select the Force Quit command from the Apple menu (**Figure 8.12**). A window will appear, displaying a list of all currently running applications. Just choose the varmint that crashed your Mac, and click the Force Quit button (**Figure 8.13**). From there, you can ignore the event and go about your computing life, free from needless repetitive restarts.

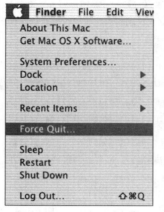

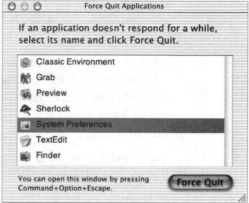

Figure 8.12

Got Mac OS X? You'll find the Force Quit command in the Apple menu.

Figure 8.13

In Mac OS X, just choose the application that's causing you grief and force it to quit.

Restarting your Mac during a crash or freeze. You should use the following method—sometimes known as a *hard restart*—only if the cursor is frozen or you cannot restart your Mac using the proper command in the Special menu (Mac OS 9 and earlier) or the Apple menu (Mac OS X).

- For most desktop Macs and many PowerBooks and iBooks, press ⌘ Control -Power On.

- For first-generation iMacs (Bondi Blue) and early PowerBooks, use your trusty straightened paper clip and locate the reset hole. On iMacs, it's located next to the power cable.

- For Blue-and-White Power Mac G3s and Power Mac G4s, use the reset button, located on the front panel of the Macintosh and marked with a triangle symbol.

- For PowerBook G3s that don't have a reset button, press Shift -Function- Control and the Power On key.

- If all else fails, gently unplug the power cord from your Mac, being careful not to jar or move the computer.

Starting up the Mac using the system-installer CD. If you experience a flashing question mark or see a broken-folder icon (a folder icon with a jagged line running through it) when you attempt to start up your Mac, you may have to use your system-installer CD to access the hard disk. (Since many of the newer Macs include a DVD drive, we will use the term *CD/DVD* here to identify both types of drives.)

If the Macintosh is on and a flashing question mark or broken-folder icon appears, simply press the CD/DVD eject button to open the loading tray. Insert the CD and close the tray. If you have a slot-loading Macintosh such as the iMac DV, simply insert the CD. You should see the happy Mac icon in a few moments. If not, restart while holding down Ⓒ on the keyboard to force the Mac to start from the CD.

If the Macintosh is off, press the power key and then immediately press the CD/DVD door on the front of the drive. Once the tray opens, insert the CD and close the tray. Press Ⓒ on the keyboard. The happy Mac should appear, and you may notice a different Desktop pattern from what you are used to seeing.

Another startup method is available to owners of Power Mac G4 models, iBooks, PowerBooks (FireWire and later), and iMacs (slot-loading and later models). Start up your Mac and hold down Option until the Startup Manager window appears. You should see a group of icons that includes circular and straight arrows, a CD icon, and a hard-disk icon. The circular arrow on the left scans for disks capable of starting up your Mac. Click the CD icon and then the straight arrow to continue the startup process.

As a last resort if all keyboard commands fail to make your Mac start from the CD, try holding down ⌘ Option Shift Delete. This procedure will force the Mac to ignore the hard disk during startup.

Keeping the peace with Apple's Extensions Manager. When it comes to troubleshooting startup problems when running Mac OS 9 or earlier, nothing comes close to the simplicity of Apple's Extensions Manager. If your Mac freezes while starting up and extensions are loading, you most likely have an extension conflict. The fastest way to resolve the problem is to restart and hold down the spacebar until the Extensions Manager window appears (**Figure 8.14**).

Because Mac OS X runs Classic programs using Mac OS 9, you can control the way extensions load (or prevent them from loading at all). As part of System Preferences, the Classic pane's Advanced tab offers Startup Options that turn extensions on or off as well as launch Extensions Manager.

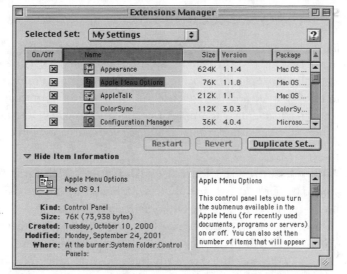

Figure 8.14

Manage extensions and control panels with Extensions Manager.

The first column displays a checkmark for every extension or control panel that is on or off. Keep in mind that these items load in alphabetical order, with extensions first, followed by control panels. Be aware of which icon appeared on the screen just before the freeze occurred—you may need to restart again and write down what you see. Because most freezes happen just after new software is installed, try removing the checkmark next to any recently installed items and then clicking the Continue button. If you successfully reach the Desktop without freezing, you have identified the suspect. The next steps are to rename and reenable the item to change the loading order.

From the Apple menu, choose Control Panels and open Extensions Manager. When the window opens, scroll down the list until you find the disabled item and then select it. Now, from the Edit menu, choose the Get Info command. The item's Get Info panel will appear. Click its name and add the letter *A* or *Z* at the beginning of the name. This forces it to load earlier or later, depending on the letter you choose. For example, if you want the DialAssist control panel to load later, you might change the name to ZDialAssist. After you rename the item, go back to the Extensions Manager window, check the box next to that item, and restart. If all goes well, that should fix your frozen Mac!

Although the Extensions Manager is a useful tool for resolving conflicts, its features are somewhat basic compared to those of a program such as Casady & Greene's Conflict Catcher (for a description, see the "Other Useful Utilities" section earlier in this chapter).

Using Mac OS X's Disk Utility

With Mac OS X, Apple created a new utility that combines its Drive Setup and Disk First Aid programs. To repair and verify Mac OS X hard disks, launch the Disk Utility application, located in the Utilities folder. From the main pane, select First Aid and then choose the function you want to use. The First Aid program is identical to Apple's Disk First Aid, so you would take exactly the same steps in either program to repair your damaged directory.

Fixing a damaged directory with Apple's Disk First Aid. As mentioned earlier in the chapter, both Disk First Aid (in Mac OS 9 and earlier) and First Aid (part of Disk Utility in Mac OS X) are low-power utilities included on the system-installer CD. When you launch these utilities, the top window panel displays your hard-disk icon and any other connected storage devices. You may choose to verify the hard disk's directory structure or repair it if the utility finds a problem—choose the disk icon in the top panel and click the Verify or Repair button. When the program is done, the displayed report identifies any found or fixed problems.

In the past, you had to start up your Mac from the system installer CD to run Disk First Aid on your hard disk, but now in Mac OS 9 you can run it anytime. In Mac OS X, you must still start up from your installer CD to repair your startup disk. The Save Results command in the File menu allows you to save the report in case you want to share it with a technical-support representative, consultant, or any fellow troubleshooter.

Using Apple's Drive Setup. Drive Setup is a hard-disk formatter for Mac OS 9 and earlier that creates logical structures on your hard disk. The main functions of the program are to set up the Macintosh file system, install a disk driver, and test media. Use this application with caution because it can erase your hard disk. This chapter details its two troubleshooting features; see Chapter 5, "Storage," for information on Drive Setup's other functions.

You can find Drive Setup in two places: on your hard disk and on the software-installer CD. In both cases, it is located in the folder called Utilities. You may launch the program from either location, but you will not be able to initialize the drive or create partitions unless you start up from the CD.

- Use Drive Setup's Test Disk command—located in the Functions menu (**Figure 8.15**)—to check the physical functions of your hard disk. This operation will read every sector to find out whether the disk has any bad blocks.

- The Update Driver command replaces the current disk driver that controls communication between the hard disk and your Macintosh. Select the disk in the List of Drives window and then choose Update Driver from the Functions menu. You must restart your Mac after the procedure is completed.

Figure 8.15

Use Drive Setup's Test Disk command in the program's Functions menu to check your hard disk.

Testing Your Hard Disk with Mac OS X's Drive Setup

Mac OS X's Disk Utility includes the Drive Setup program. This subset of the application differs radically from the stand-alone version of Drive Setup. For one thing, the program no longer includes the Update Driver function. However, it can still scan the hard-disk media for bad blocks.

To test your hard disk, launch Disk Utility, click the First Aid tab, and select your hard disk in the panel to the left. The click Verify.

Zapping the PRAM. The PRAM—pronounced "pea-ram"—is a separate clock chip that retains settings for some control panels, such as Date & Time, and keeps track of the designated startup disk. When the computer shuts down, a small battery located inside the Macintosh maintains these settings. Occasionally, they become corrupt, which can cause noticeable problems with the Date & Time, Mouse, Monitors, and Keyboard control panels, as well as make your Mac lose track of the startup disk.

If you ever want to impress a fellow Mac user, just mention zapping the PRAM in casual conversation and watch the reaction. The zapping process returns your Mac's settings to the Apple factory defaults that were assigned to your Macintosh when it was new. Although this description sounds extreme, the operation will not damage your Macintosh or its data in any way. You will, however, have to change various settings in the control panels back to your specific preferences once the process is complete.

Zapping the PRAM may require you to grow a third hand or request assistance from a family member, neighbor, coworker, or household pet. For an easy, no-hassle method, use Micromat's TechTool Pro program. Otherwise, follow the steps below.

1.   Make sure your Macintosh is turned off.

2.   Locate the following four keys on the keyboard: ⌘, Option, P, and R.

3.   Try holding down ⌘Option with your left thumb.

4.   Press R with your left index finger.

5.   With your right hand, switch on the Macintosh and immediately press P. Continue to hold down the four keys.

6.   The Macintosh will chime once when you turn it on and then a second time as it resets the PRAM. You can release the keys when you hear it

chime at least twice. Depending on the model of Macintosh you have, the screen will either remain gray or display the happy Macintosh icon. If the Mac hasn't chimed a second time, you'll have to try the operation again, as the exact timing can be tricky.

Common Problems and Solutions

Things can turn bad at just about any time, from right after you press the start button to right before you choose the Shut Down command.

Problems Starting Up the Macintosh

Startup problems can be some of the most frustrating moments you'll ever spend in front of your Mac. Most of the time the proper solution can get you out of a jam and back on the road to productivity. Stay cool and follow our expert advice ahead.

An icon with a flashing question mark appears. During startup, your Macintosh searches for a System Folder on your hard disk. If it cannot find one, it displays a flashing question mark in the middle of the screen that alternates between either a folder or a floppy-disk icon depending on the Mac you own. This may indicate missing or damaged system software, directory corruption, hard-disk failure, or a few other possible problems.

Start up your Mac with the system-installer CD. If a dialog box appears with the message "The Disk is damaged" or "This is not a Mac disk," your hard disk has some damaged directory structures. Whatever you do, *do not* click the Initialize button! Click Cancel or Eject. (See the section "Damaged disk error messages" later in this chapter for ideas on what to do next.)

However, if the hard disk appears and mounts on the Desktop, run the Repair operation in Apple's Disk First Aid to fix corruption. If Disk First Aid repairs the damage, try restarting again without the CD or floppy disk. Reinstall your system software from the system-installer CD if the problem persists.

If Disk First Aid is unable to fix your problem, try a third-party utility such as Symantec's Norton Utilities, Alsoft's DiskWarrior, or Micromat's TechTool Pro (see the "Disk Utilities" section, earlier in this chapter). These utilities can repair directory corruption and recover data. The safest method is to use a recovery routine to rescue the data and save it to another drive.

Finally, if your hard disk does not appear in the Disk First Aid window at all, contact an Apple Authorized Service Provider, who may be able to recover your data. Or contact a company that specializes in data-recovery services and hard-disk failures (see the "Ask the Experts" section later in this chapter).

Don't Whack Your Mac!

If there is one piece of Macintosh advice you should forget, it is the idea that giving your Mac a good whack on the side can make it magically start up when the infamous flashing question mark appears. This bit of trivia actually worked in the days of the Macintosh SE, circa 1989.

A condition known as "sticktion" prevented the hard-disk platters on the drives installed inside these Macs to spin up. Whacking the side of the Mac freed up the read-write heads that had stuck to the platters, allowing the drive to function but also typically causing media damage in the process. Any drive that developed the sticktion problem was on its way out.

Today, whacking your Mac has a more detrimental effect. Although modern disk drives have been designed to withstand a certain amount of shock, you actually risk destroying your hard disk and losing your data. Take our word for it—don't whack your Mac!

 Damaged disk error messages. If a "The disk is damaged" or "Not a Macintosh disk" error message appears, *do not* click the Initialize button or you will erase the directory on your hard disk and lose all your files and folders. You may see this message if you first experience the aforementioned flashing question mark and then start up from a System CD. The message signifies that the directory is damaged. Your options are as follows:

- Use a disk utility such as Apple's Disk First Aid to fix the damage.

- Use a third-party disk utility such as Norton Utilities to recover your data and store it on another disk.

- Erase the drive, lose everything, and hope that you can restore data from your backup.

- Seek the aid of a computer professional such as a consultant or data-recovery specialist (see the "Ask the Experts" section, later in this chapter).

 A broken-folder icon appears. When you're running Mac OS X, a folder icon with a jagged line through it may appear during startup if the system software is corrupt or the directory is damaged. Use the system-installer CD to start up and then select the Open Disk Utility command from the Installer menu. From there, choose First Aid, select your hard disk in the top panel, and run the Repair operation. If all goes well, quit First Aid and Installer, restart, and eject the CD.

However, if First Aid fails to restore your disk, you need to reinstall the system software from the CD. Should you require help extracting files from the drive, contact a consultant or data-recovery specialist (see the "Ask the Experts" section, later in this chapter).

The gray screen appears, but nothing else happens. During a normal startup of your Mac, you may notice a few seconds when the only thing that appears on your display is a gray pattern. This occurs as soon as the monitor is illuminated but before the smiling Macintosh icon (known as the *Happy Mac*) appears. Your Mac pauses at the gray screen as it tests the built-in physical memory, so you should expect a longish delay if you have large amounts of memory installed.

However, if the gray screen appears for an extended period, much longer than usual, you may have a problem. To troubleshoot this situation, start by doing nothing. In fact, you should wait a while—say, two or three minutes—to see if anything does happen. If your Mac won't budge, proceed to the next step, which is to turn off the Macintosh.

There are a few reasons for the Mac to make an extended stay at the gray screen. The first possibility is that an external peripheral, such as a SCSI hard disk or scanner, may have a damaged cable. Isolate your Mac by disconnecting any external peripherals, and attempt the startup again. Be aware of the rules of termination for external SCSI devices as mentioned in Chapter 5, "Storage."

It is also possible that your Macintosh has simply lost track of the hard disk and is "thinking" about its whereabouts. Because the location of your hard disk is stored in the Mac's PRAM, your next procedure should be to zap the PRAM, returning the machine to its factory defaults (see the "Zapping the PRAM" section, earlier in this chapter).

In addition, your hard disk may have directory corruption or a damaged disk driver. To find out, start up from the system-installer CD. Proceed with caution if you see a dialog box with the error message "The Disk is damaged, do you want to initialize it?" or "Not a Macintosh disk." Whatever you do, do not click the Initialize button or you risk erasing all of your files and folders. The appearance of either of these error messages indicates directory corruption (see the section "Damaged disk error messages," earlier in this chapter for ideas on what to do next).

If you successfully reach the Desktop and your hard disk icon does not appear, launch the Drive Setup program located in the Utilities folder and look for the name of your hard disk in the List of Drives window. Update the disk driver as described in the "Using Apple's Drive Setup" section, earlier in this chapter. If the name of your hard disk does not appear in the list, it may be physically damaged. In this case, your only options are to replace the hard disk and restore from your backup or contact a company that specializes in data recovery. If all else fails, seek professional help (see the "Ask the Experts" section, later in this chapter).

The monitor does not come on and stays dark. As always, check the obvious culprits first (see the "Question the usual suspects" section, earlier in this chapter). After you've taken a quick run through those procedures, you should zap the PRAM as described earlier. If that fails to do the trick, try connecting a monitor you know is working. (Obviously, this suggestion won't work if your monitor is built in, as with the iMac). Perhaps you could borrow one temporarily from a fellow Mac owner.

In most cases, the real suspect is likely the battery installed on your Mac's main motherboard. This powers the PRAM, which retains Date & Time and other settings when you shut down the system. After about five years, the battery wears out and you'll need to replace it. On some early Macs, a weak battery can prevent the monitor from coming on. The specific models affected by this anomaly are the Centris 660AV, LC 475, Performa 475 and 476, Performa 61XX series, Power Macintosh 6100, Quadra 605, and Quadra 660AV.

A Sad Mac icon appears. The Sad Mac icon may appear during startup, accompanied by unusual tones. Contrary to popular belief, the Sad Mac does not necessarily mean you have a hardware problem. In fact, in most cases the problem can be attributed to a corrupt hard-disk driver or damaged system software. To resolve the issue, begin by taking note of any error codes that may appear onscreen just underneath the Sad Mac. There are typically two sets of numbers and letters. Write these down for future reference in case it does turn out to be a hardware problem.

To reinstall the disk driver, you need a copy of the hard-disk formatter used to set up the drive—in most cases, Apple's Drive Setup, located on the system-installer CD (see the "Using Apple's Drive Setup" section, earlier in this chapter).

If the disk driver isn't the problem, bad memory chips may be the cause. If the problem persists, we suggest taking the system to an Apple Authorized Service Provider and having it checked.

The Mac emits unusual tones or sounds. Typically, when you press the power key to turn on your Macintosh, you hear the standard chime—a single powerful chord that tapers off as the display illuminates and the gray screen appears. If you hear unusual sounds of any kind, something may have gone awry.

What qualifies as an unusual sound? Depending on the particular model of Mac, you might hear tones that sound like the theme from *Twilight Zone,* a car crash, or breaking glass. Welcome to the Chimes of Doom—but don't fret. Not all is lost. Frequently these sounds play as a Sad Mac appears in the middle of your screen. Like the Sad Mac, they can indicate hardware trouble—but the reality is usually much less serious. You should update the disk driver, as you would in the case of the Sad Mac.

As far as unusual sounds go, besides the Macintosh itself, the only other components that should make noise are the internal fan and the hard disk. If you listen carefully, you can hear the specific rhythmic pattern your hard disk "plays" when you turn on your Mac. If a flashing question mark appears during startup and you don't hear the typical pattern, or if you hear a clicking or grinding sound, turn the Mac off immediately. These types of sounds can signify a hard-disk failure or head crash, as discussed in Chapter 5, "Storage." In this type of scenario, you will need to replace the hard disk or contact a company that provides data recovery (see the "Ask the Experts" section later in this chapter).

The Macintosh freezes at the welcome screen. Conflicting system extensions are the most common cause for a startup crash when your Mac is running Mac OS 9 and earlier. You are most likely to experience a conflict immediately after installing new software. It all comes down to a matter of your system extensions and control panels demanding the same area of memory or particular resource. In most cases, you can resolve the conflict with Apple's Extensions Manager or Casady & Greene's Conflict Catcher (see the "Other Useful Utilities" section, earlier in this chapter).

Apple's Extensions Manager lets you turn off extensions and control panels individually but will not let you change the loading order. The much more powerful Conflict Catcher not only allows you to disable or change individual files but also provides an incredible amount of information to aid in conflict resolution. The basic idea is to change the loading order of the offending extensions so they won't wage war upon each other.

To determine if you really do have an extension conflict, start up the Mac while pressing (Shift). Hold it down until the message "Extensions Off" appears underneath the words "Welcome to Macintosh." If you successfully reach the Desktop this time, you have a conflict and should proceed to troubleshoot it. However, if once more you do not reach the Desktop and your Mac freezes, the system software may be damaged, and you will need to reinstall it.

If you don't relish the idea of resolving an extension conflict on your own, Conflict Catcher can do all the troubleshooting for you. Don't get *too* excited—you'll still need to sit down and spend some time in front of your computer as the program runs. You simply enter information about the type of problem you're experiencing in the program's conflict test window. Conflict Catcher then begins the process of repetitive restarts until it discovers which extensions are not getting along.

Freezes and Other Unruly Behavior

Sometimes your Mac can be downright ornery, quitting applications, freezing up, and forcing you to restart. To tame your wild Mac, proceed through the following section.

The message "Application has unexpectedly quit" appears.
One day in the not-so-distant future, you may find yourself experiencing a situation where the application you're using suddenly disappears from your screen, replaced with an "Application has unexpectedly quit" message. This can be quite annoying, especially if you're in the middle of producing a document

and have not yet saved your work. Although this error message may appear sporadically, you can take precautions against its occurrence by increasing the memory allocation for the troublesome program.

To increase the amount of memory allocated to a specific application in Mac OS 9 or earlier, select the program's icon in the Finder. Then choose the Get Info command in the File menu (or press ⌘ⓘ). Select Memory from the Get Info pane's Show pop-up menu. The memory window reveals the application's requirements to function properly and displays the Suggested, Minimum, and Preferred Size in kilobytes (noted as *K*). Although there is no precise method for determining exactly how much memory you should allocate, we recommend adding 1 MB at a time in the Preferred Size field. For example, a program is using almost 2 MB of memory when the size is set to 2,000 Kbytes. To allocate an additional 1 MB or so, change Preferred Size to 3,000 Kbytes.

 Mac OS X handles memory allocation for applications, relieving you of the duty of assigning memory.

If increasing the memory allocation fails, a visit to the Mac OS 9 or earlier System Folder might be in order. Once inside, open the Preferences folder and locate the problematic application's preference file. Most of the time it's OK to remove this file because your Mac automatically creates a new one when the application next launches. For safety's sake, store the preference file temporarily in a folder. We suggest you create a folder on the Desktop called Removed From Prefs and drag the file to this location. That way, if things don't improve, you can put the old file back.

As a last resort, you might consider reinstalling your dubious application from the source CD. This may be the only way to fix an application that has become corrupt.

The bomb icon appears onscreen (TL). If you're wondering what could be worse than a system freeze, here's one answer: a system crash, or a *bomb*. Typically, an alert box appears with a bomb icon. The message starts by apologizing for the intrusion—but that probably doesn't make you feel any more kindly inclined toward it.

Like a freeze, a bomb puts an end to whatever you were doing. Actually, dealing with bombs is quite similar to dealing with freezes, except that in Mac OS 9 and earlier, the force-quit option is unlikely to work. The Restart button that may appear in the bomb box also only works sporadically. Still, you should try these options, especially if you are using Mac OS X, which has a better chance of overcoming such problems.

If the force-quit option fails, restart your Mac—with luck, the system crash won't repeat. If it does, the most likely cause is an extension conflict or software that's buggy or corrupted.

The error message "The file cannot be opened because the program cannot be found" appears. Typically, this message indicates that you don't have the program needed to open the file you just double-clicked. If you are certain the program is installed on your Mac, you should rebuild the Desktop and attempt to open the file again (see the "Desktop Rebuilding—No Hammer Required" section, earlier in this chapter, for instructions).

Another solution is to use the File Exchange control panel featured in Mac OS 9 and earlier and select the "Translate documents automatically" check box under the File Translation tab. This option attempts to open the file even if the original program that created it is not installed. If all else fails, reinstall the necessary program on your hard disk.

Programs and files have lost their custom icons. Occasionally files and folders may lose their custom icons and display generic ones. The main reason is possible corruption of the Desktop files, part of Mac OS 9 and earlier. The easiest solution is to rebuild the Desktop, prescribed as monthly maintenance (see the "Desktop Rebuilding—No Hammer Required" section, earlier in this chapter).

In addition, you can use a disk-utility program such as Apple's Disk First Aid or Symantec's Norton Utilities to fix *bundle bits*. Sometimes the bundle bit gets switched off by mistake, or the software programmer may have forgotten to turn it on. In either case, most disk utilities can resolve the problem and return your icons to their old selves (see the "Disk Utilities" section, earlier in this chapter).

The cursor is frozen onscreen. Once your Mac experiences a crash where the cursor freezes, you can't do much except decide on the best method of restarting. Still, take a shot at using the force-quit method described in this chapter, especially if you're using Mac OS X. In Mac OS 9 and earlier, if you manage to exit the crashed program and free your cursor, restart your Mac as a safety precaution. Here are the shortcuts for doing battle with a frozen Mac:

Action	Keyboard Shortcut
Stops any operation in progress	⌘.
Brings up a force-quit window	⌘ Option Esc
Shuts down or restarts iMacs and Power Mac G3s and some G4s	⌘ Option Shift-Power
Restarts most Macs	⌘ Control-Power
Restarts the Mac	Reset button

Are You Really Locked Up?

Sometimes it can be difficult to determine if your Macintosh is really frozen or if you should just wait patiently for it to finish a task. One way to get a visual cue is to check the box next to the "Flash the time separators" option in Mac OS 9's Date & Time control panel under Clock Options or in Mac OS X's Menu Bar Clock tab (**Figure 8.16**). This option is accessible via System Preferences.

This setting makes the colon that divides the hours and minutes blink. The next time you think your Mac is frozen, glance at the time in the menu bar and see if the colon is still blinking. If it isn't, it may be time to force-quit a stubborn application or restart.

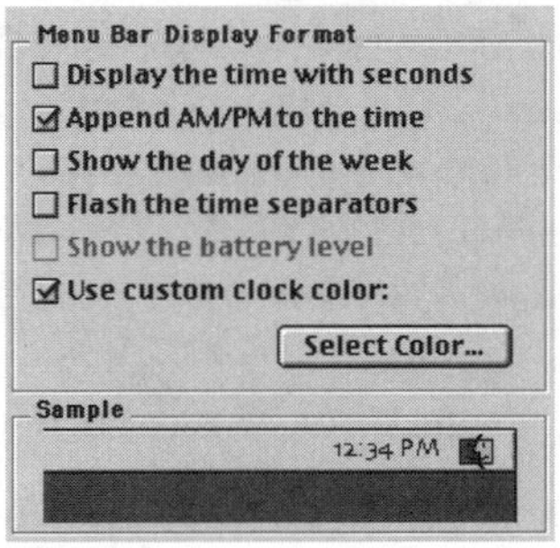

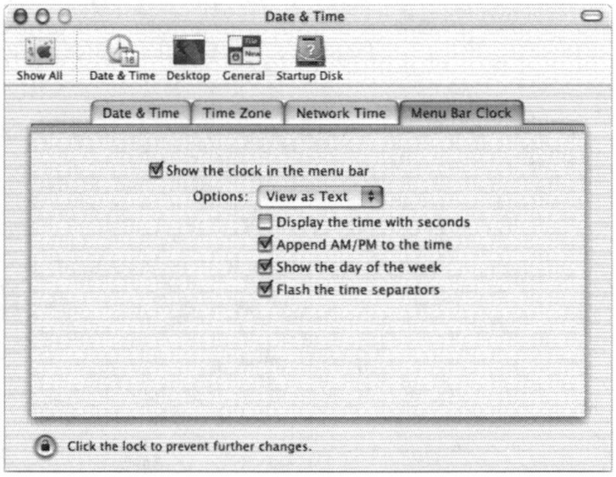

Figure 8.16

Use the "Flash the time separators" option (Mac OS 9, left; Mac OS X, right) to check up on your frozen Mac.

Error codes demystified (well, almost). When you experience a system crash or an application quits unexpectedly, the accompanying error message often lists a code number such as Type 1 or an equally mysterious expression such as "unimplemented trap" or "FPU not installed." You may well wonder what the heck all of this means.

More printers' ink has been wasted answering this Macintosh question than any other. The plain truth is that these messages are meant to guide programmers, who use them to debug software and have little usefulness for the rest of us. Still, we know you won't be satisfied until you learn more about what these messages mean (and, yes, you can occasionally glean some helpful information from them). So here's a quick tour of the subject.

First, it helps to know that these codes (or IDs) come in two flavors: positive and negative. Positive error codes most often accompany system crashes or unexpected quits. Negative error codes occur after a variety of less disruptive problems, such as failure to copy or delete a file.

Positive error codes. Type 01 ("Bus Error"), 02 ("Address Error"), and 03 ("Illegal Instruction") are the most common errors on 680X0 Macs. They mean that your Mac tried to access a memory location that does not exist or executed an improper program instruction. Sometimes you can prevent further errors of this type by increasing the memory allocation of the application in use at the time of the crash.

Otherwise, the exact cause varies according to when the error occurs. If it occurs right as startup begins, it's probably a problem with an externally connected SCSI device (possibly an incompatible disk driver). If it occurs while the extensions are loading, it's likely due to an extension conflict (typically the extension that is trying to load when the crash occurs). If it happens while you're in the Finder, chances are it comes from corrupted system software. If it happens while you're in any other application, it probably stems from a bug in the application itself.

Type 09, 10 ("Unimplemented Trap," "No FPU Installed," "Bad F-Line Instruction"), and 11 ("Miscellaneous Hardware Exception") are the most common errors on Power Macs. The "No FPU Installed" and "Bad F-line Instruction" messages may appear if the software mistakenly calls for an FPU while running in emulation mode on a Power Mac (there is no FPU in emulation mode). It also may appear whenever the Mac can't figure out what error message to use. The "Miscellaneous Hardware Exception" error typically occurs anytime a Power Mac is running a native application and an error occurs that would have caused a Type 01 or 03 error on a 680X0 Mac.

In most cases, if the problem is specific to a single application, it again indicates a bug or corruption in the software. Try the solutions just previously described. Otherwise, for more randomly occurring Type 11 errors, zapping the PRAM (see the "Zapping the PRAM" section earlier in this chapter) sometimes helps. Defective memory (SIMMs, DIMMs, and especially RAM caches) are also a common source of Type 11 errors. To check for this, you'll have to remove the suspect memory cards and see if the errors go away.

Errors between 04 and 14 are most likely due to bugs in application software. Other errors between 15 and 31 most often stem from a corrupt System file.

Negative error codes (TL). With luck, these codes may point you in the right direction. For example, if you get a message that says you can't copy a file because of a –34 ("Disk is Full") error, this does suggest why the copy attempt failed. Although we can't list every negative error code here (there are hundreds), we can supply a list of the common categories.

System file errors (–33 to –61) are probably the most common category. These include –39 ("unexpected end of file"), –41 ("memory full") and –42 ("too many files open"). Several shareware utilities, such as Bleu Rose's **Black & Bleu** ($29; www.bleurose.com), provide a complete list of all error code numbers and their technical names. Apple also offers detailed descriptions on its Web site (http://karchive.info.apple.com/article.html?artnum=60755).

Removable-Cartridge Woes

Removable-cartridge drives such as Iomega Zip and Jaz require special attention when troubleshooting. Follow the path described below to help regain access to your cartridges or CDs.

The removable cartridge won't mount. Removable media such as Iomega Zip, Jaz, SyQuest, and magneto-optical drives all require a system extension to mount cartridges on the Desktop when operating under Mac OS 9 and earlier. To confirm that the needed extension is in your System Folder, open Extensions Manager and review what's installed. Some examples of common driver extensions are Iomega Driver, SyQuest Utilities, and FWB Tools. Even if you do not have any of these extensions, there are some additional ways to mount a cartridge.

Try inserting your cartridge into the drive before starting up your Mac. This method will almost always work with any external drive connected to the Macintosh SCSI bus (see Chapter 5, "Storage," for an explanation of SCSI devices).

You hear a clicking sound and no disk icon appears. If you own an Iomega Zip drive, you may experience a situation where the drive clicks repeatedly when you insert a cartridge and the disk icon never appears on the Desktop.

This problem has been dubbed the Click of Death, as it makes your cartridge and data inaccessible while potentially destroying subsequent cartridges in the process. While the Click of Death itself is specific to Iomega Zip drives, it should be noted that most types of removable media are susceptible to this type of failure.

If a cartridge appears to have experienced the Click of Death, you should first switch off the drive by unplugging the power cord. Hold down the eject button on the drive while you plug the drive back in, and keep holding it until the cartridge pops out. If this method fails, unplug the power cord and insert a straightened paper clip into the eject hole located in the back of the drive.

To make sure the Zip drive is not damaged, insert a blank cartridge (don't insert a cartridge that was stuck). If the cartridge does not mount and begins clicking, the drive may be broken and you'll have to replace it. However, if the cartridge icon appears on the Desktop, launch the Iomega Tools program from your hard disk and choose the icon with the pencil eraser. The Erase/Initialize Disk options window appears. Click the long erase button to reformat the cartridge. This will erase it and confirm that the drive is working correctly.

If you need to recover files from the damaged cartridge, your only option is to contact a firm that specializes in data recovery (see the "Ask the Experts" section, later in this chapter).

A CD/DVD or floppy disk is stuck in the drive. Almost every kind of drive that uses removable media has some method for extracting a trapped disk. This can include an eject button, an emergency eject hole that accommodates a paper clip, or sometimes both. For most older Macs with built-in floppy drives, you restart while holding down the mouse button to kick out a stubborn disk.

Another method for freeing a jammed disk involves simply restarting the Mac while pressing the eject button on the front of the drive. This works with most built-in drives such as CD-ROM, DVD, Zip, or Jaz. Of course, you can fall back on using the eject hole if that fails.

The eject hole is located on the front panel of most removable drives. You may need to carefully pull down the CD-ROM or DVD-ROM door on Blue-and-White and G4 Macs to see the hole. Insert the straightened end of a paper clip approximately $\frac{1}{2}$ inch into the hole until you feel some resistance. Push in gently—keeping the paper clip straight—until your rebellious disk pops out.

Printing Trouble (TL)

Is your printer giving you nothing but trouble? We'll help get your printer rolling again in this section.

A document won't print. When your printer mysteriously refuses to cough up output, the fault usually lies with the Macintosh, not with the printer.

Make sure your printer is on and its cable is connected to your Mac. For a laser printer, give it about a minute or so to warm up before trying to print. If you run into a problem, you will get an alert message that asks if you want to try printing again. After making sure everything is ready, go ahead and try again—it should work this time.

For AppleTalk-connected printers, make sure AppleTalk is turned on. In most cases, you turn this on from the Chooser or the AppleTalk control panel. If you have a Mac that uses a Control Strip, you can turn it on from there. In Mac OS X, go to the AppleTalk pane in Network System Preferences.

If you have an AppleTalk printer and a PCI Power Mac or other model that uses the AppleTalk control panel, make sure the selected port (printer or modem) is the one to which your printer cable is connected. For other Macs, connect the printer *only* to the printer port.

Go to the Chooser and select the correct driver for your printer. If you don't see the driver for your printer in the Chooser window, check to see if it was moved to the "Extensions (disabled)" folder. If so, move it back to the Extensions folder. Otherwise, you'll probably have to reinstall the printer software. For AppleTalk printers, your printer's name should appear in the Chooser window after you select the driver. Click the name.

If you are trying to connect to a printer via Printer Share, make sure both the printer and the Mac to which it connects are turned on. Then make sure the Printer Share extension is installed and Printer Share is turned on in the Chooser's Setup options.

If you are using LaserWriter 8 and everything else you've tried has failed, go to the Preferences folder, locate the LaserWriter 8 preferences file, and delete it. Now go back to the Chooser and select Setup for the printer.

With computers running Open Transport, starting up with extensions off will prevent you from running any AppleTalk-connected printer (such as most LaserWriters). If you try to select such a printer from the Chooser, you will get an error message saying, "The printer port is in use. AppleTalk cannot be made active now." You need to reenable the Open Transport extensions to print.

If you start up with extensions off and you use the Desktop Printer extensions, the Desktop Printer icons on the Desktop appear with X marks over them. You can still print, but you don't have access to the special Desktop Printer features. Similarly, if you have installed QuickDraw GX, starting up with extensions off disables it. Zapping the PRAM sometimes solves these sorts of printing problems.

If all of the previous steps still fail to get your Mac to print, you may have corrupt printer software. Reinstall the software and try again.

PostScript errors. If you get a message that says a PostScript error occurred while printing, it almost always means you have a corrupt document, your document uses a corrupt font, or you ran out of memory while trying to print.

One simple cure that often works with corrupt word-processing documents is to highlight all the text using Select All and then change the font to some more acceptable font. Then try printing again. If this works, you can try reselecting your original font—it may work. If the problem is specific to a certain page, you can limit these font changes to just that page.

The easiest way to solve PostScript errors due to memory problems is to shorten the document (by breaking it into two or more separate documents) or simplify it (by using fewer fonts, for example). Also, you can turn off background printing from the Chooser. Then try printing again.

[*For more on diagnosing printing problems, see Chapter 6, "Printing."—Ed.*]

Ask the Experts

So you say you gave it your best shot and you still have trouble? Wondering where you should go next? Fear not! The solution you seek may be just a telephone call or mouse-click away.

Using the Built-in Mac OS Help

There you are with your elbows on the table and your head in your hands, staring glumly at the Desktop. Right there under your nose—actually under the Help menu—is the Help Center, which Apple has organized so well that you can get actually get help on Help itself. Selecting the Mac Help command displays a list of topics you can click to find the desired answer (**Figure 8.17**). But don't ignore the really useful Search field at the top of the main window. Type your latest debacle or discover power tips of the inner Mac circle.

Figure 8.17

You say you need help? Choose from the main help topics or type your subject and click Search.

Getting Help from Apple

When you purchase a new Mac, you get an entire 90 days of technical support at no charge. That means you have permission to call Apple as many times as you want free during the first three months you own your Mac. Take advantage of this service, because after the 90-day period you're going to have to shell out $49 per incident unless you've purchased an AppleCare Protection Plan. The good news is that it's pretty unlikely you'll need to contact Apple beyond the 90 days unless something goes drastically wrong with the hardware.

If it does, Apple won't charge you because the hardware portion of your Mac is covered for one year. In the United States, you can reach Apple support at 800/500-7078. In Canada, it's 800/263-3394.

The AppleCare Solution

If you don't have a Mac-savvy friend or family member, the AppleCare Protection Plan gives you the extra cushion of support you need whenever something goes "bump in the Mac." It covers almost any kind of situation you may experience—from basic installation questions to the replacement of any and all parts that make up your Macintosh.

The plan also includes access to a special Web site and a CD containing Micromat's TechTool Deluxe, used to test and diagnose troublesome Macs. You can conveniently purchase AppleCare at any time, even after your first year of ownership. At the time of this writing, three-year AppleCare Protection Plans run $149 to $349. You can get the latest pricing and other information at www.apple.com/support/products/proplan.html.

Finding Help on the Web

Self-help via the World Wide Web has become one of the most convenient methods for healing whatever ails your Mac. After all, it does offer some real advantages over telephone support. You won't have to remain on indefinite hold or get lost during a call transfer. Keep in mind that you can print Web pages and save them for future use. Typing www.apple.com/support/ in your browser will take you directly to Apple's main support area on the Internet.

Two of the most informative troubleshooting Web sites *not* run by Apple are Ric Ford's MacInTouch (www.macintouch.com) and Ted Landau's MacFixIt (www.macfixit.com). Landau contributed to this edition of *The Macintosh Bible* and is the author of the comprehensive troubleshooting tome *Sad Macs, Bombs, and Other Disasters* (also published by Peachpit Press).

Even if you aren't troubleshooting your Mac, visiting these sites daily will keep you so up to date that your Mac-loving friends will worship you as a guru!

Seeking Solutions with Sherlock

Besides exploring your hard disk, Apple's Sherlock can perform intelligent Internet searches (**Figure 8.18**).

Sherlock has the ability to scour multiple Web sites simultaneously and organize results by relevance in a hit list. Just launch Sherlock, select the Internet channel (the world icon in the first set of panels), type your topic, and click the search button.

You can also go directly to the source and focus your efforts using the built-in Apple Tech Info Library plug-in. Select the Apple channel (the Apple icon) and place a check in the Apple Tech Info Library box. Although this method provides the most focused results, Sherlock unfortunately doesn't rate them by relevance.

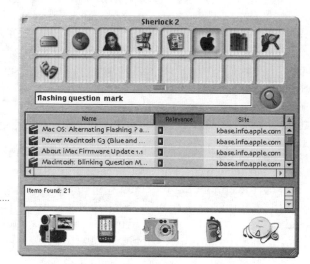

Figure 8.18

Sherlock can do more than just search your hard disk.

Apple's Discussions Area

If you believe two heads are better than one, you'll really appreciate Apple's Discussions area (**Figure 8.19**). As part of Apple's support Web site, the Discussions area features a free-flowing interchange of ideas between Mac users and Apple staff. When you post a message, the resolution to your problem may come from a user like you who has experienced the same situation or from one of Apple's qualified technicians. Either way you'll get a response that just might do the trick. To visit the Discussions area, go to http://discussions.info.apple.com. Note that you need to set up an Apple ID before you can enter this part of the Web site.

Figure 8.19

Get help from experts and other Mac users in Apple's Discussions area.

Hire a Macintosh Consultant

Although you wear most of the hats if you're an entrepreneur, your duties don't have to include Macintosh maintenance, setup, and troubleshooting. For an hourly fee, you can hire an expert to come to your home or office and attend to these tasks while you focus your energies on your business's day-to-day operations.

Finding a qualified Macintosh consultant used to be a challenge, but with the advent of the Internet, Apple has greatly simplified the process. Just launch your browser, surf over to http://experts.apple.com, and select Hire a Consultant.

Visit an Apple Authorized Service Provider

When you're ready to transport your Macintosh to the shop for a little repair work or upgrading, you'll need to locate an Apple Authorized Service Provider or Apple reseller. Whomever you choose must be Apple authorized or you risk voiding your warranty. A good place to start is the store where you purchased your Mac, as most have a service department capable of ordering Apple parts.

If you bought your Mac through an Internet or mail-order company, you can still get service through any Apple Authorized Service Provider or Apple reseller. You can find the closest one by visiting www.buy.apple.com and clicking the Find a Service Provider Near You button.

Of course, if your Mac is seriously ill and you don't have access to the Internet, you can fall back on the telephone directory (remember the big book with the yellow pages?). Once again, make sure the shop you choose is Apple Authorized.

Join a Macintosh User Group

Forget any preconceived ideas you might have about Macintosh user groups (MUGs for short). You'll find the makeup of each MUG so diverse that you could get hooked on the social benefits alone. With a consistent theme of Mac solidarity, each group has its own subset of novices, experts, consultants, and everything in between.

Most groups hold monthly meetings to demonstrate new products and frequently raffle off software donations. Members have an opportunity to discuss the latest Macintosh developments as well as some of their own challenges. You'll make many acquaintances at a MUG—and when trouble strikes, you'll need all the Mac friends you can get.

To find a MUG in your area, go to www.apple.com/usergroups/. With hundreds of these groups in the United States, you're likely to find one wherever you are.

Data Recovery—Your Final Resort

Data recovery is a specialized service that you may turn to as your absolute last resort when everyone and everything else has failed to save the precious files you didn't back up. **DriveSavers** (www.drivesavers.com) and **Ontrack Data International** (www.ontrack.com) are the leaders in this small but vital industry. By incorporating proprietary software and years of experience, these companies are capable of coaxing lost data from hard disks and other types of media when no one else can. They can even achieve successful recoveries from Macs destroyed in floods, fires, and other disasters.

Before using a service of this kind, evaluate your data loss and consider the amount of time and money necessary to re-create it. Ask yourself some important questions: Is it more cost effective to hire temporary personnel to input the missing data? Do printed copies of the material exist? How quickly is the current project needed? You may consider data recovery expensive, but sometimes regaining critical data is worth almost any price.

You can find a data-recovery company through advertising in a Macintosh publication such as *Macworld, Mac Home Journal,* or *MacAddict.* In addition, if you have access to a functional computer with an Internet connection, search for the term *data recovery* in Apple's Knowledge Base (http://kbase.info.apple.com/) or on the Web.

PART 2

Getting Productive

Editors' Poll: Which Productivity Programs Do You Use All the Time?

DM: I'm a longtime user of the standard trio of Microsoft Office applications. And I'm tired of hearing so-called knowledgeable power users repeat the folklore of their being Windows ports—each is now an excellent Mac program. I've been faithful to Power On Software's Now Contact and Up-to-Date information managers. Over the past few years, I've increased my use of Adobe Acrobat, until now it's my default printer driver.

BF: As a writer, it's Word, but I also use video-related programs such as iMovie 2 a great deal.

AD: E-mail (Eudora Pro), Word (of course), and Internet Explorer. Nothing else comes close.

CB: I make my living with the word processor (Word 2001), e-mail client (Eudora and Entourage), and Web browser (iCab and Internet Explorer). Because I spend a good portion of my day trying to breath life back into comatose Macs, I use a fair smattering of troubleshooting utilities—Alsoft's Disk Warrior and Casady & Greene's Conflict Catcher 8 are among my favorites. And Ambrosia's Snapz Pro is a must-have for anyone who needs to take lots of screenshots.

GS: As someone who struggles to earn a living as a writer, I live in Microsoft Word, which still gets my vote as the best word processor on the planet (on any platform). My favorite utilities include GraphicConverter and Snapz Pro X, both again related to my regular workday routine.

JOG: If my machine is on, I am almost guaranteed to be using e-mail and a Web browser. Currently those would be Entourage and Explorer. My other main applications are BBEdit and Interarchy for Web publishing and Limewire for all kinds of stuff.

MC: I have a tolerate-hate relationship with Microsoft Word.

KT: When I'm in the middle of a design project, I use Acrobat Distiller (and sometimes Acrobat itself) for preparing proofs for clients. I handle correspondence with either PageMaker or InDesign, and one or both is usually open all the time, as are Eudora and a Web browser. I use Excel for all sorts of purposes, even sometimes including number-crunching—but mainly for text editing, tagging, and other weird purposes its developers probably didn't envision.

JF: When I want to be productive, I go work in the garden. I think the greatest productivity tool that could be made for a computer would be the one that induces users to read carefully. If people actually read the e-mail I sent them, for example, instead of just skimming them (or whatever they do), I could cut the number of letters I write ("As I said in my last message…") in half.

JR: I depend on word processing, but I think I write more in e-mail software. My e-mail application is open all the time. I also use an HTML editor daily for my Web site and some graphics editors for simple chores. Web browsers and Sherlock are my main research tools.

JO: Outlook Express—I launch my e-mail program first whenever I sit down. Internet Explorer—after skimming my mail, I often head to the Web to check what's new on Ric Ford's excellent MacInTouch Web site. Microsoft Word 2001—I do a lot of writing (on Macs and PCs) and find it gives me the best cross platform functionality with Word 2000. Quicken—I spend a fair amount of time managing my finances, and Quicken seems to do most everything I need.

ML: Word, Excel, FileMaker Pro, and Entourage. You can bash Microsoft all you want, but you can't beat the power of Word and Excel for Word processing and spreadsheet tasks—if power is what you need. And Entourage…well, I use it, but I'm still not sold on it.

SS: My three constant software productivity companions are InTouch (long gone, but still running flawlessly in Mac OS 9), Entourage, and Adobe Acrobat.

9

Word Processing

Marty Cortinas is the chapter editor and author.

You're ready to put that Underwood in the closet, and you're determined that your next letter to Mom will slide out of your Mac's printer. Sure, you could use SimpleText or TeachText or Stickies to write her a note. But what you'll really want is a program called a word processor to produce that letter.

A word processor can help you craft the letter, from setting the margins to checking your spelling. This chapter is all about word processors.

In This Chapter

Getting Started

Defining exactly what a word processor is can be a tricky business. So many applications can perform a variety of tasks that it's difficult to draw boundaries. For example, the spelling-check and formatting options in many e-mail programs make them a viable option when you need to do some writing in a pinch.

For the purposes of this chapter, if a program has extensive tools for manipulating words, it's a word processor. The distinction lies in the program's being able to change what is written, rather than being able to change how it looks. If the program's main function deals with something else—such as sending e-mail or producing page layouts—it is not a word processor. So, by this logic, Microsoft Word, Nisus Writer, and AppleWorks qualify. Adobe Acrobat, QuarkXPress, and Adobe GoLive do not.

Choosing a Word Processor

If you don't have a word processor, your first question probably will be, "Which one should I get?" This should actually be your second question, because the answer depends on what you want to use the word processor for.

If you are going to do some simple tasks such as writing letters, creating fliers, or crafting essays, you can stick to a simple, inexpensive word processor. AppleWorks would probably be fine.

If you need to do heavy-duty editing and create things such as indexes, outlines, or bibliographies, a program such as Word or Nisus Writer is the correct call. If you need to collaborate with others, especially if they are working on different platforms, you'll probably end up with Word.

The bottom line is that word processors are not created equal. Unless you have a lot of disposable income, you must define your needs before you pick a word processor.

Working with Text

With a typewriter, you type and the words pretty much stay where they are on the page. Word processing is a lot more flexible; you can easily move, alter, or delete text.

Inserting Text

Before you can process words, you have to get them into the Mac. Let's forget about preexisting text, such as that file your boss just gave you, and start from scratch. You create a new document and are greeted by white space. Now what? Well, you type.

Notice that everything you type is entered at the insertion point, which is represented by a vertical flashing bar. In fact, everything you do happens at the insertion point. Selections start there, and paste operations happen there. Typing and deleting are based at the insertion point. To move the insertion point, you can click with the mouse somewhere else in your document or you can use the arrow keys.

 If you want to move the insertion point below the end of your text, down to where all that inviting white space is, you might have to add some paragraph marks or returns to get there. Although a large enough window will show space beyond the end-of-file marker, the program doesn't recognize it as such— there's no there there. (If you want to get really metaphysical, there is an infinite amount of white space after the end, but the window only shows part of it.) So to put some text farther down, you'll have to push down the end-of-file marker with line feeds of some sort.

Aside from typing text, you can also import existing documents using the commands in your word processor. Or you can use cut and paste to swipe text from another source. If you are the futuristic type, you can buy an application that types what you speak (this is called *voice-recognition software*). [*For a glimpse at the state of voice-recognition software on the Mac, see Chapter 12, "Personal and Business Management." —Ed.*] In any case, you're still going to have to master the basics of the insertion point and selecting text.

Selecting Text

If you wish to perform an action on a piece of text, such as deleting it, copying it, or styling it, you must first select it. You can select text by clicking and then dragging across it (**Figure 9.1**). If the selection you want runs for several lines, you don't need to move the pointer over every single word—just click at the beginning and drag to the end of the selection via the shortest route. You can even select backward. When you release the mouse button, all text between the starting point and the ending point will be selected. If you didn't quite select what you wanted, you can hold down (Shift) and click or use the arrow keys to modify your selection.

You have other ways to select text, depending on the application you're using. For the most part, double-clicking will select one whole word. Microsoft Word, for example, will let you select columns of text using (Option)-drag. Nisus Writer does a neat trick called *noncontiguous selection* (selecting unconnected blocks of text). Consult the help files of the application you're using for any specialized selecting.

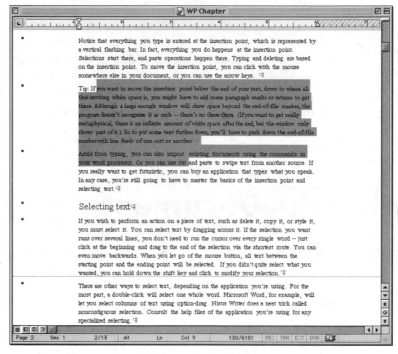

Figure 9.1

The highlighted text has been selected. Any actions you perform now will be applied only to the selected text.

To deselect text, simply click outside the selected text. If you use an arrow key, you will instantly move to the beginning or end of the selection, which will then be deselected.

If you find that you can't quite get the selection exactly the way you want it, this may be because the program insists on "helping" by selecting only entire words. Dig into the program's preferences to turn off this feature. In Word 98, for example, go to Tools > Preferences, and under the Edit tab, make sure you don't have a check in the box next to "When selecting, automatically select entire word." In Word 2001, reach the Edit tab through Edit > Preferences.

Now that you have text selected, what can you do with it? You can style it—that is, change its appearance through the use of fonts and the like. You can copy it. You can cut it. Depending on your purposes, you can cut text in two ways. If your intention is to cut the selection to move it somewhere else, you'll want to use ⌘X. This will remove the selected text and place it in the Clipboard; ⌘V will paste it wherever you want. (These are not specifically features of word processors but are commands you can use in any Mac program.) If your goal is to delete the offending selection forever, just start typing. The words you type will take the place of the selection, which won't move to the Clipboard. (If you accidentally delete something in this way and you wanted to save it, don't despair. Most applications nowadays have an undo feature, usually ⌘Z. The newer versions of Word give you multiple levels of undo, so you can go back several steps to redo a misstep.)

 A few Mac OS 9 control panels modify how type selection works. General Controls lets you set the insertion point's blink rate. The delay until repeat and the key-repeat rate can be set using the Keyboard control panel. And under the Appearance tab of the Appearance control panel (yes, the name is repeated) you can choose the highlight color for selected text. In Mac OS X, use the Keyboard System Preferences to set key-repeat rate and delay until repeat; through the Highlight Color pop-up menu of the General System Preferences you can pick a highlight color.

Styling the Document

Word processing is not only about the words themselves but how they look on the page. There's formatting, line breaks, margins, graphics, and more to consider.

Formatting

Formatting means setting the fonts, point sizes, and styles (such as bold or italic) of selected characters. When you format an entire paragraph, you can also set other parameters, such as margins, indents, space before and after, leading, and tabs.

For example, as I type the draft of this chapter, I am using regular 10-point Times with a left indent of 1.08 inches, 13-point line spacing, 6 points of space before each paragraph, and four tab stops. That's what Word tells me, at least (**Figure 9.2**).

You should think of formatting as what is done to characters once they are in the document. When you type in a document, the program records them as they are entered and then changes their appearance as you apply format changes. This can give weird results if you don't understand the logic. For example, let's say I type some goofy word with a capital in the middle of it, like "AppleWorks." If I then apply the all-caps format, I get "APPLEWORKS." However, typing "AppleWorks" and then applying the all-caps format is *not* the same thing as simply typing "APPLEWORKS," because deep in the Mac's reptilian brain, it knows that in the first case only the "A" and the "W" are capped. So if I then apply a new style to the two all-capped (but different) words, I get two different results: The first word reverts to upper- and lowercase, the second remains all uppercased (**Figure 9.3**).

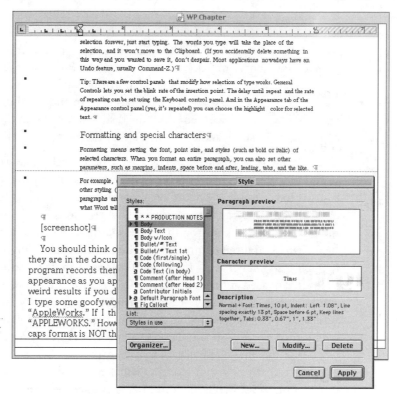

Figure 9.2

The Style dialog box shows the different formatting options you can apply to your paragraphs.

Figure 9.2

The Style dialog box shows the different formatting options you can apply to your paragraphs.

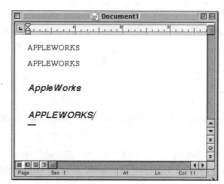

Figure 9.3

Although you may get the same results both ways, typing in all caps and applying the all-caps format are not the same thing.

Recent Mac operating systems feature font smoothing, which is another word for anti-aliasing. Smoothing blurs the edges of letters to make them look less jagged. This works especially well at larger point sizes, but to sensitive eyes it is annoying at the smaller sizes. Mac OS 9's Appearance control panel allows you to turn this feature off or to set a threshold at which smoothing starts. In Mac OS X, you can't turn anti-aliasing off but you can set a threshold at which text smoothing starts in the General System Preferences pane. Some Mac OS X applications—such as the OmniWeb browser from the Omni Group—also give you the option to forgo font smoothing.

Special Characters

Most word processors allow the writer to be specific about how words and punctuation behave in a document through the use of special characters. The most common of these are those little horizontal lines between words: hyphens and dashes. You can use two types of dashes (em and en), but for the most part you won't be concerned about the distinction between the two. (Although copyeditors do know and care—that's why they get paid the big bucks.)

 The hyphen, on the other hand, is a versatile animal in the word processor. It not only serves its usual purpose when you use it in your writing but can be used to control how a word breaks at the end of a line of text. Depending on how your paragraphs are formatted, when you get to the end of a line, the program will either drop the entire word down to the next line or try to hyphenate it. You can control where the word breaks by inserting an optional hyphen, also known as a *soft hyphen.* A soft hyphen won't show up in a word unless it's needed at the end of a line. Many programs allow you to use the soft hyphen in front of a word to prevent it from being hyphenated at all. A relative is the *nonbreaking* hyphen. This hyphen is used in a word that is hyphenated already—it simply tells the program not to break the hyphenated word over two lines. The *nonbreaking space,* on the other hand, goes between two words that you want to keep together on the same line. Consult the documentation of your chosen word processor to access these options, which are usually invoked using a keyboard combination.

Line breaks: Why should I care? If you start writing with your word processor right out of the box, you might wonder what all this talk of line breaks is about. After all, you've been typing all this time and you've never seen the computer add a hyphen to any of your words. The reason is that the default justification of paragraphs is ragged right, which means that every line starts in the same place on the left but varies on the right, depending on how many characters are in the line, and each line ends with a whole word. If you change the justification to flush right, the lines will end at the same vertical point on the right but vary on the left. If you change the setting to "justified," both sides of your paragraphs will line up. To accomplish this, the Mac adjusts the amount of white space between words so each line starts and ends at the same vertical point. When the white-space trick doesn't quite work, a word at the end of the line has to be hyphenated. The program will usually make an educated guess about the best place to break a word, but it's often a bad guess. Using special characters such as the soft hyphen can help the program make the right decisions.

Text Styles and Templates

Word processors make it easy for you to change the way words look. You can select individual words and change their appearance, and you can define a way that certain types of documents (such as business letters) look. The tools that allow you to do this are text styles and templates.

Styles. A style is a set of parameters, such as point size, font, font style, text alignment, and line spacing, that you can apply in one quick step. Usually you apply a style to entire paragraphs or to selected text. An example of where you would use styles is a small newsletter. You could have one style for the body text and another for headlines. One of the great advantages of styles is that many word processors allow you to change the look of a style and apply those changes globally in one step. So if you are writing the Great American Novel and your editors decide that they prefer 14-point Courier to 12-point Times, you don't have to scroll through your document paragraph by paragraph to make the change. Simply edit the appropriate style and update it.

Templates. A template is a blueprint for documents, and it usually contains information about menus, toolbars, palettes, shortcuts, formatting, layout, and styles. For example, most word processors come with a collection of templates for business letters, brochures, presentations, and the like.

Templates are handy tools, especially when you are working with other users. With templates, you can make sure that everyone is working on the same page. In the making of this book, for example, the writers were given a template to ensure that everyone was using the same fonts for the text, captions, and headlines. Instead of telling everyone the specific parameters for each item, a template containing all that information was distributed.

 Take care with templates. When dealing with templates, it is important to make sure you are using them, not modifying them. In Word 2001, for example, if a coworker gives you a template for a business letter, you should not just open it and start typing. If you do this, you will be modifying the template, which is not what you want to do. Store the template in your Templates folder; it then will show up in the Project Gallery, which lets you create a new document based on the template. You can also attach the template to an existing document, which gives you access to all the styles in the template (**Figure 9.4**).

Figure 9.4

In Microsoft Word you can attach a template to an existing document.

Graphics

If you're doing more than simple writing, you'll probably need to include some pictures with your work. Thankfully, most word processors handle basic graphics easily, although you won't get the versatility of a program made especially for the task, such as QuarkXPress. You can easily insert graphics and modify how they behave with text. For example, you can arrange for the text to wrap around your graphic or even have the graphic sit below or above the text.

Views. To use graphics effectively, you must be comfortable with switching between various views in your word processor. In Word, most folks usually work in the Normal view, but graphics aren't visible there. Page Layout view shows how your work will look when it is output. Nisus Writer approaches the matter a little differently, dividing graphics and text into separate layers.

Image formats. Many word processors come with a collection of clip art that can be plopped into your document. You can also include your own pictures. Keep in mind how your work is going to be output, however. While JPEG and GIF images are popular, especially on the Web, because of their relatively small file sizes, they are not always the best option for other documents. If you plan to print your work, a better option is a TIFF or similar high-resolution format.

HTML

Speaking of the Web, word processors today often offer the option to save your documents in HTML format, the language of the Web. Although this seems like a good idea, try to avoid it. Word processors are not made to create Web content, and it often shows. The code created by these programs is usually bloated, which is not desirable on the Internet. However, if you need a Web page in a pinch, it works.

Hyperlinks and Bookmarks

In Word, you have to be a little careful about terminology. For example, there's the case of *hyperlinks* and *bookmarks.* In some other applications, a bookmark is an Internet address. That's not the case in Word; a bookmark is a location in a document you name for future reference. You use bookmarks to navigate to a location, mark page ranges, create cross-references, and do other similar things. For example, you can select some text and use the Insert > Bookmark command to name the selection. Now you can use the bookmark command to navigate to that named bookmark. It is important to realize that the bookmarks allow you to move only within one document. A hyperlink is "hot" text (or even an image) that takes you to another location when you click it. For example, a hyperlink can point to a Web site, an e-mail address, another Office document, or somewhere else in the current document (**Figure 9.5**).

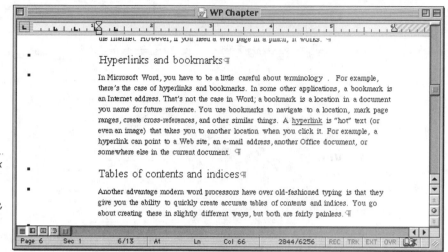

Figure 9.5

There is a bookmark and a hyperlink in this paragraph. The bookmark is invisible, and the hyperlink is a different color and underlined.

Structure and Organization

Jack Kerouac wrote the manuscript of *On the Road* without paragraphs or punctuation on a 120-foot strip of Teletype paper. (His editor must have loved him.) You and I probably can't get away with that, and we must have some structure to our documents. Fortunately, we have tools that Kerouac and his typewriter did not. Word processors make it easy to add footnotes, headers, tables of contents, and many other organizational features.

Tables of Contents and Indexes

Another advantage modern word processors have over old-fashioned typing is that they give you the ability to quickly create accurate tables of contents and indexes. You go about creating these in slightly different ways, but both are fairly painless.

Tables of contents. Tables of contents are usually derived from the hierarchy set up by the use of styled headings (**Figure 9.6**). In Word, you can also create a table of contents from any outline you may have created for the document. Generally, you pick a menu option, fiddle with the settings, and bingo—you've got a table of contents.

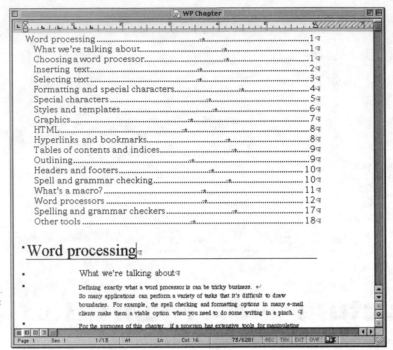

Figure 9.6

This table of contents was derived from the headings of this chapter.

Indexes. These are a little trickier, as they are more comprehensive. First, you need to decide what is worth listing in an index. Unfortunately, this means you have to read what you've been writing. When you decide that a word or term is worth indexing, you mark it in a special manner. After you've done this for the entire work, you can generate an index. It's a bit of work but still much quicker than compiling an index by hand. Not all word processors have indexing features; you have been warned.

Outlining

Outlining allows you to see the structure of your document, as long as you have been using styles to define different parts of it. In Word, for example, the Outline view lets you collapse text under topics and subtopics and assign different levels to each section. You can also generate a numbered list outlining your document.

Currently, only Word provides powerful outlining tools as part of its base package.

Headers and Footers

Headers and footers are pieces of text that appear at the top and bottom of each page of a printed document. For example, they might include a title, page number, and date. Most programs go beyond that simple functionality, however, and allow the use of multiple variables to produce dynamic headers and footers. For example, if you were creating a member directory for a local organization, you could include headers that show the first and last entries of each page, like those found in dictionaries or phone books. You can also create a unique header and footer for the first page or for different sections of a document. You can make it so the headers change depending on whether the page number is odd or even. Basically, if you can think of an application for headers and footers, you can accomplish it.

Using Tools

Word processing is not just typing and formatting. There are tools to cut down on errors and to make repetitive tasks less taxing.

Spelling and Grammar Checking

Once you've written your document, you'll want to make sure you don't embarrass yourself by misspelling something, and that's where the spelling checker comes in. As much as spelling checkers can do, it is important to remember what they can't do: spell. A spelling checker simply compares the words in a document with its dictionary; if a word isn't in the dictionary, it is flagged. Most spelling checkers at this point will suggest a replacement for the unknown word or phrase. (Word suggests that "Marty Cortinas" should be "merry courtesan.") As you can see, the efficiency of the spelling checker is directly influenced by the quality of the dictionary.

 You can edit most dictionaries. Take advantage of this to add your name, names of friends or businesses, or any other proper names you use a lot.

Another shortcoming of spelling checkers is that an incorrect spelling can be a correct spelling for another word, and the checker won't catch it. If you are talking about Bambi's mom, you may write "She's a dear," when you meant "She's a deer." Both are "right," but one is wrong in the context. The spelling checker won't catch it, so you must maintain your vigilance even though the word processor has "checked" your spelling.

Several stand-alone spelling checkers are available in the Mac market, several of which I discuss below. You might wonder why you would want to buy such a product when it seems that every program that uses words has a built-in spelling checker. As paradoxical as it appears, that is the exact reason why you might want to buy a stand-alone product. Instead of relying on several individual dictionaries in various stages of customization, you can work with one. If you type your name in Nisus Writer and OK it in your spelling checker, you won't have Word flagging your name as wrong.

Grammar checking is a little more sophisticated, and today's grammar checkers do an amazing job, considering the technical hurdles. However, I find that grammar checkers are more trouble than they're worth. If you have problems with grammar, however, they can be quite helpful, although it still pays to keep a close eye on them—they're not always right.

What's a Macro?

A macro is a stored set of instructions you can use to perform a task automatically. They are particularly useful for performing repetitive tasks. For example, if you routinely insert a table of specific proportions into your documents, you can save a lot of work by making a macro for it. In Word, you can use the macro recorder to copy the steps you take and then assign a shortcut key or menu command to trigger the steps. So instead of your going through the trouble of pulling down the Insert menu, choosing Index and Tables, and fiddling with the settings in the dialog box, the macro lets you simply press a shortcut key.

Although you can "record" a macro, there are limits to what a macro can contain. Figure that if you can perform an operation using only the keyboard and menu selections, you can make it into a macro. The minute the mouse enters the picture, a macro is pretty much out of the question. Still, within those limits, much can be done; you are limited mainly by your imagination and your macro-designing skill. And macros don't just have to be serious labor-saving devices. I've seen amusing "personality tests" that are actually macros.

Macros are powerful time-savers, but that power comes at a cost, at least in Microsoft Word. Word's macro capabilities tap into Visual Basic, a programming language. Although that allows macros to perform all sorts of neat tricks, it also opens the door for the evil that is the macro virus.

A macro virus lives among the macros in a document or template, and it is usually designed to be triggered whenever the affected document is opened. It can then find its way to your global template and infect every file you open. As an added feature, this infection ability is cross-platform, so the virus can move from Windows to Mac to Windows again. Soon your coworkers will refer to you as Typhoid Mary.

There are two ways to prevent this. One is to purchase a commercial antivirus package, such as Symantec's Norton AntiVirus (www.symantec.com). The other is to have Word disable macros in any suspect document. Actually, Word can't tell what is suspect and what is not. Once you activate the macro-virus protection in the general preferences, the program will simply alert you that a document has macros and give you the option to disable them. If the document is from a trusted source, go ahead and run them. If you're not sure, turn them off.

Does Mac OS X change anything? As far as word processing goes, Mac OS X will have little impact on how you do your work, at least compared with the way it handles graphics applications. Aside from the memory protection you get with Mac OS X and the interface changes, you'll notice hardly anything different from previous operating systems. Heck, it's only typing.

Word Processors

So you're ready to write. Now what do you do? Unless you're perfectly happy with Stickies, you'll have to get a word processor. Although there's not a ton available, you do have some choices to make.

Microsoft Word for Mac

Microsoft Word for Mac, by Microsoft Corp.(www.microsoft.com), is the 800-pound gorilla of the word-processing world. The latest version, Microsoft Word for Mac 2001, is available by itself ($399, upgrade $149) or as part of the Office 2001 for Mac suite, which also includes Microsoft Excel, Entourage, and PowerPoint. In many cases, when people talk about word processing, they are talking about Word. Naturally, this has its good points and its bad points.

The main disadvantage is that for many businesses and almost any collaborative projects, you don't have a choice of word processors. It's Word or nothing. For many years, Word was merely tolerated in the Mac community. It didn't help matters that the program came from the same company that produced Windows, the rival personal-computing platform (or "the enemy," as some people call Microsoft). Each new version of Word seemed to drift further and further away from what users considered the Mac experience. The nadir came in the early 1990s with the release of Word 6 for the Mac, which was not only overburdened with toolbars and buttons but was a pig of an application. It demanded a lot of RAM to run and took seemingly forever to start up. Word 6 was so reviled that many conspiracy theorists pointed to it as a sort of Trojan horse, sent by Microsoft to undermine the Macintosh.

OK, so Word 6 was bad. (So bad, in fact, that the company I worked for at the time refused to "upgrade" and stuck with the old, reliable Word 5.1.) But a funny thing happened in 1997. Steve Jobs had come back to Apple, and that summer he kicked up quite a ruckus by marking the clone market for death and creating an alliance with Microsoft. Microsoft paid Apple some money and promised to actively develop programs for the Mac, and Apple dropped some patent lawsuits and made Microsoft Internet Explorer the default Web browser on new Macs. [*These actions, of course, were unrelated. —Ed.*]

You can argue all you want about whether making peace with Microsoft was a good move by Jobs, but you can't that Word for the Mac is a much better product now. Microsoft not only has put together a fine Macintosh team but has let the team members loose. Before the Apple deal, the feature sets in Word and the other Office products were already converging, with the result that the products were looking and acting more and more like Windows programs, even on the Mac. If there were any cool new features, you could be sure they would be available for Windows months if not years before Mac users got a taste. Nowadays, the Microsoft Mac products are more faithful to the Mac aesthetic, and many of the cool new features start life on the Mac.

So that's good. Another good thing is that the current versions of Word, on both the Mac and Windows sides, share file formats. That makes Word the perfect vehicle for trading files across platforms. No good deed goes unpunished though, so that biplatform capability has the drawback of allowing the nefarious among us to distribute macro viruses that much more easily.

If you're a single user who doesn't do a lot of work with others, or someone who needs a word processor every once in a while, Word is probably too much—like using a bulldozer instead of a spoon. However, if you're in business, you don't have a choice: It's Word.

Making Word less helpful. Microsoft Word includes several tools to make your work go more smoothly. Unfortunately, almost all of them are enabled when you first start up the program, and this can be more of a detriment than a benefit. You may find yourself typing some simple notes to yourself, when the Word Assistant will burst in and announce, "It looks like you are writing a letter. Would you like help?" Aside from the creepiness you may feel from having the computer "watch" what you're doing, this intrusion can often just be a waste of time because no, you don't want any help, and you have to make the assistant go away.

Other times, Word may not even ask but will go ahead and format what you're typing in a manner it believes is correct. Now it's a double waste of time because you have to go back and fix what Word did. So how do you keep Word on a leash?

The top of most folks' Word hit lists has a space reserved for the Office Assistant, the little animated computer named Max (**Figure 9.7**). Max can be helpful by offering context-sensitive tips, but unless you are completely new to Word, he becomes a bother rather quickly. He's easily silenced; just choose Turn Assistant Off from the Help menu.

More pernicious is Word's habit of automatically formatting certain words or paragraphs. For instance, if you write something that appears to be a Internet link, whether it's a URL or an e-mail address, Word will make it into a live hyperlink. Getting Word to stop doing this is a little more involved than it should be, but easy enough to fix.

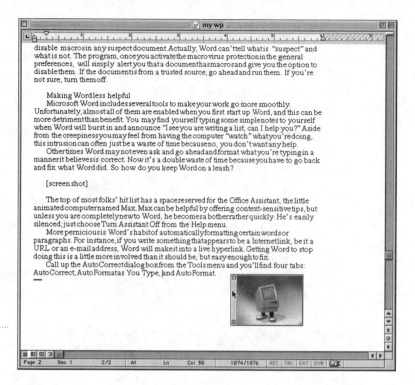

disable macros in any suspect document. Actually, Word can't tell what is "suspect" and what is not. The program, once you activate the macro virus protection in the general preferences, will simply alert you that a document has macros and give you the option to disable them. If the document is from a trusted source, go ahead and run them. If you're not sure, turn them off.

Making Word less helpful

Microsoft Word includes several tools to make your work go more smoothly. Unfortunately, almost all of them are enabled when you first start up Word, and this can be more detriment than benefit. You may find yourself typing some simple notes to yourself when Word will burst in and announce "I see you are writing a list, can I help you?" Aside from the creepiness you may feel from having the computer "watch" what you're doing, this intrusion can often just be a waste of time because no, you don't want any help.

Other times Word may not even ask and go ahead and format what you're typing in a manner it believes is correct. Now it's a double waste of time because you have to go back and fix what Word did. So how do you keep Word on a leash?

[screen shot]

The top of most folks' hit list has a space reserved for the Office Assistant, the little animated computer named Max. Max can be helpful by offering context-sensitive tips, but unless you are completely new to Word, he becomes a bother rather quickly. He's easily silenced; just choose Turn Assistant Off from the Help menu.

More pernicious is Word's habit of automatically formatting certain words or paragraphs. For instance, if you write something that appears to be a Internet link, be it a URL or an e-mail address, Word will make it into a live hyperlink. Getting Word to stop doing this is a little more involved than it should be, but easy enough to fix.

Call up the AutoCorrect dialog box from the Tools menu and you'll find four tabs: AutoCorrect, AutoFormat as You Type, and AutoFormat.

Page 2   Sec 1   2/2   At   Ln   Col 38   1874/1876   REC TRK EXT OVR

Figure 9.7

It's Max the Office Assistant. Friend or foe?

Figure 9.8

Here's the AutoFormat As You Type tab. Note the AutoFormat tab on the far right. Often, changes you make here will also need to be made there.

Open the AutoCorrect dialog box from the Tools menu and you'll find four tabs: AutoCorrect, AutoFormat As You Type, AutoText, and AutoFormat. Somewhere deep in the bowels of the Microsoft programming hutch, there is a coder who can explain why there are two AutoFormat tabs. I cannot. But I can tell you that to fix many of the annoying automatic functions in Word, you must make changes under both tabs.

Let's take the Internet link as an example. If you choose the AutoFormat tab and uncheck the "Internet paths with hyperlinks" option under Replace, you might think Word won't insert hyperlinks anymore. You'd be wrong. Move to the AutoFormat As You Type tab, and you'll find almost the same option under "Replace as you type" (**Figure 9.8**). Uncheck that box as well, and you'll banish automatic hyperlinks forever. The moral of the story is that you often have to look in more than one place to change Word's behavior.

Nisus Writer

This program, by Nisus Software ($99.95; www.nisus.com), is currently the only viable professional alternative to Microsoft Word. That alone is more than enough reason for some folks to buy it. However, Nisus Writer has more going for it than not being Word.

Nisus Writer has some interesting interface tools, such as multiple clipboards (for those pesky repetitive cut-and-paste jobs) and *noncontiguous selection.* So what is noncontiguous selection? In other programs, the text you select has a discrete beginning and end, and anything between is selected. In other words, there is only one block of selected text. Nisus Writer lets you have more than one block of selected text not adjacent to one another. For example, you can do a search for all occurrences of the word *the* in your document, and Nisus Writer will select them all. You can then do anything to this noncontiguous selection that you could do to a regular selection, such as bolding or changing fonts (**Figure 9.9**). Nisus Writer also has full multilanguage support and a ridiculously over-powered searching capability.

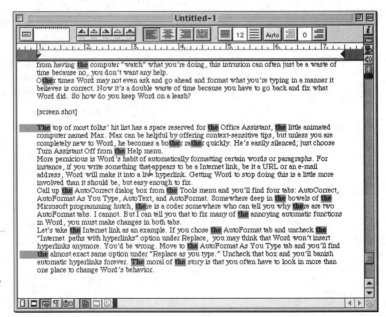

Figure 9.9

Nisus Writer can make noncontiguous selections, as in this example, where I found every the *in the document.*

There are drawbacks to Nisus Writer. If you need outlining, you're out of luck. And forget about cross-platform work or reading Word files. Still, as long as you don't need Word compatibility and you're working in a relatively insular environment or alone, Nisus Writer is strong competition for Word.

AppleWorks

The word-processor portion of Apple Computer's AppleWorks—bundled with the company's iBooks and iMacs and available at the Apple Store for $79—is worth a quick mention here; it is covered in depth in Chapter 12, "Personal and Business Management." If you need simple word processing at a small price, it's hard to go wrong with AppleWorks—plus you get spreadsheet, database, painting, drawing, and presentation modules (www.apple.com/appleworks).

What About WordPerfect?

Although WordPerfect is doing bang-up business on the Windows platform, Corel (www.corel.com) long ago gave up on developing WordPerfect for the Mac. OK, the company never really began working on a Mac version when it acquired the WordPerfect franchise from Novell in 1996. Despite this neglect, a sizable contingent of folks remain loyal to the Mac version of WordPerfect. Some of these people admit that the current version, WordPerfect 3.5, leaves much to be desired, but they apparently prefer a flawed WordPerfect to the current Word. In fact, there is a drive to get Corel to bring back WordPerfect to the Mac. The reasoning is that there is a Linux version of WordPerfect, and the Mac installed base is larger. And Corel hasn't abandoned the Mac entirely; it has a full line of graphics products for the Macintosh. So will WordPerfect come back? Consider this: You can download the current version for free (legally!) from various places on the Internet. I'd say that means WordPerfect for Mac is dead.

Movie Magic Screenwriter 2000 and Dramatica Pro

Although a mainstay such as Microsoft Word can handle most of your writing needs, it doesn't necessarily cover all of them. This product line, from Screenplay Systems (www.screenplaysystems.com), is a perfect example of filling a niche.

Presentation of the material in a script for television or the movies demands a lot of attention to detail. There are conventions for handling scene headings, action, camera angles, character names, dialogue, transitions, and a host of other elements. Screenwriter 2000 ($269) takes care of all that formatting for you.

Screenplay Systems has a host of related products for the budding or professional creative writer. Dramatica Pro ($269) is a sort of companion program to Screenwriter 2000. It's aimed at writers who are trying to craft a story. It helps refine plot points and scene creation through questions and examples.

Scriptware

Scriptware, from Cinovation ($299.95; www.cinovation.com), is another word processor for screenwriters. Long the most popular software of its kind on the Windows platform, it made the move to the Mac in late 1997. The highlight of the program is the way it understands the formatting of a script. The company calls it an "easier than a typewriter" typing system. Scriptware sees what you are typing and can make the appropriate style changes to the text. For example, it knows that "ext" indicates a scene heading and applies the appropriate changes. You can also easily manage cast names; the Tab key calls up a list of cast members that you can enter into the script with one keystroke.

Not being a screenwriter, I can't vouch for one program over the other, so if you'd like to know more, download the demos and give them a whirl.

Tools

Even though today's Macintosh word processors can do a lot of things, they can't do everything, and some things they can do are done better by others. Here's a look at some of these options.

Spelling and Grammar Checkers

Although most programs already have a built-in spelling checker, there is some advantage to adopting an outside program. You have more control over your dictionaries, and you don't have to correct the same mistake over and over in different programs. Here is a rundown of some of the more popular stand-alone spelling and grammar checkers.

Spell Catcher for Macintosh. Casady & Greene's popular stand-alone spelling checker ($49.95; www.casadyg.com) does pretty much what you'd expect, but it also has a cool little tool called a *shorthand glossary*. The shorthand glossary lets you type a shorthand version of a phrase, and Spell Catcher automatically expands it for you. For example, if you're tired of typing "for example" all the time, you could set up "eg" as shorthand for it. Just type "eg," and Spell Catcher turns it into "for example."

Grammarian 2. Also from Casady & Greene ($49.95), Grammarian 2 is an interactive grammar checker, meaning that it can alert you to mistakes it finds as you type. If you find this annoying, you can easily run batch checks, which also provide you with statistics such as grade levels. Grammarian lets the user adjust its sensitivity through a dialog box containing settings for writing styles and rules; there you can toggle searches for clichéd phrases, euphemisms, and the like.

Spellswell Plus. This program, by Working Software ($14.95; www.working. com), is billed as an Internet spelling checker, but I'm puzzled as to exactly why. My best guess is because it works with a host of Internet-related applications such as Microsoft Outlook Express, Netscape Navigator, and Qualcomm Eudora Pro. Or maybe because it can check spelling in HTML documents— it does this neat trick by ignoring text between < and > characters. Spellswell Plus acts like a built-in spelling checker when it's used with the programs it supports.

Other Tools

EndNote. EndNote, from ISI ResearchSoft ($299.95; www.isiresearchsoft.com), is a stand-alone program for creating bibliographies. It allows you to search online bibliographic databases, organize references, and consequently produce a bibliography. The program comes with more than 200 predefined connection files for online databases to make it easier to get up and searching.

EndNote has an add-in for working with Microsoft Word but not for any other word processor on the Mac. Once installed, the add-in provides a set of menu tools to create bibliographies directly in Word.

Co:Writer 4000. This program, from Don Johnston ($325; www.donjohnston. com), is designed for students with disabilities that make typing difficult. At heart it is a word-prediction tool. The user begins to type, and the program provides a list of predicted words, which the program reads aloud to aid recognition. The program also checks grammar as the words are written. Co:Writer's built-in dictionaries can be supplemented quickly with customized or topic-specific word lists made from simple text files. For example, if a student enjoys writing about sports, he or she can create a dictionary of team names from a list.

10

Spreadsheets

Maria Langer (ML) is the chapter editor and author.

Sharon Zardetto Aker (SA), Christian Boyce (CB), Elizabeth Castro (EC), Dennis Cohen (DC), and Eve Gordon (EG) contributed to earlier editions of **The Macintosh Bible,** *from which portions of this chapter are taken.*

The first breakthrough software package for the personal computer, VisiCalc, was a spreadsheet program. It became wildly successful and made people realize that perhaps there was money in selling software. Thirty years later, spreadsheets have grown up quite a bit. Used for more than just addition and subtraction, spreadsheets now solve complex financial analysis problems, create 3D graphs, and generate monthly reports. We'll tell you just what you can expect from today's spreadsheets, get you started with some spreadsheet basics, and give you a collection of tips you can use with your spreadsheet software package.

In This Chapter

What Is a Spreadsheet?

Imagine an accountant's worksheet filled with columns and rows of numbers. Now put that worksheet inside a computer, add the ability to change inputted and calculated values instantly, and throw in a few extras—such as built-in formulas, charting capabilities, and database sorting. What you'll have when you're finished is a spreadsheet.

Spreadsheets Explained (ML)

A spreadsheet software package is like a word processor for numbers. You use it to organize, calculate, and present numerical information neatly. The resulting document is usually a spreadsheet—often called a *worksheet*—but can also be a chart.

Like a paper worksheet, an electronic worksheet is laid out in a grid. *Rows,* labeled with numbers, and *columns,* labeled with letters, intersect at *cells.* Each cell has an *address* or *reference* that consists of the column letter and the row number. So you'd find cell C16 at the intersection of column C and row 16.

To use a spreadsheet you enter *values* and *formulas* into cells. A value can be text, a number, a date, or a time. It's often called a *constant value* because it won't change unless you change it. A formula is a calculation that you want the spreadsheet to perform for you. You begin a formula with an equal sign (=) and follow it with a combination of values, cell references, operators, and functions—more on those later.

The beauty of a spreadsheet is that if properly constructed, it can calculate the results of complex formulas in less time than it takes to bat an eye. And if you change any of the values referenced by a formula, the results change instantly. It sure beats an accountant with pencil-stained fingers and a ten-key calculator.

Real-World Spreadsheets

The best way to see what spreadsheet software is all about is to look at some real-life examples. With spreadsheets like the ones on the next few pages, you can calculate totals and averages, create a loan amortization table, perform what-if analyses, manage and report data, and create charts. These examples are just a small sampling of what's possible—with a little imagination and practice, you'll soon be taking spreadsheets to their limits.

Simple calculations (CB). Here's a simple little AppleWorks spreadsheet that does some straightforward mathematics (**Figure 10.1**). When you enter expense information into the white cells, the spreadsheet calculates totals and averages for each category (the light gray cells) and totals for each month (the darker gray cells). It does this by using formulas in the gray cells that refer to values entered in the white cells.

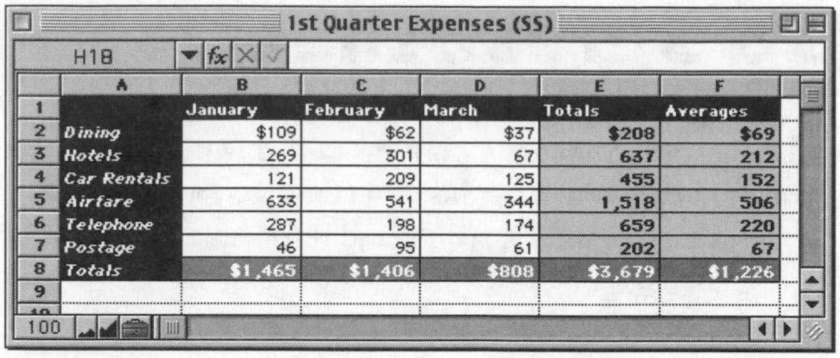

1st Quarter Expenses (SS)

	A	B	C	D	E	F
1		January	February	March	Totals	Averages
2	Dining	$109	$62	$37	$208	$69
3	Hotels	269	301	67	637	212
4	Car Rentals	121	209	125	455	152
5	Airfare	633	541	344	1,518	506
6	Telephone	287	198	174	659	220
7	Postage	46	95	61	202	67
8	Totals	$1,465	$1,406	$808	$3,679	$1,226

Figure 10.1

This simple AppleWorks spreadsheet calculates totals and averages for the numbers entered into the white cells.

Complex calculations (EG/ML). Not every formula you write or spreadsheet you create will be simple. By combining simple formulas with more advanced functions, you can create more complex spreadsheet models, such as a loan amortization table (**Figure 10.2**). Using good spreadsheet design, the one in the figure includes an input, or assumption, area where you enter the amounts you already know: the amount or principal of the loan, the interest rate, and the loan term. The monthly payment is calculated based on Microsoft Excel's built-in PMT function.

What-if analysis (EG/ML). Probably the most powerful feature of a spreadsheet is its ability to recalculate results quickly when you make changes to referenced values. This is known as *what-if analysis* because by changing a value, you're saying "*What* happens *if* this number changes?" (**Figure 10.3**).

Based on the previous loan amortization table, what if you decide to borrow less money, change the loan term, or find a better interest rate? It's easy to see how these changes will affect the monthly payment. Just change the information in the appropriate cell and—presto—the spreadsheet reflects your change.

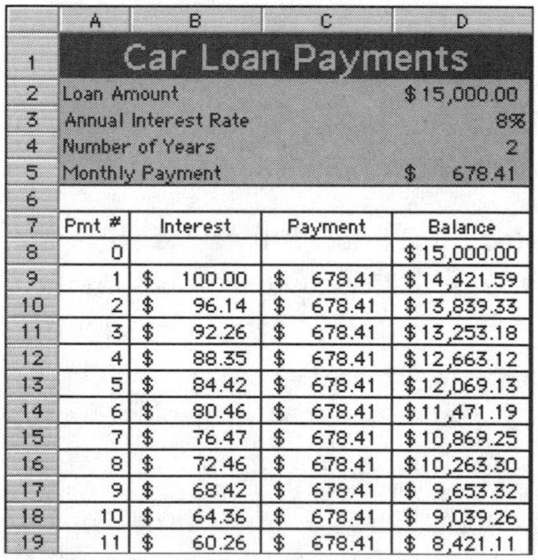

	A	B	C	D
1	Car Loan Payments			
2	Loan Amount			$15,000.00
3	Annual Interest Rate			8%
4	Number of Years			2
5	Monthly Payment			$ 678.41
6				
7	Pmt #	Interest	Payment	Balance
8	0			$15,000.00
9	1	$ 100.00	$ 678.41	$14,421.59
10	2	$ 96.14	$ 678.41	$13,839.33
11	3	$ 92.26	$ 678.41	$13,253.18
12	4	$ 88.35	$ 678.41	$12,663.12
13	5	$ 84.42	$ 678.41	$12,069.13
14	6	$ 80.46	$ 678.41	$11,471.19
15	7	$ 76.47	$ 678.41	$10,869.25
16	8	$ 72.46	$ 678.41	$10,263.30
17	9	$ 68.42	$ 678.41	$ 9,653.32
18	10	$ 64.36	$ 678.41	$ 9,039.26
19	11	$ 60.26	$ 678.41	$ 8,421.11

Figure 10.2

You can build a loan amortization table by combining simple and complex formulas, taking advantage of Excel's built-in financial functions.

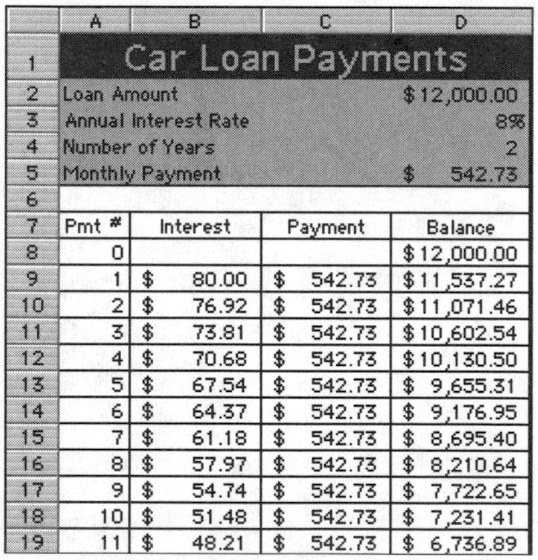

	A	B	C	D
1	Car Loan Payments			
2	Loan Amount			$12,000.00
3	Annual Interest Rate			8%
4	Number of Years			2
5	Monthly Payment			$ 542.73
6				
7	Pmt #	Interest	Payment	Balance
8	0			$12,000.00
9	1	$ 80.00	$ 542.73	$11,537.27
10	2	$ 76.92	$ 542.73	$11,071.46
11	3	$ 73.81	$ 542.73	$10,602.54
12	4	$ 70.68	$ 542.73	$10,130.50
13	5	$ 67.54	$ 542.73	$ 9,655.31
14	6	$ 64.37	$ 542.73	$ 9,176.95
15	7	$ 61.18	$ 542.73	$ 8,695.40
16	8	$ 57.97	$ 542.73	$ 8,210.64
17	9	$ 54.74	$ 542.73	$ 7,722.65
18	10	$ 51.48	$ 542.73	$ 7,231.41
19	11	$ 48.21	$ 542.73	$ 6,736.89

Figure 10.3

Using what-if analysis, you can change the amount of the loan in cell D2, and the entire worksheet changes instantly.

Using Data Tables for What-If Analysis (EG)

Another way to approach the loan scenario is to build a data table showing ranges of interest rates and different terms. The spreadsheet in **Figure 10.4**, for instance, shows the different monthly payments for a loan based on interest rates ranging from 5 percent to 15 percent and loan terms ranging from one year to five years.

Figure 10.4

If you want to see a range of loan monthly payments based on different interest rates and loan periods, use a data table.

		Car Payment by Interest Rate & Loan Period				
Loan Amount				$ 15,000		
Annual Interest Rate				8%		
Number of Years				2		
				Years		
		1	2	3	4	5
	5%	$ 1,284.11	$ 658.07	$ 449.56	$ 345.44	$ 283.07
I	6%	$ 1,291.00	$ 664.81	$ 456.33	$ 352.28	$ 289.99
N	7%	$ 1,297.90	$ 671.59	$ 463.16	$ 359.19	$ 297.02
T	8%	$ 1,304.83	$ 678.41	$ 470.05	$ 366.19	$ 304.15
	9%	$ 1,311.77	$ 685.27	$ 477.00	$ 373.28	$ 311.38
R	10%	$ 1,318.74	$ 692.17	$ 484.01	$ 380.44	$ 318.71
A	11%	$ 1,325.72	$ 699.12	$ 491.08	$ 387.68	$ 326.14
T	12%	$ 1,332.73	$ 706.10	$ 498.21	$ 395.01	$ 333.67
E	13%	$ 1,339.76	$ 713.13	$ 505.41	$ 402.41	$ 341.30
	14%	$ 1,346.81	$ 720.19	$ 512.66	$ 409.90	$ 349.02
	15%	$ 1,353.87	$ 727.30	$ 519.98	$ 417.46	$ 356.85

Database management (DC/ML). Spreadsheets are also useful for simple database functions. By setting up columns for different categories, or *fields,* of information and rows for the data, or *records,* you can organize, sort, summarize, and otherwise analyze data. Here's an example that shows the scores for the members of a bowling league (**Figure 10.5**).

Figure 10.5

This Excel worksheet contains a database of scores for members of a bowling league. By using database features like sorting and subtotaling, you can quickly analyze the information.

	Name	Date	Game 1	Game 2	Game 3	Series	Avg
The Pinheads – Bowling Stats							
	Cohen	5-Jan	184	201	173	558	186
	Cohen	12-Jan	167	186	184	537	179
	Cohen	19-Jan	213	195	197	605	202
	Cohen	26-Jan	175	175	171	521	174
	Cohen Total		739	757	725	2,221	
	Cohen Average		185	189	181	555	
	Langer	5-Jan	178	176	200	554	185
	Langer	12-Jan	177	185	180	542	181
	Langer	19-Jan	169	161	189	519	173
	Langer	26-Jan	182	180	170	532	177
	Langer Total		706	702	739	2,147	
	Langer Average		177	176	185	537	
	Gordon	5-Jan	177	177	174	528	176
	Gordon	12-Jan	186	200	183	569	190
	Gordon	19-Jan	195	165	198	558	186
	Gordon	26-Jan	202	185	187	574	191
	Gordon Total		760	727	742	2,229	
	Gordon Average		190	182	186	557	
	Team Total		2,205	2,186	2,206	6,597	
	Team Average		184	182	184	550	

Charting (CB). A picture is worth a thousand words, and when the picture stands in for numbers it's probably worth even more. You can use the charting features of spreadsheet software to make sense of a mystifying bunch of numbers. The column and pie charts in **Figures 10.6** and **10.7** show two examples of how to display a spreadsheet's results graphically.

Figure 10.6

The column chart quickly tells you that airfare is the biggest expense, that telephones and hotels are the next biggest, and that the rest of the expenses hardly make a difference. Try getting information like that quickly from raw numbers!

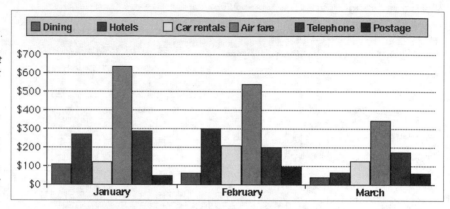

Figure 10.7

The pie chart makes it easy to see that airfare is nearly half of the total expenses for January.

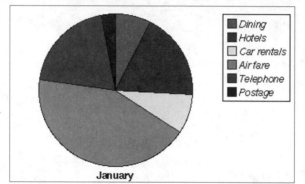

Basic Chart Types (SA/ML)

With the wide range of chart types and styles that spreadsheets have to offer, you may find it tempting to go crazy. Colors and styles might be a matter of taste, but keep in mind that certain types of charts are best used for certain types of data. Here are the four basics:

- A *line chart* shows how something changes over time, with multiple lines charting multiple items.
- A *bar chart* is useful for comparing differing items, either with no time component or with the same time component.
- A *pie chart* shows how various components make up a whole—it shows the components in relation to each other and to the whole but gives no indication of how large the whole actually is.
- A *stacked bar chart* resembles a pie chart somewhat in that both show you the relationship of the parts to the whole, but stacked bars also let you compare different wholes and see the overall size or numbers of each.

Spreadsheet Software (ML)

If you're shopping for spreadsheet software, you won't have many choices to consider. It seems that every year, another spreadsheet package drops off the face of the earth. Only two viable options are left, so let's take a look at them.

Microsoft Excel is undoubtedly the most feature-packed spreadsheet package ever created. It goes beyond the basics of spreadsheets and charts by offering hundreds of built-in functions, extensive database features, drawing tools, a wide range of formatting capabilities, and a comprehensive macro language.

The power of Excel goes beyond what it *can* do to *how* it does it. This well-thought-out package includes many features that make data entry easier or more accurate. Its dialog boxes are well organized and easy to use and understand (with a few exceptions not worth detailing here). It includes extensive online help with hypertext links, making it easy to navigate from topic to topic and find the information you need. Surprisingly, its heavy feature load does not affect its performance.

Although some people think I'm partial to Excel because I've written seven books about it, that's not true. I can objectively look at Excel and its alternatives and tell you that Excel is the best and most powerful spreadsheet package around. But is it for everyone? Of course not! The vast majority of folks who use their Macs at home or school don't need even half of Excel's bells and whistles. But if you're in corporate finance, science, or other industries where heavy-duty number crunching and presentation is a must, I doubt if you'll find a better spreadsheet solution for your needs than Excel.

In case you're wondering what Excel will cost in terms of dollars, disk space, and RAM, hold on to your hat. You'll pay about $350 for the software, which will take up at least 32 MB of hard-disk space and 16 MB of RAM. (If you use Microsoft Word for word processing, you can save money by purchasing Microsoft Office, which includes both programs, plus PowerPoint and Entourage.) But serious number crunchers will probably think Excel is worth the price.

AppleWorks is an integrated software package that includes word processing, spreadsheet, database, drawing, painting, and presentation modules. A "do-it-all" package, AppleWorks handles spreadsheet functions well, but not as well as a specialist like Excel. Still, for most home and school users and small-business owners, the spreadsheet module of AppleWorks has everything needed to get the job done, including built-in functions, extensive formatting capabilities, and linked charting. Because it's an integrated package, you can "draw" word-processing and other types of documents right on your spreadsheet without additional software.

One of the most attractive features of AppleWorks is its price: less than $100. It requires a Mac with 24 MB of RAM and at least 40 MB of hard-disk space. But remember—that's for the entire package, not just the spreadsheet module. Seems like quite a bargain to me.

Using Spreadsheets (ML/CB)

Ready to try your hand at creating a spreadsheet? It's not difficult, but there are a few tricks to learn. Read this section and you'll soon be using spreadsheets with style and verve, at least to the point where you can impress your friends and pets.

Spreadsheet Basics

Let's start with a few basics you'll use whenever you create a spreadsheet.

Moving around. You can't put anything into a cell until you *activate* it. You can tell a cell is activated by looking at its border: An activated cell's border is thick or colored. You can activate a cell in two ways:

- Position the mouse pointer (which will look like a fat plus sign [+]) over a cell and click once. You have to click—just moving the mouse pointer over a cell does not activate it.

- Use a keyboard key to move to a cell. Here are the most commonly used keystrokes:

This key...	Selects this cell...
→ or Tab	The cell to the right of the current cell
← or Shift Tab	The cell to the left of the current cell
↓ or Return	The cell below the current cell
↑ or Shift Return	The cell above the current cell

Cell references. When you select or activate a cell, the spreadsheet program reports the active cell's reference in the upper-left corner of the window. As mentioned earlier, the cell reference consists of the letter (or letters) of the cell's column and the number of the cell's row. (There are alternative ways to describe cell locations, but nobody uses them because they're confusing.) Although you can select more than one cell simultaneously by dragging through several cells at once, only one cell is active at a time. Remember, the active cell is the one with the border, the one where whatever you type will appear.

Cell ranges (SA/ML). A group of cells is a *range*. You refer to a range by the addresses of the cells at its beginning and end, separated by a colon (Excel) or a pair of periods (AppleWorks). For example, *A1:A5* describes the first five cells in the first column in Excel and *A1..E5* is a five-by-five-cell grid in the upper-left corner of an AppleWorks spreadsheet.

Kinds of entries. There are two kinds of entries: those you type in (values), and those that compute values (formulas).

Entering values. Activate the cell into which you want to put a value, type what you want to appear in the cell, and then do one of the following:

- Press ⟨Return⟩ to enter the value. Depending on what spreadsheet program you are using, this may also activate the next cell down.

- Press ⟨Enter⟩ to enter the value and leave the same cell active.

- Press ⟨Tab⟩ to enter the value and activate the next cell to the right.

- Click the checkmark button near the top of the window. That's the Enter button and it works the same way as pressing ⟨Enter⟩, entering the value and leaving the cell active.

 If you make a mistake while entering a value (or a formula, for that matter) you can start over by clicking the X button near the top of the window. That's the Cancel button. If you prefer keyboard shortcuts, ⟨Esc⟩ does the same thing.

When You Enter Too Much ... (CB/ML/DC)

For long entries, the cell width determines what appears in the cell:

- If you type a number (or date or time) that doesn't fit into a cell, the cell's contents turn into a series of number signs (#####).

- If you type more text than can fit in the cell and nothing is in the cell to its right, the text overflows to the right so you can see all of it. Even if text appears to overflow into other cells, that text is still contained in only one cell.

- If you type more text than can fit in the cell and something is entered into the cell to its right, the text appears truncated in the cell in which you entered it. This doesn't mean the text is cut off—it isn't. It just doesn't show onscreen.

In most cases you can properly display lengthy numbers or text by making the column wider. Just drag the right boundary of the column heading at the top of the column.

Another way you can make lengthy text fit in a cell is to turn on the *word wrap* feature for that cell. Both Excel and AppleWorks offer this feature.

Editing entries. You can change the contents of a cell in two ways:

- Activate the cell and type something different into it.

- Activate the cell, click in the *formula bar* (Excel) or *entry bar* (AppleWorks) at the top of the window where the cell's contents appear, and use standard word-processing techniques to edit what's there.

No matter how you edit an entry, don't forget to press ⟨Return⟩ or ⟨Enter⟩ or click the Enter button to complete it.

Creating formulas. Just putting numbers and words into neat rows and columns is fine, but spreadsheets are built to compute. You can tell your spreadsheet to add two cells, calculate sales tax, or figure out what day of the week it will be 100 days from now. In fact, you can do just about anything that involves math—and some things that don't. But to do these fancy things, you must know how to create formulas.

You must remember one thing to enter a formula successfully: All formulas start with an equal sign—no exceptions!

To enter a formula, select the cell where you want the formula's results displayed, type an equal sign, type the formula, and complete the formula by pressing [Return] or [Enter] or clicking the Enter button.

Here's an example. Let's say you have a number in cell A1 and another number in cell A2. You want to add them and put the answer in cell A3. Select cell A3, type *=A1+A2* (no spaces!), and press [Return]; the result appears in cell A3.

You do have other ways to enter the parts of formulas. For example, you can enter a cell reference in a formula by clicking the cell. To write the above formula by clicking, just click in cell A3, type an equal sign, click in cell A1, click in cell A2, and click the Enter button. The answer appears in cell A3.

This method is especially useful for preventing typing errors—the less you type, the less chance you have of making mistakes!

As you may have noticed, the plus sign appears by default if you click a cell without first specifying an operator. What you may also notice is that if you forget to complete the formula by pressing [Return] or [Enter] or clicking the Enter button, any cell you click in is added to the formula in the formula bar or entry bar. That's why it's important to complete each entry properly before continuing to other cells.

Those Darned Error Messages (EC/ML)

When you write a formula incorrectly, the spreadsheet program usually tells you by displaying an error message in a dialog box or within the cell. Here's a table of some of Excel's error messages—other spreadsheets offer similarly vague expressions.

`#DIV/0!`	Your formula is trying to divide by zero, which is a no-no.
`#N/A`	One of the referenced values is not available.
`#NAME?`	You've used an unrecognizable cell or range name. If you didn't mean to use a cell or range name, you've probably spelled a function name incorrectly.
`#NUM!`	Your formula uses a number incorrectly.
`#REF!`	Your formula references an invalid cell. This can happen if you delete cells after writing the formula.
`#VALUE!`	Your formula uses an incorrect argument or operator. Check for extra or missing commas and parentheses and for proper function names.

Why Use Cell References? (ML)

A well-constructed spreadsheet includes cell references in its formulas whenever possible to make modifications easier.

The two samples here (**Figures 10.8** and **10.9**) illustrate how these references can simplify modifying spreadsheets.

You can write formulas that include the percentage rate as a constant within the formula, like this: =B2*15%.

	A	B	C
		Sales	
1	**Name**	**Amount**	**Commission**
2	Christian	145.00	21.75
3	Eve	95.00	14.25
4	Dennis	79.00	11.85
5	Maria	130.00	19.50
6	Jeremy	201.00	30.15
7	Roslyn	138.00	20.70
8	Nancy	123.00	18.45

Figure 10.8

To change the commission rate in this spreadsheet, you would have to edit the contents of the formulas in cells C2 through C8. That's seven changes! And if you forget to make a change, the spreadsheet will produce incorrect results.

But it's a lot more convenient to write formulas that reference a cell containing the percentage rate, like this: =B4*C1.

	A	B	C
1	**Commission Rate:**		**15%**
2			
3	**Name**	**Sales** **Amount**	**Commission**
4	Christian	145.00	21.75
5	Eve	95.00	14.25
6	Dennis	79.00	11.85
7	Maria	130.00	19.50
8	Jeremy	201.00	30.15
9	Roslyn	138.00	20.70
10	Nancy	123.00	18.45

Figure 10.9

In this spreadsheet, you'd only have to change the contents of cell C1 to recalculate all commissions in column C correctly. So you're making one change that's impossible to miss. Which method would you prefer?

*2 + 3 + 5 * 10 = ?* (EG/ML)

The answer is 55. Why? Well, in spreadsheets, mathematical operations don't happen in their order of appearance—they occur in a specific order, which is shown in the table below. In the example above, the spreadsheet multiplies 5 by 10 first and then adds 2 and 3 to get 55.

Operation	Operator
Parentheses	( )
Exponents	^
Multiplication	*
Division	/
Addition	+
Subtraction	-

To force an operation to occur first, put it in parentheses. In the example above, if you wanted to add 3 and 5 first, you would use the formula 2+(3+5)*10. The spreadsheet would first add 3 and 5 to get 8 then multiply that by 10, and then add 2, with the result of 82. See what a difference a couple of parentheses can make?

Beyond the Basics

So far, we've given you enough information to get you started with just about any spreadsheet program. Here are a few additional techniques and concepts to consider as you hone your spreadsheet skills.

Functions (CB). Remember high school math? No? Fortunately, the people who make spreadsheet software do remember, and they've loaded their programs with handy calculations called *functions.* Here are some of my favorites, the ones I use over and over again. You've seen some of them in action earlier in this chapter.

SUM sums (adds) a bunch of numbers. It's especially handy for totaling a column or a row.

AVERAGE calculates the average of a range of cells. As with most functions, it's a lot easier to use the function than to calculate averages yourself.

MAX looks at a range of cells and returns the largest value. You could do this by looking at the cells yourself, but the MAX function is faster, and it never makes mistakes.

MIN determines which cell in a range is the smallest.

IF—my favorite—gives you supreme power and flexibility. It evaluates a condition (such as "Is B10 greater than 5000?") and performs a calculation (or returns a result) based on whether the condition is met (true) or not met (false). Creative use of this function can add intelligence to your spreadsheets.

PROPER changes the first character of text to a capital letter.

SIN—as in *sine,* not "Thou shalt not." It's trigonometry, the high school math subject you understood either completely or not at all. Fortunately, spreadsheets excel (hey, a spreadsheet pun!) at trigonometry. If you have an angle, the sine is a function away. **COS** gives you cosines, and **TAN** produces tangents.

WEEKDAY returns the day of the week on which a certain date falls. The answer you'll get is a number from 1 to 7 representing the day of the week. (The actual result depends on the settings in the Date & Time control panel or System Preferences pane.)

SQRT—that's *square root,* not *squirt*—calculates square roots.

PMT figures out how much the periodic payments will be when you borrow a certain amount of money at a certain rate of interest for a certain length of time.

Copying formulas (ML). You can create a spreadsheet like the expense summary or loan amortization tables shown earlier without entering each formula down the columns. How? By copying similar formulas. The spreadsheet software changes cell references as necessary so the copied formulas are correct. Of course, this technique has its limitations (see the sidebar "Absolute References" below), so check the formulas you copy to make sure they're correct.

Formatting (ML). Of course, all spreadsheet software offers the ability to format your spreadsheets and charts with fonts, colors, styles, borders—you name it. The spreadsheets shown throughout this chapter offer good examples. With a little creativity, you can make a spreadsheet look like a million bucks—even if it's reporting a $68 million loss.

Printing (ML). When you print a spreadsheet, what emerges from your printer depends on several factors:

- Did you specify a print area? A print area is the rectangular selection of cells that will print. If you don't specify a print area, most software will print the entire spreadsheet, inserting page breaks wherever necessary to get it all on paper.

- Did you insert manual page breaks? You can specify where you want one page to end and the next to begin, to eliminate page-break surprises.

- Did you set page orientation, margins, or scale? By fiddling around with these page-setup options, you can squeeze a relatively large spreadsheet onto standard-size paper—or magnify spreadsheet cells for use in a presentation.

- Did you set print titles? If your spreadsheet is lengthy, you may want to print row or column headings as titles on each page. You must tell the spreadsheet software which columns or rows to use as titles.

These options vary from one spreadsheet package to another. Explore the Page Setup and Print dialog boxes of your spreadsheet software to see how their settings affect your printouts.

Absolute References (EG)

You can use two kinds of references in your formulas: *relative* (as in D5) or *absolute* (as in D5). The only time the kind of reference matters is when you copy a formula. A relative reference changes relative to where you paste it. (For example, if a formula sums the four cells immediately above it, when the formula is copied to a new location, the pasted-in formula will sum the four cells immediately above its new location.) An absolute reference always refers to the same cell no matter where you paste it. This is probably the most complex concept you'll encounter in dealing with spreadsheets, but once you master it, it can help you quickly create error-free spreadsheets.

Tips (ML/EC/CB/SA/EG/DC)

Because there's more than one spreadsheet package out there, we've done our best to come up with a few generic tips you can use with any software package. We've also rounded up some application-specific tips that will come in handy for Excel and AppleWorks users.

General Spreadsheet Tips

Use arrow keys to change the active cell, but use the scroll bar to change the view of the spreadsheet. Although you can use the scroll bars to change your view of a spreadsheet, using the scroll bars does not change the active cell.

Pay attention to the mouse pointer. Spreadsheets change the mouse pointer to provide visual clues about things you can do.

- The mouse pointer appears as a white cross (or fat plus sign) when it's in the spreadsheet area—click to select a cell, row, or column; drag to select multiple cells; or click to add a cell to a formula if the formula or entry bar is active.

- The mouse pointer appears as a standard I-beam insertion point when it's in the formula or entry bar—click to edit the contents of the formula or entry bar.

- The mouse pointer appears as a thick black bar with arrows when it's between column or row headings—drag to change the width of the column or height of the row.

- The mouse pointer appears as a standard arrow pointer when you move it out of the spreadsheet window—use it to pull down a menu, scroll with a scroll bar, move or resize a window, or switch to another open window or application.

Turn a formula into a text value. If you're having trouble entering a formula correctly and your spreadsheet keeps beeping at you each time you try to move to another cell, delete the equal sign from the beginning of the formula and press `Enter`. The spreadsheet accepts what remains as mere text, allowing you to move on to other things. Later (when you're older and wiser), you can come back to fix the thing up. Why not just delete the formula and start from scratch later? Because often you'll get close to getting a formula right—to throw it all away is to waste the time and effort you've already put into it.

Use `Shift`-click to select cells. Select the first cell of a range, then hold down `Shift` and click in the last cell of the range or use the arrow keys to extend the selection.

Select all cells with your mouse. Click in the empty box at the top-left corner of the worksheet window (to the left of column A and above row 1). This selects every cell in the spreadsheet.

Create a data-entry area. Select the range of cells in which you want to enter data. Then, when you complete an entry by pressing ⟨Return⟩ or ⟨Enter⟩, you'll automatically move to the next cell in the selection. This is quicker than activating cells one at a time.

Understand the difference between relative and absolute references. You indicate that all or part of a cell reference is absolute by putting a dollar sign ($) before it. To remember what that symbol means in a cell reference, think of the word *always*. So, for example, you can think of D5 as *always D, always 5*—or *always D5*.

Make a column the best width. To make a column just wide enough to display the longest item in the column, double-click the line to the right of the column letter in the column-heading area.

Use drawing tools to annotate spreadsheets and charts. You can draw attention to spreadsheet results by drawing circles and arrows right on the spreadsheet. Use a text-box tool, if available, to add notes.

Use contextual menus. Hold down the ⟨Control⟩ key and click a selection. A pop-up menu with commands you can use on the selection appears.

Transpose rows and columns. You organized your spreadsheet with months in columns and categories in rows, and then you decide that you really wanted categories in columns and dates in rows. What do you do? Transpose them. Select the cells you want to transpose, and use the Copy command to copy them. Then choose the Paste Special command, and turn on the Transpose check box. Click OK to transpose the rows and columns.

Split the screen so headings stay put when you scroll. Drag the little black bar at the very top of the vertical scroll bar down as far as you wish to split the screen—you can then scroll either the top or the bottom half of the window. Horizontal splitting works the same way—look for the split bar to the left of the horizontal scroll bar.

Hide columns or rows. Hiding a column or row is a good way to get something out of your way temporarily. To hide a column or row, set its column width or row height to 0. It disappears! Your only clue to the fact that there are hidden rows or columns in the spreadsheet is the missing letters or numbers in the headers. Displaying a hidden column or row is a little trickier—you can't easily select a column or row if you can't see it. One way is to use the Go To command to select a single cell in the column or row and then set the column width or row height to something other than 0.

Excel Tips

Edit directly in the cell. If you want to change the contents of a cell without having to use the formula bar, double-click the cell.

Make noncontiguous selections. You can select cells or blocks of cells that aren't next to each other (to apply formatting, say) by selecting the first cell or block and then holding down ⌘ while you select subsequent cells.

Move a selection block. If you've selected a block of five cells in a row to apply some formatting and then want to select another five cells two rows down to apply some more formatting, don't reach for the mouse. Instead, move the selection block: [Option][Tab] moves the block to the right and [Shift][Option][Tab] moves it to the left, and [Shift][Option][Return] and [Option][Return] move it up and down, respectively.

Select referenced cells. If the current cell has a formula in it, you can select all the cells to which the formula directly refers by pressing ⌘[. Pressing ⌘[Shift][instead will select all cells to which the formula refers, even indirectly.

Move cells with drag and drop. You can drag a cell or a range of cells by its border to move it to a new position. Hold down [Shift] while dragging to insert it between other cells. Hold down [Option] while dragging to copy it to the new location.

Use AutoFill to enter data into adjacent cells. Enter a value or formula in the first cell, press [Enter] to complete the entry, and then drag the fill handle (the little box in the bottom-right corner of the cell) to extend a box around the other cells you want to contain the same value or formula. If the original cell contains a day, month, or other component of a familiar series, Excel completes the series for you.

Enter the current time or date quickly. To enter the current date in an Excel cell, press ⌘-. To enter the current time, press ⌘;.

Use AutoSum to add columns or rows. Select the cell at the bottom of a column or the right side of a row you want to total. Then double-click the AutoSum button, the one with the sigma (Σ) on it. Excel guesses which cells you want to total and writes a formula complete with the SUM function and references to the cells. You can use this feature in a variety of ways—even to total more than one column or row at a time.

Use Natural Language Formulas. This Excel feature enables you to write formulas using column and row headings to refer to cells. For example, in this little spreadsheet, the formulas in cells B10, C10, and D10 are *=SUM(FY00)*, *=SUM(FY01)*, and *=SUM(FY02),* respectively (**Figure 10.10**). Neat, huh?

Figure 10.10

Natural Language Formulas make it possible to write formulas without using cryptic cell references.

	A	B	C	D
1	**Wickenburg Division Sales**			
2	**(in thousands)**			
3		FY00	FY01	FY02
4	Janet	$ 109	$ 60	$ 37
5	Steve	245	301	67
6	Maria	154	209	125
7	Mike	351	541	344
8	Dianna	58	198	174
9	Keri	24	95	61
10	Totals	$ 941	$ 1,404	$ 808

Name cells. You can also give cells or ranges custom names, which make it easier to write formulas and use the Go To command.

Use the Formula palette to write formulas using functions. The Formula palette not only provides online help to help you understand functions but takes you every step of the way through the creation of a formula with one or more functions.

Change relative references to absolute references with a keystroke. If you've already entered a cell reference in a formula and want to change the reference type, select the cell reference and press ⌘T until Excel places the absolute reference dollar sign(s) where you want them.

Float a toolbar. Position the mouse pointer anywhere on a toolbar other than on a button and drag the toolbar down from the top of the screen. You'll get a floating toolbar that you can put anywhere you like. Drag it back up (or down or to the side) to dock it again.

Tear-off toolbar menus. If a toolbar button's drop-down menu has a move handle—a gray bar along its top or side edge—you can tear the menu off the toolbar. Simply drag the menu away from the button to display the menu as a floating toolbar.

Rename sheets. You can change the name of a worksheet in an Excel workbook file by double-clicking the sheet tab for the sheet, entering a new name, and pressing Return.

Move or copy sheets by dragging. You can change the order of sheets in a workbook by simply dragging tabs to new positions. You can copy a worksheet by holding down Option as you drag the tab. You can move (or copy) a sheet to another workbook by dragging (or Option-dragging) its tab from one workbook file to another.

Experiment with the macro feature. It enables you to perform repetitive tasks quickly or create custom functions. To get started, let Excel's macro recorder write the macro for you. This is a nice—although limited—use of macros that can familiarize you with the macro language.

Apply basic formatting from the keyboard. You can apply all the basic number-formatting choices to a cell by using keyboard commands:

General	⌘ Shift ~	Two decimal places,	⌘ Shift !
Currency	⌘ Shift $	1000 separator,	
Percentage	⌘ Shift %	and minus sign (–)	
Exponential	⌘ Shift ^	for negatives	
Date	⌘ Shift #		
Time	⌘ Shift @		

Use the Format Painter. A cell's format includes text formatting (font, size, and style), alignment (left or centered), and number formats (dollar signs and the number of decimals). You can use the Format Painter to copy formatting and apply it to other cells. Start by selecting the cell that contains the formatting you want to copy. Click the Format Painter button in the Standard toolbar. Then select the cells to which you want to apply the formatting. To apply formatting to multiple cell selections, double-click the Format Painter button; press Esc when you want to stop painting.

Apply conditional formatting. Suppose you want all values over a certain amount to appear in green or bold or with a yellow background? Use the Conditional Formatting dialog box to define the conditions and related formatting (**Figure 10.11**). Excel does the rest based on spreadsheet contents.

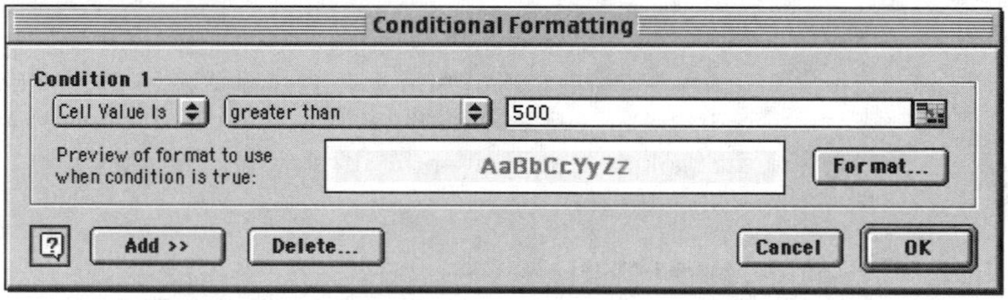

Figure 10.11

The Conditional Formatting dialog box makes it easy to set up the conditions under which to apply formatting.

Use the Range Finder feature. While you're editing a formula that refers to one or more cell ranges, the range names are color-coded in the formula bar to match Range Finder frames around the ranges in the spreadsheet. To change a range in the formula, grab the appropriate Range Finder handle and drag to surround more or fewer cells—the formula changes to reference the new range. This works with charts, too; when a chart series is selected, adjustable Range Finder frames appear around associated spreadsheet ranges. Just drag the frame's handle to change the chart.

Switch worksheets—or workbooks—without using the mouse.

Use these shortcuts instead:

Next worksheet   Option →

Previous worksheet   Option ←

Next workbook   ⌘ M

Previous workbook   ⌘ Shift M

Copy a selection as a graphic. You can copy a selected section of the spreadsheet to the Clipboard as a PICT graphic (which will include gridlines and row and column headings) and then paste it into any program as a graphic. Just hold down Shift and choose Copy Picture from the Edit menu.

Select multiple worksheets. You can select more than one worksheet at a time to perform certain global operations such as deleting the worksheets, running a spelling check, or turning off all the gridlines. Start by clicking the tab of the first worksheet to include in the selection. Then:

- To select multiple contiguous worksheets, hold down Shift and click the tab of the last worksheet. This selects all worksheets in between.

- To select noncontiguous worksheets, hold down ⌘ and click their tabs.

- To select all worksheets, hold down Control, click any worksheet tab, and choose Select All Sheets from the contextual menu that appears.

Enter the same data in the same cells of multiple worksheets.

First select the tabs of the worksheets in which you want to enter the data. Then enter the data in the top worksheet. It appears in all selected worksheets.

AppleWorks Tips

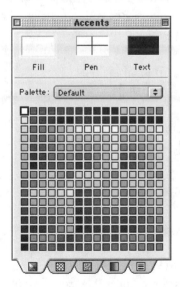

Figure 10.12

The Accents window offers a variety of colorful formatting options for cell backgrounds and lines.

Put some life in your spreadsheets.

Select a range of cells to color, and then use the Accents window options to add background colors, patterns, and other formatting effects (**Figure 10.12**). Can't see black text against your colored background? Pick a text color for selected cells with the Text Color command under the Format menu.

Customize the button bar. Use options in the Customize Button Bar dialog box to specify which buttons appear on the button bar and in what order they appear.

Zoom out to see more of your work at once. Click the small-mountains button at the bottom left of a spreadsheet window to zoom out; click the big-mountains button to zoom in. Besides displaying your current magnification level, the number in the bottom-left corner of the window is a pop-up menu that lets you zoom as far as you want in a single move.

Select all data with your mouse (SA/ML). Hold down Option while clicking in the empty box at the intersection of the column and row headings. This selects everything from cell A1 to the farthest cell containing data. (Holding down Option also changes the Edit menu's Select All command to Select All Data.)

Use the Fill Special command to type stuff for you. Need to enter a series of months into adjacent cells? Click in a cell that contains the first month of the series, and drag to the right or down as far as you want to go. Then choose Fill Special from the Calculate menu. This works for all kinds of series.

Copy and paste formatting. Select a cell with formatting you want to copy to other cells. Then choose Copy Format from the Edit menu. Now select the cells to which you want to copy the formatting, and choose Paste Format from the Edit menu. This copies the formatting of the first cell to the other cells. It's much easier than choosing formatting options such as font, size, color, or style by hand, and it always works perfectly.

Use the Lock Title Position command to keep column titles in sight (DC). Not only does this prevent column titles from scrolling out of the window but it ensures that column titles print on each page. It's also a handy way to identify a range of cells.

Set the arrow-key action. By default, the arrow keys move you around in the entry bar for editing cell contents. But you can change that through the Edit menu's Preferences command and make the arrow keys move you from one cell to another instead. (While you're in there, you can change the action of the Enter key, too.)

Reverse the arrow-key action. Whichever way you've set the preferences for the arrow keys, pressing Option reverses it temporarily. So, if an arrow key normally lets you edit in the edit bar, pressing an arrow key with Option will let you move from cell to cell, and vice versa.

Auto-enter absolute references. If you're clicking or dragging in cells to enter their names into a formula, you can make the references absolute by holding down ⌘ and Option while clicking or dragging in the cells.

Activate the entry bar. If you're working from the keyboard and have selected a cell, don't click in the entry bar to activate it so you can edit the cell contents. Instead, press Option→ to put the insertion point at the end of the entry bar or Option← to put the insertion point at the beginning of the entry bar.

Move a selection without dragging and dropping. You can move a selected cell or a block of cells by holding down ⌘ and (Option) while clicking where you want the selection moved. As with a drag-and-drop move, this doesn't change any of the cell references in formulas you may be moving.

Use AutoSum to add columns or rows. Select the range of cells you want to total, as well as the empty cell where you want the total to appear. Then double-click the AutoSum button (the one with the sigma [Σ] on it). AppleWorks writes a formula with the SUM function and references to the cells.

Reverse the axes in a chart. When your chart's axes are reversed—the *x*-axis is where you want the *y*-axis and the *y*-axis is where you want the *x*-axis— you can switch them. Use the General panel of the Chart Options dialog box to change the Series in option.

11

Databases

Steve Schwartz is the chapter editor and author.

If you're still keeping track of important names and addresses, stacks of recipes, or a mountain of CDs using a word processor or spreadsheet, you're a prime candidate for a *database program*.

In this chapter, we'll show you how databases organize information. We'll also give you a rundown of the most popular software available so you can decide which program is right for you. Finally, scattered throughout the chapter you'll find tips for getting the most from your database program.

In This Chapter

What Is a Database Program?

Generically speaking, a *database* organizes information by dividing it up into small, discrete pieces called *fields*. An address book might consist of name, address, and phone-number fields; a checkbook might include check number, payee, description, and amount fields. A computer can use these fields to sift quickly through huge amounts of data—to help you find a particular name or check number or to arrange a client list by ZIP code, for example.

A database arranges fields into *records*. A record consists of the complete collection of fields for one person, item, or entity in the database. For example, in an address-book database, each person or company has a separate record. Thus, when you want to enter address information for Sarah Johnson, you create a new record for her and fill in the name, address, and phone-number fields with her information. Later, if you need to know Sarah's phone number or mailing address, you simply search for and display her record. All of Sarah's address data is collected in one place—her record.

The address book and checkbook mentioned above are both *databases*. You create, view, and manipulate databases with a database program, such as FileMaker Pro, 4th Dimension, Helix RADE, or Panorama (see "Choosing a Database Program," later in this chapter). The tricky part is that many people use the term *database* when speaking about both the files and the programs. To make things easy for you, we'll refer to the files as *databases* and the programs as *database programs*.

You can use any of the programs discussed in this chapter to create custom databases, where you can organize and present your information in any way you like. Some examples of homegrown databases are recipe files and video-cassette catalogs, but you can also create contact managers, checkbook registers, and bookkeeping databases. If you'd rather just concentrate on entering data—leaving the design work to others—you'll be pleased to learn that many database programs include a variety of *templates* (preformatted databases that you can immediately put to use in your home or business).

 Some stand-alone programs such as Now Contact (see Chapter 12, "Personal and Business Management") are actually single-purpose database programs, usually marketed as *personal information managers*. If your needs are fairly limited in scope, these programs can save you time, effort, and money compared with a full-fledged database program.

What a Database Program Can Do

Word processors and spreadsheets can also hold information such as names and addresses, recipes, and the contents of your CD collection. So why would you want to use a database program to organize that information? The answer lies in the way a database stores information. It stores the information for each item as a discrete piece of data (that is, a *field*)—for example, a first name, check number, or recipe ingredient. This data segmentation allows the database program to access and manipulate the information quickly and easily, which in turn allows you to consult individual parts of your data, sort it in a specific order, and then output portions of it (or the whole thing).

You can view information stored in a database in many ways—selected, sorted, and presented according to your current needs. For example, suppose you have a list of names and addresses. A database enables you to sort the list by last name to create a printed phone directory. Later you can sort by ZIP code to print labels for a bulk mailing. You can also quickly find the portions of your data with which you want to work—for example, all clients in the Northeast or just those who haven't placed an order in the last six months. These tasks would be much more difficult to accomplish with a list stored in a simple text document.

You'll generally perform two types of work with a database program: designing databases, and entering and viewing the information.

Designing a Database

When you create your own database, it is up to you to decide how to divide up the information, how to enter it, and how to display or output it. If you use a little forethought and planning, you'll make entering and utilizing the information easy for yourself and other users.

Defining fields. The fields in a database divide the information into smaller, discrete pieces so the program can sift through the data more efficiently. You should create a field for each important piece of information that differs in some way from the *other* information you want to record.

One good example is a Last Name field. In an address database, all your records will have a Last Name field, clearly distinguishable from the other information fields in the record (Address, ZIP Code, Telephone Number, and so on). Another example might be a Type of Meal field in a recipe database. Each recipe will be of a certain type, such as Dessert, Main Course, or Appetizer). The Type of Meal information clearly differs from the other fields (Ingredients, Directions, Prep Time, Cooking Time, and so on).

You specify the kind of information acceptable in a field by assigning a *type* to that field. Most programs provide half a dozen or more field types, such as Text, Numeric, and Date. You might also want to specify default data for some fields (for example, today's date in a Last Modified field) and validation criteria (only allowing numbers from 1 to 12 for a Month field).

In addition to list-style databases (such as an address book), database programs also allow you to perform simple and complex computations with *calculation fields*.

You could create a Total field that summed items on an invoice, for example. Using the program's built-in functions, you could even instruct the database to make decisions based on the data entered for each record. An IF function, for instance, could tell the database to assign one of two sales-commission amounts to a record based on the size of the sale, the customer's average purchases, or the salesperson's seniority.

Creating layouts. The second step in creating your own database is designing layouts. You should create different layouts for different purposes: data entry, viewing lists on screen, mailing labels, displaying or printing various reports, and so on (**Figure 11.1**). You'll have to decide which fields to put in each layout and where to place them. Usually you'll place field labels next to the fields so you can remember what information they contain (or need to contain).

Depending on the database program you choose, layout creation may seem like using a graphics program. The process generally involves dragging elements around the screen, changing their size, drawing lines, and aligning objects.

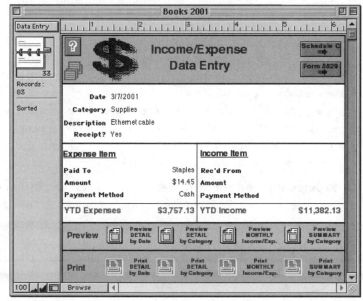

Figure 11.1

This data-entry layout, which I created in FileMaker Pro, makes it a snap to record my income and expenses. Each page of the layout is a separate record.

Entering and Viewing Information

After you've defined your fields and created the layouts, you can begin to enter data, search or sort the database, and output it in practically any format.

Entering information. Of all the tasks involved with databases, this is by far the easiest—and the dullest. You simply create a new record and start typing, tabbing from one field to the next. When you've filled in the information for one record, you create a new record and repeat the process. Many database programs save your data automatically whenever you create a new record, make changes to a layout, or modify the database structure, just as many accounting programs do to avoid potential data loss. Others—especially those that keep all data in memory to run faster—require that you periodically issue a Save command.

Most programs also allow you to import existing information from word processors, spreadsheets, and other databases so you can avoid retyping old data. The original information must be divided into fields (usually that means it's *tab-* or *comma-delimited*—commas or tabs separate the fields) and records (generally by ending each record with a Return) so the database knows where to put each piece of information.

Sorting. All databases allow you to put your records in order according to your specified criteria. For example, you can sort an address database by last name or ZIP code (or by both), or sort your recipe database by ingredients, preparation time, or category. In addition to using any criterion or a combination of criteria, you can usually sort in ascending, descending, or custom order (for example, high, medium, and low).

Searching. Searching lets you instantly find records containing certain information. For example, you can locate a client after entering his or her ID code, or find all of the recipes that contain salmon and heavy cream. Searching yields all the records that satisfy all or part of the given criteria, depending on the logical operators you use. For instance, if you're looking for a PR person whose first name you've long forgotten, you could search for all people with Anderson in the Last Name field. To make it even easier to identify the correct person, you might search for all Andersons whose Department field contains "PR."

Previewing and printing data. The simplest way to output data is to show it on the screen (called *previewing* in many programs). For example, you can examine an individual record or preview a multipage report. Database programs are especially useful in this area because they allow you to print your data in almost any way you can imagine. You can create mailing labels, directories, monthly summaries, form letters, or fax templates, for example.

Summary reports are one of the more complicated and powerful database features. In this type of report you can list a catalog of baseball cards by card type and then by year, and have the database calculate the value of each year's collection.

Using macros or scripts. Most database programs let you create macros or scripts to speed up and automate your work. To generate monthly mailing labels, you might normally search for all active clients, sort them by ZIP code and last name, and then print them using a layout called Mailing Labels. You can create a macro or script named Print Monthly Mailing to perform all these steps automatically. The next time you need to print mailing labels, you just run the script.

Many Mac database programs are also scriptable using AppleScript, a component of the Mac system software. With AppleScript, you can create multistep procedures within the database program, as well as script actions that involve multiple programs. For example, you might design a script that takes summary data from one of your databases, exports it to Microsoft Excel, and then graphs the data.

Flat-File vs. Relational Databases

Half a dozen years ago, two types of database programs existed: *flat-file* and *relational*. Today, almost all database programs are fully relational, allowing you to create flat-file *or* relational databases as your needs dictate.

Suppose you have an invoicing database. To have each client's name and address appear on an invoice, the database must either contain fields for this information or link to another database that stores client addresses.

In a flat-file database program, you include all the necessary fields in a single database. Thus, the address information would be an integral part of the invoicing database. A relational database can make a link (based on a key field such as a client ID) to information in a client database that stores the address data. Whenever you look at or print an invoice, the program consults the client file and displays the latest address information for that client ID.

The primary advantage of a flat-file database is ease of learning. Understanding how relations work, on the other hand, can be conceptually difficult. The advantages of relational databases include speed and avoiding data duplication. Instead of copying or retyping address information into every database that requires it, you can place it all in a separate database and then simply refer to it.

Choosing a Database Program

In the following sections, we examine four of the leading Macintosh database programs (or families of programs): FileMaker Pro, 4th Dimension, Panorama, and Helix RADE.

FileMaker Pro 5.5

Like most other database programs, FileMaker Pro (www.filemaker.com) started out as a flat-file database program. In recent releases, the company has enhanced FileMaker to support relational databases fully, provide connectivity tools for linking to non-FileMaker databases, enable users to publish and interact with databases on the Web or on an intranet, and simplify sharing databases across a workgroup.

FileMaker has long been the preferred database program of Macintosh owners, and its market share attests to this. While FileMaker has always made it supremely easy for users to design beautiful and highly functional databases, recent versions have added very little that enhances it for designers. The major thrust of revisions has been to target corporate users by providing additional workgroup, Web publishing, and security features. The main reason for non-corporate users to upgrade is to ensure file compatibility. FileMaker 3 and 4 databases are compatible with each other. and version 5.0 and 5.5 databases are also compatible with each other, but not with databases created in 3 or 4. Thus, if you need to work with either 5.0 or 5.5 databases, you might as well upgrade to 5.5. If, however, you're designing databases for yourself or other individual users, you can safely stick with almost any version (3 or higher).

Here's a summary of the new features introduced in FileMaker Pro 5.5:

- Version 5.5 is compatible with Mac OS X, while still supporting Mac OS 8.1 through 9.2.1. Mac OS X users can import Adobe Acrobat PDF files into Container fields.

- Instant Web Publishing now allows scripted buttons in the header or footer (Table View); such scripts can consist of as many as 3 steps chosen from the 20 supported ones. You can specify a startup script that automatically executes the first time a user opens a Web-published database. You can also sort by clicking column headings, replace the default navigation controls with buttons, and set data-access controls on a record-by-record basis.

- FileMaker can now send data to ODBC sources, such as Microsoft SQL Server and Oracle databases. Version 5.5 includes a new Execute SQL script step, and you can store SQL statements in fields for importing and exporting ODBC data.

- Comments in scripts appear in italics. The Send Mail script step adds support for Microsoft Entourage 2001 and Microsoft Outlook Express 5.

- You can hide toolbars and disable the related menu items.

- You can import named ranges from Excel worksheets.

- You can set "Number of characters" as a validation option for Text, Number, Date, or Time fields.

- New security features can prevent users from creating new databases or changing passwords, and allow you to set record-by-record access privileges.

While most users are familiar with FileMaker Pro (the best-selling database program for the Macintosh), they may not be aware that FileMaker Pro is actually a *family* of software products. Its members include the following:

FileMaker Pro 5.5 ($249) is a cross-platform program for designing databases and performing data entry in any FileMaker database. FileMaker Pro also allows small networked workgroups (as many as ten people) to share databases. Using the provided Web Companion plug-in, you can host databases on the Web or on a company intranet (ten guests in any 12-hour period).

FileMaker Server 5.5 ($999) is the program you need if your workgroup contains more than ten people or if more than that number need to connect to a database simultaneously.

FileMaker Pro 5 Unlimited ($999) serves a similar function to FileMaker Server but is for hosting FileMaker databases on the Web or on an intranet.

FileMaker Developer 5 ($499) provides tools that enable you to create stand-alone databases for the Mac or PC (referred to as *run-time applications*). If you intend to create databases that you wish to sell or to deploy widely in your company, you should consider FileMaker Developer.

FileMaker Mobile Companion for Palm OS ($49) enables you to view, edit, delete, and add data to a FileMaker Pro database using any Palm PDA (personal digital assistant) or Palm-compatible device.

At this writing, FileMaker had released FileMaker Pro 5.5. As was the case with all previous releases, the company will release the other programs in the family within the next six months or so. The sections that follow discuss mainly the 5 version rather than the unreleased 5.5 version of the other products in the family.

FileMaker Mobile Companion for Palm OS. Did you ever wish you could take your FileMaker Pro databases on trips or customer visits—*without* dragging along a PowerBook? If you own a Palm-compatible PDA, now you can. FileMaker Mobile provides the Palm and conduit software required to load databases created in FileMaker Pro 5 and higher onto a Palm handheld; view, create, and edit records on the Palm; and synchronize changes between the Palm and desktop databases.

To enable data exchange with your PDA, you perform a few simple steps. First, open the database in FileMaker Pro and choose File, then Sharing. Next, enable Mobile Companion for Palm OS. Click the Settings button and then set options for the database (**Figure 11.2**). You can choose as many as 20 fields to share, as long as each is a Text, Number, Date, or Time field. Next, if you have specified that synchronization will only include records in the current found set, you perform a Find to select the desired records. (You can have as many as 5,000 records in the Palm version of the database.) Finally, with the database still open, perform a HotSync with your PDA.

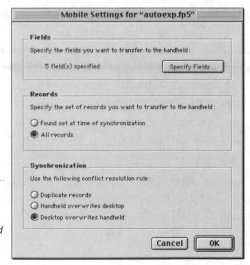

Figure 11.2

These are the basic settings you can establish for any database you intend to load into your Palm PDA.

Don't make the mistake of thinking this is FileMaker on a Palm. FileMaker Mobile lacks most of FileMaker Pro's features. What you *can* do in the Mobile version is browse the selected fields in form or list view (scrolling left or right as necessary); sort the list by any field; perform Finds; and create, edit, and delete records. The program does all these things well. However, its limitations make it better suited for some types of databases than for others:

- Other field types, such as Calculation, Summary, and Global, may not be among the chosen fields.

- Even if assigned to a field in your FileMaker Pro database, value lists are not available in Mobile. Similarly, Mobile doesn't allow check boxes, radio buttons, or pop-up lists. If the desktop version of the database relies on value lists, edited and newly created Palm records may require editing after you transfer them back to the desktop database.

- While you can sort records on the Palm, it sorts Date and Time fields numerically rather than chronologically.

- On the Palm, Mobile truncates long field names *from the left*—occasionally making them hard to read.

FileMaker Server 5.5. Contrary to what you might think, FileMaker Server is *not* a shareable network version of FileMaker Pro. In fact, Server doesn't even include a copy of FileMaker Pro. Even if you install Server, you still need a separate copy of FileMaker Pro for each user in the workgroup. FileMaker Server has one function—it *serves* shared FileMaker databases to people on the network. For instance, the members of your sales department might all require access to a database that shows the company's current inventory or all customer invoices.

Although FileMaker Pro 5.5 does have built-in networking, this feature is designed only for small workgroups. Sharing a database that's installed on your Mac can have a major impact on your computer's performance. Server, however, gets around these limitations, as well as the ten-user limit imposed by FileMaker Pro's built-in networking. First, because the shared databases will reside on a computer you've chosen to use as a file server, you don't have to worry about a performance hit on your Mac. Second, rather than a limit of 10 guests, Server can handle 250 simultaneous guests and can host as many as 125 open databases at the same time. Finally, sharing databases with Server is much faster than it is with FileMaker Pro. The network administrator can monitor Server's performance remotely from any copy of FileMaker Pro on the network. Server can also automate database backup.

Like FileMaker Pro, FileMaker Server 5.5 is a cross-platform program. In fact, FileMaker Server 5.5 includes both the Mac and Windows versions on the same CD, letting you choose the platform on which you want to install it.

FileMaker Server 5.5 adds support for Linux, Mac OS X, and Windows 2000. It also includes LDAP (Lightweight Directory Access Protocol) support and optional guest authentication by a Windows Domain controller.

FileMaker Pro 5 Unlimited. This isn't the greatest name for a product, since it tells you nothing about its function. Essentially, Unlimited is Server for Web-published FileMaker Pro databases. As mentioned previously, when you use FileMaker Pro to publish a database on the Web or on an intranet, only ten users can access the database in any 12-hour period. If additional users attempt access, they get locked out. While this may work for extremely small workgroups and infrequently accessed databases, it's woefully insufficient for many other users. FileMaker Unlimited is intended for large workgroups and Web sites; it doesn't impose a limit on the number of simultaneous Web guests or visitors during any 12-hour time period. For improved performance, Unlimited can also connect to the following Web servers:

- Mac Web servers: 4D's Web Star 4.0, AppleShare IP 6.2, Apache 1.3.6 on Mac OS X Server 1.02.

- Windows Web servers: Microsoft IIS 4.0, Microsoft PWS 4.0, Netscape Enterprise Server 3.6.2.

As is the case with FileMaker Server 5, Unlimited includes both Mac and Windows versions of the server software.

FileMaker Developer 5. Don't let the name confuse you. You don't *need* FileMaker Developer to develop databases for yourself or your company or to sell them to others. But does it help? You bet! FileMaker Developer 5 includes standard copies of FileMaker Pro 5 for Macintosh *and* Windows, as well as tools that simplify the development process. The biggie for most developers is the FileMaker Developer Tool, a program you use to create *stand-alone templates*—databases that users who don't own FileMaker Pro can run. If you're designing databases you intend to sell, this expands your potential market to every Macintosh and Windows user. Other important and useful features in Developer 5 include documentation for custom Web-programming solutions using CDML (Claris Data Markup Language), XML (Extensible Markup Language), JDBC (Java Database Connectivity), and ODBC (Open Database Connectivity); and the ability to create applications that run in kiosk mode. New features announced for 5.5 include a script debugger and a tool for examining and documenting a database's structure.

FileMaker Pro Tips

If you need to share one of your FileMaker 5.0 or 5.5 databases with a Windows user, append .fp5 to the filename (as in FaxForm.fp5). This three-character extension tells Windows the file is a FileMaker Pro 5 or 5.5 database.

FileMaker automatically saves your work as you go along. (You've probably noticed there isn't a Save command—that's why.) Before making changes to the database's structure or design, as well as before performing any function that might harm the integrity of your data (such as a mass deletion or import of records), it's a good practice to make a backup of the database. From the Finder, Control-click the database icon and choose Duplicate. You can also accomplish this from within FileMaker Pro by choosing Save a Copy As from the File menu.

FileMaker Pro 5.5 supports both *lookups* and *relationships.* How do you decide which one to use? When triggered, a lookup performs a onetime *copy* of data from a second file. A relation, on the other hand, *displays* the related data rather than actually copying it; what you see changes to reflect the most current data. If you want FileMaker to look up data once and then leave it unchanged (say, when you're recording an item amount for an invoice), use a lookup. If you want data to change as necessary (for example, displaying a customer's current phone number rather than the one that was initially available when you created the record), use a relation.

FileMaker Pro automatically switches back to the Pointer tool as soon as you finish using most of the layout-mode tools. You can use the same tool indefinitely by double-clicking its icon in the tool panel. Or if you want to lock tools with a single click, check "Always lock layout tools" in the Layout tab of the Applications Preferences dialog box (from the Edit menu, choose Preferences, and then Application).

You can create dotted lines for your layouts by applying any of the dozen or so dotted pen patterns to a line. (You'll find these patterns in the top two rows of the pen pattern palette.)

If it's been a while since you updated FileMaker Pro, it's important to know that value lists are no longer field specific, as they were in FileMaker Pro 3. The Define Value Lists command under the File menu defines every value list individually. You can associate a single value list with as many fields as you like. (You can even reuse lists in *other* FileMaker databases.) For instance, if you've created a questionnaire database, you can create one value list containing Yes and No as choices, and then associate it with every yes-or-no question.

To publish your databases on the Web using the Web Companion, you must have a *static IP address.* Whenever you connect to the Internet, your ISP (Internet service provider) assigns an IP address that identifies your computer. Unfortunately, every time most users reconnect to the Internet, their ISP assigns them a *new* IP address from the available pool. People connect to your FileMaker databases by typing your IP address, found in the TCP/IP control panel in Mac OS 9 (**Figure 11.3**) and Network System Preferences in Mac OS X, into the browser. If your address is constantly changing, they'll have a hard time connecting. Contact your ISP to determine if you can get a *static*—permanent and unchanging—IP address.

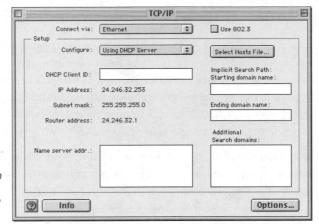

Figure 11.3

After connecting to the Internet, you can find your IP address in Mac OS 9's TCP/IP control panel.

You can test a Web-destined database on your own Mac without an active Internet connection. After you've performed the steps to publish the database, launch your Web browser and type http://localhost/ in the browser's Address field (**Figure 11.4**).

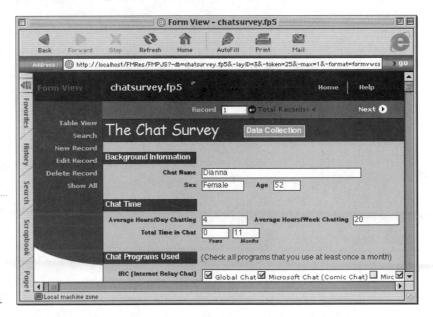

Figure 11.4

The Instant Web Companion's support for Cascading Style Sheets allows Web-published databases to look very much as they do in FileMaker Pro.

If you need some help with a tricky FileMaker Pro concept or scripting problem, consider subscribing to the free FileMaker Pro Talk mailing list sponsored by Blue World (maker of Lasso, professional software tools for designing and serving data-driven Web sites). Many of the sharpest FileMaker developers routinely follow this list, and they're often willing to lend a hand. Visit www.blueworld.com/blueworld/lists/ for the sign-up info. Unless you want to be flooded with dozens of individual e-mail messages per day, sign up in Digest mode. This is a *very* popular mailing list.

4th Dimension 6.7

4D's 4th Dimension (www.4D.com)—4D for short—is a fast, powerful, cross-platform, programmable relational-database program. Unlike the other database programs discussed in this chapter, 4D targets developers more than end users. Sure, you can use it to create flat-file or relational databases for your own use or for members of a small workgroup, but if that's all you have in mind, many simpler programs will do the job.

4D Standard Edition 6.7.1 ($349) includes 4D and Unlimited Interpreted Runtime, enabling you to create databases that run as stand-alone applications. Like FileMaker Pro, 4D Standard Edition also has built-in Web publishing and serving capabilities. Users can interact with your databases over the Internet or on their company intranets using their Web browsers.

As is the case with many programs, as a new owner of 4D, you'll need to stock up on printer paper and ink cartridges, because as far as printed documentation goes, 4D includes only brief "Installation" and "Quickstart" guides. The Quickstart manual walks you through the creation of a simple relational database; shows you how to create charts, reports, and labels; and then lets you publish and test the database on the Web. All the other documentation is on the CD in printable Acrobat and Web-browser formats. Can you make do with just reading the manuals onscreen? Of course ... but would you *want* to? That's not the way most people want to learn complex programmable applications.

On the other hand, as the argument goes, providing printed copies of all the manuals would increase the shipping weight and size of the box, as well as necessitate a bump in price. (Of all the databases mentioned in this chapter, only FileMaker Pro includes a general user manual. All the others rely on CD-based documentation.)

 Nevertheless, what 4D desperately needs is a simple document that explains what each of the 4D components does and how they all work together. If there *is* such a document—on the CD or on 4D's Web site—I didn't see it. Without this information, it's easy to become hopelessly lost at the outset. The learning curve doesn't have to be *this* long.

You use 4D to create single-user databases. If people need to share your 4D databases, you can buy **4D Server Standard Edition** ($999), which enables your single-user databases to function as multiuser ones. Server can support as many as 100 simultaneously connected copies of 4D Client on a Mac, Windows, or mixed-platform network.

4D's support of plug-ins extends its connectivity options. For example, a 4D database can serve as a front end for any ODBC-compliant database, enabling you to execute SQL queries and extract data from non-4D databases. Other database programs can do the opposite—pulling data from 4D tables. 4D also has extensive Internet functionality. You can publish secure databases on the Web (via SSL), as well as send and receive e-mail or connect to an FTP server from within a 4D database.

Like FileMaker Pro, 4D is actually an array of related products. You might also be interested in the **4D Developer Edition** ($799), **Advanced Kit for 4D** ($590), **4D Server Developer Edition** ($1,590), or **Expansion Pack for 4D Server Developer Edition** ($799). There are many additional pricing options for individual, network, and Web users. For example, the 4D Web Edition bundles a copy of 4D Standard Edition and Adobe GoLive 5.0, as well as a 4D Web Extension license for testing your Web-based solutions. The company also publishes the **4D WebStar Server Suite 4** ($399), which enables you to publish your databases on the Web, provide e-mail accounts, and serve Web pages. Visit www.4d.com/products/StdPricing.html for pricing information on the 4D product line.

One big concern of many users is that when their favorite software is released in a Mac OS X version, they'll get stuck with yet another expensive upgrade. That won't be the case with 4D. If you buy 4D Standard Edition 6.7, the upgrade to the Mac OS X version will be free.

New features introduced in version 6.7 include the following:

- 4D databases are now WML (Wireless Markup Language) compatible, allowing users with PDAs and mobile phones to connect to them.

- As in FileMaker Pro, 4D's Web-published databases support CSS, so a database will look similar whether you view it in 4D or in a browser. Web-published databases can also support XML, CGI, and SSL (Secure Socket Layer).

- Designers can add 4D tags to Web pages to create custom Internet and intranet solutions.

- A feature called *form inheritance* simplifies form design. When you make a change to a base form (for instance, modifying a company address or logo), the change ripples down to all related forms.

FileMaker Pro and 4D have both been around the block a few times: FileMaker first shipped in 1985 and 4D made its U.S. debut in 1987.

Panorama 4.0

ProVUE Development's **Panorama 4** ($299; www.provue.com) is a cross-platform, programmable, relational database program. The newest version runs on both Macs and Windows PCs. Either type of computer can access Panorama databases over a mixed-platform network.

Speed—one of Panorama's most-touted features—continues to be a selling point in this version. While most database programs are disk based (reading from the disk as they require more data, as well as automatically saving new data and changes to disk), Panorama is RAM based; that is, the computer's memory holds all data until you perform a manual Save. ProVUE claims that many operations are now twice as fast as they were in version 3.1. The company especially focused on improving the speed of sorting, searching, and selecting data, as well as displaying SuperMatrix objects and matrices.

Panorama has many features that distinguish it from the competition. For example, you can turn on *clairvoyance* for any field. When you begin typing into a field, Panorama checks all previously entered data for that field and tries to finish typing for you. If you enter "San F" in a City field, Panorama might complete it as "San Francisco." Clairvoyance is extraordinarily useful; I've wished for years that other database programs would offer it.

If you have a lot of important databases that you use regularly, keeping them organized and handy can really be a production. In Panorama 4, you can store them all in the Favorite Databases wizard (**Figure 11.5**).

Figure 11.5

You can easily open any database recorded in the Favorite Databases wizard. You can also view the file's notes, its disk location, and a list of all its defined fields and forms.

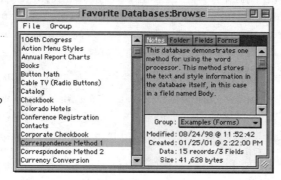

It's always been simple to script repetitive actions in Panorama. In fact, you can create many scripts (called *macros*) by simply turning on the Recorder and recording your actions. Better still, you can also *edit* macros. For example, if you want to re-sort a database by a different field after viewing a report, you can copy a sort step from the current macro, paste it in as the final step, and then just substitute the correct field name.

Other significant new features in Panorama 4 include the following:

- This version provides extensive documentation (but in PDF format only), as well as three hours of tutorials that you can view in QuickTime Player. If you need a printed copy of the documentation—all 1,800 pages of it— you can purchase one from ProVUE for $85.

- Panorama includes 21 wizards—ready-to-use databases that perform general functions (calendar, address book, and task timer, for example) and help you construct and test databases. It also provides several dozen additional sample databases.

- When you're creating or editing a procedure, error messages now appear in the window's status bar rather than in a separate dialog box. This makes it easier to continue working. When you're single-stepping through a procedure to test or debug it, the result of each step also appears in the status bar.

- Panorama 4 includes a complete online reference to all programming statements and functions.

- Credit cards have an internal *checksum* that allows validation of a number for simple data-entry errors, such as transposed digits. You can use the new *cardvalidate* statement to ensure that a number is potentially valid.

- You can set a procedure to execute every second or every minute. This allows you to create animations, timers, and other types of timed events. You can also calculate time intervals and delays as small as ¹⁄₆₀ of a second.

- Using the Custom Menu Editor wizard, you can create custom menus from within Panorama (rather than having to use a utility such as ResEdit).

- If you already have Panorama 3.1 databases, 4.0 can open them without any modification—enabling you and others to continue working with them in version 3.1. And if you want to upgrade these old databases to version 4, you can run them through the included Panorama Platform Converter utility.

 If only one person in your company will be developing databases (the others are designated as users), you just need to buy one full copy of Panorama 4 for the developer. Everyone else can use Panorama Direct ($90) to access the databases and perform data-entry tasks.

Helix RADE 5.0

A full-featured, programmable database program, **Helix RADE,** short for Rapid Application Development Environment ($150; www.helixtech.com), offers the least expensive way for Mac owners to get into database creation.

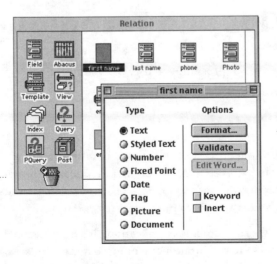

But even having previously worked with other database programs won't prepare you for Helix's unique, visual way of doing things.

A Helix database—its field definitions, formulas, forms, views, and data—is referred to as a *collection*. To construct a collection, you drag icons into a work area. You can double-click most icons to reveal a dialog box in which you can define or set options for that icon (**Figure 11.6**).

Figure 11.6

Double-click a field icon to set its field type, formatting, and validation options.

 You can change the name of any icon whenever you like. The new name will automatically propagate throughout the collection.

At present, Helix RADE includes no printed documentation, tutorials, or sample data files. If you aren't already familiar with the program's way of doing things, you'll have to read the 750-page PDF manual. Although there *is* a brief tutorial, it provides only the barest introduction. After working through it, you won't be ready to create your own databases. You'd do well to visit Helix's FTP site (ftp://ftp.helixtech.com) and download some of the sample files available there, as well as search the Internet for other examples.

Version 5.0 includes these new features:

- The Client/Server version supports communication over TCP/IP.
- By enabling Ramjet, you can load an entire Helix database into memory—dramatically speeding up most activities.
- This version has additional keyboard shortcuts and navigation keys.
- Helix Utility now includes Data Damage Repair, enabling it to correct all errors in a collection (unless it discovers damaged records or fatal errors).

Helix RADE Tips

Want to really make your database stand out? Using Custom Helper (a utility available from Helix Technology), you can create a custom help file for any database, which users can access from the top of the Apple menu.

Following a crash with an open Helix database, critical reconstruction data is stored in the Trash. To rebuild the database, you *must* run it *before* emptying the Trash!

Database Tips and Techniques

Regardless of which program you use, you'll find the following tips helpful for designing and working with databases.

General Tips

If you're still in the process of choosing a database program, don't buy more program than you need or can handle. Because of their complexity and advanced feature sets, some database programs are meant for corporate developers; others are more appropriate for end users and casual developers.

Because they're such complex applications, it's not unusual for any major database release to go through one or more minor updates. Whether you've just purchased a database program or have been using it for a year or more, you should check the company's Web site periodically for downloadable updates. (Minor updates are often free.)

When people buy a database program, they often have a specific need in mind—not an overwhelming desire to conquer a complex application. If this describes you, before buying a database program, check the Internet for ready-made solutions to your problem. You may find a commercial or share-ware program that does the trick. Or you may discover a free or inexpensive template that you can use with a particular database program, making your buying decision that much simpler. (Note that database programs often include free templates. One of them may be exactly what you need!)

Some databases—if you're storing graphics or a large number of records—can strain the program's default memory setting. Consult the database program's documentation for suggestions on how much memory you should allocate to the program. To view or alter a program's memory allocation in Mac OS 9, highlight the program icon. From the File menu, choose Get Info, and then Memory. Increase the number in the Preferred Size field (**Figure 11.7**). In Mac OS X, the system handles memory allocation for you.

Figure 11.7

You can change the amount of memory available to an application in its Get Info dialog box.

Design Tips

Databases differ from standard paper files (which serve as the basis for many business and education databases) in that it's more efficient to break database fields into as many discrete components as possible rather than combining them into a single field. For example, rather than defining a single Name field (as you might do with a paper form), you should create separate fields for Salutation (Mr., Ms., Mrs., Dr.), First Name, Middle Initial, Last Name, and Suffix (M.D., Ph.D., Jr.). Doing so ensures that the data will be entered in a consistent form.

Not every database needs or merits the extra work required to create custom data-entry forms. If the default form will do the trick (and the database won't be staring you in the face every day), your job is done. On the other hand, if your chosen database program allows custom forms and you (or others) will be using a given database regularly, some extra design work will pay off. Think carefully about how best to organize the fields, set a custom tab order, specify field-validation criteria, and make every layout easy on the eyes.

If your database program allows you to make multiple layouts, resist the temptation to jam everything in your database into a single layout. For instance, it usually makes sense to create separate layouts for data entry and for each type of report you'll generate. Data-entry forms are generally great for recording data but a poor choice for printed reports. Who wants to see a single record printed on each page? If you create a separate report layout, you can exclude data you don't need to see, display summary information (such as totals and record counts), and organize the data in useful ways (say, grouping sales figures by employee or division).

 If your database is so complex that it requires more than a couple of layouts, consider adding a main-menu layout that lets you choose what to do next. At its simplest, it might contain buttons for data entry, reports, and help information. A more complex menu system could incorporate several sub-menus, enabling you to select specific types of reports, for example.

 Unless your database is extremely simple, you should take advantage of the database program's documentation features. (A couple of years from now, do you *really* want to have to examine code to figure out how a complex procedure or report works?) For example, you can use available features to add comments to your scripts and macros, create dialog boxes or pop-up menus that explain data-entry requirements for important fields, or create a separate help-file database that users can open by clicking a button in your database.

 If your database requires that you enter the same information in multiple records—for instance, customer-address information in an invoice database—it pays to "think relational." By keeping the repeated data in a separate related file, you can avoid retyping it.

Mac OS X Databases

Longtime Mac databases FileMaker Pro and 4th Dimension have made the move to Mac OS X. But not all Mac OS X databases started life on this side of the fence. With Mac OS X's Java and Unix underpinnings, a broad group of developers, including former Next programmers, can easily bring their applications to the Mac.

Here are a few of the databases that run natively on Mac OS X—and which started life somewhere else. Most are industrial-strength applications and are probably more than you need to organize your *Mystery Science Theater 3000* video collection.

FrontBase, from FrontBase (www.frontbase.com) is a relational database that the company has designed for Internet-based applications.

MySQL, from MySQL (www.mysql.com), is a popular open source database management system. The company politely asks that you call its product "My Es Queue El" and not "My Sequel."

OpenBase, from OpenBase International (www.openbase.com), offers a relational database, a server, and developer and porting tools for Mac OS X along with Linux, Solaris, and Windows platforms.

Apple's Mac OS X application guide (www.apple.com/macosx/applications/) can direct you to specific database tools.

12

Personal and Business Management

Steve Schwartz is the chapter editor and author.

The applications discussed in this chapter are broadly classified as *business software*.

Roughly speaking, these programs are designed to help you handle important business functions, manage your time and appointments, or deal decisively with business data. Even if you aren't a businessperson, don't skip this chapter; home users and students will also find many of these programs useful.

In This Chapter

Integrated Software

If you're looking for the Swiss Army knife of Macintosh applications—one set of programs that does it all—*integrated software* is the answer. These programs combine many of the basic software tools that people use every day. Depending on the integrated suite you choose, you'll get a collection of interrelated programs, such as a word processor, a spreadsheet, a database, an e-mail and newsgroup client, drawing tools, and a presentation program.

When I wrote about integrated software in the *Macintosh Bible,* sixth edition, only two serious contenders were in the category: Microsoft Office and ClarisWorks (now known as AppleWorks). Well, nothing has changed. If you want integrated software for your Mac, you *still* have the same two choices. Both products, however, are mature, widely available, and widely used.

So which one should you choose? Because of its high price and advanced capabilities, Office 2001 may be more than many home and small-business users need. For a fraction of the price, AppleWorks 6 provides the basic tools that many users require. But if you need to ensure compatibility with others (whether across a network, on Windows, or with others around the country) and require more advanced tools for creating and formatting documents, Office may be the better choice.

Microsoft Office 2001

The programs included in **Microsoft Office 2001 for Mac** ($499; Microsoft Corp., http://shop.microsoft.com) are Word (word processing), Excel (spreadsheet), PowerPoint (presentations), Internet Explorer 5 (Web browser), and a new addition, Entourage. This program is an e-mail client, newsgroup reader, and personal information manager (PIM) that combines many of the features of Microsoft Outlook Express (Mac) and Microsoft Outlook (Windows). Although most Office users will quickly adopt Entourage as their new e-mail program, it also includes a host of capabilities for getting your business, school, or personal life in order. You can use the Tasks section to keep track of your to-do list; the Address Book to record detailed contact information on the people you know and correspond with; the Notes section to record critical tidbits of information; and the Calendar to remind you of meetings, appointments, birthdays, and other important events. In my opinion, the addition of Entourage is one of the most compelling reasons to upgrade to Office 2001.

As we went to press, Microsoft was finishing work on **Microsoft Office v. X for Mac.** It should be available by the time you read this and will sell for $499.

You can set a reminder for any Calendar or Task event. Even though the Calendar is directly accessible only in Entourage, the Reminders window (**Figure 12.1**) will pop onscreen if you're running *any* Office application.

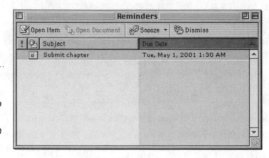

Figure 12.1

When a Calendar or Task event gets close, the Reminders window appears. Click Dismiss to make it go away, Snooze to pick another time to be reminded again, or Open Item to edit or delete the event.

The Office 2001 applications are all stand-alone programs. Not only do they launch and run separately from each other but there is no requirement that you even install or use the entire suite. For example, although most of you will adopt Internet Explorer as your default Web browser, you don't have to do so. It isn't linked to the other applications. On the other hand, the core products—Word, Excel, PowerPoint, and Entourage—are linked together by the new Project Gallery. When you need the capabilities of an Office application that isn't currently running, you can use the File > Project Gallery command (⌘ Shift P) to launch that application or open one of its documents.

If you're looking for reasons to buy or upgrade to Office 2001, here are some of the features Microsoft introduced or enhanced:

New General Features

- The Project Gallery (**Figure 12.2**) acts as a general interface for launching the Office applications as well as for creating new blank documents and ones based on templates.

- The floating Formatting Palette (View > Formatting Palette) enables you to assign formatting options to selected text and objects without having to pull down menus or remember keyboard shortcuts.

- Office 2001 supports *identities,* allowing multiple users to share a single copy of Office while keeping their documents and personal data separate.

- Office includes an extensive Clip Gallery of images you can add to your documents (Insert > Picture > Clip Art). You can add your own images to the Clip Gallery as well as download additional free ones from Microsoft's Web site by clicking the Online button in the Clip Gallery dialog box.

- Office offers direct support for scanners and digital cameras, enabling you to scan or transfer an image directly into an Office document (Insert > Picture > From Scanner or Camera).

- Office includes its own Clipboard (View > Office Clipboard), allowing you to cut or copy multiple items. Each item is available for pasting into documents from the same application or other Office applications.

- Office includes the Encarta World English Dictionary (Tools > Dictionary), allowing you to look up word definitions.
- The File > Save as Web Page command enables you to create Web pages easily from any Office document. A handy Preview command lets you view the pages onscreen before saving them as HTML files.

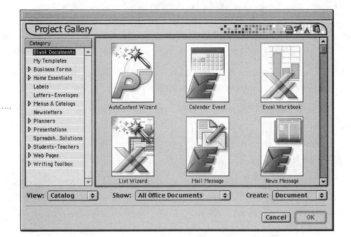

Figure 12.2

It doesn't matter which part of Office you're running, you can use the Project Gallery to create a new document in any Office application.

New in Word 2001

- The new Data Merge Manager makes it easier to do mail merges. Support is provided for merging with the Entourage Address Book and with FileMaker Pro files.
- Word 2001 contains its own set of drawing and graphics tools. There's new support for *picture bullets*—Web-style graphics you can use for bullet points, instead of than the standard bullet or dingbat characters.
- Table support has been beefed up; you can now make nested tables, for example.
- Word can now open Web pages as well as save documents as Web pages, and documents can include Web objects—such as scrolling text and clickable check boxes.

New computer users are frequently baffled by a blank word-processing document. They want to start by centering a title, for example, but can't figure out why the insertion point is frozen in the upper-left corner of the page. You can click *anywhere* on a Word 2001 page and immediately start typing; Word will automatically insert the required returns and tabs for you.

New in Excel 2001

- Excel has a new *autocomplete* feature that speeds up data entry. Rather than retyping an item (such as the name of a city), you can choose its name from the pop-up list that appears.
- A new calculator lets you create and edit formulas.

Because spreadsheets are often used to create lists, Excel 2001 introduces the new List Manager. A wizard can help you create the list, specify headings, and create any necessary formulas. Lists can be floating or embedded and are easily sorted by any column.

New in PowerPoint 2001

- As you're creating a presentation, the new tripane view lets you see your slides, notes, and outline at the same time.

- Rather than having to create tables in Word or Excel, you can use PowerPoint's new built-in table feature.

- Presentations can now have multiple masters.

- To make it easier to share your presentations with people who don't have PowerPoint, you can save them as QuickTime movies (playable on either a Mac or a PC).

- When a presentation you've saved as a Web page is viewed, it automatically scales itself to match the screen size and resolution of the viewer's computer.

AppleWorks 6

If you're on a budget or don't want or need all of the whiz-bang features of Microsoft Office, **AppleWorks 6** ($79; Apple Computer Inc., http://store. apple.com) is for you. Long a favorite of teachers, students, small-business owners, and home users, AppleWorks can readily meet your basic word-processing, spreadsheet, graphics, and—new in version 6—presentation needs.

AppleWorks 6 includes applications (referred to as *environments*) for word processing, spreadsheets, drawing, painting, and presentations. The Communications environment from earlier versions has disappeared but will be missed by few; it was only useful for connecting to other computers or bulletin board systems, not the Internet. Unlike the Office applications, the AppleWorks environments really *are* integrated. When you need to create a document in a different environment, you never leave AppleWorks; you just switch environments within the program. You can embed different types of documents within almost any AppleWorks document. For example, when writing a memo in the word-processing environment, you can embed separate frames that include a spreadsheet table or a scanned picture. When you click inside any of the embedded frames, AppleWorks displays a set of menus and tools appropriate for working within that environment. Slick.

Among the other notable features introduced in AppleWorks 6:

- AppleWorks 6 was designed to run under Mac OS X. So if you're thinking of taking the leap to the new system software, AppleWorks is ready to go. (But it still runs fine under earlier versions of the Mac OS, too.)

- A tabbed Starting Points window (**Figure 12.3**) serves as AppleWorks' new interface for creating documents, selecting templates, and accessing Web content. Other interface changes include a Clippings window (replacing the older Libraries palette) for organizing clip art and an enhanced Tools window (adding support for tables).

- Unlike previous versions, AppleWorks 6 takes advantage of an Internet connection. When you want to add a graphic image to a document, for example, you can yank clip art directly from Apple's Web site.

- An *autosave* feature lets you instruct AppleWorks to automatically save copies of your open documents at regular intervals, reducing the likelihood that you'll lose data if your Mac crashes.

- Mail merge can now merge database data to a single file, to multiple files, or directly to the printer.

- The improved spreadsheet environment lets you create formulas that reference cells in *other* worksheets, simplifies the formula-creation process by allowing you to choose functions from the Insert Function dialog box, and automatically adds closing parentheses to formulas if you forget to type them.

- Rather than create tables using a spreadsheet frame, you can use the new table feature. (However, once you finish creating a table, it changes to a bitmapped graphic, which is impossible to edit.)

 Although it's a solid, inexpensive program for new users, little in Apple Works 6 (or its predecessor, AppleWorks/ClarisWorks Office) makes it a must-have upgrade. The removal in this version of most of its file translators, in fact, represents a loss of compatibility with many other programs.

Figure 12.3

The first new feature you'll see in AppleWorks 6 is the Starting Points window. By clicking its tabs, you can create a new document in any environment, summon an Assistant, open a template, check Apple's Web site for new materials, or open a document you recently worked on.

Work Smarter with Drag and Drop

Both AppleWorks 6 and Office 2001 are fully *drag-and-drop enabled*. If you aren't familiar with this Mac system software feature, it's the equivalent of a cut and paste or copy and paste but is accomplished in a single step rather than two. Using drag and drop, you select some text or a graphic object, for example, and then you can drag it to one of these locations:

- A new spot in the same document
- Another open document in the same program
- Another open document in another drag-and-drop–enabled program
- The Desktop, to create a text or graphic clipping file

To perform a drag-and-drop operation, start by selecting some text or an object. Next, click the selected material, drag it to its new location, and then release the mouse button. When you drag an item to a new location in the same document, the equivalent of a cut and paste is performed; that is, the item is *moved*. When you drag an item to a new location in a different document, the equivalent of a copy and paste is performed; that is, the item is *duplicated*.

Where and how can you best use drag and drop? Try it anywhere that it makes sense to you. For example, you can use drag and drop to move cells to a new location in an Excel worksheet or to copy text from an Entourage e-mail message into a note or task description.

Office 2001 Tips

- What if you don't need the entire Office suite? You can purchase or upgrade the individual programs, if you prefer. The upgrade price for Office is slightly less than the cost of upgrading any two of the included applications. If you need only one program, such as Word, you can save money by upgrading it alone. If you plan to upgrade any two programs, however, upgrading the Office suite becomes a better buy—especially when you consider that you get a capable e-mail and PIM program tossed in as part of the deal.

- If you've set up Office for multiple users (called identities), remember that each user must go to Entourage at the start of every session and change to his or her identity (using the dialog box that appears when you choose File > Switch Identity, as shown in **Figure 12.4**). This is important for all Office components—not just Entourage—because the active identity determines whose documents are whose as well as which Calendar and Address Book to use, for example.

Figure 12.4

Even though all Office components use "identities," Entourage is the only one in which users can switch from one identity to another.

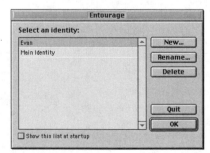

- If you want to insert a name, mailing address, e-mail address, or phone number from your Address Book into a Word document, enable the Contact toolbar (View > Toolbars > Contact).

- Looking for just the right word? Try Control-clicking a word in a Word document. A pop-up menu appears, enabling you to replace the word with a synonym or look up the word's definition in the Office dictionary.

- The Office Clipboard isn't visible from within Entourage. However, if you open the Office Clipboard in another Office program and perform a cut or copy in Entourage, the item is added to the Office Clipboard— where you can paste it into Word, Excel, or PowerPoint documents.

- When you view an e-mail group in Entourage's Group window, you can alphabetize the names of group members. Unfortunately, Entourage sorts by first name rather than last. To view the group membership arranged by last name, start by assigning a special Category to each group member (such as the group's name). Then filter the list in the Address Book window to show only the people to whom you've assigned that special category. You can also use the Find function to search for people with that category designation and then save the search results as a Custom View—which you can use to view or print an alphabetized list of the current group members whenever you like.

- If you need to move Entourage data from one computer to another (or just want to back some of it up), you can drag most of the folder icons from the Folder List onto the Desktop, creating what Microsoft refers to as an Mbox file. To move the data into another copy of Entourage, drag the Mbox file into the Folder List.

- Office 2001 includes Internet Explorer 5. It's identical to the version you can download (or have previously downloaded) from Microsoft's Web site.

- When originally released, IBM ViaVoice Enhanced Edition (see "ViaVoice for Mac: Enhanced Edition" later in this chapter) was *not* compatible with Word 2001. If you want the two products to work together, visit the IBM or Microsoft Web site to download the free ViaVoice update.

AppleWorks 6 Tips

- Be sure to periodically check the Software section of Apple's Web site for downloadable AppleWorks updates (go to http://asu.info.apple.com and search for "AppleWorks"). Update 6.0.4 added an RTF (rich text format) translator, enabling you to exchange documents with Word users. Update 6.1 added the ability to read and write Word and Excel files, enhanced formatting tools, and improved Internet performance when downloading templates.

- You can move text or objects from one spot in an AppleWorks document to another by using cut and paste or drag and drop. You can *copy* elements from one spot to another (leaving the originals intact) by holding down Option while dragging the selected text or objects to the desired destinations.

- If you've upgraded from AppleWorks 5, ClarisWorks 5, or ClarisWorks Office (all the same program but with different names), you can import its spreadsheet table styles into AppleWorks 6. In the Styles window, click Import, select the More Table Styles file (located in the AppleWorks Styles or ClarisWorks Styles folder from the previous version of the program), and choose the styles you'd like to import.

- Want to create a cool wallpaper pattern (formerly called a *texture*) that you can use to dress up your Paint documents? Although you can still design one by hand, you can also create one by simply pasting a copied image (from another program, an AppleWorks document, or the Scrapbook, for example) into the Wallpaper Editor window. To open the Wallpaper Editor, choose Options > Edit Wallpaper.

Personal and Small-Business Finance

Need a little help managing your money, balancing your checkbook, doing your personal or small-business income taxes, or tracking your portfolio? Here are several of the most popular Mac programs for managing your finances.

Quicken 2001 Deluxe

Unless you're new to computing, you've heard of Intuit Corp.'s **Quicken** ($59.95; www.intuit.com). On both the Mac and PC platforms, the name Quicken is synonymous with financial management for the home and small-business user. Like the previous versions (and there's a new one every year), Quicken 2001 Deluxe lets you track your checking, savings, money-market, and credit-card accounts. When you make transactions in these accounts, you enter the data into Quicken—either by launching the program or by running the stripped-down QuickEntry utility. As you enter more and more information, Quicken automatically memorizes your most common transactions and lets you reuse the information in subsequent transactions with the same person or company. If Quicken notices a particular transaction that recurs on a regular basis (such as a mortgage payment), it offers to create a scheduled transaction—automatically recording it each month or simply reminding you when the payment is due. When your statement arrives, Quicken makes it a snap to reconcile the account. And by assigning a category to each transaction (such as Groceries, Telephone, and Social Security), you can use Quicken's report and graph features to get a handle on your spending patterns, prepare a budget, or get ready for tax time.

Over the years, Intuit has enhanced Quicken to track many other types of financial information. You can use its portfolio features to record, update, and follow stocks and mutual funds (**Figure 12.5**). You can also record a home inventory, enabling you to quickly generate a list of your possessions and their values should a disaster occur. If you have any outstanding loans, you can keep track of them, too.

Quicken 2001 offers a variety of financial calculators and planners, enabling you to determine whether conditions are right to refinance your mortgage or whether you're carrying sufficient life insurance, for instance. It also includes an Emergency Record Organizer, a retirement planner, and planning calculators for loans and college expenses.

Like the previous version, Quicken 2001 makes excellent use of the Internet. You can download a daily update of the values of your investments, research securities, and pay bills electronically (if you've registered for online banking with your bank). Quicken 2001 adds the ability to export your portfolio to the Web, letting you examine it from anywhere you have Internet access. Other new features include a global search-and-replace function and a 401(k) adviser.

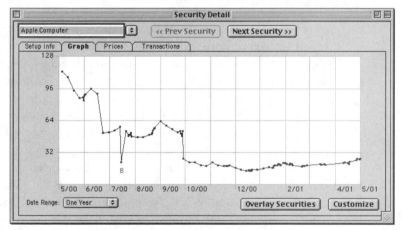

Figure 12.5

With current and historical quotes available at the click of a button, Quicken 2001 allows you to easily track your current holdings as well as stocks you may be interested in buying.

Like so many other current applications, Quicken 2001 doesn't come with a printed manual—although one is provided as an Adobe Acrobat file on the CD. If you're upgrading from a previous version of Quicken, a quick glance through the PDF manual will suffice. If you're a new user, on the other hand, stock up on inkjet cartridges. It will take two of them to print the 500-plus pages.

Quicken TurboTax

Same product, new name! In 2001, Intuit's MacInTax—my favorite tax-preparation program—was renamed TurboTax to match its well-known Windows counterpart. You have three versions to choose from: **TurboTax** ($29.95, base product), **TurboTax Deluxe** ($39.95, with additional money-saving advice and videos), and **TurboTax Home & Business** ($64.95, for sole proprietorships). The latter two versions each entitle you to a free copy of the tax software for one state—on CD or downloaded from Intuit's Web site.

 TurboTax is an Internet-enabled program. Before filing this year's taxes, you can ask TurboTax to check for program and form updates. An Internet connection also lets you download relevant tax data from some financial institutions, consult the Intuit Web site for additional help, or chat with an online tax adviser (for an additional fee).

TurboTax can import filing information from last year's TurboTax or MacInTax as well as import data from Quicken or any financial software that can create TXF files. Of course, if your tax data isn't in an appropriate format, you can enter it manually. Doing so for a personal return or a sole proprietorship isn't really that time consuming. And although it won't save you much time, TurboTax 2000 can import W-2 and 1099 information from participating employers and financial institutions, such as T. Rowe Price.

After you gather up the year's tax data and papers, you can do your taxes by answering questions in an interview format or by entering numbers directly onto onscreen tax forms, or you can combine the two approaches. Most users will want to stick with the EasyStep interview, in which you answer questions, check check boxes, and enter tax data as it's requested. As you enter each piece of information, you can see it appear in the correct lines of the actual IRS forms (shown in the bottom half of the window). TurboTax continuously calculates your tax and displays it in the upper-right corner of the window. It's fun watching how your tax liability changes as you progress through the interview. Since the program remembers where you stopped the interview, there's no need to complete your taxes in one session; you can always pick up where you left off. When you're done, you can print federal and state forms—as well as any worksheets—on any inkjet or laser printer. If you're in a rush to receive a refund, you can take advantage of the program's electronic-filing capability ($11.95 for a federal return and $5.95 for a state return).

 One of TurboTax's strengths is its wealth of helpful tax information. Because it includes the IRS's instructions, you can find the information you need in a flash. The most common tax questions (such as "Which is the correct filing status for me to use?") can be resolved by clicking the help text in the main window.

I've always done my own taxes, and I started using MacInTax about seven years ago. Now I'd *never* go back to doing them by hand.

PowerTicker 2.1

Do you have an investment portfolio, or are you thinking about dabbling in the stock market? You can use **PowerTicker 2.1** ($29.95; Galleon Software, www.galleon.com)—the successor to Aladdin Systems' MacTicker, which was recently acquired by Galleon Software—to download streaming quotes from the Internet. You can display real-time quotes (with the usual 15-minute delay) for selected stocks, mutual funds, and currencies in a scrolling ticker, in individual windows, and in Mac OS 9's Control Strip (**Figure 12.6**). You decide which investments to display, how often the quotes are updated, the quote sources used, and the colors that show whether an item is up, down, or unchanged. Other features include manual updates, alerts for gains and losses (based on a fixed dollar amount or percentage change), and multiple tickers for displaying the activity in different investments. For example, you could create one ticker that lists the current items in your portfolio, another for prospective investments, and a third showing activity on key exchanges, such as the Dow or Nasdaq. If you click the globe icon in an investment window, your Web browser launches to a Yahoo Finance page for the investment, providing additional information and statistics.

Figure 12.6

According to PowerTicker, everything is down. (But nothing is down far enough to make me want to hunt for a window from which to jump.)

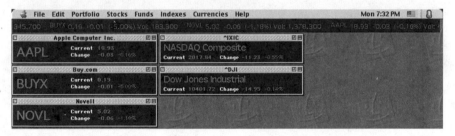

PowerTicker is extremely customizable. Unfortunately, the customization settings and preferences are scattered throughout the program. When you need to make a change, you may find yourself clicking here and there before finding the desired screen, button, or menu command.

Although watching scrolling quotes is fun and informative, you can also use PowerTicker to track your portfolio. You can view a report that shows your gains and losses for the day as well as the change to date from any investment's purchase price.

Personal and Small-Business Finance Tips

Quicken 2001 Deluxe. To update or not to update—*that* is the question. Like clockwork, there's a new version of Quicken every year. Unlike tax software that *must* be updated because of annual changes, Quicken doesn't need to be updated unless you find the new features compelling. Many users can happily use an older version of Quicken for several years before succumbing to the urge to upgrade.

TurboTax Deluxe 2000. If you're importing the previous year's MacInTax or TurboTax data, be sure to update or delete every imported item. Otherwise, you run the risk of including deductions, W2s, and 1099s that aren't relevant to the current tax year or that contain incorrect figures (for example, last year's).

PowerTicker. Successful quote downloading depends on PowerTicker being in sync with the chosen online quote sources. If a specific type of quote (Canadian stocks, for example) refuses to update or shows "N/A," either choose a new quote source or check Galleon's Web site for updated source files (http://www.galleon.com/powerticker/).

PowerTicker. Although PowerTicker is a supremely cool program, it has free competition from many Web sites, such as http://finance.yahoo.com. Many sites let you request quotes, track the performance of multiple portfolios, and view up-to-the-minute news that affects your investments.

Statistics

Although *statistics programs* are specialized applications not meant for novices, many businesses make heavy use of them to analyze sales data and project trends, examine customer demographics, perform market research, and do data mining. The Mac population is tiny when compared with the Windows market, but there is no shortage of heavy-duty statistical packages for the Mac. Below, you'll find my impressions of two such powerhouses: SPSS Base 10.0 and Stata 7.

SPSS Base 10.0

Want to do some serious computing with your Mac? Formerly a mainframe application found mainly in university and corporate computing centers, SPSS Inc.'s **SPSS Base 10.0** ($999; www.spss.com) has successfully made the transition to desktop computers. SPSS enables statisticians, market researchers, and scientists to perform sophisticated statistical analyses on personal and corporate data sets.

You enter and edit your data in the two-tabbed SPSS Data Editor. In the Data View grid, you enter or import your data. In Variable View, you define the variables: creating longer descriptive labels (variable names are restricted to eight characters), adding value labels, and specifying missing value codes. To perform analyses or generate charts, you choose commands from menus and set options in dialog boxes. The analyses and charts are automatically displayed in a scrolling, cumulative Output window. You can also export output as HTML.

If you want to do data mining, SPSS's OLAP (On-Line Analytical Processing) support enables you to view data as cubes and slice them by any combination of grouping variable values. Double-click an OLAP report in the Viewer window, and pop-up menus appear for each grouping variable, letting you view data such as employee salaries or sales figures for any combination of gender, race, and education level. You can easily rearrange analyses that result in pivot tables or cubes by dragging icons—representing variables—between rows, columns, and layers.

SPSS provides extensive help. In most dialog boxes, for example, you can ⌘-click any statistical option to learn what it does. There's also an excellent printed tutorial, an Applications Guide that explains the different analyses, a guide to using the interactive graphics feature to create charts, and a user's guide. Of the manuals, however, only the tutorial is Mac specific. A Statistics Coach helps you determine the appropriate types of analyses for your data, and a Results Coach is available to help you interpret the output.

Stata 7

In recent years, Mac users have been treated to several user-friendly statistics packages. Because these are complex programs for people with demanding statistical needs, anything that makes them easier to use is generally welcomed. However, rather than changing to an interactive, menu- and dialog-driven package as many other companies have done, Stata Corp.'s **Stata 7** ($995; www.stata.com) looks and works like a batch-driven mainframe application. To do almost anything with Stata—such as requesting an analysis or generating a graph—you type command strings into a Command window. Although there *are* menus and a toolbar, they're almost superfluous. Learning the procedural language and its syntax is critical to accomplishing tasks with Stata. The Getting Started manual does an excellent job of walking you through the Stata essentials. In addition, you can view the program's handful of noninteractive tutorials onscreen. After that, it's time to buddy up to the manuals.

Because Stata includes a complex procedural language for you to master, you'll be happy to learn that it is profusely documented—to the tune of 15 pounds of manuals. Although you can usually find what you need to know about command syntax in the online help, nothing beats a hefty manual when you want to learn a topic in detail.

All text output is routed to a single scrolling window. Graphs appear in another window; each one you request replaces the previous one. You can save yourself some typing by abbreviating command, option, and variable names. You can also reexecute any previously typed command from the current session by clicking it in the ever-present Review window, editing as necessary to change the variables or command options.

Stata's graphs will suffice for most users, but compared with SPSS's, it has fewer graph types, you can't change them interactively, and they're all two-dimensional.

Where Stata 7 really shines is in its programmability and extensibility. First, if you want to perform a series of complex analyses (perhaps repeatedly), you can create a *do-file*—a text file that contains the list of commands to execute. Second, by using Stata's procedural language, you can extend the program's capabilities. Because Stata is widely used in research and university environments, statistical add-ons of this sort are readily available as Internet downloads from within Stata. In fact, you can download program updates in the same manner.

Although Stata is difficult to master, once you have the basics down, you'll find it no more difficult to use than any other program. The question you must ask yourself, of course, is whether you'd prefer Stata's command-line approach to that of a menu- and dialog-driven package.

Stata is available not only for Mac and Windows but also for Unix. And unlike many application vendors, Stata Corp. routinely releases new versions of the program for all three platforms simultaneously.

Statistical-Application Tips

- Not every analysis you conduct will use a complete data set. If data collection is still under way, you intend to analyze multiple samples, or you need to run the same analyses on new data sets (once a month, for example), you don't have to reinvent the wheel. In both SPSS and Stata, you can save a sequence of commands to execute as a batch.

- Although still by no means cheap, Stata and SPSS are available to students and faculty for special prices. Check the respective Web sites for details.

Other Business Applications

You might be interested in some noteworthy business applications that—because of their special purposes—aren't quite so easy to categorize. Like so many current Mac programs, many of the following are now one of a kind.

IntelliNews 3.0

News junkies, rejoice! If newspapers or magazines aren't timely enough for you, and you're tired of wading through irrelevant material on the Internet, **IntelliNews 3.0** ($20; Aladdin Systems, www.aladdinsys.com) can help provide

just the news you want. Using your Internet connection, IntelliNews downloads the latest news, technology, sports, science, financial, entertainment, and
Mac headlines from a variety of Web sources (**Figure 12.7**). If you're a sports
fan, you can restrict the headlines to a particular sport, such as golf, football,
or baseball. Double-click any headline that interests you, and your Web
browser launches to display the full story.

Figure 12.7

As shown by this list
of headlines that
IntelliNews gar-
nered from the Web,
it's a snap to keep
up with news in the
Mac world.

IntelliNews is a godsend for movie lovers. In addition to presenting brief
reviews of current movies, it also tells you the show times for movies at local
theaters. Surprisingly, this feature even works for me—a resident of Lizard
Spit, Arizona. (Well, it used to work for me. I just checked again, and now the
closest theater IntelliNews can find is 70 miles away. Guess it's back to video
rentals and microwave popcorn.)

Hot enough for you? You can also use IntelliNews to keep up with the
weather for your city, a place to which you'll be traveling, or almost any spot
in the world. In addition to viewing a text summary of weather conditions,
you can request a gorgeous graphic satellite view of the United States that
shows precipitation, temperatures, and wind-chill readings, for example.

Although IntelliNews can use other news sources, the instructions are presented only as tiny help balloons; there is no other help system. Making such
changes lies beyond the ability of most users.

Now Up-to-Date & Contact 4.0

Over the past few years, PIM (personal information manager) software for the
Mac has all but disappeared. Although your address-book needs can be handled
by an e-mail program or a FileMaker Pro database, the process of scheduling
appointments and tasks, tracking your to-do list, and the like is beyond the

scope of anything but a full-fledged PIM. Power On Software Inc.'s **Now Up-to-Date & Contact 4.0** duo ($119.95; www.poweronsoftware.com) appears to be the last of the stand-alone Mac PIMs. (Entourage 2001—part of the recently released Office 2001 suite, discussed in "Microsoft Office 2001" earlier in this chapter—*is* an honest-to-goodness PIM, but it's only available as part of Office.)

Now Up-to-Date & Contact are two separate but interrelated programs. Now Up-to-Date is a calendar-based scheduling, to-do, and reminder program; Now Contact stores addresses and other important contact information. Miniature versions of the programs are available in the menu bar (QuickDay and QuickContact) and the Apple menu (QuickPad). You can use QuickDay and QuickContact to check today's scheduled events and tasks, respond to reminders, create new events, search for and view contact records, dial phone numbers, and record new contacts. With the QuickPad desk accessory's free-form data-entry window, you can quickly create new contacts, events, and notes.

Although Now Up-to-Date & Contact have just about every PIM-related feature most users will want, they do show their age in one inconvenient way. Although you can store clickable Web and e-mail addresses in contact records—you can even drag and drop to copy them from your browser or e-mail program—no standard fields are reserved for them. You must define custom fields, which suggests this feature was an afterthought. If you have to import your records from another address-book program or PIM, adding Web and e-mail addresses gets messy.

If you're on a network, you'll appreciate the programs' data-sharing and scheduling capabilities. You can share selected events and contacts with other users. Rather than have everyone keep copies of employee and vendor addresses, for example, you can store the contact information on a network server—making it available to everyone on the network. If you're in charge of administering the contact database, you can create password-protected categories that allow users to see but not alter contacts assigned those categories. You can also use Now Up-to-Date to schedule group meetings. If every affected employee indicates his or her "unavailable times" during the week, the program can select the optimal time for an upcoming meeting.

Now Up-to-Date & Contact have excellent phone-dialing and call-tracking capabilities—features that are often missing from PIMs. Most users will instruct Now Contact to either dial through their modems or play tones through their speakers. (To use speaker-based dialing, you just put the telephone handset near your speaker.) You can dial from within Now Contact, QuickContact, or QuickPad. To make things even simpler, you can add frequently called numbers to QuickContact's drop-down menu, where you can dial by simply selecting them. If you want a permanent record of your calls, you can add them—complete with notes and time stamps—to the call log in any person's contact record.

Among other noteworthy program features:

- You can mark important calendar events with sticky notes or clip art.

- Event reminders appear even when the Now applications aren't running.

- You can attach a contact to an event, providing the address and phone number of the person you're meeting, for example. You can also attach URLs to events.

- You can also attach documents to events or contacts.

- You can create multiple contact files—keeping your work contacts separate from your personal ones, for instance.

- Now Contact has two nice features to help speed data entry. When you're entering a company address with *automatic address entry* enabled, the program looks for existing contacts for that company and suggests reusing its address data. When *automatic typing* is enabled, the program does a similar search of all data for the closest possible match.

- Now Contact has a built-in word processor with which you can create letters and faxes, as well as merge documents.

 Power On said version 4.1 of Now Up-to-Date & Contact will run on Mac OS X. Check the company's Web site for updates.

Informed Designer & Filler 3.0.2

Sure, you can design business forms in a database program. But if you work for a company that's serious about forms and you appreciate forms-specific features you won't find in any database program, you're a candidate for Shana Corp.'s **Informed Designer** ($1,495; www.shana.com).

Informed Designer & Filler are actually two separate programs. You use Designer to create the forms and Filler to fill them out. When you buy Designer, it includes one free license for Filler. You can purchase additional licenses for $225 each (quantity discounts are available). Because Informed Designer & Filler are cross-platform products, you don't have to be concerned about whether your forms will work properly on every computer in your company. The CD is also cross-platform, providing both Mac and Windows versions of the software.

If you've ever created a database in FileMaker Pro, you're well on your way to understanding how Designer works; its layout tools and techniques are very similar. You design forms visually—drawing rectangular fields (called *cells*), sizing them, and dragging each one into the proper position. To create line items in most database programs, you have to draw and align a series of repeating fields. Since line items are common components in many forms, Designer lets you define them in one fell swoop as a *table*. You can also embellish your forms with graphics (such as a company logo); Designer 3.0 supports most popular graphic formats. After setting the basic elements of the form, you can name, type, and specify the data type for each cell (text, character, number, name, date, time, Boolean, picture, or signature). Forms can also include *lookups* (drawing cell data from an external database), and cells can have attached value lists or be presented as a series of check boxes.

As mentioned, many features distinguish Informed Designer & Filler from most database programs. Following are some of the most important ones:

Designer Features

Conditional tabbing. You use this feature to skip past irrelevant parts of a form, based on entries in a particular cell. If the user enters one value in a given cell, pressing Tab moves the pointer to cell X; if he or she enters another value in the same cell, Tab moves the pointer to cell Y.

Expandable table rows. Rather than hide overflow text entered in a table cell, the row can expand to show the additional text.

Autoshrinking type. This feature provides another way to avoid truncating overflow text. Filler can automatically reduce the point size of the cell's type to make it all fit.

Cell and table styles. You don't have to exercise your artistic abilities when drawing a cell or table. Just choose one of the many provided styles.

Signature cells. Using an online digital-signature service, you can designate one or more cells in which a user can officially sign off on the entire form (or selected cells).

Color indicators. To make it easy for the data-entry person to see required and recommended cells, Filler can display them with a highlight color.

Help messages. You can attach a custom help message to any cell, showing anyone entering data the type of information that's expected.

Custom menus. You can add custom menu options or remove standard ones. You can also create commands to execute AppleScripts, JavaScripts, or Informed plug-ins.

Form distribution. If multiple users have to fill out a form, you can store it in a *distribution center*—a special folder on the network file server. Whenever someone fills out the form, the distribution center automatically lets the person know if a newer version of the form is available.

Filler Features

Memorized values. To avoid repetitive typing, certain cell values—specific to the person entering data—can fill in automatically, such as the person's name, department, and employee ID number.

Form routing and submission. Forms are commonly routed to several people in a company. Using a provided e-mail plug-in, you can easily route forms to the appropriate individuals. A completed form can automatically be submitted to an external database via an AppleScript, an Apple event, ODBC (Open Database Connectivity), or HTTP.

Attachments. When submitting a form, you can optionally include attached files, such as supporting documents and memos.

Form tracking. Using any database supported by Informed plug-ins (such as Oracle, Sybase, and other ODBC databases), Filler can determine where a particular form is in the routing process.

Overall, it's easy to recommend Informed Filler & Designer. Although the new pricing structure will put the applications out of the reach of many mom-and-pop operations, larger networked organizations will be surprised how easy it is to design, fill out, and manage their forms using this package.

ViaVoice for Mac: Enhanced Edition

IBM ViaVoice for Mac: Enhanced Edition ($141; IBM Corp., www.ibm.com) is the newest release of this speech-recognition and dictation system for the Macintosh. Like the first version (ViaVoice: Millennium Edition), this one requires the processing power of a Power Mac G3 or G4 to turn your speech into text. (Note that you must have a real G3 or G4; it doesn't work with older Macs you've upgraded by adding a processor card.) New to this release is the ability to dictate text directly into Word 2001 as well as the replacement of the Millennium Edition's serial headset with a USB one.

Bug of the Year! No matter how many times and ways I tried to install ViaVoice, it failed, with the same error message—it was unable to find a particular folder on the installation CD. A search of the IBM Web site revealed the problem, which in my opinion is the silliest bug I've ever come across: I was in the wrong time zone! It was necessary for me to set the Date & Time control panel for New York City, perform the installation, and then reset Date & Time for my own southwestern city. IBM's 2.0.3 update CD corrects this problem. To order the CD, visit http://www-4.ibm.com/software/speech/support/us_vvmac203.html.

After you install ViaVoice, your first task is to train it to recognize your voice and speech patterns. To accomplish this, you can read *aloud* several prepared stories that vary in length from 5 to 35 minutes as well as ask it to analyze any text-only documents you have lying around.

After the initial training, you can dictate text directly into supported applications (such as Microsoft Word 2001 and the AppleWorks 6 word processor) or into the provided accessory, SpeakPad. If errors occur, you correct them manually or using voice commands. As you make corrections, you can improve ViaVoice's recognition capabilities by training it to recognize the missed words—similar to the way you add new words to a program's spelling dictionary. ViaVoice can also perform other actions via voice commands, such as "Launch Microsoft Word," "New document," "Surf the Web," or "Jump to (a particular URL)."

In versions 2.0.2 and 2.0.3, ViaVoice can dictate directly into Word 98, Word 2001, Internet Explorer 4.5 or later, the AppleWorks 6 word processor, and Outlook Express. Although you can't dictate into other programs, you can dictate into SpeakPad (**Figure 12.8**) and then transfer the text to the applications via cut and paste or drag and drop. ViaVoice also has a *transfer* command that you can use to move text from SpeakPad into America Online and Eudora as well as the other supported applications.

Dictating directly into Word 2001 was disappointing. It crashed or died every few sentences and had an extraordinarily hard time keeping up with even slow dictation. Dictating into the AppleWorks 6 word processor, on the other hand, was *much* better. With virtually no lag, AppleWork's performance was almost on par with the snappy response of SpeakPad.

Figure 12.8

Poe would have loved this! To correct the few errors in this SpeakPad rendition of "The Raven," I had to train ViaVoice to understand the words dreary *and* 'tis, *and pick one word from the Correction window.*

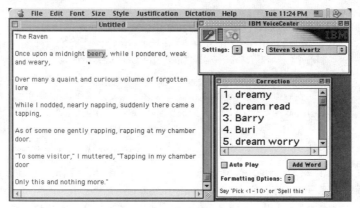

Will I keep ViaVoice on my Mac? Probably. Although it does have a moderately difficult learning curve, after only the first few days of use I was able to perform almost hands-free text entry and editing. And as I train it to understand more of the unusual words I often use in my writing, its recognition continues to improve. (I suspect it will get even better when I get rid of this sinus infection, too!)

If you have a friend or relative with a repetitive-stress injury, arthritis, or a visual impairment, consider giving him or her ViaVoice. Although it isn't perfect and still has some rough edges, you'll be amazed how far voice-recognition software has advanced in the past few years.

Other Business Applications Tips

Informed Designer & Filler. If you're working with an existing form, you can use a scan of it as a background, enabling you to place and size the data cells precisely. To print your data on the actual forms (ignoring the scanned image), set Printing Preferences in Informed Filler to "Print data only."

ViaVoice Enhanced Edition. You'll make much better progress with ViaVoice if you practice and learn the editing commands. If you can't remember them, print out the CommandRefCard.pdf file, located in the Documents folder.

ViaVoice Enhanced Edition. When dictating with ViaVoice, it's best to do only one paragraph at a shot. Stop and make any necessary corrections before continuing. This approach allows you to catch any serious errors while the dictated text is still fresh in your mind. It also gives ViaVoice a chance to catch up (if it's lagging behind). And if you really aren't sure what you originally said, you can use the Playback command to listen to the text as it was originally dictated—in your own voice.

ViaVoice Enhanced Edition. Actually, you *can* use ViaVoice in unsupported applications, but don't expect it to work 100 percent. I've had limited success dictating directly into Entourage message windows and SimpleText documents.

13
Utilities

Gene Steinberg is the chapter editor and author.

All right, so what's a utility?

This may date me, but my concept of a utility is someone who plays several positions on the baseball diamond; hence, the term *utility infielder* seems apt. One day he'll be at shortstop, the next day at third base. You get the picture.

So how does that relate to a computer and the category of utility software?

On a computer, utilities are programs that often defy definition, but, like the baseball equivalent, may serve a variety of functions. They range from applications that diagnose your Mac's hard drive to ones that provide some sort of Desktop decoration or Finder enhancement and just about everything in between. They provide essential and sometimes not-so-essential support services for other software and, of course, for your Mac. Although you won't use some of them very often, you will find others downright indispensable for special purposes. As for the rest, they add needed functions your Mac doesn't offer and they just, well, make your Mac look nicer.

With thousands of utilities out there, I can't hope to cover even a small part of what's available. Instead, I've made a few arbitrary decisions about what to select, focusing on some of the key players in a few popular software categories. The reactions to these programs are strictly my own. Feel free to disagree.

In This Chapter

Screensavers

Years ago, the theory ran like this: You needed a screensaver to protect your Mac's display from the burn-in phenomenon. It made sense, since when you look at the tiny ATM machine at a bank, you see images of the display burned into the screen itself.

So you bought a screensaver to protect your investment in your Mac's display. This made even greater sense in the days when even a basic 13-inch monitor cost upward of a thousand bucks. Now, with prices of similar-size products running below a couple hundred dollars, the issue of protecting the screen no longer seems quite so compelling.

In the old days, millions of Mac users ran screensavers of flying toasters and animated spaceships on their displays. There were active development programs to allow Mac users to create add-ons to Berkeley Systems' After Dark and competitors, such as BitJugglers' UnderWare.

After Dark gets minimal support these days, as its developer focuses on such hot-ticket items as its You Don't Know Jack series. BitJugglers is long gone.

But the real question is this: Do you really risk damage to your Mac's display if you don't use a screensaver? I posed that question to one of the larger display manufacturers, NEC Technologies. Its response? Monitors these days adhere to a worldwide standard called Display Power Management System (DPMS). This standard allows a display to slip into sleep mode after a preselected period of inactivity (you set it in the Energy Saver control panel on your Mac). Letting your display go to sleep when idle will definitely prolong its life. An activated screensaver produces a pretty picture, and the image's varying texture may prevent burn-in, but your monitor remains on when the screensaver runs, and that doesn't prolong its life—or save energy.

SETI@home

Whether or not you believe a screensaver makes any difference in the longevity of your Mac's display, wouldn't it be a fascinating experiment to use a screensaver for a valuable purpose?

A recent survey published in *Life* magazine indicated that 54 percent of poll respondents believe there is intelligent life in the universe. Some 30 percent actually believe we have already been visited (by those mysterious things called UFOs). The success of such movies as *Contact* and *Independence Day* indicates a continuing interest in the prospects of alien life, if only in fiction.

In the real world (as opposed to the reel world), scientists are conducting an ongoing search for evidence of life on other worlds. It's called the Search for

Extraterrestrial Intelligence (SETI). This enterprise uses a bank of radiotelescopes in Central America to check radio signals from the stars in the hope that one of those signals would display clear signs of a guiding intelligence—as depicted in *Contact,* for example (or in the low-budget film *The Arrival*).

Some of the folks behind this laudable effort got the bright idea of harnessing the power of millions of personal computers around the globe to assist in analyzing these radio signals. All these systems have to do is run a special utility, SETI@home, which connects to the SETI servers on a regular basis to retrieve a packet of data. Once the computer receives this data, it examines the packet for evidence of intelligence and then logs in to the server to send the results back to SETI and retrieve still more data to process.

The entire cycle can take anywhere from 10 to 30 hours (give or take a few) to finish. It all depends on how fast your Mac runs and on how much data the servers send for processing (it's not always the same). SETI@home runs either as a screensaver, which appears automatically after a selected idle period, or as an application (your choice). It can also do the number crunching in the background, but that defeats the purpose, since it has to juggle for processor time with your other applications.

Getting involved. To participate in the great worldwide search for ET, join an existing SETI@home team. Several popular Web sites already have programs in place. One is run by late-night broadcaster Art Bell (www.artbell.com) and another by PowerBook maven Jason O'Grady (www.go2mac.com/articles/read.cfm?id=45) [*Jason also contributed to this* Macintosh Bible; *see his section on Apple's portables in Chapter 2, "The Macintosh Family." —Ed.*]. Once you join a team, just download and install the software, and you're ready to make contact.

Macro Software for the New Millennium

Despite the great power of personal computers, you still have to do an awful lot of work manually. When you launch an application or document, you may have to dig through several nested folders to find the items you want. Even if you have made aliases on the Desktop or in the Mac OS 9 and earlier's Apple Menu or in Mac OS X's Dock, once the programs open, plenty of manual work remains. To create a new document, you visit the File menu and select New (or type ⌘N in most programs), bringing up a blank document window. Then you may have to go to the Page Setup or Document Setup box to set page dimensions. Next, you visit the Save dialog box to name your document and find a location for the file.

A macro program can end such simple drudgery and let you actually get some useful work done. Macro software takes a series of commands or steps and puts them on automatic pilot. You launch a little application (or applet) by clicking a button or typing a keyboard shortcut, and then the steps invoked by those shortcuts go into play.

Depending on the program you use to create these macros, you may have to type the codes in the macro language (as in AppleScript) or simply call up a Watch Me mode and perform the actions to have your macro constructed behind the scenes. The Mac OS 9 Finder supports this feature.

Some programs—such as Microsoft Word, AppleWorks, and Adobe Illustrator and Photoshop—come equipped with built-in macro-like functions (the latter two programs call these features *actions*). But you don't have to depend on a program's own features. There are other options.

 One useful feature of a macro program is the ability to batch process. Say, for example, you want to edit a bunch of pictures in Photoshop in precisely the same fashion. You can designate a special folder for that process and then set up your macro program to handle all the files identically. AppleScript can perform such shortcuts, using its Folder Actions feature. Folder Actions (a feature that, as of this writing, hasn't made it to Mac OS X) allows you to put items in a folder, and then, by opening that folder, trigger the script to do its stuff.

AppleScript. This program has the benefit of coming absolutely free as part of every standard Mac OS installation of recent years; there's even a very capable version for Mac OS X. AppleScript works with many Mac programs, so it's extraordinarily flexible. Yes, you do have to learn its English-like scripting language in many cases, but a Record feature in Script Editor lets you build a script by simply performing the proper steps and saving the result as an application. Not all programs support this feature, but where it's available (as it is in the Finder), you'll find yourself on the easy track to enjoying AppleScript's benefits. [*For more on AppleScript, see Peachpit's* AppleScript for Applications: Visual QuickStart Guide.*—Ed.*]

QuicKeys. One of the earliest desktop automation tools was CE Software's QuicKeys (www.cesoft.com; $49.95). This program is highly flexible and extensible, which is both its great advantage and its shortcoming. It works with AppleScript but uses its own routines to extend its macro-creation capability to almost any application out there.

QuicKeys creates macros that either work across the board (*universal* macros) or are limited to specific programs (such as the Finder). A series of separate extensions lets you customize the range of the program's capabilities at the expense of hogging a little extra system RAM.

If there's a downside to all this power, it's the manual, which just isn't as user friendly as it could be. More than once, I've seen users (not all computer novices, either) sitting there with QuicKeys installed, not knowing where to go next. You'll find more information and a demonstration version at the company's Web site, including the latest edition, which runs on Mac OS X.

Fortunately, the newest versions of QuicKeys have a helper application, QuicKeys Setup Assistant, which guides you through the basics of macro creation. Once you get accustomed to the routine, you'll feel more inclined to tap its power. Another great feature is the fully customizable toolbar palette, so you can activate your macro by clicking a button. You don't have to struggle to remember which keyboard shortcut you established (or frantically hunt for that printed macro list you left in another office by mistake).

A Macro Blast from the Past

One of the most powerful macro programs of years gone by was Tempo II Plus, from Ric Barron's Affinity Microsystems. This extremely powerful program offered programming-like features that could automate some of the most complex procedures imaginable.

One of my clients used the program for years, employing dozens and dozens of shortcuts to process form letters for insurance and educational purposes. Just watching him at work was amazing. He would press a couple of keys, and new documents would fly open, text entries would miraculously appear, the bottom of the document would be reached, additional information would appear, and new documents would open.

As he readied one document, another would also be printing, so a constant stream of paper emerged from his little laser printer.

A Casualty of the Times

In past editions of *The Macintosh Bible,* Tempo got high marks. Although the program had its quirks and conflicts, it was eminently useful for anything from simple procedures to complex batch processing of image files.

Tempo is no more. Barron has closed his company and moved on to other pursuits (at last report, he was marketing a video-editing product). However, Tempo lives on as dedicated users, including that client of mine, continue to mine its wealth of powerful features.

Even that client still religiously processes his complicated documents with Tempo, on a Power Macintosh G4, running Mac OS 9.1. This did require placing one of the components of the program, the Tempo II Plus 3.0 extension, in both the System Folder and the Extensions folder to allow it to function. In addition, he can't use the Microsoft IntelliMouse's custom actions to generate a macro. Go figure.

OneClick. Another variation on the macro theme is OneClick from WestCode Software (www.westcodesoft.com; $29.98 online). On the surface, it's just a floating palette for launching applications, offering buttons for your favorite programs. But OneClick's power extends way beyond that humble exterior. Each of those buttons can contain shortcuts to activate a variety of tasks. If you don't favor button clicking, it offers keyboard shortcuts too, just like QuicKeys. Version 2.0 also incorporates a "Record a Shortcut" component, so it can record your steps and build a macro based on them. Unfortunately, support for Mac OS X was not on the horizon at the time this book was written.

 OneClick has a devoted group of followers, some of whom have developed their own custom button palettes. You'll find a selection of these at WestCode's Web site, along with a demonstration version of OneClick. Some of these palettes are offered as shareware; if you like what the creators have done, they deserve your support.

KeyQuencer. Last but surely not least on our survey of macro software is Binary Software's KeyQuencer (www.binarysoft.com; $49.95). Unlike the other contenders in this derby, this program best suits power users. If the built-in shortcuts don't fit your tasks, you have to write your own. As of this writing, KeyQuencer lacked an automatic recording feature, so you have to write your own macros from the ground up. However, Binary promises that future versions will deliver more robust macros, with a version that is speedier and more reliable under a variety of Mac OS versions, but Mac OS X plans were uncertain when I wrote this chapter. A shareware version limits you to 50 active macros and a reduced feature-command set. At least you can get a functional version to see whether this program suits your needs. The company's Web site has more information.

Another Route to Keyboard Launching (Maybe)

Most of the time, a macro program launches a program via a simple keyboard command. That's no better than trying to staple a sheet of paper with a sledgehammer. There are more efficient ways to get the job done.

Beginning with Mac OS 8.5, Apple lets you set Function Key assignments in the Keyboard control panel. Just press this button and you can configure the Control Panel to launch any application or file with the press of a single button or hot key.

With Mac OS X 10.1, you have some of these capabilities through the Keyboard System Preferences.

Since a few programs already use the function keys, you may want to configure the Function Keys feature to access your hot keys *only* when you press Option simultaneously.

Disk-Repair Programs

A good diagnostic and repair program is as indispensable as your system software in making sure your Mac continues to offer reliable performance.

Disk First Aid (or Disk Utility). The great thing about Apple's Disk First Aid is that it's free and ships with the Mac OS (for Mac OS X, it's part of Disk Utility, an application that also includes the functions of Drive Setup, Apple's disk formatting application). The other great thing is that it lets you check and repair drive-directory problems on a startup disk (except for Mac OS X, unfortunately). Disk First Aid accomplishes this magic by closing all your open applications and then, in effect, suspending changes to the hard-drive directory until it does its work. Although Disk First Aid may not repair quite as many directory problems as the commercial utilities, don't sell it short. It gets the job done, and it's free. But the other programs are valuable because they offer many more features, as you'll see.

Disk First Aid doesn't just do its stuff when you launch the program. It also runs automatically at startup if you force your Mac to do an emergency restart using the reset function (or if you pull the plug by mistake), as long as you're running Mac OS 8.5 or later. Under Mac OS X, the disk check (indicated by the "Checking Disks" label on the startup screen) is done every time your Mac starts up, whether forced or not. By the way, you'll see a similar feature on a Windows system if you force a restart on one of *those* computers.

 The automatic scan feature of Disk First Aid only works on a startup drive. So if you have more than one drive partition or drive running on your Mac, you'll want to run Disk First Aid manually after a forced restart. Also, don't turn off the option in the General control panel that issues a warning when you restart your Mac or it is shut down improperly, or you'll lose the automatic scanning feature as well. Fortunately, the disk check process under Mac OS X is done for all available volumes.

DiskWarrior. One of a handful of cool utilities from Alsoft, DiskWarrior (http://alsoft.com; $69.95) is designed to do just one thing and do it well—diagnose and repair problems with the hard-drive directory. Rather than just fix the existing directory, this program rebuilds it from scratch, which Alsoft claims delivers more reliable performance and a more solid result. You have to run DiskWarrior from another drive (Alsoft gives you a CD that starts up most recent Macs as part of the package). After the program goes through its diagnostic routine, you get a report and the option to replace the drive's directory. If you click the Replace button, the program does precisely that, removing the existing directory and installing the optimized version. This program is especially valuable when you get recurring disk damage, with the same errors reported over and over even after you fix them. This has saved many folks the drudgery of reformatting the drive.

Alsoft's DiskWarrior gives you an opt-out option. You can use its Preview feature to examine the impact of its drive-directory replacement (**Figure 13.1**). In cases of severe directory damage, this is a helpful feature, because you get a chance to see whether any important files will disappear, and you can opt to either stick with what you have or back up the files before you continue.

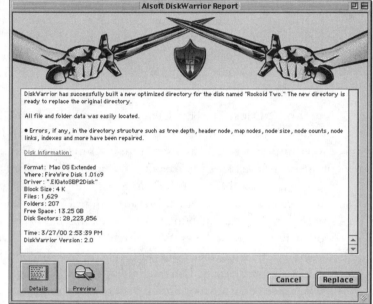

Figure 13.1

Once DiskWarrior checks your drive, you have the option to preview the fix before replacing the drive's directory.

TechTool Pro. MicroMat (www.micromat.com; $97.98) unabashedly markets its TechTool Pro as a bigger, badder answer to Norton Utilities. It can not

Figure 13.2

TechTool Pro checks both the hard drives and the hardware on your Mac.

only diagnose hard-drive directory problems and optimize your drive but also run your Mac through a bunch of hardware tests (**Figure 13.2**). It'll check your RAM, ROM, graphics cards, serial ports, network access, and Internet performance. The current version includes a virus-detection component, but the ability to detect all those Word and Excel macro viruses hadn't been added. One great feature of this utility (and of Norton Utilities, by the way) is its ability to retrieve files you've deleted by mistake. TechTool Pro accomplishes this miracle by creating an invisible folder of recently deleted items (you set its capacity in the TechTool Protection control panel). That way you don't actually delete the file—hence you can easily retrieve it intact. If you sign up for the AppleCare extended service program from Apple, you get a free version of this program, TechTool Deluxe. That version, however, doesn't check or optimize your hard drive.

TechTool Pro offers MultiTester and Navigation windows for fast access to its powerful features. The one pictured in Figure 13.2 is the Navigation window, which allows one-click access to the individual test routines. In the MultiTester window, you can customize each test suite. Don't worry that you'll get into confusing areas—TechTool clearly explains each option onscreen in the various test windows or in the manual.

Norton Utilities. The best-selling program for hard-drive diagnostics is still Symantec's Norton Utilities (www.symantec.com; $99.95). It doesn't offer the most features; in fact, it has lost features over the years. But it can handle most of the hard-drive issues you're apt to encounter. The package consists of several separate utilities, all of which you can access from a single screen (**Figure 13.3**). The Speed Disk component of Norton Utilities 6 can also optimize a hard drive's directory. Although the feature is reminiscent of the way DiskWarrior works, it's not identical. DiskWarrior replaces your hard drive's directory with an optimized version, rather than just repair the existing one. Norton Utilities's bag of tricks includes the Unerase application, which allows you to retrieve a file you deleted by mistake. So this feature can work effectively, make sure you have the Norton FileSaver extension installed—this tracks the files you delete (but it doesn't put them in any special place, as TechTool Pro does). If you manage to catch the mistake in time (before newly copied files over-write the old ones), you should be able to retrieve deleted files intact.

Figure 13.3

Norton Utilities is a set of integrated utilities with a sharp focus on disk repair and recovery.

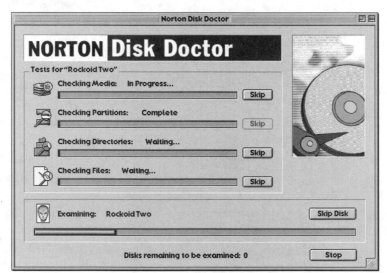

The Disk Doctor component of Norton Utilities shares an important feature with Apple's Disk First Aid: It can check and repair drive-directory damage on your startup drive. That means you don't have to run to a bookcase or scramble through the bottom of a desk drawer for a startup disk if Norton Utilities finds serious directory problems. TechTool Pro can pull off that trick, too, but not with Mac OS 9 or later (because of file-system changes). Unfortunately, none of the available utilities, so far, can fix a disk in place under Mac OS X.

Through the years, Symantec has lightened Norton Utilities's feature count by removing component after component. The backup module is history, along with Directory Assistance, an Open and Save dialog-box enhancer that some preferred to the now-departed Now SuperBoomerang, considered the most famous Open and Save dialog-box enhancer.

Drive 10. Do you want a genuine, Mac OS X–only drive-repair program? The first kid on the block again came from that upstart company MicroMat. Sporting a spiffy interface in the spirit of TechTool Pro, Drive 10 ($69.95) does one thing and one thing well: providing comprehensive diagnosis and repair. The interface is clear and clean, and it runs pretty fast (**Figure 13.4**). However, as with Apple's own DiskUtility, you can't check the startup disk. You have to restart from another drive or use the MicroMat's startup CD.

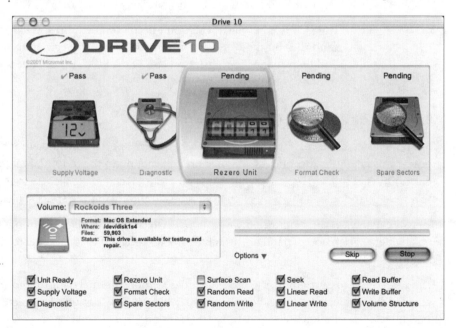

Figure 13.4

Drive 10 is the first official Mac OS X drive diagnosis application.

Compression Programs

Even if your Mac has a huge hard drive and you have the speediest possible access to the Internet, you need compression software.

Compression software uses a special algorithm to make files smaller. In addition to the obvious advantages of using hard-drive space more efficiently, a compressed file can shave a hefty percentage of time off moving files to or from the Internet.

It wasn't so many years ago that you had to think long and hard about which compression method you wanted for your Mac. The sixth edition of *The Macintosh Bible,* published in 1996 (an eternity ago in computer time of course), listed four product families in this category, and even then it didn't mention them all (it excluded a fairly popular entry, DiskDoubler Pro).

Today, just two product families are on the market. The rest are casualties of the fundamental change in storage efficiency and the higher speed of Internet file transfers. When hard drives typically maxed out at just a few hundred megabytes of data, any technique that could reduce file size was valuable—in fact, essential. Now that the smallest hard drives on new Macs span several gigabytes, compression has become less important.

But that doesn't mean you don't need compression software. If you intend to send files on the Web, for example, anything you can do to make a file smaller will help speed the transfer process. This little survey covers the compression options you'll want to consider.

An Overview of File Compression

In simple terms, compression software works by using a special software algorithm to check for redundant data. The algorithm creates a shortcut pointing to the redundant information, thus making the file smaller. Typically a compression program can make files 25 to 90 percent smaller. How much depends on the type of compression algorithm and the specific file involved.

There are two types of compression. One is *lossless,* which reduces file size without actually discarding any data. When you expand or extract the file, it's restored to its original form, complete with custom icons.

Using the other, *lossy* method, the program looks for nonessential data, or information you wouldn't miss unless you checked very carefully. It's primarily designed for pictures and movies. JPEG files, for example, are compressed in this fashion.

In fact, the popular DVD movie format uses a lossy compression technique that can fit an entire movie onto a $5\frac{1}{4}$-inch CD-type disc. The encoding process actually discards more than 90 percent of the information in a movie, but the visible difference when compared with the original is very slight (as long as compression is done correctly).

Compact Pro. This early shareware compression program from Bill Goodman still has a loyal following. It's $25, and though its menu is spare, it includes the essential features—optional password protection, self-extracting files, and the ability to segment archives so you can fit larger files on smaller media (**Figure 13.5**). What's more, it's thoroughly reliable and runs just fine under Mac OS 9 and in the Classic environment under Mac OS X. Compact Pro is also an example of how a capable programmer can write tight code and not stuff (forgive the pun) your hard drive with extra files. In fact, the last-released version used just 512 Kbytes of RAM (even on a Power Mac) and occupied just 336 Kbytes of disk storage space. Goodman probably doesn't earn much money from this program these days, but I hope he'll seriously consider a creating a version for Mac OS X. Check www.cyclos.com for the latest version.

Figure 13.5

Compact Pro, a shareware compression utility, is simple to use, yet it gives you top-notch performance.

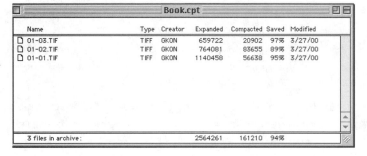

An Overview of the StuffIt Family

The compression standard-bearer on the Mac platform, StuffIt from Aladdin Systems (www.aladdinsys.com; $79.95), isn't just one program but comes in several variants, depending on whether you buy the retail version or just use the versions that come packaged with all new Macs these days. I'll try to separate the confusion from the confusion here.

StuffIt's history is an all-American success story. It began life as shareware, the brainchild of a 15-year-old high-school student, Raymond Lau. Later it became a commercial program, with loads and loads of extra features added. It's also an industry standard. Almost every compressed Mac file you'll find on America Online (AOL) or in the rest of the online world comes in StuffIt format, except for the odd file from devoted followers of other compression programs (most of which are no longer produced).

Apple even bundles two StuffIt components, DropStuff and StuffIt Expander, with its Mac OS 9 and earlier operating system releases (as long as you install the Internet-access component of the system software) and on your new Mac. Mac OS X includes a native version of StuffIt Expander.

Here are the basic features of the program:

- StuffIt in its various forms creates an archive, a single file that can contain one or more compressed files.

- StuffIt can segment files, dividing them into smaller pieces so they fit on smaller media. For example, if you have a 400 MB archive but only 100 MB Zip disks on which to store them, you can turn the archive into four segments. When the pieces arrive on a larger drive, StuffIt rejoins them and then expands them.

- StuffIt extracts files in many popular compression formats, including TAR (for Unix-based files) and Zip (the popular DOS-based compression system).

- StuffIt can create self-extracting archives, which contain the expansion program in the compressed file itself so you don't need to have a copy of StuffIt on hand to extract the file. This feature adds a little to the file size but not enough to fret over.

- The retail version of StuffIt adds a robust security feature: password protection. You can set up your files so that only someone who knows the password can expand them.

 StuffIt can also extract archives created in Compact Pro and in DiskDoubler (but you need to have a copy of DiskDoubler at hand), so it's sort of a chicken and egg situation. What to do? See if someone has a copy of DiskDoubler Expander for you to use (this was the free extractor version of the program).

StuffIt Deluxe. This is the full-featured retail version of the program. It does all of its work in a single application window with a Finder-like interface but offers extra frills to simplify the compression process (**Figure 13.6**). One of those frills is True Finder Integration, a menu-bar option that lets you access the program's major features at the Finder level without touching the application itself. The Deluxe package includes both DropStuff and StuffIt Expander.

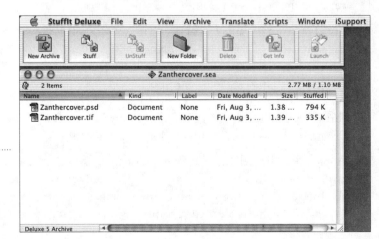

Figure 13.6

StuffIt Deluxe provides all the file-compression tools you've ever dreamed of—and then some.

True Finder Integration is sensitive to changes in various Finder versions. Whenever Apple updates the Mac operating system, more than likely you'll have to await an update from Aladdin to prevent crashes or other untoward behavior. With the newest version of StuffIt, Aladdin has added back in the Magic Menu portion to Mac OS X.

DropStuff. The shareware version ($30) of StuffIt is a simple application that offers drag-and-drop compression with a reasonable subset of StuffIt Deluxe's capabilities. It lacks segmenting capabilities but offers most of the other important features of the retail program.

StuffIt Expander. It's free, and if you never need to compress a file, this may be all the compression software you'll ever have to deal with. StuffIt Expander's drag-and-drop interface handles many of the same compression formats as the Deluxe version's.

Web browsers are usually set up to use StuffIt Expander as a helper application. So when you download a compressed file, it expands automatically without requiring that you do anything. If this isn't happening under Mac OS 9 and earlier systems, check your browser's preferences, the Internet control panel, or the Internet Config application and make sure your version of StuffIt is listed as a helper application for the various forms of compressed archives.

StuffIt Spacesaver. Consider this the last of a dying breed. Like AutoDoubler, it's a background compression program that works with most of the files on your drives, except for system-related components and other exceptions you select. It also fools the Finder into showing the files in their uncompressed form, as long as the Spacesaver extension is active. It's packaged with StuffIt Deluxe but requires separate installation. Unless you have an older, smaller hard drive and need that disk space desperately, there's little reason to use this program anymore. This is another utility that hasn't migrated to Mac OS X.

The Short Happy Life of a Utilities Developer

There are easier things to do than write utilities. Developers often get their utilities to perform magic by taking advantage of undocumented or even unauthorized system services in the Mac OS. Because of this trick, however, when Apple updates its OS, utilities are often the first to break, making utility vendors scramble to rewire their software. And if a utility is extremely useful (say, Now Menus and Now SuperBoomerang), Apple will eventually work some sort of equivalent capability into its OS, such as the revised Open and Save dialog boxes that came with Mac OS 8.5.

DropZip. If you create compressed archives for the DOS and Windows platforms, you can either force the recipients to get the Windows version of StuffIt Expander or stick with what they have, a Zip utility of one sort or another. Although several Mac-related Zip programs exist, DropZip ($20) is the only one that has functioned reliably with all sorts of files I've tried. It's part of StuffIt Deluxe and just another compelling reason to consider upgrading to the full version of the program.

MindExpander. This freeware utility comes from the geniuses at MindVision (www.mindvision.com), whose popular Vice application is the core of program installers from a variety of companies (including Adobe and AOL). MindExpander offers StuffIt Expander some competition. During the installation process, it even gives you the option to substitute MindExpander for StuffIt to handle the compressed files you receive from the Internet. If you want to look over this choice for yourself, pay a visit to the company's Web site.

The Sad Fate of DiskDoubler

Although StuffIt owns the Mac compression-software market nowadays, this wasn't always true. At one time, a little upstart program called DiskDoubler from Salient Software, the brainchild of Lloyd Chambers and Terry Morse, held sway in the market. At the beginning, DiskDoubler was the simplest compression program out there. It put up a convenient menu that handled all the program's chores.

Its developer even managed to sell a user license to Apple Computer, and within short order DiskDoubler was the most popular game in town.

DiskDoubler's popularity brought with it a demand for sequels. On the heels of DiskDoubler came AutoDoubler, an early example of background file compression. While your Mac idled, AutoDoubler would compress your files; then it would extract them when you opened them. What's more, it was transparent to the user because of the way the program worked with Apple's Finder (Spacesaver users will find this feature familiar). Your drive looked exactly the same and the document icons looked the same, but they were really compressed, so you got more data on the very same drive.

Then came CopyDoubler, a program that sped up Finder copies, did scheduled copying, and also featured Smart Replace, which only replaced the files on another disk that had changed (making it a simple, reliable, no-frills backup method).

Eventually the company was sold, first to Fifth Generation Systems, and then to Symantec, which eventually allowed the whole DiskDoubler suite to die out. A lack of compatibility between DiskDoubler's Finder menu and Mac OS 8 put the nail in the coffin, though the DiskDoubler application still functions quite nicely with the latest Mac OS versions, including Mac OS 8, Mac OS 9, and, in the Classic environment of Mac OS X.

By the way, the copy component in Connectix's Speed Doubler duplicated and perhaps surpassed CopyDoubler's core functionality, but Speed Doubler apparently died with the advent of Mac OS 9.

The End of Driver-Level Compression

Once upon a time, some compression programs worked on the drive level, not the file level. Programs such as eDisk and Stacker worked with the hard-drive device's driver to shrink files while copying them to a drive and to expand them as they opened. In the days of 100 MB and 200 MB drives, having drives seem to grow at least twice as large, at the expense of some speed, seemed like a sensible trade-off. Performance was reduced, sometimes slightly, sometimes noticeably, depending on the speed of the Mac and the speed of the drive.

Unfortunately, such programs incurred some severe risk factors. For one thing, the standard disk-repair programs could inflict permanent damage on a drive's directory when they tried to make repairs, because they weren't compatible with the compression drivers. If the files themselves were damaged, those same drive-repair utilities would be unable to help. Although the compression programs themselves came with utilities for such problems, the jury was always out as to how robust these were.

With hard drives getting bigger and faster, the need to compress a whole drive went the way of the dodo bird. Today, you can buy internal drives with 60 GB or more of storage for a couple hundred dollars, so there's no reason to use any of those old programs, if you still have one on hand. The fact that the companies have gone out of business is another warning sign.

I cannot overemphasize this point: If you still have one of those driver-level programs around, don't use it—instead, back up your data and reformat your drive in the normal way, without using the compression program's own formatting feature. If you need more space, buy a bigger drive.

The Ultimate Extensions Manager

For several years, Apple has offered a free program to manage the stuff in your System Folder—Extensions Manager. Based on a freeware utility, Extensions Manager can toggle on or off control panels, extensions, startup items, and items that are loose System Folder components. You can also create startup sets in case the items required to run one program influence the way another program works. The Mac OS–specific sets (Base and All) can isolate conflicts by restricting your startup programs to Apple's. You can even get basic information about what a strangely named extension does and then decide whether you need it.

Conflict Catcher. This product from Casady & Greene (www.casadyg.com; $79.95) does a whole lot more than the Extensions Manager. Designed by programmer Jeffrey Robbin, Conflict Catcher is a tour de force (**Figure 13.7**). It builds upon the basic capabilities of Extensions Manager and can toggle the items in the Apple Menu Items, Contextual Menu Items, Control Strip Modules, and Fonts folders. You can also check the Internet Search Sites folder (used for Apple's Sherlock search tool) and the Location Manager Items folder.

Conflict Catcher is smart enough to disable a program it knows will conflict with another because they perform the same function. So if you're using FWB's CD-ROM ToolKit to run your Mac's CD drive, Conflict Catcher will turn off Apple's CD driver. I'm just going to list a few of its greatest features; if I seem to go on interminably, it's because Conflict Catcher is a marvelous piece of work. I recommend downloading the limited-time trial copy from Casady & Greene's Web site—then see for yourself if you want to buy a copy. Even though there seems no need for such a program under Mac OS X, it can still work quite well in the Classic environment (just be sure to get the 8.0.9 update to avoid seeing a serial number prompt each time Classic launches).

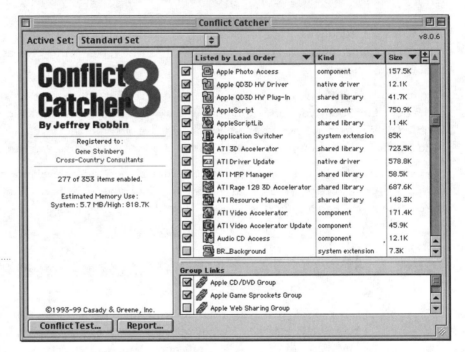

Figure 13.7

You can manage extensions and check for conflicts with Casady & Greene's Conflict Catcher.

 In addition to taking care of the basic System Folder items, Conflict Catcher can handle the plug-ins for many of your favorite productivity applications, such as Adobe Illustrator, Adobe Photoshop, Microsoft Internet Explorer, Netscape, and Quark's QuarkXPress (Quark calls them XTensions). You can also include other add-on folders using the program's simple preferences panel.

 The stock and trade of Conflict Catcher has been its legendary Conflict Test. This feature helps you isolate repeatable system problems by systematically turning System Folder components off and on using its own clever internal logic. Over five or ten restarts, Conflict Catcher will often find your culprit. It can even help you find *multiple conflicts,* created by the interaction of several programs.

The prospect of having to perform a clean install got you down? Conflict Catcher 8 introduced a Clean-Install System Merge feature that does precisely as advertised. When you run a clean system install via Apple's Mac OS installer, you get a brand-new System Folder, and the older one is relabeled Previous System Folder. Conflict Catcher goes to work comparing the two and reports the differences to you. Once you examine the list, you can move over your non-Apple extensions, Internet preferences, and other key items you need to restore your System Folder to full functionality.

Backup Software

Next to hard-drive diagnostic software, backup applications are perhaps the most indispensable products. Although you may view backups as drudgery and a task you prefer to put off until next week or next month, the first time you lose a file, you will appreciate the value of that extra work.

Perhaps you think only large businesses need to back up—but almost every Mac user has a file he or she would want to preserve in case of emergency. It could be your personal Quicken checkbook, or your TurboTax or Kiplinger TaxCut income tax return, or perhaps that important cake recipe you intended to save for your child's next birthday. Maybe it's that new novel you're working on, hoping some big publisher will fall in love with it and make you the next Tom Clancy (hmmm, that sounds like me).

Regardless, you'll want to know that you can restore your precious files should your house catch file, your office fall prey to theft, or a power outage catch your file in midsave.

Backing Up the Cheap Way

You don't *have* to buy extra software to back up your files. If you just copy the essential ones to a second drive on a regular basis, you'll be reasonably safe. You might consider storing a second copy in another location in the event that something happens to your office or home. This is fine for simple backups, but because this is a chapter about software, I'd be remiss not to mention some of the options available. I'll start with my favorite.

A Brief Look at Backup Software

Without a doubt, Dantz Retrospect (www.dantz.com) is my favorite backup utility. I've used it without fail for several years—ever since I got the backup religion (which was shortly after I had to juggle a few book contracts and became paranoid about the possibility of losing files). Paranoia is a great incentive to do something important you might have otherwise overlooked.

Retrospect comes in three forms, depending on your needs and the sort of software bundle you get. The program is packaged free with some backup drives. Once you discover all the great things this program can do and how easy it is to use, you'll wonder how you got along without it or maybe thank your stars that you didn't suffer data loss along the way (**Figure 13.8**).

Figure 13.8

Retrospect can deliver the goods when it comes to getting reliable backups.

Retrospect Express. This is the low-cost, no-frills version ($49). But it doesn't scrimp on the essentials—far from it. This utility is tremendously powerful and only misses out on a few features compared with its higher-cost siblings. Let's first see what it does, and then I'll tell you what it *doesn't* do.

First off, it's scriptable. Before you start fretting over visions of writing complex commands in some arcane language, let me explain that the feature is called EasyScript—and rightly so. All you have to do is answer a few simple questions about the sort of backup you want, where it's coming from and where it's going, and then how often and when you want to do it. Once you answer these questions, Retrospect Express performs two basic kinds of backups. A full backup simply means that everything you want duplicated goes into a special file, called a *storage set.* You can even back up your entire drive, and Retrospect will store a snapshot of that drive, a picture of its contents and exact folder layout. If the worst occurs and you need to restore your files, Retrospect will restore the entire disk, with all files, folders, and desktop icons positioned exactly the way they were at the last backup. In this respect, this feature is exactly like the Restore CD feature that comes with new Macs these days. Of course, Apple's Restore CD (or CDs, since some models have up to four) only restore the computer to shipping condition; they can't touch the files and applications you've added.

You have a wide variety of options for backup media. You can use another hard drive, another partition on your current drive (this isn't something I'd recommend, because if a drive goes down, the partitions all go with it), or a removable device, such as a Zip, Jaz, Peerless, or SuperDisk—or even a CD.

Now we come to the program's limitations. Unfortunately, Retrospect Express doesn't support tape drives, nor does it offer network backups.

You can easily get around Retrospect Express's lack of support for networks by backing up everything to a network server (or any computer you designate for that function) and then using Retrospect to back up the server. This means you have to remember to send the files to the network so Retrospect makes a copy.

Retrospect Desktop Backup. The middle of the product line ($149) is so close in setup to Retrospect Express that it may be difficult to tell them apart at first glance. But this higher-end version of the program fills in small holes in the feature set. It does support tape drives and it can perform network back-ups automatically when you install a client or workstation version on each Mac in your network. You don't get 20 separate disks; you just get one copy of the workstation version, plus user licenses for each *seat,* or networked Mac.

Retrospect also comes in Windows versions. So if you must flirt with the Dark Side of the personal computing world, and you have labored to set up a cross-platform network, you'll be pleased to know that you can handle all of your backup chores with just one program.

Of course, you have to buy a separate user license to back up from each Mac (the software checks the serial numbers across the network), but the price is modest enough to make this an essential purchase. Even if you received the basic version of the program bundled with a backup device, you can easily get extra user licenses from the publisher or your dealer.

Retrospect Workgroup and Server Backup. Those top-of-the-line versions include the regular software and 20 client licenses (Workgroup; $299) and 100 client licenses (Server; $499), so you have a full network package in one box. There's no other difference between this and the regular version of Retrospect Destkop Backup.

You can also configure Retrospect Personal Backup to back up your keystrokes, so if you lose a document because of a crash or corruption, you can at least retrieve the text portion and get back to work.

Intego Personal Backup. If you don't need network support or the ability to work on tape drives, Intego (www.intego.com; $39.95), developer of two popular security programs, produces this ultrasimplified backup utility. You manage everything, including backup scheduling, from a single control panel.

What About Mac OS X?

Backups under Mac OS X are another story entirely. As you may have observed, there are many "invisible" files placed on your drive during the installation of Apple's latest operating system. Worse, there is support for additional file systems, such as the Unix-based UFS. Present-day backup utilities won't see all of these files, and hence your backups may be incomplete. What to do?

Fortunately, the developers of backup software were, at the time I was writing this chapter, fully aware of this disparity. Dantz, for example, was tying up loose ends on the Mac OS X 10.1 version of its Retrospect backup software.

In the meantime, if you do not have a Mac OS X–savvy backup program on hand, you can still do manual backups of your documents, applications, and Users folder, by copying the files to another drive. That way, you can gain a reasonable amount of protection, at least until you buy a full-fledged backup program.

Virus Software Profiled

The renewed popularity of the Mac platform has, sad to say, given new life to the moribund Mac virus threat. Although the problem isn't nearly as compelling as what Windows users face, it nonetheless poses a serious danger. And with Mac OS X's Unix underpinnings, Mac users are now open to the Unix viruses they once safely ignored.

In the old days, you had several antivirus programs from which to choose—freeware, shareware, and commercial. For various reasons, most have departed.

 Even if your old antivirus software works just fine with the newest Apple system versions (Mac OS 8.5 and later, Mac OS X), it's still not a good idea to continue using them. The key reason is that you probably can't update the virus-detection definitions of these programs. Since computer viruses arise unpredictably, you need to update your virus program regularly to find the additional strains.

Those virus protection programs left standing, however, can capably protect your Mac, if you use them correctly.

Norton AntiVirus. Originally, this program was called SAM, short for Symantec AntiVirus Utilities for Macintosh. In an effort to keep its product line's moniker consistent across platforms, Symantec changed the name. The program ($69.95) has added new features, and its latest versions scan faster. By default, it will scan files downloaded from the Internet to minimize the risk in handling e-mail file attachments. Symantec is also good about delivering virus definition updates once a month, protecting you from the latest and most virulent threats to your Mac.

Norton AntiVirus has a LiveUpdate feature (which it shares with Norton Utilities). You can set it up to connect to Symantec's Web site on a regular basis to retrieve program and virus-definition updates.

Norton AntiVirus creates an invisible scan file when it checks a drive. The next time you run the program, it checks the reference file and only scans those files that have changed. This greatly speeds up performance on rescans.

There's a version for Mac OS X. That way, you can continue to protect your Mac from possible virus infections in the new environment. While many Mac viruses are limited to the Mac OS 9 and earlier, AppleScript and macro viruses may affect either.

Well, this is both good and bad: Norton AntiVirus checks the items in your System Folder as you start up your Mac, and can add lots of seconds to the startup process. Alas, you can't turn off this feature. It's the price you pay for security.

The initial Mac OS X release of Norton AntiVirus couldn't do background scanning, nor automatically scan removable disks when inserted. You have to run the application manually on occasion to keep yourself protected. Symantec promised that the other features would be restored in a later release.

Virex. The most popular commercial alternative to Norton AntiVirus, Network Associates's Virex (www.nai.com; $49), matches its competitor almost feature for feature. It offers SpeedScan, which sets up a reference file so the program only has to examine changed files to provide secure protection against viruses. The program updates automatically each month, and—like its competition— it will check downloaded files. I find myself leaning ever so slightly toward this program because it doesn't have to check your System Folder at each startup (hence your startups go faster). A Mac OS X version was being developed when this book was written; the early beta versions, like Norton AntiVirus for Mac OS X, weren't able to do background or automatic scans.

Although the automatic update is a useful tool to keep your program current, the one Virex offers, called eUpdate, often doesn't work. In addition, Virex's confusingly organized Web site sometimes makes you go through hoops to get needed software updates fixing program bugs.

VirusBarrier. A little company called Intego is trying to gain one up on the giants in the Mac utility industry. First it came out with NetBarrier, a personal firewall application, and then VirusBarrier, a nicely designed alternative to Norton AntiVirus and Virex. VirusBarrier ($49.95) has all the features you expect, such as fast scanning and automatic updates for new virus definitions. A Mac OS X version is promised.

Surveying Security Software

If your Mac is set up at your home or in a small office, you probably don't think much about security. You know everyone who has access to your Mac, and you do (one hopes) trust them to act responsibly.

But we live in a dangerous world where the integrity of one's personal property isn't guaranteed. Even in a home or small office, someone could break in and steal your computer and then have access to all of your personal records (financial and otherwise).

If you work in a larger office, there are many reasons why you might want to restrict access to certain files, especially those containing confidential business records or information you maintain on a need-to-know basis.

You'll want to explore some security options to protect your Macs and your files.

Mac OS 9's Enhanced Security

Starting with Mac OS 9, Apple took the hint about the need for greater security measures and offered three ways to make your Mac more secure:

Finder-level encryption. Select a file and then from the Finder's File menu choose the Encrypt option. You'll get a prompt to create a password and secure the file. You'll need that same password to extract the file.

Keychain Access. The Keychain Access application lets you store all user-access passwords in a single control panel, accessed by still another password. If you are, like most folks, constantly dealing with various password requests to open documents or access a Web site, it's nice to know you can retrieve your passwords via a single command.

Keychains require support from third-party programmers, so check to see if your programs support this feature.

Multiple Users. Whether you share your Mac with a coworker or a child, you may wish to create a customized user environment for each individual. You can use the Multiple Users Control Panel to limit another user to specific programs, files, and even the contents of certain disks.

Your password is your voice. The Voiceprint component of Multiple Users is an option you can use to store a recording of yourself and use that to access your user environment. Fortunately, you can revert to a written password in case a cold or sore throat prevents your Mac from recognizing you.

Mac OS X Is a Multiple User System

 By default, Mac OS X is, because of its Unix core, an operating system for multiple users. After you install Mac OS X and step through the Setup Assistant, you establish your initial user account, which makes you the owner or administrator of your Mac.

Once your computer is set up, you can easily added extra users and decide whether to give each user administrative access.

What do you lose if you don't have administrator access? Well, first of all, network and other settings in the System Preferences application that have padlock icons on the setup screens. Second, you can only access the contents of your personal home folder, not the folder of any other user.

But you are also able to create your own custom desktop, configure your copy of your favorite Web browser with your own bookmarks or favorites, and even install your own person set of fonts (Mac OS X has four font-related folders in all, but that's the province of Chapter 18, "Fonts").

Security Software Profiled

If you find the Multiple User environments of Mac OS 9 and Mac OS X too limiting, or if you have an older operating system, Apple pretty much abandons you when it comes to offering a secure environment. Although they occupy a much smaller playing field these days, several programs deliver a good range of security options.

Power On Software (www.poweronsoftware.com), the folks who bring you Action Utilities, also produce a pair of handy utilities (including one acquired from Symantec) that provide a pretty extensive range of security.

On Guard. This program is useful for single Macs or for large office situations, since it can manage user access across a network ($59.95). You can control the access of each individual user to files, folders, programs, and disks. One option prevents a user from downloading files off the Internet, if you use Netscape. Since this feature can also prevent access to another browser, such as Microsoft Internet Explorer, it's a pretty robust level of protection.

DiskLock. Symantec formerly produced this program, but support languished in recent years until Power On took it over and enhanced it ($89.95). As the name implies, DiskLock can restrict access to a disk or you can customize the level of protection for files and folders. The highest security level offered includes DES encryption, which is as solid as it comes.

In addition to Personal Backup, Intego offers two programs—highly rated by computer magazines—that have stood the test of time. (In case you're wondering, these programs all used to be published by ASD Software, which later sold them off to Intego.)

DiskGuard. Available in a single-user or remote form (for networks), DiskGuard ($49.95) offers two levels of protection. The master password grants you access to everything. The user password delivers access only to a specific user's files and folders.

FileGuard. This program takes security to a much higher level by allowing you to customize an extensive level of user privileges to meet your specific needs. A remote version suits network situations. FileGuard ($59.95) also lets you encrypt files before you transfer them and provides several levels of security, up to full Triple DES encryption.

The Obligatory ResEdit Section

No chapter on Mac utilities is complete without a discussion of Apple's free application-resource editor, ResEdit. This program takes full advantage of the way Mac OS 9 and earlier software is designed. Every Mac OS 9 and earlier application has a *resource fork,* containing all the visible parts of the program, such as its dialog boxes, menus, icons, buttons, and other interface elements. It also has a data fork, containing the core program code, which you don't want to mess with unless you have at least some knowledge about writing software.

If you don't like the keyboard shortcuts a program offers, or the way a menu is labeled, or the presentation of its graphics elements, ResEdit gives you the chance to change a few things to your taste. But you can't just jump in and change things around without a measure of caution. One wrong move, and the program will fail to run or will crash without mercy.

However, if you observe a few cautions, you can have a merry old time making your favorite programs work a little more to your liking.

Before you jump in and modify a program, you may also want to check its options for setting preferences. Some applications actually let you modify toolbar buttons and keyboard shortcuts (Microsoft Word and Adobe InDesign are prime examples), so you don't need to fool around with a third-party program.

While ResEdit continues to function with pre-Mac OS X applications, don't think about trying it with Mac OS X applications. All you can do is just damage the file.

Before You Start

Even if your favorite application has features that allow you to make it look exactly the way you want, you might be tempted to look over ResEdit anyway, just to experiment and see what sort of damage—er, improvements you can make.

 ResEdit has not been updated in several years. The latest release version, 2.1.3, came out in 1994. Although it seems to work all right with recent programs, if you find it keeps quitting on you or otherwise fails to run properly, the best thing to do is *give up*. It's just not worth the aggravation for a few minor program modifications.

Even if ResEdit seems to work fine, take these additional precautions before proceeding:

Make a copy of the file you're editing. Don't attempt to modify the original file. This is especially true if you decide to fiddle with the Finder or System files. Make a copy and work on that. That way, if you do something wrong, you can easily restore the original.

Don't erase or create anything. Each item you see when you open a file in ResEdit is essential for that program to function. Although you can modify a handful of items, removing a key resource can result in dire consequences for that program. It may run all right, but you could find it crashing unexpectedly.

Don't try to reprogram an application. Becoming a software engineer requires training and practice, and the software license may even prohibit modifications to a program. You can, however, play with the following items during your explorations of ResEdit's possibilities, so long as you observe the proper cautions: DITL, DLOG, ALRT (for dialog boxes); MENU, CMNU (for menus); STR# (the words in a dialog box or menu); PICT (the pictures you see in a program); CURS (the style of cursors a program uses); ICON, ics4, ic8, and so forth (for icons); and SND (for sounds).

A Fast Exercise with ResEdit

ResEdit comes without any documentation to speak of, so you're largely on your own. That's because Apple intended it as a tool for programmers of its Mac OS 9 and earlier, allowing them to check and make minor modifications to their applications, although plenty of Mac users peek into it from time to time.

Here's one way to use ResEdit to make a program behave more efficiently. This particular routine can add keyboard shortcuts to almost any application. Once again, make your changes in a copy of the program and not in the original, in case your handiwork produces undesirable results.

1. Launch ResEdit.

2. Go to the Open dialog box in ResEdit and locate and open the copy of the application you want to modify.

3. Find the MENU resource icon, and double-click it.

4. Double-click the icon representing the menu you want to modify. For example, choose the File menu if you want to add a keyboard command to the Save As feature (some programs have it already, most don't).

5. Click the Save As command and look for a box labeled Cmd-Key. Type a [Shift][S]. You'll see the shortcut added to the menu picture.

6. Choose Quit from the File menu, and then click the Yes button to save your changes.

7. Launch the copy of your application and make sure the keyboard shortcut not only appears but actually works. In this example, [⌘][Shift][S] should produce the Save As dialog box.

 Even if your ResEdit venture is successful, it's a good idea to keep a copy of the original application in case troubles arise later (or you just want to set things back to the way they were).

File Launchers

When you set up a new Mac with Mac OS 9, you already have a convenient method for launching your favorite applications and files with a single click—Launcher. This floating palette has buttons representing applications, files, folders, and disks. You can place any item that can appear as an icon in Launcher (**Figure 13.9**).

 Launcher is easy to set up and use, but for some reason the standard Mac OS 9 and earlier installation fails to turn it on. No problem. If you don't see Launcher on your desktop, go to the General control panel and check the box labeled "Show Launcher at system startup." To bring up Launcher before the next restart, just start it directly from the Control Panels folder.

 Mac OS X doesn't include Launcher: The Dock has taken over some of its capabilities. However, you can still run Launcher in the Classic environment if you like.

Figure 13.9

Just because it's free doesn't mean Launcher isn't a handy utility to have around.

Here's how to configure Launcher to your taste:

- To add an item, simply drag its icon to the Launcher window. Launcher doesn't actually store the file but creates an alias for it in the Launcher Items folder (within the System Folder). You can easily resize the window to accommodate the additional items.

- To remove an item from Launcher, hold down (Option) and then drag the item directly to the Trash. You may have to close and open Launcher to refresh it, and then the item will disappear.

 A Mac OS bug predating Mac OS 8.5 sometimes makes it impossible to remove an icon from Launcher. Should this happen, just open the System Folder, look for the Launcher Items folder, and drag the offending alias to the Trash. The next time you refresh Launcher, the icon will be gone.

 To change button size, just hold down ⌘ when clicking Launcher, and choose the Small, Medium, or Large button. The setting works best when set to Medium, but feel free to experiment.

 You can add separate buttons for additional lists of Launcher items. Just create a new folder and place a bullet (•) and a space ahead of the name. Put your additional Launcher aliases into the Launcher Items folder, inside the System Folder, and the whole shebang will appear as a separate accessible list in Launcher, identified by a button. Items dragged directly to the Launcher palette automatically go in whatever category you have open at the time.

A Look at More Launchers (and Docks)

The Launcher has the great benefit of costing nothing and may indeed be all you need in a launching dock. But the other options offer a far greater range of features that really stretch the frontiers of application and file launchers.

DragStrip. A former shareware program, this is Aladdin Systems's (www.aladdinsys.com; $20) variation on the program-launching theme. It has separate palettes for *running processes*—meaning the programs you have open (including background applications)—and for quick access to your files, applications, and folders. You can customize buttons by design and color, and the convenient drag-and-drop interface makes it easy to build custom palettes. Unlike some other programs, it runs strictly as an application rather than a system extension. If you wish DragStrip to launch at startup, just put an alias of the program in the Startup Items folder.

 You can configure the Process palette to hide other open applications when you access any single application from the palette.

 The sixth edition of *The Macintosh Bible* noted that one of the features missing from DragStrip was the ability to resize the palette as you add or remove items from the strip. Aladdin Systems hasn't fixed this shortcoming.

DragThing. A useful launching program, James Thomson's DragThing (www.dragthing.com; $25) comes in shareware form. In addition to handling files, applications, and folders, the program can store URLs for your favorite Web sites. DragThing has a host of options for customizing the shape and color of buttons and how they display. It also supports AppleScript and offers a healthy collection of built-in scripts to activate keyboard shortcuts. As with DragStrip, you can have it automatically install an alias for the program in the Startup Items folder so it launches when you start up your Mac.

 You can configure DragThing to hide open applications automatically when you access another application via the Process strip (the same as with DragStrip).

Choosing between these handy launchers is difficult. They have similar feature sets, but DragThing wins out by virtue of its simple support for AppleScript, ability to add URLs, and greater array of customization options. What's more, the latest version is Carbonized, meaning it runs under Classic, Mac OS 8.6 and later, and Mac OS X.

 The Dock. If you install Mac OS X, you won't see Launcher (unless you work in the Classic environment and enable Launcher). The Dock serves as the repository for applications, files, folders, and disks (**Figure 13.10**). It has a host of cool features, such as the ability to magnify icons when the pointer hovers over them, automatic resizing of icons, and the ability to disappear entirely until you point to the area where the Dock resides.

Figure 13.10

The Dock is Mac OS X's all-purpose launching area, putting all of your favorites a click away.

In response to tons of user requests, Apple added the ability to center the Dock at the left and right of the screen for Mac OS X 10.1 and later. If you haven't bothered to upgrade your initial Mac OS X setup, this additional feature (and the incredible performance boost and support for CD burning) may help change your mind.

Some Cool (or at Least Useful) Utilities

It's almost impossible to cover the breadth and scope of Mac utilities. There are so many thousands of programs to choose from that I have had to make a personal and arbitrary selection, simply addressing the ones that I find compelling. This final section of this chapter will cover some of the programs that appeal to my unusual sensibilities.

CapsOff. Amazing what ten bucks can deliver these days. Long ago, a Mac keyboard had a real detent for the Caps Lock feature. You got a tactile message when you were in all-caps mode. Unfortunately, on new keyboards Caps Lock is a mere toggle, with only a little light that goes on to identify which mode you're in. If you don't look down and you accidentally press the wrong key, you'll find yourself typing paragraphs of capitals before you know it. This is especially irritating in a chat room, where everyone will start wondering what you're yelling about. The CapsOff shareware program, from Redpoint Software (www.redpointsoftware.com), is designed to remedy this situation. You can set CapsOff to flash an icon and even play a sound when [Caps Lock] is engaged. And while we're on this topic, whatever happened to that old Caps Lock extension from Apple? Back in the days of the original PowerBooks, this little extension gave you a useful menu-bar display; alas, the Mac OS, from 8 on, no longer supports it.

Action Utilities. In the heady days of Mac System 7, the most powerful set of system-enhancement utilities around was Now Software's Now Utilities, a bunch of clever modules that took the Mac Finder to new frontiers. However, it fell on hard times, and promised updates for Mac OS 8 and later never seemed to happen. Some of the folks who founded Now Software went off to create a new utility maker, Extensis, where they have been making a bunch of great add-ons for such programs as Adobe Illustrator, Adobe Photoshop, and QuarkXPress. You'll even notice that the personalization dialog boxes in all the Extensis programs are the same as those for Now Utilities.

As for the original Now Utilities and Now Up-to-Date (a personal information manager), they were all sold off to Qualcomm, maker of cellular phones, and Eudora, one of the original Internet e-mail programs. There the programs languished (with the exception of an aborted attempt to update Now Up-to-Date). Finally an upstart company, Power On Software (www.poweronsoftware.com) —maker of On Guard, a security program—accomplished two feats within a very short time. First, it came up with its own answer to Now Utilities— Action Utilities. Then it bought all the original Now programs from Qualcomm.

If you still have an old Mac around with System 7, you'll be pleased to know that Now Utilities is still available, but you'll want to consider its successor instead. The final versions of Now Utilities had a poor track record for stability. Besides, Action Utilities ($89.95) has more to offer:

Each component of Action Utilities is available separately. What's more, you can download 30-day demos; if you like what you see, you can then purchase a user license directly from the company. Check the company's Web site for more information.

Action Files. This was the first of the new utilities that Power On released. Although a different programming team designed it, in many respects Action Files descends directly from SuperBoomerang. Like SuperBoomerang, it extends the capabilities of Open and Save dialog boxes way beyond anything Apple can offer (even with its new Navigation Services version that premiered in Mac OS 8.5) (**Figure 13.11**). It puts a Finder-like menu in these dialog boxes, where you can access pull-down menus of recently opened documents and folders (as well as add permanent menus for easy access). Like SuperBoomerang, it rebounds to the last opened document in a folder. A File menu adds file searches (unfortunately, Action Files can't search the *content* of files, as SuperBoomerang can) and basic file management, such as renaming, making aliases, and trashing files. The biggest question is what Power On Software will do for Mac OS X.

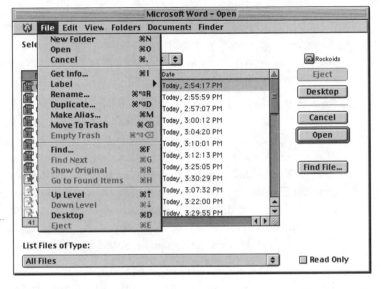

Figure 13.11

Action Files puts the Open and Save dialog boxes into overdrive.

Action WYSIWYG. This isn't just another font-menu modifier that lists fonts in the actual typeface and groups them into font families. It also helps you keep font menus at a manageable size, even if you are a font junkie and have a big library. Its trick is to split the menu into multiple panes so you can pretty much get a full font menu on any normal-size Mac display. As with the original Now WYSIWYG and Adobe Type Reunion, symbol and dingbat fonts appear in a generic style so you can see their names.

Action Menus. Pop-up menus everywhere—that's the hallmark of this utility. It replaces the Apple Menu Options control panel with submenus in the Apple menu but goes beyond that with special menu-bar icons for drive- and folder-specific pop-up menus. You can summon a pop-up menu via a keyboard command. With the help of Action Files, Action Menus delivers pop-up menus at each side of the menu bar for recent files, folders, and applications. You can configure every element of this program, from the basic icons to the number of items displayed.

Action GoMac. This is a commercial version of the popular shareware program, which delivers a Windows-style Start menu at the bottom of your Mac's display. It's an acquired taste, and one I haven't acquired, though many folks swear by this program. You can configure the contents of your Start menu to display just the programs you want and to get out of the way until you bring your mouse to the bottom of the screen. If this reminds you of Mac OS X's

Dock, you may be right. Task managers are a nice idea, even if they originated on other computing platforms.

Default Folder. Another useful Open and Save dialog box enhancer, available from St. Clair Software (www.stclairsoft.com; $25) as shareware, Default Folder adds four buttons to these dialog boxes, displaying pop-up menus of recent and favorite folders. File lists also rebound to the last opened document in a folder. You can also use it to create new folders and to move and trash files. While not as feature-packed as Action Files, it is a useful alternative—and cheaper.

Speed Doubler. This used to be an indispensable program. The ultraclever folks at Connectix (www.connectix.com) designed it to address some limitations in Apple's system software. For one thing, it gave you speedier emulation of older 680X0 software on Power Macs. It also offered a more efficient disk cache and provided copying features (such as Smart Replace, which replaces changed files but bypasses others) that Apple should have added to the Mac OS years ago. But SpeedDoubler has not kept up with the times; instead Connectix folded most of Speed Doubler into CopyAgent, its backup software ($39). Connectix had decided not to update Speed Doubler for Mac OS 9.

However, if you are using an older Mac operating system, you'll appreciate Speed Doubler 8. Connectix finally spun off an enhanced version of the program's copying component, perhaps as a modern-day answer to CopyDoubler, another orphaned program. For simple, scheduled backups, this could be a first-rate solution. The successor, Connectix CopyAgent, inherits its copying features, but that program will, apparently, never migrate to Mac OS X.

PopChar Pro. Say you want to add an accent to a word such as *résumé* or a copyright or trademark symbol. So you open up Apple's Key Caps, select a font, search for the character you want, and click the appropriate keyboard shortcut to create that character. Then you copy and paste it from the Key Caps text box into your document. Is there no better way? Yes, there is—PopChar Pro by Uni Software Plus. This handy utility puts up a menu-bar icon; click it to display a floating palette of special characters in the font you're using. Just click the character you want, and it pops up at the insertion point in your document. If you do lots of heavy-duty word processing or desktop publishing, you'll wonder how you managed without it.

SnapZPro. So how do book and magazine writers get all those perfectly cropped screen shots that show various programs in action? True, you can use the Finder's own screen-capture ability (which disappeared in Mac OS X 10.0 to 10.0.4 but returned in 10.1). But this feature is awkward, and it doesn't give you the opportunity to name files as you create them. Dealing with generic designations such as Picture 1, Picture 2, and so on gets annoying, especially when you have to open up a bunch of these files to see just what you captured. Ambrosia Software's SnapZPro (www.ambrosiasw.com; $49) does let you name your files, and it successfully captures pictures from many games—but that's only a small part of what this program does. It can also capture pictures on your Mac for QuickTime movies, and you can save your pictures in several formats, not just PICT—but also GIF, JPEG, PNG, TIFF, or MOV (for those movie captures). The best recommendation I can give this program is that I use it for all my books and magazine articles. The best news of all is the arrival SnapZPro X, which does everything the Mac OS 9 version did—and more. Check it out!

Yes, I know I'll get cards and letters now about the other 4,000 utilities I didn't cover in this chapter [*Yes: Send them to Gene and not to me.—Ed.*]. Well, maybe for the next edition.

PART **3**

Getting Creative

Editors' Poll: Has the Web Changed How Designers Approach Their Work?

DR: Because of its interactive nature, the Web has forced designers to understand how users interact with information. It's no longer enough to create a piece based on how people passively view it; now, a design has to encompass the next step—how the viewer will go past the initial design, deeper into the piece. Web design is one of the most demanding kinds of design work.

ML: Designers have changed the way Webmasters approach their work. The Web used to be the place to get information quickly. Now it's a place to waste bandwidth and time waiting for large graphics and embedded multimedia files to load. Not everyone has a T1 connection to the Net.

GS: I was schooled in traditional typography and design, and the transition to the Web has been a tremendous upheaval. The unpredictability of the Web is a big factor. You can control what comes off the printing press, but you can't control how a browser will mangle your Web site. So you are forced to compromise, so that the maximum number of people can see a reasonable approximation of your site's design and content without having to go out and seek a different browser.

SS: Just as we saw a huge influx of would-be desktop publishers leaping onto the bandwagon when layout software for the masses was introduced, we're now seeing a similar effect in Web design. Although many truly beautiful, awe-inspiring, and informative Web sites are out there, they are far outnumbered by gaudy, amateurish ones. As happened with desktop publishing, though, one of two things will happen. Either we'll get design templates that allow a novice to create a presentable Web site or people will realize that for a business site to look its best, they'll have to pay a professional designer.

JF: It has deranged designers' minds to the point that they have started to think that printed pages should look like Web pages.

DM: The influence of the browser on all content—print, television, multimedia, packaging, you name it—has been a curse. Everything today looks like a Web page or an element. Yech! This trend has ignored that each media type has its own strengths and design paradigms for delivering information. Why would anyone want to read a whole article in white text on a dark blue background? That may be fine for a display that pumps out light in the text but it's horrible for small text on a reflective media such as paper. Or why clutter a television screen—still a low-resolution device—with a passel of moving elements and text that blunts the impact of the clip.

JR: The influence of the Web is exaggerated. The iMac had more influence on consumer product design than the Web. I use the Web all the time, but it hasn't been the driving force in society and art that people make it out to be. It's not replacing books, it's not replacing retail stores, it's not replacing schools or libraries. The biggest design influence of the Web has been in the design of Microsoft Windows, where folders now act like Web browsers. Is this good?

KT: The Internet has made some things faster and more convenient for designers—clients can (and do) send text files and some photos electronically, and designers can return PDFs for approval and then send files for output. This saves paper, cuts down faxing and FedEx bills, and tightens turnaround times (which may or may not be a blessing). The effect of the Web is more problematic. Although designers can now buy and download fonts, clip art, stock photos, and other elements from Web sources, this easy access, coupled with pressure on the bottom line, has increased the use of generic art for much design work—to the detriment of visual and technical quality. (This is especially likely when clients pick up photos from the Web and expect to have them used in print work.) The effect of the Web on designers is a mixed bag, at best.

14

Graphics

Gene Steinberg is the chapter editor and author.

Even if you're an experienced artist, adapting to drawing on a personal computer is akin to entering an alien world, where you must master the foreign language of dots (or pixels) and objects so you can make pretty pictures. Fortunately, you can easily learn these skills, and once you adapt to the new techniques, you might even want to toss away your pen and pencil or paintbrush—or at least consider your newfound tools worthy additions to the older ones.

In this chapter, I first briefly describe the elements that make up a computer graphic. Then I cover some of the more popular graphics applications you'll want to consider for your illustrations. Finally, I present a set of hints and tips to help you get the most out of these programs.

In This Chapter

Bitmapped Graphics

The original imaging model of the Mac was called QuickDraw. This technology produces a picture that consists of little dots, or *bitmaps* (meaning a collection of tiny dots that use bits of computer memory to display). Each of these tiny dots is filled with a single color or just black or white. When combined, the little dots or pixels make up the picture you see on your Mac's display.

 For Mac OS X, Apple has embraced a technology based on Adobe's Portable Document Format, a vector-based imaging technique. In addition to providing ultrasharp display with built-in anti-aliasing (you may also see it called edge, text, or font smoothing), the new imaging model allows you to drag objects around the screen in real time, which means you can see the actual objects rather than just an outline.

One of the original Mac graphics programs, MacPaint, used bitmaps to create the shapes composing your illustration. Programs of this sort are called *paint* programs, because they work rather like real-world painting. With regular painting, you use your brush to cover up the parts of the picture you want to change or you rub off the paint and replace it with another picture. In a paint program, you have features such as the eraser tool that you can use to remove unwanted portions of your artwork.

Of course, MacPaint is history, but the paint component of AppleWorks incorporates an expanded version of its basic feature set. The very same basic techniques, greatly expanded, also form the basis of graphics programs such as Adobe's Photoshop.

Although the image is made up of little bits, most programs let you select and manipulate the entire shape, resizing and reshaping it to your taste. You can produce excellent illustrations in this fashion, but they have a serious short-coming. Because each dot is a fixed size, if you enlarge an illustration, the quality simply gets worse. The edges become jaggy, details get fuzzy—and the greater the size, the more blatant the effect.

The other graphics type, known as *vector* or *object-oriented* graphics, create the picture with shapes based on lines, rectangles, and curves, rather than with pixels. Because vector graphics consist of mathematically based shapes, you can easily scale them to any size without changing quality and print them at your printer's maximum resolution. For example, the artwork will appear at 300 dots per inch (dpi) on a 300 dpi printer and 1200 dpi on a 1200 dpi printer. Consider, in contrast, what happens to 300 dpi bitmapped artwork when you blow it up 800 percent (call it a nightmare in the making).

PostScript printers, which work best with such pictures, actually *convert* vector graphics to bitmaps during the processing or rasterizing of the document; only the printer's native resolution limits output quality.

Another huge advantage of vector graphics compared with bitmapped graphics is storage space. A vector graphic stays the same size regardless of the resolution at which you print it. The size of a bitmapped graphic changes depending on the number of pixels in it. Large color photos and other full-color pictures, for example, can occupy many, many megabytes of storage space.

Vector graphics made their debut back in 1986 in a program called MacDraw. As with MacPaint, AppleWorks incorporated and enhanced MacDraw's capabilities. For professional illustration, however, computer-based artists use programs such as Adobe's Illustrator and Macromedia's FreeHand, sometimes Deneba's Canvas, and (often if they're converts from the Windows platform) Corel's CorelDRAW.

I'll profile all these programs and some others (see the section "A Look at All-in-One Graphics Programs" later in this chapter).

 Graphics programs such as Macromedia FreeHand and Adobe Illustrator are considered PostScript illustration programs because the files made from these programs use the PostScript language and can print to a PostScript device (usually a laser printer with a built-in PostScript processor) at the maximum possible resolution.

A Short Story About a Dude Named Bézier

Would you believe that the PostScript page-description language owes a lot to a technique developed for car manufacturing?

Although its cars never really caught on in the United States, Renault is one of the biggest car companies in the world (and it's a big stockholder in Nissan, the Japanese auto giant). This isn't a book on automobiles or personal finance—I'm only mentioning this company because of the importance of one of its employees, a mathematician and engineer by the name of Pierre Bézier. It is from the work of this man that we get the term *Bézier curve*.

Bézier wanted to simplify the controls for machines that build auto parts. In the early 1970s, he invented a technique for making a curve that employs four points for each part of the curve. Each segment is made up of four parts: two endpoints and two anchor points.

Although the process is far from intuitive, once you master this business of manipulating points and handles, you can create all sorts of shapes, from the simple to the complex.

More than a decade later, the guiding lights of Adobe Systems, Chuck Geschke and John Warnock, used Bézier curves as part of the architecture for the PostScript page-description language. PostScript quickly became the standard for the printing and publishing industries.

Graphics File Formats

One of the most confusing aspects of working with graphics programs is the multiple file formats with which you must contend. In addition to a specific program's native formats, you'll encounter a handful of standards for bitmapped and vector files that can make the process of handling such files a chore (and sometimes a downright pain). Although most of the popular graphics programs can easily read and save files in many formats, handling the variety of files you get from a customer or over the Internet can tax your patience.

In this section, I boil down the list of popular graphics formats to those you'll encounter most often. I've included a few popular Windows-based formats in the mix, because cross-platform file handling is a reality even the most devout Mac user must face from time to time. I'll put the DOS file extensions in parentheses so you can easily recognize these files when you see them.

BMP (.bmp). This is the standard DOS or Windows bitmapped file format. It's the Windows equivalent of PICT, which I'll describe in a moment. You create this type of file when you use the print-screen feature in Windows to capture the image on your screen. Most Mac graphics programs (even AppleWorks) can read and export BMP files.

GIF (.gif). Short for Graphics Interchange Format, this is a standard format (originally created by an online service, CompuServe) for Web-based graphics and for any purpose where file size counts. It is pronounced with either a hard or a soft *g,* depending on whom you ask. Its biggest disadvantage is that the format can handle only 256 colors, and high-quality color images may take on a distinctly dithered aspect. But for the Web and for black-and-white artwork, it's just fine. In addition, you can animate GIF files to enhance the look of your Web site.

EPS (.eps). This composite file, also known as Encapsulated PostScript, stores both PostScript data for device-independent printing (meaning a printer outputs the file at its maximum resolution) and QuickDraw information for screen display. As with any PostScript file, you can scale it to any size, up or down, and print it at the highest resolution your printer can support—that is, if you have a printer with PostScript capability. If not, all you see is the jaggy, low-resolution QuickDraw image. EPS files are frequently inserted, or placed, in a page-layout program, such as Adobe's InDesign or Quark's QuarkXPress.

 You can buy PostScript software for many inkjet printers from companies such as Epson and Hewlett-Packard. These programs include Adobe's PressReady (which although discontinued, may still be available at your computer dealer), Birmy's PowerRIP, Epson's Stylus RIP Server, and Strydent's StyleScript (also discontinued, sad to say). These programs actually let you use your low-cost inkjet as a real PostScript printer. But they also consume lots of your Mac's memory and can be downright slow on an older Mac (not to mention buggy).

You'll also want to check with the companies to see whether their programs support your particular printer. As this book was written, only Birmy's software was being rewritten for Mac OS X.

JPEG (.jpg). This is a high-quality compressed image format (the name, an abbreviation for Joint Photographic Experts Group, is pronounced "jay-peg"). You can choose from several levels of compression in most programs that handle the format. The highest-quality setting produces images almost indistinguishable from the original, but they take up a considerable amount of disk storage space. The lower-quality settings cause the images to deteriorate noticeably. JPEG images don't usually suit text but are otherwise far superior in quality to GIFs (although they lack animation capabilities).

PICT (.pct). This is the standard classic Mac image format, which has the added potential to store both bitmap and vector attributes in the same file. Most Mac OS 9 and earlier programs save in this format. It's also the standard format for Mac OS 9 screen captures (although some programs let you save those in other formats).

TIFF (.tif). Short for Tagged Image File Format, this bitmapped image format is prominent in the publishing industry. A TIFF file may include black-and-white, grayscale, and color illustrations and photos. Although TIFFs offer extremely high image quality, file sizes can grow incredibly large. A big color photo, for example, may consume many megabytes of storage space. Both Macs and Windows-based computers can handle the format, but it's not as common on the Windows platform. This is also the standard format for screen captures in Mac OS X (and in Mac OS X 10.1, Apple restored the helpful ⌘ Shift -3 and ⌘ Shift -4 keyboard shortcuts for taking screen captures, which were missing in the earlier versions of its new OS).

Picking the Optimum Graphics File Format

Because most graphic programs support the majority of the formats I've listed, it doesn't make a difference which one you use, right? Not quite. Some formats are more suitable for one purpose, less so for others. Here are some examples:

Printing and publishing. Because of its scalability, EPS works best for line art. Photographs work best in TIFF format.

World Wide Web. JPEG works best for Web photos because of its ability to display in millions of colors with excellent quality (except at the highest levels of image compression). For Web logos, banners, graphics, and animations, you're best off with GIF despite its quality limitations.

Photos and artwork for family and friends. As long as you're not sending the files to someone using a Windows-based computer, PICT is just fine. Or just stick with the standard format provided with a specific program. When you want to send pictures to family, friends, or business contacts, JPEG is ideal, with the following caution: Each time you resave a JPEG image, more compression is applied. Save it several times and the quality deteriorates noticeably. It's best to use JPEG for the end product, the file you're sending to someone else. And don't forget to add the .jpg extension to the file name if you'll be sending your image to Windows users.

An Overview of the Key Players

The previous (seventh) edition of *The Macintosh Bible* emphasized three professional-level programs available at the time: Adobe's Illustrator and Photoshop and Macromedia's FreeHand. However, the graphics-software landscape has changed markedly, and you no longer have to depend on just these programs for superb quality. The field now offers strong competition if you want to explore some alternatives. For the sake of continuity, I'll start with an overview of the major entrants. Then I'll show you some other choices.

Professional graphic designers around the world use these three tools to produce the images you see in many of your favorite books and magazines. Web sites and even film and TV productions also use graphics created or edited in these programs.

The high-end programs have several features in common. These three applications can create and read documents in a variety of file formats, and they have superlative color-handling features. You can apply colors using the very same color palettes (from Pantone and other companies) that your printing house uses to run your job. You can also print full-color separations, a necessary feature for professional-quality printing.

Adobe Illustrator. This has been the standard-bearer among illustration programs since it first appeared in the late eighties (www.adobe.com; $399). At its heart, it's a PostScript drawing program, which means it creates vector-based artwork saved in the PostScript language. As software designers compete to outdo each other in terms of features, Illustrator has also taken on more and more of the aspects of bitmapped (or raster) drawing programs (**Figure 14.1**).

Beginning with Illustrator 9.0, for example, Adobe added the capability to create transparent drawings and text, a feature that brings the program closer and closer to the capabilities of another popular Adobe application, Photoshop. You can save your illustrations not only in the popular Web graphic formats GIF and JPEG but also in Macromedia's Flash (SWF) format, often used for Web-based animation.

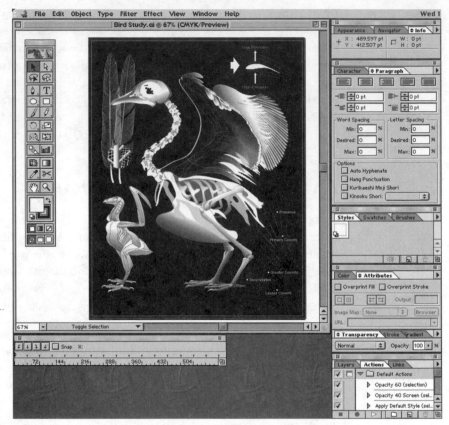

Figure 14.1

Adobe Illustrator has grown tremendously from its humble beginnings to emerge as the centerpiece for any artist's graphics-software bookshelf.

Other Web-based features include the ability to create buttons for your Web site with live drop shadows and shapes—meaning that you can create text for the shadow or shape, and the text will grow or shrink in size depending on its text content.

Like most Adobe programs, Illustrator promises—and delivers—integration and consistency. Adobe has taken Apple's integrated system environment to heart. Having mastered one Adobe graphics program, you can move on to another application from this clever company and apply much of what you learned.

On top of all that whiz and sizzle, Adobe Illustrator 9.0 is the leader among PostScript drawing programs. It provides an extensive range of tools designed to create professional-caliber illustrations, and offers extensive color support. [*As we were going to press, Adobe announced Illustrator 10. The company said the revision of the graphics program will run natively on Mac OS X 10.1; it may be available by the time you read this.—Ed.*]

After you get past the complexities of drawing using Illustrator's wide variety of pen and pencil tools to create handles and paths, you'll find this program a rich creative environment. It also offers a fairly extensive range of text capabilities, approaching those of a dedicated page-layout program. It is perfectly possible to create ads and brochures within the Illustrator environment. Long, multi-page documents with complicated text designs are not its strong suit, however, because the program puts all of a document's pages into a single large paste-board, making navigation less than intuitive. It lacks style sheets, master pages, and the other elements you would generally need for longer documents. For those, you must look elsewhere; some examples are coming up next.

Like some other Adobe graphics programs, Illustrator lets you automate complex, repeating functions using its Actions macro utility. It will record your activities and allow you to plug in program functions and build scripts you can access via a single keystroke.

Macromedia FreeHand. This program is Illustrator's major competition (www.macromedia.com; $399). Through the years, Adobe and Macromedia (or the former distributor of the program, Aldus, which sold it off when Aldus was sold to Adobe) have competed head on for the minds and hearts of graphics artists everywhere. Even the version numbers keep pace; for example, within weeks after FreeHand 9 came out, Adobe introduced Illustrator 9. The latest version is FreeHand 10 (**Figure 14.2**).

Each program has its own adherents, but many folks simply buy both and let the dictates of the particular job determine which one they use.

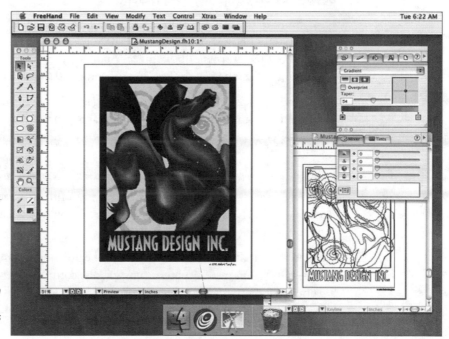

Figure 14.2

FreeHand was once second best to Illustrator in many respects, but Macromedia has worked hard to make it equal and in some ways exceed the capabilities of its major competitor.

FreeHand's most immediate advantage over Illustrator is its wider range of text-handling tools. As with page-layout and word-processing applications, FreeHand lets you create your own paragraph-level style sheets. You create additional pages in your document in much the same fashion as you would in a page-layout program, but you don't have the ability to use master pages. In theory, at least, FreeHand is better than Illustrator for multiple-page documents.

In other respects, you'll find more similarities than differences. Version 10 of FreeHand greatly expands Web integration. You can output files in HTML, using the same format as Macromedia's Dreamweaver Web-authoring software, and in SWF, the format used for Flash animations. If you opt to go all the way, you can buy a special package, called **Flash 5 FreeHand 10 Studio** ($499), which includes both of these programs. Best of all, FreeHand was the first major graphics program to migrate to Mac OS X using Carbon. What this means is that FreeHand 10 runs fine if you use it in Mac OS 9 and inherits the spiffy user interface features and enhanced stability when you use it in Mac OS X.

Even if you aren't doing Web art right now, you'll find that FreeHand offers expanded traditional drawing tools, including more-precise drawing with the FreeHand tool; an improved Autotrace feature, which gets more-accurate results from scanned artwork; and Perspective Grid, which eases the process of building 3D effects in a 2D program.

Is anything missing? I'd love to see a macro feature to match the ones in Illustrator and Photoshop. True, FreeHand does have built-in AppleScript support, but the process of building an AppleScript is a whole lot more complex than the Actions feature FreeHand's competition boasts.

FreeHand 10 includes a multiple master pages feature (as many as 32,000 supported in a single document!), which makes it extremely useful for large, graphics-rich documents. This is one area where FreeHand has a big leg up on Illustrator.

Choosing the best graphics program is definitely a matter of personal preference. Macromedia eases the process by making a fully functioning 30-day version of FreeHand available at its Web site. If you like what you see, you can buy the full version directly from the site.

Adobe Photoshop. This is the standard-bearer among photo-editing programs, but it's not just for photos (www.adobe.com; $609). At its core, it's a paint program (with a few vector-based drawing tools), which means you can actually use it to create artwork from scratch (**Figure 14.3**).

Figure 14.3

This illustration, depicting an alien from one of the Attack of the Rockoids science-fiction novels written by me and my son, was done entirely in Photoshop by well-known science fiction artist Robert Ross. The freehand-style textures were drawn using a graphics tablet fitted with a pen attachment.

Once you've completed your drawing or brought in your scanned image, you can access the huge array of special effects and image-enhancement tools that make Photoshop the choice of graphics professionals in many fields, including the motion-picture industry.

Some of the key features of version 6.0—the one shipping when I wrote this chapter—are listed under the umbrella of vector support, which is explained further in the coming paragraphs.

In addition to incorporating enhanced layer- and image-manipulation tools, Adobe is co-opting some of the better features of Illustrator in its flagship photo-editing program. To enhance Photoshop's power, you can even utilize vector-based images within pixel-based images, which definitely enhances your creative possibilities.

But the biggest new feature is Photoshop's enhanced text capabilities. Previously, I would have used the word *feh* (picked up back in my old hometown of Brooklyn, New York) to describe the range of text tools available. In the past, you had to use an awkward dialog box to enter text; now you can click directly on the image to add text.

In a sense, Adobe has taken the fairly decent text tools from Illustrator and plugged them into Photoshop. So you have Character and Paragraph palettes, along with hyphenation controls (at least for the English-language version of the program).

You can immediately see the biggest difference: An overhaul of Photoshop's interface has made the application easier to use and more accessible, and you now have the option to set up a palette well, where you can organize the palettes you use most often.

Adobe also continues to enhance Photoshop's Web-graphics tools. You have the ability to optimize Web graphics for the best combination of quality and file size. You can also create transparent GIF files, useful for logos and banners, plus JavaScript rollovers (images that change when you move the pointer over them) and animations.

All told, Photoshop provides all the things you need to retouch and enhance photos, giving you the equivalent of a darkroom on your Mac. However, feature bloat has begun to make Illustrator and Photoshop resemble each other in some ways. Although professional graphic designers often buy both, you should consider whether one program might not be enough.

Like Illustrator, Photoshop includes the Actions macro feature to automate complex, repeating operations.

The Mac OS X Equation

Will your favorite graphics program appear in a Mac OS X-savvy version? When Apple CEO Steve Jobs first introduced the striking and colorful Aqua interface for the new operating system at San Francisco's Macworld Expo in January 2000, he paraded several major Mac software developers around the stage. Each of them pledged its support for Mac OS X and its intention to port the crucial applications.

The only question is how long this will take. Depending on the complexity of an application, porting it can take weeks or months. AppleWorks 6 was one of the first important Mac programs rewritten for Mac OS X. As this book was going to press, Microsoft was putting the final touches on Office X for Mac, and Adobe was working on bringing its key applications to the new environment. [*In fact, Adobe said a Mac OS X version of Illustrator would ship by the end of 2001 and a version of InDesign for Mac OS X would be available in the first quarter of 2002.—Ed.*]

If you can't wait for the Mac graphics applications to make the trip, you might want to check out Stone Design's Create, which only runs under Mac OS X. I cover Create in a bit.

Graphics on the Cheap

The programs mentioned in "An Overview of the Key Players" and the various alternatives I discuss in "A Look at All-in-One Graphics Programs" all share a common shortcoming. They are expensive, costing several hundred dollars apiece. If you are a professional graphics artist, the cost of admission is part of the price of doing business. But if you just want to do simple graphics for a small company brochure or a club newsletter, it isn't worth spending money on features you'll simply never use. More to the point, the more power you have in a program, the more difficult a learning curve you'll face.

Fortunately, some of the alternatives won't cost a lot. In fact, a few are absolutely free.

If you own a scanner, for example, no doubt it came with photo-editing software. Although the more expensive scanners usually include the full Adobe Photoshop package, the inexpensive models give you software that's not as flexible but will do a good job for most purposes.

Adobe Photo Deluxe. Although many digital cameras scanners still package Photo Deluxe on their CDs, Adobe has dispatched this application to software heaven. That's too bad, because Photo Deluxe is an awfully good program if you just need to do simple image manipulation. One of its best features, removal of red-eye from a photo, works more easily than the Photoshop equivalent. Photo Deluxe also offers an ultrasimple user interface as standard issue, with simplified buttons and controls (a regular interface with normal menus is the option), so that you can move easily from scanning to retouching to saving without cracking open a manual.

Adobe Photoshop Elements. Imagine having a lot of the major features of Photoshop for a fraction of the price. Photoshop Elements (a revamped version of Photoshop LE) comes with many lower-priced scanners and is available as a separate package from your favorite Mac dealer (www.adobe.com; $99). It has the look and feel of the full version without some of the high-end features. But it's also lots easier to learn, with a Hints palette that helps you figure you what those highly sophisticated image-editing tools do and a Recipes palette that shows you how to deal with a complicated set of steps to ease the learning curve. Like Photo Deluxe, there's a red-eye feature.

 Some scanners still include the predecessor to Elements, Photoshop LE. Don't feel deprived, though. LE can handle a lot of your routine work, such as touching up scanned photos and creating and editing images, with precision.

AppleWorks (formerly ClarisWorks). Are you skeptical as to whether Apple's low-cost application suite can handle your graphics? Well, if you're in the professional publishing industry, your fears may be justified. But for simple artwork, the latest AppleWorks (version 6 as of this writing) has both draw and paint features that will definitely get the job done. It offers vector-graphics features, such as Bézier curves, that let you perform a surprising variety of tasks (www.apple.com; $79). However, as you might expect, it has bare-bones color support.

Graphic File Converters

Maybe you aren't interested in creating professional artwork. Perhaps you just want to do a few simple touchups, or resize an image, or convert files from one format to another. Two programs—one ultracheap, the other rather costly—provide an extensive array of file-conversion features.

DeBabelizer. This program from Equilibrium is a high-end application for handling complex image-processing texts (www.equilibrium.com; $479.95). According to its developer, it can automate some 300 image-editing commands, which makes it ideal for batch processing. It can also optimize graphic files for the best combination of quality versus image size (perfect for Web-based art), and it claims to be the "world's most powerful file converter," able to translate files in more than 100 file formats.

DeBabelizer Lite. If paying a price close to that of a high-end graphics program seems like a bit much, you might want to take a look at the low-cost version, with its file-conversion and -optimizing features ($49.95). DeBabelizer Lite also has graphics-editing tools that perform a reasonably wide range of image-manipulation chores, from basic color adjustments to scaling, cropping, and rotating.

GraphicConverter. Although the maker of DeBabelizer boasts about the number of file formats it can read and convert, the crown probably belongs to Thorsten Lemke's shareware program, GraphicConverter (www.lemkesoft.de; $35). The manual for the version I tried while writing this chapter, 4.0.9, listed more than 140 supported file formats; it has also been Carbonized to run native under Mac OS X. The program is updated so often that this file-format number will probably grow, assuming there are more file formats around to translate. It also offers batch-processing capabilities and the ability to handle basic image-editing chores, such as scaling and color correction. If it has a shortcoming, it's the lack of a proper Help menu. You have to search through some rather con-voluted menu commands to find all the powerful features or pore through a long and dense electronic manual. This shouldn't deter you from considering this program, however—it's a worthy candidate. Give it a try, but make sure you pay the developer if you decide to keep using it. (I used GraphicConverter to do final editing and scaling of all the illustrations in this chapter!)

Using a Desktop-Publishing Program for Drawing

In the old days, it was all so simple. You did your illustrations in a program such as FreeHand or Illustrator (sometimes in Canvas) and then imported or placed your completed artwork in Adobe PageMaker or Quark's QuarkXPress. Unless you labored long and hard, the page-layout programs were at best suitable for just simple shapes, such as boxes or squares.

How times have changed.

Over time, Quark began to add to the feature pot in its QuarkXPress page-layout program. First it tossed in the ability to create various polygons. Then, with an obvious wink and nod toward dedicated users of Illustrator (published by its major competitor), Quark incorporated some Illustrator-style tools beginning in version 4. These included Bézier tools for picture boxes and text on a path, plus a freehand tool (**Figure 14.4**). New in version 4.1 is a scissors tool. As in Illustrator, some of the tools include submenus for selecting further options.

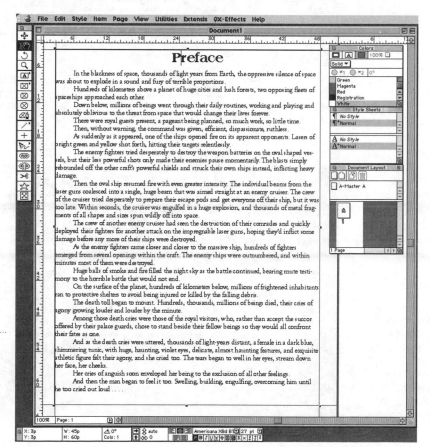

Figure 14.4

Because Adobe is Quark's major competitor, it's no wonder that QuarkXPress has taken on some Illustrator-type drawing tools.

Each of these tools, along with QuarkXPress's extensive support for color and its blend tool, reduces the need to go to an outside illustration program to create many types of drawings. This doesn't mean you won't find a dedicated drawing application a better choice, but for many drawings you may find it's no longer necessary.

As this book was written, Quark was working on long-awaited version 5 of its premier desktop-publishing program and indicated that the top features would include table-creation tools and enhanced Web-publishing capabilities and, again with a nod toward graphic artists, layer management. If you are lucky, you can catch a public beta version of the program at www.quark.com (at least until the final version is released).

In its efforts to make InDesign a compelling alternative to QuarkXPress for professional page layout, Adobe has also been working hard to lessen InDesign's dependence on Illustrator (**Figure 14.5**). InDesign's drawing features appear to be a subset of Illustrator's.

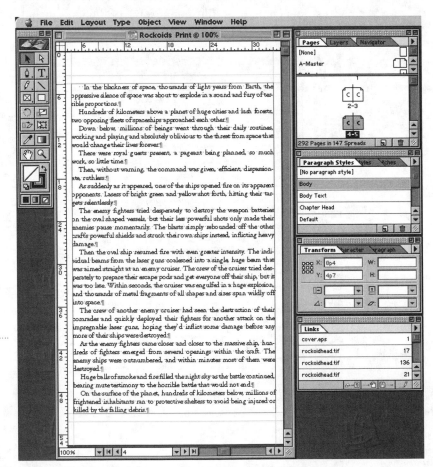

Figure 14.5

Adobe created InDesign to be the "Quark killer," the program that would combat QuarkXPress's dominance in the publishing and printing industries.

Both have pen tools with submenu options, and both also have eyedroppers and pencil tools of one sort or another. Although Illustrator has the scissors tool and charting options that InDesign lacks, InDesign can handle many of the drawings you formerly would have done in Illustrator and then ported into your page-layout program. In addition, InDesign can open Illustrator documents without requiring any conversions.

This doesn't mean you should give up on FreeHand and Illustrator and let your page-layout program handle everything from illustration to word processing and the final product—at least not yet. As Adobe and Quark contend hotly to raise the bar in this arena, you can expect to see better, more advanced drawing tools in the future that bridge whatever feature gap remains.

Then you may want to rethink what approach to take.

A Look at All-in-One Graphics Programs

When FreeHand and Illustrator first came out, their makers specifically designed them to fulfill just one purpose—creating high-quality digital artwork. As time went on, each program began to leapfrog the other with more and more features borrowed from other programs. For example, the once-rudimentary text tools were enhanced to closely resemble those of dedicated page-layout programs (in the same way that layout programs took on enhanced drawing capabilities).

Two other programs offer integrated graphics capabilities.

Deneba's Canvas (www.deneba.com; $375) began life as an integrated drawing and painting program, offering a decent collection of features from both types of software (**Figure 14.6**). Over the years its feature set has expanded greatly, as Deneba has tried to give its users four applications in one, calling it a "program for every project."

You get quite a powerful set of vector-drawing, image-editing, page-layout, and Web-design features, all rolled into one program—and it doesn't skimp much on features either. Although prior versions tended to be complex, bloated, and slow, Canvas 8 is reasonably quick and doesn't hog a huge amount of memory or disk space.

With so many features available, it's not surprising that the program has 21 floating palettes in the Window menu for accessing key features. A convenient docking palette lets you easily store all your palettes for one-click access.

Figure 14.6

Canvas 8, which also runs native under Mac OS X, has so many standard features that mastering the program can take a while, but it's definitely worth the effort.

Sprite technology. This feature allows you to use plug-ins on vector artwork or on an illustration that contains mixed vector, bitmap, and text elements. It's designed not just to blur the differences between these techniques but to give you greater flexibility in creating a professional drawing.

Page layout. Sporting an interface reminiscent of Adobe PageMaker, Canvas lets you create multipage publications with master pages, automatic headers and footers, and other features that may help you avoid a trip to another program, at least for shorter documents. A handy document-layout palette manages page creation and removal. The first-rate text-handling features put character- and paragraph-level style sheets close at hand. In this respect, Canvas exceeds the abilities of FreeHand and Illustrator for page layout.

Color printing. Canvas is no slouch here, with the ability to print four-color separations and extensive color-matching capabilities. A Collect for Output feature (similar to what you'll find in InDesign and QuarkXPress) eases the process of preparing your documents for high-resolution color output. If all this has a downside, it's that you may have to look a bit for a prepress facility or service bureau that actually supports this program.

AppleScript support. No doubt taking its cue from Adobe's Actions feature, Deneba has added AppleScript support to Canvas. Using its Sequences feature, you'll be able to record and play back complicated steps to simplify production of sophisticated graphics.

If Canvas looks attractive to you, visit its Web site and download the limited-time demo, and see if it suits your needs.

Introducing Canvas SE. If the high-end version of Canvas seems like a bit much for your needs, consider the low-cost version, Canvas Standard Edition ($99). On the surface it looks very much like a previous edition of Canvas, version 7. It also works similarly, except for the lack of some precision high-end features, such as the ability to make color separations and match spot colors. In addition, the program's text tools are scaled down considerably over what the high-priced spread offers.

Canvas SE also supports a severely limited number of graphics file formats, although it includes all the ones I mentioned (see the "Graphics File Formats" section earlier in this chapter). But at less than $100 per copy, it may be a worthwhile alternative to its big sibling (or to one of the low-cost graphics programs mentioned in "Graphics on the Cheap" earlier in this chapter).

Unlike most programs, it doesn't have any serial number in the box. You first have to register online and then wait for the number to show up via e-mail before you can enter it in the program's startup screen.

Don't look for telephone support at this price point. To get support for Canvas SE, you have to access the publisher's user forums and knowledge base. However, the manual is reasonably well written, so you might be able to get by.

If you like Canvas SE but find that you need the professional version's features, you'll be pleased to know that Deneba offers a low-cost upgrade to version 8, its professional product. You have the choice of downloading the basic version of the software or paying a higher price for the boxed version, which includes the printed manual, clip art, and fonts.

If you have used graphics in Microsoft Windows, you may be familiar with yet another graphics program, CorelDRAW.

CorelDRAW. CorelDRAW 8, Corel's initial foray into the Mac marketplace, sold a decent number of copies, according to the Corel, but never captured the hearts and minds of Mac graphics professionals. It's not that CorelDRAW 8 was a bad program; in fact, most reviewers gave it decent marks.

Unlike other applications brought over from Windows, such as the early versions of WordPerfect, CorelDRAW from the first looked remarkably Mac-like and even could use AppleScript to automate complex operations. The original release, though, could be sluggish and suffered from various bugs.

(Maintenance updates addressed many of these problems.) The program benefited from aggressive pricing and plenty of extras, such as a huge font library, to help drive sales.

Corel continues to be aggressive with Corel Graphics Suite 10 (www.corel.com; $569), a tour-de-force package that includes CorelDRAW 10 (the vector graphics program), Corel Photo-Paint 10 (which competes with Adobe Photoshop), and Corel R.A.V.E. (an animation application).

Each of these applications runs natively in Mac OS X. The suite includes an extensive collection of file import/export filters to allow you to move freely from such programs as Adobe Illustrator and Photoshop. If you're in the publishing industry, you'll appreciate the integrated preflight capability and improved PDF support. In addition, a host of utilities greatly expand the value of the bundle. CorelTrace 10 does what its name implies, takes bitmap artwork—acquired by your scanner, for example—and converts it to vector art. The suite comes with a Mac OS X version of DiamondSoft's Font Reserve font management program as well as Canto Cumulus desktop LE 5.0 (for managing your digital artwork) and a small collection of KPT plug-ins. The package is rounded out with 2,000 clip-art images, 500 stock photos, and 2,000 TrueType and PostScript fonts.

Time will tell whether Corel can grab a reasonable share of the Mac marketplace with its revised CorelDRAW and companion software, particularly against such strong competition.

 Stone Design Create. Another program captures the elements of several programs in one—and it's no lightweight, except in terms of the minimal space it occupies. Stone Design's Create fills just about 2 MB on your hard drive (**Figure 14.7**). But before you go out and get a copy, consider this caveat: Stone Design wrote Create for Mac OS X, and it will not work on Macs running OS 9 and earlier.

Figure 14.7

Designed strictly for Mac OS X, Stone Design's Create combines several graphics and page-layout functions in a single, easy-to-use program.

However, when you take the Mac OS X plunge, you'll find that Create, in addition to taking up little space on your hard drive, presents an extremely attractive interface and some compelling features that may indeed make it your illustration program of choice (www.stone.com; $149).

In one sense, it's similar to Canvas, offering both illustration and page-layout features. In addition, it can generate Web pages automatically, letting you easily export your artwork in HTML. And it is scriptable via AppleScript.

The program does lack some color-management tools. Its heavy reliance on the built-in features of Mac OS X means you don't have access to the advanced color palettes that let you match the colors in your document with your printer's, nor can you print color separations. However, Create's emphasis on Web-based and 3D artwork and its simple, compelling interface make it an attractive alternative for many graphics-oriented jobs.

You won't find this program readily available and boxed at many dealers, so check out Stone Design's Web site to learn more about Create and the company's other offerings.

As of this writing, Stone Design was offering demonstration versions of its programs at the Web site. They're definitely worth a try.

A Brief Look at Graphics Add-Ons

With graphics programs offering so many incredible features to create and enhance your artwork, it would seem developers can't add any more to increase a program's flexibility.

However, you can expand these programs still further by harnessing plug-ins (called Xtras in FreeHand), which allow you to enhance existing features or add totally new ones. There's a ready market for utilities designed to take your favorite graphics program to places it has never gone before.

One of the major suppliers of such utilities is Extensis (www.extensis.com). This company makes many clever add-ons for QuarkXPress and Photoshop that add professional-grade improvements. Here's a quick overview of some of these plug-ins:

Intellihance Pro ($199). Imagine having access to as many as 25 enhancements to a photo or other piece of artwork in Photoshop. Just select a single command, and Intellihance Pro goes to work to deliver the best possible image quality. You can also customize each of its tools. True, you could do all this work in Photoshop, given enough time, energy, and patience, but being able to handle it all in a single operation is a real plus.

Intellihance is great for instant tune-ups, but the standard settings are sometimes a little overeager when it comes to a scanned photo. The standard range of enhancements can make a photo *too* sharp, and if there are any specks on the scanned picture, you'll get a snowflake effect. Forget about fixing pimples.

Mask Pro ($299.95). A mask is an object you use to cover portions of artwork you don't wish to see. For example, you can use a white overlay atop your illustration to give it a unique effect or merge it with another piece of artwork for a special design. Mask Pro enhances your ability to create a mask in Photoshop by making it easier to select the edges of your artwork and providing more-professional results, with fewer ragged edges.

PhotoFrame ($199.95). This plug-in lets you add custom border and edge designs for Photoshop. It includes more than 1,000 prebuilt frames, and you can easily modify them to suit your taste.

PhotoGraphics ($149.95). This program affords you a neat set of vector graphic features in Photoshop. You can handle basic vector shapes, apply fills and strokes (outlines), and produce text on a path—for example, letters that go around a circle.

PhotoTools ($149.95). This adds a bunch of special effects that enhance Photoshop documents for print, multimedia, and Web purposes. One of the best features of version 3.0 is GIF animation, which lets you create advanced animations from photos.

 To explore any of these products further, pay a visit to the Extensis Web site and download a limited-time demonstration version. If you like what you see, just order the user license and you can unlock the demo by entering the serial number. You can also order the company's CD, which includes demos of all these programs to try out before purchasing.

Clip Art—Is It Worth It?

In the old days of traditional typesetting, artists used to buy packages of canned artwork, better known as *clip art*. Such material consisted of books containing high-quality prints of professional artwork you could copy or alter to suit your purposes. Rather than reinvent the wheel, for example, you'd check your handy clip-art book for various wheel pictures.

Some of the firms that produced those clip-art books actually sold subscriptions, sending updates every month or thereabouts with new and exciting designs. Such products were a boon for both experienced artists and amateurs. Whether the rush of deadlines or lack of talent prevented you from producing the artwork you needed, you always had that clip-art book to fall back on.

The advent of desktop publishing on personal computers relegated that sort of artwork to floppy disk and later to CD. Many firms offer such packages, and sometimes it comes bundled with your favorite software. The nice thing about clip art is that you don't have to go out and seek permission to use the material or pay royalties. That's part of the package, as is the right to alter it. What you *don't* get is originality. The same artwork you have is available to millions of others—and it would be embarrassing to use a piece of clip art in your company's ad or brochure and then spot it in a rival's publication.

In previous editions of *The Macintosh Bible,* editors gave their advice on picking a clip-art collection. Here are my suggestions, which may differ from those previously voiced (at least it gives you a reason to buy the new edition of this book every few years!):

- Pick the right format: If you're going to use the material for a printed document, choose clip art in EPS for drawings and TIFF for photos. JPEG is all right for the latter, but the loss of quality may be noticeable in some collections. For Web art, GIF and JPEG are just fine.

- Although clip-art packages are often updated, the new version usually includes both the original images plus the new ones. You may well get 60,000 images, many of which you already have. So when choosing a package, you might prefer to select from a variety of vendors.

- Although low-cost color inkjet printers are spreading far and wide across the Mac landscape, many people still use regular laser printers for documents. Although the newest laser printers do a dandy job with grayscale artwork and photos, full-color clip art is apt to suffer. You might need to test the clip art before you try incorporating it in your document or at least be prepared to play around with the color rendition in your graphics software (assuming it can handle color editing).

- Don't expect miracles. I have tens of thousands of clip-art images in boxes on bookshelves in my home office, but few of them merit a second glance. It's a case of quality versus quantity, and you'll want to choose this sort of material carefully.

- Sometimes you won't find a photo anywhere in your clip-art packages to suit the job. For example, I once had to design a videotape cover for a low-budget movie. I searched far and wide for a lighthouse photo among my clip-art collections, and none were satisfactory. In some cases, the image seemed all right but was too small, and I couldn't scale it upward and get acceptable quality. Finally I had to bite the bullet and arrange to have a photographer do the job for me. This doesn't, of course, mean that no clip-art collection has a good photo of a lighthouse; however, you won't always find the perfect picture for your purposes. (And don't write to me suggesting some clip-art alternatives; the photographer won't give a refund.)

- Don't expect absolutely perfect artwork without further fiddling. For drawings, you want to be able to open, ungroup, and edit the files so you can adjust them to fit your needs. If the file consists of several pictures that make up a single illustration (such as a computer and a desk), ideally you'd like to be able to separate the two so you can choose one or the other.

- What's the good of having 750,000 truly magnificent drawings and photos if there's no reference book or search system to help you retrieve the ones you want? If you want to browse, there's nothing better than the old-fashioned way—a printed book with a complete index, allowing you to examine the printed illustrations and get a feel for how they will look in your documents or on your Web site. If the documentation is strictly electronic, this last element of the collection may be a downer. The images never look the same on your Mac's display. True, you can print an image, but browsing through a lot of them can be time consuming (and costly, if you're using one of those inkjet printers that suck up large quantities of ink).

Clip-art collections. Collections of clip art have lost a lot of their popularity, because so many programs provide at least some artwork you can use. Check the last edition of *The Macintosh Bible,* for example, and you'll see that we're no longer including some clip-art collections listed. In addition to the usual changes, acquisitions, mergers, and businesses going under, few Mac catalogs now include such packages. I checked half a dozen before writing this chapter, from some of the major Mac mail-order houses, and only one offered any clip-art collections (Nova Development). I list the URL for each publisher's Web site in the following descriptions so you'll have no problem locating the collections that interest you.

One of the largest collections of clip art comes from Nova Development (www.novadevelopment.com). Its top-of-the-line product is called Art Explosion. The last edition of this book listed 250,000 images. Boy, how time flies! Today's top-end version, **Art Explosion 750,000** ($199.95), consists of 750,000 images on 48 CDs and a two-volume image catalog that spans 1,800 pages. This package includes a reasonable mixture of illustrations in a handful of formats—vector art, TIFF, JPEG, Web graphics, animations, fonts, and more.

If poring through 750,000 clip-art images seems a bit much, try a smaller, more manageable collection. The first step down is **Art Explosion 525,000** ($149.95), and then there's **Art Explosion 250,000** ($99.95). There are also special-purpose collections. **Print Explosion** ($59.95) is useful for greeting cards, signs, and banners. **Art Explosion T-Shirt Factory** ($99.95) is useful for what the name implies.

The Image Club Clip Art collections, formerly marketed by Adobe, have been sold to EyeWire (www.eyewire.com). Several dozen collections are on CD, each with a specific focus. You'll find animal images, arts and entertainment, business, flags, food and dining, and more. As with Nova Development's packages, **Image Club Clip Art** ($9.95 a set) comes in various file formats, so you can find just the right illustration to suit your needs. You'll also want to check out **Art Parts** ($169.95), another CD collection for your copy-and-paste pleasure.

From Microware (www.mwcdrom.com) comes a product called **MasterClips 150,000**. It's a full-featured mixture of vector art, TIFF and JPEG images, animations, videos, and 2,000 TrueType fonts. Although this package seems impressive in itself, the company's Windows-only products seem to offer a lot more, with collections containing as many as a million images. True, you can easily convert most of these to Mac format with a program such as GraphicConverter, but it would be a fairly inexpensive process to make a dedicated Mac version. The other collection from Microware with a Mac orientation is **MasterPhotos**—75,000 royalty-free photographs in both color and black and white, for Mac and Windows users.

One of Corel's other major Mac products is the **Corel Mega Gallery,** a package that offers more than 110,000 files. Of these, 50,000 are vector based and another 60,000 are designed for Web use. A convenient online search tool, full-color 1,000 TrueType and PostScript fonts, and sound and video files round out this impressive product. Although they may not look as comprehensive as Nova Development's offerings, the fonts alone may entice you to consider this offering.

I should warn you that the viewing software for Corel's clipart collection is buggy, and I've seen it crash several Macs running Mac OS 9. Unfortunately the collection is saved in a proprietary format, so you can't just view it with a separate graphics application without first converting it with the viewer.

Although it seems rather pricey for what it offers, **Clipables** (www.clipables.com) is a well-executed package with 1,100 full-color vector-art images of supremely high quality that you can edit and adapt for your needs. This company appears to have strived hard to maintain quality over quantity, and it has succeeded admirably. Clipables also offers special-purpose collections for Travel & Vacation and one called Editions, which includes borders, backgrounds, and decorations.

One of the oldest existing collections comes from a longtime Mac publisher, Dubl-Click Software (www.dublclick.com), which has also published such utilities as MenuFonts. **WetPaint** ($29.95), strictly a collection of bitmapped images, is a bit long in the tooth—but if you find that some of the other packages offer an overwhelming quantity of images, this one might suit your needs. You can either buy a boxed set or order and download the product directly from Dubl-Click's Web site.

Dubl-Click still sells each piece of its collection on 800 Kbyte floppy disks. This is unfortunate, and not just because you'll have to dig around to find a floppy drive that can read them. Yes, you can get a CD containing the entire package with all its collections, but then you may be stuck with lots of images you don't really need, and unfortunately the package isn't cheap compared with the competition.

Painting and Drawing in AppleWorks

You don't have to be a professional illustrator or spend hundreds of dollars to buy software that creates professional-looking artwork. You already have a program that will perform many tasks—AppleWorks. This program comes free with the iMac and iBook, and it's inexpensive enough so that even if you never exploit the capabilities of all its modules, you'll find it handy to have around.

AppleWorks 6 includes 25,000 clip-art images.

Only a handful of these clip-art files come with the software's CD. You have to download the rest of the collection from Apple's Web site, using the program's Web Starting Point and picking your categories of interest. With so much free space for extras on the CD, I wonder what Apple was thinking when it came up with this awkward method of accessing the entire collection.

In this section, I cover some handy ways to get the most out of AppleWorks' illustration tools. You'll also find it easy to apply some of these methods to other graphics-related programs, so you'll have a leg up on harnessing their power, too.

Once you've learned a cool set of steps to spruce up your AppleWorks graphics, you can record them as a macro. Just choose Macros from the Edit menu and Record Macro from the submenu to begin creating your automated routine. You'll also find some useful AppleScript shortcuts in the Scripts menu.

Painting and Drawing Hints and Tips

All of these have been tried and tested with AppleWorks 6, but most will work in earlier versions of the program.

Make a duplicate. You can create a duplicate of any selected item this way: Hold down Option and then drag the item. Presto! You now have two copies.

The Option method of duplicating an item is part of most graphics programs.

Fast eyedropper access. The eyedropper tool lets you quickly copy the attributes of a selected item, such as the outlines and fills of a drawing and the color of a painting. You can access the eyedropper by pressing Tab, regardless of which tool you are using. Press Tab again to switch back to whatever tool you were using previously.

Polygon shortcuts. Use the polygon tool to create multisided shapes. When you hold down Shift, you can constrain (or hold) a shape to exact 45-degree angles. Just click your starting point or double-click to end the shape. If you wish to create an exact number of sides in the drawing layer or *environment,* first click the polygon tool, then choose Polygon Sides from the Edit menu, and select the number of sides you want your shape to have. For the paint mode, just double-click the polygon tool to produce the dialog box where you specify the number of sides (don't ask why it's different in each mode—who knows?).

If you loved the tear-off palettes in older versions of this program, sorry— they're gone. In addition to the toolbars, AppleWorks has an Accents palette (available from the Window menu), which shows color and line options, and a Styles palette (available from the Format menu).

Dotted lines. If you need dashed or dotted lines—say, for a coupon— AppleWorks doesn't make it easy, but it can be done after a fashion. In the drawing layer, first select the Accents palette and choose the thickness setting for your lines. Then click the Patterns palette to give the line the style you want. In the painting environment, first select a paintbrush and then choose Edit Brush Shape from the Options menu. From here, just pick the shape you want and click the Edit button. This last option actually lets you toggle each pixel in a line. Click the bitmaps in the line to create the separations or gaps. Once you paint your line, it'll take on the style you selected.

To paint or draw a straight line, hold down ⎣Shift⎦ **while drawing the line.**

AppleWorks Color-Editing Shortcuts

AppleWorks doesn't have the color-matching abilities of the high-end illustration programs, and it can't print color separations. But it offers fairly decent control of color selection and styles. Here's how it works:

1. Open the Accents palette and double-click any color you want to edit.

2. You'll see a scrolling list that contains a list of color-configuration options. For the most part, just moving a slider will change colors. Choose the color scheme from the following:

    CMYK Picker lets you configure a color based on a four-color model.

    Crayon Picker gives you a choice of 60 colors from a screen that looks like a box of crayons.

    HLS Picker presents a color wheel that affords you three color settings— one for Hue Angle, another for Saturation, and a third for Lightness.

    HTML Picker is designed for Web pages. The sliders let you choose from the standard range of Web colors, and the actual HTML code appears in a list for your coding pleasure.

    RGB Picker works in the same fashion as your Mac's display. Selections are based on the three primary colors: red, green, and blue.

3. Once you've edited the color, click OK. The selected color appears in the color palette, ready for you to use in your document.

If you want to save a custom color or pattern setting for other documents, follow these steps:

1. Once you've selected your new color or pattern, click the pop-up menu in the palette and select Save As.

2. Give your palette a descriptive name so you can identify the color later on (Shocking Blue or whatever applies).

3. Click Save. From here on, you can choose that color scheme from the Accents pop-up menu for any of your AppleWorks illustrations.

AppleWorks Drawing Tips

The following tips apply primarily to the drawing environment in AppleWorks, but you'll find that many of these suggestions apply with equal facility to other programs.

Retain a selected tool. Normally, when you click a tool and then use it to perform a function, such as creating a circle, it's deselected as soon as you finish creating the shape, and it reverts to the selection tool. But what if you want to continue using the same tool? Just double-click the selected tool, and it gets a blue background to show that you've selected it for repeated use. It will remain selected until you click a different tool.

Change shape quickly. No, this isn't something out of a *Star Trek* movie. It's a way to refine an image to include accurate, custom attributes. If you create a drawing with the rectangle or rounded-rectangle tool, just double-click the shape and you'll see a dialog box in which you can set the radius of the corners and whether to round the object's sides.

Constrain your drawing. This is a standard tool available in most drawing programs that helps ensure precision. Just hold down (Shift) when you draw an object to constrain it to exact angles or squares or circles. For example, a rough oval becomes a perfect circle and a rectangle becomes a square.

 If you hold down (Shift) while moving one or more objects, you'll restrict the movement to an exact horizontal or vertical line or to a 45-degree angle.

Master your master pages. AppleWorks has one important feature in common with page-layout programs—the ability to create a master page containing items that appear in all other pages of your document. Here you can place items that you want to appear on all pages—folios, page numbers, images, whatever you wish. To use this feature, follow these steps:

1. From the Options menu, choose Edit Master Page.

2. Use your drawing or text tools to create the objects you want to appear on all pages in your document.

3. Once the master page is ready, return to the Options menu and choose Edit Master Page again to return to your normal page. From here on, the master-page elements will appear on all the pages in your document.

 If you don't want the master-page elements to appear on a specific page of your document, you can cover them up with a rectangle or other object the same color as the page background.

AppleWorks Painting Tips

Painting, drawing—what's the difference? You can create illustrations with both, right? So why should you choose one over the other? The painting environment affords you some extra color tools that can really give your illustrations some pizzazz. When you start a paint document, you can take advantage of an extra set of tools. Among these are the magic wand for selecting complex shapes, plus a paintbrush, paint bucket, spray can, and pencil. Each of these tools allows you to apply special blending, color, and tint effects to your drawings.

Once you get used to these added tools, you'll discover a whole new dimension of illustration possibilities.

Precise illustration positioning. The ability to move objects around freely is both a blessing and a curse. If you need to place an object in a special location, try the autogrid feature. This creates a set of automatic alignment points where the items you drop snap into place. To activate the feature, just go to the Options menu and then select Turn Autogrid On. This feature also works in the drawing layer.

 If you want to fine-tune your grid to a specific size, simply choose Grid Size from the Options menu. Set a grid increment that lets you accurately position the elements of your illustration.

 Although the autogrid feature helps you refine the position of illustrations, it can be a bit inhibiting, because the grid increments prevent free movement. If you don't want a specific element to snap into a fixed location, return to the Options menu and choose Turn Autogrid Off. Don't worry—this won't change the way you've positioned other parts of the illustration. You can activate autogrid again via the same steps for those elements you do want to snap into place.

 High-end graphics programs, such as Canvas, have a guides feature, which allows ultraprecise positioning. You just display the ruler, place the pointer within the ruler, and then drag a guide to the appropriate position on the page. The built-in snap-to guides in these programs allow the elements of your illustration to simply drop into place.

Selecting paint images. One thing you'll find different about a paint document is that it doesn't have any corners and handles you can select to move or change an object's shape. This makes object movement more awkward, but the process works fine once you get used to it. Here's how it's done:

1. For a rectangular object, click the selection rectangle in the lower half of the tool palette. The pointer will change to a crosshair.

2. Drag the crosshair pointer to the start of the area you wish to select, and then drag to cover the area. Hold down ⌘ to include nonwhite areas inside the selected area.

3. Drag the selected item to its new location.

To select an irregular image, use the lasso tool instead. You can select painted items and bypass the blank space between them by double-clicking the lasso.

Tips and Tricks for Adobe Photoshop

Hands down, Photoshop is at the top of the photo-editing-software heap. Whether you get the free version (full or limited edition) with a new scanner or you've bought the retail package, prepare for a real treat. Since it's a professional graphics tool, however, you may find it takes a while to master some of its best features. I'll cover a few of the really useful ones here:

TWAIN or plug-in—which to choose. Scanning software may come either as a Photoshop plug-in or as a TWAIN driver. Does it make a difference which you choose? If the software comes in both forms, choose the plug-in format. It'll usually launch faster—sometimes a lot faster. This may not mean much if you're scanning a few documents, but if you are handling many pieces of artwork, you can save a lot of time. (TWAIN, which reportedly stands for Technology Without an Interesting Name, was designed as a unified standard to give software a single resource for add-on features, such as activating scanning software. However, most Mac programs simply don't support the feature.)

Exporting transparent images. An assistant or wizard is a great way to simplify a complex process. In its Help menu, Photoshop has an assistant called Export Transparent Image, which lets you select and then export transparent illustrations (**Figure 14.8**). These images are great for Web use or for a document you create with a page-layout program. Once you call up the Export Transparent Image assistant, just follow the instructions and you'll make simple work of a formerly difficult task. You just pick the steps that apply to your particular needs, and the assistant guides you through the process of making the image transparent and then exporting it in the proper file for print or Web.

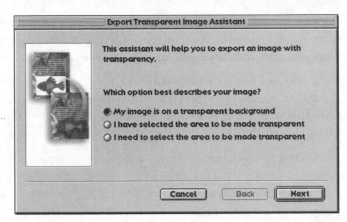

Figure 14.8

Adobe has created a special Export Transparent Image assistant that defines transparent areas and then exports the files.

Multipurpose tools. As with many Adobe programs (and QuarkXPress, for that matter), many of Photoshop's tools have submenus with two or more variations for the tool. A quick way to run through them is to hold down (Option) while clicking a tool. Each time you click, you'll see a different hidden-tool display.

Whoever designed the hidden tools for these programs didn't realize how they would benefit from sticky menus. You still have to click and hold the mouse to see all the available hidden tools, even though sticky menus debuted in the Mac operating system several years ago when Apple rolled out Mac OS 8.

Tool options. Some tools have special options—for example, the magic wand tool has options for the tolerance of the selection and anti-aliasing. A quick way to find out whether a particular tool has any options is to simply double-click it—you'll then see them displayed in the Options palette.

Convenient multiple undos. One of the features missing from older versions of Photoshop was the ability to undo more than a single action. Adobe's clever answer is the History palette, which puts up a display of all the operations you've performed on your artwork. Just click any item in the palette to revert to that particular step in the image-editing process.

Photoshop sucks up RAM, as you might expect of any high-energy graphics program. You can reduce the amount of RAM required by clearing the history once you are certain you don't want to revert to a previous version of the photo. Just hold down (Option) when you choose the Clear History option from the History menu, and you'll permanently erase the history.

Actions palette shortcuts. Photoshop (and Illustrator) offer the *actions* macro feature, which can record a series of steps you take or store any available menu-bar command. A good way to experiment with actions is to try out the ones already included. Photoshop 6.0, for example, comes with a dozen prebuilt Actions. Just look for the Actions folder inside the Adobe Photoshop Only folder. To add Actions to Photoshop, choose Load Actions from the

Actions menu (the submenu in the palette) and then select the ones you want to try. Once you get through this list, you may find you have all or most of what you need without having to create any of your own.

For fast access to your recorded actions, open the Actions menu and choose the Button mode. Any action is now just a single click away. You can also learn the keyboard command connected to an action by selecting the appropriate shortcut and then choosing Action Options from the Actions menu.

Restoring preferences. Like any complicated program, Photoshop has many preference settings that can have a large impact on how the program looks and acts. If you go a little too far in tweaking these, you might want to restore the preferences to their original condition. Version 6.0 puts the preferences in the most logical location, the Preferences folder (inside the System Folder). Once you open the Preferences folder, open the Adobe Photoshop Settings folder and remove the Adobe Photoshop 6 Prefs and Color Settings files. The next time you launch Photoshop, the program will restore the default (factory) settings.

Getting rid of palettes. Heavy-duty graphics programs can fill your screen with a plethora of palettes—and soon you find you can barely see the image you're working on. You can easily dismiss any individual palette by clicking its close box, but if you want to delete several at a time, that involves several steps. Instead, just press Tab and all the palettes and the toolbar vanish. Another press of Tab, and you get them back. This is a boon for any Mac user stuck with a small monitor (or any owner of an iMac or Apple laptop).

Try out Option for extra choices. Option is a great way to exploit secret features of the program. For example, you can use the eyedropper tool to fix your artwork's foreground color. But if you hold down Option, this affects the background color instead. When you hold down Option while dragging an object, you make a copy (this works the same way in AppleWorks). Experiment with Option to see what treasures it will reveal.

Get another view of your artwork. If you're lucky enough to have a large display (or even luckier, the gorgeous wide-screen Apple Cinema Display), this technique can give you a different perspective on your project. Just choose New Window from the Window menu to bring up a second window showing the very same document. You can establish separate zoom settings for each window and click between them to check your changes quickly at various views. This trick also works with a multiple-monitor setup.

15

Web and HTML Design

Gene Steinberg is the chapter editor and author.

It might seem downright strange to begin a chapter on Web-page design by explaining that you don't need to know a lick of HTML (Hypertext Markup Language) to make a pretty good-looking Web page. However, you don't need to master HTML code any more than you need to know what your word-processing software is doing behind the scenes when you're producing the next Great American Novel or preparing a club newsletter.

More and more applications let you design your site from stem to stern in WYSIWYG (what you see is what you get) style, in the same fashion that you would create a document in your favorite word-processing or page-layout program. This means you can create your Web page using a visual interface tool without having to dirty your hands with HTML's nuts and bolts.

On the other hand, if you want to create a first-class Web site that's easy for users with different Web browsers to access and that really looks good, even a little knowledge of how to fine-tune HTML is bound to help, so we'll look at the basics of HTML, too.

In This Chapter

The One-Two-Three Process for Building Web Pages

Most big Internet service providers (ISPs), such as America Online (AOL), CompuServe, EarthLink, Prodigy Internet, and even Apple Computer (as part of its iTools feature), give you several megabytes of free storage space for setting up a Web site. Such facilities, though not intended to help you establish a business site on the Web, are perfect for personal Web sites where you can share information with your family and friends—photos, news and views, and perhaps even your first attempt at an online newsletter.

In addition to giving you storage space, many of these services provide some sort of simplified online Web authoring tool that lets you create a simple Web page in just a few minutes.

Although the instant Web authoring tools have different names, they share several common features. For our purposes, I'll cover **Click-n-Build,** EarthLink's tool for instant Web-page creation (**Figure 15.1**).

Figure 15.1

Click-n-Build your way to your own personal Web page, courtesy of EarthLink.

Unfortunately, EarthLink (Apple's recommended ISP) seems to hide this oh-so-useful feature from its more than 4 million members, burying direct access on your EarthLink Personal Start Page. First you have to access the page itself, via http://start.earthlink.net (if you haven't previously used it, you have to enter your user name and password to bring it up). Click the Support tab and then scroll down to the My Web Site area to access the links that allow you to create or modify a Web page.

Once you get going, you must agree to the ISP terms governing the pages (mostly these tell you not to create objectionable sites, such as those showing or peddling pornographic or hateful material) and then you can proceed with the actual creation process.

First you pick one of the standard design layouts, entering your text in predefined text areas. Then you choose the pictures you want from the ISP's collection of clip art or your own.

Follow the step-by-step instructions, which clearly explain what you need to do. After each operation, you can preview your Web page without actually publishing it (that is, making it available on the Internet). That way you can make sure your page looks just right before you release it to the world.

Once you are satisfied that your Web site meets your expectations, simply click the Finished button and then Publish—in minutes, you have a Web site available to anyone with Internet access.

 AOL's Web-site creator, 1-2-3-Publish, is so simple (it involves just seven steps) that you may find it limiting. Worse, AOL saddles you with its own Hometown ad banner, which promotes the service's features and merchandise.

Web Authoring: Moving Beyond the Basics

When you're ready to extend your creativity to build the simplest possible Web site (which is probably why you're reading this chapter), you may already have the software at hand to build a pretty decent-looking Web page—your favorite word processor. AppleWorks 6, Microsoft Word 98, and the new Word 2001 (and the in-development Word for Mac OS X), for example, have the ability to save documents in HTML format.

So what *is* HTML? It is a language that adds special text commands to a document. These commands tell your Web browser how to display a Web page. They range from simple instructions determining the appearance of text to complex commands detailing the locations of graphics and the complicated issues of Java scripting and special formats. The concept of using text to specify the format of a page isn't new. Several decades ago, people coded typesetting computers using a similar process (I was one of them, which I suppose shows my age).

If you want to truly master HTML's intricacies, I suggest that you get a copy of Elizabeth Castro's definitive book, *HTML 4 for the World Wide Web, Fourth Edition: Visual QuickStart Guide* (Peachpit Press). It's a truly outstanding reference that I use regularly.

In those days, to change the look of your text, you would insert a set of instructions within a bracket or using a special key on your keyboard to specify point size, type style, and so on.

HTML is platform independent, which means a document or file created with HTML doesn't have to restrict itself to a specific operating system, as long as an HTML-aware browser application is available. That's also the shortcoming of the language and the source of great headaches for Web designers. Different browsers or different versions of the same browser may vary (sometimes extensively) in the way they interpret the contents of a page (see the sidebar "The Frustrating Differences in How Web Sites Look," later in this chapter).

Documents coded in Adobe's PostScript page-description language are set up similarly. If you opened such a document with a text editor (or using Word's All or All Documents option), you'd see that it consists largely of text-based commands that define page size, margins, font parameters, and so forth. This is true even for documents made in a PostScript illustration program, such as Adobe Illustrator.

The Limits of Word Processors for Web-Page Creation

When you save your word-processing document as HTML, the application inserts the commands behind the scenes (it doesn't burden you with them). For a Web page that consists strictly of text, this is fine and dandy. But the best-looking Web sites include a variety of elements—not just text but also pictures, animations, frames (two or more pages that are designed to fit on the same page, with some sort of separation), and possibly a link to a sound or video file. When you create a page with all these components, you end up with a lot more than just one file. Each element you add consists of a totally separate file. Your core HTML document simply references these files (in somewhat the same way as a page-layout program references the illustrations you place or import into a document).

A word processor that has the ability to convert your regular documents to HTML simply adapts it to fit HTML's formatting requirements. Microsoft Word even has a View Source option that lets you examine and tear apart the HTML, fine-tuning it to suit your needs (again, that requires some knowledge of the language). Unlike a dedicated HTML editor, however (see the section "An Overview of HTML Editors: The Key Players" later in this chapter), a word processor doesn't provide a simple way to specify sophisticated commands, and the HTML code it generates can be rough, often with strange codes or coding errors. This may cause display problems when people view it using different browsers across various computing platforms.

 Macromedia's powerful HTML editor, Dreamweaver, actually has a special command to clean up the sloppy HTML code in a document translated by Word.

Using Graphics Software to Edit HTML

Another option is your favorite graphics program (see Chapter 14, "Graphics," for more on this subject).

Adobe **Illustrator** ($399; www.adobe.com), for example, has options to convert your illustrations into Web-optimized graphics. Macromedia **FreeHand** ($399; www.macromedia.com) goes a lot further, saving both text and graphics. Stone Design's Mac OS X graphic suite, **Create** ($695 but sometimes offered for $149; www.stone.com), also excels at HTML editing.

 FreeHand's HTML Output Assistant gently guides you through the process of coping with the different requirements of print and Web output so you can be assured of good results.

 Deneba's **Canvas** ($375, or $325 for the downloadable version from www.deneba.com) also has a powerful Web Publishing wizard that makes easy work of transferring your document to HTML and optimizing the graphics. A nearly identical feature comes with the Canvas 7 Standard Edition, which means you can purchase a full-featured print- and Web-savvy illustration program for just $99.95 ($85 for the downloadable version).

 While this book was being written, Deneba posted a public preview (or late beta) version of Canvas 8 for Mac OS X. The program sports dozens upon dozens of new features, and it's worth a trial to see if you want to use its huge range of creation tools for your Web publishing and graphics work.

Note: At press time, Corel Corporation, the financially beleaguered Canadian software maker, had just released a Mac version of CorelDraw 10, with the promise of greatly enhanced HTML features and full support for Mac OS X. You might also find CorelDraw 8 for the Mac at closeout prices, but it's slow and buggy, and many buy it strictly because of its rich collection of free fonts.

An Overview of HTML Editors: The Key Players

Once you get the HTML bug and you're looking to do something more sophisticated than what an ISP's instant-page feature or a word processor can handle, you'll want a dedicated HTML program.

It is possible to write all your HTML code yourself in text form, even in Apple's SimpleText program (or Mac OS X's TextEdit). But this takes dedication and lots of time to master the nuts and bolts. You probably want a program that can do it all for you, both behind the scenes by writing tight HTML code and in a form where you can see the fully formatted document, closely resembling what those who visit your Web site will see.

In the following pages, I provide an overview of several major HTML editing programs. I show you where they might suit your purposes and where they might fall down on the job. If a company has a demo version, you'd do best to give it a test run before ordering a copy. That way you can see if it really meets your needs. I also cover some of the programs that have gone to software heaven. The number of Mac HTML editors has shrunk since the last edition of *The Macintosh Bible* appeared, so I concentrate strictly on those programs you can order or download.

Gone but Not Forgotten

When Apple jettisoned FileMaker (which became a separate company), most of the other Claris products got killed off, except for ClarisWorks, which Apple brought in house and renamed AppleWorks. One of those casualties was Claris HomePage (renamed FileMaker HomePage), a perfectly functional HTML-editing program that offered a simple, visually accessible interface. Despite the fact that FileMaker is no longer offering or supporting the program, thousands of Web sites still use it, so if you happen to find a copy at a local Mac user group store or from a dealer who handles older software, don't dismiss this product—it may be all you need.

Another program no longer developed for the Mac is Adobe's PageMill. Since Adobe acquired GoLive, the company has committed its resources to developing that program instead. However, because PageMill was bundled on many iMacs, taking advantage of it is a no-brainer. It is more flexible than HomePage and almost as easy to learn as a simple word processor.

Another casualty of poor sales and company specialization was Symantec's Visual Page.

Almost Still There

Although it'll likely never progress beyond version 1.0 (since it apparently wasn't a huge sales success), the Mac version of Microsoft's FrontPage is still available from dealers. If you work in a cross-platform office, you'll be pleased to know it's compatible with the Windows version, though it has fewer features. The fact that Microsoft apparently isn't updating it reduces its value if you want to keep abreast of the latest and greatest Web technologies. However, the program's WYSIWYG editing features are fairly easy to master (despite some confusing Microsoft-style elements to its interface), and you may want to consider it. If you find a copy of the Mac Office 98 Gold edition, you'll find FrontPage included at no extra cost (it's not in Office 2001 for the Mac).

You'll appreciate the From Existing Content wizard, which lets you import your existing site and take advantage of FrontPage's editing and site-management tools.

Adobe GoLive

When Adobe acquired **GoLive** ($299) in 1999, the company did what it does to all its graphics software—gave it the look and feel of an Adobe application. This is a double-edged sword. If you like the Adobe interface, you'll feel right at home in the latest version, GoLive 5. If you don't take to the multiple-palette layout, you might want to consider another program (never fear, I'll cover other options).

In GoLive's favor, it's remarkably easy to adapt to, particularly if you want to explore the intricacies of HTML only when absolutely necessary. I first began using this application for my own Web site (www.macnightowl.com, although my Webmaster has since moved to Macromedia's Dreamweaver, which is described below) when CyberStudio published it in the early days. Despite Adobe's extensive revisions, GoLive is a comfortable working environment that will seem fairly familiar even if your prior experience with HTML is via a word processor.

 GoLive's 360 Code—nope, it doesn't create circles. It allows you to move your documents between GoLive and a text-based editor such as BBEdit from Bare Bones Software (see the section "HTML the Old-Fashioned Way" later in this chapter).

 If you must share files with Web designers who work in that other platform, you'll be pleased to know that GoLive 5.0 is available in a near-identical Windows version, and both offer enhanced collaborative features for workgroups.

 If you look at tables as an alien language, GoLive's Table Window feature simplifies the task so it's no harder than it would be in a word processor. You can also create custom table styles and repeat recurring themes to give your site a unique look.

Regular users have been clamoring for quite some time for the Smart Objects feature. Unlike even simple programs such as Claris (and then FileMaker) HomePage, GoLive never allowed you to edit pictures in the program—you could only link to them. You had to edit them in another program, such as Adobe Photoshop. The Smart Objects feature lets you perform on-the-fly edits to pictures created in Adobe programs such as Illustrator, LiveMotion (a Web animation tool), and Photoshop.

At the risk of making this section sound like an ad for GoLive, version 5.0 features more than 100 enhancements that appeal to novices and professional users alike. I'm a happy camper.

Macromedia Dreamweaver

Macromedia's **Dreamweaver** ($299) is the other leading WYSIWYG page-building software. Dreamweaver is more attuned to the professional HTML coder and features three display options: WYSIWYG only—for those who don't want to see the code, HTML source code in a split screen above the WYSIWYG display, or source code only. This way you can fine-tune your site as you create or edit it without having to close one window and open another (as you must do in GoLive).

Dreamweaver includes slick capabilities. You can create rollovers, letting you animate a button when a user interacts with it, for example. With the application's timeline, you create simple animations without having to use a special Web design tool such as Flash. And Dreamweaver gives you an efficient way to store and update reusable content through the use of its assets-management tools.

(In fact, the program is so powerful my Webmaster ended up choosing it for the redesign of my Mac Night Owl Web site and my science-fiction site, www.rockoids.com.)

The newest edition of Dreamweaver, version 4, offers many helpful features. For example, you can draw tables and table cells wherever you want, and the program adds the adjacent cells and fills them with invisible content to make your table complete.

Dreamweaver has a large community of users, many of whom write extensions—small applications that help you easily perform tasks, such as reformatting tables. Many of these extensions are free. You can find out more at www.macromedia.com/exchange/dreamweaver/.

Of course, as with most design tools, you have to have a large enough display to see all the open windows at once (**Figure 15.2**).

Dreamweaver has an attractive, accessible interface with a learning curve that won't cause the novice user to throw up his or her hands in frustration.

The software is deep enough, however, that professional coders will be quite happy with it. The extensive Help menu will guide you through the hard parts, and a comprehensive tutorial will get you up and running in a very short time.

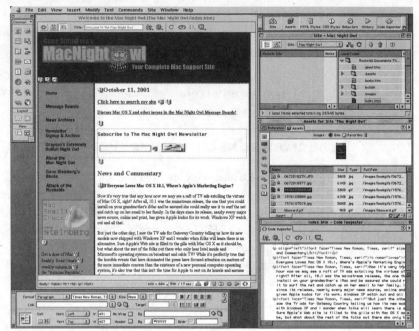

Figure 15.2

As with many design tools, put the page and the palettes together, and you'll lust for a 22-inch display.

SoftPress Freeway

This application, from the United Kingdom's SoftPress Systems Ltd. ($249; www.softpress.com), tends to get lost in the shuffle because of all the attention Dreamweaver and GoLive attract. On the surface, this Web tool offers extraordinary power, particularly in terms of its interface, which may remind you of QuarkXPress, the popular page-layout program. In fact, if you're a devoted QuarkXPress user, you'll probably adapt to Freeway in no time. The interface is also filled with convenient palettes to help you develop your site with the utmost precision.

Freeway seems like a dream come true. It's designed to free you from the drudgery of learning HTML coding, since it does everything behind the scenes like other WYSIWYG programs. But it has its quirks and problems, some of which present serious barriers.

Alignment palettes and other navigation features allow you to position the elements on your Web site with great accuracy.

Like QuarkXPress, Freeway uses frames or boxes to contain text and graphics. You can use the picture box for placement, sizing, cropping, and rotation of pictures.

For some unaccountable reason, Freeway requires that you install the graphics element of Apple's QuickDraw GX software. But if you do that, you get bogus messages about having the wrong fonts installed. Since QuickDraw GX support has vanished from the Mac OS, this can be a source of irritation. The publisher was planning to remove the GX requirement for version 4.

Freeway has difficulty importing existing sites. When I brought my own Web site into the program, Freeway scrambled all the text and layouts. To be blunt, I didn't have the patience to fix the problems (there were just too many to make repair worthwhile). The program works best when you build a site from scratch.

HTML experts will note that the code generated doesn't comply with the latest standards, and you get little or no direct access to the underlying source code.

Freeway's page-layout approach to Web authoring may well be the wave of the future; it does for the Web what page-layout and word-processing software did for print documents. However, even the version shipping when this book was published (3.1) has serious flaws that SoftPress needs to address before this program can realize its great potential.

HTML the Old-Fashioned Way

Before WYSIWYG Web tools came into existence, you did all your Web authoring in a text-based program. Even today, professional designers still depend heavily on applications such as BBEdit from Bare Bones Software ($119; www.barebones.com). Coding by hand has its advantages, since you have complete control over every element of your site. However, as graphic designers rely more and more on WYSIWYG applications to do their stuff, the days of HTML text editors are probably numbered. For one thing, programs such as GoLive and Dreamweaver give you direct access to the source code. In addition, it's simply much faster for most users to enter the text and graphics and choose the formatting from palettes and menus.

If you're a shareware fan, you may want to look for programs such as **Alpha** ($30; shareware via VersionTracker.com) and **PageSpinner** ($29.95; www.optima-system.com), designed for folks who prefer code over WYSIWYG.

Other Web Tools of the Trade

You can rely on Web-authoring software to help you build your Web site, but you will soon find that a couple more tools will help you complete your job faster and easier. In this section, I cover a collection of special-purpose utilities that handle Web graphics and attempt to optimize Web performance (more or less). I also cover a few clip art collections that can add little flourishes to your site.

Graphic Editors

Although programs such as Dreamweaver and GoLive offer expanded graphics-editing tools, a separate graphics program can provide more features and additional ways to stretch your creative powers. Here are some of the choices:

GraphicConverter. Thorsten Lemke's shareware application ($30; http://lemkesoft.com) can read and convert so many graphic formats, the mind boggles. It also offers basic editing tools. Because it's shareware, download a copy and give it a trial. If you like it, though, you'll want to pay your fee directly to Lemke so he can continue to develop and expand this great application. It runs on Mac OS X, too.

GifBuilder. For animated GIFs, this program is first rate (freeware; http://homepage.mac.com/piguet/gif.html) and its creator has released a version for Mac OS X. It's not hard to use: Just drag your GIF file to the program's icon to access its animation features.

Adobe ImageReady. Originally a separate program, Adobe's tool for creating Web graphics now comes bundled with Photoshop, and the programs link to each other. Use it to optimize Web graphics and create simple animations.

TypeStyler. Long ago, if you wanted a quick headline or a special effect for your lettering, you'd find a worthy tool in TypeStyler, once published by Brøderbund (along with that company's games and PrintShop). For reasons too complex to list here, Brøderbund unceremoniously dumped the program and left Ken and Karen Stillman, authors of the program, hanging out to dry. The clever couple recruited brother Dave Stillman and the rest of the family and began publishing it themselves. The new **TypeStyler 3** ($295, but sometimes offered for $149.95 as an introductory special; www.typestyler.com) is Web-savvy, boasting the ability to add simple animations as well as various type effects, both simple and highly complex. It also has dozens of prebuilt effects you can easily adapt to your purposes. What's more, you won't face a difficult learning curve. In about three minutes flat, I built a simple logo for my site with see-through effects in the lettering. This program is simply marvelous (and the people who produce it are marvelous too and deserve your business). Check out the Web site for a demo and more information. And, yes, they were working hard on a Mac OS X version, with lots more features, when this book was written.

Web Clip Art

Most of the clip-art collections mentioned in Chapter 14, "Graphics," come in JPEG versions that you can adapt for Web use. You'll find handy buttons for common functions, decorative bars, and so forth.

Among the finest clip-art collections are those from Nova Development Corporation (www.novadevelopment.com). However, two of the more interesting products were not being listed at the company's Web site when I consulted it for this book. But if you can find a copy, check out **Web Explosion 20,000**, which features buttons, bullets, and backgrounds. With a little judicious mixing and matching, you can give your site a unique look. **Animation Explosion**, from the same company, will give your site movement and form, with convenient special effects that add the spit and polish of a professional Web presence.

Nova Development has dedicated itself to the Mac platform for years and is a regular presence at Macworld Expos. One hopes these two packages are not earmarked for extinction.

Web Optimizers

Wouldn't it be a dream come true if a program existed that could examine your Web site and clean up the code? You wouldn't have to spend hours fine-tuning everything to get rid of unnecessary code that might slow down display of your site.

Several shareware programs promise to perform this function. Basically, they examine your HTML files and then strip out redundant or unnecessary codes, reducing file size so your page loads faster. Two of these programs can also optimize your graphics (largely by eliminating the Mac OS resource fork, which doesn't affect how they look).

Web-Tool Shareware Isn't Always Shareware at All

In the old days, shareware software came fully featured, without any limits (well, perhaps a few), and the authors or publishers depended on the honesty of their customers to earn a living. Alas, few folks actually pay for shareware; it's a sad fact of life. It's discouraging to would-be programmers who hope to build a nice part-time income from such ventures.

In answer to this dilemma, some programmers have turned their shareware into demos, providing limited functionality unless you buy a user license. Sad, but an economic necessity. Unfortunately, it also means that you can't really test some of these programs until you order a user license.

One of these programs, as you'll see below, actually does a pretty good job of making your Web pages more efficient, so stay tuned.

VSE Web Site Turbo. This $49.95 tool (http://vse-online.com/) promises reductions of 20 to 50 percent and claims to optimize GIF and JPEG images to load as quickly as possible. The information file on this program lists top ratings from several Web sites, claiming extraordinary results. It's worth a try, but don't expect to get it to do anything real before you pay the fee. The so-called "unregistered demo version" simply "mixes up the text on the optimized version of your Web pages so you cannot publish them on your Web server." However, it might be what you need if you're willing to pay for the user license.

OptimaHTML. Here's a real winner (it's $10 from www.maczsoftware.com). This shareware utility has a simple interface and does the job without messing up all the careful formatting you created for your pages. You can also customize its treatment of particular HTML strings, in case you want to tell it to retain some codes or delete others for which you have no need. Once the job is done (it takes barely a second or two), you can view the finished page or picture in the program itself or in your selected Web browser. For my two Web sites, I got savings of 5 to 15 percent on the HTML pages, and as much as 80 percent on the pictures—all without affecting the design or quality of the graphics. The only downside is that the standard optimization process deletes the line returns that separate sections of your page, which means you may end up with one continuous line of text a mile wide (but you can always save the original for further editing and another optimization pass).

A Very Short Course on HTML

With so many options for creating and editing a Web site without exposing yourself to HTML codes, this section of the chapter may seem superfluous. On the other hand, there are so many variables in Web authoring and so many areas where imprecise code can mess up the way your site appears that it's important to know at least the basics.

HTML employs text-based commands to format your Web page. In fact, the pages themselves are all text, and (if they're not too large) you can even open them in Mac OS 9's SimpleText (some folks hand-tune their HTML that way). The commands are instructions that tell your Web browser how the page should look.

If you've ever been exposed to old-fashioned text-based word processors, which were prevalent before Apple existed, or to traditional typesetting, you'll see a passing resemblance between HTML and the way you coded those documents.

For example, HTML consists of an opening tag that appears before the material you're formatting and a closing or end tag that appears at the end of the material.

To separate HTML from regular text, you place the commands within angle brackets, beginning with the less-than sign (<) and concluding with the greater-than sign (>).

The Frustrating Differences in How Web Sites Look

With a word-processing or desktop-publishing document, you can be reasonably assured that the document will look the same on your monitor and printed out as long as you have the right fonts and linked pictures. Not so with Web sites.

Every single Web browser out there interprets Web pages in a unique way. That means the Web site you laboriously created and fine-tuned may look perfectly fine in the latest Macintosh version of Microsoft Internet Explorer but may fall flat on its face in the comparable version of Netscape Communicator.

Even worse, when you view the very same site in a Windows version of these browsers, you may see additional differences—some slight, some significant. Part of the problem on the Windows side is that the display size is typically 96 dots per inch (dpi), as opposed to 72 dpi on a Mac (although high screen-resolution settings have altered that old industry-wide desktop-publishing standard). In addition, Windows uses larger font sizes to accommodate the higher standard screen resolution. All these factors can combine to give your Web pages a totally different look from what you had planned.

Furthermore, as emerging Web standards change, you can bet that what looked fine in your browser or Web authoring program will undergo still more unexpected alterations.

What Should You Do?

If your target audience is apt to be using the latest browser versions, you can probably just check out your pages in the current software and be confident that most of the visitors to your site will see acceptable results.

However, if you want the widest possible audience, consider that many users have old Macs, old PCs, and older versions of browsers, which are less able to display the latest commands. You will want to test your pages using these parameters to see if they still look acceptable.

Some designers will set up their sites with alternative versions of a page. For example, if a browser can't display features such as frames or animations, users can click a button to see another version; if they have the right browser, the page can display in all its glory.

One example where using a browser-specific tag can have unwanted results is Netscape's <BLINK> tag. A rapidly flashing button or title may seem cool, but most folks find the result downright annoying. I tried it at my site once and got several extremely heated complaints. Avoid using it.

One basic tag, `<i>`, specifies italic text. Everything following that simple command is *italic*. To switch back to roman text, you simply close the tag with a slash, like this: `</i>`. Of course, this command structure can get quite involved when you expand your HTML arsenal to specify the attributes of linked Web sites or graphics.

An example of a more complex command is this one, which links my Web site to another page on another site and then provides a title that appears tooltip style on most browsers other than Netscape (except for Netscape 6):

```
<a href="http://www.rockoids.com" title="Attack of the Rockoids Is
Coming!">
```

A List of Basic HTML Tags

I make no pretense of offering a complete course in HTML. But I do cover the basics of HTML tags. Once you get the hand of it, some practice and regular reference to a book such as Elizabeth Castro's fine work will do wonders to increase your knowledge and abilities.

The beginning of a Web site. First things first. Every Web document must have some basic tags that identify it to your browser, and you must enter additional tags in a specific order.

You begin a Web page with a header that identifies it, much as you'd set up a PostScript or PDF file. A PDF file, for example, contains a header labeled `%PDF-1.4` (the latter part is the version number).

To start your page, enter the `<HTML>` tag. You'll close your page with an `</HTML>` tag at the bottom. The latter, like all end tags, contains the telltale slash that indicates a closing command. Once you've established at the beginning of the page what kind of page you're building, you then need to separate the heads from the body copy. You can repeat these tags as needed throughout the page. Here's the way you'd set up your basic page:

```
<HTML>
<HEAD>
<TITLE>Gene's Fabulous Web Page</TITLE>
<BODY>
```

Use the area following the `<BODY>` tag for the main text of your document. Of course, the process doesn't end here. Your code will include tags that specify the text style. If you want to include graphics or links to other sites, which entails more-complex commands. You'll use special tags to add tables, frames (multiple pages within a single page), and elaborate effects such as JavaScripts and animation.

Your Web page concludes with this:

```
</BODY>
</HEAD>
</HTML>
```

All right. That's the easy stuff. You can use the tags in the table "Common Web Tags" to build a simple page with text and headlines from scratch, without a WYSIWYG Web tool. Now we move on to some of the more sophisticated tags (still basic, but more comprehensive).

Common Web Tags

<H1>	Opens a heading. There are six levels of headings in regular HTML, with number 1 being the largest.
</H1>	Closes that number 1 head.
<P>	Specifies the beginning of a paragraph in your body copy.
</P>	Ends the paragraph. An extra return usually separates paragraphs on a Web page for easy reading. Some folks use paragraph indents instead. You'll want to try both to see which works best for you.
<B>	Makes the text that follows it bold.
</B>	Changes bold text back to roman.
<UL>	Starts an unordered list, such as this bulleted list.
<LI>	Formats the text that follows the bullet so it's indented within the bullet.

The next level. Once you get past the basic formatting instructions, you'll start adding *attributes,* elements that provide special instructions describing the command's use. You can, for example, specify a background color for your Web page. Otherwise, you get a drab gray background.

One of the simplest colors to use is plain white. I'll show you the code and then tear it down to explain how it's set up:

```
<body bgcolor="white">
```

That's an easy one. The attributes—in this case, the background color—appear after the equal sign (=), enclosed in double quotes (""). You can specify basic colors by name alone or by hexidecimal format, as in the following example:

```
<BODY BGCOLOR="#FFFFFF">
```

More-complex shades always get a number rather than a name.

To insert a picture, you'd use an *image tag,* which is simply a reference to the picture and its location. This is similar to how a page-layout program such as QuarkXPress handles pictures behind the scenes, by storing a *reference* to the file rather than inserting the file itself.

For example, I used to use this tag to summon the logo for my site (until I changed it to a more complicated version consisting of banners, tables, and whatnot):

```
<img src="nightlogo.gif">
```

Nothing mysterious here—this command is just describing the source, or SRC, of the image, a file named NIGHTLOGO.GIF. If the picture is in another folder, you'd specify the path or location of the folder:

```
<IMG SRC="IMAGEFOLDER/NIGHTLOGO.GIF">
```

Don't forget that to make your pictures appear on a page, you must upload the actual images to your Web storage space, not just to the text page. Popular Web authoring tools such as Adobe GoLive and Macromedia Dreamweaver can handle all these site-management chores, so visitors always see the latest images at your site.

Commonsense Tips for a Good-Looking Web Site

As with any artistic endeavor, you don't became a crack Web designer overnight, even if you have the most expensive software, a powerful Mac, and a huge collection of clip art from which to choose. Even if you can handle print designs with aplomb, you'll find that designing for the World Wide Web entails trade-offs and some new design considerations, simply because this medium lacks the precision of the print world.

The Basics

Here are some basics to consider when you begin your Web authoring journey:

See how others do it. There is no secret as to how your favorite Web site is designed. You can easily view the source code whenever you want. Just bring up the site in your favorite Web browser and then use its source feature to display the information. With Internet Explorer, for example (and with AOL's bundled Web browser), just ⌘-click the page and choose the View Source option from the contextual pop-up menu. For Netscape users, the command is called Page Source in the View menu. Either way, with a little background in HTML you can easily learn the secrets of the top Web designers. You can then adapt some of those tags to your own site and see how they work.

Although examining source code is a great way to learn your craft, just remember not to attempt to copy and publish copyrighted content, such as the text or pictures at a site, because that would definitely run you afoul of the author's intellectual-property rights.

Make it simple. So many wonderful HTML tags and great special effects are available that it's tempting to try each one on your site. Don't! All those extra commands, pictures, and animations can slow the site to a crawl. Remember that not everyone has a cable modem or DSL; the vast majority of users still make Internet connections via analog modems, and not all of these are the latest 56Kbps designs (which, in fact, seldom approach the maximum connection speed). It's common for folks to just pass by a site that takes forever to generate its content. If your site is devoted to a top-grossing movie, perhaps your visitors will be willing to endure the wait. Otherwise, they'll go elsewhere. The best thing to do is test the page with a Web browser at every step of the way and see what content takes longest to appear. Scale down graphics as much as possible; your graphics software's optimizing tools can make them smaller. Use animation only when you really need it. Your visitors will thank you for your efforts by staying around to check out your site.

Keep pages short. Believe it or not, some Mac users aren't comfortable with scroll bars or paging down. If a single page gets too long, visitors may never read a great part of the content simply because they don't bother to move down the page. Although it's true that you might need a certain length to cover the necessary content (and many Web sites, including the popular CNN.com, are lengthy), try to use links rather than length wherever possible. I've seen pages 20 screens deep and more. Whew!

Don't depend on pictures for navigation. One of the most popular Web sites—Apple's (www.apple.com)—uses picture after picture to link you from its home page to the rest of the site (the site even requires the latest version of QuickTime for its animation). The rest of us, though, should provide clear text labels as well and not make users depend on pictures to get around. Some folks with older browsers or slow Internet connections may actually turn off graphics (in the browser's preferences) to speed up display. Try looking at your site without pictures and see if you can still get around easily.

Make text short and easy to read. You may have an awful lot to say, but saying it online is not the same as saying it in print. For one thing, it's just harder to read on a computer display, even if your site visitors have the latest model with ultrasharp text. You'll want to avoid smaller font sizes and unusual typefaces (which may not even translate to someone else's browser). Keep the paragraphs short and sweet. If you feel compelled to publish your Great American Novel online, divide it into smaller sections or chapters. Keep each section easy to read and digest. You may even want to test it out with a friend (an objective one) to see if he or she reports any problems reading the material.

Check your spelling. Make sure your word-processed or page-layout documents don't have typos, and use your Web tool's spelling checker (if it has one) for the same purpose. Nothing reflects more poorly on your content than a raft of spelling mistakes. If you work with a tool that lacks a spelling checker, try Casady & Greene's Spell Catcher ($29.95; www.casadyg.com), which puts an interactive spelling checker, dictionary, and thesaurus in every program you use. Check out the Web site for a limited-time demo.

Test, test, and test again. Even the simplest Web site may have a very different look as you move from browser to browser, from version to version, and from one computing platform to another. You'll want to test your site in as many environments as possible to make sure visitors can easily read and see your content. If you have friends who own a PC (or, heaven forbid, you own one yourself), make sure your site looks right on those machines, too. Even if your target audience is all Macintosh, many of your potential visitors may need to view the site on another computing platform from time to time. Whenever a new browser version (or even a totally new product) comes out, be first in line to get a copy so you can see how it affects your site's appearance.

It's not just the text that may look different on another computing platform. Even the gamma (the midtones) may differ, which means the picture that's perfect on the Mac is too dark under Windows. If you can't test your site with a Windows PC, try the freeware GammaToggleFKEY ($5 from www.acts.org/roland/thanks/), a useful tool that will invoke a PC's gamma setting so you can see how things change.

After making changes to your site, save the document before opening it in a browser. Otherwise you'll only see the older version of the file.

One handy tool in the arsenal of a Web designer who doesn't have a Wintel computer around is a Windows emulator—Connectix's Virtual PC ($99 to $249, depending on the Windows OS; www.connectix.com). (Alas, the other well-known emulator, FWB's SoftWindows, has been discontinued.) Although an emulator is nowhere near as fast as the real thing, you aren't playing 3D games with it. You just want to view your site under Windows to make sure it looks right. One Virtual PC version includes Linux, so you can view your content under Unix as well.

Practice your craft. Having the latest and greatest Web authoring tools, the most powerful multiprocessor Mac, or even that gorgeous Apple Cinema Display won't guarantee that you will become a great Web designer. It takes study, practice, and still more practice to hone your skills. The basic chores of learning your Web application and HTML aren't hard (though the latter can be a tedious pursuit). The rest just takes time and patience. Seek advice from professionals if you know some. Many of the best Web designers are happy to give a little advice to help a newcomer along—it makes the Web a better place, after all.

Make navigation easy. If your site consists of just one page, the question of moving from one item to another is not all that difficult, as long as you don't make your page too wide or too long. But if you have a lot of content to deliver, divide it into additional pages. It's important to make it easy for your site visitors to move from one place to another and then back again. Otherwise they'll follow link after link through several pages and then get totally lost. Put a clearly labeled link back to the introductory or home page on each page of your site.

A Web site is like a puzzle that you want to make easy to solve. Wherever a guest goes, he or she should be able to get back to the starting point without any difficulty. If moving to different areas of your site requires a number of steps, try to create a direct path instead, from beginning to end. Each page should have links for all related pages (don't forget that home page). Put the links in visible places, with large, clear, cleanly organized buttons. If you use a title for your link, label clearly what it points to. For a large site, consider adding a search engine (this isn't as hard as it seems) or creating a site map—basically, an index listing all the links at your site, organized by topic or alphabetically.

 Wouldn't it be nice if you had a built-in search engine, just like those the big sites boast? Well, many of those major companies team up with search engines such as Excite.com to provide searching capabilities. You don't have to spend an arm and a leg to make your site searchable. In fact, you don't have to spend anything. One possibility is the Virtual Search Engine, from Curry Guide Services (http://services.curryguide.com/free/vse/). Unfortunately, a really good free engine, MyComputer's SiteMiner (www.siteminer.com), was discontinued because it became too costly to maintain, and it's now only available in a paid "Professional" version, but it also includes Google for Web searches, so it may be worth checking out (pricing starts at $19.95 per month).

Use a target to simplify navigation. Even if your site has all the right ease-of-use features, sometimes folks still get lost in an endless sea of links. Once a browser window displays a new page, it's not always apparent how to get back. This is particularly true if you point to content on another site. A way to avoid this confusion is to set up as part of your link a <TARGET> tag, which opens that page in a totally separate browser, making it easy for your visitors to get back to you. Here's the simple command: <A target=window href="targetname"</A>. The rule of thumb is to set up external links—those that lie outside your site—to open in a separate window.

 You can easily use one of the interactive palettes in Web authoring tools such as GoLive to set your target page. In Dreamweaver, it's available direct from the Properties palette.

Getting the Right Color

Mac and Windows computers don't see the world the same way. For simplicity's sake, and to support older displays, Web designers use the old 8-bit (256-color) browser-safe standard, which goes right back to the days of the earliest color Macs. The problem is that the 256 colors a Mac displays are not quite the same as those you see on a PC. This doesn't mean red becomes blue on that other platform; in fact, both do support 216 of the same colors, which form the core of the browser-safe palette. It is from these colors that Web designers make their selections.

Fortunately, you don't have to figure out which of those 216 colors you can use. Just about all graphics programs and WYSIWYG Web tools support the Web-safe color palette. A simple selection from a pop-up menu should get you a listing of the correct hues.

Is Your GIF Transparent?

Well, not normally. Even if your image fills just a portion of the document, its background is generally set to white. That's perfectly fine, if the background on your Web page is white. But if you've set your background to gray or some other color, the white area can be downright disturbing. Is there a way to keep this problem from messing up your site? There is.

Some HTML tools can handle the transparency chores for you and some can't. You use a magic wand tool to select an area you want to change. If your HTML program offers this ability, you just select the wand, click the area you wish to make transparent, and delete the background. Poof!

 Adobe Photoshop has an Export Transparent Image wizard that steps you through the process of selection and saving the document in the proper form, so you don't have to figure it out yourself. It's available from the program's Help menu.

Stick to a Simple Background

The default background on an HTML page is drab gray. White is easiest on the eyes, but you might want to try something different—perhaps even a small illustration—to provide a decorative background or wallpaper effect.

Here's a command for creating a background (I used it once to provide a starry backdrop on my science-fiction page, www.rockoids.com):

```
<body bgcolor="black" background="starbg.gif" text="white">
```

In the above command, the image file, starbg.gif, is a little picture showing stars against a black background. As with wallpaper or a tiles, it repeats over and over again to cover the length and breadth of the Web page.

Although these backgrounds make it easy to create some spectacular effects at your Web site, make sure the source file is small enough to display quickly (it only needs to load once regardless of how often it repeats). You could use a single large file to create a background, at the expense of making the page take a lot longer to load.

Linking and Anchoring

As you add content to your Web site, you'll want to include links to other pages or even to other sites. You handle this via an HTML link, which a site visitor can click to access more content. The neat thing about the way HTML works is that you're not limited to a specific physical location for your link. It can point to an item on your site or to a site on the other side of the world. To your visitors, it's just one click away. This is one of the nice things about the World Wide Web's global community.

About that anchor—you don't toss it into the sea, but the principle is the same. When you specify an anchor, it creates an instant jump point that allows a visitor to access that particular area without having to scroll through an entire page to see it.

Here's a typical anchor link: www.macnightowl.com/index.htm#bullish. This URL points directly to a portion of the opening or index page of my Web site that contains the anchor "bullish."

Internet Explorer 5 handles anchors in a somewhat flaky—and frustrating—fashion. If the anchor point occurs near the top of the page, it will take you right to the top and not to the anchor (most of the time, anyway). Occasionally this also happens when the anchor is located later in the page. Under Netscape versions prior to 6.0, if the anchor appears in a part of your page that's placed within a table, the page will open at the bottom (a refresh is required to move it to the proper position). Argh!

Exploring Grids and Tables

As in a word-processing document, in a Web page you use a table to organize your content in easily digestible portions, and even to place text and picture elements side by side. The table also lets you set your page to a fixed width, so you can make sure the material appears in the intended size (allowing for the variables in display size and resolution settings, of course).

Fortunately, WYSIWYG Web tools actually let you build tables almost as easily as you can with a word processor. First you access the table feature, and then you specify the rows and columns and perhaps the table's overall dimensions. After that, it's generally a matter of inserting the various text and picture elements within each cell, making a little adjustment here and there, and presto—you have a table!

Some HTML programs, such as GoLive and Dreamweaver, can even import the tabbed text directly from a spreadsheet program, such as Microsoft's Excel, and format it into a table for you.

Making GIFs Move

One really neat thing about GIFs is that you can animate them. You see an image, and then it undergoes a change—perhaps it turns into a small animated movie. A title may switch or an image may change, morphing into a different style. You set up an animated GIF similarly to a movie. You create a separate image for each stage of the action and then combine them all into a fluid (or reasonably so) animation. That may seem terribly complicated, but several handy programs make the process quite easy.

Don't overdo it. As with any artistic pursuit, the impact of an animated GIF is a product of your imagination and skills. But the best advice is to keep it simple. Every extra effect you add simply increases file size, and this can determine whether someone remains at your site or departs in annoyance at how long it's taking to load.

If your potential audience include lots of AOL or CompuServe 2000 members, you face an additional limitation. The built-in Web browser for their software, based on Internet Explorer, sets an option called *use compressed images* by default (it's present in the Windows version, too). When a member uses that option (and most folks do not normally fiddle with their preference settings), image quality is apt to nosedive, and Web-based animations may disappear altogether.

You can set an animated GIF to repeat or loop so it displays the same pattern over and over again. This can get annoying, particularly for folks who visit your site frequently. You may want to limit the number of repeats or just leave a long delay for the initial frame so the repeating pattern isn't too obvious.

Also limit the number of frames in your animation, because each frame increases file size. The larger the file, the more time it takes the browser to download the artwork. I've seen some wonderful animations that made me lose patience while I waited for them to load. The world's greatest animation won't help if your audience has left by the time it displays. Although such special effects may work when you have a large, dedicated audience—as with a site devoted to, say, a music star—for the rest of us, less is more.

You can use a frame that contains a blurred version of the artwork to substitute for several frames, simulating motion without taking up too much disk space. The blurring effect will give the animated GIF an added feeling of rapid motion.

Some Frame Advice

A *frame* splits your Web page into two or more sections, sometimes with separate scrolling areas. On some sites it looks just terrific, since it lets you navigate through the content more easily. But it can also cause problems. For one thing, if you click a Web link in a frame, it usually opens up within that frame, even if it's on another site—yet you still see the other frame at the original site. Talk about confusing!

If you want to use this feature, do so with caution. Overuse of frames can easily confound rather than help your site visitors.

A Web site that contains frames consists of one page that defines the layout, called the *frameset,* plus a separate file for each HTML page to which the site links. The most convenient way to set up a frameset is to put some simple navigational buttons for your content on the left or at the top or bottom of the site, and suppress scrolling for this frame. Keep the scroll bars on the main portion of the page, and make that area as large as possible, since that's what your visitors want to see. Consider, too, that not all Mac users have big screens. A user who has an iMac or a Mac with an even smaller display will have an awfully hard time viewing your page without generous use of scroll bars, even if it's all in one frame.

You can put multiple frames on your site, but this just makes it more difficult for site visitors to see the content. Set up your site with a link to a frameless version for those who have older browsers that cannot view frames. Although it would be nice if everyone had the latest and greatest hardware and software, millions of users out there (Mac OS, Windows, and Unix) have older computers that can't support current browser versions or just aren't inclined to deal with the hassles and possible conflicts of an update. For these members of your potential audience, frames are unviewable.

My personal viewpoint may not sit well with those who want their Web sites to offer all the latest bells and whistles, but I believe in the "keep it simple" concept. Make the Web site simple and convenient for the largest number of visitors; if necessary, give them the option to view the content in different ways. That lets you take advantage of features such as frames and animation for those who can view that content, and streamline the site for others.

Getting There by Percentages

When you create a Web site, normally the page flows into your browser and fills the available space, without regard to the width of the document window, the browser you use, or even the settings of your Mac's display. You can specify exact sizes, using a grid or table to set fixed limits on the width of the page. But that's a double-edged sword. If a visitor to your site has an ultrasmall display, the width of the page may extend beyond the edges, forcing your guest to scroll to the right or left to see it all—a downright annoying phenomenon if he or she just wants to read some text or see the cute little button you stuck at the left corner for ease of navigation.

On the other hand, if you make your page too narrow, it ends up with a whole lot of white space on each side when viewed on a large display.

One way around this, other than to set no specifications at all (which you can't do with a table), is to use percentages instead. If you want a block of text to fill all of the available space in a browser window, you'd enter 100 percent in the source code.

Here's an example from my own Mac Night Owl Web site (at least before I switched to percentages for some pages):

```
<table cool width="600" height="5154" border="0" cellpadding="0"
cellspacing="0" gridx="16" gridy="16">
```

As you can see, I specify a width of 600 pixels, sufficient to accommodate even a small display—iMac users will have no trouble whatever seeing my content at its full size.

Keep in mind that the width of a pixel isn't set in stone. In the old days of the Mac, with a screen resolution of 72 dpi, 600 pixels added up to about 8.33 inches. But on a Windows computer, at a setting of 96 dpi, 600 pixels would fill 6.25 inches. For most Mac users, the actual width would fall somewhere between these extremes (which means you can't predict the actual size).

However, those with larger displays may find the white border annoying, so I could just as well specify that command this way:

```
<table cool width="100%" height="5154" border="0" cellpadding="0"
cellspacing="0" gridx="16" gridy="16">
```

If I wanted to guarantee a fixed amount of white space around the page, I'd make it 90 percent.

Some WYSIWYG Web tools, such as GoLive, let you specify table widths by percentage so you can see the result without having to move back and forth between the authoring tool and a browser window.

As with any new approach to designing your Web site, you'll want to experiment with both the fixed width and percentage approaches to see which works best for you.

16
Multimedia

. . . .

Michael E. Cohen is the chapter editor and author.

OK, this is the fun stuff.

It's words. It's pictures. It's sound. It's animation. It's video. It's interactive.

It's anything from the simple slide show you play on your Blue Dalmatian iMac's screen ("Here's me and Marge at the Grand Canyon …"—*click*—"… and there's Aunt Ruthie riding a donkey …"—*click*) to the CD-based, full-screen, interactive motion-picture extravaganza, complete with director's commentary, trivia game, alternate scenes, picture-in-picture, Web links … which you can *also* play on your Blue Dalmatian iMac. It's something you make to amaze your friends, impress your teacher, inform your business associates, convince your clients, woo your mate, and occupy your leisure hours (and any other spare hours you happen to have lying around).

It's what every Mac has been capable of doing since that day in 1984 when the first 128K Macintosh rolled onstage and said, "Hello." And it still does it better than just about any computer on the planet.

It's multimedia. And (did I mention this?) it's the fun stuff.

In This Chapter

Multimedia Defined (More or Less)

Multimedia is one of those concepts that gets really fuzzy around the edges; broadly speaking, it's a presentation that combines more than one medium.

On your Mac, multimedia usually comes in the form of a document that combines at least two (and usually more) of the following: text, pictures, sound, animation, video, and interactivity. A Web page that combines text, links, and graphics is a simple form of multimedia; so is a PowerPoint presentation; so is a QuickTime movie or a HyperCard stack or a Director project or a Flash file.

So, you may be wondering, is this chapter multimedia? After all, it does combine text and pictures—two media. One *could* say that it is, but it's not a really interesting kind of multimedia (though this *will* be an interesting chapter): the really interesting kinds, the ones we're going to discuss, don't live on paper but in your Mac.

Mac Mine Multimedia

When the Mac first debuted in non-Orwellian 1984, it was a unique device: a small, friendly box that displayed everything, including text, as a graphic (most other computers needed a special graphics card to do that); that could play music and even speak (most other computers could barely emit a few thin beeps); and that featured an exotic pointing device called a *mouse* that made drawing images, although a bit awkward, possible for the nonprogrammer.

As the Mac evolved, it learned new tricks: how to display color, how to use multiple screens, how to take in and produce stereo sound, and how to play video. And it grew roomier and speedier: Where the first Mac had 128 Kbytes of RAM, 400 Kbytes of floppy disk storage, and a processor that ran at a blazing 8 MHz, the current models sport gigabytes of hard-disk storage, contain dozens (and often hundreds) of megabytes of RAM, and run about a hundred times faster. And a good thing, too, because multimedia loves lots of RAM, big color displays, rich sound, heaps of storage, and sizzling processing speeds.

Multimedia also loves an operating system that understands its needs: While other computers often require special driver software to play multimedia, every Mac comes knowing how to play multimedia … and even more important, how to assemble the components that make it.

Not that the Mac is the perfect multimedia machine: Some current models lack standard multimedia features such as audio inputs or outputs, and many are not flexible enough to add the specialized hardware components that the picky professional clan of multimedia producers requires. But all current Macs can play multimedia just fine, and you can inexpensively trick out just about any of them to handle all but the most demanding multimedia-production tasks.

The QuickTime Multimedia Engine

QuickTime has been part of the Macintosh experience for ten years, and it has evolved from an interesting add-on technology that could play grainy video the size of a postage stamp (which, ten years ago, was *way* cool) to a sophisticated multimedia architecture inextricably interwoven with the Macintosh operating system. Try starting up a modern Macintosh with QuickTime disabled … you won't like the experience.

QuickTime is much, much more than a media player (the pundits of the technology press notwithstanding)—it is a set of services and features that make an astonishing variety of multimedia experiences possible, and not just on the Mac. QuickTime for Windows provides almost exactly the same high-quality multimedia services to that humble but aspiring family of operating systems.

Among the features you'll find the following (as of QuickTime version 5.0.2):

- 15 video compressors
- 12 audio compressors
- 36 file importers
- 21 file exporters
- 16 built-in video effects
- A browser plug-in
- An image-viewing program
- The obligatory free media player, which, for an additional $29.99, morphs into a surprisingly useful multimedia-editing utility

QuickTime also provides a file structure so versatile that it has been adopted by the International Organization for Standardization as the file structure for MPEG 4, the latest cross-platform multimedia standard. Some cross-platform media-streaming servers can deliver QuickTime; it supports a spectrum of media types, including virtual reality and interactive vector-based sprites; and it makes available the programming hooks or *application programming interface* (API) that let software developers quickly add QuickTime support to their products.

It is, of course, possible to make multimedia on the Mac without QuickTime … but why would you want to?

 If you haven't yet done so, download and install the *full version* of QuickTime (www.apple.com/quicktime/). Then whip out your credit card and give Apple $29.99 for a QuickTime Pro registration. Don't argue—it's worth it.

The Media Bestiary

Naturally, to make multimedia you'll need to know something about each media type you'll use. This is not to say you must become intimate with all of them: Each medium, after all, tends to come in several formats (with each format offering its own special quirks and subtleties), and, adding to the fun, new formats are born all the time. This sort of thing makes multimedia professionals giddy, and few of them can keep track of all the details in their heads (and the ones who can are just plain *sick*). The rest of this chapter is your personal field guide to the critters of Media Country.

Audio Fundamentals

Sound is just quivering air—the faster the quiver, the higher the sound; the more violent the quiver, the louder the sound. Sound pitch, or *frequency,* is measured in units called *hertz* (abbreviated as Hz), and a thousand of those units are called a *kilohertz* (abbreviated as kHz). The best human ears can hear frequencies ranging from a low, throbbing 20 Hz to a squealing 20 kHz. Sound intensity is often measured in *decibels,* and the range from the softest sound to the loudest in any given recording is called the *dynamic range*.

Audio data stored on the Mac (or any other computer) usually contains the information needed to re-create both the frequency and the intensity of the sound in any given instance. Most simply, this means measuring the intensity of the sound at regular intervals (usually thousands of times a second) and recording the intensity as a number. Given the rate of measurements (the *sampling rate*) and the measurements themselves, your Mac can easily re-create the sound waves.

The quality of any digital sound on your Mac ultimately depends on two factors: how many measurements you take per second (the more measurements, the higher the frequency you can reproduce) and how precise each of those measurements is (the more precise, the smoother the sound). But the more measurements you take and the more information you store in each measurement, the more disk space or memory is required. With sound (and as we'll see later, with video), you often find yourself making tradeoffs between quality and storage.

To get a sense of the numbers involved, let's look at the standard audio CD. It stores two channels of sound. Each channel consists of 44,100 samples per second, and each sample takes up 16 bits (2 bytes) of storage (which can hold a number between 0 and 65,535). This means *each second* of CD-quality sound requires more than 176 Kbytes of disk space, and a single minute takes up 10 MB.

When you face numbers like these, you can well understand why audio compression was invented. Some common sampling rates and sizes for a single channel of uncompressed audio appear below:

Sample Rate	Sample Size	Storage for 1 Minute of Sound
11.025 kHz	8 bit	645 Kbyte
22.050 kHz	8 bit	1.26 MB
44.100 kHz	8 bit	2.52 MB
11.050 kHz	16 bit	1.26 MB
22.050 kHz	16 bit	2.52 MB
44.100 kHz	16 bit	5.04 MB

Uncompressed Audio Formats

Uncompressed audio comes in several standard packages. Here are a few common ones you might encounter:

AIFF. A basic cross-platform format developed by Apple, AIFF can support samples of various sizes at all common sampling rates. Just about every program for digital-audio editing on the Mac can handle AIFF sound.

SND. This is the original Macintosh sound format. Your system alert sounds are stored in SND format, and it is *the* format you'll use if you need to store a sound in a file's resource fork (see Chapter 22, "Cross-Platform Compatibility," for details on resource forks and what they're for). This was once the dominant audio format on the Mac, but most multimedia now uses other (usually cross-platform) formats. One cool thing about SND files: You can play them by simply double-clicking them in the Finder—no player required.

WAV. The common Windows audio format. Though it was once bothersome to use WAV files on a Mac, that's no longer true: QuickTime Pro, for example, handles this format with ease.

8- or 16-Bit Sound?

Back when disk space and RAM were at a premium, it made some sense to keep the sample rate down to 8 bits. However, when you only have 8 bits per sample, you can only record 256 distinct levels between the softest and the loudest sounds. The effect? Even at a high sampling rate, 8-bit audio seems fuzzy and crackly. For example, even though audio stored at 11 kHz and 16 bits can only reproduce half the frequency range of audio stored at 22 kHz and 8 bits, the 11 kHz recording will usually sound a lot better. Today, storage is cheap and plentiful, so there's little reason to skimp on the sampling rate.

QuickTime. In addition to accepting any of the above formats (and many more besides), QuickTime can store uncompressed audio data in its own file format, and it can handle just about all of the commonly used sample sizes and rates. If your multimedia project is at all QuickTime based, you'll probably want to keep your sound in QuickTime audio format (**Figure 16.1**).

Figure 16.1

The QuickTime Player plays an audio file.

About Audio Compression

Uncompressed audio can eat up a lot of space quickly, and although today even the humblest iMac ships with many gigabytes of storage, that space isn't infinite. If you want to keep a lot of audio on your hard disk, you need to make it as small as possible … and if you're planning to pass it along over the Internet, you *really* need to make it as small as possible (some of us still have modems!). That's where compression comes in.

Audio tends to resist compression: The data is complicated and varies constantly, and there's usually not much in the way of redundant information to eliminate. Consequently, most audio-compression schemes are designed to throw away nonredundant data (this is called *lossy* compression) … but once enough of the data is gone, you really start to notice its absence. The best audio compressors work hard to find just the right chunks of data to eliminate or to represent in a simpler form, without degrading the sound too severely.

Once audio is compressed, it must be *decompressed* for playing: The more sophisticated the compression, the more processing is required to decompress the audio. However, the harder a decompressor has to work your Mac's processor, the less time the Mac has available to *play* the decompressed sound. The latest generation of audio compressors and decompressors (when paired, they're called *codecs*) require a fast processor to work effectively, and seem happiest using nothing less than a PowerPC G3 (or a blistering Pentium III).

Capture raw, cook it later: Because audio compression blithely discards information, you should delay compressing your audio data for as long as possible. Instead, bite the bullet and capture the best raw (that is, uncompressed) sound your system can handle. When you finish editing and otherwise manipulating your audio, that's when you want to compress it.

Compressed Audio Formats

Thanks in large part to the Internet explosion, stuffing high-quality audio into tiny packages has become a top priority for the digital technology and entertainment industries. Many (often proprietary) audio codecs have made their way to market recently (although a few hung around just long enough to squeeze the fruit before leaving).

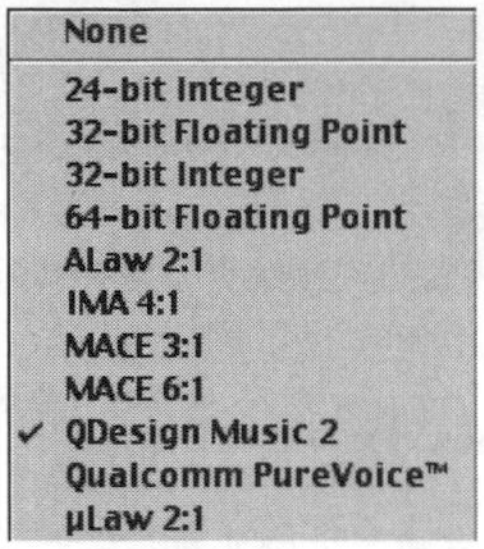

Figure 16.2

This QuickTime menu shows the audio compressors available to the program.

```
None
24-bit Integer
32-bit Floating Point
32-bit Integer
64-bit Floating Point
ALaw 2:1
IMA 4:1
MACE 3:1
MACE 6:1
✓ QDesign Music 2
Qualcomm PureVoice™
µLaw 2:1
```

The latest audio-compression schemes available on our Macs generally fall into three categories: those for which QuickTime has a codec, those formats QuickTime can decompress but not compress, and third-party proprietary formats that haven't been licensed (or reverse engineered) for QuickTime at all (**Figure 16.2**).

AU (QuickTime has codec). This format—common on Unix systems—comes in two standard variants, A-Law and µLaw. AU stores data in 8-bit chunks, but in a logarithmic format roughly equal to 14 bits of ordinary sample data. It only compresses the audio by half and is not very useful for high-quality sound (not surprising, since it was originally developed for voice data on the telephone).

IMA 4:1 (QuickTime has codec). Developed by the International Multimedia Association, this format reduces audio to about a quarter of its uncompressed size. The format is relatively simple, so the processor doesn't have to work very hard (good for older machines but not for Internet delivery), and it offers pretty good quality as long as you're not a raging audiophile (if you are, you probably don't even like *uncompressed* CD audio).

MACE (QuickTime has codec). Don't go there, sister, this one's obsolete.

QDesign Music (QuickTime has codec). Developed by QDesign Corporation (www.qdesign.com), this codec uses a proprietary psychoacoustic method to compress recorded music. The compression method is slow (usually taking several minutes to compress one minute of sound), and the decompressor requires at least a 100 MHz PowerPC. But it's worth it: This format can reduce audio files to a hundredth of their uncompressed size and still deliver acceptable quality. If you plan to use this codec frequently, you should consider getting the professional version at $399—it provides many more compression settings and is optimized to work with the PowerPC G4's Velocity Engine.

Qualcomm PureVoice (QuickTime has codec). From the digital-phone folks, the PureVoice codec works best with, well, pure voice: It reproduces human speech very nicely, and reproduces music and sound effects not so nicely. PureVoice can compress voice data in real time to less than 60 Kbytes for a full minute and still deliver telephone quality, perfect for that marathon reading of *Finnegans Wake* you want to e-mail to all your friends.

MP3 (QuickTime has decompressor). This is the codec that gives the Recording Industry Association of America nightmares. Many people call it MPEG 3, but that's incorrect: It is actually the MPEG 1, Layer 3, audio format. It performs best when compressing audio to a rate of about 16 Kbytes per second of sound (not nearly small enough for modem-speed streaming but acceptable for swapping files over the Internet). Although you can stream MP3 over the Internet to users with fast connections, the arrangement of the data in an MP3 file is not very friendly to the streaming process: You'll really notice any data drop-outs. It seems odd that Apple doesn't support an MP3 encoder in QuickTime, especially given that the company *does* provide a dandy one with iTunes, but sometimes Apple is just *so* inscrutable.

MP3 and the Coming Revolution

Maybe that title's a bit strong, but the MP3 audio codec has given the entertainment industry (and particularly the recording industry) a violent case of the revolving clammy-damps. What makes MP3 so important is that it is an easily available codec that can compress a CD-quality audio file by a factor of 10 and still provide very high fidelity. The MP3 codec made it possible for companies such as Napster and MP3.com to distribute music files to a very large audience—often before they worked out the copyright and licensing issues with the record companies (providing rich opportunities for both the legal profession and the press). Even more upsetting to music-copyright owners, the MP3 format has made it possible for *anyone* with a computer and a CD drive to create high-quality digital copies of music and share them with a few thousand of their closest friends.

So popular has this activity become that Apple now ships recordable CD drives with most of its computers and has produced the nifty (and free) iTunes program, which can play MP3 files, encode or *rip* them from audio CDs, and even record or *burn* duplicate audio CDs using the MP3 files it just ripped. Suddenly the pirate flag that flew over the original Macintosh development team's headquarters takes on a whole new historical significance.

RealAudio (unavailable to QuickTime). This proprietary format is designed for streaming audio from a remote server, although RealPlayer will let you play RealAudio files stored on your hard disk as well. The player comes in two forms: the free RealPlayer or its pay-for-play big brother, the $29.99 **RealPlayer Plus** (**Figure 16.3**). (Many users buy the Plus version because finding the link to the free player on Real's Web site at www.real.com is like playing an endless game of "Where's Waldo"—the link is tiny and seemingly moves every few days.) The format is extremely common on the Web; RealAudio is still the most widely used streaming format. Its compression is quite good, and at some data rates the quality slightly exceeds the best that any currently available QuickTime codec can provide. RealNetworks provides the $199.95 **RealSystem Producer** on the Mac for compressing QuickTime and other formats into RealAudio.

However, the format does not integrate well with other applications: Your choices are pretty much either the RealPlayer application itself or the Web browser plug-in that comes with it. If you want to extract the sound from a RealAudio file and convert it to some other format, forget it. The RealAudio format is like a Roach Motel—sounds go in but they don't come out. Finally, if you happen to have a server and want to stream RealAudio files, prepare to get a Windows machine (the RealServer software doesn't run on Macs) and to dig deep into your retirement fund. The server software price is high, and goes up as you increase the number of users you want to serve.

Figure 16.3

The free RealPlayer —note its clean, unobtrusive design.

Windows Media (unavailable to QuickTime). This is Microsoft's answer to both QuickTime and RealAudio. The current Mac version of the free **Windows Media Player** (often referred to as *WMP*) supports five audio codecs comparable in quality to the ones QuickTime and RealAudio provide (www.microsoft.com/mac). The format is becoming very common in the Windows-using world and on the Internet because Microsoft is backing it strongly. The company has specifically targeted customers who are concerned about protecting intellectual property rights. The format features both Microsoft's Digital Rights Manager and its Windows Media Rights Manager. WMP on the Mac lets you play the format (though the player seems to be in perpetual beta release), but if you want to develop multimedia for it or serve WMP files, Microsoft offers no Mac options: The folks in Redmond very much want you to both develop your multimedia on and serve it from Windows. (All right, stop laughing … they're *serious!*)

Capturing Audio

Sound (like love) is all around us; the trick with sound is to get it inside your Mac and keep it there (what you do with love is your business). The process of getting sound into your Mac is variously called *capturing, digitizing,* or *ripping.* Sound sources come in a lot of forms, so it shouldn't be surprising that there are a lot of different ways to capture it.

Capturing CD audio. If you have QuickTime Pro and a CD drive, this couldn't be simpler (**Figure 16.4**). Put in the CD. Open QuickTime Player. From the File menu, choose Import. In the Open File dialog box, select the CD and choose a track. Then click the Convert button. You'll see a Save File dialog box. Give the file a name and save it on your hard disk. If you like, before you save it you can click the Options button, which lets you choose just a portion of the track, set the sample rate and size, and choose between mono and stereo capture. The captured file will be in uncompressed AIFF format, so expect each minute to devour 10 MB.

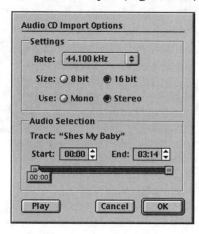

Figure 16.4

QuickTime Pro offers many capture options.

iTunes: A Ripping Good 'Ware

Apple's free iTunes software (www.apple.com/iTunes/) may be targeting the Napster-loving, CD-burning, MP3-toting youthful hordes of the twenty-first century, but it's also a slick tool for the multimedia developer who wants to bring some CD audio quickly into a project (**Figure 16.5**).

For starters, iTunes serves as a free CD cataloging program (no small thing, as keeping track of digital media is one of the essential tasks in multimedia development). Just pop a CD in your Mac and open iTunes. If you are online, it will immediately establish a direct link to Gracenote's CDDB music-recognition service (www.cddb.com) and attempt to retrieve the name of the CD, the artist, and the titles of all the tracks—and it almost always succeeds. But if CDDB comes up dry (or if you're just a roll-your-own kind of gal or guy), you can enter that information yourself. What's more, your Mac will remember the information the next time you insert the CD.

Even more useful is iTunes' capturing or ripping capability. Just click the program's Import button and stand back: iTunes will rip the CD, track by track, into MP3 format—quickly, too. Even a modest 233 MHz iMac (Rev. B) can rip a track in half the time it takes to play it (a midrange Power Mac G4 will suck in the tunes at rates better than 7:1). If MP3 isn't your compression cup of tea, you can set iTunes's preferences to rip to AIFF or WAV format at various sampling rates and sizes. The preferences also let you tune MP3 compression settings for a range of data rates and set a number of other encoding options.

iTunes: A Ripping Good 'Ware continued

Figure 16.5

Ripping a song with iTunes is easy.

So Where Are the Tunes?

iTunes stores the ripped files (which it calls *songs*) in its Music folder. It sorts the files into folders and subfolders alphabetically, first by artist and then by title. iTunes stores songs in the album folders and names them after the tracks (using either the names it fetched from CDDB or the ones you entered), so it's very easy to find the track when you want to use it in a project. Just [Control]-click any song in your iTunes library and choose Show Song File—the Finder will open the song's folder and highlight the file (**Figure 16.6**).

Sound capture, compression, and cataloging: not bad for the price. (Oh, yes, iTunes does a few *other* things, too, but those are mostly for fun.)

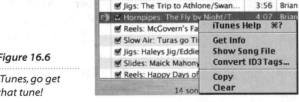

Figure 16.6

iTunes, go get that tune!

Capturing analog audio. You must first convert analog audio (such as the output of a cassette deck) into digital information before you can save it on your Mac—unlike CD audio. Luckily, if you have one of the many Macs that came with the PlainTalk microphone, you already have an analog-to-digital converter. The microphone jack on your Mac is actually a line-in jack, compatible with most consumer audio equipment, that provides good enough quality for many multimedia projects.

Demanding audio professionals will want to bypass the Mac's built-in audio input and outfit their Power Mac towers with a dedicated capture board that's compatible with high-end studio equipment (if you know what S/PDIF, ADAT optical, and MIDI I/O mean, you're one of those people). Digidesign (www.digidesign.com) is one of the product leaders in this area (it's owned by Avid, which also makes professional Mac-based video-editing systems). If you want to set up a home recording studio, the **Digi ToolBox XP** capture system will get you started for $545. On the other hand, if you're an extreme audiophile and money (at least, $11,995 of it) is no object, you may want to go all the way to Digidesign's top-of-the-line **Pro Tools/24 MIX**[3] 24-bit digital-audio production system.

If your needs fall somewhere in between—and you have a USB-equipped Mac running Mac OS 9 or later—Edirol's $430 **Roland ED UA-30** might be right for you (www.edirol.com). It provides RCA line level, ¼-inch mike-guitar, and S/PDIF optical inputs; it has a front-panel mixer; and it doesn't require a Mac with PCI slots.

Once you have the hardware figured out, you'll still need software to handle the actual capturing. The high-end capture boards usually come with their own software for this, but at the lower end you'll have to look around for suitable applications. You needn't look very far, since several shareware and freeware solutions are readily available. Among the freeware solutions is **Coaster** (www.visualclick.de/), a direct-to-disk recording utility that can handle 44.1 kHz stereo input and produce standard AIFF files. It also provides useful

Where's My Mike, Jack?

Some of the latest Macs, including the newest Power Mac G4s, omit both the previously standard audio-input jack and the microphone. Apple surely has its reasons (the profit margin is certainly involved), but that omission makes multimedia production trickier. However, third-party developers have come up with alternatives that provide audio input via the now-standard USB connectors on modern Macs. For example, Griffin Technology's surprisingly inexpensive **iMic** add-on ($35; www.griffintechnology.com) provides cleaner sound input than the older analog input and doesn't require any special driver software. (The microphone-free Tangerine iBook on which I'm writing this chapter loves its iMic and never leaves home without it.)

additional features, such as clipping detection, accurate level meters, and click elimination. A $35 shareware fee gets you **Felt Tip Sound Studio** (www.felttip.com/products/soundstudio). Not only does it perform audio capture but it also provides good basic sound-editing capabilities, audio filters, and pitch shifting (now you can make Barry White a tenor!). The $25 **Amadeus II** shareware application (www.unige.ch/math/folks/hairer/martin) can capture, edit, filter, and analyze your sound files; this one's best for working with a bunch of short sound samples.

MIDI—What It Is

Anyone who plays electronic instruments probably knows more about this standard than we can cover here, but for the rest of us, MIDI stands for *Musical Instrument Digital Interface* and is a long-established standard way to interconnect electronic music devices so they can exchange information. As the name indicates, this information is digital, so it's not surprising that your Mac can understand and manipulate MIDI data. The data is not digitized sound but, rather, information about a musical performance: which keys the player pressed, for how long, and so on. You can store such data very compactly and manipulate it very easily—a MIDI file representing ten separate instruments playing, say, a minute-long piece typically takes up just a few kilobytes on disk.

MIDI files contain *sequences,* and a sequence can contain one or more *channels,* where each channel represents the performance of a single instrument, and each instrument has a corresponding *program* number. In the electronic music world, MIDI data usually goes to a synthesizer, which plays the sequence using its own sounds (these can be either hardware generated or predigitized sound samples).

Although the basic MIDI standard lets a musician assign any instrument to a MIDI program number, another standard called *General MIDI* helps musicians work together by assigning specific instruments to specific program numbers. For example, in General MIDI 0 is always a piano sound and 12 is a vibraphone. Using this specification, musicians can exchange MIDI files and get reasonably comparable results on their different playback systems.

Figure 16.7

You can change a MIDI channel's instrument with QuickTime Pro.

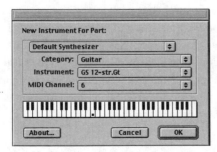

Macs can both play and produce MIDI. Among its many other features, QuickTime provides MIDI playback support, allowing Apple's QuickTime Player to open any standard MIDI file and play it back using QuickTime's built-in Roland GS samples, which adhere to the General MIDI specification. QuickTime Player Pro even lets you change the instruments assigned to each channel (**Figure 16.7**).

Making MIDI. Hooking a MIDI instrument (such as a keyboard) to your Mac is more complicated than it used to be. On older Macs with serial ports, you could hook an inexpensive MIDI interface device to one of the Mac's two serial ports (each port can support 16 MIDI channels). However, today's modern Macs don't have serial ports—but they do have USB ports, and several manufacturers have produced MIDI USB interfaces. Mark of the Unicorn (www.motu.com) provides a range of USB-based MIDI interfaces, from the **Fastlane** model ($79) to the full-featured Pro Tools–compatible **MIDI Timepiece AV** ($595).

MIDI files consist of sequences, and the programs used to write them are *sequencers*. Generally, you have to know a good deal about music to use them, and even the simplest sequencers provide much music-making power. One widely used MIDI sequencer is Steinberg's **Cubase VST** (www.steinberg.net) at $195; another is Mark of the Unicorn's **Performer** ($295). Many others are available as well, and musicians apparently never tire of discussing the features and quirks of the sequencer du jour.

Creating scores. MIDI can also take the drudgery out of transcribing music; the MIDI data contains the notes played, the duration of those notes, and the volume … and that's just what a musical score is all about. After all, why labor to write down your music when you can just play it and have your Mac lay out the score? The top-of-the-line product for such interactive music notation is Coda's **Finale 2001** ($545; www.codamusic.com), which provides unlimited staves, professional notation, and seemingly endless features (with the concomitant seemingly endless learning curve). A less complex (and less expensive) notation program that understands MIDI is Ars Nova's **SongWorks II** ($125; www.ars-nova.com).

Uses. Aside from its obvious uses for musicians and composers, MIDI fits right into many multimedia projects. Games often use MIDI tracks to provide background music, Web sites occasionally play background MIDI sequences (and we really wish they wouldn't), and because QuickTime can easily play MIDI, interactive QuickTime projects often use MIDI samples for button-click sounds and other effects.

MIDI also has other, nonmusical uses as well—technicians have even used it to control the lighting during stage shows … you know, *analog* multimedia.

Playing Audio

Digital audio is not much use if you can't hear it, but fortunately there are plenty of ways to play digital audio on your Mac. Once again, QuickTime Player is your friend: It can play many of the formats apt to end up on your Mac, including streaming versions. And as we've seen earlier in this chapter, players for both RealAudio and Windows Media are available for your Mac as well.

 Keep your installers. RealPlayer and Windows Media Player can both play some of the same formats QuickTime can, and installing either of these packages will often reassign those media formats to the new player; the file that launched QuickTime yesterday may suddenly launch RealPlayer today. Though a polite installer will ask if you want to reassign the file types, not all installers are polite. To make sure QuickTime will continue to play the files you want it to, you may need to reinstall QuickTime after installing RealPlayer or Windows Media.

In the last year or two, the MP3 format has rocketed to stardom and MP3 players have proliferated wildly. The various MP3 players have their vociferous fans and detractors, and the available offerings are changing very rapidly. Aside from Apple's QuickTime Player (which can play MP3s) and iTunes (which can play them, encode them, catalog them, and give you a dandy light show), currently popular MP3 players include Casady & Greene's **SoundJam MP** (Plus version $39.95; also comes as freeware; www.soundjam.com), Panic's **Audion 2** player and encoder ($32.95; www.panic.com/audion/), and the **Macast** multimedia player, which can play MP3s and many other formats ($24.95 for the full version, also available as freeware; www.macast.com).

Editing Audio

If you plan to use digital audio in a multimedia project, chances are you'll need to edit the sound at some point.

If you simply need to trim a sound file or splice two sounds together, all you really require is QuickTime Player Pro. The editing commands are very similar to what you'll find in a word processor: Position the slider where you want to start (or end), shift-click to select a range, and then choose Cut, Copy, or Clear from the Edit menu. You can paste a sound from one file to another by simply cutting or copying it from the source, selecting the location in the destination file, and choosing Paste from the Edit menu.

However, QuickTime Player Pro doesn't have the editing chops for detailed work, and you'll want to use a more full-featured audio editor on these projects. Such editors will let you mix multiple tracks, filter sounds, add audio effects, and edit sounds down to a fraction of a second. Two previously mentioned shareware products, Felt Tip Sound Studio and Amadeus II, can take you quite a bit further than QuickTime Player Pro for very little cost.

QuickTime files can point to other files. That is, when you copy media from one file to another in QuickTime Player Pro, all you are really copying is a reference to the sound's location in the first file. You'll need to have both files on your disk to play the edited piece. (This is actually very useful while you are working on a project because it saves a lot of disk space and processing time while you experiment with different versions.) If you want your edited sound to end up in one file, save the file as self-contained: From the File menu, choose Save As and click the "Save as self-contained" button in the file dialog box.

The tools that professional sound editors use usually come in a complete package that includes audio hardware, such as Digidesign's previously discussed suite of products. If you want to experience Digidesign's audio-editing approach, try a free reduced version of the Pro Tools editing software (http://download.cnet.com/downloads/0-10216-100-3296394.html), which can handle eight separate audio tracks (as well as 48 MIDI tracks). For a professional-quality editor that falls between the shareware and freeware offerings and the really big-ticket suites, you might consider Bias's **Bias Deck VST** ($399; www.bias-inc.com), which lets you edit as many as 999 tracks and play back 64 of them simultaneously.

Video Fundamentals

As you probably know already, movies don't really move; they're simply sequences of still pictures that go by so fast they fool your brain into thinking it's seeing motion. This is true whether you're sitting in your neighborhood cineplex watching the latest summer blockbuster, at home watching Steve Irwin taunt a crocodile on your television, or in front of your Mac, watching the latest movie trailers on Apple's QuickTime Web site.

You probably know, too, that everything you see on your Mac's screen is made up of *pixels* (picture elements)—dots of color, usually 72 to 96 of them per inch. Just as a quick succession of still pictures can fool the brain into perceiving motion, an array of small, closely spaced dots can fool it into perceiving a seamless picture.

The quality of a video experience depends on the *frame rate* (how many still images are displayed each second), the *bit depth* of each image (how many bits of storage each pixel takes up, which dictates the range of colors each pixel can display), and the *frame size* (the number of pixels, horizontally and vertically, that make up each image). The faster the frame rate, the deeper the image, and the larger the frame, the better looking the video … but the more storage is required and the harder your Mac's processor and other components must work to display the video.

Let's look at some numbers. Suppose we want to display video that's roughly equivalent to American television quality. The picture will be 640 pixels wide and 480 pixels tall, each pixel will require 3 bytes (24 bits) of storage to provide a full range of color, and the frame rate will match the TV standard of 30 frames per second (fps). (Broadcast professionals may quibble, calling for 720 by 480 pixels to account for digital video's rectangular pixels, 32 bits of color to provide an alpha channel, and a frame rate of 29.97 fps, which is actually what American TV standards dictate—but let's not quibble.) This means each image will require 900 Kbytes, and a single second of video will consume a walloping 26 MB. Even today's fastest, most spacious Macs would be hard pressed to handle that.

Fortunately, they don't have to. Many technical compromises are made to deliver an analog TV signal to you, and even so-called uncompressed digital video can take advantage of these compromises to lower the data rates to a somewhat more manageable 10 MBps (if you understand what 4:2:2 quantization means, you are ahead of the curve).

Architectures, Formats, and Codecs

We've been calling QuickTime, Real, and Windows Media *formats,* but a more accurate description would be *architectures*. An architecture is a comprehensive, flexible scheme for combining disparate media types, employing multiple codecs, interpreting and producing various file formats, and delivering media content to the end user. Although this distinction was not so important when we were discussing audio, it becomes more important when we consider video. Since most videos tend to have accompanying audio, they are already inherently multimedia, combining two very different forms of data that must be synchronized and integrated. That's what an architecture does.

Compressing Time and Space

Video exists in time (the duration of the video) and space (the size of the frame). Most video-compression schemes therefore work with both time and space when crunching video down to a practical size.

Spatial compressors try to reduce the size of individual frames, using a variety of means (usually lossy)—for example, removing redundant information or combining areas of similar color.

Temporal compressors examine nearby frames and only store the differences between frames. They usually use a *key frame* (which contains a complete image), followed by a sequence of *difference frames* (which contain only data that differs from the key frame); eventually the differences are big enough to warrant the creation of a new key frame.

Most video codecs use both spatial and temporal compression (and a host of other tricks, too).

As with audio, digital video on the Mac tends to fall into three categories: video for which the QuickTime architecture has a codec, video QuickTime can play but not create, and third-party proprietary codecs that haven't been licensed (or reverse engineered) for QuickTime at all.

Sorenson Video (QuickTime has codec). Sorenson provides very tight compression and is particularly good at low data rates; you can get very respectable results at rates as low as 10 KBps. Conversely, at data rates higher than 100 KBps, the codec begins to impose a considerable load on the CPU. Sorenson Video takes a lot more time to compress than to decompress, and requires a fast processor (120 MHz or better). This is the current standard QuickTime video codec for Web delivery and streaming video. A $499 Pro version is available from Sorenson Media (www.sorenson.com) that compresses faster, takes advantage of the PowerPC G4 Velocity Engine, and provides a wealth of compression options. Version 2 of Sorenson Video comes with QuickTime 4, and QuickTime 5 adds Sorenson Video 3, a new compression format that provides substantially better performance.

Cinepak (QuickTime has codec). In the early nineties, this was the leading codec for QuickTime video, providing 10:1 compression ratios. You may not want to use this on new videos, but it's good to have around for older materials.

Apple Video (QuickTime has codec). Known sometimes by the nickname "Road Pizza," this was the first QuickTime codec. It compresses quickly and doesn't require much CPU horsepower, making it good for tests and quick mock-ups. It compresses about 7:1.

M-JPEG (QuickTime has codec). Not to be confused with MPEG, M-JPEG is a JPEG-based codec, good for capturing, editing, and storing high-quality material. It only does spatial, not temporal, compression, and isn't suited for delivery purposes. You may want to edit in M-JPEG, then compress the edited file using a more powerful codec like Sorenson Video.

H.263 (QuickTime has codec). Designed for videoconferencing applications, this codec compresses quickly and relatively efficiently. It only supports a few discrete frame sizes, and is best for talking-head material and other video with relatively little change between frames.

Apple Animation (QuickTime has codec). Use this for animated materials (especially images with unvarying colored areas and with small differences between frames). The compressor provides several quality settings, and at a 100 percent quality setting it is lossless but can still cut down on size. You'll probably use this as an intermediate format and apply a different compressor to your final product.

DV (QuickTime has codec). Digital cameras use this format, which compresses during filming. The data rate is a fixed 3 MBps, and the format allows you to transfer data between the Mac and the camera via a FireWire connection with no data loss. Apple's iMovie and other video-editing programs use this format, so you can shoot video, edit it on the Mac, transfer it back to the camera, and then show it on your TV. For multimedia work, you'll usually recompress DV with a tighter codec when you finish editing your video.

Apple None (QuickTime has codec). Not a codec at all, this provides no compression and creates huge files but is good if you need to archive perfect-quality video or apply various filters and effects to it. You want a very fast Mac with a boatload of storage when you work with this one.

 Because video consists of a sequence of pictures, it is possible to use any image codec (even those designed for still images) to store video data. QuickTime is especially flexible in this regard: If you want to, QuickTime can store your video as a sequence of Windows bitmapped (BMP format) images! You may not ordinarily need to do something this weird, but it's nice to know you can.

Indeo (QuickTime has codecs). First popularized on Windows, Indeo began as a codec for Microsoft's AVI video format. Indeo 3, 4, and 5 are successive versions of the codec, but are not interchangeable; 3 is the oldest and is roughly comparable to Cinepak; 4 and 5 are more recent developments and are designed to work with a later Microsoft video architecture, DirectShow. Indeo 5 (as one might expect from a codec designed by Intel) takes advantage of the MMX processing available on Pentium CPUs and does not work as smoothly on the Mac (there's no reason why it can't, but if you were Intel, would you go to all that trouble?). The Indeo 3 and 4 codecs are both built into QuickTime; an Indeo 5 codec for QuickTime is available separately from Apple.

MPEG 1 (QuickTime has decompressor). The Motion Pictures Expert Group developed this standard for both audio and video compression (that's where MP3 came from). It was designed to play high-quality video and audio at data rates around 150 KBps, but requires a good deal of processing horse-power to decompress, originally requiring additional hardware on an add-in card. Today's fast processors have no problem with its computational requirements, and it is a popular cross-platform format for delivering video but almost useless as an editing format.

MPEG 2 (unavailable to QuickTime). A successor to MPEG 1, this is the DVD video/audio format. It uses a higher data rate than its predecessor (between 300 KBps and 1 MBps) and requires even more computational power to decode. Most DVD players and drives have special MPEG 2 decoding hardware to handle the load, although the latest Power Mac G4s are powerful enough to decode it entirely in software. Apple's new iDVD and DVD Studio Pro packages can produce MPEG 2 files (and even burn them to DVD), but multimedia development doesn't currently use this format often.

MPEG 4 (unavailable to QuickTime). There are two versions of the MPEG 4 codec: the legitimate one just finalized by the Motion Pictures Expert Group, and a codec that Microsoft developed, based on an early draft of the standard. Microsoft has since renamed its codec and now calls it Windows Media Video, but the company has achieved its objective: Many people now think MPEG 4 is a Microsoft technology. MPEG 4 is actually an architecture designed to support audio, video, and interactivity (the MPEG 4 file format, in fact, is based upon the QuickTime architecture, although there is not as yet an MPEG 4 codec available to QuickTime).

Real (unavailable to QuickTime). Like RealAudio, this is designed for the RealPlayer and primarily distributes streaming video. The video codec, based on Intel's Indeo Video Interactive codec, is quite scalable: the RealSystem Server can selectively drop information from the Real video stream to accommodate narrow bandwidths or network congestion, giving good results at a wide range of connection speeds. On the Mac, RealSystem Producer converts QuickTime (or other) video files to Real video format.

Compressing Video

Even at the dawn of a new millennium, video compression remains an art and not a science: The right way to do it varies from video to video and depends very much upon the intended use. Here are some tips and guidelines:

Know your audience. The compressor you choose for your video depends as much upon its special virtues as it does upon the end user. For example, Sorenson Video *can* look great at 100 KBps, but if your audience consists of elementary-school teachers running five-year-old Macs, they simply won't have the CPU power to handle it. In many cases you'll want to make separate versions of your video and compress each using different settings—or even different codecs—to create versions that the entire spectrum of your intended audience can use. This is especially true for Web-based delivery (many people out there are still using modems).

Experiment. Even if you think you have *the* ultimate recipe for compressing video, do yourself a favor—extract a minute or two of your video and compress it several different ways, using different data rates, compression options, and even codecs. Sometimes the settings that worked perfectly for one video don't suit another. You should look especially hard at action sequences and video effects (such as dissolves and wipes), because that's where compressors often have the most trouble producing good results.

You don't need 30 fps. Just because your TV gives you 30 fps (well, 29.97) doesn't mean you must use that frame rate. You can save a lot of space by simply choosing a lower frame rate when you compress. You can drop down to around 10 fps before the motion looks obviously jerky, and even that rate (or lower ones) may be acceptable for some materials. If you drop frames, choose a frame rate that lets you drop them evenly (that is, choose a final frame rate that evenly divides into the source frame rate). For example, if your source material is at 30 fps, choosing 15 fps when you compress lets you drop every other frame.

Shrink and crop. Full-screen video is not always necessary or even desirable, and it can easily eat up disk space and processing power. For multimedia, something smaller than a 640-by-480-pixel frame size is usually practical, and even when it isn't, you can often cut the frame dimensions in half when you compress and then double the frame size for playback. You might also consider cropping the source video before compressing it—most TV producers use a safe area, well inset from the edges of the frame, simply because many TVs are not properly adjusted and chop off some of the picture's top, bottom, or sides. If your source material was originally intended for broadcast, a little judicious cropping can save storage space. (Note that many codecs work best when the frame dimensions are even multiples of 4 or 16, so you should crop or shrink the frame with your codec in mind.)

Use high-quality source material. All things being equal, the better your source video, the more efficient (and better-looking) the final compressed version. A codec will compress everything, including distortion and static, and because most codecs tend to look for areas of uniform appearance to compress (either within a frame or within adjacent frames), static makes the codec work harder. If you must capture and compress from VHS tape, don't use long or extended play speeds, since these settings sacrifice more of the picture quality. Compressing from original digital source material is always preferable. And don't even think about recompressing video already compressed for delivery (for example, with Sorenson or MPEG 1). It will take a long time and produce questionable results. In fact, even recompressing material originally compressed with M-JPEG, as we suggested above, is at best a compromise (though usually an acceptable one).

Compressing with QuickTime Pro

If you pay Apple the $29.99 fee to upgrade QuickTime Player to the Pro version, you get access to the File menu's Export command, your gateway to QuickTime's compression features (**Figure 16.8**).

To use these features, open an audio or video file and export it. In the Save File dialog box, you'll see two pop-up menus. The first, Export, lets you save the file in a variety of file formats (including some popular Windows formats). The second, Use, offers a list of prepackaged settings for compression and export. The available presets change depending on the export format you choose; the QuickTime movie settings provide many useful presets for both streaming and CD-based movies.

And if that isn't enough control for you, click the Options button in the Save File dialog box. This brings up another dialog box where you can specify exact settings for video and audio compression, as well as set detailed streaming options. If you're a pro on a limited budget, you shouldn't do without QuickTime Pro.

Figure 16.8

QuickTime Pro offers a myriad of compression presets.

Trade money for time. For occasional compression tasks on the Mac, QuickTime Player Pro or RealSystem Producer can often meet your needs. But if you have to do a lot of compression, and you don't want to become a dedicated expert, a few strategic investments will save time and effort, and provide better-quality results. For example, you might consider getting the professional version of Sorenson Video. The **Sorenson Pro** codec costs $499, but it compresses faster than the version that comes with QuickTime, provides additional features (such as variable bit-rate encoding, which can result in better-looking output), and lets you adjust a wide range of compression options. **Cleaner 5**, from Terran ($599; www.terran.com), is another sound investment: This product *knows* compression inside and out, providing a wide variety of built-in settings and wizards to get the best results possible, and it can create QuickTime, Real, Windows Media, and MPEG files. Cleaner can also handle batch processing, so you can sleep the sleep of the just while your Mac toils all night long compressing files (**Figure 16.9**).

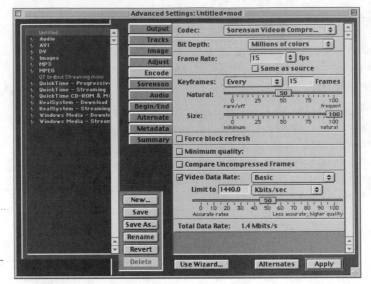

Figure 16.9

Cleaner 5's advanced settings can handle just about any compression task for you.

Capturing Video

With the introduction of FireWire as a standard Mac accoutrement, Apple made video capture much easier. Between iMovie and FireWire, the Mac has sparked a desktop-video revolution that may rival the desktop-publishing revolution.

Setting up for capture. Today's Macs have fast processors and large, speedy hard disks, but video capture can tax even those. It is still prudent to take a few steps to ensure a flawless capture.

- Turn off CPU-hungry extensions and network connections. Some extensions work continually in the background, taking small chunks of processing time away from the capture process. Also, if you have AppleTalk turned on, the Mac will be checking the network periodically, and while it's doing that, it won't be working on your video.

- Capture your video at the final frame *size* you wish to use. If you're planning to show your video in a 180-by-120-pixel window, it doesn't make sense to capture it at a larger size; this will merely consume disk space and processing time. Worse, if you plan to show your video in, say, a 320-by-240 window and you capture it at 180 by 120, it will look terrible scaled up.

- Capture your video at the final frame *rate* you wish to use. You should capture video at some even divisor of the TV standard—30 fps—for the best playback. Usually 15 fps is a good choice. Otherwise you may encounter jerky motion, dropped frames, and other oddities.

- Fill the holes. That is, put a CD in the CD drive and a disk in any other drives. Seriously. Every so often your Mac likes to check all attached drives to see if there's anything in them. This check takes a little time, and you can't spare any time when capturing video. Once a disk is in a drive, the Mac doesn't check again until you remove the disk.

Capturing digital video with FireWire. Here's the simplest way: Connect your DV camera and your Mac with a FireWire cable. Click iMovie's Import button. There's no step three.

But iMovie may not be everyone's cup of tea. Although it's simple, that simplicity comes at the price of eliminating many useful capture options. If you'd like a bit more control over your captures (or can't afford $49), download Apple's free **HackTV** (http://developer.apple.com). Written as an example for developers who want to learn how to do QuickTime programming, this unassuming application provides enough basic capture options to suit the casual user's needs: frame size, frame rate, audio-capturing format, and more.

Capturing analog video. Capturing video from a non-FireWire device usually requires a capture card to digitize the video; if your Mac has slots, you certainly want to look into getting one of them. Aurora Video Systems sells the **Fuse** card ($499; www.auroravideosys.com), which can handle both composite and S-Video inputs and capture NTSC signals as well as the European PAL and SECAM video formats. It also provides video outputs so you can transfer your edited video to a standard VCR.

If your Mac has USB but no card slots, you can still capture analog video: Eskape Labs offers the USB-based **MyVideo** peripheral ($249; www.eskapelabs.com), which can digitize 320-by-240-pixel 30 fps video from any NTSC, PAL, or SECAM analog source. If you need a larger frame size, you're out of luck, but for many multimedia projects you may not need anything more.

Another cardless analog capture solution for those with FireWire Macs is the Sony **DVMC** ($320; www.sony.com). This FireWire device converts analog video to digital and vice versa.

Finally, if you have a FireWire Mac and a DV camera that accepts analog input (and many do), you're in business: Just dub your analog video onto a DV tape in your camera, and transfer that video to the Mac. Once again, there's no step three.

Why You Can't Transfer Digital Video from a DVD

Although DVD is digital (that's what the first *D* in DVD stands for), you can't transfer the data directly to your Mac and recompress it for use in a multimedia project. The entertainment industry worked very hard to make sure that DVD data is encrypted and that DVD players don't supply digital outputs compatible with computer equipment. Bypassing the encryption is completely illegal, thanks to the Digital Millennium Copyright Act, for which industry heavyweights lobbied fiercely—even decrypting the data for backup purposes or other personal use (as the "Fair Use" copyright law usually allows) can land you in legal difficulties. If you must capture video from a DVD, you'll have to do it by taking the signal from the DVD player's analog outputs (composite or S-Video), then redigitizing it, with a resulting loss in quality.

Playing Video

Each of the three major desktop-video architectures (QuickTime, Real, and Windows Media) comes with its own free player and provides browser plug-ins that let you see its video formats in a Web browser. In addition, both RealPlayer and QuickTime Player also come in Pro versions for a fee.

RealPlayer Plus ($29.99) provides access to additional streaming content, claims superior video performance, and offers more sophisticated audio- and video-playback controls than the free version.

Windows Media Player provides basic playing capabilities for various Microsoft formats not otherwise available. The player can also handle old-style QuickTime video (before version 3).

QuickTime Pro also costs $29.99, but the price buys you little above the free player's capabilities when it comes to playing video (the Pro version *does* let you choose a full-screen presentation mode). What the money *does* buy is access to editing features, format conversion, compression … in other words, a complete basic tool kit for QuickTime editing and multimedia construction.

 Because QuickTime is a system-level architecture, you can incorporate it easily into other applications and play QuickTime movies inside Microsoft Word, SimpleText, and many other programs. In particular, Apple's long-neglected but still viable HyperCard software comes with a QuickTime Tools stack that lets you add QuickTime support in your stacks for both playing and editing QuickTime media.

QuickTime Skins

Although some media players let you dress them in custom skins (visual appearances, including controls), QuickTime 5 thinks different. It adds skins to the movie instead of to the player: In essence, each movie can come with its own player. All you need is QuickTime Pro 5, a graphics editor, and Flash or LiveStage Pro to create your own controls. Apple has a tutorial on creating skin tracks on its Web site (when last seen, the URL was www.apple.com/quicktime/products/tutorials/mediaskins/).

Editing Video

Editing can involve anything from simply trimming the ends of captured videos to overlaying multiple images, adding floating captions, adding complex dissolves and wipes, mixing soundtracks—in short, full-on professional work. The Mac has editing tools that span the range.

As we've already seen, QuickTime Pro transforms the Player into a multimedia tool kit. The Pro version of QuickTime Player lets you add, delete, and export tracks; cut, copy, and paste within or between movies; add special visual effects; and add text captions.

Apple's **iMovie 2** ($49 for download, provided free to purchasers of new Macs; a free downloadable version for Mac OS X owners is also available; www.apple.com) provides a friendly, easy-to-master editing interface for the video hobbyist, which includes a clip shelf for holding all of your captured or imported clips, audio-editing features, special visual- and audio-effects panels, a simple title editor, and a dual-mode timeline that lets you see your project as a sequence of clip thumbnails or view it as a set of tracks.

An order of magnitude pricier, Digital Origin's **CineStream 3,** previously known as Edit-DV ($499; www.digitalorigin.com), is an entry-level professional tool, with features to match: three-point editing, chroma- and luma-keying, support for nonsquare pixels and EDL (edit decision list), and more. This product also provides great support for producing streaming Web videos in QuickTime, Real, and Windows Media formats.

The grandmother of all Mac-based video-editing packages, Adobe's **Premiere 6.0** ($549; www.adobe.com/premiere/) bills itself as the best video-editing tool around. Although that's arguable, Adobe has added digital-video support, streaming format output, and a refined user interface to this low-end professional package. Add in a collection of video effects, storyboard editing, audio mixer and filters, and other professional features, and you have a very competitive editing tool.

Apple has its own entry in the professional arena: **Final Cut Pro 2** ($999; www.apple.com/finalcutpro/). This program builds upon QuickTime to add real production value, including media-management tools, real-time compositing and effects (by way of supported PCI cards), and support for Adobe After Effects filters. And of course it has all the capabilities of its competitors in this price range.

Stepping up to a higher plateau, you'll find **Media 100's** set of pro editing packages (www.media100.com). The hardware-and-software packages in the Media 100 i product line range in price from $3,500 to $18,000. For the money you get the ability to edit almost any format of video, produce interactive streaming output, and generally work in the big leagues. The company recently went on a subsidiary buying spree and purchased Digital Origin (CineStream), Terran (Cleaner 5), and several other digital-video companies, propelling it to the forefront of vendors of digital-video content-creation tools.

Finally, Avid's line of digital-video editing products is still the Hollywood standard, with Hollywood-style prices (www.avid.com). Its **Media Composer** products, commonly used in commercial broadcast production, cost around $50,000 for a basic system, and prices go up quickly. For the slightly less well heeled, the company also offers a product line aimed at corporate users and Web professionals, **Avid Xpress**. You'll still need deep pockets—prices start at $10,000—but the money buys a package that lets you do almost anything short of cutting a big-budget motion-picture spectacular. However, if you only need to edit DV format, Avid provides the much less expensive **XPress DV** (only $1,699).

Animation

Whether traditional two-dimensional or cutting-edge three-dimensional animation is your preference, the Mac has tools to release your inner Chuck Jones or John Lasseter.

Like video, animation is simply a series of pictures shown rapidly enough to fool the eye into seeing motion. A 2D animation usually involves drawing pictures—lots of them—and then assembling them in the right order. 3D animation, on the other hand, requires digital construction of models (using *nurbs* and *wire frames*), then instructing the animation software to move the model around, light it, and so on.

2D

If all you want from a 2D animation package is to make some animated GIFs for a Web page, you can't go wrong with Yves Piguet's free **GifBuilder** (http://homepage.mac.com/piguet/), which lets you stitch together a sequence of pictures in a simple, Web-based animated GIF format. Though bare-bones, it has features to control timing and repetition, and can optimize file size. For just a little money, the **VSE Animation Maker** ($19.95; http://vse-online.com) can produce animated GIFs as well; here you get a built-in paint program.

More-expensive 2D packages can save time spent on tedious tasks such as *in-betweening* or *tweening* (that is, drawing the intermediate frames between the manually drawn key frames). One relatively inexpensive program, Beatware's **eZ-Motion** ($99.99; www.beatware.com), provides text-animation tools, tweening features, filters, and templates to get you started. And it not only produces animated GIFs but can also export animations to QuickTime and other useful formats.

Probably the most popular Web-oriented animation tool is Macromedia's **Flash 5** ($399; www.macromedia.com). The package provides vector-based animation support, timelines, soundtracks, and the ability to add interactivity via its ActionScript programming environment. Many Web sites have begun to use Flash to provide animated site-navigation interfaces. Macromedia has made the Flash file format available to developers (such as Apple), which allows QuickTime to import Flash animations and interactivity directly into QuickTime movies.

Professional 2D animators will want to look at Linker Systems' **Animation Stand** (www.animationstand.com). A demo version, which limits your animations to a small 256-by-192-pixel frame, provides a quick look at the package's powerful and diverse feature set: special optical effects, multiplane camera control, automatic cel painting, 3D shading, audio editing, and even production-cost reporting. A professional edition, suitable for television production work, costs $595, but if the silver screen is your target, $5,995 for the Cinema edition makes your Mac into the next Termite Terrace.

3D

Usually, 3D animation requires a powerful computer—you will want a Power Mac G3 or better system if you intend to do it at all seriously. The reason is simple: 3D work requires your Mac to calculate and draw (or *render*) each frame of your work based upon a very complex mathematical description of all the objects in it. These calculations can make your processor sweat big time. Professional 3D animators use *render farms*—vast assemblies of computers all working together to render the frames of an animation—and it is not uncommon for a single frame to take hours to render.

Although a fully tricked-out 3D animation setup can cost as much as you are willing to spend, you can start out for free. Strata Software makes a freeware version of its product Strata 3D available as a 22 MB download (www.strata.com), or you can pay $24.95 to have the company ship a CD and manual. The program gives you everything you need to start serious 3D design work: modeling tools, camera control, special effects, textures, graphics tools, and lighting controls. Strata also sells a professional version, Strata 3D Pro ($595), which adds high-end texturing, modeling, animation, and rendering capabilities to the basic package.

Newtek offers a comparable package, **Inspire** ($495; www.newtek.com), which offers 2D and 3D tools, and comes with an onscreen tutorial, a library of 1,600 objects, and compatibility with many third-party graphics packages, as well as QuickTime. Or you can vault to the high end with Newtek's **LightWave 6.5** at $2,495. This one, targeting film and video professionals, gives you the ability to sculpt digital clay and introduces proprietary modeling aids the company calls IntelligEntities, such as *skelegons, endomorphs,* and *MultiMeshes.*

QuickTime VR

Sometimes you just have to be there … but when you can't, virtual reality brings you closer. Apple's flavor of virtual reality, known as QuickTime VR, uses QuickTime's ability to store multiple images in a single file to create 360-degree panoramas or pictures of objects (**Figure 16.10**). You simply take a bunch of pictures and use a QuickTime VR authoring tool to stitch the pictures together. QuickTime VR lets you pan around an image or spin an object, zoom in and out, add background sound effects, and build *multinode* environments (these allow you to embed hot spots in your VR; when clicked, these move the viewer from place to place or from view to view within the VR environment).

Figure 16.10

QuickTime does virtual reality.

Apple will be happy to sell you the $395 QuickTime VR Authoring Studio, which provides all the basic tools you need to build a VR movie. A company called VR ToolBox (www.vrtoolbox.com) sells a $299.99 package, the **VR Worx 2.0,** that also provides a good set of VR construction tools.

Look Up, Look Down …

Older versions of QuickTime VR stored a VR movie as a group of pictures arranged in a cylinder: You could spin around, but couldn't look straight up or down. Now, QuickTime 5 improves on QuickTime VR with the addition of a new format, *cubic VR,* which lets you build VR scenes from floor to ceiling. Now the sky's no longer the limit.

Graphics

From its very beginning, the Mac was a digital-graphics powerhouse, and in fact the Mac is still the top choice among designers of digital graphics. Elsewhere in this book you'll find a wealth of information about the types of graphics you can create on a Mac and the tools you can use to make them. Although most multimedia involves graphics at some point, there's not a whole lot one can say about graphics that is specific to multimedia. Here are a few pointers, however.

When preparing graphic materials for multimedia, remember that multimedia is intended for the screen, not the printed page. This means you should use appropriate color settings: The CMYK color space is intended for print; use RGB if your destination is the screen. Nor do you need high resolutions (such as 300 dots per inch) for your graphic materials: The screen is only about 72 dpi, and all the extra resolution simply takes up space and processing power. Also, no matter what program you use to create your graphics, you should save them in a format that multimedia-authoring or presentation programs can use: JPEG, GIF, TIFF, and PICT are the most common, although some programs can also handle native Adobe Photoshop formats.

Text Is a Medium, Too

Text may not seem eye-poppingly exciting, and the hype that surrounds multimedia often ignores it—but text is a very useful medium, capable of conveying complex information in a flexible and compact format. For example, this entire chapter, which is more than 14,000 words long, can fit in just a few hundred kilobytes (in contrast, the illustrations take up several megabytes). Text is also searchable, indexable, and often the only medium that can make your point effectively. Few multimedia packages, however, treat text with the respect it deserves, often reducing the text to a graphic image or providing only the most primitive of text-entry and -editing tools.

When preparing text for multimedia use, it is best to stick with common formats: HTML and Microsoft's Rich Text Format (RTF) are two standards that retain font, style, and some layout information; if a package supports formatted text at all, chances are it will support one of these. Also, keep in mind that the way your text looks (and in multimedia, looks are important) depends on the fonts you use, and most multimedia formats don't include fonts. If your multimedia package does not let you embed the fonts you used when creating the text, your audience may see something very different from what you intended.

Often you're best off either sticking with very common fonts (such as Times New Roman or Arial—yes, these are Windows fonts, but Mac users usually have them, too), or providing the necessary fonts along with your project.

If you intend to make your multimedia creation work on both Macs and Windows machines, and your text is really text and not just a graphic representation, keep in mind that the two platforms don't handle text exactly the same way. The biggest inconsistency has to do with size. Text is measured in units called *points* **(roughly one 72nd of an inch). Because Macs started out with a screen resolution of 72 pixels per inch, most Mac programs assume that 1 point is equal to 1 pixel. Not so in the Windows world, where the standard screen resolution is 96 pixels per inch—hence, a 12-point character will be 16, not 12, pixels tall. This discrepancy can play havoc with your layout, especially when you want to fit text into an area with a specific pixel dimension. Therefore, if you lay out your project's text on a Mac, make sure you allow for the Windows "magnification" effect to avoid unsightly surprises.**

QuickTime Text Tracks

QuickTime's text-track format lets you embed text in a movie and synchronize it to other tracks. Text tracks can enhance a movie in many ways. You can use them to create chapter markers so users can go to specific points in your movie. You can use them to create subtitles or running textual commentaries that enhance the visual and audio aspects of your QuickTime masterpiece. You can use them to make your movie searchable: The QuickTime Player's Find command can search text tracks. Text tracks can scroll, contain hypertext links, and provide karaoke capability. Text tracks in a movie embedded on a Web page can even send commands to the Web browser to open a new page or run a JavaScript command. Text may be a humble medium, but QuickTime makes it mighty.

Some Assembly Required

Once you've got all of your digital-media *assets* together (that is, your pictures, texts, videos, and sounds), you will probably want to assemble them into a unified presentation or program of some sort. That's when you'll need a *multimedia authoring tool*. There is no one-size-fits-all tool, however; all of them have their strengths and weaknesses, and which one you choose depends on what you want to create.

Multimedia-authoring tools often use a controlling metaphor to describe and define how they integrate media. Some tools use a book metaphor, others use a slide show, still others rely on a timeline. Here's a look at some of the many Mac multimedia-authoring tools, arranged by metaphor.

The Bit Budget

Multimedia projects usually involve compromises. While you may want CD-quality audio and full-motion, full-screen video (who doesn't?), that's not always practical—if you'll be delivering your project over the Web or running it on first-generation Power Macs, something has to give. What gives, and how much it gives, varies depending on the situation.

For example, a CD-ROM can only hold 650 MB of data, but most modern CD drives can transfer it into the computer at speeds well above 1 MBps. On the other hand, a Web server may have a lot more storage space available but much lower data-transfer speeds: A user connected with a 56 Kbps modem can only receive 4 or 5 KBps, and even a broadband (DSL or cable modem) user can only receive between 50 and 100 KBps.

Savvy multimedia producers have a bit budget for their projects. The budget keeps track of how much storage space each asset takes up and how long it takes to deliver that asset to the user. The budget need not be elaborate—you can implement it in a spreadsheet, in a database, or on little scraps of paper in a folder. What matters is that you have one—and use it.

Slide Rules

A number of multimedia-authoring tools are designed for creating sophisticated slide shows. Replacing the venerable overhead projector and foils, digital-multimedia slide shows have become the staple (and occasionally the bane) of the modern business or classroom presentation.

AppleWorks. AppleWorks 6 is Apple's general-purpose office suite, but it also functions as a useful multimedia-authoring tool. It has a word processor for preparing text, a drawing module for creating charts and diagrams, a paint module for creating illustrations and retouching images, and—to tie it all together—a presentation module for making slide shows. The program also comes with clip art and templates to get you started.

AppleWorks presentations build on a slide-show metaphor: The program calls each screen you make a *slide,* and the controls for moving from one slide to the next should be familiar to anyone who has used a slide projector. You can set slide shows to run automatically and to loop (useful for kiosk presentations).

The program offers several tools and features to make slide-show construction easier. You can name each slide so you can find it quickly in a complex presentation. You can create *master slides*—templates that provide a common design for related slides. You can add speaker notes to each slide and print them out.

As you might expect of an Apple product, the program makes good use of QuickTime. AppleWorks lets you easily add QuickTime video or audio to your slides; in addition, it uses QuickTime to provide transitions as you move from one slide to the next; the current version has 25 different visual effects for transitions.

AppleWorks is truly a bargain package for multimedia developers: it ships free on all iMacs and iBooks; for the rest of us it costs $79.

 Even if you don't intend to make a single AppleWorks presentation, you may want to get this program anyway: AppleWorks includes a spreadsheet and a database module, both of which you can use to keep track of your media assets and to track your bit budget.

PowerPoint 2001 for Mac. Microsoft (www.microsoft.com/mac/products/ office/2001/) provides the predominant presentation program in the Windows world, and—courtesy of Microsoft's Macintosh Business Unit—it is available on the Mac, too. You can get it either bundled as part of Microsoft Office ($499) or as a separate purchase ($399). So ubiquitous is this program in the business world that PowerPoint has become synonymous with business presentations (**Figure 16.11**).

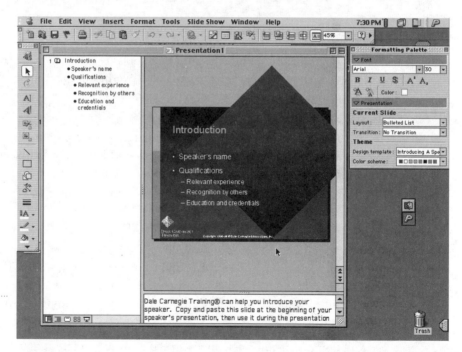

Figure 16.11

PowerPoint offers multimedia for the suits.

Like AppleWorks, PowerPoint conceives of its screens as slides and provides tools to manage them, including a Slide Finder. Also like AppleWorks, PowerPoint lets you create master slides and apply their formatting to previously created slides. The program offers a rich library of clips and templates to assist you if you have little in the way of artistic skills (or if you are just having one of those creativity-free days). It also lets you view your presentation as an outline, making navigation easy.

PowerPoint supports standard image formats for the Web (including animated GIFs). It supports QuickTime as well, letting you place QuickTime video or audio on a slide and use QuickTime effects for slide transitions. You can even save your PowerPoint presentation as a QuickTime movie, either self contained or along with a set of assets for later editing.

Finally, PowerPoint can publish your presentation to the Web, converting the presentation outline into a home page with links to all of the slides.

Making Books

Books are great devices for information storage and display: They provide an ordered sequence of text and graphics, and they can contain indexes and cross-references. So it's only natural that many multimedia tools leverage the power of this tried-and-true technology.

Acrobat. Adobe's Acrobat 5.0 package ($249; www.adobe.com) has developed from a program designed solely to reproduce exactly the look of a printed document into something rich and strange. Today's Acrobat files can contain hypertext links, interactive forms, and QuickTime media—yet they still look like printed documents. This is hardly surprising, because Acrobat uses Adobe's sophisticated printing technology to create its documents in Portable Document Format (PDF). You prepare the document aspect of your project in a word processor or a drawing program, and use Adobe's PDFWriter print driver to create the PDF file. Then you use the Acrobat program itself to add nonprinting features such as links, audio, and video. Acrobat allows you to embed all the fonts in your PDF files so they will look exactly as they should on both Macs and Windows computers. Adobe's free Acrobat Reader can open and read PDF files (the Preview program in Mac OS X can also read PDF files, though Preview may not have access to all of Acrobat's special multimedia features). Acrobat PDFs are one of the most popular ways to distribute electronic books, and Adobe has built an entire e-commerce system to support its publishers.

TK3. From some of the people who pioneered the electronic book at the Voyager Company in the early nineties, this package from Nightkitchen (www.nightkitchen.com) is designed to create complex and elegant interactive multimedia books. Like Acrobat, Nightkitchen provides a free TK3 Reader to go with the for-pay authoring tool, TK3 Author. Unlike Acrobat, Nightkitchen does not start from print (though it does embed fonts for portability). TK3 Author lets you *flow* a main text (in HTML or Microsoft's RTF format) into the book and then adorn that text with annotations, which can either pop up in separate windows or stick to the page. Annotations are the key to using the program. Almost everything you see other than the main text itself *is* an annotation in a TK3 book, and those annotations can be text, pictures, audio, video, or even other minibooks (called *complex annotations*). Books have automatically generated tables of contents, are extensively searchable, and offer useful (and customizable) navigation tools. TK3 can create very powerful multimedia publications without requiring that you learn how to script or program. You can download a 30-day free demo, buy a year's worth of use along with technical support and any upgrades for $59, or buy the program outright for $149.

HyperCard. This Apple creation was one of the first multimedia-authoring tools, and although Apple has not done much in the way of supporting it in the last few years (a Mac OS X–native version seems unlikely), it is still widely used for quickly creating multimedia on the Mac. Built on the metaphor of a stack of cards, the program by itself supports text, black-and-white graphics, visual transitions, and interactivity. Add-on features provided by Apple let you add color and QuickTime support to HyperCard stacks. What's more, HyperCard lets you add almost any functionality via external commands (called XCMDs) and external functions (called XFCNs)—you can find many XCMDs and XFCNs on the Web, or you can even write them yourself in C or some other traditional programming language. But you don't need to learn C to teach HyperCard new tricks: It includes a simple but powerful scripting language, called HyperTalk, that lets you do anything from creating simple flip-book animations to developing software prototypes. Developers have authored many critically and commercially successful multimedia products in HyperCard, including the original Myst and Voyager's Macbeth. Because it is not a cross-platform program, most multimedia producers in the last few years have moved to other authoring tools, but HyperCard still has many fans. Apple sells version 2.4.1 from its online store ($99; http://store.apple.com).

SuperCard. This program began as a third-party attempt to remedy HyperCard's limitations by integrating color, better drawing tools, and multiple windows, and has had a difficult journey through life, including ownership by a succession of companies—the latest is IncWell Digital Media Group ($144.95; http://incwell.com/SuperCard/). Now at version 3.6.3, SuperCard provides many of the same features as HyperCard and some additions, including a more powerful programming interface. Like HyperCard, this is a Mac-only product, though you can tailor some stacks to work with IncWell's FlameThrower Web-server software ($295, or $395 bundled with SuperCard), which allows viewing of these stacks in a Web browser.

Play It As It Lays

Books are about *space*—they order information by stacking pages upon each other. Movies are about *time*—they depict a process by playing one frame after another. The following multimedia tools use time as their ordering principle.

Director. No one could have predicted at the beginning that VideoWorks, a simple animation program, would become Macromedia's Director, the pre-eminent multimedia powerhouse ($1,199; www.macromedia.com). But after adding a scripting language called Lingo (based on HyperTalk) and an explosion of multimedia-authoring features, the ugly duckling grew up to become … well, a really big, *strong* ugly duck. Director builds multimedia using a timeline and stage metaphor, with various multimedia objects (sprites, graphics, sounds, and videos) as cast members, entering and leaving the stage at various points on the timeline. In Director, you can attach scripts to each cast member, controlling its behavior and the behavior of others. You can also attach scripts to individual frames on the timeline; these scripts run when you reach that point in the movie. Director calls its assemblages of cast members and scripts *movies,* which can be confusing when you realize that one kind of cast member in Director movie is a QuickTime movie (the program supports some 40 media types). In fact, a *lot* about Director may confuse the beginning multimedia author, but you'll find much arcane Director lore readily available on Macromedia's Web site, and active Director user groups can also help the initiate. Director 8 comes bundled with Shockwave, which prepares Director movies for Web delivery; Fireworks (for graphics editing); and Peak LE (for audio editing).

LiveStage Pro. This package is a totally hip product—literally: Totally Hip's LiveStage Pro is the QuickTime developer's coolest friend ($699; www.totallyhip.com). The program was designed to take advantage of nearly all the features that Apple built into QuickTime but never bothered to provide tools to access. Did you know that QuickTime can do math? That you can script it? That it can handle tweening? It can do all this and a lot more, and LiveStage makes these features available. Like Director, LiveStage has a scripting language (QScript), a stage, sprites (graphic characters that can move onstage and respond to user actions), and a timeline; but unlike Director, LiveStage produces QuickTime movies that any QuickTime-compatible program can play. Not as confusing as Director to learn (possibly because it is newer than Director and has had less time to accrete features), LiveStage lets you assemble any QuickTime-supported media into interactive multimedia presentations; visit Totally Hip's Web site to see just how hip QuickTime can be.

QuickTimes at Media High

Among QuickTime Pro's many capabilities are its media-integration tools. The QuickTime Player lets you cut and paste tracks and track sections; adjust their placement, orientation, and size; and modify their time scale. The latest version of QuickTime Pro also offers extensive support for AppleScripts, making it possible to automate the building of complex multimedia projects. A description of all Pro Player's feature could fill a book … and in fact it has: *QuickTime 5 for Macintosh and Windows: Visual QuickStart Guide,* by Judith Stern and Robert Lettieri (Peachpit Press).

General Delivery

You can put multimedia in slide shows, you can stuff it into books, you can make movies out of it … or you can put it into boxes.

iShell. A highly evolved descendant of Apple's old Apple Media Tool, Tribeworks' iShell 2 (www.tribeworks.com) handles the multiple personalities of multimedia by letting you arrange it in containers and then put these containers into other containers. You can control your containers by scripting them to handle events such as mouse clicks. The interface is drag and drop: You drop both media and event handlers on containers. iShell supports both CD-based and Web-based projects, and can handle many media types, relying upon QuickTime extensively to do so. It can also extend its capabilities with add-on modules, available from Tribeworks when you become a Tribe member. iShell is free, but the company offers yearly subscriptions at various levels and costs. A Silver Membership costs $975 for the first year and gets you tech support, manuals, and a run-time license; a $2,750 Gold Membership gets you a software development kit, unlimited run-time licenses, and much more extensive technical support.

The Web. Maybe you've heard of it: the World Wide Web. It began as a way for particle physicists to share scientific articles and within a decade became by far the most popular integration and delivery platform for multimedia.

The Web is built upon *pages* but is hardly booklike in its arrangement: Each page is independent and only connected to other pages by explicitly supplied links. At the same time, the Web is the most textual of all multimedia: Each page is nothing more or less than text—text users can read; text that tells the Web browser where to find and how to present graphics, audio, video, and other interactive media; or text that forms scripts to handle events.

How to build a Web page is a topic much too broad to handle in this chapter, but an author must keep a few general points in mind when creating multimedia Web pages. First, the bit budget is critical; more than half the Web users in the country still connect to the Internet with a modem, so you must keep the amount of media on each page small enough so your audience can open it in a reasonable period of time. Second, what kinds of media you can use depend on what your viewers have installed on their machines. Most browsers can display text and graphics, but other media rely on particular plug-ins. QuickTime, Real, and Windows Media Player all require plug-ins. Third, the fonts you use for text (and ultimately the languages you can display) depend on what fonts your viewers have on their machines and how they've configured their browsers. In short, because so much of multimedia on the Web depends on the audience and not on the author, ultimately you should design your Web pages only as a suggestion, not as an order. Within those limitations, you have extraordinary expressive freedom and a potentially enormous audience.

17

Page Layout

- -

Kathleen Tinkel (KT) is the chapter editor and coauthor.

Phil Gaskill (PG) is the chapter coauthor.

Page layout is as old as printing, but it has gotten a lot easier over time.

In the Middle Ages, early printers carved images and bold letters in blocks of wood. (If they made a mistake, they had to sand it out, mortise in a plug of fresh wood, or start over.)

At the dawn of the Renaissance, Gutenberg assembled pieces of movable metal type (but first he had to engrave punches and hand-cast all the type).

By the end of the 19th century, typesetting-machine operators could set type from a keyboard (not a smoothly clicking one like ours, but still an improvement over picking up thousands of little bits of metal type and arranging them backwards in a chase). They also remelted type metal (before that, redistribution—putting small pieces of type back in cases so it could be reset—was a major labor item). When photo-offset lithography began to take over printing after the second world war, graphic designers pasted typeset galleys on art boards, ready for the printer's process camera. (Reprinting was as easy and cheap as reusing negatives.)

Today we flow text and images onto a Mac's virtual pages and never need to get our hands dirty. The desktop-publishing software available today is so easy to use that we may be tempted to take its power for granted. Page-layout programs make it easy to edit and format text, arrange text on the page, add rules and other graphic elements, import scanned photos and line art, and specify color and output settings for printing on your desktop inkjet or laser printer, on a commercial offset press, or even on the Web. In this chapter we talk about page layout and the programs available for doing it on the Mac.

In This Chapter

Page Layout and Desktop Publishing (KT)

Thanks to modern technology, any Mac user with an idea and a design can sit at the computer and arrange pages of type, digitized photos, graphics, and other elements. A few mouse clicks let you reproduce your pages faithfully, printing a few copies on an in-house desktop inkjet or laser printer or hundreds or thousands of copies by sending files to an outside service for output on such high-end equipment as imagesetters, computer-to-plate systems, or high-capacity direct digital printers.

What makes this miracle possible is page-layout software—programs designed for setting type and for mixing text and images freely on the page. There are at least nine of these programs for the Mac, although Quark's QuarkXPress, Adobe PageMaker, and Adobe's new InDesign are the best known and most used. If Gutenberg, Garamond, and Goudy were alive today, they'd probably be using one of those three programs, exulting in levels of control and ease of use that could scarcely have even been imagined in 1440, 1550, and 1930, the years when those famous printers were working.

Page-layout programs are also the best tools for creating Adobe Acrobat PDF (electronic book) files when you want to preserve the design and format of a document.

Some optimists try to use a word-processing program such as Microsoft Word to lay out publications for printing. That's really the hard way, however, as you can see in the "Word for Page Layout?" sidebar, later in the chapter. A page-layout program is the right tool for the job. It saves time, gives you more control over the pages, and produces better-quality type.

What Is Page Layout?

Unlike word processors, with their riverlike approach to text, page-layout programs deal with objects: blocks (or frames) of text; imported bitmap and vector graphics; and rules, circles, rectangles, and polygons drawn in the program. This emphasis on the page rather than text is a fundamental difference. You begin by specifying the size and shape of your finished page (the trim size), which may not be the same as the standard paper sizes supported by your printer. You set explicit margins, columns, and other boundaries to order the pages. And you have both WYSIWYG and numeric control over type and typography, the placement of elements on the page, their size, and how they will look when printed.

A few of the essential functions that all page-layout programs support:

Document. Allows publications of any useful size, from miniature books and business cards up through banners, signs, and other large formats, with a single page or many that can be printed on one or both sides. Provides space for images or color to bleed (print beyond the trim lines) and for crop marks and other printer markings. Provides a working view that shows trim lines (printable area), margins, and text columns, and the gutters between them. Shows pages as you intend them to be read, with spreads shown as facing pages with a useful range of zoom-in ratios for detailed work. Provides master pages for control of repeating elements and variations of the basic layout.

Graphics. Accepts standard formats of graphic files (at least EPS, TIFF, and JPEG and preferably others from both major platforms). Has the ability to crop, resize, and rotate imported images and has some sort of mask or clipping-path function. Includes drawing tools for rules, circles, rectangles, and polygons, with control over line weights and ability to fill these objects with color (or not) and assign color separately to outlines. Supports all industry-standard color spaces: CMYK (for commercial printing), RGB (for film recorders, some inkjets, and conversion to and from Web pages), and more.

Text. Provides word-processing functions, including a spelling checker and search-and-replace tools that work with text content and type attributes. Supports import of plain ASCII text as well as common word-processor formats (Word, primarily) from both Mac and Windows, retaining user-selected formatting that can include styles. Filters text and replaces double hyphens and typewriter (or straight) quotation marks and apostrophes with typographic characters (em dashes and curly quotes).

Pages. Lets you set up columns and flow type automatically from column to column and page to page. Has rulers, nonprinting grids and guides, and numeric controls of all elements on the page, with access through keyboard shortcuts as well as menus or palettes. Capable of creating newsletterlike documents, with stories starting on one page and jumping to other pages. Allows text to flow controllably around images, sidebars, callout text, and other elements. Supports folios (automatic page numbering) and running heads and feet.

Typography. Gives you control of hyphenation and all aspects of the spacing of type—between words and characters (including automatic and manual kerning) and between lines and paragraphs. Supports paragraph styles.

Technical control. Lets you control output specs for a wide range of devices: Specify screen resolutions, transfer functions, color specs, and other output functions and print separations or composite pages to PostScript and non-PostScript printers (inkjets, for example), as well as to high-resolution equipment at output services. The software will also *preflight* (or check for output quality of) files and gather all needed files, including fonts, for remote output.

Surveying the Field (KT)

Any Mac user with a scintilla of interest in desktop publishing or page layout has heard of the high-end big three: Quark's **QuarkXPress** ($869, upgrade from version 4.0 or 4.1 free, upgrade from versions prior to 4.0 $306.15, competitive upgrade from PageMaker $499; www.quark.com), **Adobe PageMaker** ($499, upgrade $79; www.adobe.com), and **Adobe InDesign** ($699, upgrade from version 1.0 $99, upgrade from PageMaker or PageMaker Plus $299). If you need to produce work destined for commercial printing, the search can easily begin and end with that short list. In fact, some would short-circuit the process and tell you to choose QuarkXPress, known affectionately as Quark and more cynically as QuirkXPress—the de facto standard among designers at ad agencies and publishing houses, and at commercial print shops and output services. But you do have other options.

If you produce software manuals, textbooks, or other long technical works, you should consider **Adobe FrameMaker** ($799, upgrade $209). PageMaker and XPress are both capable of producing books (in fact, most books today seem to be typeset with XPress), but FrameMaker is the champ when it comes to tables, and it is the only layout program with built-in support for cross-referencing and footnotes.

Graphic artists with the demanding job of creating supermarket ads, flyers, coupons, and other detailed pieces on a short timetable should consider **MultiAd Creator** ($299; www.creatorsoftware.com), or if you are running Mac OS X, **Creator LE** ($99), both of which are designed for this specific purpose. (Creator LE is simplified for the nondesigner and has simpler code than its big sister, thanks largely to speed and graphics functions supplied by Mac OS X.)

But maybe you don't intend to make page layout your life's work. In that case, a less full-featured (some would say less bloated) program might be perfect for you. **SoftLogik PageStream** ($249, upgrade from previous versions $60 to $100, competitive upgrade $150; www.grasshopperllc.com), long established on the Amiga platform; the venerable Mac program **Diwan Ready,Set,Go!** ($150, updaters free; www.diwan.com), now with a new publisher and a new Arabic version (the publisher also sells Arabic fonts); and **Deneba Canvas Pro** ($375, competitive upgrade $199.95; www.deneba.com), a program that began as a bitmap and vector graphics program for the Mac but now has capable page-layout functions built in.

Interestingly, the layout, typesetting, and output functions in these three pretty much rival those in the major applications. Their drawbacks? Well, they have fewer users, either on the Mac or among graphic designers or others who specialize in page layout. Except for Canvas, the programs tend to have fewer exotic bells and whistles. You won't find articles detailing tips and tricks in

Macworld or other magazines. And they may not be supported at many output services, which means that instead of supplying application files as you can with XPress or PageMaker, you may have to learn how to create print files—PostScript or Acrobat PDF—when you send your files.

There is also an inexpensive, very unsophisticated Mac layout program called **Staz Redneck Publisher** ($29.95; www.stazsoftware.com). Although it's a nifty bit of programming that seems to adhere strictly to Mac interface guidelines, it doesn't offer any typographic controls or much other finesse, it lacks a zoom function (except in its drawing module), and it generally cannot be recommended for page-layout work (or even as a learning tool). We mention it only because of its charm (seriously), and because it does ship with a collection of useful templates (Avery labels, perforated business cards, postcards, and other standard forms).

The New Big Three: QuarkXPress, PageMaker, and InDesign (PG/KT)

XPress, PageMaker, and InDesign share most of the same capabilities, but each has a distinctive working style, and each of them has individual strengths and weaknesses.

General Approach

Although these programs evolved by copying features from each other, each has strengths and weaknesses, and all manage to retain their own feel and working style.

Initial default settings. InDesign has the best settings right out of the box, possibly because being newer, it has less legacy rubbish to sustain. But software engineers and marketing experts set the defaults, and every user needs to review—and revise—all the settable functions after installing a new version of one of these programs (and periodically thereafter).

A few defaults are positively dangerous: PageMaker's Save Faster option and XPress's text inset and suboptimal Optimum word-space settings. (See the "Fixing the Dreadful Defaults" section, later in the chapter.)

Frames. XPress is still resolutely based on frames—you draw a text or picture box and then fill it with text or a graphic. InDesign is also frame-based but is more casual about it—what you put into a frame determines whether it is a text or image box, and you can import text or graphics and it will automatically create the frame for you. PageMaker, long known as a frameless, free-form program, now has frames as an option. Longtime PageMaker users generally save the frames for when they want to add a background tint or to have an outline or border that prints.

Extensibility. XPress is the extensions champ. Quark originated the notion of third-party extensions (which it calls XTensions), and XPress has the largest selection. Some are amazing in what they do (and cost more than XPress); others may perform only one task and are inexpensive or free.

PageMaker has fewer third-party plug-ins. InDesign also has only a few at this point—many of them from companies that also develop for XPress (ShadowCaster, from A Lowly Apprentice Production, for example).

Long-document support. PageMaker and XPress ship with book, indexing, and automatic table-of-contents functions. The book function not only assembles individual files (chapters) in one print operation, automatically repaginating in response to revisions, but lets you index and create a table of contents across the whole book. To accomplish these tasks with InDesign requires the Sonar plug-ins from Virginia Systems.

Screen display. PageMaker and InDesign offer the user several high-quality options for how the program shows imported graphics onscreen. The default setting is adequate, and even better previews can be chosen.

XPress needs improvement in this area—its previews don't give a clear enough view when you need to position, size, or crop an image.

Story editor. You can edit text manually on layout pages in all three programs, but PageMaker allows you to use search-and-replace, spelling-checker, and other global functions only in a special plain-text story-editor view. This is usually a time-saver; you can make changes to multiple stories and the software moves quickly without having to deal with laid-out pages. But when you want to see the effect of a change, it's a nuisance. The other programs do not have a built-in plain-text editor—you edit text in layout view, which allows you to observe the effects of changes while you work but may also slow down the process as revisions ripple through the text.

Master pages. All three programs have master pages, a sort of template that helps keep even a large document consistent without a lot of repetition.

InDesign's override option lets you decide whether master-page items should be locked or editable on the regular pages. PageMaker is strict about this— except for guides, master-page elements are completely locked and cannot even be selected on regular pages. Elements from XPress's master pages can all be edited on the regular pages. Only InDesign lets you base one master page on another—changes made to the parent ripple down through the based-on templates.

Spreads. XPress and InDesign allow spreads of more than two pages. PageMaker is limited to two. InDesign has a nifty function that prevents designated spreads from being split apart when changes are made to the pagination. There's nothing like it in PageMaker or XPress.

Eyedropper tool. Borrowed from graphics programs, InDesign's tools include an eyedropper tool that can pick up not only colors (and other fill and stroke attributes) but also text attributes and then apply those attributes to other text.

Layout adjustment. Both PageMaker and InDesign (but not XPress) have this sometimes handy (but disastrous if misused) function, which gives you the option to have elements rearranged automatically when page dimensions are revised, either on a regular page or by making changes to master-page templates.

Layers. Both InDesign and PageMaker support layers, which are handy for creating customized variants of a brochure or other documents. Items on layers can be handled together, and a layer may be hidden or revealed at print time. XPress has not had this feature but will include it in XPress 5 when it is released.

Sections. InDesign and XPress, but not PageMaker, support this feature, which enables you to have front matter with one series of page numbers (lowercase roman numerals, for example) and then begin the main with an arabic number 1. In PageMaker, you must create two documents and then assemble them with the book function for indexing and printout.

Moving and scaling. All three programs provide for precise numeric positioning and resizing of objects.

PageMaker and InDesign have an extremely useful "proxy"—a schematic diagram in the control palette that lets you select a point (corner, side, or center) to be used as the location from which transformations will occur. The object remains fixed at the selected point when you enlarge/reduce, rotate, or otherwise shift the object.

Align and distribute. XPress and PageMaker let you specify the size of gutters between objects. InDesign does not.

Bézier drawing tools. InDesign and XPress have these, a handy subset of the functions found in standalone vector drawing programs such as Adobe Illustrator, Macromedia FreeHand, and Deneba Canvas. For all but the simplest work, most users will probably also need one of the vector drawing programs as well, however.

Step and repeat. InDesign and XPress have it, by name. PageMaker's "power paste" can be used to accomplish something similar: Select Copy, and then (Option)-Paste; shift the copy the desired direction and amount, and then each subsequent (Option)-Paste pastes the object with the same relative shift in position.

Lock. Both InDesign and PageMaker let you lock the size and position of an object—nothing can be changed unless you first unlock it.

XPress's "lock" function prevents accidental moves with the mouse but will let you move a locked item by using the Measurements palette or the Modify dialog box. This will be fixed in XPress 5.

Group. All three programs let you group two or more objects. PageMaker's group function supports only a single level (if you include groups in a new group, all end up in a single group and ungrouping will leave a heap of separate pieces). PageMaker also lets you group a single item—kind of an oxymoron, but it then allows you to apply a text wrap to text, something the program otherwise does not support. The grouping in XPress and InDesign is less illogical.

Search and replace. All three programs search on text, styles, and some type attributes (the particulars vary by program).

InDesign can search on several paragraph attributes the others cannot, including paragraph indent, paragraph spacing, drop caps, composer version (of course—only InDesign has multiple composition modes), "keep" options, and text color. (PageMaker can also search on color; XPress cannot.)

PageMaker's search function works only in the Story Editor.

Packaging/preflighting. All three programs package (assemble) document files and graphics necessary for output. PageMaker and InDesign also include fonts; XPress will include fonts in version 5. Both PageMaker (as part of the Save for Service Provider plug-in) and InDesign check files before packaging them for output. Both InDesign and PageMaker also check placed EPS graphics and list any included fonts.

Text and Typography

There's more to typography than placing text on the page and letting it flow. The three programs have their own approaches to setting type.

Styles. All three programs have paragraph styles; XPress and InDesign also support character styles.

Composition methods. InDesign alone has a multiline composer, which evaluates a user-specified number of lines and number of alternatives when determining how to control hyphenation and spacing in justified type. XPress and PageMaker use only a single-line composer, which is also an option in InDesign.

Justification. InDesign is unusual in that it lets you select a justified paragraph alignment with the last line centered or flush right rather than flush left (useful for academic abstracts and ornamental typography).

Hyphenation controls. XPress and InDesign let you specify minimum word length and number of characters before and after the hyphen. PageMaker lacks this specific control, but if you invest a lot of tedious effort in customizing the hyphenation dictionary, you can get PageMaker to provide nearly the same result. All three programs have user-editable hyphenation dictionaries. XPress hyphenation is primarily based on a set of algorithms, and PageMaker and InDesign default to a dictionary. Then PageMaker lets you choose between two methods—Manual plus dictionary or Manual plus dictionary and algorithm. XPress uses a separate spelling dictionary; PageMaker and InDesign use one dictionary for spelling and hyphenation. Both XPress and PageMaker are likely to exhibit hyphenation idiosyncrasies. XPress sometimes breaks a word at other than a syllable and is prone to breaking contractions before the *n't*. PageMaker too is likely to break after a two-letter syllable and often fails to hyphenate proper (capitalized) nouns at all. (If this is your house style, you may like this, but it often leads to dreadful spacing.)

True tracking. Both PageMaker and XPress can adjust type spacing globally by means of predefined (modifiable) tracks.

PageMaker's multiple tracks are applicable to selected text or within paragraph styles. XPress's single track applies to the specified font wherever it appears in the document.

Almost no one uses XPress tracks, and only a minority use PageMaker's. This may be why Adobe decided not to include this useful feature in InDesign. InDesign does support the same sort of on-the-fly "tracking" that XPress users rely on (and, truth to tell, so do many PageMaker users, who know it as "range-kerning"). This is unfortunate—true tracking, PageMaker style, not only adapts automatically to type size but is configurable and storable for reuse.

Built-in kern pair editor. XPress lets you adjust kerning in live text and have the changes applied globally to that font in the document. The actual font remains unchanged. (Unexpectedly, PageStream has a similar feature.) PageMaker ships with KernEdit, a standalone editor that actually modifies fonts, making them work the same way in any application. Modifying fonts is typographically sound. It enables you to get the same results from any application, for one thing. But it is also much more work than making needed adjustments within the program, as you can do with XPress, and the KernEdit application is old and prone to crashing.

Automatic character substitution. InDesign and XPress replace *fi* and *fl* with the appropriate ligatures (PageMaker does not). If a small-caps or expert font is open, InDesign also swaps small-caps and old-style figures. InDesign also supports the extended OpenType character set and makes other automatic substitutions if such a font is available.

Text wrap. All three programs allow you to set how text flows around intrusions. Only InDesign allows text to flow around not only the outside of another element but also its interior.

Vertical justification. Both XPress and InDesign support it.

Drop caps. XPress and InDesign permit more than one character in their automatic drop caps. PageMaker allows only one.

Optical alignment. InDesign offers the option of optical alignment, which allows punctuation marks and sprawling letters (A and W, for example) to protrude slightly into the gutter. Used with discretion, this technique can make the margin look straighter; used carelessly, it can create columns of type that appear to have random whiskers down the side. Neither of the other programs has anything like it.

Kerning. All three programs support automatic pair kerning, based on metrics defined in fonts.

InDesign and PageMaker offer optical kerning, which ignores the font's kern pairs and adjusts spacing based on the way the characters look and fit. In careless hands, this function can be dangerous, but is useful for fonts that are badly spaced to begin with. The PageMaker function (which you get to by selecting text and then choosing Expert Kerning from the Type menu) came first and calls for manual settings. InDesign's optical kerning (select Optical instead of Metric in the kerning section of the Character palette) is integrated with the program and can be included in stylesheets.

Color

All three programs support most industry-standard color libraries. PageMaker and InDesign support color management and give you options as to which to use (if any). XPress includes its own Quark CMS, which claims to support ColorSync.

Production Features

The craft of layout has always included responsibility for some aspects of print production, but today's page-layout software is also the primary production tool.

Automation. All three programs support tags (ASCII codes that are interpreted by XPress, PageMaker, or InDesign when text is imported). PageMaker and InDesign can read XPress tags as well as their own. InDesign and XPress are AppleScriptable. PageMaker has its own scripting language, which can be called by AppleScripts but also works across platforms.

Data merge. PageMaker has this word-processing tool, useful for creating mass mailings. It's new in version 7.

HTML export. Both InDesign and PageMaker can do this, although the results won't thrill most people who know anything about HTML. XPress 4 can export text stories as HTML but not the entire page or document without a third-party extension. XPress 5 is expected to have more substantial support for HTML.

PDF export. InDesign creates its own PDF files. PageMaker automates the process using the bundled Acrobat Distiller. For XPress, you must create a PostScript file and run your own copy of Acrobat Distiller.

Illustrator/Photoshop file import. PageMaker and InDesign let you place native files from these two Adobe programs. This eliminates the need to create and track EPS and TIFF files. It's one of the ways Adobe helps its various products work together (both PageMaker and InDesign also work well with Adobe Acrobat).

Making Your Decision

PageMaker and XPress have grown up together, and InDesign was designed to compete with them. As a result, they're all capable of doing something like 90 percent of the work for 90 percent of users. Your decision is easy only if you must have a function supported in only one of these programs.

If page layout is a secondary function for you, PageMaker may be the right choice. It's extremely flexible, is widely used in corporate settings, has hoards of users who can offer peer support, and output services that accept PageMaker files are easy to find.

Most new users should probably choose XPress. It is universally accepted by commercial printers and output services and is widely used in ad agencies, publishing houses, and design firms, which makes it easier either to get a job with one of these companies or to work as a freelancer for them. The myriad users also offer useful peer support in online venues, magazine articles, and the workaday world, which can be extraordinarily useful.

However, it is unreasonable today to expect to have "permanent" software. It would make sense for PageMaker and XPress users to invest in InDesign and learn how to use it. (This is certainly true for those whose work is typo-graphically demanding.) That way, no matter what may happen in the future, you'll be prepared.

So: Our best advice is to hedge your bets.

High-Powered Specialists (KT)

You can produce almost any sort of publication with any of the standard page-layout programs. The ability to lay out business cards, brochures, signs, simple packaging, magazines, books, and whatever else you may need to throw at them in the course of a day's work is what makes programs such as XPress, PageMaker, and InDesign useful. But if your work is specialized, you may be able to save time and get better results with one of these programs.

Adobe FrameMaker 6.0

If you specialize in producing long documents—especially textbooks, computer manuals, academic treatises, or other "technical" books—you should be using FrameMaker. Adobe bought the Frame Corporation in the mid-1990s but was using this focused workhorse to produce its software manuals long before buying the company.

FrameMaker doesn't work or feel much like the standard layout programs. It's a sort of hybrid, with the powerful features of high-end word processing as well as page-layout functions. It uses the equivalent of master pages and templates, paragraph and character styles, and other predefined options to automate most of the production process. But among its standard tools are many that don't exist in the other layout programs at all (or only exist in inchoate form, or only expensively, by means of plug-ins or extensions), including automated table-making, cross-referencing, an equations editor, conditional text, and footnotes. Inserting markers for these functions as well as for automatic generation of a table of contents, glossaries, or an index is relatively painless in FrameMaker.

If there's a method of automating document production, FrameMaker has it, including a scripting language, tags, and a version designed for SGML, the heavy-duty tagging language—of which HTML is a subset—widely used by government and academic publishers. The program continues to sustain work-alike versions for Windows and Unix as well as for the Mac. The current version has extensive support for reconfiguring documents for Acrobat PDF, HTML, or XML.

FrameMaker has a reputation for being hard to learn. We didn't find it hard to learn so much as it is very different from the other page-layout programs. Once you buy into FrameMaker's way of thinking, it's logical and fairly easy to use.

MultiAd Creator 6.0.1

We've noted in the past several editions of *The Macintosh Bible* that MultiAd Creator was a well-kept secret, and as far as computer and design venues are concerned, it's still true. Creator is marketed directly to ad-making pros and advertising businesspeople as part of a comprehensive package of services that includes content development, clip-art subscriptions, placement services, and direct-mail printing and management. MultiAd has been supplying advertising producers for years—it didn't spring up in recent times as a software company. (It began as a Mac-only company, and even though MultiAd now offers a Windows version, Creator has a very good Mac feel to it.)

Although MultiAd Creator now supports multiple pages, it still doesn't attempt to compete with XPress, PageMaker, InDesign, or similar layout programs. You would probably find it especially frustrating to use for most other sorts of work, especially long documents. Its typography can be superb, but it seems designed to allow for (and require a certain amount of) manual tweaking. And even though the standard layout programs have added many of Creator's essential functions—drawing tools and clipping paths, for example—they don't compete with it, either. Creator's strength is its focus on ad production. It ships with hundreds of ornamental borders, including all the standard dashed-line borders essential for coupons. It creates starbursts and other vector graphics at the click of the mouse, as you'd expect. It provides for good control over all aspects of color, including trapping; lets you easily define a mask (clipping path) affecting one or several objects; and has special features that automate the creation of coupons.

If you think Creator might be useful for you, MultiAd offers fully functional downloadable demos of both versions at www.creatorsoftware.com.

Other Possibilities (KT)

We're always interested in software of exceptional value, a category that includes these three page layout programs: PageStream, Ready,Set,Go!, and Canvas. It's not merely that they cost less than most of the better-known alternatives but that they are all capable of producing commercial-caliber work, with output as printable as that of the major programs. Despite their capabilities, these programs are somewhat anonymous. You don't usually see collections of "tips & tricks" articles for them, and you may have to coax your printer or output service to accept your files (or supply Acrobat PDF or PostScript print files) for output.

Soft-Logik PageStream 4.0.9

We first heard about this program from its favorable reviews when it ran only on the Commodore Amiga platform—back when the Amiga was a contender. A few years later, the developer brought it out for the Mac. PageStream is essentially frame-based (like XPress), but it also allows for free-form text blocks (something like PageMaker's).

The free-form blocks cannot be linked, however, and if you change their height or width, the text within the block is rescaled to fit.

In addition to a complete set of standard text-formatting functions, PageStream also has some fairly advanced features, including an eyedropper tool (like InDesign's) that copies and pastes attributes for text as well as graphic elements, and a kern pair editor similar to the one in XPress (changes to a text pair apply to all instances of that pair in the document). And, echoing PageMaker, it has a set of tracks (Very Loose, Loose, Normal, Tight, Very Tight), although they don't work the way PageMaker's do. It will create numbered and bulleted lists (and lets you define the font and character to use as the bullet). Its output functions include object-level trapping and simple imposition as well as a Collect for Output function that places the layout file plus graphics (but not fonts used) in a folder for sending to the printer.

The program exports Acrobat PDF files using its own software (although graphic-rich documents will probably still require Acrobat Distiller). It also exports HTML-encoded text and will import HTML as well. Indexing is built in, as is generation of tables of contents and lists of figures. It has many organizational tools, including sections.

PageStream is reasonably priced. The programmer (himself) offers technical support via e-mail. For more information: www.grasshopperllc.com.

Deneba Canvas Pro 7.0

Canvas, which has been around in one form or another since the Mac's early years—it deserves a Mac software stick-to-itiveness award—can't seem to get any respect. It's a capable Bézier drawing program whose essential features compare favorably with those in Adobe Illustrator and Macromedia FreeHand. It's a useful bitmap editor; though not the equal of Adobe Photoshop, it has sufficient image-editing, retouching, color-correcting, and painting tools to suffice for most print (and Web) production work. More interesting for desktop publishers, the program also includes a respectable set of page-layout features that put Canvas, if not in the XPress, PageMaker, or InDesign class, close enough for booklet, brochure, newsletter, ad, and letterhead work (which is all that many users ever need). If that isn't enough, the Pro version includes hundreds of decently made fonts from URW and a collection of clip art.

Canvas lets you type or paste text into predrawn columns, as in a frame-based layout program, but you can also type in a drawn object, on a vector path, or directly on the page. The program allows you to apply unusual effects to typeset text (to extrude the letters or apply a drop shadow, or both, for example), but Canvas will convert the text to paths (drawings) behind the scenes, so it will not be editable afterward. Canvas doesn't distinguish page-layout documents from any others; you can add a text frame (with one or multiple columns, including columns of varying width) to any page, add pages (specifying whether they are one- or two-sided and whether they should appear as spreads). It supports master pages, layers, grids and guides, and other page-layout essentials.

This program is almost unbelievably feature-laden. Canvas 7 is described here, but you can download a 15-day demo version of Canvas 8 if you want to experiment with it, at www.deneba.com.

Word for Page Layout? (PG)

Microsoft touts Word as a page-layout program. But can it really do the kinds of things InDesign, PageMaker, and XPress can do? Can Word play with the big boys? In a word (pardon the play on, er, words), the answer is a resounding no.

Word's main problem is that it's merely a word processor—a sort of souped-up text editor. It thinks of text as a river that flows smoothly along and gets broken up into pages at print time. Because of this, it's difficult to accomplish the common desktop-publishing task of starting a story on page 1 and then jumping it to the back of the book. To be fair, it's not impossible (with Word 98 or later, anyway). You can create blank pages with Word's page-break commands and then come back and "float" graphics and text boxes (yes, Word does have text boxes, of a sort) on those empty pages, making sure they're not anchored to the text stream that contains the page breaks. It's not even a huge hassle, really; it's just dumb that you have to do it this way.

Word can import graphics. It can even crop them and resize them—but not easily. If you want freely positionable graphics (as opposed to graphics that are anchored to, or in line with, text), you must check Float Over Text with the Insert Picture from File command.

What if you want to place that image at the bottom of a page? Word's positioning facilities are minimal. There are no guides. Let me say that again: There are *no* guides—if you want a guide to help you align objects, draw a rule. You won't be able to have objects snap to this "guide," of course. And don't forget to delete the rule before printing.

If you really know Word, you can look in the Format Picture dialog box, in the Format menu, with a picture to ascertain the position of an object. Then—probably by trial and error—you can figure out what numbers to type into the dialog box so that your picture appears where you want it. Whew—this would take just a few seconds in a page-layout program.

The worst problem is that Word does a lousy job of setting type. You cannot set type if you cannot control hyphenation and spacing of words and characters, especially in justified text. If Word has these settings, they're well hidden from users—which is too bad, because Word sets homely type. It isn't much improved by Word's late-blooming support for automatic pair-kerning (recognizing the kern pairs in your fonts), or even by its pathetic manual kerning, with coarse increments ($1/10$ of a point compared with PageMaker's $1/100$ or XPress's $1/20,000$ of a point). If you're setting headlines in a huge point size, Word's kerning may work, but it's useless with text sizes.

Bottom line: Word is a limited and clumsy page-layout tool that produces lousy-looking pages.

Diwan Ready,Set,Go! 7.2

Diwan's Ready,Set,Go! looks a great deal like versions of the software formerly distributed by Manhattan Graphics and Letraset. Although the interface is a little old-fashioned, the program has all the essentials of page layout and type-setting that most users need, with recent incremental enhancements that keep it up to date with newer OS versions (at least through Mac OS 9.1 at the time of this writing).

The most interesting changes are included in Ready,Set,Go! Global, which takes advantage of Apple's AAT (Apple Advanced Typography) features and can set text properly in several non-Latin scripts, including Japanese, Chinese, and Arabic. It can even mix one of the supported languages with English (or another European language) on the same line. (A demo copy of the Global version is available at www.diwan.com/ready/prsg.htm/.)

Fixing the Dreadful Defaults (PG/KT)

The first thing you should do after installing (or reinstalling) one of these layout programs is change at least the worst of the initial default settings.

To change default settings, launch the program but do not open or create a document. (Changes made with an open document will apply to that file only, which is useful for customizing settings for particular jobs.) As soon as you have finished making changes, quit, and the changes will be written to the appropriate preferences files.

Then make a backup copy of the defaults file. Find the file (listed by application below), duplicate it, and save the copy. The next time you need to reinstall, you can simply replace the new, out-of-the-box preferences file with your backup defaults copy.

InDesign. Replace two files—InDesign Defaults and InDesign SavedData—both located in the Version 1.5 folder in the Adobe InDesign folder in the Preferences folder in the System Folder.

PageMaker. The defaults file is named Adobe PageMaker 6.5 (or 7.0) Prefs, and it's located in the Preferences folder in the System Folder.

XPress. The defaults file is named XPress Preferences, and it's in the same folder as the XPress application file, which theoretically can be anywhere on your hard disk or disks. If you know where your QuarkXPress folder is, you know where your defaults file is.

Here are some of the defaults we routinely change in current versions of these three programs. Some settings are merely annoying, but a few are downright dangerous.

InDesign 1.5.2

InDesign has, in general, the fewest settings that need changing, and none of them are of the terribly stupid variety. However, we do change these.

Preferences

General. These are essentially fine. Change the image-display option if you find that EPS and other placed graphics are hard to see clearly. You may want to choose absolute page numbering. Tool tips are useful until you've learned the program (at which point they become very annoying).

Text. The superscript/subscript and small-cap defaults are fine until you need to use them—then you're likely to need to adjust them for a particular font. If you really dislike anti-aliased type, you can turn that off. Leave the other two settings alone (for print work you will always want typographer's quotes and the correct optical size).

Composition. Increase both the look-ahead and consider-up-to numbers to 10 or 15 or even higher. (The faster your computer, the more speed you can spare for composition. If the higher values slow down your computer, you can reduce them slightly.) Keeping the substituted-font option on is important especially for opening PageMaker or XPress files that may include styled italics or bold type instead of the named italic, bold, or bold-italic fonts. We also suggest highlighting H&J violations, as it warns you if your settings are making too many spacing problems that InDesign cannot resolve.

Units & Increments. We prefer using a page-based ruler origin just because most page elements are measured on the page (even if they are viewed on the whole spread). Experienced designers and typesetters make sure to use picas for both horizontal and vertical units, unless you need to measure column inches (usually for newspaper work). The keyboard increments are up to you; the default values are fine.

Grids. Retain the setting to keep grids in back; the others are a matter of personal preference.

Guides. Guides in front (the default) is recommended.

Dictionary. Turn on the "Recompose all stories when modified" option and retain the "User dictionary and document" setting.

Edit Shortcuts (from Edit menu). If you're a QuarkXPress user, choose the QuarkXPress 4.0 set. Customize the commands in the menus according to your own preferences, assigning keystrokes to the commands you use the most.

Object: Text Frame Options. Set the columns for each job—if you'll be creating lots of two- or three-column text boxes, for example, change this setting so you won't have to modify each box individually. You may prefer using leading for the First Baseline Offset rather than Ascent.

Paragraph Palette

Multi-line Composer. Make sure this option is checked, not Single-line Composer—unless you have a very slow Mac or you just don't care.

Justification. The default values are perfectly acceptable but will often need adjustment for particular fonts. You can widen the ranges if InDesign is having trouble composing text (Word Spacing to 75/100/175 and Letter Spacing to –2/0/2). If you like to experiment with type sizes, setting Auto Leading to 100% is convenient.

Hyphenation. Change "Words longer than" to 5, and let words break after the first two letters. The other default settings are OK (though you may want to reduce the Hyphenation Zone to 1 or 1p6 and increase the Hyphen Limit to 3).

PageMaker 6.52/7.0

PageMaker is still the most flexible of these programs. XPress has matched most of PageMaker's special functions (or will have done once version 5 is released), but PageMaker is still the program to buy if you expect to do all sorts of work from business cards to books. Its index and TOC generation are very good, and so is its trapping (even if you do need a Ph.D. in color processing to use it effectively).

Preferences

General. Most of these are a matter of personal preference, but one is crucial: Change the option to Save Smaller. The Save Faster setting creates increasingly larger files that are prone to fatal damage. Designers and typesetters will want to change measurements to picas and opt to show loose/tight lines. Standard mode is fine for displaying graphics; change it to high resolution if you want a clearer view of imported graphics. Guides are usually best in front (the default setting). Click More.

General: More. If you see too much greeked text (gray lines instead of letters), turn the greek threshold down to 6 pixels. Don't elect to turn pages when autoflowing unless you want to waste a lot of time. Use typographer's (or smart) quotes. Turn the TrueType display to "Preserve character shape" to avoid having cropped characters. If you have trouble reading the default 12-point type, increase the size of the story editor font to 14 or 16 point but leave it as Geneva or you're likely to have problems with a misplaced cursor.

It's usually helpful to display paragraph marks (which really means to display invisibles) and style names. You can leave the three Graphics settings as they are. Increase the PostScript printing setting to Maximum. Now go back to the main Preferences dialog box and click "Map fonts."

General: Map fonts. For most print work, it is better to use PANOSE as the primary font-mapping process with ATM in a secondary role. To do this, first deselect PANOSE, then turn ATM on, and then turn PANOSE back on. Leave 50 as the tolerance level unless you find it's not working well. The big thing is knowing this feature is here at all; it's *very* powerful. Now click Spellings.

General: Map fonts: Spellings. This is a translation table between Windows fonts and Mac fonts. If you receive Windows PageMaker files in your work-flow, this will be indispensable; otherwise, ignore it. The hard part is finding the correct names of PC versions of the fonts—you can then edit this table. It will save hours of work on every cross-platform job. Return to the "Map fonts" dialog box and click Exceptions.

Preferences: General: Map fonts: Exceptions. This looks like the previous table, but it changes an incoming font to another one present on your Mac. This function is for PageMaker files that specify a font you don't have. It's another powerful feature that saves lots of time.

Element Menu

Link Options. Another crucially bad default: You do not want to store imported graphics in your PageMaker files. It makes your files too big and fragile. You can turn on this option on a case-by-case basis, so if you really want to keep small repeating files (such as logos) in a PageMaker file, you can. But it is generally a bad setting.

Frame Options (from the Frame pop-up menu in the Element menu). Change the default inset to zero. If you are using a border with text, the ugliness will remind you to change the inset (typically 1 pica left and right) when you need to.

Document Setup (File menu). Notice there are a couple of items here that you might not expect to find. One is "Adjust layout" (an option that is also in the Layout > Column Guides dialog box). Before using this you need to set the preferences (File > Preferences > Layout Adjustment). Then if you should change the size of the page or number of columns in an existing document, you can use this powerful (though potentially dangerous) function. Document Setup also includes Restart page numbering, for use when setting up PageMaker publications that are used in a book.

Edit Tracks (from Type > Expert Tracking). Just wanted to mention that this powerful feature is here. For most work, you only need the Normal track (or you can define one of the others—"Very loose" is most logical—for automatically letter-spacing caps and small caps). The default tracks work for average text fonts (such as the ubiquitous Times and Palatino), but you may need to change the settings for other typefaces. This is one of PageMaker's secret typographic weapons, well worth learning and using.

QuarkXPress 4.11

Over the years XPress has come to set the standard for page-layout programs. It's not that the XPress way is necessarily best, but hordes of designers and output specialists have adapted to it, so any different behavior (even that of PageMaker's, which came before) seems nonstandard.

Preferences

Application. The second tab (Interactive) contains the setting for Smart Quotes, which is a good thing; the settings for delayed item dragging, which is good; and the setting for drag-and-drop text, which is bad. The third tab (Save) contains settings for Auto Save and Auto Backup, both of which can create problems; Auto Library Save, which is normally a very good thing (unless you're adding lots of items to a library all at once); and Save Document Position, also a good thing. The last tab (XTensions) contains a radio button that you should *always* choose: Show XTensions Manager at Startup: Always.

Document: General. Designers and typographers will want picas as the measurement units. As a matter of convenience, select Guides In Front and use Page for Item Coordinates. Always set Auto Picture Import to On (verify) and Auto Constrain to Off unless you really know what you're doing. You'll normally want Accurate Blends, and you certainly want 72.0 points to the inch. Some of these are already set this way, but you might as well check them anyway.

Paragraph tab. Unless you know what you're doing, turn Maintain Leading Off (you can always turn it on when you need it). Make sure the Mode is Typesetting, and that the Hyphenation Method is Expanded.

Character tab. Turn on Standard Em Space, Accents for All Caps, and Ligatures.

Now we get to one of the foolish settings you absolutely, positively must fix:

Document Preferences: Tool tab. Double-click the Text Box icon, and choose the Text tab. Change the Text Inset: 1 pt to 0 pt. Immediately. Whew! Now you can relax. That 1-point setting is one of the two dumbest, most useless settings in XPress. (The other is in H&Js.) For a particular job (or text box) you might want 6 or 12 points, but no one ever needs a 1-point inset.

Runaround tab. It's usually convenient to set the defaults for Type: Item and Picture Box all to zero. This lets you insert into a column a text or picture box of the same width, which can come in handy when you need to insert a picture box in the text stream.

H&Js (from the Edit menu). Change the Standard H&J for Space to 80%/100%/150% (or the last could be 133% for classically tight word spacing); and change the settings for Char to –2%/0%/2% (or 0/0/0 for classical setting). The program's initial defaults are so bad that we're mentioning them twice. With this change you will have undone the single most nonsensical default value in XPress. (See the "Improving the H&Js" sidebar below for the rest of the diatribe.) It's also a good idea to set the Flush Zone to 6 points, and turn off Single Word Justify.

After clicking OK, duplicate the Standard H&J, call it "No hyphenation," and edit it so that Auto Hyphenation is off, all the Space values are 100%, and all the Char values are 0%. Use this H&J for ragged—flush left, centered, or flush right—text. Base all other H&Js on one of these.

Kerning Table Edit (from the Utilities menu). Some fonts, even some from Adobe, have problematic kern pairs. If you use a font frequently, and don't mind grappling with a poor interface, you can make changes to its kern pairs so they will apply in new XPress documents. Just edit the kern pairs with no document open. (The changes are not recorded in the font, so they will apply only to XPress documents.) Kerning edits can be exported and imported into existing XPress documents, as well.

Tracking Edit (from the Utilities menu). XPress's tracking function is a little-known secret—most users just select a bunch of text and use keyboard shortcuts to modify spacing on the fly. However, the program does provide a track for each font, and it's always on as long as automatic pair-kerning is on. The default settings are zero, however, which means that no tracking changes are applied. Tracking is a powerful tool when you need to use a font designed for (10- to 12-point size range) in a headline—the track can be set to automatically tighten the letter-spacing as the type size increases, to ameliorate that weak and sloppy look that otherwise occurs. To use this, choose a font and edit the track: Smaller point sizes need very little positive tracking, text sizes need no change at all, and larger sizes need negative tracking. You make these changes by moving points on a line graph. The result should be a straight line, or close to it, but at a slight angle, moving from small positive values at, say, 6 or 8 point, through zero at 10 or 11 to larger negative values at 24 or larger sizes. (You'll have to experiment.) If you do this with no document open, the tracking will affect the font in all new documents.

Improving the H&Js (PG/KT)

All the page-layout programs ship with H&Js (hyphenation and justification settings) that cause more problems—in the form of typesetting that ranges from bad to mediocre—than they solve. If you care about the way type looks on your pages, you'll always have to do some manual tweaking, but we think the programs should try to minimize the need for much of this tedious work.

Background

Every font has a space character (sometimes referred to as a *spaceband* for historical reasons) that was designed with a specific width. The width is not the same in all fonts—designing the space is a critical aspect of designing the font as it relates to the fit of letters and words overall. Thus the word-spacing values discussed later in this sidebar refer to the width of a character in the font, expressed as a percentage.

The letter-spacing values are a bit more complicated. There is normally no space between letters—the bounding box (a PostScript term; it more or less replicates the block on which the old metal characters sat) of one letter fits snugly against the next. Digital type has an advantage over metal—we can move these boxes around, even overlap them without having to saw or file away metal as in the old days. But we still need something to measure. When we refer to character spacing or letter-spacing, we are applying a percentage of some other unit to the fit. In most programs this unit is the word space; in XPress, the unit is the zero character. The normal letter-space is thus 0% (no adjustment).

In classical typography, all justification adjustments were made to word spacing, none to letter fit. You can see why—the printer would have had to insert bits of spacing metal between some pieces of type and cut away metal from others. It was simply not done. Since the 1970s, when type became nonphysical (photo images, later digital data), it has become fashionable at times to set letters tightly, especially in advertising work. Against this one can only argue for good taste (and relatively natural spacing).

Here are the initial settings and two sets of enhancements: Phil's and Kathleen's. Phil's are much more practical; Kathleen's assume some manual tweaking (especially to get rid of consecutive hyphens) to make the text work out.

continues on next page

Deneba Canvas

	SPACING SETTINGS (%)		
	Original	Phil's	Kathleen's
Word	100, 100, 150	80, 100, 150	80, 100, 133
Letter*	100, 100, 150	95, 100, 110	100, 100, 100

	HYPHENATION		
	Original	Phil's	Kathleen's
Minimum word	6	5	5
Character before	3	2	2
Character after	2	3	3
Consecutive	3	2	6

*It appears that Canvas bases its letter-spacing adjustments on the em.

InDesign

InDesign came the closest to shipping with a perfectly workable set of default values. We would be happier working with these values than with the default values that come with any other of these applications.

InDesign has a sophisticated feature—the multiline composer, a text-composition routine that examines more than one line at a time. Using InDesign's single-line composer (thus basing composition on each line as if it were alone on the page) can create ugly stripes of loose and tight lines, which calls for a lot of manual tweaking if you care about typography.

	SPACING SETTINGS (%)		
	Original	Phil's	Kathleen's
Word	80, 100, 133	80, 100, 150	80, 100, 133
Letter*	0, 0, 0	–2, 0, 2	0, 0, 0

	HYPHENATION		
	Original	Phil's	Kathleen's
Minimum word	8	4	4
Character before	3	2	2
Character after	3	3	3
Consecutive	2	2	6

	COMPOSER		
	Original	Phil's	Kathleen's
Number of lines	5	10	12
Number of alternatives	5	10	12

*Letter-space adjustments are a percentage of word space in the font.

FrameMaker

FrameMaker's Spacing dialog box has a nice feature—when you select a font, the width of its space character pops into view. This is helpful for deciding how much adjustment may be needed. FrameMaker only allows you to turn Automatic Letter Spacing on or off.

	SPACING SETTINGS (%)		
	Original	Phil's	Kathleen's
Word	90, 100, 110	80, 100, 150	80, 100, 133
Letter	Off	On	Off

	HYPHENATION		
	Original	Phil's	Kathleen's
Minimum word	5	5	5
Character before	3	2	2
Character after	3	3	3
Consecutive	2	2	6

PageMaker

The program allows you to choose from three options: Manual only (no word hyphenates unless you add a discretionary or regular hyphen to it); Manual plus dictionary (which takes advantage of the ranked list); and Manual plus algorithm (all three).

	SPACING SETTINGS (%)		
	Original	Phil's	Kathleen's
Word	75, 100, 150	80, 100, 175	80, 100, 133
Letter*	–5, 0, 25	–5, 0, 10	0, 0, 0

	HYPHENATION		
	Original	Phil's	Kathleen's
Minimum word	N/A	N/A	N/A
Character before	N/A	N/A	N/A
Character after	N/A	N/A	N/A
Consecutive	3	2	No limit
Manual plus ...	Dictionary	Algorithm	Algorithm

*Letter-space adjustments are a percentage of word space in the font.

continues on next page

PageStream

This program hides its word- and character-spacing settings in the Preferences: Tracking dialog box.

	SPACING SETTINGS (%)		
	Original	Phil's	Kathleen's
Word	80, 100, 133	80, 100, 150	80, 100, 133
Letter*	–10, 0, 20	–5, 0, 10	0, 0, 0
	HYPHENATION		
	Original	Phil's	Kathleen's
Minimum word	6	5	5
Character before	3	2	2
Character after	2	3	3
Consecutive	3	2	6

*Letter-space adjustments are a percentage of the em.

QuarkXPress

QuarkXPress has the strangest set of default values of any of these programs. Once you've fixed them, XPress sets acceptable type.

That 110% value for Optimum word spacing is a very, very, very bad value. It means that XPress normally uses a word space that's 10% wider than the font designer intended. What ego! What chutzpah! What wrongheadedness! What a slap in the face to font designers!

	SPACING SETTINGS (%)		
	Original	Phil's	Kathleen's
Word	85, 110, 250	80, 100, 150	80, 100, 133
Letter*	0, 0, 4,	–2, 0, 2,	0, 0, 0
	HYPHENATION		
	Original	Phil's	Kathleen's
Minimum word	6	5	5
Character before	3	2	2
Character after	2	3	3
Consecutive	No limit	2	No limit

*Letter-space adjustments are a percentage of the en.

Redneck Publisher

Unfortunately, Redneck Publisher has absolutely no typographic controls, and very few other controls, either. In fact, it doesn't even have the controls needed to specify the width of a text box. This is a cute, inexpensive little program, but it's best used with the templates that come with it to make calendars, certificates, greeting cards, what have you. Don't try to use it to do serious— or even semiserious—typesetting.

18

Fonts

Jim Felici (JF) is the chapter editor and coauthor.

Erfert Fenton (EF) is the chapter coauthor.

The first time I saw a Mac—back in 1983, after swearing a blood oath to Apple not to disclose what I'd seen—I thought, my god, it's a little typesetting machine! It had fonts built right into it, just like a $100,000 typesetter from Mergenthaler/Linotype.

As it turned out, those early Mac fonts produced pretty ugly type—bitmapped at 72 dots per inch for Apple's ImageWriter printers—but in a couple of years, PostScript fonts from Adobe and LaserWriter printers from Apple finally made the Mac into the typesetting system I had hallucinated a few years earlier.

The Mac's use of type—the central role, in fact, that type played in the whole Mac experience—made it the darling of the graphic arts community. It also made the once arcane practice of typography so accessible that soon after Adobe released its first fonts (and T-shirts to go with them), a gal stopped me outside a Bob's Big Boy in the rural California hills and—after giving my shirt the once-over—said with a flash of recognition, "Ahh, fonts."

We've come a long way. (JF)

In This Chapter

The ABCs of Fonts and Typefaces (JF)

The terms *font* and *typeface* are often used interchangeably, but they don't mean the same thing.

A typeface is a work of art—a set of letters, numerals, symbols, and punctuation marks that share a common design style and are meant to be used together. Times Roman is a typeface. What you see on a printed page is type set in a particular typeface.

A font is a piece of software that describes to a computer how it should draw the letters of a particular typeface. In other words, a font is the means for getting the image of a typeface onto the page (or screen, or whatever). You use a Times Roman font to create Times Roman type.

When you see a printed page, then, you can ask "What typeface is that?" or "What font did you use to print that?" But you can't ask "What font is that?" because the font is in the computer, not on the page.

I know all this sounds a little pedantic, but I'm a type guy—I can't help myself.

A Little Crucial Jargon

Type has a language all its own, and although you'll hear a lot of type talk in this chapter, here are a few basic terms and concepts that will help you make sense of the whole thing.

Many typefaces are designed to be part of a *family,* a group of faces that share common design characteristics so they work well together. A family usually consists of at least four members, which vary according to the thickness (or weight) of the strokes that compose the letters' parts and the angle at which the letters are poised. A typical typeface family consists of several variants.

Regular (roman). This is what you're reading now, the normal face used for text, whether in newspapers, books, or magazines. Most Mac Style and Format menus refer to this member of the family as Plain (although you'll never see a typeface named, say, Garamond Plain).

Italic (oblique). This is a slanted variation of about the same weight as the regular member of the family. True italics have a calligraphic quality, but some are essentially inclined (oblique) versions of the roman face.

Bold. The characters in a bold typeface are thicker and heavier than those of the regular family member and look darker on the page.

Bold italic. This variation combines the heavy weight of the family's bold member and the inclined posture of the italic or oblique member.

Some typeface families have dozens of members (**Figure 18.1**), which vary in weight (from extralight to extrabold), character width (from condensed or compressed to extended or expanded), and special effects such as outlining.

Futura Light
Futura Light Italic
Futura Book
Futura Book Italic
Futura Medium
Futura Medium Italic
Futura Heavy
Futura Heavy Italic
Futura Bold
Futura Bold Italic
Futura Extra Black
Futura Extra Black Italic
Futura Condensed Light
Futura Condensed Medium
Futura Condensed Bold
Futura Condensed Extra Black

Figure 18.1

A typeface family can contain dozens of members, differing from each other in weight, width, and angle. The basic family consists of four members: regular, italic, bold, and bold italic.

Typefaces are categorized in many ways, but the principal ones you need to know are *serif* and *sans serif.* Serifs are little adornments at the ends of the letters' main strokes (**Figure 18.2**). Arguments arise as to whether these adornments derive from the ancient letters made with pens or those carved with chisels, but without a doubt they have a practical value: They make characters easier to identify, which in turn makes text easier to read. Times Roman is a serif face.

Sans Serif

Figure 18.2

A major division among typefaces is between sans serif faces (left) and serif faces (right). In general, serif faces are more legible, so they're favored for use in long text passages.

Sans serif faces—you guessed it—have no serifs, giving them a clean, modern, machined look. Helvetica is a sans serif face. Some typeface families have both serif and sans serif members (**Figure 18.3**).

Figure 18.3

Some typeface families contain both serif and sans serif members, making them adaptable to a wide range of designs and uses.

Officina Sans
Officina Sans Italic
Officina Sans Bold
Officina Sans Bold Italic

Officina Serif
Officina Serif Italic
Officina Serif Bold
Officina Serif Bold Italic

Thou Shalt Not Steal

Fonts are software, and as with most other software you're supposed to pay for them before you use them. Now, fonts—like postage stamps and Beanie Babies—seem to bring out the collector's impulse in people. Some folks just can't have too many of them. That's fine as long as you own them legitimately. But when you copy fonts you didn't pay for, you're not just gypping Microsoft or Apple or some other corporate giant—you're also gypping type designers, who are trying to eke out a living on royalties that come from the use of their typefaces. Fonts are cheap. Pay for them. Support your local type designer.

How Fonts Work

When Gutenberg invented movable type more than 500 years ago, he created fonts consisting of sets of metal stamps designed to be arranged in rows, inked, and pressed against paper to make an image of the type. This technology required casting of a separate set of letters for each type size. So in the days of metal type, a font not only represented a specific typeface but also represented that typeface in a specific *size*.

Then along came offset printing, a technology that created the inked images of pages photographically on flat printing plates. The natural next step was to create type photographically as well, and the first computer typesetting systems used fonts that resembled film negatives. These systems projected light through stencillike images of the letters and exposed them on photosensitive film. This technique rapidly gave way to software fonts, which drew images on the photographic surface by various techniques, the latest being laser beams.

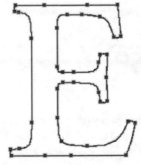

Figure 18.4

A font character outline is essentially the same as any other piece of vector art, consisting of paths and control points.

The great majority of the fonts used these days are called *outline fonts*. They store a collection of mathematical mumbo-jumbo that describes the shapes of all the *glyphs* (the official word for character and symbol shapes) in a font. You can then scale this outline (**Figure 18.4**) to any size you specify and fill it in with any color you want (basic black continues to be the most popular).

Most digital devices fill in these characters with an array of dots, and the density of this array is called the device's *resolution*. The resolution of a Mac monitor, for example, is usually 72 or 96 dpi. Laser and inkjet printers have resolutions ranging from 300 dpi to 1200 dpi and more. Imagesetters, such as those used to set the type in this book, have resolutions of several thousand dpi. The higher the device's resolution, the smaller the dots and the finer the type rendering can be.

The resolution of a computer screen is so low that it's easy to see individual dots (called *pixels* in the case of monitors). When you're trying to draw type in normal text sizes with dots as big as these, it can be hard to make characters legible. They tend to look lumpy and misshapen. As sophisticated as the technology is for scaling font outlines, at small sizes it just doesn't work so well. For this reason, outline fonts often comes with a set of *screen fonts,* sets of characters that—like Gutenberg's metal type—have been hand drawn at a specific, fixed size. These screen fonts are hand drawn dot by dot for optimal legibility, and each dot is assigned a specific position on an imaginary grid, giving them their alternate name: *bitmapped fonts.*

 Although bitmapped screen fonts may seem old-fashioned, in Mac OS 9 and earlier, you should use them if you have them, especially in sizes of 14 points and below. They're more legible, and because of that, they're easier on the eyes.

Your program's Font menu will usually tell you the point sizes for which you have screen fonts installed. If your program offers a menu of type sizes, the ones available as screen fonts appear in outline form (**Figure 18.5**). Sizes that have no corresponding screen fonts appear in solid black.

Figure 18.5

A program's Font menu often shows which screen fonts are available. Here the popular screen font sizes are listed at the top, with the sizes of the installed screen fonts displayed in outline format.

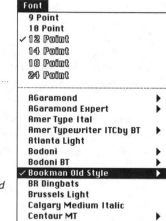

What's in a Name?

Screen fonts usually have pretty straightforward names—Garamond, Rockwell, Frutiger—but printer fonts have much more elaborate naming schemes. Though these names follow a set of conventions, that doesn't always make them more intelligible. For example, you can probably figure out that NewCenSchBolIta stands for New Century Schoolbook Bold Italic. But what about SnellBTBla? It's Snell Black, and the BT stands for Bitstream, the type's manufacturer. SpartHeaCla? That's Spartan Heavy Classified (used for classified ads). When in doubt about what a font name means, just click the mystery font's icon and use Get Info in Mac OS 9 and earlier and Show Info in Mac OS X to see the complete name.

Another problem with these filenames is that when a Font menu is arranged alphabetically, members of typeface families are spread hither and yon. B Times Bold (Times Roman Bold) is near the top of the menu, while Times can be yards farther down, near the end of the list. The most popular program for bringing order to your Font menu in Mac OS 9 and earlier is Adobe's Type Reunion, which comes as part of the Adobe Type Manager, or ATM, Deluxe package. (Adobe said it doesn't plan to create a version of ATM that runs on Mac OS X.) Type Reunion gathers the members of a font family into a single Font menu entry, providing a fly-out sub-menu that lists the members individually. This is a great service—you want it (**Figure 18.6**).

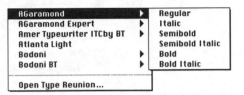

Figure 18.6

Adobe's Type Reunion makes short work of lengthy font menus by reorganizing family groups into single entries that appear as fly-out submenus. Type Reunion has condensed the entire list on the left into the short list on the right.

What's in a Font?

Fonts consist of a lot of program code, but you only need to know about four basic kinds of information they contain:

- The first is the set of outline descriptions, the drawings of the letters themselves. This collection of glyphs is known as the font's *character set*. Most Mac fonts use a standard collection known as the Standard Apple Character set (**Figure 18.7**).

abcdefghijklmnopqrstuvwxyz.,:;' " \ | / ?
ABCDEFGHIJKLMNOPQRSTUVWXYZ
1234567890-=§±!@#$%^&*()_+[ ] { }¡™
£¢∞§¶•ªº–≠∑`´®†¥π " " ' 'ß∂ƒ©˙Δ°¬…«Ω
≈√∫˜µ≤≥÷ / ¤‹›fifl‡°·——œŒ„'‰ˇ¨ˆ∏˝æÆ»
¸◊₁¯˘¿ÀÁÄÂÃÅàáäâãåÇçÈÉËÊèéëêÌÍÏÎ
ìíïîÑñÒÓÖÔÕØòóöôõøÙÚÜÛùúüûŸÿ

Figure 18.7

These are the characters in the Standard Apple Character set, the one used by almost all Mac fonts.

- The second kind of data in a font is a table that lists how wide each of the characters is. Your applications use these widths to calculate how to position type on a page—for example, how many characters can fit on a line. In other words, your application pays no attention to what the characters look like; it just adds up their widths, and when the total reaches the line length you've specified, it breaks the line and starts a new one.

- Another list inside the font describes how to adjust the spacing between individual pairs of characters when they land next to each other on a line. This adjustment is called *kerning,* and it compensates for the differences between the shapes of adjoining letters, such as a capital *T* and a small *o.* A value in the font's kerning table tells your application how much to tuck the *o* underneath the arm of the *T* to make the spacing look more even. (For more details, see the "Kerning" section later in this chapter.)

- Fonts also contain lists of instructions called *hints* that tell the System (or the printer software) how to position the dots that make up a character image so letters are as legible as possible. Hints are important to making text-size screen type readable. The more dots used to draw a character—either because it's a large character or a high-resolution display device—the less important these hints become. But at screen resolutions, they're crucial.

How the Mac OS Handles Type

Part of the Mac OS takes care of handling fonts for your applications. When you ask for 12-point Garamond in your word processor and start typing, the System puts characters of the right size and face onscreen.

In addition to serving up type in the right face and size, the System can perform some basic type tricks and offers shortcuts that make setting type easier. In fact, the System directly supplies much of what appears in any application's Font or Style menu and often controls many of a program's character formatting tools as well. Font Styles, for example, are usually System creations, and they include typeface variations including outline, shadow, strikethrough, and underscore.

One of the handiest of these features allows you to specify which members of a typeface family to use without having to name specific fonts.

For example, if you just start typing in a word processor, it will set type using that program's *default* font, the one that comes up automatically if you don't specify a particular font. This will almost always be the regular or plain member of this typeface family (usually New York). By using your program's formatting menu or standard Mac keyboard shortcuts, you can shift to the bold (⌘ Shift B), italic (⌘ Shift I), or bold italic (⌘ Shift B, then ⌘ Shift I) member of this font family. You can then select the entire passage of text and change it to the plain or regular member of an entirely different typeface family, and all the bold, italic, and bold italic you've applied will follow suit using fonts from this new family.

Installing and Removing Fonts

A lot of programs—particularly font managers (see the "Managing Fonts" section later in this chapter) alter how the Mac System serves up fonts, but let's take a look at the basic setup first.

For the System to handle fonts correctly, they have to be in their appointed place. For Mac OS 9 and earlier, this is easy: inside the Fonts folder within the System Folder.

 For Mac OS X, you can drop them off in several locations: inside the Fonts folder within the Library folder on the startup disk (for fonts that are available to all users of the computer); inside the Fonts folder within the Library folder of each user's home folder (for fonts that are available just to that user); inside the Fonts folder within the Library folder of the Network folder (for fonts shared among users on a local network), and in the Fonts folder in the System Folder in the Mac OS X Classic environment.

Installing fonts is simple: In Mac OS 9 and earlier, just drag them onto the icon of the System Folder, and the System will file them for you automatically; in Mac OS X, drag them to the appropriate Fonts folder. This goes for both outline and screen fonts. If you want to remove fonts from your System, just drag them out of the Fonts folder and store them elsewhere.

 Normally the System won't let you remove fonts from the Fonts folder while programs are running. It's trying to protect these applications from looking for a font that's not there and having some kind of fit.

The reason these fits happen is that most applications check only when launching to see what fonts are available in the Fonts folder. If a application tries to use a font that you've removed in the meantime, it may lose control of itself, and we don't want that. Likewise, if you add fonts to the Fonts folder while programs are running, the System will give you the warning that these fonts "will not be available to currently running applications until they have quit." What the System means is until they've quit and restarted, but you get the idea.

A few programs, mainly publishing applications, keep a constant eye on the Fonts folder, so if you add fonts while they're running, the new fonts will appear in their Font menus immediately (despite the System's warning). This is easy enough to check: Add a font to the System while your program is running, click OK to accept the System's warning, and see if the font has appeared in your application's Font menu.

Inside the Fonts Folder

If you look inside the Fonts folder in Mac OS 9 and earlier, you'll see two basic kinds of icons: printer fonts and suitcases (**Figure 18.8**).

Figure 18.8

A sampler of font icons and font file names. Top row (left to right): TrueType suitcase, Adobe PostScript, OpenType. Middle row: Adobe Multiple Masters, generic PostScript Type 1, Bitstream PostScript. Bottom row: Monotype PostScript, screen font suitcase, individual screen font.

An open Fonts folder in Mac OS X can be a little more bewildering. You'll see printer fonts and suitcases, but you may also see files whose names include a handful of extensions. The files that end in .otf, for example, are OpenType fonts. Those that have a .dfont extension are members of a new font format Apple uses with Mac OS X. In the .dfont format, the font resources are stored in the data fork of the file. TrueType fonts have a .ttf extension, and TrueType collections end with .ttc.

Suitcases are special folders for screen fonts (as well as other kinds of System resources). They also hold TrueType fonts (see the "TrueType" section later in this chapter), whose suitcases may contain both printer and screen fonts, although the latter are not always supplied.

If you double-click a screen font suitcase in Mac OS 9 and earlier, it will open as a new window, just like any other folder, and you can see the screen fonts listed inside.

Screen fonts can function correctly if taken out of their suitcase and placed directly in the Fonts folder—but they can also cause untold havoc left exposed like this, creating hassles that range from printing problems to System crashes. If you don't want a lot of extraneous screen fonts on your System, you can drag them out of their suitcases and trash them, but you should store even a single screen font in a suitcase.

If you double-click a font file contained inside a suitcase, a little preview window will open showing a sample of the typeface that file represents. If the file is a screen font, you will see it displayed at its nominal size. If the file is a TrueType font, you'll see samples in a range of sizes (**Figure 18.9**).

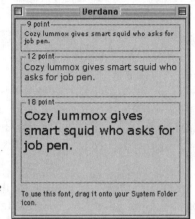

Figure 18.9

Double-clicking the icon of a TrueType font opens a sample showing the typeface at several sizes.

Prior to Mac OS 9, the System only allowed you to have a total of 128 suitcases in the Fonts folder. Each one of these suitcases could hold 16 MB of fonts. To get around those limitations, a breed of programs called font managers sprung up (for more on this, see the section "Type Management Software," later in this chapter). In Mac OS 9, Apple raised that number to 512 suitcases. Mac OS X has no hard ceiling for how many fonts and suitcases you can have; your only limit is how much RAM you have.

Font Formats

Life would be too simple if there were only one font format, and the competitive nature of the computer business ensures that life never remains simple for very long. Although for years Adobe's PostScript fonts were the de facto font format for the Mac, Apple (not happy to be beholden to another company for such a key System element) set about creating its own font format—TrueType—in collaboration with Microsoft. Over the past few years, to create a single font standard again and to make fonts easier to use, Adobe and Microsoft have collaborated on a hybrid font format—OpenType—intended to combine the best of PostScript and TrueType and eliminate the confusion that multiple font standards have created.

The System handles these various font formats slightly differently.

PostScript Fonts

The System can still treat PostScript fonts like poor relations, even though they are by far the most popular fonts for the Mac, especially in the publishing community. To help out, in Mac OS 9, ATM makes PostScript fonts equal citizens; Mac OS X, with its ATM-like capabilities, also gives them equal status.

For the Mac system to deliver a PostScript font to a program, at least one size screen font for that typeface must be in the Fonts folder. For correct output of that type on a printer, the corresponding printer font must be in that folder as well. But onscreen type requires only the screen font.

When you ask for a particular typeface in a particular point size while you're working in a program, the System peeks into the Fonts folder to see if what you want is there. If it sees a screen font for that typeface there, that's a good start. If a screen font for the specific point size you want is there as well, you're golden—the Mac will use the characters from that font to display your text onscreen.

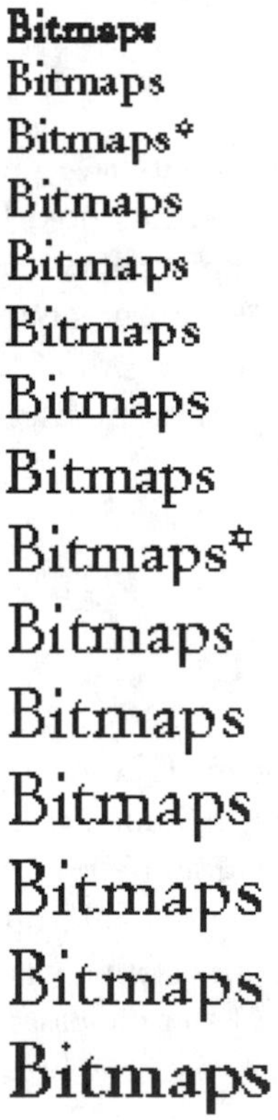

If the System finds the screen font in the right typeface but not the right point size, it will scale the characters from a screen font of another size to the one you asked for and display them onscreen. These scaled bitmaps usually look dreadful—lumpy and misshapen, although still legible (**Figure 18.10**).

This arrangement has additional subtleties. For example, for your basic four-member typeface family (say, Helvetica Regular, Italic, Bold, and Bold Italic), merely having the Regular screen font in the Fonts folder allows the System to display type in the other three family faces as well. This is because the Regular screen font of a PostScript typeface family contains information that describes how wide all the characters in the other three fonts are.

Screen type created this way won't look as good as the real Bold, Italic, and Bold Italic screen fonts (**Figure 18.11**), but it will be in the ballpark, and you'll get accurate line endings because the System uses the characters' true widths to fit your text into lines. This type will print correctly too, assuming that the necessary printer fonts are available at printing time.

Figure 18.10

Screen type created by scaling bitmapped screen fonts is not a pretty sight. The samples marked with asterisks come from screen fonts for those sizes; the rest are created by scaling those screen fonts to other sizes.

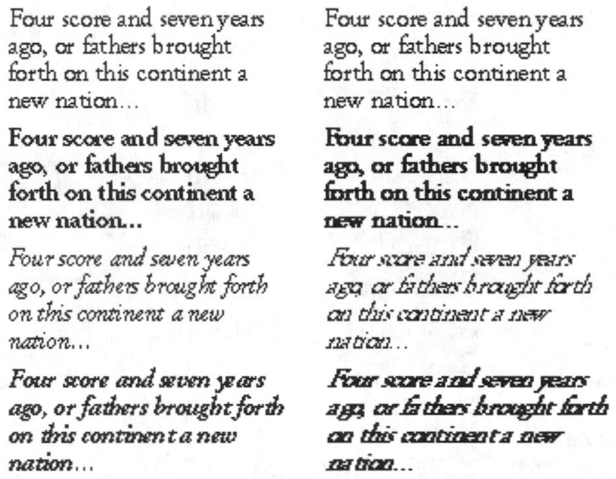

Four score and seven years
ago, or fathers brought
forth on this continent a
new nation...

Four score and seven years
ago, or fathers brought
forth on this continent a
new nation...

**Four score and seven years
ago, or fathers brought
forth on this continent a
new nation...**

**Four score and seven years
ago, or fathers brought
forth on this continent a
new nation...**

*Four score and seven years
ago, or fathers brought forth
on this continent a new
nation...*

*Four score and seven years
ago, or fathers brought forth
on this continent a new
nation...*

***Four score and seven years
ago, or fathers brought forth
on this continent a new
nation...***

***Four score and seven years
ago, or fathers brought forth
on this continent a new
nation...***

Figure 18.11

The screen type at left was created from four separate screen fonts: regular, bold, italic, and bold italic. The type on the right has all been created from a single screen font: the regular member of the family. It's legible, but just barely.

The PostScript Font Name Game

PostScript fonts are often called PostScript Type 1 fonts. There are actually many flavors of PostScript fonts, but you don't have to consider most of them. PostScript Type 1s are the top-of-the-line PostScript fonts. They are fully hinted and produce the best results onscreen and on the page.

At one time, Adobe charged type vendors a fee for the secret of how to create Type 1 fonts. If they didn't want to license the technology, they could only create Type 3 fonts, which looked good at high resolutions but fairly crummy on medium-resolution devices, such as 300-dpi laser printers. When Apple and Microsoft launched TrueType, Adobe started giving away the recipe for Type 1 fonts.

PostScript fonts also come in several other varieties, including Type 2 and Type 42, the ones built into OpenType fonts.

Adobe Type Manager. ATM was Adobe's answer to Apple's lack of solid support for PostScript fonts.

In Mac OS 9 and earlier, this program does several things.

First and foremost, it uses PostScript outline fonts to generate the type you see on the Mac's screen. This means screen type is much smoother and easier to read, because it's based on the same character outlines used for printing—it's not an interpolation of another bitmap. ATM gives you the option of using those screen fonts you may have installed, and this is a good idea, because as they were designed by hand (not by machine), they are the most legible versions. At point sizes for which you don't have screen fonts, ATM creates good-looking bitmaps for display onscreen (**Figure 18.12**).

Smooth? Smooth!
Smooth? Smooth!
Smooth? Smooth!
Smooth? Smooth!
Smooth? Smooth!
Smooth? Smooth!
Smooth? Smooth!
Smooth? Smooth!
Smooth? Smooth!
Smooth? Smooth!
Smooth? Smooth!
Smooth? Smooth!
Smooth? Smooth!
Smooth? Smooth!
Smooth? Smooth!

Figure 18.12

ATM uses outline fonts to generate screen type on the fly (right), creating much smoother type than when screen type is scaled from bitmaps (left).

ATM doesn't create whole new screen fonts, though. It creates bitmaps only for the characters you type, and it stores these in memory so it doesn't have to redraw them every time you need them. This speeds things up considerably. ATM lets you specify how much memory—that is, how large a *memory cache*— to dedicate to saving these bitmaps. It will suggest a value automatically, but if you routinely create documents using lots of typefaces, you may want to increase the size of your cache, which you do in ATM's control panel (**Figure 18.13**). Remember, though, that ATM reserves all this memory in advance; it doesn't just take memory as it needs it. So when you enlarge ATM's cache, you are depriving other applications of access to that memory.

Figure 18.13

In the ATM control panel, you can control how much memory to use for preserving the screen type that the program has created. The more ATM can save, the less it has to redraw on demand and the faster your programs can run.

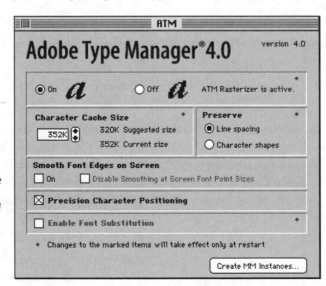

ATM also allows you to print PostScript fonts to a non-PostScript printer. Normally, PostScript type for printing is scaled and rendered in a special PostScript interpreter, an onboard computer built into PostScript printers. But ATM will do this job in your Mac if you have a non-PostScript printer, so you can use your PostScript fonts on any printer you like.

The high-octane Deluxe version of ATM can make your screen type look even smoother using a technique called *anti-aliasing* (ATM uses the term *font smoothing*). Basically this means ATM uses gray pixels in addition to black ones to draw your screen type, adding the gray pixels around the edges of characters to fill in gaps and reduce their jagged appearance (**Figure 18.14**). This can be effective and actually makes it possible to identify one typeface from another even at small sizes onscreen. (With most black-and-white screen bitmaps at text sizes, it's nearly impossible to tell one typeface from another.)

Figure 18.14

When you turn on ATM's or the System's font-smoothing (or anti-aliasing) option, screen type gets even smoother. Adding gray pixels smooths out the jaggies, as seen in the enlarged letter at the bottom.

The downside of anti-aliasing is that these gray pixels make the type look slightly fuzzy, which gives your eyes a real workout as they're constantly trying to draw the images into focus. Personally, I find the slightly jaggy, unsmoothed ATM type easier on my eyes, at least in common text sizes.

In Mac OS 8.5, Apple added font smoothing to the system, letting you manage anti-aliasing for TrueType fonts in the Appearance control panel.

With Mac OS X, Apple decided to take in-house much of the work ATM performs. The 2D imaging model in Mac OS X, called Quartz, is based on Adobe's PDF (Portable Document Format) and provides many of the capabilities ATM gave to Mac OS 9 and earlier users, including anti-aliasing the PostScript type you see on the screen. Mac OS X also handles printing PostScript fonts to non-PostScript printers. Because of Mac OS X's PostScript-like features, Adobe is not rewriting ATM for Apple's new OS.

Multiple Master fonts. Modern outline fonts are slick, but in some ways they're more primitive than the ones Gutenberg used. Early type designers realized they had to design small type differently from large type. These pioneers saw that for legibility they needed to make small type somewhat heavier and somewhat wider, with somewhat taller lowercase letters than in larger type. But modern computer type design mostly ignores this crucial fact—even today, the majority of fonts create characters with the same proportions at whatever size you choose.

Usually this single master outline is designed to look best at about 12 points. The type from a master outline of this size looks thin and weak when reduced in size and heavy and thick when enlarged.

But Multiple Master fonts can contain any number of outlines. For example, a Multiple Master font could have one master outline for use at small sizes (say, 6 point for footnotes and such), another at 12 point (for reading text), and another at 36 point (for headlines and titles). Multiple Master–savvy programs can then create custom instances of such a font—a 24-point version, for example, whose features average those of the 12- and 36-point masters. It's a clever scheme and desirable for the typographical connoisseur (**Figure 18.15**).

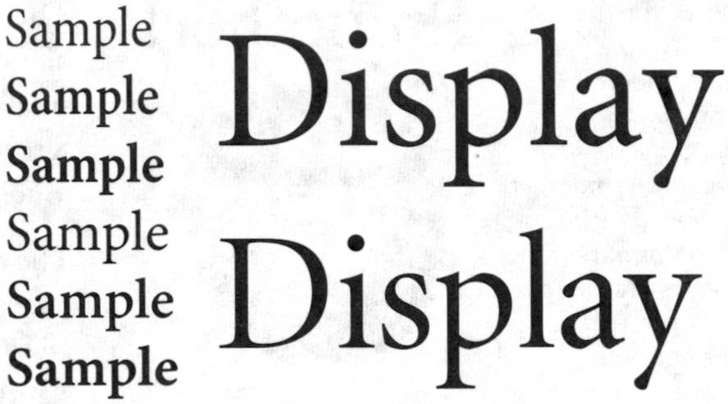

Figure 18.15

All these samples come from a single Multiple Master font. The top three samples (left) are condensed versions of the ones below. In each threesome, the top one came from a 72-point master outline, the middle one from an 11-point master outline, and the bottom one from a 6-point master outline. The proportions of the characters change for maximum legibility at all sizes. The type from the 72-point master (below, right) is more finely modeled than the one just above it from the 6-point master.

Sample
Sample
Sample
Sample
Sample
Sample

Display
Display

Multiple Master fonts can also contain other master outlines that vary in weight or angle. In this way, one font could generate an infinite number of typeface instances, ranging in weight from light to bold or in slant from upright to oblique. In other words, you can get a whole family of typefaces from a single font.

The problem with Multiple Master fonts is that they're a lot of work to create, making them expensive to develop and to buy. In an era when the retail value of fonts has gone through the floor, few users are willing to pay the extra cost for a Multiple Master font, although they are popular in professional publishing circles. Relatively few faces have been released in this format.

 When we finished this chapter, Mac OS X couldn't yet properly work with Multiple Master fonts.

TrueType

Much to Apple's chagrin, TrueType never did become popular on the Mac. But it did turn the Windows OS of Microsoft—its collaborator in developing the format—into a powerful publishing platform and helped Microsoft steal a large part of one of Apple's traditional markets. The PostScript interpreter that Microsoft was developing as part of the deal (to squeeze Adobe out of the picture) never materialized, leaving Apple holding the bag.

Unlike PostScript fonts, which consist of a separate file for each typeface in a family plus suitcases of screen fonts for each one, TrueType fonts come packed in a single suitcase. This may or may not contain screen fonts. Often several family members are combined into a single font file within that suitcase (such as Geneva or Courier). This makes font housekeeping somewhat easier.

Best of all, with TrueType you don't need to have (or buy) anything like ATM, because the System itself scales and renders TrueType fonts. Mac OS 9 and Mac OS X can also anti-alias type as ATM does, using gray pixels in addition to black ones to create smooth screen type. In Mac OS 9, you can activate this feature in the Appearance control panel. In Mac OS X, you can control it through the General pane of System Preferences; Mac OS X calls it text smoothing. Unlike ATM, however, Mac OS 9 and X lets you specify a point size above which this smoothing kicks in, allowing you to continue to read text-size type in clear, simple black and white.

One of TrueType's claims to fame is its sophisticated *hinting* technology. This allows a TrueType font, like a PostScript Multiple Master font, to vary outline shapes according to point size. Also like a Multiple Master font, a single TrueType font can generate type in a range of weights or widths (or both at the same time). This was a feature of so-called TrueType GX fonts, but these never became popular (they were too complicated to make), and with Mac OS 9 Apple has dropped support for the QuickDraw GX imaging technology required to use them.

Another problem with TrueType fonts is that most imagesetters (the high-resolution typesetters professional publishers use) are based on the PostScript imaging technology and don't handle TrueType fonts well. Often TrueType fonts have to be converted into PostScript format during the imaging process, and this can gum up the works. For the Macintosh publishing community, PostScript is still the font format of choice.

The Freebies

Here's a list of the fonts you get free when you buy a copy of Mac OS 9 or a PostScript printer. The Mac OS 9 fonts are all in TrueType format; the PostScript printer fonts are—naturally enough—in PostScript format.

Mac OS X comes with more than two dozen fonts—including Baskerville, Big Caslon, Copperplate, Didot, and Zapfino—in a mix of TrueType and OpenType formats. And because it uses the Unicode character format (which can handle many more characters than the older ASCII format), Mac OS X includes a handful of Japanese fonts.

Mac OS 9 System Fonts	*PostScript Core Fonts*
Apple Chancery	Helvetica
CAPITALS	ITC Avant Garde*
Charcoal	ITC Bookman Oldstyle*
Chicago	ITC New Century Schoolbook*
Courier	ITC Zapf Dingbats (✺❑✌✔)*
Gadget	ITC Zapf Chancery Medium Italic*
Geneva	Palatino Symbol (Ω♣◊≈)
Helvetica	Times Roman
Hoeffler Ornaments (⚬⚭⚮⚬)	
Hoeffler Text	* ITC stands for International Typeface Corp.,
Monaco	which created these typefaces.
New York	
Palatino	
Sand	
Symbol (Ω♣◊≈)	
Techno	
Textile	
Times	

OpenType

In an attempt to resolve the "font war" between PostScript and TrueType, Adobe and Microsoft (Apple having effectively lost the custody battle for TrueType) collaborated on a master font format called OpenType. This consists essentially of a TrueType shell that can contain TrueType font data, PostScript font data, or both. The idea is that an OpenType font file will work on any computer, any operating system, and any output device. You don't need a Windows version or a Mac version of the font file—any OpenType font will operate on either platform.

OpenType fonts are more complex to make than TrueType or PostScript fonts. More important, though, font vendors can choose among various flavors of OpenType fonts. The OpenType specification allows a vendor to create an OpenType font with no TrueType content—just a TrueType "wrapper"—that essentially acts like a PostScript font. Likewise, the font could contain TrueType content but no PostScript content. Both types retain cross-platform file compatibility, but what's inside may not be evident.

New versions of ATM (4.6 and beyond) support the PostScript-flavored OpenType fonts on Mac OS 9 and earlier (that is, OpenType fonts with file names ending in .otf), and the System should support them directly if they contain TrueType font data (that is, if their filenames end in .ttf). Mac OS X handles both types of fonts natively, without ATM. On the PC side, Windows 2000 supports OpenType as a native font format, just as it does for TrueType fonts.

Another potential benefit of OpenType fonts is that they support a huge character set: as many as 64,000 characters, as opposed to the 256 contained in standard PostScript and TrueType fonts. This means a single font could support a range of languages and contain a host of alternate characters. However, no one knows yet exactly how this will work and what a standard extended character set might look like.

As of this writing, only a handful of OpenType fonts are available on the retail market, and most of them come from Adobe. Check the company's Web site (www.adobe.com) for samples. Some of the fonts that come with Mac OS X are OpenType.

The Name Game

Beware of having multiple fonts with the same names installed on your Mac. Some font names are copyrighted or trademarked, but many are not. Thus it's easy to end up with two or more fonts named, say, Bodoni on your Mac. In addition, many typefaces may have unique filenames but appear under the same name in the Font menu as another font.

Case in point: When you buy the Mac operating system, you get TrueType versions of the PostScript fonts that come with all PostScript printers, such as Times, Helvetica, Courier, and Symbol. Since these fonts contain identical characters, usually this doesn't present a problem. But some programs—and under some conditions the Mac OS itself—stumble over fonts with duplicate filenames, so you end up with missing type, incorrect type, or printing problems. And when you see these fonts in the Font menu, you don't know which font format you're getting.

Fonts: How to Use 'Em

There are several ways to select a particular typeface for text.

First, with your program's text cursor (the familiar I-beam) blinking and ready, you can go to the Font menu and select a font to use. Though you haven't typed a single character, you've now assigned that font to that cursor position, and as soon as you start typing, your text will appear in the typeface you chose. If you move your cursor to a new position, though, the program will forget your font choice.

Another way to use a font is to select a passage of text and then choose a font from the Font menu. When you click OK, the selected text will appear in that font.

 Mac OS X includes a new tool called the Font panel to help you select a font. (The built-in Mail and TextEdit applications use it, for example.) It works the same way, however: From the Font panel, you can either select the font first or select the passage of text first. The Font panel is available to Cocoa applications and not Carbonized applications (**Figure 18.16**).

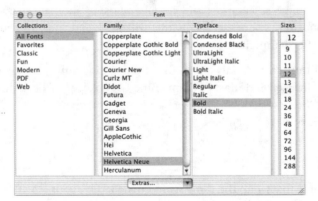

Figure 18.16

The Font Panel in Mac OS X allows you to select and style type as well as create your own type collections.

No matter how you use fonts, you end up with a zone of text in which that font is in effect. If you move your cursor into that zone and start typing, the type appears in that face.

 But remember, word spaces are not just blanks—they're typeset characters, formatted in a typeface. In fact, not all word spaces are the same, as the fonts you use actually *define* their widths. This may not seem important, but if you inadvertently format a word space using the wrong font, you may get error messages from printers and applications that try to use a file containing it. When a printer or program comes across a call for a specific font, it expects to find that font available, even if the font's just for a word space.

Having chosen to work with a specific typeface, you'll probably use other members of its family, such as italic or bold. The easiest way is by using keyboard commands, tool bar buttons, or Style menu options to switch to the bold, italic, and bold italic members. These commands don't request a specific font—instead, they simply ask the System for the bold (or italic, or bold italic) member of the *font family currently in use.* This means if you select the whole passage of text and assign a new font to it, all of the family members will be pressed into service according to how you previously formatted the text. If you change the whole passage from Times to Helvetica, Times Italic becomes Helvetica Italic and Times Bold becomes Helvetica Bold. This slick technique works for all kinds of fonts, and it's faster than running off to the Font menu every time you want a different typeface.

These controls work as *toggles,* which means each control works as an on-off switch. Choosing Bold from the menu or clicking the Bold toolbar button makes selected text bold; a second click of the same command changes it back to regular text. The same goes for italic.

You may get funny results if the text you select already uses fonts from two members of the same family. For example, if you choose some text that's half regular and half bold, issuing the bold command may either turn the regular into bold or turn the bold into regular (remember the toggle effect). Depending on what you're after, you may have to issue the formatting command twice: once to get all the text formatted the same way, and the second time to get it into the typeface you want.

 How you format your text affects how you can search for it using your program's search-and-replace command. Let's say you formatted your type in Palatino and used the style commands or keyboard shortcuts to access other family members. If you then want to search for all the text set in Palatino Italic, you must tell your program to search for type *styled* as italic (Figure 18.17). If you ask the program to search for type formatted using the Palatino Italic font, it won't find any. This is because you formatted the text with generic italic, bold, and bold italic commands. The use of specific fonts happens behind the scenes.

Likewise, if you've formatted your text by selecting specific fonts from the Font menu, you must ask your program's search facility to look for text set in that specific font. If you ask it to find Palatino styled as italic, it won't find any.

Figure 18.17

Not all italics are created equal. From a Find and Replace standpoint, an italic created from an italic font (bottom) is distinct from an italic created by applying the italic style to a roman typeface (top).

Change Character Attributes		
Find what:		**OK**
Font:	Bookman Old Style	**Cancel**
Size:	Any ▷ points Leading: Any ▷ points	
Horiz scale:	Any ▷ % size Track: Any	
Color:	Any Tint: Any ▷ %	
Type style:	Italic	
Change to:		
Font:	Bookman Old Style Italic	
Size:	Any ▷ points Leading: Any ▷ points	
Horiz scale:	Any ▷ % size Track: Any	
Color:	Any Tint: Any ▷ %	
Type style:	Normal	

Other Typeface Styles

In addition to giving you the ability to switch among members of a font family, Mac programs' Style or Format menus give you a range of other ways to alter the appearance of the type you set. Not all of these are as slick as they might appear at first glance.

Underline. This option creates a solid line underneath text. It imitates what people used to do for emphasis on typewriters. But on a typewriter, at least you could choose which letters to underline and which ones not to. Except in a few programs, the Mac's underscore runs under every character—even letters with descenders, such as *g* or *y,* which it runs right through. This is not pretty. People used underlining on a typewriter because they didn't have the option of italics; you should use italics instead. If you do opt for underlining, use it only with text set in all capitals, which usually has no descenders.

 If you really love your underlining, choose a program that can skip descending letters and (better yet) lets you vary the thickness of the underline.

Outline. The outline feature looks good onscreen, less good on a laser or inkjet printer page, and terrible on a high-resolution imagesetter. That's because the outline itself is created not as a scalable object but as an array of pixels—a bitmap.

 Since higher-resolution devices have smaller pixels, the outline itself becomes fainter and fainter at higher resolutions, until it almost completely disappears on an imagesetter. This is one special effect best reserved for onscreen use.

Strikethrough. This is a variation of underlining in which the line passes right through the midsection of the letters on a line. It generally indicates a recommended or intended deletion of the text so formatted. It can be handy for clarifying editorial changes in a manuscript.

 Shadow. For the same reasons as in the case of Outline, Shadow doesn't work well at high resolutions. Save it for onscreen use.

Small caps. This is another one to avoid if possible (see the section "The Seven Deadly Typographic Sins" later in this chapter).

 In addition to the usual typeface styles, Apple has built in to Mac OS X a handful of typography tricks you'd normally find in a professional page-layout program. TextEdit—Mac OS X's replacement for SimpleText—for example, takes advantages of these and lets you kern letters and control ligatures. Although these typographic tools are part of the system software, third-party software developers have to write Cocoa applications to use them. Create from Stone Design is a good example of an application that uses Mac OS X's typographic features.

The Question of Attributes

To simplify typesetting concepts, the first word-processing programs divided typographic attributes into three kinds: those that apply to whole documents, those that apply to paragraphs, and those that apply to single characters or ranges of characters.

 These divisions, which persist today, are highly arbitrary and have little precedent in real typesetting practice, where you can apply almost any typographic variable to a single character. Advances in desktop publishing technology now allow you to apply some paragraph attributes to characters as well.

More confusingly, not all programs agree on the definition of paragraph and character attributes. Some programs, for example, can only apply style sheets to whole paragraphs, while others can apply them to single words or characters.

Fonts and Printing

Creating the image of a page for printing is complicated. The printer must calculate the placement of every dot used to create the printed image. PostScript printers and non-PostScript printers have differing approaches to the task. Chapter 6, "Printing," takes this subject up more fully—but here's a quick overview to get you started.

PostScript Printing

PostScript printers use a built-in computer with software (called a PostScript interpreter) designed to handle the work. Your Mac just sends the printer all the information about the page and then goes on to its next task. One thing the printer needs is font information.

For a PostScript printer to image a page properly, it needs the outline information (stored in the fonts) for every character and symbol used in the text or used in illustrations that contain text. Every PostScript printer has some fonts built in, and some have hard disks on which they can store many other fonts. If the PostScript interpreter does not find the fonts used in a document while processing the page, it will call back to the Mac that sent the file and ask if the fonts are there. If they are, the Mac downloads them to the printer, which stores them in memory until the job is done. Then the printer forgets the fonts.

If neither the printer nor the Mac has the appropriate fonts, you've got a problem—one the printer usually resolves by substituting Courier for the missing fonts.

Font Downloading

A PostScript printer can store fonts in three places: in ROM (the chips built in to the printer), in RAM (in the printer's memory), or on the printer's hard disk (if it has one). If you just tell your Mac to print, it starts a dialogue with your printer about which fonts the printer has already—either built in or stored on its hard disk—and which need to come from the Mac.

The Mac downloads any fonts the printer needs into the printer's memory. This is called *automatic downloading,* and it's the easiest way to get the job done. The only penalty you pay is the seconds you have to wait while your Mac sends the fonts to the printer. Once the printer has completed the job, it flushes the fonts from its memory to make room for the next job.

Now, the next bunch of fonts may well be the same ones you just used. In office settings, where everyone uses the same set of "house fonts," this is often the case. So instead of having everybody pay this little time penalty to download fonts automatically, you can opt to download fonts manually. To do this, you use a special utility program to download fonts into the printer's memory, where they stay until the printer is turned off. Called *permanent downloading,* this is a handy option. The Mac OS used to come with one such program, the LaserWriter Font Utility, and if you have a copy left from those old days, it will still work. Adobe's Font Downloader, which comes with ATM, does the same thing. However, unless you notice this uncommon problem, you shouldn't have to worry about this.

A problem can arise when the printer doesn't have enough memory to support everyone's font needs. When the printer runs out of memory, you lose your job and you may have to restart the printer. The lesson: Don't permanently download fonts unless you know there will be enough memory left for others' printing needs.

Even a single job—if it uses enough fonts—can cause a PostScript printer to run out of memory. To avoid this, Apple has built an option into the Page Setup/PostScript Options dialog box for Unlimited Downloadable Fonts. It sounds like a good idea, but don't use it unless you have to—that is, don't use it until either a document has failed to print because of a memory shortage or you're sure it's going to happen. This option works by allowing only one font to load into printer memory at a time. When a different font is called for, the printer deletes the one in memory and downloads the new one. In a simple paragraph with six italicized words scattered through it, this would mean 13 separate font downloads. You can see what could happen: a four-page document would take ten minutes to print.

Type and Non-PostScript Printing

Printers without onboard computers use your Mac to do their thinking for them. Your Mac does all the image processing and merely sends a stream of data to the printer telling it where to put which dots.

The Mac OS itself renders TrueType fonts, but in Mac OS 9 and earlier, ATM must process any PostScript fonts. And with its PostScript-like capabilities, Mac OS X handles PostScript fonts. Otherwise, what you see on the page will be a crudely smoothed version of the onscreen type.

Font Embedding

Just as documents can run into trouble on a printer because of missing fonts, the same thing can happen when they travel to another computer. For this reason, more and more applications allow you to embed fonts within a document. This can add a lot to the size of your file, but at least you're assured of its looking the way you want it to when it arrives at its destination.

Some typeface designers are leery of this process, as it's fairly easy to crack into a file containing embedded fonts, remove the fonts, and use them. This, of course, is theft. For this reason, the TrueType and OpenType specifications contain a setting that a font designer can activate to prevent font embedding. If you then try to embed that font in a document, you'll get an error message.

PostScript fonts have no such embedding shield, so make sure you read your software license agreement when buying PostScript fonts to see if you have the right to embed fonts in your documents. You usually do.

Cross-Platform Issues

Until OpenType (or something like it) becomes a cross-platform font standard, sending typographically formatted documents from a Mac to a PC or vice versa will be fraught with potential problems and fonts will remain in the forefront.

Fortunately, in building Windows, Microsoft had the good sense to create a core font set that corresponded to the one used on the Mac. They're not the same typefaces, but they have character widths identical to those of their Mac analogs, so you can use files created in the Mac version of a typeface in Windows and end up with nearly the same results (**Figure 18.18**).

Apple is moving in the same direction with Mac OS X. The new operating system can use Mac and Windows TrueType fonts—along with OpenType and PostScript fonts—which hopefully will make sharing documents across platforms easier.

Times New Roman	Times Roman
Arial	Helvetica
Arial Narrow	Helvetica Narrow
Bookman Old Style	ITC Bookman Old Style
Century Gothic	ITC Avant Garde
Century Schoolbook	ITC New Century Schoolbook
Book Antiqua	Palatino
Monotype Corsiva	*ITC Zapf Chancery Medium Italic*
Courier	Courier
Symbol (Ω♣◊≈)	Symbol (Ω♣◊≈)
Monotype Sorts (✐❑✇✔)	ITC Zapf Dingbats (☎❑✇✓)

Figure 18.18

The basic Windows font set (left) looks similar to the basic Mac PostScript font set (right). The widths of all the characters in analogous fonts are the same, so the formatting of a document using these fonts remains the same when it moves from one platform to the other. The operating system will map any of these fonts automatically to its equivalent on the alternative platform.

Finding the Characters You Need

There aren't enough keys on the Mac keyboard to give you easy access to all the characters of even a simple PostScript or TrueType font.

Key Caps—under the Apple menu in Mac OS 9 and earlier and in the Utilities folder inside the Applications folder in Mac OS X—can help you find what you're after. Just launch the program and choose from the Key Caps menu the font whose character set you want to investigate. Since nearly all Mac fonts have the same character set and the same keyboard assignments for getting at those characters, if the typeface you're looking at is too faint or too hard to read onscreen (the Key Caps window is really much too small), pick a more legible typeface, such as Charcoal (**Figure 18.19**).

Figure 18.19

Key Caps, under the Apple menu in Mac OS 9 and in the Applications folder in Mac OS X, shows which characters are assigned to which keys. You can copy text typed in the window to your documents.

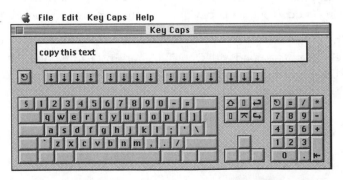

With your hands off the keyboard, you'll see all the characters available in the unshifted keyboard layout. Hold down (Shift), and the Key Caps display will change to reflect what you'll get if you type a key while shifting the keyboard. The same goes for (Option) (labeled (Alt) on some Mac keyboards) and for (Shift)(Option). These keystrokes give you a view of all four keyboard "rails" (to use an old typesetting term).

But even more characters lurk behind those keys. Certain characters are only accessible through a two-part keystroke sequence. In most text fonts, these include characters capped with the following accents: grave (`), acute (´), circumflex (^), umlaut or dieresis (¨), and tilde (˜).

To get these compound characters (they're actually assembled for you on demand, using an accent character and a separate consonant or vowel character), you first type the key sequence for the accent and then the letter to which you want to apply that accent. The accent appears only after you've typed the letter.

Here are the keystrokes to set the accents:

(Option)(`)	` (grave)
(Option)(E)	´ (acute)
(Option)(I)	^ (circumflex)
(Option)(U)	¨ (umlaut or dieresis)
(Option)(N)	˜ (tilde)

So to type an e with an accent acute, as in *cliché,* first type (Option)(E). Nothing will appear to happen. Then type e. Bingo—the accented *é* will appear.

Here's the whole list of accented characters you can create using this technique:

À, Á, Ä, Â, Ã, à, á, ä, â, ã, È, É, Ë, Ê, è, é, ë, ê, Ì, Í, Ï, Î, ì, í, ï, î, Ñ, ñ, Ò, Ó, Ö, Ô, Õ, ò, ó, ö, ô, õ, Ù, Ú, Ü, Û, ù, ú, ü, û, Ÿ, ÿ

The same technique works in many symbol (or pi) fonts, including Zapf Dingbats:

(Option)(`) + (A)	❷	(Option)(U) + (U)	❬
(Option)(N) + (A)	❸	(Option)(E) + (A)	❭
(Option)(N) + (O)	❹	(Option)(`) + (A)	❰
(Option)(U) + (A)	❲	(Option)(I) + (A)	❱
(Option)(E) + (E)	❯	(Option)(U) + (A)	❳
(Option)(N) + (N)	❮	(Option)(N) + (A)	❩
(Option)(U) + (O)	❵	(Option)(U) + (Y)	❯

And don't forget Symbol:

Option ` + A	¢	Option N + O	⊆
Option N + A	C	Option U + Y	¬

Well, maybe you *can* forget Symbol.

The Curse of the Little Box

Some older Mac System fonts (prior to Mac OS 9, that is) didn't have complete character sets. When typing using one of these faces (New York, Chicago, and Geneva, to be specific), you may suddenly see little rectangles onscreen instead of the characters you thought you'd typed. These little boxes are placeholders for characters the font's character set doesn't include.

To see the characters you want, just switch to another font.

Expert Sets

Some typeface families come with auxiliary fonts called *expert sets* (**Figure 18.20**). The characters typically found in expert sets include old-style numbers (sometimes called *nonlining numbers,* these don't all sit on the baseline), swash characters (with flamboyant extended strokes), true small capitals (better proportioned than those scaled down from a text-size master outline), fractions (and small numerals for building them), and extra ligatures (usually ffl and ffi).

Figure 18.20

Typical expert set characters include (top row) small capitals, (second row) fractions and old-style numbers, (third row) fraction elements and ligatures, and (bottom two rows) swash characters.

A B C D E F G H I J K L M N O P Q R S T U V W X Y Z
¼ ½ ¾ ⅛ ⅜ ⅝ ⅞ ⅓ ⅔ 1 2 3 4 5 6 7 8 9 0
1 2 3 4 5 6 7 8 9 0 ₁₂₃₄₅₆₇₈₉₀ ffi ffl ct
A B C D E F G H I J K L M N
O P Q R S T U V W X Y Z

Few font families include expert sets, but if you're serious about typography, they're worth seeking out. The new OpenType sets do include auxiliary fonts.

Character Set Enigmas

Just about every Mac text font contains the same collection of characters, but not all of these belong to that font. For reasons known only to Apple, some of the characters that appear to be part of each font are actually borrowed from the Symbol font. This is why some characters in every font don't seem to match the design of the rest (unless you use them with Times Roman, which supplies the design motif for Symbol).

The list of such borrowed characters includes ∂, Δ, π, Π, Σ, Ω, $\neq$, ∞, $\leq$, $\geq$, $\int$, $\sqrt{}$, $\approx$, $\Diamond$, and (of course) .

Handy Characters

You should know about a few handy characters lurking in special Mac fonts. Ever had a craving to set the Mac Command symbol (⌘)? You'll find that and much more by using Key Caps—under the Apple Menu in Mac OS 9 and earlier and in the Utilities folder inside the Applications folder in Mac OS X. To peek inside the Chicago and Charcoal TrueType System fonts, hold down Control: You'll see a bunch of handy symbols for this and other keyboard actions, such as Delete (Delete and Del) , Shift (Shift) and the cursor key directions (←, →, ↑, and ↓).

How to Talk Type

Type has its own vocabulary, with roots that go back centuries and span many cultures and languages, mingling German, Italian, and English with a lot of French. The word *font,* for example, comes from the French language and means "fount" or "source" (although these days in France a font is inexplicably called a *police de caractères*).

Most of this vocabulary relates to either the positioning of type on the page or the features of characters themselves. You could delve into a ton of arcane stuff here, but this section includes just what you need to know to use your programs' type controls.

The Measure of Type

Type has its own measuring system. Actually, it has two measuring systems: one absolute and one relative. Let's look at the simpler absolute one first.

The basic measuring units in typography are picas and points. There are 12 points to the pica. When Adobe Systems invented PostScript, it tidied up what had been a near equivalence between these measurements and standard English measurements and made it exact. Thanks to Adobe, these days there are exactly 6 picas (72 points) to the inch. Designers often use picas and points to measure distances on a page, while they use points to describe the size of type and the spacing between lines. The shorthand notation used to designate points is the single prime mark ('), so you can write 16' instead of 16-point or 16 points.

This measuring scheme is based on the system of movable type invented by Gutenberg in the sixteenth century. Back then—and this is still the case in some hand-printing facilities—each letter was cast on a metal block, and all the blocks of a given size were the same height so they would align neatly in rows. The height of such a block was the point size of the type (**Figure 18.21**).

Figure 18.21

In handset type, each letter was cast on its own lead block, as represented here. On the left is a solid setting, in which the point size of the type is equal to its leading. In the specimen on the right, extra lead spreads the lines of type apart.

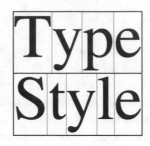 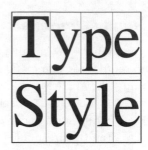

Today the blocks of metal are gone but the concept remains, and the point size of type is the distance, measured in points, from just above the tallest (or ascending) letters—such as an *l* or *F*—to just below the lowest (or descending) letter—such as a *g* or *y*. Type size used to be measured in whole-point increments, but with today's publishing software, you can set sizes in tenths, hundredths, or even thousandths of a point.

Typographers also use relative units to express sizes and distances. These units have no fixed value; their values float according to the size of the type they're used with (**Figure 18.22**).

Figure 18.22

Typography relies on relative measuring units, as illustrated here by the horizontal increments that describe the widths of these characters. The W here, for example, is 20 units wide. This measuring system can describe the width of type independent of its size; shrink the type and you shrink the units as well. The widths of characters in a font are measured using relative units in this fashion.

The most basic of these relative units is the *em*. Despite what it sounds like, the em is not based on the width of the letter *M*. Instead it is equal to the size of the type with which you use it. For example, when you're setting 12-point type, an em is 12 points. Paragraph indents are often expressed in ems, which relates the size of the indent to the size of the type. Enlarge the type, and the size of the indent changes correspondingly.

Other relative spaces are the *en* (half an em) and the *thin space* (typically half an en but usually customizable in a publishing program).

This may sound abstract, but understanding relative spaces is crucial to using the typographic controls of publishing software, because spacing adjustments such as kerning, tracking, and hyphenation and justification settings are all expressed in relative units (see the section "Hyphenation and Justification," later in this chapter).

Type in Motion

Type on a computer is said to *flow.* When you add type to an empty column, frame, or shape, it flows in like water to fill that shape (except that it fills from the top down instead of the bottom up). When you're typing a line of text that becomes full and the type starts a new line, the type has *wrapped.* If you add more words at the beginning of this text or change its size or typeface, the text *reflows* and *rewraps* as all the line endings change.

Baselines and Leading

The fundamental point of reference for type is the *baseline,* an invisible line (akin to the one printed in notebooks) on which most letters appear to sit.

The distance from a baseline to the one below it is called *leading* and is usually measured in points (**Figure 18.23**). It gets its name from the days of handset type, when the blocks of type were made of lead alloy. When typesetters set rows of these blocks representing lines of type directly above each other, the type was said to be *set solid.* The term persists today.

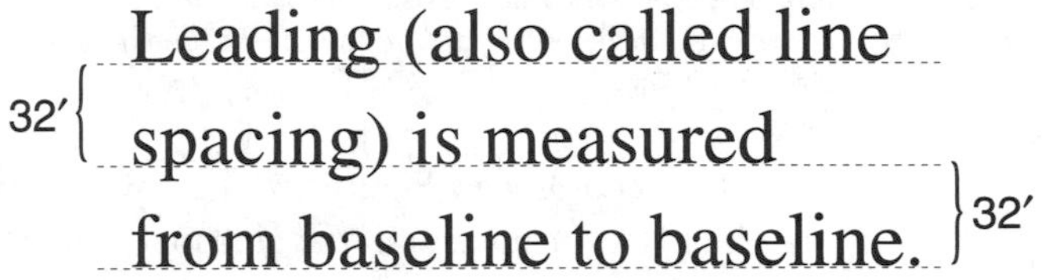

Figure 18.23

Leading (or line spacing) is always measured from the baseline of one line of type to the baseline of another line of type before or after it. Here, 24-point type is set on 32 points of leading.

32′ { Leading (also called line
spacing) is measured
from baseline to baseline. } 32′

If typesetters wanted more space between those lines, they added lead or used extra leading. The old-timers did it with thin strips of metal; we do it with the leading or line spacing command in our Mac programs. Either way, the net effect is to push the baselines of successive lines further apart.

If you were setting 12-point type, a *solid* set would be 12 points of leading. In 16-point type, a solid set is 16 points of leading, usually written as 16/16 and pronounced "16 on 16" (meaning 16-point type with 16-point leading).

Solid-set type usually looks too tight, though, and most word processors and publishing programs use a default setting that adds leading automatically. This automatic leading is usually 120 percent of the point size, so 10-point type set with automatic leading would end up as 10/12 (or 10 on 12). In practice, you'll probably want to set specific values for text leading. Generally, use less leading in narrow columns and more leading in wider ones.

Before the desktop publishing revolution, the computerized system for setting type treated leading as a character attribute. In today's desktop programs, though, leading is almost always a paragraph attribute. If you change the leading anywhere in a paragraph, the leading of the whole paragraph changes. To change the positions of individual characters relative to the baseline, programmers cooked up the notion of the *baseline shift*. This character attribute allows you to take one or more characters in a line and make them rise above or sink below the baseline without affecting the leading in the rest of the paragraph. It can be handy in making fractions, for example, where you have to elevate little numbers off the baseline to create the numerators.

Alignments

Spatial relationships are everything in type, and a lot of them are based on how elements align. The most basic of these, as we've seen, is *base alignment,* the alignment of letters within a line of text. But there are other frames of reference as well (**Figure 18.24**).

Align-o-Matic™

Figure 18.24

Typical vertical alignment points include the ascender line (for top-aligning characters such as this trademark symbol), the x-height (the tops of the lowercase letters), the baseline, and the descender line.

The ascent line in Figure 18.24 shows a line that coincides with the tops of the tallest characters in the alphabet. Some characters, such as trademark symbols, are commonly set to bump up against this invisible ceiling. They're said to be *top-aligned.* There's also a descent line, which marks the point below the baseline to which descending letters reach. Not many items *bottom align,* although it's a handy capability for setting mathematical equations. Another commonly used alignment point, the *x-height,* is at the tops of the lowercase letters.

When you set type, you specify a maximum length for lines. The official term for this length is *measure,* but word processors have popularized this as simply *line length.* Because lines of type are usually stacked to form columns, the line length or measure is also sometimes referred to as the *column width.*

The last of these terms makes it easier to visualize how lines of type align. Imagine the column as a tall rectangle, with the left and right sides representing its margins. Type set so that each line completely fills the column from margin to margin is *justified.* To get type to justify, your program has to stretch or squeeze the spaces between letters and characters to make every line the same length.

If all the lines of type you set start hard against the left margin, that type is *flush left.* This term usually implies that the lines are not all the same length—that is, they're not justified—giving the right margin a ragged appearance.

That irregularity is called a *rag,* and the full description for type set this way is *flush left, ragged right.*

You can also set type *flush right, ragged left* or *centered.*

A final option is *force-justified.* The last lines of justified paragraphs usually end short of the right margin. But in force-justified text, you can force even this last line to fill the measure. This isn't very useful except in one-line settings, where you can force a line to stretch, creating the spaced-out effect you often see in advertisements. Programs that offer forced justification usually have you specify a zone just inside the right margin, so that only if the last line of a paragraph reaches into that zone will it be force justified. This tidies up your margins.

Hyphenation and Justification

The process your program goes through to fit text into lines is called *hyphenation and justification,* or *H&J* for short. (From a mechanical perspective, justification is the process of fitting type into lines, no matter how the margins are aligned.)

A program has a limited bag of tricks for getting type to fit into lines. It can stretch or compress the spaces between words, stretch or compress the spaces between letters, or break a word in half and hyphenate it. (A scheme to subtly alter character widths to assist in H&J will be introduced in Adobe's InDesign 2.0 when it's released in early 2002.) Or it can use a combination of these techniques.

In any case, the goal of the process is to create lines with consistent color; that is, lines with consistent, even spacing. Lines set too loose look pale; lines set too tight look dark. These variations in color are distracting and unattractive. They also make text harder to read because the reader's eyes can't lock into the rhythm that evenly spaced type creates.

Your programs give you some control over how these options are exercised (professional publishing programs, of course, offer the most control). At best, you get to tell the program the following:

- How wide the spaces between letters and words should ideally be (usually defined as 100 percent of "normal," which is a value defined within the font).
- How wide you are willing to let these spaces stretch (usually expressed as a percentage of normal; standard values range from 120 to 150 percent or more).
- How narrow you will allow these spaces to be squeezed (rarely less than 85 percent of normal).
- How many hyphenated lines in a row you will allow (three is the traditional maximum).

- The minimum number letters of a word that must appear on a line before it can be hyphenated (two or three is the norm).

- The minimum number of letters following the hyphen that can be carried down to start the next line (usually three).

The number of letters you allow before and after a hyphen is important. The smaller these numbers, the more flexibility the program has in breaking words. For example, if you say that at least three letters of a word must precede any hyphen and at least three must be carried to the next line, a word such as *abalone* can break in only one way: aba-lone. But if you reduce those limits to two letters, you get more options: ab-alone, aba-lone, abalo-ne. Having more hyphenation options makes it easier for your program to maintain consistent type color, because it reduces the need to alter spacing. Two or three letters is the norm, while one is universally regarded as too few. A-men.

When a program is setting a line of type, it puts as many words onto the line as will fit. When it comes to a word that won't fit, it juggles hyphenation and spacing variations until it comes up with a way to fill the lines and keep your spacing as close to normal as possible.

 If the type you're setting has too many loose or tight lines, it's probably because you need to adjust the H&J values specified in your program.

[*For more on H&J, including settings for specific page-layout applications, see Chapter 17, "Page Layout." —Ed.*]

A Handy Hyphenation Trick

No program is always going to hyphenate correctly all the time. Sometimes they hyphenate words—especially proper names and products—improperly or not at all. You can help your program along by adding a hyphen yourself—but don't use a normal hyphen right off the keyboard. Known in the trade as a *hard hyphen,* this indeed allows a line to break, but it also becomes part of your text forever. If some other editing or design change causes your text to reflow, the hyphen will still be there, probably in midline somewhere, converted from a solution into a typo.

Instead, use a *soft hyphen,* sometimes called a *discretionary hyphen.* You can usually create a soft hyphen with ⌘- (this may vary from program to program), and when typed in a word, it tells your program to break the word there if it can and then add a hyphen. If the text reflows to make that line break unnecessary, the hyphen disappears.

Tracking

The word *tracking* refers to the overall spacing of the characters in a passage of text. If you want the characters closer together, tighten the tracking. If you want them farther apart, loosen the tracking.

Why would you do this? The main reason is to improve the type's appearance and make the reader's eyes happy.

In a kind of optical illusion, small type always looks more tightly spaced than large type. For this reason, typographers tighten the tracking of large type to draw the characters closer together and loosen the tracking of small type to make it less crowded and easier to read. Because typefaces vary so much in their designs, there's no set rule about how much you should tighten or loosen tracking at specific type sizes. But with display type—the big type used for headlines and titles—you can often tighten tracking by as much as 20 percent before it starts to look too crowded (**Figure 18.25**).

Tracking

Tracking

Tracking

Tracking

Tracking

Figure 18.25

All these samples appear to have the same spacing between characters, but in fact the tracking has been progressively tightened from one size to the next. The spacing between the characters in the largest sample is 10 percent tighter than that of the smallest one.

In most programs, you set tracking (sometimes called *track kerning*) by selecting a range of text and applying a tracking value, usually expressed either as a percentage (plus or minus) of normal spacing or an adjustment based on fractions of an em (usually thousandths).

Desktop publishing programs often allow you to set up tracking changes to happen automatically. When using them, you can specify that at certain point sizes the tracking value in effect will change. For example, you could have tracking loosen automatically below 9 points. Then above, say, 18 points you could have it tighten somewhat, and at 36 points tighten again. The idea is to have all the type on the page look as if it has the same spacing, and the only way to achieve this is to use different tracking settings for different type sizes.

Tracking also has many practical problem-solving uses. For example, if you have a line of type that's obviously set too loose, with word spaces stretched to the point of ugliness, you can often get the line to break at another point by tightening its tracking. Likewise, you can usually correct tight lines by loosening their tracking.

 Tracking can also act as a copy-fitting tool. It can squeeze a headline into a narrow space or fit a block of text that's too long or too short into its appointed space on the page. The only guideline is visual common sense: Avoid making the tracking of type so tight or loose that it contrasts obviously with other type on the page.

Kerning

Kerning is the adjustment of the space between two specific letters, often required because the shapes of adjoining letters may make them appear to be too close together or (more commonly) too far apart. The problem usually occurs when one character with a concave shape appears next to another with a convex shape. You can solve some typical kerning problems by adjusting the widths of spaces between individual characters (**Figure 18.26**).

Figure 18.26

The irregular shapes of letters creates uneven spacing, particularly obvious here between the T and the o in the upper sample. In the lower sample, the letter pairs have been kerned to produce more even spacing.

Toys

Toys

If this fiddling sounds like a process that could go on forever, you're right. But today's fonts have largely automated kerning. Every font you buy contains a table of kerning adjustments—created by the typeface's designer—for specific letter pairs. There are usually several dozen to more than a thousand such adjustments listed within each font, and most applications that handle text these days use these values as you set your type. Sometimes you may have to turn on kerning yourself in the program's Preferences or Options dialog box.

A thousand kern pairs may sound like a lot, but the total number of possible kerning pairs in a 256-character font ranges into the tens of thousands. Inevitably pairs of letters and other characters (such as punctuation) that may need adjusting will appear in your pages but not in those kerning tables. For example, I used to set type for KQED television, and not surprisingly the rare KQ letter combination is not in any font's kerning table.

You then have to make some kerning adjustments manually, and publishing programs in particular give you sophisticated controls for making subtle adjustments using keyboard commands. Word processors, in contrast, usually give you only the option to adjust the tracking for the range of the two characters you want to kern. This is awkward, as it usually means a trip to a dialog box for every adjustment and readjustment.

The key to kerning well is to make the spacing of all characters look even. Don't try to get two letters to fit together as tightly as possible. Instead, tighten just enough to make the spacing of the bad pair look close to that in the rest of the word or line.

The Sad Lot of Widows and Orphans

The terms *widow* and *orphan* are among type's most colorful. A widow occurs when the last line of a paragraph doesn't fill out the column fully. There is nothing wrong with widows per se, but you have to be on the lookout for *bad* widows—lines so short that they almost make it look as if a whole line space separates paragraphs. One-word widows are a problem, as are widows not much longer than the paragraph indent of the line that follows. Hyphenated widows—consisting of just part of a hyphenated word—are a definite no-no.

Not many programs offer good widow controls, although few allow a hyphenated widow. If you find a bad widow, try loosening the tracking of the paragraph to make the widow longer or tightening it to draw the widow up onto the previous line.

An orphan is a fragment of a paragraph that ends up at the bottom or top of a page or column. This always presents a problem—for example, when the last line of a column or page is the first line of a paragraph, the paragraph indent makes the column look dented at the corner and out of square, and likewise if the last line of a paragraph ends up at the top of a column or page.

At the top of a column, a two-line orphan looks awkward if the second line is short (in effect, the unhappy combination of an orphan and a bad widow).

Preventing orphans is not easy. Most programs try to do it through a system of so-called *keeps* rules, which let you specify that a certain number of lines at the beginning and end of each paragraph be kept together so they're not splintered into orphans. This works, but it also makes some pages shorter than others because each page can't contain the same number of lines.

The only real solution to the orphan problem is *vertical justification*. This is just beginning to appear in a useful form in professional publishing programs. Vertical justification alters the leading between lines over the length of the entire column to push orphans onto the next page or to draw additional lines onto the page to make the orphan longer. This also works as a copy-fitting device, expanding the length of the text to fit a given space.

Managing Fonts

Fonts multiply like rabbits. The Mac OS gives you fonts. Applications give you fonts. And you'll find it hard to pass by those cheap CDs full of fonts. The next thing you know, you've got hundreds of them all over the place.

It's no wonder that font management has become a big issue and that there are so many programs out there to whip your fonts into line.

There are two main reasons to manage your fonts. First of all, it reduces System overhead (having gobs of fonts on hand saps your Mac's energy) and shortens your Font menu so you can find and choose fonts more quickly and easily. Also, in Mac OS 9 there is a limit as to how much stuff the System will let you cram into the Fonts folder (512 suitcases). If you exceed this limit, things start to go haywire. You may, for example, suddenly find that all of your dialog box inputs appear in the Symbol font. This is a wake-up call that tells you the System is teetering on the brink of a crash. Mac OS X doesn't have a suitcase limit.

The Do-It-Yourself Approach

The simplest method of font management is to keep only those fonts in your Fonts folder that you'll actually be using. Just store the others in some other folder: For Mac OS 9 and earlier, that would be outside your System Folder; for Mac OS X, that would be outside the various Fonts folders you can keep them in. You can then add them back as needed. In the case of some older applications, you may need to restart the program to get it to recognize fonts you added while the program was running. This is not a big deal and will ultimately save time compared to scrolling through mile-long Font menus whenever you want to change a typeface. If you are working in the Classic environment of Mac OS X, you have to restart Classic after dragging fonts into the System Folder.

As part of your housekeeping, you may be tempted to rename certain font files. Take care! You can rename suitcases holding screen fonts, but do not rename TrueType fonts or PostScript printer fonts—their filenames are specific and important, and changing them could cause all sorts of font confusion, substitutions, and even System crashes.

Type Management Software

Type management programs do several things. First and foremost, they allow you to organize your fonts into collections, or sets, that you can install in one fell swoop. You can create a set of fonts for a particular job, for example, or for a particular client. One font can belong to several sets.

Second, type management programs can pluck out duplicate fonts (which can befuddle the System) as well as weed out and often fix corrupted screen fonts.

Third, they can install (the word they usually use is *activate*) fonts as they're called for in the applications of files you open (assuming the application is compatible with this function—not all are). Open a file that uses Beppo Black? Bingo! Your font manager activates it automatically. This helps to keep your fonts menu from becoming overwhelming.

 Although Adobe is not revamping ATM for Mac OS X, other font-management software—including DiamondSoft's Font Reserve, Alsoft's MasterJuggler Pro, and Extensis's Suitcase—are moving over to Apple's new operating system. And Mac OS X's Font Panel can group fonts together but doesn't let you activate fonts, as third-party font managers can.

Here's a summary of the most popular Mac font managers and what they do.

Extensis Suitcase (www.extensis.com; $99.95). Suitcase from Extensis is a suite of programs from various vendors, including Extensis's Suitcase (for installing and deinstalling font sets), Insider Software's FontAgent (see below), and Dubl-Click Software's MenuFonts (for WYSIWYG Font menus that list fonts in their true typefaces).

DiamondSoft Font Reserve (www.diamondsoft.com; $89.95). The Cadillac of font managers, Font Reserve from DiamondSoft creates a database of the fonts you have on hand, allowing you to search your font library by design style, manufacturer, format, or any other number of criteria, including those you invent yourself. The program holds your fonts in a "vault," protecting the originals against corruption and using copies of the fonts when you need them. It fixes corrupted fonts before allowing them into the vault. The program also has excellent preview functions, which makes it as good for finding the typefaces you want as for managing the fonts that generate them.

Adobe Type Manager Deluxe (www.adobe.com; $65). ATM Deluxe from Adobe combines the type rendering capabilities of ATM with a solid font management program that allows you to build, install, and uninstall sets of fonts. Every time you start the program, it peruses your entire font library to make sure everything is A-OK: All printer fonts have screen fonts (and vice versa), no fonts are corrupted, no fonts have identical names, and so on. Adobe is not revising ATM for Mac OS X, but the tool will still work in Mac OS 9 and earlier and in Mac OS X's Classic environment.

Alsoft MasterJuggler Pro (www.alsoft.com; $39.98). This solid, basic font manager can also manage other System resources, such as sounds. It culls fonts it suspects are damaged and can round up and make copies of fonts you want to send to a service bureau along with files for typesetting.

Insider Software FontAgent (www.theinside.com; $69.95). FontAgent from Insider Software scours your entire hard disk looking for printer and screen fonts, uprooting duplicates, finding PostScript printer fonts that lack screen fonts (and screen fonts with no corresponding printer fonts), sorting screen fonts by family (and putting them in a single folder if you like), and finding and fixing corrupted screen fonts. It's a great housekeeping aid.

Making Your Own Fonts

Many of the tools typeface designers use for creating Mac fonts are themselves Mac programs you can buy and use.

Typeface design and font manufacture are complicated jobs. None of these programs will teach you how to design a typeface, for example, or how to create the character spacing that makes type look good on the page. But you may have reason to use these programs even if you never design a typeface of your own. Because they can import artwork created in other applications, you could use the programs, for example, to add your company's logo to your house font.

Fontographer (www.macromedia.com; $349.00). Still popular with small and independent font foundries, Fontographer from Macromedia has been virtually neglected by Macromedia since that company bought Altsys some years back (mainly to get its mitts on the rights to the FreeHand drawing program, which Altsys developed). It's still a solid program and fairly easy to use considering the complexity of the task.

FontLab (www.pyrus.com; $399.00). Pyrus has aggressively continued to upgrade FontLab, which migrated from Windows to the Mac. It is particularly good at hinting TrueType fonts, but it can also do everything that Fontographer can do with PostScript fonts, including creating Multiple Master fonts.

Troubleshooting

It seems like everything having to do with computers only gets more complicated and more fraught with technicalities over the years. Not so with fonts. They have become far easier to use and far more reliable.

Most font errors come from sloppy housekeeping habits—that is to say, they're your fault—but some others are out of your control.

Crummy-looking, lumpy type. This happens when your printer can't find the necessary printer font and prints a smoothed version of the type as it appears onscreen. It means you have the screen fonts installed but not the printer fonts.

Courier substitution. This is a variation on the theme above. It can happen when the printer fonts you need are not installed or when you get a document from someone else and you have neither the necessary screen fonts nor the printer fonts installed.

Wrong typeface. There is a remote possibility that two fonts will have the same internal ID number (applications usually handle fonts by number rather than name). In this case, the wrong font may appear. Most software is smart enough to prevent this by issuing its own temporary ID numbers to avoid duplications. Font managers do the same thing. If this happens to you, the only solutions are to keep only one of the problem fonts on your Mac at a time or to buy a font management program (such as one mentioned earlier) capable of renumbering fonts to avoid ID conflicts.

Corrupt screen fonts. Screen font files carry vital data about how the System and your programs should handle type. Your Mac reads these files over and over every day. Sometimes in this process they become damaged, or *corrupted* in the jargon of high-tech. Corrupt fonts can cause an amazingly diverse range of problems, few of which seem related to type: System freezes, crashes, and corrupted documents that your applications will refuse to open or read and that may crash your System when you *do* try to open them. Some font management programs and font utilities can weed out corrupt screen fonts. But if you don't have such a program, you have to find the culprit by trial and error. If you remember which fonts you were using when the problem first appeared, try removing them from the Fonts folder and replacing them with fresh versions from the original disks. If that doesn't work, you may have to remove all your fonts and replace them from scratch.

Typesetting Tips

There's typing, and then there's typesetting. Anyone can buy a few fonts, whack away at the keyboard, and print a publication. But not just anyone can make a document aesthetically pleasing and easy to read. That's where the art of typesetting comes in. In this section you'll learn some advanced tips for making your publications look like the work of a professional typesetter.

The Seven Deadly Typographic Sins

We'll start by pointing out some common mistakes almost every beginning desktop publisher makes. See if you've committed any of the following sins.

1. Two spaces after a period. This is probably the most common typographic sin. You'll see it in ads, newsletters, and even books. Simply because the Elders used to do it, many modern typesetters place not one but *two* spaces between sentences in a paragraph. The Elders were justified in putting two spaces after a period, because in the olden days they used typewriters, which generated *monospaced* fonts, in which each character was the same width (a few such—Courier, for example—still exist). With monospaced fonts it made sense to place two spaces between sentences; otherwise, a paragraph became a wall of uniformity, with one sentence blending into the next. But typewriters haven't been in vogue for, oh, a generation or so, so it's high time people let go of the old ways and stopped being so spaced out. Period.

Bonus sin: Two hyphens for a dash. Your old Underwood might make you type two hyphens to represent a dash, but your word processor or page layout program should have a setting that automatically converts two hyphens into a dash (known in typesetting terms as an *em dash* because it's one em wide—for more on ems, see the section "The Measure of Type" earlier in this chapter). If your word processor doesn't have this feature, you can type an em dash by pressing ⟨Shift⟩⟨Option⟩⟨-⟩.

2. Straight quotes. Nothing cries out "AMATEUR TYPESETTER!" more loudly than a set of straight quotes (except maybe using capital letters for emphasis—but that's another story). Your keyboard gives you access to perfectly good typographer's, or curly, quotes. Use them. These days most word processors are smart enough to generate curly quotes automatically; if you find yourself typing straight quotes, check your word processor's settings and enable curly quotes (many programs call this feature "Smart Quotes").

3. Text on a busy background. Black text on a white background? Boring! You may think that text on a colored or patterned background is the way to go if you want your message to stand out. But that way is fraught with danger, as you'll see by hitting eight or ten Web pages at random. Many Web designers feel obliged to prove their creativity by placing text—often smallish text—on a festively patterned background, which makes the page virtually unreadable.

This particular peccadillo is not limited to the Web. Many publications are rife with eye-catching but illegible text on patterned backgrounds. Even white text on a black background can be hard to read. If you're using a typeface with thin strokes, delicate serifs, or other subtleties, the black ink can bleed right over the thin parts, making for a melted-looking mess. If you do place text on a black, colored, or patterned background, make sure you use a robust typeface that's readable against your chosen texture (**Figure 18.27**).

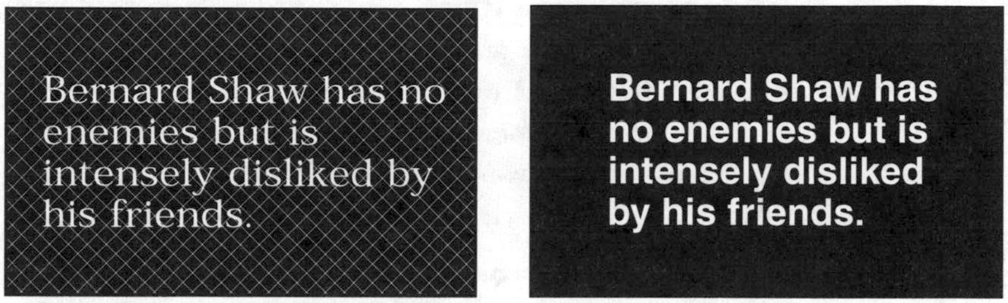

Figure 18.27

A delicate typeface can disappear on a background (left); use a more robust one (right).

Bernard Shaw has no enemies but is intensely disliked by his friends.

Bernard Shaw has no enemies but is intensely disliked by his friends.

If you come across a Web page that's hard to read (say, 12-point red text on a red-and-orange paisley background), you can magically make the text readable by highlighting it, which places it on a plain background. Alas, this tip doesn't work for printed pages.

4. Narrow justified columns. Let's say you're laying out your monthly newsletter. And let's say you use justified columns (see the "Alignments" section earlier in this chapter). So far, so good. In one of your articles you include a large illustration, and you make one of the columns an inch wide so the image fits on the page. Bad idea. When you use really narrow justified columns, all the hyphenation in the world can't save your publication from looking awkward. You'll end up with gaps, ultrawide tracking (see the "Tracking" section earlier in this chapter), and a possible plethora of hyphens. If possible, reformat your document to eliminate the narrow column. You may even be justified in redesigning your newsletter to use unjustified text.

5. A lack of leading. You've seen him on the street corner—the scruffy, bearded loner passing out his four-page manifesto. He has a lot to say, so he uses small type with almost no space between the lines; ascenders run into descenders and the overall effect is dark and ominous, sort of like his gaze. You don't want to turn into this fellow, do you? Good. Then listen up. When you're typesetting your manifesto, make it light, airy, and inviting (thus winning more converts to your cause) by using sufficient leading.

Because typefaces vary (a willowy face with long ascenders and descenders might warrant extra leading, for example), there's no hard and fast rule for how much leading to apply. Your best bet is to print a paragraph at several settings and see what looks best for your publication.

Some word processors automatically use a leading that's the same as the selected point size (11 points of leading for an 11-point font, for example). Typesetters call this *set solid* and avoid it like the plague. As a general rule, in book-width columns 11-point type should have at least 2 points of leading (11/13); 12-point type generally needs at least 3 points of leading (12/15). At shorter line lengths you can get by with less leading.

6. Inappropriate styles. Some word processors offer shadowed or outlined styles in their Style or Format menus or palettes. These styles were cute back in 1984, but these are the 00s (pronounce it as you wish); using them these days is the typographic equivalent of wearing a straw boater, a bow tie, and spats to a rave. (If you want some technical reasons to hate 'em, see the "Other Typeface Styles" section earlier in this chapter.)

7. Inappropriate or mismatched fonts. Some typesetting beginners find a font they love and feel they *have* to use it no matter what the circumstances. Black-letter headlines with a modern, sans serif face—no problem! An entire article in a script face—how elegant! A 9-point caption in a barely legible grunge font—cutting edge! These people should be ashamed of themselves. Well, no, they shouldn't—they're beginners. But you, dear reader, should exercise some common sense when choosing which faces to use. When in doubt, you're pretty safe using a classic serif face (Palatino, Times, Caslon, Janson, Garamond, or the like) for text and a bold sans serif face (Helvetica, Gill Sans, Futura, Avant Garde Gothic) for headlines.

Advanced Type Tips

Now that you know how to avoid some common typographic faux pas, it's time to improve your typesetting skills with some advanced techniques.

Ligatures. One way to tell a typist from a typesetter is to look at the Big Picture. A well-set page is pleasing to the eye and easy to read, with wide enough columns (but not too wide, or the reader's eye will get tired on the long trek across a line) and proper leading. Another way is to look at the details, including ligatures. *Ligatures* are connected pairs (or sometimes threesomes) of letters, found in many text faces. The most common ligatures are *fi* and *fl*.

Here are some examples without (top) and with (bottom) ligatures:

All five of the florists ordered the flounder.

All five of the florists ordered the flounder.

To create the *fi* ligature, press Shift Option 5. For the *fl* ligature, press Shift Option 6. (A handy way to remember the difference is that the word *five* starts with the letters *f-i*.) The easiest way to add ligatures is to use your word processor's Find and Replace feature (select Match Case or you'll wipe out the uppercase *F*s.)

A program that places ligatures automatically also keeps track of the fact that these characters actually represent two letters, which enables the program to hyphenate correctly if a word should break between the two letters. But when you use Find and Replace to insert ligatures, your program will no longer recognize them as representing two letters and will fail to hyphenate properly.

Old-style numbers. Another way to make your publications look professional is to use *old-style numbers*. Take a look at the numbers in a typical text font. Chances are they sit squarely on the baseline, the imaginary line on which the bottoms of letters fall. In addition, regular numbers are often monospaced and are generally the same height as capital letters. All of this makes them stick out like a sore thumb. If your document contains a lot of numbers, such as dates, it will look much nicer with old-style numbers, which are generally about the height of lowercase letters and proportionally spaced rather than monospaced. In addition, some of them dip below the baseline. In short, old-style numbers are designed to look like text rather than like numbers.

The Hoefler Text font that comes with your Mac OS 9's System software includes old-style numbers. (In Mac OS X, Big Caslon can give you a similar look). Here's a sample:

> In 1987, only 652 Americans were unaware of the existence of old-style numbers. In 2001, that number had risen to nearly 43 million.

Small caps. You use small caps for abbreviations such as A.M., P.M., B.C., and A.D. Like the old-style numbers just described, small caps are designed to blend in with the overall size of a typeface so they don't stand out in a block of text.

Some programs offer a small caps option in a Style menu or checklist; however, the characters this option produces aren't true small caps but shrunken regular caps. To get true small caps, use an expert set (see the "Expert Sets" section earlier in this chapter) or one of the new OpenType Pro faces. Both expert sets and OpenType Pro faces include special characters such as small caps and old-style numbers that make your type look professional.

Don't use fancy formatting in a document you intend to make into a Web page. Saving the document in Web-ready format will transform special characters such as ligatures, em dashes, and curly quotes into gibberish.

Friendly Characters

There are a handful of characters lurking in every font that you should know about and make a habit of using. Some of the keystrokes may seem weird, but typing them soon becomes second nature.

En dash. An en dash is half as wide as an em dash. Unlike the em dash, the en dash (–) is used as a connector. It commonly indicates spans of time, as in 1989–90. It also looks better as a fake minus sign than a hyphen does (although the real minus sign [−] appears only in the Symbol font, at the hyphen position on the keyboard). You'll find the en dash at Option -.

Fraction bar. Found at Shift Option 1, the fraction bar (∕) is used for building fractions. It's different from the virgule (/, popularly known as the slash) in that it has a different angle, sits on the baseline, and kerns automatically. This last feature means the little numerator and denominator numbers you set next to it will snuggle up against it for better spacing. You can set the numerator by reducing the number's point size and using a baseline shift to top-align it. For the denominator, simply reduce the number to the same point size as the numerator; it should sit on the baseline as other text characters do (**Figure 18.28**).

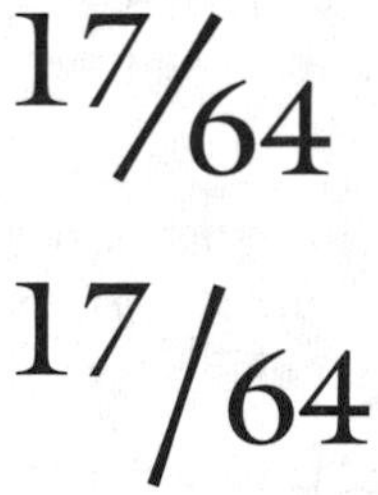

$$17\!/\!64$$

$$17/64$$

Figure 18.28

The special fraction bar character has been used in the upper sample to make a correct fraction. The lower sample was created using a virgule (or slash), which not only extends below the baseline but also produces bad spacing.

Ellipsis. This is the official name for the three dots used to indicate … um, a pause or omission (as often seen in movie review blurbs: "Fab … boffo … a laugh riot!"). You can also set these as three periods in a row, but they might wind up breaking at the end of a line. The one-character ellipsis (Option ;) will always stay in one piece.

The only problem with this character is that it spaces the dots much more tightly than in traditional typography. If you prefer a wider-setting ellipsis, you'll need the nonbreaking space. This invisible character comes in handy. A nonbreaking space (Option -spacebar) is just like a word space, but it's not a legal place for your program to break a line. Two or more characters joined by a nonbreaking space always travel as a unit. This would be useful for the three-dot ellipsis or for a four-dot ellipsis that includes a period ending a sentence. Here comes one now…

Enhancing Type

You have thousands upon thousands of Macintosh fonts from which to choose (see the "Where to Buy Fonts" section later in this chapter for a list of vendors). Even so, you might not find exactly the style or effect you're looking for. Don't despair. Because Mac fonts are essentially computer data, you can use a variety of programs to modify their shapes, angles, colors, and many other attributes.

If you have a PostScript graphics program such as Adobe Illustrator or Macromedia FreeHand, you can create any number of effects that modify a single character or a block of text. To a lesser extent, you can modify text in a page layout program—for instance, expanding or condensing it. You could stretch a headline vertically to make it tall and narrow or horizontally to make it wide.

TypeStyler (www.typestyler.com; $150). If you want to have fun with fonts, try Strider Software's TypeStyler. This type-manipulation program lets you bend, twist, shape, outline, fill, emboss, or blur text. You can add shadows, apply a metallic or wood-grain finish, fill a word with a pattern or other graphic, or apply a neon glow. Use the program's preset shapes and effects or tailor them to your own needs.

TypeStyler 3 allows you to add animated font effects to your Web page. These include bouncing or pulsing letters, glows, spins, zooms, and fades. You select an animation effect from the Web menu and edit it as you like, preview the effect onscreen, and then click a button to have TypeStyler generate the HTML and JavaScript code to paste into your Web page.

Headline Studio (www.fractal.com). Another program that can add special effects to the fonts on your Web page is Headline Studio, which was acquired in 2001 by Fractal from MetaCreations. Apply effects such as walk-ins, fades, and dissolves to a letter, a word, or a line of text. You can preview your effect (and even check out how it will look at different modem speeds) before telling Headline Studio to create a GIF animation. Fractal said it is not offering Headline Studio for sale but is providing technical support. Fractal must have sort of a plan for Headline Studio, however, because it bought the software, so check the company's Web site for news on the product.

How to Buy Fonts

If you're getting tired of the fonts that came with your Mac, you have your pick of thousands of fonts from dozens of vendors. How do you find out what's available? Well, a good place to start is the font vendors list in the "Where to Buy Fonts" section later in this chapter. Some of these companies offer printed catalogs of their font collections, usually for a fee. More and more, however, font companies are showing and selling their wares on the Web (Web addresses are listed for all font vendors, with the exception of a few holdouts who don't have Web sites). Most companies provide onscreen samples of their fonts; some have utilities that can print samples on your home printer.

If you have access to the Web, your best bet is to go to a vendor's site and see what it has to offer. Most sites let you click a button that sends an e-mail message to customer service if you have questions. Once you find a font or family you like, do some comparison shopping; some vendors have permission to sell other companies' fonts, and you might find a better deal if you shop around.

When you find the font you want, you can purchase it in one of several formats.

Floppy disk. In the early days of fonts, most fonts were packaged on floppy disks. Some still are. However, these newfangled Macs don't even have floppy-disk drives, so you might want to consider other options.

CD-ROM. Some font vendors offer their collections on CD-ROM. In some cases you can buy the entire collection outright, usually for hundreds of dollars. In other cases you buy a locked CD-ROM and receive a code to unlock the fonts you want when you pay for them with your credit card.

Online sales. The latest trend in font sales is to buy them online. You go to a font vendor's Web site, choose the font you need, enter your credit card information, and download the font to your hard drive. You can then install it just as you would any other font.

 To entice you to their Web sites, many font vendors let you download a free sample font. What are you waiting for?

Where to Buy Fonts

The following is a list of font vendors. Some are small, independent digital foundries with a dozen fonts to offer; others are huge resellers with more than 10,000 fonts for sale. You can visit most of them on the World Wide Web and take a look at online samples before you buy.

You'll also find online lists of font vendors at www.philsfonts.com/phils/sections/ linkfont.html, which takes you to a listing of font vendors and resources courtesy of Phil's Fonts. (Just a warning: The contact information in this section was accurate as we went to press, but Web addresses are changeable and may be different when you look for the companies.)

Active Images (www.comicbookfonts.com). You need not be a rocket scientist to figure out what kind of fonts these folks offer; the Web address should give you a clue. (Favorite font names: IncyWincySpider, Running with Scissors, Brontoburger.)

Adobe Systems (www.adobe.com/type). As the developer of PostScript, Adobe put Macintosh fonts on the map. Adobe offers text, display, decorative, script, symbols, original designs, revivals—you name it and this company probably has it (with the exception of wacky new designs; for that you need to go to some of the other foundries in this listing).

Agfa Monotype (www.monotype.com). These two type (and typesetting equipment) giants have teamed up and now offer around 7,000 well-crafted fonts from a variety of designers.

Richard Beatty Designs (704/696-8316). Mr. Beatty has created lovely digital versions of dozens of classic typefaces, including several by Frederic Goudy.

Berthold Types (www.bertholdtypes.com). Not one of your flash-in-the-pan, upstart foundries, Berthold has been in business for more than 140 years. (Favorite typeface name: Akzidenz-Grotesk—which is neither an accident nor grotesque, in case you were wondering, but comes from an old German term for sans serif type. It's the model on which Helvetica is based.)

Bitstream (www.bitstream.com). As its name implies, Bitstream is a modern type foundry (*bit* is computerese for *binary digit*); it has been in operation since the early 1980s. Bitstream provides not only digital fonts but font technology, including a utility that lets you display fonts in your Web pages with the formatting intact. (Favorite font name: Old Peculiar.)

Carter & Cone Type (800/952-2129). The Carter in Carter & Cone is none other than Matthew Carter, renowned type designer and founder of Bitstream. Faces include the gorgeous Mantinia, inspired by the letterforms of the Renaissance artist Mantegna, as well as Sophia, suggested by alphabets from sixth-century Constantinople. None of your grunge fonts here.

Castle Systems (www.castletype.comwww.bertholdtypes.com). This small foundry offers Art Deco revivals, traditional faces, pictorial fonts, decorative and display fonts, and specialty fonts such as a collection of 101 ampersands (& a sequel with 101 more ampersands). (Favorite font name: Tambor Adornado.)

Cool Fonts (www.cool-fonts.com). If you want a font that has "an edgy mutated feel," looks like "what's left when you fall asleep with a lit cigarette in your mouth," or is "cosmic '60s space cartoon retro," you've come to the right place. If you're looking for something a little more sedate, Cool Fonts does offer one it bills as "grunge with class." (Favorite font names: Jean Splice, Killer Ants, Goombah.)

Deniart Systems (www.deniart.com). Not your everyday faces, these: Deniart's fonts are inspired by Egyptian hieroglyphs, Mayan pictographs, inscriptions from ancient tablets found on Easter Island, and alchemy symbols, among other exotica. Also your one-stop shopping source for Tolkien elvish runes. (Favorite font names: RongoRongo, Hypnotica, Sublimina.)

DS Design (www.dsdesign.com/kidtype.htm). Here's a niche market: fonts based on kids' handwriting. But hey, if you have a niche, scratch it; these fonts are delightful because they were drawn by genuine, certified kids.

DsgnHaus (www.dsgnhaus.com). Would you like to buy a vowel? Then DsgnHaus is the place to go, with more than 10,000 fonts for sale from more than a dozen sources. (Favorite font names: Aaaaaaargh Caps, Acme Whatever, Ashtray Empty, Aunt Mildred—and that's only the *A*s.)

Emigre (www.emigre.com). In the 1980s, Emigre was among the font avant garde (not to be confused with the Avant Garde font—little typographic joke there). It has stayed alive and now offers modern faces from some two dozen designers. (Favorite font names: Arbitrary Sans, Big Cheese, Not Caslon.)

Exploding Font Company (explofont@aol.com). These guys have fonts called Gutter and Drunk. A refined bunch they ain't. However, they do offer some energetic and eye-arresting designs, from edgy to retro in style. (Favorite font names: Ammonia, Mantisboy, Space Toaster.)

Font Bureau (www.fontbureau.com). This small foundry originally furnished typefaces for newspapers and magazines. Now its fonts are available to you as well. Font Bureau consistently turns out fresh, clean, innovative designs. (Favorite font names: Garage Gothic, Fobia, Epitaph.)

Font Diner (www.fontdiner.com). What fun! Choose from a menu of retro fonts that are "cooler than the middle of a TV dinner brownie." If you're old enough to remember the 1950s and 1960s, you'll be overcome with nostalgia. Young whippersnappers should enjoy these amusing faces as well. (Favorite font names: Devilette, Spaghetti Western, American Cheese.)

Fonthead Design (www.fonthead.com). Fonthead offers six volumes of delightful decorative and display fonts to liven up your publications. (Favorite font names: Gritzpop, Holy Cow, Pesto.)

The Fontry (www.signweb.com/fontry). From the 70-year-old designs of Alf R. Becker to fonts inspired by the lettering on race cars, this foundry offers an eclectic collection of fun designs. (Favorite font names: After Disaster, Marbles & Strings.)

FontShop (www.fontfont.de). With more than 1400 fonts, FontShop International is one of the leading sources of contemporary text and display faces. Although font designers are often unknown and unappreciated, FontShop's Web site includes biographies of all its designers. (Favorite font names: Brokenscript, LetterGothicSlang, Fancy Writing.)

Galápagos Design Group (www.galapagosdesign.com). Although Galapagos Design Group formed in 1994, these designers are no newcomers. The senior staff has an average of 20 years of type design experience. (Favorite font names: ITC Backyard Beasties, Big Clyde.)

GarageFonts (www.garagefonts.com). GarageFonts emerged in 1993, primarily to distribute the experimental fonts used in *Raygun* magazine. Its faces continue to be on the cutting edge, thanks to a talented group of international designers. (Favorite font names: Achilles Blur, Acid Queen, Bitchin Camero, Bo-Legged Lou; Drunk Robot Pimp—to name a few.)

Hoefler Type Foundry (www.typography.com). An island in a sea of grunge, the Hoefler Type Foundry offers classical designs with attention to detail. For example, the complete Hoefler Text family (originally developed for Apple) offers 27 fonts, including swashes, ornaments, and other special characters.

International Typeface Corporation (ITC) (www.itcfonts.com/itc). In its 25 years, ITC has always appreciated the hard work that goes into type design, as evidenced by the fact that you can search for a font on its Web site by font name or designer. ITC's 1000-plus fonts are the products of more than 200 designers.

LetterPerfect (www.letterspace.com). LetterPerfect has been around since 1986, almost as long as the Mac. It offers around 50 original display and decorative faces with a distinctive flair.

Makambo.com (www.makambo.com). Makambo offers more than 1000 fonts from many contemporary designers. It has a refreshingly realistic view of type design. One of the font categories on its Web site is "Trendy: Type that's fashionable today, but may not be tomorrow." Yes, only time will tell if Buckethead, Boochie, or Electric Weasel will join the pantheon of great typefaces.

MindCandy Design (www.mindcandy.com). Seven type foundries and assorted designers have teamed up to bring us more than 150 fresh faces. This is the place to go if you want your publication to stand out from the crowd. (Favorite font names: Autumnull, Bureaucracy [Federal, Municipal, and State variants], Chupacabra, Sibley Potato.)

P22 Type Foundry (www.p22.com). You've probably asked yourself on occasion, "Now where can I get a font that's made up of actual scanned and rearranged insect parts?" You're in luck! P22 offers just such a font, Infestia. Hey, it's art. Or parts. Whatever. Here you can also find a font based on Leonardo da Vinci's handwriting—forward and backward, of course—and many other eclectic selections.

Phil's Fonts (www.philsfonts.com). Phil's Fonts offers not only a huge collection of fonts from more than 75 foundries but links to dozens of foundry Web sites and other online type resources as well as an online typography magazine.

Precision Type (www.precisiontype.com). Here you'll find more than 13,000 fonts from more than 70 foundries. Precision Type also offers a font-matching service: Fax the company a sample of a mystery font, and the company's experts will try to identify it. Precision Type also offers a good printed type catalog with plenty of samples ($40).

Psy/Ops Type Foundry (www.psyops.com). Hmmmm. Psychological operations? Is this the right Web site? It is. According to the welcome page, "type is a powerful behavior-modification tool." These guys are out there, "generally celebrating the obscure." (Favorite font names: Oxtail, Table Manners.)

Quadrat Communications (www.quadrat.com). This one-person design firm offers some intriguing faces, including a graceful sans serif face called Clear Prairie Dawn.

Scriptorium/Ragnarok Press (www.ragnarokpress.com/scriptorium). If you remember the 1960s (and who does?), you'll enjoy Earthpig, a font reminiscent of the psychedelic lettering on Fillmore concert posters. Another fun font is Doppelganger, which sports shadowy twins of each letter.

Shift (www.shiftype.com). Minimalist.

Stone Type Foundry (415/704-3253). Sumner Stone was once the director of typography at Adobe but followed his muse to his own design studio, where he has created some fine typeface families, including ITC Stone and Silica.

T-26 (www.t26font.com). Some of these fonts are short on legibility—they might be made up of dots or squares or minimalist lines—but all are long on inventiveness and attitude. (Favorite font names: Quagmire, Kennel District, Who's Frank, Bad Angel.)

Three Islands Press (www.typequarry.com). This small foundry offers some excellent handwriting fonts as well as a label-gun–style font. (Favorite font names: Treefrog, Speed Bump, Horsefeathers.)

Tiro Typeworks (www.tiro.com). Designed with the professional typographer in mind, Tiro offers some serious faces, such as Aeneas, inspired by modern interpretations of classical Roman capitals, and Plantagenet, celebrating the English vernacular style.

Treacyfaces/Headliners (www.treacyfaces.com). Joe Treacy's font collection comprises 400 carefully crafted fonts, some of which have 5000 kerning pairs. In these days of sometimes slapdash fonts, it's good to see someone taking the time to do it right.

TypeArt Foundry (www.typeart.com). Lively decorative, display, and specialty faces, and the best label-gun–style font ever. (Favorite font names: Amnesia, Bighead, Typochondriac, Deviant Plain.)

Vintage Type Font Foundry (www.vintagetype.com). Pining for your old Underwood typewriter? Pine no more; these folks offer lots of vintage typewriter fonts. Also some novelty and scruffy faces. (Favorite font names: Lucifer's Pension, Necrotic Fluid.)

Will-Harris House (www.will-harris.com). In addition to several of font maven Daniel Will-Harris's own designs, his Web site includes Esperfonto, a step-by-step guide to choosing the right typeface for a particular job as well as additional design and typography tips. The site also includes a link to Webfonts.com, where you can get the latest scoop on using fonts on the Web.

Building Your Typeface Library (EF)

People sometimes ask me which fonts are essential for a good typeface library. That's a tough one. For one thing, everybody's tastes are different. For another, it depends on how you'll be using the typefaces; a face that is fine for a book might not look good on the Web, for example. What I *can* do is show you some of my favorite faces for a variety of purposes. I hope you like them.

Text

When it comes to a text face for a book or magazine, I like Adobe Jenson, an Adobe Original by Robert Slimbach.

abcdefghijklmnopqrstuvwxyz
ABCDEFGHIJKLMNOPQRSTUVWXYZ
1234567890&

For a sans serif text face, I enjoy ITC Goudy Sans, created for Monotype by the redoubtable Fred Goudy in the early 1930s.

abcdefghijklmnopqrstuvwxyz
ABCDEFGHIJKLMNOPQRSTUVWXYZ
12334567890&

For a semiserif face, give me Hermann Zapf's Optima. (Optima is basically a sans serif face but has slightly flared strokes that give it character.)

abcdefghijklmnopqrstuvwxyz
ABCDEFGHIJKLMNOPQRSTUVWXYZ
1234567890&

Headline

For headings, you can't go wrong with that old standby, Gill Sans Bold, from Agfa Monotype. It was originally created for Monotype by Eric Gill in the late 1920s.

abcdefghijklmnopqrstuvwxyz
ABCDEFGHIJKLMNOPQRSTUVWXYZ
1234567890&

Script

Caflisch Script, by Robert Slimbach of Adobe, is attractive but not too ornate, making it quite readable.

abcdefghijklmnopqrstuvwxyz

ABCDEFGHIJKLMNOPQRSTUVWXYZ

1234567890&

Display

You see it everywhere. It won't make your document stand out from the crowd, but you can't deny that Lithos, by Carol Twombly of Adobe, is already a classic.

ABCDEFGHIJKLMNOPQRSTUVWXYZ
1234567890

Handwriting

David Siegel's Graphite (Adobe) is a strong, legible face based on hand-printed letters.

abcdefghijklmnopqrstuvwxyz

ABCDEFGHIJKLMNOPQRSTUVWXYZ

1234567890¢

Decorative

The mind boggles in this category, since there are so many faces to choose from. But I like ITC Anna, by Daniel Pelavin, which has a Deco flavor.

ABCDEFGHIJKLMNOPQRSTUVWXYZ
1234567890&

Those are just a few of my personal favorites. Once you begin exploring the 15,000 or more available digital fonts, you'll no doubt come up with your own list of favorites. Happy hunting!

19

Fun!

Bart G. Farkas (BF) *is the chapter editor and coauthor.*

Ruffin Bailey (RB), *Michael M. Eilers* (ME), *and Greg Kramer* (GK) *are the chapter coauthors.*

All work and no play makes Mac a dull box! We know you have your *serious* reasons for buying that Mac, but deep down there's part of you that wants to have some fun. Come on, admit it. Do you think all that computing power is there for you to write e-mails to Grandma?

You don't have to be a hard-core gaming enthusiast to hunger for a little diversion. Whether you want to play a quick game of solitaire to pass the time or a frenetic all-night session of multiplayer Unreal Tournament, there's something for everyone with a Mac and an appetite for fun.

We're here to help you get started having fun with your Mac or, if you've already dipped your toes, to show you how to get the most out of your machine. You'll find in this chapter an overview of the Mac entertainment universe, descriptions of the best titles in all categories of game and hobby software, and helpful primers about specialized hardware you can use to play the biggest and newest games. So loosen up and have some fun with us.

In This Chapter

About Mac Gaming

Contrary to what you may have heard, the Mac is indeed a toy. A wonderful, powerful toy. Sure it's as good as (read: *better than*) those dull, user-hostile PCs for serious work, but the Mac has its wild side. Just look at it: the glorious colors of the iMac, the elegant design of the Power Mac G4, the classic beauty of the older Macs, the smiling face that greets you every time you start up. "Play with me," it says.

Why wouldn't you want to play with your Mac? Computer gaming in general has never been more vibrant and exciting than it is today. Gaming is the fastest-growing entertainment industry in the world. And whether you know it or not, your Mac is ready and willing to be a part of it.

Mac Gaming, Y2K and Beyond

There has never been a better time to play games with your Mac. If you haven't been paying attention for the last few years, you might have thought that Mac gaming was hurting; it was. So minor an area was it that regular readers of this book may have noticed that the 7th edition relegated this topic to a tiny section.

In the last couple of years, however, things have changed, thanks mostly to Apple itself. The Mac's manufacturer has publicly committed to gaming, winning the confidence of many in the PC-dominated gaming industry, including Quake creator and legendary Mac-basher John Carmack—his company, Id Software; released Quake III Arena for the Mac within a month of the PC version. As proof of Apple's pledge, all new desktop Macs come with built-in high-end video acceleration; even PowerBooks and iMacs contain hardware capable of playing most new games. No PC maker can boast as much.

Still, you may have heard a nasty rumor of the PC's superiority as a game platform; it's mostly not true … mostly. Now that the hardware gap is closing, much of this argument is flaking away like so much old, blistered paint. Still, not all games released for the PC are ever ported to, or rewritten for, the Mac, and precious few are actually developed for it. Most games are still released to the Mac after a delay, sometimes a substantial one. The good news is that this market reality acts as a filter for the preponderance of truly awful games and pointless rip-offs of successful titles. For the most part, Mac gamers do get the best games—and nowadays, the Mac gets them faster.

Can you play games on your Mac? Oh yes! For all but the most hard-core game hobbyist, the Mac is a great choice for those who want to have fun at their computers. And in many important ways (ease of use, for example) the Mac is superior to the PC.

Most important, for those of us who demand the quality and elegance of the Mac to do the important work of our lives, there's no need to deny our thirst for old-fashioned, frivolous fun.

How to Buy Games (GK)

Time was that the only way to buy games for your Mac was through one of the handful of catalog companies. Not anymore.

With the Mac's resurgence has come more availability at retail stores. CompUSA's Mac store-within-a-store has a solid selection of the most popular Mac games. The national chain Best Buy has a small slate of Macintosh entertainment software. Don't overlook your local software stores or Mac specialty stores or local Apple store.

Your best source, though, is arguably the Internet. The emergence of Internet commerce has liberated retailers from the traditional rationalization for not carrying Mac software: limited shelf space. With no shelves, there's no limit to how much Mac software an Internet site can stock.

There's more to Mac gaming, however, than commercial titles you can buy at the store. The Mac gaming community has always been fertile ground for a vibrant shareware and freeware market. Top-caliber games of all genres can be found all over the Internet from developers small and (relatively) large, and for prices far below those of commercial games. We highlight several of the best titles and shareware companies in this chapter.

Shareware Sources (GK)

Shareware can be found all over the Internet. You can look to the Web sites of the larger shareware companies (such as Ambrosia, www.ambrosiasw.com; Monkey Byte, www.monkeybyte.com; and Freeverse, www.freeverse.com) or any of the Mac-game news sites we discuss later.

The easiest sources, however, are the Mac software–download clearinghouses. Search any of these sites for direct links to the games you desire. The best-known sites are VersionTracker.com (www.versiontracker.com), CNET's Download.com (http://download.cnet.com) and ZDNet's Macdownload.com (www.macdownload.com).

News About Mac Gaming (GK)

Several print magazines that cover the general Mac market provide news and reviews of Mac games—these include *Macworld, Mac Home Journal,* and *MacAddict.*

For more complete coverage and fresher news, however, you must look to the Internet. The paucity of Mac coverage in mainstream gaming magazines has spawned scores of online publications that cover nothing but gaming on the world's best computer platform. The best-known and most established are Inside Mac Games (www.insidemacgames.com), MacGamer.com (www.macgamer.com), and MacCentral's MacGaming.com (www.macgaming.com).

All three sites offer links to other sites, downloads, feature articles, interviews, and previews of upcoming titles. Inside Mac Games offers subscriptions to its voluminous CD-ROM version.

This shortlist doesn't begin to scratch the surface of what's out there. Several newer and more specialized sites exist for almost every taste. It doesn't take long to find what you want on the Internet.

Gaming on Pre-PowerPC Macs (GK)

The sad truth is that owners of older Macs, those manufactured before 1995 and based on the older 680X0 processors, will not be able to play most of the games discussed in this chapter.

We'd love to have the space to cover the entire universe of Mac gaming, but out of necessity we are focusing on only the most current games. This usually means games that won't run on anything slower than a PowerPC. Some games may even be limited to PowerPC G3 and G4 Macs, and others all but require 3D acceleration.

For a complete list of games playable on 680X0 Macs, check out the Mac 68K Games Web site at www.Mac68kGames.com. The site stopped being updated as of February 1, 2000, but its information is still up and accurate. For information on networkable games for older Macs, check out Networkable Mac Games at www.macgamer.com/netgames/netgames/index.html.

Online Commercial Game Sources (GK)

There are far too many online sources for Macintosh games to list here. Some of the best, however, deserve mention. Outpost.com (www.outpost.com) features free overnight shipping on all items. Good prices and bundles can be found at MacMall (www.macmall.com), Club Mac (www.clubmac.com) and MacWarehouse (www.macwarehouse.com). CompUSA's online incarnation (www.compusa.com) carries the most popular Mac game titles.

Finally, don't forget the big Internet general stores such as Amazon.com (www.amazon.com) and Buy.com (www.buy.com).

Game Titles

Whether you're looking for a little mental stimulation via a nice game of chess or want to get your pulse racing with an action game, chances are Mac game makers have what you're looking for. Here's an overview of what's available.

Action Games (GK/ME)

More than any other genre in Mac gaming, action games show how far the Mac has come as a gaming platform. The action category has been nothing less than action packed, with a slate of superlative games. Prepare yourself for sleepless nights, numb arms, crossed eyes, and hazardously raised adrenaline levels as soon as one of these games enters your life.

First-person shooters. One of the most popular genres of action gaming is the *first-person shooter*. These real-time three-dimensional (3D) games live by the motto "Kill or be killed," and they offer amazing amounts of eye candy as well as gripping combat fraught with gore and mayhem. They will also test every possible limit of your system, from the speed of your graphics card to the depths of your Mac's memory. You will need a 300 MHz PowerPC G3 or faster processor and a graphics card with a minimum of 6 MB of VRAM to enjoy most shooters.

Like a couple of heavyweight prizefighters, one old and experienced, the other young and brash, the Unreal and Quake franchises are slugging it out for dominance in the action-game market. Their fight spilled over into the Mac world when both of these A-list games were released for the Mac weeks after their PC debuts.

Since 1997, all installments (each a classic in its own right) of both games have become available for the Macintosh. Players looking for the older titles or playing with pre-G3 Power Macs can get a taste of the action with **Quake** ($19.99; MacSoft, www.wizworks.com/macsoft/), **Unreal** ($19.99; MacSoft), and **Quake II** ($19.99; Activision, www.activision.com). Each game is best enjoyed with, but does not require, 3D acceleration.

The latest installments of both games seek to create the ultimate multiplayer experience, focusing more on online play than on player-versus-computer action. **Unreal Tournament** ($39.99; MacSoft) boasts superb online play in a variety of free-for-all and team games. Its maps are, well, unreal, and its weapons subtle and powerful. Though Unreal Tournament doesn't include a solo game in the traditional sense, it does allow you to play through a lengthy and increasingly difficult "career" of deathmatches against "bots" (computer-controlled opponents). These artificially intelligent opponents are the crown jewel of Unreal Tournament: No game can come up to their complexity and subtlety. Although no computer player can match the unpredictability and ingenuity of a human player, these bots come darned close and can even automatically adjust to your skill level.

Quake III Arena ($39.99; Activision); not to be outdone, takes its familiar formula and adds to it a large cocktail of stimulants and hallucinogens. The gameplay is faster and gorier than ever, and the new graphics engine constructs the most stunning arenas you've ever seen. Solo play entails deathmatching against challenging computer-controlled bots, and multiplay pits you against human opponents in standard deathmatch and (to a lesser extent) capture-the-flag contests. Quake's bots aren't as clever as Unreal's, but the game's online play is more than a match for that of its outstanding competition.

Not all first-person shooters involve bullet-riddled bloodshed. **Descent 3** ($19.95; www.graphsim.com) is a zero-g shooter, in which you pilot a tiny spacecraft loaded to the gills with powerful weaponry through 3D mazes, stalked by fiendish robot opponents. Featuring a full range of motion—you can fly in any direction, at any angle—this game has complex controls and gut-wrenching visuals as well as a fascinating plot. Although it takes some time to master flying your craft, the experience of hurtling through surreal underground passages while being pursued by intelligent killer robots is not to be missed. This game also features online play, with the same caveats as the previous games. You must have 3D hardware acceleration to play, and a robust processor is recommended.

The Marathon series from Bungie Studios is a trio of classic shooters that for quite some time defined the entire genre for Mac users. Available as part of the **Bungie Mac Action Sack** ($19.95; www.bungie.com), Marathon, Marathon 2, and Marathon Infinity compose the holy trinity of Mac shooters, with slick gameplay, excellent (for the time) visuals, and a totally engrossing plot. Tests of mental mettle as well as your trigger finger, these puzzle-filled titles will take you across the universe and into the depths of space in an attempt to protect the helpless Earth against an invasion of insectlike aliens. This series has the added advantage of being able to run on quite modest hardware, back to the very first PowerPC-based machines. Also included in the Sack are Pathways into Darkness, Minotaur: The Labyrinths of Crete, and Abuse.

Thinking action. First-person shooters are not the only titles the action genre has to offer—many great games emphasize speed and reaction time and don't focus on putting an enemy in the crosshairs.

If you are the sort who would rather have more puzzles and less of a body count, then all four installments of the **Tomb Raider** series ($14.95 to $39.95; Aspyr Media, www.aspyr.com) are what you are looking for. Following the Indiana Jones–esque exploits of heroine and protagonist Lara Croft, you travel through caverns, over ruins, and inside pyramids. Viewed from a third-person perspective, Lara can run, jump, climb, push, and pull as she makes her way through a complex maze of obstacles and puzzles. There is indeed some bloodshed—alarmingly, Lara seems to specialize in killing endangered species such as bears, tigers, and wolves—but there are also extensive travels over complex landscapes and gorgeous cities. Each title is longer, more detailed, and more spectacular than the last, and all will run on a 266 MHz G3 or faster.

Ambrosia Software's **Ferazel's Wand** ($30, www.ambrosiasoftware.com) is a brilliantly realized combination of reaction-time-testing death traps and complex puzzles. With crisp hand-animated graphics and great sound, this side-scrolling 2D adventure follows the exploits of the last of the Habnabbits on a lonely quest to defeat the evil creatures that have invaded their underground home. This full-length adventure will keep you engrossed for a long, long time.

High-speed action. If you would rather have speed than puzzles, **Star Wars: Episode I Racer** ($19.95; LucasArts, www.lucasarts.com) is a thrill ride and a half. Set in the Star Wars universe but within the limits of a classic racing game, this gorgeous 3D-accelerated title looks great on almost any G3-equipped Power Mac, thanks to clever programming. You'll want a joystick for this one, definitely—and a good set of stereo speakers so you can enjoy the sound effects and music. As you howl through canyons, over desert plains, and inside undersea tunnels, the illusion of speed is fantastic. It's a white-knuckle experience every time.

If you want a fast-paced game with a classic arcade feel, Logicware's **Jazz Jackrabbit 2** ($29.95; www.logicware.com) is the title for you. With gameplay that features a little Sonic the Hedgehog, a little Super Mario, and a whole lot of speed, this attractive, spunky game is addictive. Choose a long solo game or play head to head against another player on the same machine in split-screen races or competitions. And of course, you can play Jazz on the Internet in chaotic deathmatch-style mayhem or one-on-one races against the clock. This game runs well on modest hardware and is an excellent bargain-bin find.

Those big spinning rocks are back in MacSoft's update of the arcade classic **Asteroids** ($29.99), but this ain't no chintzy bleep-bleep early-1980s arcade game. This new incarnation has all the inexplicably addictive and sweat-gland–stimulating action of the original, complete with optional 3D acceleration and a host of new gameplay enhancements.

Fighting. Macintosh fighting games are a rare breed indeed. Although few one-on-one fighters are available, **Oni** ($39.95; published by Gathering of Developers (www.godgames.com/main.php) and developed by Bungie, should satisfy even the most intense combat jones. Like traditional fighters, Oni allows you to engage in blistering hand-to-hand combat with dozens of basic and special moves—including my favorite, the neck-snapping Running Lariat. But wait, there's more: In classic John Woo fashion, your heroine,

Konoko, can whip out any of ten potent weapons to perforate the game's two dozen-plus enemy types. Finally, all of this action is wrapped around a compelling (if not groundbreaking) 14-level storyline. Oni is loads of fun but practically pleads for a multiplayer mode. One hopes that online play will be added in the future.

Action/strategy. Blizzard's **Starcraft** ($9.95; www.blizzard.com) and **Starcraft: Brood War** ($19.95) not only are two of the best-selling games of all time but are among the best strategy games ever made. The Starcraft games are the perfect blend of action, strategy, resource management, cool cinematics, and tactical challenges. The storyline is fantastically engrossing and pulls you deeper into the game with every mission. The cinematics are award winning, and in fact you can purchase a DVD of the Starcraft cinematics from Blizzard ($14.95). It has some 50-odd single-player missions to play through, and there's an endless world of challenges in the multiplayer games, either head to head or against many opponents over Battle.net.

Sports Games (RB)

The year 2001 was a high-water mark for Mac sports gamers. EA Sports, arguably the most recognized name in sports video games and simulations, has found its way back to our operating system of choice. But EA's Madden isn't the only game Mac sports fanatics have to enjoy.

Football. **Madden 2000** ($19.95; Aspyr Media) for the Mac is a great game, hands down. If you love the crunching of the gridiron and the battles in the trenches, playing Madden 2000 on your Mac will make you feel like you've died and gone to heaven. Each NFL team is represented, and every player on every team is modeled according to height, weight, and ability—making this the most realistic NFL simulation on the market for any system. You can even play online against your friends, though for best results you'll need a DSL or cable high-speed connection. If you want to join an online league, check out www.thepfl.com, and you'll find the information you need.

EA Sports didn't skimp on the Macintosh version of Madden 2000; this one's a winner. Nor should you be worried about playing a game that's a year or two old. You can download current rosters at www.maddenmania.com.

Golf. Our second headliner is **Links LS** ($54.95; www.microsoft.com), brought to the Mac by the company Mac users love to hate, Microsoft. This time, though, it's done Mac users a huge favor. Links LS is an impressive game, including 3 beautiful courses for play (Latrobe Country Club, Kapalua Plantation, and Kapalua Village) with more than 25 more courses available. Links LS makes even a duffer feel like a pro. Check out the trial version at www.microsoft.com/games/linksmac/default.htm, and get ready for Links 2002, which Microsoft announced for the Mac.

Another option for Mac golfers is **Jack Nicklaus 4** ($9.99), from MacSoft. Every bit as beautiful to play as Links LS, it also includes a course designer to help you create the perfect challenge. You can find information about this game at www.wizworks.com/macsoft/jack04/jack_01.html.

Soccer and team management. Soccer and baseball are not as well represented on the Mac as they could be, which just means you have to look a little harder to get your fix. **ActuaSoccer,** by Gremlin, is a great old game that you can still find through some Mac-game specialists such as Mac-o-Rama (www.mac-o-rama.com), but it won't run on Mac OS 8 and later.

If you don't mind simply managing rather than directly controlling your cyberteams, Feral's **Championship Manager 00/01** is the game for you (http://feral.co.uk/english/cm0001/). It has every team from 16 world leagues, and its scope is second to none.

If controlling the action is your thing and you don't mind sacrificing some realism, take at least two looks at Humongous Entertainment's **Backyard** series (www.humongoussports.com). There are Backyard games for soccer ($9.99, $19.99) and baseball ($9.99, $19.99), and even football ($19.99), though there you're better off with Madden. The Backyard series might aim at a younger crowd, but as any Nintendo Entertainment System vet can tell you, it doesn't take a Major League Baseball license to make a great game. Humongous makes sure that what's missing in realism is made up for in gameplay. Switch the difficulty level to "hard" from the start, and play ball.

The great outdoors. For the outdoors enthusiast, MacSoft offers two hunting games, **Deer Hunter** ($14.99; www.wizworks.com/macsoft/ deerhunt/deerhunt.htm) and **Rocky Mountain Trophy Hunter** ($9.99; www.wizworks.com/macsoft/rmth/rmth.html). Both of these are relatively inexpensive games that simulate hunting many species of game with several weapons. For the angler, Sierra's **MacPak** ($9.99; www.gamedb.com/ssps/ 0/1/00008) includes **Trophy Bass,** one of the most intricately detailed fishing sims around.

If strategy is your thing, take a look at **Strat-O-Matic** (www.strat-o-matic.com). The company doesn't offer games controlled by a joystick, but it does offer extremely in-depth simulations of baseball and basketball that allow you to manage and coach major-league teams.

Shareware sports. There are also many shareware sports games for the Mac, including fringe sports such as bowling, pool, cricket, and even curling. The best place to get the skinny on all these downloadable games is Mac Game Database at www.gamedb.com. Check out its sports section, and you'll be sure to keep your modem busy for quite some time to come.

Emulation

As a final option, you can always cheat and use Connectix's **Virtual Game Station** (www.connectix.com/products/cvgs.html) to play tried-and-true PlayStation sports games on your Mac. Although Connectix stopped shipping the emulator in June 2001, Virtual Game Station is still a great option for those who have it, and it will let you walk down to the corner store and do the seemingly impossible: rent a game for your Mac. Games in specialized niches such as NCAA football and major professional sports such as Major League Baseball are just waiting to be played on a G3 or better Mac. Just two quick warnings: (1) Make absolutely sure your Mac meets Virtual Game Station's system requirements, and (2) check that the game you rent or purchase is on Connectix's recommended-games list. If you follow that advice, you'll be surprised just how much game you can get out of your Mac!

Role-Playing Games (BF)

Role-playing games (RPGs) were born as pen-and-paper contests with complicated record keeping and expensive dice and game sets. But now, even the most modest Mac can handle the statistics and mapping that made these games somewhat of a chore to play, leaving you free to simply enjoy the pleasure of adventuring with a surrogate personality, in search of treasure and conquest.

This diverse genre offers games ranging from traditional RPG simulations to real-time hack-and-slash games, with some hybrids. The Mac platform, in particular, has a bevy of shareware RPGs with amazing quality and complexity—and some of them even allow you to create your own adventures. In any case, RPG gaming is well suited (with one obvious exception—Diablo II) to those with less powerful systems and those who prefer games that involve lots of thought and little dependence upon raw reaction time.

Let's start off with a selection of shareware games, many of them for the Mac only.

Spiderweb Software has many such games to offer, all of them with engrossing storylines and excellent interfaces. The three-part **Exile** series ($45; www.spiderwebsoftware.com) and the fourth installment, Blades of Exile ($30), is a set of deceptively simple two-dimensional (2D) RPG games in the Ultima style. These games make up for a lack of flash with deep plots and long, branching quests. Prepare to take notes and sketch maps, as these games are a time commitment!

Avernum ($25) and **Avernum 2** ($25) are other excellent Spiderweb offerings. Avernum is a remake of the original Exile; it features a new graphics engine, new quests, and a simplified interface. It will still run on the humblest iMac and offers all the great writing and detail we expect from Jeff Vogel's creations.

Nethergate ($30) is a thrilling adventure from Spiderweb in which you can play Romans fending off barbarian hordes or Celts seeking to rid their land of Roman invaders. The intricate plot and detailed graphics complement this title well, but its difficulty may discourage some players.

Cythera ($25; Ambrosia Software) is another great shareware RPG. Featuring the flexible Delver engine, this good-looking, polished title has a unique interface and lots of classic RPG gaming. With an emphasis on puzzles over straight combat, this simulated 3D (overhead view) RPG is an instant classic.

Realmz ($20; Fantasoft, www.fantasoft.com) is a few years' worth of adventuring in itself. This RPG includes tools to help you make your own adventures, and dozens of quests and entire scenarios are available for download. Although Realmz's artwork and interface look a bit dated, the humble charm of this RPG is complemented by many maps, weapons, spells, and monsters. Additional Realmz scenarios are available at $13 each from the Fantasoft Web site.

Jewel of Arabia (shareware; Quarter Note Software, www.qnote.com), is a highly original shareware offering set in the ancient Middle Eastern world of the Djinn, surrounded by all the myths and legends of the desert. With crisp graphics and a complex plot, this is a game for people who are tired of dungeons and have always wanted their own genie in a bottle.

Baldur's Gate ($24.95; BioWare, www.bioware.com; Mac port by Graphic Simulations) is the first serious commercial RPG to hit the Mac platform in a long time, and it was a long time coming. This gorgeous, complex RPG adheres to strict Advanced Dungeons and Dragons rules and features a long, involved solo story as well as multiplayer support. With a fantastic array of spells, weapons, and foes, this one is a must-have for any RPG fan. The simulated 3D viewpoint and diverse environments make this game a pleasure to behold.

Diablo II ($39.95; www.blizzard.com) is the follow-up to Blizzard Entertainment's fabulously popular Diablo, and like its predecessor, it was ported to the Mac with full functionality; you can play on Battle.net against anyone in the world. Diablo II has 5 character classes, each with 30 distinct skills. Considering that you can only choose one character class, and you'll only get about 25 skill points to put into developing your 30 skills, there's literally an unlimited replay factor in this game. If you liked Diablo, and you like a game that's perfectly balanced in terms of play (the game is great no matter which character class you take), Diablo II is perhaps *the* game of the decade. Diablo II: Lord of Destruction ($34.95; requires original Diablo II game) adds a new act to the Diablo II universe, as well as thousands of new items, enemies, and gameplay wrinkles that will keep Diablo aficionados playing for years to come.

The original **Diablo** ($19.95) seems a bit long in the tooth these days, but it has the benefit of being able to run on almost any modern Mac at full speed. With much more emphasis on hack and slash than cogitation, this real-time RPG will test your reflexes and quick thinking rather than your mapmaking skills. For those who don't need a deep plot, though, Diablo is a thrill. Online play extends the life of this title considerably, but some participants in the online version of the game unfortunately tend to cheat, lessening the value of others' achievements.

Heroes of Might and Magic III, from 3DO ($29.95; www.3do.com), is a hybrid title: part RPG, part turn-based strategy game. Playable as a series of quests or single-map skirmishes, this engrossing game covers all the bases with quests, magic, weapons, armor, and of course lots of combat. With nifty visuals and great sounds, this game should appeal to RPG fans as well as to those who love strategy. This title supports online play, although games tend to take a long time to finish, even with few allies or opponents.

Puzzle, Board, and Card Games (ME)

Although action games and shooters may be the flagship titles of the gaming industry, the actual sales numbers lie elsewhere—not everyone derives pleasure from drawing virtual blood or racing a car around a track at ungodly speed. For those who prefer a more sedate, intellectual type of gaming, many titles feature brain-teasing challenges or games of luck. From simple solitaire to digital versions of your favorite game show, this is one genre that is exploding with titles.

Conquest. Risk II, by MacSoft ($29.99), is a visually stunning remake of the classic Hasbro board game of strategic combat. Although inspired by the classic, Risk II takes the exquisitely balanced battle for the conquest of the world way beyond the board to a gorgeous, complex, and engrossing game. You can play the classic rule set against the computer, play with friends and family as the game officiates, or even play online. You can also explore some of the new game modes such as tournament play and Same Time mode, in which all moves occur simultaneously, so that wisely anticipating your opponent's attacks is a vital skill. The game itself is attractive, with colorful graphics and animation, movies, and detailed stats screens. The online play isn't perfect— if a player quits before the end, the game stops prematurely—but for fans of the Risk board game this is the ultimate version. And best of all, there are no cards or pieces to lose.

Board strategy. Part Reversi, part Chinese checkers, part Tetris, **The Alchemist** is an intriguing, gorgeous game from the Russian developer Computer Systems Odessa ($19.99; www.cs-odessa.com.ua). Rival alchemists battle for control of a playing field, using combinations of color-coded flasks that change color in "reactions." The goal is to match a pattern on the playing field while being handed random pieces and shapes; the pseudo-3D grids are increasingly challenging. Great eye candy and good background music give this game a relaxed, meditative feel.

Classic board games. No gamer's collection would be complete without a version of **Monopoly** ($29.99), and luckily the Hasbro game's digital incarnation by MacSoft is even better than the classic family favorite's original form. It doesn't have any tiny game pieces or paper money to lose, and it offers a customizable game board and Internet play—so anyone who thought Monopoly was all played out is surely mistaken. The game includes ten game boards based on major U.S. cities, support for six players, 3D animated player tokens and board elements, and various rule sets. If you have no one to play against, add a computer opponent or two. You can also play the classic rule set or a simpler "quick game" mode for an instant challenge.

For those who want to show off their vocabulary rather than their real-estate acumen, the computer version of the Hasbro classic **Scrabble** ($29.99; MacSoft) is your game. While its primary attraction might be the built-in dictionary to verify scoring words, it also offers 3D-style graphics, Classic and Tournament modes of play, six levels of skill, and support for four players (computer or human). You also get Internet play, hint guides, and a customizable soundtrack. Scrabble with no tiles to lose is a parent's dream come true.

Chess. The game **Chessmaster 6000** ($39.95; Mindsoft, http://shop.store. yahoo.com/chessexpress/ches60formac.html) can be a patient tutor or a merciless opponent who will wipe you off the board. This game has all the elements that serious students of chess will desire, from replays of classic matches to a huge library of opening moves. With the assistance of an interactive "coach" that assesses your moves, you'll be a champion in no time—at least in your own home. The game's various 2D and 3D boards, along with voice and visual hints, will appeal to those just learning the game as well.

Card games. Solitaire and other card games are extremely popular with computer gamers, and there are far too many titles to list here. Freeverse Software (www.freeverse.com) alone offers eight card games for download and play. Its 3D series, which features online play, computer opponents, and humorous graphics and sound, includes games such as **3D Bridge Deluxe, 3D Euchre Deluxe, 3D Hearts Deluxe, 3D Spades Deluxe,** and **3D Setback aka Pitch** ($19.95 per game). Each game is presented with its classical rule set as well as several variations, and each has a tutorial mode to teach you how to play the game effectively against the computer or real-world opponents. For those who prefer solitaire, Freeverse offers **Burning Monkey Solitaire 2** ($14.95), a decidedly nontraditional approach to the traditional time-waster, with great graphics and sound. Also available are **Classic Cribbage** ($19.95) and **Classic Gin Rummy** ($14.95), for those who want an old-fashioned game without chatty opponents. You can download these games from the Freeverse Web site, or you can get them all on CD-ROM and only register the ones you want to keep.

If you would rather have all of your card games in one place, **Hoyle Card Games** ($29.95; Sierra Attractions, www.sierraattractions.com) is a huge collection of card-game favorites including poker, solitaire, gin rummy, go fish, memory match, bridge, cribbage, hearts, spades, euchre, old maid, pinochle, crazy eights, war, canasta, and pitch. Although the graphics aren't flashy, they are certainly functional, and the games come with classic and alternate rule sets, hints, and tips.

An ancient game of strategy and luck, **Mah Jong Parlour** ($9.95; Aspyr Media) is both a solo strategy and a complex multiplayer game. Although the rules are easy to learn, they are quite tough to master and will challenge even seasoned players. You can play solo or over the Internet with as many as four players, at varying levels of difficulty. Attractive graphics and low system requirements make this one a must for those looking for an Eastern approach to gaming.

Hoyle Word Games ($29.95; Sierra Attractions) is a collection of brain teasers that offers codes to break, anagrams to unscramble, and new versions of classics such as hangman, crosswords, and word-yahtzee to try. With a built-in dictionary and a well-documented manual, this compendium of games not only delivers classic and variant versions of each puzzle but also provides insight into the history and origin of each. Solo or against an opponent, you can increase your word power while having fun.

Puzzle games. For a radical departure from sedate, wait-your-turn puzzle games, try **Burning Monkey Puzzle Lab** ($19.95; Freeverse Software). Its colorful graphics, fantastic sound, and head-to-head action will keep you glued to the computer for hours. Inspired by classics such as Tetris and Columns, this game features four modes of play, computer opponents to challenge, customizable rule sets, and fantastic hand-illustrated graphics. Once you have tested your skills against the likes of Jones the Mouse, take your chops online and challenge players on the HMS Freeverse online server. Relax with the meditative Zen mode at the end of the day, or try out your own custom rule sets in the Lab.

A collection of computer puzzle games wouldn't be complete without an actual puzzle game, and this one's a doozy. **Puzz3D: The Orient Express** ($19.95; Wrebbit, www.wrebbit.com) isn't just a computer form of a flat puzzle, it is a 3D puzzle constructed from specially designed pieces. An exact copy of a real-world puzzle, this game also has a storyline and characters (played by real actors) that tell the story of the fabled Orient Express, a train that ran from Paris to Istanbul.

The game contains minipuzzles to be solved that unlock each "car" of the train puzzle. Wrebbit also offers a **Bavarian Castle** ($19.95), a **Victorian Mansion** ($19.95), and a replica of **Notre Dame Cathedral** ($19.95) to solve as well. No pieces to lose, multiple views and angles, and varying levels of difficulty make these titles a puzzle lover's dream.

For those who like a little Star Wars with their games, **Pit Droids** ($19.95; Lucas Learning, www.lucaslearning.com) is an attractive collection of puzzles that will challenge players young and old. Using a variety of switches, gates, signs, and tools, you guide the pit droids from one point to another while avoiding all manner of crazy obstacles. When you get tired of the random puzzles, you can construct your own with the built-in editor and share them with others online. Fans of *Star Wars: Episode I* will find all the classic sights, sounds, and characters from this Lucas film.

Television. Why not start off with the most famous trivia game in the world: **Who Wants to Be a Millionaire,** second edition ($19.99; Disney Interactive, http://disney.go.com/DisneyInteractive/). Although often dismissed by trivia buffs, this game show has certainly earned its reputation as the foremost trivia challenge with the biggest cash prize. Hosted by a digitized version of the well-dressed Regis Philbin, the game offers 600 questions not featured on the show and all the tools: polling the audience, phoning a friend, and the 50-50 lifeline. With all the show's tension and atmosphere, this one makes a great party game.

Although the jackpots of Alex Trebek's trivia challenge **Jeopardy** ($29.99; MacSoft) are considerably smaller, purists find the questions much more challenging and the banter much less annoying. With all the classic elements of the game show (including Alex's voice and chatter), video daily doubles, and a wide variety of opponents, this one is sure to make you study the encyclopedia just for fun. You can play Classic, Solo, or Tournament mode and have the point of view of actually being on the set, facing off against Alex and the judges. With 3,500 answers to choose from in hundreds of categories, this one will challenge you for seasons to come.

If you prefer a more irreverent approach to trivia gaming, the monster **You Don't Know Jack Jumbo** ($39.99; Sierra Attractions) is the ultimate collection of quiz party games. Although you can play solo, this game really shines as a party game with friends (or complete strangers, over the Internet). With topics from sports, television, movies, literature, history, and more, this huge collection will shower you with wacky questions and endless verbal abuse from the nutty announcer. The game offers unusual modes of play and tons of challenges that may make it the best reason yet to move the computer into the living room.

Online and Network Gaming (ME)

Most games allow you to battle artificial-intelligence opponents of one sort or another, but let's face it—there just isn't as much fun to be found humiliating faceless automatons as there is in howling triumphantly as you blow your coworkers out of their virtual boots. Nothing provides the visceral thrill of gaming quite like testing your skills against a human opponent, regardless of the rules or setting. Luckily, nothing networks as easily as a Macintosh system, and you have many options to choose from.

Easily hundreds of games support network play, from card and chess games to high-tech shooters with buckets of blood. Rather than discuss the games themselves, we'll cover methods and types of network gaming.

Server-client issues. With the majority of online games, one computer—whether it is far away over the Internet or in the same room—must act as the server that coordinates and connects the game players. This is known as *hosting* a game. Usually a person can play on the server computer as well as use it as a host, so you only need two computers to play a two-player game. However, with CPU-intensive games such as first-person shooters or real-time strategy games, the time that the host computer uses to play the game cuts into the time that the computer has to coordinate and serve the game. The result can be choppy network performance and a poor experience for all involved. In this case you want to set up a *dedicated* server—a machine that hosts the game but is not used by any of the players—and if you can spare the hardware (and the game supports it), this is always the better option.

Also, many games are peer-to-peer, which means that no server is required. These tend to be slower-paced games, such as card, board, and trivia games.

Can my Mac be a server? Your Mac's ability to host or serve games depends on your hardware and bandwidth as well as the game involved. For simple chess or card games, almost any CPU or network connection will do; for intense action games, you want the fastest machine and the biggest network bandwidth you can get. Typical host systems (local or Internet) have lots of RAM, an Ethernet connection of 10Base-T or greater, and (for an Internet server) 256 Kbps DSL or greater, with a T1 or T3 being ideal. Few action games allow reliable hosting over a modem connection. Also, the server must not be behind a firewall or protected by network security measures of any kind.

The best way to find out if your system would make a good host is just to give it a try. Note that many games, especially action-oriented titles such as Quake III Arena, run better on PC servers with Windows or Linux. This is due to many factors, from the architecture of the Mac OS to the internal design of the game itself. Another essential ingredient for game hosting (if you want to do it more than once or leave a server on permanently) is a static IP address.

If your IP is dynamically assigned, it will be tough for players who like your server to find it again in the future.

LAN gaming. A local area network (LAN) is a set of networked machines that share a hub or server. For information on how to set one up, refer to Chapter 20, "Networking." The advantage of LAN gaming over other types is twofold: First, you can see (or at least hear) your opponents and apply the required amount of trash talk and yells of victory or screams of defeat. Second and more important, LAN gaming eliminates the problem of latency (or *lag*) that other networking situations can face (see the "Lag" section below). Thus, for games in which this is critical, all gamers have a level playing field. LAN games can take place across a wide variety of platforms, and they use protocols such as TCP/IP, AppleTalk, and IPX.

Examples of LAN games range from board and trivia games to the latest strategy games and shooters. Almost without exception, any game that can be networked supports LAN play. Unfortunately, the steps you take to play a LAN network game vary widely from game to game, so there are no general guidelines to follow—just keep that manual in hand and try, try again. It is worth noting that most games will not play outside a local AppleTalk zone, and almost none will work through a firewall.

Internet gaming. Playing games on the Internet can be a source of limitless entertainment or endless frustration. All the strengths of Internet gaming— unlimited numbers of opponents, a different contest every time, new levels or maps to try, new teammates to join—are countered by the drawbacks, such as bandwidth or lag problems, slow servers, cheaters, and cretins who shoot you in the back. Gaming on the Internet mirrors the real world, except that there are no referees and no repercussions for bad behavior. If you're willing to take the bad with the good, the Internet can provide endless ways to test your skills and pass the time.

Lag. Latency, or *lag,* is an unavoidable part of Internet gaming. Due to the design of the Internet itself, *packets* of information may take any number of routes to get from the server to your computer, and vice versa. These packets can get jammed up like train cars at a switching station when an Internet gateway fails to operate quickly enough or the traffic is too high. This causes gaps in the stream of information the game requires and introduces lag into gameplay. Packets that stay jammed up too long time out, and your client game declares them lost; what happens when a chunk of needed data is missing depends on the game itself.

Lag is inevitable in any Internet gaming situation regardless of the speed of your Internet connection, due to the way the Internet processes data. However, the slower your Internet connection, the more susceptible your computer is to lag, and the more it will hurt your game when it happens. Just how much it will hurt depends heavily on the game's design. Low-bandwidth amusements—such as card, board, and trivia games—probably need to trade data with another player only when you move or when you chat with the other players, so lag will most likely never be an issue unless your connection actually fails. For games that require a continuous stream of information, such as Diablo II, Unreal Tournament, and Total Annihilation, a slow connection or lots of network traffic will guarantee a choppy, interrupted experience.

Another critical issue that affects Internet play is the distance between your computer and the server. The farther the server is from your local network, the more Internet gateways the network data stream has to go through and the greater the chance that those packets will get sidetracked or lost. Generally the distance and amount of lag you can expect are expressed in *ping*—a measure of the time it takes a signal to travel from you to the server and back. Each game measures ping slightly differently, but in general the higher the ping, the worse the game will perform with that server.

You have three solutions to lag problems. The first is to run the game as fast as possible on your system, by either upgrading your CPU and RAM or just choosing a game that runs fast. If a game runs poorly on your system, the CPU has less time to compensate for lost data and also may send out network packets to the server in an erratic fashion. The second solution is to upgrade your Internet connection to the fastest method you have available and can afford, such as DSL, cable, or a dedicated network connection. Finally, if neither of those solutions is available to you or solves the problem, then just choose a different game more suited to your system's limitations.

Finding opponents (or teammates). Once you have a game you want to play and an Internet connection, joining an online game can be a point-and-click experience. But it is often tough to find network opponents, especially those who want to play a game on terms you find acceptable. That is where various connection services become critical.

Many games come with built-in Internet play. First-person shooters such as Unreal Tournament and Quake III Arena have a built-in game browser that automatically finds Internet servers and gives you detailed statistics on who is playing on a given server, what the rules are, and what map they are playing. Other types of games such as Diablo II and Descent 3 have special company-run servers set up expressly for connecting gamers with each other; for example, Blizzard Software's Battle.net is a place for Diablo I and II players to meet, greet, and tackle quests online. To learn how to take advantage of these services, consult your game's manual.

Other services. For games that don't have a built-in browser, other methods are available. Online game services may be general, they may support many games, or they may be dedicated to only one game or type of game.

GameRanger (www.gameranger.com) is currently the only general game-connection service on the Mac platform; at last count this free multigame browser supported 43 games. As the service is Mac only, you can expect to find like-minded players, but beware—you may find the conversation and language a little unsavory at times. The service also browses servers for popular games such as Unreal Tournament and Quake III Arena, if you don't find the built-in browsers for those games to your liking. The only price you have to pay for using GameRanger is putting up with occasional fits of juvenile behavior.

HMS Freeverse is a server and game-connection service that Freeverse Software (www.freeverse.com) created for playing its excellent collection of shareware card and puzzle games. Free to registered users of Freeverse games, HMS Freeverse connects players of Burning Monkey Puzzle Lab, Classic Cribbage, and the entire 3D game collection (3D Bridge Deluxe, 3D Hearts Deluxe, and so on). Although the server only supports Freeverse games at present, there are hints that it may support more games in the future.

MacFIBS (www.fibs.com/macfibs/) is the Mac OS client for the First Internet Backgammon Server, a free service for fans of (you guessed it) backgammon. Players can chat, watch a match in progress, or find an opponent to battle. Special features such as custom rule sets and playing boards are supported. Although online play is free, the client itself is not; the author requests a $20 shareware fee.

For those who prefer the classic game of chess, there is **Fixation** (www3.sk. sympatico.ca/cknelsen/fixation/fixation.html). Fixation is the Mac OS client for the ICC, FICS, USCL, and chess.net servers that provide cross-platform, global connections to chess opponents. Fixation, which is freeware, has many advanced options.

For older games with no built-in browser or server support, players must exchange IP addresses or know the IP address of the server they want to use. Methods for doing this vary widely, from e-mail and ICQ (a form of Internet chat) to special Web pages that list game servers. Again, the method to use depends heavily on the game itself, and your best bet is to consult the game's manual. A good secondary resource for this information is the game's fan pages; just type the name of the game into any online search engine such as Yahoo or Google and you'll find dozens (perhaps hundreds) of pages dedicated to almost any game you can imagine.

Simulation Gaming (ME/GK)

Although many gaming genres reveal the computer's strengths as an entertainment device—for instance, you can't lose the pieces from a virtual chessboard—nothing showcases the power of computing like games that attempt to replicate reality itself. Known as *simulation,* or *sim,* games, the titles in this genre aren't necessarily concerned with high scores or getting past level X; instead, intellect takes precedence over reflexes, and your goals are personal, not arbitrarily constructed by some game designer. Sim games place you in another world, one that works by logical rules, and allow you to experience that world unconstrained. Sim games range from flight sims (one of computing's earliest goals was to simulate flying a plane), to economic and social sims, to world-conquest sims. Although this genre is broad, the common goal is to allow the player to explore a virtual world with great freedom. No one hunts you with a gun, and you don't have any magic keys to find or obscure plot points to follow. Freedom is the rule, and intellectual challenges await.

Flight sims. The flight-simulation genre has always been sparsely populated on the Mac platform. This was most likely due to a combination of low demand and poor access to good 3D hardware, which was a problem for the Mac platform until recently. What differentiates a flight sim from a typical arcade or action game is the developer's attempt to replicate the experience of flying an actual plane, whether it be a Learjet or a P52 Mustang.

Even though Macs and their 3D hardware have come a long way in a few short years, flight sims are still among the most demanding games in terms of system resources. After all, the game is simulating an entire world, not just a plane. The combination of landscapes, skyscapes, flight modeling, and advanced navigation systems will bring any computer to its virtual knees; thus, this genre is best ventured into by those with powerful systems and 2000 or 2001 or later video cards such as the ATI Radeon Mac Edition.

In terms of visual impact and uncompromising realism, **Fly 2K** ($19.99; Gathering of Developers) is the top of the line. This civilian (noncombat) flight sim combines gorgeous skies and breathtaking landscapes with extremely realistic cockpit instrumentation and the latest navigational gear. With four midsize aircraft replicated in perfect detail, GPS and Navaid support, five major U.S. cities with detailed skylines replicated from satellite maps, and 30,000 navigational waypoints covering the entire globe, you will be hard-pressed to run out of places to go or things to do. Serious armchair pilots can simulate systems failures, poor weather conditions, nighttime or dusk landings, and other such piloting challenges. The game features *volumetric* clouds you can fly into (and get lost in), true elevation (mountains, canyons, and everything in-between), and airports in 200 countries.

If that isn't enough for you, developer Terminal Reality has released a sequel called **Fly II,** published by MacSoft. This version features improved game graphics, a new fleet of aircraft including the Bell 407 helicopter and the Pilatus PC-12 Jetprop and extremely detailed landscapes, and it requires 3D hardware and OpenGL. What the flight sim **X-Plane** ($39.99; Laminar Research, www.laminarresearch.com) lacks in commercial polish and packaging it makes up for in sheer depth and breadth. A true flight sim that builds upon the classical principles of avionics, X-Plane can simulate any type of aircraft you can think of, from the autogyro (an early form of the helicopter) to the NASA space shuttle, and everything in between. Harrier jump jets, engineless gliders, and the Concorde are just a few of the exotic aircraft you can pilot in any conditions, anywhere in the world and beyond. The game is modifiable, so you can change an aircraft's flight behavior or even world characteristics such as the value of gravity or the atmosphere's density. That's right—you can simulate flying a glider on Mars! You can even land a shuttle from orbit at Mach 5. The developers of X-Plane constantly update it with new features; by the time you read this they probably will have added dozens of new simulations and features. The latest version includes network play, so you can fly with other pilots, and simulated storms that include hail and cloud-to-cloud lightning. Although this title is for serious flight-sim junkies only, those who live for this kind of stuff will be in nirvana. Again, a good hardware 3D card (16 MB or more) and OpenGL support are required.

If you want to experience realistic flight but feel the need to blast a fellow pilot out of the air as you do so, you have many options.

SkyFighters 1945 ($39.95; Bullseye Software, www.dogfightcity.com) is a fun-oriented World War II flight sim with online play, and **WarBirds** ($9.95 per month; iEntertainment Network, http://ientertain.iencentral.com) is a more serious sim that features huge virtual battlefields with hundreds of online opponents. Both games emphasize fun over realism and thus will tax your system less. With the games' authentic World War II planes, sounds, and flight physics, you can almost hear the aircraft whizzing through the sky. And you never have any shortage of opponents to put in the gun sight.

If you would rather do your flying outside a planetary atmosphere, **Terminus** ($9.99; Vatical Entertainment, www.vatical.com/flash/flashmain.htm) is a space-flight sim of an entire outer-space experience. The game's Newtonian spaceflight physics—meaning the ships don't steer like biplanes, as they did in *Star Wars*—and dynamic supply-and-demand trading economy allow you to experience a future world where spaceflight is the norm and the solar system has been conquered. There is a long solo plot to explore that you can take on in four careers: as a space pilot for Earth, as one for Mars, as a pirate, or as a humble merchant. You can also play a freestyle game in which your career becomes whatever you make of it, as you accept missions, collect bounties, trade goods for cash, and buy new equipment. And when you get bored with solo play, there are online missions to fly as cooperative or combat simulations with functioning, persistent economics and vast areas to explore. Although the 3D engine is complex and the visuals spectacular, the game will run on most systems and can be played online with just a modem connection. The game's free-form nature lets you make your own way in the galaxy—a refreshing break from linear games where the only decision is which bad guy to kill next.

Economic sims. Rather than simulating the laws of physics, these sims replicate the laws of commerce and the foibles of human character. Although conquest is the ultimate goal, how you go about accomplishing this is up to you, which is why sims of this type are so engrossing. You will also need the skills of foresight, intuition, and logical design to make your economic empire grow.

Railroad Tycoon II, by Gathering of Developers, is a simulation of the railroad empires, from the heady days of the first "steel horses" in the 1800s to the bullet trains of 2000 and beyond. Featuring authentic period footage, sounds, and of course the classic trains, this sim pits you against fellow robber barons in an attempt to take over the rail system of the United States (or the United Kingdom, or China, or many other countries) and build a fortune as well as an empire. With crisp pseudo-3D graphics, great sound, and tons of trains, this one is a model-railroad fan's dream. The economic simulation is intense, from simple supply and demand to stock market transactions and hostile takeovers. But if economics isn't your thing, don't worry—there is a "sandbox" mode, which allows you to build your own perfect railroad from the available tracks, bridges, towns, and resources, without the game's usual restrictions. You can even build the landscape that the trains run on, controlling the elevation, vegetation, and details such as mountains and water. Two versions of the game are available: the original Railroad Tycoon II ($19.99) and Railroad II Gold ($19.99). The Gold version includes the Second Century expansion pack, which features modern and future trains and city features.

If you would rather be riding the rails of a five-loop roller coaster than an antique railway, **Sim Theme Park** ($34.95; Aspyr Media) is the game for you. A detailed simulation of an amusement park, this title lets you construct and manage your own dream park from the T-shirt stands to the log flume. You can work in one of four themes: Space Zone, Lost Kingdom, Land of Wonders, and Halloween, each rendered in glorious, colorful 3D graphics. You can micromanage the park from top to bottom, from the amount of salt on the fries to how often maintenance cleans up the mess from kids who get sick on your roller coaster. You can even design your own rides and then take them for a spin from the rider's perspective. Although the 3D graphics do demand a competent system (a PowerPC G3 or G4 at 233 MHz or faster, and at least 64 MB of RAM), this one is a family pleaser.

Empire builders. This subgenre of sim gaming crosses the line into war and strategy games but still relies on the simulation of realistic environments and human behavior as the basis for gameplay. Your goal might be complete conquest or merely building a sustainable society that prospers over time. Although these sims range from historical and local to literally out of this world, they will challenge both your ability to lead and your ability to rule— two distinct concepts.

Sid Meier's Alpha Centauri ($19.95; Aspyr Media) features seven unique factions of human explorers attempting to establish colonies on a planet. As leader of one of those factions, you must balance exploration, resource gathering, diplomacy, and warfare to allow your faction to flourish. You will be able to starve or crowd out rivals, smooth-talk them into attacking your foes, or crush them in open war—it's your choice. The game is turn based, which gives it a chesslike element of strategy, and can be played online or even over e-mail. When you exhaust all the options, be sure to grab the expansion pack, **Sid Meier's Alien Crossfire** ($9.95; Aspyr Media), which adds hostile alien races and seven new factions to the mix as well as new technologies, resources, and artifacts to discover. The graphics are quite nice, and the turn-based nature of the game will allow it to run on any PowerPC G3 machine, including the humblest iMac.

Spanning the whole of human history from our stone-tool days to the year 3000, **Civilization: Call to Power** ($29.99; MacSoft) is an ambitious and breathtaking sim of empire-building and conquest. Explore the world, discover new technologies, engage in diplomacy, and conduct warfare in an attempt to make your empire the dominant force on the globe. With crisp 16-bit graphics and turn-based play, this title allows an in-depth exploration of not only our planet but also human character. Attack your foes outright, or woo them with diplomacy, subterfuge, propaganda, or even religious conversion.

Life Simulations. Life is complex, but not so complex that it can't be boiled down into a really fun computer game. Yes, we're aware that quite a bit is lost in the translation, but that's not really the point. If you want life, live it. If you want a game about life, then have we got some titles for you.

SimCity. Maxis Software pretty much invented the genre of life simulations with its flagship game, SimCity. There have been many variations on this game's basic formula (some successful, some not, some from other developers, some from Maxis itself), but few have matched the elegance and complexity of SimCity. There's no winning or losing in SimCity—you build a city by zoning its raw terrain and fulfilling its need for services, and then you use the tools at your disposal to shape the city to fit your imagination. The latest installment, **SimCity 3000 Unlimited** ($39.95; Electronic Arts, http://simcity.ea.com/us/guide/), is a beautiful and delightfully complex evolution of the franchise's original concept. The graphics have been wonderfully enhanced, making your cities feel more alive than ever. Several new features offer challenges to ambitious mayors, such as trash collection, negotiations with neighboring cities, and the development of clean, high-tech industry and agriculture. Dozens of old features have been streamlined and updated to shore up previous installments' shortcomings and add layers of complexity; water and power grids have been simplified; and the transportation system is easier than ever. All this complexity, however, comes with a massive hardware price tag. You'll certainly need a PowerPC G3 processor, and I heartily recommend at least 128 MB of RAM to accommodate the game's constant and ever-increasing computations. Anything less will render the game more frustrating than stimulating.

The Sims. Not one to rest on its laurels, Maxis has done nothing less than revolutionize the life simulation. If the SimCity games allow you to play mayor, Maxis's new title, **The Sims** ($49.95; Aspyr Media), lets you play god. Well, the god of one little suburban household, at least. A Sim is a simulated person who resides within the game. You can't directly tell the Sims what to do, but you can influence them in indirect ways, making for a unique gaming (simulating) challenge. If that isn't enough to keep you engrossed, you can add the expansion pack **Livin' Large** ($29.95; Aspyr Media) for even more Sims fun. With new furniture, new art and architecture, new houses, much more neighborhood space, and tons of new Sims to choose from, this is practically a whole new game. Special "magical" objects, such as a genie's lamp and a chemistry set, allow you to change the lives of your Sims in amusing ways. Create Gothic castles, rock-and-roll mansions, and 1950s-modern apartments that would make Martha Stewart flip her wig. You also get new career tracks for your Sims to follow (including rock star and journalist) and tons of new decorative elements to purchase.

Emulation (RB)

The astounding power and performance of the PowerPC G3 and G4 processors don't just give Mac users more speed—they give us the ability to do tasks that seemed impossible with humbler hardware. The G3 pushed open the door to emulation—the art of fooling your system into thinking it is another piece of hardware altogether. You can make your Mac into a Sony PlayStation, a Nintendo 64, a SuperNES, or any of hundreds of arcade cabinets, using the power of the PowerPC G3 or G4 chip to run virtual game-system hardware—in software—on your Mac.

Mainstream emulators. The most impressive feat by far is running Windows 95, 98, or 2000 on your Mac; **Virtual PC,** by Connectix ($199 for Windows 98 and $249 for Windows 2000; www.connectix.com), is designed to enable this. Even the most powerful Mac cannot run PC software at the speed of an equivalent Wintel machine, but most 2D games and applications run acceptably on a high-end G3 system. However, 3D-based games are out of the question. Virtual PC is expensive, but it is useful for much more than playing games.

MacMAME (www.macmame.org) is an emulator with a mission: to preserve the legacy of the coin-op arcade game by emulating hundreds of kinds of hardware and thousands of games that are now disappearing due to neglect and disrepair. From Asteroids to Zaxxon and everything between, all the classics are playable, including many unknown or undistributed games. It takes a PowerPC G3 or G4 machine to run these titles full speed, and playing them with the keyboard just isn't the same, but the nostalgia quotient is high. MacMAME is in constant development, and it adds support for new games and more accurate emulation all the time. However, there is a catch—ROMs (the hardware chips that arcade machines use for storage) are not readily available, and it is currently illegal to possess or distribute ROMs for a game you do not own. If you are able to locate ROM images, you can try them for a 24-hour period, after which you must delete them.

Other emulators. The same issue applies to a host of console emulators. **DGen** (Sega Genesis, www.bannister.org/software/dgen.htm), **sixtyforce** (Nintendo 64, www.sixtyforce.com), **SNES9X** (SNES, www.emulation.net/ snes/index.html), and **Virtual Gameboy** (Game Boy, www.emulation.net/ gameboy/index.html) allow you to run classic consoles on your Mac. Most of these emulators are freeware; ROM images are scarce, difficult to find, and illegal to distribute or download unless you own the actual game. The Web site Emulation.net (www.emulation.net) is a one-stop shop of emulation information, MacMAME has its own site at www.macmame.org, and Connectix shows off its products at www.connectix.com.

Hardware (GK)

There was a time when Macs boasted superior gaming hardware. Unlike DOS-based PCs, every Mac came with onboard video hardware and audio. PC users were long limited to simple bloop-bloop sounds, but Mac gamers could hear more elaborate effects. That advantage soon evaporated as the PCs raced ahead, and the gap has been widening ever since, in favor of the PC.

With the resurgence of the Mac, that trend is finally reversing; you are reading this at the dawn of a golden era of Macintosh gaming hardware. We still lack the copious choices and gee-whiz gadgetry our PC cousins take for granted, but it's a start—one that positions us to play all the newest games.

Video Cards

The most basic form of gaming hardware is the video card. It wasn't so long ago that 3D graphics cards were only for hard-core gamers. Now they're mandatory.

Owners of Macs without AGP (Accelerated Graphics Port) slots have only a few choices. Although graphics-card pioneer 3dfx has been devoured by nVidia, its strongest competition, the former company's last Mac products are still sparsely available. The technology is a bit out of date by the blisteringly fast standard of gaming hardware, but you could do worse than the **3dfx Voodoo5 5500 PCI** ($129.99; www.outpost.com). A warning: There is no guarantee that nVidia will support the drivers for this card or update them for compatibility with future Mac operating systems, so caveat emptor.

A better bet for PCI-only Macs is the **Radeon 32MB PCI** ($199.95; ATI, www.outpost.com). This outstanding card offers fantastic performance and will likely be the last PCI graphics card you'll ever need. It'll cost you more than the Voodoo5, but its future is more assured.

Buyers of new Macs, however, are the lucky ones. If your Mac has an AGP slot, the world is your oyster. Basic Power Mac G4s and iMacs come with the still potent ATI Rage 128 graphics card. For a bit more money, however, you can have your new Power Mac G4 built with the latest in 3D acceleration. You can choose from the economical **nVidia GeForce2 MX** ($100; Build-to-Order from Apple, www.apple.com/games/hardware/), the **ATI Radeon** ($100; Build-to-Order from Apple), or the state-of-the-art **nVidia GeForce 3** ($450; Build-to-Order from Apple).

If you already own an AGP-based Mac, you can purchase the **ATI Radeon AGP** ($199.95; ATI technologies, www.ati.com) to replace your built-in card.

Audio

The most exciting bit of audio hardware news to hit the Mac is the first-ever release of a third-party sound card. The **Sound Blaster Live** ($149.95; Creative Labs, www.creativelabs.com) dramatically enhances your PCI-based Mac's ability to output high-quality sound. Although the technology is hardly cutting edge, the difference is striking. If this one succeeds, look for a wider selection of sound hardware in the years to come.

What good is great sound without great speakers? Here are a few of the latest and greatest options. The **SoundSticks,** from audio giant Harman Kardon ($199; Harman Multimedia, www.harman-multimedia.com; available from the Apple Store, www.apple.com), come with the iSub subwoofer and a supercool transparent case. The **Monsoon iM-700** ($169; Sonigistix, www.sonigistix.com) delivers great sound with a subwoofer and a pair of compact flat-panel speakers. Finally, Creative Labs can fill any audiophile's need with its full line of **Cambridge SoundWorks** speakers (starting at $59.95).

Controllers

When Apple added USB (Universal Serial Bus) support a few years ago, gamers tentatively cheered. Could this mean that our anemic selection of input devices and game controllers was about to widen? The answer has proved to be a satisfying if not resounding yes.

The market has expanded dramatically. Several companies have recognized that going to the trouble of writing Macintosh drivers for their devices opens up a whole new market with minimal time and expense. However, many have not. Make sure the device you're considering has both a USB connector *and* Macintosh-compatible drivers.

Gamepads. The selection of gamepads is extensive. Some of the best are the **Destroyer Tilt GamePad** ($29.99; Gravis, www.gravis.com), **Xterminator Gamepad** ($49.95; Gravis, www.outpost.com), **FireStorm Dual Analog Gamepad** ($24.99; Guillemot, http://us.thrustmaster.com), **Firestorm Digital Gamepad** ($14.99; Guillemot), **WingMan Gamepad Extreme** ($39.95; Logitech, www.logitech.com), and **iShockII** ($49; Macally, www.macally.com).

Racing wheel. For driving aficionados, look into the **NASCAR Pro Digital 2 Racing Wheel** ($59.99; Guillemot). The set comes with both the driving wheel and floor pedals.

Flight-sim devices. Need hardware for that realistic flight-simulation experience? No problem. Check out the **Flight Sim Yoke USB LE** ($109.95; CH Products, www.chproducts.com), **Top Gun AfterBurner Force Feedback Joystick** ($89.95; Guillemot), and **Top Gun AfterBurner Joystick** ($59.99; Guillemot).

Mice and trackballs. For those who prefer the traditional mouse or trackball for their games, the selection has become extensive. Seriously consider the outstanding Intellimouse Optical mice and trackballs from Microsoft. Particularly impressive are the **IntelliMouse TrackBall Optical** ($44.95) and **IntelliMouse Optical** ($39.95). Their rollerball-free design and array of customizable buttons give these controllers the advantage over traditional multibutton mice and the otherwise strong one-button **Apple Pro Mouse** ($59; Apple). Look also at the products from Logitech (www.logitech.com) and Kensington (www.kensington.com).

PART 4

Extending Your Reach

Editors' Poll: What Do You Do Online?

JC: Google, Google, Google! Search with Google, and spend money on Amazon.

MC: The Web is my primary source of news, so most of my browsing time is spent at news sites such as The New York Times, Washington Post, and Nando. If you're stuck in a town with a third-rate newspaper, you can still get quality national and world coverage on the Web. Plus you have easy access to more than one source of news without getting ink stains on your hands.

BF: As a gaming guru of sorts I spend a fair amount of time playing online multiplayer games, largely for work.

ML: E-mail, Web browsing for specific information (I don't "surf"), shop to buy. If you live on the edge of nowhere like I do, the ability to shop and buy online saves a lot of driving time.

KT: Assist clients by converting design jobs for use on the Web. Help manage the Publishing Production forum on CompuServe (an amalgam of the former Desktop Publishing, Adobe, Quark, and Corel forums), where I have worked for 12 years. Search for information—it's more efficient than the library so long as you keep your wits and critical faculties about you. E-mail, neatly avoiding as much spam as possible. Shop, especially for old books. Monitor newsgroups and mail lists on typography, cooking, wine, and home coffee roasting. Attempt to build my own Web site.

DM: After working in a library for more than a decade, I admit to being fascinated by search engines and search optimization. As the Web expands, finding the information you need is getting more difficult—not easier. The greatest source of ready information has become a digital garbage heap. The Web's condition is a professional challenge and a source of depression.

JF: Except for the hours I spend writing personal letters, I consider all the time I spend in front of a computer to be billable time. I surf not, nor do I chat. When I need an airline ticket, I find the best itinerary and price and bring it to my travel agent, who always finds a better deal. When I need to shop for something, I support my local merchants by buying from them.

JR: I communicate, do research, read news, download software. I bank and buy computer hardware online. However, I'm not a fan of online shopping. I have purchased books, but I still prefer bookstores.

JO: Reading and research. The sites I go to most often are My Yahoo—to catch up on news, scores, and the stock market; MacInTouch—to see what's happening in (or troubling) the Macintosh community; VersionTracker—to check for updated versions of the applications and utilities I use; WSJ to read the Wall Street Journal if I left my print copy at home; Boston.com to read what's happening locally. Whenever I need to find something I tend to use Sherlock or go directly to Google.

SS: The Internet is such a major part of my everyday life that I couldn't imagine being without it. I use it to make submissions to my editors, do research, Web surf, keep my software up to date, communicate with friends and family, and hunt for a girlfriend … not necessarily in that order.

MEC: As a Webmaster and interactive media specialist in a large urban university, I spend most of my workday online, doing Web design and publishing as well as producing interactive streaming media. I browse for news, technical information, academic research, and amusement (what is a day without an episode of Helen, Sweetheart of the Internet?).

CB: In addition to the usual e-mail and web browsing, I spend a fair amount of time moderating *Macworld* magazine's public forums (http://macworld.zdnet.com/cgi-bin/ubb/Ultimate.cgi). During the days following the tragic events of September 11, 2001, the people who frequent these forums turned from Mac users seeking cures for a recalcitrant computer to caring individuals trying to make sense of senseless events. In those few days I learned a lot of wonderful things about online communities and those who participate in them.

20

Networking

John Rizzo is the chapter editor and author.

Before the dot-com craze, before e-mail, before the Web, Macs were networking. In the mid-1980s Macs were networked together, exchanging files and sharing printers at a time when most PC users were considering whether to switch from command-line DOS to this new Windows thing. These days, networking is sending e-mail, doing file sharing and group scheduling, and sharing Internet access among a group of Macs.

The secret of Mac networking success has always been a combination of built-in hardware and operating-system features—built-in networking hardware controlled by operating-system software Apple designed specifically for it. Mac OS 9 gives you networking features such as file sharing, e-mail, and browsing software, and it can communicate over cables or through the air.

Mac OS X gives your Mac more network capabilities than ever before, adding the ability to communicate on Windows and Unix networks. However, network configuration is different in Mac OS X than in Mac OS 9. If you think you know Mac networking but don't know Mac OS X, you have some new things to learn. You'll find Mac OS X information in each of the sections in this chapter.

There's a lot you can do with networks, and there are a lot of ways to do it—which is why entire books are written on networking. In this chapter, you'll get a foundation in network basics and learn how to set up your Mac for most common networking tasks.

This chapter starts with a high-level description of some of the pieces of a network. After that, I describe how to get your network up and running. (For specifics on connecting to the Internet, see Chapter 21, "The Internet.")

In This Chapter

Networking in a Mac: A Primer

A *local network* is the computer network in your room, building, or campus. Local networks are also called *local area networks*. The *area* seems to have been included to make the acronym *LAN* pronounceable. But since networking has enough unavoidable acronyms, I'll just stick to the term *local network* in this chapter.

You can think of the Internet as a connection of local networks all around the world. Your local network has a lot of similarities to the Internet. It uses some of the same network protocols, and you can use some of the same network services, such as a Web server or e-mail, locally or globally via the Internet. On local networks, Mac users often employ file sharing to move files between computers. On the Internet, FTP servers are more commonly used for file sharing. However, Mac OS X includes FTP that can also be used locally. Your Mac is also bilingual and speaks AppleTalk.

Most of the Mac's networking infrastructure—the built-in hardware and system software—is used for local networks as well as for the Internet. Getting your Mac ready for the Internet is similar to getting it ready for a local network. In some cases, one configuration works for both.

Network Foundation: Protocols

You can think of a network as a discussion between computers using one or more network *protocols* as the common language. The discussion takes place over the network media, which is usually the Ethernet cables—or the air, in the case of AirPort, Apple's wireless networking technology. Your Mac is a native speaker of two network protocols, TCP/IP (Transmission Control Protocol/Internet Protocol) and AppleTalk. AppleTalk can run at the same time as TCP/IP.

Both AppleTalk and TCP/IP are able to handle network software communication such as e-mail, group-scheduling programs, and print-sharing software—it's up to the software manufacturer to implement the protocols. However, Internet software only runs on TCP/IP.

You don't need to configure AppleTalk beyond turning it on and off. TCP/IP is not as user friendly and does need to be set up before it will work. Configuring TCP/IP is the first thing you do after plugging in to your network (or connecting wirelessly). TCP/IP is not always easy to set up, but in part because of its use on the Internet, is now used more than AppleTalk.

Turning on AppleTalk or configuring TCP/IP is an enabling step, but it doesn't allow you to actually do anything yet. Next, you need to set up your *network services*—the tools that let you perform network tasks.

Network Services: Servers and Clients

Network services are the functional features that perform your work. For instance, file service lets you see files on other computers and move files around. E-mail is a network service, as is whichever group-calendar program you may use.

Network services run in two parts—the server software and the client software—which communicate with each other. The server software provides the service to other computers. It can run on a dedicated server computer that is not doing double duty as a user's workstation. Server software can also run on your Mac, providing a service (such as the ability to access your files) for other users. Dedicated servers are faster than server software running on a user's Mac and can handle more simultaneous connections to clients.

The client software is what you, the user, typically work with. For instance, Microsoft Outlook is an e-mail client. It communicates with an e-mail server, either on your local network or on the Internet. Sometimes client software is invisible to you. For example, the Mac OS's Software Update application can run behind the scenes to check Apple servers for new versions of your system software.

The user versions of Mac OS come with both client and server software for various tasks. For instance, there's a file-sharing client that lets you access other computers. You don't see an application that is a file-sharing client because the functionality is integrated into the Mac OS. The Mac OS also has an integrated file-sharing server, which you don't see as a separate application. When you turn on file sharing to allow other users to access your Mac, your Mac is acting as a server.

The table "Integrated Network Services in Mac OS 9 and Mac OS X" lists the basic network services that are integrated into Mac OS 9 and Mac OS X. (It doesn't list the e-mail client, Web browsers, or other network software that come with Mac OS—these aren't integrated services.) The network services in Mac OS X are generally beefier than those in Mac OS 9. Setting them up is a bit easier as well. (I describe the difference between Web serving and Web sharing in the section "Built-In File Sharing and Web Services.")

You can see from the table that Mac OS X has several more network services than Mac OS 9. It has clients for accessing Windows file-sharing servers and for accessing Unix NFS (network file server) servers and has a server for allowing other computers to access files using FTP.

We'll look at the configuration and use of all these built-in, integrated network services. But first, we're going to go back to the beginning of the network story and discuss the network media, over which communication occurs.

Integrated Network Services in Mac OS 9 and Mac OS X

Feature	Mac OS 9	Mac OS X
File sharing over AppleTalk	yes	yes (Mac X 10.1 and later; client and server)
File sharing over TCP/IP	yes	yes (client and server)
Windows file sharing client	no	yes (Mac OS X 10.1 and later)
Printing over AppleTalk	yes	yes
Printing over TCP/IP	yes	yes
Web server/sharing	yes	yes
FTP server	no	yes
Unix NFS file sharing client	no	yes

Wires and Wireless: Setting Up Network Media

This used to be the point in *The Macintosh Bible* where we'd start talking about how to plug in your Macs. Since the appearance of AirPort on the networking scene a few years ago, you no longer need to "plug in" to get connected, as wireless networking is an attractive alternative to using your Mac's built-in Ethernet port. Or you can create a network of mixed media, wireless and wired. Regardless of the media, any network software that works on one network medium will work on the other.

 Mac OS X is more advanced than Mac OS 9 and earlier when it comes to the network media. Mac OS X supports *multihoming,* a feature that allows it to connect over multiple network media types at the same time. Mac OS 9 and earlier can only speak over one type of medium at a time.

Wired or Wireless?

When you begin planning a network, you should seriously think about whether you want to go with an Ethernet network, a wireless network, or some combination of the two. Ethernet networks are still simpler to set up than wireless AirPort networks, and they don't require users to log in to the network. Wireless networks can be more convenient, especially with iBooks and PowerBooks that are used in different locations or aren't located next to a wall socket. For instance, some schools are putting their computer labs on carts. A teacher wheels a cart full of iBooks into an AirPort-equipped classroom and unloads the iBooks, and soon the students are all cruising the Internet.

The comparative cost of each type of network medium varies. If you're just stringing cables across the floor, Ethernet is less expensive than AirPort. However, if you need to route wires through walls or between floors, the labor costs can easily exceed the cost of the AirPort hardware.

Ethernet is also faster. AirPort is limited to 11 Mbps. This is fast enough for Internet connection and simple network tasks, but if you are transferring mass quantities of files, you might need the 100 Mbps that today's Macs can now handle or the gigabit Ethernet in Power Mac G4s.

Ethernet

Ethernet is like a public highway. You can run any protocol on it using any software on any computer running any operating system. Macs have been running on Ethernet for a long time. Your Mac has a built-in Ethernet port with a standard connector. Ethernet comes in various compatible flavors that differ in the bandwidth they can support.

Ethernet bandwidth. The total *bandwidth* of a network is the maximum amount of traffic it can carry at one time. Bandwidth is related to speed but is not the same thing. The more Macs you have on a network, the more traffic is on the network, and the more bandwidth is taken up. The more bandwidth is used, the slower the performance for each user.

You can think of bandwidth as the width of a hallway in a popular train station. At rush hour, hallway number one, which is 10 feet wide, can allow 100 people per minute to pass through it. Hallway number two, which is 20 feet wide, can allow 200 people per minute to pass through. You might say that hallway two is "faster," because you don't have to wait as long to get through, but really, it's just wider, or has more bandwidth.

So it is with Ethernet. Another reason why bandwidth is not equivalent to speed is network overhead. At 100 Mbps, if you move a file that is 100 Mb in size (12.5 MB), it won't reach its destination in 1 second. (You may have noticed that a 56 Kbps modem connection actually moves 3 or 4 Kbits of data every second.) This is partly because about a third of network bandwidth is used for carrying data and commands that keep communications organized and identified. Additionally, you never actually get 100 percent use of the bandwidth because of something called packet collisions—pieces of data bumping into each other as on a crowded freeway.

Apple uses three Ethernet bandwidths in various Mac models:

10Base-T, providing 10 Mbps

100Base-T, providing 100 Mbps (also called Fast Ethernet)

1000Base-T, providing 1 Gbps (commonly known as Gigabit Ethernet)

The Mac's Ethernet port can sense the bandwidth at which the network is operating and will choose the appropriate speed to send and receive data. There is no setup or configuration required. However, you do need to make sure you buy an Ethernet hub that supports the bandwidths at which you want to run. (There's more about hubs in the next section.)

If you want to increase the Ethernet bandwidth of an older Mac through its expansion slot, you can add an Ethernet network interface card (sometimes called a *NIC*). For instance, you can add a Gigabit Ethernet card to the first Power Mac G4 models, which support only 10/100Base-T. Older Power Macs, such as the Power Mac 7600 and the 8500, came with built-in 10Base-T. You can upgrade these with a NIC as well. Just make sure the card comes with driver software for the Mac OS.

Cables and connectors. All Macs produced since the mid-1990s have an Ethernet port that consists of some networking electronics on the motherboard and an RJ-45 connector. An RJ-45 plug on an Ethernet cable looks like a slightly fatter telephone connector, usually made of clear plastic (**Figure 20.1**).

The typical cable used in Ethernet networks is known as *Category 5* cable (or just *Cat 5*). This is of a higher quality than Category 3 cable, which can work with 10Base-T networks. For 100Base-T, Cat 5 is required. This designation is usually on the cable.

Figure 20.1

An RJ-45 Ethernet connector.

You can connect two Macs directly with a special Ethernet cable known as a *crossover cable*. (Most Ethernet cables you see in stores are not crossover cables, so be careful.) However, with more than two Macs, you need an *Ethernet hub*. This is a little box that all the computers on the network plug into using *Ethernet patch cables* (**Figure 20.2**).

You can mix 10Base-T, 100Base-T, and Gigabit Ethernet as long as the hub supports these bandwidths. Hubs don't have to be expensive, but be careful about bargains. If you buy a 10Base-T hub, you will be limited to 10 Mbps bandwidth, even though your Macs support 100 Mbps or more.

Figure 20.2

An Ethernet hub.

Extinct Ethernet

If you have an old Mac sitting around, you may have an AAUI (Apple Attachment Unit Interface) connector instead of a standard RJ-45. The AAUI connectors are compatible with your hub-based, 10Base-T Ethernet network, provided you have a small AAUI–to–RJ-45 transceiver box. A lot of old Macs (of the vintage Power Mac 7500 or 8500) have both an RJ-45 port and an AAUI port. If you have one of these Macs, you can ignore the AAUI port.

Older types of Ethernet that predate 10Base-T may not be at all compatible. One was called *thick Ethernet* (or *Thicknet*), and the other was called *thin Ethernet* (also called *Thinnet* or *10Base2*). These used coaxial cables, similar to cable TV cable, but Thicknet was thicker than Thinnet (which really wasn't all that thin). The cable was strung from one computer to the other, which was much less convenient than using hubs. This and the high cost of the coaxial cables eventually led to the replacement of Thinnet and Thicknet by 10/100/1000Base-T. You may still see thick or thin Ethernet used as a network "backbone" in some networks, but even this is becoming increasingly rare.

LocalTalk

Pre-iMac Macs have another type of networking hardware called *LocalTalk*. The LocalTalk port was the same as the printer port—the port did double duty. Apple dropped LocalTalk when it introduced the iMac because LocalTalk had many drawbacks. It was slow (240 Kbps), could not handle many Macs (32 maximum), and could not run TCP/IP—it could only run AppleTalk. (This is why the LocalTalk ports on older network laser printers were sometimes called AppleTalk ports.) There is no point in trying to get new devices on a LocalTalk network, but you can get older network devices on Ethernet. (This might be a laser printer or an old Mac with no Ethernet port.) You can do this with a LocalTalk-to-Ethernet bridge such as Farallon's EtherMac iPrint Adapter.

Networking Without Wires: AirPort

Mac support of wireless networking began with the first iBook model. Today, every iMac, iBook, PowerBook, and Power Mac has a slot for an AirPort card and a built-in antenna for sending and receiving data. You can also buy a pre-installed AirPort card when you order a new Mac. Mac OS 9 and Mac OS X both support AirPort networking. And networking software and protocols that work over Ethernet will work over AirPort wireless networks.

AirPort implements an industry standard called IEEE 802.11 Direct Sequence Spread Spectrum (DSSS). The standard uses low-power radio frequencies that can travel a short distance through walls, although large structures can block the signal. The current specification describes a maximum bandwidth of 11 Mbps.

AirPort is called AirMac in Japan.

Apple calls its IEEE 802.11 DSSS products AirPort, but other companies make compatible cards and access points. At press time, however, Apple was saying that the Apple AirPort card was the only card compatible with Mac OS X, probably because the card vendors had not yet created a Mac OS X driver for the card. It is reasonable to expect that these drivers will eventually be created, possibly by the time you read this book.

AirPort uses encryption to prevent someone with an iBook outside your window from eavesdropping on your network traffic. This means that users have to log in to an AirPort network. You can do this from the AirPort Control Strip module.

AirPort networks use an encryption standard called Wired Equivalency Privacy (or WEP). Data being transmitted through the air between a Mac and an access point, such as the AirPort Base Station, is encrypted using an encryption key that both the Mac and the Base Station have. This is why you use a password to join a wireless network—the password tells the Base Station to send your Mac an encryption key. WEP is just used locally over the air and not over the Internet. You can turn WEP encryption off in the Base using the AirPort Admin Utility from either Mac OS 9 or Mac OS X.

AirPort Network Configurations

Most wireless networks require a wireless access point such as Apple's AirPort Base Station, a kind of wireless hub and Internet gateway roll into one (**AirPort Base Station,** $299; **AirPort card,** $99; www.apple.com). However, you can run an AirPort network without a Base Station. You have three basic ways to configure an AirPort network:

- Two Macs (maybe more) without an AirPort Base Station (computer-to-computer)
- As many as ten Macs with an AirPort Base Station
- As many as ten Macs with an AirPort Base Station, using one Mac as a base station and Internet connection

PowerBook and iBook users can maximize battery life by turning off power to the AirPort Card using the AirPort Control Strip module in Mac OS 9 or the AirPort Dock item in Mac OS X.

A two-Mac AirPort network. Just as you can use an Ethernet cable to connect two Macs directly without a hub, you can connect a few AirPort-equipped Macs directly without any other hardware. This is called *computer-to-computer mode* (**Figure 20.3**). This can save you the cost of an AirPort Base Station and enable you to create a spontaneous network if, say, you and a friend happen to meet with your iBooks on the subway.

Figure 20.3

You can set the AirPort Control Strip module for two Macs, no Base Station, in Mac OS 9.

Apple recommends that you use computer-to-computer mode for only two Macs, but you should be able to get more than two Macs communicating if they are close together. The drawback to having more than two Macs is that performance may suffer. Apple says the two computers need to be within 150 feet (45 meters) of each other.

You can use the Control Strip's AirPort module on both computers to switch from using the AirPort Base Station to using direct computer-to-computer communications.

When you are running Mac OS 9 in computer-to-computer mode, the AirPort Control Strip module will indicate this by showing two Mac icons with three dots in between (**Figure 20.4**). (These are images of the original Macintosh, for those youngsters who don't recognize them as Macs.) When you are not in computer-to-computer mode, the module shows five dots and no Macs.

Figure 20.4

The Control Strip's AirPort module in computer-to-computer mode.

 In Mac OS X, you can get into computer-to-computer mode by clicking the AirPort icon in the Dock and selecting Create Computer to Computer network.

 In Mac OS X version 10.1, you can also use the AirPort status menu item to select computer-to-computer mode. This is a menu in the upper right of the screen. Choose Open Internet Connect from the AirPort menu. In the dialog box that appears, choose AirPort from the Configuration menu. Then choose Create Network from the Network pop-up menu (**Figure 20.5**). In the sheet that rolls down, enter your network name; choose a password; and from the pop-up menu select a channel (this is the channel the members of your network will use).

Figure 20.5

From the AirPort status menu item (left), choose Open Internet Connect to set up a computer-to-computer mode connection (right).

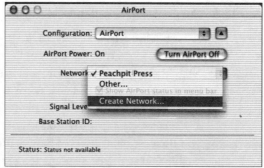

You can also install the AirPort menu by dragging and dropping it. Go to /System/Library/CoreServers/Menu Extras/. Now drag the file AirPort item to the right of the top menu, next to the time. To remove it, hold ⌘ while you drag it off the menu and then release the mouse button. It will disappear in a puff of smoke.

AirPort doesn't use WEP encryption in computer-to-computer mode. You can tell this is so because you don't need a password to join the network. This could be a problem in a public setting, as someone across the room with an iBook could join your network. If you are doing file sharing in computer-to-computer mode in a public place (such as a library), you may want to make sure guest access is disabled in the File Sharing control panel of Mac OS 8 and 9 or in the Sharing pane of Mac OS X's System Preferences.

Of course, you need to have TCP/IP or AppleTalk or both turned on and configured for AirPort (see the section "Setting Up an AirPort Base Station").

AirPort Base Station

The AirPort Base Station used for most AirPort networks is a multifunctional device. It's a wireless hub, it's an Internet gateway, it's an Ethernet bridge, and it comes with a set of Ginsu knives! (Well, no, it doesn't actually come with Ginsu knives, but you get the idea.) You can use other IEEE 802.11 access points with your AirPort network—Lucent, for example, offers one—but many don't have all the functionality of the AirPort Base Station.

Wireless access point. The simplest function of the Base Station is to act as a wireless hub—when it receives a signal from your computer, it broadcasts the signal to the other computers. This is what the industry calls a *wireless access point*.

Apple recommends using one AirPort Base Station for every ten users, though you usually can squeeze in a few more Macs. The drawback, though, is that performance can suffer with more than ten users if everyone is active. For bigger networks, you can use multiple Base Stations (or buy a bigger access point from another vendor such as Lucent or 3Com).

Ethernet-to-wireless bridge. The AirPort Base Station can also act as a bridge to connect an Ethernet network to Macs running AirPort. When you plug an Ethernet hub in to the Base Station's Ethernet port, you enable the computers on the wired network to communicate with those on the wireless network.

Use the AirPort Admin Utility to set this up (in Mac OS X, you find it in the Utilities folder inside the Applications folder; in Mac OS 9, navigate through the Applications (Mac OS 9) folder to the Apple Extras folder to the AirPort folder to reach it). The Base Station (or Base Stations) must have the box next to "Enable AirPort to Ethernet bridging" checked.

Internet gateway. The Base Station uses a standard technique called network address translation (NAT) to act as an Internet gateway. With NAT, you only need one IP address that is visible to the Internet. All the Macs on the network get an IP address from the Dynamic Host Configuration Protocol (DHCP) server in the AirPort Base Station. NAT passes traffic from the Internet to the Macs and sends the traffic from the Macs to the Internet. A NAT gateway provides security, in that the Internet can't directly see the Macs on your network. It also is less expensive than leasing multiple Internet IP addresses for all your Macs from your Internet service provider.

The AirPort Base Station has a built-in modem to connect to the Internet using a dial-up account. You can also use the Base Station's Ethernet port to connect to a high-speed Internet connection, such as a cable modem or DSL modem.

DHCP server. The DHCP server in the Base Station assigns IP addresses to Macs automatically over the network. Using the AirPort Admin Utility, you can set a Base Station to act as a DHCP server by selecting the "Distribute IP addresses" check box. (See the sections "Setting DHCP in Mac OS 9" and "Setting DHCP in Mac OS X.")

Setting up an AirPort Base Station

You can set up the Base Station using AirPort Admin Utility or the AirPort Setup Assistant. The AirPort Setup Assistant is a more automated tool than AirPort Admin Utility and is useful when setting up the Base Station for the first time. For instance, the Assistant can transfer your Mac's Internet settings to the AirPort Base Station.

AirPort Admin Utility is better for making changes to Base Station settings. You can also use it to configure multiple AirPort Base Stations at the same time. (If you want to set up an AirPort Base Station from Mac OS X, you'll need at least version 10.1.)

To get your Base Station up and running in Mac OS 9 or Mac OS X 10.1 or later:

1. Plug in the AirPort Base Station power cord. This will turn it on.

2. Plug your Internet connection into the AirPort Base Station (either a phone line to the modem port or a high-speed line to the Ethernet port).

3. Start with your Mac set up to connect to the Internet. That is, don't switch it to use AirPort. The Setup Assistant will do this for you.

4. Launch the AirPort Setup Assistant. (The Assistant can be found in the Mac OS 9 Assistants folder inside Apple Extras, or in the Mac OS X Utilities folder. If you don't have it on your Mac, install it from the CD that came with the Base Station.)

5. Follow the Assistant's directions as they apply to your situation. If you already have AirPort running on other Macs or have a Base Station turned on, you'll see a dialog box (**Figure 20.6**). If this is the case, choose "Set up an AirPort Base Station" and click the right arrow. If you don't see this dialog box, you haven't turned on the Base Station (that is, you've skipped step 1).

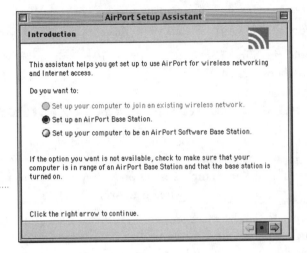

Figure 20.6

You'll see this dialog box only if you already have AirPort turned on.

After you finish, you'll notice that the AirPort Setup Assistant has created new TCP/IP and AppleTalk configurations set to use AirPort instead of Ethernet. (These will appear in the TCP/IP control panel in Mac OS 9 and earlier, or in the Network pane of System Preferences in Mac OS X.) The new TCP/IP configuration will be set to get its IP address from the Base Station's DHCP server. (See the section "Setting DHCP in Mac OS X," later in the chapter, for more about multiple configurations and DHCP.)

Joining AirPort Networks

Your Mac is now connected to the AirPort Base Station. If you have a high-speed Ethernet Internet connection, you should be able to open your Web browser or other software and access the Internet.

If the Base Station is using a modem connection, you'll have to tell it to dial in.

To join a wireless AirPort network in Mac OS 9:

1. From the Apple menu, choose AirPort (or go to the AirPort Control Strip module and select Open AirPort).

2. Click Connect.

If the Base Station is using WEP encryption, you'll have to type in a password in a field that appears when you log in.

If you have multiple AirPort networks, you can use this dialog box to choose a network to join. You do this from the "Choose network" pop-up menu. The Mac will remember this setting when you shut down.

There are several ways to join an AirPort network in Mac OS X. Here's one:

1. Open Internet Connect (located in the Applications/Utilities folder).

2. From the Configuration pop-up menu, choose AirPort.

3. From the Network pop-up menu that appears, choose your network.

You could also join a network from the AirPort item in the Mac OS X menu bar. Just choose Open AirPort.

Connecting Additional Macs to AirPort

So far you've got one Mac communicating wirelessly to the Internet via the AirPort Base Station. Now you can add other Macs to the wireless network. Just open the AirPort Setup Assistant on each Mac and select "Set up your computer to join an existing wireless network."

Make sure that all the Macs on the AirPort network and the AirPort Base Station are running the same version of the AirPort software. With different versions, the Macs may not be able to communicate with each other.

Using a Mac as a Base Station

You can designate one of the Macs as an access point using software running on the Mac. This software feature is referred to as an AirPort software access point and is installed with the AirPort software. This Mac will act as the wireless hub and as the connection to the Internet. As with computer-to-computer mode, you don't use a hardware Base Station, but you do get other Base Station features, including the ability to share Internet access with other Macs The software access point works with a dial-up modem as well as high-speed connections.

You have several ways to configure your Mac as a software Base Station in either Mac OS 9 or Mac OS X. One method is to use the AirPort Setup Assistant. In the first screen, choose "Set up your computer to be an AirPort Software Base Station." (If the software doesn't detect a Base Station, this will be the only choice.) Then follow the directions.

If your Mac is already using AirPort, you can also use the AirPort Admin Utility. When AirPort opens, click the Software Base Station button. A new window opens (**Figure 20.7**). You can give your network a name and enable WEP encryption (as you can with a hardware Base Station).

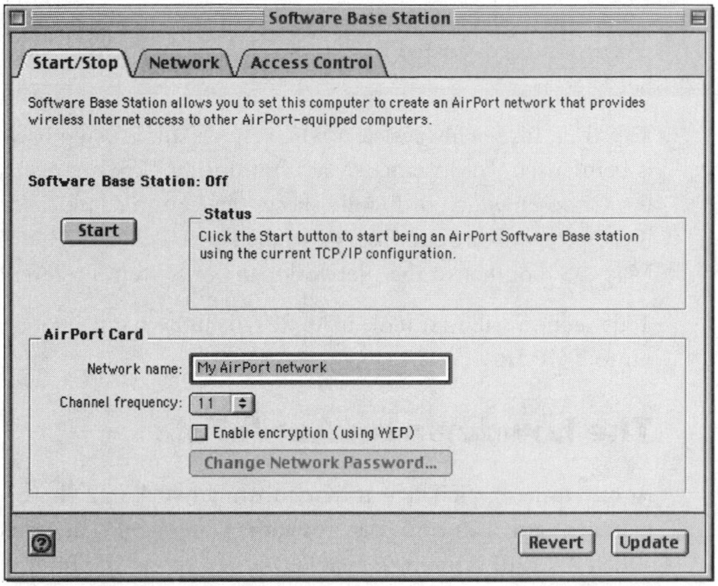

Figure 20.7

Setting up a Mac to be a Software Base Station.

Interference. If you are having trouble making an AirPort connection, there may be some interference between you and the Base Station or Mac you are trying to communicate with. Devices that generate signals near the 2.4 Hz frequency used by AirPort can cause interference. These include some cordless telephones and microwave ovens. Nearby power lines can also generate interference.

Some building materials may cause problems. Metal (as in steel beams) can cause the most interference. Concrete can also be a problem, and brick walls can weaken signals. Wood-and-plaster walls don't pose much of an interference threat.

Setting Up AppleTalk and TCP/IP

Whether you use Ethernet or AirPort, you will need TCP/IP or AppleTalk to do anything. These are the network transport protocols that enable your Mac to talk to other network devices and to the Internet. Other, more specific protocols work "on top" of the transport protocols. For instance, there are protocols for printing, file sharing, e-mail, and the various other tasks you might do on a network. But these specific protocols are mostly invisible to the user. You need to set TCP/IP; with AppleTalk, you merely turn it on.

However, don't confuse AppleTalk with AppleShare. These are two different things and not necessarily tied together. AppleTalk is a network transport protocol, as is TCP/IP. AppleShare is what Apple calls *file sharing over the network*.

AppleShare can occur over AppleTalk or over TCP/IP. AppleShare is a network service, and is discussed later in the chapter (see "Built-In File Sharing and Web Services").

To a user, it's not always clear when AppleTalk is being used and when TCP/IP is being used. For instance, Macs running AppleShare over TCP/IP show up in the Chooser, which ordinarily shows devices on AppleTalk networks. To check if the protocols are running, go to the AppleTalk and TCP/IP control panels in Mac OS 8 or 9 or to the Network pane of System Preferences in Mac OS X.

This section will first look at AppleTalk and what it's good for and then move on to TCP/IP.

The Lowdown on AppleTalk

At one time, AppleTalk *was* Macintosh networking. There were cables and printers named after it; Mac networks were AppleTalk networks. Later, Apple added TCP/IP support to enable Macs to access the Internet. But this support was incomplete, and the performance wasn't good. In 1995, Apple rewrote the Mac OS's networking software, calling it Open Transport. Open Transport made TCP/IP a core protocol equal to AppleTalk. Mac OS X makes even more use of TCP/IP with additional IP-based network services.

Pros and cons of AppleTalk. For the past few years, Apple has been adding more TCP/IP-based services, such as Web sharing and FTP file sharing, while not expanding AppleTalk. In fact, Apple announced that it was moving away from AppleTalk altogether. It carried out this plan in the first versions of Mac OS X (10.0 through 10.0.4), which do not do file sharing over AppleTalk — only printing. This was actually the same level of AppleTalk support as found in Windows NT and 2000 Workstation. However, the outcry from users was such that Apple restored file sharing over AppleTalk in version 10.1.

Apple's shift toward TCP/IP was part of the company's move to adopting industry standards in its operating-system software. The rise of the Internet has made TCP/IP the industry standard for network transport protocol. Additionally, AppleTalk is inferior in some ways. For one, AppleTalk is slower than TCP/IP. It sends data in smaller packets than TCP/IP can and thus takes longer to transmit. TCP/IP can stream data continuously, something AppleTalk cannot do. And while TCP/IP is ubiquitous, AppleTalk isn't usually found on Windows or Unix PCs.

The main benefit of AppleTalk is that it is much easier to set up than TCP/IP, as we'll see in the next section, and is the first choice for home and small-office networks of Macs running Mac OS 9 and earlier. AppleTalk is also still preferable to TCP/IP for printing to network laser printers for Mac OS X or Mac OS 9 and earlier. (USB printers can be shared over TCP/IP.)

Setting up AppleTalk in Mac OS 9 or earlier. There's not a lot to do to set up AppleTalk. Unlike TCP/IP, AppleTalk doesn't require you to configure addresses on each Mac—it's self-addressing. Configuring AppleTalk in Mac OS 9 and earlier is a two-step process:

1. Turn AppleTalk on.

2. Choose a network medium (Ethernet or AirPort).

You can turn on AppleTalk in the Chooser, the AppleTalk control panel, or the AppleTalk Control Strip module.

It's easiest to turn AppleTalk on and off in the Control Strip. You can identify the AppleTalk Control Strip module by the icon of the original Macintosh connected to a network cable (**Figure 20.8**).

Figure 20.8

The AppleTalk Control Strip module.

To use the Chooser to turn on AppleTalk, go to the Apple menu, open the Chooser, and click the Active button next to AppleTalk.

To turn on AppleTalk using the AppleTalk control panel, open it in Advanced mode and click Options. In the AppleTalk Options dialog box, select Active (**Figure 20.9**).

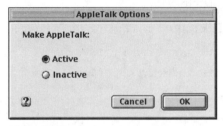

Figure 20.9

The AppleTalk Options dialog box.

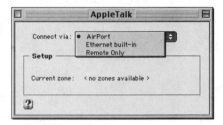

Figure 20.10

Choosing network media in the AppleTalk control panel.

To choose your network medium, open the AppleTalk control panel. In the "Connect via" pop-up menu you will see multiple choices, depending on your Mac hardware. Three choices are shown here (**Figure 20.10**):

AirPort. This only appears if you have an AirPort card installed. Most Macs will change this setting to AirPort automatically when you install an AirPort card.

Ethernet built-in. All Macs have this setting.

Remote Only. This selection allows AppleTalk connection via modem but shuts off AppleTalk to the Ethernet port. Using this setting is better than turning off AppleTalk altogether. Turning off AppleTalk prevents some aspects of file sharing from functioning correctly.

Two other choices are possible in the AppleTalk "Connect via" menu:

Infrared Port (IrDA). This is used for Macs with infrared ports. You can use this setting to print wirelessly to an AppleTalk network printer that supports IrDA or to do file sharing with another Mac via an infrared port. The PowerBook G4 has an IrDA port, as did the original iMac. (On some very old PowerBooks, the phrase in parentheses is "IRTalk" instead of "IrDA." IRTalk was an Apple-only infrared technology, and you can't use it to connect to a newer Mac with IrDA.)

Printer Port or Modem/Printer Port. You'll see this only on old Macs with a LocalTalk port.

Once you select your network medium, close the AppleTalk control panel to have your selection take effect.

Advanced AppleTalk Settings in Mac OS 9 and Earlier

The AppleTalk control panel has an Advanced user mode that lets you view or change some options. You'll rarely, if ever, need to use it, but it's there if you do. There's also an Administrator mode that is the same as Advanced mode but lets you lock the settings with a password.

To switch the AppleTalk control panel to Advanced mode:

1. Open the AppleTalk control panel.
2. Go to the Edit menu and select User Mode (or press ⌘Ⓤ).
3. Click Advanced.
4. Click OK.

You'll now see a bigger AppleTalk control panel (**Figure 20.11**). Manually setting a node number for a Mac can be useful in certain troubleshooting situations. If you select the "User defined" check box, you can enter an AppleTalk node number and network range, which together form the Mac's AppleTalk address. (The node number must be from 1 and 253, the network number from 0 to 65534.) Like IP addresses, the combination of network number and node address must be unique. Close the AppleTalk control panel after making any changes to put them into effect.

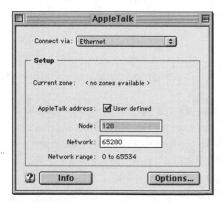

Figure 20.11

The AppleTalk control panel in Advanced mode.

AppleTalk zones. Zones are probably the most misunderstood aspect of AppleTalk. The concept of AppleTalk zones is tied to AppleTalk *routers*— a device or software running on servers that connects network segments together. Routers are used in large networks. Some routers for TCP/IP also support AppleTalk, and Microsoft includes software AppleTalk routers with Windows NT Server and Windows 2000 Server.

So how are routers and zones linked? When a network administrator configures an AppleTalk router, he or she can also choose to create AppleTalk zones. This is purely optional. If you see zones in your Chooser, you have an AppleTalk router. If you don't have zones, you don't have a router.

To help you decide whether your AppleTalk network needs zones, consider the following:

- If you don't have a large network, you don't need AppleTalk zones.
- Zones only appear with AppleTalk and are not used with TCP/IP.
- An AppleTalk zone is a logical creation, not a physical one.

This last point goes to the heart of the issue. An AppleTalk zone does not correspond to a network segment but is a logical grouping of servers and shared network printers, regardless of physical location. The purpose of a zone is only to organize large numbers of servers, Macs with file sharing turned on, and printers into several lists of AppleTalk network resources. These lists are presented to the user in the Chooser as zones. For instance, a network administrator might put all of the printers for the marketing department in a "marketing" zone.

Setting the Default Zone on a Mac

Each Mac will find a default zone to belong to (depending on how the routers are set up). You can change the default zone for each Mac in its AppleTalk control panel. This is the zone used for file sharing. That is, if your Mac has file sharing turned on, it will appear in the list of servers for that zone in the Chooser (as described in "Log In to an AFP File Server or Another Mac," below).

To set a zone in Mac OS 9 or earlier:

1. Open the AppleTalk control panel.
2. Choose a zone from the "Current zone" pop-up menu.
3. Close the AppleTalk control panel.

If you don't have any zones on the network, you won't have a "Current zone" pop-up menu. Instead, there will be the phrase "No zones available."

 You can also choose a default zone in Mac OS X.

Setting up AppleTalk in Mac OS X

Configuring AppleTalk in Mac OS X is completely different from the procedure in Mac OS 9 and earlier. You do it in the Network pane of System Preferences.

In Mac OS X, configuring AppleTalk (and TCP/IP) is done in the reverse order of the process in Mac OS 9. Instead of picking the protocol first (in an AppleTalk or TCP/IP control panel) and then choosing a medium, in Mac OS X you choose the medium first and then choose the protocol. You also have to choose a network medium before you can turn on AppleTalk.

Open System Preferences, and click the Network icon. Select a media option from the Show pop-up menu (**Figure 20.12**). (The Show pop-up menu is called Configure in Mac OS X 10.0 to 10.0.4.)

When you choose a type of network medium, the tabs of the Network window change—that is, you get one set of tabs if you choose Built-in Ethernet, another if you choose AirPort. Both have an AppleTalk tab.

There is no AppleTalk tab in the Network window when you choose Internal Modem in the Configure menu, because Mac OS X doesn't support AppleTalk connections over a modem.

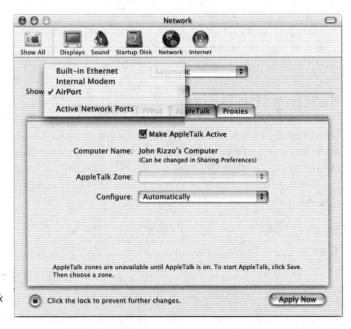

Figure 20.12

Choosing network media for AppleTalk in Mac OS X.

The AppleTalk tab of Built-in Ethernet and AirPort is the same. At the top is a check box for Make AppleTalk Active. There's a menu where you can select an AppleTalk zone if you have zones configured on AppleTalk routers. The Configure pop-up menu (under the AppleTalk Zone menu) lets you select Manually for setting AppleTalk addressing. This is equivalent to the Advanced User mode in the Mac OS 9 control panel and lets you type in AppleTalk node and network numbers (**Figure 20.13**).

When you're finished configuring AppleTalk, click the Apply Now button (or Save button in some versions). You can now select a default zone from the AppleTalk Zone pop-up menu if you have zones on the network.

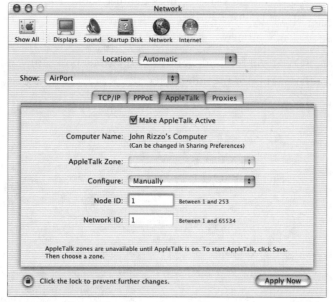

Figure 20.13

Manually configuring AppleTalk in Mac OS X.

You can also print over AppleTalk. I discuss configuring Mac OS X to print to AppleTalk printers in the section "Sharing Printers."

AppleTalk with PPPoE in Mac OS X

There is one exception to the above procedure: If you have PPPoE (Point-to-Point Protocol over Ethernet) turned on for a DSL Internet connection, you won't be able to turn on AppleTalk using the Built-in Ethernet setting. Instead, you'll have to create a new configuration.

After you open System Preferences, click the Network icon, unlock the pane by clicking the lock in the lower left of the window, and type a password (if necessary).

1. Click the Show pop-up menu near the top of the Network pane and choose Active Network Ports.

2. Click the New button.

3. A sheet will slide down asking you to create a new configuration for a specific port. Select Built-in Ethernet from the Port pop-up menu.

4. Give your configuration a recognizable name, such as Ethernet with AppleTalk (**Figure 20.14**).

5. Click OK on the sheet.

6. Click Apply Now.

7. Click the Show menu again. Your new configuration (Ethernet with AppleTalk) now shows up as a choice, along with Built-in Ethernet and AirPort (**Figure 20.15**).

8. Select your new configuration. You can now make AppleTalk active.

Mac OS X will run both your new AppleTalk port setup and your PPPoE-configured port at the same time.

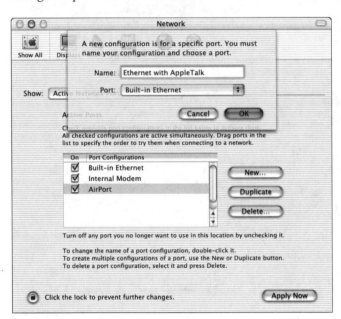

Figure 20.14

Giving your new configuration a name.

Figure 20.15

Your new configuration shows up as a selection in the Network pane.

The Lowdown on TCP/IP

Many users new to TCP/IP networking want a simple answer to the question, "How do I set up my Mac for IP networking?" Unfortunately, no simple answer works for everyone. How you configure TCP/IP depends on the type of network you have, how it is set up, and how you are connected to the Internet. Hopefully, by the time you finish this section, you'll be able to figure out what applies to your situation.

Your TCP/IP setup is based on the *IP address,* an identifying number that each computer has. You can either designate the IP (Internet Protocol) address yourself or set your Mac to get an address from one of several other sources. Depending on which you choose, you may have to specify several other related items.

Every Mac needs an IP address to identify itself on the network. Getting an IP address for your Mac is the central issue of setting up TCP/IP and is your first decision to make. These issues apply equally to Mac OS X and to Mac OS 9 and earlier.

A Mac can get an IP address in several ways. It can get an address from a DHCP server (such as the AirPort Base Station) or a PPP (Point-to-Point Protocol) server, or it can give itself an IP address. All these methods are called *dynamic addressing* because the IP can change whenever the Mac starts up. It can also change several times during the course of a day.

Static addressing is when the IP address doesn't change. Static addressing is manual addressing—you have to type an IP address and other information. This is more difficult, not only because of the typing involved but because you need to know the rules of IP addressing for the network to work.

We'll first look at the easy method, dynamic addressing, and then move on to static addressing.

Dynamic Addressing and Self-Configuration

The easiest way to configure TCP/IP in any Mac is to set it to use DHCP, which will work with or without a DHCP server. A DHCP server is software that gives IP addresses to computers on a network. These addresses can change every few hours or stay the same. DHCP servers can run on network servers such as Windows 2000 or XP Server or in Internet gateway software and hardware such as the AirPort Base Station.

If there is no DHCP server, the Mac will pick its own IP address, consistent with all the rules. This is similar to the way AppleTalk works, except that here you have to *tell* the Mac to go and do it. With TCP/IP, you have to configure the Mac to get its IP address via DHCP.

Another common dynamic-addressing scheme you can choose is using PPP. Your Mac gets an IP address from an Internet service provider's PPP server or PPPoE server (in the case of a DSL connection). You normally don't use PPP to get an IP address on a local network.

Two other choices for dynamic IP addressing are BootP and RARP, which behave similarly to DHCP but are older. If you don't have a BootP or RARP server, you should ignore these settings.

Along with the IP address, dynamic addressing also sets other data, such as the subnet mask. You may still have to enter certain information, such as the Name server (or DNS server) address.

Setting DHCP in Mac OS 9

In Mac OS 8 through Mac OS 9, you use the TCP/IP control panel to set DHCP:

1. In the "Connect via" pop-up menu, choose your network medium, such as Ethernet, AirPort, or PPP. (PPP here indicates a modem connection.) If you have third-party DSL connection software, you'll also see it listed here.

2. In the Configure via pop-up menu, select the method of getting an IP address (**Figure 20.16**). You may have a choice of manual, PPP Server, DHCP Server, BootP Server, or RARP Server, depending on the "Connect via" setting.

3. If you have a small network with no Internet connection, you may be finished with setup. If not, fill in any other fields as necessary (see "Other IP Configuration Settings," below), and close the TCP/IP control panel.

 AppleTalk (MacIP) can also appear in the "Connect via" menu. This allows you to connect to the Internet by "tunneling" IP through AppleTalk protocols. It's a holdover from the days when TCP/IP was uncommon on Mac networks.

Figure 20.16

Setting DHCP in the TCP/IP control panel in Mac OS 9.

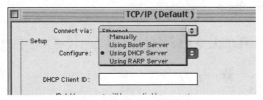

Setting DHCP in Mac OS X

 TCP/IP configuration in Mac OS X is different than in Mac OS 9, not only because of the new user interface but because TCP/IP support is improved in Mac OS X. In Mac OS 9 and earlier, you can create multiple TCP/IP configurations (for instance, dial-up, a local Ethernet setup, or a DSL Internet connection). You can switch between them, using one configuration at a time.

Mac OS X includes a feature called *multihoming,* which lets the Mac use multiple configurations at the same time and communicate over multiple network media simultaneously. It also lets you configure multiple IP addresses for different connections, even over the same Ethernet port.

1. Open System Preferences, and click the Network icon.

2. In the Show pop-up menu, select your network medium (Built-in Ethernet, AirPort, Internal Modem, and so on; **Figure 20.17**).

3. Make sure the TCP/IP tab is selected.

4. In the Configure pop-up menu in the TCP/IP pane, select the method of getting an IP address. You'll have a choice of PPP, DHCP, BootP, and possibly other methods. (The exact list changes with different network media and some of your other settings.)

5. Click Apply Now.

 If you have "Connect using PPPoE" checked in the PPPoE tab, you won't be able to choose DHCP. You'll have to create another configuration, described a little later in the chapter.

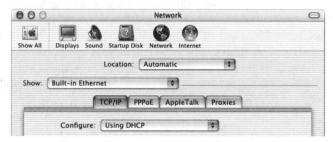

Figure 20.17

Setting DHCP in the Network pane of System Preferences in Mac OS X.

Static addressing. If you are going to set IP addresses manually, you need to follow some rules. This can be tricky—the Using DHCP setting works well in many situations (even without a DHCP server) and is a lot easier. However, if you need to set IP addresses manually, read on.

An IP address is in the form of four numbers from 0 to 255, separated by periods. For example, this is a valid IP address:

169.254.2.192

If your Macs aren't connected to the Internet, or they use a gateway, you can assign IP addresses from one of several private address ranges. A private IP address is one that isn't in use on the Internet.

Every computer *directly* connected to the Internet must have a unique IP address—no other computer anywhere on the planet that is directly connected to the Internet can have the same IP address. Because this would be difficult to manage, and because being directly connected to the Internet opens up some security problems, many networks use some sort of Internet gateway.

The Internet sees only the IP address of the gateway. The computers on the network use IP addresses that the world standards groups have designated as private addresses that the Internet can't directly see. (The Internet sees only the gateway, such as an AirPort Base Station or software Base Station running on a Mac.)

There are several private address ranges. One is the range that Macs give themselves when you set them to use DHCP (described in the previous section), which makes them a good choice for static addressing. These are IP addresses that start with 169.254. The range is:

169.254.0.0 to 169.254.254.255

Note that the last number can be 255, but the one before it can only go as high as 254.

Two other private ranges are:

10.0.0.1 through 10.255.255.254

192.168.0.1 through 192.168.0.254

If you manually configure the IP addresses of your Mac for a local network, you can use IP addresses from any of these ranges, as long as all the Macs on the network are in the same range. Also, two computers on your network can have the same IP address. Again, you cannot use these addresses to connect directly to the Internet, but you can use them to connect indirectly to the Internet through a gateway (such as an AirPort Base Station).

If you are configuring a server for the Internet, you will type an IP address given to you by your service provider. In this case, the IP address is not "private" but is in a range that can be seen on the Internet.

When you type an IP address, you may also have to give the Mac a subnet mask number, depending on your other settings. (If the Subnet Mask field appears, you need to type it yourself.) A subnet mask number is part of the addressing scheme that helps identify your Mac on a TCP/IP network. All Macs must have the same subnet mask. For a small local network, the subnet is usually:

255.255.0.0 or 255.255.255.0

In the next couple of sections, I look at how Mac OS 9 and Mac OS X handle static addressing. I assume you are running Ethernet, since that is typically where static addressing is used. However, you can also use it with an AirPort connection.

Static IP Addressing in Mac OS 9

To configure static IP addresses in Mac OS 9 and earlier:

1. Open the TCP/IP control panel. Set "Connect via" to Ethernet.

2. Select Manually in the Configure pop-up menu. Additional data-entry fields appear (**Figure 20.18**).

3. Type an IP address.

4. Type a subnet mask number.

5. Fill in any other required fields (see the section "Other IP Configuration Settings").

6. Close the TCP/IP control panel.

7. Click Save when prompted.

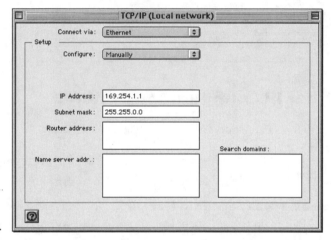

Figure 20.18

Static IP addressing in Mac OS 9 (basic user mode is shown).

Static IP Addressing in Mac OS X

To configure static IP addresses in Mac OS X:

1. Open System Preferences, and click the Network icon.

2. Choose Built-in Ethernet from the Show pop-up menu (**Figure 20.19**).

3. In the TCP/IP pane, select Manually from the Configure pop-up menu.

4. Type an IP address.

5. Type a subnet mask number.

6. Fill in any other required fields (see the next section).

7. Click Apply Now, and quit System Preferences.

Figure 20.19

Static IP addressing in the Network pane of System Preferences in Mac OS X.

Other IP Configuration Settings

Whether you are configuring your IP address dynamically (PPP, DHCP, or BootP) or statically, you may need to fill in some other fields. In Mac OS 9, these items go in the TCP/IP control panel. In Mac OS X, these items go in the TCP/IP tab of the Network pane of System Preferences.

 Domain Name Servers in Mac OS X. DNS servers associate IP addresses with IP domain names (such as apple.com). You will need to fill in this field if you are configuring a direct Internet connection or your local network has a domain server. You can leave this field blank if you are configuring a Mac for a small local network.

Name server addr. in Mac OS 9 or earlier. *Name server* here refers to the domain name servers. Here is where you type the IP addresses of DNS servers. This field is always shown, but you may not need to fill it, as described in the previous section.

 If you forget what these fields are for, in Mac OS 9 you can turn on balloon help (Help > Show Balloons). When you point to the field, a text balloon will describe it.

 Router address in Mac OS 9 or Router in Mac OS X: This appears only when you select Manually in the Configure menu and is used on large networks that have IP routers (not AppleTalk routers). It will be the router's IP address. If you have been given a static IP address from an Internet service provider, you will need this. If you have a small local network, you can leave this field blank.

Search Domains. This field typically contains the domain name of your ISP (such as mindspring.com). If you are part of a large local network, you many have one or more domain names to type as well. As with the other fields, you'll have to get these from your network administrator.

In Mac OS 9 and earlier, the "Connect via" menu offers the choice of AppleTalk (MacIP). This is a way to tunnel TCP/IP through AppleTalk networks. It is mostly a holdover from an earlier time when AppleTalk networks were more prevalent.

Creating and Using Multiple Configurations

In Mac OS 9 and earlier and in Mac OS X, you can create and save multiple TCP/IP configurations. For instance, you might want one for a DSL (PPPoE) Internet account, another for a backup dial-up Internet account, another for AirPort or Ethernet. You could also have multiple dial-up configurations for different locations on an iBook or PowerBook. In Mac OS 9, you can only run one configuration at a time. In Mac OS X, it is possible to run multiple configurations simultaneously.

In Mac OS, a TCP/IP configuration comprises all the IP settings for one type of access. Instead of messing with the settings, you just switch between them—at least, that's how it is in Mac OS 9 and earlier. In Mac OS X, it's even easier: You create as many configurations as you need, and that's it—they can all run at the same time, if you like.

You can create multiple configurations in the AppleTalk control panel as well. However, there is little need to do this with AppleTalk, as there is little to configure.

Multiple IP configurations in Mac OS 9. After you create your first TCP/IP configuration in Mac OS 9 and earlier, you create a second with the TCP/IP control panel open. You duplicate your current settings, create a new name for the duplicated settings, edit the settings, and save them.

1. Select Configurations from the File menu (or press ⌘K).

2. In the Configurations window, select your configuration. (Only one will appear if you've created only one.)

3. Click Duplicate.

4. A window opens asking you to name the new configuration. Give it a name that makes sense to you (such as dial-up link, New York office LAN, or DSL).

5. Click OK. You return to the TCP/IP control panel, but the title of the window is your new connection name.

6. Make the relevant settings changes.

7. Close the TCP/IP control panel.

8. Click Save when prompted.

Now when you want to switch between configurations, open the TCP/IP control panel and select Configurations from the File menu. Select the configuration you want to use, and click Make Active (**Figure 20.20**).

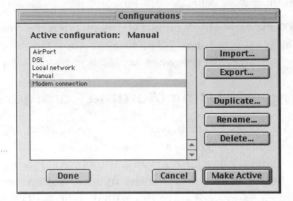

Figure 20.20

This Mac has several TCP/IP configurations.

Multiple configurations in Mac OS X. You don't have to switch between network configurations in Mac OS X (here they are called *port configurations*). Unlike Mac OS 9, Mac OS X can run multiple port configurations simultaneously. For instance, if you have one configuration to use Ethernet with a DSL Internet connection, you may want a second Ethernet configuration for a local network. Or, on a PowerBook or iBook, you may want multiple Ethernet setups or multiple dial-up settings for different locations.

To add a TCP/IP configuration in Mac OS X:

1. Open System Preferences, and click the Network icon.

2. The Show pop-up menu in the Network pane presents you with two or three configuration options: Built-in Ethernet, Internal Modem, AirPort (if you have an AirPort installed).

   If you want to configure one of these, select it now and configure it as needed, and go to step 9. If you want to create a new configuration, go to step 3.

3. Select Active Network Ports from the Show pop-up menu.

4. Click New. A sheet slides down asking you to create a new configuration for the port.

5. Click the Port pop-up menu on the sheet, and select Built-in Ethernet.

6. Give your configuration a recognizable name.

7. Click OK on the sheet.

8. Click the Show tab again. Your new configuration now shows up as a choice, along with Built-in Ethernet, AirPort, and Internal Modem (**Figure 20.21**).

9. Click Apply Now.

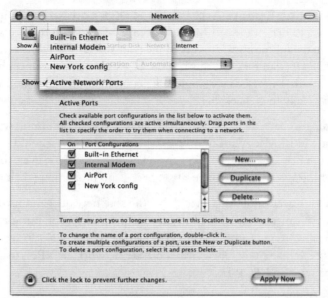

Figure 20.21

Your new configuration shows up along with the network media choices.

You can now change the order of the port configuration by dragging the configuration names up or down when you select Active Network Ports in the Show pop-up menu). Why do this? Because it determines the order in which they appear in the Internet Connect application. This can be handy, as having the configuration you use most at the top of the list means that it becomes the default in the Internet Connect application's Configuration pop-up menu, so you don't have to make a menu choice every time you connect.

As mentioned before, all of the Mac OS X network configurations can run simultaneously. However, you may not want them to. If you are configuring a PowerBook or iBook, the multiple configurations may be for different locations. You can turn port configurations off by selecting Active Ports in the Show pop-up menu of the Network pane and clicking the On check box next to a configuration's name (shown in Figure 20.21). When you turn a configuration off, the Show menu will no longer list it.

Finally, you can create several locations using the Location pop-up menu in the Network pane. By creating multiple locations, you not only save the configurations themselves but designate which ones are turned off and the order in which they are listed.

Remote Access: Dialing in to Your Mac

You can enable other Macs to dial directly in to your Mac for sharing files, printing, or accessing other network services. In Mac OS 9 and earlier, this can be done with AppleTalk or TCP/IP or both.

Mac OS X handles dial-in access only via TCP/IP.

Enabling Remote Access in Mac OS 9 and earlier. You can allow other Macs to dial in to your Mac using your Mac's Remote Access control panel. The default protocol used is AppleTalk. You also have the option of enabling TCP/IP (via PPP), but this is more of a security risk, as most hackers are working with TCP/IP. Since AppleTalk is not the protocol of the Internet, it is much less likely to be hacked.

You also have the choice of enabling access to an entire network or just the individual Mac. With network access turned on, you could print to a network printer or access a file server from another Mac. However, the network access setting is a security risk because there is no protection (such as a firewall).

Setting access for "this Mac only" (not the network) and using AppleTalk doesn't mean that your computer will be hack-proof, but it is the safer way to allow remote access. For secure remote access, you can set up a server with a firewall and possibly a virtual private network, or VPN, using third-party software and TCP/IP.

To enable a Mac to allow remote access:

1. Open the Remote Access control panel.

2. From the Remote Access menu select Answering.

3. In the Answering window, select the "Answer calls" check box (**Figure 20.22**). (You don't need to select "Allow TCP/IP clients to connect using PPP," as you'll be dialing in using AppleTalk.)

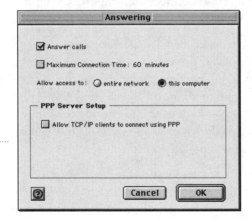

Figure 20.22

Setting remote access using the Mac OS 9 Remote Access control panel.

4. Click OK, and close the Remote Access control panel.

5. Now open the File Sharing control panel, and make sure that file sharing is turned on.

6. In the Users and Groups pane, double-click a user name or create a new user. If you want to dial in, double-click your name (identified as the "owner").

7. In the window that appears, select Remote Access from the Show pop-up menu. Now check the box next to "Allow user to dial in to this computer."

On the Mac that is dialing in, set up the Remote Access control panel with your desktop Mac's telephone number, your user name, and your password.

 Enabling Remote Access in Mac OS X. Remote dial-in access in Mac OS X is different from that in Mac OS 9. Mac OS X lets you dial in from a text-based terminal application. It also lets you enable other users to send Apple events to your computer, such as those used by AppleScript.

To enable remote terminal access in Mac OS X:

1. Open System Preferences, and click the Sharing icon.

2. Click the Application tab.

3. If you want to enable dial-in from a text-based terminal application, check the box next to "Allow remote login."

4. To enable other users to send Apple events to you, check the box next to "Allow Remote Apple Events." If you want Mac OS 9 users to be able to do the same, check the box below this one.

Built-in File Sharing and Web Services

The Mac provides several ways to share files. The traditional file-sharing service in Macs uses the AppleShare-compatible Apple File Protocol (AFP). You go to the Chooser and log in to a Mac or a server, and a network volume mounts on your desktop. In Mac OS X, you use the Connect to Server command in the Go menu.

In early versions of Mac OS, AFP only ran over AppleTalk. In Mac OS 9, AFP file sharing can run over both AppleTalk and TCP/IP. In Mac OS X 10.0 to 10.0.4, AFP file sharing ran only over TCP/IP. Apple restored AFP over AppleTalk with version 10.1 of Mac OS X.

Another Mac file-sharing method is called Web sharing. With this method your Mac becomes a mini Web server. Other computers access your files using a Web browser.

Mac OS X has some other file-sharing technologies. It includes SMB/CIFS, the Windows equivalent of AFP, which lets you log in to Windows servers. Mac OS X also has a built-in FTP server (users with FTP client software can access files on FTP servers) and an NFS, or Network File System, client. The NFS client lets you log in to NFS servers running on Unix or Linux machines to share files.

Log in to an AFP File Server or Another Mac

AppleShare-based AFP file sharing in Macs remained nearly unchanged for more than ten years until Mac OS X came along. With Mac OS X it has changed completely. In Mac OS 9 and earlier, you log in to another Mac using the Chooser or the Network Browser. In Mac OS X, you use the Connect to Server Command in the Go menu.

To log in to an AFP file server, you'll need to have AppleTalk turned on, or you may need TCP/IP configured.

Computers that support AFP file service over TCP/IP include Macs with Mac OS 9 or later, Apple's AppleShare IP, Windows 2000 Server and Windows XP Server with Services for Macintosh installed, and Linux servers with Netatalk installed. If you have Windows NT Server, you'll have to use AppleTalk.

The Chooser

The Chooser of Mac OS 9.2.1 is an old interface feature, originating in 1985 as a tool for selecting printers. (Mac OS X does not have a Chooser.) Today's Chooser hasn't changed much. It offers a mishmash of objects to select: nonnetwork and AppleTalk printers, AppleTalk-based file servers and Macs with file sharing turned on, and certain TCP/IP file servers and Macs. *All* of the file-sharing entities seen in the Chooser are AppleShare-based AFP entities.

 Strangely enough, Macs running Mac OS X versions 10.0.0 through 10.0.4 with file sharing turned on will show up in the Chooser of Mac OS 9 users. This is strange because the Chooser usually spots AppleTalk devices, and these old versions of Mac OS X do not use AppleTalk for file sharing.

To log in to another Mac or file server offering AFP file sharing:

1. Open the Chooser. Make sure that AppleTalk is set to Active.

2. Click the AppleShare icon.

3. In the area called "Select a file server" you'll see a list of computers offering file service via the AFP protocol (**Figure 20.23**). These could be Macs with file sharing turned on, Mac servers, Windows servers running Services for Macintosh, or a third-party AFP server. Select one and click OK.

4. The log-in window appears (**Figure 20.24**). Type a name and password, or select Guest.

5. A list of shared folders or drives appears. Choose one or more to mount, and click OK.

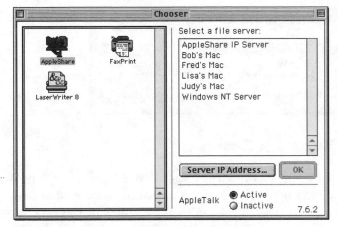

Figure 20.23

Selecting a file
server or Mac in the
Mac OS 9 Chooser.

Figure 20.24

The Chooser's log-in
window.

New projects

Figure 20.25

A mounted
network volume.

The shared volume appears on your desktop, acts like a disk, and has an icon
similar to that in **Figure 20.25**.

If you have full access privileges, you will be able to copy files to the disk and
see everything on it. Your access may be restricted, however. (See "Enabling
Others to Access Your Files," below, for more on access privileges.)

 **Once a network volume is mounted on the desktop, you can make an alias
of it. The next time you want to log in to it, just double-click the alias, and the
log-in screen will appear.**

If your network has AppleTalk zones set up, you will see them in the lower-left
of the Chooser. In this case, you'll have to select a zone before selecting a file
server in step 3 above.

Type the IP address of an AFP server. Some file servers running AFP
over TCP/IP will appear in the Chooser, but some may not. If a server isn't
showing up, try typing its IP address to access it: Click the Chooser's Server IP
Address button, and type an address in the dialog box that opens (**Figure 20.26**).

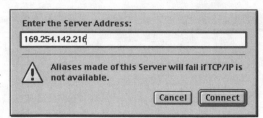

Figure 20.26

Typing an IP address to access an AFP file server in the Chooser.

Network Browser

The Network Browser in Mac OS 9 and earlier was supposed to be an update to the Chooser, but it wasn't particularly successful. It displays additional types of servers but doesn't really simplify the process of logging in to a server.

To log in to a file server using the Network Browser:

1. Select Network Browser from the Apple menu.

2. The Network Browser opens. Click the triangle next to either AppleTalk or Local Network (**Figure 20.27**).

3. If a list of computers appears, double-click one of them.

4. The same log-in window that you get from the Chooser appears (Figure 20.24). From here, the procedure is the same as logging in via the Chooser.

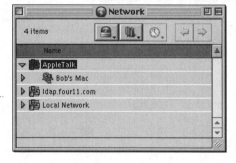

Figure 20.27

Selecting an AFP file-sharing computer with the Network Browser.

 You can use the Network Browser to add a server volume to the Favorites menu. To add an item, click the second button from the left—the Favorites button— at the top of the Network Browser. When you select a network volume in a favorites list, the log-in window appears.

Mac OS X Log in to AFP and NFS Servers

 Mac OS X doesn't have a Chooser. Instead, it offers the Connect to Server command in the Finder's Go menu (**Figure 20.28**). You can use the Connect to Server dialog to log in to AppleShare-compatible AFP servers as well as NFS servers, which usually run on a Unix or Linux host.

Figure 20.28

The Mac OS X Connect to Server dialog.

Mac OS X versions 10.0 to 10.0.4 cannot connect to AFP servers running on AppleTalk. You need at least version 10.1 of Mac OS X.

Here you can browse for AFP volumes or type in the names of AFP and NFS file servers or type IP addresses of AFP servers. (You can't browse for NFS servers.) The Connect to Server dialog also remembers the computers you've accessed recently. You can choose a server to log in to from this list.

You can't use the Network icon in the Finder's Computer view to access AFP and NFS servers. Only files on Unix networks will appear here.

When you type a server name or address and click Connect, or choose a server from the pop-up menu, you will be prompted for a name and a password. After you type these, the network volume will appear on the desktop and in the Finder's Computer view (**Figure 20.29**). As with Mac OS 9, this icon behaves as a mounted disk, letting you copy items to and from it, if you have the access privileges.

Figure 20.29

A mounted AFP network volume in Mac OS X; this is equivalent to the icon in Figure 20.25.

Log in to SMB (Windows) Servers

Server Message Block (SMB) is the file sharing protocol most commonly used with Windows networks. With Mac OS X 10.1 and later, you can log in to a Windows file server, a Windows PC with file sharing turned on, or a Linux machine running an SMB server:

1. Select the Connect to Server command in the Finder's Go menu.

2. In the Connect to Server window that appears, type an address for the server in this form:

Smb://computername/share

where *share* is the directory on the server you'd like to access.

3. Click Connect.

4. In the log-in window that appears, type your user name and password and the name of the Windows workgroup if you have one on your network.

5. Click OK.

Enabling Others to Access Your Files

Mac OS 9 and Mac OS X give you several ways to share files. The one you may be familiar with is traditional Mac file sharing, or AppleShare-based AFP file sharing.

Both Mac OS 9 and X have Web sharing, which is a newer form of file sharing that isn't as convenient but allows non-Mac users to access files on your Mac through a Web browser. Mac OS X can also share files using a built-in FTP server.

AFP-based file sharing. To enable users to access files on your Mac using traditional Mac file sharing, you need to take several steps. And because Mac OS 9 and Mac OS X are so different, the basic premises of what you can share and who can access it are different in these two systems.

Turn on File Sharing in Mac OS 9

You can initiate file sharing in two places in Mac OS 9: the File Sharing Control Strip module or the File Sharing control panel. (This control panel is called the Sharing Setup control panel in versions before Mac OS 8.)

First make sure that AppleTalk is turned on in the AppleTalk control panel or that TCP/IP is configured.

Don't turn off AppleTalk, or your Mac won't show up in other Macs' Choosers. If you want to keep AppleTalk off the network, use the Remote Only setting in the AppleTalk control panel.

1. Open the File Sharing control panel. Make sure it contains an owner name, a password, and a computer name.

2. In the Start/Stop pane, click Start to turn on file sharing. (File sharing can also be turned on in the Control Strip.)

3. If you want to share files over TCP/IP, check the box next to "Enable File Sharing clients to connect over TCP/IP" (**Figure 20.30**). If you see the message "IP address unavailable," then you haven't properly configured TCP/IP for a local network.

IP file sharing is not available in the Mac systems before Mac OS 9.

4. Go to the Finder and select the icon of a folder or drive to share. Choose Get Info > Sharing from the File menu.

5. In the Get Info window, check the box next to "Share this item and its contents."

If you want others to be able to access your Mac (in addition to yourself), you'll need to set access privileges and possibly create users or groups. I cover how to do that in a bit.

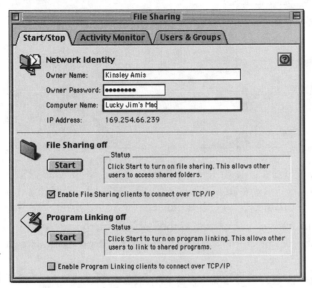

Figure 20.30

Turning on File Sharing in Mac OS 9.

Turn on File Sharing in Mac OS X

As with other settings in Mac OS X, you start configuring file sharing from the System Preferences application. First, make sure that TCP/IP is correctly configured or that AppleTalk is turned on in Mac OS X version 10.1 and later. You should also turn on AppleTalk if you want your Mac to appear in the Connect to Server and Chooser windows of other Mac users. Even if you are using TCP/IP, AppleTalk will enable browsing when turned on. (If file sharing is on, turn it off before you turn on AppleTalk.)

To turn on file sharing:

1. Open System Preferences, and select the Sharing icon.

2. In the Sharing pane, make sure the Computer Name field is filled in.

3. Click the File & Web tab.

4. Click the Start button under the words File Sharing Off in the top section (**Figure 20.31**).

5. Quit System Preferences.

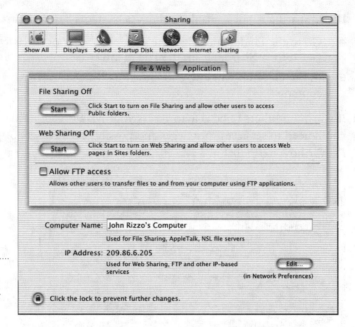

Figure 20.31

The Sharing pane in the System Preferences of Mac OS X.

Now it gets a little different from configuring in Mac OS 9. As the administrator, you can log in to your Mac's entire hard disk from another Mac (running Mac OS 9 or Mac OS X). However, other users who are not designated as administrators can only access the Public folder inside your home folder or their own home directories on your computer. (More about users in the next section.)

Users and Groups in Mac OS 9

After turning on file sharing, you're the only person who can access your files from another Mac. If you want other people to have access, you can create *users*. Different users can have different levels of access privileges. You can set it up so that some users can access certain folders or disks while other users access other folders. You can also set access privileges so that a user might be able to copy files to your Mac but not copy your files to his or her own Mac.

In Mac OS 9, file-sharing users are not the same as users of the Mac, as defined in the Multiple Users control panel. Network users are defined in the Users & Groups tab of the File Sharing control panel (**Figure 20.32**).

There will be two users to start with—you, the owner; and a user called Guest. People who log in as Guests don't need a password. Guest access is disabled by default, but you can turn it on by double-clicking the Guest user and by choosing Sharing in the Show pop-up menu. Then check the box next to "Allow guests to connect to this computer" (**Figure 20.33**), and close the Guest box.

Guest access makes network administrators nervous because of the lack of security. But if you have just a few Macs or a home network, and you'd rather not deal with passwords, Guest access is convenient.

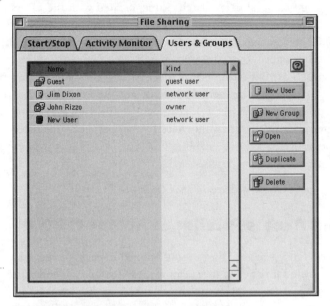

Figure 20.32

Creating File Sharing users.

Figure 20.33

Enabling Guest access.

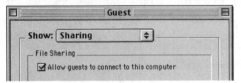

You can add new users by clicking the New User button under the Users & Groups tab in the File Sharing control panel. Giving a new user access to your Mac is the same as enabling Guest access, except you can add a password. Click the New User button, and in the New User dialog box that opens, choose Sharing from the Show pop-up menu. Check the box next to "Allow user to connect to this computer." Choose Identity from the Show pop-up menu. Type a password in the Password field.

 If you ever want to see who is logged in to your Mac, use the Activity Monitor pane of the File Sharing control panel. If you see someone who shouldn't be logged in, select that person's name here and use the Disconnect button to boot 'em off.

You can also use the New Group button in the File Sharing control panel's Users & Groups pane to create *groups*. You can give a group a set of access privileges for a shared folder. Instead of applying to one user, group access privileges apply to multiple users. Click the New Group button; a New Group window appears. Drag the users' icons from the Users & Groups pane into the group window, give the group a name, and close the window. The new group's name appears in the Users & Groups pane.

Users in Mac OS X

Unlike Mac OS 9, Mac OS X does not separate file-sharing users from users of your Mac—all users are the same, created with the Users pane of System Preferences. (Users also get FTP access.) Creating a user also creates a home folder for the user on your Mac, something you may not want to do. However, you don't need to create users in Mac OS X, since you can't give users access to much of your hard disk. If this is your Mac and you are a registered administrator, then you can get access to the entire hard disk. Other users are generally restricted to the Public folder in your home folder. Users who are not designated administrators cannot access other parts of your hard disk. Your Public folder also defaults to enabling Guest access. This is why you don't have to create users.

You can't create groups in Mac OS X file sharing.

Set Access Privileges in Mac OS 9

Access privileges are the settings applied to each shared folder or disk that determine if network users can read, write, or read and write files. To set access privileges, select the shared folder or disk by clicking it once. Go to the File menu and select Get Info. In the Get Info window that opens, choose Sharing from the Show pop-up menu (**Figure 20.34**). The figure shows sharing for a hard drive, but the procedure is the same for sharing a folder.

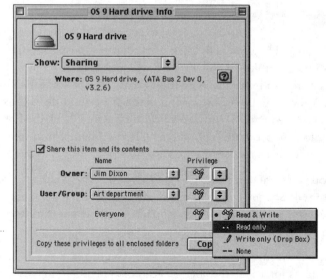

Figure 20.34

Setting access privileges for a shared hard drive or folder.

You can limit the access privileges for the Mac's owner (which is usually you if this is your Mac), for all users on the network, and for certain users or groups.

From the pop-up menus you can choose "Read & Write" (glasses and pencil icons), "Read only" (glasses icon), or "Write only (Drop Box)" (pencil icon). A write-only folder is called a *drop box*—users can copy files into it, but they can't open the folder to see what's inside.

Prior to Mac OS 8, you set access-privilege choices by selecting check boxes next to options instead of using pop-up menus.

Usually, you'll want to give the owner (yourself) read and write privileges. However, you can designate other people to be the owner of this shared folder if you wish.

Close the Get Info window when you're finished. You can set up sharing for additional folders the same way.

Set Access Privileges in Mac OS X

Setting access privileges in Mac OS X is similar to the procedure for Mac OS 9, except you are more limited as to what you can share. You can't share your entire disk, and it's best to share folders inside your home folder. (Again, as an administrator, you can get access to your entire hard disk over the network.)

In Mac OS X you select a folder in the Finder, choose File > Show Info (the Mac OS X equivalent of the Get Info box of earlier Mac OSs), and choose Privileges from the Show pop-up menu (**Figure 20.35**).

Figure 20.35

Setting access privileges for a shared folder in Mac OS X.

Using the FTP Server in Mac OS X

You can also share files through the Mac OS X built-in FTP server. One benefit of FTP is that any computer user (not just Mac users) can access your files with a Web browser or FTP client (such as Fetch).

To start up the FTP server in Mac OS X:

1. Open System Preferences, and click the Sharing icon.
2. In the Sharing pane select the File & Web tab.
3. Check the box next to "Allow FTP access."

Unlike Mac OS 9 and Mac OS X AFP file-sharing access, Mac OS X FTP sharing doesn't let you set guest access (which is called *anonymous user* access in FTP-speak). To access your Mac's files via FTP, people must be set up as users in the System Preferences' Users pane. Users get access to whatever folders you have set access privileges for as long as they are in your home folder or the users' home folder.

You can log in to the Mac OS X FTP server using an IP address shown in the Sharing pane of System Preferences. For example:

ftp://169.254.66.238

Type your name and password, and leave the Account field blank.

Web-based File Sharing and Mini Web Servers

You have two ways to make files available to users with Web browsers:

Web Personal NetFinder (Mac OS 9 only). Folks on a network can use a Web browser to view a Finder-like list of Mac folders and files in a Web browser. Users can open folders and download the files from the Mac. These include non-HTML files, such as word-processor, graphics, and desktop-publishing documents.

Mac OS X replaced Personal NetFinder with an FTP server, which is simpler to set up. (The Mac OS X FTP server is described in the previous section.)

Personal Web Sharing (Mac OS 9 and Mac OS X). This turns a folder containing HTML files (Web files) into a mini Web server. Users view HTML pages in a Web browser.

Web Sharing and Web Serving in Mac OS 9

Enabling either Personal Web Sharing or Personal NetFinder starts with the Web Sharing control panel. The procedure is similar, except that in the case of Web Sharing you select an HTML file to be the home page of your mini Web site.

To share files:

1. Open the Web Sharing control panel (**Figure 20.36**). Click the top Select button to choose a folder or hard drive to share; in the dialog box that opens, navigate to the folder and click Select.

2. In the Web Sharing control panel, click the Select button next to Home Page. When a dialog box appears asking you to "Select a document in the web folder to use as your home page," click None. This is the Personal NetFinder option.

3. You can select "Give everyone read-only access" if you like.

4. Click Start.

Instead of setting read-only access for everyone, you can determine access by selecting "Use File Sharing to control user access." With this selected, you must have File Sharing running in the File Sharing control panel. You can then limit access to a user or a group. However, write privileges here are limited to replacing HTML files of the same name already in the computer (if the browser supports uploading).

If you want to create a mini Web server via Personal Web Sharing, choose a folder containing HTML pages (such as the Web Pages folder that comes with Mac OS 8.x and 9.x). You then use the Web Sharing control panel to select one of your HTML files as a home page. Next, select the "Give everyone read-only access" option, and click Start to publish the Web site.

Figure 20.36

Don't select a home page when you're setting up Web Sharing to share your files with other users.

Turn on Web Sharing in Mac OS X

Web Sharing in Mac OS X is faster than in Mac OS 9 because it uses the industry-standard Apache Web server. However, you don't have to deal with Web-server software, and turning a folder containing HTML files into a mini Web server is easier than in Mac OS 9.

1. Place your Web site files in the Sites folder inside your home folder.

2. In System Preferences, click Sharing.

3. In the Sharing pane select the File & Web tab.

4. Click the Web Sharing button.

That's it. In their Web browsers, users can type the IP address shown in the Sharing window and view the Web pages in the Sites folder of your home folder.

Sharing Printers

Since 1985, Macs have had the ability to share laser printers. In fact, sharing laser printers was the first reason to create a Mac network. Not all laser printers are network printers, but those that are—such as some of the trusty old Apple LaserWriters and Hewlett-Packard LaserJets—can plug in to a network directly and don't need to be connected to a Mac or a server. Many network laser printers use AppleTalk, but some use TCP/IP.

Since 1985, inkjet technology has improved while prices have crashed, making inkjet printers far commoner than laser printers. Apple took its first stab at sharing inkjet printers on a network with Grayshare, software that once came with Mac OS. However, Grayshare only worked with the old Apple StyleWriters.

Today, Mac OS 9 comes with USB Printer Sharing. It can share USB inkjet printers from a variety of manufacturers over a network. The USB Printer Sharing software uses TCP/IP, while the old Grayshare used AppleTalk. (Epson and Hewlett-Packard also sell software that enables their inkjet printers to be shared over a network.)

 At the time of this writing, Mac OS X did not have the ability to share USB printers over a network.

Mac OS 9 USB Printer Sharing utility. The USB Printer Sharing utility can share USB printers with other Mac users on the network. It consists of an extension file and a control panel. USB Printer Sharing first shipped with Mac OS 9.1. You can install it on Mac OS 9.0 and 9.0.4 after downloading it from Apple's support site (www.info.apple.com/support/downloads.html).

All the Macs that are going to use the printer need Mac OS 9.x and the Printer Sharing software. You'll also have to install the printer's driver on all the Macs that need to access the printer.

Printer Sharing works over an Ethernet or AirPort wireless network but uses TCP/IP instead of AppleTalk. This means that the Macs need to have TCP/IP set up in the TCP/IP control panel.

To share a USB printer connected to your Mac:

1.   Plug the printer into the Mac's USB port, and turn it on.
2.   Open the USB Printer Sharing control panel, and in the Start/Stop pane click Start (**Figure 20.37**).

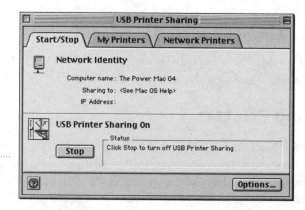

Figure 20.37

The USB Printer Sharing control panel.

3. Now go to the My Printers pane, and click the Share check box next to your printer's name.

4. Drag the printer to your desktop. This creates an Internet location file.

5. Move this file to the other Macs on the network using file sharing or e-mail.

6. On the other Macs, drag the Internet location file into the Network Printers pane of the Printer Sharing control panel.

Users on the other Macs can now select the shared printer in their Choosers.

Networked laser printers in Mac OS 9. The easiest-to-use network laser printers are AppleTalk printers, which are also PostScript printers. You don't need to configure them for sharing—just plug them in to the network. Network printers can have an Ethernet port or the older LocalTalk port (see the "Extinct Ethernet" sidebar, earlier in the chapter.)

Network laser printers show up in the Chooser when you click the LaserWriter 8 driver icon. LaserWriter 8 is a generic PostScript driver and should work with any PostScript printer. Other drivers, such as those from Adobe or HP or those that came with the printer, may offer additional functions.

Since TCP/IP isn't as simple as AppleTalk, it takes more effort to connect to a TCP/IP printer.

TCP/IP Printers

If your network laser printer supports IP, you can use TCP/IP instead of AppleTalk. There are drawbacks, however. TCP/IP doesn't report as much information back to the user as AppleTalk can, so you may not get the printer-out-of-paper error message that you do with AppleTalk.

You need Mac OS 8.1 or later. Here's how you set up IP printing:

1. Open the Desktop Printer Utility on your Mac's hard disk (or on your Mac OS CD-ROM).

2. Under Create Desktop, click Printer (LPR) and then OK. (LPR refers to the *line printer remote* protocol, originally from Unix.)

3. In the next window, click your printer on the list of PostScript Printer Description files and then click Select.

4. The next window that opens lists your printer along with an "unspecified Internet printer."

5. In the next window, enter the IP address or domain name of the printer. (If you haven't configured the printer yourself, you'll need to get this info from your network administrator.)

Networked laser printers in Mac OS X. Mac OS X recognizes USB printers right away, but you have to tell it to connect to network laser printers. You do this with the Print Center utility, located in the Utilities folder inside the Applications folder.

1. Launch Print Center. The Printer List window opens. You'll see your USB printer listed if you have one.

2. Click the Add button, and click the pop-up menu, which reads Directory Services. You're given a choice of printer connections: AppleTalk, LPR Printers using IP, and USB.

3. If you have an Apple LaserWriter, select AppleTalk. After a few seconds, your printer will show up in the Printer List window (**Figure 20.38**).

4. Click Add, and you're done.

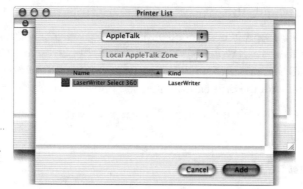

Figure 20.38

Adding a network laser printer to Print Center's print list in Mac OS X.

If you have a non-Apple laser printer you may have to do some work before you open Print Center. If Mac OS X doesn't include the PPD (PostScript Printer Description) files for your printers, you'll have to supply them yourself. Hewlett-Packard has a Mac OS X printing-software package that installs a set of PPD files for all LaserJets in Mac OS X. (At press time this was at www.hp.com/cposupport/printers/software/ljmacosx_en.hqx.html.) The HP installer says it's putting them in the Applications folder, but this is incorrect. It puts them here:

System/Library/Printers/PPDs/Contents/Resources/English.lprog

(If you downloaded PPDs in languages other than English, you'll find them in the appropriately named .lprog folder.) You can also copy your PPD files from Mac OS 9 to the above directory (they are in the Printer Descriptions folder in the Extensions folder inside the System folder).

With the PPD files in place, go back to Print Center. Your printer should show up in Print Center when you click Add Printer. If it doesn't, use the "LPR Printers using IP" option instead of AppleTalk. You'll need the printer's IP address.

21

The Internet

. . . .

Jonathan A. Oski (JO) is the chapter editor and coauthor.

*Timothy Aston (TA), Andrea Dudrow (AD), Tara Marchand (TM), and Phil Strack (PS)
are the chapter coauthors.*

*Steven Bobker (SB), Joseph O. Holmes (JH), and David J. Swift (DJS) edited earlier
editions of* **The Macintosh Bible,** *from which portions of this chapter are taken.*

The Internet has become so interwoven with personal computing that the boundary between your desktop and the Net is a blur. Apple's initiatives to integrate the Macintosh user experience with the Internet—such as through its unique iTools—have proved to be visionary and are still unequaled on any other mass-market desktop platform. Despite all the changes that the Internet has already gone through, the turmoil that started in late 2000 has led many Internet industry observers to say that the Internet is still in its infancy and we are likely to see continual rapid evolution of the medium, its services, and how it integrates with our computing experience.

In this chapter you'll learn how to get your Mac connected to the Internet—how to make sure you have the right hardware and software, choose an Internet service provider (ISP), and pick the right plan. Web browsers provide the foundation for most of your use of the Internet. You will learn how to pick the browser that best suits your needs and how to tune your browser preferences for maximum functionality and performance. Choosing an electronic-mail (e-mail) application or service is another important step in maximizing your Internet experience; we go over the nuances of the popular e-mail applications to help you ferret out the package that works best for you.

The Mac OS and Apple's Web site offer many great services. Sherlock makes searching the Internet part of the Macintosh experience. Apple's iTools services offer a suite of features to Mac users such as free Web disk space, hosting, and content filtering.

Read on to get started using your Mac on the Internet and make the most of your Internet experience.

In This Chapter

Getting Connected (TM)

As recently as 1996, getting connected to the Internet was a difficult proposition. Mac users were forced to seek out, install, and configure their own networking software, since most of it didn't come with the operating system. Setting up modems often meant editing raw scripts, a task not for the faint of heart. Finally, wrestling with the proprietary settings of different vendors' equipment and the often Mac-hostile support departments of ISPs caused endless headaches.

Connecting a Mac to the Internet is much easier today. The system software now includes everything necessary for networking, and Apple has simplified its configuration with the Internet Setup Assistant. The company also includes third-party Internet applications, such as Microsoft Internet Explorer, on the hard drives of new computers. In addition, the Mac's hardware is more Net-friendly than it used to be. For example, new machines are equipped with modems, and all include the hardware required to connect directly to a high-speed network.

Another benefit to prospective Internet surfers is the quantity and quality of access options. The number of ISPs increased dramatically during the 1990s, and in the past year many companies have started to offer high-speed Internet access through such services as digital subscriber line (DSL), cable modem, or integrated services digital network (ISDN).

The bottom line is, connecting a Mac to the Internet still isn't quite as easy as using a telephone, but it is getting closer.

What You'll Need

To successfully connect to the Internet, your Mac needs to meet certain hardware requirements, and it should also contain a basic set of Internet software.

Hardware. At a minimum, you'll want a Macintosh equipped with a PowerPC processor, preferably a G3 or G4 chip. The Mac should also have at least 64 MB of memory (RAM) if you are running Mac OS 9 and 128 MB if you are using Mac OS X: More is better. Finally, as a general rule, your Mac's hard drive ought to have a capacity of at least 1 GB. Although you may be able to upgrade your computer's RAM or hard drive, if the processor is too slow, you're better off getting a new machine. The iMac was designed for people unfamiliar with the Internet (and computers in general), but it's also an excellent choice for experienced users. To view Web pages at a reasonable size and resolution, you'll need at least a 15-inch monitor—and a 17-inch monitor is ideal. Less important—but still nice—are external speakers, which improve the experience of audio and multimedia.

The most basic, and common, way to connect is known as *dial-up,* which involves using a *modem* (technically called a *modulator-dem*odulator) over existing analog phone lines. Modems that transfer data at a rate of 56 Kbps are the norm, and many new Macs come equipped with them, but you may be able to get away with using a 33.6 or even 28.8 Kbps modem. Most modems can also transmit and receive faxes, with the appropriate software. Modems are available for every model of Mac, old or new, and can be hooked up externally or internally. Mac-friendly modem manufacturers include Global Village (www.globalvillage.com) and 3Com U.S. Robotics (www.usr.com).

High-speed, dedicated network connections using DSL, cable modem, or ISDN usually require that your Mac have an Ethernet port. Again, new Macs come with these built in, but for older machines that don't, you can purchase Ethernet cards or adapters by manufacturers such as Asanté (www.asante.com) and Farallon (www.proxim.com). These connection methods frequently require additional, external hardware, which is often sold or leased by the service provider. DSL is a newer type of connection that digitally transmits data over phone lines; cable modem is usually provided by the same company that offers cable TV services; and ISDN is an older kind of high-speed access that also operates over phone lines.

Software. The oldest version of the Mac OS you should use with Internet-enabled Macs is System 7.6.1. Mac OS 8 is even better, and the latest versions of the Mac OS—9 and X—are ideal, because they include such amenities as Sherlock, which allows the use of multiple Web search engines at once. Mac OS X takes things a bit further in terms of ease of use. You can use one System Preferences panel, Network, to configure all your Internet connection settings.

To make a dial-up connection to the Internet, your Mac needs several pieces of software, which are included in the Mac OS: In Mac OS 9, you need Remote Access (inelegantly called OT/PPP in older versions of the operating system) and the TCP/IP control panel; in Mac OS X, you need Internet Connect and the Network System Preferences panel. Remote Access and Internet Connect enable your modem to dial in to your ISP, and TCP/IP allows your computer to communicate with other machines on the Internet, once a connection is established. Many ISPs distribute software installers that automatically configure all the networking software, and some also provide customized Web browsers and e-mail packages.

 The most popular of these automated configuration tools is Internet Setup Monkey from Rockstar Software (www.rockstar.com). It does a great job of making all the setting changes for you in one fell swoop. (JO)

Once you're connected, you'll probably be interested in two main activities: surfing the Web and sending and receiving e-mail. The most basic Internet application is the Web browser, and the two most popular are Microsoft

Internet Explorer and Netscape Navigator (the browser component of Netscape Communicator). Internet Explorer, currently at version 5, comes bundled with Mac OS and on new Macs. It offers a host of specialized features, including an auction manager, a page holder, and a scrapbook. Communicator, which offers many features in addition to the Navigator browser, is currently at version 4.78; Navigator, as of this writing, is available in version 6.1. [*Although version 6 has been out for some time now, the version 6.0 uptake was slow. Most users complained about poor performance or improper display of certain sites built for earlier versions of Navigator or Internet Explorer.—JO*] Navigator (which used to be the name of the whole product) was the de facto browser in the early years of the commercial Internet. Today it's less popular than Internet Explorer, but it's still a viable program and is preferred by those who don't want to use a Microsoft product. (However, Mac users might want to think twice about scorning Microsoft Internet programs, since the company's offerings for the Mac OS are surprisingly strong.) Whichever browser you choose, you shouldn't use a version earlier than 4.0.

Unless you choose to use Netscape Communicator, which includes a full-featured e-mail module, you will need to select an e-mail application. Two of the most popular are Microsoft Outlook Express and Qualcomm Eudora. Like Internet Explorer, Outlook Express comes bundled with the Mac OS and new Macs. Eudora is often favored by e-mail power-users. It's available in three forms that vary in price and features. Both Outlook Express and Eudora include standard amenities such as address books and filters. Web-based e-mail services are also popular. Some of the most widely used services are offered by Hotmail, Yahoo, and Netscape. These accounts offer the convenience of being accessible from any location via a Web browser.

(See the sections "Using Your Browser" and "E-mail," below, for in-depth discussions of these features.)

Choosing a Method and a Provider

Before you go online, you must decide on a connection method. The most popular is dial-up; less common, but increasingly popular, are DSL, cable modem, and ISDN. You will also need an account with an ISP. These companies essentially set up high-capacity connections to the Internet and then rent out their bandwidth to consumers and businesses.

Connection options. Dial-up access typically costs $20 to $30 per month, compared with DSL, cable, and ISDN, which often cost between $50 and $70 per month for consumer-level access. If you're in a reasonably large metropolitan area, chances are good that you will be able to sign up for either DSL or cable-modem service. If it's available, and if you're serious about surfing the Internet, DSL or cable Internet access is the way to go: The connections are significantly faster than those provided by dial-up modem, and in most cases they are more convenient. However, dial-up access is still useful for connecting on the go, from different locations.

Dial-up Internet access has been available for many years and is the mostly widely used method. The first major ISPs to offer this service started to appear in the early 1990s, and nowadays the service is available everywhere. Many dial-up packages include one or more e-mail accounts plus room on a server for a personal Web site. Depending on whether your ISP is a local or a national provider (see the following section), you're given a list of phone numbers you can use to connect. Each time you want to connect to the Internet, you have to tell your computer to dial the modem. If you plan to dial up frequently and for long periods of time, you may want to have separate voice and data lines.

DSL access is becoming more and more popular as its availability increases. It is usually offered by special DSL providers who have partnerships with particular ISPs, mostly in major metropolitan regions. A DSL connection is always on—you don't have to worry about dialing in and hanging up. DSL is available in different flavors, but the most common is asymmetrical DSL, or ADSL. Unlike other types of connections, ADSL has faster download and slower upload speeds, meaning you'll be able to retrieve files from the Internet more quickly than you'll be able to transmit files from your computer to another system. Also, different levels of DSL service provide different download and upload rates. Consumer-level packages typically offer slower speeds (starting at 384 Kbps download, 128 Kbps upload) than those targeted for businesses (as fast as 1.5 Mbps download, 384 Kbps upload). DSL operators often provide DSL modems and sometimes Ethernet cards, if necessary, to customers. Regardless of who your provider is, your local phone company will need to split your phone line before DSL is actually installed. If line sharing isn't available in your area, the phone company can install a second line that will be dedicated to the DSL connection or prepare an existing second line for DSL access.

 You should be aware that the DSL industry fell on hard times in 2000 and 2001. If you're going to go with DSL, select your ISP very carefully. Many users were suddenly left without an ISP when DSL providers such as NorthPoint and HarvardNet declared bankruptcy in 2000. (JO)

Cable modem is another fairly new, increasingly popular option. As you might expect, it's offered by the same companies that provide cable television and it runs over the same wires. Service providers will also often supply customers with the necessary cable-modem and additional hardware. Like DSL hookups, cable-modem connections are always on, and they're generally rated faster than DSL. However, there's one caveat: As more people in an area use cable modems, the lines get congested, and all users' speeds drop.

Rounding out the major Internet connection methods is ISDN. Before DSL and cable-modem services became widespread, ISDN was the only type of high-speed access available to consumers, but it has been eclipsed by the newer services. It's also slower, operating at speeds of between 64 and 128 Kbps. Unlike dial-up and DSL, ISDN operates over special digital phone lines, which you must order from your phone company, and as with dial-up, you must manually initiate the connection.

Local vs. national providers. When choosing an ISP, you need to decide how much you want to pay and what services you require. Another important decision is whether to go with a local or a national provider. Each has its pluses and minuses. For instance, local companies may be able to provide more personalized service, but they may not have the resources that bigger companies do. Also, local ISPs may not have as many dial-up numbers, in as many places, as national providers.

America Online is the largest ISP in the United States, claiming more than 31 million subscribers. The company offers its own, proprietary Internet software that includes e-mail and Web-browser capabilities as well as custom content and advertisements; however, AOL subscribers can use other programs, such as Internet Explorer, with the company's service. AOL's popularity is not surprising: The service is easy to use, and free CDs containing AOL's software are everywhere. But some more sophisticated Net users find AOL's lack of high-speed connection options (it's only a dial-up ISP—you can access the service from a high-speed connection but you'll be paying twice for your Internet service) and its restrictions too limiting.

In January 2000 Apple inked a deal with EarthLink, the No. 2 Internet service provider, which claims 4.9 million subscribers. EarthLink is now the default ISP on new Macintoshes. Unlike AOL, EarthLink offers DSL service in addition to standard dial-up service, and it doesn't require special software. AOL and EarthLink provide large numbers of dial-up phone numbers around the country, and for frequent travelers, these national services can be a boon.

For homebodies who have decided against a large company, a local ISP may be the best choice—if you can find one, as many small ISPs gradually have been bought out by larger providers. Local ISPs often have better reputations for customer service than larger companies.

 A couple of good resources to use when searching for an ISP are The List (http://thelist.internet.com) and www.thedirectory.org. (JO)

Ten Questions to Ask an ISP (SB)

The most important factor in effectively using the Net is finding the best possible Internet service provider. When picking an ISP, you need to get the right answers to several questions. Here are the top 10 questions and some answers.

1. What's the monthly cost? About $22 a month for unlimited hours is fair. You should consider hourly connect-time charges only if there isn't a local ISP that offers unlimited hours.

2. Does the ISP provide at least 5 MB of storage for a personal home page? [*In my experience, 5 MB is generous; 2 MB seems to be typical.—JH*] [*It is also worth finding out who manages your Web pages. Can you upload changes directly, or does someone on the ISP staff publish them after you have copied them to the server?—JO*]

3. What is the server software? It's likely to be some flavor of Unix, but you might get lucky and find an ISP running a Mac-based operation. If you plan an elaborate Web site, running it on a Mac-based server will be beneficial.

4. What are the technical-support hours and policies? Are there specialists in Mac technical support?

5. Who supplies the software, and can popular tools such as Eudora, NewsWatcher, and Netscape Communicator be used, or are you restricted to proprietary software? Although using the popular tools is slightly more difficult, they offer many more options and the ability to quickly stay on top of the technology as it advances.

6. Are dial-in locations local calls? Is toll-free service or some low-cost method available for checking in while traveling? How many dial-in numbers are there?

7. Does the news feed get all Usenet groups, and does it ever "miss" messages? Most ISPs miss some; you want to miss as few as possible. [*I've also noticed that some ISPs try to play censor and refuse to carry certain newsgroups. If you want them all, make sure the provider doesn't censor any.—JO*]

8. Do all call-in nodes support V.90 modems at 56 Kbps? You don't want anything else, even if you currently have a slower modem.

9. Can you run CGI scripts—scripts that run on the server to enable more powerful capabilities such as forms—and if so, in what language? The programming language PERL is ideal on Unix-based servers.

10. Is there a trial period? What happens if you sign up and then get solid busy signals from dawn to midnight?

Using Your Browser (AD)

If you want to explore the World Wide Web, you're going to need software to do it with. That's what a Web browser lets you do.

Web Basics

Nearly everyone has heard of the World Wide Web. But what exactly is this so-called Web, and how is it different from this Internet we've also heard so much about? Well, it's pretty simple, really. The Internet, which came about 20 years before the Web, is what it sounds like: an interconnected network of computers all over the world. When you dial up your Internet service provider, you are taking a place on that network, and from there you can access any other computer, or server, on that network.

HTML. The Web is one means of using the Internet (e-mail is another). Since text is much easier to send over the Internet—it takes up less space, or bandwidth, than images, and every computer can understand it regardless of operating system—a while back some clever academic figured out a way to use text to represent graphic layouts, containing images and colors. This is accomplished with HTML (Hypertext Markup Language) tags, or bits of text, to denote various graphic elements such as font, color, and page-layout characteristics. You use a Web browser to translate the HTML sent over the Internet into the graphic images it represents. (If you want to see what a Web page looks like before your browser makes it all pretty, choose Page Source from your browser's View menu in Navigator or Source from the View menu in Internet Explorer; **Figure 21.1**).

Figure 21.1

Choose Source from Internet Explorer's View menu (left) to see a Web page's underlying HTML code (right).

URLs. Every site on the Web has an address, also called a *URL* (for Uniform Resource Locator). You visit a site by telling your Web browser to look up that address on the Internet. A Web address usually, but not always, looks something like this: *www.webaddress.com*. Almost every Web site also has links to other sites. These are special hot spots on a page that will take you to another page when you click them. Links are usually underlined and appear in a different color from the rest of the text. In addition, when you move your mouse pointer over a link, it will turn into a pointing hand.

Browsers. There are two "major" Web browsers (called major because almost everyone uses one or the other of them) and a smattering of other ones (see "Alternative Browsers," later in the chapter). The major browsers are Microsoft Internet Explorer and Netscape Navigator (see the "Software" section of "What You'll Need," earlier in this chapter, and the sections detailing both browsers' features, later).

The good news for all of us is that both of these browsers are free. You can download them from Microsoft (www.microsoft.com/mac/) and Netscape (http://home.netscape.com/products/). If you prefer to have your software on CD, both Microsoft and Netscape offer this option for less than $10.

The browser you choose really depends on your preference. Traditionally, Mac users have tended to choose Navigator, because it's been around longer and it's not a Microsoft product. However, version 5 of Internet Explorer supports more Web standards (these are the technologies that the World Wide Web Consortium, a panel of Web experts, has developed so that every Web page will appear the same in every browser window) than version 4.7 of Navigator. Navigator 6.1, however, looks to be pretty much neck and neck with Internet Explorer: There are not enough differences between the two to base your decision on anything other than pure preference. Or you can do what I do: use both.

Managing Bookmarks (AD)

The more you browse the Web, the more Web pages you will come across that you'd like to visit again. Of course, you will bookmark those pages so you don't lose their URLs (by pressing ⌘D in either Navigator or Internet Explorer). Eventually you will end up with quite a collection of bookmarks, and you'll probably want to organize them somehow, so you don't have to scroll through the entire list every time you're looking for a specific Web address. In this section, I use the generic term *bookmarks* to refer to what Navigator calls Bookmarks (**Figure 21.2**) and what Internet Explorer calls Favorites (**Figure 21.3**).

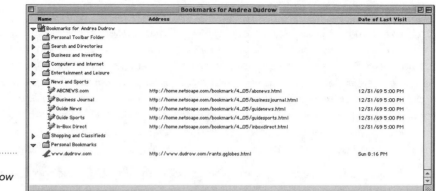

Figure 21.2

Working in the Bookmarks window in Navigator.

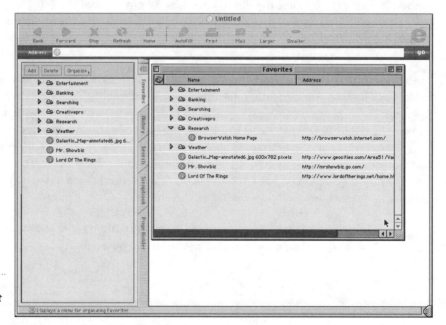

Figure 21.3

Organizing Favorites in Internet Explorer.

Luckily, Internet Explorer and Navigator each handles bookmarks in relatively the same fashion, so if you learn how to use them in one browser, you can easily use them in the other. To make it even easier, you can think of the bookmarks window as being something like your Mac's Finder. Just as you want to organize your files and programs into different folders so you always know where everything is, you will want to organize your bookmarks in specific folders so you know where they are.

In Internet Explorer you can create and organize bookmarks and folders directly within the Favorites panel in the Explorer Bar; in Navigator you open the Bookmarks window by choosing Edit Bookmarks from the Bookmarks menu. You can also work with Internet Explorer in this way by choosing Open Favorites Window from the menu that appears when you click and hold the Organize button in the Favorites Panel or by choosing Organize Favorites from the Favorites menu.

continues on next page

Managing Bookmarks continued

Both browsers have options for creating new bookmark folders in their respective bookmark windows. I find it's best to organize bookmarks by topic, so I have folders in my browser with such names as Entertainment, Banking, Searching, Cooking, and Weather. Once you have created and named the folders you want, you can drag and drop bookmarks into specific folders. If you are doing this directly within Internet Explorer's Favorites panel in the Explorer Bar, be sure to click and hold a bookmark before dragging it, so Internet Explorer doesn't think you are trying to load that URL. You can also put folders within folders, as you can do in the Finder. Both browsers let you put dividers between groups of bookmarks or folders to help organize them.

If you are using Internet Explorer, you can add a bookmark to a specific spot in your bookmark hierarchy by dragging the @ sign that's next to the bookmark's Web address in the Address box to the place where you'd like the site to live in the Favorites panel of the Explorer Bar. In Navigator you can do this by dragging the bookmark icon that's next to the Web address into the desired spot in the open Bookmarks window. This saves time organizing and will keep your bookmarks from becoming an unruly mess.

In addition, both major browsers let you specify certain bookmarks to appear on a bar at the top of your browser, underneath the Address box. In Internet Explorer this area is called Toolbar Favorites; in Navigator it's called a Personal Toolbar. Each browser comes with a folder with this name in its bookmarks window—simply drag the URLs of your favorite sites into this folder to have them appear on the toolbar. Personally, I don't find that this option offers any additional convenience, so I've configured both of my browsers not to show this toolbar. You do this in Navigator by deselecting Personal Toolbar in the Show section of the View menu, and in Internet Explorer by deselecting Favorites Bar in the View menu.

 Another great tool for managing URLs is Alco Blom's URL Manager Pro ($25; www.url-manager.com). It's inexpensive and powerful.

Setting Internet Options

If you are using Mac OS 8.6 or later, you have probably noticed a control panel simply called Internet (**Figure 21.4**). In Mac OS X, it is a System Preferences panel. This handy little innovation lets you enter all the settings for your Internet applications in one place. Of course you can also enter your settings in each of your programs—e-mail client, Web browsers, newsgroup clients—but why make more work for yourself when your computer will do it for you?

The handiest feature of the Internet control panel is that you can create multiple sets of Internet information. For instance, if you do most of your work on a PowerBook, you can have a set to use while you are at home logged in to your personal ISP, another set for using at work when you are plugged in to a network, and still another set to use if you are traveling and need to connect to the Internet from a hotel room or someone's house. Since I try never to leave my house, I have just one set.

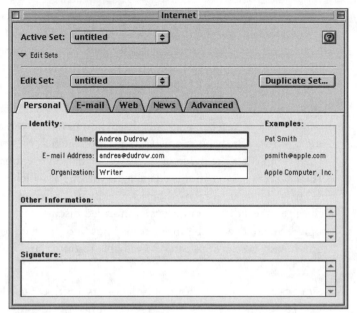

Figure 21.4

The Internet control
panel in Mac OS 9.

Personal. Mac OS 9's Internet control panel has five tabs; Mac OS X has four. Under the tab called Personal you enter information about yourself: your name as you would like it to appear in Internet communications such as e-mail, your e-mail address (this is generally your *username@isp.com,* but you may, like me, have an e-mail address other than your default one, and in this case you would enter the address at which you want people to send you mail), and your organization (I enter my title here instead; Figure 21.4). The Internet panel in Mac OS X lacks this tab.

E-mail. Under the E-mail tab in Mac OS 9 and the Email tab in Mac OS X, you enter your user account ID (the user name your ISP gave you), your incoming-mail-server name (this is often *pop.isp.com,* but check with your ISP to make sure), your e-mail password (you've also set this with your ISP), and your outgoing mail-server name (usually *smtp.isp.com,* but again, check with your ISP). In this panel you can also set your default mail application. You may have more than one mail application on your Mac—both Internet Explorer and Netscape Communicator come with e-mail clients, and you may prefer a different one. The one you specify here will be the one that opens when you click any links on the Web that send e-mail messages.

Web. The next tab is the Web tab, where you can specify a home page (this is the page your browser will go to when you click the home button) and a default search page (we will talk more about searching on the Web in the section "Where to Visit"). You can also tell your computer where to put files you have it download from the Web. I like my downloaded files to go directly to my Desktop so that I always know what I'm getting. You may prefer to specify a folder on your hard drive. You can also set a default Web browser under the Web tab. This will be the browser your Mac opens when you tell it to find a certain Web page by searching the Web from Sherlock, for instance. This doesn't mean you have to use only that browser—you can always open another one by clicking its application icon in your hard drive.

News. Thousands and thousands of newsgroups are out there, each with a different topic. These are text-only discussion lists, and you access them using a browser or through a news application such as NewsWatcher. In this part, you can enter the name of the news server you use most often (see the "Usenet" section, later in this chapter) or the one at which you are a registered user. These days many things are taking the place of newsgroups, including e-mail discussion lists and threaded discussions on Web sites, and people who are new to the Internet may not find the need to use them. Nonetheless, newsgroups can be a valuable resource, and it can't hurt to check them out.

Advanced. Mac OS 9's control panel offers a fifth tab used to specify advanced Internet settings such as screen fonts, firewall information, file helpers (programs that are invoked automatically when certain file types are downloaded—StuffIt for compressed files is a good example), and hosts (for telnet, gopher, archie, and so on).

 iTools. Mac OS X's Internet panel has an iTools tab. Here, you can set your iTools member name and password. At the bottom of the panel is a Sign Up button that gets you started with iTools.

Managing Security, Cookies, Passwords (AD)

Do you remember those commercials a few years back that depicted a group of people sitting around talking, their conversation going something like this?

"Do you think it's safe?"
"I don't think it's safe."
"Well, I think it's safe."

They were talking about submitting credit card numbers over the Internet. We all know now that submitting credit card information over the Web is about as safe as using a credit card in a real-world store—the inherent risks are just not enough to keep most people from purchasing items on the Web. Of course, just as in the real world, you'll want to make sure you feel good about a store before you give it your money.

Security

You'll also always want make sure that your connection to the Web site you are purchasing from is secure. This means that any information you send over the Internet will be encrypted so that third parties can't intercept it in transit. You have a few ways of doing this. First, if you use Internet Explorer, make sure your browser's security preferences are set to tell you when you are entering a page that is secure (go to the Preferences window, click Security, and choose from the notification options). Netscape automatically tells you, whenever you submit a form, whether it is secure or not. You can also find out if a page is secure by looking at the little padlock icon in the bottom-left corner of both browsers—if the padlock is closed, you're in a secure site; if not, the site is not secure.

Still, I like to be selective about when and where I enter my credit card numbers on the Web. Some sites—Travelocity.com (www.travelocity.com), for instance—let you try out their services a couple of times as a guest and then require you to give them your credit card number. I don't like to give anyone my credit card number unless it is for a specific purchase, so I have a sneaky way of getting around that requirement. This is where cookies come in.

Cookies

Cookies are bits of information that sites you visit leave behind on your computer so that the next time you visit, they will know who you are. When using cookies first came into practice, many folks derided them as invasions of privacy. There are, however, many valid reasons to accept cookies. As discussed elsewhere in this chapter, lots of portal sites on the Web let you personalize them—you tell them what kinds of news and information you are most interested in. The only way these sites can remember who you are is by leaving a cookie behind. This is also how sites such as Travelocity.com remember how many times you've already been there as a guest without entering your credit-card information.

If you use Internet Explorer, you can view all the cookies you have downloaded (you'll be surprised at how many there are) and delete the ones you don't want around anymore, such as the ones from Travelocity.com in this example (**Figure 21.5**). Do this by clicking Cookies in the menu at the left in your Preferences window. You can also use this screen to configure Internet Explorer to notify you of incoming cookies so you can accept or reject them, or just have it download them in the background, as I have my browser set to do.

Figure 21.5

You can use the Cookies screen of Internet Explorer's Preferences window to see which cookies you have downloaded and delete any you don't want, as well as to set the cookie notification.

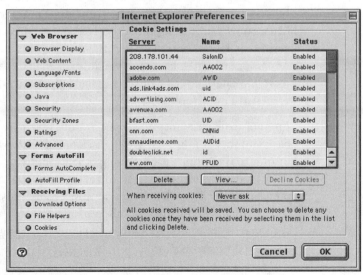

continues on next page

Managing Security, Cookies, Passwords   *continued*

If you are using Netscape, click Advanced in the Preferences window to tell the browser when to accept cookies and when not to. Netscape, however, won't let you view and delete the cookies you've already accepted.

Passwords

Many Web sites also ask you to set a user name and password for yourself so that you can sign in whenever you visit. In fact, so many sites require passwords that if you're not careful you can end up with a whole jumble of passwords without knowing which corresponds to which site. I only have three or four passwords I use every time I'm asked to set one; that way I have a greater chance of picking the right one when signing in to a site (I use one mostly for Web-based e-mail, one for online banking, and so on). Most sites will also let you set a prompt to remind yourself of your password if you forget—something like your mother's maiden name or the city where you were born.

You can use various Web-based services and software to remember all your user names and passwords, but you're better off using passwords you'll be able to remember—but make sure they include letters, numbers, and symbols to make them harder to guess. You should also consider changing your passwords periodically to protect against an instance where someone else knows your password.

Microsoft Internet Explorer

For the past few years Microsoft has devoted more energy to developing software for the Mac, and one of the results has been a much more Mac-like look and feel to some Microsoft products. Internet Explorer 5.0, Macintosh Edition (www.microsoft.com/mac/), which you can download free from Microsoft's Web site, is one of these products. Version 5's toolbar icons have a gelatinous look to them (for the true aficionados among you, this look, called Aqua, appears in the icons and windows of Mac OS X), and you can configure them to match the color of your Macintosh (choices include the iMac colors as well as PowerBook Black).

Internet Explorer comes with basic buttons on the toolbar—arrows for moving back and forward through a Web session and buttons to stop a page from loading and to print a page, among others—but you can add new buttons to your toolbar by choosing Customize Toolbars from Internet Explorer's View menu (**Figure 21.6**). When you do this, a page loads in your browser that shows you all the toolbar buttons available; you can add these buttons to your version of Internet Explorer by simply dragging them from the browser window onto the toolbar.

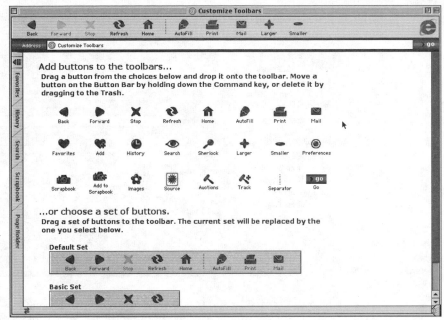

Figure 21.6

You can customize Internet Explorer's toolbar icons by choosing Customize Toolbars from the View menu.

Internet Explorer Preferences control panel. Before you start surfing the Web, you'll want to configure Internet Explorer's preferences to the settings you prefer. Choose Preferences from the Edit menu. On the left side of the Preferences window is a menu of the aspects of Internet Explorer for which you can set preferences. There are a few, and it isn't necessary to change all of them from their default settings. We'll go through them, one by one.

The first selection under the Web Browser heading is Browser Display (**Figure 21.7**). If you set a home page in the Internet control panel (see "Setting Internet Options," later in this chapter), that page should appear in the Home Page section here (it opens when you click the Home button in the toolbar). At the bottom of this section is a box you can check if you want Explorer to load that page automatically when it starts up. If your home page is a place you will go to every time you open your browser—a search or news page, for instance— check the box. Since my home page is my personal Web site, which I don't need to see every time I open Internet Explorer, I prefer to have the browser start out with a blank page. In the Toolbar Settings section you can specify whether you'd like icons and text or just one or the other on your toolbar.

The next screen, Web Content, lets you specify colors for links and text on Web pages you visit. Of course, many Web pages will override these color preferences, so don't expect to see them everywhere you surf. The rest of this screen lets you set preferences for things such as sounds, scripting, plug-ins, and images. I generally leave these settings on their defaults (except that I hate it when Web pages play sounds, so I turn that option off).

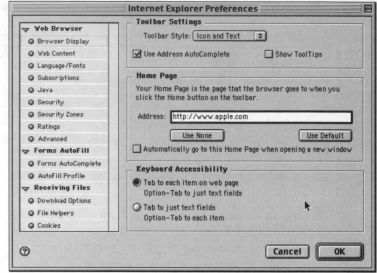

Figure 21.7

The Browser Display screen in Internet Explorer 5's Preferences window.

This is followed by the Language and Fonts screen. Language is easy enough—set the one you understand (that's English for me). What you set in the Fonts section depends on what fonts you have installed in your Mac. When Web designers make Web pages, they generally specify a group of fonts for each section of their text. For instance, they might set a paragraph to be viewed in a sans-serif font, but since they can't tell which sans-serif fonts are installed on your computer, the Web page looks for just that—any sans-serif font. The Fonts section of the Language and Fonts screen is where you tell the browser which sans-serif font to use when a page specifies this group.

Next comes the Subscriptions screen. Let's say there's a Web site you visit frequently. Wouldn't it save you time if you knew when the content on that site had changed? That way you wouldn't have to wait for it to load in your browser to find out if there was any new information on it. Internet Explorer lets you subscribe to sites and notifies you when those sites' content changes. You subscribe to a site by choosing Subscribe from the Favorites menu in Internet Explorer when that site is loaded in your browser window. Then you can go to the Subscriptions screen of your Preferences window and tell Internet Explorer how often you would like it to check those sites for changes and how you would like the browser to notify you. In addition, you can always choose Update Subscriptions from the Favorites menu to immediately check for changes.

In the Java screen you can turn Java on or off. Java is a language for writing applications that can be used with any operating system, as long as a Java Virtual Machine is present. You're in luck, because the Mac OS comes with one of these virtual machines. Internet Explorer automatically knows to use this virtual machine, and when you have the Enable Java box checked, you can use Java applications on the Web, within your browser's window. (Many interactive games you can play over the Web are Java-based. Others are made with Shockwave or Flash. There's more about this in the "Plug-Ins" sidebar.) A few years back, when Java technology wasn't as stable as it is now, I routinely left this box unchecked. Today, however, you can check it without fear of incompatibilities. Unless you are a Java expert, however, you're probably better off leaving the rest of the options in this screen on their default settings.

In the Security screen you can tell Internet Explorer to alert you when you enter pages and submit forms that are not secure. If you are new to the Web, you might want to keep all these options checked so that you can get a sense of what kinds of things are handled securely (that is, coded so they can't be intercepted out in the ether between your computer and the computer it is talking to—the one hosting the Web site you are visiting). However, these alerts can get annoying after a while, so you'll probably want to eventually turn them off.

We won't go into the Security Zones or Ratings screens; unless you really know what you're doing, you should probably leave these at their default settings, as they won't affect your browsing experience much.

 If you are getting annoyed by frequent security messages when browsing to sites, your security settings are most likely too restrictive. Try changing them to the next lowest level to see if some of the messages disappear. (JO)

You will, however, want to take a look at the Advanced screen of the Internet Explorer Preferences window (**Figure 21.8**). Indeed, it's unclear why Internet Explorer calls this screen Advanced, as it contains settings most people will want to configure for themselves. First of all, you can set Internet Explorer to remember Web sites you have visited, in case you want to return but haven't added them to your Favorites (this is covered in "History" in a page or two). These links will appear on the History panel of your Explorer bar (we also talk about the Explorer Bar later). I have mine set to remember the last 150 sites I've visited; if you browse the Web a little less than I do (which is quite a bit), you may want to have Internet Explorer remember fewer sites.

 If you don't want to leave tracks to the sites you've visited, you should clear your history. This is handy when you share a computer with others (in a computer lab or at home, for example) and don't want anyone who is snooping to find out where you've been. (JO)

You'll also want to configure cache settings here. *Cache* is a section of space on your hard disk that Internet Explorer sets aside to hold information about Web sites you have already visited. This way, if you return to that Web site, your computer doesn't have to download all of its elements all over again— they are already there. Set a size for this space on your hard disk; I have mine set at 5 MB. Remember, elements on Web pages generally aren't very big, which is how they can download quickly enough to keep you interested, so you don't really need too much cache space to hold them.

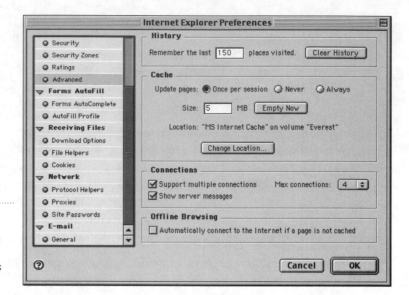

Figure 21.8

You can use the Advanced screen of the Preferences window to set Internet Explorer's cache size.

If you use Mac OS 9 and have a broadband or other high-speed Internet connection, you should consider placing your browser cache on a RAM disk. Use Mac OS 9's Memory control panel to create a 5 MB RAM disk, and then set your Internet preferences to use this space for cache. (JO)

You can also use the Advanced screen to configure Internet Explorer to support multiple connections. This is handy if you'd like to download more than one file at a time or visit more than one Web page. There is also a setting for offline browsing here; see the sidebar "Offline Browsing" for details.

In the Forms Autofill screens you can enter information about yourself. Then, if you are filling out an online form, you can simply click the Autofill button in Internet Explorer's toolbar to enter this information in the corresponding sections of the online form. This feature appeared in Internet Explorer 4.5 for the Mac, and I find it immeasurably handy not to have to type my name and address every time a form asks for this information.

In the Download Options screen, under Receiving Files in the menu, you can set the folder where Internet Explorer will deposit files it downloads from the Internet. As I mentioned earlier, I prefer my downloads to go directly to the Desktop. You generally won't need to make any changes to the File Helpers screen, so we'll skip over this part, as well as the Cookies screen, which we discuss in the sidebar "Managing Security, Cookies, Passwords."

You can probably skip the rest of the settings in the Preferences window, as they are either already configured with the information you entered in the Internet panel or are simply not necessary to most browsing needs.

Now we're finally ready to start surfing the Web with Internet Explorer. Start by entering the address you want to visit in Internet Explorer's Address box (this is the blank space to the right of the @ symbol right under the toolbar). If there is already an address there—for the last site you visited, for instance—you can press ⌘L to automatically select that address and replace it with another.

Explorer Bar. The Explorer Bar is the multitabbed section on the left side of your browser window with five tabbed panels—Favorites, History, Search, Scrapbook, and Page Holder—that provide helpful features for your Web-browsing experience. To expand or close the Explorer Bar, click any tab.

If there are Web sites you visit frequently, you'll want to add these to the Favorites panel (**Figure 21.9**). You can do this by choosing Add Page to Favorites from the Favorites menu, by clicking the Add button in the Explorer Bar's Favorites panel, by clicking the Add button in the toolbar if you have chosen to add this one using the process described above, or simply by pressing ⌘D. (See the sidebar "Managing Bookmarks" for more on organizing your Favorites.)

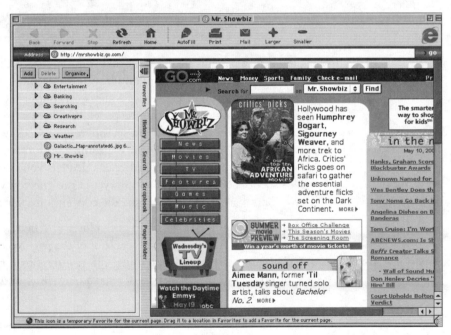

Figure 21.9

You can add a URL to a specific place in Internet Explorer's Favorites panel by dragging and dropping it.

The History panel in the Explorer Bar shows a list of the Web sites you've been to; the list is as long as you've told Internet Explorer to make it in the Advanced screen of the Preferences window. So you don't have to scroll through the whole list (mine is 150 sites long!), Internet Explorer automatically organizes the sites in folders based on the dates you visited them (**Figure 21.10**).

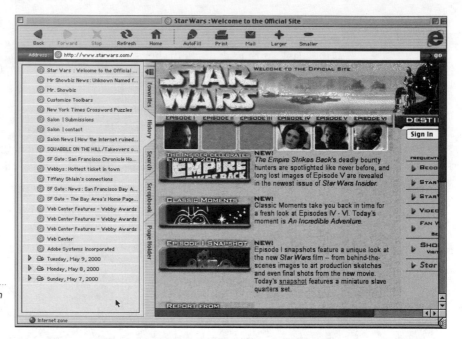

Figure 21.10

The History panel in Internet Explorer's Explorer Bar.

After the History panel is the Search panel. You can search the Web by typing the address of a search engine in the Address box (see the section "Where to Visit," below), but Internet Explorer also lets you conduct searches from this panel. Click the Search tab to open the panel. You'll see a list of various kinds of searches you can conduct. You can set different services to use for each of these types of searches by clicking the Customize button at the top of this panel. When you do this, a dialog box opens that lets you choose from lists of various services (**Figure 21.11**). However, if the one you want to use isn't there, you can always go to its Web site the conventional way.

The Scrapbook panel is new in Internet Explorer 5. When you click Add in this panel, Internet Explorer takes a snapshot of the page you are currently visiting. I haven't yet had occasion to use this feature, but I imagine it would come in handy if I wanted a picture of what a frequently updated Web site looked like on a day, say, last week.

The Page Holder panel can come in handy if you have chosen to conduct a Web search. When you search, you'll get a list of links for Web pages. If you follow any of those links, you'll generally have to click Internet Explorer's Back button to move back to the search page and the rest of the links. This is where the Page Holder comes in handy. Click the Add button at the top of this panel, and your search results will move into the Page Holder panel; any link you click will open in the main window. Click Links to view only the links in your search results page.

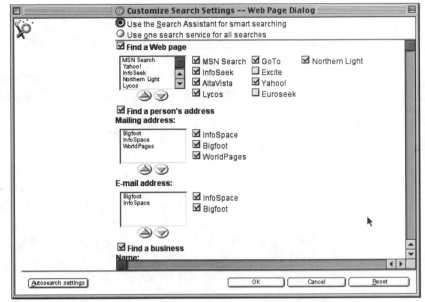

Figure 21.11

To customize
Internet Explorer's
Search panel, click
Customize and then
choose from the
search options in
the window that
opens.

A few other notes for using Internet Explorer. If you have a slower
Internet connection and don't want to wait for all those images to load, you
can simply turn them off in the Web Content screen of the Preferences window (uncheck the box next to "Show pictures"). Then, if you want to see the
images at any time, choose Reload Images from Internet Explorer's View menu.

You'll find, while browsing the Web, that there are lots of great, if low-resolution,
images on sites that you visit. If you want to download one of these images to
your computer, click it and hold. In the pop-up menu that appears, choose
Download Image to Disk (**Figure 21.12**). Be sure to check on any applicable
copyrights before you use any of these images.

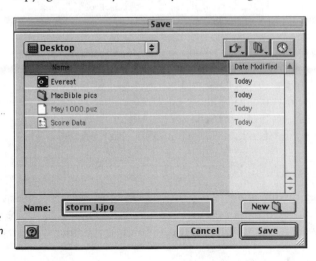

Figure 21.12

To download an
image from a Web
site, click and hold
on the image,
choose Download
Image to Disk from
the pop-up menu,
and save the image
to your hard drive in
this dialog box.

Netscape Navigator

Netscape Navigator was at one time the preferred Web browser of most Mac users. Netscape was seen as a sort of David to Microsoft's Goliath, and Mac users, who had already decided not to use Windows, traditionally tended to keep their machines as free of Microsoft products as possible. All this has changed, not only because Microsoft has actually put a lot of effort into producing good Mac-specific software but because Netscape itself is now part of a huge corporate juggernaut: America Online.

When AOL announced that it had purchased Netscape back in 1998, many people were surprised. However, the acquisition made good sense for both companies: The proprietary browser that AOL was distributing to its millions of customers wasn't nearly as well developed as Navigator and didn't adhere to many Web technology standards (those World Wide Web Consortium guidelines for developing Web pages). Also, Navigator was fighting a losing battle with Microsoft's Internet Explorer for a majority share of the Web-browser market.

Today, with AOL behind it, Netscape has the marketing and financial power (as well as the ready-made customer base of AOL subscribers) it needs to make sure that Navigator continues to be a player on the Web-browser circuit. Though version 6 (available as a free download at www.netscape.com) is the first full revision of the browser in years, Navigator has managed to keep its sometimes tenuous hold on its portion of the market. By the way, the reason Netscape decided to skip version 5, the company says, is that the new version ended up with so many new things packed into it that it deserved a higher number.

Speaking of all those extra features, those of you with older computers that may be slower or have less RAM installed than most modern machines may want to stick with Internet Explorer or a previous version of Navigator. Navigator 6.1, at a recommended 28 MB or RAM, is a bit of a memory hog, and the combination of all its new features may cause it to move too slowly for comfort on computers more than a few years old.

Since Navigator and Internet Explorer do basically the same thing—that is, translate text-based code into pictures and Web sites—it's relatively easy to use one if you already know how to use the other. With version 6, Netscape has made its browser even more similar to Internet Explorer than before, so switching between the two is even easier. However, there are several differences in the way the two handle basic functions, and it can't hurt to familiarize yourself with both browsers.

To begin with, you'll notice that although the buttons on Navigator's toolbar look different from the buttons on Internet Explorer's toolbar, they have the same names and for the most part do the same things (**Figure 21.13**).

Figure 21.13

The toolbar buttons on Navigator 6.1 look different from Internet Explorer's but do most of the same things.

In version 6, Netscape lets you change the toolbar button set. You change toolbar buttons in the browser's Preferences window, as I discuss in a bit. A button you won't see on Internet Explorer is My Netscape, which takes you to a page on Netcenter, Netscape's portal site (a portal site is one from which you can access a whole range of information, such as weather, sports, news, and Web-based e-mail services; **Figure 21.14**).

Figure 21.14

Netcenter, the portal site you are taken to if you click the My Netscape, Search, or Shopping button in Navigator.

All manner of portal sites are out there, and most allow you to customize them so that you get just the information you want whenever you load them; you don't have to use Netcenter if you don't want to. We'll talk more about portal sites in the "Search Engines" section, later.

Navigator 6 (also known as Netscape 6) may take some getting used to for those who have used a previous version or who are used to Internet Explorer. The History panel, for instance, which appears as a regular menu item or toolbar icon in both Internet Explorer 5 and Navigator 4.7, is located in the Tools submenu of the Tasks menu in Navigator 6. Also, though Navigator 6 has an expandable toolbar called My Sidebar on the left side of the browser window that looks similar to the Explorer Bar in Internet Explorer, Navigator 6's is used to store content from other Web sites (more on how to configure this later), whereas the Explorer Bar is used to store your own settings, such as Favorites and History.

Navigator 6 has also changed the location of the Security button. In version 4.7 it appeared as a padlock icon in the toolbar—in the new version it is a much smaller icon in the bottom right-hand corner of the browser window. However, clicking this will still call up security information for the Web page you have loaded. This can be good stuff to know if you plan to do something such as submit a credit-card number over the Web, although almost any site that offers shopping has a secure method of doing this.

Let's look at Netscape's Preferences window, which is a little bit different from Internet Explorer's but not that different from the Preferences window in Netscape 4.7 (**Figure 21.15**). The Appearance screen lets you decide which parts of Communicator you want to be displayed when you start up the program. In addition to Navigator, Communicator comprises an e-mail client and a (somewhat primitive but easy-to-use) Web-page editor for making your own site. Since I use other software for these things, I have only Navigator checked here.

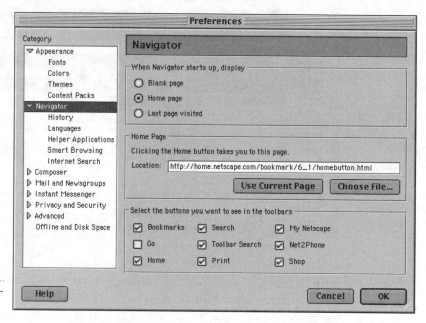

Figure 21.15

The Preferences window in Navigator.

The Fonts and Colors sections are almost exactly the same as those in Internet Explorer's Preferences window. I generally leave these on their default settings, but you can override the fonts and colors specified by the Web page's designer and replace them with your own choices.

New in version 6 is the Themes section of the Preferences window. You may have already noticed that Navigator 6 has a whole new look and feel—the buttons and icons have all been redesigned. If you don't like the new look, however, you can switch back to the old icons by choosing the Classic theme in this section. If you want another new look, you can download additional themes from the download area of Netscape's Web site.

The Navigator screen lets you decide whether you want the browser to go to a specific page upon opening it or start with a blank page. Again, I like to start with a blank page since I never know where I'll want to go on any given day. You can also type in the URL of your home page here; this is the page Navigator will load when you click the Home button in the toolbar.

Navigator treats the History function a little differently than Internet Explorer does. With Navigator, you tell it how many days you want it to remember the Web sites you've been to, while you tell Internet Explorer how many Web sites to remember. There are pros and cons to both methods; it really comes down to which you prefer. Navigator also lets you specify a number of Web sites to remember in the location bar—that's the space at the top of the browser window where you type the URL of the site you want to visit. Clicking the arrow to the left of that space will call up a list of previously visited sites—as many as you like.

In the Smart Browsing section of the Preferences window, you can enable something called Internet Keywords, which will allow you to enter phrases like "shop clothes" into the location bar and find Web sites that will allow you to do just that. The nifty little What's Related feature from Navigator 4.7 is standard on version 6 (you can't turn it on or off as you could in the previous version). To the right of the address box is a button called What's Related (**Figure 21.16**). When you click this, a pop-up menu appears, containing a list of sites related to the one you are currently visiting. This can be nice if you are new to the Web and would like a sampling of the variety of sites out there.

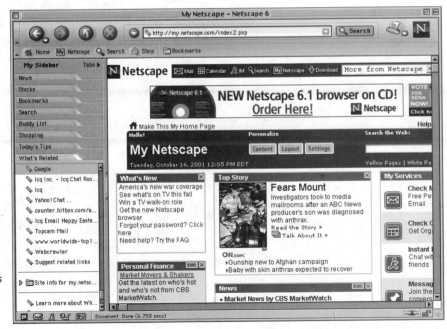

Figure 21.16

Click the What's Related tab to get a pop-up menu that gives you information about Web sites that may be similar to the one you are visiting.

We'll skip the settings for mail and newsgroups, as those are covered elsewhere in this chapter, and move to the Advanced screen. Here you can enable technologies such as Java and JavaScript (a technology for creating interactive Web elements). If you want to get the most out of your Web-browsing experience, I recommend keeping all of these on. The only exception might be if you have an extremely slow Internet connection and can't wait for different data types to download. In that case, you'd want to keep these turned off and download items on a case-by-case basis.

In the next section you can set your cache—the amount of space on your hard drive that you want Navigator to set aside for storing elements from Web pages it has downloaded. I don't like to set aside more than 5 MB (about 5,000 KB) for cache.

When it comes to actually surfing the Web with Navigator, you'll find it's similar to Internet Explorer. To get to a Web site, you type the address in the address box under the toolbar; in Navigator you can also press ⌘ Shift L to open the Open Location dialog box, which lets you type a URL to visit (**Figure 21.17**). As with Internet Explorer, pressing ⌘ D in Navigator adds the current page to your Favorites (except that Netscape calls them Bookmarks). In both browsers you can click the Reload button if you think some elements of a Web page are missing.

Figure 21.17

You can type the URL you wish to visit in the Open Location dialog box; when you click Open, Navigator will load that Web page.

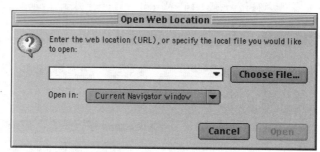

One of the major new features in Navigator 6 is the My Sidebar panel. You'll notice that this area comes preconfigured with a variety of tabs (for example, the What's Related tab and the Search tab, which lets you choose Web search engines to search simultaneously—a big timesaver). You are by no means required to keep those tabs—click the Tabs button in the top right of the panel to change the tabs that appear there. Selecting Customize Tabs in the menu will call up a window with a list of possible tabs, including any type of content you can think of—from wedding dresses to gardening to celebrity style (**Figure 21.18**).

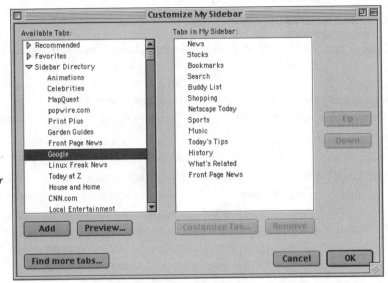

Figure 21.18

One of the great new features of Netscape 6 is the My Sidebar panel. It can be customized to include personal preferences for what content you use on a frequent basis (click the Tabs button and then Customize Tabs in the menu to get the Customize Sidebar window).

Finally, Navigator 6 has one more place you can click to navigate around and find content on the Web—the small buttons near the top of the browser window that read Home, My Netscape, Search, Shop, and Bookmarks (**Figure 21.19**). Clicking one of these will take you to a page full of search engines or shopping sites, or help you manage your bookmarks.

Figure 21.19

The small buttons near the top of the browser window can help you navigate the Web and manage your bookmarks.

Offline Browsing (AD)

There are many reasons why you might want to look at a Web page without being connected to the Internet. You could be using a connection that charges per unit of time, or you might have Internet access only at school or at work and want to view a Web page on a computer at home. Luckily both Navigator and Internet Explorer let you download a copy of a Web page—all of the images, HTML code, and links—so that you can look at it while you are disconnected.

To download a copy of a Web page in Internet Explorer, choose Save As from the File menu. In the dialog box that appears, select Web Archive from the Format menu and then click Options. In the Site Download Options dialog box that opens, you can choose which elements and links from a Web page you would like to download and save for later viewing (**Figure 21.20**). Remember that most Web pages have lots of links, and downloading all the information on the other end of those links could take up a considerable amount of space. Internet Explorer lets you specify how many links deep in a page you want to go and which data types you would like to download. Unfortunately Navigator does not offer a Web archive download option, so you're stuck with either text or source code, and no images.

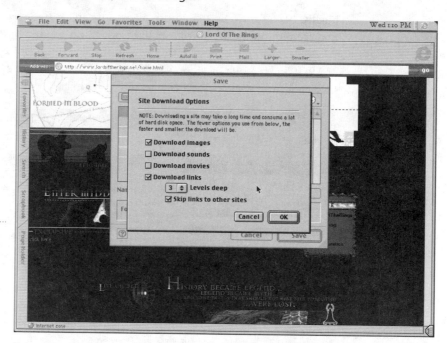

Figure 21.20

In the Site Download Options dialog box in Internet Explorer you can specify options for downloading Web pages to view offline.

Both browsers, however, let you switch between online and offline modes (**Figure 21.21**). To transfer into offline mode, simply choose Offline > Work Offline from Internet Explorer's File menu or Offline from Navigator's File menu. If you want to reconnect to the Internet, choose Work Online from the File menu in both browsers.

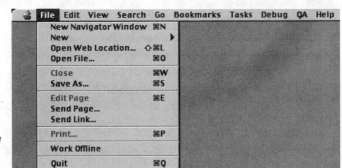

Figure 21.21

Choose File > Work Offline to work in Navigator while you are not connected to the Internet.

Alternative Browsers

Some of you out there who, after testing out Navigator and Internet Explorer, won't like either of them very much. Or perhaps you just don't like using products made by huge corporations and want to support some of the smaller developers. Never fear, several alternative Web browsers are available for the Mac (I call them alternative because they each have a very small percentage of the browser market share). Some of these browsers aren't free like Navigator and Internet Explorer, since they are made by smaller companies that can't afford to give their products away, but none of them is very expensive.

iCab. This browser is made by a German company called, you guessed it, iCab (www.icab.de). This is a Mac-only browser in preview release as of this writing. Rest assured, however, that iCab's preview release is quite stable, so it is worth trying out if you're not happy with Navigator or Internet Explorer. A final Pro version will cost $29, and there will also be a free version for downloading.

The iCab browser takes up less space on your hard drive than either of the major browsers, which might come in handy if you own an older Mac with a smaller hard drive. It's also a good browser to consider if you plan to do any HTML coding yourself (HTML code is very easy to learn, and it's a lot of fun to write your own code and then watch it turn into pretty pictures in a Web browser). When you load your HTML into iCab, a little face smiles if the code is correct and frowns if there are problems. In addition, iCab can act like either Navigator or Internet Explorer, displaying pages exactly the way those browsers would (since they each have their own idiosyncrasies, pages often look slightly different in them). The downside is that iCab doesn't yet support all of the Web standards of the major browsers.

The iCab browser does not offer support for Java at this time, so it limits what you can do on some sites. (JO)

Mozilla. Mozilla (www.mozilla.org) is another browser you might want to check out if you plan to do any Web designing. Mozilla is actually an open-source version of Netscape Navigator (**Figure 21.22**). This means that the underlying code that makes up the browser is available for developers to download and play around with. If you want to change any aspect of the browser, you can submit those changes to Netscape at www.mozilla.org, and a team of developers there will decide whether to incorporate them into future versions of Navigator.

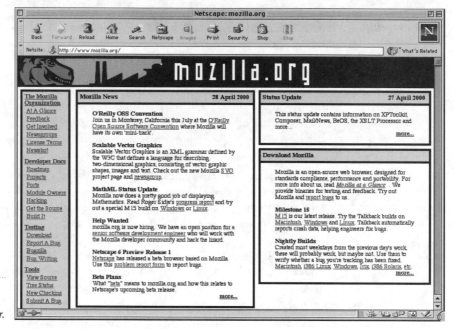

Figure 21.22

Mozilla is an open-source version of Netscape Navigator.

 OmniWeb. If you want a browser for Mac OS X, check out OmniWeb (www.omnigroup.com). OmniWeb isn't new: A version for Mac OS X (or Rhapsody) has been around for several years—its first public beta was in late 1997—and it is now up to version 4.0.5. It's also free.

There are a few other alternative browsers for the Mac, and more in the works. Opera, a Norwegian company (www.opera.com/mac), is currently developing three versions of its Opera Web browser for the Mac. To find out more about Mac-compatible Web browsers and related news, as well as to get updates to the major browsers, check out BrowserWatch (www.browserwatch.internet.com).

Everyone has an opinion about which Web browser is the best; try out as many as possible and decide for yourself.

How to Read a URL (JH)

Before you dig any deeper into this chapter, you'll need to know a little about Internet addresses, known as URLs, for Uniform Resource Locators. Most people pronounce it "you are ell," though some folks pronounce it "earl" (which is why otherwise literate people may sometimes write "an URL"). Every accessible resource on the Net has its own unique URL, and you can learn about what a URL points to by reading it piece by piece (**Figure 21.23**).

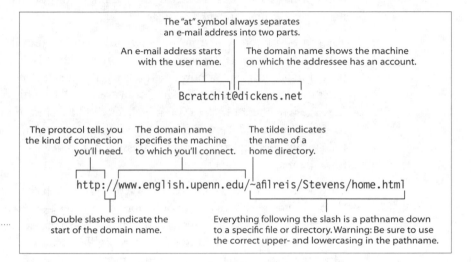

Figure 21.23

Anatomy of two URLs.

URLs are divided into three parts. First comes the protocol, a few letters that specify both the resource at the address as well as the tool that will reach it (such as *http*). After a separator—either two forward slashes (//) or the "at" sign (@)—comes the domain name, which spells out the host computer or network on which the resource is located. Finally, beginning with a slash, you'll find the file path through the host's hierarchy of directories all the way down to the resource itself.

E-mail—look for the @. If the separator is an @, it's an e-mail address.

Every Internet e-mail address begins with the addressee's *user name,* the unique name assigned at the service or company. For example, Bob Cratchit may have picked his own user name, "bcratchit," on his Internet service provider, Dickens Internet Services. On the other hand, his office network at Scrooge Inc. may have assigned him the user name "bobc."

The portion following the @ separator, known as the domain name, is the host on which that user has an e-mail account. The domain name breaks down into subdomains, specifying first the organization or company, then typically the machine, and then a final three-letter domain type: *com* indicates a commercial organization; *net,* an Internet service provider; *gov,* a U.S. government site;

edu, an educational institution, such as a college or university; *org,* a nonprofit organization; and *mil,* the military. (You can find a guide to country codes at www.ics.uci.edu/pub/websoft/wwwstat/country-codes.txt.) Thus Tiny Tim's e-mail address at Oxford University might be ttim@oxford.edu.

Domains aren't just picked willy-nilly—a host must purchase and register a domain name with an organization known as InterNIC (www.internic.net). If you'd just love to have ebeneezer@scrooge.com as your e-mail address, don't print up your business cards just yet. Someone else may already have registered the domain name Scrooge.

You can e-mail someone from anywhere in the online universe by addressing a message to *username@service.xxx.* Thus you'd write to Bob Cratchit at bcratchit@dickens.net or bobc@scrooge.com. You must know Cratchit's exact user name and the exact name of his service. One little typo and your message will bounce back to you undelivered or disappear into the ether forever. Your friend Tiny Tim may have an account on America Online, but simply guessing at his e-mail address, with ttim@aol.com, will probably miss the mark.

Now let's say that, by coincidence, someone else also picked the user name "bobc." That creates no confusion as long as he's on a different service, because his e-mail address remains unique: If Bob's provider is Heaven Connections, his address is the unique bobc@heavens.net. No service will allow two users to pick identical user names.

Two notes: You needn't worry about uppercase and lowercase in e-mail addresses. BCratchit@scrooge.com and bcratchit@Scrooge.COM are considered identical e-mail addresses. And a space in a user name in an online service ("bob cratchit" on America Online) is simply dropped for Internet purposes ("bobcratchit").

Other Internet URLs—look for the //. If the first part of the URL is followed by a double slash (//), then the leading protocol tells you what sort of address it is: *http* indicates a World Wide Web page; *ftp* is an FTP site from which you can download a file (see the "FTP" section, later in the chapter); *gopher* is a Gopher site, and *wais* is a searchable text database called WAIS, for Wide Area Information Services. Gopher and WAIS are tools that preceded the World Wide Web and were useful for finding information using a menu-based approach (gopher) or searching through indexed material (WAIS). Web-site domains usually begin with "www," as in http://www.peachpit.com. Similarly, FTP sites usually begin with "ftp." Many Web browsers will understand a URL that is missing the protocol "ftp://" or "http://" as long as the domain name begins with "ftp" or "www." As with e-mail addresses, a single typo in a URL and you're nowhere.

Finally, slashes after the domain name are used to show the path down through various directories (as with the Mac's folders) to the file's location. Thus if you go to the address ftp://ftp.acns.nwu.edu/pub/newswatcher/, you'll see a list of all the files that reside inside the "newswatcher" directory, which is in the "pub" (for public) directory at the Northwestern University FTP site. When you see a tilde (~) at the beginning of a Web URL path, you've spotted the Unix identifier for the home directory of the account. While most of the URL isn't case-sensitive, upper- and lowercasing does matter in the pathname. That's the first thing to examine when you get a "404 Not Found" error in your Web browser.

Plug-Ins (AD)

Back in the early days of the Web, say 1995 or so, Web pages were little more than images and text. Eventually, developers came up with ways to make the Web more interactive, employing video and audio files, for example, and even interactive games you could play with opponents on other computers on the Internet. The only problem was that HTML wasn't built to handle this sort of technology, so a lot of these features required you to have additional browser components, called *plug-ins*. The good news was that almost every plug-in was available for free (Web designers want you to be able to look at their sites, after all), but you still had to download and then install the plug-ins you wanted before you could go back to the Web site you were trying to visit in the first place.

Initially, site designers tended to shy away from using too many elements that required plug-ins. These days, things have changed. Most popular plug-ins are now automatically installed either as part of Mac OS or as part of either Navigator or Internet Explorer. Here's a look at some of the most common plug-ins and the kinds of media you can view using them.

Shockwave

Both Shockwave and Flash are interactive Web technologies developed by Macromedia. Shockwave is the name used to describe multimedia created with Macromedia's software. To view Shockwave content, which includes games, cartoons, and other interactive presentations, you need to download the Shockwave player from Macromedia's Web site, www.macromedia.com. However if you're using the most recent version of Internet Explorer, your browser is already equipped to handle Shockwave content. If you are using Navigator 4.7, however, you'll have to download the Shockwave player from www.shockwave.com; it is included in Netscape 6. While you're there, check out some of the games and cartoons for a glimpse of how far the Web has come in a few short years. I just finished watching an episode of the TV cartoon show *South Park* myself (**Figure 21.24**).

continues on next page

Plug-Ins *continued*

Figure 21.24

An episode of South Park *demonstrates the interactive Shockwave format.*

Flash

Macromedia Flash is equally as cool and even more widely used than Shockwave media. Some Web designers specialize in creating Flash content these days. Since Flash is based on vector images, which are smaller and take up much less bandwidth than other types of images, Flash has become quite popular for creating Web multimedia such as animations and interactive menus. Again, Internet Explorer 5 comes with the Flash plug-in; you'll have to download it from www.macromedia.com if you're using Navigator 4.7 but it is included in Netscape 6.

Streaming Media

You can also watch short movies and listen to audio tracks on the Web. You've probably heard the terms *streaming video* and *streaming audio*. These refer to video and audio files you can play in your Web browser while they are being downloaded, or streamed, to your computer, as opposed to having to wait until the entire file has downloaded to your hard drive. These days most types of video and audio can be streamed over the Web.

QuickTime

A lot of the video and audio you'll run across on the Web is in Apple's QuickTime format (www.apple.com/quicktime/; **Figure 21.25**). You'll need QuickTime Player to view these files, but since you have a Mac, chances are that player is already installed on your computer. Your QuickTime Player also lets you listen to audio files in the popular MP3 format.

Figure 21.25

Viewing the QuickTime movie trailer of Star Wars: Episode I on the QuickTime Web site.

Real Player G2

RealNetworks has a competing multimedia format that you can access using the RealPlayer G2. You'll find things such as live Webcasts in this format most often; to access this type of content you must download the free player from www.real.com.

PDF

Another format you'll often find on the Web is PDF (Portable Document Format), a technology developed by Adobe (www.adobe.com) that lets you view formatted documents as they originally appeared, without their having to be transferred into a browser-readable format. Mac OS 9 comes with the free Acrobat Reader, which you'll need to view these documents. Mac OS X also has Preview, which can view PDF files.

E-mail (PS)

It's hard to imagine not having at least one e-mail account these days. The explosive use of the Internet has brought e-mail to the masses. You may have an account on your company's e-mail system that's connected to the Internet, a home account through your ISP, an account with a free Web-based e-mail provider, or all of the above. In just a few short years, e-mail has become as widely used and accepted as the telephone—a task, for the latter, that took the majority of a century.

Virtually every new computer sold today ships with some form of e-mail program, and the Mac is no exception. In this section we take a look at a few of the options available to the Mac for connecting, communicating, and managing e-mail. This section focuses primarily on Internet e-mail and not commercial workgroup-based e-mail programs (such as Microsoft Exchange or Lotus Notes), and it assumes that you have already obtained an e-mail account with your ISP. (If you have Web access but are unsure as to whether you have an e-mail account, you should check with your ISP. Most ISPs bundle at least one e-mail mailbox with Internet access services.) If your Mac is connected to the Internet, then you're on your way to being able to communicate using e-mail.

You have a lot of options to choose from, so in this section we consider a few of the most popular e-mail clients for the Mac today. I also provide some background, terms, and tips for managing your e-mail, and help you determine what kind of e-mail client works best for you.

What to Ask Your ISP

All the e-mail clients discussed in this section require some basic information for initial setup. This information is the same for all the clients, and most of it comes from your ISP. So, while there isn't the space to cover this in detail for each client, I tell you what information to get from your ISP so you have everything you need to get your e-mail client set up and running. The four questions you should ask your ISP are:

1. What are my account name and password? Most ISPs will let you select these yourself and give you the means to change your password later. Your account name is usually used as part of your e-mail address.

2. What is my e-mail address? This address is usually in the format of *accountname@ispname.com* or *.net*.

3. What is the address of the POP server or host? You need this address to retrieve your mail from your ISP and is usually in the format of *POP.ispname.com* or *.net*.

4. What is the address of the SMTP server or host? You need this to send e-mail that you compose; it usually is in the format of *SMTP.ispname.com* or *.net*.

Outlook Express

Beginning with the release of Mac OS 8, Apple has included an e-mail client with the other Internet tools that it ships. Microsoft Outlook Express 5 (www.microsoft.com/mac/) is the e-mail manager bundled with Internet Explorer and is a stripped-down version of Microsoft's Outlook product. Outlook Express, a free download from Microsoft's Web site, supports POP and SMTP, and has several other features that make managing e-mail a pretty simple process.

Microsoft has made the installation process as simple as dragging a folder to your hard drive. Once you click the downloaded file and accept the license agreement, a window will open with the folder for Outlook Express. Just drag that folder to the location on your Mac where you want to install it, and release the mouse button. The installation will copy all the necessary files to the correct places.

Once the installation is complete, double-click the Outlook Express alias to start the program. While Outlook Express is launching, it will search for Microsoft Office's proofing tools for its spelling checker. If you do not have Office installed, you may be greeted with an error message that asks if you would like to search for them (**Figure 21.26**). If you have another compatible spelling checker, you can point it to that one; otherwise, click "Don't ask again."

Figure 21.26

When installing Outlook Express, the program searches for your current proofing tools (such as the spelling checker in Microsoft Office). This dialog box lets you pick an alternate.

Setting up Outlook Express. When the main Outlook Express window opens, its Setup Assistant appears and guides you through the setup of your e-mail account or accounts. Most of the information you need to put in comes from the answers to the four questions at the beginning of this section you asked your ISP. Click through the Assistant's screens and fill in the fields. Once you're done, Outlook Express has all the information it needs to start managing your e-mail.

The Outlook Express main window is divided into three sections, or panes, containing folders, the details of a selected folder, and a message-preview pane for quick display of a highlighted message (**Figure 21.27**).

Figure 21.27

Outlook Express's main window is divided into three panes. You can resize the individual panes by dragging their borders.

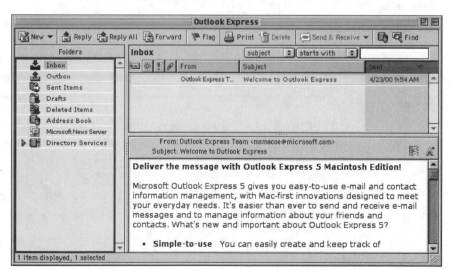

Creating a new message. To create a new message, click New in the upper-left corner of the main window, and select Mail Message from the pop-up menu. Two new windows appear—an untitled message window and a small addressing window. In the messaging window enter the address of the person to whom you want to send a message, and press Return.

If you want to send your message to more than one address, press Tab after typing the first address, and another address box will appear. This can be repeated for as many addresses as you need to add. If you frequently send e-mail to the same group of addresses, you can set up a group mailing list so that you only have to type one address. When you've added all the addresses, press Return.

Type a short description for your message in the Subject box, and you are ready to write your message. Outlook Express supports plain text, rich text format (allowing type styles such as bold and italic), and HTML for messages (**Figure 21.28**). When you have finished writing your message, you're ready to send it.

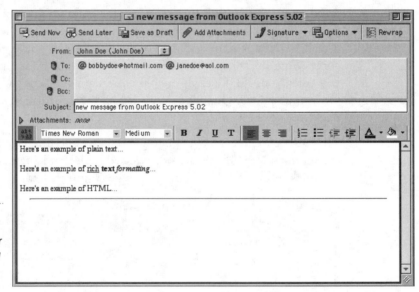

Figure 21.28

Outlook Express supports various formatting styles for messages, including plain text, Rich Text Format, and HTML.

Sending and receiving messages. You have a couple of options for sending your message. You can click Send Now or Send Later. The difference between these options is that Send Now immediately tries to connect to your ISP's SMTP server to send the message and Send Later puts all your completed messages into the Outbox so that they are sent all at once when you connect to your ISP. (If you pay a connect charge to access your ISP, this is definitely the way you want to go.)

Eudora

Qualcomm's Eudora 5.1 (www.eudora.com) comes in three licensing modes and can be downloaded from the Web site (there is a short optional survey, but the only information you're required to fill in to get the download link is an e-mail address). Which mode you decide on determines how much the client costs. (Don't worry—a fully functional mode won't cost you anything but a little extra Desktop real estate.) The three modes are free sponsored mode (default), paid mode, and light mode.

Sponsored mode is the full Pro version of Eudora and is free, with the caveat that when the client is running, it will display advertisements in a corner of your Desktop.

Paid mode is the full Pro version of Eudora. If you don't like the ads in the corner of your screen, you can pay $39.95 and get the Pro client sans ads.

Light mode is free without ads, but you don't get the full feature set that you get with the Pro versions. Light is a great mode if you don't require advanced features and only want to do basic e-mail.

Setting up Eudora. When you run Eudora for the first time after installation, you are presented with the Settings window. This is where you fill in the fields with the information from the four questions that you asked your ISP. (Unlike Outlook Express, Eudora doesn't have a setup assistant to walk you through the setup.) Access the Settings window from the Special menu; here, you set the preferences for the whole client, including many options (**Figure 21.29**).

Note that in Eudora's Settings window, on the Getting Started screen, in the Mail Host box, the program is looking for the address of the POP server of your ISP. If you click Hosts in the menu on the left to display the Hosts screen, you can enter the addresses of both your ISP's POP and SMTP servers.

Figure 21.29

To configure or change your Eudora settings, choose Settings from the Special menu and then click the appropriate icon in the window's left pane to display or change the relevant settings.

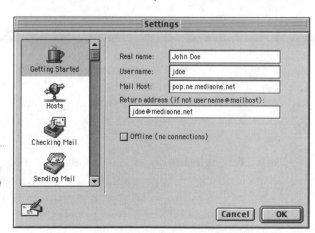

Getting around in Eudora. Access Eudora's basic features largely through the Icon bar that appears when you launch the program. (**Figure 21.30**).

Figure 21.30

Eudora's floating icon bar contains the tools for navigating the program.

You view messages in the inbox and outbox in separate windows, each with its own message-preview feature, and you can sort them by clicking one of the column headings at the top of the window (**Figure 21.31**).

Figure 21.31

After you select a folder from the icon bar, a window appears that displays a list of items in the folder; you can select and preview items in the folder. The list of items can be sorted by clicking the column headings.

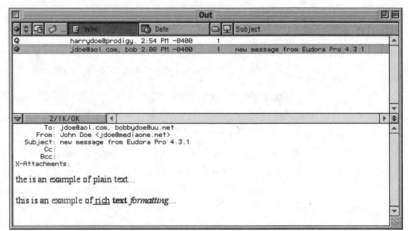

The horizontal bar that splits the window contains the mailbox-size information, represented by three numbers separated by slashes—2/1K/0K in Figure 21.31.

The first number (2) is the amount of messages in the mailbox. The second number (1K) is the total amount of disk space the messages require. The third number (0K) is the amount of unused disk space within that mailbox.

The third number grows when you delete messages from your mailbox; deleting messages creates the unused-space number. (The unused space will be removed automatically if the number gets too big.) To remove the wasted space in your mailbox manually, just click the mailbox's size display. (If you have multiple mailbox files in which you would like to clean up wasted space, you can take care of all of them at once by holding down (Option) while performing the same process.)

Say a few syllables. Eudora supports a function called Speak, which is accessible from the Edit menu. If you have a message selected (it doesn't need to be open—this also works in preview mode), you can select Speak and have Eudora read message back to you using the Mac OS's built-in speech technology, if your Mac supports it. If it's a message you received, the address of the person who sent you the message is read first, then the subject of the message, and finally the body of the message. If it's a message you are preparing to send, the program will read back the name of the person to whom you are sending it, the subject, and the body of the message.

QuickMail Pro

You can obtain QuickMail Pro 2.1 for Mac, from CE Software ($39.95; www.cesoft.com), through the company's Web site. QuickMail Pro comes in both client and server versions; be sure to get the client version. (Since we're concentrating on Internet e-mail here, we'll be looking at the client only.) Once you pay for the program, CE Software provides an activation key to allow you to use it. (Put this key in a safe place in case you ever have to reinstall the client.)

QuickMail Pro Assistant. You set up the QuickMail Pro client using the Account Assistant, which appears the first time you launch the client after installation. To set up Internet e-mail, you must select the "Configure the account manually" option. As you click through the pages of the Account Assistant, it prompts you for the information from the four questions at the beginning of this section your ISP answered. The only additional piece of information you will need is your activation key, which is the first thing the Account Assistant asks you for.

The main event. QuickMail Pro's main window resembles the Mac OS Finder, with its list of folders whose contents can be viewed by clicking small triangles to the left of the folders (**Figure 21.32**).

Figure 21.32

QuickMail Pro's main window lists all folders in a hierarchical display much like the Finder's. Unread items appear in bold, and you can open an item by double-clicking it.

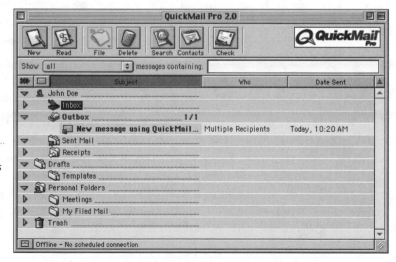

The message-preview function (called Message Peek in QuickMail Pro) is not enabled by default; however, it's easy to enable. Just click the icon in the lower-left corner of the main window, and the window will be split into two panes. (If you do not have a message highlighted when you click this option, you will see no contents in the lower pane. To see a preview, just highlight a message in the top pane.)

A quick way to enable the Message Peek function in QuickMail Pro is to press Control P. **Press** Control P **again to hide it.**

QuickMail has a type-ahead feature that fills in the rest of the address for you if you enter the first few letters of an e-mail address that is in your contacts list. To add addresses to the contacts list, just click the Contacts icon bar of the main window. A new Address Book window, called Main Address Book, appears (**Figure 21.33**).

Figure 21.33

QuickMail Pro's Address Book let's you store frequently used e-mail addresses. You can edit or add to the Address Book by clicking the Contacts icon in the icon bar of the main menu.

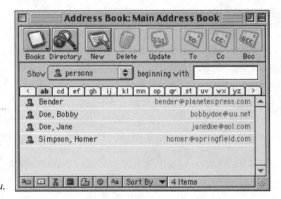

You can sort the Address Book several ways by selecting options from the Sort By pop-up menu at the bottom of the Address Book window. You can also display more detailed views of your contacts by clicking the buttons to the left of the Sort By menu.

Pausing the pointer over any of the buttons for a second or two displays a brief description of the fields they will add to the current contacts display.

You can create multiple address books for easy organization of e-mail addresses and contact information (you might create separate address books for personal and business contacts, for example). Most full-featured e-mail clients offer some kind of contact-management feature like this one so that you can more easily access, store, and sort your frequently used e-mail addresses, as well as extended address information such as full name, postal address, and associated phone numbers.

To create a contact entry in QuickMail Pro, click New in the icon bar at the top of the window. A new window opens, containing a series of tabbed forms with several fields where you can enter all the pertinent information for the new contact (**Figure 21.34**).

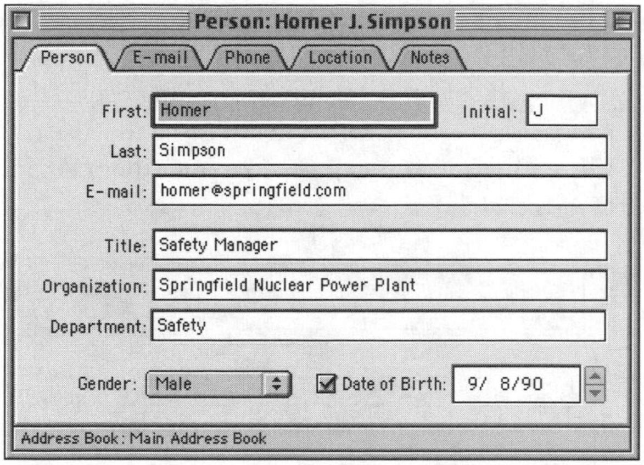

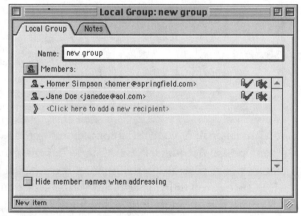

Figure 21.34

QuickMail Pro's Address Book can store a variety of information about your contacts. The tabbed interface lets you select the type of information you want to specify.

To create groups, go to the File menu and select New > Local Group. In the window that appears, you can name the group and add the group's members (**Figure 21.35**). (You can use the type-ahead feature here or click the Members icon to select names from your contact list.) When you are finished, close the window; you are prompted to indicate the address book in which you would like to save the new list.

Figure 21.35

Use Local Group to send messages to a list of contacts. Selecting New > Local Group from the File menu calls up the group dialog box, where you can add or delete members.

PowerMail

PowerMail 3.0 ($49, single license; www.ctmdev.com) isn't quite as feature-rich as some of the other e-mail clients we've looked at here, but if all you need is a simple e-mail client without a lot of bells and whistles, then this is a safe bet. Once you've provided payment, you receive a registration code that you must enter when you install the client.

The setup. Perform the easy PowerMail installation by dragging a folder to your hard disk. There is no installer to run, and the installation doesn't require a restart. When you launch PowerMail for the first time, you are greeted with a three-paned window (called the Mail Browser) and an icon bar above it. The Mail Browser can be set to display three panes with a short list of folders on the left side, three panes with a long list on the left side, or two panes (no message-preview pane). It doesn't run any assistants that prompt you for your ISP settings, so you will need to enter them before you can use the client (**Figure 21.36**).

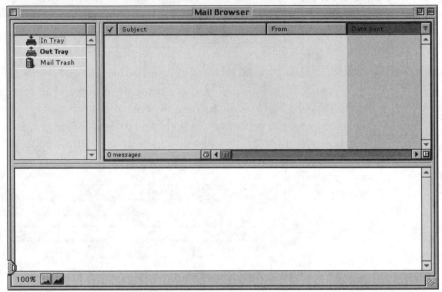

Figure 21.36

The main PowerMail user interface is composed of a floating icon bar (top) and the Mail Browser window (bottom). You can specify the size and arrangement of the panes.

You can enter all of your ISP information by going to the Setup menu and selecting Mail Accounts. PowerMail, by default, carries over any information you may have provided in the Internet control panel in the System Folder in Mac OS 9. If you didn't specify any settings for e-mail when you entered that information, you can do it here, but you will need to remove the check from the "Use default internet settings" box to enable all the fields. (PowerMail also allows you to launch the Internet Setup Assistant or Internet control panel from the Setup menu.)

Signatures. PowerMail's signature feature lets you store multiple text snippets that you can append to the end of e-mails. Signatures are a great way to reduce the typing of repetitive information you might add to many of the e-mails you send. If you regularly end your e-mails with a thank you and your name, address, title, company name, phone number, and so on, you can put it all in a signature and have it automatically appended to your e-mails.

To create a signature, select Signatures from the Setup menu. In the Signatures window, click the pen icon in the lower-left corner, and in the Signature screen, type a description and enter the information you'd like to include (**Figure 21.37**).

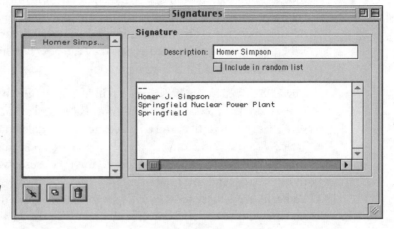

Figure 21.37

PowerMail allows you to maintain a collection of signatures—your contact information and the closing phrases at the end of your messages.

Importing and exporting. Access PowerMail's import and export features by going to the File menu and selecting Database > Import or Database > Export. Both offer assistants to step you through the process of moving e-mail and addresses in and out of PowerMail (**Figure 21.38**).

The assistants come in handy if you are upgrading from a previous version of PowerMail, moving data out of PowerMail for use in a PDA (personal digital assistant), or switching to PowerMail from a competing e-mail client (several of them are covered in this section). The export options include allowing you to extract your Address Book to a delimited text file and to pull out the entire contents of your mailbox (all messages).

Figure 21.38

If you are switching to PowerMail from another package, the Import Assistant helps you import messages and contacts from the other application.

Being efficient. Like most other e-mail clients, PowerMail offers some utilities to keep your program running smoothly. E-mail mailboxes can become less efficient over time as you delete messages. What happens is, when you delete messages, you create small pockets of unused space in your message indexes. Since a typical message has additional information associated with it, such as its status (read or unread), priority, and time and date, it keeps track of these associations by maintaining indexes of all the related information. When these pockets of space occur, they can affect an index's ability to report a mailbox's related information correctly.

PowerMail's client tools include a reindexing feature that maintains the integrity of the messages' related information and a compacting tool that squeezes out all of the unused space created by deleted messages. The tools are easy to use, and although there are no hard and fast rules as to how often they should be run, it's a good idea to use them somewhat regularly. (The frequency depends on how many messages you receive, store, and delete.) You can access these tools by choosing Database from the File menu and then making your selection from the submenu (**Figure 21.39**).

Figure 21.39

To help ensure the integrity of your PowerMail database, you should compact the database and update indexes from time to time.

Netscape Communicator

It might seem slightly odd at first to include Netscape Communicator in our discussion of e-mail (especially compared with the clients we've looked at so far) because when most people hear the name Netscape, the first thing that comes to mind is Web browsing. Although it's true that Communicator grew up as a Web browser (called Navigator in a past life, as the browser still is), it has evolved into a full suite of components able to take advantage of many of the services that the Internet has to offer, including e-mail. The current version of Communicator can be downloaded free of charge from www.netscape.com/download/index.html.

When you run Communicator for the first time, you are actually opening the Navigator Web browser, but getting to the e-mail client is easy and you can do it in a couple of ways. The first way is by selecting Mail from the Tasks menu; the second is by clicking the small envelope icon in the bottom-left corner of the browser window. Since the e-mail client runs separately from the browser, it opens in a new window, called Mail. The first time it's launched, Mail runs a handy Account Wizard to step you through setting up your ISP information. Once you complete all the screens, the wizard brings you back to the Mail window so you can start using your new e-mail client (**Figure 21.40**).

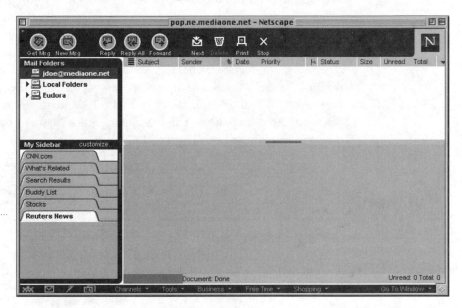

Figure 21.40

Netscape Communicator 6's user interface displays mail folders, messages, and a preview window.

Integration. The Communicator e-mail client is unique among the clients we've looked at so far. Although the program has a basic feature set and offers the same messaging functions available in other e-mail clients, Netscape has taken the concept of the e-mail client to a new level by tightly integrating browsing, e-mail, and instant messaging into a single unified console.

Instant messaging takes the concept of e-mail a step further by eliminating the time it takes to send a message. Instant messaging allows the intended recipient of your message to actually see the message, in real time, as you type it. (It also allows the recipient to respond immediately to the message.) An easy way to think of it is as a telephone conversation typed out. (See the "Chatting/Conferencing" section, later in the chapter.)

As the lines between traditional e-mail and instant messaging continue to blur, you're likely to see more makers of e-mail clients follow Netscape's lead by incorporating multiple methods of electronic messaging into their programs.

A new look. Another thing that differentiates Communicator from most of the other Macintosh e-mail clients we've looked at is its appearance—it looks the least Mac-like. Netscape has completely redesigned Communicator around its new Gecko Technologies and made it compliant with all the current Internet standards. As a result of the redesign, Communicator looks identical on both Macs and PCs.

Multiple accounts. As with some of the other clients, Communicator allows you to manage multiple e-mail accounts using the same client. If you have accounts on multiple ISPs, or you have one ISP but more than one family member using the account, you can manage all of them from a single Communicator window. Each new account you add shows up as an additional folder in the Mail Folders pane of the Communicator window. To add accounts to the Netscape client, go to the Edit menu and select Mail/News Account Settings. (This option only appears if you are in the mail client of Netscape. To open the mail client, go to the Task menu and select Mail.) When the Account Settings window appears, click New Account to launch the account setup wizard (**Figure 21.41**).

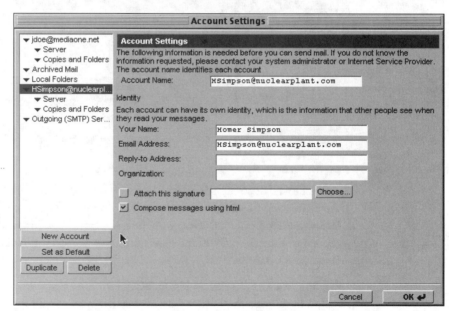

Figure 21.41

Netscape Communicator's settings are configured in the Account Settings window. You can maintain multiple accounts and view the mail from all of them in one window.

If the account wizard looks familiar, it should—we used it when we first set up the Communicator client. You will need to have the ISP information for each additional account you are setting up.

If you have multiple accounts set up and you want one specific account to always open whenever you launch the Communicator client, just highlight the account in the folder list on the left side of the window and click Set as Default.

If you want to have accounts from multiple ISPs, you may need to set up multiple dialing profiles to get to each one. You can do this by creating additional configurations in the Remote Access control panel. (For more information, see the "Getting Connected" section, earlier in the chapter.)

Mac OS X's Own Mail

If you don't want to stray far from Apple software, Mac OS X comes with its own e-mail application, prosaically named Mail. Mail's icon is in the Dock by default, but you can also find it in the Applications folder. During the Mac OS X setup, the installer probably asked you if you wanted to use Mail and prompted you for settings. If not, the first time you launch Mail, it presents you with a Mail Setup window, where you can enter your name, e-mail address, and other account information.

Mail uses the built-in capabilities of Mac OS X: For example, through Mail's Font panel, you can take advantage of the system's advanced text-handling tools. Mail also hooks into Mac OS X's Address Book to store contact information.

Browser-Based (Free) E-mail Services

Several ISPs and Internet content providers provide e-mail services at their Web sites without requiring you to install a client. These e-mail services are accessible via a browser and are usually available free of charge when you sign up for a provider's portal services. (These are also typically free. For more on portal services, see "Where to Visit," later in the chapter.) If you already have an ISP and are connected to the Internet for Web browsing, then you have everything you need to use a browser-based e-mail service. Now you may be saying, "Hold on! Nobody gets anything for free. What's the catch?" OK, there is a catch: Although the e-mail service is actually free (the service providers make their money through advertising revenue), you may still need to pay for your ISP connection.

Access e-mail from anywhere. One of the big advantages of these "free" e-mail services is that they are accessible from any Internet-connected computer with a browser. You don't need to be connected to a specific ISP or use a client with your particular account settings. You only need to connect to a Web site and log in, and your e-mail is waiting for you.

Hotmail. Microsoft was one of the first providers to offer browser-based e-mail, with its Hotmail service, which is now part of MSN. To set up a Hotmail account, go to www.hotmail.com and click the sign-up link (**Figure 21.42**).

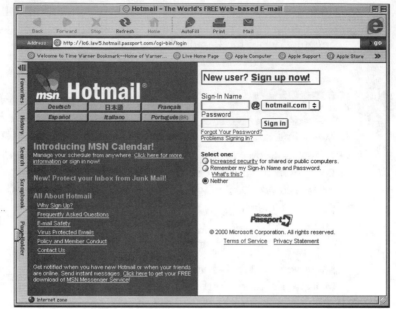

Figure 21.42

Microsoft's Hotmail is one of the free Web-based e-mail services that offer an alternative to Macintosh e-mail clients.

When you click that link, you are directed to a page where you fill out a form that requires some basic information; you then select an e-mail name. (Your e-mail address becomes *e-mailname@hotmail.com*.) Once you fill out all the information and Hotmail verifies the e-mail name you have chosen, you are signed up and directed to your online mailbox (**Figure 21.43**).

Figure 21.43

Hotmail uses your browser window to display message lists and features. Web-based browsers generally don't offer the flexibility of dedicated client applications.

The inbox in Hotmail is presented as a table of hyperlinks, each one representing a message that has been sent to you. To read a message you click a link. You are provided 2 MB of storage for your mailbox, which may not seem like a lot, but you can receive an awful lot of plain text messages before you reach that limit.

Yahoo. Similar to Hotmail in format, Yahoo Mail is another free, browser-based e-mail option. When you create an account for Yahoo's portal services and get your own personalized content page, a mailbox is also assigned to your account. Yahoo allocates 6 MB of storage for each free e-mail box and offers most of the same mail-handling features that Hotmail offers. You can sign up at www.yahoo.com.

Netscape. In addition to offering a full-blown e-mail client for your Mac (as part of Communicator), Netscape has a browser-based free e-mail option that's part of its Netcenter portal. It offers the same type of e-mail service and feature set as Hotmail and Yahoo, and you can sign up for an account by going to www.netscape.com and clicking Mail.

What's not to like? OK, browser-based e-mail is a pretty good deal, but it has a couple of minor drawbacks. The biggest is probably that you have to manage all of your mail while connected to the Internet. This is particularly troublesome if you have an iBook or PowerBook and want to get caught up on some of your e-mail messages while traveling or not near an Internet connection. However, the good news is that you don't have to remember any additional ISP settings for your e-mail client. So if you don't want pay for an off-the-shelf e-mail package and the features of browser-based e-mail suit your needs, then it's a great way to go.

If you simply want to check your POP mailbox without signing up for a separate mail account, you should visit MailStart (http://www.mailstart.com), a technology demo for MailStart's **WebBox,** which allows you to consolidate your mail from as many as five accounts and also manage your contacts and calendar. For full functionality you'll need to pony up the $10 yearly fee for the service, but if you travel a lot you will find it well worth this small sum.

One of the caveats to free browser-based e-mail is that there is a greater risk of exposure to solicitation. Most of these e-mail services are advertising-revenue driven, which is why they can be provided free of charge. When you're signing up for an account, be sure to read all the fine print before clicking the submit button. Many of these service providers partner with all kinds of businesses whose sole purpose in life is to push advertising and marketing information, via e-mail, in your particular demographic direction.

Managing Mail (PS)

We've looked at a lot of tools for the Mac with features that can help you manage your e-mail, but we haven't actually looked at how to manage e-mail. The following features are useful for sifting through the deluge of messages you're likely to get once you start to give out your e-mail address. Most of them are available in the clients we've discussed in this section, but some are implemented better than others. Since most clients are available for free or in a trial or demo version, take a couple for a test drive and play with their feature sets. This approach offers a couple of benefits: It helps you to identify the features you are likely to use most often, and you get to see which client has best implemented the features that are most important to you.

Folders. One of the first steps to managing anything, whether it's e-mail or your sock drawer, is to get organized. Most e-mail clients offer the ability to sort messages in a variety of ways. Many also allow you to create hierarchical folders to categorize messages by sender or by subject. You can even use folders to design and manage an e-mail workflow kind of scenario. You can set up folders for messages that you've received but not read, read but not researched, and researched but not yet replied to.

Filters. Another capability of the more robust e-mail clients is the ability to filter messages by particular criteria. You may not want any messages over a particular size to be downloaded because you are accessing your mailbox from a slow dial-up connection, or you may not want messages uploaded that don't meet a certain set of conditions. (In this context download and upload refer to the transmission of messages from or to your Internet mail servers.) Filters also allow you to weed out any spam you might receive, such as unsolicited online marketing or sales offers (**Figure 21.44**).

Figure 21.44

Once you start using e-mail on a regular basis, you might get over-whelmed by the number of messages—and spam—you receive. Mail filtering allows you to process messages as they arrive—it files them in folders or ignores them, using rules that you specify using Boolean operators. This is PowerMail's Filters window.

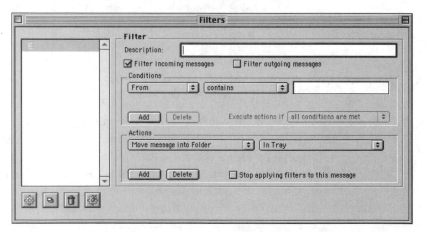

Schedulers. Maybe you have created several e-mail messages based on the timing of other events, and you only want the messages sent based on those events. If you know when the events are going to take place, you can set up schedules to deliver your messages automatically. This can be useful if you know you are not going to be available to send the messages yourself.

Address books. Managing your e-mail is not just about keeping all those messages neat and organized. It's also about managing the information associated with those messages, such as the addresses of their senders or people you might correspond with on a regular basis. Just about every e-mail client available for the Mac offers some kind of address book or contact manager that stores and organizes not only e-mail addresses but, in most cases, postal addresses, phone numbers, company names, and so on (**Figure 21.45**).

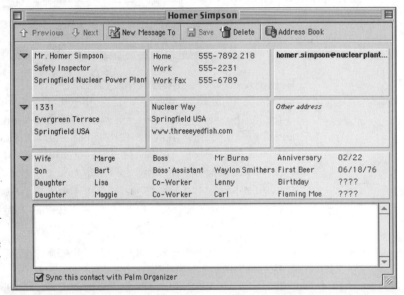

Figure 21.45

Some e-mail packages, such as Outlook Express, provide limited personal-information-management capability. This screen from Outlook Express's Address Book shows the variety of contact information you can manage.

Mailing lists. Mailing or distribution lists are simply sets of e-mail addresses grouped together. If you have certain addresses to which you send a lot of the same e-mail, you can set them up in a mailing list and address your messages to the list. The client will look up who is in the list and distribute the message to all the recipients. This can save you huge amounts of time that you would otherwise spend typing in the same addresses, over and over, every time you send messages to these recipients.

Signatures. Another feature that saves keystrokes is the ability to create predefined signatures. You can save a snippet of text as a signature, or create a cool graphic with text for a signature, and have it automatically appended to every message you compose.

Searching. Can't find an e-mail because you created a lot of folders to get more organized and forgot which one you dropped that all-important message into? Not to worry. The search capabilities available in the current crop of e-mail clients offer an easy way to quickly find what you're looking for. You can typically search on just about any part of a message (addresses, message text, attachments, and so on) and get some speedy results (**Figure 21.46**).

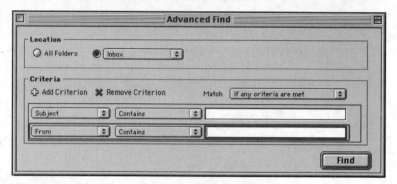

Figure 21.46

Once you accumulate a lot of messages, the find feature of your e-mail client, as shown in Outlook Express's Advanced Find window, can help you find messages you may have received some time ago. You can make your search more specific by adding more criteria.

Bringing it all together with rules. You can combine many of the management options—such as filters, mailing lists, schedulers, and folders—in rules. With rules, you can use an e-mail client's features to automate tasks and functions much the way that AppleScript automates functions within the Mac OS. (Think of a rule as a macro for your e-mail client.) When you define rules, you are actually telling the client to use a specific function or set of functions to react to a particular event. You don't actually write macros when creating rules; you generate most by selecting some criteria information and telling those criteria what event to act upon.

Most of the popular e-mail clients let you create rules and allow you to run them manually, all the time, or at a scheduled time. The one caveat regarding rules is that in most cases the e-mail client must be running for rules to work. (Workgroup-based e-mail products such as Microsoft Exchange and Lotus Notes have server-side rules that can run whether the client is operating or not.) This can be an issue if security is a concern. If you send and receive confidential e-mail, you don't want to have to leave your e-mail client open and unattended so the rules you've set up can run.

To create rules, you select criteria based on an event (if something happens…) and set an action that responds to the event (…then do this). In the WorkMail rule example shown in **Figure 21.47**, I've instructed Outlook Express to check for all unread messages from anyone with an e-mail address containing @mediaone.net. If it finds any messages meeting that specific criterion, Outlook Express should change the color of the message, mark it as read, and move it to a folder called Business. Notice that I've checked the Enabled box. This means the rule is considered active, so once I click OK, it immediately goes to work on any messages that fit the criteria defined. You can be as vague as or detailed as you like when setting up a rule. If you need to be more specific for a given circumstance, simply define additional criteria and additional actions.

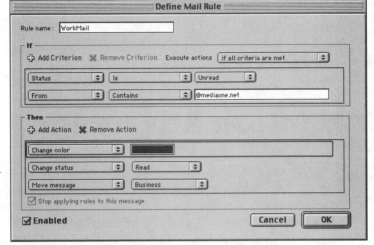

Figure 21.47

Rules in Outlook Express can perform a function similar to filters, as shown in Figure 21.44.

E-Mail, Chat, and Discussion Etiquette: Ten Rules (JH, DJS)

If you've ever visited France and watched American tourists shouting orders in English at scowling Parisians, you know that it pays to do your homework and learn the local lingo. Violate the rules of Internet behavior and you'll be branded a clueless newbie, a newcomer who doesn't have the decency even to pick up the basics. OK, you're warned. Study these few rules and you just may be mistaken for a veteran in your discussion group.

1. DON'T TYPE IN ALL CAPS! It's hard to read, and it looks like YOU'RE SHOUTING!

2. It is OK to type like a banshee e. e. cummings; all lowercase is fine, if perhaps a trace too hip. Always put two carriage returns at the end of each paragraph. And keep the paragraphs short.

3. Quote a relevant piece of a message to which you're replying—just enough to give needed context, but not the entire message. Nothing looks more idiotic than quoting an entire enormous message, followed by your reply: "Thanks for the tip!"

4. Don't delete messages to which you reply. In a public message forum, the original message helps others follow the conversation.

5. Address people by their first names—it may not be proper in a business letter, but it's standard online.

6. Stay out of flame wars. Just stay out. Life's too short, and nothing ever, not ever, gets settled. Remember: The best way to extinguish a flame is to deprive it of fuel. Corollary: You'll never have the last word, because there's always a fool with even more time to waste.

continues on next page

E-Mail, Chat, and Discussion Etiquette: Ten Rules continued

7. Reread your messages before you send them or post them. You'll be surprised how often you reconsider and decide to tone down the language.

8. Use smileys and emoticons, but sparingly. It's sometimes important to give readers a clue to your state of mind, but you might try writing so that they're not needed. You don't see Dave Barry peppering his column with little smiley faces, do you?

9. Give back as you take. Seek help, but don't forget to help others.

10. Finally, give the clueless newbies a break.

The Macintosh Advantage (JO)

 Internet and messaging applications for the Macintosh are cool, but they're not the ones that really differentiate the Macintosh Internet experience. Not too long ago, Apple enhanced the integration of the Mac OS with the Internet on a couple of fronts. iTools, a suite of Internet-based utilities that can appear seamlessly blended with the Macintosh Desktop, and Sherlock, an extensible search tool that lets you comb the Internet without opening a browser, are two examples that showcase the Mac's superiority as an Internet station (**Figure 21.48**). (You need to be running Mac OS 9 or Mac OS X to use iTools and Sherlock.)

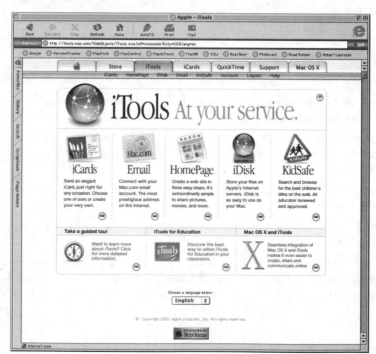

Figure 21.48

Apple has created a real affinity between the Mac OS and the Internet with iTools. Some of the nicest benefits to iTools are its free Web hosting and e-mail.

Want Some Free Disk Space?

The iTools collection consists of iCards, HomePage, iDisk, and Email. You can access the entire suite of tools from your browser by going to http://itools.mac.com. iDisk begins as 20 MB of *free* personal storage space on Apple's Internet servers. You open your iDisk from Apple's iTools Web site, and it quickly appears on your Desktop as if it were a shared volume on a local network. You can use your iDisk just as you would any other Macintosh disk. By default, Apple provides several folders on the disk to help you organize documents, music, movies, pictures, and other material. Although you have 20 MB of free when you sign up for iTools (at no cost), you can add space up to 1 GB in various increments for just $1 per megabyte per year. The uses for iDisk are tremendous. Since you can access it from any Macintosh with an Internet connection, you can use your iDisk to store files that you want to be able to open while you are away from home or work. Through a folder called Public, you can share files with other people. (All they need to know is your iTools user name to access anything in your Public folder.)

Apple also shares some of its software (and that of leading Mac OS X developers) with you via iDisk. In a folder called Software you'll find some of the latest updates, tools, and applications for both Mac OS 9 and Mac OS X. For example, you can get the latest version of iTunes, AOL Instant Messenger, and the popular game Klondike by opening the Software folder and dragging the application or installer directly to your local hard disk.

You can create an alias to your iDisk to make access easier. Depending on your Apple Menu settings, it will show up in the list of servers that you recently accessed if you have this feature enabled.

 OS X users can easily mount their iDisks from the Go menu in the Finder, and they can include their iDisks in the Dock for quick access.

How About a Free Web Site?

iDisk is also integral to another iTool, HomePage. Using the HomePage iTool, you can easily create your own Web site with nothing more than a few mouse-clicks. Apple provides predefined templates for photo albums, iMovies, invitations, shared files, résumés, and more. The default URL that is created for your site is *http://homepage.mac.com/<username>*. For example, you could tell your friends to surf to http://homepage.mac.com/jsmith to easily share family photo albums or movies or to point them to an invitation to an upcoming reunion or get-together (**Figure 21.49**).

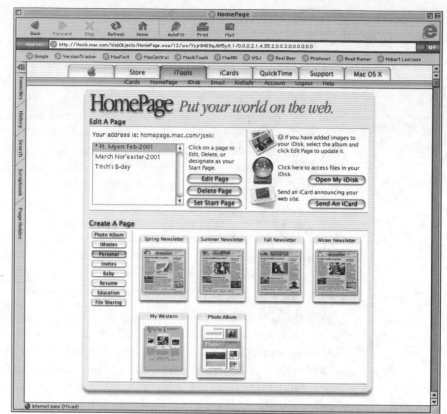

Figure 21.49

iTools' HomePage lets you create Web pages with text and pictures in just minutes. You can copy pictures from your digital camera to your iDisk and then easily create a Web family album.

The elegance of the HomePage iTool is its ease of use. If you have a digital camera or another source of digital images that you'd like to share, simply copy the images to your iDisk, click the Photo Album button in your HomePage iTool, specify a theme from the long list of predefined templates (such as beach, birthday, and graduation), and then indicate where on your iDisk the images are located. HomePage will automatically create captions for the album using the filenames for the pictures. You can change any of the headings, but to save this extra effort, name your files ahead of time.

You can have as many pages as you want on your iTools HomePage. The HomePage tool lets you specify the page that you want to appear by default when someone goes to your site; the other pages you've created are shown as hyperlinks at the top of the page. This makes it easy for your visitors to navigate your HomePage site, and you don't have to know a shred of HTML to make all this happen.

Free E-mail and Other Goodies

Want some more free tools from Apple?

Email. iTools is another provider of free Web-based e-mail. When you become an iTools member, an account with the address *<username>@mac.com* is automatically created for you. Unlike the other free e-mail services covered earlier in this chapter, iTools lets you access your mac.com mailbox using any standard e-mail client, such as Outlook Express or Netscape Communicator, which are included with Mac OS 9, or the built-in Mail application that comes with Mac OS X. You can store 5 MB of messages and attachments on the mac.com server, or if you prefer, you can have your mac.com e-mail automatically forwarded to another account. Setup of your mail client follows the standard conventions for the programs we discussed earlier in this chapter, but if you need some assistance, the iTools help facility can walk you through setup for Outlook Express, Communicator, or another mail client. The limited space you get with your mac.com mailbox can be restrictive if you don't delete your mail frequently, but Apple's limits are in line with those of other free mail services on the Internet. The forwarding and Auto Reply features can help you direct your mac.com messages to the right place.

Customized electronic postcards. iCards, one of the few iTools that are accessible from non-Macintosh clients, is simply a free electronic postcard service. A few other sites on the Net offer similar functionality—allowing you to send a short note that contains a picture to someone via e-mail—but iCards offers a unique customization option to iDisk users. Using iCards' "Create your own" option, you can use any JPEG or GIF file stored on your iDisk as the graphic for an iCard. This certainly lets you add a nice touch to your iCards that is unavailable with most, if any, other Web-based e-postcard services.

Using the Mac OS Master Sleuth

Elsewhere you have learned how Sherlock, the Mac OS's built-in search engine, can help you find files and content on your Mac, but did you know that the same great utility can help you find items on the Internet? You know how to start Sherlock already—press ⌘F in the Finder; in Mac OS 9, select Sherlock 2 from the Apple menu; in Mac OS X, select Find from the File menu. When you start the utility, Sherlock remembers the last "channel" (these are the icons in the bar at the top of Sherlock's window) you used to perform a search; if you want to change channels, just click a different icon. When first installed, Sherlock has several channels preconfigured for you. These include Internet, People, Shopping, News, Apple, Reference, My Channel, and Entertainment. You can easily organize these to suit your needs—see the sidebar "Channel Surfing." When you click a channel icon, the list of search sites for that channel will appear in the top pane of Sherlock's window (**Figure 21.50**). From this point, you can choose which search sites to use when you let Sherlock do its thing.

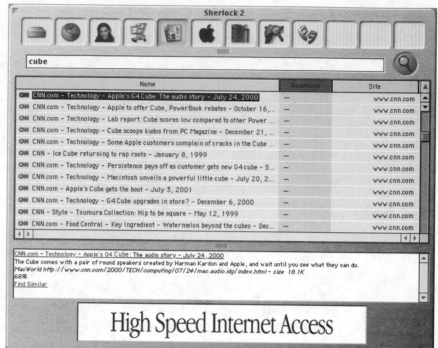

Figure 21.50

Sherlock lets you search not only your hard drive but reference material on the Web. You can customize any of the panes at the top of Sherlock's window to hold pointers to your favorite collections of search sites.

To start an Internet search, enter a word or phrase in the text box to the left of the magnifying-glass icon, and then click the icon or press Return. The search site list is replaced with a list of results that match your search criteria—much like the results from a conventional Web-based search engine such as Google, Yahoo, or AltaVista (**Figure 21.51**). On each item, you see the source of the "hit" and a title for the result. The beauty of Sherlock is that you can now search all these sites at the same time. The relevance bar to the right of the item indicates how well the item matches your search criteria.

When you click an item in the hit list, you will see it displayed in greater detail at the bottom of the window. If you click any of the highlighted text in the detail section, your browser will open to the Web page where Sherlock found its match. You can also pick which sites you want Sherlock to use (**Figure 21.52**).

You can save searches that you use regularly by selecting Save Search Criteria from Sherlock's File menu. You can then reexecute your search by double-clicking this file (or opening it from Sherlock directly).

Microsoft has yet to incorporate anything into Windows that comes close to mimicking the seamless integration and ease of use that Sherlock offers. Many popular Web search engines cried foul when Sherlock was first released in Mac OS 8.5 because there was a potential loss of advertising revenue from users skipping right over the ads on their sites. Happily for us, Apple now links you to the source site to see the full content of the items you find.

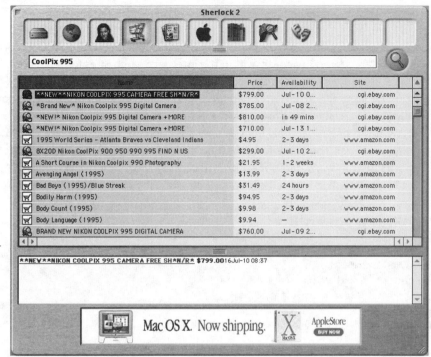

Figure 21.51

Sherlock can make shopping a snap. Here we searched across a variety of sites, including eBay and Amazon.com, for a Nikon CoolPix 995 digital camera.

Figure 21.52

In Sherlock, you can include the sites you want in your search by clicking the check boxes next to them (click the globe icon to get the Internet search-engine list).

Channel Surfing

Channels are a way for you to organize your Sherlock searches by topic and scope. Each channel's source files are stored in a folder within the Internet Search Sites folder in your System Folder (in Mac OS 9 and earlier). You can create or change your own channels in Sherlock by selecting the appropriate command from the Channels menu in Sherlock. Sherlock does a good job of ensuring that the source files (the files with the extension .src in the various channel folders) are up to date, and it will download new ones as they are updated. You can create your own Sherlock source files as well. The brute-force method involves using a text editor, such as Bare Bones Software's BBEdit (www.barebones.com), to create a file that looks like this for Apple's Web site:

```
#
# Apple search Plugin for Sherlock
# © 2000 Apple Computer, Inc.
#
<search
name="Apple.com"
description="Searches the Apple web site."
action="http://search.apple.com/s97is.vts"
method="GET"
update="http://si.info.apple.com/updates/Apple.src.hqx"
updateCheckDays="3"
bannerLink="http://www.apple.com"
bannerImage='<img src="http://www.apple.com/main/elements/sherlockbar.gif" alt="Apple Computer">'
  >
<input name="Action" value="Search" />
<input name="Collection" value="Apple" />
<input name="ResultTemplate" value="sherlock.hts" mode="results" />
<input name="ResultMaxDocs" value="9" mode="results" />
<input name="ResultTemplate" value="webx2.hts" mode="browser" />
<input name="ServerKey" value="Primary" />
<input name="queryText" user />
<interpret
resultListStart="<!–IL–>"
resultListEnd="<!–/IL–>"
resultItemStart="<!–IS–>"
resultItemEnd="<!–/IS–>"
relevanceStart="<!–REL–>"
relevanceEnd="<!–/REL–>"
/>
</search>
```

An easier way to create source files is to use a tool such as Martin Productions' free **Sherlock Creator.** You can get this tool, which greatly simplifies source-file creation, at www.ekera.com/products/sch.tpl.

If you simply prefer to have source files turned on or off, a variety of tools can manage the contents of these system files, including Casady & Greene's **Conflict Catcher** ($69.95; www.casadyg.com).

FTP (JH)

Not surprisingly, the Internet offers the universe's largest collection of software, available for download by a process known as FTP, which stands for File Transfer Protocol, a set of rules dating back to the early days of the Internet. You can use FTP to download (and upload) files from thousands of sites all around the Internet, many of them universities, which make software libraries available to the general public.

Accessing and Navigating FTP Sites

You can access public FTP sites on which you have no account by means of anonymous FTP—give "anonymous" as your user name and your e-mail address as your password. Then just supply the URL—the host name and the path to the file you're seeking. If you're not allowed in, try this trick: Use "anonymous" for your user name and the "at" sign (@) for your e-mail address.

After the software—either your Web browser or a specialized FTP program such as Fetch—takes you to the FTP site, don't worry if you don't immediately spot the file you want. Most FTP sites are organized in nested directories similar to the Mac's folders, enabling you to navigate up and down the hierarchy to look for files. Clicking a period takes you to the root or top directory, and clicking a double period takes you one level higher in the directory hierarchy (**Figure 21.53**). Feel free to poke around. Look for directories named "pub" (for public), "incoming," and of course "Mac." Look for files titled "readme" for useful information.

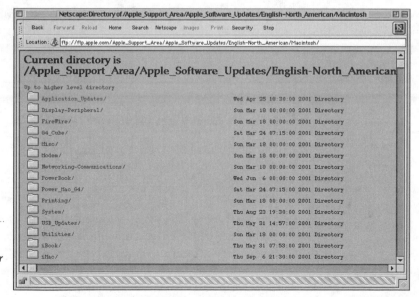

Figure 21.53

A typical FTP directory, as seen in a Web-browser window. Click "Up to higher level directory" to move back up the hierarchy.

FTP Etiquette

It's common courtesy to limit your downloading to off hours—evenings and weekends as measured locally at the FTP site. Try to use a local site. And when possible, download from a mirror site, a less busy copy of the original site.

Help for Serious Downloaders

Several utilities are available to ease the process of searching for and downloading software. Most Web browsers allow you to FTP files—just pop the FTP address into the browser's address box—but a dedicated utility is much easier and faster. My favorite by far is the shareware classic **Fetch** ($25; ftp.dartmouth.edu/pub/software/mac/ for older versions or http://fetchsoftworks.com/ for newer ones), which is extremely easy to use (**Figure 21.54**). Fetch displays lots of information in a friendly way, so you know just what's happening (though don't take its estimate of remaining download time too seriously). It makes terrific use of drag and drop, and I often find it's smarter than me—drag a long URL to its dialog box and it splits it up to put the pathname in the correct text box. Fetch can also do almost all the uploading and maintenance work for a Web page.

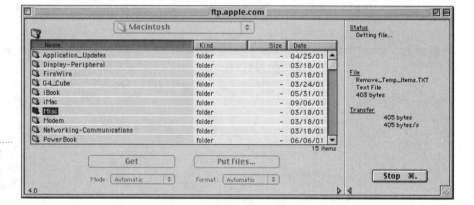

Figure 21.54

Fetch displays lots of information on the progress of an FTP download.

Where in the World Is carmen.sgo?

Archie is the name of the special databases that keep track of the locations of files on Internet sites all around the world. These databases reside on a few publicly accessible servers. Although you can search an Archie server manually (ugh!), one terrific utility automates the process: Stairways Software Pty Ltd FTP tool **Interarchy** 5.0 ($45; www.interarchy.com). Interarchy searches the servers for files but lets you download the files once you've found them. Of course, Interarchy can also download files from FTP sites (**Figure 21.55**). [*Interarchy makes FTP uploads and downloads a matter of dragging icons the way we've always done in the Finder. A smart, deep, and fast program.—DJS*]

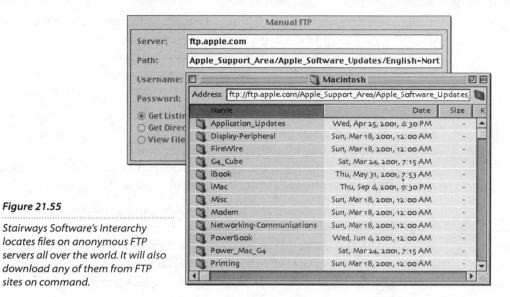

Figure 21.55

Stairways Software's Interarchy locates files on anonymous FTP servers all over the world. It will also download any of them from FTP sites on command.

Usenet (TA)

Before we embark on an updated discussion of Usenet and the many popular Mac-based software products that access it, here is a definition of Usenet:

> *Usenet is a collection of user-submitted notes or messages on various subjects that are posted to servers on a worldwide network. Each subject collection of posted notes is known as a newsgroup. There are thousands of newsgroups and it is possible for you to form a new one. Most newsgroups are hosted on Internet-connected servers, but they can also be hosted from servers that are not part of the Internet. Usenet's original protocol was Unix-to-Unix Copy (UUCP), but today the Network News Transfer Protocol (NNTP) is [primarily] used.*—From WhatIs.com

Browsers can contain newsreader components that allow you to access Usenet via NNTP. Newer versions of Netscape Communicator (from AOL) have this feature. Microsoft's Outlook Express combines a newsreader with a POP e-mail client. Also, you can find applications built to serve the newsreader function almost exclusively (such YA-NewsWatcher—see "Software for Accessing Usenet," later in this section). On the Web, Critical Path (formerly RemarQ) and other sites provide a subject-oriented directory as well as a search approach to newsgroups and help you register to participate in them. These sites use HTTP protocols, allowing you to navigate and participate in Usenet through your browser.

Being a vast network of message boards, Usenet is widely considered the original network for online discussion and sharing of rich media (such as photos and graphics). These days, Usenet is becoming more easily accessible and searchable through friendly Web-based connections. Before services such as these came along, Usenet's text-intensive interface made access and participation difficult, especially for nontechnical people.

One of the ways Critical Path makes Usenet easy to digest is by renaming message boards for easy identification. For example, the Usenet name for one message board about travel in Europe is rec.travel.europe. Critical Path calls the board European Travel to make it easier for people to find and identify.

 Another popular Web-based alternative for searching and reading Usenet content is hosted by Google, the awesome search engine. The service, formerly known as Deja News, can be accessed at http://groups.google.com. It is a comprehensive Usenet archive that you can search without a newsreader client.

Software for Accessing Usenet

You have almost two dozen newsreader clients to choose from, but three of the more popular are YA-NewsWatcher (we tested version 5.1), Microsoft Outlook Express (we tested version 5.02), and Netscape Communicator (we tested version 4.72).

Each product is quite different in scope, with Communicator including an Internet browser (Navigator), an e-mail client, and a Usenet newsreader. Neither Outlook Express nor YA-NewsWatcher incorporate an Internet browser but you can set them up to launch Internet Explorer when you select a hyperlink in a news item. Outlook Express is primarily an e-mail client and newsreader (see the e-mail section for more detail on Outlook as an e-mail client). NewsWatcher is primarily a newsreader, with some basic messaging functionality.

All three products are available for free.

YA-NewsWatcher. Although it focuses almost exclusively on Usenet news, YA-NewsWatcher (short for Yet Another NewsWatcher) was lacking in screen presentation and simplicity. However, if you are already using a browser and a primary e-mail client (which most of us are), this product has an extensive feature set for the pure news user. By not containing redundant browsing and e-mail functions, this product will appeal to many as a comprehensive newsreader and a worthy tool in their software toolboxes.

When you launch YA-NewsWatcher, the Preferences window (accessible from the Edit menu) provides many options to customize the environment, with the News Server Entry panel being the most important. Here you enter the news server's domain name or IP address (you need these before you can actually go to any newsgroups; you can get the name or address from your ISP). Once this is done, you can easily connect and download newsgroups. YA-NewsWatcher lacks setup wizards, though, and it's difficult to identify where you have to enter the needed information to begin a Usenet session. Once YA-NewsWatcher is underway, though, you'll appreciate many of its useful features. A Status window always gives a view of what the application is doing at any given time (including connection to a host and message downloading). This is helpful when the system is busy performing a network-intensive task. You can also easily cycle between open windows for easy navigation.

A Newsreading options panel lets you limit the number of articles fetched at a time. View options are extremely granular and set via the Subject Windows panel. Here you can set sort order, thread indicators (to view or not to view message threads), and priority labels.

YA-NewsWatcher also has an extensive filtering function, helping you filter messages from specific, user-defined newsgroups. You can also filter on message subjects, messages from certain individuals or groups, or even other news-hosting services.

YA-NewsWatcher is a full-featured newsreader and easy to use and customize once you've properly set it up.

Microsoft Outlook Express. Outlook Express, a combination e-mail client and Usenet newsreader, boasts an integrated e-mail/newsreader interface that portrays Usenet messages in much the same way it displays e-mail messages. The commonality between the e-mail inbox folder and a Usenet news group folder is apparent in the screen views of both. Messages are organized using the column headers From, Subject, Sent, and Size. This is helpful because Usenet discussion groups use messages and responses similarly to the way e-mail does, albeit in a threaded discussion format. Providing this consistent view of Usenet is one of Outlook Express's greatest strengths, giving a familiar look and feel to a sometimes daunting array of groups, messages, and attachments.

Setup is simplified through an extensive array of wizards that you will be quite comfortable with if you are a Microsoft Office user. Upon startup, you are prompted for setup specifics on the news and mail services before being brought into the application for first-time use. This reduces the opportunities for confusion. Many Office-like features appear in Outlook Express, with similar menu layouts and Word-like shortcuts. This also reduces confusion (for Microsoft Office users especially).

Other useful features include default-encoded attachments using AppleDouble format. This allows attachments to be easily decoded and read by both Macintosh and Windows operating systems. Other encoding formats are available as well (BinHex, UUencode). Outlook Express supports users who share a computer by providing separate inboxes and by storing separate account and preference information for each user. Outlook Express also supports the multiuser functionality available in Mac OS 9 and later. It has an extensive help function that guides the user through a thoughtful array of timesaving tips and features.

Outlook Express is a mature and full-featured newsreader, with a clean look and feel. The presentation consistency with other Microsoft products makes it familiar and easy to use, something you will appreciate if you are new to Usenet.

Netscape Communicator. Communicator is a browser application that also includes an e-mail client and a Usenet newsreader. Although these two modules don't take center stage, they are still stars in their own right. Accessible via the Communicator menu, messaging and newsgroups are integrated much the same way Outlook Express integrates the two functions, which is through a consistent presentation of the mail and Usenet message folders. A hierarchy of message folders is presented in the window's left pane, with the selected message folder open in the top-right pane and a preview pane on the bottom right. This is almost identical to Outlook Express's presentation.

The Preferences window is extremely useful, giving access to all the presentation and usability options contained in all three modules: browser, e-mail, and newsreader. The organization of the window is clean and easy to navigate, giving the user one place in which to customize the entire program. Although it is lacking the extensive wizards setup functionality of Outlook Express, Communicator is easy to set up and use.

Communicator provides filtering capability at the message level, allowing the user to screen unwanted content. Although not as extensive as YA-NewsWatcher's filter, it is still useful, especially at the message level.

Communicator is the most full-featured of the products we tested. Mature and all-encompassing, it has a host of useful and user-friendly features that make it a capable newsreader. If you are looking to have your browsing, e-mail, and newsreader capabilities bundled into one product, this is the one for you.

Chatting/Conferencing (JO)

We've been able to talk to one another using telephones for some time now, so why are so many people, especially teenagers, using instant-messaging systems to converse? Who knows?

The Instant Messenger client from America Online (AOL) has popularized the instant-messaging phenomenon. Using instant-messaging applications, two or more people can "chat" in real time by typing and sending messages back and forth. One attraction of these services is that they're free. AOL's

Instant Messenger has the largest following, but Microsoft has MSN Messenger, Yahoo has Yahoo Messenger, and a host of products, such as ICQ (www.icq.com/download/ftp-macppc.html), use Internet Relay Chat (IRC) as a message-exchange transport (**Figure 21.56**). The unfortunate problem with these messaging tools is a lack of interoperability. Microsoft and Yahoo have tried to make their products work with the popular AOL Instant Messenger system, but AOL has thus far thwarted their attempts by changing its code and blocking non-AOL clients at every pass.

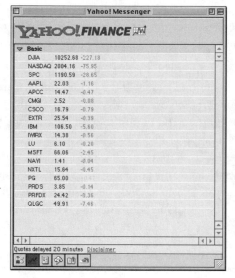

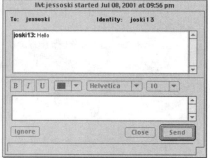

Figure 21.56

Among the clients that offer instant messaging are Yahoo Messenger (shown here), MSN Messenger, and ICQ.

 A variant of typing messages back and forth is videoconferencing, using products such as CUseeMe. With a small desktop video camera you can create a virtual videophone, and suddenly the Jetsons have nothing on you.

Getting Started

You can download a copy of the client software for AOL Instant Messenger, Yahoo Messenger, or MSN Messenger from the America Online, Yahoo, and Microsoft Mactopia Web sites, respectively:

AOL Instant Messenger
www.aol.com/aim/home.html

Yahoo Messenger
http://messenger.yahoo.com/intl/us/

MSN Messenger
www.microsoft.com/mac/messenger/messenger_default.asp?navindex=s15

 If you look carefully, you can even get Carbonized versions of some of these products for Mac OS X.

Once you have downloaded and installed the client software, you need to register and then find some buddies. To communicate with one or more of your friends who use the same messaging system, you need to know their screen names, system names, or e-mail addresses. All the products provide a means to search for your buddies using a variety of demographics, but it's best to exchange e-mail or a phone call to ensure that you have their correct messaging names.

You can group messaging buddies in folders and store them on your buddy list. When they are online, their names will appear in the Online portion of the list. You can even configure the software to alert you when one of your buddies appears online so you can pounce on him or her with a greeting.

To start a chat session using AOL Instant Messenger, you select someone on your buddy list who is online and click the IM button. A window appears for your conversation, where you can type whatever you like and then press Enter (not Return) or hit the Send button to send the message (**Figure 21.57**). You can change the appearance and emphasis of your messages using the same character formatting (such as fonts, bold, underline, italics) you use in word-processing and other Macintosh applications. To display emotions in your message text, you can pick from a good collection of icons. Another way to embellish your messages is to include "images." These can be short movie clips, recorded sounds, or still images.

This is not the free-for-all you might expect. If there are people you do not wish to chat with, you can send them warnings or block them entirely.

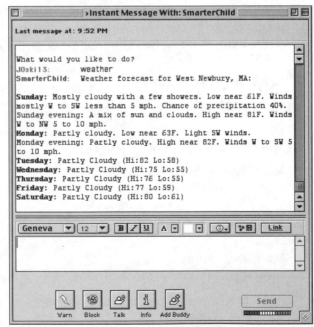

Figure 21.57

Instant messaging, popularized by America Online's Instant Messenger (shown here), makes it easy to chat with one or more people in real time.

Getting Involved

Once you've gotten comfortable with simple keyboard conversations, you can try your hand at multiple conversations or group chats. You can chat one-on-one with several people simultaneously, as long as you can keep track of the various conversations. Just open multiple windows and type separate conversations into each window. If you have a group of people whom you want to talk with together—as in a conference call—you can select the individuals from your buddy list and click the Chat button to create an impromptu meeting room for a group discussion.

Should you wish to lurk or get on your soapbox in a free-form chat room, you can select from a variety of community chats hosted on AOL Instant Messenger. Topics range from pets to popular movies, music to television shows, artists to basketball. You should be aware of the proper protocol for discussion, as these rooms are often monitored, and use of improper or abusive language will often result in censorship.

Finally, if you have a computer equipped with a microphone and speakers—as most Macs have—you can talk back and forth with someone. The voice quality is poor, so you should not expect this method to substitute for a telephone conversation—unless you're accustomed to talking to someone overseas with a poor phone connection.

Meet George Jetson

Those of you who can remember the 1960s probably recall the notion that the videophone was a bold example of what technology of the future would bring us. The promise was that one day you would be able to see the person with whom you were talking. Here in the beginning of the 21th century, videophones have not yet become a household phenomenon, but a Mac equipped with a Web cam or other video camera can serve as a crude videoconferencing system. In addition to the camera, you will need some software to conduct your video chats. Cornell University created a product called **CUseeMe** some time ago. CUseeMe is no longer being developed for the Mac—although you can still download older versions of the software on the Web—but a great freeware alternative called **iVisit** is available from Eyematic Interfaces (www.eyematic.com). Another voice option is Internet "soft phones." These applications can turn your microphone-equipped Macintosh into a telephone. With software such as **Net2Phone** (www.net2phone.com), you can place calls to anyone over the Internet using a technology called Voice over IP (VoIP). (Net2Phone says it has a Macintosh version of its client software in the works.) These applications are part of the growing trend toward using our high-speed data networks to transmit voice (and video) traffic. The application digitizes and compresses your speech and then transmits it over a TCP/IP connection to the desired endpoint. If you're calling a conventional land or cell phone, a gateway converts your call back to a standard call—otherwise the soft phone you are calling handles the job. Pricing for these services runs from free to a few cents per minute. They can provide a lower-quality alternative to using the public switched-telephone network for your calls. Quality is a function of the amount of congestion on the Internet and the level of compression used for your call. Although soft phones are no substitute for calling across town, if you want to save some money talking to those far away—both domestically and internationally—these applications show considerable promise.

Where to Visit (AD)

Now that you know what the Web is and how to access it, the next question is where to go—what sites to visit.

When the Web first became popular, and most big companies (and even the little ones) started building their own Web sites, these sites were often known as "brochureware" because they consisted of little more than an electronic pamphlet, or brochure. In the past few years, many of these companies have moved to add more content to their sites. *Content* is the word most people use to refer to the meat of a Web site—the stuff that keeps you coming back.

Apple's Web Site

In addition to the features we discussed earlier in "The Mac Advantage," you have several other reasons to visit Apple's Web site (www.apple.com). Apple maintains a comprehensive set of technical notes that can help you resolve problems you might experience with both Mac hardware and software. Click the Support tab from any page on Apple's Web site, and you can get to these technical notes or download updates to any of Apple's system or application software. Apple's online Store is a good place to visit to buy a new Mac or add accessories or software to one that you already own. Apple also maintains a special location to showcase its QuickTime streaming video content. The QuickTime tab take you a page on the site where you can view trailers for forthcoming or recently released movies and connect with one of the many streaming video channels featured on the site (**Figure 21.58**). Finally, Apple features its latest operating system, Mac OS X, on its site. The tab devoted to Mac OS X is a good resource for viewing news, tips, and tutorials on the operating system and the applications that have been or will soon be released for it.

Figure 21.58

Clicking the QuickTime button on Apple's Web site brings you to this page where Apple showcases its QuickTime Player and QuickTime TV streaming video channels.

The biggest problem most people have with the Web is deciding where to go and finding out what sites exist. Since the Web is just that, a web, it isn't organized in any human-readable fashion, the way a newspaper or magazine might be. So finding things on the Web can be difficult. Most people tend to find sites for an area or two they are interested in and then find other sites by following links on the ones they already know about. Another way people find out about good sites is by word of mouth.

Search engines, which we'll discuss in a bit, are good at finding specific information but can often be inadequate guides to the Web sites you'd like to keep coming back to.

Other Mac-Related Sites

A whole bunch of sites out there supply you with news and information about your Mac, let you download software, offer tutorials and tips for using your computer, and generally provide a place to hang out in cyberspace with other Mac users.

One of my favorite Mac sites is **www.woz.org,** run by Apple cofounder Steve Wozniak (**Figure 21.59**). Called Woz by just about everyone, this father of Apple answers e-mail from fans and other curious parties (you can learn quite a bit about Apple lore by reading through this correspondence), maintains a library of links to Mac resources on the Web, and discourses on his various interests, which include an all-consuming passion for the game Tetris. Beyond doubt, the best part of this site is the Woz Cam—you can actually watch Woz as he works away in his office and can even pan and zoom around the room.

Figure 21.59

Steve Wozniak's Web site, Woz.org.

Another notable Mac-specific site is **MacDirectory** (www.macdirectory.com), where you can get Mac-related news and technical support and find Mac resellers and consultants. Another, **Macinstein** (www.macinstein.com), is a Mac-only search engine that has links to virtually every Mac-related item or service you could hope to find. Many sites deal specifically in Mac- and Apple-related news. **MacCentral** (http://maccentral.macworld.com/) and **MacInTouch** (www.macintouch.com) do their best to bring you breaking news about issues that affect your Mac, such as software updates, Apple financial results, and new hardware.

Search Engines

The best way to find specific information on the Web is by using a search engine. Many search engines are also now portal sites (or many portal sites now also have search engines), so in many cases they can be one-stop shops for just about everything you need on the Web. Of course one of the first and most famous search engines is **Yahoo** (www.yahoo.com). This site has so much going on that it is actually pretty short on charm these days (Web surfers often joke that this site, which is the most popular on the Web, is also the ugliest), but it is nonetheless useful.

Additional search engines include:

Ask Jeeves (www.ask.com)   **Google** (www.google.com)

Dogpile (www.dogpile.com)   **HotBot** (www.hotbot.com)

Excite (www.excite.com)   **LookSmart** (www.looksmart.com)

Go.com (www.infoseek.com)   **Lycos** (www.lycos.com)

Of course, there are many more, and each works a little differently from the others. **Ask Jeeves** and **LookSmart,** for instance, allow you to submit search queries in what's called "natural language"—that is, the way you might ask a person where to find something. To use the others you must enter criteria, or keywords, in that site's search syntax. Most of these sites use standard syntaxes, such as Boolean operators, but you should always click the search tips button or link to find out how each site works. Often your search terms will yield a whole slew of results that have nothing to do with what you're looking for. This will probably happen until you become more skilled at refining your search terms. To get you started, however, here are a few tips that should help you out on most search sites:

 If you are searching for a name or other multiword term, such as *Albert Einstein* or *Mac software,* you should put it in quotation marks. Otherwise, most search engines will look for sites that contain either one or the other word.

 The word *not* can come in handy. Search for the term *Apple* and you could get results that have nothing to do with the computer company. Instead, try something like *"Apple NOT orchard"* to narrow the results.

 In many search engines, you can use an asterisk to tell the engine to look for a word that ends in a number of ways. For instance, if you search on *cat** you will get results for catalogues, cater, cathode, catholic, and catch, among others. This can be useful if you are looking for Mac sites, because simply typing *Mac** will cover the word *Macintosh* as well.

 Remember that you can always search within the results of your first search. It is often best to start out with broad search terms and then look within those results for narrower terms.

 Some sites, such as Dogpile, will automatically submit your search terms to a variety of search engines, modifying them so that they adhere to those engines' preferred syntax. I find sites such as this handy because I can search multiple sites without actually having to go to them. Of course, you can also do this with Internet Explorer's Search panel or by clicking the Search button in Navigator's toolbar.

Don't expect every search engine to be able to find every site on the Web. Searching is an inexact science, and it often takes engines a long time to find out about sites. Search engines work by sending little virtual robots out on the Web to crawl around and look for new sites. Most Web sites have something called *metadata* buried in their HTML code, and this data tells the search bots what that site is about (and is generally the text a search engine will turn up next to a link to that site). Most search engines will also let you submit your site for them to index, so that a search for you will call up your Web site, for instance, but this can take a long time to accomplish.

The important thing about searching the Web is to not get discouraged if you end up with a lot of results you don't want. With a little patience you can narrow them down or come up with better search terms.

Daily News, Magazines, and More

Besides searching for specific information, the Web is good at providing you with the kind of news you would get in a daily newspaper. In fact, so many news sites are on the Web, I almost never pick up an actual paper anymore. Why pay for a subscription to *The New York Times* when I can read almost the entire paper on the Web for free? In addition to the sites run by newspapers and magazines you can find sites run by news networks such as CNN and online-only news organizations.

You can usually find the day's bigger news headlines at portal sites such as the search engines mentioned earlier. In addition, most of the search engines offer an option to search news, as opposed to the entire Web. This means they will search wire reports from such services as Reuters and the Associated Press as well as press releases that businesses have submitted to those services.

Some good sites to try for your daily news dose are:

CNN.com (http://cnn.com). I like it because it offers video clips of many news items.

NPR (www.npr.org/news). The news site for National Public Radio.

BBC News (http://news.bbc.co.uk). The British Broadcasting Corporation.

LATimes.com (www.latimes.com). The *Los Angeles Times* on the Web.

The New York Times on the Web (www.nytimes.com). *The New York Times.*

Newcity.com (www.newcity.com). An alternative news portal.

You can also find a growing crop of online magazines, which because they are on the Web, have an unlimited amount of space for content. Perhaps the most popular of these is Salon.com (www.salon.com). A general-interest magazine with a terrifically talented group of writers, Salon covers everything from entertainment to politics to technology. Others to check out are Feed.com (www.feedmag.com), and the Microsoft-run Slate (www.slate.com). And if you like satire, don't miss The Onion (www.theonion.com), a send-up of modern news that is one of the more entertaining stops on the Web.

If there's one thing true of the Web, it's that it has at least one of everything on it, and usually more than one. There are sites devoted to anything you could possibly imagine as well as answers to any question you could ask.

Though it can often be hard to find just what you're looking for, especially if you are new to the Web, it is out there, and with a little perseverance and the willingness to go to new places and try a few new things, you'll find it.

Honors Internet (JO)

Making the most of your Internet experience with a Macintosh poses some additional challenges and opportunities. The increasingly popular broadband networking options, both via cable modem and DSL, provide a great way to leverage a home network. But before you consider one of these high-speed, always-on connections, you need to ensure that your Macintosh, or home network of computers, is protected from unauthorized access—or worse, tampering. The Internet's vast, uncontrolled nature has its bright and dark sides. The wealth of information available to you (and your family) via the Internet grows by the day. Likewise, content that you might find objectionable also seems to grow at an almost equally rapid rate.

Sharing the Wealth

The advent of affordable, easy-to-install home and small-office (SOHO) networking technology has made it easy for two or more computers to share information and peripherals (such as printers). Although an Internet connection is not really a peripheral, much of the same logic applies to sharing one. Whether you have a dial-up or a broadband connection to the Internet, it is impractical to have multiple computers in your home connect to the Internet simultaneously. You will either need additional phone lines for each simultaneous connection or separate, expensive broadband connections to each of your computers.

During the past few years, some elegant software and hardware products have emerged that allow many computers to share a single Internet connection, much as businesses have been doing for years. These products depend on a device called a *router* that intelligently transmits packets from one network (the Internet) to another network (your home or SOHO network). Initially, these products appeared as software that you run on a Macintosh. Some examples are Sustainable Softworks's **IPNetRouter** (from $89; www.sustworks.com) and Vicomsoft's (www.vicomsoft.com) **SurfDoubler** (from $54.99) and **Internet Gateway** (from $149). SurfDoubler is strictly for the home user and allows a maximum of three computers to share a single connection. Internet Gateway can support unlimited users. IPNetRouter not only offers routing for an unlimited number of computers but provides some other key services, such as Dynamic Host Configuration Protocol (DHCP) support, filtering, and port mapping. You can use these link-sharing products with a dial-up connection or Ethernet connection to a cable modem or DSL router.

For those seeking a easier, plug-and-play alternative, a wide variety of products labeled DSL/cable modem routers and hubs have begun to appear on the market. Coming from network-equipment providers such as **Linksys** (www.linksys.com), **NetGear** (www.netgear.com), and **Asanté** (www.asante.com), these products are an appliance version of the software products mentioned earlier. They're typically restricted to broadband connections, so you can't use them to share a dial-up link, but they are priced competitively—starting at $80 or so. The nice feature of these products is that they are easy to set up and use. Administration is commonly done through a Web browser, and default configurations should suffice for many users. As an added protection, they do provide some firewall functionality as well restrict unauthorized access to your home network from most common types of intrusion attempts.

The Digital Watchdog

Having a high-speed, always-on connection to the Internet is convenient. It allows you to use your Macintosh as an Internet appliance with relative ease because you avoid the time-consuming process of dialing your ISP every time to want to find something on the Internet. As is usually the case, the reward does not come without some risk. Having your Macintosh persistently connected to the Internet can make it a target for attack—even though we all know that Macs traditionally have been more resilient than most when it comes to security vulnerabilities. You can add a layer of protection to your Macintosh by installing a personal firewall. To thwart those who may try to snoop, borrow, or damage information on your Mac, these applications restrict incoming access via TCP/IP. Some examples of personal firewall applications are **Norton Personal Firewall,** from Symantec ($69.95; www.symantec.com/sabu/nis/npf_mac/), **IPNetSentry,** from Sustainable Softworks (www.sustworks.com), and **NetBarrier,** from Intego ($59.95; www.intego.com). These products are easy to install and set up, even for the average user, and they provide you with a log of all the attempts made to access your Mac. If you have a high-speed connection in your home or small office, or you travel frequently to visit customers or stay in hotels with high-speed access, a personal firewall can give you an added level of security.

The Good Without the Bad and Ugly

Allowing your children unfettered Internet access to your computer can be like letting them run loose in Times Square at night. If you've ever mistakenly typed the wrong URL when using a browser, you are apt to have come across some objectionable content—the logic goes, if it happened to you, it will probably happen to your kids. You can reduce the likelihood that this will happen by installing a content-filtering application on your Macintosh. Two of the best content-filtering applications are SurfControl's **Cyber Patrol** ($49.95; www.surfcontrol.com) and Intego's **ContentBarrier** ($39.95; www.intego.com).

Cyber Patrol is a ratings-based approach to content filtering. When you install the software, you specify the types of content you want to filter. Content can range from sexual or pornographic material to violent or illegal topics. You can specify filters on a user-by-user basis and pick any combination of topics to limit. When a user tries to go to a Web site, the Web address is compared with a list maintained by SurfControl. If the site is allowed, you can see it—if not, you are presented with a message saying that the content is not permitted. You can limit other Internet use as well, such as news, e-mail, and messaging. If you are interested in limiting Internet access time or limiting access at certain times of day, Cyber Patrol will also let you add these filters. The CyberNot list is updated automatically when you subscribe to the service so your filters can track the ever-changing content on the Internet.

Intego's ContentBarrier follows a similar approach and many will appreciate its cleaner user interface (**Figure 21.60**). It supports multiple users, lets you regulate the times that Internet access is allowed, and can prevent the user from supplying personal information to those with whom you might be unwilling to share it.

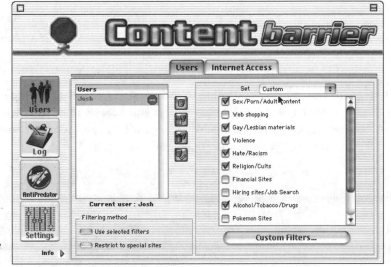

Figure 21.60

ContentBarrier lets you set up filters for all the folks who use your Mac.

These approaches to content filtering are by no means foolproof. The SurfControl approach in particular relies upon the CyberNot Oversight Committee to categorize sites with potentially objectionable material. With new sites appearing all the time, it is hard for the committee to stay ahead of some sites that may contain material you would rather your child not view. There is no substitute for supervised browsing to prevent the presentation of unwanted content.

Sharing with Your Peers

Remember the Napster phenomenon that took place during 2000 and 2001? This system, based on a peer-to-peer file-sharing model, enabled users to share files, in this case digital music, with the world. Napster's approach was not entirely peer-to-peer since it depended on directory servers that tracked content and the sites on which it was stored. In case you missed it, a massive copyright storm erupted and Napster shut down its service with the hope of reinventing itself.

Concurrent with the ascension of Napster, other true peer-to-peer file-sharing systems began to emerge. Unlike Napster, which was focused solely on music, these others demonstrated that anything could be shared—images, music, video, applications, and documents. One of the more popular is Gnutella, an open, decentralized, peer-to-peer search system that is used to find and share files. Gnutella is not an application, it is a protocol for sharing information on a peer-to-peer basis. Client applications, of which there are many, reach out to other Gnutella systems, telling them what they have when queries are sent over the Internet. (This is a simplification of the process—you can find more information at http://gnutella.wego.com/.)

There are a few Gnutella client/server applications for the Macintosh. LimeWire (www.limewire.com) and Mactella (www.cxc.com) are two popular freeware examples (**Figure 21.61**). They're both available for both Mac OS 9 and Mac OS X. The beauty of Gnutella is that it allows you to share virtually anything.

 It would be irresponsible to recommend freely sharing copyrighted content with the world: It is illegal to post and download content without the assent of the copyright holder. You can generally restrict access and limit what you share by tweaking the application's settings.

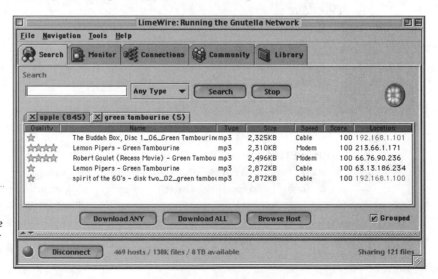

Figure 21.61

With the LimeWire client you can access Gnutella, one of the most popular systems for peer-to-peer file sharing.

22

Cross-Platform Compatibility

John Rizzo is the chapter editor and author.

Don't worry, they said. Go ahead and buy a Mac—it can do everything a PC can and more. Now you're having trouble working collaboratively with your Windows-using colleagues. You can't open a file someone sent you, or you can't run a program someone wants you to, or you can't connect to a network.

This may sound like blasphemy in the *Macintosh Bible,* but here goes: The Mac has limitations. The cruel fact is, Windows PCs work better with other Windows PCs than Macs do. Let's face it—it's a Windows world, and it's up to you to deal with it.

The good news is that you *can* deal with it. With a few extra utilities and some know-how, you can join the Windows world without leaving the comfort of the Mac. Sometimes the solutions are simple, other times they're not. But there *are* solutions for most cross-platform problems.

Most Mac-PC compatibility issues have to do with using PC files and creating files your Windows colleagues can use. This chapter describes the differences between Mac and PC files and their most common cross-platform problems.

Another major area of cross-platform problems is networking—a fuzzy area that is difficult to get a handle on. But you can add some tools to your Mac to get it talking Windows.

Some of the problems I describe in this chapter also apply to dealing with Linux and Unix users, and I point it out when they do. Mac OS X tends to have fewer problems with Linux and Unix, since it has Unix built into its core.

In This Chapter

Working with Files

Files are the stuff that your work is made of. (At least, they are on a computer.) And files are where many of your cross-platform problems lie. Most people don't realize that a lot of the problems with files downloaded from the Internet are actually cross-platform file problems.

Some of the file incompatibilities you may run into have to do with the fact that Mac files are intrinsically different from Windows and Linux files. This section first deals with some basic differences between Mac files and files created on other computers and how these differences cause cross-platform problems. I then proceed to specific problems with using files that PC users send you and problems with files you send to PC users.

Note on cross-platform terminology: Most PCs do Windows, but many Intel-based PCs are running Linux. When I refer to *PC*, the statement can apply to Windows or Linux. I use the term *Windows* to refer to issues specific to that operating system.

What's in a Mac File

Macintosh files are a bit more complex than Windows files. Mac files have some invisible components that Windows, Unix, and Linux files don't have and consequently don't support. (Mac OS X is one flavor of Unix that does support these Mac file attributes.) Special server software designed to support Mac clients can handle these Macintosh file components, even if the servers are running Windows and Linux. However, non-Mac desktop machines don't support Mac file attributes, and neither do many servers for Internet e-mail, Web, FTP, and other services. These operating systems will simply ignore and lose the Mac file attributes. This can have various results, from the loss of a file's icon to the destruction of the file.

So what are these mysterious, unseen file attributes? There are several, but the most important is the resource fork, which holds code. Then there are the type and creator codes, which help the Mac identify a file.

Generic Icon

Figure 22.1

A generic file icon can indicate a missing file fork as well as missing type and creator codes.

File forks. Traditional Mac files (or Mac OS 9 and earlier files) consist of two *forks*—a *data fork* and a *resource fork*. The data fork contains the data contents of a file—the text, formatting, graphics, and sound you created. The resource fork contains programming code and file resources, such as the file's icon.

If you move a file from a Mac to a PC and then back to a Mac, the file will lose its icon—the icon becomes generic (**Figure 22.1**). (The same is true if you move a Mac file to Unix, Linux, or many Internet servers and back.) This is because the file has lost its resource fork.

The loss of an icon in a document file is not fatal—you can still open the file from the Open dialog box of an application that supports the file format. But if an *application* loses its resource fork, the program won't work. That's because the resource fork is where the application keeps the executable programming code that makes the application an application.

Self-expanding archives and self-mounting disk-image files also contain code in their resources. These consist of small programs that decompress the archive or mount the disk image on the desktop. If the resource fork of these types of files is lost, the embedded program is lost, and the file won't open.

This means merely moving these types of files to PCs and back to Macs can destroy them. To prevent this, some software creates files that combine the resource and data forks. These types of files are said to be *flat*. All Windows files are flat. Some Mac software can create flat files. QuickTime files, for instance, are flat and can run across platforms on Macs and PCs.

Apple is encouraging Mac OS X developers to make new software that creates flat files. That is, the applications will put the resources in the data fork. This will make the files more portable and able to move around the Internet and to Windows PCs without problems. Mac OS X can also use files with file forks (separate resource and data forks).

As time goes on, we may see the use of file forks diminish and eventually fade away. However, at this time you will find that most files created in Mac OS X do have data and resource forks, as do all files created in Mac OS 9 and earlier.

Type and creator codes. The type and creator codes are important Macintosh file attributes that PCs lose along with the resource fork. A file's *creator code* tells Mac OS which application to launch when you double-click the file. The *type code* identifies the file format, such as JPEG, plain text, or Microsoft Word 2001. Together, a file's type and creator codes determine a file's icon and what application will launch when you double-click the file.

If you know the type and creator codes, you can add them back in if they've disappeared. The table "Codes and Their Descriptions" shows a few common type and creator codes. Note that type and creator codes are case-sensitive.

Mac OS X–native files don't always need type and creator codes—new Mac OS X–native software can create files without them. Mac OS X can use type and creator codes or use the filename extensions.

Codes and Their Descriptions

Type Codes	Description
APPL	application
CWSS	AppleWorks spreadsheet
CWWP	AppleWorks word-processing file
PDF	PDF file
TEXT	text (generic) file
W8BN	Microsoft Word 98 file
XLS8	Microsoft Excel 98 file
Creator Codes	**Description**
8BIM	Adobe Photoshop
BOBO	AppleWorks 6
CARO	Acrobat Reader
MOSS	Netscape Communicator
MSWD	Microsoft Word
ttxt	SimpleText
XCEL	Microsoft Excel

In Mac OS 9 and earlier, you can use Sherlock to read the type and creator codes of a file. Unfortunately, as of this writing, Mac OS X's Sherlock could not do this trick. Here is how to do it in Mac OS 9:

1. Open Sherlock and click Edit.
2. Drag the file you are interested in from the Finder to Sherlock's More Search Options window.
3. Look under Advanced Options. The "file type" and "creator" fields will display the codes of the file.

In **Figure 22.2** Sherlock displays a PDF file with its codes intact. A file created on a PC with no codes might show random characters or question marks in the "file type" and "creator" fields (**Figure 22.3**).

You can change or add type and creator codes to files with other tools, such as Apple's ResEdit or MacLinkPlus (see "Editing Type and Creator Codes," below).

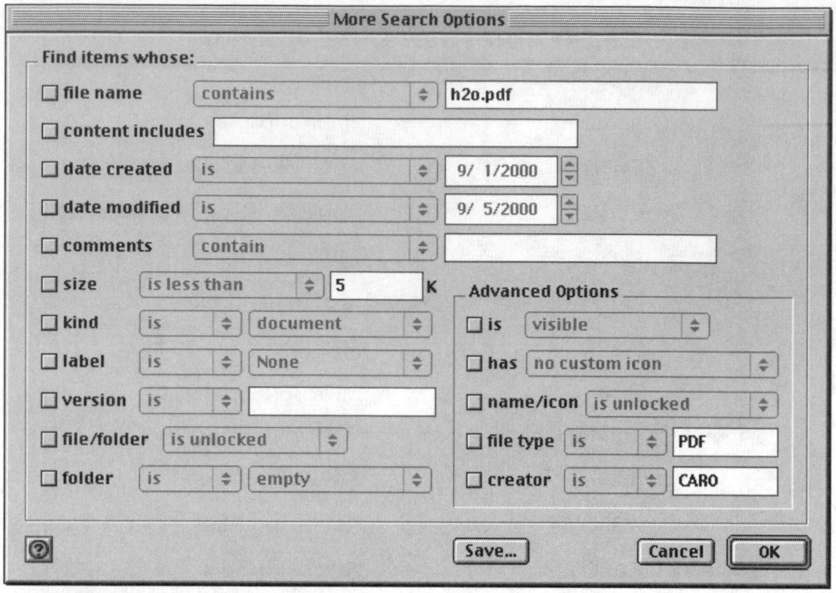

Figure 22.2

Use Sherlock to read a file's type and creator codes.

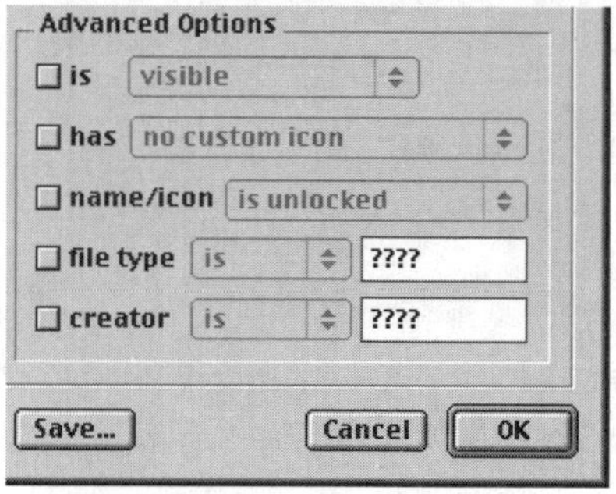

Figure 22.3

A file with no type and creator codes might appear this way in Sherlock.

Extension mapping in Mac OS 9 and earlier. Other operating systems don't use type and creator codes. To identify files, Windows and Linux mostly use the file's filename extension—the characters after the dot at the end of a filename. Files created on Windows often have a generic icon when copied to a Mac.

Mac OS 9 and earlier has a feature that can associate, or map, the file extension to type and creator codes. The purpose of this Mac software is to find an application to open a PC file when you double-click it. Two control panels do extension mapping:

- The File Exchange control panel works with files copied to your hard drive from PC-formatted disks (**Figure 22.4**).

- The File Extension Mappings menu in the Internet control panel (click the File Mapping icon in the Advanced panel) works with files downloaded from the Internet (**Figure 22.5**).

This isn't a particularly useful feature, however, which may explain why it wasn't included in the first versions of Mac OS X. One problem is that both control panels list applications you may not have—if you don't have the application, the file mapping does nothing for you.

You can add file mappings for your applications if they aren't listed. You can also edit file mappings. For instance, the default setting for files ending in .jpg (JPEG files) is QuickTime's PictureViewer. You could change this to Adobe Photoshop if you like—this makes Photoshop launch when you double-click files ending in .jpg that don't have type and creator codes and that you either download from the Internet or copy to your hard drive from a PC disk.

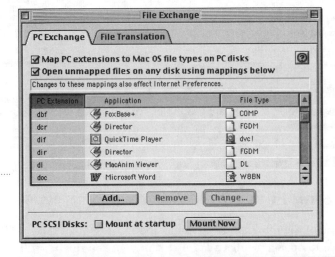

Figure 22.4

The File Exchange control panel handles extension mappings of files on PC disks.

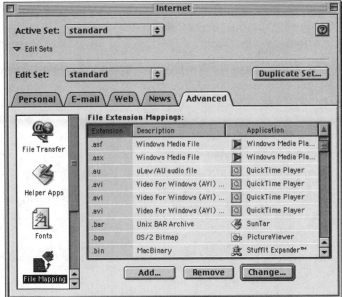

Figure 22.5

The Internet control panel handles extension mappings of files downloaded from the Internet.

You can edit extension mappings in either the Internet or File Extension control panel. The two have a nearly identical interface in Mac OS 9. However, if you want to change both at the same time, do your editing in the File Exchange control panel:

1. From the list, select the extension you would like to edit.

2. Click the Change button. A new window called Change Mapping appears (**Figure 22.6**).

3. Scroll through the list of applications, and pick one that has the ability to open the file.

4. Click the Change button.

The Mac's file-extension software doesn't always work, as there are loopholes. You can set Web browsers to not use the Internet control panel, for instance. And remember, if you don't have the software to open a PC file, extension mapping doesn't help—which brings us to the next section.

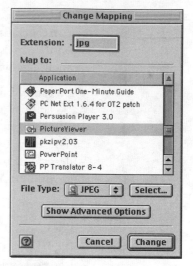

Figure 22.6

You can edit extension mapping in the File Exchange control panel.

Using Files from Windows

One of the most annoying things about living in a PC world is not being able to open a file that a PC user sent you. You might get this file as an attachment to an e-mail message. Or maybe you copied it from your local network or downloaded it from the Internet or dragged it from a Zip disk. Unfortunately, there isn't a single cause of this problem. But here are some likely suspects:

The file was created with a program you don't have. For example, someone sends you a Microsoft Word file, but you don't have Word and use AppleWorks instead.

The fix for this is to use translation software to convert the file.

Wrong (or no) type-creator code. In this case, you do have an application that can open your file, but your Mac doesn't know it.

Extension mapping might work here. If it doesn't, there are tools you can use to add the correct type and creator codes (see "Editing Type and Creator Codes," later in the chapter).

Encoding. The sender's e-mail software encoded it in a format your software can't decode.

You'll have to use software tools that can decode PC or Linux and Unix encoding formats. (See "Receiving E-mail Attachments: Encoding and Compression" later in the chapter.)

Compression. The sender's e-mail software compressed the file in a format your software can't decode.

Some of the same software that can decode PC attachments can also decompress PC compression formats.

The file was corrupted. This is rare and is most likely not your problem, but it does happen with files from Mac or PC users. If this is the case, all you can do is ask the sender to resend the file.

Remember, for now we are talking about PC files coming to your Mac. We'll talk about sending Mac files to PC users later in the chapter (see "Translating Mac Files to PC Formats" later in the chapter).

Translating files. You get a file and none of your applications can translate and open it. This kind of problem isn't really related to differences between the Mac and Windows. If someone sends you a Word file and you don't have Word, it doesn't much matter whether it was created on a PC or on a Mac—the result is the same: You can't open it.

You might also run into a problem if you have an older version of an application. For instance, if you have AppleWorks 5 and someone gives you a file created with AppleWorks 6, you won't be able to open it.

The tool you need is a file translator, software that reads the file you can't open and creates a new file in a format your computer can read. Some file translators are separate utilities. Others are files that work with applications such as AppleWorks.

MacLinkPlus Deluxe. DataViz's **MacLinkPlus Deluxe** ($99.95; www.dataviz.com) is the king of file translators. It has been around the longest (since the 1980s) and can translate the widest variety of PC and Mac files. This includes files created with old or new word processors and spreadsheets and some database formats. MacLinkPlus Deluxe can translate between various versions of AppleWorks and Microsoft Office. It also translates between common graphics formats, including GIF, JPEG, TIFF, BMP, WMF, and Mac and Windows EPS.

MacLinkPlus translates PC files into Mac formats and Mac files into PC formats. It translates file details such as text formatting, footnotes, page numbering, tables, hyperlinks, margins, columns, and embedded graphics. Its translation ability is limited by the features your application supports. For instance, since AppleWorks spreadsheets don't support pivot tables, MacLinkPlus translates Excel pivot tables into ordinary tables.

MacLinkPlus can also decode e-mail attachments and decompress compressed archives from PC users. (For more about e-mail attachments, see "E-mail: Use PC Compression and Encoding," below.)

If you only need to read or print a Word file and not edit it, check out the inexpensive shareware utility icWord ($19.95; www.icword.com). It allows you to view Word files, much as Acrobat Reader lets you view PDFs. icWord will also print Word files.

You can use MacLinkPlus Deluxe in several ways to translate a file. In the Finder, you can ⸤Control⸥-click a file to bring up the pop-up menu. You then select MacLinkPlus in the contextual menu, choose Translate to > Mac Format, and select the Mac file format you want the new file to use.

For the full range of options, use the MacLinkPlus application (**Figure 22.7**). I like to keep an alias of MacLinkPlus on my Mac desktop. I can then drag any file—or a folder full of files—on the icon to launch MacLinkPlus with my file loaded. The utility will try to identify the file and let me peek inside.

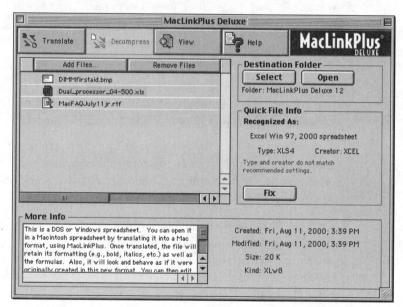

Figure 22.7

The MacLinkPlus application can recognize Windows files and preview and translate them.

To look at the contents of the file without translating it, select the file in the MacLinkPlus Deluxe window and click View. A new window opens, displaying the unformed text (or graphic) inside the file. (This doesn't work too well with spreadsheets, however, as all the cells and formulas get jumbled together.)

If you decide to translate the file or folder full of files, click Translate. In the window that appears, select the file format for the new file from one of the pop-up menus. Type a name for the new file, and click Translate.

AppleWorks. If you have AppleWorks 6.1 or later for Mac OS 8, Mac OS 9, or Mac OS X, you have translators for Word and Excel files. (Some earlier versions of AppleWorks and ClarisWorks included file translators, but version 6.0 did not.) In fact, these AppleWorks translators are MacLinkPlus translators. You don't get *all* of the MacLinkPlus translators or the MacLinkPlus Deluxe application, but you do get the ability to open and save in Word for Macintosh 6 and Word for Macintosh 98; Word for Windows 6/95 and Word for Windows 97/2000; Excel for Macintosh 5 and Excel for Macintosh 98; and Excel for Windows 5 and Excel for Windows 97/2000. The translators also let you save AppleWorks files in HTML and RTF (Rich Text Format).

AppleWorks enables you to use the MacLinkPlus translators directly from its Open and Save dialog boxes. Here's how to open a Word or Excel file in AppleWorks 6.1 or later:

1. Choose the Open dialog box from the File menu.
2. Choose "Word processor" or "Spreadsheet" from the Document Type pop-up menu.
3. Click the File Format pop-up menu, and select the Windows application (**Figure 22.8**).
4. Select the PC file you want to translate.
5. Click Open.

The translator will create a new AppleWorks version of the PC file, keeping the original intact.

To save an AppleWorks document as a Word or Excel file, choose Save As from the File menu. Now click the File Format pop-up menu and select the desired format. Click Save, and a new file is created.

Figure 22.8

The AppleWorks 6 Open dialog box lets you open files generated on both PCs and Macs; here Excel for Windows 97, 2000 is selected.

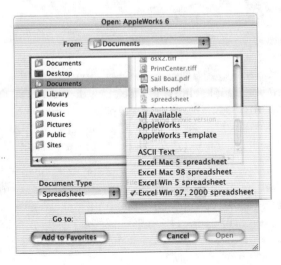

QuickTime multimedia translators. Mac OS 8, Mac OS 9, and Mac OS X come with a set of QuickTime file translators that can translate a variety of PC and Mac graphics and sound formats. There isn't a translation utility, but you can access the translators from several locations, such as QuickTime Player.

The QuickTime translators also show up in the AppleWorks 6 Open and Save dialog boxes. In the AppleWorks Open dialog box, when you choose a Painting or Drawing Document Type, the File Format pop-up menu lists dozens of multimedia file formats followed by "[QT]" to indicate that QuickTime translators will convert the file (**Figure 22.9**).

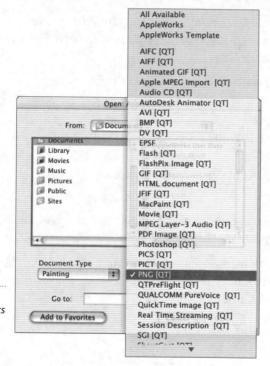

Figure 22.9

You can access QuickTime's graphics and sound file translators from within AppleWorks.

You'll also find that QuickTime translators show up in a dialog box that may appear when you double-click a PC file. This dialog lists all the applications on your hard drive, some along with the phrase "with QuickTime translation." When MacLinkPlus Deluxe is installed, the applications may also appear with the phrase "with MacLinkPlus translation" (**Figure 22.10**).

You have to know which application is appropriate to open your file. Not every application will be able to open the file even after QuickTime (or MacLinkPlus) translates it. If you don't want this long list of applications to appear, you can go to the File Exchange control panel. Click the File Translation tab and check the box next to "Don't show choices if there's only one."

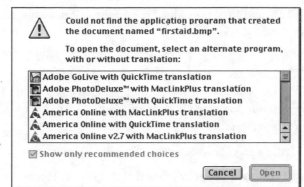

Figure 22.10

This dialog box may appear if you double-click a PC file. It shows the translators you have installed, including QuickTime and MacLinkPlus.

GraphicConverter. An inexpensive shareware file-translation utility from developer Thorsten Lemke, **GraphicConverter** ($30; www.lemkesoft.de/) picks up with graphics formats where MacLinkPlus leaves off. It can translate dozens of PC, Mac, and Unix graphics formats.

GraphicConverter also adds some graphics-editing tools, features that MacLink-Plus and QuickTime don't have. Editing tools are often needed for translating graphics files, which don't always translate exactly. GraphicConverter is not a Photoshop replacement, but it has some handy selection and draw and paint tools as well as effects such as dithering, gamma correction, and other color manipulations.

To convert a file, open it from the GraphicConverter dialog box, or drag the file on top of the GraphicConverter icon in the Finder. Choose Save As from the File menu, and select the type of file from the Format pop-up menu. GraphicConverter will create a new file in the specified file format.

Fonts and translation. File translators don't translate fonts. Instead, they try to match fonts, specifying a font similar to the original. The results can vary. If you want to see the same fonts on both a Mac and a PC, make sure both machines have a similar font installed. For instance, if both are working with Microsoft Office, make sure the PC document is specifying the fonts that come with Office.

Fonts themselves are not cross-platform. You can sometimes purchase font families that come in both Macintosh and Windows versions. You'll need to install them before you create your documents.

Some utilities can translate between Mac and Windows font families. These utilities translate the font files themselves, not the fonts specified within files. The idea is to translate a font and then install it on each computer. Then you can pass around files that specify the fonts.

TransType, from FontLab ($49.95; www.fontlab.com/html/transtype.html), is a commercial font-translation utility that converts between Mac and PC TrueType fonts or Mac and PC PostScript Type 1 fonts. (It does not convert between TrueType and Type 1 fonts.)

Another font translator is **TTConverter** ($10), a shareware utility from Chris Reed. TTConverter converts between Mac and PC TrueType fonts. It doesn't handle Type 1 fonts. As of this writing, TTConverter didn't have its own Web site, but you can download it at www.geocities.com/SiliconValley/Way/4789/ TTConverter15.hqx.

If this URL changes, search for TTConverter at www.versiontracker.com.

Editing type and creator codes. If you do have an application that can open your file but your Mac doesn't know it, changing or adding type and creator codes may help. For example, you may have received a file enclosed as an e-mail message that has a generic icon. This file may have no type or creator code, or it may have a garbled, nonsense code. Double-clicking the file might bring up some application choices or might not. You can play around with extension mapping (see "Extension Mapping in OS 9 and Earlier," earlier in the chapter), but if you are going to use the file a lot or want to distribute it to other Mac users, changing the type and creator code will make the Mac instantly launch the right application every time.

You may be able to open this file by launching an application that can open it and then opening the file from the Open dialog box. However, you may have trouble doing this if the file has garbled codes.

You can edit a file's type and creator codes with utilities. First, find out what the correct codes should be, on a similar file that has a Mac icon, using Sherlock (see "Type and Creator Codes," earlier in the chapter). Then you can use a utility such as MacLinkPlus Deluxe or ResEdit to edit the codes in the problem file.

MacLinkPlus Deluxe. If you have MacLinkPlus Deluxe for file translation, you can also use the utility to edit type and creator codes. When you open a file with the MacLinkPlus Deluxe utility, it will tell you the file's type and creator codes in the Quick File Info section (Figure 22.7). If the codes are incorrect, MacLinkPlus will tell you so. You can change the type and creator codes with a click of the Fix button. MacLinkPlus reads the file and makes a guess but doesn't always set the codes you want. If you want to change the codes, go to the MacLinkPlus File menu and select Set Type and Creator. A new box pops up where you can edit the codes (**Figure 22.11**).

Figure 22.11

....

You can edit type and creator codes by selecting Set Type and Creator from the File menu in MacLinkPlus.

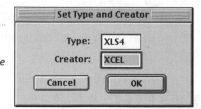

ResEdit. Apple's free ResEdit utility also lets you edit type and creator codes in Mac OS 9 and earlier. However, be careful not to muck around too much with ResEdit—it can be dangerous to your files, even corrupting them. Here's how to edit type and creator codes:

1. Launch ResEdit. Close the Open dialog box that appears.
2. From the File menu, select Get File/Folder Info.
3. Select your file from the menu of files that appears.

   A new window appears containing entry fields for Type and Creator (**Figure 22.12**).
4. Type the codes in the fields.

ResEdit is available at the software download area of Apple's web site (http://www.info.apple.com/support/downloads.html).

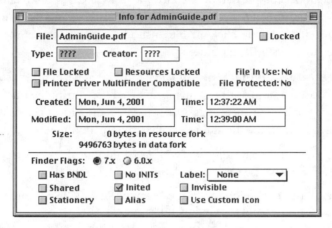

Figure 22.12

You can use ResEdit to edit type and creator codes. The question marks show this file has no codes.

Receiving e-mail attachments: encoding and compression. Many of the problems with opening e-mail attachments from Windows users are caused by the use of PC encoding or compressing standards your e-mail software doesn't understand. Unrecognizable encoding or compression can also be a problem when downloading files from the Internet. Compression can be a problem with any method of moving files, including copying files from a disk or local network. E-mail attachments can also be both compressed and encoded, in that order.

The symptoms of either problem appear when you try to open the file. Often you can open it, but the file looks like garbled random characters. You need to decode the file yourself, using one of many utilities available.

Decode with StuffIt Expander. The first thing to try is StuffIt Expander, which comes with Mac OS 8, 9, and X. Drag your problem file on top of the StuffIt Expander icon in the Finder. This sometimes works when double-clicking the file doesn't. However, sometimes StuffIt Expander just can't recognize the file, particularly if the e-mail message headers are mixed in with the encoded file.

You can try cleaning up the file manually:

1. Open it with a text editor (Word, AppleWorks, or SimpleText will work).

   If you see the line "Content-Type: text/plain," the file is a MIME/Base64-encoded file. Delete everything above this line. (MIME/Base 64 is the most common type of encoding used on the PC.)

   If you see a line that begins with the characters "begin 644," it's a Uuencoded file. Delete everything before this line.

2. Now use the Save As command to save the file as a text-only file (and not a Word or AppleWorks file if you are using those programs).

3. Drag the file onto StuffIt Expander.

StuffIt Expander for Mac OS X does a better job with Unix encoding and compression standards than Expander for Mac OS 9. Unfortunately, double-clicking a compressed or encoded file in Mac OS X often launches the Mac OS 9 version of StuffIt Expander, which causes Classic to launch. To prevent this, don't double-click the file. Instead, drop it on top of the Mac OS X version of StuffIt Expander.

Decode with MacLinkPlus. I've found that MacLinkPlus Deluxe tends to do a better job of recognizing encoded files, stripping out e-mail headers, recognizing the encoding format, and decoding it, all automatically. You don't have to open the file and manually strip out anything.

You decode and decompress with MacLinkPlus the same way you would translate a file (see the "Translating Files" section, above):

1. Drop the file on top of the MacLinkPlus Deluxe utility icon (or drag it into the utility's window if it's open).

2. Select the file, and click Decompress. (This works for decoding as well.)

StuffIt Deluxe. Aladdin Systems has its own "Deluxe" program as well. StuffIt Deluxe is the commercial version of StuffIt Expander ($79.95; www.aladdinsystems.com). In addition to decoding and decompressing PC files, it can also encode and compress in a variety of Mac, Windows, and Unix standards. This includes self-expanding Windows archives (EXE archives), one compression format MacLinkPlus Deluxe doesn't yet support.

Decoding with StuffIt Deluxe is the same as decoding with StuffIt Expander—you drag your file on top of the StuffIt Expander icon in the Finder. StuffIt Deluxe installs more behind-the-scenes encoding and compression engines than the version of StuffIt Expander that comes with Mac OS.

Moving software (applications) from PC to Mac. Here's another common problem: You have a PC at work with a fast Internet connection and a Mac at home with a slow modem Internet link. To take advantage of your office's fast link, you want to download Mac software on the PC and move it to your Mac on a Zip disk. But when you get the software to your Mac, the computer doesn't recognize it.

Notice that we are now talking about executable software rather than data files. This cause of this problem goes back to the resource fork Mac files have (see the "File Forks," section, earlier in this chapter). Windows will ignore the application file's resource fork—where the programming code is kept—and only send the data fork on to the Mac. Half an application just won't run on a Mac.

The solution is to *not* decode or decompress it in Windows. Keep the file in its archive, move it to the Mac, and then decode it or decompress it (or both) on the Mac. Disabling decoding and decompression may require you to muck about in the Properties dialog boxes of your Windows Web browser or e-mail client.

 Windows software does not run on a Mac unless you are running Windows on your Mac with an emulator such as Virtual PC. Filenames for Windows software end in .exe.

How to Create Files for a PC

When sending a file to a PC user, you can use some of the same techniques I described for opening PC files, only in reverse. These include file translation, encoding, and compression. However, there is a difference: You are in control. You have to choose file formats and encoding and compression standards. You also have a new issue to deal with: naming your files so that PCs will be able to read them.

Translating Mac files to PC formats. The techniques for translating files into PC formats are the same as for translating PC files into Mac formats. (Refer to the earlier discussions in "Using Files from Windows" on using file-translation tools, such as those that come with AppleWorks and MacLinkPlus Deluxe.) If you are using Microsoft Office, PC users will be able to read and edit the files you create.

You do have an alternative to translating a file into a specific PC-application file format: Turn it into a PDF file. Just about everyone has the free Acrobat Reader, which reads PDF files. This is one of the best ways to send a file to Windows users or to a group of mixed Mac and Windows users—as long as the file doesn't need to be editable. The file will look just the way you want it to when opened on the PC, including any fancy layouts or embedded graphics.

You can create a PDF file in Mac OS 8 and 9 with the full version of Adobe Acrobat (as opposed to Acrobat Reader, which only reads PDF files). You can also find less costly shareware PDF creation utilities—for example, **PrintToPDF,** from developer Jim Walker ($20; www.jwwalker.com/pages/pdf.html).

In Mac OS X, you can save any file as a PDF file using the Print dialog box (**Figure 22.13**).

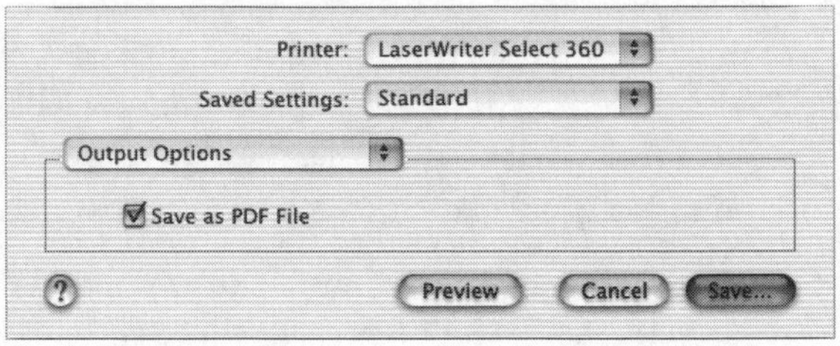

Figure 22.13

In Mac OS X, you can save any file as a PDF document using the Print dialog box.

1. With the document open, choose Print from the File menu.
2. Choose Output Options from the lower pop-up menu.
3. Click the Save as PDF File check box.
4. Click Save.

Another cross-platform format you can use is RTF, or rich text format. The benefit is that an RTF document is editable. The drawback is that the format supports only basic formatting and is for text-based files. AppleWorks and Word can save files as RTF files, and both Mac and PC versions of these programs can read RTF.

PC filenames. When naming files that will run on a PC, you need to observe certain rules. Otherwise, the file may not open on the PC. In some cases, if you incorrectly name it, the file can disappear from the view of PC users when posted to a local file server.

Here are the rules:

Don't use "illegal" characters. These include slashes (/ and \); most punctuation including the question mark (?), colon (:), semicolon (;), quotation mark ("), and comma (,); square brackets ([,]) and angle brackets (<, >); and plus and equal signs (+, =).

Always end a filename with the appropriate extension such as .doc, .txt, or .jpg.

Don't use more than one period (dot) in a filename. Use a dot only before a filename extension.

Don't use spaces in names. Filenames that end with a space are particularly problematic.

E-mail: Use PC compression and encoding. We talked about decoding earlier in the section on receiving e-mail attachments in "Using Files from Windows." The same issue comes up when you send a file to a PC user. You have to make sure to use encoding that the PC e-mail software will be able to decode. Otherwise, your file will look like a garbled mess.

To guarantee that a Windows user can decode your e-mail attachment, use the MIME/Base64 encoding format. If you are sending a file to a mixture of Mac and PC users, you can try the AppleDouble format. UUencode is good for Linux and Unix users; some Windows users might be able to handle UUencode as well. When in doubt, use MIME/Base64 for Windows users.

Some Mac users may also be able to handle MIME/Base64 and UUencode, but these formats won't retain a file's Mac icon or resource fork. The best bet for sending enclosures to Mac users is to use BinHex encoding.

Setting encoding is easy to do in Microsoft Outlook Express 5 and later, which comes with Mac OS 9. You do it in a new message window (**Figure 22.14**). Here's how:

1. After you attach a file to an e-mail message, click the triangle next to Attachments to open the Attachments list. This should display your attachment and its size.

2. Click the "Encode for" bar below the Attachments list.

   A drop-down menu opens listing encoding formats.

3. Under "Encode for," choose your encoding format—Windows (MIME/Base64) is the best choice for Windows users.

4. Under Compression, select None.

If the filename doesn't have a filename extension, you can check "Append Windows extensions to file names." However, the file shown in Figure 22.14 already has the .pdf file extension, so we can leave this box unchecked.

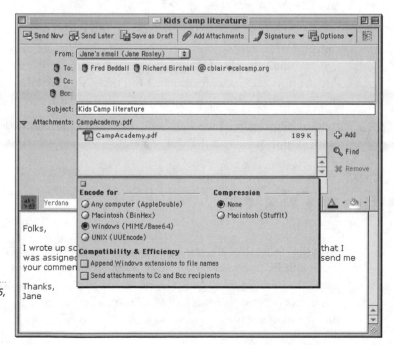

Figure 22.14

In Outlook Express 5, you can easily set the encoding for a Windows user.

If you've already attached a file and closed the message window and now want to change the encoding, you'll have to go back and open the message window. You can do this by clicking Drafts in Outlook's Folders list at left and then double-clicking the message name in the message-list window.

If you have a version of Outlook Express earlier than version 5, it's worth your while to go to the Microsoft Web site and download a free copy of the latest version (www.microsoft.com/mac, on the Downloads page). However, if you want to stick with Outlook Express versions 4.5 and earlier, here's how to choose Windows encoding:

1. Choose Preferences from the Edit menu.

2. Under Outlook Express, choose Message Composition in the left-hand column.

3. Near the bottom of the window you'll see a pop-up menu called "Attachment encoding." Choose Base64 (MIME) from the menu.

 Unfortunately, the Mac OS X Mail application does not have settings for encoding. If you want a file to get to a PC user, you should use another mail application that does.

You may wonder why we set compression to "off" in the example with Outlook Express 5. That's because Mac e-mail software defaults to compressing files using StuffIt (with the filename extension .sit), a format most PC software doesn't recognize. The free **StuffIt for Windows** and **StuffIt for Linux** (www.aladdinsystems.com) can decompress StuffIt files, but you can't count on PC users' having a copy.

If the file you are sending is large and you think it should be compressed, then compress it first in Zip format. (E-mail attachments are always compressed first and then encoded.) You can compress in Zip format using Tom Brown's **ZipIt** utility ($20; www.maczipit.com); make sure MacBinary is turned off in the Preferences settings. If you can't Zip it, then turn compression off.

 Unlike compression, encoding does not make a file smaller. In fact, encoding often slightly increases the size of a file.

Sharing Disks

With the rise of the Internet, e-mail, and cross-platform local networks, sharing disks with PC users just isn't as important as when the floppy disk was the main method of moving files. But it is still handy to move CDs, Zip cartridges, and other media between Macs and PCs. You can even move hard drives between the two platforms.

Disk Formats

The main issue with sharing disks between Macs and PCs is that of *disk format,* the method used to lay down information on disk storage devices. It shouldn't come as a surprise that Macs and PC use different disk formats for many storage types.

The standard disk format used in Mac hard drives is Mac OS Extended, also known as HFS+ (Heirarchical File System Plus). (Mac floppy disks are formatted in an older version called HFS.) Mac OS X also supports hard disks formatted in UFS (Unix File System). As mentioned in Chapter 1, "Working with Your Mac," you can create an Mac OS X startup disk formatted with either HFS+ or UFS. You would use UFS if you wanted the Mac for Unix-type tasks, such as running a Web server or developing Unix software.

 You will often see the Unix file format UFS confused with UDF (Universal Disc Format), the format used for DVD discs. These are *not* the same format. Unfortunately, the confusion is common, even on reputable computer Web sites and in print.

PC hard disks running Windows 95, 98, or Me or Linux are formatted with FAT (File Allocation Table). FAT has been around for a while and is available in several versions, such as FAT16 and FAT32. Linux running on Intel-based hardware also uses FAT-formatted hard drives.

Windows NT, Windows 2000, and Windows XP can also use a newer disk format known as NTFS (NT File System). NTFS is mostly used for hard drives. If you have a Zip disk or other removable media from a PC, it is probably formatted as a FAT volume.

 If you see references to "DOS-formatted" disks in the Mac help system and elsewhere, be aware that this is Apple's term for FAT. Yes, this is confusing, since most PCs run Windows, not DOS, which is why I stick to the standard use of FAT.

Optical media can be formatted with HFS+ or FAT, but they are more likely to be formatted with optical standards—ISO 9660 for CDs and UDF for DVDs. Mac OS supports these optical-disc formats.

Reading PC Magnetic Disks

Mac OS has had the ability to read FAT-formatted magnetic disks for many years. (It cannot read NTFS-formatted drives.) For PC floppy disks and hard drives, the system software that handles this in Mac OS 9 and earlier is the File Exchange control panel. You don't have to open this control panel to mount FAT-formatted PC disks—just insert (or plug in) a disk, and it will mount on the Desktop. If the disk isn't mounting, make sure the File Exchange control panel is installed and turned on in the Extensions Manager control panel.

Mac OS X 10.0 through 10.0.4 did not come with support for PC disks. You'll need Mac OS X 10.1 or later to use FAT-formatted disks.

Blank Zip cartridges usually come preformatted as FAT disks, although Mac-formatted Zip disks are available. However, the File Exchange control panel is not responsible for reading FAT-formatted Zip or Jaz disks. This is the job of the Iomega Driver file in the Extensions folder. If you are having a problem mounting a Zip or Jaz cartridge, this is the file to reinstall.

Preparing a Magnetic Disk for Use on a PC

If you want to create a disk that a PC user will be able to use, you should format it as a FAT disk. You can do this in Mac OS 9.x and earlier, and Mac OS X 10.1 gives you the option to use the MS-DOS File System.

An alternative to giving FAT disks to PC users is to enable Windows to read and format Mac disks by adding HFS+ support to the PC. You can do this with several products, including MediaFour's MacDrive ($49.95; www.mediafour.com) or DataViz's MacOpener ($49.95; www.dataviz.com). Both support a wide range of disk types and integrate with the Windows interface.

In Mac OS 9 and earlier, select the disk in the Finder, and choose Erase Disk from the Special menu. (This can be a floppy disk or a hard disk.) In the Format pop-up menu, select DOS. Give the drive a name that is 11 characters or less. Click Erase, and you now have a FAT-formatted drive (**Figure 22.15**).

Figure 22.15

The Finder's Erase command can format a FireWire drive in FAT format and give it a shorter name.

Blank Zip cartridges usually come formatted as FAT disks. If you do need to format a Zip or Jaz cartridge, don't use the Finder's Erase command. Instead, use the Iomega Tools utility, located in the Iomega folder you may have installed with your drive.

Reading Optical Media: CDs and DVDs

The File Exchange/PC Exchange control panel doesn't enable Macs to read PC CDs. Optical disks have other system-extension files that enable the Mac to read them:

- Foreign File Access.
- ISO 9660 File Access.
- High Sierra File Access.
- Audio CD Access (for playing music CDs).
- UDF Volume Access (for mounting DVDs; another set of extension files lets your Mac play DVD movies).

If you are having problems mounting a CD on the desktop, check the Extensions Manager control panel in Mac OS 9 to make sure you have these files installed and turned on.

Joliet CDs. Joliet is a Microsoft expansion of the ISO 9660 standard that supports filenames longer than 8.3 (eight characters plus the three-character extension). Joliet supports filenames up to 64 characters long and spaces in filenames. The Mac OS doesn't support Joliet and displays filenames on Joliet discs in truncated 8.3 without spaces. You may also have trouble accessing files on Joliet CDs.

Fortunately, you can add software to Mac OS 9 and earlier to make it Joliet-aware. **Joliet Volume Access** is a extension file for Mac OS 9 created by Thomas Tempelmann (www.tempel.org/joliet/). With this extension file installed, the Finder will display filenames up to 31 characters. For filenames longer than 31 characters, the full name is viewable in the file's Get Info box. Joliet Volume Access before version 2.0 is free. Versions 2.0 and later are shareware.

 At the time of this writing, indications were that Apple was working on Joliet compatibility for a later release of Mac OS X. If this occurs, the Mac OS X Finder will be able to display a full 64-character Joliet filename.

Networking Macs and PCs

You can do quite a lot with Macs and PCs on the same network. Sometimes you need to add some software to accomplish your goals—other times you can use features built into your computers.

When creating a cross-platform network, you should start by asking yourself what it is you want to do. The reply "Connect my Mac and PC" won't help you find the right answer—it's too vague and has no real meaning. You need to get specific as to what you want to accomplish—access a virtual private network, share files, or go wireless, for instance. Each is a different problem with a different solution. Sometimes the fix is in hardware, sometimes it's in software.

These days, the network hardware is the easy part. It's mostly cross-platform, or rather, platform independent. Often, it is software that will solve your Mac-PC networking problem. This section begins with hardware issues and then moves on to software solutions.

Cross-platform networking is a large subject area, worthy of a book the size of the one you are reading. In this section, I cover the basics and point you in the right direction for locating answers to cross-platform networking problems. First you might want to review Chapter 20, "Networking," to see how Mac networking works. You can find more help on cross-platform networking at my Web site, MacWindows (www.macwindows.com). Finally, this chapter assumes that you know how to set up your PC for networking. After all, this is the *Macintosh Bible.*

Connecting Network Hardware

The hardware that moves the bits along the cables or through the air is inherently cross-platform. There's no such thing as "Mac-compatible Ethernet" or a "PC-compatible hub." As with peripherals such as printers, both Macs and PCs use the same hardware—it's the software driver that's different. If a driver is required, it has to be specific to the operating system.

Remember, connecting the hardware is just the first step. After this, you'll have to consider the software you need to use.

Ethernet. Ethernet is the main way to connect Macs and PCs. The same rules described in Chapter 20 apply to cross-platform networks. Most PC makers don't build Ethernet into their machines as Apple does with Macs, but you can get an Ethernet card for the price of inexpensive shareware.

You connect Macs and PCs to the same Ethernet hub, or you can directly connect one Mac to one PC. When you do, take care to use the right cable. There are two types:

Patch cable. This is the cable to use if you have an Ethernet hub.

Crossover cable. Use this type if you are directly connecting one Mac to one PC.

The only difference between the two is that the wires are reversed in the crossover cable. Most cables you see in stores are patch cables. If you want a crossover cable, you may have to ask for it.

Wireless networks. AirPort is Apple's implementation of the IEEE 802.11 Direct Sequence Spread Spectrum (DSSS) wireless networking standard. PCs can be on the same wireless network using 802.11 cards from Lucent, 3Com, Dell, and other companies.

PCs can connect to your AirPort Base Station to connect to the Internet or to Macs using AirPort. Some people also use the AirPort Base Station to connect a wireless Mac network with PCs on an Ethernet network.

The AirPort Base Station is not the only 802.11 wireless access point. You can use others such as those from Lucent and 3Com. However, check before you buy, as not all wireless access points include Internet connectivity. Other access points can be trickier to get running than the AirPort Base Station for Macs and PCs. Because of this, and because Apple's is still one of the least expensive wireless access points, I'd recommend using the AirPort Base Station with cross-platform wireless networks.

The best way to proceed is to get your AirPort Base Station set up and running from a Mac using Apple's AirPort Admin Utility. When configuring the wireless settings on the PC, you may need the name of the network that you've given for the AirPort Base Station.

 Apple doesn't ship PC configuration software with the AirPort Base Station, but you can find programs that work from a PC. FreeBase (http:// freebase.sourceforge.net/), written by Rop Gonggrijp, is a free Windows utility that can do the job. Another is Jonathan Sevy's AirPort Base Station Configurator, written in Java (http://edge.mcs.drexel.edu/GICL/people/ sevy/airport/).

Once the Macs and PCs are connected to the wireless network, any cross-platform network software that runs on Ethernet will run on the wireless network.

LocalTalk. LocalTalk is a slower type of network that was used in older Macs. (If you haven't heard of LocalTalk, don't worry.) LocalTalk was never an industry standard and was only used by Apple. So how do you set up a cross-platform LocalTalk network? Forget it. Now that LocalTalk is history on the Mac, you can no longer find LocalTalk interface cards for PCs. Use Ethernet. If you have an older network device (such as a laser printer), add it to your Ethernet network with a LocalTalk-to-Ethernet bridge such as Farallon's **EtherMac iPrint Adapter** ($102.00; www.farallon.com).

Network Protocols

Protocols are where you start getting into the acronym soup of networking: TCP/IP, AFP, SMB, and so forth. You can think of network protocols as working in layers. At the bottom are basic transport protocols, such as TCP/IP and AppleTalk. On top of these are protocols that perform certain functions, such as file sharing, browsing, or connecting to various types of servers. We won't get too deep here, but it is important to know a little about protocols when trying to understand how Macs and PCs can communicate.

Transport protocols. TCP/IP is the main transport protocol for connecting Macs with PCs. Mac OS, Windows, and Linux all come with TCP/IP. Mac OS 9 and Mac OS X also come with AppleTalk, which is an alternative. (Mac OS X before version 10.1 can only print using AppleTalk.) Although Windows and Linux don't come with AppleTalk support, you can get software that helps Windows communicate via AppleTalk—most notably Miramar's **PC MacLAN** ($199.00; www.miramar.com). However, with Apple moving away from AppleTalk, the software vendors, including Miramar, have added TCP/IP support.

Another transport protocol in decline is IPX, which at one time was the basis of Novell NetWare networks. It supported Macs with software called MacIPX. Novell has since moved on to TCP/IP. However, you still occasionally run into IPX on multiplayer network games, which will provide a copy of MacIPX. This becomes rarer with each passing year.

 One cross-platform network product, Thursby's **MacSOHO** for home networks ($49; www.thursby.com), enables Macs to communicate using NetBEUI, an old PC protocol. The benefit of NetBEUI is that it is simple to set up. NetBEUI is also secure since it cannot be routed across the Internet.

Using TCP/IP in cross-platform networks. The biggest drawback to TCP/IP is that each computer needs a unique IP address (see Chapter 20, "Networking," for more information). Large networks usually have a DHCP server to assign IP addresses. Some Internet gateway hardware (devices that allow you to share an Internet connection with a network of computers) includes a DHCP server.

For a small network without any servers, you can also set Mac OS and Windows to get IP addresses using DHCP. When they don't find a server, the computers will give themselves IP addresses. I cover this procedure for the Mac in Chapter 20. In Windows, this is done through the Network control panel.

File-sharing protocols. You connected a Mac and a PC to Ethernet, you set up TCP/IP on both, but you can't move files between the two. Why not? Because you haven't dealt with the file-sharing protocols. Mac OS and Windows use different file-sharing protocols, which means that the built-in file sharing in Macs is not compatible with that of Windows. PCs normally don't show up in the Chooser (or the Mac OS X Connect window), and Macs don't normally show up in the Windows Network Neighborhood.

Macs use the Apple File Protocol (AFP), and Windows machines use the Server Message Block/Common Internet File System (SMB/CIFS). AFP and SMB can run over a variety of transport protocols (such as TCP/IP, AppleTalk, or IPX), although TCP/IP is the most common. However, you need to be aware of both the transport protocol and the file-sharing protocol when doing cross-platform networking.

For instance, Windows NT Server can support Mac file sharing using AFP, but only over AppleTalk. Mac OS X before version 10.1 can connect to AFP file servers, but only over TCP/IP. Therefore, Mac OS X before version 10.1 cannot access files on Windows NT Servers. Mac OS X 10.1 and later supports AFP over AppleTalk.

We'll look at some of the solutions for cross-platform file sharing in the next section.

Cross-Platform Network File Sharing

As we mentioned in the last section, Macs OS and Windows use different file-sharing protocols. To get around this, you can adopt one of the following strategies:

- Use a product that installs SMB on Macs.

  Example: Thursby's **DAVE** ($149; www.thursby.com).

  When to use: This strategy makes sense with a few Macs in a mostly Windows network.

- Use a product that installs AFP on Windows.

  Example: Miramar's PC MacLAN.

  When to use: This strategy makes sense with a few Windows PCs on a mostly Mac network.

- Use a server-based product that supports AFP for Mac clients and SMB for Windows clients.

  Example: Mac OS X Server, Windows 2000 or XP Server running Services for Macintosh, or a Windows server running a third-party server, such as Cyan Soft's **MacServerIP** (www.cyansoft.de) or Group Logic's **ExtremeZ-IP** (www.grouplogic.com).

  When to use: The server-based strategy is the most economical when large numbers of computers are involved.

- Use a third protocol, such as the FTP or Web protocols.

  Example: Web sharing in Mac OS.

  When to use: You're looking for a quick way to move a file from a Mac to a PC.

The first three strategies require buying third-party software. The products I listed are tops in their categories in terms of features and reliability. Other products are available as well.

You can implement the fourth strategy for free using Mac OS's Web-sharing feature.

Web sharing, FTP sharing: Free file sharing with a PC. If you want to move files from your Mac to a PC without adding any software, Web Sharing is the way to do it. With Web sharing turned on, a PC user (or a Mac user, for that matter) can access a folder on the Mac by using a Web browser. Typing the Mac's IP address in the Web browser brings up the contents of the shared folder. PC users can then download a file from your Mac.

Web sharing is the same regardless of what kind of computer is accessing your Mac. As long as the other users have a Web browser, they'll be able to see the folder or drive you've designated. For details on enabling Web sharing in Mac OS 9 and Mac OS X, see Chapter 20, "Networking."

 Another free method is to use the FTP server built into every copy of Mac OS X. PC users can download files from the Mac using a Web browser or FTP client software. A description on how to enable the FTP file-sharing feature of Mac OS X is also described in Chapter 20.

Running Windows on Your Mac

When all else fails, you can run Windows itself on your Mac—provided you install an *emulator.* A PC emulator is a complex application that tricks Windows or x86-based Linux into thinking it is running on a real PC. A PC emulator is not a replacement for a real PC—it's not as fast or as compatible—but it does give you access to Windows programs on your Mac.

Emulation Products

Three emulators are available for Macs: **Virtual PC,** from Connectix ($99 to $329, depending on the operating system; www.connectix.com); **Real PC,** from FWB Software ($35.95; www.fwb.com); and **Blue Label PowerEmulator,** by Lismore Software Systems ($39.95; www.lismoresoft.com). FWB discontinued another, SoftWindows, in 2001.

Virtual PC is the premier PC emulator. It is the only one you can buy with Windows or Linux preinstalled. (The others come with DOS. If you have your own copy of Windows, you can buy Virtual PC with DOS and save a substantial sum on the purchase price.) Virtual PC is also the fastest emulator and offers the most features. For instance, starting with version 4, Virtual PC lets you run multiple Windows or Linux operating systems at once. Virtual PC is the only PC emulator that can run with Mac OS X.

What Emulation Does and Doesn't Do

Emulators (and Virtual PC in particular) are designed to run Windows business software such as databases, communications, or office suites. This is what they do best. That's because business software tends to stick to Windows programming conventions. Software that bypasses Windows to make direct calls to hardware will be problematic or incompatible with emulators. Business software also doesn't make a lot of demands on hardware the way video-editing or game software can.

Virtual PC can also participate on Windows networks using a variety of Windows networking software. The other PCs and servers see a Mac that's running Virtual PC as just another PC. Because Virtual PC uses so much RAM and hard-disk space, it's best to seek a native Macintosh networking solution first. But if you can't find one, or you need to run some Windows software in conjunction with a network, Virtual PC will serve your needs.

Virtual PC can run Linux, but that support varies with each version of Virtual PC and of Linux. New versions of Linux often don't work with current versions of Virtual PC. You should check with Connectix for which versions of Linux to use with your version of Virtual PC.

Emulators support standard PC peripherals, such as printers, scanners, and storage devices. They tend to have problems with more specialized equipment, such as hardware devices that convert USB signals to other signals.

Gaming

Unfortunately, Virtual PC is not great for running Windows games. It no longer supports accelerated graphics cards, as version 3 did. Games often run slowly, and you can have problems with sound. Some games won't run at all.

A better choice for a gaming emulator might be Connectix's Virtual Game Station, if you can find it or have a copy, which emulates a Sony PlayStation. (Connectix stopped selling the emulation software in 2001.) Because there is less to emulate in a PlayStation than in a PC running Windows, Virtual Game Station's gaming performance is better than Virtual PC's. Many of the games for PCs are available for the PlayStation. Of course, an even better choice is to buy the games when they are ported to the Mac. Or buy a PC.

What You Need

Got RAM? You'll need it to run an emulator. That's because you're running two operating systems at the same time, so you'll need enough memory for both. Just how much RAM depends on what versions of Windows and Mac OS you are running. You'll need less RAM with older operating systems, such as Mac OS 8 and Windows 95 and 98. The minimum with these operating systems is 64 MB. With Mac OS 9 and Windows Me, you can bump up the RAM requirement to a minimum of 128 MB. With Windows 2000 or XP and Mac OS X, start at 256 MB.

You'll also need some processing power. Emulation works best on Macs with PowerPC G3 or G4 processors, but the faster your Mac, the faster Windows will run.

You will also need enough free hard-disk space to support Windows and your Windows applications. With Windows 98, this is about a gigabyte. You'll need more for Windows Me, 2000, or XP.

Tips for Emulation

The main goal when running an emulator is to maximize performance. Here are some tips that can help you get the greatest possible speed out of your emulated PC:

Leave enough memory free for your emulator. If necessary, quit other applications before launching the emulator.

Defragment your Mac hard disk with a utility such as Norton Utilities. This is important. An emulator will install a large disk image of a PC boot drive. This file can be a gigabyte or more—a large file by any standard. If this file is fragmented, performance in your Windows or Linux environment will suffer.

Defragment your PC virtual C drive from within Windows using the Windows defragging tool.

Leave some free space in your PC C drive. Windows will slow down if the C drive is nearly full.

Turn off Processor Cycling in PowerBooks and iBooks. This is done in the Advanced Settings area of the Energy Saver control panel. Processor Cycling is a battery-conservation method that slows down the processor. It also slows down Windows.

Try not to tax the "Pentium processor." Of course, there *is* no Pentium processor with an emulator, which is the point. Don't run multiple Windows tasks at the same time or use unnecessary multimedia settings. Taxing the PC "hardware" will slow performance much more than it would on a real PC.

Pentium Cards

For many years, you could run Windows on your Mac with hardware—a real Pentium chip and RAM on a card. At one time this was a much faster option than an emulator. However, with Macs getting faster all the time, the advantage of expensive hardware became smaller and smaller. The nail in the coffin for Pentium cards was the introduction of the iMac. The most popular Mac model no longer had an expansion slot, greatly reducing the potential market for Pentium cards. You can't buy a new Pentium card anymore. They've all been discontinued.

However, the old cards still work, for the most part —if you have a Mac that can take an expansion card. For instance, if you have an old Apple PC Compatibility Card (or just bought one on eBay), you might consider upgrading the ancient Apple software. Apple doesn't make the software anymore, but you can buy a third-party replacement called **pcSetup** from FVDCS Inc. ($39.95; www. pcsetup2x.com). It lets you run the Apple card with Mac OS 8 and 9 (but not Mac OS X).

Orange Micro's OrangePC cards were better and faster (and more expensive) than other Pentium cards. Orange Micro also no longer supports the cards or updates the software, but if you have an OrangePC card, you can still get information, manuals, and last versions of the software at Orange Micro's Web site (www.orangemicro.com).

A
Buying Macs

Christopher Breen is the appendix editor and author.

OK: So now you understand how a Mac works, why you use Microsoft applications, what to do if your Power Macintosh doesn't start up, and how to be polite online. But you actually need a Mac to apply this knowledge.

Whether you are a student just heading off to college or a filmmaker editing your video, Apple has a computer for you.

This chapter walks you through which Macs you should consider, based on what you want to spend and how you intend to use your machine.

In This Appendix

A Short History Lesson

If the point hasn't been made clearly enough elsewhere in this tome, let's underscore it here: All things Macintosh have changed radically in the past couple of years. When the last edition of *The Macintosh Bible* appeared, dozens of computers on the market were capable of running the Mac OS. Some of these computers were made by Apple, and others bore the names of such companies as Power Computing, Umax, Motorola, DayStar, Radius, APS, and PowerTools. When Steve Jobs returned to Apple as interim CEO in 1997, the licenses required to continue the manufacture of these "clones" were unceremoniously killed. Jobs made no secret of the fact that the cloners were taking sales away from Apple and that Apple would no longer stand for it (he failed to mention, however, that at this time Apple's Macs were generally more expensive and less powerful than their cloned counterparts).

But Jobs did more than kill the clones. He took what can be politely described as Apple's "confused" product line and streamlined it. Instead of offering one line of computers for students, another to be sold through warehouse retail outlets, another for businesspeople, another for businesspeople who need a laptop, and yet another for red-headed businesspeople who need a tiny laptop on every other Wednesday, Jobs declared that Apple would offer just four Mac models—these four Mac models were eventually revealed to be the Power Mac, iMac, PowerBook, and iBook.

The Grid

When Jobs launched this strategy, he unveiled the now-famous "grid" that divides desktop and portable Macs into professional and consumer models. The grid looks like this:

	Desktop	Portable
Professional	Power Macintosh	PowerBook
Consumer	iMac	iBook

The thinking behind the grid is that you can make your decision without having to know the specifics of a particular Macintosh model. Instead, you look at the kind of user you are and—based on your needs and budget— buy the appropriate Mac. For example, if you're a student and want a Mac for your dorm room, the iMac is the logical choice. If you want to take your Mac to class with you, choose the iBook instead.

Not Quite So Simple

Since the birth of the grid, things have become a bit confused. On July 19, 2000, Jobs stepped outside the grid and unveiled the Power Mac G4 Cube—a beautiful, futuristic Macintosh that was designed to appeal to the tastes of the Bang & Olufsen crowd. In many ways the Cube was as limited as an iMac (the Cube had no slots), but it lacked the iMac's convenient built-in monitor, yet it nonetheless sported the Power Mac name and a Power Mac's price ($1,800). Despite Apple's expectations (and subsequent price reductions), Cube sales never took off, so the company shelved the stylish Mac in the summer of 2001.

But what about the countless iMac models—many of which are powerful enough to be used by professionals? Or the iBook introduced in May 2001 that was robust enough—and offered such high-end options as a CD-RW burner—to tempt those professional users who might otherwise have chosen a Titanium PowerBook G4?

You can readily understand why Apple abandoned the grid as a marketing concept when multiple configurations of the various Mac models appeared. But where does that leave you as a Mac buyer?

Understanding Your Needs

Given that your choice of Mac isn't the slam-dunk decision the grid implies, how do you determine which Mac is right for you? For most people, budget is of primary importance. If you've earmarked no more than $1,200 for a Mac, monitor, and printer, your decision is pretty well made: You'll be buying an iMac or a used Mac.

But in addition to the depth of your pockets, consider the kind of work you intend to do with this machine over the next couple of years. If your work demands little from your Mac—e-mail and word processing, for example—go for one of the less expensive Macs and you'll be happy with your computer for a long time to come. If, on the other hand, you work in the graphics or desktop-video business, you need the fastest Mac that Apple can build, with a huge hard drive and tons of RAM—and you'll still wish it were faster. And if you need to burn DVDs that will run on commercial DVD players, you should look for a Mac model that features the SuperDrive—a CD/DVD burner made by Pioneer that, as we go to press, is available in the top two models of the Power Mac G4.

Expandability is another important consideration. All Mac models include USB and FireWire ports, but only the Power Mac G4s include PCI slots—slots that allow you to add video or sound cards. Also, the processors in Apple's laptops cannot be upgraded. If you'd like to add a faster processor to your Mac someday, look to the Power Mac G4s that include the Zero Insertion Force (ZIF) slot—a slot that allows you to easily remove and replace the Mac's processor.

So Which Mac Is Right for You?

With these three factors in mind—budget, requirements, and expandability—let's see if we can find the perfect new Mac for you. But before we do, allow us to issue this important caveat: The world doesn't stop just because words have been committed to print. We fully understand that new Mac models will be introduced after we've fluffed this little book's pillow and put it to bed. Although the following examples apply to the Macs available as of this writing, you can generally apply the same rules to later generations of Macs.

For the Budget-Conscious Desktop User

Currently the cheapest new Mac you can get is the base-model Indigo iMac. For your $799 you get a 500 MHz PowerPC G3 processor, 64 MB of RAM, a 20 GB hard drive, a 56K modem, an ATI Rage 128 Ultra graphics chipset with 16 megabytes of video RAM, a CD-ROM drive (for creating CDs), and a built-in 15-inch monitor. Like all iMac models, this iMac has two FireWire ports, two USB ports, a 10/100Base-T Ethernet port, and a VGA video-out port, and it can accept an AirPort wireless networking card. This is a perfectly fine Mac for general use—e-mail, Web browsing, word processing, home finances, and game playing. Your grandmother or your kids would probably be tickled to own this machine. For $999, you can move to 128 MB of RAM and a CD-RW drive and pick between Indigo and Snow.

For another $300 you can have one of the mid-line iMacs, which come in Snow and Graphite and move to a 600 MHz G3 processor and double the storage, with a 40 GB hard drive, and 256 MB of RAM. This is a great iMac that would be particularly attractive to someone interested in editing home movies taken with a digital camcorder.

 All iMacs (all Macs, in fact) come with Mac OS X as well as the latest version of Mac OS 9. Mac OS X, however, is a RAM-hungry operating system, and the 128 MB of RAM included in the $999 model is the minimum you need to comfortably run both Mac OS X and the Classic environment.

For the Budget-Conscious Portable User

Apple's entry-level iBook model can hardly be termed dirt cheap at $1,299, but it's a very capable laptop with its 500 MHz PowerPC G3 processor, a 15 GB hard drive, two USB ports, and one FireWire port; and it has a sleek white finish. The least expensive PowerBook G4 (with a 550 MHz G4, 256 MB of RAM, and 20 GB hard drive) is $900 more than the iBook, so if you're on a budget and want a brand-new Mac portable, this is your only choice.

For the Middling-Budget Desktop User

At this point you hit the great divide. For $1,499 you can own the top-of-the-line iMac, which differs from the mid-line iMac in its inclusion of a 700 MHz PowerPC G3 processor and a 60 GB hard drive.

Another $200 more than that (we're up to $1,699 now) gets you the low-end QuickSilver Power Mac G4 introduced in the summer of 2001, equipped with a 733 MHz PowerPC G4, 128 MB of RAM, a 40 GB hard drive, a CD-RW drive, nVidia GeForce 2 MX graphics card with 32 MB of video RAM, and four PCI slots. Unlike the iMac, this Mac doesn't come with a built-in monitor, stereo speakers, or software other than the usual System Software discs. However, if you already own a monitor and a shelf-full of software, and you like the expandability that comes with four open PCI slots and an upgradable processor, the Power Mac G4 may be the better choice.

For the Middling-Budget Portable User

Apple has included some flexibility in the iBook line as well. The $1,499 iBook model includes a faster system bus (100 MHz vs. 66 MHz) than the entry-level model, a 600 MHz PowerPC G3 processor, and a DVD-ROM drive—an attractive option for those who like to watch movies of their choosing on long plane trips. The $1,599 model includes a CD-RW drive, and the $1,699 iBook sports a DVD-ROM/CD-RW combo drive and a 20 GB hard drive.

For the Performance-Is-Primary Desktop User

Those who require high performance from their Macs—meaning you who work with graphics, video, audio, or serious number-crunching applications or who are *serious* gamers—will leave the iMac behind and look to the Power Mac G4 line. Which flavor of Power Mac you buy will depend on your budget and your perception of just how relevant that "time is money" concept is to you. Currently, the Power Mac G4 line includes PowerPC G4 processors running at 733, 800, and 867 MHz. In general, the more megahertz you buy, the more RAM and hard-drive space you get as well. What is deceiving, however, is that the fastest-megahertz Mac may not run applications the quickest.

Although the 867 MHz Power Mac G4 carries the highest megahertz rate, the $2,499 machine actually runs a bit slower in certain applications than the $3,499 dual-processor 800 MHz Power Mac G4. Applications such as Adobe Photoshop that are designed to run faster with more than one processor are sprightlier on this dual-processor Mac than on the 867 MHz model. And because Mac OS X is written to take advantage of multiprocessor Macs, this difference may be even more pronounced in the future.

The 867 MHz Power Mac G4 steps up from the entry-level 733 MHz Power Mac by moving to a 60 GB hard drive and the SuperDrive CD-RW/DVD-R device.

With the dual-processor 800 MHz Power Mac G4, you get 256 MB of RAM, an 80 GB hard drive, and 64 MB of video RAM. The high-end box also comes with the SuperDrive device and a video card that lets you use two monitors at once.

For the Performance-Is-Primary Portable User

 The $2,199 550 MHz Titanium PowerBook G4 and the $2,999 PowerBook G4 model—with its 667 MHz processor, 30 GB hard drive, and 512 MB of RAM—are great laptops, but if you want the most a laptop can offer, be prepared to pay $3,299 for the 667 MHz PowerBook G4. It includes 512 MB of RAM; a 48 GB hard drive; an ATI Rage Mobility 128 video card with 16 MB of video RAM; and ports for making 10/100Base-T Ethernet, FireWire, and USB connections. As we go to press, it's the fastest PowerBook in the land—and one of the most attractive, with its luxuriously wide screen and Titanium case.

Buying a Used Mac

Ah, so you're looking for a bargain? You say your cousin Bob has a sweet little Mac Plus he's willing to let you have for $500? Before laying down the dough for a used Mac, keep the following in mind.

Of Processors and Slots

The Mac made a couple of major technological leaps in the past several years. Two of the most important were the switchover from the 680X0 Motorola processor to the PowerPC processor, and the change from Apple's proprietary NuBus slot to the ubiquitous PCI slot.

If you're looking for a used Mac capable of handling the demands of modern computing, you'll seek one with both a PowerPC processor and PCI slots. Not only are 680X0-based processors too weak to handle most modern applications, but many of today's programs won't even run on these older processors. And owning a NuBus Mac nowadays is about as worthwhile as having a Mac with no slots at all. NuBus cards haven't been made in ages, and if you need add-on cards for these Macs, you'll spend considerable time tracking down used parts. Unless you're a hobbyist or historian—or you can get one of these computers for an absolute song—the older used Macs just aren't worth buying.

What You Need

To run moderately demanding applications such as word processors, Web browsers, and e-mail clients, you need a PowerPC 603e processor or better. (What's better? A PowerPC 604, 604e, G3, or G4.) If you work with graphics and QuickTime, adjust this up to a 150 MHz 604 or better, and if you're a gamer, it's a 266 MHz G3 or better for you.

Because today's applications consume RAM and hard-disk space like there's no tomorrow, you should try to find a Mac with at least 32 MB of RAM—though you'll be much happier with 64 MB, and if you intend to run Mac OS X, you need at least 128 MB—and a 6 GB hard drive. If you can't find such a Mac, be prepared to upgrade. If the Mac won't accept more than 32 MB of RAM, look elsewhere.

 A final consideration is how well you expect your Mac to be able to keep up with modern system software—specifically, Mac OS X. If you have some variety of Mac that originally bore a PowerPC G3 processor—a Power Mac G3, iMac, PowerBook G3, or iBook—it will run Mac OS X. Note, however, that the Beige Power Mac G3 models are sometime finicky about accepting Mac OS X. Older Macs equipped with G3 processor upgrades may be compatible with Mac OS X—as we go to press, manufacturers of such upgrade cards are working on patches to make their products compatible with Mac OS X. Of course there's no reason on earth that you have to run Mac OS X. Software that works with Mac OS 8 and 9 will be around for quite awhile.

Where to Shop

Apple maintains tight control over distribution of its hardware and requires retailers to charge a certain price for its products. Therefore, you can forget about shopping around for a "cheap" new Mac. They just don't exist. That doesn't mean, however, that you can't save a few bucks by being a smart shopper.

As with shopping for books, CDs, or pepperoni pizza, you can shop for a Mac online, over the phone, or the old-fashioned way—from a local retailer. Here are some of your options:

The Apple Store

Apple maintains two different stores—the virtual, Web-based Apple Store and the bricks-and-mortar Apple Stores found in 25 locations around the United States. All Apple Stores sell Apple hardware and software as well as a selection of peripherals from third parties.

Which to choose? Obviously, if you don't live near a major metropolitan area graced with a real live Apple Store, you'll opt for its virtual counterpart. And choosing to do so may not be all that terrible a burden. Although retail Apple Stores are a brand-new concept as we go to press, we can guess that there will be times when the online Apple Store has access to hardware that's more difficult to get at the retail outlets. Also, the online Apple Store allows you to build Macs to your specifications. The retail Apple Stores may not offer this kind of flexibility.

The downside to the online shopping experience is that you can never be quite sure when your products will be delivered—Apple, like nearly every mail-order company you're likely to encounter, occasionally has problems with items being out of stock. And even if an item is ready to be shipped, you must pay shipping charges if you want that item quickly. UPS Ground shipping, which takes three to seven business days, is free. Express shipping, which takes two business days, is not.

Besides the option to Take It Home Right Now, retail Apple stores offer other advantages. For example, you can test-drive a variety of Mac models and see how they perform with peripherals such as printers, scanners, and digital cameras. Plus, these retail stores carry a load of Mac software—software that's not available from the online store. And finally, retail Apple stores are staffed by folks who understand and love the Mac. If you have a problem or question, you can talk with one of the employees holding court at the Genius Bar—a location in each Apple Store where a Mac guru is waiting to help you with your Mac trials and tribulations.

Catalog Sales

You can also purchase Macs through catalog outfits such as MacConnection, MacWarehouse, and MacZone. Although these places may knock off a few bucks from Apple's price, they more than make up for it in shipping and handling charges. They may also offer "specials" such as an extra 64 MB of RAM, but such offers usually involve an installation charge that costs as much as the item itself. Finally, if you purchase a Mac from one of these places and it's defective, you have to go through the hassle of repacking and shipping it back to the place of purchase.

Every so often, these companies will offer bundles—a printer offered at a discount if you buy it with an iMac, for example—that can save you money. Often these same bundles are available elsewhere—even at the Apple Store. Check around before biting on one of these promotions.

Local Dealers

Although the retail version of the Apple Store has taken a piece out of local dealers, some remain, and some are very, very good. Talk with your Mac buddies to see who in your area offers good service and support.

Unfortunately, some stores may offer a less-than-spiffy Mac-buying experience. Huge chain stores such as Best Buy, Sears, and CompUSA are fine if that's all you have to choose from, but the people who work there generally know more about the washer-dryer combo in the corner than a Macintosh. Frankly, in most cases you're better off dealing with the online Apple Store than shopping at one of these places.

Short Shopping Tips

Take these tips with you when you shop:

Pay by credit card. If you have a problem (your new Mac catches fire, for example) and the dealer is reluctant to resolve it, you can instruct your credit card company to withhold payment until things are worked out to your satisfaction.

Know what you want. After tripping through the pages of this book, you'll know more about Macs than 90 percent of the salespeople you're likely to encounter. Do your homework before shopping, and resist a salesperson's attempt to sell you something you don't need.

Become a student. Many institutions of higher learning offer students Macs at a discount. Get an education *and* get a Mac on the cheap! How cool is that?

Extended warranties are usually no deal. Invariably if a Mac is going to break, it will do so in the first couple of weeks. New Macs are covered by a one-year warranty. Extended warranties are rarely worth the money. On more-delicate Macs such as iBooks and PowerBooks, it *might* be worth purchasing Apple's AppleCare extended warranty. Only you know how much abuse you're likely to inflict on your portable pal.

Don't worry about repairs. Some folks refuse to buy a Mac at a store such as Fry's or CompUSA because they're understandably nervous about the competence of the store's service department. Don't worry about it. You can take your Mac to *any* Apple Authorized Service Provider—and more often than not, the dealer will return your Mac to Apple for servicing anyway. The only reason you'll need to return to the point of purchase is if the Mac is defective.

Glossary

3D Three-dimensional. Normal graphics use two dimensions, height and width (x- and y-axes), while 3D graphics add depth (z-axis) to the original dimensions.

A

active window The topmost window; the window that is currently receiving mouse and keyboard input. Pre–Mac OS X, that window can be identified by the horizontal lines in its title bar.

ADB Apple Desktop Bus. (*See* Apple Desktop Bus.)

AGP Accelerated Graphics Port, the slot for a video card on newer Macs.

AIFF Audio Interchange File Format, the standard sound format on the Mac.

AirPort Apple's wireless networking technology. There are AirPort cards, which fit into Macs, and AirPort Base Stations, which communicate with the cards.

alert box A box that appears when the user is about to do something dangerous or if something has gone wrong.

alias A file that points to another item, such as a file, folder, or application. When you double-click an alias, the item it points to is opened. In the Mac OS 9 Finder, an alias is distinguished by an italicized name and a small arrow in its icon. In Mac OS X, you just get the arrow. (These are called *shortcuts* in Windows.)

all-in-one An adjective describing a desktop computer system in which the monitor and CPU are housed in one unit. All iMacs are all-in-one Macs. Although portable computers such as the PowerBook have the monitor, keyboard, and CPU contained in one unit, they are not considered all-in-one machines. Why? Maybe the same reason that *flammable* and *inflammable* mean the same thing.

AltiVec *See* Velocity Engine.

Amelio, Gilbert Apple CEO, 1996–97. Best known for acquiring NeXT Software and bringing back Steve Jobs, who eventually took his job.

anti-aliasing The blurring of certain pixels to smooth out an image. Usually used to make screen fonts easier to read.

Apple Desktop Bus A low-speed serial bus that connects peripherals such as keyboards and mice to the Macintosh. This has been supplanted by USB. (*See* Universal Serial Bus.)

Apple Guide An older version of the internal Macintosh help system. Replaced in Mac OS X by Help Viewer.

Apple menu In Mac OS 9 and earlier, a menu for accessing utilities, recent items, and aliases. In Mac OS X, a menu for accessing systemwide commands (such as shut down and log out), preferences, and recent documents and applications.

Apple Remote Access Software that allows your Mac to connect to a nonlocal network.

AppleScript A simple scripting language you can use to automate your Mac.

AppleShare IP Apple's commercial server software.

AppleTalk Apple's local area network (LAN) architecture. Macs can use it to communicate with each other and with network peripherals.

application A program designed for end users. (Meaning normal, everyday people.) Example: Microsoft Word.

Application menu The Finder menu on the far right side of the menu bar in Mac OS 9 and earlier. It allows the user to move between running applications. In Mac OS X, it is to the right of the Apple menu and gives users access to preferences for the application the user is currently using.

Aqua The name of the interface in Mac OS X, so called because of its translucent blue highlights.

ASCII A code for designating characters in which each letter or symbol is assigned a number. Its long name is American Standard Code for Information Interchange. Thus, ASCII files are text only, with no added styles like bold or italic.

B

balloon help A feature of the Mac OS 9 and earlier that pops up cartoon balloons of descriptive text when the pointer pauses over an item.

bandwidth The amount of data a system can deliver over a set period of time. High bandwidth is good.

beta version A prerelease version of software or hardware for testing purposes only.

BinHex Binary-to-hexadecimal. BinHex is a process for converting Mac OS files into ASCII files. It's mostly used for transferring files via e-mail or FTP.

blessed System Folder In operating systems before Mac OS X, this is a valid System Folder (it's got a Finder and a System). It can usually be identified by the little Mac OS symbol on its folder icon

browser An application for accessing and displaying pages on the World Wide Web.

BSD Berkeley Software Distribution. Mac OS X uses BSD, the version of the Unix operating system developed at the University of California, Berkeley. BSD runs on top of the Mach kernel. *See also* Mach.

bug A programming glitch. (If someone finds a productive use for the glitch, the company responsible for the bug might call it a feature.)

bus The connection that transmits data between the CPU and internal components, such as drives and video cards. Current Macs use the PCI expansion bus, and older Macs use NuBus.

byte A unit of storage capable of holding one character, which is 8 bits.

C

cable modem A modem enabling you to connect to the Internet via the same lines used by cable television.

cache A storage mechanism used to speed up computing. There are disk caches and memory caches. A disk cache stores recently used data in a memory buffer, speeding up its retrieval. A memory cache stores often-used instructions in high-speed static RAM instead of slower dynamic RAM.

Carbonized A Carbonized application has been rewritten by its developer using the Carbon set of APIs, which allows it to run on most Mac OS 8 and 9 systems and on Mac OS X systems. *See also* Classic *and* Cocoa.

CD-R Compact Disc-Recordable. Discs you can write to only once.

CD-ROM Compact Disc–Read-Only Memory. The discs on which most programs and music are available.

CD-RW Compact Disc-Rewritable. Discs you can write to multiple times.

Chooser In Mac OS 9 and earlier, used to select printers and servers. In Mac OS X, you choose printers with the Print Center.

Classic A Classic application is one written for Mac OS 9 or earlier but not rewritten for Mac OS X. (More technically, the developer has not used Apple's Carbon APIs to rewrite the application.) Classic applications run in the Classic environment of Mac OS X and on Mac OS 9 and earlier.

client A Mac program that connects to a server. For example, e-mail programs are clients, as they connect to mail servers to send and receive messages.

clip art Generic images used to illustrate documents. Many programs, such as AppleWorks, come with collections of royalty-free clip art.

Clipboard A special section of memory dedicated to items you cut and paste. When you use the Cut command, the selection is placed in the Clipboard. Paste places what is in the Clipboard at the insertion point.

clone A non-Apple computer built to run the Mac OS.

close box The box in the upper-left-hand corner of a Mac OS 9 and earlier and Mac OS X window. It closes the window but doesn't necessarily close the application. *See also* Mac OS X window buttons.

Cocoa In Mac OS X, a development environment for writing Mac OS X applications. A Cocoa application can easily take advantage of Mac OS X's built-in services, such as the Font Panel. A Cocoa application, however, can't run on Mac OS 9 and earlier systems. *See also* Carbonized *and* Classic.

contextual menu Provides access to commands associated with an item. When the user presses the Control key while clicking an item, a contextual menu appears next to the item.

control panel A small memory-resident program for adjusting properties of your Mac or the behavior of certain applications. In Mac OS X, you use System Preferences to set many of the properties of your Mac.

Control Strip A toolbar in Mac OS 9 and earlier containing modules for adjusting settings on the Mac.

CPU Central processing unit. The brains of the computer. In current Macs, the CPU is a PowerPC processor.

crash An incident that causes a program or computer to cease functioning. The cause can be due to faulty software coding or a hardware malfunction.

cross-platform An adjective describing something compatible with more than one type of computer system. For example, Microsoft Word files are cross-platform because they can be used on Macintosh or Windows computers.

cursor A graphic symbol that indicates where a user-initiated action will take place. On the Mac, the cursor is often an arrow. *See* pointer.

D

Darwin The open-source component of Mac OS X.

database A software program for storing, retrieving, and manipulating multiple pieces of information.

default A setting that is chosen if a user does not specify another. For example, the default home

page for some Web browsers is the developing company's site.

defragment To reorganize a file so that it occupies contiguous clusters on a disk.

Desktop The main area of the Mac OS; the part that contains icons for drives, files, folders, and in Mac OS 9 and earlier, the Trash.

dialog box An alert that asks for user input.

disc and disk When you're talking about CD or DVD or other optical media, it is a disc. When referring to magnetic media such as those used in hard drives or Zip drives, it's a disk.

disclosure button The triangle that reveals more options or contents when you click it. Apple says you can also call it a disclosure triangle.

display A monitor. Shorthand for *display screen*.

Dock In Mac OS X, the Dock is a strip of icons representing running applications, frequently used items, and the Trash.

double-click A sequence of two consecutive clicks.

download To retrieve a file from another computer over the Internet.

driver A piece of software that facilitates communication between a piece of hardware and the operating system.

DSL Digital Subscriber Line, a high-speed way to connect to the Internet over phone lines.

DVD Digital Video Disc, a type of CD-ROM that can hold nearly 5 GB of data per disc, enough for a feature-length movie.

dynamic RAM RAM that needs to be constantly refreshed to retain its contents. Slower than static RAM.

E

e-mail Electronic mail, the transmission of messages over a network.

emulation Mimicking another program or hardware device in software. For example, the Macintosh program Virtual PC emulates the Windows environment, allowing you to run Windows programs on the Mac. *See also* native software.

encryption The encoding of data so that it is unintelligible to unauthorized parties.

F

FAQ Frequently asked questions, which in itself is a bit of shorthand. An FAQ is a list of frequently asked questions and answers about a specific subject. It is a timesaving device so that folks in the know, be they technical support staff or newsgroup veterans, don't keep answering the same basic questions.

file A discrete collection of data that has a unique name.

file server A storage device on a network dedicated to holding files.

File Transfer Protocol A means of moving files from one computer to another over the Internet. The common abbreviation is FTP.

FileMaker Pro A database application from FileMaker Inc., formerly known as Claris.

Finder The main application of the Mac OS. The Finder manages the Mac's files and folders.

FireWire A communications standard developed by Apple. It transmits data, video, audio, and power over a single line, and can transfer data as fast as 400 MBps (more than 30 times faster than USB), making it a popular choice for digital audio and video professionals. How popular? In 2001, Apple won an Emmy Award for FireWire's impact on the TV industry. Sony calls it i.Link, and others refer to it as IEEE 1394.

flame A vitriolic post on a public message board.

G

gigabyte A gigabyte is 1,073,741,824 bytes, not a jillion.

GUI Graphical user interface. An interface that uses a computer's graphical capabilities to make the computer easier to use. A GUI usually features menus and icons representing disks and files. Commands are sent to the computer via mouse clicks. The antithesis of a GUI is a command-line interface, where the user types in commands after a prompt, such as C:>. DOS and Unix use a command-line interface.

H

hard disk A magnetic storage medium for computer data. Also called a *hard drive.* The word *hard* is used to differentiate it from floppy disks. In common usage, a hard disk is the big disk inside your Mac.

hardware The physical elements of the computer. The processor, the printer, the disks, or the monitor, for example.

HFS *See* Hierarchical File System.

HFS+ Hierarchical File System Plus.

Hierarchical File System Usually referred to as HFS, this was the standard file format for the Macintosh, which Apple now officially calls the Mac OS X Standard Format. HFS + is the standard for Mac OS 8 and 9 and X, and Apple calls it Mac OS Extended Format.

home folder In Mac OS X, each user of the system gets a home folder to store files, music, documents, pictures—things like that. You don't actually see something called a "Home" folder because the system names it after the user: Marty, for example.

HTML Hypertext Markup Language, the language used to create Web pages.

I

iBook Apple's consumer-oriented portable computer.

icon Apple's free convicted-felon software… no, wait—an icon is a graphic representation of a file, application, or folder.

iDisk Apple's free Internet storage-space service.

iMac The all-in-one consumer Macintosh that comes in several cheery colors.

iMovie Apple's basic moviemaking software.

insertion point The place where items are placed in documents when you type or paste. It's usually a blinking vertical bar.

installer A special program made to place a program on your Macintosh. Installers usually put several files in specific locations, saving the user a lot of hassle.

interface The means by which a user communicates with the computer. The Mac uses a graphical user interface. *See also* GUI.

Internet A global network that connects millions of computers.

IP Internet Protocol, a communications standard.

ISDN Integrated services digital network, a way to send data over phone lines. ISDN supports speeds of 64 Kbps to 128 Kbps; faster than your standard 56 Kbps modem but slower than DSL or a cable modem.

ISP Internet service provider, a company that sells access to the Internet. America Online is a big ISP, as is EarthLink.

iTunes Apple's free music recording, cataloging, and playback program.

J

Java A cross-platform programming language developed by Sun Microsystems. The theory is that a developer could write a program in Java and have it work on Windows machines and Macs without altering it.

Jobs, Steve Apple interim CEO (or iCEO) and then CEO, 1997 to present. One of the fathers of the Mac.

K

kilobyte A kilobyte is 1,024 bytes, not exactly 1,000 as would seem logical. Abbreviated as Kbyte.

M

Mac OS Note the space. The official name of the Macintosh operating system.

Mac OS X The X is the Roman numeral ten and pronounced "ten."

Mac OS X window buttons The buttons in the top-left corner of a Mac OS X window. The left button (red) is the Close button. The middle button (yellow) is the Minimize button, which places the file or folder in the Dock. The right button (green) is the Zoom button.

Mach Mac OS X uses the Mach kernel, originally created at Carnegie Mellon University. The kernel handles such tasks as memory allocation and scheduling what tasks the computer is doing. *See also* BSD.

macro A sequence of commands activated by a single command. A shortcut. A macro in Microsoft Word, for example, might open a new document and put your name and address at the top.

megabyte A megabyte is 1,048,576 bytes, not 1 million. Abbreviated as MB.

megahertz A frequency measurement equaling 1 million cycles per second. The speed of microprocessors is expressed in megahertz. Abbreviated as *MHz.*

menu A list of commands from which the user can choose.

microprocessor A chip that contains a central processing unit (CPU). The PowerPC, the heart of the Macintosh line, is a microprocessor. But if you call it a *processor* or a *CPU,* people will know that you mean microprocessor.

modem A device that allows computers to communicate over phone lines. The name is short for *modulation-demodulation.*

monitor A video display for a computer.

motherboard The main circuit board of a computer. It holds the CPU and slots for expansion.

mouse The Mac's pointing device; a peripheral that controls the movement of the cursor on the screen.

MP3 Short for MPEG 1, Layer 3 (MPEG itself is short for Moving Picture Experts Group), a scheme for compressing audio. It has quickly become the standard for digital audio.

multimedia Content that uses more than one medium for communication as in video and audio.

multiprocessing Using more than one processor to complete a task. Some high-end Macs have two CPUs; special programming can take advantage of the extra processing power.

N

native software Software designed to run on a particular microprocessor. Apple has designed Mac OS X to run specifically on PowerPC G3 and G4 processors, and Mac OS X's Mail application is designed to run specifically on Mac OS X: Both are native software for the PowerPC G3 and G4 processors. Through emulation software, an application designed to run on one processor can be tricked into thinking it is running on another one. *See also* emulation.

network A collection of interconnected computers and devices.

Newton An Apple technology for handheld devices that incorporates handwriting recognition. The short-lived device was called Newton MessagePad.

O

online To be connected to the Internet or a local network.

open source Descriptive term for software whose underlying code has been made available by its developer for modification. Parts of Mac OS X and all of Linux are open source.

operating system Software that controls the functions of a computer. An operating system tracks input from a keyboard and mouse, sends output to display devices, negotiates resources among running programs, monitors files and folders, and controls peripherals, among other things.

OS Operating system.

P

parallel port An interface that transmits data several bits simultaneously. *Compare with* serial port.

parameter RAM Persistent memory that holds system-configuration data, such as date, time, and desktop settings. Also known as PRAM. Unlike regular memory, which forgets everything the moment the power is cut, PRAM is powered by a separate battery so it remembers its contents.

PCI Peripheral Component Interconnect, an expansion bus. Macs have PCI expansion slots for things such as video cards or SCSI cards.

pixel A single point in an electronic image.

Platinum appearance The gray, beveled style for menus, icons, windows, and controls that Apple introduced with Mac OS 8.

plug-in An extra piece of software that adds functions to another program. For example, plug-ins in Adobe Photoshop add ways for users to manipulate images.

pointer The arrow-shaped cursor.

POP Post Office Protocol, the method most e-mail programs use to retrieve messages from a server.

pop-up menu A menu that appears when an onscreen item is clicked. The menu disappears when an action is selected.

PowerBook Apple's line of professional portable computers. Oddly enough, these were called PowerBooks even before the advent of the PowerPC chip, so there are non-PowerPC PowerBooks.

Power Macintosh A desktop Mac with a PowerPC processor. Note that *Power Macintosh* is two words, unlike *PowerPC* and *PowerBook,* and the latter Mac machine may or may not have a PowerPC processor. Yes, it's confusing.

PowerPC The name of the processor used in the Power Macintosh line and manufactured by Motorola and IBM.

PRAM Parameter RAM.

Print Center In Mac OS X, you use this to select printers. It replaces parts of the Chooser, found in Mac OS 9 and earlier.

protected memory A memory scheme that sets aside unique space for each application so that if one program crashes, it will not affect the others. This is a feature of Mac OS X.

protocol A standardized format for transmitting data between devices.

Q

QuickTime Apple's software for playing audio and video on a computer. It's actually more complicated than that; it's also a media-authoring platform and a file format. But if you're like most of us—a regular old computer user—it's just a media player.

R

RAM Random Access Memory, which allows any byte in memory to be accessed randomly. Well, isn't that self-referential? Random access means to be able to get something without disturbing its neighbors. For example, if you wanted to fetch byte 10, you could just nab byte 10 instead of moving aside bytes 1 through 9 on your way to 10. Still not working for you? OK, imagine that you have been given the gift of teleportation. You are in San Francisco and want to go to New York. Close your eyes; think New York; open your eyes and you are there. You didn't have to travel through Missouri to get there, you just went there. That's how random access works.

RAM disk A portion of RAM set aside to act as if it were physical storage, like a disk drive. The opposite of virtual memory. *Compare with* virtual memory.

read-me file A document that contains important information for the user, usually about the pitfalls of installing software.

resolution A measurement of the clarity of an image. Resolutions are given for monitor displays (how many pixels are on the screen), printer output (dots per inch), and image files (number of pixels).

S

Scrapbook A Mac OS 9 and earlier built-in application for storing often-used graphics, sounds, and movies.

screensaver An application that displays images, animation, or other information when the computer has been idle for a specified amount of time. Screensavers were created to prevent pixel burn-in, which afflicted older monitors. They changed the image so one wouldn't get permanently etched into the screen. This is no longer a danger, but the name and the application have remained.

scroll bar The bar on the side or bottom of a window that controls what part of a document is displayed.

SCSI Small Computer System Interface, a parallel interface standard for connecting peripherals. Pronounced "skuzzy."

Sculley, John Apple CEO, 1983–93.

serial port An interface that transmits data one bit at a time. Compare with *parallel port*.

server A computer on a network that manages network resources.

shareware Free-distribution software that users pay for only if they decide to continue using it. Most shareware is written by smaller developers.

Sherlock Apple's disk- and Internet-searching utility.

sleep A low-power mode in which the Mac's screen and drives are turned off.

SMTP Simple Mail Transfer Protocol, the method most e-mail servers use to deliver messages.

software Computer code or data. If it can be stored electronically, it is definitely software. If you can copy it, it is probably software.

Spindler, Michael CEO of Apple, 1993–96. His nickname was "The Diesel" because of his hard-driving personality.

startup disk The disk used to start up a computer, or a disk capable of starting up a computer. You can designate which disk is used via the Startup Disk control panel in Mac OS 9 and in the Startup Disk of System Preferences in Mac OS X.

static RAM RAM that does not need to be refreshed to keep its contents. Faster and more reliable than dynamic RAM, but more expensive.

System file The main Mac OS file in Mac OS 9 and earlier.

System Folder The folder that holds files crucial to the running of Mac OS 9 and earlier. In Mac OS X, it's just called System.

T

TCP/IP Transmission Control Protocol/Internet Protocol, used to make connections on the Internet.

Terminal An application that lets you use Mac OS X's command-line interface.

title bar The top border of a window, which contains its name.

trackball A pointing device that consists of a ball held in a stationary base.

trackpad A pointing device. The user moves the pointer by dragging a finger across the surface of the trackpad.

Trash The holding area for items you want to delete from your computer.

U

undo A command that takes back the previous command, "undoing" it. For example, if you delete a word from a sentence, Undo puts it back. The shortcut for Undo is usually ⌘Z.

Universal Serial Bus USB for short. USB is a technology for connecting peripherals—such as pointing devices and printers—to your computer. Apple has standardized on USB, supplanting the Apple Desktop Bus and traditional serial ports. Not only is USB 1,000 times faster than ADB and more than 50 times faster than Apple's old serial ports, it's "hot-swappable," which means you can disconnect or connect devices without powering down or restarting the computer.

Unix An operating system. Mac OS X is based on a version of Unix. *See also* BSD.

upload To transfer a file to another computer over the Internet.

URL Uniform Resource Locator. A URL is the address of a specific spot on the Internet. For example, the URL for Peachpit's home page is www.peachpit.com.

utility A program that performs a specific task (such as managing extensions) or supplements the functions of other programs (such as an add-on spelling checker).

V

Velocity Engine An addition to the PowerPC processor architecture, implemented on the G4 chip. It is built to speed up tasks such as graphics processing, and developers have to write special code to take advantage of it. Also known as *AltiVec*.

virtual memory A method for making an operating system behave as if it has more RAM available than it actually has. In Mac OS 9 and earlier, this is accomplished by treating a user-specified amount of hard-drive space as "RAM." In Mac OS X, virtual memory is always on, and the Mach kernel maintains virtual memory.

virus A malicious program that attaches itself to or replaces another program to reproduce itself, generally without the knowledge of the target computer's user.

W

Web Short for *World Wide Web*.

window A rectangular, movable display box in a graphical user interface (GUI). Windows can hold documents, folder contents, and applications, among other things.

wizard A help program that guides a user step-by-step through a task, such as the creation of a document or the setting of Internet preferences.

World Wide Web A collection of interconnected servers on the Internet that use the Hypertext Transfer Protocol (HTTP). This allows documents written in Hypertext Markup Language (HTML) to link to other documents and files, so the viewer can quickly jump from one to another using a browser.

worm A malicious program that replicates itself. Unlike a virus, it does not attach itself to a host program.

Z

zoom box The second box from the left in the title bar of a window in Mac OS 9 (it looks like a box with a smaller box inside) and the third button from the left in Mac OS X. Clicking the zoom box makes the window expand to the size of the whole screen (or a reasonable facsimile) or return to its original size. *See also* Mac OS X window buttons.

Index